AMERICAN
GOVERNMENT

AND POLITICS
TODAY

AMERICAN
GOVERNMENT

AND POLITICS TODAY

2013–2014 EDITION

Steffen W. Schmidt
Iowa State University

Mack C. Shelley, II
Iowa State University

Barbara A. Bardes
University of Cincinnati

Lynne E. Ford
College of Charleston

WADSWORTH
CENGAGE Learning

Australia • Brazil • Japan • Korea • Mexico • Singapore • Spain • United Kingdom • United States

American Government and Politics Today, 2013–2014 Edition
Steffen W. Schmidt, Mack C. Shelley, Barbara A. Bardes, Lynne E. Ford

Publisher: Suzanne Jeans

Executive Editor: Carolyn Merrill

Development Editor: Jennifer Jacobson, Ohlinger Publishing Services

Assistant Editor: Scott Greenan

Editorial Assistant: Eireann Aspell

Marketing Manager: Kyle Zimmerman

Senior Marketing Communications Manager: Linda Yip

Production Manager: Suzanne St. Clair

Print Buyer: Fola Orekoya

Rights Acquisition Specialist: Jennifer Meyer Dare

Production Service: Integra Software Services, Inc.

Photo Researcher: Bill Smith Group

Text Researcher: Christie Barros

Art Director: Linda May

Cover Designer: Rokusek Design

For product information and technology assistance, contact us at
Cengage Learning Customer & Sales Support, 1-800-423-0563
For permission to use material from this text or product,
submit all requests online at **www.cengage.com/permissions**
Further permissions questions can be emailed to
permissionrequest@cengage.com

Library of Congress Control Number: 2012947224

ISBN-13: 978-1-133-60213-2

ISBN-10: 1-133-60213-4

Wadsworth
20 Channel Center
Boston, MA 02210
USA

Cengage Learning is a leading provider of customized learning solutions with office locations around the globe, including Singapore, the United Kingdom, Australia, Mexico, Brazil, and Japan. Locate your local office at:
international.cengage.com/region

Cengage Learning products are represented in Canada by Nelson Education, Ltd.

For your course and learning solutions, visit **www.cengage.com**

Purchase any of our products at your local college store or at our preferred online store **www.cengagebrain.com**

Printed in the United States of America
1 2 3 4 5 6 7 14 13 12

BRIEF CONTENTS

CONTENTS

© Dimitris Stephanides / iStockphoto 12741677

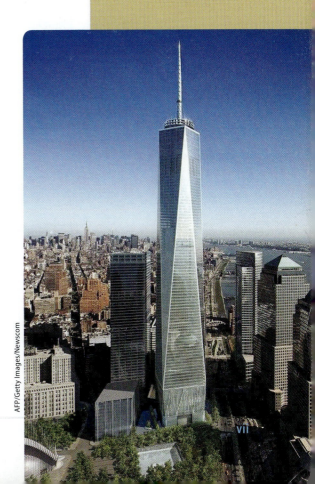

AFP/Getty Images/Newscom

CHAPTER 2 FEATURES

Politics with a Purpose
How to Form a More Perfect Union? 40

Beyond Our Borders
What Makes a Constitution? 51

You Can Make a Difference
How Can You Affect The U.S. Constitution? 59

© Ramin Talaie/Corbis

© Dimitris Stephanides / iStockphoto 12741677

Chapter 3: Federalism 62

© Dimitris Stephanides / iStockphoto 12741677

BRIAN KERSLEY/UPI / Landov

PART 2: CIVIL RIGHTS AND LIBERTIES

Chapter 4: Civil Liberties 94

WHAT IF . . . *ROE V. WADE* WERE OVERTURNED? 95

Chapter 5: Civil Rights 134

© Dimitris Stephanides / iStockphoto 12741677

© dbimages/Alamy

PART 3: PEOPLE AND POLITICS

Chapter 6: Public Opinion and Political Socialization 179

© Dimitris Stephanides / iStockphoto 12741677

© White House Photo/Alamy

Chapter 7: Interest Groups 210

© Dimitris Stephanides / iStockphoto 12741677

Douglas Graham/Roll Call/Getty Images

Chapter 8: Political Parties 242

CHAPTER 8 FEATURES

Politics with a Purpose

Beyond Our Borders

You Can Make a Difference

AP Photo/Dave Weaver

Chapter 9: Voting and Elections 279

© Dimitris Stephanides / iStockphoto 12741677

SKIP BOLEN/EPA/Newscom

Chapter 10: Campaigning for Office 305

© Dimitris Stephanides / IStockphoto 12741677

CRAIG LASSIG/EPA/Newscom

PART 4: POLITICAL INSTITUTIONS

Chapter 11: The Congress 339

CHAPTER 11 FEATURES

© Dimitris Stephanides / iStockphoto 12741677

TIM SLOAN/AFP/Getty Images

Chapter 12: The President 377

Brendan Hoffman/Getty Images

© Dimitris Stephanides / iStockphoto 12741677

Chapter 13: The Bureaucracy 412

CHAPTER 13 FEATURES

Beyond Our Borders
Privatizing the U.S. Military Abroad 431

Politics with a Purpose
Holding Government Accountable 439

You Can Make a Difference
What the Government Knows About You 441

© Dimitris Stephanides / iStockphoto 12741677

New house News Service/Landov

Chapter 14: The Courts 444

CHAPTER 14 FEATURES

Beyond Our Borders
The Legal System Based on *Sharia* 448

Politics with a Purpose
Political Struggles Fought in the Court 450

You Can Make a Difference
Volunteer in the Courts 470

JONATHAN ERNST/Reuters/Landov

© Dimitris Stephanides / iStockphoto 12741677

PART 5: PUBLIC POLICY

Chapter 15: Domestic Policy 474

Chapter 16: Economic Policy 507

WHAT IF . . . THE FEDERAL GOVERNMENT WERE REQUIRED TO BALANCE ITS BUDGET? 508

Scott Olson/Getty Images

© Dimitris Stephanides / iStockphoto 12741677

© Dimitris Stephanides / iStockphoto 12741677

©Everett Collection Inc/Alamy

PART 6: STATE AND LOCAL POLITICS

Chapter 18: State and Local Government 571

The new 2013–2014 edition of *American Government and Politics Today* includes significant revisions and reflects our commitment to producing the most up-to-date text possible. The 2012 election reflected deep divisions in the American citizenry over the future direction of the nation. President Barack Obama, who had won election in 2008 with a strong majority, faced former Massachusetts Governor Mitt Romney, the Republican nominee, in a battle over social values and economic ideology. Barack Obama came into office on a wave of enthusiasm and wide support among the public for his historic candidacy. However, the economic recession which began in 2008 became a sustained economic downturn which lasted through his first term. In 2010, Republicans regained control of the House of Representatives and a national movement, the Tea Party, rose to encourage a different economic policy from that of the president and the Democratic party. The 2012 election campaign drove home the the differences between the two major parties and the two presidential candidates. In the end, President Barack Obama and Vice President Joe Biden were re-elected by a 51 to 48 percent margin. The incumbents received strong support in all but two states they had won in 2008 (Indiana and North Carolina). The Romney-Ryan ticket fought hard to win the "battleground" states but were unable to overcome the president's well-organized plan to get out the vote. Democrats capitalized on changing demographics in the electorate and attracted a larger share of the vote total from young people, women, Latinos, and African Americans than in previous elections. Nearly 6 billion dollars was spent on the 2012 election.

The changes we have made to this edition are not limited to bringing the text up to date. We have also made major revisions based on the latest research. The entire textbook is more focused on showing students how participation in the system can result in political change. For instance, each chapter's *Politics with a Purpose* feature highlights political change brought about by citizens, groups, or organizations. Finally, pedagogy in the profession has evolved over time and is now focused more than ever on documenting student learning. This edition will make doing so easier than ever.

2012 Election Results Included and Analyzed

Our experience has been that students respond to up-to-date information about political events. Consequently, we have included results of the November 2012 elections as well as discussion of how the social media are used by the candidates and parties in the campaign. We also analyze how these results will affect our political processes at the national, state, and local levels. While we have updated all of the text to be consistent with these results, in particular we have added throughout the text numerous special subsections dedicated to the elections.

The Interactive Focus of This Text

Whether the topic is voter participation, terrorism, or the problems that face the president, we constantly strive to involve the student reader in the analysis. We make sure that the reader comes to understand that politics is not an abstract process but a very human enterprise. We emphasize how different outcomes can affect students' civil rights and liberties, employment opportunities, and economic welfare.

Throughout the text, we encourage the reader to think critically and to engage directly with the ideas and topics presented in the book. The features titled *Beyond Our Borders* encourage students to think globally. We further encourage interaction with the political system by ending each chapter with features titled *You Can Make a Difference*, which show students not only what they can do to become politically involved, but also why they should care enough to do so. In addition, these chapter-ending features highlight one young politically involved individual or point out actions that students can take themselves to change the system.

APLIA

The online learning solution Aplia is now available with *American Government and Politics Today.* Aplia helps students learn the essential concepts of introductory American government and apply them to real life through the use of interactive coursework that strengthens their critical thinking and comprehensive reading skills. Students receive immediate, detailed explanations for every answer. Homework and class assignments help students come to class better prepared. Grades are automatically recorded in the instructor's Aplia gradebook. Questions are visually engaging and require students to analyze information and apply key concepts; instructors are also able to assign open-ended essay questions that require students to think critically. Exercises, assignments, and questions are tied to each chapter's Learning Outcomes, which are described below.

The organization of the book and supplementary materials make assessment of student learning easier for instructors, departments, and institutions. The learning outcomes for each chapter are supported by Aplia interactive coursework and can be assessed by the instructor through the graded Aplia exercises and/or through test items keyed to the learning outcomes. This linkage will make assessing student learning easier for the instructor and make it possible for departments to assess American government course outcomes by aggregating individual section results.

Special Pedagogy and Features

The 2013–2014 edition of *American Government and Politics Today* contains many pedagogical aids and high-interest features to assist both students and instructors. The following list summarizes the special elements that can be found in each chapter:

- **Learning Outcomes**—Chapter-opening learning outcomes help students target their reading. The outcomes are linked to sections of each chapter and revisited directly in the chapter summary. They are tied to the introduction to American government outcomes that are expected from most courses across the country and help instructors meet and exceed the expectations for what the learner must know and be able to do at the end of the course.

- **What If...?**—These chapter-opening provocative questions are drawn from current events and prompt lively classroom discussion by putting critical thinking skills into practice with real-life dilemmas such as "What If Taxes Never Increased and Local Services Disappeared?" (new, Chapter 1); "What If One State's Same-Sex Marriages Had to Be Recognized Nationwide?" (updated, Chapter 3); "What If *Roe v. Wade* Were Overturned?" (Chapter 4); "What If Birthright Citizenship Were Repealed?" (new, Chapter 5); "What If All Interest

Groups Were Regulated by the Government?" (new, Chapter 7); "What If Political Parties Had Actual Members?" (new, Chapter 8); "What If Voting on the Internet Became Universal?" (updated, Chapter 9); "What If Congress Had Time Limits?" (new, Chapter 11); "What If There Were No Executive Privilege?" (updated, Chapter 12); "What If Every Federal Agency Reported to the People?" (new, Chapter 13); and "What If We Had Universal Health Care?" (rewritten, Chapter 15).

- **Politics with a Purpose**—Highlighting how a group or individual has influenced our political system, these boxes succinctly incorporate a literature review of key scholarship on the topic and offer a balance of positive and negative, modern and historical examples. Examples include "When Passions Mobilize," featuring a new discussion of the Occupy Wall Street movement (revised, Chapter 1); "The Innocence Project," about students fighting wrongful convictions (Chapter 4); "YouTube, Jon Stewart, and Stephen Colbert: Changing Politics for the Better?" describing the power of social media as it relates to KONY 2012, the film and campaign by Invisible Children to bring the Ugandan war criminal Joseph Kony to justice (revised, Chapter 6) and "How to Organize a Group" (new, Chapter 7).

- **Beyond Our Borders**—This feature discusses a topic such as globalization, the war on terrorism, immigration, or comparative government that is relevant to the chapter. New or rewritten *Beyond Our Borders* features in this edition are "Importing Workers: Challenging Cultures in Europe," which focuses on the debate over what to do about undocumented immigrants who have come to the United States for employment and a better life (revised, Chapter 1); "What Makes a Constitution?" which discusses new constitutions written around the world (new, Chapter 2); "Taking American Rights Overseas," which gets students to consider how their rights as U.S. citizens may or may not apply to other legal systems (new, Chapter 4); and "Everyone Has a Mayor!" which discusses the services that towns and villages provide that a nation cannot and how local governments are organized in different nations (new, Chapter 18).

- **Margin Definitions**—For all important terms. All terms and definitions are compiled in a complete glossary at the end of the book as well.

- **Did You Know?**—Margin features presenting various facts and figures that add interest to the learning process.

- **You Can Make a Difference**—These chapter-ending features show students ways to become politically involved. In the new edition, these features continue to highlight one young adult or organization in particular who has made or is making a difference. For example, the Chapter 4 box, "Your Civil Liberties: Searches and Seizures," features the case of Savana Redding—the Arizona eighth-grader who was strip-searched at school; the Chapter 7 box discusses how students can reduce gun violence on their campuses, and the Chapter 15 box, "Doing Your Part: Sustain the Planet," offers a wealth of ideas for students to get involved with conservation efforts.

- **Key Terms**—A chapter-ending list with page numbers of all terms in the chapter that were boldfaced and defined in the margins.

- **Chapter Summary**—A point-by-point summary of the chapter text.

- **Selected Print, Media, and Online Resources**—An annotated list of suggested scholarly readings, as well as popular books, films, and Web sites relevant to chapter topics, with several new entries in each chapter.

Appendices

Because we know that this book serves as a reference, we have included important documents for the student of American government to have close at hand: **The Constitution of the United States**—A fully annotated copy of the U.S. Constitution appears as the second appendix. In addition, we have included the **Declaration of Independence** and *Federalist Papers* **Nos. 10 and 51.**

A Comprehensive Supplements Package

We are proud to be the authors of a text that has the most comprehensive, accessible, and fully integrated supplements package on the market. Together, the text and the supplements listed as follows constitute a total learning and teaching package for you and your students. For further information on any of these supplements, contact your Wadsworth Cengage Higher Education sales representative.

Supplements for Instructors

PowerLecture DVD with ExamView® and JoinIn® for Schmidt, Shelley, Bardes, and Ford's American Government and Politics Today: 2013–2014 Edition, 16e

ISBN-13: 9781285075105

An all-in-one multimedia resource for class preparation, presentation, and testing, this DVD includes Microsoft® PowerPoint® slides, a test bank in both Microsoft® Word and ExamView® formats, online polling and JoinIn™ clicker questions, an Instructor Manual, and a Resource Integration Guide.

The book-specific **PowerPoint® slides** of lecture outlines, as well as photos, figures, and tables from the text, make it easy for you to assemble lectures for your course, while the **media-enhanced PowerPoint® slides** help bring your lecture to life with audio and video clips, animated learning modules illustrating key concepts, tables, statistical charts, graphs, and photos from the book as well as outside sources.

The **test bank**, updated by Heather Ramsier of Valencia College, offered in Microsoft Word® and ExamView® formats, includes 60+ multiple-choice questions with answers and page references along with 10 essay questions for each chapter. ExamView® features a user-friendly testing environment that allows you to not only publish traditional paper- and computer-based tests, but also Web-deliverable exams. **JoinIn™** offers "clicker" questions covering key concepts, enabling instructors to incorporate student response systems into their classroom lectures.

The **Instructor's Manual**, updated by John Osterman of San Jacinto College, includes learning objectives, chapter outlines, summaries, discussion questions, class activities and projects suggestions, tips on integrating media into your class, and suggested readings and Web resources. A **Resource Integration Guide** provides a chapter-by-chapter outline of all available resources to supplement and optimize learning. Contact your Cengage representative to receive a copy upon adoption.

Aplia for Schmidt, Shelley, Bardes, and Ford's *American Government and Politics Today:* 2013–2014 Edition, 16e

ISBN-13: 9781285074238 (Printed Access Card; available in bundle)
ISBN-13: 9781285074245 (Instant Access Code for student purchase)
ISBN 13: 9781285488363 (Book with Aplia bundle)

Easy to use, affordable, and effective, Aplia helps students learn and saves you time. It's like a virtual teaching assistant! Aplia helps you have more productive classes by providing assignments that get students thinking critically, reading assigned material, and reinforcing basic concepts—all before coming to class. The interactive questions also help students better understand the relevance of what they're learning and how to apply those concepts to the world around them.

Visually engaging videos, graphs, and political cartoons help capture students' attention and imagination, and an automatically included eBook provides convenient access. Aplia is instantly accessible via CengageBrain or through the bookstore via printed access card.

Please contact your local Cengage sales representative for more information, and go to www.aplia.com/politicalscience to view a demo.

Political Science CourseMate for Schmidt, Shelley, Bardes, and Ford's *American Government and Politics Today:* 2013-2014 Edition, 16e

ISBN-13: 9781285074771 PAC (Printed Access Card)
ISBN-13: 9781285074740 IAC (Instant Access Code)
ISBN 13: 9781285484624 (Book with CourseMate bundle)

Cengage Learning's Political Science CourseMate brings course concepts to life with interactive learning, study tools, and exam preparation tools that support the printed textbook. Use **Engagement Tracker** to assess student preparation and engagement in the course, and watch student comprehension soar as your class works with the textbook-specific Web site. An **interactive eBook** allows students to take notes, highlight, search, and interact with embedded media. Other resources include video activities, animated learning modules, simulations, case studies, interactive quizzes, and timelines.

The American Government NewsWatch is a real-time news and information resource, updated daily, that includes interactive maps, videos, podcasts, and hundreds of articles from leading journals, magazines, and newspapers from the United States and the world. Also included is the **KnowNow! American Government Blog**, which highlights three current events stories per week and consists of a succinct analysis of the story, multimedia, and discussion-starter questions. Access your course via www.cengage.com/login.

The Wadsworth News DVD for American Government 2014

ISBN-13: 9781285053455

This collection of two- to five-minute video clips on relevant political issues serves as a great lecture or discussion launcher.

Free Companion Website for Schmidt, Shelley, Bardes, and Ford's *American Government and Politics Today:* 2013–2014 Edition, 16e

ISBN-13: 9781285074382

This password-protected website for instructors features all of the free student assets plus an instructor's manual, book-specific PowerPoint® presentations, JoinIn™ "clicker" questions, Resource Integration Guide, and a test bank. Access your resources by logging into your account at www.cengage.com/login.

Election 2012: An American Government Supplement

ISBN-13: 9781285090931 (Printed Access Card; available in bundle)
ISBN-13: 9781285420080 (Instant Access Code)
ISBN-13: 9781285090924 (Single Sign On)
Written by John Clark and Brian Schaffner, this booklet addresses the 2012 congressional and presidential races, with real-time analysis and references. Access your course via www.cengage.com/login. This electronic module can be purchased separately or bundled with the textbook.

CourseReader: American Government 0-30 Selections

ISBN-13: 9781111479954 PAC (Printed Access Card)
ISBN-13: 9781111479978 IAC (Instant Access Code)

CourseReader: American Government allows you to create your reader, your way, in just minutes. This affordable, fully customizable online reader provides access to thousands of permissions-cleared readings, articles, primary sources, and audio and video selections from the regularly updated Gale research library database. This easy-to-use solution allows you to search for and select just the material you want for your courses.

Each selection opens with a descriptive introduction to provide context, and concludes with critical-thinking and multiple-choice questions to reinforce key points. CourseReader is loaded with convenient tools like highlighting, printing, note-taking, and downloadable MP3 audio files for each reading.

CourseReader is the perfect complement to any political science course. It can be bundled with your current textbook, sold alone, or integrated into your learning management system. CourseReader 0-30 allows access to up to 30 selections in the reader.

Please contact your Cengage sales representative for details, or please visit us at **www.cengage.com/login**. Click on "New Faculty User" and fill out the registration page. Once you are in your new SSO account, search for "CourseReader" from your dashboard and select "CourseReader: American Government" Then click "CourseReader 0-30: American Government Instant Access Code" and click "Add to my bookshelf." To access the live CourseReader, click on "CourseReader 0-30: American Government" under "Additional resources" on the right side of your dashboard.

Custom Enrichment Module: Latino-American Politics Supplement

ISBN-13: 9781285184296
This revised and updated 32-page supplement uses real examples to detail politics related to Latino Americans and can be added to your text via our custom publishing solutions.

For Students, When Requested By Your Instructors

Political Science CourseMate for Schmidt, Shelley, Bardes, and Ford's *American Government and Politics Today: 2013–2014 Edition, 16e*

Cengage Learning's Political Science CourseMate brings course concepts to life with interactive learning, study tools, and exam preparation tools that support the printed textbook. The more you study, the better the results. Make the most of your study time by accessing everything you need to succeed in one place. Read your textbook, take notes, watch videos, read case studies, take practice quizzes, and more—online with CourseMate. CourseMate also gives you access to the American Government **NewsWatch Web site**—a real-time news and information resource updated daily, and **KnowNow!**—the go-to blog about current events in American government.

Purchase instant access via CengageBrain or via a printed access card in your bookstore. Visit www.cengagebrain.com for more information. CourseMate should be purchased only when assigned by your instructor as part of your course.

Aplia for Schmidt, Shelley, Bardes, and Ford's *American Government and Politics Today*: 2013–2014 Edition, 16e

Easy to use, affordable, and convenient, Aplia helps you learn more and improve your grade in the course. Through interactive assignments, including videos, graphs, and political cartoons, you can better understand the essential concepts of American government and how they apply to real life.

Aplia helps prepare you to be more involved in class by strengthening your critical-thinking skills, reinforcing what you need to know, and helping you understand why it all matters. For your studying convenience, Aplia includes an eBook, accessible right next to your assignments.

Get instant access via CengageBrain or via a printed access card in your bookstore. Visit www.cengagebrain.com for more information. Aplia should be purchased only when assigned by your instructor as part of your course.

Free Companion Web site for Schmidt, Shelley, Bardes, and Ford's *American Government and Politics Today*: 2013–2014 Edition, 16e

Access chapter-specific interactive learning tools, including flashcards, quizzes, and more in your companion website, accessed through www.CengageBrain.com.

For Users of the Previous Edition

As usual, we thank you for your past support of our work. We have made numerous changes to this text for the 2013–2014 edition:

- We have rewritten much of the text, added numerous new features, updated the book to reflect the results of the 2012 elections, and eliminated what had been Chapter 11, "The Media and Cyberpolitics," in the previous edition. As updating the role of media in politics was a goal of this new edition, we incorporated such coverage in other chapters where it is most relevant. As a result, the new edition includes 18 total chapters, rather than 19.
- New and updated coverage of a multitude of topics includes the economic recession and its impact on the future of today's students, social media, the power of interest groups, the influence of Hispanic voters, new state-imposed barriers to voting, recent Supreme Court rulings on immigration and health care, and in-depth coverage of the 2012 elections, including the influence of Super PACs, the impact of redistricting on the composition of the House of Representatives, and women's roles in and reactions to 2012 campaign politics.

- *What If…?*— New or revised *What If* features include the following: "What If Taxes Never Increased and Local Services Disappeared?" (new, Chapter 1); "What If One State's Same-Sex Marriages Had to Be Recognized Nation-wide?" (updated, Chapter 3); "What If Birthright Citizenship Were Repealed?" (new, Chapter 5); "What If All Interest Groups Were Regulated by the Government?" (new, Chapter 7); "What If Political Parties Had Actual Members?" (new, Chapter 8); "What If Voting on the Internet Became Universal?" (updated, Chapter 9); "What If Congress Had Time Limits?" (new, Chapter 11); "What If There Were No Executive Privilege?" (updated, Chapter 12); "What If Every Federal Agency Reported to the People?" (new, Chapter 13); and "What If We Had Universal Health Care?" (rewritten, Chapter 15).

- *Politics with a Purpose*—Updated or new Politics with a Purpose boxes include "When Passions Mobilize," featuring a new discussion of the Occupy Wall Street movement (revised, Chapter 1); "YouTube, Jon Stewart, and Stephen Colbert: Changing Politics for the Better?" describing the power of social media as it relates to KONY 2012, the film and campaign by Invisible Children to bring the Ugandan war criminal Joseph Kony to justice (revised, Chapter 6) and "How to Organize a Group" (new, Chapter 7).

- New or rewritten *Beyond Our Borders* features in this edition are "Importing Workers: Challenging Cultures in Europe," which focuses on the debate over what to do about undocumented immigrants who have come to the United States for employment and a better life (revised, Chapter 1); "What Makes a Constitution?" which discusses new constitutions written around the world (new, Chapter 2); "Taking American Rights Overseas," which gets students to consider how their rights as U.S. citizens may or may not apply to other legal systems (new, Chapter 4); and "Everyone Has a Mayor!" which discusses the services that towns and villages provide that a nation cannot and how local governments are organized in different nations (new, Chapter 18).

- **New political science scholarship**—New citations in every chapter highlighting cutting-edge research and the latest scholarship are included. Figures and tables have been updated with the most recent data available, some added at press time.

Significant Changes Within Chapters

Each chapter contains updated data in figures and tables; updated citations; new photographs; updated entries for print, media, and online resources; and whenever feasible, the most current information available on the problems facing the nation.

In addition, significant chapter-by-chapter changes have been made as follows:

Chapter 1 (One Republic—Two Americas?)—This chapter has been recast around the question, "Can America honor past promises and still meet future challenges?" It looks at whether our democratic republic is nimble enough to take on new problems such as unemployment in a global economy or the education gap in a knowledge economy even as it must continue to fund Social Security and care for veterans returning from Iraq and Afghanistan. Another prevalent theme looks at what the "American Dream" holds for today's college students and whether the rules have changed or if it just feels that way to some people. The Occupy Wall Street movement caught fire because of this angst and spread quickly across the country, thanks to social media. Has the economic recession contributed to the making of "two Americas"? This chapter looks more deeply at the role of political ideology in shaping attitudes about the role of government and challenges students to think critically about why they need to know about and understand how government works—their futures depend on it.

Other changes in this chapter include the following: a new box, "What if Taxes Never Increased and Local Services Disappeared?"; a rewritten Beyond Our Borders box that focuses on the debate over what to do about undocumented immigrants who have come to the United States for employment and a better life; a new discussion of the Occupy Wall Street movement in the Politics with a Purpose box; and two new figure "supercaptions" that carefully guide students through how to make the most of the visual features of the textbook, including figures, tables, photographs, and political cartoons. The authors walk students through how to read, interpret, and analyze visual elements of each chapter, stressing how they are carefully selected to present information that is critical to their understanding of the content in each chapter.

Chapter 2 (The Constitution)—A new Beyond Our Borders box, "What Makes a Constitution?" discusses new constitutions written around the world.

Chapter 3 (Federalism)—Presents a variety of new policy issues that bring into stark focus the evolving relationship between the national and state governments: economic recession, terrorism, immigration, public employee rights, environmental regulation, and access to health care, among others. A rewritten and thoroughly updated opening box, "What if One State's Same-Sex Marriages Had To Be Recognized Nationwide?" includes an analysis of the future of the Defense of Marriage Act. The chapter also includes a discussion of the 2012 challenge to the Affordable Care Act and the commerce clause.

Chapter 4 (Civil Liberties)—Includes updated discussion of school voucher programs, the Ten Commandments on public property and the teaching of evolution, the FCC, and new coverage of Wikileaks. A new Beyond Our Borders box, "Taking American Rights Overseas," gets students to consider how their rights as U.S. citizens may or may not apply to other legal systems. Content on the Westboro Church has been added to the section, "The Right to Assemble and to Petition the Government." The chapter also includes new discussion of the incredible growth of modern wireless technology as an opportunity and challenge for law enforcement officials and as it presents potential threats to civil liberties.

Chapter 5 (Civil Rights)—Includes new material on voter identification laws and other challenges to voting rights and the elimination of "don't ask, don't tell." Other changes include the following: a new opening box, "What if Birthright Citizenship Were Repealed?"; new discussion on preventing voter fraud; and a reconsideration of affirmative action in higher education, including new coverage of the Supreme Court's review of the constitutionality of a broad affirmative action program used to admit the freshman class at the University of Texas at Austin.

Chapter 6 (Public Opinion and Political Socialization)—An updated Politics with a Purpose, "YouTube, Jon Stewart, and Stephen Colbert: Changing Politics for the Better?" describes the power of social media as it relates to KONY 2012, the film and campaign by Invisible Children to bring the Ugandan war criminal Joseph Kony to justice. In addition, there is new coverage of social media and social networking as tools that influence the dynamics of public opinion formation and expression; new material considering the role of the economic recession on the political socialization process and the expression of public opinion throughout the 2012 primary and general election campaigns; new analysis of how technological advances in communication and changes in how people use telephones have made gathering public opinion data more difficult; updates to the discussion of the "Obama Effect" in how the United States is perceived abroad; presentation of new research from the Pew Research Center on how the prolonged economic recession has combined with U.S. involvement in multiple conflicts overseas to reshape our understanding of political ideology; and new discussions of the empowerment of women and girls as the 21st century's moral imperative, the effect of the upheavals and revolutions around the world in recent years on the political socialization of young people, and the 2012 tactics to sharpen the gender gap.

Chapter 7 (Interest Groups)— Rewritten to focus on the impact of interest groups in every aspect of politics and policymaking and to consider whether interest groups have become so professionalized and elite-driven that they have few ties to their grassroots supporters; new opening box "What if All Interest Groups Were Regulated by the Government?"; new Politics with a Purpose box, "How to Organize a Group"; new figure "Profiles of Power—Four Influential Interest Groups"; updated Beyond Our Borders box, "Lobbying and Foreign Interests"; updated discussions of indirect and direct lobbying techniques and generating pressure to influence government; expanded You Can Make a Difference box with more on the gun control issue.

Chapter 8 (Political Parties)— New 2012 election coverage including analysis of the outcome, partisan trends, the role economics and social values played in the election, discussion of the Democratic and Republican issues; new opening box, "What if Political Parties Had Actual Members?"; updated section "Red State, Blue State; expanded discussion of local party organizations; expanded Beyond Our Borders box on multiparty systems; and new speculation on the impact of the evolving rivalry between the parties on independents.

Chapter 9 (Voting and Elections)—Rewritten opening box "What if Voting on the Internet became Universal?"; updated section on plans for improving voter turnout; updated section "Current Eligibility and Registration Requirements" now includes discussion of the debate over requiring photo identification to vote; rewritten Beyond Our Borders, "Why Would Compulsory Voting Increase Turnout?"

Chapter 10 (Campaigning for Office)—Revised to address the new facts of campaigning, from the creation of Super PACs to the use of social media in campaigns and of data-mining techniques to find all the voters. Includes updated opening box, "What if Spending Limits Were Placed on Campaigns?"; new and updated sections on the media and political campaigns, advertising, management of news coverage, debates, the Internet, and financing campaigns (content moved from old Chapter 11 and updated); new coverage of Super PACs and their role in campaign financing, given the new rules; repositioned and updated Tables 10–1 and 10–2 to connect to discussion of PACs and 527s, respectively; rewritten Politics with a Purpose box, "Campaign Funds: How Many Sources Are There?" that moves the discussion beyond 527s; new coverage of the case *FreedomNow .org v. FEC* and how it has led to the creation of Super PACs, including a new table, "Top 10 Super PACs in Expenditures in First Six Months of 2012"; streamlined recap of the 2008 presidential primary contest; and a new section, "The 2012 Primary Season"; new discussion of the 2012 convention activities; new coverage of campaigns as they led up to the 2012 general elections.

Chapter 11 (The Congress)—A new section on how the increased polarization of the members of Congress has led to new processes including the frequent threat of the filibuster and the ability of the majority to control the action of each respective house; new opening box, "What if Congress Had Time Limits?"; new coverage of recent judicial and executive appointments in the section on powers of the Senate; updated section on party control of Congress that reflects the outcome of the 2012 elections; a detailed illustration of redistricting after the 2010 census using the state of Ohio.

Chapter 12 (The President)—Updated opening box, "What if There Were No Executive Privilege?" that now includes coverage of communications in the Department of Justice's "Fast and Furious" operation; Beyond Our Borders box, "Do We Need a President *and* a King?" that has been brought up to date with regard to Putin and Medvedev; updated content on how the White House uses social media; and updated content about how President Obama created more than 40 positions in the Executive Office of the President to advise him on specific issue areas and to coordinate the work of cabinet departments.

Chapter 13 (The Bureaucracy)—New box, "What if Every Federal Agency Reported to the People?"; updated coverage of the issues facing the postal service; expanded and updated coverage of the practice of using private contractors in theaters of war.

Chapter 14 (The Courts)—Expanded section on the politics within the Supreme Court and the 2012 decisions on the Affordable Care Act and Arizona's immigration law; updated discussion of the decline in the number of cases heard by the Supreme Court.

Chapter 15 (Domestic Policy)—Refocused, as all policy chapters have been, to approach policymaking in difficult times, reflect the connection between domestic and global policy, and highlight why policy matters to students—all within the framework of past promises and future challenges; expanded environmental politics coverage, with even greater treatment of sustainability. In addition, the chapter is now framed in terms of the U.S. policy agenda and how it has changed over time; completely rewritten opening box, "What if We Had Universal Health Care?"; section on policy-making process that explains how the Affordable Care Act moved through the entire process of policymaking to policy evaluation; completely rewritten sections on environmental policy and the environmental movement; updates to content on the country's war on toxic emissions; new section on sustainability; updated section on global climate change; new section on energy policy that includes new figures, "U.S. Energy Consumption by Economic Sector, 2010" and "Sources of Electricity Generation, 2011"; updated content on nuclear power; updated content on American attempts at immigration reform; deleted section on crime in the 21st century; new section, "The Range of Federal Public Policies"; new box, "You Can Make a Difference: Doing Your Part: Sustain the Planet."

Chapter 16 (Economic Policy)—New opening discussion of the causes of the 2008 recession and economic collapse; rewritten and clarified discussion of the government's tools to influence economic prosperity; new section relating economic theories to policy decisions; expanded and updated section on globalization and world trade; and a new section on facing the future in the years following the recession.

Chapter 17 (Foreign Policy and National Security)—Early portion of the chapter reorganized to cover how Congress balances the presidency and domestic sources of foreign policy; new discussions of the concepts of moralist foreign policy and realist foreign policy; new map and discussion of the Mideast and the

Arab Spring; updated discussion of the war on terrorism and new discussion of the concept of "preemptive war"; updated discussion of the Iraq War and a new section on the "necessary" war in Afghanistan, including an analysis as each wound to an end; updated discussion of the United States and regional conflicts; new content on Hugo Chavez and Venezuela; and new coverage of recent conflicts in African nations.

Chapter 18 (State and Local Government)—Additional information on emergency management; update on different states' approaches to undocumented immigrants; new content on the recall process and the case of Governor Scott Walker of Wisconsin; updated table on state expenditures; updated discussion of state and local government revenue; expanded discussion on balancing state budgets.

The 2013–2014 edition of this text is the result of our working closely with reviewers, who each offered us penetrating criticisms, comments, and suggestions. Although we have not been able to take account of all requests, each of the reviewers listed will see many of his or her suggestions taken to heart:

Terri Towner
Oakland University

Dr. Elsa Dias
Pikes Peak Community College

Heather Ramsier
Valencia College

Zack Sullivan
Inver Hills Community College

Sharon Sykora
Slippery Rock University

Christopher Gilbert
Gustavus Adolphus College

Narges Rabii
Saddleback College

Chris Cooper
Western Carolina University

Daniel Sweeney
University of Scranton

Acknowledgments

Since we started this project several years ago, a sizable cadre of individuals has helped us in various phases of the undertaking. The following academic reviewers offered numerous constructive criticisms, comments, and suggestions during the preparation of all previous editions:

Krista Ackermann, Allan Hancock College

Martin J. Adamian, California State University, Los Angeles

Danny M. Adkison, Oklahoma State University, Stillwater

Ahrar Ahmad, Black Hills State University, Spearfish, South Dakota

Sharon Z. Alter, William Rainey Harper College, Palatine, Illinois

Hugh M. Arnold, Clayton College and State University, Morrow, Georgia

William Arp III, Louisiana State University, Baton Rouge

Kevin Bailey, North Harris Community College, Houston, Texas

Evelyn Ballard, Houston Community College, Texas

Orlando N. Bama, McLennan Community College, Waco, Texas

Dr. Charles T. Barber, University of Southern Indiana, Evansville

Clyde W. Barrow, Texas A&M University, College Station

Louis Battaglia, Erie Community College

Shari Garber Bax, Central Missouri State University, Warrensburg

Dr. Joshua G. Behr, Old Dominion University, Norfolk, Virginia

David S. Bell, Eastern Washington University, Cheney

David C. Benford, Jr., Tarrant County Junior College, Fort Worth, Texas

Teri Bengtson, Elmhurst College

Dr. Curtis Berry, Shippensburg University, Shippensburg, Pennsylvania

John A. Braithwaite, Coastline Community College, Fountain Valley, California

Lynn R. Brink, North Lake College, Irving, Texas

Barbara L. Brown, Southern Illinois University at Carbondale

Richard G. Buckner, Santa Fe Community College, New Mexico

Kenyon D. Bunch, Fort Lewis College, Durango, Colorado

Ralph Bunch, Portland State University, Oregon

Carol Cassell, University of Alabama, Tuscaloosa

Dewey Clayton, University of Louisville, Kentucky

Frank T. Colon, Lehigh University, Bethlehem, Pennsylvania

Frank J. Coppa, Union County College, Cranford, New Jersey

Irasema Coronado, University of Texas at El Paso

James B. Cottrill, Santa Clara University, California

Robert E. Craig, University of New Hampshire, Durham

Doris Daniels, Nassau Community College, Garden City, New York

Carolyn Grafton Davis, North Harris County College, Houston, Texas

Paul B. Davis, Truckee Meadows Community College, Reno, Nevada

Richard D. Davis, Brigham Young University, Salt Lake City, Utah

Ron Deaton, Prince George's Community College, Largo, Maryland

Marshall L. DeRosa, Louisiana State University, Baton Rouge

Michael Dinneen, Tulsa Junior College, Oklahoma

Gavan Duffy, University of Texas at Austin

Don Thomas Dugi, Transylvania University, Lexington, Kentucky

George C. Edwards III, Texas A&M University, College Station

Gregory Edwards, Amarillo College, Texas

Mark C. Ellickson, Southwestern Missouri State University, Springfield

Larry Elowitz, Georgia College, Milledgeville

Jodi Empol, Montgomery County Community College, Pennsylvania

John W. Epperson, Simpson College, Indianola, Indiana

Victoria A. Farrar-Myers, University of Texas at Arlington

Daniel W. Fleitas, University of North Carolina at Charlotte

Elizabeth N. Flores, Del Mar College, Corpus Christi, Texas

Joel L. Franke, Blinn College, Brenham, Texas

Barry D. Friedman, North Georgia College, Dahlonega

Robert S. Getz, SUNY–Brockport, New York

Kristina Gilbert, Riverside Community College, Riverside, California

William A. Giles, Mississippi State University, Starkville, Mississippi

Donald Gregory, Stephen F. Austin State University, Nacogdoches, Texas

Forest Grieves, University of Montana, Missoula

Dale Grimnitz, Normandale Community College, Bloomington, Minnesota

Paul-Henri Gurian, University of Georgia

Stefan D. Haag, Austin Community College, Texas

Justin Halpern, Northeastern State University, Muskogee, Oklahoma

Willie Hamilton, Mount San Jacinto College, San Jacinto, California

Matthew Hansel, McHenry County College, Crystal Lake, Illinois

Jean Wahl Harris, University of Scranton, Pennsylvania

David N. Hartman, Rancho Santiago College, Santa Ana, California

Robert M. Herman, Moorpark College, Moorpark, California

Richard J. Herzog, Stephen F. Austin State University, Nacogdoches, Texas

Paul Holder, McLennan Community College, Waco, Texas

Michael Hoover, Seminole Community College, Sanford, Florida

J. C. Horton, San Antonio College, Texas

Alice Jackson, Morgan State University, Baltimore, Maryland

Robert Jackson, Washington State University, Pullman

Willoughby Jarrell, Kennesaw State University, Kennesaw, Georgia

Loch K. Johnson, University of Georgia, Athens, Georgia

Donald L. Jordan, United States Air Force Academy, Colorado Springs, Colorado

John D. Kay, Santa Barbara City College, California

Charles W. Kegley, University of South Carolina, Columbia

Bruce L. Kessler, Shippensburg University, Shippensburg, Pennsylvania

Robert King, Georgia Perimeter College, Clarkston, Georgia

Jason F. Kirksey, Oklahoma State University, Stillwater

Nancy B. Kral, Tomball College, Tomball, Texas

Dale Krane, Mississippi State University, Starkville, Mississippi

Samuel Krislov, University of Minnesota, Minneapolis, Minnesota

William W. Lamkin, Glendale Community College, Glendale, California

Harry D. Lawrence, Southwest Texas Junior College, Uvalde, Texas

Ray Leal, Southwest Texas State University, San Marcos

Sue Lee, Center for Telecommunications, Dallas County Community College District, Texas

Alan Lehmann, Blinn College, Brenham, Texas

Terence Lenio, McHenry County College

Carl Lieberman, University of Akron, Ohio

Orma Linford, late, formerly of Kansas State University, Manhattan

James J. Lopach, University of Montana, Missoula, Montana

Eileen Lynch, Brookhaven College, Dallas, Texas

William W. Maddox, University of Florida, Gainesville, Florida

S. J. Makielski, Jr., Loyola University, New Orleans, Louisiana

Jarol B. Manheim, George Washington University, District of Columbia

J. David Martin, Midwestern State University, Wichita Falls, Texas

Susan J. Martin, Indiana University of Pennsylvania

Bruce B. Mason, Arizona State University, Tempe

Thomas Louis Masterson, Butte College, Oroville, California

Steve J. Mazurana, University of Northern Colorado, Greeley

James D. McElyea, Tulsa Junior College, Oklahoma

Thomas J. McGaghie, Kellogg Community College, Battle Creek, Michigan

William P. McLauchlan, Purdue University, West Lafayette, Indiana

Stanley Melnick, Valencia Community College, Orlando, Florida

Robert Mittrick, Luzerne County Community College, Nanticoke, Pennsylvania

Helen Molanphy, Richland College, Dallas, Texas

James Morrow, Tulsa Community College, Oklahoma

Jeanine Neher, Butte Glen Community College

Keith Nicholls, University of South Alabama, Mobile, Alabama

Sandra O'Brien, Florida Gulf Coast University, Fort Myers, Florida

Stephen Osofsky, Nassau Community College, Garden City, New York

John P. Pelissero, Loyola University of Chicago, Illinois

Neil A. Pinney, Western Michigan University, Kalamazoo

George E. Pippin, Jones County Community College, Ellisville, Mississippi

Walter V. Powell, Slippery Rock University, Slippery Rock, Pennsylvania

Michael A. Preda, Midwestern State University, Wichita Falls, Texas

Jeffrey L. Prewitt, Brewton-Parker College, Mt. Vernon, Georgia

Mark E. Priewe, University of Texas at San Antonio

Charles Prysby, University of North Carolina at Greensboro

Donald R. Ranish, Antelope Valley College, Lancaster, California

John D. Rausch, Fairmont State University, Fairmont, West Texas A&M

Renford Reese, California State Polytechnic University, Pomona

Curt Reichel, University of Wisconsin, Madison, Wisconsin

Russell D. Renka, Southeast Missouri State University, Cape Girardeau

Donna Rhea, Houston Community College—Northwest, Texas

Steven Rolnick, Western Connecticut State University

Paul Rozycki, Charles Stewart Mott Community College, Flint, Michigan

Bhim Sandhu, West Chester University, West Chester, Pennsylvania

Gregory Schaller, Villanova University, Villanova, Pennsylvania; and St. Joseph's University, Philadelphia, Pennsylvania

Pauline Schloesser, Texas Southern University, Houston

Eleanor A. Schwab, South Dakota State University, Brookings

Charles R. Shedlak, Ivy Tech State College, South Bend, Indiana

Len Shipman, Mount San Antonio College, Walnut, California

Scott Shrewsbury, Minnesota State University, Mankato

Alton J. Slane, Muhlenberg College, Allentown, Pennsylvania

Joseph L. Smith, Grand Valley State University, Allendale, Michigan

Michael W. Sonnlietner, Portland Community College, Oregon

Gilbert K. St. Clair, University of New Mexico

Robert E. Sterken, Jr., University of Texas, Tyler

Carol Stix, Pace University, Pleasantville, New York

Gerald S. Strom, University of Illinois at Chicago

Maxine Swaikowsky, Hubbard High School

Joseph Swarner, Garfield High School, Seattle, Washington

Regina Swopes, Northeastern Illinois University, Chicago

John R. Todd, North Texas State University, Denton, Texas

Ron Velton, Grayson County College, Denison, Texas

Richard Vollmer, Oklahoma City Community College, Oklahoma

Albert C. Waite, Central Texas College, Killeen, Texas

Benjamin Walter, Vanderbilt University, Nashville, Tennessee

B. Oliver Walter, University of Wyoming, Laramie

Mark J. Wattier, Murray State University, Murray, Kentucky

Stella Webster, Wayne County Community College—Downtown, Detroit, Michigan

Paul Weizer, Fitchburg State College, Fitchburg, Massachusetts

Thomas L. Wells, Old Dominion University, Norfolk, Virginia

Jean B. White, Weber State College, Ogden, Utah

Lance Widman, El Camino College, Torrance, California

Allan Wiese, Minnesota State University, Mankato

J. David Woodard, Clemson University, Columbia, South Carolina

Robert D. Wrinkle, Pan American University, Edinburg, Texas

In preparing this edition of *American Government and Politics Today*, we were the beneficiaries of the expert guidance of a skilled and dedicated team of publishers and editors. We would like, first of all, to thank Sean Wakely, executive vice president, Cengage Arts & Sciences, for the support he has shown for this project. We have benefited greatly from the supervision and encouragement given by Carolyn Merrill, executive editor; and P. J. Boardman, editor-in-chief.

Jennifer Jacobson at Ohlinger Publishing Services, our developmental editor, also deserves our thanks for her many aspects of project development. We are also indebted to editorial assistant Eireann Aspell, and previously Scott Greenan, for their contributions to this project.

We are grateful to Josh Allen, our content production manager, Amber Allen, managing editor at Integra Software Services, and Linda May, for a remarkable design and for making it possible to get the text out on time. In addition, our gratitude goes to all of those who worked on the various supplements offered with this text, especially Laura Hildebrand, who coordinated the media. We would also like to thank Lydia Lestar, marketing manager, for her tremendous efforts in marketing the text.

Any errors remain our own. We welcome comments from instructors and students alike. Suggestions that we have received in the past have helped us to improve this text and to adapt it to the changing needs of instructors and students.

STEFFEN SCHMIDT • MACK SHELLEY • BARBARA BARDES • LYNNE E. FORD

About the Authors

STEFFEN W. SCHMIDT

Steffen W. Schmidt is a professor of political science at Iowa State University. He grew up in Colombia, South America, and studied in Colombia, Switzerland, and France. He obtained his PhD from Columbia University, New York, in public law and government.

Schmidt has published 12 books and more than 122 journal articles. He is the recipient of numerous prestigious teaching prizes, including the Amoco Award for Lifetime Career Achievement in Teaching and the Teacher of the Year award. He is a pioneer in the use of Web-based and real-time video courses and is a member of the American Political Science Association's section on computers and multimedia. He is on the editorial board of the *Political Science Educator* and is the technology and teaching editor of the *Journal of Political Science Education*.

Schmidt has a political talk show on WOI Public Radio, where he is known as Dr. Politics, streaming live once a week at **www.woi.org**. The show has been broadcast live from various U.S. and international venues for 17 years. Schmidt is a frequent on-air commentator for U.S. elections on CNN en Español. He is the cofounder, associate editor, and chief political and foreign correspondent for a new Internet magazine, InsiderIowa.com.

MACK C. SHELLEY II

Mack C. Shelley II is a professor of political science and statistics at Iowa State University. His BA is from American University in Washington, DC; he received his MA and PhD at the University of Wisconsin–Madison. After two years at Mississippi State University, he arrived at Iowa State in 1979. He has served as co-editor of the *Policy Studies Journal* and has numerous publications on public policy, including *The Permanent Majority: The Conservative Coalition in the United States Congress; Biotechnology and the Research Enterprise* (with William F. Woodman and Brian J. Reichel); *American Public Policy: The Contemporary Agenda* (with Steven G. Koven and Bert E. Swanson); and *Quality Research in Literacy and Science Education: International Perspectives and Gold Standards* (with Larry Yore and Brian Hand).

BARBARA A. BARDES

Barbara A. Bardes is professor *emerita* of political science and former dean of Raymond Walters College at the University of Cincinnati. She received her BA and MA from Kent State University and her PhD from the University of Cincinnati. She held a faculty position at Loyola University in Chicago for many years before returning to Cincinnati, her hometown, as a college administrator. Bardes has written articles on public opinion and foreign policy and on women and politics. She also has authored *Thinking about Public Policy* and *Declarations of Independence: Women and Political Power in Nineteenth Century American Fiction* and co-authored *Public Opinion: Measuring the American Mind*.

LYNNE E. FORD

Lynne E. Ford is professor of political science and associate provost for curriculum and academic administration at the College of Charleston in Charleston, South Carolina. She received her BA from The Pennsylvania State University and her MA and PhD in government and political behavior from the University of Maryland–College Park.

Ford's teaching and research interests include women and politics, elections and voting behavior, political psychology, and civic engagement. She has written articles on women in state legislatures, the underrepresentation of women in political office in the American South, and work-family policy in the United States. She has also authored *Women and Politics: The Pursuit of Equality* and *The Encyclopedia of Women and American Politics*. Ford served as department chair for eight years and she has led a number of campuswide initiatives, including reform of general education and faculty compensation, and civic engagement.

1 One Republic— Two Americas?

In April 2012, One World Trade Center reached a height of 1,271 feet, making it once again the tallest building in New York City. The tower, built at Ground Zero of the September 11, 2001, terrorist attacks, was designed to represent the resilience of the American spirit. Although the building will not be completed until 2014, the design includes a mast that would bring its total height to 1,776 feet.

AFP/Getty Images/Newscom

LEARNING OUTCOMES

After reading this chapter, students will be able to:

■ **LO1** Define the institution of government and the process of politics.

■ **LO2** Identify the political philosophers associated with the "social contract," and explain how this theory shapes our understanding of the purpose of government and the role for individuals and communities in the United States.

■ **LO3** Describe the U.S. political culture, and identify the set of ideas, values, and ways of thinking about government and politics shared by all.

■ **LO4** Compare and contrast types of government systems, and identify the source of power in each.

■ **LO5** Define political ideology, and locate socialism, liberalism, conservatism, and libertarianism along the ideological spectrum.

1

What If...

TAXES NEVER INCREASED AND LOCAL SERVICES DISAPPEARED?

BACKGROUND

The power to tax and spend is a defining function of government. Taxation is a concurrent power, meaning that the federal, state, and local governments can all collect taxes. Taxes on property, goods and services, and income provide revenue for government to operate. Dating back to the earliest days of the republic, the government's power to tax has provoked strong negative reactions. The Boston Tea Party in 1773, the Whiskey Rebellion in 1794, and California's 1978 Proposition 13, known as the "People's Initiative to Limit Property Taxation," are all examples of popular rebellions. More recently, the Tea Party protests have brought attention to questions about the government's power to tax and the appropriate size and role of government. In the 2010 elections, many fiscally conservative candidates promised to eliminate tax increases and shrink the size of government. In reality, eliminating tax increases means cutting state and local budgets and eliminating services that people have come to expect. How should communities respond? What happens to schools, roads, police and fire protection, and other public services when local governments can no longer afford to pay for them?

TAXES PAY FOR LOCAL SERVICES WE EXPECT

The tax system allows government to redistribute revenue in a variety of ways. For example, intergovernmental transfers provide money collected by state and federal governments to local governments, accounting for roughly 40 percent of local operating dollars. Cities and towns make up the rest of their budget through property taxes, local sales taxes, and various user fees and charges. In an economic recession, people buy fewer goods and services. This means that local governments collect less revenue from sales taxes and need to make up the deficit by other means or cut budgets. Local budget cuts often mean that services to citizens are dramatically reduced or eliminated altogether.

Local governments—counties and cities—usually take responsibility for parks and recreation services, police and fire departments, housing services, emergency medical services, municipal courts, transportation services (including public transportation), and public works (streets, sewers, trash collection, snow removal, and signage).

NO TAXES, NO SERVICES: TOUGH CHOICES

In conservative Colorado Springs, Colorado, home of the "Taxpayer's Bill of Rights," voters rejected a tax increase to restore a budget deficit caused by declining sales tax revenues. The city turned off one-third of its streetlights to save electricity costs. The city also locked public restrooms, reduced bus service, and stopped maintaining the city parks.

In New Jersey, Republican governor Chris Christie cut $3 billion from the state budget in his first two years in office. As a result, Trenton, New Jersey, fired one-third of the police force (103 officers). Between January 2011 and January 2012, gun-related assaults increased by 76 percent, robberies with a firearm increased by 55 percent, car thefts more than doubled, and break-ins more than tripled. The domestic violence unit was eliminated.

In Kansas, when the Shawnee County district attorney's office announced that in order to save money it would no longer prosecute misdemeanor cases, including domestic violence, the city council of Topeka feared that it would be forced to pick up the costs of prosecution. Facing its own budget crisis, the council considered decriminalizing domestic battery to avoid paying the costs of prosecution.

FOR CRITICAL ANALYSIS

1. *The U.S. tax system is designed to collect and redistribute revenue. Public goods and services paid for by tax revenue are therefore available to all in most cases (police protection, snow removal) or to those in the community who qualify because of special needs (legal aid to the poor, Medicaid). Some services or facilities are financed with "user fees." In other words, you pay only for what you as an individual use (toll roads, parking meters). Consider the local government services just mentioned. In your view, is it better to pay for each with tax revenue or user fees? How does your answer relate to your perspective on the appropriate role for government?*

2. *Although we all live in the same country, will choices about who has access to public goods and services mean that we are creating two Americas? What kind of country do you want to live in?*

ALTHOUGH IT HAS BECOME POPULAR to complain about government, we could not survive as individuals or as communities without it. The challenge for you as an individual, and for us as a society, is to become invested enough in the American system and engaged enough in the political process so that the government we have is the government we want and deserve. This is a tremendous challenge because, until you understand how our system works, "the government" can seem like it belongs to somebody else; it can seem distant, hard to understand, and difficult to use when there is a problem to solve or hard decisions to make. Nevertheless, democracies, especially this democracy, derive their powers from the people, and this fact provides each of you with a tremendous opportunity. Individuals and groups of like-minded individuals who participate in the system can create change and shape the government to meet their needs. Those who opt not to pay attention or fail to participate must accept what others decide for them—good or bad.

Complicating matters further is the simple truth that although we all live in the same country and share the same political system, we may experience government differently. This leads us to hold different opinions about how big or small government should be, what kind of role government should play in our individual daily lives, what kinds of issues are appropriate for policymakers to handle, and what should be left to each of us alone.

For example, let's look at the arguments over health care and health insurance. At the heart of this complicated debate is the question of how best to pay for and provide access to health care for every citizen. In 2009, this country's federal, state, and local governments, corporations, and individuals spent $2.5 trillion, or about $8,047 a person, on health care.[1] Health insurance costs are rising faster than wages or inflation. Costs like this are not sustainable and drain the economy of resources needed elsewhere. The Patient Protection and Affordable Care Act was signed into law in 2010, although many of its provisions will take five years to implement. The Affordable Care Act is large and complicated because the issue is large and complicated.

Several aspects of the law are favored by nearly everyone, such as providing access to insurance for people with pre-existing conditions or allowing children to stay on their parents' insurance until age 26. However, the law also requires people to be insured, either through their employer or by purchasing insurance, so that the costs and risks are spread across the entire population. Failure to do so results in a penalty. The law's insurance mandate seems at odds with the value we place on individual responsibility; yet health care is something everyone requires, and the costs are more manageable if everyone is included.

We resolve these and other conflicting values using the political process, and institutions of government are empowered to make decisions on our behalf. In the case of health care, the conflict has been resolved by the judiciary. The U.S. Supreme Court scheduled an unprecedented six hours of oral arguments over the course of three days in March 2012. The justices faced a number of critical questions including whether or not the law's requirement that individuals carry health insurance was within the powers granted to Congress in the constitution. On June 28, 2012, the Supreme Court issued a 5-4 decision upholding nearly all of the health care law,[2] including the minimum coverage provision. Chief Justice John Roberts wrote the majority opinion. President Obama called the ruling "a victory for people all over this country whose lives will be more secure" since

did you know?

The Greek philosopher Aristotle favored enlightened despotism over democracy, which to him meant mob rule.

---

1. Centers for Medicare and Medicaid Services, accessed at www.cms.gov.
2. National Federation of Independent Business, et. al. v. Sebelious, Secretary of Health and Human Services, et.al. 567 U.S. ___ (2012)

nearly 30 million Americans who currently lack health insurance will eventually be covered as a result of the law.

Sir Winston Churchill, British prime minister during World War II, once said, "No one pretends that democracy is perfect or all-wise. Indeed, it has been said that democracy is the worst form of government except all those other forms that have been tried from time to time."[3] Our system isn't perfect, but it is more open to change than most. This book, along with your instructor and your course, offers essential tools to learn about American government and politics today so that you are prepared to take your place among the many people who have changed this country for the better.

What are your dreams for the future, and what role do you believe the government can and should play in helping you realize your dreams? There was a time when we all aspired to live the "American Dream"—when we believed that government played an essential role in ensuring that the opportunity to achieve the American Dream was available to everyone. Members of each successive generation brimmed with confidence that if they worked hard and followed the rules, they would live richer and more successful lives than the generation before them. Public policy has historically been an effective tool to promote economic growth, educational equity, homeownership, and job security. Is that still true today?

There are some troubling signs, to be sure. Significant inequality in income and wealth exists in the United States, and rather than shrinking, the gap has widened for your generation and your parents' generation. In 1979, the richest 1 percent accounted for 8 percent of all personal income; by 2010, their share had more than doubled, to 17.4 percent.[4] The global economic recession, the unemployment rate, rising home foreclosures, and corporate relocation of jobs overseas all present government with significant challenges. Moreover, people's trust in nearly all institutions (government, media, banks, business, churches, and organized labor) has fallen over the past decade (see Figure 1-1 on page 7). Native-born citizens know less than ever about the very political system they hope will restore their confidence in the future; one in three failed the civics portion of the naturalization test (answering only 6 of 10 questions correctly) in a national telephone survey.[5] Can people effectively engage in political activity to change their lives for the better when they know so little about the governmental system?

There are also some hopeful signs. According to the Center for the Study of the American Dream at Xavier University, a majority of Americans surveyed (63%) remain confident that they will achieve the American Dream despite the current challenges. More than 75 percent believe they have already achieved some measure of it. Those surveyed defined the American Dream in terms of a good life for their family (45%), financial security (34%), freedom (32%), opportunity (29%), the pursuit of happiness (21%), a good job (16%), and homeownership (7%). How does this definition fit with your own? Are you surprised that homeownership is last on the list? How might the mortgage crisis and the persistent economic recession influence how we define our future dreams? Interestingly, the study found that Latinos and immigrants are most positive about the possibility of achieving the American Dream and are more optimistic about the future of the country than the population as a whole. Finally, a majority of Americans view immigration as an important part of keeping the American Dream alive and believe that immigration continues to be one of America's greatest strengths.

3. House of Commons speech on November 11, 1947.
4. Facundo Aleredo, Tony Atkinson, Thomas Piketty, and Emannuel Saez, "The World Top Incomes Database," accessed at http://g-mond.parisschoolofeconomics.eu/topincomes/#Home
5. "U.S. Naturalization Civics Test: National Survey of Native-Born U.S. Citizens, March 2012," conducted by the Center for the Study of the American Dream, Xavier University, accessed at http://www.xavier.edu/americandream/programs/National-Civic-Literacy-Survey.cfm

What is the state of America today? Given the economic and educational disparities evident in the United States today, are we one America or two? Are you confident that your life will be better than that of your parents and grandparents? Can the problems we face as a nation today be addressed by the political system? Is the American republic up to today's challenges? These will be central questions in our analysis of American government and politics today.

Politics and Government

Before we can answer any of these provocative questions, we have to define some terms. For example, what is politics? **Politics** is the process of resolving conflicts and deciding "who gets what, when, and how."[6] Although politics may be found in many places outside of government (for example, in your family or your workplace), for the purposes of this book, when we talk about politics we are referring to conflicts and decisions found at the federal, state, and local levels regarding the selection of decision makers, the structure of institutions, and the creation of public policy. Politics is particularly intense when decisions are made that hit close to home, such as decisions about how to spend local and state tax dollars (see the What if? feature that opened the chapter). Equally intense are political decisions that yield leaders for our country. Elections at the national and state levels attract the most media attention, but thousands of elected and appointed officials make up the government and render decisions that impact our lives.

What is the government? **Government** is the term used to describe the formal **institutions** through which decisions about the allocation of resources are made and conflicts are resolved. Government can take many forms, come in many sizes, and perform a variety of functions, but at the core, all governments rule. To govern is to rule. Governments can, as a matter of their authority, force you to comply with laws through taxes, fines, and the power to send you to prison. The inherent power of government is what led the founders of the United States system to impose limitations on the power of government relative to the rights of individuals. Likewise, the power of government leads Americans to be wary of too much government when less will do.

Why Is Government Necessary?

Americans may not always like government, but they like the absence of government even less. Governments are necessary at a minimum to provide public goods and services that all citizens need but cannot reasonably be expected to provide for themselves. National security and defense are obvious examples. But governments do far more than provide for the common defense. As you will learn in Chapter 2, our founding documents such as the Declaration of Independence and the Constitution are predicated upon and convey through their language a set of shared political values. Government reinforces those values regularly. For example, one of our defining values is belief in the rule of law. By this we mean that laws determined through the political process are enforced uniformly and that no individual, regardless of wealth, privilege, or position, is above the law. Government includes a system of justice administered by institutions known as the courts to maintain this important value. We will return to this discussion of fundamental values later in this chapter. In addition to providing public goods and services and reinforcing shared values, governments are necessary to provide security so that liberty may flourish.

■ **Learning Outcome 1:**
Define the institution of government and the process of politics.

Politics
The process of resolving conflicts and deciding "who gets what, when, and how." More specifically, politics is the struggle over power or influence within organizations or informal groups that can grant or withhold benefits or privileges.

Government
The preeminent institution in which decisions are made that resolve conflicts or allocate benefits and privileges. It is unique because it has the ultimate authority within society.

Institution
An ongoing organization that performs certain functions for society.

■ **Learning Outcome 2:**
Identify the political philosophers associated with the "social contract," and explain how this theory shapes our understanding of the purpose of government and the role for individuals and communities in the United States.

---

6. Harold Lasswell, *Politics: Who Gets What, When, and How* (New York: McGraw-Hill, 1936).

Divine Right of Kings
A political and religious doctrine that asserts a monarch's legitimacy is conferred directly by God and as such a king is not subject to any earthly authority, including his people or the church.

Social Contract
A theory of politics that asserts that individuals form political communities by a process of mutual consent, giving up a measure of their individual liberty in order to gain the protection of government.

Our contemporary understanding of why government is necessary has been shaped by Enlightenment thinkers from 17th and 18th-century Europe. During the Age of Enlightenment, also known as the Age of Reason, philosophers and scientists challenged the **divine right of kings** and argued that the world could be vastly improved through the use of human reason, science, and religious tolerance. Essential to this argument was the belief that all individuals were born free and equal, and imbued with natural rights. Individuals were in control of their own destiny, and by working with others, a society could shape a government capable of both asserting and protecting individual rights. English **social contract** theorists such as Thomas Hobbes (1588–1679) and John Locke (1632–1704) were particularly influential in shaping our theory of government. Hobbes was far more pessimistic about human nature than Locke. Hobbes believed that without government and the rule of law, people would revert to a state of nature, and individuals would be left to fight over basic necessities, rendering life "solitary, poor, nasty, brutish, and short."[7] To avoid such a fate, Hobbes argued for a single ruler, a Leviathan, so powerful that the rights of the weak could be protected against intrusion by the strong. By contrast, John Locke had a more positive view of human nature. He took basic survival for granted, believing that all humans were endowed with reason— an internal code of conduct. Therefore, individuals are willing to give up a portion of their individual liberty in order to gain the protection of government through the social contract. Government is formed to protect life, liberty, and property; however, if a government compromises its legitimacy by violating the social contract, it is the people's duty to end the abusive government and replace it with a new form.

It is within this theoretical framework that we understand the necessity for government: to provide security, to protect liberty and enforce property rights, and to maintain legitimacy by exercising authority consistent with the fundamental values of those governed. Consent of the governed is the basis for power and legitimacy in American democracy.

Fundamental Values

■ **Learning Outcome 3:**
Describe the U.S. political culture, and identify the set of ideas, values, and ways of thinking about government and politics shared by all.

The authors of the American Constitution believed that the structures they had created would provide for both democracy and a stable political system. They also believed that the nation could be sustained by its **political culture**—the set of ideas, values, and ways of thinking about government and politics that are shared by all citizens. A critical question facing America today is to what extent do all citizens continue to share in a single political culture? Does the widening wealth and income gap threaten to undermine our shared political values as well as our confidence in government? We live under one republic, but are we increasingly two Americas? There is considerable consensus among American citizens about concepts basic to the U.S. political system. Given that the population of the United States is made up primarily of immigrants and descendants of immigrants with diverse cultural and political backgrounds, how can we account for this consensus? Primarily, it is the result of **political socialization**—the process by which beliefs and values are transmitted to successive generations. The nation depends on families, schools, houses of worship, and the media to transmit the precepts of our national culture. With fewer people going to church and a widening educational gap that strongly correlates with economic disparities, we may need to reexamine the ways in which our political culture is transmitted. On the other hand, you can find these fundamental values reaffirmed in most major public speeches given by the president and other important officials in American politics.

Political Culture
The set of ideas, values, and ways of thinking about government and politics that is shared by all citizens.

Political Socialization
The process through which individuals learn a set of political attitudes and form opinions about social issues. Families and the educational system are two of the most important forces in the political socialization process.

---

7. Hobbes, Leviathan: Revised student edition (Cambridge Texts in the History of Political Thought) Cambridge University Press; Rev Stu edition (August 28, 1996)

Confidence in Institutions Declines: How Do We Know?

Figure 1–1 ▶ Confidence in Institutions Declines

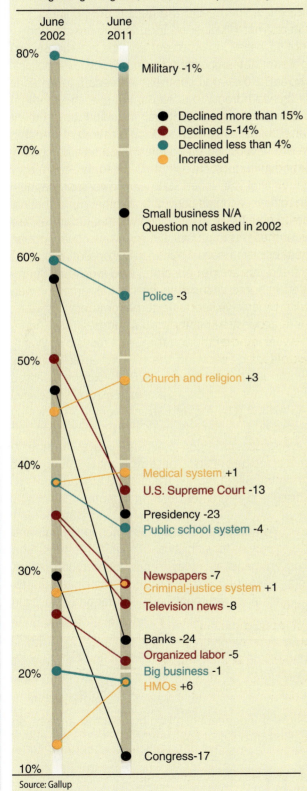

Gallup polling shows a loss in faith in institutions in the past 10 years, including steep declines regarding Congress, bank, and the presidency.

June 2002   June 2011

80%

Military -1%

- ● Declined more than 15%
- ● Declined 5-14%
- ● Declined less than 4%
- ● Increased

70%

Small business N/A
Question not asked in 2002

60%

Police -3

50%

Church and religion +3

Medical system +1
U.S. Supreme Court -13

40%

Presidency -23
Public school system -4

Newspapers -7
Criminal-justice system +1
Television news -8

30%

Banks -24
Organized labor -5
Big business -1
HMOs +6

20%

Congress-17

10%

Source: Gallup

Throughout this book, you will find a number of visual features including figures, tables, photographs, and political cartoons. These visual features are carefully selected to present information that is critical to your understanding of the content in each chapter. Therefore, you must study the visuals carefully. In addition, you may be tested on this information.

The figure to the left presents Gallup polling data on the public's loss of confidence in major institutions at two points in time. (Gallup Poll regularly conducts public opinion polls in more than 140 countries around the world. You'll often see these polls referenced in the mass media.) Begin by reading the title of the figure and the descriptive information—the caption—right below the title. Together, the title and caption summarize the information that you need in order to understand the graphic. Captions below photographs and cartoons have a similar function. Figure 1—1 shows two points in time, indicating a change in public attitudes. Other ways to show change over time include line graphs.

This figure communicates a lot of information. On the left vertical axis, you will find the scale indicating the percentage of people who express a great deal or quite a lot of confidence in each institution. To display the magnitude of the change (decline or increase) in confidence, the authors have used four colors. The key for the colors is found on the right, near the top. Yellow, for example, represents an increase in confidence. Black indicates the most dramatic loss of confidence in the institution between 2002 and 2011. Read the graphic starting on the left and moving to the right and follow the line connecting the two dots. Like many figures, tables, and photographs, this visual presents you with descriptive data. Descriptive information provides an answer to *what* or *who* questions but does not typically answer *why* or *how* questions. Analysis (determining why or how) is a form of critical thinking. The accompanying text may provide theories or results from other research, and sometimes you will find questions for critical anlaysis. Synthesizing all of the information to create a new explanation or understanding is the most important skill you can develop in college.

© Win McNamee/Getty Images

Secretary of Homeland Security Janet Napolitano testifies before a congressional committee.

Liberty
The greatest freedom of individuals that is consistent with the freedom of other individuals in the society.

Order
A state of peace and security. Maintaining order by protecting members of society from violence and criminal activity is the oldest purpose of government.

We will return to these important questions throughout the book, but particularly in Chapter 6.

Liberty. As you recall, the advancement and protection of individual liberty is central to the social contract theory of government. **Liberty** is among the natural rights articulated by John Locke and later by Thomas Jefferson in the Declaration of Independence ("life, liberty, and the pursuit of happiness"). In the United States, our civil liberties include religious freedom—both the right to believe in whatever religion we choose and freedom from any state-imposed religion. Liberty, as a political value, has two sides to it—one positive (the freedom to) and one negative (the freedom from). The freedom of speech—the right to political expression on all matters, including government actions—is an example of a positive liberty. Freedom of speech is perhaps one of our most prized liberties, because a democracy could not endure without it. The right to privacy is a more controversial liberty claim. The United States Supreme Court has held that the right to privacy can be derived from other rights that are explicitly stated in the Bill of Rights. The Supreme Court has also held that under the right to privacy, the government cannot ban either abortion[8] or private sexual behavior by consenting adults.[9]

Positive freedoms are not absolute, and individual liberty can be limited in some circumstances such as times of war. When Americans perceive serious external or internal threats, they have supported government actions to limit individual liberties in the name of national security. Such limits were imposed during the Civil War, World War II, and the McCarthy era of the Cold War. Following the terrorist attacks on the World Trade Center and the Pentagon on September 11, 2001, Congress passed legislation designed to provide greater security at the expense of some civil liberties. In particular, the USA PATRIOT (Uniting and Strengthening America by Providing Appropriate Tools Required to Intercept and Obstruct Terrorism) Act gave law enforcement and intelligence-gathering agencies greater latitude to search out and investigate suspected terrorists. These and many other basic guarantees of liberty are found in the Bill of Rights, the first 10 amendments to the Constitution, and will be discussed in greater detail in Chapter 4.

Order and the Rule of Law. As noted earlier in this chapter, individuals and communities create governments to provide for stability and order in their lives. John Locke justified the creation of governments as a way to protect every individual's property rights and to organize a system of impartial justice. In the United States, laws passed by local, state, and national governments create order and stability in every aspect of life, ranging from traffic to business to a national defense system. Citizens expect these laws to create a society in which individuals can pursue opportunities and live their lives in peace and prosperity. People also expect the laws to be just and to apply to everyone equally. However, the goal of maintaining **order** and security can sometimes run counter to the values of liberty and equality.

Individualism. The Declaration of Independence begins with a statement on the importance of the individual in our political culture: "When in the Course of

---

8. Roe v. Wade, 410 U.S. 113 (1973).
9. Lawrence v. Texas, 539 U.S. 558 (2003).

human events, it becomes necessary for one people to dissolve the political bands which have connected them with one another, and to assume among the Powers of the earth, the separate and equal station to which the Laws of Nature and of Nature's God entitle them,..." By a "separate and equal station," Jefferson was distinguishing the belief in the rationality and autonomy of individuals from the traditions of aristocracies and other systems in which individuals did not determine their own destiny. Individualism asserts that one of the primary functions of government is to enable individuals' opportunities for personal fulfillment and development. In political terms, individualism limits claims by groups in favor of the individual. Therefore, it should come as no surprise that a universal right to health care is not a part of the American constitution.

Equality. Thomas Jefferson wrote in the Declaration of Independence, "We hold these truths to be self-evident, that all men are created equal...." The proper meaning of equality, however, has been disputed by Americans since the Revolution.[10] Much of American history—and world history—is the story of how the value of **equality** has been extended and elaborated.

Political equality reflects the value we place on the individual. At our founding, political leaders excluded some people from the broad understanding of a politically autonomous person. African Americans, women, Native Americans, and most men who did not own property were excluded from the equal extension of political rights. Under a social contract theory of government, individuals must freely enter the compact with others on an equal basis. Although Enlightenment philosophers believed in the inherent equality of all persons, they did not define all individuals as full persons. Recall that the Constitution counted slaves as three-fifths of a person, for example. For a period of our history, a married woman was indivisible from her husband and could not act as a full person.[11] Today, of course, we believe all people are entitled to equal political rights as well as the opportunities for personal development provided by equal access to education and employment. In reality we still have work to do to be sure that opportunities afforded by society and protected by government can be fully realized by everyone in society.

Recently some cultural observers and scholars have begun to question whether political and social equality can coexist with economic inequality. In a book titled *Why Nations Fail*, Massachusettts Institute of Technology economist Daron Acemoglu argues that "when economic inequality increases, the people who have become economically more powerful will often attempt to use that power in order to gain even more political power. And once they are able to monopolize political power, they will start using that for changing the rules in their favor."[12] Many people point to the U.S. Supreme Court's decision in *Citizens United v. Federal Election Committee*[13] and the growth in Super PAC spending in federal elections as evidence of the growing political influence of a few very wealthy individuals and interests. According to Alan Krueger, chairman of President Obama's Council of Economic Advisers, the size of the middle class has steadily declined over the last three decades. Whereas in 1970 a little over half of all American households had an

Equality
As a political value, the idea that all people are of equal worth.

© Library of Congress, Prints & Photographs Division, U.S. News & World Report Magazine Collection [LC-U9- 10363-5]

A high point of the civil rights movement of the 1950s and 1960s was the March on Washington on August 28, 1963, led by Martin Luther King, Jr. Nearly 250,000 people participated in the event. The following year, Congress passed the Civil Rights Act of 1964, one of the most important civil rights acts in the nation's history. Why does the mandate of equal treatment for all groups of Americans sometimes come into conflict with the concept of liberty?

10. Gary B. Nash, *The Unknown American Revolution: The Unruly Birth of Democracy and the Struggle to Create America* (New York: Viking, 2005); and Alfred F. Young, ed., *Beyond the American Revolution: Explorations in the History of American Radicalism* (DeKalb, IL: Northern Illinois University Press, 1993).
11. British Common Law known as "coverture" meant that once married, a woman's identity was "covered" by her husband's, leaving her no independent rights.
12. Acemoglu, Daron and James Robinson. *Why Nations Fail: Power, Prosperity, and Poverty.* New York: Crown Publishers, 2012.
13. 558 U.S. 08-205 (2010)

income within 50 percent of the median, today the figure is just over 40 percent. Put differently, the share of all income accruing to the top 1 percent increased by 13.5 percent from 1979 to 2007. This is the equivalent of shifting $1.1 trillion of annual income to the top 1 percent of families. More troubling, as income inequality has increased, year-to-year and generation-to-generation economic mobility (the opportunity to improve one's economic standing) has declined. Can the values of political and social equality withstand the significant erosion of economic equality that has accompanied the great recession? What will this mean for you as you contemplate your role as a political and economic citizen in the United States? Civil rights and the value of equality will be discussed further in Chapter 5.

Property. The value of reducing economic inequality is in conflict with the right to **property**. This is because reducing economic inequality typically involves the transfer of property (usually in the form of money) from some people to others. For many people, liberty and property are closely entwined. A capitalist system is based on private property rights. Under **capitalism**, property consists not only of personal possessions but also of wealth-creating assets, such as farms and factories. The investor-owned corporation is in many ways the preeminent capitalist institution. The funds invested by the owners of a corporation are known as *capital*—hence, the very name of the system. Capitalism is also typically characterized by considerable freedom to make binding contracts and by relatively unconstrained markets for goods, services, and investments. Property—especially wealth-creating property—can be seen as giving its owner political power and the liberty to do whatever he or she wants. At the same time, the ownership of property immediately creates inequality in society. The desire to own property, however, is so widespread among all classes of Americans that egalitarian movements have had a difficult time securing a wide following here.

As with the other values shaping our political culture, even individual property rights are not absolute. **Eminent domain** allows government to take private land for public use in return for just compensation. Weighing the public's interest against the interest of private landowners is a delicate political judgment. Typically, eminent domain is used to acquire land for roads, bridges, and other public works projects. However, a 2005 Supreme Court ruling allowed the city of New London, Connecticut, to "take" homeowners' property and turn it over to private developers, who used the land to build an office park and expensive condominiums.[14] In this atypical case, the majority ruled that economic stimulus and the increase in city tax revenues fulfilled the public use requirement for eminent domain takings. Since the ruling, several state and local governments have passed laws to forbid the kind of takings at issue in this case.

Why Choose Democracy?

Today, 196 nations exist in the world. Nearly all have some form of government that possesses authority and some degree of legitimacy. Governments vary in their structure and how they govern. The crucial question for every nation is who controls the government. The answer could be a small group, one person—perhaps the monarch or a dictator—or no one.

At one extreme is a society governed by a **totalitarian regime**. In such a political system, a small group of leaders or a single individual—a dictator—makes all political decisions for the society. North Korea is an example of a totalitarian state. Citizens are deprived of the freedom to speak, to dissent, to assemble, and

---

Property
Anything that is or may be subject to ownership. As conceived by the political philosopher John Locke, the right to property is a natural right superior to human law (laws made by government).

Capitalism
An economic system characterized by the private ownership of wealth-creating assets, free markets, and freedom of contract.

Eminent Domain
A power set forth in the Fifth Amendment to the U.S. Constitution that allows government to take private property for public use under the condition that just compensation is offered to the landowner.

■ **Learning Outcome 4:**
Compare and contrast types of government systems, and identify the source of power in each.

Totalitarian Regime
A form of government that controls all aspects of the political and social life of a nation.

---

14. Kelo v. City of New London, 545 U.S. 469 (2005).

ANDRE PAIN/EPA/Landov

to seek solutions to problems. Individual needs, including food, are subsumed by the interests of the ruler and the regime. Famine, widespread malnutrition, and illness exist as a result of the country's "military first" policy. Running afoul of the regime can often mean imprisonment or death. The death of Kim Jong Il in 2011 is unlikely to bring change as he is succeeded by his son, Kim Jong Un, continuing an unbroken 63-year reign that began with Kim Jong Il's father, Kim Il Sung. Totalitarianism is an extreme form of authoritarianism.

Authoritarianism is also characterized by highly concentrated and centralized power maintained by political repression. Authoritarianism differs from totalitarianism in that only the government is fully controlled by the ruler, leaving social and economic institutions to outside control. The contemporary government of China is often described as authoritarian. China is ruled by a single political party, the Communist Party. Policies are made by Communist Party leaders without input from the general population. The Chinese market economy is expanding rapidly with little government intrusion or regulations, but signs of political dissent are punished severely. Internet access is monitored and political content restricted.

Many of our terms for describing the distribution of political power are derived from the ancient Greeks, who were the first Western people to study politics systematically. One form of rule by the few was known as **aristocracy**, literally meaning "rule by the best." In practice, this meant rule by leading members of wealthy families who were, in theory, the best educated and dedicated to the good of the state. The ancient Greeks had another term for rule by the few, **oligarchy**, which means rule by a small group for corrupt and self-serving purposes.

The Greek term for rule by the people was **democracy**, which means that the authority of the government is granted to it from the people as a whole. Within the limits of their culture, some of the Greek city-states operated as democracies. Today, in much of the world, the people will not grant legitimacy to a government unless it is based on democracy.

If totalitarianism is control of all aspects of society by the government, **anarchy** is the complete opposite. It means that there is no government at all. Each individual or family in a society decides for itself how it will behave, and there is no institution with the authority to keep order in any way. As you can imagine, examples of anarchy do not last very long. A state of anarchy may

Authoritarianism
A type of regime in which only the government is fully controlled by the ruler. Social and economic institutions exist that are not under the government's control.

Aristocracy
Rule by "the best"; in reality, rule by an upper class.

Oligarchy
Rule by the few in their own interests.

Democracy
A system of government in which political authority is vested in the people. Derived from the Greek words *demos* ("the people") and *kratos* ("authority").

Anarchy
The absence of any form of government or political authority.

characterize a transition between one form of government (often totalitarian or authoritarian and repressive) and one where people want more power but do not yet have political institutions to structure popular participation. The interim period can be chaotic and violent, as in Somalia and to a lesser degree in Tunisia, Egypt, Libya, and Yemen following the Arab Spring rebellions.

Direct Democracy as a Model

The system of government in the ancient Greek city-state of Athens is usually considered the purest model of **direct democracy**, because the citizens of that community debated and voted directly on all laws, even those put forward by the ruling council of the city. The most important feature of Athenian democracy was that the **legislature** was composed of all of the citizens. Women, foreigners, and slaves, however, were excluded because they were not citizens. This form of government required a high level of participation from every citizen; participation was seen as benefiting the individual and the city-state. The Athenians believed that although a high level of participation might lead to instability in government, citizens, if informed about the issues, could be trusted to make wise decisions. Greek philosophers also believed that debating the issues and participating in making the laws was good for the individual's intellectual and personal development.

Direct democracy has also been practiced in Switzerland and in the United States in New England town meetings. At New England town meetings, which can include all of the voters who live in the town, important decisions—such as levying taxes, hiring city officials, and deciding local ordinances—are made by majority vote. Some states provide a modern adaptation of direct democracy for their citizens; representative democracy is supplemented by the **initiative** or the **referendum**— processes by which the people may vote directly on laws or constitutional amendments. The **recall** process, which is available in many states, allows the people to vote to remove an official from state office.

Because of the Internet, Americans have access to more political information than ever before. Voters can go online to examine the record of any candidate. Constituents can contact their congressional representatives and state legislators by sending them e-mail. Individuals can easily and relatively inexpensively find like-minded allies and form political interest groups using social networking sites such as Facebook, Google+, and countless others. During the 2008 presidential campaign, the Obama campaign pioneered new uses of the Internet to connect supporters, solicit campaign donations, and maintain nearly constant contact between likely voters and the campaign.

Direct Democracy
A system of government in which political decisions are made by the people directly, rather than by their elected representatives; probably attained most easily in small political communities.

Legislature
A governmental body primarily responsible for the making of laws.

Initiative
A procedure by which voters can propose a law or a constitutional amendment.

Referendum
An electoral device whereby legislative or constitutional measures are referred by the legislature to the voters for approval or disapproval.

Recall
A procedure allowing the people to vote to dismiss an elected official from state office before his or her term has expired.

In 2011 Governor Scott Walker introduced a budget bill that promised to save the state an estimated $330 million over three years by, among other things, requiring public employees to pay a larger share of their health insurance and pension plans. The bill also greatly reduced bargaining rights for many state employees. Beginning in February of 2011, as many as 100,000 protesters converged on the state capitol to oppose the Wisconsin budget repair bill. The bill passed and opponents vowed to mount a recall. Wisconsin law requires 540,000 signatures to force a recall vote. The Government Accountability Board certified 900,939 recall petition signatures. The recall vote took place on June 5, 2012 and Governor Walker prevailed with 53 percent of the vote over Democrat Tom Barrett.

In 2012, social media provided voters with new forms of real-time engagement through breaking campaign news, the debates, and election night returns. President Obama's victory tweet of "4 more years" set a record for re-tweets. Facebook motivated people to get to the polls; seeing that friends had already voted worked as a form of peer pressure to do likewise. In the last week of campaign 2012, Twitter released a political engagement map that allowed users to track tweets about specific candidates or issues around the country.

There are limits, however, to how much political business people currently want to conduct using technology, largely because of security concerns. Although Colorado offered its citizens the opportunity to vote online in 2000, the Pentagon cancelled a plan for troops overseas to vote online in 2004 due to Internet security concerns. Several states, however, do allow for voter registration online. Florida, Virginia, and California allowed voters abroad to download a ballot for the 2012 Republican primary and mail it back.

The Limits of Direct Democracy

Although they were aware of the Athenian model, the framers of the U.S. Constitution had grave concerns about the stability and practicality of direct democracy. During America's colonial period, the idea of government based on the consent of the people gained increasing popularity. Such a government was the main aspiration of the American Revolution, the French Revolution in 1789, and many subsequent revolutions. At the time of the American Revolution, however, the masses were still considered to be too uneducated to govern themselves, too prone to the influence of demagogues (political leaders who manipulate popular prejudices), and too likely to subordinate minority rights to the tyranny of the majority.

James Madison defended the new scheme of government set forth in the U.S. Constitution, while warning of the problems inherent in a "pure democracy":

> A common passion or interest will, in almost every case, be felt by a majority of the whole ... and there is nothing to check the inducements to sacrifice the weaker party or an obnoxious individual. Hence it is that such democracies have ever been spectacles of turbulence and contention, and have ever been found incompatible with personal security or the rights of property; and have in general been as short in their lives as they have been violent in their deaths.[15]

Like other politicians of his time, Madison feared that direct democracy would deteriorate into mob rule. What would keep the majority of the people, if given direct decision-making power, from abusing the rights of minority groups?

A Democratic Republic

The framers of the U.S. Constitution chose to craft a **republic**, meaning a government in which sovereign power rests with the people, rather than with a king or monarch. To Americans of the 1700s, the idea of a republic also meant a government based on common beliefs and virtues that would be fostered within small communities. The rulers were to be amateurs—good citizens who would take turns representing their fellow citizens.

The U.S. Constitution created a form of republican government that we now call a **democratic republic**. The people hold the ultimate power over the government through the election process, but policy decisions are made by elected officials. For the founders, even this distance between the people and the government was not sufficient. The Constitution made sure that the Senate and the president

Republic
A form of government in which sovereignty rests with the people, as opposed to a king or monarch.

Democratic Republic
A republic in which representatives elected by the people make and enforce laws and policies.

---

15. James Madison, in Alexander Hamilton, James Madison, and John Jay, *The Federalist Papers*, No. 10 (New York: Mentor Books, 1964), p. 81. See Appendix C of this textbook.

would be selected by political elites rather than by the people, although later changes to the Constitution allowed the voters to elect members of the Senate directly.

Despite these limits, the new American system was unique in the amount of power it granted to ordinary citizens. Over the course of the following two centuries, democratic values became increasingly popular, at first in the West and then throughout the rest of the world. The spread of democratic principles gave rise to another name for our system of government—**representative democracy**. The term *representative democracy* has almost the same meaning as *democratic republic*, with one exception. In a republic, not only are the people sovereign, but there is no king. What if a nation develops into a democracy but preserves the monarchy as a largely ceremonial institution? This is exactly what happened in Britain. Not surprisingly, the British found the term *democratic republic* to be unacceptable, and they described their system as a representative democracy instead.

Principles of Democratic Government. All representative democracies rest on the rule of the people as expressed through the election of government officials. In the 1790s in the United States, only free white males were able to vote, and in some states they had to be property owners as well. Women did not receive the right to vote in national elections in the United States until 1920, and the right to vote was not secured in all states by African Americans until the 1960s. Today, **universal suffrage** is the rule.

Because everyone's vote counts equally, the only way to make fair decisions is by some form of **majority** will. But to ensure that **majority rule** does not become oppressive, modern democracies also provide guarantees of minority rights. If political minorities were not protected, the majority might violate the fundamental rights of members of certain groups, especially groups that are unpopular or that differ from the majority population, such as racial minorities.

To guarantee the continued existence of a representative democracy, there must be free, competitive elections. Thus, the opposition always has the opportunity to win elective office. For such elections to be totally open, freedom of the press and speech must be preserved so that opposition candidates may present their criticisms of the government.

Yet another key feature of Western representative democracy is that it is based on the principle of **limited government**. Not only is the government dependent on popular sovereignty, but the powers of the government are also clearly limited, either through a written document or through widely shared beliefs. The U.S. Constitution sets down the fundamental structure of the government and the limits to its activities. Such limits are intended to prevent political decisions based on the ambitions of individuals in government rather than on constitutional principles. Wisely, the founders created constitutional limits on government that actually rely on human nature and ambition. Consider the counsel of James Madison in Federalist #51:

> *Ambition must be made to counteract ambition. The interest of the man must be connected with the constitutional rights of the place. It may be a reflection on human nature that such devices should be necessary to control the abuses of government. But what is government itself but the greatest of all reflections on human nature? If men were angels, no government would be necessary. If angels were to govern men, neither external nor internal controls on government would be necessary.*[16]

Representative Democracy
A form of government in which representatives elected by the people make and enforce laws and policies; may retain the monarchy in a ceremonial role.

Universal Suffrage
The right of all adults to vote for their representatives.

Majority
More than 50 percent.

Majority Rule
A basic principle of democracy asserting that the greatest number of citizens in any political unit should select officials and determine policies.

Limited Government
The principle that the powers of government should be limited, usually by institutional checks.

---

16. James Madison, in Alexander Hamilton, James Madison, and John Jay, *The Federalist Papers*, No. 51 (New York: Mentor Books, 1968). See Appendix C.

As neither is the case, constitutional democracy in the United States is based on an intricate set of relationships—federalism, separation of powers, and checks and balances. Each will be discussed in more detail in later chapters.

Who Really Rules in America?

Americans feel free to organize, to call and e-mail their representatives, and to vote candidates in and out of office. We always describe our political system as a democracy or democratic republic. However, do the people of the United States actually hold power today? Political scientists have developed several theories about American democracy, including *majoritarian* theory, *elite* theory, and theories of *pluralism*. Advocates of these theories use them to describe American democracy either as it actually is or as they believe it should be.

Majoritarianism

Many people believe that in a democracy, the government ought to do what the majority of the people want. This simple proposition is the heart of majoritarian theory. As a theory of what democracy should be like, **majoritarianism** is popular in concept among ordinary citizens. However, majorities can sometimes mobilize around issues with outcomes harmful to minorities. Even if much of the decision making in American government is done on the basis of majorities, it is rarely unchecked. For example, in 2008 a majority of voters (52%) in California approved Proposition 8, amending the state constitution to ban same-sex marriage. This action prompted a flurry of actions in state and federal appellate courts. On February 7, 2012, a federal appeals court struck down California's ban, making it increasingly likely that the issue will be heard by the U.S. Supreme Court. Many scholars, however, consider majoritarianism to be a surprisingly poor description of how U.S. democracy actually works. In particular, they point to the low level of turnout for elections. Polling data have shown that many Americans are neither particularly interested in politics nor well informed. Few are able to name the persons running for Congress in their districts, and even fewer can discuss the candidates' positions.

Elitism

If ordinary citizens do not really indicate policy preferences with their votes, then who does? One answer suggests that elites really govern the United States. Rather than opting out of participation, ordinary Americans are excluded. **Elite theory** is usually used simply to describe the American system. Few people today believe it is a good idea for the country to be run by a privileged minority. In the past, however, many people believed that it was appropriate for the country to be run by an elite. Consider the words of Alexander Hamilton, one of the framers of the Constitution:

> *All communities divide themselves into the few and the many. The first are the rich and the wellborn, the other the mass of the people.... The people are turbulent and changing; they seldom judge or determine right. Give therefore to the first class a distinct, permanent share in the government. They will check the unsteadiness of the second, and as they cannot receive any advantage by a change, they therefore will ever maintain good government.*[17]

Some versions of elite theory posit a small, cohesive, elite class that makes almost all of the important decisions for the nation,[18] whereas others suggest that voters

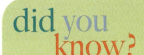

did you know?

In 2010, more babies were born to minority parents than to Caucasian parents, the first time that has happened in U.S. history.

Majoritarianism
A political theory holding that in a democracy, the government ought to do what the majority of the people want.

Elite Theory
A perspective holding that society is ruled by a small number of people who exercise power to further their self-interest.

---

17. Alexander Hamilton, "Speech in the Constitutional Convention on a Plan of Government," in *Writings*, ed. Joanne B. Freeman (New York: Library of America, 2001).
18. Michael Parenti, *Democracy for the Few*, 7th ed. (Belmont, CA: Wadsworth Publishing, 2002).

Politics with a Purpose
WHEN PASSIONS MOBILIZE

"We the People" has profound meaning in the 21st century. A quick Internet search reveals literally millions of Web sites with "citizens against" and just as many more with "citizens for" in their titles.

People organize into groups in order to influence the system and affect changes in public policy. Many groups mobilize to keep watch on government power. Some groups address specific policy problems—the environment, handgun violence, or urban gas well drilling—while others have bigger issues, such as reducing taxes or the national debt. In recent months, several interest groups have mobilized either against the Obama administration's approach to health care reform and increased government spending or in support of the president's initiatives. While it is true that such groups may have ties to a political party or to an existing political organization, many people who join do so out of real passion and may have little political experience.

In 2009, the fastest-growing groups organized under the label of the Tea Party, although there was no real national organization at first. Tea Partiers rallied, marched on Washington, and went to town halls to object to the health reform legislation. Some local groups got involved in local politics, while others chose to work only on national issues. Sometimes groups can form out of crowds gathered to make a political statement.

Occupy Wall Street's origin can be traced to *Adbusters*, an anti-consumerism magazine based in Vancouver, British Columbia. In July 2011, the magazine included the following message "#OCCUPY WALLSTREET. September 17th. Bring tent. www.occupywallstreet.org." With that as the catalyst, social media spread the call to community organizers around the country. Generally speaking, the group was mobilized against corporate influence on democracy, the lack of legal consequences for those who had brought about the global economic crisis, and the increasing economic inequality between the richest 1 percent and the other 99 percent.

Usually those who join such groups to express specific views are better educated, older, and more likely to be involved in community affairs, but not always. One of the earliest organizers of the Tea Party in Washington State was Keli Carender, a young performance artist who has a ring in her nose and a teaching degree. Carender does not fit the profile of an organizer. She began by protesting government spending by herself and then started to organize rallies. Occupy Wall Street, on the other hand, worked hard to avoid all of the typical signs of organized political activity—there was no single leader or organizer associated with the cause. Instead, the group attracted followers who felt an affinity with its slogan, "We are the 99 percent," and social media made it possible for the protests to spread from Wall Street to cities all over the country.

It is interesting to consider how organizations such as the Tea Party or Occupy Wall Street contribute to public debates on the issues and to examine the role of the media in the growth of such organizations. Do you think that citizen organizations can become too extreme when passions run high? What is your passion? What are the issues about which you care most deeply? Chances are good that other similarly motivated individuals would welcome your help!

choose among competing elites. New members of the elite are recruited through the educational system so that the brightest children of the masses allegedly have the opportunity to join the elite stratum. One view suggests that the members of the elite are primarily interested in controlling the political system to protect their own wealth and the capitalist system that produces it.[19] Studies of elite opinion, however, have also suggested that elites are more tolerant of diversity, more willing to defend individual liberties, and more supportive of democratic values than are members of the mass public.

Pluralism

A different school of thought holds that our form of democracy is based on group interests. As early as 1831, the French traveler and commentator Alexis de

19.   G. William Domhoff, *Who Rules America?* 4th ed. (New York: McGraw-Hill Higher Education, 2002).

Tocqueville noted the American penchant for joining groups: "As soon as the inhabitants of the United States have taken up an opinion or a feeling which they wish to promote in the world, they look out for mutual assistance; and as soon as they have found one another out, they combine. From that moment they are no longer isolated men, but a power seen from afar. ..."[20]

Pluralist theory proposes that even if the average citizen cannot keep up with political issues or cast a deciding vote in any election, the individual's interests will be protected by groups that represent her or him. Theorists who subscribe to **pluralism** see politics as a struggle among groups to gain benefits for their members.

Many political scientists believe that pluralism works very well as a descriptive theory. As a way to defend the practice of democracy in the United States, however, pluralism has problems. Poor citizens are rarely represented by interest groups. At the same time, rich citizens are often overrepresented, in part because they understand their own interests. As political scientist E. E. Schattschneider observed, "The flaw in the pluralist heaven is that the heavenly chorus sings with a strong upper-class accent."[21] There are also serious doubts as to whether group decision making always reflects the best interests of the nation.

Critics see a danger that groups may become so powerful that all policies become compromises crafted to satisfy the interests of the largest groups. The interests of the public as a whole, then, would not be considered. Critics of pluralism have suggested that a democratic system can be virtually paralyzed by the struggle among interest groups. We will discuss interest groups at greater length in Chapter 7.

Political Ideologies

A political **ideology** is a closely linked set of beliefs about politics. Political ideologies offer their adherents well-organized theories that propose goals for the society and the means by which those goals can be achieved. At the core of every political ideology is a set of guiding values. The two ideologies most commonly referred to in discussions of American politics are *liberalism* and *conservatism*. In the scheme of ideologies embraced across the globe, these two, especially as practiced in the United States, are in the middle of the ideological spectrum, as noted in Table 1–1.

Pluralism
A theory that views politics as a conflict among interest groups. Political decision making is characterized by bargaining and compromise.

Ideology
A comprehensive set of beliefs about the nature of people and about the role of an institution or government.

did you know?
The phrase "In God We Trust" was made the national motto on July 30, 1956, but had appeared on U.S. coins as early as 1864.

■ **Learning Outcome 5:**
Define political ideology, and locate socialism, liberalism, conservatism, and libertarianism along the ideological spectrum.

Table 1—1 ▶ The Traditional Political Spectrum

	SOCIALISM	LIBERALISM	CONSERVATISM	LIBERTARIANISM
How much power should the government have over the economy?	Active government control of major economic sectors	Positive government action in the economy	Positive government action to support capitalism	Almost no regulation of the economy
What should the government promote?	Economic equality, community	Economic security, equal opportunity, social liberty	Economic liberty, morality, social order	Total economic and social liberty

20. Alexis de Tocqueville, *Democracy in America*, Volume II, Section 2, Chapter V, "Of the uses which the Americans make of Public Associations" (available in many editions, and as full text in several Web locations)
21. E. E. Schattschneider, *The Semi-Sovereign People* (Hinsdale, IL: The Dryden Press, 1975; originally published in 1960).

The Traditional Political Spectrum

A traditional method of comparing political ideologies is to array them on a continuum from left to right, based primarily on how much power the government should exercise to promote economic equality, as well as the ultimate goals of government activity. Table 1–1 shows how ideologies can be arrayed in a traditional political spectrum. In addition to liberalism and conservatism, the table includes the ideologies of socialism and libertarianism.

Socialism falls on the left side of the spectrum. Socialists play a minor role in the American political arena, although socialist parties and movements are very important in other countries around the world. In the past, socialists typically advocated replacing investor ownership of major businesses with either government ownership or ownership by employee cooperatives. Socialists believed that such steps would break the power of the very rich and lead to an egalitarian society. In more recent times, socialists in Western Europe have advocated more limited programs that redistribute income.

On the right side of the spectrum is **libertarianism**, a philosophy of skepticism toward most government activities. Libertarians strongly support property rights and typically oppose regulation of the economy and redistribution of income. Libertarians support *laissez-faire* capitalism. (*Laissez-faire* is French for "let it be.") Libertarians also tend to oppose government attempts to regulate personal behavior and promote moral values.

In the Middle: Liberalism and Conservatism

The set of beliefs called **conservatism** includes a limited role for the government in helping individuals. These values usually include a strong sense of patriotism. Conservatives believe that the private sector probably can outperform the government in almost any activity. Believing that the individual is primarily responsible for his or her own well-being, conservatives typically oppose government programs to redistribute income or change the status of individuals. Conservatism may also include support for what conservatives refer to as traditional values regarding individual behavior and the importance of the family.

The set of beliefs called **liberalism** includes advocacy of government action to improve the welfare of individuals, support for civil rights, and tolerance for social change. American liberals believe that government should take positive action to reduce poverty, to redistribute income from wealthier classes to poorer ones, and to regulate the economy. Those who espouse liberalism may also be more supportive of the rights of women and gays and diverse lifestyles. Liberals are often seen as an influential force within the Democratic Party, and conservatives are often regarded as the most influential force in the Republican Party.

The Difficulty of Defining Liberalism and Conservatism

While political candidates and commentators are quick to label candidates and voters as "liberals" and "conservatives," the meanings of these words have evolved over time. Moreover, each term may represent a quite different set of ideas to the person or group that uses it.

Liberalism.   The word *liberal* has an odd history. It comes from the same root as *liberty*, and originally it simply meant "free." In that broad sense, the United States as a whole is a liberal country, and all popular American ideologies are variants of liberalism. In a more restricted definition, a *liberal* was a person who

---

Socialism
A political ideology based on strong support for economic and social equality. Socialists traditionally envisioned a society in which major businesses were taken over by the government or by employee cooperatives.

Libertarianism
A political ideology based on skepticism or opposition toward almost all government activities.

Conservatism
A set of beliefs that includes a limited role for the national government in helping individuals, support for traditional values and lifestyles, and a cautious response to change.

Liberalism
A set of beliefs that includes the advocacy of positive government action to improve the welfare of individuals, support for civil rights, and tolerance for political and social change.

believed in limited government and who opposed religion in politics. A hundred years ago, liberalism referred to a philosophy that in some ways resembled modern-day libertarianism. For that reason, many libertarians today refer to themselves as *classical liberals*.

How did the meaning of the word *liberal* change? In the 1800s, the Democratic Party was seen as the more liberal of the two parties. The Democrats of that time stood for limited government and opposition to moralism in politics. Democrats opposed Republican projects such as building roads, freeing the slaves, and prohibiting the sale of alcoholic beverages. Beginning with Democratic president Woodrow Wilson (served 1913–1921), however, the party's economic policies began to change. President Franklin Delano Roosevelt won a landslide election in 1932 by pledging to take steps to end the Great Depression. Roosevelt and the Democratic Congress quickly passed several measures that increased federal government intervention in the economy and improved conditions for Americans. By the end of Roosevelt's presidency in 1945, the Democratic Party had established itself as standing for positive government action to help the economy. Although Roosevelt stood for new policies, he kept the old language—as Democrats had long done, he called himself a liberal. We will discuss the history of the two parties in greater detail in Chapter 8.

Outside the United States and Canada, the meaning of the word *liberal* never changed. For this reason, you might hear a left-of-center European denounce U.S. president Ronald Reagan (served 1981–1989) or British prime minister Margaret Thatcher (served 1979–1990) for their "liberalism," meaning that these two leaders were enthusiastic advocates of *laissez-faire* capitalism.

Conservatism. The term *conservatism* suffers from similar identity problems. In the United States and Western Europe, conservatives tended to believe in maintaining traditions and opposing change. Conservatives were more likely to support the continuation of the monarchy, for example. At the end of World War II, Senator Robert A. Taft of Ohio was known as "Mr. Conservative," and he steadfastly opposed the Democratic Party's platform of an active government. However, he was not a spokesperson for conservative or traditional personal values.

Today, conservatism is often considered to have two quite different dimensions. Some self-identified conservatives are "economic conservatives" who believe in less government, support for capitalism and private property, and allowing individuals to pursue their own route to achievement with little government interference. Recent presidential campaigns have seen great efforts to motivate those individuals who might be called "social conservatives" to support Republican candidates. Social conservatives are much less interested in economic issues than in supporting particular social values, including opposition to abortion, support for the death penalty or the right to own firearms, and opposition to gay marriage. Given these two different dimensions of conservatism, it is not surprising that conservatives are not always united in their political preferences.

Libertarianism. Although libertarians make up a much smaller proportion of the population in the United States than do conservatives or liberals, this ideology shares the more extreme positions of both groups. If the only question is how much power the government should have over the economy, then libertarians can be considered conservatives. However, libertarians advocate the most complete possible freedom in social matters. They oppose government action to promote conservative moral values, although such action is often favored by other groups on the political right. Libertarians' strong support for civil liberties seems to align them more closely with modern liberals than with conservatives. Ron Paul,

did you know?

A 2007 study by the Organisation for Economic Co-operation and Development (OECD) found income inheritance in the United States to be greater (and therefore economic mobility lower) than in Denmark, Australia, Norway, Finland, Canada, Sweden, Germany, Spain, and France.

AP Photo/Charlie Riedel

Ron Paul, a candidate for the 2012 Republican presidential nomination, is very popular among college students because of his libertarian positions emphasizing personal freedom.

a congressman from Texas and a candidate for the Republican presidential nomination in 2008 and 2012, is known for his libertarian positions. Although Paul has never won the Republican nomination, he is very popular among college students, most likely because of his positions in favor of personal freedoms, liberalizing drug laws, and bringing home troops serving abroad.

The Challenge of Change

The United States faces enormous internal and external challenges. In the next 50 years, not only will the face of America change as its citizens age, become more diverse, and generate new needs for laws and policies, but the country will also have to contend with a decline in economic dominance in the world. Other nations, including China and India, have much larger populations than the United States and are assuming new roles in the world. The United States and its citizens will need to meet the challenges of a global economy and mitigate the impact of global environmental change. Technology has transformed the way we live, learn, and work. All of these challenges—demographic change, globalization, ubiquitous technology, and environmental change—will impact how the American political system functions in the future.

Demographic Change in a Democratic Republic

The population of the United States is changing in fundamental ways that will impact the political and social system of the nation. Long a nation of growth, the United States has become a middle-aged nation with a low birthrate and an increasing number of older citizens who want the services from government they were promised. Social Security and Medicare are among the few government entitlements remaining, and any suggestion that either program be changed elicits immediate political action by older citizens and their interest groups. In communities where there is a large elderly population whose children are grown and gone,

did you know?

Russia is expected to lose 30 million people by 2050 and will have a population of only 118 million, compared to the predicted 420 million for the United States.

Beyond Our Borders

IMPORTING WORKERS: CHALLENGING CULTURES IN EUROPE

One of the most controversial issues in American politics is the debate over what to do about undocumented immigrants who have come to the United States for employment and a better life. An estimated 11 million individuals reside in the United States without legal status. Some conservatives believe that the best solution is deporting the undocumented people to their respective native countries. Others, including President Barack Obama and moderate leaders of both parties, have argued that the United States should recognize its need for workers and implement a system by which individuals can come to this country to work and someday earn a right to citizenship. Immigration is a major source of population growth and cultural change in the United States. The political focus on undocumented immigrants can overshadow the tremendous benefits of immigration. For example, immigrants are among the founders of many prominent American technology companies, such as Google, Yahoo, and eBay.

Nations, especially in Europe, have long admitted immigrants as unskilled and semiskilled workers to fuel their economies and increase their populations. Immigrants make up about 12 percent of the population of Germany and 15 percent of that of Austria. Luxembourg has a 37 percent immigrant population and Switzerland, about 23 percent. For many decades, Great Britain has allowed individuals who were subjects of the British Commonwealth to enter the country, while France extended legal residency to many French citizens from its former colonies in North Africa.

All nations face a dilemma in how to balance the cultural energy immigrants bring with the tensions associated with integration and assimilation processes. Immigrants may find limits to employment, education, and housing. Nonwhite and Muslim residents claim they are the subject of unwarranted police attention through racial or religious profiling. The clashes sometimes turn violent. Young people rioted in France in the last few years over the lack of employment opportunities for nonwhite French residents, while the Netherlands has seen outbreaks of violence by Muslim residents against other Dutch citizens. Many of these states are engaged in serious internal discussion about how to socialize new residents to the culture of their new home and how

Sergey Brin, co-founder and president of Google, was born in Moscow, Russia. When Brin was six, his family entered the United States with the assistance of HIAS, the Hebrew Immigrant Aid Society. In honor of the 30th anniversary of his family's immigration, Brin gave $1 million to HIAS, which he credits with helping his family escape anti-Semitism in the Soviet Union.

to ensure that immigrants can find economic opportunities for themselves and their children, while at the same time challenging the prejudice and racism sometimes found in the native population.

FOR CRITICAL ANALYSIS

1. *How can the inevitable tensions created when new ideas and customs confront established cultures be resolved? What role is appropriate for government in this process?*

2. *To what extent should nations ensure that immigrants accept the cultural and political values of their new home? In what specific ways does multiculturalism benefit political, social, and economic development?*

Figure 1–2 ▶ The Aging of America

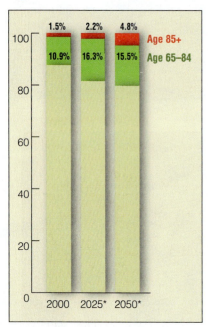

*Data for 2025 and 2050 are projections.
Source: U.S. Bureau of the Census.

Hispanic
Someone who can claim a heritage from a Spanish-speaking country other than Spain. This is the term most often used by government agencies to describe this group. Citizens of Spanish-speaking countries do not use this term to describe themselves.

Latino
Preferred term for referring to individuals who claim a heritage from a Spanish-speaking country other than Spain.

did you know?

It is estimated that people of Hispanic origin will make up almost one-quarter of the U.S. population by 2025.

increasing taxes in support of public education is a difficult proposition. Both the aging of the population and its changing ethnic composition will have significant political consequences.

Like other economically advanced countries, the United States has in recent decades experienced falling birthrates and an increase in the number of older citizens (see Figure 1–2). The "aging of America" is a weaker phenomenon than in many other wealthy countries, however. Today, the median age of the population is 36.7 in the United States and 40.0 in Europe. By 2050, the median age in the United States is expected to decline slightly to 36.2. In Europe, it is expected to reach 52.7. As is already the case in many European nations, older citizens demand that their need for pensions and health care dominate the political agenda. Young people in the United States, at times apathetic about politics, could use their vote to reorient the policy agenda. In the 2012 presidential contest, people younger than 30 made up a larger share of the electorate than those 65 and older.

Ethnic Change

As a result of differences in fertility rates and immigration, the ethnic character of the United States is also changing. Non-Hispanic white Americans have a fertility rate of just over 1.8 per two people; African Americans have a fertility rate of 2.1; and Hispanic Americans have a current fertility rate of almost 3.0. Figure 1–3 shows the projected changes in the U.S. ethnic distribution in future years.

A large share of all new immigrants are Hispanic. A **Hispanic** or **Latino** is someone who can claim a heritage from a Spanish-speaking country (other than Spain). Today, most individuals who share this heritage prefer to refer to themselves as Latino rather than Hispanic; however, government agencies such as the Census Bureau use the terms Hispanic and *non-Hispanic white* for their tables. In this book, Hispanic is used when referring to government statistics, while Latino is used in other contexts.

Latinos may come from any of about 20 primarily Spanish-speaking countries, and, as a result, they are a highly diverse population. The three largest Hispanic groups are Mexican Americans at 58.5 percent of all Latinos; Puerto Ricans (all of whom are U.S. citizens) at 9.6 percent of the total; and Cuban Americans at 3.5 percent. The diversity among Hispanic Americans results in differing political behavior; however, the majority of Latino Americans vote Democratic.

Barack Obama captured the majority of the Latino vote in 2008 and in 2012. Between the two presidential elections, the Latino population grew and grew more Democratic, particularly in states like Colorado, New Mexico, and Nevada. In Colorado, for example, Latino voters made up 14 percent of the electorate, and three-quarters voted for Obama. Nationally, the Latino share of the electorate rose to 10 percent of the whole, and President Obama attracted 71 percent of their support compared to 27 percent for Governor Romney. Similarly, Obama attracted a higher percentage of votes from African Americans (93 percent) and Asian Americans (73 percent) than did the Republican candidate. As the nation's population grows more diverse, political parties and candidates will need to attend carefully to the new demographic reality in America.

The United States is becoming a more ethnically diverse nation in every way. Nothing could be more telling than the election of Bobby Jindal, an American of Indian descent, as the governor of Louisiana in 2007. A former Republican congressman, Jindal did not represent any major ethnic group in that state but ran on a platform of effective government and an end to corruption. The campaign of

Figure 1-3 ▶ **Distribution of U.S. Population by Race and Hispanic Origin, 1980–2075**

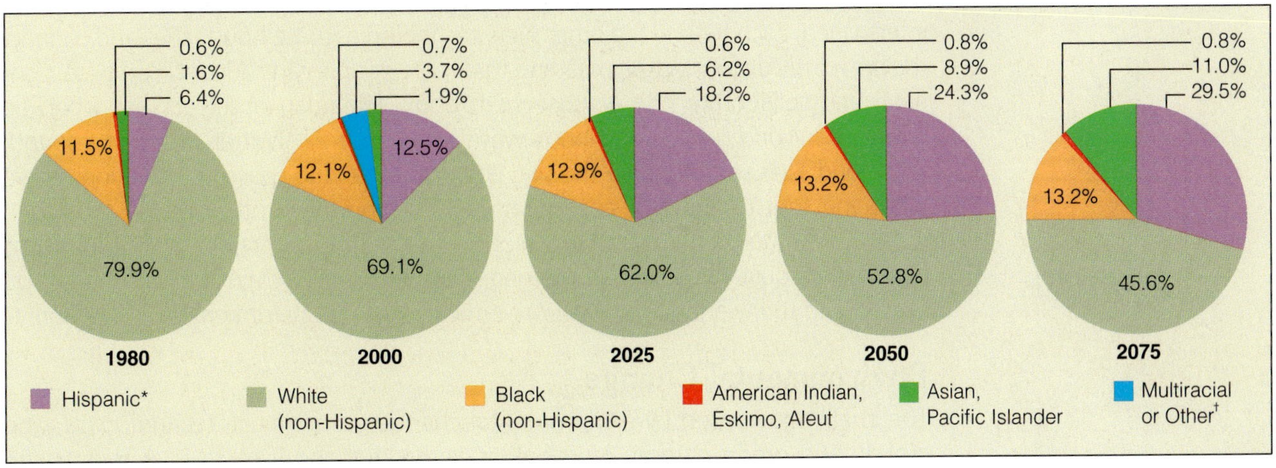

Data for 2025, 2050, and 2075 are projections.
*Persons of Hispanic origin can be of any race.
†The "multiracial or other" category in 2000 is not an official census category but represents all non-Hispanics who chose either "some other race" or two or more races in the 2000 census.
Source: U.S. Bureau of the Census.

Jindal—and even more significantly of Barack Obama for president of the United States—may signal the end of white dominance in political leadership at state and national levels. A multiethnic, multiracial society, however, poses some real challenges in keeping the various groups from exacerbating racial differences to obtain benefits for themselves. If the United States could achieve a higher level of economic equality for all Americans, group differences could be minimized.

Globalization

Globalization of the world economy has advanced rapidly. The power of the American economy and its expansion into other parts of the world spurred similar actions by the European, South American, and Asian nations. Huge international corporations produce and market products throughout the world. American soft drinks are produced and sold in China, while Americans buy clothing manufactured in China or the former states of the Soviet Union. Jobs are outsourced from the United States to India, the Philippines, or Vietnam, while other nations outsource jobs to the United States. Companies such as General Electric employ design teams that collaborate in the design and production of jet engines, with employees working around the clock, across all time zones.

Globalization brings a multitude of challenges to the United States and all other nations, beginning with the fact that no single government can regulate global corporations. Globalization changes employment patterns, reducing jobs in one nation and increasing employment in another. Products produced in low-wage nations are cheaper to buy in the United States, but the result is little control over quality and consumer safety. An economic recession triggered by one nation's economic decline now affects the entire globe, as evidenced by the growing financial crisis among several European Union members, including Greece and Spain.

The Technology Revolution

The revolution in our lives brought about by rapidly changing technology has transformed the way we communicate with one another, where and how we work, and even where and how we learn. You may be reading this book electronically, and you

did you know?

In 2012, New Hampshire became the first state to have an all-woman delegation in Congress. The state also elected a female governor, Maggie Hassan.

may even be completing this course online. In 2005, Thomas Friedman wrote a book titled *The World Is Flat*, in which he signaled that globalization and technology are intertwined, each fueling the other. New technologies erase boundaries and connect the previously unconnected, meaning that more people can suddenly compete, connect, and collaborate.[22] In a subsequent book, Friedman observed that when he wrote *The World Is Flat*, "Facebook wasn't even in it … 'Twitter' was just a sound, the 'cloud' was something in the sky, '3G' was a parking space, 'applications' were what you sent to colleges, and 'Skype' was a typo."[23] In other words, the world becomes "flatter" every day. What sort of education and training will tomorrow's workforce require? What role will colleges and universities play? Will the degree you are earning today enable you to work effectively in a transformed global economy?

Environmental Change

The challenges posed by environmental change are political, technological, and global. The great majority of scientists agree that the climate is changing and global warming is taking place. Many scientists and global organizations are focusing their efforts on measures to reduce humankind's contribution to global warming through carbon emissions and other actions. While the Bush administration balked at joining in the imposition of the measures on all nations until developing nations such as China and India were included, the Obama administration has signaled strong support for an international treaty to reduce global warming. Signing any kind of treaty on this matter is a serious issue for the United States because, as we will see in Chapter 2, according to our Constitution, treaties override U.S. law. American citizens would have their own lives determined by these treaties whether they approve of these policies or not.

While many scientists are working on the technologies to slow global warming, others believe that it is more important to concentrate on mitigating the impact of global warming, whatever the cause. The United States, like many other nations, has a concentration of population on the seacoasts: How should policies change in the face of rising seas and more hurricanes and coastal damage? Global warming is predicted to have more immediate and dire consequences on nations in Africa, where droughts will cause millions to starve. Should the United States play a much greater role in ameliorating these disasters and others caused by global warming in the near future, or should our policy priorities focus on technologies to change our lifestyles years from now?

What will all of these changes mean for you, your generation, and the nation? Is the American government nimble enough to recognize the challenges we will face in the future in time to meet them? What will doing so mean for the commitments we have made to previous generations and the promises we make to one another as a single nation? Can the United States continue to replicate and embrace a single political culture, or have we become two Americas? These and other questions will guide our exploration of American government and politics today.

South Carolina Governor Nikki Haley campaigns on behalf of Republican nominee Mitt Romney. Haley is the first woman to serve as Governor of South Carolina and one of two Indian-American governors in the country. The other is Bobby Jindal, Governor of Louisiana.

© ZUMA Press, Inc./Alamy

22. Thomas Friedman, *The World is Flat: A Brief History of the Twenty-first Century*. New York: Ferrar, Straus, and Giroux, 2005.
23. Thomas L. Friedman and Michael Mandelbaum. *That Used to be Us: How America Fell Behind in the World it Invented and How We Can Come Back*. New York: Ferrar, Straus, and Giroux, 2011.

Social Networking Is a Global Phenomenon: How Do We Know?

Young people, in particular, are using the Internet for social networking. Figure 1—4 below presents three important pieces of information. First, the bar for each country tells you what percentage of those using the Internet are using it for social networking and what percentage are not. For example, in the United States, 82 percent of the public use the Internet, but only 46 percent use it for social networking. The column on the far right gives the percentage of the public that does not use or have access to the Internet or e-mail.

Table 1—2 presents social networking usage by age range. Typically, when you read information presented as percentages in a table, either a row or column sums to 100 percent. In this case, it does not. This table presents a division of age based on the total for each country that uses social networking. So, for example, we learned from Figure 1—4 that 46 percent of those who use the Internet use social networking. Of that 46 percent, 77 percent are between the ages of 18 and 29; 55 percent are between the ages of 30 and 49; and 23 percent are 50 and older. The far right column represents the size of the gap between the oldest and youngest social network users.

Look carefully at both the figure and the table. What conclusions can you draw about the spread of technology across the globe? What conclusions might you draw about the relationship between age and use of social networking? These figures are from 2010. If information was available for 2012, would you imagine that it would look similar?

Figure 1-4 ▶ Social Networking Usage

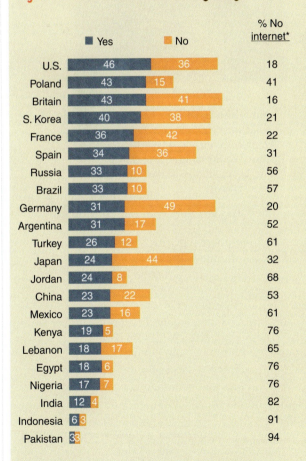

	Yes	No	% No internet*
U.S.	46	36	18
Poland	43	15	41
Britain	43	41	16
S. Korea	40	38	21
France	36	42	22
Spain	34	36	31
Russia	33	10	56
Brazil	33	10	57
Germany	31	49	20
Argentina	31	17	52
Turkey	26	12	61
Japan	24	44	32
Jordan	24	8	68
China	23	22	53
Mexico	23	16	61
Kenya	19	5	76
Lebanon	18	17	65
Egypt	18	6	76
Nigeria	17	7	76
India	12	4	82
Indonesia	6	3	91
Pakistan	3	3	94

*Respondents who do not use the internet or email. Based on total sample. "Don't know/Refused" not shown. Samples in China, India and Pakistan are disproportionately urban.

Pew Research Center Q66.

Table 1—2 ▶ Social Networking Use by Age and Country (based on total)

COUNTRY	18–29 %	30–49 %	50+ %	OLDEST-YOUNGEST GAP
United States	77	55	23	−54
Germany	86	36	8	−78
Britain	81	58	16	−65
France	78	40	13	−65
Spain	74	36	12	−62
Poland	82	57	12	−70
Russia	65	36	10	−55
Turkey	55	22	3	−52
Jordan	47	12	6	−41
Lebanon	39	12	3	−36
Egypt	37	8	8	−29
S. Korea	81	42	6	−75
Japan	63	31	6	−57
China	49	21	4	−45
India	20	6	6	−17
Indonesia	14	2	0	−14
Pakistan	5	1	0	−5
Brazil	59	29	10	−49
Argentina	54	33	10	−44
Mexico	47	16	6	−41
Kenya	26	13	8	−18
Nigeria	21	15	7	−14

Source: Pew Research Center (Q66). Accessed at: www.pewglobal.org/files/2010/12/Pew-Global-Attitudes-Technology-Report-FINAL-December-15-2010.pdf

You Can Make a Difference

SEEING DEMOCRACY IN ACTION

One way to begin to understand the American political system is to observe a legislative body in action. There are thousands of elected legislatures in the United States at all levels of government. You might choose to visit a city council, a school board, a township board of trustees, a state legislature, or the U.S. Congress.

WHY SHOULD YOU CARE?

State and local legislative bodies can have a direct impact on your life. For example, local councils or commissions typically oversee the police, and the behavior of the police is a matter of interest even if you live on campus. If you live off campus, local authorities are responsible for an even greater number of issues that affect you directly. Are there items that the Sanitation Department refuses to pick up? Have crimes been committed in your neighborhood? You might get more action by lobbying your city councilperson. Even if no local issues concern you, you can still benefit from observing a local legislative session. You may discover that local government works rather differently than you expected. You might learn, for example, that the representatives of your political party do not serve your interests as well as you thought—or that the other party is much more sensible than you had presumed.

WHAT CAN YOU DO?

To find out when and where local legislative bodies meet, look up the number of the city hall or county government building in the telephone directory and call the clerk of the council, or check on the Internet for the meeting times. In many communities, city council meetings and county board meetings can be seen on public-access TV channels.

Before attending a business session of the legislature, try to find out how the members are elected. Are the members chosen by the at-large method of election, so that each member represents the whole community, or are they chosen by specific geographic districts or wards? Is there a chairperson or official leader who controls the meetings? What are the responsibilities of this legislature?

When you visit the legislature, keep in mind the theory of representative democracy. The legislators or council members are elected to represent their constituents (those who live in their geographic area). Observe how often the members refer to their constituents or

Courtesy of Luke Scott

Luke Scott, 18-year-old councilman from Wellston, Ohio, is sworn in as city councilman by Ohio secretary of state Jennifer Brunner. Early in 2012, Scott decided to throw his hat in the ring for state representative of the 93rd Ohio House District.

to the special needs of their community or electoral district. Listen for sources of conflict within a community. If there is a debate, for example, over a zoning proposal that involves the issue of land use, try to figure out why some members oppose the proposal.

If you want to follow up on your visit, try to get a brief interview with one of the members of the council or board. Ask the member how he or she sees the job of representative. How can the wishes of constituents be identified? How does the representative balance the needs of the ward or district with the good of the entire community? You might even consider running for the council yourself. In 2009, Luke Scott, then a senior in high school, decided that his small Ohio town was in decline and that the city council needed to consider how to change this situation. He decided to run for election to the council and was elected. A freshman political science major at Ohio University, he commutes to school from Wellston, Ohio. As Scott explained his decision to run, "I believe my hometown is worth fighting for."* If, like Scott, you get elected to office in your community you won't be alone. There is a national organization called the Young Elected Officials (YEO) Network for those 35 and younger.

* www.ohiodailyblog.com, August 5, 2009; www.yeonetwork.org/

Key Terms

anarchy 11
aristocracy 11
authoritarianism 11
capitalism 10
conservatism 18
democracy 11
democratic republic 13
direct democracy 12
divine right of kings 6
elite theory 15
eminent domain 10

equality 9
government 5
Hispanic 22
ideology 17
initiative 12
institution 5
Latino 22
legislature 12
liberalism 18
libertarianism 18

liberty 8
limited government 14
majoritarianism 15
majority 14
majority rule 14
oligarchy 11
order 8
pluralism 17
political culture 6
political socialization 6

politics 5
property 10
recall 12
referendum 12
representative democracy 14
republic 13
social contract 6
socialism 18
totalitarian regime 10
universal suffrage 14

Chapter Summary

1. Governments are necessary at a minimum to provide public goods and services that all citizens need but cannot reasonably be expected to provide for themselves. National security and defense are obvious examples. Our founding documents such as the Declaration of Independence and the Constitution are predicated upon and convey through their language a set of shared political values. Government reinforces those values regularly.

2. Politics is the process of resolving conflicts and deciding "who gets what, when, and how." Government is the institution within which decisions are made that resolve conflicts or allocate benefits and privileges. It is unique because it has the ultimate authority within society.

3. Political philosophers Thomas Hobbes and John Locke believed governments were formed on the basis of consent. Individuals, all equal and endowed with reason, give up a portion of their individual liberty in order to gain the protection of government through the social contract. Government is formed to provide security and protect life, liberty, and property. Consent to be governed can be withdrawn if government becomes too powerful or abuses fundamental political values such as liberty, equality, individualism, the rule of law, and property rights.

4. Governments can vary in form depending on who controls the government. In a democracy, authority is held by the

people as whole. In totalitarian and authoritarian regimes, control is exercised by a single individual or a small group. Greek terms are often used to indicate how widely power is distributed. An aristocracy is "rule by the best," while an oligarchy is "rule by a few," and democracy is understood as "rule by the people." The United States is a representative democracy, where the people elect representatives to make the decisions.

5. Theories of American democracy include majoritarianism, in which the government does what the majority wants; elite theory, in which the real power lies with one or more elites; and pluralist theory, in which organized interest groups contest for power.

6. Popular political ideologies can be arrayed from left (liberal) to right (conservative). We can also analyze economic liberalism and conservatism separately from cultural liberalism and conservatism. However, other ideologies on the left (communism) and the right (fascism) also exist in the world.

7. The United States faces significant change and challenges ahead. Among these are demographic changes in the nation, the impact of globalization and the technology revolution, and the threats of environmental change. This is set against a backdrop of rising economic inequality that may undermine the opportunity for social mobility and progress in ways we have not experienced as a people before.

Selected Print, Media, and Online Resources

PRINT RESOURCES

Acemoglu, Daron, and James Robinson. *Why Nations Fail: The Origins of Power, Prosperity, and Poverty.* New York: Crown Publishers, 2012. The authors, one an economist and the other a political scientist, argue that nations thrive when they develop inclusive political and economic institutions and fail when institutions concentrate power and opportunity in the hands of only a few. Economic growth cannot be sustained in countries with limited political participation, nor can open political systems be maintained when large economic inequalities exist.

Fineman, Howard. *The Thirteen American Arguments: Enduring Debates That Define and Inspire Our Country.* New York: Random House Trade Paperbacks, 2009. Fineman, the senior Washington correspondent for *Newsweek*, describes questions that have divided Americans since the Revolutionary War.

Friedman, Thomas L., and Michael Mandelbaum. *That Used to Be Us: How America Fell Behind in the World It Invented and How We Can Come Back.* New York: Farrar, Straus, and Giroux, 2011. Friedman and Mandelbaum argue that America faces four challenges on which our future depends: globalization, the information technology revolution, chronic deficits, and excessive energy consumption. Drawing on America's core values and from hundreds of examples, the authors argue that the country can regain its footing.

Hodgson, Godfrey. *The Myth of American Exceptionalism.* New Haven, CT: Yale University Press, 2009. A respected British commentator, Hodgson argues that America's history and political philosophy have always been influenced by European philosophy, more than most Americans will admit.

Lasswell, Harold. *Politics: Who Gets What, When and How.* New York: McGraw-Hill, 1936. This classic work defines the nature of politics.

Noah, Timothy. *The Great Divergence: America's Growing Inequality Crisis and What We Can Do About It.* New York: Bloomsbury Press, 2012. An examination of the causes and consequences of the growing income gap, with nonpartisan recommendations on how to reverse the trend.

Obama, Barack. *Dreams from My Father: A Story of Race and Inheritance.* New York: Three Rivers Press, 2004. President Obama's best-selling autobiography ends before his rise to national prominence. He describes the sense of isolation he felt due to his unusual background and his attempts to come to grips with his multiethnic identity.

Tocqueville, Alexis de. *Democracy in America.* Edited by Phillips Bradley. New York: Vintage Books, 1945. Life in the United States is described by a French writer who traveled through the nation in the 1820s.

Zukin, Cliff, Scott Keeter, Molly Andolina, Krista Jenkins, and Michael X. Delli Carpini. *A New Engagement? Political Participation, Civic Life and the Changing American Citizen.* Oxford: Oxford University Press, 2006. An examination of political participation across generational cohorts. The authors conclude that nonvoting among the young is not a sign of apathy, but rather that young people engage by volunteering and being active in their communities.

MEDIA RESOURCES

All Things Considered—A daily broadcast of National Public Radio (NPR) that provides extensive coverage of political, economic, and social news stories.

Europe in One Room—An Emmy Award–winning film that demonstrates Fishkin's idea of deliberative democracy with a forum including European Union citizens speaking 21 languages who come together to make decisions about their common problems.

ONLINE RESOURCES

American Conservative Union—information about conservative positions: www.conservative.org

Americans for Democratic Action—home of one of the nation's oldest liberal political organizations: www.adaction.org

Bureau of the Census—a wealth of information about the changing face of America: www.census.gov

Center for the Study of the American Dream—located at Xavier University, a research center dedicated to the study of the American Dream: past, present, and future: www.xavier.edu/americandream/

Pew Research Center—a nonpartisan repository for facts on the issues, attitudes, and trends shaping American and the world. Pew is a research center and does not take positions on policy: www.pewresearch.org

University of Michigan—a basic "front door" to almost all U.S. government Web sites: www.lib.umich.edu/govdocs/govweb.html

U.S. Government—access to federal government offices and agencies: www.usa.gov

2 The Constitution

© Ramin Talaie/Corbis

An Occupy Wall Street protestor holds his copy of the Constitution at a rally in Union Square, New York City.

LEARNING OUTCOMES

After reading this chapter, students will be able to:

■ **LO1** Explain the theoretical and historical factors that influenced the writers of the U.S. Constitution.

■ **LO2** Describe the structure of the Articles of Confederation, and explain why the confederation failed.

■ **LO3** Identify and explain the compromises made by the delegates to come to agreement on the U.S. Constitution.

■ **LO4** Explain the rationale for, and give examples of the separation of powers and the checks and balances in the U.S. Constitution.

■ **LO5** Demonstrate understanding of the formal and informal processes for amending the U.S. Constitution.

29

What If...

THE CONSTITUTION HAD BANNED SLAVERY OUTRIGHT?

BACKGROUND

Slavery came to the American colonies not long after the first settlers arrived. In the earliest days of the Virginia colony about half of the immigrants were indentured servants, meaning that at some point they could earn enough or fulfill the terms of their contract to be freed. Even African Americans were often considered in this category. However, by the 1650s, great plantations had formed in the southern states and they needed agricultural labor. In 1654, a Virginia court found that John Casor, an African American, was a "property," owned for life by another black colonist. Shortly after this case, law established that the children of slaves were also property. As the agricultural needs of the country grew, so did the trade in slaves. By the end of the Revolutionary War, the new nation had nearly 650,000 slaves.

WHAT TO DO ABOUT THE SLAVERY ISSUE?

One of the most hotly debated issues at the Constitutional Convention concerned slavery. Most northern colonies had already abolished slavery, and the argument over the morality of owning human property was well known. Given the language of the Declaration of Independence, "All men are created equal,… that they are endowed by their Creator with certain unalienable rights, that among them are life, liberty, and the pursuit of happiness," why did the writers of the U.S. Constitution have so much difficulty with the issue of slavery? As you will learn in this chapter, the Constitutional Convention eventually agreed to two huge compromises to gain approval of the final document: Slaves would count as only three-fifths of a person for purposes of representation and the slave trade could not be banned until after 1808. The debate over slavery—or, more specifically, over how the founders dealt with it—continues to this day. Some contend that those delegates who opposed slavery should have made greater efforts to ban it completely.*

DID THE FOUNDERS HAVE NO OTHER CHOICE?

Some historians argue that the founders had no choice. The South was an important part of the economy, and the southern states depended on slave labor for their agricultural production. Virginia, perhaps the most powerful of the southern states, counted nearly 300,000 slaves in its population in 1790; North Carolina, South Carolina, and Maryland each counted about 100,000 in that census. Although political leaders from Virginia, such as George Washington, had serious doubts about slavery, the delegates from those states may never have agreed to the Constitution if slavery had been threatened—meaning that these states would not have joined the new nation. The founders believed, as James Madison said, "Great as the evil is, a dismemberment of the Union would be worse.…If those states should disunite from the other states,…they might solicit and obtain aid from foreign powers."** Benjamin Franklin, then president of the Pennsylvania Society for the Abolition of Slavery, also feared that without a slavery compromise, delegates from the South would abandon the convention.

CRITICS ARGUE THAT ETHICS SHOULD HAVE PREVAILED

Critics of the founders' actions nonetheless believe that any compromise on slavery implicitly acknowledged the validity of the institution in 1860. According to these critics, the delegates who opposed slavery had a moral obligation to make greater efforts to ban it. At the time, many delegates felt that slavery would eventually end. Would the southern states actually have left the Union if slavery were banned? Would they have tried to form a separate nation? If slavery had been banned in 1789 or shortly thereafter, would the southern states have adapted to a paid labor system rather than expanded the slave population to 4 million by 1860? It was, of course, the importance of slaves to the economy of the southern states as well as the moral opposition to slavery that brought the nation to civil war and led to many of the issues of race that the nation still struggles with today.

*See Paul Finkelman's criticism of the founders' actions on the slavery issue in *Slavery and the Founders: Race and Liberty in the Age of Jefferson*, 2nd ed. (Armonk, NY: M. E. Sharpe, 2001).

**Speech before the Virginia ratifying convention on June 17, 1788, as cited in Bruno Leone, ed., *The Creation of the Constitution* (San Diego, CA: Greenhaven Press, 1995), p. 159.

FOR CRITICAL ANALYSIS

1. Do you think that antislavery delegates to the convention should have insisted on ending slavery throughout the new nation?

2. Do you think the nation would have survived without the southern states?

3. How would our nation be different if slavery had been abolished in 1789?

NO MATTER WHICH POLITICAL PARTY occupies the White House or holds a majority in the Congress, the opposition is likely to claim, sooner or later, that some action taken or law passed violates the Constitution. Groups ranging from the Tea Party to the Occupy movement rally under the banner of the Constitution. Why is this *old* document such a symbol to Americans? Why hasn't it been changed more drastically or replaced since 1789? You may think that the Constitution is not relevant to your life or to modern times, but it continues to define the structure of the national and state governments and to regulate the relationship between the government and each individual citizen.

The Constitution of the United States is a product of the historical period in which it was written, a product of the colonists' experiences with government. Many of its provisions were grounded in the political philosophy of the time, including the writings of Thomas Hobbes and John Locke. The delegates to the Constitutional Convention in 1787 brought with them two important sets of influences: their political culture and their political experience. In the years between the first settlements in the New World and the writing of the Constitution, Americans had developed a political philosophy about how people should be governed and had tried out several forms of government. These experiences gave the founders the tools with which they constructed the Constitution. Milestones in the nation's early political history are shown in Table 2–1.

The Colonial Background

In 1607, the English government sent a group of farmers to establish a trading post, Jamestown, in what is now Virginia. The Virginia Company of London was the first to establish a permanent English colony in the Americas. The king of England gave the backers of this colony a charter granting them "full power and authority" to make laws "for the good and welfare" of the settlement. The colonists at Jamestown instituted a **representative assembly**, setting a precedent in government that was to be observed in later colonial adventures.

Jamestown was not an immediate success. Of the 105 men who landed, 67 died within the first year. But 800 new arrivals in 1609 added to their numbers. By the spring of the next year, frontier hazards had cut their numbers to 60. Of the 6,000 people who left England for Virginia between 1607 and 1623, 4,800 perished. This period is sometimes referred to as the "starving

did you know?

The first U.S. Census, taken in 1790, showed that almost 20 percent of Americans were enslaved people.

Representative Assembly
A legislature composed of individuals who represent the population.

■ **Learning Outcome 1:**
Explain the theoretical and historical factors that influenced the writers of the U.S. Constitution.

Table 2–1 ▶ Milestones in Early U.S. Political History

YEAR	EVENT
1607	Jamestown established; Virginia Company lands settlers.
1620	Mayflower Compact signed.
1630	Massachusetts Bay Colony set up.
1639	Fundamental Orders of Connecticut adopted.
1641	Massachusetts Body of Liberties adopted.
1682	Pennsylvania Frame of Government passed.
1701	Pennsylvania Charter of Privileges written.
1732	Last of the 13 colonies (Georgia) established.
1756	French and Indian War declared.
1765	Stamp Act; Stamp Act Congress meets.
1774	First Continental Congress.
1775	Second Continental Congress; Revolutionary War begins.
1776	Declaration of Independence signed.
1777	Articles of Confederation drafted.
1781	Last state (Maryland) signs Articles of Confederation.
1783	"Critical period" in U.S. history begins; weak national government until 1789.
1786	Shays's Rebellion.
1787	Constitutional Convention.
1788	Ratification of Constitution.
1791	Ratification of Bill of Rights.

time" for Virginia. Climatological researchers suggest that this "starving time" may have been brought about by a severe drought in the Jamestown area, which lasted from 1607 to 1612.

Separatists, the *Mayflower*, and the Compact

The first New England colony was established in 1620. A group of religious separatists who wished to break with the Church of England came over on the ship *Mayflower* to the New World, landing at Plymouth (Massachusetts). Before going onshore, the adult males—women were not considered to have any political status—drew up the Mayflower Compact, which was signed by 41 of the 44 men aboard the ship on November 21, 1620. The reason for the compact was obvious. This group was outside the jurisdiction of the Virginia Company of London, which had chartered its settlement in Virginia, not Massachusetts. The separatist leaders feared that some of the *Mayflower* passengers might conclude that they were no longer under any obligations of civil obedience. Therefore, some form of public authority was imperative. As William Bradford (one of the separatist leaders) recalled in his accounts, there were "discontented and mutinous speeches that some of the strangers amongst them had let fall from them in the ship; That when they came a shore they would use their owne libertie; for none had power to command them."[1]

The compact was not a constitution. It was a political statement in which the signers agreed to create and submit to the authority of a government, pending the receipt of a royal charter. The Mayflower Compact's historical and political significance is twofold: It depended on the consent of the affected individuals, and it served as a prototype for similar compacts in American history. According to Samuel Eliot Morison, the compact proved the determination of the English immigrants to live under the rule of law, based on the *consent of the people*.[2]

The signing of the compact aboard the *Mayflower*. In 1620, the Mayflower Compact was signed by almost all of the men aboard the *Mayflower* just before they disembarked at Plymouth, Massachusetts. It stated, "We…covenant and combine ourselves togeather into a civil body politick…; and by virtue hearof to enact, constitute, and frame such just and equal laws…as shall be thought [necessary] for the generall good of the Colonie."

The Granger Collection, New York.

1. John Camp, *Out of the Wilderness: The Emergence of an American Identity in Colonial New England* (Middleton, CT: Wesleyan University Press, 1990).
2. See Morison's "The Mayflower Compact," in Daniel J. Boorstin, ed., *An American Primer* (Chicago: University of Chicago Press, 1966), p. 18.

More Colonies, More Government

Another outpost in New England was set up by the Massachusetts Bay Colony in 1630. Then followed other settlements in New England which became Rhode Island, Connecticut, New Hampshire, and others. By 1732, the last of the 13 colonies, Georgia, was established. During the colonial period, Americans developed a concept of limited government, which followed from the establishment of the first colonies under Crown charters. Theoretically, London governed the colonies. In practice, owing partly to the colonies' distance from London, the colonists exercised a large measure of self-government. The colonists were able to make their own laws, as in the Fundamental Orders of Connecticut in 1639. The Massachusetts Body of Liberties in 1641 supported the protection of individual rights and was made a part of colonial law. In 1682, the Pennsylvania Frame of Government was passed. Along with the Pennsylvania Charter of Privileges of 1701, it foreshadowed our modern Constitution and Bill of Rights. All of this legislation enabled the colonists to acquire crucial political experience.

British Restrictions and Colonial Grievances

The conflict between Britain and the American colonies, which ultimately led to the Revolutionary War, began in the 1760s when the British government decided to raise revenues by imposing taxes on the American colonies. Policy advisers to Britain's young King George III, who ascended to the throne in 1760, decided that it was only logical to require the American colonists to help pay the costs for their defense during the French and Indian War (1756–1763). The colonists, who had grown accustomed to a large degree of self-government and independence from the British Crown, viewed the matter differently.

In 1764, the British Parliament passed the Sugar Act. Many colonists were unwilling to pay the tax imposed by the act. Further regulatory legislation was to come. In 1765, Parliament passed the Stamp Act, providing for internal taxation—or, as the colonists' Stamp Act Congress, assembled in 1765, called it, "taxation without representation." The colonists boycotted the purchase of English commodities in return. The success of the boycott (the Stamp Act was repealed a year later) generated a feeling of unity within the colonies.

The British, however, continued to try to raise revenues in the colonies. When Parliament passed duties (taxes) on glass, lead, paint, and other items in 1767, the colonists again boycotted British goods. The colonists' fury over taxation climaxed in the Boston Tea Party, when colonists dressed as Mohawk Indians dumped close to 350 chests of British tea into Boston Harbor as a gesture of protest. In retaliation, Parliament passed the Coercive Acts (the "Intolerable Acts") in 1774, which closed Boston Harbor and placed the government of Massachusetts under direct British control. The colonists were outraged—and they responded.

The Colonial Response

New York, Pennsylvania, and Rhode Island proposed the convening of a colonial congress. The Massachusetts House of Representatives requested that all colonies hold conventions to select delegates to be sent to Philadelphia for such a congress.

The First Continental Congress

The First Continental Congress was held at Carpenters' Hall on September 5, 1774. It was a gathering of delegates from 12 of the 13 colonies (delegates from Georgia did not attend until 1775). At that meeting, there was little talk of independence.

King George III
(1738–1820) was king of Great Britain and Ireland from 1760 until his death on January 29, 1820. Under George III, the British Parliament attempted to tax the American colonies. Ultimately, exasperated at repeated attempts at taxation, the colonies proclaimed their independence on July 4, 1776.

© King George III, c.1762-64 (oil on canvas), Ramsay, Allan (1713-84) / National Portrait Gallery, London, UK / The Bridgeman Art Library International

The Congress passed a resolution requesting that the colonies send a petition to King George III expressing their grievances. Resolutions were also passed requiring that the colonies raise their own troops and boycott British trade. The British government condemned the Congress's actions, treating them as open acts of rebellion.

The delegates to the First Continental Congress declared that in every county and city, a committee was to be formed whose mission was to spy on the conduct of friends and neighbors and to report to the press any violators of the trade ban. The formation of these committees was an act of cooperation among the colonies, which represented a step toward the creation of a national government.

The Second Continental Congress

By the time the Second Continental Congress met in May 1775 (this time all of the colonies were represented), fighting had already broken out between the British and the colonists. One of the main actions of the Second Continental Congress was to establish an army, naming George Washington as commander in chief. The participants in that Congress still attempted to reach a peaceful settlement with the British Parliament. One declaration of the Congress stated explicitly that "we have not raised armies with ambitious designs of separating from Great Britain, and establishing independent states." But by the beginning of 1776, military encounters had become increasingly frequent.

Public debate was acrimonious. Then Thomas Paine's *Common Sense* appeared in Philadelphia bookstores. The pamphlet was a colonial best seller. (To do relatively as well today, a book would have to sell between 9 and 11 million copies in its first year of publication.) Many agreed that Paine did make common sense when he argued that

> *a government of our own is our natural right: and when a man seriously reflects on the precariousness [instability, unpredictability] of human affairs, he will become convinced, that it is infinitely wiser and safer, to form a constitution of our own in a cool and deliberate manner, while we have it in our power, than to trust such an interesting event to time and chance.*[3]

Students of Paine's pamphlet point out that his arguments were not new—they were common in tavern debates throughout the land. Rather, it was the near poetry of his words—which were at the same time as plain as the alphabet—that struck his readers.

Declaring Independence

On April 6, 1776, the Second Continental Congress voted for free trade at all American ports with all countries except Britain. This act could be interpreted as an implicit declaration of independence. The next month, the Congress suggested that each of the colonies establish a state government unconnected to Britain. Finally, in July, the colonists declared their independence from Britain.

The Resolution of Independence

On July 2, the Resolution of Independence was adopted by the Second Continental Congress:

> *RESOLVED, That these United Colonies are, and of right ought to be free and independent States, that they are absolved from allegiance to the British*

---

3. *The Political Writings of Thomas Paine,* Vol. 1 (Boston: J. P. Mendum Investigator Office, 1870), p. 46.

Crown, and that all political connection between them and the state of Great Britain is, and ought to be, totally dissolved.

The actual Resolution of Independence was not legally significant. On the one hand, it was not judicially enforceable, for it established no legal rights or duties. On the other hand, the colonies were already, in their own judgment, self-governing and independent of Britain. Rather, the Resolution of Independence and the subsequent Declaration of Independence were necessary to establish the legitimacy of the new nation in the eyes of foreign governments, as well as in the eyes of the colonists. What the new nation needed most were supplies for its armies and a commitment of foreign military aid. Unless it appeared to the world as a political entity separate and independent from Britain, no foreign government would enter into a contract with its leaders.

July 4, 1776—The Declaration of Independence

By June 1776, Thomas Jefferson (at the age of 33) was writing drafts of the Declaration of Independence in the second-floor parlor of a bricklayer's house in Philadelphia. On adoption of the Resolution of Independence, Jefferson argued that a declaration clearly putting forth the causes that compelled the colonies to separate from Britain was necessary. The Second Congress assigned the task to him, and he completed his work on the declaration, which enumerated the colonists' major grievances against Britain. Some of his work was amended to gain unanimous acceptance (for example, his condemnation of the slave trade was eliminated to satisfy Georgia and North Carolina), but the bulk of it was passed intact on July 4, 1776. On July 19, the modified draft became "the unanimous declaration of the thirteen United States of America." On August 2, it was signed by the members of the Second Continental Congress.

Universal Truths. The Declaration of Independence has become one of the world's most famous and significant documents. The words opening the second paragraph of the Declaration are known most widely:

> *We hold these Truths to be self-evident, that all Men are created equal, that they are endowed by their Creator with certain unalienable Rights, that among these are Life, Liberty, and the Pursuit of Happiness—That to secure these Rights, Governments are instituted among Men, deriving their just Powers from the Consent of the Governed, that whenever any Form of Government becomes destructive of these Ends, it is the Right of the People to alter or abolish it, and to institute new Government.*

Natural Rights and a Social Contract. The assumption that people have **natural rights** ("unalienable Rights"), including the rights to "Life, Liberty, and the Pursuit of Happiness," was a revolutionary concept at that time. Its use by Jefferson reveals the influence of the English philosopher John Locke (1632–1704), whose writings were familiar to educated American colonists, including Jefferson.[4] In his *Two Treatises on Government*, published in 1690, Locke had argued that all people possess certain natural rights, including the rights to life, liberty, and property, and that the primary purpose of government was to protect these rights. Furthermore, government was established by the people through a

Natural Rights
Rights held to be inherent in natural law, not dependent on governments. John Locke stated that natural law, being superior to human law, specifies certain rights of "life, liberty, and property." These rights, altered to become "life, liberty, and the pursuit of happiness," are asserted in the Declaration of Independence.

---

4. Not all scholars believe that Jefferson was truly influenced by Locke. For example, Jay Fliegelman states that "Jefferson's fascination with Homer, Ossian, Patrick Henry, and the violin is of greater significance than his indebtedness to Locke," in Jay Fliegelman, *Declaring Independence: Jefferson, Natural Language, and the Culture of Performance* (Palo Alto, CA: Stanford University Press, 1993).

Social Contract
A voluntary agreement among individuals to secure their rights and welfare by creating a government and abiding by its rules.

social contract—an agreement among the people to form a government and abide by its rules. As you read earlier, such contracts, or compacts, were not new to Americans. The Mayflower Compact was the first of several documents that established governments or governing rules based on the consent of the governed. In citing the "pursuit of happiness" instead of "property" as a right, Jefferson clearly meant to go beyond Locke's thinking.

After setting forth these basic principles of government, the Declaration of Independence goes on to justify the colonists' revolt against Britain. Much of the remainder of the document is a list of what "He" (King George III) had done to deprive the colonists of their rights. (See Appendix A at the end of this book for the complete text of the Declaration of Independence.)

Once it had fulfilled its purpose of legitimating the American Revolution, the Declaration of Independence was all but forgotten for many years. According to scholar Pauline Maier, the Declaration did not become enshrined as what she calls "American Scripture" until the 1800s.[5]

The Rise of Republicanism

Although the colonists had formally declared independence from Britain, the fight to gain actual independence continued for five more years—until the British general Charles Cornwallis surrendered at Yorktown in 1781. In 1783, after Britain formally recognized the independent status of the United States in the Treaty of Paris, Washington disbanded the army. During these years of military struggles, the states faced the additional challenge of creating a system of self-government for an independent United States.

Some colonists had demanded that independence be preceded by the formation of a strong central government. But others, who called themselves Republicans, were against a strong central government. They opposed monarchy, executive authority, and virtually any form of restraint on the power of local groups.

Unicameral Legislature
A legislature with only one legislative chamber, as opposed to a bicameral (two-chamber) legislature, such as the U.S. Congress. Today, Nebraska is the only state in the Union with a unicameral legislature.

Confederation
A political system in which states or regional governments retain ultimate authority except for those powers they expressly delegate to a central government. A voluntary association of independent states, in which the member states agree to limited restraints on their freedom of action.

State
A group of people occupying a specific area and organized under one government; may be either a nation or a subunit of a nation.

From 1776 to 1780, all of the states adopted written constitutions. Eleven of the constitutions were completely new. Two of them—those of Connecticut and Rhode Island—were old royal charters with minor modifications. Republican sentiment led to increased power for the legislatures. In Pennsylvania and Georgia, **unicameral** (one-body) **legislatures** were unchecked by executive or judicial authority. Basically, the Republicans attempted to maintain the politics of 1776. In almost all states, the legislature was predominant.

■ **Learning Outcome 2:**

Describe the structure of the Articles of Confederation, and explain why the confederation failed.

The Articles of Confederation: The First Form of Government

The fear of a powerful central government led to the passage of the Articles of Confederation, which created a weak central government. The term **confederation** is important; it means a voluntary association of *independent* **states**, in which the member states agree to only limited restraints on their freedom of action. As a result, confederations seldom have an effective executive authority.

In June 1776, the Second Continental Congress began the process of drafting what would become the Articles of Confederation. The final form of the Articles was achieved by November 15, 1777. It was not until March 1, 1781, however,

---

5. See Pauline Maier, *American Scripture: Making the Declaration of Independence* (New York: Knopf, 1997).

that the last state, Maryland, agreed to ratify what was called the Articles of Confederation and Perpetual Union. Well before the final ratification of the Articles, however, many of them were implemented: The Continental Congress and the 13 states conducted American military, economic, and political affairs according to the standards and the form specified by the Articles.[6]

Under the Articles, the 13 original colonies, now states, established on March 1, 1781, a government of the states—the Congress of the Confederation. The Congress was a unicameral assembly of so-called ambassadors from each state, with each state possessing a single vote. Each year, the Congress would choose one of its members as its president (that is, presiding officer), but the Articles did not provide for a president of the United States.

The Congress was authorized in Article X to appoint an executive committee of the states "to execute in the recess of Congress, such of the powers of Congress as the United States, in Congress assembled, by the consent of nine [of the 13] states, shall from time to time think expedient to vest with them." The Congress was also allowed to appoint other committees and civil officers necessary for managing the general affairs of the United States. In addition, the Congress could regulate foreign affairs and establish coinage and weights and measures, but it lacked an independent source of revenue and the necessary executive machinery to enforce its decisions throughout the land. Article II of the Articles of Confederation guaranteed that each state would retain its sovereignty. Figure 2–1 illustrates the structure of the government under the Articles of Confederation; Table 2–2 summarizes the powers—and the lack of powers—of Congress under the Articles of Confederation.

Figure 2–1 ▶ The Confederal Government Structure under the Articles of Confederation

Congress
Congress had one house. Each state had two to seven members, but only one vote. The exercise of most powers required approval of at least nine states. Amendments to the Articles required the consent of all the states.

Committee of the States
A committee of representatives from all the states was empowered to act in the name of Congress between sessions.

Officers
Congress appointed officers to do some of the executive work.

The States

Accomplishments under the Articles

The new government had some accomplishments during its eight years of existence under the Articles of Confederation. Certain states' claims to western lands were settled. Maryland had objected to the claims of the Carolinas, Connecticut, Georgia, Massachusetts, New York, and Virginia. It was only after these states consented to give up their land claims to the United States as a whole that Maryland signed the Articles of Confederation. Another accomplishment under the Articles was the passage of the Northwest Ordinance of 1787, which established a basic pattern of government for new territories north of the Ohio River. All in all, the Articles represented the first real pooling of resources by the American states.

Weaknesses of the Articles

Despite these accomplishments, the Articles of Confederation had many defects. Although Congress had the legal right to declare war and to conduct foreign policy, it did not have the right to demand revenues from the states. It could only *ask* for them. Additionally, the actions of Congress required the consent of nine states. Any amendments to the Articles required the unanimous consent of the Congress and confirmation by every state legislature. Furthermore, the Articles did not create a national system of courts.

Basically, the functioning of the government under the Articles depended on the goodwill of the states. Article III of the Articles simply established a "league

did you know?

The Articles of Confederation specified that Canada could be admitted to the Confederation if it ever wished to join.

---

6. Robert W. Hoffert, *A Politics of Tensions: The Articles of Confederation and American Political Ideas* (Niwot, CO: University Press of Colorado, 1992).

Table 2-2 ▶ Powers of the Congress of the Confederation

CONGRESS HAD POWER TO	CONGRESS LACKED POWER TO
Declare war and make peace.	Provide for effective treaty-making power and control foreign relations; it could not compel states to respect treaties.
Enter into treaties and alliances.	Regulate interstate and foreign commerce; it left each state free to set up its own tariff system.
Establish and control armed forces.	Compel states to meet military quotas; it could not draft soldiers or demand revenue to support an army or navy.
Requisition men and revenues from states.	Collect taxes directly from the people; it had to rely on states to collect and forward taxes.
Regulate coinage.	Compel states to pay their share of government costs.
Borrow funds and issue bills of credit.	Provide and maintain a sound monetary system or issue paper money; this was left up to the states, and monies in circulation differed tremendously in value.
Fix uniform standards of weight and measurement.	
Create admiralty courts.	
Create a postal system.	
Regulate Indian affairs.	
Guarantee citizens of each state the rights and privileges of citizens in the several states when in another state.	Establish an enforcement division to ensure those rights.
Adjudicate disputes between states on state petition.	

of friendship" among the states—no national government was intended.

Probably the most fundamental weakness of the Articles, and the most basic cause of their eventual replacement by the Constitution, was the lack of power to raise funds for the militia. The Articles contained no language giving Congress coercive power to raise revenues (by levying taxes) to provide adequate support for the military forces controlled by Congress. When states refused to send revenues to support the government (*not one state* met the financial requests made by Congress under the Articles), Congress resorted to selling off western lands to speculators or issuing bonds that sold for less than their face value. Due to a lack of resources, the Continental Congress was forced to disband the army, even in the face of serious Spanish and British military threats.

Shays's Rebellion and the Need for Revision of the Articles

Because of the weaknesses of the Articles of Confederation, the central government could do little to maintain peace and order in the new nation. The states bickered among themselves and increasingly taxed each other's goods. At times they prevented trade altogether. By 1784, the country faced a serious economic depression. Banks were calling in old loans and refusing to give new ones. People who could not pay their debts were often thrown into prison.

By 1786, in Concord, Massachusetts, the scene of one of the first battles of the Revolution, three times as many people were in prison for debt as for all other crimes combined. In Worcester County, Massachusetts, the ratio was even higher—20 to 1. Most of the prisoners were small farmers who could not pay their debts because of the economic chaos.

In August 1786, mobs of musket-bearing farmers led by former Revolutionary War captain Daniel Shays seized county courthouses and disrupted the trials of debtors in Springfield, Massachusetts. Shays and his men then launched an attack on the federal arsenal at Springfield, but they were repulsed. Shays's Rebellion demonstrated that the central government could not protect the citizenry from armed rebellion or provide adequately for the public welfare. The rebellion spurred the nation's political leaders to action. As John Jay wrote to Thomas Jefferson,

did you know?

Daniel Shays incurred the debts that led to Shays's Rebellion because he never received pay for serving in the Revolutionary War.

Changes are Necessary, but what they ought to be, what they will be, and how and when to be produced, are arduous Questions. I feel for the Cause of Liberty. … If it should not take Root in this Soil[,] Little Pains will be taken to cultivate it in any other.[7]

Drafting the Constitution

Concerned about the economic turmoil in the young nation, five states, under the leadership of the Virginia legislature, called for a meeting to be held at Annapolis, Maryland, on September 11, 1786—ostensibly to discuss commercial problems only. It was evident to those in attendance (including Alexander Hamilton and James Madison) that the national government had serious weaknesses that had to be addressed if it were to survive. Among the important problems to be solved were the relationship between the states and the central government, the powers of the national legislature, the need for executive leadership, and the establishment of policies for economic stability.

Those attending the meeting prepared a petition to the Continental Congress for a general convention to meet in Philadelphia in May 1787 "to consider the exigencies of the union." Congress approved the convention in February 1787. When those who favored a weak central government realized that the Philadelphia meeting would in fact take place, they endorsed the convention. They made sure, however, that the convention would be summoned "for the sole and express purpose of revising the Articles of Confederation." Those in favor of a stronger national government had different ideas.

The designated date for the opening of the convention at Philadelphia, now known as the Constitutional Convention, was May 14, 1787. Because few of the delegates had actually arrived in Philadelphia by that time, however, the convention was not formally opened in the East Room of the Pennsylvania State House until May 25.[8] Fifty-five of the 74 delegates chosen for the convention actually attended. (Of those 55, only about 40 played active roles at the convention.) Rhode Island was the only state that refused to send delegates.

Who Were the Delegates?

Who were the 55 delegates to the Constitutional Convention? They certainly did not represent a cross section of American society in the 1700s. Indeed, most were members of the upper class. Consider the following facts:

1. Thirty-three were members of the legal profession.
2. Three were physicians.
3. Almost 50 percent were college graduates.
4. Seven were former chief executives of their respective states.
5. Six were owners of large plantations.
6. Eight were important businesspersons.

They were also relatively young by today's standards: James Madison was 36, Alexander Hamilton was only 32, and Jonathan Dayton of New Jersey was 26.

did you know?

The 1776 constitution of New Jersey granted the vote to "all free inhabitants," including women, but the large number of women who turned out to vote resulted in male protests and a new law limiting the right to vote to "free white male citizens."

---

7. Excerpt from a letter from John Jay to Thomas Jefferson written in October 1786, as reproduced in Winthrop D. Jordan et al., *The United States*, combined ed., 6th ed. (Englewood Cliffs, NJ: Prentice Hall, 1987), p. 135.
8. The State House was later named Independence Hall. This was the same room in which the Declaration of Independence had been signed 11 years earlier.

Politics with a Purpose

HOW TO FORM A MORE PERFECT UNION?

"We the People of the United States, in Order to form a more perfect Union, establish Justice, insure domestic Tranquility, provide for the common defense, promote the general Welfare, and secure the Blessings of Liberty to ourselves and our Posterity, do ordain and establish this Constitution for the United States of America." Did you ever wonder what the framers of the Constitution meant by "a more perfect union"? Or why establishing justice and insuring domestic tranquility would be at the top of their list? The framers were reacting to the then-current problems created by the Articles of Confederation.

Adopted in 1781, the Articles of Confederation governed the emerging nation until our existing Constitution replaced it in 1787. Although the central government had very little power, the Articles held competing and disparate interests together for the first years of the nation's independence.

Any time political rules are changed, there are winners and losers. Some wish to maintain the status quo and others want change. Whether to amend or replace the Articles of Confederation was a dispute between those who enjoyed power under the Articles and those who found their weaknesses too dangerous and unprofitable. Under the Articles, the Congress had very little power. It could not regulate commerce or foreign trade nor levy taxes, and it had to depend on the states to begin to pay down the war debt. To deal with the difficulty of deficits without power to tax, Congress simply printed more money. This led to inflation, a lack of trust in the printed currency, and reliance on gold and silver.[a]

Members of Congress, as well as those whose economic interests were hurt by the economic instability, were frustrated. In addition to the aforementioned problems, the national government could not effectively regulate trade (all 13 states could negotiate separate trading arrangements with each other and with foreign governments). For people such as seaport merchants, large plantation owners, and commercial farmers who depended on trade, this was a trying and unstable situation.[b]

On the other hand, some people did approve of the Articles. Smaller farmers and those who lived inland depended less on trade and were more likely to believe the state governments were sufficient to solve their problems. Like Thomas Jefferson and Patrick Henry, many feared a strong national government and preferred a less active government that would keep taxes low and provide debt relief. With the success of the Articles in creating the Northwest Territory, a contingent in state governments was suspicious of national encroachment on their power.

So, why would states give up the enormous power they enjoyed under the Articles of Confederation? Initially, they did not. As early as 1786, calls were made to reform the Articles, and it was through crises such as the rebellion led by Daniel Shays in Massachusetts that those favoring a stronger national government were able to organize to form a Constitutional Convention. Meeting in 1787, they deliberated for months in secret to draft a document that was acceptable to the participants. The new Constitution was ratified in July 1788 through intense efforts to persuade state leaders (including promises of positions in the new government), a promise of greater protection of civil liberties, and lobbying efforts modern politicians would recognize. [c]

[a] www.loc.gov/rr/program/bib/ourdocs/articles.html, accessed September 22, 2008.
[b] Robert A. McGuire, "Review of Keith L. Dougherty," *Collective Action under the Articles of Confederation*, EH.Net Economic History Services, April 11, 2002, http://eh.net/bookreviews/library/0469.
[c] Lee Epstein and Thomas G. Walker, *Constitutional Law for a Changing America*, 5th ed., 2 vols. (Washington, DC: CQ Press, 2004).

The venerable Benjamin Franklin, however, was 81 and had to be carried in on a portable chair borne by four prisoners from a local jail. Not counting Franklin, the average age was just over 42. What almost all of them shared, however, was prior experience in political office or military service. Most of them were elected members of their own states' legislatures. George Washington, the esteemed commander of the Revolutionary War troops, was named to chair the meeting. There were, however, no women or minorities among this group. Women could not vote anywhere in the confederacy and, while free African Americans played an important part in some northern states, they were certainly not likely to be political leaders.[9]

The Working Environment

The conditions under which the delegates worked for 115 days were far from ideal and were made even worse by the necessity of maintaining total secrecy. The framers of the Constitution believed that if public debate took place on particular positions, delegates would have a more difficult time compromising or backing down to reach agreement. Consequently, the windows were usually shut in the East Room of the State House. Summer quickly arrived, and the air became heavy, humid, and hot by noon of each day. Also, when the windows were open, flies swarmed into the room. The delegates did, however, retire to a nearby tavern and inn, the Indian Queen, each evening to discuss the day's events.

Factions among the Delegates

What we know about the actual daily work of the convention comes from the detailed personal journal kept by James Madison. A majority of the delegates were strong nationalists—they wanted a central government with real power, unlike the central government under the Articles of Confederation. George Washington and Benjamin Franklin preferred limited national authority based on a separation of powers. They were apparently willing to accept any type of national government, however, as long as the other delegates approved it. A few advocates of a strong central government, led by Gouverneur Morris of Pennsylvania and John Rutledge of South Carolina, distrusted the ability of the common people to engage in self-government.

Among the nationalists, several went so far as to support monarchy. This group included Alexander Hamilton, who was chiefly responsible for the Annapolis Convention's call for the Constitutional Convention.

Still another faction consisted of nationalists who were less democratic in nature and who would support a central government only if it was founded on very narrowly defined republican principles. Many of the other delegates from Connecticut, Delaware, Maryland, New Hampshire, and New Jersey were concerned about only one thing—claims to western lands. As long as those lands became the common property of all of the states, they were willing to support a central government.

Finally, there was a group of delegates who were totally against a national authority. Two of the three delegates from New York quit the convention when they saw the nationalist direction of its proceedings.

Politicking and Compromises

The debates at the convention started on the first day. James Madison had spent months reviewing European political theory. When his Virginia delegation arrived ahead of most of the others, it got to work immediately. By the time George Washington opened the convention, Governor Edmund Randolph of Virginia was prepared to present 15 resolutions. In retrospect, this was a masterful stroke on the part of the Virginia delegation. It set the agenda for the remainder of the

■ **Learning Outcome 3:**
Identify and explain the compromises made by the delegates to come to agreement on the U.S. Constitution.

---

9. For a detailed look at the delegates and their lively debates, see Carol Berkin, *A Brilliant Solution: Inventing the American Constitution* (New York: Harcourt, 2002).

convention—even though, in principle, the delegates had been sent to Philadelphia for the sole purpose of amending the Articles of Confederation. They had not been sent to write a new constitution.

The Virginia Plan.

Randolph's 15 resolutions proposed an entirely new national government under a constitution. It was, however, a plan that favored the large states, including Virginia. Basically, it called for the following:

Bicameral Legislature

A legislature made up of two parts, called chambers. The U.S. Congress, composed of the House of Representatives and the Senate, is a bicameral legislature.

1. A **bicameral** (two-chamber) **legislature**, with the lower chamber chosen by the people and the smaller upper chamber chosen by the lower chamber from nominees selected by state legislatures. The number of representatives would be proportional to a state's population, thus greatly favoring the states with larger populations, including slaves, of course. The legislature could void any state laws.
2. The creation of an unspecified national executive, elected by the legislature.
3. The creation of a national judiciary, appointed by the legislature.

It did not take long for the smaller states to realize they would fare poorly under the Virginia plan, which would enable Virginia, Massachusetts, and Pennsylvania to form a majority in the national legislature. The debate on the plan dragged on for many weeks. It was time for the small states to come up with their own plan.

The New Jersey Plan.

On June 15, lawyer William Paterson of New Jersey offered an alternative plan. After all, argued Paterson, under the Articles of Confederation, all states had equality; therefore, the convention had no power to change this arrangement. He proposed the following:

1. The fundamental principle of the Articles of Confederation—one state, one vote—would be retained.
2. Congress would be able to regulate trade and impose taxes.
3. All acts of Congress would be the supreme law of the land.
4. Several people would be elected by Congress to form an executive office.
5. The executive office would appoint a Supreme Court.

Supremacy Doctrine

A doctrine that asserts the priority of national law over state laws. This principle is rooted in Article VI of the Constitution, which provides that the Constitution, the laws passed by the national government under its constitutional powers, and all treaties constitute the supreme law of the land.

Basically, the New Jersey plan was simply an amendment of the Articles of Confederation. Its only notable feature was its reference to the **supremacy doctrine**, which was later included in the Constitution.

The "Great Compromise."

The delegates were at an impasse. Most wanted a strong national government and were unwilling even to consider the New Jersey plan, but when the Virginia plan was brought up again, the small states threatened to leave. The issues involved in the debate included how states and their residents would be represented. Small states feared that the Virginia plan with its powerful national government would pass laws that would disadvantage smaller states. The larger states, aware that they would be the economic force in the new nation, absolutely opposed a government in which smaller states had the balance of power. Roger Sherman of Connecticut proposed a solution that gave power to both the small states and the larger states. On July 16, the **Great Compromise** was put forward for debate:

Great Compromise

The compromise between the New Jersey and Virginia plans that created one chamber of the Congress based on population and one chamber representing each state equally; also called the Connecticut Compromise.

1. A bicameral legislature in which the lower chamber, the House of Representatives, would be apportioned according to the number of free inhabitants in each state, plus three-fifths of the slaves.
2. An upper chamber, the Senate, which would have two members from each state elected by the state legislatures.

© Bettmann/CORBIS

George Washington presided over the Constitutional Convention of 1787. Although the convention was supposed to start on May 14, 1787, few of the delegates had actually arrived in Philadelphia by that date. The convention formally opened in the East Room of the Pennsylvania State House (later named Independence Hall) on May 25. Only Rhode Island did not send any delegates.

This plan, also called the Connecticut Compromise because of the role of the Connecticut delegates in the proposal, broke the deadlock. It did exact a political price, however, because it permitted each state to have equal representation in the Senate. Having two senators represent each state in effect diluted the voting power of citizens living in more heavily populated states and gave the smaller states disproportionate political powers. But the Connecticut Compromise resolved the large-state/small-state controversy. In addition, the Senate acted as part of a checks-and-balances system against the House, which many feared would be dominated by, and responsive to, the masses. However, another important piece of the debate needed a resolution: How were slaves to be counted in determining the number of members of Congress allotted to a state?

The Three-Fifths Compromise. Part of the Connecticut Compromise dealt with this problem. Slavery was still legal in many northern states, but it was concentrated in the South. Many delegates were opposed to slavery and wanted it banned entirely in the United States. Charles Pinckney of South Carolina led strong southern opposition to a ban on slavery. Furthermore, the South wanted slaves to be counted along with free persons in determining representation in Congress. Delegates from the northern states objected. Sherman's three-fifths proposal was a compromise between northerners who did not want the slaves counted at all and southerners who wanted them counted in the same way as free whites. Actually, Sherman's Connecticut plan spoke of three-fifths of "all other persons" (and that is the language of the Constitution itself). It is not hard to figure out, though, who those other persons were.

The Three-Fifths Compromise illustrates the power of the southern states at the convention.[10] The three-fifths rule meant that the House of Representatives and the electoral college would be apportioned in part on the basis of *property*—specifically, property in slaves. Modern commentators have referred to the three-fifths rule as valuing African Americans only three-fifths as much as whites.

did you know?

During the four centuries of slave trading, an estimated 10 million to 11 million Africans were transported to North and South America—and that only 6 percent of these slaves were imported into the United States.

10.   See Garry Wills, *"Negro President": Jefferson and the Slave Power* (New York: Houghton Mifflin, 2003).

A slave auction in the South, about 1850.

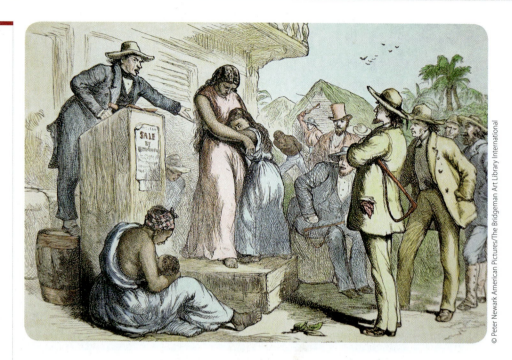

Actually, the additional southern representatives elected because of the three-fifths rule did not represent the slaves at all. Rather, these extra representatives were a gift to the slave owners—the additional representatives enhanced the power of the South in Congress.

The Three-Fifths Compromise did not completely settle the slavery issue. There was also the question of the slave trade. Eventually, the delegates agreed that Congress could not ban the importation of slaves until after 1808. The compromise meant that the matter of slavery was never addressed directly. The South won 20 years of unrestricted slave trade and a requirement that escaped slaves in free states be returned to their owners in slave states. Could the authors of the Constitution have done more to address the issue of slavery?

Other Issues. The South also worried that the northern majority in Congress would pass legislation that was unfavorable to its economic interests. Because the South depended on agricultural exports, it feared the imposition of export taxes. In return for acceding to the northern demand that Congress be able to regulate commerce among the states and with other nations, the South obtained a promise that export taxes would not be imposed. As a result, the United States is among the few countries that do not tax their exports.

There were other disagreements. The delegates could not decide whether to establish only a Supreme Court or to create lower courts as well. They deferred the issue by mandating a Supreme Court and allowing Congress to establish lower courts. They also disagreed over whether the president or the Senate would choose the Supreme Court justices. A compromise was reached with the agreement that the president would nominate the justices and the Senate would confirm the nominations. These compromises, as well as others, resulted from the recognition that if one group of states refused to ratify the Constitution, it was doomed.

Working toward Final Agreement

The Connecticut Compromise was reached by mid-July. The makeup of the executive branch and the judiciary, however, was left unsettled. The remaining work of the convention was turned over to a five-man Committee of Detail, which

■ Learning Outcome 4:
Explain the rationale for, and give examples of the separation of powers and the checks and balances in the U.S. Constitution.

presented a rough draft of the Constitution on August 6. It made the executive and judicial branches subordinate to the legislative branch.

The Madisonian Model—Separation of Powers.

The major issue of **separation of powers** had not yet been resolved. The delegates were concerned with structuring the government to prevent the imposition of tyranny—either by the majority or by a minority. Madison proposed a governmental scheme—sometimes called the **Madisonian model**—to achieve this: The executive, legislative, and judicial powers of government were to be separated so that no one branch had enough power to dominate the others, nor could any one person hold office in two different branches of the government at the same time. The separation of powers was by function, as well as by personnel, with Congress passing laws, the president enforcing and administering laws, and the courts interpreting laws in individual circumstances.

Each of the three branches of government would be independent of the others, but they would have to share power to govern. According to Madison, in Federalist #51 (see Appendix C), "the great security against a gradual concentration of the several powers in the same department consists in giving to those who administer each department the necessary constitutional means and personal motives to resist encroachments of the others."

The Madisonian Model—Checks and Balances.

The "constitutional means" Madison referred to is a system of **checks and balances** through which each branch of the government can check the actions of the others. For example, Congress can enact laws, but the president has veto power over congressional acts. The Supreme Court has the power to declare acts of Congress and of the executive unconstitutional, but the president appoints the justices of the Supreme Court, with the advice and consent of the Senate. (The Supreme Court's power to declare acts unconstitutional was not mentioned in the Constitution, although arguably the framers assumed that the Court would have this power—see the discussion of judicial review later in this chapter.) Figure 2–2 outlines these checks and balances.

Madison's ideas of separation of powers and checks and balances were not new. The influential French political thinker Baron de Montesquieu (1689–1755) had explored these concepts in his book *The Spirit of the Laws*, published in 1748. Montesquieu not only discussed the "three sorts of powers" (executive, legislative, and judicial) that were necessarily exercised by any government but also gave examples of how, in some nations, certain checks on these powers had arisen and had been effective in preventing tyranny.

In the years since the Constitution was ratified, the checks and balances built into it have evolved into a sometimes complex give-and-take among the branches of government. Generally, for nearly every check that one branch has over another, the branch that has been checked has found a way of getting around it. For example, suppose that the president checks Congress by vetoing a bill. Congress can override the presidential veto by a two-thirds vote. Additionally, Congress holds the "power of the purse." If it disagrees with a program endorsed by the executive branch, it can simply refuse to appropriate the funds necessary

American School, (19th century); Musee Franco-Americaine, Blerancourt, Chauny, France/Giraudon/ The Bridgeman Art Library

James Madison (1751–1836) earned the title "master builder of the Constitution" because of his persuasive logic during the Constitutional Convention. His contributions to the *Federalist Papers* showed him to be a brilliant political thinker and writer.

Separation of Powers
The principle of dividing governmental powers among different branches of government.

Madisonian Model
A structure of government proposed by James Madison in which the powers of the government are separated into three branches: executive, legislative, and judicial.

Checks and Balances
A major principle of the American system of government whereby each branch of the government can check the actions of the others.

did you know?

Alexander Hamilton wanted the American president to hold office for life and to have absolute veto power over the legislature.

Figure 2-2 ▶ Checks and Balances

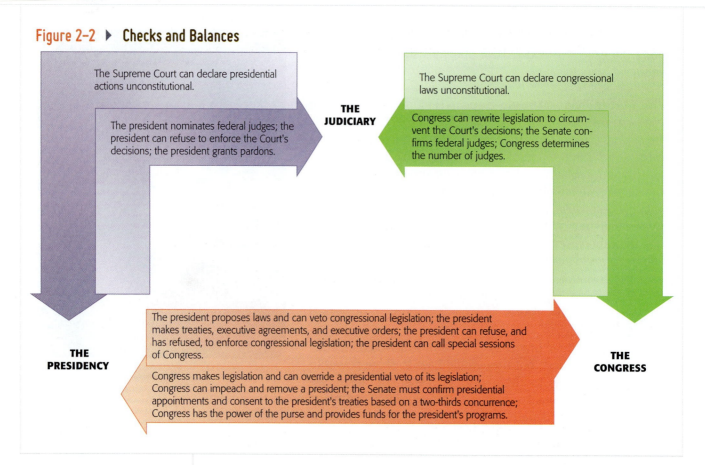

to operate that program. Similarly, the president can impose a countercheck on Congress if the Senate refuses to confirm a presidential appointment, such as a judicial appointment. The president can simply wait until Congress is in recess and then make what is called a "recess appointment," which does not require the Senate's approval. Recess appointments last until the end of the next session of the Congress.

The Executive. Some delegates favored a plural executive made up of representatives from the various regions. This was abandoned in favor of a single chief executive. Some argued that Congress should choose the executive. To make the presidency completely independent of the proposed Congress, however, an electoral college was adopted. To be sure, the **electoral college** created a cumbersome presidential election process (see Chapter 9). The process even made it possible for a candidate who came in second in the popular vote to become president by being the top vote-getter in the electoral college, which happened in 2000 and in three prior contests. The electoral college insulated the president, however, from direct popular control. The seven-year single term that some of the delegates had proposed was replaced by a four-year term and the possibility of reelection.

A Federal Republic. The Constitution creates a **federal system** of government that divides the sovereign powers of the nation between the states and the national government. This structure allows for states to make their own laws about many of the issues of direct concern for their citizens while granting the national government far more power over the states and their citizens than under the Articles of Confederacy. As you will read in Chapter 3, the Constitution expressly granted certain powers to the national government.

Electoral College
A group of persons called electors selected by the voters in each state and the District of Columbia; this group officially elects the president and vice president of the United States. The number of electors in each state is equal to the number of each state's representatives in both chambers of Congress.

Federal System
A system of government in which power is divided between a central government and regional, or subdivisional, governments. Each level must have some domain in which its policies are dominant and some genuine political or constitutional guarantee of its authority.

For example, the national government was given the power to regulate commerce among the states. The Constitution also declared that the president is the nation's chief executive and the commander in chief of the armed forces. Additionally, the Constitution made it clear that laws made by the national government take priority over conflicting state laws. At the same time, the Constitution provided for extensive states' rights, including the right to control commerce within state borders and to exercise those governing powers that were not delegated to the national government.

The Final Document

On September 17, 1787, the Constitution was approved by 39 delegates. Of the 55 who had originally attended, only 42 remained. Three delegates refused to sign the Constitution. Others disapproved of at least parts of it but signed anyway to begin the ratification debate.

The Constitution that was to be ratified established the following fundamental principles:

1. Popular sovereignty, or control by the people.
2. A republican government in which the people choose representatives to make decisions for them.
3. Limited government with written laws, in contrast to the powerful British government against which the colonists had rebelled.
4. Separation of powers, with checks and balances among branches to prevent any one branch from gaining too much power.
5. A federal system that allows for states' rights, because the states feared too much centralized control.

The Difficult Road to Ratification

The founders knew that **ratification** of the Constitution was far from certain. Because it was almost guaranteed that many state legislatures would not ratify it, the delegates agreed that each state should hold a special convention. Elected delegates to these conventions would discuss and vote on the Constitution. Further departing from the Articles of Confederation, the delegates agreed that as soon as nine states (rather than all 13) approved the Constitution, it would take effect, and Congress could begin to organize the new government.

The federal system created by the founders was a novel form of government at that time—no other country in the world had such a system. It was invented by the founders as a compromise solution to the controversy over whether the states or the central government should have ultimate sovereignty. As you will read in Chapter 3, the debate over where the line should be drawn between states' rights and the powers of the national government has characterized American politics ever since. The founders did not go into detail about where this line should be drawn, thus leaving it up to scholars and court judges to divine their intentions.

The Federalists Push for Ratification

The two opposing forces in the battle over ratification were the Federalists and the Anti-Federalists. The **Federalists**—those in favor of a strong central government and the new Constitution—had an advantage over their opponents, called the **Anti-Federalists**, who wanted to prevent the Constitution as drafted

Ratification
Formal approval.

Federalist
The name given to one who was in favor of the adoption of the U.S. Constitution and the creation of a federal union with a strong central government.

Anti-Federalist
An individual who opposed the ratification of the new Constitution in 1787. The Anti-Federalists were opposed to a strong central government.

from being ratified. In the first place, the Federalists had assumed a positive name, leaving their opposition the negative label of *Anti*-Federalist.[11] More important, the Federalists had attended the Constitutional Convention and knew of all the deliberations that had taken place. Their opponents had no such knowledge, because those deliberations had not been open to the public. Thus, the Anti-Federalists were at a disadvantage in terms of information about the document. The Federalists also had time, power, and money on their side. Communications were slow. Those who had access to the best communications were Federalists—mostly wealthy bankers, lawyers, plantation owners, and merchants living in urban areas, where communications were better. The Federalist campaign was organized relatively quickly and effectively to elect Federalists as delegates to the state ratifying conventions.

The Anti-Federalists, however, had at least one strong point in their favor: They stood for the status quo. In general, the greater burden is always placed on those advocating change.

The *Federalist Papers*.

In New York, opponents of the Constitution were quick to attack it. Alexander Hamilton answered their attacks in newspaper columns over the signature "Caesar." When the Caesar letters had little effect, Hamilton switched to the pseudonym Publius and secured two collaborators—John Jay and James Madison. In a very short time, those three political figures wrote a series of 85 essays in defense of the Constitution and of a republican form of government.

These widely read essays, called the *Federalist Papers*, appeared in New York newspapers from October 1787 to August 1788 and were reprinted in the newspapers of other states. Although we do not know for certain who wrote every one, it is apparent that Hamilton was responsible for about two-thirds of the essays. These included the most important ones interpreting the Constitution, explaining the various powers of the three branches, and presenting a theory of *judicial review*—to be discussed later in this chapter. Madison's Federalist #10 (see Appendix C), however, is considered a classic in political theory; it deals with the nature of groups—or factions, as he called them. Despite the rapidity with which the *Federalist Papers* were written, they are considered by many to be perhaps the best example of political theorizing ever produced in the United States.[12]

The Anti-Federalist Response.

The Anti-Federalists used such pseudonyms as Montezuma and Philadelphiensis in their replies. Many of their attacks on the Constitution were also brilliant. The Anti-Federalists claimed that the Constitution was written by aristocrats and would lead to aristocratic tyranny. More important, the Anti-Federalists believed that the Constitution would create an overbearing and overburdening central government hostile to personal liberty. (The Constitution said nothing about freedom of the press, freedom of religion, or any other individual liberty.) They wanted to include a list of guaranteed liberties, or a bill of rights. Finally, the Anti-Federalists decried the weakened power of the states.

The Anti-Federalists cannot be dismissed as unpatriotic extremists. They included such patriots as Patrick Henry and Samuel Adams. They were arguing what had been the most prevalent contemporary opinion. This view derived from

---

11. There is some irony here. At the Constitutional Convention, those opposed to a strong central government pushed for a federal system because such a system would allow the states to retain some of their sovereign rights (see Chapter 3). The label *Anti-Federalists* thus contradicted their essential views.
12. Some scholars believe that the *Federalist Papers* played only a minor role in securing ratification of the Constitution. Even if this is true, they still have lasting value as an authoritative explanation of the Constitution.

the French political philosopher Montesquieu, who, as mentioned earlier, was an influential political theorist at that time. Montesquieu believed that liberty was safe only in relatively small societies governed by direct democracy or by a large legislature with small districts. The Madisonian view favoring a large republic, particularly expressed in Federalist #10 and #51 (see Appendix C), was actually the more *un*popular view at the time. Madison was probably convincing because citizens were already persuaded that a strong national government was necessary to combat foreign enemies and to prevent domestic insurrections. Still, some researchers believe it was mainly the bitter experiences with the Articles of Confederation, rather than Madison's arguments, that persuaded the state conventions to ratify the Constitution.[13]

The March to the Finish

The struggle for ratification continued. Strong majorities were procured in Delaware, Pennsylvania, New Jersey, Georgia, and Connecticut. After a bitter struggle in Massachusetts, that state ratified the Constitution by a narrow margin on February 6, 1788. By the spring, Maryland and South Carolina had ratified by sizable majorities. Then on June 21 of that year, New Hampshire became the ninth state to ratify the Constitution. Although the Constitution was formally in effect, this meant little without Virginia and New York—the latter did not ratify for another month (see Table 2–3).

Did the Majority of Americans Support the Constitution?

In 1913, historian Charles Beard published *An Economic Interpretation of the Constitution of the United States*.[14] This book launched a debate that has continued ever since—the debate over whether the Constitution was supported by a majority of Americans.

Beard's Thesis. Beard's central thesis was that the Constitution had been produced primarily by wealthy property owners who desired a stronger government able to protect their property rights. Beard also claimed that the Constitution had been imposed by undemocratic methods to prevent democratic majorities from exercising real power. He pointed out that there was never any popular vote on whether to hold a constitutional convention in the first place.

Furthermore, even if such a vote had been taken, state laws generally restricted voting rights to property-owning white males, meaning that most people in the country (white males without property, women, Native Americans, and slaves) were not eligible to vote. Finally, Beard pointed out that even the word *democracy* was distasteful to the founders. The term was often used by conservatives to smear their opponents.

Table 2-3 ▶ Ratification of the Constitution

STATE	DATE	VOTE FOR—AGAINST
Delaware	Dec. 7, 1787	30—0
Pennsylvania	Dec. 12, 1787	43—23
New Jersey	Dec. 18, 1787	38—0
Georgia	Jan. 2, 1788	26—0
Connecticut	Jan. 9, 1788	128—40
Massachusetts	Feb. 6, 1788	187—168
Maryland	Apr. 28, 1788	63—11
South Carolina	May 23, 1788	149—73
New Hampshire	June 21, 1788	57—46
Virginia	June 25, 1788	89—79
New York	July 26, 1788	30—27
North Carolina	Nov. 21, 1789*	194—77
Rhode Island	May 29, 1790	34—32

*Ratification was originally defeated on August 4, 1788, by a vote of 84–184.

13. Of particular interest is the view of the Anti-Federalist position contained in Herbert J. Storing, *What the Anti-Federalists Were For* (Chicago: University of Chicago Press, 1981). Storing also edited seven volumes of the Anti-Federalist writings, *The Complete Anti-Federalist* (Chicago: University of Chicago Press, 1981). See also Josephine F. Pacheco, *Antifederalism: The Legacy of George Mason* (Fairfax, VA: George Mason University Press, 1992).
14. Charles A. Beard, *An Economic Interpretation of the Constitution of the United States* (New York: MacMillan, 1913; New York: Free Press, 1986).

State Ratifying Conventions. As for the various state ratifying conventions, the delegates had been selected by only 150,000 of the approximately 4 million citizens. That does not seem very democratic—at least not by today's standards. Some historians have suggested that if a Gallup poll could have been taken at that time, the Anti-Federalists would probably have outnumbered the Federalists.[15]

Support Was Probably Widespread. Much has also been made of the various machinations used by the Federalists to ensure the Constitution's ratification (and they did resort to a variety of devious tactics, including purchasing at least one printing press to prevent the publication of Anti-Federalist sentiments). Yet the perception that a strong central government was necessary to keep order and protect the public welfare appears to have been fairly pervasive among all classes—rich and poor alike.

Further, although the need for strong government was a major argument in favor of adopting the Constitution, even the Federalists sought to craft a limited government. Compared with constitutions adopted by other nations in later years, the U.S. Constitution, through its checks and balances, favors limited government over "energetic" government to a marked degree.

The Bill of Rights

The U.S. Constitution would not have been ratified in several important states if the Federalists had not assured the states that amendments to the Constitution would be passed to protect individual liberties against incursions by the national government. The idea of including certain rights in the Constitution had been discussed in the convention. There were those who believed that including these rights was simply unnecessary, whereas others suggested that carefully articulating certain rights might encourage the new national government to abuse any that were not specifically defined. Some rights, including the prohibition of *ex post facto lawmaking*, were included in the document. *Ex post facto lawmaking* is passing laws that make one liable for an act that has already taken place. Also prohibited were *bills of attainder*, through which a legislature could pass judgment on someone without legal process. However, many of the recommendations of the state ratifying conventions included specific rights that were considered later by James Madison as he labored to draft what became the Bill of Rights.

A "Bill of Limits"

Although called the Bill of Rights, essentially the first 10 amendments to the Constitution were a "bill of limits," because the amendments limited the powers of the national government over the rights and liberties of individuals.

Ironically, a year earlier Madison had told Jefferson, "I have never thought the omission [of the Bill of Rights] a material defect" of the Constitution. But Jefferson's enthusiasm for a bill of rights apparently influenced Madison, as did his desire to gain popular support for his election to Congress. Madison promised in his campaign letter to voters that, once elected, he would force Congress to "prepare and recommend to the states for ratification, the most satisfactory provisions for all essential rights."

Madison had to cull through more than 200 state recommendations.[16] It was no small task, and in retrospect he chose remarkably well. One of the

---

15. Jim Powell, "James Madison—Checks and Balances to Limit Government Power," *The Freeman,* March 1996, p. 178.
16. For details on these recommendations, including their sources, see Leonard W. Levy, *Origins of the Bill of Rights* (New Haven, CT: Yale University Press, 1999).

Beyond Our Borders
WHAT MAKES A CONSTITUTION?

When Americans think of the Constitution, most visualize an old handwritten document that is protected in our National Archives. They may also reflect on the basic principles of the Constitution—checks and balances, separation of powers, the Bill of Rights—that structure how the national government carries out its work. However, the United States Constitution was written more than 200 years ago for a relatively small, mostly rural nation. Constitutions are still being written, in some cases for the first time, and in others, such as in Egypt, to reflect a major change in political power.

WHAT SHOULD BE INCLUDED?

In February 2012, associate justice of the Supreme Court Ruth Bader Ginsburg visited Egypt and gave an interview broadcast on YouTube. Ginsburg's remarks were criticized by some because she suggested that the Egyptians, as they write their new constitution, not use ours as a model. While she praised many aspects of the American document, she recommended that the Egyptians look at newer charters including that of South Africa, the Canadian charter of rights and freedoms, and the Kenyan constitution.

Justice Ruth Ginsburg discusses law and constitutions with Egyptian students after the overthrow of the former ruler, Hosni Mubarak.

What kinds of models is the justice suggesting? What provisions are included in these new constitutions that make them more appropriate to a nation like Egypt? It is important to remember that nations that are struggling to write constitutions face conditions far different than those faced by the Founding Fathers in 1789. In Egypt, for example, the 30-year rule of Hosni Mubarak was ended by the "Arab Spring" protests of Egyptians seeking a more democratic nation and the end of a repressive military regime. In South Africa, the 1996 constitution had to deal with the end of apartheid and provide a way to unify a country that had been divided by race for a century. In Iraq, the new constitution was written to allow rights and authority for the three major sectarian and ethnic groups. In Egypt and South Africa, an additional problem is the existence of a vast majority of economically disadvantaged citizens who need basic sanitation and housing.

Justice Ginsburg called attention to the South African constitution's bill of rights. It is, in comparison to the U.S. Constitution, very inclusive and modern in its interpretation of human rights. All of the political rights included in the American model are there but, in addition, citizens are guaranteed the freedom to travel; the right to housing; the right to basic education; the right to food, water, and social assistance from the government; and the right to unionize. The government may not discriminate on the basis of race, gender, sex, pregnancy, religion, ethnic or social origin, sexual orientation, and so on. To date, the Supreme Court of the United States has declared that race, religion, and ethnic origin but little else have that protected status.

WHAT IS THE GOAL?

After a war, the victorious nation or coalition of allies may decide that the defeated country should have a new constitution, one that will make another war less likely. After World War II, General Douglas MacArthur, the commander of the Pacific forces, occupied Japan and gave strong direction to the writing of the new Japanese Constitution. That document, which is still in force and has never been amended, makes it clear that the Japanese imperial family has no political power at all. The Basic Law of Germany was also written after the Allied victory in World War II and contains provisions that are intended to prohibit the rise of a political movement like that of Adolf Hitler.

IS IT A REAL CONSTITUTION?

During the Cold War between the United States and the Soviet Union, the Soviet republics held elections and called themselves democratic nations. They all had written constitutions to which they strictly adhered. However, the elections were not contested, and no opposition candidates or political parties emerged. Newspapers and other media were strictly controlled, as was any

(Continued)

AP Photo/U.S. Embassy Egypt

iStockphoto.com/Kyoshino iStockphoto.com/mattjeacock

(Continued)

access to external information. Today, all of the former Soviet republics have new constitutions, and many are democracies with the same freedoms as other nations in Western Europe or the United States.

Similarly, the People's Republic of North Korea has a fairly new constitution (1998) and claims to be democratic. However, the military and the premier, Kim Jong Un , direct all aspects of life there, including limiting the frequencies available on radios and televisions to those approved by the government. So, it seems that just having a written document outlining the structures of government and freedoms of the people may not be enough to guarantee any form of democratic government, at least in the sense that we know it. As Justice Ginsburg put it, "The spirit of liberty has to be in the population."*

*"Ruth Bader Ginsburg Talks Constitution, Women and Liberty on Egyptian TV," www.Huffingtonpost.com/2012/02/01. February 1, 2012.

If you would like to read the constitution of any country in the world, go to confinder. richmond.edu.

Another site provides resources to constitution-makers: constitutionmaking.org is linked to a research project about constitutions. That site, maintained by Zachary Elkins of the University of Texas and Tom Ginsburg of the University of Illinois, is www.comparativeconstitutionsproject.org.

FOR CRITICAL ANALYSIS

1. *Do you think the United States could have survived without a written constitution?*

2. *How important is it for the people of a nation to have approved their constitution?*

3. *How can you tell if a nation is following the letter and the spirit of its constitution?*

rights appropriate for constitutional protection that he left out was equal protection under the laws—but that was not commonly regarded as a basic right at that time. Not until 1868 did the states ratify an amendment guaranteeing that no state shall deny equal protection to any person. (The Supreme Court has since applied this guarantee to certain actions of the federal government as well.)

The final number of amendments that Madison and a specially appointed committee came up with was 17. Congress tightened the language somewhat and eliminated five of the amendments. Of the remaining 12, two—dealing with the apportionment of representatives and the compensation of the members of Congress—were not ratified immediately by the states. Eventually, Supreme Court decisions led to reform of the apportionment process. The amendment on the compensation of members of Congress was ratified 203 years later—in 1992!

No Explicit Limits on State Government Powers

On December 15, 1791, the national Bill of Rights was adopted when Virginia agreed to ratify the 10 amendments. On ratification, the Bill of Rights became part of the U.S. Constitution. The basic structure of American government had already been established. Now the fundamental rights and liberties of individuals were protected, at least in theory, at the national level. The proposed amendment that Madison characterized as "the most valuable amendment in the whole lot"—which would have prohibited the states from infringing on the freedoms of conscience, press, and jury trial—had been eliminated by the Senate. Thus, the Bill of Rights as adopted did not limit state power, and individual citizens had to rely on the guarantees contained in a particular state constitution or state bill of rights. The country had to wait until the violence of the Civil War before significant limitations on state power in the form of the Fourteenth Amendment became part of the national Constitution.

Altering the Constitution: The Formal Amendment Process

The U.S. Constitution consists of 7,000 words. It is shorter than any state constitution except that of Vermont, which has 6,880 words. One of the reasons the federal Constitution is short is that the founders intended it to be only a framework for the new government, to be interpreted by succeeding generations. One of the reasons it has remained short is that the formal amending procedure does not allow for changes to be made easily. Article V of the Constitution outlines the ways in which amendments may be proposed and ratified (see Figure 2–3).

Two formal methods of proposing an amendment to the Constitution are available: (1) a two-thirds vote in each chamber of Congress or (2) a national convention that is called by Congress at the request of two-thirds of the state legislatures (the second method has never been used).

Ratification can occur by one of two methods: (1) by a positive vote in three-fourths of the legislatures of the various states or (2) by special conventions called in the states and a positive vote in three-fourths of them. The second method has been used only once, to repeal Prohibition (the ban on the production and sale of alcoholic beverages). That situation was exceptional because it involved an amendment (the Twenty-first) to repeal an amendment (the Eighteenth, which had created Prohibition). State conventions were necessary for repeal of the Eighteenth Amendment, because the "pro-dry" legislatures in the most conservative states would never have passed the repeal. (Note that Congress determines

■ **Learning Outcome 5:**
Demonstrate understanding of the formal and informal processes for amending the U.S. Constitution.

Figure 2–3 ▶ The Formal Constitutional Amending Procedure

There are two ways of proposing amendments to the U.S. Constitution and two ways of ratifying proposed amendments. Among the four possibilities, the usual route has been proposal by Congress and ratification by state legislatures.

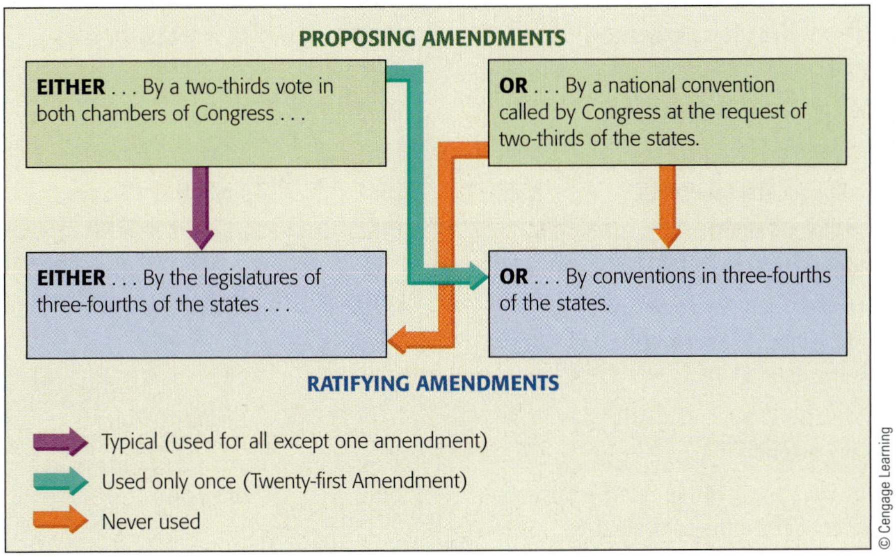

PROPOSING AMENDMENTS

EITHER . . . By a two-thirds vote in both chambers of Congress . . .

OR . . . By a national convention called by Congress at the request of two-thirds of the states.

EITHER . . . By the legislatures of three-fourths of the states . . .

OR . . . By conventions in three-fourths of the states.

RATIFYING AMENDMENTS

➡ Typical (used for all except one amendment)
➡ Used only once (Twenty-first Amendment)
➡ Never used

© Cengage Learning

the method of ratification to be used by all states for each proposed constitutional amendment.)

Many Amendments Are Proposed; Few Are Accepted

Congress has considered more than 11,000 amendments to the Constitution. Many proposed amendments have been advanced to address highly specific problems. An argument against such narrow amendments has been that amendments ought to embody broad principles, in the way that the existing Constitution does. For that reason, many people have opposed such narrow amendments as one to prohibit the burning or defacing of the American flag.

Only 33 amendments have been submitted to the states after having been approved by the required two-thirds vote in each chamber of Congress, and only 27 have been ratified—see Table 2–4. (The full, annotated text of the U.S. Constitution, including its amendments, is presented in Appendix B at the end of this book.) It should be clear that the amendment process is much more difficult

Table 2–4 ▶ Amendments to the Constitution

AMENDMENT	SUBJECT	YEAR ADOPTED	TIME REQUIRED FOR RATIFICATION
First to Tenth	The Bill of Rights	1791	2 years, 2 months, 20 days
Eleventh	Immunity of states from certain suits	1795	11 months, 3 days
Twelfth	Changes in electoral college procedure	1804	6 months, 3 days
Thirteenth	Prohibition of slavery	1865	10 months, 3 days
Fourteenth	Citizenship, due process, and equal protection	1868	2 years, 26 days
Fifteenth	No denial of vote because of race, color, or previous condition of servitude	1870	11 months, 8 days
Sixteenth	Power of Congress to tax income	1913	3 years, 6 months, 22 days
Seventeenth	Direct election of U.S. senators	1913	10 months, 26 days
Eighteenth	National (liquor) prohibition	1919	1 year, 29 days
Nineteenth	Women's right to vote	1920	1 year, 2 months, 14 days
Twentieth	Change of dates for congressional and presidential terms	1933	10 months, 21 days
Twenty-first	Repeal of the Eighteenth Amendment	1933	9 months, 15 days
Twenty-second	Limit on presidential tenure	1951	3 years, 11 months, 3 days
Twenty-third	District of Columbia electoral vote	1961	9 months, 13 days
Twenty-fourth	Prohibition of tax payment as a qualification to vote in federal elections	1964	1 year, 4 months, 9 days
Twenty-fifth	Procedures for determining presidential disability and presidential succession and for filling a vice presidential vacancy	1967	1 year, 7 months, 4 days
Twenty-sixth	Prohibition of setting minimum voting age above 18 in any election	1971	3 months, 7 days
Twenty-seventh	Prohibition of Congress's voting itself a raise that takes effect before the next election	1992	203 years

than a graphic depiction such as Figure 2–3 can indicate. Because of competing social and economic interests, the requirement that two-thirds of both the House and Senate approve the amendments is difficult to achieve. Thirty-four senators, representing only 17 sparsely populated states, could block any amendment. For example, the Republican-controlled House approved the Balanced Budget Amendment within the first 100 days of the 104th Congress in 1995, but it was defeated in the Senate by one vote.

After approval by Congress, the process becomes even more arduous. Three-fourths of the state legislatures must approve the amendment. Only those amendments that have wide popular support across parties and in all regions of the country are likely to be approved.

Limits on Ratification

A reading of Article V of the Constitution reveals that the framers of the Constitution specified no time limit on the ratification process. The Supreme Court has held that Congress can specify a time for ratification as long as it is "reasonable." Since 1919, most proposed amendments have included a requirement that ratification be obtained within seven years. This was the case with the proposed Equal Rights Amendment, which sought to guarantee equal rights for women. When three-fourths of the states had not ratified in the allotted seven years, however, Congress extended the limit by an additional three years and three months. That extension expired on June 30, 1982, and the amendment still had not been ratified. Another proposed amendment, which would have guaranteed congressional representation to the District of Columbia, fell far short of the 38 state ratifications needed before its August 22, 1985, deadline.

On May 7, 1992, Michigan became the 38th state to ratify the Twenty-seventh Amendment (on congressional compensation)—one of the two "lost" amendments of the 12 that originally were sent to the states in 1789. Because most of the amendments proposed in recent years have been given a time limit of only seven years by Congress, it was questionable for a time whether the amendment would take effect even if the necessary number of states ratified it. Is 203 years too long a lapse of time between the proposal and the final ratification of an amendment? It apparently was not, because the amendment was certified as legitimate by archivist Don Wilson of the National Archives on May 18, 1992.

The National Convention Provision

The Constitution provides that a national convention requested by the legislatures of two-thirds of the states can propose a constitutional amendment. Congress has received approximately 400 convention applications since the Constitution was ratified; every state has applied at least once. Fewer than 20 applications were submitted during the Constitution's first hundred years, but more than 150 have been filed in the last two decades. No national convention has been held since 1787, and most national political and judicial leaders are uneasy about the prospect of convening a body that conceivably could do as the Constitutional Convention did—create a new form of government. The state legislative bodies that originate national convention applications, however, do not appear to be uncomfortable with such a constitutional modification process; more than 230 state constitutional conventions have been held.

Informal Methods of Constitutional Change

Formal amendments are one way of changing our Constitution, and, as is obvious from their small number, they have been resorted to infrequently and are very difficult to pass and ratify. If we discount the first 10 amendments (the Bill of Rights), which were adopted soon after the ratification of the Constitution, only 17 formal alterations have been made to the Constitution in the more than 200 years of its existence.

Just looking at the small number of amendments vastly understates the ability of the Constitution to adjust to changing times. The brevity and ambiguity of the original document have permitted great alterations in the Constitution by way of varying interpretations over time. As the United States grew, both in population and territory, new social and political realities emerged. Congress, presidents, and the courts found it necessary to interpret the Constitution's provisions in light of these new realities. The Constitution has proved to be a remarkably flexible document, adapting itself repeatedly to new events and concerns.

Congressional Legislation

The Constitution gives Congress broad powers to carry out its duties as the nation's legislative body. For example, Article I, Section 8 of the Constitution gives Congress the power to regulate foreign and interstate commerce. Although the Constitution has no clear definition of foreign commerce or interstate commerce, Congress has cited the *commerce clause* as the basis for passing thousands of laws that have defined the meaning of foreign and interstate commerce.

Similarly, Article III, Section 1 states that the national judiciary shall consist of one supreme court and "such inferior courts, as Congress may from time to time ordain and establish." Through a series of acts, Congress has used this broad provision to establish the federal court system of today, which includes the Supreme Court, the courts of appeal, and district courts. This provision allows Congress to create a court such as the Foreign Intelligence Surveillance Act (FISA) court to review requests for wiretapping suspected terrorists.

In addition, Congress has frequently delegated to federal agencies the legislative power to write regulations. These regulations, numbering in the tens of thousands, become law unless challenged in the court system. Nowhere does the Constitution outline this delegation of legislative authority.

Presidential Actions

Even though the Constitution does not expressly authorize the president to propose bills or even budgets to Congress,[17] presidents since the time of Woodrow Wilson (president from 1913 to 1921) have proposed hundreds of bills to Congress each year. Presidents have also relied on their Article II authority as commander in chief of the nation's armed forces to send American troops abroad into combat, although the Constitution provides that Congress has the power to declare war.

The president's powers in wartime have waxed and waned through the course of American history. President Abraham Lincoln instituted a draft and suspended several civil liberties during the Civil War. During World War II, President Franklin Roosevelt approved the internment of thousands of Japanese American citizens.

---

17. Note, though, that the Constitution, in Article II, Section 3, does state that the president "shall from time to time … recommend to [Congress's] consideration such measures as he shall judge necessary and expedient." Some scholars interpret this phrase to mean that the president has the constitutional authority to propose bills and budgets to Congress for consideration.

President George W. Bush significantly expanded presidential power in the wake of the terrorist attacks of 2001, especially in regard to the handling of individuals who could be defined as "enemy combatants." The creation of the detention facility at Guantánamo Bay, Cuba, made it possible for those prisoners to be held and interrogated by the military under the full control of the executive branch. After 2010, when President Obama faced a divided Congress, he too began to use executive power more liberally, supporting the writing of regulations to protect the environment and making recess appointments when his appointees could not be confirmed.

Presidents have also conducted foreign affairs by the use of executive agreements, which are legally binding documents made between the president and a foreign head of state. The Constitution does not mention such agreements.

Judicial Review

Another way of changing the Constitution—or of making it more flexible—is through the power of judicial review. Judicial review refers to the power of U.S. courts to examine the constitutionality of actions undertaken by the legislative and executive branches of government. A state court, for example, may rule that a statute enacted by the state legislature is unconstitutional. Federal courts (and ultimately, the United States Supreme Court) may rule unconstitutional not only acts of Congress and decisions of the national executive branch but also state statutes, state executive actions, and even provisions of state constitutions.

Not a Novel Concept. The Constitution does not specifically mention the power of judicial review. Those in attendance at the Constitutional Convention, however, probably expected that the courts would have some authority to review the legality of acts by the executive and legislative branches, because, under the common-law tradition inherited from England, courts exercised this authority. Alexander Hamilton, in Federalist #78, explicitly outlined the concept of judicial review. Whether the power of judicial review can be justified constitutionally is a question that has been subject to some debate, particularly in recent years. For now, suffice it to say that in 1803, the Supreme Court claimed this power for itself in *Marbury v. Madison*,[18] in which the Court ruled that a particular provision of an act of Congress was unconstitutional.

Allows the Court to Adapt the Constitution. Through the process of judicial review, the Supreme Court adapts the Constitution to modern situations. Electronic technology, for example, did not exist when the Constitution was ratified. Nonetheless, the Supreme Court has used the Fourth Amendment guarantees against unreasonable searches and seizures to place limits on the use of wiretapping and other electronic eavesdropping methods by government officials. The Court has needed to decide whether antiterrorism laws passed by Congress or state legislatures, or executive orders declared by the president, violate the Fourth Amendment or other constitutional provisions. Additionally, the Supreme Court has changed its interpretation of the Constitution in accordance with changing values. It ruled in 1896 that "separate-but-equal" public facilities for African Americans were constitutional; but by 1954, the times had changed, and the Supreme Court reversed that decision.[19] Woodrow Wilson summarized the Supreme Court's work when he

---

18. 5 U.S. 137 (1803). See Chapter 15 for a further discussion of the *Marbury v. Madison* case.
19. *Brown v. Board of Education of Topeka,* 347 U.S. 483 (1954).

described it as "a constitutional convention in continuous session." Basically, the law is what the Supreme Court says it is at any given time.

Interpretation, Custom, and Usage

The Constitution has also been changed through interpretation by both Congress and the president. Originally, the president had a staff consisting of personal secretaries and a few others. Today, because Congress delegates specific tasks to the president and the chief executive assumes political leadership, the executive office staff alone has increased to several thousand persons. The executive branch provides legislative leadership far beyond the expectations of the founders.

Changes in the ways of doing political business have also altered the Constitution. The Constitution does not mention political parties, yet these informal, "extraconstitutional" organizations make the nominations for offices, run the campaigns, organize the members of Congress, and in fact change the election system from time to time. The emergence and evolution of the party system, for example, has changed the way the president is elected. The entire nominating process with its use of primary elections and caucuses to choose delegates to the party's nominating convention is the creation of the two major political parties. The president is then selected by the electors who are, in fact, chosen by the parties and are pledged to a party's candidate.

A recent book by Bruce Ackerman argues that the rise of political parties and growth of the executive represent the failure of the Founding Fathers to understand how the government would develop over time. He proposes that the only reason that the system has maintained its checks is the development of the Supreme Court into the guarantor of our rights and liberties.[20] Perhaps most striking, the Constitution has been adapted from serving the needs of a small, rural republic to providing a framework of government for an industrial giant with vast geographic, natural, and human resources.

---

20. Bruce Ackerman, *The Failure of the Founding Fathers: Jefferson, Marshall, and the Rise of Presidential Democracy* (Cambridge, MA: The Belknap Press, 2005).

You Can Make a Difference

HOW CAN YOU AFFECT THE U.S. CONSTITUTION?

The U.S. Constitution is an enduring document that has survived more than 200 years of turbulent history. It is also a changing document, however. Twenty-seven amendments have been added to the original Constitution. How can you, as an individual, actively influence constitutional amendments?

www.dotrights.org is a Web site established by the American Civil Liberties Union to help people understand their right to privacy and their protections against the government in the use of the Internet.

WHY SHOULD YOU CARE?

The laws of the nation have a direct impact on your life, and none more so than the Constitution—the supreme law of the land. The most important issues in society are often settled by the Constitution. For example, for the first 75 years of the republic, the Constitution implicitly protected the institution of slavery. If the Constitution had never been changed through the amendment process, slavery might still be legal today.

Since the passage of the Fourteenth Amendment in 1868, the Constitution has defined who is a citizen and who is entitled to the protections the Constitution provides. Constitutional provisions define our liberties. Today, the national debate is over whether undocumented individuals who live and work here should also be protected. The First Amendment protects our rights to free expression and the right to assemble to protest government. Few other nations have such extensive guarantees for free speech and yet, those guarantees make possible the huge campaign donations of interest groups and individuals. All of these are among the most fundamental issues we face.

WHAT CAN YOU DO?

One way that you can affect the Constitution is by protecting your existing rights and liberties under it. In the wake of the September 11 attacks, several new laws have been enacted that many believe go too far in curbing our constitutional rights. If you agree and want to join with others who are concerned about this issue, a good starting point is the Web site of the American Civil Liberties Union (ACLU) at **www.aclu.org**. Click on the Take Action button to see the latest news on constitutional issues and see what actions you could take. One of the most recent campaigns launched by the ACLU is "Protect Your dotRights,"

meaning protecting your privacy rights on the Internet and on social networking sites. Take a look at this page to see what the issues are and how you can better protect your privacy on the Internet.

Do you feel that your vote makes a difference? Many voters are beginning to feel disenfranchised by the political process in presidential elections through the effects of the electoral college. A 2007 poll found that 72 percent of Americans favored replacing the electoral college with a direct election.* The Every Vote Counts Amendment proposes to abolish the electoral college and would provide for the direct popular election of the president. If you would like to further investigate Every Vote Counts, go to **www.washingtonwatch.com**, a forum for monitoring proposed legislation in Washington, D.C. Visit the Take Action box, where you can comment on the amendment, alert your friends and colleagues about the issue, and write your representative in Congress.

At the time of this writing, national coalitions of interest groups are supporting or opposing several proposed amendments. Constitutional amendments are difficult to pass, needing supermajorities in the House and Senate, as well as three-fourths of the state legislatures. The National Popular Vote Bill seeks to reform the electoral college through individual state legislatures, which may change state laws regarding the distribution of electoral votes. With the National Popular Vote Bill, all state electoral votes would be awarded to the presidential candidate winning the popular vote in all 50 states and the District of Columbia. Check out National Popular Vote, Inc., a nonprofit group, at **www.nationalpopularvote.com**, for more information regarding this bill. Its Web site offers numerous ways to become informed and take action. You can even check the bill's progress in your own state.

* The Washington Post–Kaiser Family Foundation–Harvard University Survey of Political Independents, Public Opinion and Media Research Program, *Kaiser Family Foundation*, July 1, 2007, p. 14; www.kff.org/kaiserpolls/7665.cfm.

Key Terms

Anti-Federalist 47
bicameral legislature 42
checks and balances 45
confederation 36
electoral college 46

Federalist 47
federal system 46
Great Compromise 42
Madisonian model 45

natural rights 35
ratification 47
representative assembly 31
separation of powers 45

social contract 36
state 36
supremacy doctrine 42
unicameral legislature 36

Chapter Summary

1. The first permanent English colonies were established at Jamestown in 1607 and Plymouth in 1620. The Mayflower Compact created the first formal government for the British colonists. By the mid-1700s, other British colonies had been established along the Atlantic seaboard from Georgia to Maine.

2. In 1763, the British tried to impose a series of taxes and legislative acts on their increasingly independent-minded colonies. The colonists responded with boycotts of British products and protests. Representatives of the colonies formed the First Continental Congress in 1774. The delegates sent a petition to the British king expressing their grievances. The Second Continental Congress established an army in 1775 to defend the colonists against attacks by British soldiers.

3. On July 4, 1776, the Second Continental Congress approved the Declaration of Independence. Perhaps the most revolutionary aspects of the Declaration were its assumptions that people have natural rights to life, liberty, and the pursuit of happiness; that governments derive their power from the consent of the governed; and that people have a right to overthrow oppressive governments.

4. Based on their understanding of natural rights and the social contract and their experience with an oppressive British regime, all of the colonies adopted written constitutions during the Revolutionary War. Most of these gave great power to their legislatures and restrained the power of the executive.

5. At the end of the Revolutionary War, the states had signed the Articles of Confederation, creating a weak central government with few powers. In this government, each state had one vote and there was no executive. The Congress had no power to raise revenue and virtually no way to amend the Articles. The Articles proved to be unworkable because the national government had no way to ensure compliance by the states with such measures as securing tax revenues.

6. General dissatisfaction with the Articles of Confederation prompted the call for a convention at Philadelphia in 1787. Although the delegates ostensibly convened to amend the Articles, the discussions soon focused on creating a constitution for a new form of government. The Virginia plan and the New Jersey plan did not garner widespread support. The Great Compromise offered by Connecticut helped to break the large-state/small-state disputes dividing the delegates. The Three-fifths Compromise, which counted slaves as three-fifths of a person for purposes of representation, was adopted to keep the southern states from leaving the union. The final version of the Constitution provided for the separation of powers, checks and balances, and a federal form of government. The principles of separation of powers and the checks and balances were intended to prevent any one branch of the government from becoming too powerful.

7. Fears of a strong central government prompted the addition of the Bill of Rights to the Constitution. The Bill of Rights secured for Americans a wide variety of freedoms, including the freedoms of religion, speech, and assembly. It was initially applied only to the federal government, but amendments to the Constitution following the Civil War made it clear that the Bill of Rights would apply to the states as well.

8. An amendment to the Constitution may be proposed either by a two-thirds vote in each house of Congress or by a national convention called by Congress at the request of two-thirds of the state legislatures. Ratification can occur either by a positive vote in three-fourths of the legislatures of the various states or by a positive vote in three-fourths of special conventions called in the states for the specific purpose of ratifying the proposed amendment. The process for amending the Constitution was made very difficult to ensure that most of the states and the majority of both houses agree to the proposed change. Informal methods of constitutional change include congressional legislation, presidential actions, judicial review, and changing interpretations of the Constitution.

Selected Print, Media, and Online Resources

PRINT RESOURCES

Ackerman, Bruce. *The Failure of the Founding Fathers: Jefferson, Marshall, and the Rise of Presidential Democracy.* Cambridge, MA: Belknap Press, 2005. In this book, the author sees the contested election of 1800 as exposing the failure of the new Constitution to account for the rise of presidential power and the appearance of political parties.

Armitage, David. *The Declaration of Independence: A Global History.* Cambridge, MA: Harvard University Press, 2007. The author examines the history of the Declaration of Independence and then looks at its impact on the peoples and governments of other nations.

Bailyn, Bernard. *To Begin the World Anew: The Genius and Ambiguities of the American Founders.* New York: Knopf, 2003. In a series of essays, a two-time Pulitzer Prize–winning historian discusses the themes of order and liberty in the *Federalist Papers* and the advantages of the founders' provincialism.

Breyer, Stephen G. *Active Liberty: Interpreting Our Democratic Constitution.* New York: Knopf, 2005. Supreme Court Justice Stephen Breyer offers his thoughts on the Constitution as a living document. He argues that the genius of the Constitution rests in the adaptability of its great principles to cope with current problems.

Dahl, Robert A. *How Democratic Is the American Constitution?* New Haven, CT: Yale University Press, 2002. This book compares the U.S. Constitution with the constitutions of other democratic countries in the world.

Gibson, Alan. *Understanding the Founding: The Crucial Questions.* Lawrence: The University Press of Kansas, 2007. The author looks at several oft-debated questions concerning the motivation and political views of the Founding Fathers.

Hamilton, Alexander, et al. *The Federalist: The Famous Papers on the Principles of American Government.* Benjamin F. Wright, ed. New York: Friedman/Fairfax Publishing, 2002. This is an updated version of the papers written by Alexander Hamilton, James Madison, and John Jay and published in the *New York Packet*, in support of the ratification of the Constitution.

Philbrick, Nathaniel. *Mayflower: A Story of Courage, Community and War.* New York: Penguin, 2007. The author investigates many of the myths surrounding the first colony in New England and sheds light on some little-known history.

MEDIA RESOURCES

In the Beginning—A 1987 Bill Moyers TV program that features discussions with three prominent historians about the roots of the Constitution and its impact on our society.

John Locke—A 1994 video exploring the character and principal views of John Locke.

Thomas Jefferson—A 1996 documentary by acclaimed director Ken Burns. The film covers Jefferson's entire life, including his writing of the Declaration of Independence, his presidency, and his later years in Virginia. Historians and writers interviewed include Daniel Boorstin, Garry Wills, Gore Vidal, and John Hope Franklin.

ONLINE RESOURCES

Avalon Project digital documents relevant to law, history, and diplomacy including James Madison's notes on the Constitutional Convention debates, taken from his daily journal: www.yale.edu/lawweb/avalon/

Emory University School of Law U.S. founding documents, including the Declaration of Independence, scanned originals of the U.S. Constitution, and the *Federalist Papers*: www.law.emory.edu/erd/docs/federalist

FindLaw.com comprehensive resource for legal information: www.findlaw.com/casecode/state.html

National Constitution Center information on the Constitution—including its history, current debates over constitutional provisions, and news articles: www.constitutioncenter.org

University of Oklahoma Law Center houses several U.S. historical documents online: www.law.ou.edu/hist

3 Federalism

BRIAN KERSEY/UPI /Landov

In 2011 thousands of Wisconsin public employees occupied the State House in opposition to the "Wisconsin budget repair bill" backed by Governor Scott Walker. The bill, designed to close the state budget deficit, required public employees to pay more toward their pensions and health insurance and limited collective bargaining rights for some public employees. A federal system provides for multiple levels of government and therefore multiple points of access for citizen involvement.

aplia

LEARNING OUTCOMES:

After reading this chapter, students will be able to:

■ **LO1** Define federalism and contrast the federal system of government with the unitary and confederal systems in explaining where governmental power lies.

■ **LO2** Identify two advantages and two disadvantages of the U.S. federal system.

■ **LO3** Locate the sources of federalism in the U.S. Constitution; using the terms *vertical control* and *horizontal control*, explain how the founders intended federalism and separation of powers to limit the expansion of national power.

■ **LO4** Explain the historical evolution of federalism as a result of the Marshall Court, the Civil War, the New Deal, civil rights, and federal grant-making.

■ **LO5** Evaluate immigration policy as a challenge to modern federalism.

What If ...

ONE STATE'S SAME-SEX MARRIAGES HAD TO BE RECOGNIZED NATIONWIDE?

BACKGROUND

The full faith and credit clause of the Constitution requires states to recognize that a couple married in Iowa is also married when they move to Delaware. But what if one state recognizes same-sex marriages? Does that mean that all other states must recognize such marriages and give each partner the benefits accorded to partners in opposite-sex marriages?

Traditionally, all matters involving marriage, divorce, and the custody of children have been handled through state laws. However, the Supreme Court has overturned state laws that forbid marriages between persons of separate races (*Loving v. Virginia*, 1967) and laws that regulate sexual conduct between consenting adults in the privacy of their own dwelling (*Lawrence v. Texas*, 2003).

Gay and lesbian couples face many legal hurdles without the benefit of legal marriage when it comes to health benefits, care for an ill partner, fostering or adoption of children, and disposition of an estate. The right of same-sex couples to adopt children varies widely by state. Often, the ability to visit a seriously ill person in the hospital is reserved to relatives by blood or marriage.

A few jurisdictions in the United States have responded to the needs of gay and lesbian couples by passing legislation that allows gay marriage or legally recognized civil unions. Nine states and the District of Columbia now issue marriage licenses to same-sex couples. Maryland, Maine, and Washington became the first states to approve same-sex marriage by voter referenda in November 2012. Twelve states prohibit same-sex marriage by statute, and another 30 states via state constitution. Under the Constitution, which state laws will prevail? Does the full faith and credit clause of the Constitution apply in the case of same-sex marriage?

FEDERAL LAW INTERVENES

Prior to 1996, the federal government left the definition of marriage entirely to the states, and any union recognized by a single state was also recognized by the United States government. However, the Defense of Marriage Act (DOMA), signed into law by President Bill Clinton, specifically defines marriage as a union of one man and one woman, allowing state governments to ignore same-sex marriages performed in other states. Legally married persons in same-sex unions are also prevented by DOMA from enjoying the rights and protections afforded by the federal government to other married persons in areas such as Social Security benefits, veterans' benefits, health insurance, pensions, and immigration, raising the constitutional question of equal protection of the laws. What would happen if the United States Supreme Court ruled the Defense of Marriage Act unconstitutional? If this happened, all of the state laws that refuse to recognize same-sex marriages performed in another state would be unconstitutional as well, because the U.S. Constitution is the supreme law of the land. All state laws that distinguish between same-sex and heterosexual marriages would also become null and void. All married persons would become eligible for all federal protections and benefits.

HOW LIKELY IS CHANGE?

In the nearly two decades since the Defense of Marriage Act became law, public opinion regarding gay marriage has shifted. A poll conducted in May 2012 found that 53 percent of Americans now favor same-sex marriage, a dramatic increase from the 36 percent of Americans in support six years ago.* Thirty-nine percent of Americans today, a new low, say gay marriage should be illegal. When President Obama was elected in 2010, he opposed gay marriage, but in an interview televised in May 2012, he announced that his position had evolved and he publicly endorsed same-sex marriage. Do these shifts mean that the law will be repealed or that the U.S. Supreme Court will declare DOMA unconstitutional? No, but other signs indicate that the federal government is ready to step away from DOMA. In February 2011, President Obama instructed the Justice Department to no longer defend the constitutionality of the Defense of Marriage Act when challenged in court, even as it continues to enforce the law. The law pending in the lower courts faces multiple legal challenges, and most observers think it is only a matter of time before the U.S. Supreme Court is presented with a ripe opportunity to rule on this matter. The same poll that found a majority of Americans now support gay marriage also found that people are nearly evenly divided on whether each state should make its own laws (49%) or whether the federal government should make one law for all states (46%).

*Washington Post-ABC News poll conducted by telephone May 17–20, 2012, among a random sample of 1,004 adults, including landline and cell phone respondents. Accessed at: www.washingtonpost.com/wp-srv/politics/polls/postabcpoll_20120520.html

FOR CRITICAL ANALYSIS

1. *A federal system allows a degree of consistency across states but also variation between states on some issues. Given the issues presented by same-sex marriage, do you believe this is a question best settled by federal law or by individual states? Why?*

2. *Same-sex marriage is legal in Iowa, but legally married persons in Iowa are still not eligible for federal benefits. Under federal law about 1,100 rights and privileges accompany legal marriage, but none of those is available to married persons of the same sex in Iowa. If DOMA was eliminated allowing all married persons access to federal protections and benefits, but some states still prohibited same-sex marriage, would the issue be settled? Why or why not?*

Federalism
A system of government in which power is divided by a written constitution between a central government and regional or subdivisional governments. Each level must have some domain in which its policies are dominant and some genuine constitutional guarantee of its authority.

THE UNITED STATES IS, as the name implies, a union of states. Unlike in many other nations, the national government does not have all of the authority in the system; rights and powers are reserved to the states by the Tenth Amendment. But the situation is even more complicated than having just state governments and the national government: The nation has more than 89,000 separate governmental units, as you can see in Table 3–1.

Visitors from France or Spain are often awestruck by the complexity of our system of government. Consider that a criminal action can be defined by state law, national law, or both. Thus, a criminal suspect can be prosecuted in the state court system or in the federal court system (or both). Think about such a simple matter as getting a driver's license. Each state has separate requirements for the driving test, the written test, the number of years between renewals, and the cost for the license. In 2005, Congress passed the REAL ID Act requiring states to include a specified set of information on the license so that it can be used as an identity card for travel, but the act was opposed by several states that insisted on maintaining their own requirements. If the licenses issued by those states do not meet the new requirements by January 2013, the IDs will not be accepted at airports for travel.

Relations between central governments and local units are structured in various ways around the world. Federalism is one of these ways. Understanding **federalism** and how it differs from other forms of government is important in understanding the American political system. The impact of policies on the individual would be substantially different if we did not have a federal form of government in which governmental authority is divided between the central government and various subunits.

Three Systems of Government

Today, about 196 independent nations are in the world. Each of these nations has its own system of government. Generally, though, we can describe how nations structure relations between central governments and local units in terms of three

Table 3–1 ▶ **Governmental Units in the United States**

With more than 89,000 separate governmental units in the United States today, it is no wonder that intergovernmental relations in this country are so complicated. Actually, the number of school districts has decreased over time, but the number of special districts created for single purposes, such as flood control, has increased from only about 8,000 during World War II to more than 37,000 today.

Federal government	1
State governments	50
Local governments	89,476
Counties	3,033
Municipalities (mainly cities or towns)	19,492
Townships (less extensive powers)	16,519
Special districts (water, sewer, and so on)	37,381
School districts	13,051
TOTAL UNITS	89,527

Source: U.S. Census Bureau, 2012 Statistical Abstract, Table 428, 2007 data.

models: (1) the unitary system, (2) the confederal system, and (3) the federal system. The most popular, both historically and today, is the unitary system.

A Unitary System

A **unitary system** of government assigns ultimate governmental authority to the national, or central, government and subnational governments exercise only the powers the central government chooses to delegate. The central government can also withdraw powers previously delegated to local or regional governments. American colonists lived under Great Britain's unitary system, and this experience no doubt contributed to their fear of recreating an unchecked centralized power. The majority of countries today operate under a unitary form of government.

A Confederal System

You were introduced to the elements of a **confederal system** of government in Chapter 2, when we examined the Articles of Confederation. A confederation is the opposite of a unitary governing system. It is a league of independent states in which a central government or administration handles only those matters of common concern expressly delegated to it by the member states. The central government has no ability to make laws directly applicable to member states unless the members explicitly support such laws. The United States under the Articles of Confederation was a confederal system. Very few examples of confederal systems are found today; however, Switzerland is one modern example.

A Federal System

The federal system lies between the unitary and confederal forms of government. As mentioned in Chapter 2, in a federal system, authority is divided, usually by a written constitution, between a central government and regional, or subdivisional, governments (often called constituent governments). The central government and the constituent governments both act directly on the people through laws and through the actions of elected and appointed governmental officials. Within each government's sphere of authority, each is supreme, in theory. Thus, a federal system differs sharply from a unitary one, in which the central government is supreme and the constituent governments derive their authority from it. Australia, Brazil, Canada, Germany, India, and Mexico are examples of other nations with federal systems. (See Figure 3–1 for a comparison of the three systems.)

Why Federalism?

Why did the United States develop a federal system? We look here at that question, as well as at some of the arguments for and against a federal form of government. The delegates at the Constitutional Convention were often divided over how much power the national government should have over their respective states.

A Practical Constitutional Solution

The historical basis of our federal system was laid down in Philadelphia at the Constitutional Convention, where advocates of a strong national government debated states' rights advocates. This dichotomy continued through to the ratifying conventions in the several states. The resulting federal system was therefore

Unitary System
A centralized governmental system in which local or subdivisional governments exercise only those powers given to them by the central government.

Confederal System
A system consisting of a league of independent states, each having essentially sovereign powers. The central government created by such a league has only limited powers over the states.

did you know?

In Florida, Michigan, Mississippi, North Carolina, North Dakota, Virginia, and West Virginia, male-female unmarried cohabitation is against the law and punishable by a short jail term, a fine of up to $500, or both.

■ Learning Outcome 2:
Identify two advantages and two disadvantages of the U.S. federal system.

Figure 3-1 ▶ **The Flow of Power in Three Systems of Government**

In a unitary system, power flows from the central government to the local and state governments. In a confederal system, power flows in the opposite direction—from the state governments to the central government. In a federal system, the flow of power, in principle, goes both ways.

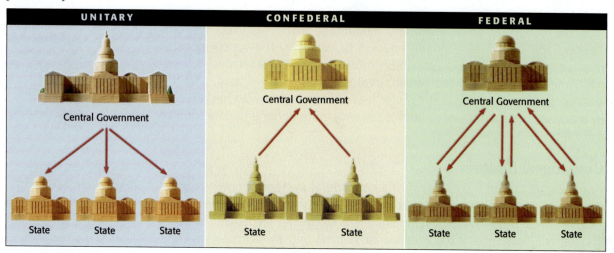

one of many compromises.[1] Supporters of the new Constitution were political pragmatists—they realized that without a federal arrangement, the new Constitution would not be ratified. The appeal of federalism was that it retained state traditions and local power while establishing a strong national government capable of handling common problems.

Even if colonial leaders had agreed on the desirability of a unitary system, size and regional isolation would have made such a system difficult operationally. At the time of the Constitutional Convention, the 13 colonies taken together were much larger geographically than England or France. Slow travel and communication contributed to the isolation of many regions within the colonies. It could take several weeks for all of the colonies to be informed about a particular political decision. A federal form of government that allows many functions to be delegated by the central government to the states or provinces makes sense. Finally, federalism brings government closer to the people. It allows more direct access to, and influence on, government agencies and policies, rather than leaving the population restive and dissatisfied with a remote, faceless, all-powerful central authority.

Benefits for the United States. In the United States, federalism has yielded many benefits. State governments long have been a training ground for future national leaders. Many presidents first made their political mark as governors. The states have been testing grounds for new government initiatives. As United States Supreme Court Justice Louis Brandeis once observed: "It is one of the happy incidents of the federal system that a single courageous state may, if its citizens choose, serve as a laboratory and try novel social and economic experiments without risk to the rest of the country."[2]

Examples of programs pioneered at the state level include unemployment compensation, which began in Wisconsin, and air pollution control, which was

---

1. For a contemporary interpretation of this compromise and how the division of power between the national government and the states has changed, see Edward A. Purcell, *Originalism, Federalism and the American Constitutional Enterprise: A Historical Inquiry* (New Haven, CT: Yale University Press, 2007).
2. *New State Ice Co. v. Liebmann*, 285 U.S. 262 (1932).

Figure 3-2 ▶ States with No State Income Tax

States with no income tax are shown in green, and states that tax only dividends and interest but not income are shown in yellow.

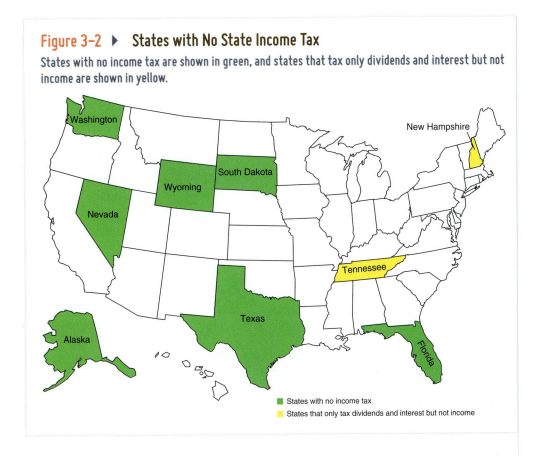

initiated in California. Statewide health care plans have been pioneered in Hawaii and Massachusetts. Today, states are experimenting with policies ranging from education reforms to environmental policies to homeland security defense strategies. States employed different strategies for dealing with the impact of the recession. Some focused on attracting new industries, while others invested in education and training opportunities for their residents. Indeed, states have widely different schemes for financing government. As shown in Figure 3–2, seven states do not have an income tax, which makes them magnets for retirees.

Allowance for Many Political Subcultures. The American way of life always has been characterized by many political subcultures, which divide along the lines of race and ethnic origin, region, wealth, education, and, more recently, degree of religious fundamentalism. When the Constitution was written, the diversity of the 13 "states" was seen as an obstacle to the survival of the nation. How could the large, rural, slaveholding states ever coexist with states where slavery was illegal? What would prevent a coalition of the larger states from imposing unfair laws on smaller states and minority groups? In Federalist #51 (see Appendix C), Madison argued that adopting a federal system would protect the people from the absolute power of the national government and the will of an unjust majority. He put it this way:

> *In the compound republic of America, the power surrendered by the people is first divided between two distinct governments, and then the portion allotted to each subdivide among distinct and separate departments. Hence a double security arises to the rights of the people. The different governments will control each other, at the same time that each will be controlled by itself.*

Had the United States developed into a unitary system, various political subcultures certainly would have been less able to influence government behavior than they have been, and continue to, in our federal system.

Political scientist Daniel Elazar claimed that one of federalism's greatest virtues is in fact that it encourages the development of distinct political subcultures. These political subcultures reflect differing demands and preferences for government. Federalism, he argues, allows for "a unique combination of governmental strength, political flexibility, and individual liberty."[3] The existence of political subcultures allows a wider variety of interests to influence government. As a result, political subcultures have proved instrumental in driving reform even at the national level, as shown by the differing state approaches to such issues as same-sex marriage and gun laws. Handgun regulation runs the gamut from forbidding the ownership of handguns in the city of Chicago to allowing the open carrying of weapons in the state of Virginia.

Arguments against Federalism

Not everyone thinks federalism is such a good idea. Some see it as a way for powerful state and local interests to block progress and impede national plans. Smaller political units are more likely to be dominated by a single political interest or group, and at times in our history this influence has limited rights for minority groups. (This was essentially the argument that James Madison put forth in Federalist #10, which you can read in Appendix C of this text.) Alternatively, progressive dominant factions in states have pressured the national government for change in many areas, such as the environment.

Critics of federalism also argue that too many Americans suffer as a result of the inequalities across the states. Individual states differ markedly in educational spending and achievement, crime and crime prevention, and even the safety of their buildings. States also differ considerably on women's rights, specifically support for equal pay and free access to safe legal abortion. Not surprisingly, these critics argue for increased federal legislation and oversight. This

A California woman carries her handgun into Riley's grocery in the city of Brentwood. Her right to do so is granted by the open carry law in that state.

© IS8/ZUMA Press/Newscom

3.   Daniel Elazar, *American Federalism: A View from the States*, 2nd ed. (New York: Crowell, 1972).

involves creating national educational standards, national building code standards, national expenditure minimums for crime control, and so on.

Others see dangers in the expansion of national powers at the expense of the states. President Ronald Reagan (served 1981–1989) said, "The Founding Fathers saw the federalist system as constructed something like a masonry wall. The States are the bricks, the national government is the mortar....Unfortunately, over the years, many people have increasingly come to believe that Washington is the whole wall."[4]

The Constitutional Basis for American Federalism

The term *federal system* is not found in the U.S. Constitution. Nor is it possible to find a systematic division of governmental authority between the national and state governments in that document. Rather, the Constitution sets out different types of powers. These powers can be classified as (1) the powers of the national government, (2) the powers of the states, and (3) prohibited powers. The Constitution also makes it clear that if a state or local law conflicts with a national law, the national law will prevail.

Powers of the National Government

The powers delegated to the national government include both expressed and implied powers, as well as the special category of inherent powers. Most of the powers expressly delegated to the national government are found in Article I, Section 8, of the Constitution. These enumerated powers include coining money, setting standards for weights and measures, making uniform naturalization laws, admitting new states, establishing post offices, and declaring war. Another important enumerated power is the power to regulate commerce among the states—a topic we deal with later in this chapter.

The Necessary and Proper Clause.
The implied powers of the national government are also based on Article I, Section 8, which states that Congress shall have the power

> [t]o make all Laws which shall be necessary and proper for carrying into Execution the foregoing Powers, and all other Powers vested by this Constitution in the Government of the United States, or in any Department or Officer thereof.

This clause is sometimes called the **elastic clause,** or **necessary and proper clause,** because it provides flexibility to the U.S. constitutional system. It gives Congress all of those powers that can be reasonably inferred but that are not expressly stated in the brief wording of the Constitution. The clause was first used in the Supreme Court decision of *McCulloch v. Maryland*[5] (discussed later in this chapter) to develop the concept of implied powers. Through this concept, the national government has succeeded in strengthening the scope of its authority to meet the numerous problems that the framers of the Constitution did not, and could not, anticipate.

■ **Learning Outcome 3:**
Locate the sources of federalism in the U.S. Constitution; using the terms *vertical control* and *horizontal control,* explain how the founders intended federalism and separation of powers to limit the expansion of national power.

Elastic Clause, or Necessary and Proper Clause
The clause in Article I, Section 8, that grants Congress the power to do whatever is necessary to execute its specifically delegated powers.

---

4. Text of the address by the president to the National Conference of State Legislatures, Atlanta, Georgia (Washington, DC: The White House, Office of the Press Secretary, July 30, 1981), as quoted in Edward Millican, *One United People: The Federalist Papers and the National Idea* (Lexington: The University Press of Kentucky, 1990).
5. 4 Wheaton 316 (1819).

Politics with a Purpose

STATES LEARNING FROM EACH OTHER

Have you ever moved to a new city or town? It is a challenge to locate the goods and services you need. How do you turn on your utilities or enroll yourself or your children in school? If you attend college out of state, you may wonder if you are eligible to vote and, if you are, how to register. Or, if you wish to vote by absentee ballot in your hometown, how do you get one? Federalism is responsible for many of the differences in the answers to these questions and countless others that exist across cities and states.

The nature of power held by national, state, and local governments has changed over time. State governments, rather than the federal government, increasingly have been asked to solve the problems of their citizens' education, health care, clean air, and safe streets, to name a few. How do states accomplish these tasks? Do they decide independently, or can they work cooperatively to learn from each other how best to solve policy problems?

One way states can cope with these challenges is through associations and organizations designed to share policy ideas and provide members with support. For example, the State Legislative Leaders Foundation hosts educational programs for key state legislators so that leaders can learn from experts and each other. Other examples are mayors' groups (the United States Conference of Mayors; the National Conference of Democratic Mayors; the Republican Mayors and Local Officials organization), governors' associations (National Governors Association), and groups for state government officials (Council of State Governments).[a] These organizations provide networking opportunities for state and local officials to learn from each other.[b] In addition, these groups provide information on how students can get involved with state government and become part of the policy innovation process. Legislative internships are available in all states[c] and many states also sponsor mock student legislatures that recommend policy initiatives to the legislature itself.

This sharing of experiences has led to policy innovation and diffusion.[d] Policy entrepreneurs find new solutions to problems. States and localities adopt these policies, adapt them to their needs, and share information and ideas.[e] This diffusion of public policy occurs in areas as diverse as health care, accessibility issues for the disabled, education, and resource management, just to name a few.

[a] http://usmayors.org, www.ncdm.org, www.nga.org, www.csg.org
[b] For example, see Jill Clark and Thomas H. Little, "National Organizations as Sources of Information for State Legislative Leaders," *State and Local Government Review*, Volume 34 (1), Winter 2002, pp. 38–45; and T. Heikkila and A. Gerlak, "The Formation of Large-scale Collaborative Resource Management Institutions: Clarifying the Roles of Stakeholders, Science, and Institutions," *Policy Studies Journal*, Volume 33 (4), pp. 583–612.
[c] For information on state internships, go to National Council of State Legislatures and search for internships at www.ncsl.org.
[d] For example, see John W. Kingdon, *Agenda, Alternative, and Public Policies* (Boston: Little, Brown, and Co., 1984); M. Mintrom, "Policy Entrepreneurs and the Diffusion of Innovation," *American Journal of Political Science*, Volume 41 (3), p. 738; and M. Mintrom and S. Vergari, "Policy Networks and Innovation Diffusion: The Case of State Education Reforms," *Journal of Politics*, Volume 60 (1), February 1998, p. 126.
[e] F. Meyer and R. Baker, "An Overview of State Policy Problems," *Policy Studies Review*, Volume 11 (1), Spring 1992, pp. 75–90.

Inherent Powers. A special category of national powers that is not implied by the necessary and proper clause are the inherent powers of the national government. These powers derive from the fact that the United States is a sovereign power among nations, and so its national government must be the only government that deals with other nations. Under international law, it is assumed that all nation-states, regardless of their size or power, have an *inherent* right to ensure their own survival. To do this, each nation must have the ability to act in its own interest among and with the community of nations—by, for instance, making treaties, waging war, seeking trade, and acquiring territory.

Note that no specific clause in the Constitution says anything about the acquisition of additional land. Nonetheless, through inherent powers, the federal government made the Louisiana Purchase in 1803 and then went on to acquire Florida, Texas, Oregon, Alaska, Hawaii, and other lands. The United States grew from a mere 13 states to 50 states, plus several "territories."

The national government has these inherent powers whether or not they have been enumerated in the Constitution. Some constitutional scholars categorize inherent powers as a third type of power, completely distinct from the delegated powers (both expressed and implied) of the national government.

Powers of the State Governments

The Tenth Amendment states that the powers not delegated to the United States by the Constitution, nor prohibited by it to the states, are reserved to the states, or to the people. These are the reserved powers that the national government cannot deny to the states. States had all the power when the Constitution was written so it isn't surprising that these reserved powers are not more clearly specified, but it does lead to questions about whether a certain power is delegated to the national government or reserved to the states. State powers include each state's right to regulate commerce within its borders and to provide for a state militia. States also have the reserved power to make laws on all matters not prohibited to the states by the U.S. Constitution or state constitutions and not expressly, or by implication, delegated to the national government. Furthermore, the states have **police power**—the authority to legislate for the protection of the health, morals, safety, and welfare of the people. Their police power enables states to pass laws governing such activities as crimes, marriage, contracts, education, intrastate transportation, and land use.

The ambiguity of the Tenth Amendment has allowed the reserved powers of the states to be defined differently at different times in our history. When widespread support for increased regulation by the national government exists, the Tenth Amendment tends to recede into the background. When the tide turns the other way (in favor of states' rights), the Tenth Amendment is resurrected to justify arguments supporting increased states' rights.

Concurrent Powers

In certain areas, the states share **concurrent powers** with the national government. Most concurrent powers are not specifically listed in the Constitution; they are only implied. An example of a concurrent power is the power to tax. The types of taxation are divided between the levels of government. For example, states may not levy a tariff (a set of taxes on imported goods); only the national government may do this. Neither government may tax the facilities of the other. If the state governments did not have the power to tax, they could not operate independent of the federal government.

Other concurrent powers include the power to borrow funds, to establish courts, and to charter banks and corporations. To a limited extent, the national government exercises police power, and to the extent that it does, police power is also a concurrent power. Concurrent powers exercised by the states are normally limited to the geographic area of each state and to those functions *not* granted by the Constitution exclusively to the national government (such as the coinage of money and the negotiation of treaties).

Prohibited Powers

The Constitution prohibits or denies several powers to the national government. For example, the national government may not impose taxes on goods sold to other countries (exports). Moreover, any power not granted expressly or implicitly to the federal government by the Constitution is prohibited to it. The states are also denied certain powers. For example, no state is allowed to enter into a treaty on its own with another country.

Police Power
The authority to legislate for the protection of the health, morals, safety, and welfare of the people. In the United States, most police power is reserved to the states.

Concurrent Powers
Powers held jointly by the national and state governments

The Supremacy Clause

The supremacy of the national constitution over subnational laws and actions is established in the **supremacy clause** of the Constitution. The supremacy clause (Article VI, Clause 2) states the following:

> This Constitution, and the Laws of the United States which shall be made in Pursuance thereof; and all Treaties made…under the Authority of the United States, shall be the supreme Law of the Land; and the Judges in every State shall be bound thereby, any Thing in the Constitution or Laws of any State to the Contrary notwithstanding.

In other words, states cannot use their reserved or concurrent powers to prevent or undermine national policies. All national and state officers, including judges, are bound by oath to support the Constitution. Hence, any legitimate exercise of national governmental power supersedes any conflicting state action.[6] Of course, deciding whether a conflict actually exists is a judicial matter, as you will see when we discuss the case of *McCulloch v. Maryland*.

National government legislation in a concurrent area is said to preempt (take precedence over) conflicting state or local laws or regulations in that area. One of the ways in which the national government has extended its powers, particularly during the 20th century, is through the preemption of state and local laws by national legislation. In the first decade of the 20th century, fewer than 20 national laws preempted laws and regulations issued by state and local governments. By the beginning of the 21st century, the number had risen to nearly 120.

Some political scientists believe that national supremacy is critical for the longevity and smooth functioning of a federal system. Nonetheless, the application of this principle has been a continuous source of conflict. As you will see, the most extreme example of this conflict was the Civil War.

Vertical Checks and Balances

Recall from Chapter 2 that one of the goals of the founders was to prevent the national government from becoming too powerful. For that reason, they divided the government into three branches—legislative, executive, and judicial. They also created a system of checks and balances that allowed each branch to check the actions of the others. The federal form of government created by the founders also involves checks and balances. These are sometimes called vertical checks and balances because they involve relationships between the states and the national government. They can be contrasted with horizontal checks and balances, in which the branches of government that are on the same level—either state or national—may check one other.

For example, the reserved powers of the states act as a check on the national government. Additionally, the states' interests are represented in the national legislature (Congress), and the citizens of the various states determine who will head the executive branch (the presidency). Finally, national programs and policies are administered by the states. This gives the states considerable control over the ultimate shape of those programs and policies. For example, the states will play a major role in implementing the Patient Protection and Affordable Care Act now that the U.S. Supreme Court has determined the law is constitutional.

The national government, in turn, can check state policies by exercising its constitutional powers under the clauses just discussed, as well as under the

Supremacy Clause
The constitutional provision that makes the Constitution and federal laws superior to all conflicting state and local laws.

---

6. An example of this is President Dwight Eisenhower's disciplining of Arkansas Governor Orval Faubus in 1957 by federalizing the National Guard to enforce the court-ordered desegregation of Little Rock High School.

commerce clause (to be examined later). Furthermore, the national government can influence state policies indirectly through federal grants, as you will learn later in this chapter.

Interstate Relations

So far we have examined only the relationship between central and state governmental units. The states, however, have constant commercial, social, and other dealings among themselves. The U.S. Constitution imposes certain "rules of the road" on interstate relations. These rules have prevented any one state from setting itself apart from the other states. The three most important clauses governing interstate relations in the Constitution, all derived from the Articles of Confederation, require each state to do the following:

1. Give full faith and credit to every other state's public acts, records, and judicial proceedings (Article IV, Section 1).
2. Extend to every other state's citizens the privileges and immunities of its own citizens (Article IV, Section 2).
3. Agree to return persons who are fleeing from justice in another state back to their home state when requested to do so (Article IV, Section 2).

The Full Faith and Credit Clause. This provision of the Constitution protects the rights of citizens as they move from state to state. It provides that "full faith and credit shall be given in each State to the public Acts, Records and judicial Proceedings of every other State." This clause applies only to civil matters. It ensures that rights established under deeds, wills, contracts, and the like will be honored by any other states. It also ensures that any judicial decision with respect to such property rights will be honored, as well as enforced, in all states. The **full faith and credit clause** has contributed to the unity of American citizens, particularly as we have become a more mobile society.

Privileges and Immunities. **Privileges and immunities** are defined as special rights and exemptions provided by law. Under Article IV, "The Citizens of each State shall be entitled to all Privileges and Immunities of Citizens in the several States." This clause indicates that states are obligated to extend to citizens of other states protection of the laws, the right to work, access to courts, and other privileges they grant their own citizens. It means that if you are a student from Iowa attending college in Ohio, you have the same rights as Ohioans to protest a traffic ticket, to buy a car, to hold a job, and to travel freely throughout the state.

Interstate Extradition. The Constitution clearly addressed the issue of how states should cooperate in catching criminals. Article IV, Section 2, states that "[a] person charged in any State with Treason, Felony, or another Crime who shall flee from Justice and be found in another State, shall on Demand of the executive Authority of the State from which he fled, be delivered up, to be removed to the State having jurisdiction of the Crime." While the language is clear, a federal judge will not order such an action. It is the moral duty of the governor to **extradite** the accused. From time to time, the governor of a state may refuse to do so, either because he or she does not believe in capital punishment, which might be ordered upon conviction, or because the accused has lived a law-abiding life for many years outside the state in which the crime was committed.

Additionally, states may enter into agreements called **interstate compacts**, if consented to by Congress. In reality, congressional consent is necessary only if such a compact increases the power of the contracting states relative to other

Full Faith and Credit Clause
This section of the Constitution requires states to recognize one another's laws and court decisions. It ensures that rights established under deeds, wills, contracts, and other civil matters in one state will be honored by other states.

Privileges and Immunities
Special rights and exceptions provided by law. States may not discriminate against one another's citizens.

Extradite
To surrender an accused or convicted criminal to the authorities of the state from which he or she has fled; to return a fugitive criminal to the jurisdiction of the accusing state.

Interstate Compact
An agreement between two or more states. Agreements on minor matters are made without congressional consent, but any compact that tends to increase the power of the contracting states relative to other states or relative to the national government generally requires the consent of Congress. Such compacts serve as a means by which states can solve regional problems.

Beyond Our Borders
FLEXIBLE FEDERALISM

The United States Constitution lays out the division of powers and authority between the states and the national government, as well as creating a complex election scheme to further guarantee representation for the states, but the relative balance of power between the states and the national government has been subject to interpretation and development over time. One might say the division of powers is not always clear. Several other large, diverse countries have adopted a federal system of government. Have they been able to construct a clear division of powers between the national government and states that has lasted? Or is federalism as a system flexible enough for nations to change their internal arrangements in response to need?

Canada is a federal system with a national government and multiple provinces and territories. At its founding in 1867, the Canadian federal system differed from that of the United States in at least two major ways: (1) it was created by the United Kingdom, and the new nation owed allegiance to the British monarch; and (2) from the very beginning, provinces were divided by culture and language, with one of the largest provinces being French-speaking Quebec.

The division of powers in the Canadian system is also different from that of the United States. In general, the government has operated on the principle that all Canadians, regardless of where they live, should be taxed about equally and receive equal government benefits. The national government has power over defense, trade, transportation, and so on, whereas the 10 regional provinces have control over education, civil rights, hospitals, and all natural resources within their boundaries. In the 20th century, the Canadian national government has acquired much more power over social services, the national health system, and other direct services to the people. In contrast to the American states, provinces have won increased economic independence from the central government through their control over natural resources and the money they earn from taxing their use. Today, with the price of oil skyrocketing, the province of Alberta has become the world capital of oil sand production, and the province has earned a windfall in revenue from its natural resources.

Another large federal system is that of India, formed after the end of British rule in 1948. India adopted federalism to deal with its huge number of ethnic minorities and local cultures and languages. At the beginning, while powers were constitutionally divided between the capital of New Delhi and the states, the drive for economic development led to national control of some industries directly and considerable control over state decisions and economic initiatives. In the 1990s, India began to reform its economic system to encourage more development. One of the principles

Jeff Whyte/Shutterstock.com

The Canadian federal system is organized into three territories and ten provinces. Provinces receive their authority directly from the Constitution Act (1867) whereas territories derive their mandates and authority from the federal government. The flags pictured here represent six of the ten provinces.

of that reform was to end much of the national control of the economy and allow states to develop their own laws and incentives for development. Today, the balance of power has shifted toward the states.

FOR CRITICAL ANALYSIS

1. *What lessons can emerging democracies draw from the experiences of older federal systems like those in the United States and Canada? Under what conditions is a federal system most likely to emerge?*

2. *How has the global recession influenced the division of power and fiscal responsibility in federal systems?*

iStockphoto.com/kyoshino iStockphoto.com/mattjeacock

states (or to the national government). Typical examples of interstate compacts are the establishment of the Port Authority of New York and New Jersey by an interstate compact between those two states in 1921 and the regulation of the production of crude oil and natural gas by the Interstate Oil and Gas Compact of 1935. Recently, the federal government has attempted to mediate the dispute between Georgia and Tennessee over a prior agreement about how much water can be sent from a Tennessee lake to meet Georgia's needs.

Defining Constitutional Powers— The Early Years

■ Learning Outcome 4:
Explain the historical evolution of federalism as a result of the Marshall Court, the Civil War, the New Deal, civil rights, and federal grant-making.

Recall from Chapter 2 that constitutional language, to be effective and to endure, must have some degree of ambiguity. Certainly, the powers delegated to the national government and the powers reserved to the states contain elements of ambiguity, thus leaving the door open for different interpretations of federalism. Disputes over the boundaries of national versus state powers have characterized this nation from the beginning. In the early 1800s, the most significant disputes arose over differing interpretations of the implied powers of the national government under the necessary and proper clause and over the respective powers of the national government and the states to regulate commerce.

Although political bodies at all levels of government play important roles in the process of settling such disputes, ultimately the Supreme Court casts the final vote. As might be expected, the character of the referee will have an impact on the ultimate outcome of any dispute. From 1801 to 1835, the Supreme Court was headed by Chief Justice John Marshall, a Federalist who advocated a strong central government. We look here at two cases decided by the Marshall Court: *McCulloch v. Maryland*[7] and *Gibbons v. Ogden*.[8] Both cases are considered milestones in defining the boundaries between federal and state power.

McCulloch v. Maryland (1819)

Nowhere in the U.S. Constitution does it state that Congress has the power to create a national bank, although it does have the express power to regulate currency. Twice in the history of the nation has the Congress chartered banks—the First and Second Banks of the United States—and provided part of their initial capital; thus, they were national banks. The government of Maryland, which intended to regulate its own banks and did not want a national bank competing with its own institutions, imposed a tax on the Second Bank's Baltimore branch in an attempt to put that branch out of business. The branch's cashier, James William McCulloch, refused to pay the Maryland tax. When Maryland took McCulloch to its state court, the state of Maryland won. The national government appealed the case to the Supreme Court.

The Constitutional Questions. The questions before the Supreme Court were of monumental proportions. The very heart of national power under the Constitution, as well as the relationship between the national government and the states, was at issue. Congress has the authority to make all laws that are "necessary and proper" for the execution of Congress's expressed powers. Strict Constitution constructionists looked at the word *necessary* and contended

---

7. 4 Wheaton 316 (1819).
8. 9 Wheaton 1 (1824).

that the national government had only those powers *indispensable* to the exercise of its designated powers. To them, chartering a bank and contributing capital to it were not necessary, for example, to coin money and regulate its value.

Loose constructionists disagreed. They believed that the word *necessary* could not be looked at in its strictest sense. As Alexander Hamilton once said, "It is essential to the being of the national government that so erroneous a conception of the meaning of the word *necessary* be exploded." The important issue was, if the national bank was constitutional, could the state tax it?

Marshall's Decision. Three days after hearing the case, Chief Justice John Marshall announced the Court's decision. (Given his Federalist allegiance, it is likely he made his decision before he heard the case.) It is true, Marshall said, that Congress's power to establish a national bank was not expressed in the Constitution. He went on to say, however, that if establishing such a national bank aided the government in the exercise of its designated powers, then the authority to set up such a bank could be implied. To Marshall, the necessary and proper clause embraced "all means which are appropriate: to carry out the 'legitimate ends' of the Constitution." Only when such actions are forbidden by the letter and spirit of the Constitution are they thereby unconstitutional. There was nothing in the Constitution, according to Marshall, "which excludes incidental or implied powers; and which requires that everything granted shall be expressly and minutely described." It would be impossible to spell out every action that Congress might legitimately take—the Constitution "would be enormously long and could scarcely be embraced by the human mind."

In perhaps the single most famous sentence every uttered by a Supreme Court justice, Marshall said, "[W]e must never forget it is a constitution we are expounding." In other words, the Constitution is a living instrument that has to be interpreted to meet the practical needs of government. Having established this doctrine of implied powers, Marshall then answered the other important question before the Court and established the doctrine of national supremacy. Marshall stated that no state could use its taxing power to tax an arm of the national government. If it could, "the declaration that the Constitution…shall be the supreme law of the land, is an empty and unmeaning declamation."

Marshall's decision enabled the national government to grow and to meet problems that the Constitution's framers were unable to foresee. Today, practically every expressed power of the national government has been expanded in one way or another by use of the necessary and proper clause.

Gibbons v. Ogden (1824)

One of the most important parts of the Constitution included in Article I, Section 8, is the so-called **commerce clause**, in which Congress is given the power "[t]o regulate Commerce with foreign Nations, and among the several States, and with the Indian Tribes." What exactly does "to regulate commerce" mean? What does "commerce" entail? The issue here is essentially the same as that raised by *McCulloch v. Maryland*: How strict an interpretation should be given to a constitutional phrase? As might be expected given his Federalist loyalties, Marshall used a liberal approach in interpreting the commerce clause in *Gibbons v. Ogden*.

Commerce Clause
The section of the Constitution in which Congress is given the power to regulate trade among the states and with foreign countries.

The Background of the Case. Robert Fulton and Robert Livingston secured a monopoly on steam navigation on New York waters from the New York legislature in 1803. They licensed Aaron Ogden to operate steam-powered ferryboats between New York and New Jersey. Thomas Gibbons, who had obtained a license from the U.S. government to operate boats in interstate waters, decided to compete with Ogden, but he did so without New York's permission. Ogden sued Gibbons. The New York state courts prohibited Gibbons from operating in New York waters. Gibbons appealed to the Supreme Court.

Several issues were actually before the Court in this case. The first issue was how the term *commerce* should be defined. New York's highest court had defined the term narrowly to mean only the shipment of goods, or the interchange of commodities, not navigation or the transport of people. The second issue was whether the national government's power to regulate interstate commerce extended to commerce within a state (*intra*state commerce) or was limited strictly to commerce among the states (*inter*state commerce). The third issue was whether the power to regulate interstate commerce was a concurrent power (as the New York court had concluded), meaning a power that could be exercised by both the state or national governments, or an exclusive national power. Clearly, if such powers were concurrent, many instances of laws that conflicted with each other would occur.

Marshall's Ruling. Marshall defined commerce as all commercial intercourse—all business dealings—including navigation and the transport of people. Marshall used this opportunity not only to expand the definition of commerce but also to validate and increase the power of the national legislature to regulate commerce. Declared Marshall, "What is this power? It is the power . . . to prescribe the rule by which commerce is to be governed. This power, like all others vested in Congress, is complete in itself." Marshall also held that the commerce power of the national government could be exercised in state jurisdictions, even though it cannot reach solely intrastate commerce. Finally, Marshall emphasized that the power to regulate interstate commerce was an exclusive national power. Marshall held that because Gibbons was duly authorized by the national government to navigate in interstate waters, he could not be prohibited from doing so by a state court.

Marshall's expansive interpretation of the commerce clause in *Gibbons v. Ogden* allowed the national government to exercise increasing authority over all areas of economic affairs throughout the land. Congress did not immediately exploit this broad grant of power. In the 1930s and subsequent decades, however, the commerce clause became the primary constitutional basis for national government regulation—as you will read later in this chapter.

did you know?

The Liberty Bell cracked when it was rung at the funeral of John Marshall in 1835.

States' Rights and the Resort to Civil War

The controversy over slavery that led to the Civil War took the form of a dispute over national government supremacy versus the rights of the separate states. Essentially, the Civil War brought to an ultimate and violent climax the ideological debate that had been outlined by the Federalist and Anti-Federalist parties even before the Constitution was ratified.

The Shift Back to States' Rights

As we have seen, while John Marshall was chief justice of the Supreme Court, he did much to increase the power of the national government and to reduce that of the states. During the Jacksonian era (1829–1837), however, a shift back to states' rights began. The question of the regulation of commerce became one of the major issues in federal-state relations. When Congress passed a tariff in 1828, the

© Bettmann/CORBIS

President Lincoln meets with some of his generals and other troops on October 3, 1862. While many believe that the Civil War was fought over the issue of slavery, others point out that it was really a battle over the supremacy of the national government. In any event, once the North won the war, what happened to the size and power of our national government?

state of South Carolina unsuccessfully attempted to nullify the tariff (render it void), claiming that in cases of conflict between a state and the national government, the state should have the ultimate authority over its citizens.

Over the next three decades, the North and South became even more sharply divided over tariffs that mostly benefited Northern industries and over the slavery issue. On December 20, 1860, South Carolina formally repealed its ratification of the Constitution and withdrew from the Union. On February 4, 1861, representatives from six Southern states met at Montgomery, Alabama, to form a new government called the Confederate States of America.

War and the Growth of the National Government

The ultimate defeat of the South in 1865 permanently ended any idea that a state could successfully claim the right to secede, or withdraw, from the Union. Ironically, the Civil War—brought about in large part because of the South's desire for increased states' rights—resulted in the opposite: an increase in the political power of the national government.

The War Effort. Thousands of new employees were hired to run the Union war effort and to deal with the social and economic problems that had to be handled in the aftermath of war. A billion-dollar national government budget was passed for the first time in 1865 to cover the increased government expenditures. The first (temporary) income tax was imposed on citizens to help pay for the war. This tax and the increased national government spending were precursors to the expanded future role of the national government in the American federal system. Civil liberties were curtailed in the Union and in the Confederacy in the name of the wartime emergency. The distribution of pensions and widows' benefits also boosted the national government's social role. Many scholars contend that the North's victory set the nation on the path to a modern industrial economy and society.

The Civil War Amendments. The expansion of the national government's authority during the Civil War was reflected in the passage of the Civil War Amendments to the Constitution. Before the war, legislation with regard to slavery was some of the most controversial ever to come before the Congress. In fact, in the 1830s, Congress prohibited the submission of antislavery petitions. When new states were admitted into the Union, the primary decision was whether slavery would be allowed. Immediately after the Civil War, at a time when former officers of the Confederacy were barred from voting, the three Civil War Amendments were passed. The Thirteenth Amendment, ratified in 1865, did more than interfere with slavery—it abolished the institution altogether. By abolishing slavery, the amendment also in effect abolished the rule by which three-fifths of the slaves were counted when apportioning seats in the House of Representatives (see Chapter 2). African Americans were now counted in full.

The Fourteenth Amendment (1868) defined who was a citizen of each state. It sought to guarantee equal rights under state law, stating that

did you know?

Only after the Civil War did people commonly refer to the United States as "it" instead of "they."

[no] State [shall] deprive any person of life, liberty, or property, without due process of law; nor deny to any person within its jurisdiction the equal protection of the laws.

For a brief time after the ratification of these amendments, the rights of African Americans in the South were protected by the local officials appointed by the Union forces. Within two decades, the Fourteenth Amendment lost much of its power as states reinstituted separate conditions for the former slaves. Decades later, the courts interpreted these words to mean that the national Bill of Rights applied to state governments, a development that we will examine in Chapter 4. The Fourteenth Amendment also confirmed the abolition of the three-fifths rule. Finally, the Fifteenth Amendment (1870) gave African Americans the right to vote in all elections, including state elections, although a century would pass before that right was enforced.

The Continuing Dispute over the Division of Power

Although the outcome of the Civil War firmly established the supremacy of the national government and put to rest the idea that a state could secede from the Union, the war by no means ended the debate over the division of powers between the national government and the states. The debate over the division of powers in our federal system can be viewed as progressing through at least two general stages since the Civil War: dual federalism and cooperative federalism.

Dual Federalism and the Retreat of National Authority

During the decades following the Civil War, the prevailing model was what political scientists have called **dual federalism**—a doctrine that emphasizes a distinction between federal and state spheres of government authority. Various images have been used to describe different configurations of federalism over time. Dual federalism is commonly depicted as a layer cake, because the state governments and the national government are viewed as separate entities, like separate layers in a cake. The national government is the top layer of the cake; the state government is the bottom layer. Nevertheless, the two layers are physically separate. They do not mix. For the most part, advocates of dual federalism believed that the state and national governments should not exercise authority in the same areas.

Dual Federalism
A system in which the states and the national government each remains supreme within its own sphere. The doctrine looks on nation and state as coequal sovereign powers. Neither the state government nor the national government should interfere in the other's sphere.

A Return to Normal Conditions. The doctrine of dual federalism represented a revival of states' rights following the expansion of national authority during the Civil War. Dual federalism, after all, was a fairly accurate model of the prewar consensus on state-national relations. For many people, it therefore represented a return to normal. The national income tax, used to fund the war effort and the reconstruction of the South, was ended in 1872. The most significant step to reverse the wartime expansion of national power took place in 1877, when President Rutherford B. Hayes withdrew the last federal troops from the South. This meant that the national government was no longer in a position to regulate state actions that affected African Americans. While the black population was now free, it was again subject to the authority of Southern whites.

President Franklin Delano Roosevelt (served 1933–1945). Roosevelt's national approach to addressing the effects of the Great Depression was overwhelmingly popular, although many of his specific initiatives were controversial. How did the Great Depression change the political beliefs of many ordinary Americans?

The Role of the Supreme Court. The Civil War crisis drastically reduced the influence of the United States Supreme Court. In the prewar *Dred Scott* decision,[9] the Court had attempted to abolish the power of the national government to restrict slavery in the territories. In so doing, the Court placed itself on the losing side of the impending conflict. After the war, Congress took the unprecedented step of exempting the entire process of Southern reconstruction from judicial review. The Court had little choice but to acquiesce.

In time, the Supreme Court reestablished itself as the legitimate constitutional interpreter. Its decisions tended to support dual federalism, defend states' rights, and limit the powers of the national government. In 1895, for example, the Court ruled that a national income tax was unconstitutional.[10] In subsequent years, the Court gradually backed away from this decision and eventually might have overturned it. In 1913, however, the Sixteenth Amendment explicitly authorized a national income tax.

For the Court, dual federalism meant that the national government could intervene in state activities through grants and subsidies, but for the most part, it was barred from regulating matters that the Court considered to be purely local. The Court generally limited the exercise of police power to the states. For example, in 1918, the Court ruled that a 1916 national law banning child labor was unconstitutional because it attempted to regulate a local problem.[11] In effect, the Court placed severe limits on the ability of Congress to legislate under the commerce clause of the Constitution.

The New Deal and Cooperative Federalism

The doctrine of dual federalism receded into the background in the 1930s as the nation attempted to deal with the Great Depression. Franklin D. Roosevelt was inaugurated on March 4, 1933, as the 32nd president of the United States. In the previous year, nearly 1,500 banks had failed (and 4,000 more would fail in 1933). Thirty-two thousand businesses had closed down, and almost one-fourth of the labor force was unemployed. The public expected the national government to do something about the disastrous state of the economy. But for the first three years of the Great Depression (1930–1932), the national government did very little.

The "New Deal." President Herbert Hoover (served 1929–1933) clung to the doctrine of dual federalism and insisted that unemployment and poverty were local issues. The states, not the national government, had the sole responsibility for combating the effects of unemployment and providing relief to the poor. Roosevelt, however, did not feel bound by this doctrine, and his new Democratic administration energetically intervened in the economy. Roosevelt's "New Deal" included large-scale emergency antipoverty programs. In addition, the New Deal introduced major new laws regulating economic activity, such as the National Industrial Recovery Act of 1933, which established the National Recovery Administration (NRA). The NRA, initially the centerpiece of the New Deal, provided codes for every industry to restrict competition and regulate labor relations.

9. *Dred Scott v. Sanford*, 19 Howard 393 (1857).
10. *Pollock v. Farmers' Loan & Trust Co.*, 157 U.S. 429 (1895); *Pollock v. Farmers' Loan & Trust Co.*, 158 U.S. 601 (1895).
11. *Hammer v. Dagenhart*, 247 U.S. 251 (1918). This decision was overruled in *United States v. Darby*, 312 U.S. 100 (1940).

The End of Dual Federalism. Roosevelt's expansion of national authority was challenged by the Supreme Court, which continued to adhere to the doctrine of dual federalism. In 1935, the Court ruled that the NRA program was unconstitutional.[12] The NRA had turned out to be largely unworkable and was unpopular. The Court, however, rejected the program on the ground that it regulated intrastate, not interstate, commerce. This position appeared to rule out any alternative recovery plans that might be better designed. Subsequently, the Court struck down the Agricultural Adjustment Act, the Bituminous Coal Act, a railroad retirement plan, legislation to protect farm mortgages, and a municipal bankruptcy act.

In 1937, Roosevelt proposed legislation that would allow him to add up to six new justices to the Supreme Court. Presumably, the new justices would be more friendly to the exercise of national power than were the existing members. Roosevelt's move was widely seen as an assault on the Constitution. Congressional Democrats refused to support the measure, and it failed. Nevertheless, the "court-packing scheme" had its intended effect. Although the membership of the Court did not change, after 1937 the Court ceased its attempts to limit the national government's powers under the commerce clause. For the next half-century, the commerce clause would provide Congress with an unlimited justification for regulating the economic life of the country.

Cooperative Federalism. Some political scientists have described the era since 1937 as characterized by **cooperative federalism**, in which the states and the national government cooperate in solving complex common problems. Roosevelt's New Deal programs, for example, often involved joint action between the national government and the states. The pattern of national-state relationships during these years created a new metaphor for federalism—that of a marble cake. Unlike a layer cake, in a marble cake the two types of cake are intermingled, and any bite contains cake of both flavors.

As an example of how national and state governments work together under the cooperative federalism model, consider Aid to Families with Dependent Children (AFDC), a welfare program that was established during the New Deal. (In 1996, AFDC was replaced by Temporary Assistance to Needy Families—TANF.) Under the AFDC program, the national government provided most of the funding, but state governments established benefit levels and eligibility requirements for recipients. Local welfare offices were staffed by state, not national, employees. In return for national funding, the states had to conform to a series of regulations on how the program was to be carried out. These regulations tended to become more elaborate over time.

The 1960s and 1970s were a time of even greater expansion of the national government's role in domestic policy. The evolving pattern of national-state-local government relationships during the 1960s and 1970s yielded yet another metaphor—**picket-fence federalism**, a concept devised by political scientist Terry Sanford. The horizontal boards in the fence represent the different levels of government (national, state, and local), while the vertical pickets represent the various programs and policies in which each level of government is involved. Officials at each level of government work together to promote and develop the policy represented by each picket.

Cooperative Federalism
The theory that the states and the national government should cooperate in solving problems.

Picket-Fence Federalism
A model of federalism in which specific programs and policies (depicted as vertical pickets in a picket fence) involve all levels of government—national, state, and local (depicted by the horizontal boards in a picket fence).

---

12. *Schechter Poultry Corp. v. United States*, 295 U.S. 495 (1935).

Methods of Implementing Cooperative Federalism

Even before the Constitution was adopted, the national government gave grants to the states in the form of land to finance education. The national government also provided land grants for canals, railroads, and roads. In the 20th century, federal grants increased significantly, especially during Roosevelt's administration during the Great Depression and again during the 1960s, when the dollar amount of grants quadrupled. These funds were used for improvements in education, pollution control, recreation, and highways. With this increase in grants, however, came a bewildering number of restrictions and regulations.

Categorical Grants
Federal grants to states or local governments that are for specific programs or projects.

Categorical Grants. By 1985, **categorical grants** amounted to more than $100 billion per year. They were spread out across 400 separate programs, but the largest five accounted for more than 50 percent of the revenues spent. These five programs involved Medicaid (health care for the poor), highway construction, unemployment benefits, housing assistance, and welfare programs to assist mothers with dependent children and people with disabilities. For fiscal year 2009 the national government gave an estimated $253 billion to the states and local governments through federal grants.

Before the 1960s, most categorical grants by the national government were *formula grants*. These grants take their name from the method used to allocate funds. They fund state programs using a formula based on such variables as the state's needs, population, or willingness to come up with matching funds. Beginning in the 1960s, the national government began increasingly to offer *program grants*. This funding requires states to apply for grants for specific programs. The applications are evaluated by the national government, and the applications may compete with one another. Program grants give the national government a much greater degree of control over state activities than formula grants.

Why have federal grants to the states increased so much? One reason is that Congress has decided to offload some programs to the states and provide a major part of the funding for them. Also, Congress continues to use grants to persuade states and cities to operate programs devised by the federal government. Finally, states often are happy to apply for grants because they are relatively "free," requiring only that the state match a small portion of each grant. States can still face criticism for accepting the grants, because their matching funds may be diverted from other state projects.

Feeling the Pressure—The Strings Attached to Federal Grants.
No dollars sent to the states are completely free of strings, however; all funds come with requirements that must be met by the states. Often, through the use of grants, the national government has been able to exercise substantial control over matters that traditionally have been under the purview of state governments. When the federal government gives federal funds for highway improvements, for example, it may condition the funds on the state's cooperation with a federal policy. This is exactly what the federal government did in the 1980s and 1990s to force the states to raise their minimum drinking age to 21.

Such carrot-and-stick tactics have been used as a form of coercion in recent years as well. In 2002, for example, President George W. Bush signed the No Child Left Behind (NCLB) Act into law. Under NCLB, Bush promised billions of dollars to the states to bolster their education budgets. The funds would only be delivered, however, if states agreed to hold schools accountable to new federal achievement benchmarks on standardized tests designed by the federal government. Education traditionally had been under state control, and the

did you know?

The Morrill Act of 1862, providing for land grants to states to create public institutions of higher education, was the first example of the federal government providing grants to the states.

conditions for receiving NCLB funds effectively stripped the states of some autonomy in creating standards for public schools. President Barack Obama proposed revising NCLB but also supports federal standards for the achievement of individual schools and students.

Block Grants. **Block grants** lessen the restrictions on federal grants given to state and local governments by grouping several categorical grants under one broad heading. Governors and mayors generally prefer block grants because such grants give the states more flexibility in how the money is spent.

One major set of block grants provides aid to state welfare programs. The Personal Responsibility and Work Opportunity Reconciliation Act of 1996 ended the AFDC program. The TANF program that replaced AFDC provided a welfare block grant to each state. Each grant has an annual cap. According to some, this is one of the most successful block grant programs. Although state governments prefer block grants, Congress generally favors categorical grants, because the expenditures can be targeted according to congressional priorities.

Federal Mandates. For years, the federal government has passed legislation requiring that states improve environmental conditions and the civil rights of certain groups. Since the 1970s, the national government has enacted literally hundreds of **federal mandates** requiring the states to take some action in areas ranging from the way voters are registered, to ocean-dumping restrictions, to the education of persons with disabilities. The Unfunded Mandates Reform Act of 1995 requires the Congressional Budget Office to identify mandates that cost state and local governments more than $50 million to implement. Nonetheless, the federal government routinely continues to pass mandates for state and local governments that cost more than that to implement.

For example, the estimated total cost of complying with federal mandates concerning water purity, over just a four-year period, is in the vicinity of $29 billion. In all, the estimated cost of federal mandates to the states in the early 2000s was more than $70 billion annually. One way in which the national government has moderated the burden of federal mandates is by granting *waivers*, which allow

Block Grants
Federal programs that provide funds to state and local governments for general functional areas, such as criminal justice or mental health programs.

did you know?
State government spending in fiscal year 2012 is likely to total more than $1.4 trillion, the majority of which will be directed to five major functions: health care (31%), education (18%), welfare (13%), state pensions (11%), and transportation (8%).

Federal Mandate
A requirement in federal legislation that forces states and municipalities to comply with certain rules.

Under the No Child Left Behind Act, a school that is rated "in need of improvement" over a period of five years must be "restructured." Presumably, this could mean closing the school, as suggested by the cartoonist. The No Child Left Behind Act imposes certain federal mandates on the states in return for funding by the national government. In what way might this act represent a shift away from the federal system?

individual states to try out innovative approaches to carrying out the mandates. For example, Oregon received a waiver to experiment with a new method of rationing health care services under the federally mandated Medicaid program.

The Politics of Federalism

As we have observed, the allocation of powers between the national and state governments continues to be a major issue. In 2005, the devastation caused by Hurricane Katrina in Louisiana unleashed a heated debate about federalism, as Americans disagreed on which level of government should be held accountable for inadequate preparations and the failures in providing aid afterward. Some 1,300 people died as a result of the storm, while property damage totaled tens of billions of dollars. Many Americans felt that the federal government's response to Katrina was woefully inadequate. Much of their criticism centered on the failures of the Federal Emergency Management Agency (FEMA) in the aftermath of Katrina.

FEMA, the government agency responsible for coordinating disaster preparedness and relief efforts, was disorganized and slow to respond in the days following the storm. On their arrival in the Gulf Coast, FEMA officials often acted counterproductively—on some occasions denying the delivery of storm aid that their agency had not authorized. Many critics of the federal government's handling of Katrina pointed out that FEMA's director, Michael Brown, had no disaster management experience; he was a political appointee, earning the job through his campaign efforts to help the president.

Other Americans claimed that state and local politicians, including Louisiana Governor Kathleen Blanco and New Orleans Mayor Ray Nagin, were not adequately prepared for the storm. Local officials knew the region and its residents best, yet they failed to make proper provisions for evacuating vulnerable residents.

The real reason for the disaster was the failure of the levees that protect New Orleans from Mississippi River floods. The levees were constructed by the Army Corps of Engineers (a federal agency) and maintained by the Corps; however, those employees took orders from both federal officials and state and local politicians, including the multiple local levee boards that could and did divert funds to other purposes.[13] It was widely known that the levees needed replacement, but Congress had declined to fund the design for many years. The aftermath of Hurricane Katrina was a classic case of failure due, perhaps, to the design of our federal system of government.

What Has National Authority Accomplished?

Why have conservatives favored the states and liberals favored the national government? One answer is that throughout American history, the expansion of national authority typically has been an engine of social change. Far more than the states, the national government has been willing to alter the status quo. The expansion of national authority during the Civil War freed the slaves—a major social revolution. During the New Deal, the expansion of national authority meant unprecedented levels of government intervention in the economy. In both the Civil War and New Deal eras, support for states' rights was a method of opposing these changes and supporting the status quo.

Some scholars believe that this equation was also a subtext in the Supreme Court's defense of states' rights between the Civil War and 1937. These scholars

13. Douglas Brinkley, *The Great Deluge: Hurricane Katrina, New Orleans and the Mississippi Gulf Coast* (New York: HarperCollins, 2006).

argue that the Supreme Court, in those years, came increasingly under the influence of *laissez-faire* economics—a belief that any government intervention in the economy was improper. When the Court struck down national legislation against child labor, for example, it was not acting only in defense of the states; an underlying motivation was the Court's belief that laws banning child labor were wrong no matter which level of government implemented them.

Civil Rights and the War on Poverty.

Another example of the use of national power to change society was the presidency of Lyndon B. Johnson (1963–1969). Johnson oversaw the greatest expansion of national authority since the New Deal. Under Johnson, a series of civil rights acts forced the states to grant African Americans equal treatment under the law. Crucially, these acts included the abolition of all measures designed to prevent African Americans from voting. Johnson's Great Society and War on Poverty programs resulted in major increases in spending by the national government. As before, states' rights were invoked to support the status quo—states' rights meant no action on civil rights and no increase in antipoverty spending.

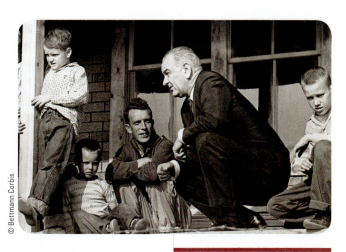

President Lyndon Johnson listens to Tom Fletcher describe some of the problems of the town. Fletcher is the father of eight children.

Why Should the States Favor the Status Quo?

When state governments have authority in a particular field, great variations may occur from state to state in how the issues are handled. Inevitably, some states will be more conservative than others. Therefore, bringing national authority to bear on a particular issue may impose national standards on states that, for whatever reason, have not adopted such standards. One example is the voting rights legislation passed under President Johnson. By the 1960s, there was a national consensus that all citizens, regardless of race, should have the right to vote. A majority of the white electorate in former Confederate states, however, did not share this view. National legislation was necessary to impose the national consensus on the recalcitrant states.

Another factor that may make the states more receptive to limited government, especially on economic issues, is competition among the states. It is widely believed that major corporations are more likely to establish new operations in states with a "favorable business climate." Such a climate may mean low taxes and therefore relatively more limited social services. If states compete with one another to offer the best business climate, the competition may force down taxes all around. Competition of this type also may dissuade states from implementing environmental regulations that restrict certain business activities. Those who deplore the effect of such competition often refer to it as a "race to the bottom." National legislation, in contrast, is not constrained by interstate competition.

A final factor that may encourage the states to favor the status quo is the relative power of local economic interests. A large corporation in a small state, for example, may have a substantial amount of political influence. Such a corporation, which has experienced success within the existing economic framework, may be opposed to any changes to that framework. These local economic interests may have less influence at the national level. This observation echoes James Madison's point in Federalist #10 (see Appendix C of this text). Madison argued that a large federal republic would be less subject to the danger of factions than a small state.

Devolution
The transfer of powers from a national or central government to a state or local government.

Federalism Becomes a Partisan Issue

In the years after 1968, the **devolution** of power from the national government to the states became a major ideological theme for the Republican Party. Republicans believed that the increased size and scope of the federal government—which began with the New Deal programs of Franklin Roosevelt and continued unabated through Lyndon Johnson's Great Society programs—was a threat to individual liberty and to the power of the states. As the Republicans became more conservative in their views regarding the extent of national government power, Democrats have become more liberal and supportive of that power.

The "New Federalism."

The architects of Lyndon Johnson's War on Poverty were reluctant to let state governments have a role in the new programs. This reluctance was a response to the resistance of many southern states to African American civil rights. The Johnson administration did not trust the states to administer antipoverty programs in an impartial and efficient manner.

Republican president Richard Nixon (served 1969–1974), who succeeded Johnson in office, saw political opportunity in the Democrats' suspicion of state governments. Nixon advocated what he called a "New Federalism" that would devolve authority from the national government to the states. In part, the New Federalism involved the conversion of categorical grants into block grants, thereby giving state governments greater flexibility in spending. A second part of Nixon's New Federalism was revenue sharing. Under the revenue-sharing plan, the national government provided direct, unconditional financial support to state and local governments.

Nixon was able to obtain only a limited number of block grants from Congress. The block grants he did obtain, plus revenue sharing, substantially increased financial support to state governments. Republican President Ronald Reagan was also a strong advocate of federalism, but some of his policies withdrew certain financial support from the states. Reagan was more successful than Nixon in obtaining block grants, but Reagan's block grants, unlike Nixon's, were less generous to the states than the categorical grants they replaced. Under Reagan, revenue sharing was eliminated.

Federalism in the 21st Century.

Today, federalism (in the sense of limited national authority) continues to be an important element in conservative ideology. At this point, however, it is not clear whether competing theories of federalism truly divide the Republicans from the Democrats in practice. Consider that under Democratic president Bill Clinton (served 1993–2001), Congress replaced AFDC, a categorical welfare program, with the TANF block grants. This change was part of the Welfare Reform Act of 1996, which was perhaps the most significant domestic policy initiative of Clinton's administration. In contrast, a major domestic initiative of Republican president George W. Bush was increased federal funding and control of education—long a preserve of state and local governments.

Also, in some circumstances, liberals today may benefit from states' rights understood as policy innovation opportunities. One example is the issue of same-sex marriages, which we examined in the What if? feature. A minority of the states has been much more receptive than the rest of the nation to same-sex marriages. Similarly, states have been incubators for sustainability and green energy initiatives, states primarily in the West have been leaders in developing death with dignity or assisted suicide laws, while still others have legalized marijuana for medicinal purposes.

Conservatives today also remain active in limiting the scope of federal power. One example is opposition to health care reform that substantially involves the government in mandating that individuals carry health insurance or pay a penalty.

Federalism and the Supreme Court Today

The United States Supreme Court, which normally has the final say on constitutional issues, necessarily plays a significant role in determining the line between federal and state powers. Consider the decisions rendered by Chief Justice John Marshall in the cases discussed earlier in this chapter. Since the 1930s, Marshall's broad interpretation of the commerce clause has made it possible for the national government to justify its regulation of virtually any activity, even when an activity would appear to be purely local in character.

Since the 1990s, however, the Supreme Court has been reining in somewhat the national government's powers under the commerce clause. The Court also has given increased emphasis to state powers under the Tenth and Eleventh Amendments to the Constitution. At the same time, other recent rulings have sent contradictory messages with regard to states' rights and the federal government's power.

Reining In the Commerce Power

In a widely publicized 1995 case, *United States v. Lopez*,[14] the Supreme Court held that Congress had exceeded its constitutional authority under the commerce clause when it passed the Gun-Free School Zones Act in 1990. The Court stated that the act, which banned the possession of guns within 1,000 feet of any school, was unconstitutional because it attempted to regulate an area that had "nothing to do with commerce, or any sort of economic enterprise." This marked the first time in 60 years that the Supreme Court had placed a limit on the national government's authority under the commerce clause.

In 2000, in *United States v. Morrison*,[15] the Court held that Congress had overreached its authority under the commerce clause when it passed the Violence against Women Act in 1994. The Court invalidated a key section of the act that provided a federal remedy for gender-motivated violence, such as rape. The Court noted that in enacting this law, Congress had extensively documented that violence against women had an adverse "aggregate" effect on interstate commerce: It deterred potential victims from traveling, from engaging in employment, and from transacting business in interstate commerce. It also diminished national productivity and increased medical and other costs. Nonetheless, the Court held that evidence of an aggregate effect on commerce was not enough to justify national regulation of noneconomic, violent criminal conduct.

One of the central questions in the 2012 challenge to the Patient Protection and Affordable Care Act also concerns the commerce power. The most controversial provision of the law known as the individual mandate, requires individuals to have health insurance either through an employer or by purchasing it through the market. The federal government has argued that Congress is authorized to enact the individual mandate under two provisions of Article I, Section 8, of the U.S. Constitution—its power to regulate commerce and its power to tax. The government argues that health care falls under the heading of commerce because the health care law addresses a pressing national problem that is economic in nature. Opponents of the law say that the requirement to buy a product or service is unprecedented, regulates inactivity rather than activity, and opens the door to allowing Congress unlimited power to intrude on individual freedom. In the decision issued on June 28, 2012, the Supreme Court upheld the law but did so under Congress's taxing authority and not the commerce clause. Chief Justice Roberts, writing for the

14.   514 U.S. 549 (1995).
15.   529 U.S. 598 (2000).

5-4 majority said the individual mandate "cannot be upheld as an exercise of Congress's power under the commerce clause," which allows Congress to regulate interstate commerce but "not to order individuals to engage in it." He continued, "In this case, however, it is reasonable to construe what Congress has done as increasing taxes on those who have a certain amount of income, but choose to go without health insurance. Such legislation is within Congress's power to tax."[16]

State Sovereignty and the Eleventh Amendment

In recent years, the Supreme Court has issued a series of decisions that bolstered the authority of state governments under the Eleventh Amendment to the Constitution. As interpreted by the Court, that amendment in most circumstances precludes lawsuits against state governments for violations of rights established by federal laws unless the states consent to be sued. For example, in a 1999 case, *Alden v. Maine*,[17] the Court held that Maine state employees could not sue the state for violating the overtime pay requirements of a federal act. According to the Court, state immunity from such lawsuits "is a fundamental aspect of the sovereignty which [the states] enjoyed before the ratification of the Constitution, and which they retain today."

In 2000, in *Kimel v. Florida Board of Regents*,[18] the Court held that the Eleventh Amendment precluded employees of a state university from suing the state to enforce a federal statute prohibiting age-based discrimination. In 2003, however, in *Nevada v. Hibbs*,[19] the Court ruled that state employers must abide by the federal Family and Medical Leave Act (FMLA). The reasoning was that the FMLA seeks to outlaw gender bias, and government actions that may discriminate on the basis of gender must receive a "heightened review status" compared with actions that may discriminate on the basis of age or disability. Also, in 2004, the Court ruled that the Eleventh Amendment could not shield states from suits by individuals with disabilities who had been denied access to courtrooms located on the upper floors of buildings.[20]

Tenth Amendment Issues

The Tenth Amendment states: "The powers not delegated to the United States by the Constitution, nor prohibited by it to the States, are reserved to the States respectively, or to the people." In 1992, the Court held that requirements imposed on the state of New York under a federal act regulating low-level radioactive waste were inconsistent with the Tenth Amendment and thus unconstitutional. According to the Court, the act's "take title" provision, which required states to accept ownership of waste or regulate waste following Congress's instructions, exceeded the enumerated powers of Congress. Although Congress can regulate the handling of such waste, "it may not conscript state governments as its agents" in an attempt to enforce a program of federal regulation.[21]

In 1997, the Court revisited this Tenth Amendment issue. In *Printz v. United States*,[22] the Court struck down the provisions of the federal Brady Handgun Violence Prevention Act of 1993 that required state employees to check the backgrounds of prospective handgun purchasers. Said the Court:

> [T]he federal government may neither issue directives requiring the States to address particular problems, nor command the States' officers, or those

16. Robert Barnes, "Supreme Court upholds Obama's health-care law," *The Washington Post*, published June 28, 2012. Accessed at www.washingtonpost.com/politics/supreme-court-to-rule-thursday-on-health-care-law/2012/06/28/gJQAar-Rm8V_story.htm
17. 527 U.S. 706 (1999).
18. 528 U.S. 62 (2000).
19. 538 U.S. 721 (2003).
20. *Tennessee v. Lane*, 541 U.S. 509 (2004).
21. *New York v. United States*, 505 U.S. 144 (1992).
22. 521 U.S. 898 (1997).

of their political subdivisions, to administer or enforce a federal regulatory program.

Other Federalism Cases

In recent years, the Supreme Court has sent mixed messages in federalism cases. At times the Court has favored states' rights, whereas on other occasions it has backed the federal government's position.

Cases involving federalism issues have drifted toward favoring the states. Despite this trend, the Supreme Court argued in 2005 that the federal government's power to seize and destroy illegal drugs trumped California's law legalizing the use of marijuana for medical treatment.[23] Yet, less than a year later, the Court favored states' rights in another case rife with federalism issues, *Gonzales v. Oregon*.[24] After a lengthy legal battle, the Court upheld Oregon's controversial "Death with Dignity" law, which allows patients with terminal illnesses to choose to end their lives early and thus alleviate suffering. More recently the Court was presented with the issue of immigration. Control of the country's borders would normally fall within the federal government's jurisdiction; however, the state of Arizona argued that the federal government was not doing enough to control illegal immigration and adopted a controversial new law in 2010. When the Court ruled on the constitutionality of the law in 2012, justices said that a state cannot act to undermine federal authority in immigration law and sided with the administration (see You Can Make a Difference for more details).

As you have read in this chapter, the federal government has provided states with financial resources through direct transfer and various forms of grants-in-aid that have enabled states to experiment with innovative solutions to problems and to address the needs of each state's residents. However, as the global recession continues to erode the financial viability of states and the federal government has fewer resources to share, how will federalism fare? If the federal government has fewer "carrots" in the form of financial incentives for state policy behavior, will it resort to "sticks" in the form of more unfunded mandates with stiff penalties for noncompliance?

AP Photo/Dana Verkouteren

■ **Learning Outcome 5:**
Evaluate immigration policy as a challenge to modern federalism.

Attorney Paul Clement speaks before the Supreme Court in Washington, Wednesday, March 28, 2012, during arguments on the constitutionality of President Barack Obama's health care overhaul.

23. *Gonzales v. Raich*, 545 U.S. 1 (2005).
24. 546 U.S. 243 (2006)

You Can Make a Difference

iStockphoto.com/kyoshino

FEDERALISM AND STATE IMMIGRATION POLICY

Until very recently, immigration policy was widely viewed as falling within the purview of the federal government. Naturalization, and by extension, determining rates of immigration and countries of origin is the responsibility of Congress. Regulating the border would also seem to fall to the federal government since it involves more than one state as well as the United States. However, citing inaction or ineffective action by the federal government, six states have enacted their own immigration laws that are more restrictive than federal statute requires (as indicated in red and orange on the map).

U.S. federal law requires all immigrants over the age of 14 who remain in the United States for more than 30 days to register with the U.S. government and to have registration documents in their possession at all times. In 2010, Arizona adopted a more restrictive law that makes it a misdemeanor crime for an immigrant to be in Arizona without required documents. The law also requires state law enforcement personnel to attempt to determine an individual's immigration status during a stop, detention, or arrest when "reasonable suspicion" exists that the individual is an illegal immigrant. State and local officials are prohibited from restricting enforcement of immigration law and stiff penalties are imposed on anyone found to be sheltering, hiring, or transporting illegal immigrants. This approach has been labeled "attrition through enforcement."

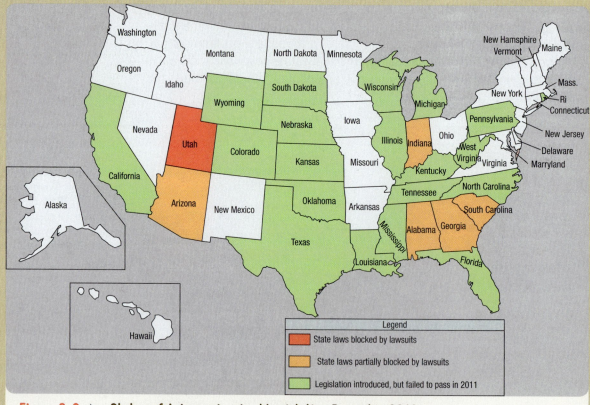

Legend

🟥	State laws blocked by lawsuits
🟧	State laws partially blocked by lawsuits
🟩	Legislation introduced, but failed to pass in 2011

Figure 3-3 ▶ **Status of Arizona-inspired Legislation Passed in 2011**

Source: National Immigration Law Center www.nilc.org

On June 25, 2012, the U.S. Supreme Court issued a split decision, upholding part of the Arizona law and rejecting other provisions on the grounds that they interfered with the federal government's role in setting immigration policy. The court unanimously affirmed the law's requirement that police check the immigration status of people they detain and suspect to be in the country illegally emphasizing that state law enforcement officials already possessed the discretion to ask about immigration status. In the same ruling, however, the court rejected parts of the Arizona law that it said undermine federal law; specifically, making it a misdemeanor for immigrants to not carry registration documents; criminalizing the act of an illegal immigrant seeking employment; and authorizing state officers to arrest someone on the belief that the person has committed an offense that makes him deportable. Justice Anthony Kennedy, writing for the majority, also indicated that the court would entertain future challenges to the "show me your papers" provision if when the law is implemented there is evidence of illegal racial or ethnic profiling. Lower courts will now revisit laws similar to Arizona's recently passed by five other states and currently on hold to determine if they are consistent with the court's ruling.

WHY SHOULD YOU CARE?

It may seem like the debate over state versus federal immigration policy is remote from your daily life; however, this may affect you for a variety of reasons, even if you were born in this country. Civil rights groups claim that the Arizona law and others like it will promote a form of "racial profiling"—the arrest and detention of individuals just because they look like foreigners. In Alabama, for example, state officials were embarrassed when foreign executives from Mercedes-Benz and Honda were stopped and detained in two separate incidents. The laws have a "chilling effect" on immigrant populations, even among those who are here legally or have become naturalized citizens. Farmers in Georgia and Alabama report that the new immigration laws are depriving them of a stable and experienced workforce, resulting in spoiled crops and higher food prices. Employers and public schools including colleges and universities are now required to document lawful presence for all employees and students. For the first time since the Depression, more Mexicans are leaving the United States than entering it. While illegal immigration causes problems in society, legal immigration is an important positive force for dynamic social and economic change in the country.

WHAT CAN YOU DO?

Research the immigration policies of your state. Think carefully about the implications of policies that promote "attrition by enforcement" for your daily life and for those around you. Will you or someone you know be more likely to be stopped or questioned by law enforcement officials as a result of these laws? Will you be required to provide identity documentation? Think carefully about how immigration policies relate to building diverse societies and to the value of tolerance on your own campus. Is this another force contributing to the creation of two Americas? Regardless of which side of this issue you may find yourself on, organizations can provide information and a way for you to get involved.

REFERENCES

Tara Bahrampour, "For First Time since Depression, More Mexicans Leave U.S. than Enter," *The Washington Post,* April 23, 2012.
Robert Barnes, "Arizona Immigration Law: Supreme Court again Examines Federal Power," *The Washington Post*, April 21, 2012.
Adam Liptak, "Blocking Parts of Arizona Law, Justices Allow its Centerpiece," *The New York Times*, June 25, 2012.
Julia Preston, "Justices to Rule on Role of States in Immigration," *The New York Times*, April 22, 2012.

Key Terms

block grants 83
categorical grants 82
commerce clause 76
concurrent powers 71
confederal system 65
cooperative federalism 81

devolution 86
dual federalism 79
elastic clause, or necessary and proper clause 69
extradite 73
federalism 64

federal mandate 83
full faith and credit clause 73
interstate compact 73
picket-fence federalism 81

police power 71
privileges and immunities 73
supremacy clause 72
unitary system 65

Chapter Summary

1. There are three basic models for ordering relations between central governments and local units: (1) a unitary system (in which ultimate power is held by the national government), (2) a confederal system (in which ultimate power is retained by the states), and (3) a federal system (in which governmental powers are divided between the national government and the states).

2. Among the advantages of federalism are that distributed decision making is effective in large geographic areas, it promotes the development and sustainability of many subcultures within the states, it allows states to serve as incubators for new policies and processes, and it limits the influence of any one group or set of interests. Among the disadvantages of federalism are that powerful states or states controlled by minority interests can limit progress or undermine the rights of minority groups. Federalism also results in inequities across states in terms of policies and spending on services like education or crime prevention.

3. The Constitution expressly delegated certain powers to the national government in Article I, Section 8. In addition to these expressed powers, the national government has implied and inherent powers. Implied powers are those that are reasonably necessary to carry out the powers expressly delegated to the national government. Inherent powers are those held by the national government by virtue of its being a sovereign state with the right to preserve itself. The supremacy clause of the Constitution states that the Constitution, congressional laws, and national treaties are the supreme law of the land. States cannot use their reserved or concurrent powers to override national policies. Vertical checks and balances allow states to influence the national government and vice versa. Horizontal checks and balances provide another form of check and balance in that governments on the same level—either state or national—may check one another.

4. The Tenth Amendment to the Constitution states that powers not delegated to the United States by the Constitution, nor prohibited by it to the states, are reserved to the states, or to the people. In certain areas, the Constitution provides for concurrent powers, such as the power to tax, which are powers that are held jointly by the national and state governments. The Constitution also denies certain powers to both the national government and the states.

5. Two landmark Supreme Court cases expanded the constitutional powers of the national government. Chief Justice John Marshall's expansive interpretation of the necessary and proper clause of the Constitution in *McCulloch v. Maryland* (1819) permitted the "necessary and proper" clause to be used to enhance the power of the national government. Additionally, his decision made it clear that no state could tax a national institution. Marshall's broad interpretation of the commerce clause in *Gibbons v. Ogden* (1824) further extended the constitutional regulatory powers of the national government.

6. The controversy over slavery that led to the Civil War took the form of a fight over national government supremacy versus the rights of the separate states. Ultimately, the South's desire for increased states' rights and the subsequent Civil War resulted in an increase in the political power of the national government.

7. Since the Civil War, federalism has evolved through at least two general phases: dual federalism and cooperative federalism. In dual federalism, each of the states and the federal government remain supreme within their own spheres. The era since the Great Depression has sometimes been labeled one of cooperative federalism, in which states and the national government cooperate in solving complex common problems.

8. The United States Supreme Court plays a significant role in determining the line between state and federal powers. Since the 1990s, the Court has been reining in somewhat the national government's powers under the commerce clause and has given increased emphasis to state powers under the Tenth and Eleventh Amendments to the Constitution. New challenges to the balance of power between the federal and state governments come from the prolonged economic recession that has limited the federal government's ability to transfer funds to states to promote policy innovation and from controversial social issues on which public opinion varies widely by state, including same-sex marriage, medical marijuana, and immigration policy.

Selected Print, Media, and Online Resources

PRINT RESOURCES

Gerston, Larry A. *American Federalism: A Concise Introduction.* New York: M. E. Sharpe, 2007. The author introduces the reader to the philosophical and historical foundations of the federal system. He examines cases of conflict throughout our history.

Hamilton, Alexander, et al. *The Federalist: The Famous Papers on the Principles of American Government.* Benjamin F. Wright, ed. New York: Friedman/Fairfax Publishing, 2002. These essays remain an authoritative exposition of the founders' views on federalism.

Karmis, Dimitrios, and Wayne Norman, eds. *Theories of Federalism: A Reader.* New York: Palgrave MacMillan, 2005. This reader brings together the most significant writings on Federalism from the late 18th century to the present.

Manna, Paul. *School's In: Federalism and the National Education Agenda.* Washington, DC: Georgetown University Press, 2006. The author examines the changing relationship between the federal government and the states with regard to our public education system.

Nagel, Robert F. *The Implosion of American Federalism.* New York: Oxford University Press, 2002. The author contends that despite the states' rights trend of recent years, which has been given force by the Supreme Court in several of its decisions, the nation faces the danger of increasingly centralized power.

Nugent, John D. *Safeguarding Federalism: How States Protect Their Interests in National Policymaking.* Norman, OK: University of Oklahoma Press, 2009. Tracing the history of federalism, the author proposes that federalism is a vital force in American politics. He shows how the states protect their interest in policy innovation through a number of tactics, including influencing federal legislation.

MEDIA RESOURCES

City of Hope—A 1991 movie by John Sayles. The film is a story of life, work, race, and politics in a modern New Jersey city. An African American alderman is one of the several major characters.

The Civil War—The PBS documentary series that made director Ken Burns famous. First shown in 1990, it marked a revolution in documentary technique. Photographs, letters, eyewitness memoirs, and music are used to bring the war to life. The DVD version was released in 2002.

McCulloch v. Maryland and Gibbons v. Ogden—These programs are part of the series *Equal Justice under Law: Landmark Cases in Supreme Court History.* They provide more details on cases that defined our federal system.

When the Levees Broke: A Requiem in Four Acts—A 2006 documentary by Spike Lee that critically examines the federal, state, and local government response to Hurricane Katrina.

ONLINE RESOURCES

Brookings—policy analyses and recommendations on a variety of issues, including federalism: www.brookings.edu

Catalog of Federal Domestic Assistance—complete listing of the federal grants that may be distributed to states and local governments: www.cfda.gov

Cato Institute—a libertarian approach to issues relating to federalism: www.cato.org

The Constitution Society—links to U.S. state constitutions, the *Federalist Papers*, and international federations, such as the European Union: www.constitution.org

Council of State Governments—information on state responses to federalism issues: www.csg.org

Emory University Law School—access to the *Federalist Papers*—the founders' views on federalism—and other historical documents: http://els449.law.emory.edu/index.php?id=3130

National Governors Association—information on issues facing state governments and federal-state relations: www.nga.org

4 Civil Liberties

Marchers demonstrate for jobs, peace, and housing at this Martin Luther King, Jr. holiday celebration.

LEARNING OUTCOMES:

After reading this chapter, students will be able to:

■ **LO1** Explain the origin of the Bill of Rights, and discuss how these rights were applied to the states.

■ **LO2** Explain how the Bill of Rights protects freedom of religion while maintaining a separation between the state and religion.

■ **LO3** Define freedom of expression, explain where it is found in the Bill of Rights, and show why it is important in a democracy.

■ **LO4** Discuss the concept of privacy rights, and give examples of how individual privacy is protected under the Constitution.

■ **LO5** Identify the rights of the accused, and discuss the role of the Supreme Court in expanding those rights.

What If ...

ROE V. WADE WERE OVERTURNED?

BACKGROUND

The Bill of Rights and other provisions of the U.S. Constitution are the ultimate protections of our civil rights and liberties. But how do these rights work in practice? How do we determine what our rights are in any given situation? One way is through judicial review, the power of the United States Supreme Court or other courts to declare laws and other acts of government unconstitutional. Supreme Court cases are often hotly contested, and the decision in the 1973 case *Roe v. Wade* is one of the most contentious ever handed down. In the *Roe v. Wade* case, the Court declared that a woman's constitutionally protected right to privacy includes the right to have an abortion. The Court concluded that the states cannot restrict a woman's right to an abortion during the first three months of pregnancy. Forty years later, however, the debate over the legality of abortion still rages in the United States.

WHAT IF *ROE V. WADE* WERE OVERTURNED?

If the Supreme Court overturned *Roe v. Wade*, the authority to regulate abortion would fall again to the states. Before the *Roe v. Wade* case, each state decided whether abortion would be legal within its borders. State legislatures made the laws that covered abortion. Some critics of the constitutional merits of *Roe v. Wade* have argued that allowing the Supreme Court to decide the legality of abortion nationwide is undemocratic because the justices are not elected officials. In contrast, if state legislatures regained the power to create abortion policy, the resulting laws would reflect the majority opinion of each state's voters. Legislators would have to respect popular sentiment on the issue or risk losing their reelection bids.

THE POSSIBILITY OF STATE BANS ON ABORTION

Simply overturning *Roe v. Wade* would not make abortion in the United States illegal overnight. In many states, abortion rights are very popular, and the legislatures in those states would not consider measures to ban abortion or to further restrict access to abortion. Some states have laws that would protect abortion rights even if *Roe v. Wade* were overturned. Access to abortions would likely continue in the West Coast states and in much of the Northeast. In much of the South and the Midwest, however, abortion could be seriously restricted or even banned. Some states have "trigger laws" that would immediately outlaw abortion if *Roe v. Wade* were overturned.

Women living in conservative states such as the Dakotas, Kentucky, and Mississippi already face serious difficulties in obtaining an abortion. In each of these states, 98 percent of the counties do not have an abortion clinic. Many women desiring the procedure already have to travel long distances. If abortion were banned, these women could still cross state lines to obtain an abortion. If 21 of the most conservative states banned abortion, only 170 clinics would be affected—less than 10 percent of the national total.

STATE CHALLENGES TO *ROE V. WADE*

Undoubtedly feeling optimistic because of President George W. Bush's conservative Supreme Court appointments (John Roberts and Samuel Alito), South Dakota's legislature passed a law in February 2006 banning abortion; however, the law was overturned in a statewide referendum. Another ballot effort to ban abortions was also defeated by South Dakota voters, in 2008. In 2008, "right-to-life" activists in a number of other states placed anti-abortion measures on the ballot. In Colorado, for example, citizens voted on whether the state constitution should declare a fertilized egg a "person" who enjoys "inalienable rights, equality of justice, and due process of law." The measure was voted down by a three-to-one margin.

With the election of Barack Obama as president, the future of *Roe v. Wade* brightened. His first Supreme Court appointment, Sonya Sotomayor, was likely to become a supporter of the decision, and in 2010, the president nominated Elena Kagan to replace Justice Stevens, likely shoring up the coalition in support of *Roe v. Wade*.

FOR CRITICAL ANALYSIS

1. *Why do you think that abortion remains a contentious topic 40 years after the Roe v. Wade decision? Should that decision be revisited? Why or why not?*

2. *How significant a role should the courts play in deciding constitutional questions about abortion? Do you feel that individual states should have a say in the legality of abortion within their own borders? Why or why not?*

"THE LAND OF THE FREE." When asked what makes the United States distinctive, Americans commonly say that it is a free country. Americans have long believed that limits on the power of government are an essential part of what makes this country free. The first 10 amendments to the U.S. Constitution—the Bill of Rights—place such limits on the national government. Of these amendments, none is more famous than the First Amendment, which guarantees freedom of religion, speech, the press, and other rights.

Most other democratic nations have laws to protect these and other **civil liberties**, but none of those laws is quite like the First Amendment, which states, "Congress shall make no law … abridging the freedom of speech, or of the press." Think about the issue of "hate speech." What if someone makes statements that stir up hatred toward a particular race or other group of people? In Germany, where memories of Nazi anti-Semitism remain alive, such speech is unquestionably illegal. In the United States, such speech may well be constitutionally protected, depending on the circumstances under which it occurred. In this chapter, we describe the civil liberties provided by the Bill of Rights and some of the controversies that surround them. We look at the First Amendment liberties, including freedom of religion, speech, press, and assembly, and then discuss the right to privacy and the rights of the accused.

Civil Liberties
Those personal freedoms that are protected for all individuals. Civil liberties typically involve restraining the government's actions against individuals.

The Bill of Rights

As you read through this chapter, bear in mind that the Bill of Rights, like the rest of the Constitution, is relatively brief. The framers set forth broad guidelines, leaving it up to the courts to interpret these constitutional mandates and apply them to specific situations. Thus, judicial interpretations shape the true nature of the civil liberties and rights that we possess. Because judicial interpretations change over time, so do our rights. On the next several pages, you will read about several conflicts over the meaning of such simple phrases as *freedom of religion* and *freedom of the press*. To understand what freedoms we actually have, we need to examine how the courts—and particularly the United States Supreme Court—have resolved some of those conflicts. One important conflict was over the issue of whether the Bill of Rights in the federal Constitution limited the powers of state governments as well as those of the national government.

Extending the Bill of Rights to State Governments

Many citizens do not realize that, as originally intended, the Bill of Rights limited only the powers of the national government. At the time the Bill of Rights was ratified, the potential of state governments to curb civil liberties caused little concern. For one thing, state governments were closer to home and easier to control. For another, most state constitutions already had bills of rights. Rather, the fear was of the potential tyranny of the national government. The Bill of Rights begins with the words, "Congress shall make no law…" It says nothing about *states* making laws that might abridge citizens' civil liberties.

In 1833, in *Barron v. Baltimore*,[1] the United States Supreme Court held that the Bill of Rights did not apply to state laws. The issue in the case was whether a property owner could sue the city of Baltimore for recovery of his losses under the Fifth Amendment to the Constitution. Chief Justice Marshall spoke for a united court, declaring that the Supreme Court could not hear the case because the amendments were meant only to limit the national government.

■ **Learning Outcome 1:**
Explain the origin of the Bill of Rights, and discuss how these rights were applied to the states.

did you know?

One of the proposed initial constitutional amendments—"No State shall infringe the equal rights of conscience, nor the freedom of speech, nor of the press, nor of the right of trial by jury in criminal cases"— was never sent to the states for approval because the states' rights advocates in the first Congress defeated it.

---

1. 7 Peters 243 (1833).

We mentioned that most states had bills of rights. These bills of rights were similar to the national one, with some differences. Furthermore, each state's judicial system interpreted the rights differently. Citizens in different states, therefore, effectively had different sets of civil rights. Remember that the Thirteenth, Fourteenth, and Fifteenth Amendments were passed after the Civil War to guarantee equal rights to the former slaves and free black Americans, regardless of the states in which they lived. It was not until after the Fourteenth Amendment was ratified in 1868 that civil liberties guaranteed by the national Constitution began to be applied to the states. Section 1 of that amendment provides, in part, as follows:

No State shall ... deprive any person of life, liberty, or property, without due process of law.

Incorporation of the Fourteenth Amendment

There was no question that the Fourteenth Amendment applied to state governments. For decades, however, the courts were reluctant to define the liberties spelled out in the national Bill of Rights as constituting "due process of law," which was protected under the Fourteenth Amendment. Not until 1925, in *Gitlow v. New York*,[2] did the United States Supreme Court hold that the Fourteenth Amendment applied one of the protections of the First Amendment, freedom of speech, to the states.

Only gradually, and never completely, did the Supreme Court accept the **incorporation theory**—the view that most of the protections of the Bill of Rights are incorporated into the Fourteenth Amendment's protection against state government actions. Table 4–1 shows the rights that the Court has incorporated into

Incorporation Theory
The view that most of the protections of the Bill of Rights apply to state governments through the Fourteenth Amendment's due process clause.

TABLE 4–1 ▶ Incorporating the Bill of Rights into the Fourteenth Amendment

YEAR	ISSUE	AMENDMENT INVOLVED	COURT CASE
1925	Freedom of speech	I	*Gitlow v. New York*, 268 U.S. 652
1931	Freedom of the press	I	*Near v. Minnesota*, 283 U.S. 697
1932	Right to a lawyer in capital punishment cases	VI	*Powell v. Alabama*, 287 U.S. 45
1937	Freedom of assembly and right to petition	I	*De Jonge v. Oregon*, 299 U.S. 353
1940	Freedom of religion	I	*Cantwell v. Connecticut*, 310 U.S. 296
1947	Separation of church and state	I	*Everson v. Board of Education*, 330 U.S. 1
1948	Right to a public trial	VI	*In re Oliver*, 333 U.S. 257
1949	No unreasonable searches and seizures	IV	*Wolf v. Colorado*, 338 U.S. 25
1961	Exclusionary rule	IV	*Mapp v. Ohio*, 367 U.S. 643
1962	No cruel and unusual punishment	VIII	*Robinson v. California*, 370 U.S. 660
1963	Right to a lawyer in all criminal felony cases	VI	*Gideon v. Wainwright*, 372 U.S. 335
1964	No compulsory self-incrimination	V	*Malloy v. Hogan*, 378 U.S. 1
1965	Right to privacy	I, III, IV, V, IX	*Griswold v. Connecticut*, 381 U.S. 479
1966	Right to an impartial jury	VI	*Parker v. Gladden*, 385 U.S. 363
1967	Right to a speedy trial	VI	*Klopfer v. North Carolina*, 386 U.S. 213
1969	No double jeopardy	V	*Benton v. Maryland*, 395 U.S. 784

2. 68 U.S. 652 (1925).

the Fourteenth Amendment and the case in which it first applied each protection. As you can see in that table, in the 15 years following the *Gitlow* decision, the Supreme Court incorporated into the Fourteenth Amendment the other basic freedoms (of the press, assembly, the right to petition, and religion) guaranteed by the First Amendment. These and the later Supreme Court decisions listed in Table 4–1 have bound the 50 states to accept for their citizens most of the rights and freedoms that are set forth in the U.S. Bill of Rights. We now look at some of those rights and freedoms, beginning with the freedom of religion.

Freedom of Religion

■ Learning Outcome 2:
Explain how the Bill of Rights protects freedom of religion while maintaining a separation between the state and religion.

Establishment Clause
The part of the First Amendment prohibiting the establishment of a church officially supported by the national government. It is applied to questions of state and local government aid to religious organizations and schools, the legality of allowing or requiring school prayers, and the teaching of evolution versus intelligent design.

In the United States, freedom of religion consists of two main principles as they are presented in the First Amendment. The **establishment clause** prohibits the establishment of a church that is officially supported by the national government, thus guaranteeing a division between church and state. The *free exercise clause* constrains the national government from prohibiting individuals from practicing the religion of their choice. These two precepts can inherently be in tension with one another, however. Public universities are constrained to allow religious groups to form on campus under the free exercise clause but may decide not to fund such student groups because of the Supreme Court's prohibition of supporting religion under the establishment clause. You will read about several difficult freedom of religion issues in the following discussion.

The Separation of Church and State— The Establishment Clause

The First Amendment to the Constitution states, in part, that "Congress shall make no law respecting an establishment of religion." In the words of Thomas Jefferson, the establishment clause was designed to create a "wall of separation of Church and State."[3]

Perhaps Jefferson was thinking about the religious intolerance that characterized the first colonies. Many of the American colonies were founded by groups that were pursuing religious freedom for their own particular denomination. Nonetheless, the early colonists were quite intolerant of religious beliefs that did not conform to those held by the majority of citizens within their own communities. Jefferson undoubtedly was also aware that established churches, meaning state-protected denominations, existed within 9 of the original 13 colonies.

As interpreted by the United States Supreme Court, the establishment clause in the First Amendment means at least the following:

> *Neither a state nor the federal government can set up a church. Neither can pass laws which aid one religion, aid all religions, or prefer one religion over another. Neither can force nor influence a person to go to or to remain away from church against his will or force him to profess a belief or disbelief in any religion. No person can be punished for entertaining or professing religious beliefs or disbeliefs, for church attendance or nonattendance. No tax in any amount, large or small, can be levied to support any religious activities or institutions, whatever they may be called, or whatever form they may adopt to teach or practice religion. Neither a state nor the federal government can, openly or secretly, participate in the affairs of any religious organizations or groups and vice versa.[4]*

---

3. "Jefferson's Letter to the Danbury Baptists, The Final Letter, as Sent," January 1, 1802, The Library of Congress, Washington, D.C.
4. *Everson v. Board of Education*, 330 U.S. 1 (1947).

© Jim Young/Reuters/Corbis

U.S. Representative Keith Ellison (D-Minn) places his hand on an English translation of the Koran once owned by Thomas Jefferson and held by his wife Kim as he is sworn in as the first Muslim member of Congress by then U.S. Speaker of the House Nancy Pelosi. His children watch the ceremony. Should members of Congress be required to be sworn in on a sacred text?

The establishment clause is applied to all conflicts about such matters as the legality of state and local government aid to religious organizations and schools, the allowing or requiring of school prayers, the teaching of evolution versus intelligent design, the posting of the Ten Commandments in schools or public places, and discrimination against religious groups in publicly operated institutions. The establishment clause's mandate that government can neither promote nor discriminate against religious beliefs raises particularly complex questions at times.

Aid to Church-Related Schools. Throughout the United States, all property owners except religious, educational, fraternal, literary, scientific, and similar nonprofit institutions must pay property taxes. A large part of the proceeds of such taxes goes to support public schools. But not all children attend public schools. Fully 12 percent of school-aged children attend private schools, of which 85 percent have religious affiliations. Many cases have reached the United States Supreme Court; the Court has tried to draw a fine line between permissible public aid to students in church-related schools and impermissible public aid to religion. These issues have arisen most often at the elementary and secondary levels.

In 1971, in *Lemon v. Kurtzman*,[5] the Court ruled that direct state aid could not be used to subsidize religious instruction. The Court in the *Lemon* case gave its most general statement on the constitutionality of government aid to religious schools, stating that the aid had to be secular (nonreligious) in aim, that it could not have the primary effect of advancing or inhibiting religion, and that the government must avoid "an excessive government entanglement with religion." The three phrases above became known as the "three-part *Lemon* test" which has been applied in most of the cases under the establishment clause since 1971. The interpretation of the test, however, has varied over the years.

did you know?

On the eve of the American Revolution, fewer than 20 percent of American adults adhered to a church in any significant way, compared with the 62 percent who do so today.

5.   403 U.S. 602 (1971).

In several cases, the Supreme Court has held that state programs helping church-related schools are unconstitutional. The Court also has denied state reimbursements to religious schools for field trips and for developing achievement tests. In a series of other cases, however, the Supreme Court has allowed states to use tax funds for lunches, textbooks, diagnostic services for speech and hearing problems, state-required standardized tests, computers, and transportation for students attending church-operated elementary and secondary schools. In some cases, the Court argued that state aid was intended to directly assist the individual child, and in other cases, such as bus transportation, the Court acknowledged the state's goals for public safety.

A Change in the Court's Position. Generally, today's Supreme Court has shown a greater willingness to allow the use of public funds for programs in religious schools than was true at times in the past. Consider that in 1985, in *Aguilar v. Felton*,[6] the Supreme Court ruled that state programs providing special educational services for disadvantaged students attending religious schools violated the establishment clause. In 1997, however, when the Supreme Court revisited this decision, the Court reversed its position. In *Agostini v. Felton*,[7] the Court held that *Aguilar* was "no longer good law." What had happened between 1985 and 1997 to cause the Court to change its mind? Justice Sandra Day O'Connor answered this question in the *Agostini* opinion: What had changed since *Aguilar*, she stated, was "our understanding" of the establishment clause. Between 1985 and 1997, the Court's makeup had changed significantly. In fact, six of the nine justices who participated in the 1997 decision were appointed after the 1985 *Aguilar* decision.

School Vouchers. Questions about the use of public funds for church-related schools are likely to continue as state legislators search for new ways to improve the educational system in this country. An issue that has come to the forefront in recent years is school vouchers. In a voucher system, educational vouchers (state-issued credits) can be used to "purchase" education at any school, public or private.

School districts in Florida, Ohio, and Wisconsin have all been experimenting with voucher systems. In 2000, the courts reviewed a case involving Ohio's voucher program. Under that program, some $10 million in public funds is spent annually to send 4,300 Cleveland students to 51 private schools, all but five of which are Catholic schools. The case presented a straightforward constitutional question: Is it a violation of the principle of separation of church and state for public tax money to be used to pay for religious education?

In 2002, the Supreme Court held that the Cleveland voucher program was constitutional.[8] The Court concluded, by a 5-4 vote, that Cleveland's use of tax-payer-paid school vouchers to send children to private schools was constitutional, even though more than 95 percent of the students use the vouchers to attend Catholic or other religious schools. The Court's majority reasoned that the program did not unconstitutionally entangle church and state, because families theoretically could use the vouchers for their children to attend religious schools, secular private academies, suburban public schools, or charter schools, even though few public schools had agreed to accept vouchers. The Court's decision raised a further question that will need to be decided—whether religious and

---

6. 473 U.S. 402 (1985).
7. 521 U.S. 203 (1997).
8. *Zelman v. Simmons-Harris*, 536 U.S. 639 (2002).

private schools that accept government vouchers must comply with disability and civil rights laws, as public schools are required to do.

Despite the United States Supreme Court's decision upholding the Cleveland voucher program, in 2006 the Florida Supreme Court declared Florida's voucher program unconstitutional. The Florida court held that the Florida state constitution bars public funding from being diverted to private schools that are not subject to the uniformity requirements of the state's public school system. The state of Arizona has taken an entirely different approach, passing legislation to allow parents to reduce their state taxes by the amount of tuition paid to a private school. In 2011, the Supreme Court ruled that, because the money was paid directly from the individual to the school and the government did not support the private school, the law could not be challenged by other taxpayers.[9] In 2012, school voucher programs in eight states and the District of Columbia served about 80,000 children; however, many of these programs were still being legally contested in state courts.

The Issue of School Prayer—Engel v. Vitale.

Do the states have the right to promote religion in general, without making any attempt to establish a particular religion? That is the question raised by school prayer and was the precise issue in 1962 in *Engel v. Vitale*,[10] the so-called Regents' Prayer case in New York. The State Board of Regents of New York had suggested that a prayer be spoken aloud in the public schools at the beginning of each day. The recommended prayer was as follows:

> *Almighty God, we acknowledge our dependence upon Thee, And we beg Thy blessings upon us, our parents, our teachers, and our Country.*

Such a prayer was implemented in many New York public schools. The parents of several students challenged the action of the regents, maintaining that it violated the establishment clause of the First Amendment. At trial, the parents lost. The Supreme Court, however, ruled that the regents' action was unconstitutional because "the constitutional prohibition against laws respecting an establishment of a religion must mean at least that in this country it is no part of the business of government to compose official prayers for any group of the American people to recite as part of a religious program carried on by any government." The Court's conclusion was based in part on the "historical fact that governmentally established religions and religious persecutions go hand in hand." In *Abington School District v. Schempp*,[11] the Supreme Court outlawed officially sponsored daily readings of the Bible and recitation of the Lord's Prayer in public schools.

The Debate over School Prayer Continues.

Although the Supreme Court has ruled repeatedly against officially sponsored prayer and Bible-reading sessions in public schools, other means for bringing some form of religious expression into public education have been attempted. In 1983, the Tennessee legislature passed a bill requiring public school classes to begin each day with a minute of silence. Alabama had a similar law. In 1985, in *Wallace v. Jaffree*,[12] the Supreme Court struck down as unconstitutional the Alabama law authorizing one minute of silence for prayer or meditation in all public schools. Applying the three-part *Lemon* test, the Court concluded that

---

9. *Arizona School Tuition Organization v. Winn.* 09-987 (2011)
10. 370 U.S. 421 (1962).
11. 374 U.S. 203 (1963).
12. 472 U.S. 38 (1985).

the law violated the establishment clause because it was "an endorsement of religion lacking any clearly secular purpose."

Since then, the lower courts have interpreted the Supreme Court's decision to mean that states can require a moment of silence in the schools as long as they make it clear that the purpose of the law is secular, not religious.

Prayer outside the Classroom. The courts have also dealt with cases involving prayer in public schools outside the classroom, particularly prayer during graduation ceremonies. In 1992, in *Lee v. Weisman*,[13] the United States Supreme Court held that it was unconstitutional for a school to invite a rabbi to deliver a nonsectarian prayer at graduation. The Court said nothing about *students* organizing and leading prayers at graduation ceremonies and other school events, however, and these issues continue to come before the courts. A particularly contentious question in the last few years has been the constitutionality of student-initiated prayers before sporting events, such as football games. In 2000, the Supreme Court held that while school prayer at graduation did not violate the establishment clause, students could not use a school's public-address system to lead prayers at sporting events.[14]

Despite the Court's ruling, students at several schools in Texas continue to pray over public-address systems at sporting events. In other areas, the Court's ruling is skirted by avoiding the use of the public-address system. For example, in a school in North Carolina, a pregame prayer was broadcast over a local radio station and heard by fans who took radios to the game for that purpose.

The Ten Commandments. A related church–state issue is whether the Ten Commandments may be displayed in public schools—or on any public property. Supporters of the movement to display the Ten Commandments argue that they embody American values and that they constitute a part of the official and permanent history of American government.

Opponents of such laws claim that they are an unconstitutional government entanglement with the religious life of citizens. Still, various Ten Commandments installations have been found to be constitutional. For example, the Supreme Court ruled in 2005 that a granite monument on the grounds of the Texas state capitol that contained the commandments was constitutional because the monument as a whole was secular in nature.[15] In another 2005 ruling, however, the Court ordered that displays of the Ten Commandments in front of two Kentucky county courthouses had to be removed because they were overtly religious.[16]

The Ten Commandments controversy took an odd twist in 2003 when, in the middle of the night, former Alabama chief justice Roy Moore installed a two-and-a-half-ton granite monument featuring the commandments in the rotunda of the state courthouse. When Moore refused to obey a federal judge's order to remove the monument, the Alabama Court of the Judiciary was forced to expel him from the judicial bench.

Forbidding the Teaching of Evolution. For many decades, certain religious groups, particularly in southern states, have opposed the teaching of evolution in the schools. To these groups, evolutionary theory directly counters their religious belief that human beings did not evolve but were created fully formed, as described in the biblical story of creation. State and local attempts to forbid the

13. 505 U.S. 577 (1992).
14. *Santa Fe Independent School District v. Doe*, 530 U.S. 290 (2000).
15. *VanOrden v. Perry*, 125 S. Ct. 2854 (2005).
16. *McCreary County v. American Civil Liberties Union*, 125 S. Ct. 2722 (2005).

© TAMI CHAPPELL/Reuters/Landov

Workers work to remove a monument of the Ten Commandments from the rotunda area of the Alabama Judicial Building where Superior Court Justice Roy Moore had refused to take it down, on August 27, 2003, in Montgomery, Alabama. Judge Moore was expelled from his seat on the bench for his refusal.

teaching of evolution, however, have not passed constitutional muster in the eyes of the United States Supreme Court. For example, in 1968, the Supreme Court held in *Epperson v. Arkansas*[17] that an Arkansas law prohibiting the teaching of evolution violated the establishment clause because it imposed religious beliefs on students. The Louisiana legislature passed a law requiring the teaching of the biblical story of the creation alongside the teaching of evolution. In 1987, in *Edwards v. Aguillard*,[18] the Supreme Court declared that this law was unconstitutional, in part because it had as its primary purpose the promotion of a particular religious belief.

Nonetheless, state and local groups around the country, particularly in the so-called Bible Belt, continue their efforts against the teaching of evolution. The Cobb County school system in Georgia attempted to include a disclaimer in its biology textbooks that proclaims, "Evolution is a theory, not a fact, regarding the origin of living things." A federal judge later ruled that the disclaimer stickers must be removed. Other school districts have considered teaching "intelligent design" as an alternative explanation of the origin of life. Proponents of intelligent design contend that evolutionary theory has gaps that can be explained only by the existence of an intelligent creative force (God). They suggest that teaching intelligent design in the schools is simply teaching another kind of scientific theory, so it would not breach the separation of church and state. Critics of intelligent design have pointed out that many of its proponents have a religious agenda. The same religious groups also once backed creationism, a set of quasi-scientific theories that support the creation narrative. Intelligent design, at its essence, proposes an original Creator, which is a religious belief and cannot be taught in the schools.

17. 393 U.S. 97 (1968).
18. 482 U.S. 578 (1987).

Religious Speech.   Another controversy in the area of church-state relations concerns religious speech in public schools or universities. For example, in *Rosenberger v. University of Virginia*,[19] the issue was whether the University of Virginia violated the establishment clause when it refused to fund a Christian group's newsletter but granted funds to more than 100 other student organizations. The Supreme Court ruled that the university's policy unconstitutionally discriminated against religious speech. The Court pointed out that the funds came from student fees, not general taxes, and were used for the "neutral" payment of bills for student groups.

Later, the Supreme Court reviewed a case involving a similar claim of discrimination against a religious group, the Good News Club. The club offers religious instruction to young schoolchildren. The club sued the school board of a public school in Milford, New York, when the board refused to allow the club to meet on school property after the school day ended. The club argued that the school board's refusal to allow the club to meet on school property, when other groups—such as the Girl Scouts and the 4-H Club—were permitted to do so, amounted to discrimination on the basis of religion. Ultimately, the Supreme Court agreed, ruling in *Good News Club v. Milford Central School*[20] that the Milford school board's decision violated the establishment clause.

The Free Exercise Clause

Free Exercise Clause
The provision of the First Amendment guaranteeing the free exercise of religion.

The First Amendment constrains Congress from prohibiting the free exercise of religion. Does this **free exercise clause** mean that no type of religious practice can be prohibited or restricted by government? Certainly, a person can hold any religious belief that he or she wants, or have no religious beliefs. When, however, religious *practices* work against public policy and the public welfare, the government can act. For example, regardless of a child's or parent's religious beliefs, the government can require certain types of vaccinations. The sale and use of marijuana for religious purposes has been held illegal, because a religion cannot make legal what would otherwise be illegal.

The extent to which government can regulate religious practices has always been a subject of controversy. For example, in 1990 in *Oregon v. Smith*,[21] the United States Supreme Court ruled that the state of Oregon could deny unemployment benefits to two drug counselors who had been fired for using peyote, an illegal drug, in their religious services. The counselors had argued that using peyote was part of the practice of a Native American religion. Many criticized the decision as going too far in the direction of regulating religious practices.

The Religious Freedom Restoration Act.   In 1993, Congress responded to the public's criticism by passing the Religious Freedom Restoration Act (RFRA). One of the specific purposes of the act was to overturn the Supreme Court's decision in *Oregon v. Smith*. The act required national, state, and local governments to "accommodate religious conduct" unless the government could show a *compelling* reason not to do so. Moreover, if the government did regulate a religious practice, it had to use the least restrictive means possible.

Some people believed that the RFRA went too far in the other direction—it accommodated practices that were contrary to the public policies of state governments. Proponents of states' rights complained that the act intruded into an area

---

19.   515 U.S. 819 (1995).
20.   533 U.S. 98 (2001).
21.   494 U.S. 872 (1990)

traditionally governed by state laws, not by the national government. In 1997, in *City of Boerne v. Flores*,[22] the Supreme Court agreed and held that Congress had exceeded its constitutional authority when it passed the RFRA. According to the Court, the act's "sweeping coverage ensures its intrusion at every level of government, displacing laws and prohibiting official actions of almost every description and regardless of subject matter."

Free Exercise in the Public Schools. The courts have repeatedly held that U.S. governments at all levels must remain neutral on issues of religion. In the *Good News Club* decision discussed previously, the Supreme Court ruled that "state power is no more to be used to handicap religions than it is to favor them." Nevertheless, by overturning the RFRA, the Court cleared the way for public schools to set regulations that, while ostensibly neutral, effectively limited religious expression by students. An example is a rule banning hats, which has been instituted by many schools as a way of discouraging the display of gang insignia. This rule has also been interpreted as barring yarmulkes, the small caps worn by strictly observant Jewish boys and men.

Freedom of Expression

Perhaps the most frequently invoked freedom that Americans have is the right to free speech and a free press without government interference. Each of us has the right to have our say, and all of us have the right to hear what others say. For the most part, Americans can criticize public officials and their actions without fear of reprisal by any branch of government.

No Prior Restraint

Restraining an activity before that activity has actually occurred is called **prior restraint**. When expression is involved, prior restraint means censorship, as opposed to subsequent punishment. Prior restraint of expression would require, for example, that a permit be obtained before a speech could be made, a newspaper published, or a movie or TV show exhibited. Most, if not all, Supreme Court justices have been very critical of any governmental action that imposes prior restraint on expression. The Court clearly displayed this attitude in *Nebraska Press Association v. Stuart*,[23] a case decided in 1976:

> A prior restraint on expression comes to this Court with a "heavy presumption" against its constitutionality.... The government thus carries a heavy burden of showing justification for the enforcement of such a restraint.

One of the most famous cases concerning prior restraint was *New York Times v. United States*[24] in 1971, the so-called Pentagon Papers case. The *Times* and *The Washington Post* were about to publish the Pentagon Papers, an elaborate secret history of the U.S. government's involvement in the Vietnam War (1964–1975). The secret documents had been obtained illegally by a disillusioned former Pentagon official. The government wanted a court order to bar publication of the documents, arguing that national security was threatened and that the documents had been stolen. The newspapers argued that the public had a right to know the information contained in the papers and that the press had

■ **Learning Outcome 3:**
Define freedom of expression, explain where it is found in the Bill of Rights, and show why it is important in a democracy.

Prior Restraint
Restraining an action before the activity has actually occurred. When expression is involved, this means censorship.

---

22.   521 U.S. 507 (1997).
23.   427 U.S. 539 (1976). See also *Near v. Minnesota*, 283 U.S. 697 (1931).
24.   403 U.S. 713 (1971).

the right to inform the public. The Supreme Court ruled 6-3 in favor of the newspapers' right to publish the information. This case affirmed the no-prior-restraint doctrine.

WikiLeaks

In recent years, an organization known as WikiLeaks, led by an Australian named Julian Assange, has made available on the Internet huge sets of documents that were held by governments around the world. Most of these documents had been "classified" by the respective governments as too sensitive to be made public. Assange, who has been indicted on other unrelated crimes, continues to live in Great Britain and direct the operation. The United States government charged the member of the U.S. military who allowed WikiLeaks to gain access to the documents with a crime, but no other action seems to be possible. The Internet has, in this case, made freedom of expression a worldwide issue.

The Protection of Symbolic Speech

Symbolic Speech
Nonverbal expression of beliefs, which is given substantial protection by the courts.

Not all expression is in words or in writing. Articles of clothing, gestures, movements, and other forms of expressive conduct are considered **symbolic speech**. Such speech is given substantial protection today by our courts. For example, in a landmark decision issued in 1969, *Tinker v. Des Moines School District*,[25] the United States Supreme Court held that the wearing of black armbands by students in protest against the Vietnam War was a form of speech protected by the First Amendment. The case arose after a school administrator in Des Moines, Iowa, issued a regulation prohibiting students in the Des Moines School District from wearing the armbands. The Supreme Court reasoned that the school district was unable to show that the wearing of the armbands had disrupted normal school activities. Furthermore, the school district's policy was discriminatory, as it banned only certain forms of symbolic speech (the black armbands) and not others (such as lapel crosses and fraternity rings).

Demonstrators burn U.S. flags in front of the World Bank headquarters in 2002, protesting the international meetings there. Why is it legal to burn the flag in protest?

© HIROKO MASUIKE/AFP/Getty Images

25. 393 U.S. 503 (1969).

In 1989, in *Texas v. Johnson*,[26] the Supreme Court ruled that state laws that prohibited the burning of the American flag as part of a peaceful protest also violated the freedom of expression protected by the First Amendment. Congress responded by passing the Flag Protection Act of 1989, which was ruled unconstitutional by the Supreme Court in June 1990.[27] Congress and President George H. W. Bush immediately pledged to work for a constitutional amendment to "protect our flag"—an effort that has yet to be successful.

In 2003, however, the Supreme Court held that a Virginia statute prohibiting the burning of a cross with "an intent to intimidate" did not violate the First Amendment. The Court concluded that a burning cross is an instrument of racial terror so threatening that it overshadows free speech concerns.[28]

The Protection of Commercial Speech

Commercial speech usually is defined as advertising statements. Can advertisers use their First Amendment rights to prevent restrictions on the content of commercial advertising? Until the 1970s, the Supreme Court held that such speech was not protected at all by the First Amendment. By the mid-1970s, however, more commercial speech had been brought under First Amendment protection. According to Justice Harry A. Blackmun, "Advertising, however tasteless and excessive it sometimes may seem, is nonetheless dissemination of information as to who is producing and selling what product for what reason and at what price."[29] Nevertheless, the Supreme Court will consider a restriction on commercial speech valid as long as it (1) seeks to implement a substantial government interest, (2) directly advances that interest, and (3) goes no further than necessary to accomplish its objective. What this means is that an advertisement that makes totally false claims can be restricted.

The issue of political campaign advertising is one that crosses the boundaries between individual free speech and commercial speech. For many years, federal law has prohibited businesses, labor unions, and other organizations from engaging directly in political advertising. As you will learn later in this book, corporations and other groups were allowed to create political action committees to engage in regulated activities. In recent years, new organizational forms were created to campaign for issues. However, nonprofit organizations were strictly prohibited from directly campaigning for candidates. In 2009, the Supreme Court overturned decades of law on this issue, declaring in *Citizens United vs. FEC* that corporations and other associations were "persons" in terms of the law and had free speech rights. According to the majority decision, Citizens United, an incorporated nonprofit group, was unfairly denied the right to pay for broadcasting a movie about Senator Hillary Clinton, a film which was intended to harm her campaign for president. President Obama reacted by asking the Congress to rewrite the campaign finance laws to restrict such forms of political advertising.[30]

Permitted Restrictions on Expression

At various times, restrictions on expression have been permitted. As we have seen after the terrorist attacks of September 11, 2001, periods of perceived foreign threats to the government sometimes lead to more repression of speech

Commercial Speech
Advertising statements, which increasingly have been given First Amendment protection.

that is thought to be dangerous to the nation. It is interesting to note that the Supreme Court changes its view of what might be dangerous speech depending on the times.

Clear and Present Danger. When a person's remarks create a clear and present danger to the peace or public order, they can be curtailed constitutionally. Justice Oliver Wendell Holmes used this reasoning in 1919 when examining the case of a socialist who had been convicted for violating the Espionage Act by distributing a leaflet that opposed the military draft. Holmes stated:

> The question in every case is whether the words are used in such circumstances and are of such a nature as to create a **clear and present danger** that they will bring about the substantive evils that Congress has a right to prevent. It is a question of proximity and degree.[31] [Emphasis added.]

According to the **clear and present danger test**, then, expression may be restricted if evidence exists that such expression would cause a condition, actual or imminent, that Congress has the power to prevent. Commenting on this test, Justice Louis D. Brandeis in 1920 said, "Correctly applied, it will reserve the right of free speech … from suppression by tyrannists, well-meaning majorities, and from abuse by irresponsible, fanatical minorities."[32]

Modifications to the Clear and Present Danger Rule. Since the clear and present danger rule was first enunciated, the United States Supreme Court has modified it. In 1925, during a period when many Americans feared the increasing power of communist and other left-wing parties in Europe, the Supreme Court heard the case *Gitlow v. New York*.[33] In its opinion, the Court introduced the *bad-tendency rule*. According to this rule, speech or other First

Clear and Present Danger Test
The test proposed by Justice Oliver Wendell Holmes for determining when government may restrict free speech. Restrictions are permissible, he argued, only when speech creates a *clear and present danger* to the public order.

In 2002, a student who held this banner outside his school in Alaska was suspended for supporting drug use with his "speech." The Supreme Court upheld the principal's decision in the 2007 case *Morse v. Frederick*, saying that public schools are able to regulate what students say about promoting illegal drug use. Do you think banning such speech is a violation of students' free speech rights? Should colleges be able to implement such a ban as well?

31. *Schenck v. United States*, 249 U.S. 47(1919).
32. *Schaefer v. United States*, 251 U.S. 466 (1920).
33. 268 U.S. 652 (1925).

Amendment freedoms may be curtailed if a possibility exists that such expression might lead to some "evil." In the *Gitlow* case, a member of a left-wing group was convicted of violating New York State's criminal anarchy statute when he published and distributed a pamphlet urging the violent overthrow of the U.S. government. In its majority opinion, the Supreme Court held that although the First Amendment afforded protection against state incursions on freedom of expression, Gitlow could be punished legally in this particular instance because his expression would tend to bring about evils that the state had a right to prevent.

The Supreme Court again modified the clear and present danger test in a 1951 case, *Dennis v. United States.*[34] During the early years of the Cold War, Americans were anxious about the activities of communists and the Soviet Union within the United States. Congress passed several laws that essentially outlawed the Communist Party of the United States and made its activities illegal. Twelve members of the American Communist Party were convicted of violating a statute that made it a crime to conspire to teach, advocate, or organize the violent overthrow of any government in the United States. The Supreme Court affirmed the convictions, significantly modifying the clear and present danger test in the process. The Court applied a *grave and probable danger rule*. Under this rule, "the gravity of the 'evil' discounted by its improbability justifies such invasion of free speech as is necessary to avoid the danger." This rule gave much less protection to free speech than did the clear and present danger test.

Six years after the *Dennis* case, the Supreme Court heard another case in which members of the Communist Party in California were accused of teaching and advocating the overthrow of the government of the United States. The ruling of the Court in this case greatly reduced the scope of the law passed by Congress. In *Yates v. United States,*[35] the Court held that there was a difference between "advocacy and teaching of forcible overthrow as an abstract principle" and actually proposing concrete action. The Court overturned the convictions of the party leaders because they were essentially engaging in speech rather than action. This was the beginning of a series of cases that eventually found the original congressional legislation to be unconstitutional because it violated the First and Fourth Amendments.

Some claim that the United States did not achieve true freedom of political speech until 1969. In that year, in *Brandenburg v. Ohio,*[36] the Supreme Court overturned the conviction of a Ku Klux Klan leader for violating a state statute. The statute prohibited anyone from advocating "the duty, necessity, or propriety of sabotage, violence, or unlawful methods of terrorism as a means of accomplishing industrial or political reform." The Court held that the guarantee of free speech does not permit a state "to forbid or proscribe advocacy of the use of force or of law violation except where such advocacy is directed to inciting or producing imminent lawless actions and is likely to incite or produce such action." The incitement test enunciated by the Court in this case is a difficult one for prosecutors to meet. As a result, the Court's decision significantly broadened the protection given to advocacy speech.

Unprotected Speech: Obscenity
Many state and federal statutes make it a crime to disseminate obscene materials. Generally, the courts have not been willing to extend constitutional protections of free speech to what they consider to be obscene materials. But what is obscenity?

34. 341 U.S. 494 (1951).
35. 354 U.S. 298 (1957).
36. 395 U.S. 444 (1969).

Justice Potter Stewart once stated, in *Jacobellis v. Ohio*,[37] a 1964 case, that even though he could not define *obscenity*, "I know it when I see it." The problem is that even if it were agreed on, the definition of *obscenity* changes with the times. Victorians deeply disapproved of the "loose" morals of the Elizabethan Age. The works of Mark Twain and Edgar Rice Burroughs at times have been considered obscene (after all, Tarzan and Jane were not legally wedded).

Definitional Problems.   The Supreme Court has grappled from time to time with the difficulty of specifying an operationally effective definition of *obscenity*. In 1973, in *Miller v. California*,[38] Chief Justice Warren Burger created a formal list of requirements that must be met for material to be considered legally obscene. Material is obscene if (1) the average person finds that it violates contemporary community standards; (2) the work taken as a whole appeals to a prurient interest in sex; (3) the work shows patently offensive sexual conduct; and (4) the work lacks serious redeeming literary, artistic, political, or scientific merit. The problem is that one person's prurient interest is another person's medical interest or artistic pleasure. The Court went on to state that the definition of *prurient interest* would be determined by the community's standards. The Court avoided presenting a definition of *obscenity,* leaving this determination to local and state authorities. Consequently, the *Miller* case has been applied in a widely inconsistent manner.

Protecting Children.   The Supreme Court has upheld state laws making it illegal to sell materials showing sexual performances by minors. In 1990, in *Osborne v. Ohio*,[39] the Court ruled that states can outlaw the possession of child pornography in the home. The Court reasoned that the ban on private possession is justified because owning the material perpetuates commercial demand for it and for the exploitation of the children involved. At the federal level, the Child Protection Act of 1984 made it a crime to receive knowingly through the mails sexually explicit depictions of children.

Pornography on the Internet.   A significant problem facing Americans and lawmakers today is how to control obscenity and child pornography disseminated via the Internet. In 1996, Congress first attempted to protect minors from pornographic materials on the Internet by passing the Communications Decency Act (CDA). The act made it a crime to make available to minors online any "obscene or indecent" message that "depicts or describes, in terms patently offensive as measured by contemporary community standards, sexual or excretory activities or organs." The act was immediately challenged in court as an unconstitutional infringement on free speech. The Supreme Court held that the act imposed unconstitutional restraints on free speech and was therefore invalid.[40] In the eyes of the Court, the terms *indecent* and *patently offensive* covered large amounts of nonpornographic material with serious educational or other value. Later attempts by Congress to curb pornography on the Internet also encountered stumbling blocks. For example, the Child Online Protection Act (COPA) of 1998 banned the distribution of material "harmful to minors" without an age-verification system to separate adult and minor users. In 2002, the Supreme Court upheld a lower court injunction suspending the COPA, and in 2004, the Court again upheld the

37.   378 U.S. 184 (1964).
38.   413 U.S. 5 (1973).
39.   495 U.S. 103 (1990).
40.   *Reno v. American Civil Liberties Union*, 521 U.S. 844 (1997).

suspension of the law on the ground that it was probably unconstitutional.[41] In 2000, Congress enacted the Children's Internet Protection Act (CIPA), which requires public schools and libraries to install filtering software to prevent children from viewing Web sites with "adult" content.

Should "Virtual" Pornography Be Deemed a Crime? In 2001, the Supreme Court agreed to review a case challenging the constitutionality of another federal act attempting to protect minors in the online environment—the Child Pornography Prevention Act (CPPA) of 1996. This act made it illegal to distribute or possess computer-generated images that appear to depict minors engaging in lewd and lascivious behavior. At issue was whether digital child pornography should be considered a crime even though it uses only digitally rendered images and no actual children are involved.

The Supreme Court, noting that virtual child pornography is not the same as child pornography, held that the CPPA's ban on virtual child pornography restrained a substantial amount of lawful speech.[42] The Court stated, "The statute proscribes the visual depiction of an idea—that of teenagers engaging in sexual activity—that is a fact of modern society and has been a theme in art and literature throughout the ages." The Court concluded that the act was overbroad and thus unconstitutional.

Unprotected Speech: Slander

Can you say anything you want about someone else? Not really. Individuals are protected from **defamation of character**, which is defined as wrongfully hurting a person's good reputation. The law imposes a general duty on all persons to refrain from making false, defamatory statements about others. Breaching this duty orally is the wrongdoing called *slander*. Breaching it in writing is the wrongdoing called *libel*, which we discuss later. The government does not bring charges of slander or libel. Rather, the defamed person may bring a civil suit for damages.

Legally, **slander** is the public uttering of a false statement that harms the good reputation of another. Slanderous public uttering means that the defamatory statements are made to, or within the hearing of, persons other than the defamed party. If one person calls another dishonest, manipulative, and incompetent to his or her face when no one else is around, that does not constitute slander. The message is not communicated to a third party. If, however, a third party accidentally overhears defamatory statements, the courts have generally held that this constitutes a public uttering and therefore slander, which is prohibited.

Campus Speech

In recent years, students have been facing free-speech challenges on campuses. One issue has to do with whether a student should have to subsidize, through student activity fees, organizations that promote causes that the student finds objectionable.

Student Activity Fees. In 2000, this question came before the United States Supreme Court in a case brought by several University of Wisconsin students. The students argued that their mandatory student activity fees—which

Defamation of Character
Wrongfully hurting a person's good reputation. The law imposes a general duty on all persons to refrain from making false, defamatory statements about others.

Slander
The public uttering of a false statement that harms the good reputation of another. The statement must be made to, or within the hearing of, persons other than the defamed party.

---

41. *Ashcroft v. American Civil Liberties Union,* 542 U.S. 656 (2004).
42. *Ashcroft v. Free Speech Coalition,* 535 U.S. 234 (2002).

helped to fund liberal causes with which they disagreed, including gay rights—violated their First Amendment rights of free speech, free association, and free exercise of religion. They contended that they should have the right to choose whether to fund organizations that promoted political and ideological views that were offensive to their personal beliefs. To the surprise of many, the Supreme Court rejected the students' claim and ruled in favor of the university. The Court stated that "the university may determine that its mission is well served if students have the means to engage in dynamic discussions of philosophical, religious, scientific, social, and political subjects in their extracurricular life. If the university reaches this conclusion, it is entitled to impose a mandatory fee to sustain an open dialogue to these ends."[43]

Campus Speech and Behavior Codes. Another free speech issue is the legitimacy of campus speech and behavior codes. Some state universities have established codes that challenge the boundaries of the protection of free speech provided by the First Amendment. These codes are designed to prohibit so-called hate speech—abusive speech attacking persons on the basis of their ethnicity, race, or other criteria. For example, a University of Michigan code banned "any behavior, verbal or physical, that stigmatizes or victimizes an individual on the basis of race, ethnicity, religion, sex, sexual orientation, creed, national origin, ancestry, age, marital status, handicap" or Vietnam-veteran status. A federal court found that the code violated students' First Amendment rights.[44]

Although the courts generally have held, as in the University of Michigan case, that campus speech codes are unconstitutional restrictions on the right to free speech, such codes continue to exist. Whether hostile speech should be banned on high school campuses has also become an issue. In view of school shootings and other violent behavior in the schools, school officials have become concerned about speech that consists of veiled threats or that could lead to violence. Some schools have even prohibited students from wearing clothing, such as T-shirts bearing verbal messages (such as sexist or racist comments) or symbolic messages (such as the Confederate flag), that might generate "ill will or hatred." Defenders of campus speech codes argue that they are necessary not only to prevent violence but also to promote equality among different cultural, ethnic, and racial groups on campus and greater sensitivity to the needs and feelings of others.

Hate Speech on the Internet

Extreme hate speech appears on the Internet, including racist materials and denials of the Holocaust (the murder of millions of Jews by the Nazis during World War II). Can the federal government restrict this type of speech? Should it? Content restrictions can be difficult to enforce. Even if Congress succeeded in passing a law prohibiting particular speech on the Internet, an army of "Internet watchers" would be needed to enforce it. Also, what if other countries attempt to impose their laws that restrict speech on U.S. Web sites? This is not a theoretical issue. In 2000, a French court found Yahoo in violation of French laws banning the display of Nazi memorabilia. In 2001, however, a U.S. district court held that this ruling could not be enforced against Yahoo in the United States.[45]

43. *Board of Regents of the University of Wisconsin System v. Southworth*, 529 U.S. 217 (2000).
44. *Doe v. University of Michigan*, 721 F. Supp. 852 (1989).
45. *Yahoo!, Inc. v. La Ligue Contre le Racisme et l'Antisemitisme*, 169 F. Supp. 2d 1181 (N.D. Cal. 2001).

Freedom of the Press

Freedom of the press can be regarded as a special instance of freedom of speech. Of course, at the time of the framing of the Constitution, the press meant only newspapers, magazines, and books. As technology has modified the ways in which we disseminate information, the laws touching on freedom of the press have been modified. What can and cannot be printed still occupies an important place in constitutional law, however.

Defamation in Writing

Libel is defamation in writing (or in pictures, signs, films, or any other communication that has the potentially harmful qualities of written or printed words). As with slander, libel occurs only if the defamatory statements are observed by a third party. If one person writes a private letter to another person wrongfully accusing him or her of embezzling funds, that does not constitute libel. It is interesting that the courts have generally held that dictating a letter to a secretary constitutes communication of the letter's contents to a third party, and therefore, if defamation has occurred, the wrongdoer can be sued.

A 1964 case, *New York Times Co. v. Sullivan*,[46] explored an important question regarding libelous statements made about public officials. The Supreme Court held that only when a statement against a public official was made with **actual malice**—that is, with either knowledge of its falsity or a reckless disregard of the truth—could damages be obtained.

The standard set by the Court in the *New York Times* case has since been applied to **public figures** generally. Public figures include not only public officials but also public employees who exercise substantial governmental power and any persons who are generally in the limelight. Statements made about public figures, especially when they are made through a public medium, usually are related to matters of general public interest; they are made about people who substantially

Libel
A written defamation of a person's character, reputation, business, or property rights.

Actual Malice
Either knowledge of a defamatory statement's falsity or a reckless disregard for the truth.

Public Figure
A public official, movie star, or other person known to the public because of his or her position or activities.

© Bettmann/CORBIS

Police Commissioner
L. B. Sullivan (second from right) celebrates his $500,000 libel suit victory in the case *New York Times Co. v. Sullivan*. From left are attorneys J. Roland Nachman, Jr., who directed the plaintiff's suit, Calvin Whitesell, Sullivan, and Sam Rice Baker.

46. 376 U.S. 254 (1964).

affect all of us. Furthermore, public figures generally have some access to a public medium for answering disparaging falsehoods about themselves, whereas private individuals do not. For these reasons, public figures have a greater burden of proof (they must prove that the statements were made with actual malice) in defamation cases than do private individuals.

A Free Press versus a Fair Trial: Gag Orders

Another major issue relating to freedom of the press concerns media coverage of criminal trials. The Sixth Amendment to the Constitution guarantees the right of criminal suspects to a fair trial. In other words, the accused have rights. The First Amendment guarantees freedom of the press. What if the two rights appear to be in conflict? Which one prevails?

Jurors certainly may be influenced by reading news stories about the trial in which they are participating. In the 1970s, judges increasingly issued **gag orders**, which restricted the publication of news about a trial in progress or even a pretrial hearing. In a landmark 1976 case, *Nebraska Press Association v. Stuart*,[47] the Supreme Court unanimously ruled that a Nebraska judge's gag order had violated the First Amendment's guarantee of freedom of the press. Chief Justice Warren Burger indicated that even pervasive adverse pretrial publicity did not necessarily lead to an unfair trial, and that prior restraints on publication were not justified. Some justices even went so far as to suggest that gag orders are never justified.

Despite the *Nebraska Press Association* ruling, the Court has upheld certain types of gag orders. In *Gannett Co. v. De Pasquale*[48] in 1979, for example, the highest court held that if a judge found a reasonable probability that news publicity would harm a defendant's right to a fair trial, the court could impose a gag rule: "Members of the public have no constitutional right under the Sixth and Fourteenth Amendments to attend criminal trials."

Gag Order
An order issued by a judge restricting the publication of news about a trial or a pretrial hearing to protect the accused's right to a fair trial.

Radio "Shock Jock"

Howard Stern offended the sensibilities of the Federal Communications Commission (FCC). That regulatory body fined Stern's radio station owner hundreds of thousands of dollars for Stern's purportedly obscene outbursts on the radio in 1992 and again in 2004. The extent to which the FCC can regulate speech over the air involves the First Amendment. But the current FCC regulation does not apply to pay-for-service satellite radio, pay-for-service cable TV, or satellite TV. To take advantage of this, in December of 2005, Stern took his show to satellite radio, thus, for now, evading FCC regulation. Why is it that what is permissible and acceptable on radio and TV today probably would have been considered obscene three decades ago?

© Getty Images

47. 427 U.S. 539 (1976).
48. 443 U.S. 368 (1979).

The *Nebraska* and *Gannett* cases, however, involved pretrial hearings. Could a judge impose a gag order on an entire trial, including pretrial hearings? In 1980, in *Richmond Newspapers, Inc. v. Virginia*,[49] the Court ruled that actual trials must be open to the public except under unusual circumstances.

Films, Radio, and TV

As we have noted, only in a few cases has the Supreme Court upheld prior restraint of published materials. The Court's reluctance to accept prior restraint is less evident with respect to motion pictures. In the first half of the 20th century, films were routinely submitted to local censorship boards. In 1968, the Supreme Court ruled that a film can be banned only under a law that provides for a prompt hearing at which the film is shown to be obscene. Today, few local censorship boards exist. Instead, the film industry regulates itself primarily through the industry's rating system.

Radio and television broadcasting has the least First Amendment protection. In 1934, the national government established the Federal Communications Commission (FCC) to regulate electromagnetic wave frequencies. The government's position has been that the airwaves and all frequencies that travel through the air belong to the people of the United States. Thus, no broadcaster can monopolize these frequencies nor can they be abused. The FCC is the authority that regulates the use of the airwaves and grants licenses to broadcast television, radio, satellite transmission, etc. Based on a case decided by the Supreme Court in 1978,[50] the FCC can impose sanctions on radio or TV stations that broadcast "filthy words," even if the words are not legally obscene. During the George W. Bush administration, the FCC acted more frequently to sanction radio and television broadcasters for the use of words, phrases, and pictures that might be considered in the category of "filthy words."

A protestor in Chicago demonstrates against the NATO meeting there in 2012. What kinds of regulations do you think should govern such protests?

---

49.   448 U.S. 555 (1980).
50.   *FCC v. Pacifica Foundation*, 438 U.S. 726 (1978). The phrase "filthy words" refers to a monologue by comedian George Carlin, which became the subject of the court case.

The Right to Assemble and to Petition the Government

The First Amendment prohibits Congress from making any law that abridges "the right of the people peaceably to assemble, and to petition the Government for a redress of grievances." Inherent in such a right is the ability of private citizens to communicate their ideas on public issues to government officials, as well as to other individuals. Indeed, the amendment also protects the right of individuals to join interest groups and lobby the government. The Supreme Court has often put this freedom on a par with freedom of speech and freedom of the press. Nonetheless, it has allowed municipalities to require permits for parades, sound trucks, and demonstrations so that public officials can control traffic or prevent demonstrations from turning into riots.

The freedom to demonstrate became a major issue in 1977 when the American Nazi Party sought to march through Skokie, Illinois, a largely Jewish suburb where many Holocaust survivors resided. The American Civil Liberties Union defended the Nazis' right to march (despite its opposition to the Nazi philosophy). The Supreme Court let stand a lower court's ruling that the city of Skokie had violated the Nazis' First Amendment guarantees by denying them a permit to march.[51]

One of the most controversial groups organizing protests in the last few years has been the Westboro Baptist Church in Topeka, Kansas, which often demonstrates at the funeral services for members of the military who were killed in enemy action in Afghanistan and Iraq. Westboro members and supporters carry signs and protest the funerals on the grounds that these deaths are the result of the nation's sins in tolerating homosexuality and what they view as other immorality. Many churches, communities, and families have attempted to limit the access of Westboro church members to the site of memorial services, but the church claims freedom of expression as its right. In 2011, the Supreme Court heard the case *Snyder v. Phelps*[52] and overturned a jury verdict against the church, upholding the right of free speech in this case.

Online Assembly

A question for Americans today is whether individuals should have the right to "assemble" online to advocate violence against certain groups (such as physicians who perform abortions) or advocate values that are opposed to our democracy (such as terrorism). While some online advocacy groups promote interests consistent with American political values, other groups aim to destroy those values. Whether First Amendment freedoms should be sacrificed (by the government's monitoring of Internet communications, for example) in the interests of national security is a question that will no doubt be debated for some time to come.

More Liberties under Scrutiny: Matters of Privacy

■ **Learning Outcome 4:**
Discuss the concept of privacy rights, and give examples of how individual privacy is protected under the Constitution.

No explicit reference is made anywhere in the Constitution to a person's right to privacy. Until the second half of the 1990s, the courts did not take a very positive approach toward the right to privacy. For example, during Prohibition, suspected

---

51. *Smith v. Collin*, 439 U.S. 916 (1978).
52. *Snyder v. Phelps*, 08-751 (2011).

bootleggers' telephones were tapped routinely, and the information obtained was used as a legal basis for prosecution. In *Olmstead v. United States*[53] in 1928, the Supreme Court upheld such an invasion of privacy. Justice Louis Brandeis, a champion of personal freedoms, strongly dissented from the majority decision in this case. He argued that the framers of the Constitution gave every citizen the right to be left alone. He called such a right "the most comprehensive of rights and the right most valued by civilized men."

In the 1960s, the highest court began to modify the majority view. In 1965, in *Griswold v. Connecticut*,[54] the Supreme Court overturned a Connecticut law that effectively prohibited the use of contraceptives, holding that the law violated the right to privacy. Justice William O. Douglas formulated a unique way of reading this right into the Bill of Rights. He claimed that the First, Third, Fourth, Fifth, and Ninth Amendments created "penumbras [shadows], formed by emanations [things sent out from] those guarantees that help give them life and substance," and he went on to describe zones of privacy that are guaranteed by these rights. When we read the Ninth Amendment, we can see the foundation for his reasoning: "The enumeration in the Constitution, of certain rights, shall not be construed to deny or disparage [belittle] others retained by the people." In other words, just because the Constitution, including its amendments, does not specifically talk about the right to privacy does not mean that this right is denied to the people.

Some of today's most controversial issues relate to privacy rights. One issue involves the erosion of privacy rights in an information age, as computers make it easier to compile and distribute personal information. Other issues concern abortion and the "right to die." Since the terrorist attacks of September 11, 2001, Americans have faced another crucial question regarding privacy rights: To what extent should Americans sacrifice privacy rights in the interests of national security?

Privacy Rights in an Information Age

An important privacy issue, created in part by new technology, is the amassing of information on individuals by government agencies and private businesses, such as marketing firms, grocery stores, and casinos, to name just a few. Personal information on the average American citizen also is filed away in dozens of agencies—such as the Social Security Administration and the Internal Revenue Service. Because of the threat of indiscriminate use of private information by unauthorized individuals, Congress passed the Privacy Act in 1974. This was the first law regulating the use of federal government information about private individuals. Under the Privacy Act, every citizen has the right to obtain copies of personal records collected by federal agencies and to correct inaccuracies in such records. However, this applies only to government agencies and has no bearing on records collected by private organization or companies.

The ease with which personal information can be obtained by using the Internet for marketing and other purposes has led to unique privacy issues. Some fear that privacy rights in personal information may soon be a thing of the past. However, for today's young adults, the concept of privacy seems to have evolved into something that individuals define for themselves. Portraits on public Web sites such as Facebook, Linked In, or other networking sites are created by the user and can protect personal data or make certain facts *very public*. The

53. 277 U.S. 438 (1928). This decision was overruled later in *Katz v. United States*, 389 U.S. 347 (1967).
54. 381 U.S. 479 (1965).

person who submits the information gets to decide. Whether privacy rights can survive in an information age is a question that Americans and their leaders continue to confront.

Privacy Rights and Abortion

Historically, abortion was not a criminal offense before the "quickening" of the fetus (the first movement of the fetus in the uterus, usually between the 16th and 18th weeks of pregnancy). During the last half of the 19th century, however, state laws became more severe. By 1973, performing an abortion at any time during pregnancy was a criminal offense in a majority of the states.

Roe v. Wade. In 1973, in *Roe v. Wade*,[55] the United States Supreme Court accepted the argument that the laws against abortion violated "Jane Roe's" right to privacy under the Constitution. The Court held that during the first trimester (three months) of pregnancy, abortion was an issue solely between a woman and her physician. The state could not limit abortions except to require that they be performed by licensed physicians. During the second trimester, to protect the health of the mother, the state was allowed to specify the conditions under which an abortion could be performed. During the final trimester, the state could regulate or even outlaw abortions, except when necessary to preserve the life or health of the mother.

After *Roe*, the Supreme Court issued decisions in several cases defining and redefining the boundaries of state regulation of abortion. During the 1980s, the Court twice struck down laws that required a woman who wished to have an abortion to undergo counseling designed to discourage abortions. In the late 1980s and early 1990s, however, the Court took a more conservative approach. For example, in *Webster v. Reproductive Health Services*[56] in 1989, the Court upheld a Missouri statute that, among other things, banned the use of public hospitals or other taxpayer-supported facilities for performing abortions. And, in *Planned Parenthood v. Casey*[57] in 1992, the Court upheld a Pennsylvania law that required preabortion counseling, a waiting period of 24 hours, and, for girls under the age of 18, parental or judicial permission. The *Casey* decision was remarkable for several reasons. The final decision was a 5-4 vote with Sandra Day O'Connor writing the opinion. While the opinion explicitly upheld *Roe*, it changed the grounds on which the states can regulate abortion. The Court found that states could not place an "undue burden" on a woman who sought an abortion. In this case, the Court found that spousal notification was such a burden. Because many other conditions were upheld, abortions continue to be more difficult to obtain in some states than others.

The Controversy Continues. Abortion continues to be a divisive issue. "Right-to-life" forces continue to push for laws banning abortion, to endorse political candidates who support their views, and to organize protests. Because of several episodes of violence attending protests at abortion clinics, in 1994 Congress passed the Freedom of Access to Clinic Entrances Act. The act prohibits protesters from blocking entrances to such clinics. The Supreme Court ruled in 1993 that such protesters can be prosecuted under laws governing racketeering, and in 1998 a federal court in Illinois convicted right-to-life protesters under these

55. 410 U.S.113 (1973). Jane Roe was not the real name of the woman in this case. It is a common legal pseudonym used to protect a person's privacy.
56. 492 U.S. 490 (1989).
57. 505 U.S. 833 (1992).

© AP Photo/Pablo Martinez Monsivais

In 2006, on the 33rd anniversary of *Roe v. Wade,* opposing sides on the abortion issue argued with each other in front of the United States Supreme Court building in Washington, D.C. What was the major argument against laws prohibiting abortion that the Court used in the *Roe* case?

laws. In 1997, the Supreme Court upheld the constitutionality of prohibiting protesters from entering a 15-foot "buffer zone" around abortion clinics and from giving unwanted counseling to those entering the clinics.[58] In 2006, however, the Supreme Court unanimously reversed its earlier decision that anti-abortion protesters could be prosecuted under laws governing racketeering.[59]

In a 2000 decision, the Court upheld a Colorado law requiring demonstrators to stay at least eight feet away from people entering and leaving clinics unless people consent to be approached. The Court concluded that the law's restrictions on speech-related conduct did not violate the free speech rights of abortion protesters.[60]

In the same year, the Supreme Court again addressed the abortion issue directly when it reviewed a Nebraska law banning "partial-birth" abortions. Similar laws had been passed by at least 27 states. A partial-birth abortion, which physicians call intact dilation and extraction, is a procedure that can be used during the second trimester of pregnancy. Abortion rights advocates claim that in limited circumstances the procedure is the safest way to perform an abortion, and that the government should never outlaw specific medical procedures. Opponents argue that the procedure has no medical merit and that it ends the life of a fetus that might be able to live outside the womb. The Supreme Court invalidated the Nebraska law on the grounds that, as written, the law could be used to ban other abortion procedures, and it contained no provisions for protecting the health of the pregnant woman.[61] In 2003, legislation similar to the Nebraska statute was passed by the U.S. Congress and signed into law by President George W. Bush. It was immediately challenged in court. In 2007, the Supreme Court heard several challenges to the partial-birth abortion law and upheld the constitutionality of that legislation, saying that the law was specific enough that it did not "impose an undue burden" on women seeking an abortion.[62]

58. *Schenck v. Pro Choice Network,* 519 U.S. 357 (1997).
59. *Scheidler v. National Organization for Women,* 126 S. Ct. 1264 (2006).
60. *Hill v. Colorado,* 530 U.S. 703 (2000).
61. *Stenberg v. Carhart,* 530 U.S. 914 (2000).
62. *Gonzales v. Carhart,* 550 U.S. (2007) and *Gonzales v. Planned Parenthood,* 550 U.S. (2007).

In a move that will likely set off another long legal battle, in 2006 the South Dakota legislature passed a law that banned almost all forms of abortion in the state. The bill's supporters hope that it will eventually force the United States Supreme Court to reconsider *Roe v. Wade*. Opponents of the bill have already filed suit.

Privacy Rights and the "Right to Die"

A 1976 case involving Karen Ann Quinlan was one of the first publicized right-to-die cases.[63] The parents of Quinlan, a young woman who had been in a coma for nearly a year and who had been kept alive during that time by a respirator, wanted her respirator removed. In 1976, the New Jersey Supreme Court ruled that the right to privacy includes the right of a patient to refuse treatment and that patients who are unable to speak can exercise that right through a family member or guardian. In 1990, the Supreme Court took up the issue. In *Cruzan v. Director, Missouri Department of Health*,[64] the Court stated that a patient's life-sustaining treatment can be withdrawn at the request of a family member only if "clear and convincing evidence" exists that the patient did not want such treatment.

What If No Living Will Exists? Since the 1976 *Quinlan* decision, most states have enacted laws permitting people to designate their wishes concerning life-sustaining procedures in "living wills" or durable health care powers of attorney. These laws and the Supreme Court's *Cruzan* decision have resolved the right-to-die controversy for situations in which the patient has drafted a living will. Disputes are still possible if there is no living will.

Physician-Assisted Suicide. In the 1990s, another issue surfaced: Do privacy rights include the right of terminally ill people to end their lives through physician-assisted suicide? Until 1996, the courts consistently upheld state laws that prohibited this practice, either through specific statutes or under their general homicide statutes. In 1996, after two federal appellate courts ruled that state laws banning assisted suicide (in Washington and New York) were unconstitutional, the issue reached the United States Supreme Court. In 1997, in *Washington v. Glucksberg*,[65] the Court stated, clearly and categorically, that the liberty interest protected by the Constitution does not include a right to commit suicide, with or without assistance. In effect, the Supreme Court left the decision in the hands of the states. Since then, assisted suicide has been allowed in only one state— Oregon. In 2006, the Supreme Court upheld Oregon's physician-assisted suicide law against a challenge from the Bush administration.[66]

Privacy Rights versus Security Issues

As former Supreme Court justice Thurgood Marshall once said, "Grave threats to liberty often come in times of urgency, when constitutional rights seem too extravagant to endure." Not surprisingly, antiterrorist legislation since the attacks on September 11, 2001, has eroded certain basic rights, in particular the Fourth Amendment protections against unreasonable searches and seizures. Several tools previously used against certain types of criminal suspects (e.g., "roving

---

63.   *In re Quinlan*, 70 N.J. 10 (1976).
64.   497 U.S. 261 (1990).
65.   521 U.S. 702 (1997).
66.   *Gonzales v. Oregon*, 126 S. Ct. 904 (2006).

wiretaps" and National Security Letters) have been authorized for use against a broader array of terror suspects. Many civil liberties organizations argue that abuses of the Fourth Amendment are ongoing.

While it has been possible for a law enforcement agency to gain court permission to wiretap a telephone virtually since telephones were invented, a roving wiretap allows an agency to tap all forms of communication used by the named person, including cell phones and e-mail, and it applies across legal jurisdictions. Previously, roving wiretaps could only be requested for persons suspected of one of a small number of serious crimes. Now, if persons are suspected of planning a terrorist attack, they can be monitored no matter what form of electronic communication they use. Such roving wiretaps appear to contravene the Supreme Court's interpretation of the Fourth Amendment, which requires a judicial warrant to describe the *place* to be searched, not just the person, although the Court has not banned them to date. One of the goals of the framers was to avoid *general* searches. Further, once a judge approves an application for a roving wiretap, when, how, and where the monitoring occurs will be left to the discretion of law enforcement agents. Supporters of these new procedures say that they allow agents to monitor individuals as they move about the nation. Previously, a warrant issued in one federal district might not be valid in another.

Moreover, President George W. Bush approved a plan by the National Security Agency to eavesdrop on telephone calls between individuals overseas and those in the United States if one party was a terrorist suspect. This plan was carried out without warrants because the administration claimed that speed was more important. Critics called for immediate termination of such eavesdropping. Congress, after criticizing the Bush plan, reauthorized it in law in 2008.

The USA PATRIOT Act. Much of the government's failure to anticipate the attacks of September 11, 2001, has been attributed to a lack of cooperation among government agencies. At that time, barriers prevented information sharing between the law enforcement and intelligence arms of the government. A major objective of the USA PATRIOT Act was to lift those barriers. Lawmakers claimed that the PATRIOT Act would improve lines of communication between agencies such as the Federal Bureau of Investigation (FBI) and the Central Intelligence Agency (CIA), thereby allowing the government to better anticipate terrorist plots. With improved communication, various agencies could more effectively coordinate their efforts in combating terrorism.

In addition, the PATRIOT Act eased restrictions on the government's ability to investigate and arrest suspected terrorists. Because of the secretive nature of terrorist groups, supporters of the PATRIOT Act argue that the government must have greater latitude in pursuing leads on potential terrorist activity. After receiving approval of the Foreign Intelligence Surveillance Court (known as FISA), the act authorizes law enforcement officials to secretly search a suspected terrorist's home. It also allows the government to monitor a suspect's Internet activities, phone conversations, financial records, and book purchases. Although a number of these search and surveillance tactics have long been a part of criminal investigations, the PATRIOT Act expanded their scope to include individuals as terrorist suspects even if they are not agents of a foreign government.

Civil Liberties Concerns. Proponents of the PATRIOT Act insist that ordinary, law-abiding citizens have nothing to fear from the government's increased search and surveillance powers. Groups such as the ACLU have objected to the PATRIOT

Act, however, arguing that it poses a grave threat to constitutionally guaranteed rights and liberties. Under the PATRIOT Act, FBI agents are required to certify the need for search warrants to the FISA Court. Rarely are such requests rejected.

In the last few years, the FBI began using another tool that it has had for several years, the National Security Letter (NSL), to avoid the procedures required by the FISA Court. The NSL allows the FBI to get records of telephone calls, subscriber information, and other kinds of transactions, although it does not give the FBI access to the content of the calls. However, as Congress tightened the requirements for warrants under the PATRIOT Act, the FBI evidently began to use the NSLs as a shortcut. While the use of NSLs has been legal for more than 20 years, recent massive use of this technique has led Congress to consider further restrictions on the FBI and its investigations in order to preserve the rights of U.S. citizens.

Opponents of the PATRIOT Act fear that these expanded powers of investigation might be used to silence government critics or to threaten members of interest groups who oppose government polices today or in the future. Congress debated all of these issues in 2005 and then renewed most of the provisions of the act in 2006. It has been renewed again in 2011 over the objections of many civil liberties organizations. One of the most controversial aspects of the PATRIOT Act permits the government to eavesdrop on telephone calls with a warrant from the FISA Court. In 2005, it became known that the Bush administration was eavesdropping on U.S. telephone calls without a warrant if the caller was from outside the United States. After almost three years of controversy, Congress passed the FISA Amendments Act in June 2008, which regulates such calls and gives immunity from prosecution to telecommunications companies.

The incredible growth of modern wireless technology is an opportunity and a challenge for law enforcement officials but carries potential threats to civil liberties. Modern wireless technology makes it possible to track offenders more easily, but is such tracking legal? Most wireless devices that we carry around—smartphones, tablets, netbooks—contain wireless receivers that connect with the Internet, and most include a GPS transmitter. If you lose your telephone, you can call your service provider and be told approximately where it is because it is signaling a nearby tower or satellite. Is the tracking of your device an invasion of your privacy?

Our total dependence on the Internet and its infrastructure for everything from our social network to finding the weather or traffic reports or looking for the best deal on a purchase brings a new set of privacy challenges. Unless the individual puts extensive privacy controls into place, purchase records are sent to advertisers, and Facebook data are sent to friends and to friends of friends and to marketers. Your location is signaled by your wireless device, as is that of your friends as you tweet. All Internet traffic is recorded; much of it is mined as a database for private companies. The government archives all of it but does not search for individuals unless, possibly, Internet and telephone messages suggest a terrorist plot.

■ **Learning Outcome 5:**
Identify the rights of the accused, and discuss the role of the Supreme Court in expanding those rights.

The Great Balancing Act: The Rights of the Accused versus the Rights of Society

The United States has one of the highest murder rates in the industrialized world. It is not surprising, therefore, that many citizens have extremely strong opinions about the rights of those accused of violent crimes. When an accused person, especially one who has confessed to some criminal act, is set free because of an apparent legal technicality, many people believe that the rights of the accused are being given more weight than the rights of society and of potential or actual victims. Why, then, give criminal suspects rights? The answer is partly to avoid convicting innocent people, but mostly because all criminal suspects have the right to due process of law and fair treatment.

The courts and the police must constantly engage in a balancing act of competing rights. At the basis of all discussions about the appropriate balance is the U.S. Bill of Rights. The Fourth, Fifth, Sixth, and Eighth Amendments deal specifically with the rights of criminal defendants. (You will learn about some of your rights under the Fourth Amendment in the You Can Make a Difference feature at the end of this chapter.)

The basic rights of criminal defendants are outlined in Table 4–2. When appropriate, the specific constitutional provision or amendment on which a right is based is also given.

Extending the Rights of the Accused

During the 1960s, the Supreme Court, under Chief Justice Earl Warren, significantly expanded the rights of accused persons. In *Gideon v. Wainwright*,[67] a case decided in 1963, the Court held that if a person is accused of a felony and cannot

TABLE 4–2 ▶ Basic Rights of Criminal Defendants

LIMITS ON THE CONDUCT OF POLICE OFFICERS AND PROSECUTORS
No unreasonable or unwarranted searches and seizures (Amend. IV)
No arrest except on probable cause (Amend. IV)
No coerced confessions or illegal interrogation (Amend. V)
No entrapment
On questioning, a suspect must be informed of her or his rights

DEFENDANT'S PRETRIAL RIGHTS
Writ of *habeas corpus* (Article I, Section 9)
Prompt arraignment (Amend. VI)
Legal counsel (Amend. VI)
Reasonable bail (Amend. VIII)
To be informed of charges (Amend. VI)
To remain silent (Amend. V)

TRIAL RIGHTS
Speedy and public trial before a jury (Amend. VI)
Impartial jury selected from a cross section of the community (Amend. VI)
Trial atmosphere free of prejudice, fear, and outside interference
No compulsory self-incrimination (Amend. V)
Adequate counsel (Amend. VI)
No cruel and unusual punishment (Amend. VIII)
Appeal of convictions
No double jeopardy (Amend. V)

67. 372 U.S. 335 (1963).

afford an attorney, an attorney must be made available to the accused person at the government's expense. This case was particularly interesting because Gideon, who was arrested for stealing a small amount of money from a vending machine, was not considered a dangerous man, nor was his intellect in any way impaired. As related by Anthony Lewis,[68] Gideon pursued his own appeal to the Supreme Court because he believed that every accused person who might face prison should be represented. Although the Sixth Amendment to the Constitution provides for the right to counsel, the Supreme Court had established a precedent 21 years earlier in *Betts v. Brady*,[69] when it held that only criminal defendants in capital (death penalty) cases automatically had a right to legal counsel.

Miranda v. Arizona. In 1966, the Court issued its decision in *Miranda v. Arizona*.[70] The case involved Ernesto Miranda, who was arrested and charged with the kidnapping and rape of a young woman. After two hours of questioning, Miranda confessed and was later convicted. Miranda's lawyer appealed his conviction, arguing that the police had never informed Miranda that he had a right to remain silent and a right to be represented by counsel. The Court, in ruling in Miranda's favor, enunciated the *Miranda* rights that are now familiar to virtually all Americans:

> *Prior to any questioning, the person must be warned that he has a right to remain silent, that any statement he does make may be used against him, and that he has a right to the presence of an attorney, either retained or appointed.*

Two years after the Supreme Court's *Miranda* decision, Congress passed the Omnibus Crime Control and Safe Streets Act of 1968. Section 3501 of the act reinstated a rule that had been in effect for 180 years before *Miranda*—that statements by defendants can be used against them if the statements were made voluntarily. The Justice Department immediately disavowed Section 3501 as unconstitutional and has continued to hold this position. As a result, Section 3501, although it was never repealed, has never been enforced. In 2000, in a surprise move, a federal appellate court held that the all-but-forgotten provision was enforceable, but the Supreme Court held that the *Miranda* warnings were constitutionally based and could not be overruled by a legislative act.[71]

Exceptions to the *Miranda* Rule. As part of a continuing attempt to balance the rights of accused persons against the rights of society, the Supreme Court has made several exceptions to the *Miranda* rule. In 1984, for example, the Court recognized a "public-safety" exception to the rule. The need to protect the public warranted the admissibility of statements made by the defendant (in this case, indicating where he had placed a gun) as evidence in a trial, even though the defendant had not been informed of his *Miranda* rights.

In 1985, the Court further held that a confession need not be excluded even though the police failed to inform a suspect in custody that his attorney had tried to reach him by telephone. In an important 1991 decision, the Court stated that a suspect's conviction will not be automatically overturned if the suspect was coerced into making a confession. If the other evidence admitted at trial is strong enough to justify the conviction without the confession, then the fact that the confession was obtained illegally in effect can be ignored. In yet another case, in

68. Anthony Lewis, *Gideon's Trumpet* (New York: Vintage, 1964).
69. 316 U.S. 455 (1942).
70. 384 U.S. 436 (1966).
71. *Dickerson v. United States*, 530 U.S. 428 (2000).

1994, the Supreme Court ruled that suspects must unequivocally and assertively state their right to counsel in order to stop police questioning. Saying "Maybe I should talk to a lawyer" during an interrogation after being taken into custody is not enough. The Court held that police officers are not required to decipher the suspect's intentions in such situations. Most recently, the *Miranda* protections

Beyond Our Borders
TAKING AMERICAN RIGHTS OVERSEAS

Many thousands of American students study abroad each year, while others go abroad to work for not-for profit organizations in developing countries or as Peace Corps volunteers, or as members of the American military. Inevitably, some young Americans (and older ones as well) come into contact with the law enforcement officials of other nations. The following question will occur to them at that moment: Do I have the same rights here as I have in the United States? The answer is complex: You probably have the same rights on paper, but the interpretation of criminal procedure may be quite different.

The rights of the accused person in the United States are defined by state law, federal law, the Bill of Rights, and the interpretations of the Supreme Court. In the nations that have similar legal systems, such as Great Britain, Canada, and Australia, your rights and the way you are treated as an accused person are quite similar to your treatment in the United States. Many European and South American nations have a different legal system based on their respective legal code. In those nations, the prosecutor and court will begin with a presumption of guilt, and your defense counsel must conclusively prove your innocence. In some countries, it may be very difficult for you to post bond and leave jail to await your trial. Even though most of the nations of the world subscribe to the Universal Declaration of Human Rights and have impressive lists of rights, your treatment will also depend on the level of development of the nation and its political status. In some nations, jails are extremely unhealthy and unsanitary places, and prisoners must arrange for their own food to be brought in. Communication with your family or your lawyer is extremely difficult, and visiting rights may be severely limited.

Consider the advice given by the U.S. State Department on the criminal justice system in Mexico: "For an accused person, the accused is ... considered guilty until proven innocent." The State Department notes that you have the right to see the American consular representative but that this person cannot help with your legal case. You are subject to the Mexican criminal code, which makes some crimes such as possession of drugs much more serious than in the United States.

Three American hikers who accidentally crossed into Iran, were held in prison for two years, accused as spies.

Matters are further complicated for travelers in nations that have ongoing civil conflicts or do not have a democratic form of government. If you are suspected of being involved with the opposition, you may be arrested, tortured, and detained without notice even though the nation has a written bill of rights. In the case of civil conflicts or outright military action against another nation, you could be detained as an enemy combatant and held as a prisoner of war or, worse yet, a spy.

It is important to be aware of the political and social situation in any country in which you travel or volunteer and to be respectful of the local government and its officials. While you are an American and our embassy will keep in touch with you, it can do little if you are in legal trouble. Before you travel to countries that are experiencing civil unrest or high criminal activity, it is a good idea to read the travel warnings posted by the U.S. State Department. If you are truly interested in the state of human rights abroad, go to the Web site of Human Rights Watch, which issues an annual report on the state of justice in most of the nations of the world, including the United States.

For the U.S. State Department, go to www.state.gov and go to travel advisories. The Web site for Human Rights Watch is www.hrw.org.

were further narrowed when the Court found that a suspect must expressly announce his or her desire to remain silent, not just sit silently during questioning.

Video Recording of Interrogations. In view of the numerous exceptions, there are no guarantees that the *Miranda* rule will survive indefinitely. Increasingly, though, law enforcement personnel are using digital cameras to record interrogations. According to some scholars, the recording of *all* custodial interrogations would satisfy the Fifth Amendment's prohibition against coercion and in the process render the *Miranda* warnings unnecessary. Others argue, however, that recorded interrogations can be misleading.

The Exclusionary Rule

Exclusionary Rule
A policy forbidding the admission at trial of illegally seized evidence.

At least since 1914, judicial policy has prohibited the admission of illegally seized evidence at trials in federal courts. This is the so-called **exclusionary rule**. Improperly obtained evidence, no matter how telling, cannot be used by prosecutors. This includes evidence obtained by police in violation of a suspect's *Miranda* rights or of the Fourth Amendment. The Fourth Amendment protects against unreasonable searches and seizures and provides that a judge may issue a search warrant to a police officer only on *probable cause* (a demonstration of facts that permit a reasonable belief that a crime has been committed). The question that must be determined by the courts is what constitutes an unreasonable search and seizure.

The reasoning behind the exclusionary rule is that it forces police officers to gather evidence properly, in which case their due diligence will be rewarded by a conviction. Nevertheless, the exclusionary rule has always had critics who argue that it permits guilty persons to be freed because of innocent errors.

This rule was first extended to state court proceedings in a 1961 United States Supreme Court decision, *Mapp v. Ohio*.[72] In this case, the Court overturned the conviction of Dollree Mapp for the possession of obscene materials. Police found pornographic books in her apartment after searching it without a search warrant and despite her refusal to let them in.

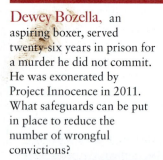

Dewey Bozella, an aspiring boxer, served twenty-six years in prison for a murder he did not commit. He was exonerated by Project Innocence in 2011. What safeguards can be put in place to reduce the number of wrongful convictions?

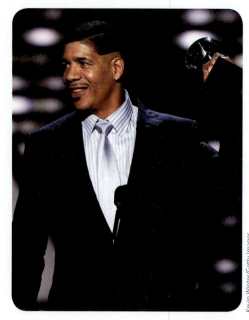

Over the last several decades, the Supreme Court has diminished the scope of the exclusionary rule by creating some exceptions to its applicability. For example, in 1984, the Court held that illegally obtained evidence could be admitted at trial if law enforcement personnel could prove that they would have obtained the evidence legally anyway. In another case decided in the same year, the Court held that a police officer who used a technically incorrect search warrant form to obtain evidence had acted in good faith and therefore the evidence was admissible at trial. The Court thus created the "good faith" exception to the exclusionary rule.

The Death Penalty

Capital punishment remains one of the most debated aspects of our criminal justice system. Those in favor of the death penalty maintain that it serves as a deterrent to serious crime and satisfies society's need for justice and fair play. Those opposed to the death penalty do not believe it has any deterrent value and hold that it constitutes a barbaric act in an otherwise civilized society.

Kevin Winter/Getty Images

72. 367 U.S. 643 (1961).

Politics with a Purpose

THE INNOCENCE PROJECT

As long as the United States has imposed capital punishment on convicted felons, there have been claims of innocence by those sentenced to die. Although police officers and judges have always known that sometimes the innocent are falsely accused and convicted, they also believe that most of the individuals were correctly prosecuted and convicted of their crimes. As most Americans know from popular television series such as *CSI* and *Bones*, new scientific techniques make it possible to find biological and chemical evidence that was completely unknown to law enforcement in the past. Most important of these new tools is the use of DNA, or deoxyribonucleic acid. DNA molecules contain all of the information about a person's or an animal's genetic makeup and are almost unique to each individual. The importance of DNA to criminal investigations is that DNA molecules found on a strand of hair or saliva on a handkerchief can be tested many years after they were deposited on that object.

In the early 1990s, law students at the Benjamin N. Cardozo School of Law at Yeshiva University began theorizing that DNA found in old evidence records could be used to establish the innocence of individuals wrongfully convicted of crimes. Led by Barry C. Scheck and Peter J. Neufeld, the students and faculty founded the Innocence Project, which is dedicated to helping exonerate innocent people and improving the legal system to avoid wrongful convictions. To date, more than 291 people have been exonerated through DNA evidence, and 17 of those were serving time on death row. A recent wrongful conviction that was overturned is that of boxer Dewey Bozella, who served 26 years for a murder he did not commit.

Why do wrongful convictions occur? Don't the safeguards of the Constitution (the right to confront witnesses, the right to an attorney, and the right to a speedy trial) protect people from wrongful imprisonment? The Innocence Project identifies a number of reasons why wrongful convictions occur. Witnesses may identify the wrong person as the suspect; individuals who are arrested may feel strongly pressured to make a confession,

especially if the prosecution offers a plea bargain for a lesser sentence; forensic science may be faulty in a particular location; the police may have acted out of discriminatory motives or failed to complete an investigation; informants or snitches may have given false information; or the free counsel offered to a defendant may be incompetent.[a] The Innocence Project is a nonprofit organization located at Yeshiva University; however, the work has spread throughout the United States and to some foreign countries. Now, 54 affiliated projects are found mostly at law schools and centers in 45 states. The centers form when students and faculty come together to begin the work in their own state. Law students provide most of the volunteer investigations into possible cases of wrongful conviction, with guidance from their faculty. Students also research the laws governing criminal procedure in their own state and then lobby for changes to reduce the chance of wrongful convictions. In 2010, Governor Strickland of Ohio signed into law a bill that was researched by a student of the Innocence Project at the University of Cincinnati law school. The student was present at the General Assembly when the bill passed. The new legislation requires preservation of DNA evidence forever in serious crimes, strengthens the requirements for police lineups, and gives incentives for the video recording of interrogations in most serious crimes. The legislation is considered groundbreaking for preserving evidence that might prevent wrongful convictions.

If you are interested in taking part in the Innocence Project or finding a center near you, log on to the national Web site, www.innocenceproject.org, and look for the list of state projects. You can learn a great deal about wrongful convictions from the organization's site and explore changes in the law that may prevent the miscarriage of justice.[b]

[a] Barry Scheck, Peter Neufeld, and Jim Dwyer, *Actual Innocence: When Justice Goes Wrong and How to Make It Right,* New York: New American Library, 2003.
[b] Saundra Westervelt and John Humphrys, *Wrongly Convicted: Perspectives on Failed Justice,* Piscataway, NJ: Rutgers University Press, 2001.

Cruel and Unusual Punishment?

The Eighth Amendment prohibits cruel and unusual punishment. Throughout history, "cruel and unusual" referred to punishments that were more serious than the crimes—the phrase referred to torture and to executions that prolonged the agony of dying. The Supreme Court never interpreted "cruel and unusual" to prohibit all forms of capital punishment in all circumstances. Indeed, several states had imposed the death penalty for a variety of crimes and allowed juries to decide when the condemned could be sentenced to death. However, many believed that the imposition of the death penalty was random and arbitrary, and in 1972 the Supreme Court agreed in *Furman v. Georgia*.[73]

The Supreme Court's 1972 decision stated that the death penalty, as then applied, violated the Eighth and Fourteenth Amendments. The Court ruled that capital punishment is not necessarily cruel and unusual if the criminal has killed or attempted to kill someone. In its opinion, the Court invited the states to enact more precise laws so that the death penalty would be applied more consistently. By 1976, 25 states had adopted a two-stage, or *bifurcated*, procedure for capital cases. In the first stage, a jury determines the guilt or innocence of the defendant for a crime that has been determined by statute to be punishable by death. If the defendant is found guilty, the jury reconvenes in the second stage and considers all relevant evidence to decide whether the death sentence is, in fact, warranted.

In *Gregg v. Georgia*,[74] the Supreme Court ruled in favor of Georgia's bifurcated process, holding that the state's legislative guidelines had removed the ability of a jury to "wantonly and freakishly impose the death penalty." The Court upheld similar procedures in Texas and Florida, establishing a procedure for all states to follow that would ensure them protection from lawsuits based on Eighth Amendment grounds. On January 17, 1977, Gary Mark Gilmore became the first American to be executed (by Utah) under the new laws.

The Death Penalty Today

Today, 33 states (see Figure 4–1) and the federal government have capital punishment laws based on the guidelines established by the *Gregg* case. State governments are responsible for almost all executions in this country. The executions of Timothy McVeigh and Juan Raul Garza in 2001 marked the first death sentences carried out by the federal government since 1963. At this time, about 3,200 prisoners are on death row across the nation.

The most recent controversy over the death penalty concerns the method by which the punishment is carried out. The 33 states that have the death penalty use a lethal injection to cause the convicted person's death. Most use a combination of three different drugs injected in an intravenous manner. Several cases have been appealed to the Supreme Court on the basis that this method can cause extreme pain and thus violates the Constitution's ban on cruel and unusual punishment. The Court has upheld the three-drug method, most recently in April 2008, although the justices wrote seven opinions in the case, indicating a lack of consensus among them.[75]

The number of executions per year reached a high of 98 in 1998, and then began to fall. Some believe that the declining number of executions reflects the waning support among Americans for the imposition of the death penalty. In 1994, polls indicated that 80 percent of Americans supported the death penalty. Recent polls, however, suggest that this number has dropped to between 50 and 60 percent, depending on the poll, possibly because of public doubt about the justice of the system. Recently, DNA testing has shown that some innocent people may have been convicted unjustly of murder. Since 1973, more than 130 prisoners have been freed from death row after new evidence suggested that

did you know?

There are 62 women on death row, and 12 women have been executed since 1976.

73.   408 U.S. 238 (1972).
74.   428 U.S. 153 (1976).
75.   *Baze v. Rees*, 553 U.S. 35 (2008).

Figure 4—1 ▶ The States and the Death Penalty: Executions 1976—2012 and the Death Row Population

Today, as shown in this figure, 33 states and the federal government and military have laws permitting capital punishment. Since 1976, there have been 1,295 executions in the United States, 52 in 2009, 46 in 2010, 43 in 2011, and 18 in the first half of 2012.

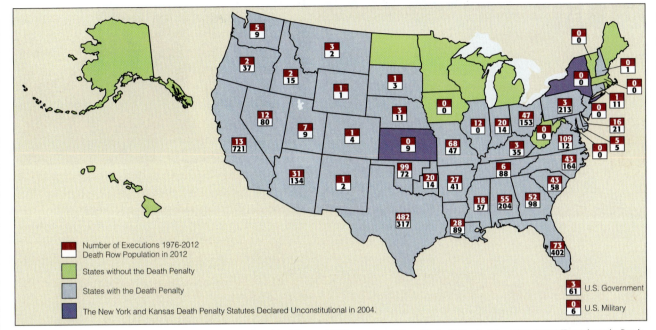

Sources: U.S. Department of Justice, Bureau of Justice Statistics, "Capital Punishment, 2006," www.ojp.usdoj.gov/bjs; Death Penalty Information Center, "Facts about the Death Penalty," May 2, 2012.

they were wrongfully convicted. It is the goal of the Innocence Project, discussed in Politics with a Purpose, to continue to investigate wrongful convictions in every state.

The number of executions may decline even further due to the Supreme Court's 2002 ruling in *Ring v. Arizona*.[76] The Court held that only juries, not judges, could impose the death penalty, thus invalidating the laws of five states that allowed judges to make this decision. The ruling meant that the death sentences of 168 death row inmates would have to be reconsidered by the relevant courts. The sentences of many of these inmates have been commuted to life in prison.

In 1996, Congress passed the Anti-Terrorism and Effective Death Penalty Act. The law limits access to the federal courts for all defendants convicted in state courts. It also imposes a severe time limit on death row appeals. The law requires federal judges to hear these appeals and issue their opinions within a specified time period. Many are concerned that the shortened appeals process increases the possibility that innocent persons may be put to death before evidence that might free them can be discovered. On average, it takes about seven years to exonerate someone on death row; however, the time between conviction and execution has been shortened from an average of 10 to 12 years to an average of six to eight years.

76. 536 U.S. 548 (2002).

You Can Make a Difference

YOUR CIVIL LIBERTIES: SEARCHES AND SEIZURES

© AP Photo/Evan Vucci, file

Savana Redding stands before the U.S. Supreme Court building on the day her case was heard. As a 13-year-old, Redding was strip-searched by school authorities looking for ibuprofen. Her parents were not asked for their consent or informed about the incident.

Our civil liberties include numerous provisions, many of them listed in the Bill of Rights, that protect persons suspected of criminal activity. Among these are limits on how the police—as agents of the government—can conduct searches and seizures.

WHY SHOULD YOU CARE?

You may be the most law-abiding person in the world, but that will not guarantee that you will never be stopped, arrested, or searched by the police. Sooner or later, most citizens will have some kind of interaction with the police. People who do not understand their rights or how to behave toward law enforcement officers can find themselves in serious trouble. The words of advice in this feature actually provide you with key survival skills for life in the modern world.

WHAT CAN YOU DO?

How should you behave if you are stopped by police officers? Your civil liberties protect you from having to provide information other than your name and address. Normally, even if you have not been placed under arrest, the officers have the right to frisk you for weapons, and you must let them proceed. The officers cannot, however, check your person or your clothing further if, in their judgment, no weaponlike object is produced.

The officers may search you only if they have a search warrant or probable cause to believe that a search will likely produce incriminating evidence. What if the officers do not have probable cause or a warrant? Physically resisting their attempt to search you can lead to disastrous results. It is best simply to refuse orally to give permission for the search, preferably in the presence of a witness, and to be polite. It is usually advisable to limit what you say to the officers. If you are arrested, it is best to keep quiet until you can speak with a lawyer.

If you are in your car and are stopped by the police, the same fundamental rules apply. Always be ready to show your driver's license and car registration. You may be asked to get out of the car. The officers may use a flashlight to peer inside the car if it is too dark to see otherwise. None of this constitutes a search. A true search requires either a warrant or probable cause. No officer has the legal right to search your car simply to find out if you may have committed a crime.

Police officers can conduct searches that are incidental to lawful arrests, however, such as an arrest for speeding or drunk driving.

If you are in your home and a police officer with a search warrant appears, you can ask to examine the warrant before granting entry. A warrant that is correctly made out will state the place or persons to be searched, the object sought, and the date of the warrant (which should be no more than 10 days ago), and it will bear the signature of a judge or magistrate. If the warrant is in order, you need not make any statement. If you believe the warrant to be invalid, or if no warrant is produced, you should make it clear orally that you have not consented to the search, preferably in the presence of a witness. If the search later is proved to be unlawful, normally any evidence obtained cannot be used in court.

Officers who attempt to enter your home without a search warrant can do so only if they are pursuing a suspected felon into the house. Rarely is it advisable to give permission for a warrantless search. You, as the resident, must be the one to give permission if any evidence obtained is to be considered legal. The landlord, manager, or head of a college dormitory cannot give legal permission. A roommate, however, can give permission for a search of his or her room, which may allow the police to search areas where you have belongings.

If you are a guest in a place that is being legally searched, you may be legally searched as well. But unless you have been placed under arrest, you cannot be compelled to go to the police station or get into a squad car.

If you would like to find out more about your rights and obligations under the laws of searches and seizures, you might wish to contact the following organization, which maintains a downloadable Know Your Rights Card.

American Civil Liberties Union
125 Broad St., 18th Floor
New York, NY 10004
212-549-2500
www.aclu.org

Key Terms

Chapter Summary

1. Originally, the Bill of Rights limited only the power of the national government, not that of the states. Gradually and selectively, however, the Supreme Court accepted the incorporation theory, under which no state can violate most provisions of the Bill of Rights.

2. The First Amendment's protection of speech, press, religion, and the right to assemble and petition government is meant to protect the fundamental rights of citizens in a democracy. If a government can suppress speech, the press, religious beliefs, or the right to join a group, it can make democratic debates and elections impossible.

3. The First Amendment protects against government interference with freedom of religion by requiring a separation of church and state (under the establishment clause) and by guaranteeing the free exercise of religion. Controversial issues that arise under the establishment clause include aid to church-related schools, school prayer, the teaching of evolution versus intelligent design, school vouchers, the posting of the Ten Commandments in public places, and discrimination against religious speech. The government can interfere with the free exercise of religion only when religious practices work against public policy or the public welfare; however, the government cannot sponsor or support religion in general or any specific religious belief.

4. The First Amendment protects against government interference with freedom of speech, which includes symbolic speech (expressive conduct). The Supreme Court has been especially critical of government actions that impose prior restraint on expression. Commercial speech (advertising) by businesses has received limited First Amendment protection. Restrictions on expression are permitted when the expression creates a clear and present danger to the peace or public order. Speech that has not received First Amendment protection includes expression that is judged to be obscene or slanderous.

5. The First Amendment protects against government interference with the freedom of the press, which can be regarded as a special instance of freedom of speech. Speech by the press that does not receive protection includes libelous statements. Publication of news about a criminal trial may be restricted by a gag order in some circumstances.

6. The First Amendment protects the right to assemble peaceably and to petition the government. Permits may be required for parades, sound trucks, and demonstrations to maintain the public order, and a permit may be denied to protect the public safety.

7. Under the Ninth Amendment, rights not specifically mentioned in the Constitution are not necessarily denied to the people. Among these unspecified rights protected by the courts is a right to privacy, which has been inferred from the First, Third, Fourth, Fifth, and Ninth Amendments. A major privacy issue today is how best to protect privacy rights in cyberspace. Whether an individual's privacy rights include a right to an abortion or a "right to die" continues to provoke controversy. Another major challenge concerns the extent to which Americans must forfeit privacy rights to control terrorism.

8. The Constitution includes protections for the rights of persons accused of crimes. Under the Fourth Amendment, no one may be subject to an unreasonable search or seizure or be arrested except on probable cause. Under the Fifth Amendment, an accused person has the right to remain silent. Under the Sixth Amendment, an accused person must be informed of the reason for his or her arrest. The accused also has the right to adequate counsel, even if he or she cannot afford an attorney, and the right to a prompt arraignment and a speedy and public trial before an impartial jury selected from a cross section of the community.

9. In *Miranda v. Arizona* (1966), the Supreme Court held that criminal suspects, before interrogation by law enforcement personnel, must be informed of certain constitutional rights, including the right to remain silent and the right to be represented by counsel.

10. The exclusionary rule forbids the admission in court of illegally seized evidence. There is a "good faith exception" to the exclusionary rule: Illegally seized evidence need not be thrown out due to, for example, a technical defect in a search warrant.

11. Under the Eighth Amendment, cruel and unusual punishment is prohibited. Whether the death penalty is cruel and unusual punishment and the circumstances under which it is appropriate continue to be debated.

Selected Print, Media, and Online Resources

PRINT RESOURCES

Behe, Michael. *Darwin's Black Box: The Biochemical Challenge to Evolution.* New York: Simon and Schuster, 2006. Considered a seminal work in the intelligent design movement, Behe's book has been updated to include further evidence for his claims that evolution does not fully explain the origins of life.

Epps, Garrett. *To an Unknown God: Religious Freedom on Trial.* New York: St. Martin's Press, 2001. The author chronicles the journey through the courts of *Oregon v. Smith* (discussed earlier in this chapter), a case concerning religious practices decided by the Supreme Court in 1990. The author regards this case as one of the Supreme Court's most momentous decisions on religious freedom in the last 50 years.

Hamadi, Rob. *Privacy Wars: Who Holds Information on You and What They Do with It.* London: Vision Paperbacks, 2009. Hamadi sounds an alarm about the current extent of surveillance in the United States. He also provides recommendations that citizens can use to protect their own privacy.

Herman, Susan N. *Taking Liberties: The War on Terror and the Erosion of American Democracy.* New York: Oxford University Press, 2011. The president of the ACLU analyzes the long- and short-term effects of the USA Patriot Act and the new legal practices that have reduced personal liberty.

Kitcher, Philip. *Living with Darwin: Evolution, Design, and the Future of Faith.* New York: Oxford University Press, 2007. This brief book looks at the history of the controversy over evolution as part of a larger conflict between religious faith and the discoveries of modern science.

Lewis, Anthony. *Freedom for the Thought We Hate: Tales of the First Amendment.* New York: Basic Books, 2008. Pulitzer Prize–winning journalist Anthony Lewis writes eloquently on the value of free expression and the resulting need for "activist judges." He provides a series of engaging stories of how the courts came to give real life to the First Amendment.

Lewis, Anthony. *Gideon's Trumpet.* New York: Vintage, 1964. This classic work discusses the background and facts of *Gideon v. Wainwright,* the 1963 Supreme Court case in which the Court held that the state must make an attorney available for any person accused of a felony who cannot afford a lawyer.

MEDIA RESOURCES

The Abortion War: Thirty Years after Roe v. Wade—An ABC News program released in 2003 that examines the abortion issue.

The Chamber—A movie, based on John Grisham's novel by the same name, about a young lawyer who defends a man (his grandfather) who has been sentenced to death and faces imminent execution.

Execution at Midnight—A video presenting the arguments and evidence on both sides of the controversial death penalty issue.

Gideon's Trumpet—An excellent 1980 movie about the *Gideon v. Wainwright* case. Henry Fonda plays the role of the convicted petty thief Clarence Earl Gideon.

God's Christian Warriors—A controversial 2007 CNN special on how evangelical Christians seek to influence American politics and society. Reported by CNN chief international correspondent Christiane Amanpour, the two-hour show is part of a broader series that includes *God's Jewish Warriors* and *God's Muslim Warriors.*

The Lord Is Not on Trial Here Today—A Peabody Award–winning documentary that tells the compelling personal story of Vashti McCollum, and how her efforts to protect her 10-year-old son led to one of the most important and landmark First Amendment cases in U.S. Supreme Court history — the case that established the separation of church and state in public schools.

May It Please the Court: The First Amendment—A set of audiocassette recordings and written transcripts of the oral arguments made before the Supreme Court in 16 key First Amendment cases. Participants in the recording include nationally known attorneys and several Supreme Court justices.

The People vs. Larry Flynt—An R-rated 1996 film that clearly articulates the conflict between freedom of the press and how a community defines pornography.

Skokie: Rights or Wrong?—A documentary by Sheila Chamovitz. The film documents the legal and moral crisis created when American Nazis attempted to demonstrate in Skokie, Illinois, a predominantly Jewish suburb that was home to many concentration camp survivors.

ONLINE RESOURCES

American Civil Liberties Union (ACLU) the nation's leading civil liberties organization provides an extensive array of information and links concerning civil rights issues: www.aclu.org

The American Library Association information on free-speech issues, especially issues of free speech on the Internet: www.ala.org

Center for Democracy and Technology nonprofit institute that monitors threats to the freedom of the Internet and provides a wealth of information about issues involving the Bill of Rights. It also focuses on how developments in communications technology are affecting the constitutional liberties of Americans: www.cdt.org

Electronic Privacy Information Center information on Internet privacy issues: www.epic.org/privacy

Foundation for Individual Rights in Education (FIRE) tracks the rights to free speech, press, religion, and assembly at the nation's colleges and universities. Find a rating for your own university's speech and conduct codes: www.thefire.org

Freedom Forum nonpartisan foundation dedicated to free press, free speech, and free spirit for all people. Includes history of flag protection and the First Amendment, as well as the status of the proposed flag amendment in Congress: www.freedomforum.org

Legal Information Institute at Cornell University Law School searchable database of historic Supreme Court decisions: www.law.cornell.edu/supct/search/

Liberty Counsel nonprofit litigation, education, and policy organization dedicated to advancing religious freedom, the sanctity of human life, and the family: www. lc.org

The Oyez Project provides summaries and the full text of Supreme Court decisions concerning constitutional law, plus a virtual tour of the Supreme Court: www. oyez.org

5 Civil Rights

A rainbow flag, a symbol of gay and lesbian rights, waves in front of the U.S. Capitol dome during the 2009 Equality Across America march in Washington D.C. Several of the most pressing civil rights issues today concern the interests of gays and lesbians and their families.

© dbimages/Alamy

LEARNING OUTCOMES

After reading this chapter, students will be able to:

■ **LO1** Define civil rights, and locate in the U.S. Constitution the obligation on government to guarantee all citizens equal protection of the law.

■ **LO2** Explain why discrimination against individuals and groups exists in the United States today.

■ **LO3** Assess the limits of state and federal law in guaranteeing equality to all people.

■ **LO4** Explain why the U.S. Supreme Court plays such an important role relative to civil rights, and identify at least two significant Supreme Court decisions that advanced civil rights in the United States.

■ **LO5** Identify and explain three significant events related to each of the campaigns for civil rights undertaken by African Americans, women, the Latino community, persons with disabilities, and the LGBTQ community.

■ **LO6** Define the goal of affirmative action, and explain why this approach is controversial in the United States.

What If...

BIRTHRIGHT CITIZENSHIP WERE REPEALED?

BACKGROUND

The Fourteenth Amendment (1868) confers citizenship on "all persons born or naturalized in the United States, and subject to the jurisdiction thereof" and was adopted as a repudiation of the U.S. Supreme Court's *Dred Scott* ruling that people of African descent could *never* be American citizens. As a concept, birthright citizenship has its origins in English common law. Although not a new idea, until just recently the idea of repealing birthright citizenship had been largely relegated to advocates of severe restrictions on immigration. However, in 2012 a group of Republican state and national lawmakers introduced legislation to repeal birthright citizenship. This time several well-known legislators were among the supporters, including Senators John McCain, Mitch McConnell, Lindsey Graham, Jeff Sessions, and Jon Kyl.

PAST CHALLENGES

In 1882 the Chinese Exclusion Act along with other restrictive state and federal laws denied Chinese and other Asians the right to own property, to marry, to return to the United States once they left the country, and to become U.S. citizens. In the case *U.S. v. Wong Kim Ark*, the Supreme Court took up the issue of birthright citizenship. The case involved a man who was born in San Francisco to Chinese parents who later returned to China. When Wong left the United States to visit his parents, he was denied reentry upon his return. The government claimed that Wong had no right to birthright citizenship under the Fourteenth Amendment because his parents remained "subjects of the emperor of China" even while living in California when he was born. In a 7-2 decision, the majority said "The amendment, in clear words and in manifest intent, includes the children born within the territory of the United States of all other persons, of whatever race or color, domiciled within the United States." This case remains the ruling precedent for challenges to birthright citizenship.

A POLITICAL STRATEGY FOR REPEAL

As you recall, the process for amending the constitution is intentionally difficult, requiring the support of two-thirds of both houses of congress and three-fourths of the state legislatures. Those advocating the repeal of birthright citizenship have opted to avoid this path and have instead proposed a two-pronged strategy. At the federal level, a bill has been introduced to reinterpret the "subject to the jurisdiction thereof" language in the Fourteenth Amendment so that noncitizens and illegal immigrants are not covered. Thus, a student who comes to the United States to attend college would not be "subject to the jurisdiction thereof" for the purposes of citizenship, and any children born to that student would not be citizens of the United States. At the state level, several states working together propose to create two types of birth certificates—one for children born to citizens of the United States and one for those born to noncitizens. Neither of these strategies is likely to pass the test of constitutionality, given the precedent set in *Wong*.

FOR CRITICAL ANALYSIS

1. In the popular press, children born to noncitizens are sometimes referred to as "anchor babies" because they presumably tie their parents to this country. However, this is a misnomer because only the child born here is a citizen. Why do you think so much opposition exists to granting citizenship to children born to noncitizen parents?

2. Given the Supreme Court's reasoning in *Wong*, is it likely that either approach to repealing birthright citizenship would be ruled constitutional?

3. Is the concept of birthright citizenship consistent with the values of America? What would be gained and lost by the nation if birthright citizenship were repealed?

DESPITE THE WORDS set forth in the Declaration of Independence that "all Men are created equal," the United States has a long history of discrimination based on race, gender, national origin, religion, and sexual orientation, among others. The majority of the population had few rights at the nation's founding. As you learned in Chapter 2, the framers of the Constitution permitted slavery to continue, thus excluding slaves from the political process. Women also were excluded for the most part, as were Native Americans, African Americans who were not slaves, and white men who did not own property. To the nation's founders, equality required a degree of independent thinking and the capacity for rational action, which they believed members of these groups did not possess. Today we believe that all people are entitled to equal political rights as well as the opportunities for personal development provided by equal access to education and employment. Thus, the story of civil rights in the United States is the struggle to reconcile our ideals as a nation with the realities of discrimination individuals and groups may still encounter in daily life.

Equality is at the heart of the concept of civil rights. Generally, the term **civil rights** refers to the rights of all Americans to equal treatment under the law, as provided for by the Fourteenth Amendment to the Constitution and by subsequent acts of Congress. Although the terms *civil rights* and *civil liberties* are sometimes used interchangeably, scholars make a distinction between the two. As you learned in Chapter 4, civil liberties are limitations on government; they specify what the government *cannot* do. Civil rights, in contrast, specify what the government *must* do to ensure equal protection and freedom from discrimination.

The history of civil rights in America therefore is the story of the struggle of various groups to be free from discriminatory treatment. Ending slavery was a necessary but not sufficient prerequisite to advancing civil rights in America. In this chapter, we first look at two movements with significant consequences for the history of civil rights in America: the civil rights movement of the 1950s and 1960s and the women's movement, which began in the mid-1800s and continues today. Each of these movements resulted in legislation that secured important basic rights for all Americans—the right to vote and the right to equal protection under the laws. Each of these movements also demonstrates how individuals working alone and with others in groups can effect significant change. Today's civil rights activists draw on insights and strategies from these earlier movements in making new claims for political and social equality. We then explore a question with serious implications for today's voters and policymakers: What should the government's responsibility be when equal protection under the law is not enough to ensure truly equal opportunities for Americans? And we will return to a question first raised in Chapter 1—can political and social equality exist in the face of a widening economic gap?

African Americans and the Consequences of Slavery in the United States

Before 1863, the Constitution protected slavery and made equality impossible in the sense in which we use the word today. African American leader Frederick Douglass pointed out that "Liberty and Slavery—opposite as Heaven and Hell—are both in the Constitution." Abraham Lincoln stated sarcastically, "All men are created equal, except Negroes."

The constitutionality of slavery was confirmed just a few years before the outbreak of the Civil War in the infamous *Dred Scott v. Sandford*[1] case of 1857. The Supreme Court held that slaves were property, not citizens of the United States, and thus they were not entitled to the rights and privileges of citizenship. The Court also ruled that the Missouri Compromise, passed by Congress in 1820, which banned slavery in the territories north of 36°30′ latitude (the southern border of Missouri), was unconstitutional. The *Dred Scott* decision had grave consequences. Most observers contend that the ruling contributed to making the Civil War inevitable.

Ending Servitude

With the Emancipation Proclamation in 1863 and ratification of the Thirteenth, Fourteenth, and Fifteenth Amendments during the Reconstruction period following the Civil War, constitutional inequality for African American males ended.

The Thirteenth Amendment (1865) states that neither slavery nor involuntary servitude shall exist within the United States. The Fourteenth Amendment (1868) says that *all* persons born or naturalized in the United States are citizens of the United States. It states, furthermore, that "[n]o State shall make or enforce any law which shall abridge the privileges or immunities of citizens of the United States; nor shall any State deprive any person of life, liberty, or property, without due process of law; nor deny to any person within its jurisdiction the equal protection of the laws." Note the use of the terms *citizen* and *person* in this amendment. Citizens have political rights, such as the right to vote and run for political office. Citizens also have certain privileges or immunities (see Chapter 4). All *persons*, however, including noncitizens, have a right to due process of law and equal protection under the law.

The Fifteenth Amendment (1870) reads as follows: "The right of citizens of the United States to vote shall not be denied or abridged by the United States or by any State on account of race, color, or previous condition of servitude." Activists in the women's suffrage movements brought pressure on Congress to include in the Fourteenth and Fifteenth Amendments a prohibition against discrimination based on sex, but with no success.

The Civil Rights Acts of 1865 to 1875

At the end of the Civil War, President Lincoln's Republican Party controlled the national government and most state governments, and the so-called radical Republicans, with their strong antislavery stance, controlled the party. From 1865 to 1875, the Republican majority in Congress succeeded in passing a series of civil rights acts that were aimed at enforcing the Thirteenth, Fourteenth, and Fifteenth Amendments even as legislatures in the Southern states moved quickly to pass laws (known as **Black Codes**) intended to limit the civil rights of African Americans and regulate their labor in ways that closely resembled slavery. For example, South Carolina's Black Code passed in 1865 stated that "all persons of color who make contracts for service or labor, shall be known as servants, and those with whom they contract, shall be known as masters."[2] Following the assassination of President Lincoln on April 15, 1865, Andrew Johnson assumed the presidency and presided over the initial period of Reconstruction. Johnson, a Southerner and former slave owner, was viewed by radical Republicans as too conciliatory toward Southern states.

did you know?

June 19th, known as Juneteenth or Freedom Day, celebrates the day in 1865 that slaves in Galveston, Texas, found out they were free three years after Lincoln signed the Emancipation Proclamation.

Black Codes
Laws passed by Southern states immediately after the Civil War denying most legal rights to freed slaves.

---

1. 19 Howard 393 (1857).
2. "Acts of the General Assembly of the State of South Carolina Passed at the Sessions of 1864–65," pp. 291–304.

An engraving of Ku Klux Klan members active in the late 1860s as Southerners rebelled against Northern influence during Reconstruction.

■ **Learning Outcome 3:**
Assess the limits of state and federal law in guaranteeing equality to all people.

Jim Crow Laws
Laws enacted by Southern states that enforced segregation in schools, in transportation, and in public accommodations.

Following the 1866 elections, in which Southern states were not allowed to vote, an emboldened radical Republican majority in Congress moved to take control of Reconstruction. The first Civil Rights Act in the Reconstruction period was passed in 1866 over the veto of President Johnson. That act extended citizenship to anyone born in the United States and gave African Americans full equality before the law. It gave the president authority to enforce the law with military force. Johnson characterized the law as an invasion by federal authority of the rights of the states. It was considered to be unconstitutional, but the ratification of the Fourteenth Amendment two years later ended that concern.

Among the six other civil rights acts passed after the Civil War, one of the most important was the Enforcement Act of 1879, which set out specific criminal sanctions for interfering with the right to vote as protected by the Fifteenth Amendment and by the Civil Rights Act of 1866. Equally important was the Civil Rights Act of 1872, known as the Anti–Ku Klux Klan Act. This act made it a federal crime for anyone to use law or custom to deprive an individual of his or her rights, privileges, and immunities secured by the Constitution or by any federal law.

The last of these early civil rights acts, known as the Second Civil Rights Act, was passed in 1875. It declared that everyone is entitled to full and equal enjoyment of public accommodations, theaters, and other places of amusement, and it imposed penalties for violators. What is most important about all of the civil rights acts was the belief that congressional power applied to official or government action or to private action. If a state government did not secure rights, then the federal government could do so. Thus, Congress could legislate directly against individuals who were violating the constitutional rights of others. As we will see, these acts were quickly rendered ineffective by law and by custom. However, they became important in the civil rights struggles of the 1960s, 100 years after their passage.

The Limitations of the Civil Rights Laws

The Reconstruction statutes, or civil rights acts, ultimately did little to secure equality for African Americans. Both the *Civil Rights Cases* and *Plessy v. Ferguson* effectively nullified these acts. The election of Rutherford B. Hayes as president in 1877 marked an end to the progressive advance of rights for African Americans during Reconstruction. He withdrew federal forces from states in the former Confederacy. Without direct oversight, Southern and border states created a variety of seemingly race-neutral legal barriers that in reality prevented African Americans from exercising their right to vote, while also adopting policies of racial segregation known as **Jim Crow laws**.

The Civil Rights Cases. The Supreme Court invalidated the 1875 Civil Rights Act when it held, in the *Civil Rights Cases*[3] of 1883, that the enforcement clause

---

3. 109 U.S. 3 (1883).

of the Fourteenth Amendment (which states that "[n]o State shall make or enforce any law which shall abridge the privileges or immunities of citizens") was limited to correcting actions by states in their *official* acts; thus, the discriminatory acts of private citizens were not illegal. ("Individual invasion of individual rights is not the subject matter of the Amendment.") The 1883 Supreme Court decision removed the federal government as a forceful advocate for advancing civil rights in all aspects of daily human interaction, and it was met with widespread approval throughout most of the United States.

Twenty years after the Civil War, the white majority was all too ready to forget about the three Civil War amendments and the civil rights legislation of the 1860s and 1870s. The other civil rights laws that the Court did not specifically invalidate became effectively null without any mechanisms of enforcement, although they were never repealed by Congress. At the same time, many former proslavery secessionists had regained political power in the Southern states.

Plessy v. Ferguson: **Separate-but-Equal.** A key decision during this period concerned Homer Plessy, a Louisiana resident who was one-eighth African American. In 1892, he boarded a train in New Orleans. The conductor made him leave the car, which was restricted to whites, and directed him to a car for non-whites. At that time, Louisiana had a statute providing for separate railway cars for whites and African Americans.

Plessy went to court, claiming that such a statute was contrary to the Fourteenth Amendment's equal protection clause. In 1896, the United States Supreme Court rejected Plessy's contention. The Court concluded that the Fourteenth Amendment "could not have been intended to abolish distinctions based upon color, or to enforce social. . . equality." The Court stated that segregation alone did not violate the Constitution: "Laws permitting, and even requiring, their separation in places where they are liable to be brought into contact do not necessarily imply the inferiority of either race to the other."[4] With this case, the Court announced the **separate-but-equal doctrine**.

Plessy v. Ferguson became the judicial cornerstone of racial discrimination throughout the United States. Even though *Plessy* upheld segregated facilities in railway cars only, it was assumed that the Supreme Court was upholding segregation everywhere as long as the separate facilities were equal, which in reality meant as long as there were separate facilities. The result was a system of racial segregation, particularly in the South—supported by laws collectively known as Jim Crow laws—that required separate drinking fountains; separate seats in theaters, restaurants, and hotels; separate public toilets; and separate waiting rooms for the two races. "Separate" was indeed the rule, but "equal" was never enforced, nor was it a reality.

Separate-but-Equal Doctrine
The 1896 doctrine holding that separate-but-equal facilities do not violate the equal protection clause.

Voting Barriers. The brief enfranchisement of African Americans ended after 1877, when the federal troops that occupied the South during the Reconstruction era were withdrawn. Southern politicians regained control of state governments and, using everything except race as a formal criterion, passed laws that effectively deprived African Americans of the right to vote. By claiming that political parties were private organizations, the Democratic Party was allowed to restrict black voters from participating in its primaries. Since most Southern states were dominated by a single party, the Democratic Party, denying blacks the right to vote in the primary effectively disenfranchised them altogether. The **white primary**

White Primary
A state primary election that restricts voting to whites only; outlawed by the Supreme Court in 1944.

---

4. *Plessy v. Ferguson*, 163 U.S. 537 (1896).

was upheld by the Supreme Court until 1944 when, in *Smith v. Allwright*,[5] the Court ruled it a violation of the Fifteenth Amendment.

Another barrier to African American voting was the **grandfather clause**, which restricted voting to those who could prove that their grandfathers had voted before 1867. **Poll taxes** required the payment of a fee to vote; thus, poor African Americans—as well as poor whites—who could not afford to pay the tax were excluded from voting. Not until the Twenty-fourth Amendment to the Constitution was ratified in 1964 was the poll tax eliminated as a precondition to voting. **Literacy tests** were also used to deny the vote to African Americans. Such tests asked potential voters to read, recite, or interpret complicated texts, such as a section of the state constitution, to the satisfaction of local registrars— who were, of course, never satisfied with the responses of African Americans. Each of these barriers to voting was, on its face, race-neutral. However, each was vigorously enforced disproportionately against African Americans by government agents and a system of racial intimidation.

Southern states, counties, and towns also passed numerous ordinances and laws to maintain a segregated society and to control the movements and activities of African American residents. In Florida, for example, no "negro, mulatto, or person of color" was permitted to own or carry a weapon, including a knife, without a license. This law did not apply to white residents. Other laws set curfews for African Americans, set limits on the businesses they could own or run and on their rights to assembly, and required the newly freed men and women to find employment quickly or be subject to penalties. The penalty sometimes meant that the men would be forced into labor at very low wages at large farms or factories against their will. Denied the right to register and vote, black citizens were also effectively barred from public office and jury service.

Extralegal Methods of Enforcing White Supremacy.

The second-class status of African Americans was also a matter of social custom, especially in the South. In their interactions with Southern whites, African Americans were expected to observe an informal but detailed code of behavior that confirmed their inferiority. The most serious violation of the informal code was "familiarity" toward a white woman by an African American man or boy. The code was backed up by the common practice of *lynching*—mob action to murder an accused individual, usually by hanging and sometimes accompanied by torture. Lynching was illegal, but Southern authorities rarely prosecuted these cases, and white juries would not convict. African American women were instrumental in antilynching campaigns, beginning in the 1890s with the work of Ida B. Wells-Barnett. As the owner and editor of *The Free Speech*, a Memphis newspaper, she used her voice to call attention to the brutality of lynching and argued in editorials that lynching was a strategy to eliminate prosperous, politically active African Americans.

Grandfather Clause

A device used by Southern states to disenfranchise African Americans. It restricted voting to those whose grandfathers had voted before 1867.

Poll Tax

A special tax that must be paid as a qualification for voting. The Twenty-fourth Amendment to the Constitution outlawed the poll tax in national elections, and in 1966, the Supreme Court declared it unconstitutional in all elections.

Literacy Test

A test administered as a precondition for voting, often used to prevent African Americans from exercising their right to vote.

These segregated drinking fountains were common in Southern states in the late 1800s and during the first half of the 20th century. What landmark Supreme Court case made such segregated facilities legal?

Bettmann/Corbis

5. 321 U.S. 649 (1944).

African Americans outside the South were subject to a second kind of violence—race riots. In the early 20th century, race riots were typically initiated by whites. Frequently, the riots were caused by competition for employment. For example, several serious riots occurred during World War II (1939–1945), when labor shortages forced Northern employers to hire more black workers.

The End of the Separate-but-Equal Doctrine

The successful attack on the separate-but-equal doctrine began with a series of lawsuits in the 1930s that sought to admit African Americans to state professional schools. Nearly three decades earlier, in 1909, influential African Americans and progressive whites, including W.E.B. Dubois and Oswald Garrison Villard, joined to form the National Association for the Advancement of Colored People (NAACP) with the express intention of targeting the separate-but-equal doctrine. Although all Southern states maintained a segregated system of elementary and secondary schools as well as colleges and universities, very few offered professional education for African Americans. Thus, the NAACP elected to begin its challenge with law schools, believing in part that it would be too expensive for states to establish an entirely separate system of black professional schools, leaving integration as the best option. To pursue this strategy, the NAACP established the Legal Defense and Education Fund (LDF). As a result of several such challenges, law schools in Maryland, Missouri, Oklahoma, and Texas were forced to change their policies regarding admittance or matriculation of law school students, paving the way for *Brown v. Board of Education* (1954).

By 1950, the Supreme Court had ruled that African Americans who were admitted to a state university could not be assigned to separate sections of classrooms, libraries, and cafeterias. In 1951, Oliver Brown attempted to enroll his eight-year-old daughter, Linda Carol Brown, in the third grade of his all-white neighborhood school seven blocks from their home rather than have her travel by bus to the segregated school across town. Although Kansas law did not require schools to be segregated by race, in practice there were separate schools for white and black children. When Linda was denied admission to the all-white school, the Topeka NAACP urged Brown to join a lawsuit against the Topeka Board of Education.

Brown v. Board of Education of Topeka[6] established that segregation of races in the public schools violates the equal protection clause of the Fourteenth Amendment. First argued in 1952 by NAACP Legal Defense Fund attorney Thurgood Marshall (appointed as the first African American to the U.S. Supreme Court in 1967), the votes were almost evenly split to uphold or strike down *separate but equal*; Chief Justice Fred Vinson held the swing vote. In 1953, Vinson died, and President Dwight Eisenhower appointed Earl Warren to replace him.

■ **Learning Outcome 4:**
Explain why the U.S. Supreme Court plays such an important role relative to civil rights, and identify at least two significant Supreme Court decisions that advanced civil rights in the United States.

These three lawyers successfully argued in favor of desegregation of the schools in the famous *Brown v. Board of Education of Topeka* case. On the left is George E. C. Hayes; on the right is James Nabrit, Jr.; and in the center is Thurgood Marshall, who later became the first African American Supreme Court justice.

Bettmann/Corbis

6. 347 U.S. 483 (1954).

Brown was reargued, and Warren wrote a unanimous decision to strike down *separate but equal*, arguing that "separate" is inherently unequal.

"With All Deliberate Speed." The following year, in *Brown v. Board of Education*[7] (sometimes called the second *Brown* decision), the Court declared that the lower courts needed to ensure that African Americans would be admitted to schools on a nondiscriminatory basis "with all deliberate speed." The district courts were to consider devices in their desegregation orders that might include "the school transportation system, personnel, [and] revision of school districts and attendance areas into compact units to achieve a system of determining admission to the public schools on a nonracial basis."

This legal strategy was only one of many African Americans found successful in their struggle for civil rights, and many difficult days lay ahead. The success of civil rights groups in *Brown* was a flashpoint, sparking an enormous backlash among segregationists. They defied the Court, closed public schools rather than integrate them, and vowed to maintain inequality in other areas such as voting. Violence and sometimes death for civil rights activists followed.

Reactions to School Integration

The white South did not let the Supreme Court ruling go unchallenged. Governor Orval Faubus of Arkansas used the state's National Guard to block the integration of Central High School in Little Rock in September 1957. The federal court demanded that the troops be withdrawn. Finally, President Dwight Eisenhower had to federalize the Arkansas National Guard and send in the army's 101st Airborne Division to quell the violence. Central High became integrated.

The universities in the South, however, remained segregated. When James Meredith, an African American student, attempted to enroll at the University of Mississippi in Oxford in 1962, violence flared there, as it had in Little Rock. The white riot at Oxford was so intense that President John Kennedy was forced to send in 30,000 U.S. combat troops, a larger force than the one then stationed in Korea. There were 375 military and civilian injuries, many from gunfire, and two bystanders were killed. Ultimately, peace was restored, and Meredith began attending classes.[8]

An Integrationist Attempt at a Cure: Busing

In most parts of the United States, residential concentrations by race have made it difficult to achieve racial balance in schools. This concentration results in **de facto segregation**, as distinct from **de jure segregation**, which results from laws or administrative decisions.

Court-Ordered Busing. One solution to both *de facto* and *de jure* segregation seemed to be transporting some African American schoolchildren to white schools and some white schoolchildren to African American schools. The courts ordered school districts to engage in such **busing** across neighborhoods. Busing led to violence in some Northern cities, such as in south Boston, where African American students were bused into blue-collar Irish Catholic neighborhoods. Indeed, busing was unpopular with many groups. In the mid-1970s, almost 50 percent of African Americans interviewed were opposed to busing, and approximately three-fourths of the whites interviewed held the same opinion.

De Facto Segregation
Racial segregation that occurs because of past social and economic conditions and residential racial patterns.

De Jure Segregation
Racial segregation that occurs because of laws or administrative decisions by public agencies.

Busing
In the context of civil rights, the transportation of public school students from areas where they live to schools in other areas to eliminate school segregation based on residential racial patterns.

---

7. 349 U.S. 294 (1955).
8. William Doyle, *An American Insurrection: James Meredith and the Battle of Oxford, Mississippi, 1962* (New York: Anchor, 2003).

The End of Integration? During the 1980s and the early 1990s, the Supreme Court began to back away from its earlier commitment to busing and other methods of desegregation. By the late 1990s and early 2000s, the federal courts were increasingly unwilling to uphold race-conscious policies designed to further school integration and diversity. In 2001, a federal appellate court held that the Charlotte-Mecklenburg school district in North Carolina had achieved the goal of integration,[9] meaning that race-based admission quotas could no longer be imposed constitutionally.

The Resurgence of Minority Schools. Today, schools around the country are becoming segregated again, in large part because changing population demographics result in increased *de facto* segregation. Even as African American and Latino students are becoming more isolated, the typical white child is in a school that is more diverse in large part due to the substantial decline in the number and proportion of white students in the population relative to the increase of nonwhites. In Latino and African American populations, two of every five students attend a school with more than 90 percent minority enrollment. Public school segregation is most severe in the western states. In California, the nation's most multiracial state, half of African Americans and Asians attend segregated schools, as do one-quarter of Latino and Native American students.[10] Most nonwhite schools are segregated by poverty as well as race. A majority of the nation's dropouts come from nonwhite public schools, leading to large numbers of virtually unemployable young people of color. The Bureau of Labor Statistics reported that in November 2008, the month President Obama was elected, the unemployment rate for African American adult and teen males was nearly twice that for white males—a remarkably persistent gap evident in Figure 5-1.

Generally, Americans are now taking another look at what desegregation means. In 2007, the Supreme Court handed down a decision that would dramatically change the way school districts across the country assigned students to schools. In cases brought by white parents in Seattle and Louisville, the court, by a narrow 5-to-4 majority, found that using race to determine which schools students could attend was a violation of the Fourteenth Amendment. White children could not be denied admission to magnet schools or other schools designed to have racially balanced populations on account of their race. Justice Anthony Kennedy was the swing vote in this case. Although he agreed with four justices in striking down voluntary plans that assigned students to schools solely on the basis of race, he also agreed with other justices in holding that integrated education was a compelling educational goal that could be pursued through other methods.[11]

An alternative being tried in over 60 school districts across the country is to integrate schools on the basis of income. A more advantaged school environment translates into higher achievement levels. On the 2007 National Assessment of Educational Progress given to all fourth-graders in math, for example, low-income students attending more affluent schools scored almost two years ahead of low-income students attending high-poverty schools. Today more than 3.2 million students live in school districts with some form of socioeconomic integration in place.[12]

9.   *Belk v. Charlotte-Mecklenburg Board of Education*, 269 F.3d 305 (4th Cir. 2001).
10. Gary Orfield, *Reviving the Goal of an Integrated Society: A 21st Century Challenge* (Los Angeles, CA: The Civil Rights Project/Proyecto Derechos Civiles at UCLA, 2009).
11. *Parents Involved v. Seattle School District No. 1*, 550 U.S (2007) and *Meredith v. Jefferson County Board of Education*, 550 U.S. (2007).
12. Richard D. Kahlenberg, "Can Separate Be Equal?" *The American Prospect*, September 16, 2009.

Figure 5–1 ▶ Unemployment Rates by Race and Hispanic or Latino Ethnicity, January 1972 to December 2011

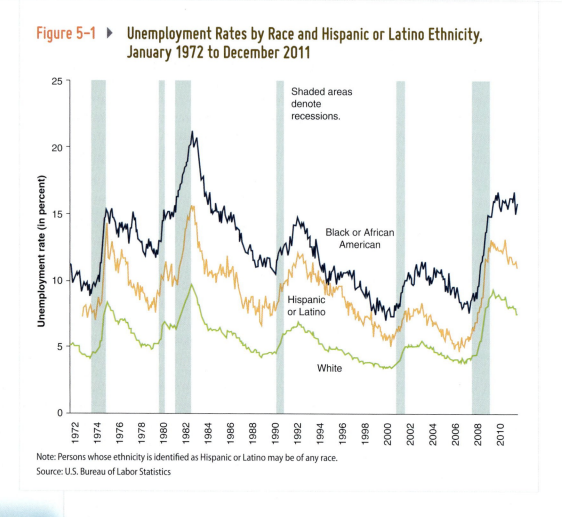

Note: Persons whose ethnicity is identified as Hispanic or Latino may be of any race.

Source: U.S. Bureau of Labor Statistics

■ **Learning Outcome 5:**
Identify and explain three significant events related to each of the campaigns for civil rights undertaken by African Americans, women, the Latino community, persons with disabilities, and the LGBTQ community.

Civil Disobedience
A nonviolent, public refusal to obey allegedly unjust laws.

The Civil Rights Movement

The *Brown* decision applied only to public schools. Not much else in the structure of existing segregation was affected. In December 1955, a 43-year-old African American woman, Rosa Parks, boarded a public bus in Montgomery, Alabama. When the bus became crowded and several white people stepped aboard, Parks was asked to move to the rear of the bus (the "colored" section). She refused, was arrested, and was fined $10, but that was not the end of the matter. For an entire year, African Americans boycotted the Montgomery bus line. The protest was headed by a 27-year-old Baptist minister, Dr. Martin Luther King, Jr. During the protest period, he went to jail, and his house was bombed. In the face of overwhelming odds, the protesters won. In 1956, a federal district court issued an injunction prohibiting the segregation of buses in Montgomery. The era of civil rights protests had begun.

King's Philosophy of Nonviolence

The following year, in 1957, King formed the Southern Christian Leadership Conference (SCLC). King advocated nonviolent **civil disobedience** as a means to achieve racial justice. King's philosophy of civil disobedience was influenced, in part, by the life and teachings of Mahatma Gandhi (1869–1948). Gandhi had led resistance to the British colonial system in India from 1919 to 1947. He used tactics such as demonstrations and marches, as well as nonviolent, public disobedience to unjust laws. King's followers successfully used these methods to gain wider public acceptance of their cause.

Nonviolent Demonstrations. For the next decade, African Americans and sympathetic whites engaged in sit-ins, freedom rides, and freedom marches. Organizations including the NAACP, the Congress of Racial Equality (CORE), and the Student Nonviolent Coordinating Committee (SNCC) organized and supported these actions. In the beginning, such demonstrations were often met with violence, and the contrasting image of nonviolent African Americans and violent, hostile whites created strong public support for the civil rights movement. In 1960, when African Americans in Greensboro, North Carolina, were refused service at a Woolworth's lunch counter, they organized a sit-in that was aided day after day by sympathetic whites and other African Americans. Enraged customers threw ketchup on the protesters. Some spat in their faces. The sit-in movement continued to grow, however. Within six months of the first sit-in at the Greensboro Woolworth's, hundreds of lunch counters throughout the South were serving African Americans.

The sit-in technique also was successfully used to integrate interstate buses and their terminals, as well as railroads engaged in interstate transportation. Although buses and railroads engaged in interstate transportation were prohibited by law from segregating African Americans from whites, they stopped doing so only after the sit-in protests.

Marches and Demonstrations. One of the most famous of the violence-plagued protests occurred in Birmingham, Alabama, in 1963, when Police Commissioner Eugene "Bull" Connor unleashed police dogs and used electric cattle prods against the protesters. People throughout the country viewed the event on television with indignation and horror. King was thrown in jail. The media coverage of the Birmingham protest and the violent response by the city government played a key role in the process of ending Jim Crow laws in the United States. The ultimate result was the most important civil rights act in the nation's history, the Civil Rights Act of 1964.

In August 1963, African American leaders A. Philip Randolph and Bayard Rustin organized a massive March on Washington for Jobs and Freedom. Before nearly a quarter-million white and African American spectators and millions watching on television, King told the world his dream: "I have a dream that my four little children will one day live in a nation where they will not be judged by the color of their skin but by the content of their character."

Another Approach—Black Power

Not all African Americans agreed with King's philosophy of nonviolence or with the idea that King's strong Christian background should represent the core spirituality of African Americans. Black Muslims and other African American separatists advocated a more militant stance and argued that desegregation should not result in cultural assimilation. During the 1950s and 1960s, when King was spearheading nonviolent protests and demonstrations to achieve civil rights for African Americans, black power leaders insisted that African

The Black Power salute was a human rights protest and one of the most overtly political statements in the 110 year history of the civil rights movement.

© World History Archive/Alamy

Americans should "fight back" instead of turning the other cheek. Some would argue that without the fear generated by black militants, a "moderate" such as King would not have garnered such widespread support from white America.

Malcolm Little (who became Malcolm X when he joined the Black Muslims in 1952) and other leaders in the black power movement believed that African Americans fell into two groups: the "Uncle Toms," who peaceably accommodated the white establishment, and the "New Negroes," who took pride in their color and culture and who preferred and demanded racial separation as well as power. Malcolm X was assassinated in 1965, but he became an important reference point for a new generation of African Americans and a symbol of African American identity.

■ Learning Outcome 3

The Escalation of the Civil Rights Movement

Police dog attacks, cattle prods, high-pressure water hoses, beatings, bombings, the March on Washington, and black militancy—all of these events and developments led to an environment in which Congress felt compelled to act on behalf of African Americans.

Modern Civil Rights Legislation

As the civil rights movement mounted in intensity, equality before the law came to be "an idea whose time has come," in the words of then Republican Senate minority leader Everett Dirksen. The legislation passed during the Eisenhower administration was relatively symbolic. The Civil Rights Act of 1957 established the Civil Rights Commission and a new Civil Rights Division within the Department of Justice. The Civil Rights Act of 1960 was passed to protect voting rights. Whenever a pattern or practice of discrimination was documented, the Justice Department, on behalf of the voter, could bring suit, even against a state. However, this act, which had little enforcement power, was relatively ineffective.

The 1960 presidential election featured Vice President Richard Nixon against Senator John F. Kennedy. Kennedy sought the support of African American leaders, promising to introduce tougher civil rights legislation. When Martin Luther King, Jr. was imprisoned in Georgia after participating in a sit-in in Atlanta, candidate Kennedy called Mrs. King to express his support, and his brother, Robert, made telephone calls to expedite King's release on bond. However, President Kennedy's civil rights legislation was stalled in the Senate in 1963, and his assassination ended the effort in his name. When Lyndon B. Johnson became president in 1963, he committed himself to passing civil rights bills, and the 1964 act was the result.

The Civil Rights Act of 1964. The Civil Rights Act of 1964, the most far-reaching bill on civil rights in modern times, forbade discrimination on the basis of race, color, religion, gender, and national origin. The major provisions of the act were as follows:

1. It outlawed arbitrary discrimination in voter registration.
2. It barred discrimination in public accommodations, such as hotels and restaurants, whose operations affect interstate commerce.
3. It authorized the federal government to sue to desegregate public schools and facilities.

4. It expanded the power of the Civil Rights Commission and extended its life.
5. It provided for the withholding of federal funds from programs administered in a discriminatory manner.
6. It established the right to equality of opportunity in employment.

Title VII of the Civil Rights Act of 1964 is the cornerstone of employment-discrimination law. It prohibits discrimination in employment based on race, color, religion, sex, or national origin. Under Title VII, executive orders were issued that banned employment discrimination by firms that received any federal funding. The 1964 Civil Rights Act created a five-member commission, the Equal Employment Opportunity Commission (EEOC), to administer Title VII.

The EEOC can issue interpretive guidelines and regulations, but these do not have the force of law. Rather, they give notice of the commission's enforcement policy. The EEOC also has investigatory powers. It has broad authority to require the production of documentary evidence, to hold hearings, and to **subpoena** and examine witnesses under oath.

Subpoena
A legal writ requiring a person's appearance in court to give testimony.

The equal employment provisions of the 1964 act have been strengthened several times since its first passage. In 1965, President Johnson signed an Executive Order (11246) that prohibited any discrimination in employment by any employer who received federal funds, contracts, or subcontracts. It also required all such employers to establish *affirmative action plans*, which will be discussed later in this chapter. A revision of that order extended the requirement for an affirmative action plan to public institutions and medical and health facilities with more than 50 employees. In 1972, the Equal Employment Opportunity Act extended the provisions prohibiting discrimination in employment to the employees of state and local governments and most other not-for-profit institutions.

The Voting Rights Act of 1965. As late as 1960, only 29.1 percent of African Americans of voting age were registered in the Southern states, in stark contrast to 61.1 percent of whites. The Voting Rights Act of 1965 addressed this issue. The act had two major provisions. The first one outlawed discriminatory voter-registration tests. The second authorized federal registration of voters and federally administered voting procedures in any political subdivision or state that discriminated electorally against a particular group. In part, the act provided that certain political subdivisions could not change their voting procedures and election laws without federal approval. The act targeted counties, mostly in the South, in which less than 50 percent of the eligible population was registered to vote. Federal voter registrars were sent to these areas to register African Americans who had been kept from voting by local registrars. Within one week after the act was passed, 45 federal examiners were sent to the South. A massive voter-registration drive drew thousands of civil rights activists, many of whom were white college students, to the South over the summer. This effort resulted in a dramatic increase in the proportion of African Americans registered to vote.

Urban Riots. Even as the civil rights movement was experiencing its greatest victories, a series of riots swept through African American inner-city neighborhoods. These urban riots were different in character from the race riots described earlier in this chapter. The riots in the first half of the 20th century were street battles between whites and blacks. The urban riots of the late 1960s and early 1970s, however, were not directed against individual whites—in some instances, whites actually participated in small numbers. The riots were primarily civil insurrections, although these disorders were accompanied by large-scale looting of stores. Inhabitants of the

President Lyndon B. Johnson is shown signing the Civil Rights Act of 1968. What are some of the provisions of that far-reaching law?

affected neighborhoods attributed the riots to racial discrimination.[13] The riots dissipated much of the goodwill toward the civil rights movement that had been built up earlier in the decade among Northern whites. Together with widespread student demonstrations against the Vietnam War (1964–1975), the riots pushed many Americans toward conservatism.

The Civil Rights Act of 1968 and Other Housing Reform Legislation. Martin Luther King, Jr., was assassinated on April 4, 1968. Despite King's message of peace, his death was followed by widespread rioting. Nine days after King's death, President Johnson signed the Civil Rights Act of 1968, which forbade discrimination in most housing and provided penalties for those attempting to interfere with individual civil rights (giving protection to civil rights workers, among others). Subsequent legislation added enforcement provisions to the federal government's rules against discriminatory mortgage lending practices. Today, all lenders must report to the federal government the race, gender, and income of all mortgage loan seekers, along with the final decision on their loan applications.

Consequences of Civil Rights Legislation

As a result of the Voting Rights Act of 1965 and its amendments, and the large-scale voter-registration drives in the South, the number of African Americans registered to vote climbed dramatically. Subsequent amendments to the Voting Rights Act of 1965 extended its protections to other minorities, including Latinos, Asian Americans, Native Americans, and Native Alaskans. To further protect the voting rights of minorities, the law now provides that states must make bilingual ballots available in counties where 5 percent or more of the population speaks a language other than English.

Some of the provisions in the Voting Rights Act of 1965 were due to "sunset" (expire) in 2007. In July 2006, President George W. Bush signed a 25-year extension of these provisions, following heated congressional debate in which many members, particularly those representing the states and counties still monitored by the Justice Department, argued that the Voting Rights Act was no longer needed.

Political Participation by African Americans. The movement of African American citizens into high elected office has been sure, if exceedingly slow. African American representatives hold 43 of the 435 seats in the House of Representatives (9.5 percent) and none of 100 seats in the U.S. Senate in the 112th Congress. The number of African American state legislators increased from 401 in 1986 to a record 628 (or 9 percent) in 2009, the latest data available. In 2008, Karen Bass was selected as the first female African American assembly speaker in California. At the local level (city and county offices), the Joint Center for Political and Economic Studies estimated that black elected officials held over 5,700 offices in 2002. In a decisive victory, Barack Obama was elected the first African American president on

13. Angus Campbell and Howard Schuman, *ICPSR 3500: Racial Attitudes in Fifteen American Cities,* 1968 (Ann Arbor, MI: Inter-University Consortium for Political and Social Research, 1997). Campbell and Schuman's survey documents both white participation in and the attitudes of the inhabitants of affected neighborhoods. This survey is available online at www.grinnell.edu/academic/data/sociology/minorityresearch/raceatt1968.

Politics with a Purpose

RESEARCH WITH IMPACT: SLAVERY REPARATIONS

Deandria Farmer-Paellmann grew up listening to stories about her ancestors, who were rice farmers in South Carolina. Her grandfather, whose own grandfather was a slave on a rice plantation on St. Helena Island, often claimed, "They still owe us 40 acres and a mule."

He was referring to a short-lived promise made by General William T. Sherman to slaves freed in 1863 by the Emancipation Proclamation that they would receive a 40-acre plot of land. The plots were drawn from "the islands from Charleston, south, the abandoned rice fields along the rivers for thirty miles back from the sea, and the country bordering the St. Johns river, Florida."[a] After Lincoln was assassinated, President Andrew Johnson revoked the order, took the land away from the freed slaves, and returned it to its original owners, who in many cases turned around and "hired" the former slaves at very low wages. Thus, the first recorded form of reparations for slavery never materialized.

Deandria Farmer-Paellmann was still interested in the issue when she enrolled in the New England School of Law. While researching a paper on slave reparations, she discovered an insurance policy from 1856 that offered slave owners in six Southern states the option of insuring the lives of their slaves so that their "property interests" could be protected in the event a slave died. A $2 policy on a 10-year-old, for example, would pay out $100 if the child died. Tom Baker, director of the Insurance Law center at the University of Connecticut School of Law, says, "It was very common. Basically, insurance and slavery go all the way back…."[b] When she found a similar document from a company that is now Aetna, Inc., the nation's largest health insurer, she contacted the company and asked for archival records related to slave insurance. This discovery and request ignited a national dialogue. In 2000, Aetna issued a public apology for its role in supporting the "deplorable practice" of slavery. The state of California passed a law requiring all insurance companies that do business in the state to submit records of any slaveholder insurance policies. As a result of the law, Farmer-Paellmann learned that Aetna wrote a policy on the life of Abel, one of her ancestors from South Carolina. This discovery provided her legal standing to pursue reparations through litigation.

In March 2002, Deandria Farmer-Paellmann and other plaintiffs filed a federal lawsuit against Aetna, a bank, and a major railroad company on the grounds that they "knowingly benefited from a system that enslaved, tortured, starved and exploited human beings" and concealed their involvement with the slave trade from consumers—an act that constitutes fraud.[c] In an interview, Farmer-Paellmann said that although she was intrigued by the idea of a national apology and federal restitution for descendants of slaves, she decided that the American public wasn't ready for a national reparations bill, and so she turned her attention to corporations.

Not all scholars and activists believe reparations are the way to settle the debts of slavery. Glenn Loury, director of Boston University's Institute on Race and Social Division, warns that a successful reparations lawsuit could end up helping white Americans feel even less responsible for slavery than they do now. Loury and others prefer progressive social policies that benefit impoverished African Americans: "What I'm advocating is politics … reparations is not a substitute for politics."[d] Randall Robinson, author of *The Debt: What America Owes to Blacks*, links the contemporary popularity of the reparations movement to scaled-back social programs and to the backlash against affirmative action policy.

Whatever the eventual outcome of Farmer-Paellmann's legal actions, her curiosity about her ancestor's slave experiences led her to do research that sparked a new public dialogue on the legacy of slavery. Several universities including Harvard, Yale, and Brown have undertaken efforts to document and make public the ways in which their endowments are connected to the slave trade. The U.S. Congress passed a resolution issuing a formal apology for the institution of slavery in 2008. Law schools across the country have hosted scholarly conferences on reparations. The question of what, if any, legal and moral responsibility today's society has toward the descendants of slaves is far from settled. Yet one woman's actions helped to put the question of reparations back onto the political agenda.

[a] Major General William T. Sherman, "Special Field Orders, No. 15," Savannah, Georgia, January 16, 1865.
[b] Virginia Groark, "Slave Policies," *The New York Times*, May 5, 2002.
[c] The bank is FleetBoston Financial Corporation and the railroad is CSX Corporation.
[d] Sasha Polakow-Suransky, "Sins of Our Fathers," *Brown Alumni Magazine*, July/August 2003.

November 4, 2008. In his acceptance speech on election night, the president-elect stressed the need for all Americans to come together regardless of race or ethnic background to solve the problems facing the nation.

The U.S. Census and Civil Rights.

The census, which calls for a count of the country's population every 10 years and which took place in 2010, is the basis for virtually all demographic information used by policymakers, educators, and community leaders. The census is related to civil rights in a number of important ways. First, it is used for determining representation for the purposes of redistricting (covered in detail in Chapter 11). In this sense, the census data also provide an important tool for enforcing the Voting Rights Act, which forbids drawing districts with the intention of diluting the concentration and thus the political power of minority voters. Census data are also used to allocate federal dollars in support of community development, education, crime prevention, and transportation. For these reasons, civil rights leaders urged full participation from within their communities. Being counted in the census equates to political and community empowerment.

Lingering Social and Economic Disparities.

According to Joyce Ladner of the Brookings Institution, one of the difficulties with the race-based civil rights agenda of the 1950s and 1960s is that it did not envision remedies for cross-racial problems. How, for example, should the nation address problems such as poverty and urban violence that affect underclasses in all racial groups? In 1967, when Martin Luther King, Jr., proposed a Poor People's Campaign, he recognized that a civil rights coalition based entirely on race would not be sufficient to address the problem of poverty among whites as well as blacks. During his 1984 and 1988 presidential campaigns, African American leader Jesse Jackson also acknowledged the inadequacy of a race-based model of civil rights when he attempted to form a "Rainbow Coalition" of minorities, women, and other underrepresented groups, including the poor.[14]

A Renewed Focus on Preventing Voter Fraud.

Under the guise of preventing voter fraud, a number of states have adopted laws likely to suppress the vote. Nine states now require government-issued photo identification. Because any form of poll tax is unconstitutional, states must pay the monetary costs associated with acquiring state-issued photo identification. Maine has abolished Election Day registration. Three states have passed laws requiring proof of citizenship as a prerequisite to voting. Five states have shortened or eliminated early voting opportunities. Florida and Texas have adopted laws that make it difficult for nonparty organizations like the League of Women Voters to register voters through registration drives. If this last change spreads to other states, registration drives on college campuses may be adversely impacted as well. Critics of these new laws argue that the burden falls disproportionately on elderly, poor, disabled, young, and minority voters. A 2012 study by the Brennan Center for Justice found that as many as 5 million eligible voters could be disenfranchised by new laws passed in the states, a number larger than the margin of victory in two of the last three presidential elections.[15]

Race-Conscious or Postracial Society?

Whether we are talking about college attendance, media stereotyping, racial profiling, or academic achievement, the black experience is different from the white one. As a result, African

did you know?

During the Mississippi Summer Project in 1964, organized by students to register African American voters, 1,000 students and voters were arrested, 80 were beaten, 35 were shot, and 6 were murdered; 30 buildings were bombed; and 25 churches were burned.

---

14. Joyce A. Ladner, "A New Civil Rights Agenda," *The Brookings Review*, Vol. 18, No. 2, Spring 2000, pp. 26–28.
15. Wendy R. Weiser and Lawrence Norden, *Voting Law Changes in 2012*, Brennan Center for Justice at New York University School of Law, accessed at: http://brennan.3cdn.net/92635ddafbc09e8d88_i3m6bjdeh.pdf

Americans view the nation and many specific issues differently than their white counterparts do.[16] In survey after survey, when blacks are asked whether they have achieved racial equality, few believe that they have. In contrast, whites are five times more likely than blacks to believe that racial equality has been achieved.[17] As a candidate for the Democratic nomination for president, Barack Obama directly addressed race in America in his "A More Perfect Union" speech delivered in Philadelphia in March 2008.[18] Since taking office, however, President Obama has been criticized by some within the civil rights community for not making the goal of racial equality a higher priority within his administration.

The president addressed racial profiling in ways no previous president could when one of the nation's preeminent African American scholars, Harvard Professor Henry Louis Gates, was arrested in his own home and charged with disorderly conduct for displaying "loud and tumultuous behavior" when he was asked by Cambridge police for identification to prove that he was indeed the homeowner. For their part, the police said they were responding to a call from a neighbor who reported seeing "two black men with backpacks" trying to enter the house. In reality that afternoon, Professor Gates had returned home from a trip to China to find his front door stuck; he and the taxi driver were trying to get it open. The president, asked at a news conference to comment on the incident, said, "What I think we know, separate and apart from this incident, is that there's a long history in this country of African Americans and Latinos being stopped by law enforcement disproportionately. That's just a fact...."[19]

In February of 2012, when unarmed 17-year-old African American Trayvon Martin was fatally shot by George Zimmerman, a 28-year-old community watch

By permission of Chris Britt and Creators Syndicate, Inc.

This cartoon highlights the issue of racial profiling; however, as you know from the description of the incident in the text, Professor Gates was confronted and later arrested in his home during daylight hours. Why would the cartoonist draw this scene at night? How is the fact that neighborhood racial segregation is still prevalent in the United States related to this incident and the way it has been portrayed by the cartoonist?

16. Lawrence D. Bobo et al., "Through the Eyes of Black America," *Public Perspective,* May/June 2001, p. 13.
17. Ibid., p. 15, Figure 2.
18. Barack Obama, "A More Perfect Union," Transcript of speech delivered, March 18, 2008, at the Constitution Center in Philadelphia, PA. http://www.npr.org/templates/story/story.php?storyId=88478467
19. "Obama Addresses Race and Gates Incident," *Washington Post,* July 23, 2009.

coordinator in the gated Florida community where the shooting took place, President Obama spoke in highly personal terms in acknowledging the racial overtones of the incident: "Obviously, this is a tragedy; we all have to do some soul searching to find out why something like this happened. But my main message is to the parents of Trayvon Martin. You know, if I had a son, he'd look like Trayvon. And, you know, I think they are right to expect that all of us as Americans are going to take this with the seriousness it deserves and that we're going to get to the bottom of exactly what happened."[20] Despite the civil rights movement and civil rights legislation, and despite the election of the first black president, many African Americans continue to feel a sense of injustice in matters of race, and this feeling is often not apparent to, or appreciated by, the majority of white America.

Women's Campaign for Equal Rights

Like African Americans and other minorities, women also have had to make a claim for equality. Political citizenship requires personal autonomy (the ability to think and act for oneself), but at the founding, the prevailing opinion about women was that they were not endowed with reason. During the first phase of this campaign, the primary political goal of women was to obtain the right to vote.

Early Women's Political Movements

The first political cause in which women became actively engaged was the movement to abolish slavery. When the World Antislavery Convention was held in London in 1840, women delegates were barred from active participation. Partly in response to this rebuff, two American delegates, Lucretia Mott and Elizabeth Cady Stanton, returned from that meeting with plans to work for women's rights in the United States.

In 1848, Mott and Stanton organized the first women's rights convention in Seneca Falls, New York. The 300 people who attended the two-day event debated a wide variety of issues important for expanding women's social, civil, and religious rights including access to education and employment, marriage and divorce reform, and most controversial of all, **suffrage**. Attendees approved a Declaration of Sentiments modeled in word and spirit on the Declaration of Independence: "We hold these truths to be self-evident: that all men and *women* are created equal." Groups that supported women's rights held similar conventions in cities in the Midwest and East.

With the outbreak of the Civil War, advocates of women's rights were urged to put their support behind the war effort and women in the North and South dedicated themselves to their respective causes. In 1866 the American Equal Rights Association (AERA) was formed to advance the cause of universal suffrage, but tensions arose immediately between those whose first priority was black male suffrage and those who were dedicated first to women's suffrage. The failure to include women in the Fifteenth Amendment resulted in the dissolution of the AERA and the formation of two rival women's suffrage organizations.

Women's Suffrage Associations

Susan B. Anthony and Elizabeth Cady Stanton formed the National Woman Suffrage Association (NWSA) in 1869 and dedicated themselves nearly exclusively

Suffrage
The right to vote; the franchise.

did you know?

Of all those in attendance at Seneca Falls, only one 19-year-old woman, Charlotte Woodward, lived long enough to exercise her right to vote.

---

20.   Michael D. Shear, "Obama Speaks Out on Trayvon Martin Killing," *The New York Times*. March 23, 2012.

to advancing women's suffrage at the federal level by way of a constitutional amendment. In their view, women's suffrage was a means to achieve major improvements in the economic and social situation of women in the United States. Unlike Anthony and Stanton, Lucy Stone, a key founder of the American Woman Suffrage Association (AWSA), continued to support the Fifteenth Amendment restricted to males but vowed to support a Sixteenth Amendment dedicated to women's suffrage. The AWSA primarily focused its efforts on the states.

In the November election of 1872, several women attempted to vote under the revolutionary legal reasoning that the Fourteenth Amendment extended citizenship rights to all persons, and voting was among the privilege and immunities of citizenship. In Missouri, Virginia Minor cast her vote and was arrested for illegal voting. In the case of *Minor v. Happersett*, the U.S. Supreme Court ruled that since the federal Constitution did not explicitly grant women the right to vote, the states were free to decide who had the privilege of voting. For suffragists, this left two options—an amendment to the U.S. Constitution or a state-by-state campaign.

For the next 20 years, the two organizations worked along similar paths to educate the public and legislators, testifying before legislative committees, giving public speeches, and conducting public referendum campaigns on women's suffrage with varying degrees of success, as indicated by the map in Figure 5–2. Organizations such as the Women's Christian Temperance Union (WCTU) joined the campaign for suffrage, arguing that only women could be counted on to cast the votes necessary to prohibit the sale and consumption of alcohol. The combination of efforts yielded the movement's first successes. The western territory of Wyoming granted women the right to vote in 1869, and several state legislatures in other regions (outside the South) took up legislation

Figure 5–2 ▶ The Suffrage Map, Early August, 1920

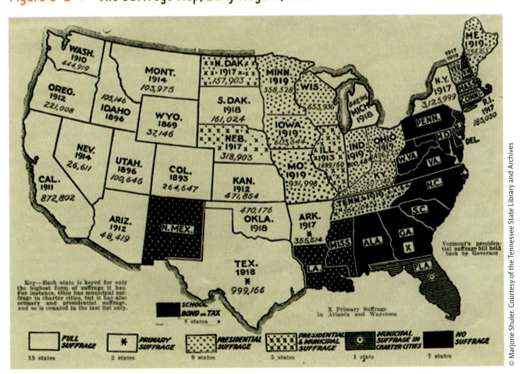

Source: From "Out of Subjection into Freedom" by Marjorie Shuler, published in *The Woman Citizen*, p. 360, September 4, 1920.

granting women the vote. Political scientist Lee Ann Banaszak calculated that between 1870 and 1890, an average of four states a year took up the question of women's suffrage.[21] In 1890, the two organizations joined forces, creating the National American Woman Suffrage Association (NAWSA), with only one goal—the enfranchisement of women—and continued lobbying in the states and western territories.

Opposition to women's suffrage came from a number of sources including the liquor industry, big business, and the church. Brewers and distillers were interested in preventing prohibition, and thus hoped to keep women from the voting booth. Industry was interested in limiting the reach of progressive policy to set wages and improve working conditions (both areas where female activists were heavily involved), and the church opposed suffrage primarily on ideological grounds. However, beginning in about 1880, the most persistent opponents of the suffrage cause emerged: other women. Suffragists at first dismissed the "antis" but later came to understand that they were a powerful, well-organized force dedicated to protecting traditional gender roles as well as women's social and economic privileges as they understood them.[22]

At the turn of the century, an impatient new generation of women introduced direct protest tactics they had observed while working alongside Emmeline Pankhurst in the British suffrage campaign. Harriet Stanton Blatch (Elizabeth Cady Stanton's daughter), Alice Paul, and Lucy Burns urged NAWSA to return to a federal amendment strategy. The new suffragists, as they were called, intended to *demand* their right to vote. They scheduled a massive parade in Washington, D.C., for March 3, 1913, timed to coincide with Woodrow Wilson's inauguration as president, scheduled for the next day. Alice Paul believed that Congress would only be persuaded to move the suffrage amendment forward if prodded to do so by the president. The parade attracted 8,000 marchers and more than half a million spectators.

Alice Paul continued to agitate for women's suffrage in ways that embarrassed NAWSA's leadership. She organized "Silent Sentinels" to stand in front of the White House with banners reading, "Mr. President, What Will You Do for Woman Suffrage?" These women were the first picketers ever to appear before the White House. When the United States joined the war against Germany in 1917, women were urged to set aside their goals in favor of the overall war

Silent Sentinels posted in front of the White House gates. The women were often arrested and attacked by onlookers, but the protests continued. Long prison terms were imposed in an attempt to scare women away. Women who could not themselves stand on the picket line sent money to support the families of those who were jailed. Women in jail organized hunger strikes only to be force-fed through the nose.

Library of Congress, Prints & Photographs Division, LC-USZ62-31799

21. Lynne E. Ford, *Women and Politics: The Pursuit of Equality.* (Boston: Cengage Learning Wadsworth, 2011).
22. Susan E. Marshall, *Splintered Sisterhood: Gender and Class in the Campaign Against Women's Suffrage* (Madison, WI: University of Wisconsin Press, 1997).

effort. Paul refused and formed the National Woman's Party (NWP) to bring even greater attention to women's disenfranchisement.

Meanwhile NAWSA members, under the leadership of Carrie Chapman Catt, were pursuing the "winning plan," which entailed a two-pronged lobbying strategy focused on both federal and state legislators. In the end, scholars agree that it was the combination of patient lobbying by NAWSA members and the more militant tactics of the NWP that resulted in Congress passing the suffrage amendment in May 1919. In Tennessee, the last state required to win ratification, the amendment passed by one vote on August 26, 1920. The Nineteenth Amendment reads: "The right of citizens of the United States to vote shall not be denied or abridged by the United States or by any State on account of sex."

■ Learning Outcome 4

The United States was neither the first nor the last to give women the vote. New Zealand introduced universal suffrage in 1893, while Kuwait allowed women to vote and seek public office for the first time in 2005. In 2011 King Abdullah of Saudi Arabia granted women the right to vote and run in future municipal elections, next scheduled for 2015 (see Table 5–1).

The Second Wave Women's Movement

After gaining the right to vote in 1920, women did not flock to the polls in large numbers, nor did many of the thousands of women who had lobbied for and against suffrage seek political office. There was little by way of an organized women's movement again until the second wave began in the 1960s. The civil rights movement of that decade resulted in a growing awareness of rights for all groups, including women. Women's increased participation in the workforce and the publication of Betty Friedan's *The Feminine Mystique* in 1963 focused national attention on the unequal status of women in American life.

In 1966, Betty Friedan and others who were dissatisfied with existing women's organizations, and especially with the failure of the Equal Employment Opportunity Commission to address discrimination against women, formed the National Organization for Women (NOW). NOW immediately adopted a blanket resolution designed "to bring women into full participation in the mainstream of American society *now*, exercising all the privileges and responsibilities thereof in truly equal partnership with men."

The second wave gained additional impetus from young women who entered politics to support the civil rights movement or to oppose the Vietnam War. Many of them found that despite the egalitarian principles of these movements, women remained in second-class positions. In the late 1960s, "women's liberation" organizations began to spring up on college campuses and women organized "consciousness-raising groups,"

Table 5—1 ▶ WOMEN'S VOTING RIGHTS AROUND THE WORLD Selected Countries, Year Women's Suffrage Granted

Year	Country
1893	New Zealand
1902	Austria
1913	Norway
1918	Canada
1919	Germany
1920	United States
1928	United Kingdom
1930	Turkey
1934	Cuba
1939	El Salvador
1944	France
1945	Japan
1947	Mexico
1948	Israel
1949	China
1950	India
1956	Egypt
1961	Rwanda
1964	Afghanistan
1965	Sudan
1971	Switzerland
1974	Jordan
1980	Iraq
1994	South Africa
2005	Kuwait
2015*	Saudi Arabia

*projected, next municipal elections scheduled for 2015
Source: Center for the American Woman and Politics

Beyond Our Borders

THE CAMPAIGN FOR WOMEN'S RIGHTS AROUND THE WORLD

Although in the last several decades women's rights have emerged as a global issue, progress has been slow. The campaign for women's rights in countries where cultural or legal practices perpetuate the inequality of women is especially difficult. December 2009 marked the 30th anniversary of the United Nations' adoption of the Convention on the Elimination of All Forms of Discrimination against Women (CEDAW), an international treaty to promote the adoption of national laws, policies, and practices to ensure that women and girls live free from violence, have access to high-quality education, and have the right to participate fully in the economic, political, and social sectors of their society. Although it has been ratified by 186 countries, the United States is one of only seven nations that have not ratified. International agreements such as CEDAW convey a set of universal ethical standards and global norms regarding human rights.

THE PROBLEM OF VIOLENCE

Most people consider the right to be free from violence as one of the most basic human rights. Women's rights advocates point out that this right is threatened in societies that do not accept the premise that men and women are equal. Some parts of India, for example, implicitly tolerate the practice of dowry killing. (A dowry is a sum of money given to a husband by the bride's family.) In a number of cases, husbands, dissatisfied with the size of dowries, have killed their wives in order to remarry for a "better deal"—a crime that is rarely prosecuted.

THE SITUATION IN AFGHANISTAN

In 2001, a startling documentary, *Behind the Veil,* was aired repeatedly on CNN. A courageous female reporter had secretly filmed Afghan women being beaten in the streets, killed in public for trivial offenses, and subjugated in extreme ways. Women's rights became a major issue in our foreign policy. Americans learned that Afghan girls were barred from schools, and by law women were not allowed to work. Women who had lost

Iraqi Girls wait for the start of class at the Eastern Secondary School in Baghdad. The role of women in the new Iraq remains uncertain. What negative consequences could result if discriminatory laws forced Iraqi women—among the region's most educated— to retreat to their homes?

their husbands during Afghanistan's civil wars were forced into begging and prostitution. Women had no access to medical care. Any woman found with an unrelated man could be executed by stoning, and many were.

NATION BUILDING AND WOMEN'S RIGHTS

After the collapse of the Taliban regime, the United States and its allies were able to influence the status of Afghan women. The draft constitution of Afghanistan, adopted in January 2004, gave women equality before the law and 20 percent of the seats in the National Assembly. Much of the country remained outside the control of the national government, however. Women continue to face abuse, including arson attacks on girls' schools, forced marriages, and reimposition of the all-covering burka garment.

Women in Iraq had enjoyed greater equality than in most Arab nations. In line with the secular ideology of the Baath Party, Saddam Hussein's government tended to treat men and women alike. A problem for the U.S.–led Coalition Provisional Authority (CPA) that governed Iraq until June 2004 was ensuring that women did not lose ground under the new regime. Some members of the Iraqi Governing Council, for example, advocated traditional Islamic laws that would have deprived women of equal rights. Women's organizations campaigned against these provisions, and they were vetoed by the CPA. The interim Iraqi constitution, adopted in March 2004, allotted 25 percent of the seats in the parliament to women. Following the 2010 election, women occupied 82 of 325 seats in parliament, or 25.2 percent (considerably higher than the 17 percent held by women in the United States).

FOR CRITICAL ANALYSIS

1. *Is it fair or appropriate for one country to judge the cultural practices of another? Why or why not?*

2. *What universal norms of gender equality, if any, should prevail? Is an international treaty such as CEDAW an effective tool to promote equality across cultures? Why has the United States failed to ratify CEDAW?*

AP Photo/Alexander Zemlianichenko

in which they discussed how gender affected their lives. The new women's movement emerged as a major social force by 1970.

Historian Nancy Cott contends that the word *feminism* first began to be used around 1910.[23] At that time, **feminism** meant, as it does today, political, social, and economic equality for women. It is difficult to measure the support for feminism at present because the word means different things to different people. When the dictionary definition of *feminist*—"someone who supports political, economic, and social equality for women"—was read to respondents in a survey, 67 percent labeled themselves as feminists.[24] In the absence of such prompting, however, the term *feminist* (like the term *liberal*) implies radicalism to many people, who therefore shy away from it. Young women have launched a third wave of feminism embracing a multitude of perspectives on what it means to be a feminist woman.[25]

The Equal Rights Amendment. Leaders of NOW and other women's rights advocates sought to eradicate gender inequality through a constitutional amendment. The proposed Equal Rights Amendment (ERA), first introduced in Congress in 1923 by leaders of the National Woman's Party, states: "Equality of rights under the law shall not be denied or abridged by the United States or by any state on account of sex." For decades the amendment was not even given a hearing in Congress, but finally it was approved by both chambers and sent to the state legislatures for ratification in 1972.

As was noted in Chapter 2, any constitutional amendment must be ratified by the legislatures (or conventions) in three-fourths of the states. Since the early 1900s, most proposed amendments have required that ratification occur within seven years of Congress's adoption of the amendment. Although states competed to be the first to ratify the ERA, by 1977 only 35 of the necessary 38 states had ratified the amendment. Congress granted a rare extension, but the remaining three states could not be added by the 1982 deadline even though the ERA was supported by numerous national party platforms, six presidents, and both chambers of Congress.

As with the antisuffrage efforts, the staunchest opponents to the ERA were other women. Many women perceived the goals pursued by feminists as a threat to their way of life. At the head of the countermovement was Republican Phyllis Schlafly and her conservative organization, Eagle Forum. Eagle Forum's "Stop ERA" campaign found significant support among fundamentalist religious groups and other conservative organizations. The campaign was a major force in blocking the ratification of the ERA, although 21 states have passed such amendments to their own constitutions.

Three-State Strategy. Had the ERA been ratified by 38 states, it would have become the Twenty-seventh Amendment to the Constitution. Instead, that place is occupied by the "Madison Amendment" governing congressional pay raises, first sent to the states in 1789 but not actually ratified until 1992. ERA supporters argue that acceptance of the Madison Amendment means that Congress has the power to maintain the legal viability of the ERA and the existing 35 state ratifications leaving supporters just three states to achieve final

Feminism
The philosophy of political, economic, and social equality for women and the gender consciousness sufficient to mobilize women for change.

did you know?
Seventy-two years passed between the time the Declaration of Independence was signed in 1776 and women first demanded the vote at the Seneca Falls Convention in 1848; it took another 72 years for women to win suffrage via the Nineteenth Amendment, ratified in 1920; and it took another 72 years before more than two women were elected to serve in the U.S. Senate at the same time (1992).

23. Nancy F. Cott, The *Grounding of Modern Feminism* (New Haven, CT: Yale University Press, 1987).
24. Nancy E. McGlen and Karen O'Connor, *Women, Politics, and American Society*, 4th ed. (Upper Saddle River, NJ: Prentice Hall, 2004).
25. See, for example, Jessica Valenti, *Full Frontal Feminism: A Young Woman's Guide to Why Feminism Matters* (Emeryville, CA: Seal Press, 2007); and Jennifer Baumgardner and Amy Richards, *Manifesta: Young Women, Feminism, and the Future* (New York: Farrar, Straus and Giroux, 2000).

ratification. The legal rationale for the three-state strategy was developed by three law students in a law review article published in 1997.[26] Support for constitutional equality remains high in the United States; however, mobilizing support for ratification of the ERA in the future may prove difficult. A 2001 poll found that although 96 percent of those polled supported constitutional equality for women and men, 72 percent mistakenly believed that the U.S. Constitution already includes the Equal Rights Amendment.[27]

Challenging Gender Discrimination in the Courts and Legislatures.

With the failure of the ERA, feminists turned their attention to national and state laws that would guarantee the equality of women. In 1978, the Civil Rights Act of 1964 was amended by the Pregnancy Discrimination Act, which prohibits discrimination in employment against pregnant women. In addition, Title IX of the Education Amendments was passed in 1972; it banned sex discrimination at all levels and in all aspects of education and dealt with issues of sexual harassment, pregnancy, parental status, and marital status. Although best known for increasing women's access to sports, the legislation's most significant impact has been on equalizing admissions to professional programs, financial aid, and educational facilities. Prior to Title IX, women's entrance into professional programs in law, medicine, science, and engineering was limited by quotas. In 1996, the Supreme Court held that the state-financed Virginia Military Institute's policy of accepting only males violated the equal protection clause, leading to the admission of women at The Citadel, the state-financed military college in South Carolina, as well.[28]

Women's rights organizations challenged discriminatory statutes and policies in the federal courts, contending that **gender discrimination** violated the Fourteenth Amendment's equal protection clause. Since the 1970s, the Supreme Court has tended to scrutinize gender classifications closely and has invalidated a number of such statutes and policies. For example, in 1977 the Court held that police and firefighting units cannot establish arbitrary rules, such as height and weight requirements, that tend to keep women from joining those occupations.[29] In 1983, the Court ruled that life insurance companies cannot charge different rates for women and men.[30]

A question that the Court has not ruled on is whether women should be allowed to participate in military combat. Generally, the Supreme Court has left this decision up to Congress and the Department of Defense. In 1994 Congress repealed the "risk rule" barring women from all combat situations. As a result over 90 percent of positions in the military are now open to women, and most experts think it is only a matter of time until full gender integration. Most recently, the navy has opened service on submarines to women, beginning in 2012. While technically women cannot be "assigned" to direct combat units, the wars in Iraq and Afghanistan have stretched the limits of that law, and more women have been "attached" to front-line units in combat support positions. Generally, the public supports increasing women's combat role. A 2009 poll found that 53 percent of those polled would favor permitting women to "join combat units, where they would be directly involved in the ground fighting."

Gender Discrimination
Any practice, policy, or procedure that denies equality of treatment to an individual or to a group because of gender.

26. Allison Held, Sheryl Herndon, and Danielle Stager, "The Equal Rights Amendment: Why the ERA Remains Legally Viable and Properly Before the States." *William & Mary Journal of Women and the Law,* Spring 1997, pp. 113–136.
27. *The ERA Campaign,* Issue #5, July 2001, accessed at http://eracampaignweb.kishosting.com/newsletter5.html.
28. *United States v. Virginia,* 518 U.S. 515 (1996).
29. *Dothard v. Rawlinson,* 433 U.S. 321 (1977).
30. *Arizona v. Norris,* 463 U.S. 1073 (1983).

Women in Politics Today

Today women make up just 18 percent of the U.S. Congress. The United States is ranked 80th among 190 nations by the Inter-Parliamentary Union based on the proportion of seats held by women in the lower house. Rwanda ranks first—in that nation, women hold 56 percent of seats in the Lower House.[31] The efforts of women's rights advocates have helped increase the number of women holding political offices at all levels of government. In 2007, Nancy Pelosi of California became the first female Speaker of the House, the most powerful member of the majority party and second in the line of succession to the presidency.

Although no woman has yet been nominated for president by a major political party, in 1984 Geraldine Ferraro became the Democratic nominee for vice president. In 2008 Hillary Rodham Clinton, senator from New York, became one of two final contenders for the presidential nomination of the Democratic Party, but ultimately lost to Barack Obama. In a surprise move, Senator John McCain chose Alaskan governor, Sarah Palin, for his running mate. However, only one woman was a candidate for the 2012 Republican presidential nomination. Congresswoman Michelle Bachman announced her campaign in June 2011 but withdrew from the race after coming in last in the Iowa caucuses in January 2012.

In recent presidential administrations, women have been more visible in cabinet posts. President Bill Clinton (1993–2001) appointed four women to his cabinet, more than any previous president. Madeleine Albright was appointed to serve as secretary of state, a first for a woman. President George W. Bush also appointed several women to cabinet positions, including Condoleezza Rice as his secretary of state in 2005.

Increasing numbers of women sit on federal judicial benches. President Ronald Reagan (1981–1989) was credited with a historic first when he appointed Sandra Day O'Connor to the Supreme Court in 1981. President Clinton appointed a second woman, Ruth Bader Ginsburg, to the Court. O'Connor retired from the Court in 2006. In 2009 President Barack Obama appointed

did you know?

As of November 2012 the United States ranked 80th of 190 nations based on the percentage of women serving in the lower house (U.S. House of Representatives), while Rwanda ranked first. Women make up just 18 percent of the U.S. House but hold 56 percent of the seats in the lower chamber of Rwanda's parliament.

The 112th Congress included 17 women in the U.S. Senate (shown here) and 75 women in the House of Representatives. The 113th Congress, elected in 2012, will have a record number of women, including 20 women in the U.S. Senate.

Photo by U.S. Senator Lisa Murkowski

31. Inter-Parliamentary Union, "Women in National Parliaments," accessed at http://www.ipu.org/wmn-e/classif.htm.

Federal Appeals Court Judge Sonia Sotomayor to fill the vacancy created by Justice David Souter's retirement. Justice Sotomayor is the first Latina to serve on the U.S. Supreme Court. In April 2010, Justice John Paul Stevens announced his retirement, giving President Obama the chance to make a second appointment to the Court. He selected Elena Kagan, the solicitor general of the United States, to fill the vacancy, thus increasing the number of women currently sitting on the Supreme Court to three.

Gender-Based Discrimination in the Workplace

Traditional cultural beliefs concerning the proper role of women in society continue to be evident not only in the political arena but also in the workplace. Since the 1960s, however, women have gained substantial protection against discrimination through laws mandating equal employment opportunities and equal pay.

Title VII of the Civil Rights Act of 1964

Title VII of the Civil Rights Act of 1964 prohibits gender discrimination in employment and has been used to strike down employment policies that discriminate against employees on the basis of gender. Even so-called protective policies have been held to violate Title VII if they have a discriminatory effect. In 1991, for example, the Supreme Court held that a fetal protection policy established by Johnson Controls, Inc., the country's largest producer of automobile batteries, violated Title VII. The policy required all women of childbearing age working in jobs that entailed periodic exposure to lead or other hazardous materials to prove that they were infertile or to transfer to other positions. The same requirement was not applied to men. Women who agreed to transfer often had to accept cuts in pay and reduced job responsibilities. The Court concluded that women who are "as capable of doing their jobs as their male counterparts may not be forced to choose between having a child and having a job."[32]

Sexual Harassment

Sexual Harassment
Unwanted physical or verbal conduct or abuse of a sexual nature that interferes with a recipient's job performance, creates a hostile work environment, or carries with it an implicit or explicit threat of adverse employment consequences.

The Supreme Court has also held that Title VII's prohibition of gender-based discrimination extends to **sexual harassment** in the workplace. Sexual harassment occurs when job opportunities, promotions, salary increases, and the like are given in return for sexual favors. A special form of sexual harassment, called hostile-environment harassment, occurs when an employee is subjected to sexual conduct or comments that interfere with the employee's job performance or are so pervasive or severe as to create an intimidating, hostile, or offensive environment.

In two 1998 cases, the Supreme Court clarified the responsibilities of employers in preventing sexual harassment. The Court ruled that employers must take reasonable care to prevent and promptly correct any sexually harassing behavior. Claims by the employer that it was unaware of the situation or that the victim suffered no tangible job consequences do not reduce liability.[33] In another 1998 case, *Oncale v. Sundowner Offshore Services, Inc.*,[34] the Supreme Court ruled that Title VII protection extends to same-sex harassment.

32. *United Automobile Workers v. Johnson Controls, Inc.,* 499 U.S. 187 (1991).
33. 524 U.S. 725 (1998) and 524 U.S. 742 (1998).
34. 523 U.S. 75 (1998).

Wage Discrimination

In 2010, largely as a result of the economic recession, women constituted the majority of U.S. workers. Although Title VII and other legislation since the 1960s have mandated equal employment opportunities for men and women, women continue to earn less, on average, than men do.

The Equal Pay Act of 1963. The issue of women's wages was first addressed during World War II (1939–1945), when the War Labor Board issued an "equal pay for women" policy largely to ensure that salaries remained high when men returned from war and reclaimed their jobs. The board's authority ended with the war. Although it was supported by the next three presidential administrations, the Equal Pay Act was not enacted until 1963 as an amendment to the Fair Labor Standards Act of 1938.

The Equal Pay Act requires employers to provide equal pay for substantially equal work. In other words, males cannot legally be paid more than females who perform essentially the same job. The Equal Pay Act did not address occupational segregation, the fact that certain types of jobs traditionally held by women pay lower wages than the jobs usually held by men. For example, more women than men are salesclerks and nurses, whereas more men than women are construction workers and truck drivers. Even if all clerks performing substantially similar jobs for a company earned the same salaries, they typically would still be earning less than the company's truck drivers.

When Congress passed the Equal Pay Act in 1963, a woman, on average, made 59 cents for every dollar earned by a man. Figures recently released by the U.S. Department of Labor suggest that women now earn 77.4 cents for every dollar that men earn, statistically unchanged from the two prior years. The wage gap is greater for minority women. In some areas, the wage gap is widening. According to the results of a General Accounting Office survey, female managers in 10 industries made less money relative to male managers in 2000 than they did in 1995.[35] A 2007 study on the gender pay gap for college graduates found that one year out of college, women working full time earn only 80 percent as much as their male peers, even among those men and women graduating with the same major and entering the same occupation. The same study found that women earn only 69 percent of men's wages 10 years out of college.[36]

The first bill President Obama signed after taking office in 2009 was the Lilly Ledbetter Fair Pay Act. The law is an example of congressional action undertaken specifically to overturn a decision by the U.S. Supreme Court. Lilly Ledbetter, an employee of Goodyear Tire and Rubber for 19 years, discovered that she was a victim of gender pay discrimination by an anonymous tip when she retired in 1998. She filed a complaint under Title VII, but in a 5-4 ruling the U.S. Supreme Court held that race and gender discrimination claims must be made within 180 days of the employer's discriminatory act.[37] As Justice Ruth Bader Ginsburg noted in her dissenting opinion, pay disparities often occur in small increments and over time, making them difficult to discover. The Ledbetter Act amends Title VII of the Civil Rights Act of 1964 by stating that the 180-day statute of limitations for filing an equal pay lawsuit regarding pay discrimination resets with each new discriminatory paycheck. It does not, however, provide

---

35. The results of this survey are online at www.gao.gov/audit.htm. To view a copy of the results, enter "GAO-02-156" in the search box. In 2004, the name of this agency was changed to the "Government Accountability Office."
36. Judy Goldberg Dey and Catherine Hill, "Behind the Pay Gap," AAUW Educational Foundation, April 2007.
37. *Ledbetter v. Goodyear Tire & Rubber* Co., 550 U.S. 618 (2007).

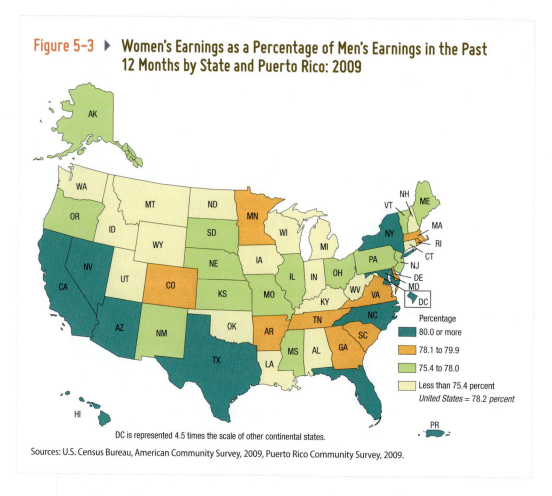

Figure 5–3 ▶ **Women's Earnings as a Percentage of Men's Earnings in the Past 12 Months by State and Puerto Rico: 2009**

Percentage
- 80.0 or more
- 78.1 to 79.9
- 75.4 to 78.0
- Less than 75.4 percent

United States = 78.2 percent

DC is represented 4.5 times the scale of other continental states.

Sources: U.S. Census Bureau, American Community Survey, 2009, Puerto Rico Community Survey, 2009.

any additional tools to combat wage discrimination or enforce provisions already in effect. Equal Pay Day, typically celebrated in April, marks the day each year on which women "catch up" to men in terms of wages. It is an occasion to call attention to the wage gap and to examine progress toward closing the wage gap between women and men (see Figure 5–3).

While women have made significant progress in the last decade toward equality in politics, education, and the workplace, traditional gender role expectations regarding children and family and the assignment of a disproportionate share of family responsibilities to women make achieving true equality a persistent challenge.

Voting Rights and the Young

The Twenty-sixth Amendment to the Constitution, ratified on July 1, 1971, reads as follows:

> *The right of citizens of the United States, who are eighteen years of age or older, to vote shall not be denied or abridged by the United States or by any State on account of age.*

Before this amendment was ratified, the age at which citizens could vote was 21 in most states. One of the arguments used for granting the right to 18-year-olds was that, because they could be drafted to fight in the country's wars, they had a stake in public policy. At the time, the example of the Vietnam War (1964–1975) was paramount. In the first election following ratification, 58 percent of 18- to 20-year-olds were registered to vote, and 48.4 percent reported voting. But by the 2000 presidential election, of the 11.5 million U.S. residents in the 18-to-20 age bracket,

50.7 percent were registered, and 41 percent reported that they had voted. In contrast, voter turnout among Americans aged 65 or older is very high, usually between 60 and 70 percent. People younger than 30 made up a larger share of the electorate in the 2012 presidential election than those 65 and older. Likewise, the share of the vote accounted for by those age 18 to 29 in 2012 rose from 18 to 19 percent.

Immigration, Latinos, and Civil Rights

■ **Learning Outcome 5**

Time and again, this nation has been challenged, changed, and culturally enriched by immigrant groups. Immigrants have faced challenges associated with living in a new and different political and cultural environment, overcoming language barriers, and often having to deal with discrimination in one form or another. The civil rights legislation passed during and since the 1960s has done much to counter the effects of prejudice against immigrant groups by ensuring that they obtain equal rights under the law.

One of the questions facing Americans and their political leaders today concerns the effect of immigration on American politics and government. This is especially true with regard to the Hispanic American or Latino community. With the influx of individuals from Latin American countries growing exponentially, issues related to immigration and Hispanic Americans will continue to gain greater attention in years to come. While those in the Latino community did not have to mount a separate campaign to gain access to constitutional suffrage like African Americans and women, they nonetheless have been subject to public and private forms of discrimination.

Mexican American Civil Rights

The history of Mexican Americans spans more than 400 years and varies by region in the United States. Many of the most important challenges to discrimination took place in Texas and California and parallel the claims to rights made by African Americans and women. For example, Mexican American children were forced to attend segregated schools, referred to as "Mexican schools," in California. In a case that preceded *Brown v. Board of Education*, the U.S. Court of Appeals for the Ninth Circuit ruled in 1947 that segregated schools were unconstitutional. In this narrow decision, the court found that while California law provided for separate education for "children of Chinese, Japanese, or Mongolian parentage," the law did not include children of Mexican descent and therefore it was unlawful to segregate them.[38] California governor Earl Warren, who would later be appointed chief justice of the U.S. Supreme Court and preside over *Brown*, signed a law in 1947 repealing all school segregation statutes.

In 1954, an agricultural worker named Pete Hernandez was convicted of murder by an all-white jury in Texas. Hernandez maintained that juries could not be impartial unless they included members of other races. The U.S. Supreme Court ruled in *Hernandez v. Texas* that Mexican Americans and other racial groups were entitled to equal protection under the Fourteenth Amendment.[39] The Court ordered that Mr. Hernandez be retried with a jury composed without regard to race or ethnicity.

In the realm of voting rights, Mexican Americans were covered under the 1965 Voting Rights Act but they did not enjoy the singular focus of federal registration oversight as African Americans did. Poll taxes (until ended by the Twenty-fourth Amendment in 1964) limited Mexican Americans' electoral participation, particularly in Texas and California. Political organizing in the 1960s and 1970s by

---

38. *Mendez v. Westminster School District*, 64 F. Supp. 544 (C.D. Cal. 1946), aff'd, 161 F. 2d 744 (9th Cir. 1947) (en banc).
39. *Hernandez v. Texas*, 347 U.S. 475 (1954).

groups such as the La Raza Unida Party, founded in Texas but active in other regions, increased minority representation at the local level. Although Mexican Americans potentially constitute a very large voting bloc, they tend to have low voter turnout rates, which scholars attribute to lower income and education rates as well as recent concerns over immigration status.

The Chicano movement is often characterized as an extension of the Mexican American civil rights movement but one focused on land rights, farmworkers' rights, education, and voting rights, as well as the eradication of ethnic stereotypes and promotion of a positive group consciousness. At first a label with negative connotations, in the 1960s "Chicano" became associated with ethnic pride and self-determination. Movement leaders such as Cesar Chavez and Delores Huerta were instrumental in founding a number of organizations that, in addition to focusing on labor rights, offered members of the community language classes, assistance in obtaining citizenship, and advocacy for Spanish language rights (see Chapter 7). The Chicano movement has galvanized and trained successive generations of community and political activists. Recent campaigns have focused on the plight of immigrant workers in low-wage jobs such as janitors, truck drivers, and domestics.

The Continued Influx of Immigrants

Every year, about 1 million people immigrate to this country, and those who were born on foreign soil now constitute more than 12 percent of the U.S. population—twice the percentage of 30 years ago.

Since 1977, more than 80 percent of immigrants have come from Latin America or Asia. Latinos have overtaken African Americans as the nation's largest minority. In 2011, 16 percent of the U.S. population identified itself as Hispanic or Latino, 13 percent as African American or black, and 5 percent as Asian. Non-Latino white Americans made up about 66 percent of the population (see Figure 5-4). If current immigration rates continue, minority groups

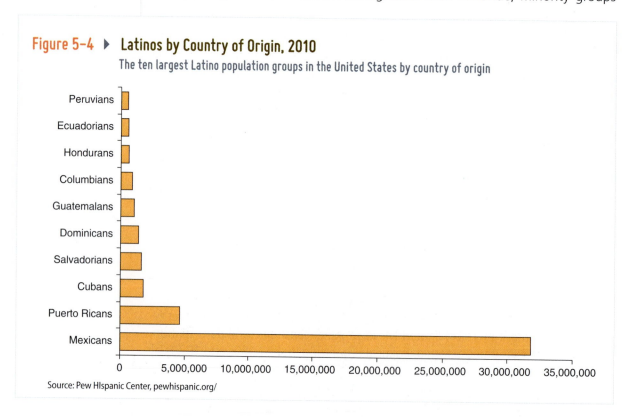

Figure 5-4 ▶ Latinos by Country of Origin, 2010

The ten largest Latino population groups in the United States by country of origin

Source: Pew Hispanic Center, pewhispanic.org/

collectively will constitute the "majority" of Americans by the year 2042, according to estimates by the U.S. Census Bureau. If Latinos, African Americans, and perhaps Asians were to form coalitions, they could increase their political strength dramatically and would have the numerical strength to make significant changes. However, as noted in earlier discussions of civil rights campaigns and social movements, coalitions are difficult to form when common interests are not immediately obvious.

Illegal Immigration

In the past few years, the issue of illegal immigration has become both a hot political issue and a serious policy concern. As many as 12 million undocumented aliens reside and work in the United States. Immigrants typically come to the United States to work, and their labor continues to be in high demand, particularly in construction and farming.

One civil rights question that often surfaces is whether the government should provide services to those who enter the country illegally. Residents of southwestern states complain about the need to shore up border control and perceive that undocumented immigrants place a burden on government-provided social services and the health care industry. Some schools have become crowded with the children of undocumented immigrants. Often, these children require greater attention because of their inability to speak English, although many are themselves native-born U.S. citizens.

On April 23, 2010, Arizona governor Jan Brewer signed a highly controversial bill on immigration designed to identify, prosecute, and deport illegal immigrants. The law makes the failure to carry immigration documents a crime and gives the police broad powers to detain anyone *suspected* of being in the country illegally. Governor Brewer said the law "represents another tool for our state to use as we work to solve a crisis we did not create and the federal government has refused to fix." On June 25, 2012, the U.S. Supreme Court issued a split decision, upholding part of the Arizona law and rejecting other provisions on the grounds that they interfered with the federal government's role in setting immigration policy. The court unanimously affirmed the law's requirement that police check the immigration status of people they detain and suspect to be in the country illegally emphasizing that state law enforcement officials already possessed the discretion to ask about immigration status. The court rejected other portions of the law that criminalized activities such as seeking employment. Leaders in the Latino community maintain that the law will increase racial and ethnic profiling and create a climate of fear among residents of the state. Justice Anthony Kennedy, writing for the majority, left the door open to re-considering the Arizona law if after implementation there is evidence that it leads to illegal racial and ethnic profiling.

The Arizona law offers an opportunity to examine generational differences in attitudes about immigration. A Brookings Institution report found that Arizona has the largest "cultural generation gap" between older Americans, who are largely white (83 percent in Arizona), and children under 18, who are increasingly members of minorities (57 percent in Arizona).[40] This gap fuels conflict over policy issues such as immigration and funding allocations for education and health care. Because older people are more likely to vote and less likely to be connected to the perspectives of youth, the gap also has the potential to further alienate young people from direct political participation. A recent

40.   William H. Frey, *The State of Metropolitan America* (Washington, DC: Brookings Institution, 2010).

poll found that Americans 45 and older were more likely than young people to restrict immigration, a finding attributed to the multicultural environment young people today inhabit.

Citizenship. Members of Congress from both parties have proposed legislation that would either immediately or gradually extend citizenship to undocumented immigrants now residing in the United States. Although not all Americans agree that citizenship should be extended to illegal immigrants, the greater Latino community in the United States has taken up the cause. Numerous protests and marches calling for citizenship occurred in 2006, with more than 1 million individuals participating in demonstrations on May 1, 2006, alone. To be sure, the citizenship question will be an important political topic for the foreseeable future.

One expedited path to citizenship for immigrants with permanent resident status and permission to work (green card holders) is through military service. Noncitizens have served in the military since the Revolutionary War, and today about 29,000 noncitizens serve in uniform. Service members are eligible for expedited citizenship under a July 2002 executive order, an opportunity realized by nearly 43,000 men and women since September 11, 2001.[41]

Accommodating Diversity with Bilingual Education. The continuous influx of immigrants into this country presents another ongoing challenge—how to overcome language barriers. Bilingual education programs, first introduced in the 1960s, teach children in their native language while also teaching them English. Congress authorized bilingual education programs in 1968 when it passed the Bilingual Education Act, which was intended primarily to help Hispanic children learn English. In a 1974 case, *Lau v. Nichols*,[42] the Supreme Court bolstered the claim that children have a right to bilingual education. In that case, the Court ordered a California school district to provide special programs for Chinese students with language difficulties if a substantial number of these children attended school in the district. However, bilingual programs have more recently come under attack. In 1998, California residents passed a ballot initiative that called for the end of bilingual education programs in that state. The law allowed schools to implement English-immersion programs instead. In these programs, students are given intensive instruction in English for a limited period of time and then placed in regular classrooms. The law was immediately challenged in court on the grounds that it unconstitutionally discriminated against non-English-speaking groups. A federal district court, however, concluded that the new law did not violate the equal protection clause and allowed the law to stand, thus ending bilingual education efforts in California.

Affirmative Action

■ **Learning Outcome 6:**
Define the goal of affirmative action, and explain why this approach is controversial in the United States.

As noted earlier in this chapter, the Civil Rights Act of 1964 prohibited discrimination against any person on the basis of race, color, national origin, religion, or gender. The act also established the right to equal opportunity in employment. A basic problem remained, however: Minority groups and women, because of past discrimination, often lacked the education and skills to compete effectively in the marketplace. In 1965, the federal government attempted to remedy this problem

---

41.   Department of Defense, MAVNI Fact Sheet, accessed at http://www.defense.gov/news/mavni-fact-sheet.pdf.
42.   414 U.S. 563 (1974).

by implementing the concept of affirmative action. **Affirmative action** policies attempt to "level the playing field" by giving special preferences in educational admissions and employment decisions to groups that have been discriminated against in the past.

In 1965, President Lyndon B. Johnson ordered that affirmative action policies be undertaken to remedy the effects of past discrimination. All government agencies, including those of state and local governments, were required to implement such policies. Additionally, affirmative action requirements were applied to companies that sell goods or services to the federal government and to institutions that receive federal funds. Affirmative action policies were also required whenever an employer had been ordered to develop such a plan by a court or by the Equal Employment Opportunity Commission because of evidence of past discrimination. Finally, labor unions that had been found to discriminate against women or minorities in the past were required to establish and follow affirmative action plans.

The *Bakke* Case

The first Supreme Court case addressing the constitutionality of affirmative action plans examined a program implemented by the University of California at Davis. Allan Bakke, a white student who had been denied admission to the medical school, discovered that his academic record was better than those of some of the minority applicants who had been admitted to the program. He sued the University of California regents, alleging **reverse discrimination**. The UC–Davis Medical School had held 16 places out of 100 for educationally "disadvantaged students" each year, and admitted to using race as a criterion for these 16 admissions. Bakke claimed that his exclusion from medical school violated his rights under the Fourteenth Amendment's provision for equal protection of the laws. The trial court agreed. On appeal, the California Supreme Court agreed also. Finally, the regents of the university appealed to the United States Supreme Court.

In 1978, the Supreme Court handed down its decision in *Regents of the University of California v. Bakke*.[43] The Court did not rule against affirmative action programs. Rather, it held that Bakke must be admitted to the UC–Davis Medical School because its admissions policy had used race as the sole criterion for the 16 "minority" positions. Justice Lewis Powell, speaking for the Court, indicated that while race can be considered "as a factor" among others in admissions (and presumably hiring) decisions, race cannot be the sole factor. So affirmative action programs, but not specific quota systems, were upheld as constitutional.

The *Bakke* decision did not end the controversy over affirmative action programs. At issue in the current debate over affirmative action programs is whether favoring one group violates the equal protection clause of the Fourteenth Amendment to the Constitution as it applies to all other groups.

Further Limits on Affirmative Action

Several cases decided during the 1980s and 1990s placed further limits on affirmative action programs by subjecting any federal, state, or local affirmative action program that uses racial or ethnic classifications as the basis for making decisions to "strict scrutiny" by the courts (to be constitutional, a discriminatory law or action must be narrowly tailored to meet a *compelling* government interest).[44] Yet in two cases involving the University of Michigan, the Supreme

Affirmative Action
A policy in educational admissions or job hiring that gives special attention or compensatory treatment to traditionally disadvantaged groups in an effort to overcome present effects of past discrimination.

Reverse Discrimination
The charge that an affirmative action program discriminates against those who do not have minority status.

43. 438 U.S. 265 (1978).
44. 515 U.S. 200 (1995).

Court indicated that limited affirmative action programs continue to be acceptable and that diversity is a legitimate goal. The Court struck down the affirmative action plan used for undergraduate admissions at the university, which automatically awarded a substantial number of points to applicants based on minority status.[45] At the same time, it approved the admissions plan used by the law school, which took race into consideration as part of a complete examination of each applicant's background.[46]

The Supreme Court will review the constitutionality of a broad affirmative action program used to admit the freshman class at the University of Texas at Austin.[47] (Justice Elena Kagan has recused herself because of her involvement in the case while working in the solicitor general's office.) The University of Texas adopted the admissions plan at issue in the case soon after the 2003 ruling in the case of *Grutter v. Bollinger* said that race could be taken into account as one of the factors in helping to achieve racial diversity. The Texas plan in this new case goes considerably further than seeking diversity across the entering class of students; the plan also seeks to achieve that goal among the major fields of study, and at the classroom level. Abigail Noel Fisher, a student who was not admitted to the Texas campus, contends that she was denied admission on account of her race while minority students with lower grade point averages than hers were admitted under the diversity plan. A couple of details in this case history indicate that while the Court may be interested in revisiting affirmative action as applied to university admissions, the justices may disagree on important points. First, University of Texas officials argued that Fisher had elected to go to another school, Louisiana State University, and has since graduated, making her ineligible to seek readmission as a freshman at UT-Austin. However, the Court first considered the petition in early January 2012 but did not agree to take the case until the docket was full, thus delaying any decision until after the fall 2012 election.

State Ballot Initiatives

A ballot initiative passed by California voters in 1996 amended that state's constitution to end all state-sponsored affirmative action programs. The law was challenged immediately in court by civil rights groups and others arguing that it violated the Fourteenth Amendment by denying racial minorities and women the equal protection of the laws. In 1997, however, a federal appellate court upheld the constitutionality of the amendment. Thus, affirmative action is now illegal in California in all state-sponsored institutions, including state agencies and educational institutions. In 1998, Washington voters also approved a law banning affirmative action in that state.

Making Amends for Past Discrimination through Reparations

Reparation

Compensation, monetary or nonmonetary (e.g., formal apology), to make amends for a past transgression or harm.

While affirmative action programs attempt to remedy past discrimination by "leveling the playing field," reparations are a way of apologizing for past discriminatory actions and providing compensation. The legal philosophy of **reparation** requires that victims of a harm be replenished by those who inflicted the harm. In criminal courts, for example, defendants are sometimes sentenced to perform community service or provide restitution to the victim in lieu of jail time. When

45. *Gratz v. Bollinger*, 539 U.S. 244 (2003).
46. *Grutter v. Bollinger*, 539 U.S. 306 (2003).
47. *Fisher v. University of Texas at Austin*, Docket number 11–435.

Library of Congress, Prints and Photographs Division, LC-USZ62-113923

Asians in America have experienced a long history of discrimination. In 1922, for example, the Supreme Court ruled that Asians were not white and therefore were not entitled to full citizenship rights (*Ozawa v. U.S.*, 1922). Following the Japanese attack on Pearl Harbor in 1941, Executive Order 9066 required the exclusion of all people of Japanese ancestry (including U.S. citizens) from the Pacific coast. Approximately 110,000 people were forcibly relocated to internment camps. In 1944, the Supreme Court upheld the constitutionality of the war relocation camps *(Korematsu v. U.S.)*, citing national security concerns during a time of war.

reparation is used relative to a class of people who experienced discrimination, such as descendants of former slaves or Japanese Americans who were interned during World War II, restitution is made by the government. In 1988, Congress passed legislation that apologized for and admitted that wartime government action against Japanese Americans was based on racial prejudice and war hysteria. Over $1.6 billion has been disbursed to Japanese Americans who were themselves interned or to their heirs.

Proposals for similar forms of restitution for the descendants of slaves in the United States have been under discussion for some time, with little consensus around the issue (see the Politics with a Purpose feature). On July 29, 2008, the U.S. House of Representatives passed a resolution (with 120 cosponsors from both parties) apologizing to African Americans for the institution of slavery, Jim Crow laws, and other practices that have denied people equal opportunity under the law. Democrat Steve Cohen from Tennessee introduced the resolution, saying, "... only a great country can recognize and admit its mistakes and then travel forth to create indeed a more perfect union...."[48] The U.S. Senate followed with a similar resolution of apology the following summer. The resolutions did not contain any mention of financial compensation for descendants of slaves.

When President Obama signed into law the 2010 Defense Appropriations Act on December 19, 2009, it included a footnote, entitled Section 8113, otherwise known as an "apology to Native Peoples of the United States." The passage of the apology resolution went largely unnoticed but served as the culmination of a five-year attempt by Senator Sam Brownback of Kansas to convince Congress to adopt a formal apology for the government's past treatment of Native Americans. The condensed resolution conveys the nation's regret "for the many instances of

48. "Congress Apologizes for Slavery, Jim Crow," National Public Radio, July 30, 2008.

violence, maltreatment, and neglect inflicted on Native Peoples by citizens of the United States," as the condensed resolution states. The resolution was not accompanied by monetary reparations or funds for new programs.

Special Protection for Older Americans

Age discrimination is potentially the most widespread form of discrimination, because anyone—regardless of race, color, national origin, or gender—could be a victim at some point in life. In an attempt to protect older employees from such discriminatory practices, Congress passed the Age Discrimination in Employment Act (ADEA) in 1967. The act, which applies to employers, employment agencies, and labor organizations and covers individuals over the age of 40, prohibits discrimination against individuals on the basis of age unless age is shown to be a bona fide occupational qualification reasonably necessary to the normal operation of the particular business. To succeed in a suit for age discrimination, an employee must prove that the employer's action, such as a decision to fire the employee, was motivated, at least in part, by age bias. Even if an older worker is replaced by a younger worker who is also over the age of 40, the older worker is entitled to bring a suit under the ADEA.[49] Most states have their own prohibitions against age discrimination in employment, and some are stronger than the federal provisions.

■ Learning Outcome 5

Securing Rights for Persons with Disabilities

Persons with disabilities did not fall under the protective umbrella of the Civil Rights Act of 1964. In 1973, however, Congress passed the Rehabilitation Act, which prohibited discrimination against persons with disabilities in programs receiving federal aid. A 1978 amendment to the act established the Architectural and Transportation Barriers Compliance Board. Regulations for ramps, elevators, and the like in all federal buildings were implemented. Congress passed the Education for All Handicapped Children Act in 1975. It guarantees that all children with disabilities will receive an "appropriate" education. The most significant federal legislation to protect the rights of persons with disabilities, however, is the Americans with Disabilities Act (ADA), which Congress passed in 1990.

The Americans with Disabilities Act of 1990

The ADA requires that all public buildings and public services be accessible to persons with disabilities. The act also mandates that employers must reasonably accommodate the needs of workers or potential workers with disabilities. Physical access means ramps; handrails; wheelchair-accessible restrooms, counters, drinking fountains, telephones, and doorways; and easily accessible mass transit. In addition, other steps must be taken to comply with the act. Car rental companies must provide cars with hand controls for disabled drivers. Telephone companies are required to have operators to pass on messages from speech-impaired persons who use telephones with keyboards.

The ADA requires employers to "reasonably accommodate" the needs of persons with disabilities unless to do so would cause the employer to suffer an "undue hardship." The ADA defines persons with disabilities as persons who have physical or mental impairments that "substantially limit" their everyday activities. Health

---

49. *O'Connor v. Consolidated Coin Caterers Corp.*, 517 U.S. 308 (1996).

conditions that have been considered disabilities under federal law include blindness, alcoholism, heart disease, cancer, muscular dystrophy, cerebral palsy, paraplegia, diabetes, acquired immune deficiency syndrome (AIDS), and infection with the human immunodeficiency virus (HIV) that causes AIDS.

The ADA does not require that *unqualified* applicants with disabilities be hired or retained. If a job applicant or an employee with a disability, with reasonable accommodation, can perform essential job functions, however, then the employer must make the accommodation. Required accommodations may include installing ramps for a wheelchair, establishing more flexible working hours, creating or modifying job assignments, and creating or improving training materials and procedures.

Limiting the Scope and Applicability of the ADA

Beginning in 1999, the Supreme Court has issued a series of decisions that effectively limit the scope of the ADA. In 1999, for example, the Court held in *Sutton v. United Airlines, Inc.*[50] that a condition (in this case, severe nearsightedness) that can be corrected with medication or a corrective device (in this case, eyeglasses) is not considered a disability under the ADA. In other words, the determination of whether a person is substantially limited in a major life activity is based on how the person functions when taking medication or using corrective devices, not on how the person functions without these measures. Since then, the courts have held that plaintiffs with bipolar disorder, epilepsy, diabetes, and other conditions do not fall under the ADA's protections if the conditions can be corrected with medication or corrective devices. The Supreme Court has also limited the applicability of the ADA by holding that lawsuits under the ADA cannot be brought against state government employers.[51]

The Rights and Status of Gays and Lesbians

On June 27, 1969, patrons of the Stonewall Inn, a New York City bar popular with gays and lesbians, responded to a police raid by throwing beer cans and bottles because they were angry at what they felt was unrelenting police harassment. In the ensuing riot, which lasted two nights, hundreds of gays and lesbians fought with police. Before Stonewall, the stigma attached to homosexuality and the resulting fear of exposure had tended to keep most gays and lesbians quiescent. In the months immediately after Stonewall, however, "gay power" graffiti began to appear in New York City. The Gay Liberation Front and the Gay Activist Alliance were formed, and similar groups sprang up in other parts of the country. Thus, Stonewall has been called "the shot heard round the homosexual world."

Growth in the Gay and Lesbian Rights Movement

The Stonewall incident marked the beginning of the movement for gay and lesbian rights. Since then, gays and lesbians have formed thousands of organizations to exert pressure on legislatures, the media, schools, churches, and other organizations to recognize their right to equal treatment.

Michael Newman/photoEdit

A man and a woman communicating in sign language at work. Sign language is not a method of representing English, but is an entirely unique language system. Despite the fact that it is not English, should sign language be exempted from the effects of English-only laws that have been adopted in some jurisdictions? Why or why not?

■ **Learning Outcome 5**

did you know?

In October 1999, Scouts Canada, the Canadian equivalent of the Boy Scouts of America, officially approved North America's first gay Scout troop.

---

50.   527 U.S. 471 (1999).
51.   *Board of Trustees of the University of Alabama v. Garrett,* 531 U.S. 356 (2001).

To a great extent, lesbian and gay groups have succeeded in changing public opinion—and state and local laws—relating to their status and rights. Nevertheless, they continue to struggle against age-old biases against homosexuality, often rooted in deeply held religious beliefs, which allow discrimination to persist. For example, in a widely publicized case involving the Boy Scouts of America, a troop in New Jersey refused to allow gay activist James Dale to be a Scout leader. In 2000, the case came before the Supreme Court, which held that, as a private organization, the Boy Scouts had the right to determine the requirements for becoming a Scout leader.[52] In 1998, a student at the University of Wyoming named Matthew Shepard was brutally beaten, tortured, tied to a fence post, and left to die near Laramie, Wyoming, because he was believed to be gay. His killers could not be charged with a **hate crime** because at the time, the state law did not recognize sexual orientation as a protected class. In 2009, Congress passed the Matthew Shepard Act expanding the 1969 federal hate crime law to include crimes motivated by the victim's actual or perceived gender, sexual orientation, gender identity, or disability.[53]

Hate Crime
A criminal offense committed against a person or property that is motivated, in whole or in part, by the offender's bias against a race, color, ethnicity, national origin, sex, gender identity or expression, sexual orientation, disability, age, or religion.

State and Local Laws Targeting Gays and Lesbians

Before the Stonewall incident, 49 states had sodomy laws that made various kinds of sexual acts, including homosexual acts, illegal (Illinois, which had repealed its sodomy law in 1962, was the only exception). During the 1970s and 1980s, more than half of these laws were either repealed or struck down by the courts. In 2003, the Court reversed an earlier antisodomy position[54] with its decision in *Lawrence v. Texas.*[55] The Court held that laws against sodomy violate the due process clause of the Fourteenth Amendment, stating: "The liberty protected by the Constitution allows homosexual persons the right to choose to enter upon relationships in the confines of their homes and their own private lives and still retain their dignity as free persons." The result of *Lawrence v. Texas* was to invalidate all remaining sodomy laws throughout the country.

Today, 20 states and the District of Columbia have laws protecting lesbians and gays against discrimination in employment, housing, public accommodations, and credit. Several laws at the national level have also been changed over the past two decades. Among other things, the government has lifted a ban on hiring gays and lesbians and voided a 1952 law prohibiting gays and lesbians from immigrating to the United States.

Gays and Lesbians in the Military

The U.S. Department of Defense traditionally has viewed homosexuality as incompatible with military service. In 1993 President Clinton announced a new policy, generally characterized as "don't ask, don't tell" (DADT). Enlistees would not be asked about their sexual orientation, and gays and lesbians would be allowed to serve in the military so long as they did not declare that they were gay or lesbian or commit homosexual acts. Military officials endorsed the new policy, after opposing it initially, but supporters of gay rights were not enthusiastic.

As a presidential candidate, Barack Obama promised to help bring an end to the "don't ask, don't tell" policy (only Congress can repeal the law). In March of 2009, Secretary of Defense Robert M. Gates announced a number of interim steps designed to make it more difficult for the military to discharge openly gay men and women. In December 2010, a bill to repeal DADT was enacted

52. *Boy Scouts of America v. Dale,* 530 U.S. 640 (2000).
53. "Obama Signs Measure to Widen Hate Crimes Law," *PBS Newshour,* October 28, 2009.
54. *Bowers v. Hardwick,* 478 U.S. 186 (1986).
55. 539 U.S. 558 (2003).

specifying that the policy would remain in place until the president, the secretary of defense, and the chairman of the Joint Chiefs of Staff certified that repeal would not harm military readiness, followed by a 60-day waiting period. The certification was sent to Congress on July 22, 2011, making the date of the law's repeal September 20, 2011. Following the repeal, discharged servicemen and servicewomen were permitted to reenlist, and several have successfully done so.

Same-Sex Marriages

Perhaps one of the most sensitive political issues with respect to the rights of gay and lesbian couples is whether they should be allowed to marry, just as heterosexual couples are.

Defense of Marriage Act. The controversy over this issue was fueled in 1993, when the Hawaii Supreme Court ruled that denying marriage licenses to gay couples might violate the equal protection clause of the Hawaii constitution.[56] In the wake of this event, other states began to worry about whether they might have to treat gay men or lesbians who were legally married in another state as married couples in their state as well. Opponents of gay rights pushed for state laws banning same-sex marriages, and the majority of states enacted such laws or adopted constitutional amendments. At the federal level, Congress passed the Defense of Marriage Act of 1996, which bans federal recognition of lesbian and gay couples and allows state governments to ignore same-sex marriages performed in other states. However, in 2009 President Obama signed an order extending health care and other benefits to the partners of gay federal employees.

The controversy over gay marriages was fueled again by developments in the state of Vermont. In 1999, the Vermont Supreme Court ruled that gay couples are entitled to the same benefits of marriage as opposite-sex couples.[57] Subsequently, in April 2000, the Vermont legislature passed a law permitting gay and lesbian couples to form "civil unions." The law entitled partners forming civil unions to receive some 300 state benefits available to married couples, including the rights to inherit a partner's property and to decide on medical treatment for an incapacitated partner. In 2005, Connecticut became the second state to adopt civil unions. Neither law entitled partners to receive any benefits allowed to married couples under federal law, such as spousal Social Security benefits.

State Recognition of Gay Marriages. Massachusetts was the first state to recognize gay marriage. In November 2003, the Massachusetts Supreme Judicial Court ruled that same-sex couples have a right to civil marriage under the Massachusetts state constitution and that civil unions would not suffice.[58] In 2005, the Massachusetts legislature voted down a proposed ballot initiative that would have amended the state constitution to explicitly state that marriage could only be between one man and one woman (but would have extended civil union status to same-sex couples). Although the highest courts in several states have upheld bans on gay marriage, in 2008 the Supreme Court of California held that the state was required to recognize gay marriages. Citizens immediately prepared petitions to put a constitutional amendment on the ballot in November of 2008 to outlaw such marriages. The campaign for and against Proposition 8, which would ban gay marriages in California, cost at least $74 million and was funded by contributions from almost every state. Ultimately, Proposition 8 was approved by a margin of 4 percent. The 18,000 marriages that took place between the

---

56. *Baehr v. Lewin,* 852 P.2d 44 (Hawaii 1993).
57. *Baker v. Vermont,* 744 A.2d 864 (Vt. 1999).
58. *Goodridge v. Department of Public Health,* 798 N.E.2d 941 (Mass. 2003).

Del Martin (L) and Phyllis Lyon (R) are married by San Francisco mayor Gavin Newsom in a private ceremony at San Francisco City Hall on June 16, 2008. Martin and Lyon, a couple since 1953, were active in the gay rights and women's rights movements. Del Martin died on August 27, 2008.

AP Photo/Marcio Jose Sanchez

California Supreme Court decision and the approval of Proposition 8 remain valid. On August 4, 2010, a federal judge declared California's ban on same-sex marriage unconstitutional, saying that no legitimate state interest justified treating gay and lesbian couples differently from others. The ruling was the first in the country to strike down a marriage ban on federal constitutional grounds rather than on the basis of a state constitution. It is widely believed that this will be the case that the U.S. Supreme Court agrees to hear (see What if? in Chapter 3). After a period of public opposition to same-sex marriage, President Barack Obama announced an evolution in his thinking in a nationally televised interview in May 2012, saying that he believes same-sex couples should be allowed to marry. His view is supported by a majority of Americans, according to poll data. Polls conducted immediately following the president's statement also found that opposition to gay marriage fell by 11 percentage points among African Americans.

Same-sex marriage is currently permitted in Massachusetts, Connecticut, Iowa, Vermont, New Hampshire, New York, as well as the District of Columbia, and Oregon's Coquille and Washington State's Suquamish Indian tribes. In November 2012, voters in Maryland, Maine and Washington state approved same-sex marriage through referenda, marking the first time that marriage rights have been extended to same-sex couples by popular vote. On the same day, voters in Minnesota rejected a constitutional amendment that would have defined marriage solely as a heterosexual union. A majority of states have explicitly banned gay marriage either by statute or by amending the state constitution. The shift in public opinion favoring gay marriage, likely because of contact with friends and others who are gay, will take some time to translate into repeals of gay marriage bans at the state level. A review of the constitutionality of the federal Defense of Marriage Act by the Supreme Court is likely to happen more quickly. On May 31, 2012, the United States Court of Appeals for the First Circuit in Boston ruled unanimously that the federal law declaring marriage to be a union solely between a man and a woman discriminates against married same-sex couples by denying them the same benefits afforded to heterosexual couples. A week later, the United States Court of Appeals for the Ninth Circuit in San Francisco refused, as a full court, to reexamine its earlier ruling that Proposition 8, California's ban on same-sex marriage, is unconstitutional. Same-sex marriage is currently accepted nationwide in Belgium, Canada, the Netherlands, Norway, South Africa, and Spain.

You Can Make a Difference

iStockphoto.com/kyoshino

DEALING WITH DISCRIMINATION

Bill Clark/Roll Call/Getty Images

When the U.S. Supreme Court used a narrow interpretation of the statute to rule against Lilly Ledbetter's claim of pay discrimination, Congress passed the Lilly Ledbetter Fair Pay Act in January 2009.

You may think you know what "discrimination" means while applying for or working at a job. But do you really understand how it applies to your life? To "discriminate" means to treat differently or less favorably, and discrimination can happen while you are at school or at work. Discrimination can come from friends, teachers, coaches, coworkers, managers, and business owners and be based on race, color, gender, religion, age, sexual orientation, or disability. Tests while applying for a job may have a discriminatory effect on being hired (tests of strength, for example, must be directly related to the requirements of the job). Genetic information, now more widely available, might some day be used by employers in making hiring decisions. Increasingly, evidence shows that employers make use of online sites such as Facebook, MySpace, blogs, and personal Web sites to learn more about applicants. While doing so may leave employers subject to "failure to hire" lawsuits if information gathered online is used to discriminate illegally, you should be very aware of how you present yourself online. Agencies at the state and federal government examine the fairness and validity of criteria used in screening job applicants and, as a result, ways of addressing the problem of discrimination are available.

WHY SHOULD YOU CARE?

Some people may think that discrimination is only a problem for members of racial or ethnic minorities. Actually, almost everyone can be affected. In some instances, white men have experienced "reverse discrimination"—and have obtained redress for it. Also, discrimination against women is common, and women constitute half the population. Therefore, knowledge of how to proceed when you suspect discrimination is another useful tool to have when living in the modern world.

WHAT CAN YOU DO?

If you believe that you have been discriminated against by a potential employer, consider the following steps:

1. Evaluate your own capabilities, and determine if you are truly qualified for the position.
2. Analyze the reasons why you were turned down. Would others agree with you that you have been the object of discrimination, or would they uphold the employer's claim?
3. If you still believe that you have been treated unfairly, you have recourse to several agencies and services. You should first speak to the personnel director of the company and explain that you believe you have not been evaluated adequately. If asked, explain your concerns clearly and provide detailed examples of behavior you believe is discriminatory.

If further action is warranted, many states and localities have antidiscrimination laws and agencies responsible for enforcing these laws. They are referred to as Fair Employment Practices Agencies (FEPAs). They can be found on your state's official government Web site and include your state attorney general; state commissions on civil rights, equal rights, equal opportunity, and antidiscrimination; and departments of labor and industry.

You can access all local and state government agencies through www.usa.gov, the U.S. government's official Web portal to all federal, state, and local government resources and services.

Finally, the U.S. Equal Employment Opportunity Commission (EEOC) enforces federal laws concerning job discrimination and harassment, processing about 80,000 complaints a year, and partners with 90 state and local agencies that investigate an additional 50,000 complaints. You can contact the EEOC anytime you feel you are being treated unfairly on the job because of race, religion, sex (including pregnancy), national origin, disability, or age. This federal agency is an extensive resource and will answer questions about job discrimination even if you do not want to file a formal complaint.

The U.S. Equal Employment Opportunity Commission
1801 L St. NW
Washington, D.C. 20507

Key Terms

affirmative action 167

Black Codes 137

busing 142

civil disobedience 144

civil rights 136

de facto segregation 142

de jure segregation 142

feminism 157

gender discrimination 158

grandfather clause 140

hate crime 172

Jim Crow laws 138

literacy test 140

poll tax 140

reparation 166

reverse discrimination 167

separate-but-equal doctrine 139

sexual harassment 160

subpoena 147

suffrage 152

white primary 139

 # Chapter Summary

1. The term *civil rights* refers to the rights of all Americans to equal treatment under the law, as provided for by the Fourteenth Amendment to the Constitution and by subsequent acts of Congress. Although the terms *civil rights* and *civil liberties* are sometimes used interchangeably, scholars make a distinction between the two. Civil liberties are limitations on government; they specify what the government *cannot* do. Civil rights, in contrast, specify what the government *must* do—to ensure equal protection and freedom from discrimination.

2. The story of civil rights in the United States is the struggle to reconcile our ideals as a nation with the realities of discrimination individuals and groups may still encounter in daily life. To the nation's founders, political equality required a degree of independent thinking and a capacity for rational action that at the time they believed were limited to a very few white males. Therefore, other groups and individuals were systematically excluded, not only from the exercise of political rights, but also from access to education and employment. Today we believe that all people are entitled to equal political rights as well as to the opportunities for personal development provided by equal access to education and employment. However, the roots of past discrimination live on in today's discriminatory practices, including racial profiling, the wage gap, the achievement gap in schools, and the "glass ceiling," which prevents women from rising to the top in business and professional firms.

3. Legal segregation was declared unconstitutional by the Supreme Court in *Brown v. Board of Education of Topeka* (1954), in which the Court stated that separation implied inferiority. In *Brown v. Board of Education* (1955), the Supreme Court ordered federal courts to ensure that public schools were desegregated "with all deliberate speed." Also in 1955, the modern civil rights movement began with a boycott of segregated public transportation in Montgomery, Alabama. Of particular impact was the Civil Rights Act of 1964 banning discrimination on the basis of race, color, religion, sex, or national origin in employment and public accommodations. The act created the Equal Employment Opportunity Commission to administer the legislation's provisions.

4. The Voting Rights Act of 1965 outlawed discriminatory voter-registration tests and authorized federal registration of persons and federally administered procedures in any state or political subdivision evidencing electoral discrimination or low registration rates. The Voting Rights Act and other protective legislation passed during and since the 1960s apply not only to African Americans but to other ethnic groups as well. Minorities have been increasingly represented in national and state politics, although they have yet to gain representation proportionate to their numbers in the U.S. population. Lingering social and economic disparities have led to a new civil rights agenda—one focusing less on racial differences and more on economic differences.

5. In the early history of the United States, women were considered citizens, but by and large they had no political rights because they were largely viewed as dependents. After the first women's rights convention in 1848, the campaign for suffrage gained momentum, yet not until 1920, when the Nineteenth Amendment was ratified, did women finally obtain the right to vote. The second wave of the women's movement began in the 1960s and the National Organization for Women (NOW) was formed in 1966 to bring about complete equality for women in all walks of life. Efforts to secure the ratification of the Equal Rights Amendment failed. Women continue to fight gender discrimination in employment. Federal government efforts to eliminate gender discrimination in the workplace include Title VII of the Civil Rights Act of 1964, which prohibits, among other things, gender-based discrimination, including sexual harassment on the job. Wage discrimination also continues to be a problem for women, as does the glass ceiling. Women make up just 17 percent of the U.S. Congress.

6. America has always been a land of immigrants and will continue to be so. Today, more than 1 million immigrants enter the United States each year, and more than 12 percent of the U.S. population consists of foreign-born persons. Demographers estimate that the foreign-born will account for 15 percent of the nation sometime between 2020 and 2025. In particular, the Latino community in the United States has experienced explosive growth. In recent years, undocumented immigration has surfaced as a significant issue for border states and the nation. Indeed, one of the pressing concerns facing today's politicians at the state and federal level is how U.S. immigration policy should be reformed.

7. The Rehabilitation Act of 1973 prohibited discrimination against persons with disabilities in programs receiving federal aid. Regulations implementing the act provide for ramps, elevators, and the like in federal buildings. The Americans with Disabilities Act of 1990 prohibits job discrimination against persons with physical and mental disabilities, requiring that positive steps be taken to comply with the act. The act also requires expanded access to public facilities, including transportation, and to services offered by such private concerns as car rental and telephone companies.

8. Gay and lesbian rights groups work to promote laws protecting gays and lesbians from discrimination and to repeal antigay laws. After 1969, sodomy laws that criminalized specific sexual practices were repealed or struck down by the courts in all but 18 states, and in 2003 a Supreme Court decision effectively invalidated all remaining sodomy laws nationwide. Gays and lesbians are no longer barred from federal employment or from immigrating to this country. Twenty states and the District of Columbia outlaw discrimination based on sexual orientation. Hate crimes based on sexual orientation or gender identity are punishable by federal law under the Matthew Shepard Act of 2009. The Obama administration issued an order extending benefits to partners of federal employees and President Obama, in a change of position, announced his support for same-sex marriage in May 2012. The military's "don't ask, don't tell" policy was repealed effective September 20, 2011.

9. Although the government has the power to assert rights and the obligation to protect civil rights, it does not always do so. Individuals and groups then organize to bring pressure on government to act. The civil rights movement started with the struggle by African Americans for equality. Before the Civil War, most African Americans were slaves, and slavery was protected by the Constitution and the Supreme Court. Constitutional amendments after the Civil War legally ended slavery, and African Americans gained citizenship, the right to vote, and other rights through legislation. This legal protection was rendered meaningless in practice by the 1880s, however, and politically and socially, African American inequality continued. Legal guarantees mean little when people's attitudes and practices remain discriminatory.

10. Affirmative action programs have been controversial because of charges that they can lead to reverse discrimination against majority groups or even other minority groups. Supreme Court decisions have limited affirmative action programs, and voters in California and Washington passed initiatives banning state-sponsored affirmative action in those states. Two Supreme Court decisions in cases brought against the University of Michigan have confirmed the principle of diversity as an important educational goal and that limited affirmative action programs are constitutional.

11. The Supreme Court is in the best position within the framework of American government to interpret the values and ideals contained in the founding documents and ensure those ideas are reflected in policy and practice. The Court is often in a good position to pull the public along as more progressive ideas are percolating throughout society by issuing rulings that speed up the timetable for social change, as it did in the *Brown v. Board of Education* (desegregating schools) decision and *United States v. Virginia* (opening VMI, the state military college, to women).

Selected Print, Media, and Online Resources

PRINT RESOURCES

Anderson, Terry H. *The Pursuit of Fairness: A History of Affirmative Action.* New York: Oxford University Press, 2004. Anderson offers an evenhanded history of affirmative action. His account extends from the administrations of Franklin D. Roosevelt and Harry Truman in the 1940s to the 2003 University of Michigan cases that have established the current constitutional parameters of affirmative action policies.

Kristoff, Nicholas D., and Sheryl WuDunn. *Half the Sky: Turning Oppression into Opportunity for Women Worldwide.* New York: Alfred Knopf, 2009. Written by two Pulitzer Prize–winning journalists, this book demonstrates that the key to solving global poverty is to improve the lives of women around the globe. The book profiles women throughout Asia and Africa who have not only coped with unimaginable forms of brutal discrimination, but created opportunities for survival for themselves and other women.

Moore, Wes. *The Other Wes Moore: One Name, Two Fates.* New York: Random House, Inc. This memoir tells the story of two boys, both named Wes Moore, who grew up in Baltimore, Maryland, within a few blocks of one another; one became a Rhodes Scholar and one is serving a life sentence in the Jessup Correctional Institution.

Morin, Jose Luis. *Latino/a Rights and Justice in the United States: Perspectives and Approaches.* Durham, NJ: Carolina Academic Press, 2009. This book offers a thorough overview of the history and modern incarnation of Latino/a civil rights and experiences within the U.S. justice system. Case studies and a focus on taking action complement the legal analysis.

Savage, Dan. *The Commitment: Love, Sex, Marriage, and My Family.* New York: Penguin, 2005. A humorous memoir exploring the definition of "family" within the context of the gay marriage policy debate.

Valenti, Jessica. *Full Frontal Feminism: A Young Woman's Guide to Why Feminism Matters.* Emeryville, CA: Seal Press, 2007. Valenti, founder of feministing.com, a wildly popular blog, explores what it means to be a young feminist today by confronting and discounting the myths so often associated with the feminist label.

MEDIA RESOURCES

Chisholm '72: Unbought and Unbossed—A documentary about the career of Congresswoman Shirley Chisholm, the first black woman to run for president of the United States. Includes archival footage and contemporary interviews.

Eyes on the Prize: America's Civil Rights Movement 1954–1985—A 14-part *American Experience* documentary first aired on public television that features both movement leaders and the stories of average Americans through contemporary interviews and historical footage.

Fight in the Fields: Cesar Chavez and the Farmworkers' Struggle—A 1997 film documenting the first successful drive to organize farmworkers in the United States; described as a social history with Chavez as a central figure, the documentary draws from archival footage, newsreels, and present-day interviews.

Lioness—A documentary film about a group of female army support soldiers who were a part of the first program in American history to send women into direct ground combat against insurgents in Iraq.

Miss Representation—A documentary exploring how the media's misrepresentations of women have led to the underrepresentation of women in positions of power and influence.

ONLINE RESOURCES

National Immigration Forum established in 1982, the National Immigration Forum is the leading immigrant advocacy organization in the country, with a mission to advocate for the value of immigrants and immigration to the nation: www.immigrationforum.org/

Pew Hispanic Center founded in 2001, the Pew Hispanic Center is a nonpartisan research organization that seeks to improve understanding of the U.S. Hispanic population and to chronicle Latinos' growing impact on the nation: www. pewhispanic.org/

Reporting Civil Rights an anthology of the reporters and journalism of the American civil rights movement hosted by Library of America: www.reportingcivilrights.loa.org/

Women's Rights National Historical Park operated by the National Park Service, the park preserves the sites associated with the first women's rights convention in 1848: www.nps.gov/wori/index.htm

6 Public Opinion and Political Socialization

© White House Photo/Alamy

President Barack Obama greets students from Medina Elementary School February 17, 2012 in Medina, WA.

aplia

LEARNING OUTCOMES

After reading this chapter, students will be able to:

■ **LO1** Define public opinion, and identify at least two ways public opinion impacts government actions.

■ **LO2** Evaluate how the political socialization process shapes political attitudes, opinions, and behavior; explain the impact of demographic characteristics on political behavior.

■ **LO3** Describe three forms of social media, and explain how social media can shape political decisions or events.

■ **LO4** Identify three factors that might distort public opinion results collected through opinion polling.

■ **LO5** Assess the impact that world opinion of the United States has on the government's domestic and foreign policy decisions.

What If ...

YOUNG PEOPLE WERE REQUIRED TO SERVE?

BACKGROUND

What if the United States adopted a policy that required all persons between the ages of 18 and 22 residing in the United States to engage in domestic or military service for a period of at least 18 months? Would national service create a stronger bond between young citizens and the nation? How might 18 months of service socialize new generations of young people to politics and political activity?

Young people typically know less about politics, express less interest in politics, and vote less often than their elders. But that isn't set in stone! Voter turnout by people under 30 reached 51 percent in 2008, the third highest turnout since the voting age was lowered to 18 years of age. In 2012, people under 30 made up a larger share of the electorate than those 65 and older. Thus, young citizens have tremendous potential to shape politics and policy *if* they get involved.

SERVICE AS POLITICAL SOCIALIZATION

The United States has a long history of citizens rendering service to their communities, including the Civilian Conservation Corps, the Peace Corps, and Volunteers in Service to America (VISTA). Teach for America recruits college graduates and trains them to teach in America's most challenged schools. During the Clinton administration, AmeriCorps, a large-scale national service program designed to place young people in service positions in communities across the country, was established. The Obama administration has significantly expanded both the AmeriCorps and VISTA programs.

Would young people be willing to serve their country? This chapter reviews what we know about the process of becoming socialized into civic and political life and, as a result, how we develop and express political opinions. Forces such as the family, schools, faith communities, the media, and peers all shape how we understand public life. Likewise, direct personal experience with politics is a developmental force. From national surveys of first-year college students, we know that roughly a third of all students believe that it is important to keep up with political affairs and that roughly a third report a very good chance that they will participate in community service or volunteer work while in college. These individuals are also more likely to remain engaged with their communities after they graduate from college. Those who oppose national service do so for a variety of reasons, including the disruption to education and career, as well as the belief that individual liberty would be violated.

TOWARD A NATIONAL POLICY

What would the nation gain from a service requirement? The U.S. military is an all-volunteer force today following the repeal of the draft in 1973. Representative Charles B. Rangel, a veteran of the Korean conflict, argued in a 2002 *New York Times* op-ed essay that the draft should be reinstated to promote the philosophy of shared sacrifice and enforce a greater appreciation of the consequences of war. Similarly, when President Bill Clinton proposed AmeriCorps, he said "Citizen service bridges isolated individuals, local communities, the national community, and ultimately, the community of all people." AmeriCorps members serve in communities across the United States for one or two years in return for an educational stipend.[a] The nation benefits from a diverse group of committed individuals performing public work that needs doing. Critics charge that national service amounts to forced voluntarism and that the compulsory nature undermines the benefits for individuals and communities.

[a]William J. Clinton, "The Duties of Democracy," in E. J. Dionne et. al., eds. *United We Serve: National Service and the Future of Citizenship* (Washington, DC: Brookings Institution, 2003).

FOR CRITICAL ANALYSIS

1. *Do you believe a national service requirement would improve young people's connection to politics and to the country? Why or why not?*

2. *You have no doubt heard the phrase, "with rights come responsibilities." What responsibilities do you have as a resident of your community, of your state, and of the nation?*

IN A DEMOCRACY, the people express their opinions in many different ways. First and foremost, they express their views in political campaigns and vote for the individuals who will represent their views in government. Between elections, individuals express their opinions in many ways, ranging from writing to the editor to calling their senator's office to responding to a blog. Public opinion is also expressed and conveyed to public officials through public opinion polls, which are reported almost daily in the media. Sometimes public opinion is expressed through mass demonstrations, rallies, or protests.

In 2003, when President George W. Bush asked the Congress to authorize the use of force against Iraq, 72 percent of the public approved. At that time, more than 80 percent of Americans either believed or considered it possible that Saddam Hussein was building an arsenal of biological and other extremely dangerous weapons. By 2005, support for the use of troops in Iraq had declined to 39 percent and, by mid-2007, had fallen to 36 percent. Senator Barack Obama made withdrawal of American troops from Iraq a priority of his campaign and claimed that if he had been in the Senate at that time, he would not have supported the authorization of the use of force. Senator Hillary Clinton, who had voted for the resolution, no longer supported the Iraqi campaign and claimed that she had been misled at the time of the debate. The approval rating of President Bush, inevitably connected with the unpopular war, fell to 30 percent or less. In the past, public opinion also has had a dramatic impact on presidents. In 1968, President Lyndon B. Johnson decided not to run for reelection because of the intense and negative public reaction to the war in Vietnam. In 1974, President Richard Nixon resigned in the wake of a scandal when it was obvious that public opinion no longer supported him. Although President Obama promised to make health care reform a top legislative priority, vacillating public opinion made it difficult to pressure even members of his own party in Congress to act. President Obama's approval ratings heading into the 2012 campaign were closely tied to the public's perception of the state of the economy, and particularly the unemployment rate. Thus, the extent to which public opinion affects policymaking is not always clear and scholars must deal with many uncertainties when analyzing its impact.

Defining Public Opinion

Among the many different publics, no single public opinion exists. In a nation of more than 300 million people, innumerable gradations of opinion on an issue may exist. What we do is describe the distribution of opinions among the members of the public about a particular question. Thus, we define **public opinion** as the aggregate of individual attitudes or beliefs shared by some portion of the adult population.

Typically, public opinion is distributed among several different positions, and the distribution of opinion can tell us how divided the public is on an issue and whether compromise is possible. When a large proportion of the American public appears to express the same view on an issue, we say that a **consensus** exists, at least at the moment the poll was taken. Figure 6–1 shows a pattern of opinion that might be called consensual. In this situation, 89 percent of adults polled by Gallup say birth control is morally acceptable. Issues on which the public holds widely differing attitudes result in **divisive opinion** (see Figure 6–2). In a poll conducted by the Henry J. Kaiser Family Foundation, Americans were asked about the health reform law passed by Congress in 2010. A full year after the law's

■ **Learning Outcome 1:**
Define public opinion, and identify at least two ways public opinion impacts government actions.

Public Opinion
The aggregate of individual attitudes or beliefs shared by some portion of the adult population.

Consensus
General agreement among the citizenry on an issue.

Divisive Opinion
Public opinion that is polarized between two quite different positions.

Figure 6–1 ▶ Consensus Opinion

From May 3–6, 2012
Question: Regardless of whether you think it should be legal, please tell me whether you personally believe that in general birth control is morally acceptable or morally wrong.

● **Morally acceptable—89%**
● **Morally wrong—8%**
● **Depends/No opinion—3%**

Source: www.gallup.com/poll/154799/Americans-Including-Catholics-Say-Birth-Control-Morally.aspx?version=print)

Figure 6–2 ▶ Divisive Opinion

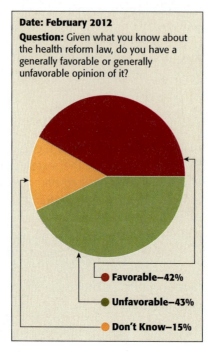

Date: February 2012
Question: Given what you know about the health reform law, do you have a generally favorable or generally unfavorable opinion of it?

● **Favorable—42%**
● **Unfavorable—43%**
● **Don't Know—15%**

Source: www.kff.org/kaiserpolls/upload/8281-F.pdf

Figure 6–3 ▶ Nonopinion

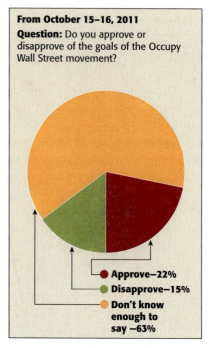

From October 15–16, 2011
Question: Do you approve or disapprove of the goals of the Occupy Wall Street movement?

● **Approve—22%**
● **Disapprove—15%**
● **Don't know enough to say —63%**

Source: USA Today/Gallup Poll www.gallup.com/poll/150896/support-occupy-unchanged-criticize-approach.aspx

Nonopinion
The lack of an opinion on an issue or policy among the majority.

passage, opinion remains divided, with 43 percent indicating an unfavorable opinion of the law and 42 percent indicating a favorable opinion. Sometimes, a poll shows a distribution of opinion indicating that most Americans either have no information about the issue or are not interested enough in the issue to formulate a position. This is sometimes referred to as **nonopinion** (see Figure 6–3). In October 2011, the Gallup polling organization asked adults whether they approved or disapproved of the goals of the Occupy Wall Street movement. While 22 percent said they approved and 16 percent said they disapproved, the majority of those asked indicated they didn't know enough to say one way or the other. Politicians may believe that the public's lack of knowledge about an issue gives them more room to maneuver, or they may be wary of taking any action for fear that opinion will crystallize after a crisis.

Public Opinion and Policymaking

Sometimes public officials have a difficult time discerning the public's opinion on a specific issue from the public's expression of general anger or dissatisfaction. The Tea Party protests present just such a dilemma. The rallies began in early 2009 to express opposition to the TARP (Troubled Asset Relief Program) bailout bill passed by Congress. Drawing on themes from the Revolutionary War era in general and the Boston Tea Party in particular, the protesters often arrive dressed as Patriots and holding handmade placards with antitax slogans. Organizers have utilized social networking sites and the Internet to call for Tea Party meetings and protests in communities large and small. They have demonstrated against health care reform and increased government spending on a wide array of social programs. Several rallies were held around the country on April 15th—widely known as tax day. This coalition of disparate groups acting under a single moniker is not "for" or "against" any single policy or program, but rather an expression of negative opinion directed at incumbents of both parties. As a result, public officials and candidates for office are having a difficult time knowing how to respond.

If public opinion is important for democracy, are policymakers really responsive to public opinion? A study by political scientists Benjamin I. Page and Robert Y. Shapiro suggests that in fact the national government is very responsive to the public's demands for action.[1] In looking at changes in public opinion poll results over time, research demonstrates that when the public supports a policy change, the following occurs: Policy changes in a direction consistent with the change in public opinion 43 percent of the time; policy changes in a direction opposite to the change in opinion 22 percent of the time; and policy does not change at all 33 percent of the time. When public opinion changes dramatically—say, by 20 percentage points rather than by just 6 or 7 percentage points—government policy is much more likely to follow changing public attitudes.

Public opinion can also serve to set limits on government. For example, consider the highly controversial issue of abortion. Most Americans are moderates on this issue; they do not approve of abortion as a means of birth control, but they do feel that it should be available. Yet sizable groups of people express very intense feelings both for and against legalized abortion. Given this distribution of opinion, most elected officials would rather not try to change policy to favor either of the extreme positions. To do so would clearly violate the opinion of the majority of Americans. In this case, as in many others, public opinion does not make public policy; rather, it restrains officials from taking truly unpopular actions. In this sense, public opinion plays a vital role in the American system.

How Public Opinion Is Formed: Political Socialization

■ **Learning Outcome 2:**
Evaluate how the political socialization process shapes political attitudes, opinions, and behavior; explain the impact of demographic characteristics on political behavior.

Most Americans are willing to express opinions on political issues when asked. How do people acquire these opinions and attitudes? Typically, views that are expressed as political opinions are acquired through the process of **political socialization**. By this we mean that people acquire their political attitudes, often including their party identification, through relationships with their families, friends, and coworkers.

Models of Political Socialization

Scholars have long believed that the most important early sources of political socialization are found in the family and the schools. Children learn their parents' views on politics and on political leaders through observation and approval seeking. When parents are strong supporters of a political party, children are very likely to identify with that same party. If the parents are alienated from the political system or totally disinterested in politics, children will tend to hold the same attitudes. Other researchers claim that political attitudes (although not party identification) are influenced much more heavily by genetics than by parental or environmental socialization.[2] And, perhaps most interestingly, in explaining differences in people's tendencies to possess political opinions at all

Political Socialization
The process by which people acquire political beliefs and attitudes.

1. See the extensive work of Page and Shapiro in Benjamin I. Page and Robert Y. Shapiro, *The Rational Public: Fifty Years of Trends in Americans' Policy Preferences* (Chicago: University of Chicago Press, 1992).
2. John Alford, Carolyn Funk, and John R. Hibbing, "Are Political Orientations Genetically Transmitted?" *American Political Science Review,* vol. 99:2 (May, 2005).

AP Photo/Charlotte Observer, John D. Simmons

The Kids Vote project involves teachers, parents, and children in encouraging children to vote on an unofficial ballot in the presidential election. Do you think this project will increase the children's desire to vote when they are adults?

regardless of their ideology, the researchers find that genetics explains one-third of the differences among people, and shared environment is completely inconsequential. Thinking about how nature (genetics) might shape political attitudes is a relatively new area of research, but it complements the nurture approach taken by generations of political socialization researchers, helping to provide answers to longstanding puzzles.

In the last few decades, more sources of information about politics have become available to all Americans and especially to young people. Although their basic outlook on the political system may be formed by genetics and early family influences, young people are now exposed to many other sources of information about issues and values. It is not unusual for young adults to hold very different views on issues. The exposure of younger Americans to many sources of ideas may also underlie their more progressive views on such issues as immigration and gay rights.

The Family and the Social Environment

Not only do our parents' political attitudes and actions affect our opinions, but the family also links us to other factors that affect opinion, such as race, social class, educational environment, and religious beliefs. How do parents transmit their political attitudes to their offspring?

Studies suggest that the influence of parents is due to two factors: communication and receptivity. Parents communicate their feelings and preferences to children constantly. Because children have such a strong desire for parental approval, they are very receptive to their parents' views. Children are less likely to influence their parents, because parents expect deference from their children.[3]

Nevertheless, other studies show that if children are exposed to political ideas at school and in the media, they will share these ideas with their parents, giving the parents what some scholars call a "second chance" at political socialization. Children can also expose their parents to new media, such as the Internet.[4]

Education as a Source of Political Socialization. From the early days of the republic, schools were perceived to be important transmitters of political information and attitudes. Children in the primary grades learn about their country mostly in patriotic ways. They learn about the Pilgrims, the flag, and some of the nation's presidents. They also learn to celebrate national holidays. Without much explicit instruction, children easily adopt democratic decision-making tools such as "taking a vote" and democratic procedures such as "the majority wins." Later, in the middle grades, children learn more historical facts and come to understand the structure and functions of government. By high school, students have a more complex understanding of the political system, may identify with a political party, and may take positions on issues. Additionally, students in grade school and high school may gain some experience in political participation: first,

3. Barbara A. Bardes and Robert W. Oldendick, *Public Opinion: Measuring the American Mind*, 3rd ed. (Belmont, CA: Wadsworth Publishing, 2006), p. 73.
4. For a pioneering study in this area, see Michael McDevitt and Steven H. Chaffee, "Second Chance Political Socialization: 'Trickle-up' Effects of Children on Parents," in Thomas J. Johnson et al., eds., *Engaging the Public: How Government and the Media Can Reinvigorate American Democracy* (Lanham, MD: Rowman & Littlefield, 1998), pp. 57–66.

through student elections and activities, and second, through their introduction to registration and voting while still in school.

Generally, education is closely linked to political participation. The more formal education a person receives, the more likely it is that he or she will be interested in politics, be confident in his or her ability to understand political issues, and be an active participant in the political process.

Peers and Peer Group Influence.

Once a child enters school, the child's friends become an important influence on behavior and attitudes. For children and for adults, friendships and associations in **peer groups** affect political attitudes. We must, however, separate the effects of peer group pressure on opinions and attitudes in general from the effects of peer group pressure on political opinions. For the most part, associations among peers are nonpolitical. Political attitudes are more likely to be shaped by peer groups when the peer groups are involved directly in political activities. For example, if you join an interest group based on your passion for the environment, you are more likely to be influenced by your organizational peers than you are by classmates.

Peer Group
A group consisting of members sharing common social characteristics. These groups play an important part in the socialization process, helping to shape attitudes and beliefs.

Opinion Leaders' Influence.

We are all influenced by those with whom we are closely associated or whom we hold in high regard—friends at school, family members and other relatives, and teachers. In a sense, these people are **opinion leaders**, but on an *informal* level; that is, their influence on our political views is not necessarily intentional or deliberate. When President Obama announced a change in his position on gay marriage, a similar positive change in public opinion among African Americans was detected by pollsters. We are also influenced by *formal* opinion leaders, such as presidents, lobbyists, congresspersons, media figures, and religious leaders, who have as part of their jobs the task of shaping people's views. Nicholas Kristof, a prominent *New York Times* reporter and author, has characterized empowerment of women and girls as the 21st century's moral imperative.[5] Secretary of State Hillary Clinton rarely misses the opportunity to urge nations, including the United States, to invest resources to empower women and girls: "[W]ithout providing more rights and responsibilities for women, many of the goals we claim to pursue in our foreign policy are either unachievable or much harder to achieve....Democracy means nothing if half the people can't vote, or if their vote doesn't count, or if their literacy rate is so low that the exercise of their vote is in question. Which is why when I travel, I do events with women, I talk about women's rights, I meet with women activists, I raise women's concerns with the leaders I'm talking to."[6] They hope to define the political agenda in such a way that discussions about policy options will take place on their terms.

Opinion Leader
One who is able to influence the opinions of others because of position, expertise, or personality.

Political Change and Political Socialization.

The political system is relatively stable in the United States. But what influences might the upheavals and revolutions around the world in recent years have on the political socialization of young people experiencing and witnessing those dramatic changes?[7] Earlier chapters have referenced the Arab Spring, for example. How will people who have learned to live under an oppressive regime like that of Muammar Gaddafi in Libya develop and learn to live in a new regime? Americans are sometimes puzzled by the slow pace of democratization once a dictator has been removed, but imagine the

did **you**
know?
CNN reaches more than 1.5 billion people in 212 countries.

---

5. Nicholas Kristof and Sheryl WuDunn, "The Women's Crusade," *New York Times Magazine*, August 17, 2009.
6. Mark Landler, "A New Gender Agenda" *The New York Times*, August 18, 2009.
7. Virginia Sapiro, "Not Your Parents' Political Socialization: Introduction for a New Generation," *Annual Review of Political Science*, Vol. 7, 2004, pp. 1–23.

difficulty of building civil society and creating new day-to-day political norms and practices when politics has always meant capriciousness and brutality. New regimes must help people establish important political dispositions such as trust and political efficacy (the belief that your engagement will yield results)—a difficult task when the agents of socialization (education, media, religion) are associated with the old regime.

The Impact of the Media

Media
Channels of mass communication.

Agenda Setting
Determining which public policy questions will be debated or considered.

Clearly, the **media**—newspapers, television, radio, and the Internet— strongly influence public opinion. This is because the media inform the public about the issues and events of our times and thus have an **agenda-setting** effect. In other words, to borrow from Bernard Cohen's classic statement about the media and public opinion, the media may not be successful in telling people what to think, but they are "stunningly successful in telling their audience what to think about."[8] The Tea Party movement may be the best example of this. Media coverage of candidates eager to affiliate with Tea Party supporters was highly influential in the 2010 midterm elections.

As part of their news function, the media also provide a political forum for leaders and the public. Candidates for office use news reporting to sustain interest in their campaigns, while officeholders use the media to gain support for their policies or to present an image of leadership. Presidential trips abroad are an outstanding way for the chief executive to get colorful, positive, and exciting news coverage that makes the president look "presidential." The media also offer ways for citizens to participate in public debate, through letters to the editor, televised editorials, or electronic mail. Americans may cherish the idea of an unbiased press, but in the early years of the nation's history, the number of politically sponsored newspapers was significant. The sole reason for the existence of such periodicals was to further the interests of the politicians who paid for their publication. As chief executive of our government during this period, George Washington has been called a "firm believer" in **managed news**. Although acknowledging that the public had a right to be informed, he believed that some matters should be kept secret and that news that might damage the image of the United States should be censored (not published). Washington, however, made no attempt to control the press.

Managed News
Information generated and distributed by the government in such a way as to give government interests priority over candor.

Today, many contend that the media's influence on public opinion has grown to equal that of the family. For example, in her analysis of the role played by the media in American politics,[9] media scholar Doris A. Graber points out that high school students, when asked where they obtain the information on which they base their attitudes, mention the mass media far more than they mention their families, friends, and teachers. A national Annenberg Policy Center study found that 55 percent of those 18 to 29 used the Internet for presidential campaign information in 2008, compared to 15 percent of those 65 and older. Three in four adults now have access to the Internet either at home or at work.[10] This trend, combined with the increasing popularity of cable satires such as *The Daily Show,* talk radio, blogs, social networking sites, and the Internet as information sources, may significantly alter the nature of the media's influence on public opinion.

did you know?

The number of people watching the television networks during prime time has declined by almost 25 percent in the last 10 years.

8. Bernard C. Cohen, *The Press and Foreign Policy* (Princeton, NJ: Princeton University Press, 1963), p. 81.
9. See Doris A. Graber, *Mass Media and American Politics*, 7th ed. (Chicago: University of Chicago Press, 2005).
10. Ken Winneg and Kate Kenski, National Annenberg Election Survey, March 28, 2008. Accessed at www .annenbergpublicpolicycenter.org.

Politics with a Purpose

YOUTUBE, JON STEWART, AND STEPHEN COLBERT: CHANGING POLITICS FOR THE BETTER?

■ **Learning Outcome 3:**
Describe three forms of social media, and explain how social media can shape political decisions or events.

"Did you watch *Colbert* last night? Have you seen the *KONY 2012* video? My friend just tweeted me the link." If this sounds familiar, you're in good company. "Viral videos" and social networking have become a part of daily life. Politicians and political campaigns are scrambling to figure out how best to take advantage of new social media.

YouTube, a video share site, has been around since 2005. Although many of the videos feature pets, children, and stunts gone wrong, some have tremendous political impact. One such example is *KONY 2012*, posted by the nonprofit group Invisible Children on March 5, 2012. In five days, the video had 100 million views on YouTube. In a survey conducted by the Pew Research Center in the days following the release, a majority of people aged 18 to 29 had heard about the film. Invisible Children reported around 66,000 views on the first day. After Oprah Winfrey tweeted about the film, views of the video climbed to 9 million—a 13,536 percent increase.[a] The film's purpose was to bring global public attention to indicted but fugitive Ugandan war criminal Joseph Kony in order to have him arrested by December 2012. Kony and his rebel group Lord's Resistance Army (LRA) are responsible for brutal guerilla warfare in northern Uganda, the Democratic Republic of the Congo and South Sudan). Invisible Children charges that Kony and the LRA are responsible for the abduction of more than 30,000 children. The film advocates curtailing compelled and coerced youth military service and the restoration of social order to the region. As a result of the film and the advocacy that followed, President Obama authorized the deployment of 100 United States military advisers to provide "information, advice, and assistance to partner nation forces" so Central African troops can eventually "remove Joseph Kony from the battlefield." Invisible Children continues its efforts today to bring Kony to justice.

In 2010 Google launched a campaign toolkit designed to help candidates use YouTube and other Google products effectively.[b] Although campaigns work hard to keep candidates from making memorable gaffes, viral videos and instant twitter feeds mean missteps live longer, with greater consequences. During the primary campaign in 2008, a remark that Barack Obama made about rural, white gun owners at a private fundraising dinner made it to the Internet within hours. Hillary Clinton used that quote to bolster a win in the Pennsylvania primary. In 2011, candidate Herman Cain gave a taped interview to the *Milwaukee Journal Sentinel* in which he appeared confused about the U.S. position on Libya, saying, "I've got all this stuff twirling around in my head." Candidate Rick Perry's debate performances provided plenty of material for late-night comedians, including the night he promised to eliminate three cabinet-level agencies but could only name two of the three. It used to be that only a few people heard or saw such mistakes, but today YouTube, Twitter, and Facebook mean that millions share in the moment.

Sometimes comedians use their craft for a more serious political purpose. In 2011, Stephen Colbert and Jon Stewart teamed up to illustrate the myriad of loopholes in American election law through performance art. Colbert created "Americans for a Better Tomorrow, Tomorrow," a Super PAC, and began raising political money. In the January 2012 filing with the Federal Election Commission, Colbert's PAC had raised more than $1 million. In January 2012, Colbert announced that he was forming "an exploratory committee to lay the groundwork for my possible candidacy for president of the United States of America of South Carolina," requiring him to transfer control of his Super PAC. He did so—to Jon Stewart. Stewart promptly renamed the PAC "The definitely not coordinating with Stephen Colbert Super PAC." Colbert was too late to get on the ballot in South Carolina's February Republican primary, so he mounted the "Rock Me Like a Herman Cain" campaign, in which he urged South Carolina voters to cast a vote for Cain as a proxy for Colbert and then quickly ended his campaign.

Does this political comedy have a purpose? Yes! According to a Rasmussen survey, 30 percent of young people aged 18 to 29 say programs like Stewart's and Colbert's that feature news reports with a comic twist are replacing traditional news outlets. A university researcher found that *The Daily Show* turned the attention of apolitical viewers to political issues like the war in Afghanistan and the presidential campaign. The most apolitical viewers were 13 percent more likely to attend to the issue very closely than were similarly inattentive nonviewers.[c] Candidates at all levels will be watching the influence of new media closely in the years to come.

[a] "Kony 2012 in Numbers," DataBlog, *The Guardian*, April 20, 2012. Accessed at: http://www.guardian.co.uk/news/datablog/2012/apr/20/kony-2012-facts-numbers?newsfeed=true

[b] Lena Rao, "YouTube Launches Campaign Toolkit for Politicians," TechCrunch, June 3, 2010. Accessed at: http://techcrunch.com/2010/06/03/youtube-launches-campaign-toolkit-for-politicians/

[c] Xiaoxia Cao. (2010) "Hearing It from Jon Stewart: The Impact of *The Daily Show* on Public Attentiveness to Politics." *International Journal of Public Opinion Research*, 22(1), 26–46.

The Influence of Political Events

Generally, older Americans tend to be somewhat more conservative than younger Americans, particularly on social issues and, to some extent, on economic issues. This is known as the **life cycle effect**. People change as they grow older as a result of age-specific experiences. Likewise, as new generations of citizens are socialized within a particular social, economic, and political context, it in turn affects individual members' more specific opinions and actions. In other words, political events and environmental conditions have the power to shape the political attitudes of an entire generation. You no doubt recall what you were doing and where you were when terrorists flew planes into the World Trade Center towers in New York City. Although you and your parents may have similarly witnessed the terror attacks, the ways that they have influenced your attitudes about the increased airport security measures that resulted might differ. When events produce such a long-lasting result, we refer to it as a **generational effect** (also called the *cohort effect*).[11]

Voters who grew up in the 1930s during the Great Depression were likely to form lifelong attachments to the Democratic Party, the party of Franklin D. Roosevelt. In the 1960s and 1970s, the war in Vietnam and the **Watergate break-in** and the subsequent presidential cover-up fostered widespread cynicism toward government. Evidence indicates that the years of economic prosperity under President Ronald Reagan during the 1980s led many young people to identify with the Republican Party. More recently, the increase in non-party-affiliated Independents may mean that although young people heavily supported Democrat Barack Obama over Republican John McCain in the 2008 election, Democrats should not count on a lifelong attachment. After a strong showing in the 2008 presidential contest, young voters were largely absent in the 2010 midterm elections, with those under 30 indicating less interest (31% compared to 53%) and little likelihood of voting (45% compared to 76%) compared to those over 30 years of age.[12]

However, young people returned to the polls in the 2012 election in numbers nearly identical to 2008. Young voters' share of the electorate increased from 18 to 19 percent, and roughly 51 percent of those under 30 cast a ballot. The majority of votes went to Barack Obama, although he pulled a lower share of the youth vote in 2012 than in 2008 (60 percent compared to 68 percent). Researchers characterize this level of turnout as the "new normal" and expect the positive turnout trend to continue in future elections as young people begin to identify voting as an expression of power.

Political Preferences and Voting Behavior

Various socioeconomic and demographic factors appear to influence political preferences. These factors include education, income and **socioeconomic status**, religion, race, gender, geographic region, and similar traits. People who share the same religion, occupation, or any other demographic trait are likely to influence one another and may also have common political concerns that follow from the common characteristic. Other factors, such as party identification, perception of the candidates, and issue preferences, are closely connected to the electoral process. Table 6–1 illustrates the impact of some of these variables on voting behavior.

Life Cycle Effect
Concept that people change as they grow older because of age-specific experiences and thus are likely to hold age-specific attitudes.

Generational Effect
A long-lasting effect of the events of a particular time on the political opinions of those who came of political age at that time.

Watergate Break-in
The 1972 illegal entry into the Democratic National Committee offices by participants in President Richard Nixon's reelection campaign.

■ Learning Outcome 2

Socioeconomic Status
The value assigned to a person due to occupation or income. An upper-class person, for example, has high socioeconomic status.

---

11. Cliff Zukin, Scott Keeter, Molly Andolina, Krista Jenkins, and Michael X. Delli Carpini, *A New Engagement? Political Participation, Civic Life, and the Changing American Citizen* (New York: Oxford University Press, 2006).
12. "Lagging Youth Enthusiasm Could Hurt Democrats in 2010," Pew Research Center for the People and the Press, October 7, 2010.

TABLE 6–1 ▶ **Votes by Groups in Presidential Elections, 1992–2012 (in Percentages)**

| | 1992 | | | 1996 | | 2000 | | 2004 | | 2008 | | 2012 | |
	CLINTON (DEM.)	BUSH (REP.)	PEROT (REF.)	CLINTON (DEM.)	DOLE (REP.)	GORE (DEM.)	BUSH (REP.)	KERRY (DEM.)	BUSH (REP.)	OBAMA (DEM.)	MCCAIN (REP.)	OBAMA (DEM.)	ROMNEY (REP.)
Total Vote	43	38	19	49	41	48	48	48	51	53	46	51	48
Gender													
Men	41	38	21	43	44	42	53	44	55	49	48	45	52
Women	46	37	17	54	38	54	43	51	48	56	43	55	44
Race													
White	39	41	20	43	46	42	54	41	58	43	55	39	59
Black	82	11	7	84	12	90	8	88	11	95	3	93	6
Hispanic	62	25	14	72	21	67	31	54	44	67	31	71	27
Educational Attainment													
Not a high school graduate	55	28	17	59	28	59	39	50	50	63	35	64	35
High school graduate	43	36	20	51	35	48	49	47	52	52	46	51	48
College graduate	40	41	19	44	46	45	51	46	52	50	48	47	51
Postgraduate education	49	36	15	52	40	52	44	54	45	58	40	56	42
Religion													
White Protestant	33	46	21	36	53	34	63	32	68	45	54	42	57
Catholic	44	36	20	53	37	49	47	47	52	53	45	50	48
Jewish	78	12	10	78	16	79	19	75	24	77	22	69	30
White fundamentalist	23	61	15	NA	NA	NA	NA	21	79	24	74	20	79
Union Status													
Union household	55	24	21	59	30	59	37	59	40	58	40	58	40
Family Income													
Under $15,000	59	23	18	59	28	57	37	63	37	73	25	NA	NA
$15,000–29,000	45	35	20	53	36	54	41	57	41	60	37	NA	NA
$30,000–49,000	41	38	21	48	40	49	48	50	49	55	43	57	42
Over $50,000	40	42	18	44	48	45	52	43	56	49	49	45	53
Size of Place													
Population over 500,000	58	28	13	68	25	71	26	60	40	71	28	69	29
Population 50,000 to 500,000	50	33	16	50	39	57	40	50	50	59	40	58	40
Population 10,000 to 50,000	39	42	20	48	41	38	59	48	51	45	63	42	56
Rural	39	40	20	44	46	37	59	39	60	45	53	39	59

NA = not asked
Sources: *The New York Times*; CNN; *The Wall Street Journal*

Demographic Influences

Demographic influences reflect the individual's personal background and place in society. Some factors have to do with the family into which a person was born: race and (for most people) religion. Others may be the result of choices made throughout an individual's life: place of residence, educational achievement, and occupation.

It is also clear that many of these factors are interrelated. People who have more education are likely to have higher incomes and to hold professional jobs. Similarly, children born into wealthier families are far more likely to complete college than children from poor families. Many other interrelationships are not so immediately obvious; for example, many people might not know that 88 percent of African Americans report that religion is very important in their lives, compared with only 57 percent of whites.[13]

Education. In the past, having a college education tended to be associated with voting for Republicans. In recent years, however, this correlation has become weaker. In particular, individuals with a postgraduate education (professors, doctors, lawyers, other managers) have become increasingly Democratic. Also, a higher percentage of voters with only a high school education, who were likely to be blue-collar workers, voted Republican in 2000 and 2004, compared with the pattern in many previous elections, in which that group of voters tended to favor Democrats. In 2012 voters with a college degree slightly favored Republican Mitt Romney over President Obama (51 percent to 47 percent). People with a high school education or less, and those with post-graduate or professional degrees, favored Obama by much larger margins (See Table 6-1).

The Influence of Economic Status. Family income is a strong predictor of economic liberalism or conservatism. Those with low incomes tend to favor government action to benefit the poor or to promote economic equality. Historically, voters in union households have tended to vote for the Democratic candidate. Those with high incomes tend to oppose government intervention in the economy or to support it only when it benefits business. On economic issues, therefore, the traditional economic spectrum described in Chapter 1 is a useful tool. The rich trend toward the right; the poor trend toward the left.

There are no hard-and-fast rules, however. Some very poor individuals are devoted Republicans, just as some extremely wealthy people support the Democratic Party. Indeed, research indicates that a realignment is occurring among those of higher economic status: professionals now tend to vote Democratic, while small-business owners, managers, and corporate executives tend to vote Republican.[14]

The combination of the prolonged economic recession and U.S. involvement in multiple conflicts overseas has reshaped the political typology, according to new research by the Pew Research Center.[15] The public's political mood is "fractious" and more unpredictable. Pew's typology divides Republicans into "Staunch Republicans" who are conservative on both economic and social issues and "Main Street Republicans"—also conservative, but less so. On the left, Pew identifies "Solid Liberals," predominantly white, who are diametrically opposed to Staunch Republicans on nearly every issue. "New Coalition Democrats" made up of nearly equal numbers of whites, African Americans, and Hispanics and "Hard-Pressed Democrats" are highly religious and more socially conservative than Solid Liberals. In the center of the new political typology are the Independents, divided into

13. The Gallup Poll, "A Look at Americans and Religion Today," March 23, 2004.
14. Thomas B. Edsall, "Voters Thinking Less with Their Wallets," *International Herald Tribune*, March 27, 2001, p. 3.
15. Andrew Kohut, "Beyond Red vs. Blue Political Typology," Pew Research Center for the People and the Press, May 4, 2011.

three categories with little to no overlap: Libertarians, Post-Moderns, and Disaffecteds. The first two are largely white, well educated, and affluent. Those in the Disaffected group are financially stressed and cynical about politics. Groups on the right side of the spectrum prefer elected officials who stick to their positions rather than those who compromise, while Solid Liberals overwhelmingly prefer officials who compromise (the other two groups on the left do not). In short, the political landscape is dynamic and makes establishing electoral coalitions based on partisanship and economic status nearly impossible today.

The 2012 campaign themes emphasized the struggling economy and job creation. Republicans believed they could win votes from Independents who had been negatively impacted by the long recession. However, even though 45 percent of voters labeled the state of the national economy as "not so good" in exit polls, President Obama won 55 percent of those votes. The president did even better among the 39 percent of the electorate who believed the economy was getting better (88 percent compared to 9 percent for Governor Romney). Although the economy was important to voters, their ultimate decision was based on a far more complex array of issues and factors.

Religious Influence: Denomination. Traditionally, scholars have examined the impact of religion on political attitudes by dividing the population into such categories as Protestant, Catholic, and Jewish. In recent decades, however, such a breakdown has become less valuable as a means of predicting someone's political preferences. It is true that in the past, Jewish voters were notably more liberal than members of other groups on both economic and cultural issues, and they continue to be more liberal today. Persons reporting no religion are likely to be liberal on social issues but have mixed economic views. Northern Protestants and Catholics, however, do not differ that greatly from each other, and neither do Southern Protestants and Catholics. This represents something of a change—in the late 1800s and early 1900s, Northern Protestants were distinctly more likely to vote Republican, and Northern Catholics were more likely to vote Democratic.[16] Between 2004 and 2008, nearly all religious groups moved toward the Democratic candidate Barack Obama, with the largest shifts occurring among Catholics (+7 percentage points) and those unaffiliated with any religion (+8 percentage points).[17] Support among Catholics, particularly among Catholic women, does not appear to have eroded as a result of the conflict over the new federal rule requiring that all health insurance plans include free contraception and the compromise position that religious organizations that object to contraception on moral grounds are not required to pay for the costs of contraception. Catholic voters favored the president by a margin of 50 to 48 percent. Although some observers speculated that white fundamentalist Protestants would not support a Mormon candidate for president, that proved not to be the case. Seventy-nine percent of self-identified Born-again Christians supported Governor Romney compared to only 20 percent for Barack Obama.

Religious Influence: Religiosity and Evangelicals. Nevertheless, two factors do turn out to be major predictors of political attitudes among members of the various Christian denominations. One is the degree of *religiosity*, or intensity in practice of beliefs, and the other is whether the person holds fundamentalist or evangelical views. A high degree of religiosity is usually manifested by very frequent attendance at church services, at least once or twice a week.

16.   John C. Green, *The Faith Factor: How Religion Influences American Elections* (New York: Praeger, 2007).
17.   "How the Faithful Voted," The Pew Forum on Religion and Public Life, November 5, 2008.

Voters who are more devout, regardless of their church affiliation, tend to vote Republican, whereas voters who are less devout are more often Democrats. In 2008, for example, people who regularly attend church regardless of denomination were more likely to support John McCain than Barack Obama (55 percent to 43 percent) compared with those who attend church less often (57 percent voted for Obama, while 42 percent voted for McCain). The exception to this trend is that African Americans of all religious backgrounds have been and continue to be strongly supportive of Democrats.

Another distinctive group of voters likely to be very religious are those Americans who can be identified as holding fundamentalist beliefs or consider themselves part of an evangelical group. They are usually members of a Protestant church, which may be part of a mainstream denomination or may be an independent congregation. In election studies, these individuals are usually identified by a pattern of beliefs: They may describe themselves as "born again" and believe in the literal word of the Bible, among other characteristics. As voters, these Christians tend to be cultural conservatives but not necessarily economic conservatives.

The Influence of Race and Ethnicity. Although African Americans are, on average, somewhat conservative on certain cultural issues such as same-sex marriage and abortion, they tend to be more liberal than whites on social welfare matters, civil liberties, and even foreign policy. African Americans voted principally for Republicans (the party of Lincoln) until Democrat Franklin Roosevelt's New Deal in the 1930s. Since then, they have nearly exclusively identified with the Democratic Party. Indeed, Democratic presidential candidates have received, on average, more than 80 percent of the African American vote since 1956. President Obama won 93 percent of the African American vote in 2012. As you learned in Chapter 1, Latinos also favor the Democrats. Latinos of Cuban ancestry, however, are predominantly Republican. Most Asian American groups lean toward the Democrats, although often by narrow margins. Muslim American immigrants and their descendants are an interesting category.[18] In 2000, a majority of Muslim Americans of Middle Eastern ancestry voted for Republican George W. Bush because they shared his cultural conservatism. In the 2004 and 2008 election campaigns, however, the civil liberties issue propelled many of these voters toward the Democrats.[19] In 2012, the emergence of the Latino vote, particularly in swing states, was the big story. Making up 10 percent of the national electorate, Latino voters overwhelmingly supported Barack Obama (71 percent). As the fastest growing population in the country, Latino voters can be expected to exercise greater political influence in future elections. Some experts predict that growing Latino populations will turn a traditionally red state like Texas into a battleground state. White voters' share of the electorate continues to decline, dropping to 72 percent in 2012.

The Gender Gap. Until the 1980s, there was little evidence that men's and women's political attitudes were very different. Following the election of Ronald Reagan in 1980, however, scholars began to detect a **gender gap**. The gender gap has reappeared in subsequent presidential elections, with women being more likely than men to support the Democratic candidate (see Figure 6–4). In the 2000 elections, 54 percent of women voted for Democrat Al Gore, compared with 42 percent of men. In 2012, Barack Obama attracted 55 percent of women's votes and 45 percent of men's votes.

Gender Gap
The difference between the percentage of women who vote for a particular candidate and the percentage of men who vote for the candidate.

---

18. At least one-third of U.S. Muslims are actually African Americans whose ancestors have been in this country for a long time. In terms of political preferences, African American Muslims are more likely to resemble other African Americans than Muslim immigrants from the Middle East.

19. For up-to-date information on Muslim American issues, see the Web site of the Council on American-Islamic Relations at www.cair.com.

Figure 6-4 ▶ Gender Gap in Presidential Elections, 1980–2012

The gender gap is defined as the difference in the proportions of women and men voting for the winning candidate. In 2012, the size of the gender gap held relatively constant at 10 percentage points with 55 percent of women but only 45 percent of men voting for Barack Obama.

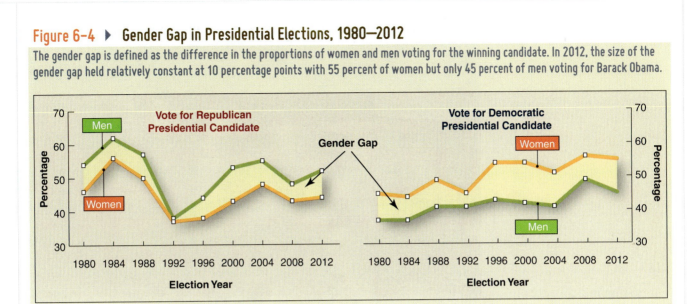

Women also appear to hold different attitudes from their male counterparts on a range of issues other than presidential preferences. They are much more likely than men to oppose capital punishment and the use of force abroad. Studies also have shown that women are more concerned about risks to the environment, more supportive of social welfare, and more in agreement with extending civil rights to gays and lesbians than are men. The contemporary gender gap ranges from about 7 to 12 percent. Obama won about the same proportion of women voters in 2012 as he did in 2008 (55 percent versus 54 percent), but Governor Romney fared much better among men in 2012 (52 percent) than did Senator McCain in 2008 (48 percent). Exit poll data shows some variation in the size of the gender gap in battleground states. In Iowa, for example, the gender gap in 2012 was 15 points, whereas in Colorado there was no evidence of a gender gap. Because more women are registered to vote and more women vote than men, as a result of the gender gap female voters can reasonably claim to have delivered victories in many electoral contests.

Reasons for the Gender Gap. What is the cause of the gender gap? A number of explanations have been offered, including the increase in the number of working women, feminism, women's concerns over abortion rights and other social issues, and the changing political attitudes of men. Researchers Lena Edlund and Rohini Pande of Columbia University, however, have identified another factor leading to the gender gap—the disparate economic impact on men and women of not being married. In the last three decades, men and women have tended to marry later in life or stay single even after having children. The divorce rate has also risen dramatically. Edlund and Pande argue that, particularly for those in the middle class, this decline in marriage has tended to make men richer and women relatively poorer. Consequently, support for Democrats is higher among single or divorced women.[20]

In 2004, observers noted that women seemed more concerned about homeland security and terrorism than men, so much so that the media coined a new term: *security moms*. The label's origins have been traced to a poll reporting that while only 17 percent of men were personally concerned that a member of their family would be the victim of a terrorist attack, 43 percent of women and 53 percent of mothers with children under 18 expressed the same concern. However,

20. Lena Edlund and Rohini Pande, "Why Have Women Become Left-Wing? The Political Gender Gap and the Decline in Marriage," *The Quarterly Journal of Economics*, Vol. 117, No. 3, August 2002, pp. 917–961.

Republican presidential candidates participate in a Republican presidential debate in Sioux City, Iowa, Thursday, December 15, 2011.

ERIC GAY/AFP/Getty Images

further analysis found that although the Democratic candidate, John Kerry, was underperforming among female voters relative to past Democrats, "security moms" did not result in George W. Bush's victory. In fact, researchers Laurel Elder and Steven Greene found that parenthood does not move men or women in a more conservative direction.[21] These studies suggest that labels the media apply to groups of voters based on demographic characteristics may not always be accurate explanations of voting behavior or political attitudes.

During the Republican presidential primaries in 2012, several issues and candidate statements converged in what became known as the "GOP War on Women." Moves to adopt increasingly severe restrictions on abortion services in several Republican-controlled states, initiatives to limit contraception insurance coverage and access, congressional budget cuts to women's health programs, and proposals to weaken the Violence Against Women Act drew lots of media attention. Sandra Fluke, a Georgetown University law school student, was barred from testifying at a Republican congressional hearing on the Obama administration's policy requiring religiously affiliated institutions to provide free contraception in student health insurance plans. When she appeared before a House Democratic panel and testified to the difficulties female students have when reproductive services are curtailed, conservative talk-radio host Rush Limbaugh accused her of "having so much sex she can't afford the contraception." On his live radio show, he called Fluke a prostitute. Many advertisers immediately dropped his radio show but he stayed on the air. Senate contests in Indiana and Missouri that had looked like certain wins for Republicans turned into Democratic victories over remarks about pregnancy resulting from rape. Missouri Rep. Todd Aiken claimed that "if it's a legitimate rape, the female body has ways to shut that whole thing down." In a late October debate, Republican candidate Richard Mourdock said that if a woman becomes pregnant from rape it is "something God intended to happen." Although the Romney campaign disavowed both comments, the damage compounded the Republican's image with women voters.

Geographic Region. Finally, where you live can influence your political attitudes. In one way, regional differences are less important today than just a few decades ago. The formerly solid (Democratic) South has steadily moved toward

21. Laurel Elder and Steven Greene, "The Myth of 'Security Moms' and 'NASCAR Dads'": Parenthood, Political Stereotypes, and the 2004 Election," *Social Science Quarterly*, Vol. 88, No. 1, March 2007, pp. 1–19.

Figure 6–5 ▶ The Purple Election Map

We have grown used to seeing the national vote portrayed using the electoral college map (see, for example, Figure 8–2 on page 252). Because the states are colored red or blue depending on which party's candidate receives the majority of votes, it appears as if all voters in the state are either Republicans (red) or Democrats (blue). Of course, we know that this is not true. Republican and Democratic voters are in every state, and states are broken down into smaller counties, where the diversity is even more apparent. One way to reveal more accurately the nuance in the vote is to use red, blue, and shades of purple to indicate percentages of votes that each party's candidate receives at the county level. In this way, the diversity of political affiliation within states is more visible. Areas that appear purple represent more balance between Republicans and Democrats.

the Republican Party in national elections. For example, only 43 percent of the votes from the southern states went to Democrat Al Gore in 2000, while 55 percent went to Republican George W. Bush. However, Gallup poll data collected over all of 2008 suggest that, across all regions, the country is becoming more Democratic. In 29 states and the District of Columbia, Democrats have a 10-point or greater advantage in party affiliation. The top 10 Republican states in affiliation include only two from the South (South Carolina and Alabama), with the heaviest concentration of Republican affiliation found in Utah, Wyoming, and Idaho.[22] Because so much variability exists in political attitudes and partisan affiliation within a single state, a map constructed at the county level looks purple rather than distinctly red (representing Republicans) or blue (representing Democrats). (See Figure 6–5).

Measuring Public Opinion

In a democracy, people express their opinions in a variety of ways, as mentioned in this chapter's introduction. One of the most common means of gathering and measuring public opinion on specific issues is, of course, through the use of **opinion polls.**

The History of Opinion Polls

During the 1800s, certain American newspapers and magazines spiced up their political coverage by doing face-to-face straw polls (unofficial polls indicating the

■ **Learning Outcome 4:**
Identify three factors that might distort public opinion results collected through opinion polling.

Opinion Poll
A method of systematically questioning a small, selected sample of respondents who are deemed representative of the total population.

22. Jeffrey M. Jones, "State of the State: Party Affiliation," Gallup, January 28, 2009.

trend of political opinion) or mail surveys of their readers' opinions. In the early 20th century, the magazine *Literary Digest* further developed the technique of opinion polling by mailing large numbers of questionnaires to individuals, many of whom were subscribers, to determine their political opinions. From 1916 to 1936, more than 70 percent of the magazine's election predictions were accurate.

Literary Digest's polling activities suffered a setback in 1936, however, when the magazine predicted, based on more than 2 million returned questionnaires, that Republican candidate Alfred Landon would win over Democratic candidate Franklin D. Roosevelt. Landon won in only two states. A major problem with the *Digest*'s polling technique was its use of nonrepresentative respondents. In 1936, at possibly the worst point of the Great Depression, the magazine's subscribers were considerably more affluent than the average American. In other words, they did not accurately represent all of the voters in the U.S. population.

Several newcomers to the public opinion poll industry accurately predicted Roosevelt's landslide victory. These newcomers are still active in the poll-taking industry today: the Gallup poll founded by George Gallup and the Roper poll founded by Elmo Roper. Gallup and Roper, along with Archibald Crossley, developed the modern polling techniques of market research. Using personal interviews with small samples of selected voters (fewer than 2,000), they showed that they could predict with accuracy the behavior of the total voting population.

By the 1950s, improved methods of sampling and a whole new science of survey research had been developed. Survey research centers sprang up throughout the United States, particularly at universities. Some of these survey groups are the American Institute of Public Opinion at Princeton, in New Jersey; the National Opinion Research Center at the University of Chicago; and the Survey Research Center at the University of Michigan.

Sampling Techniques

How can interviewing fewer than 2,000 voters tell us what tens of millions of voters will do? Clearly, it is necessary that the sample of individuals be representative of all voters in the population. Consider an analogy: Let's say we have a large jar containing 10,000 pennies of various dates, and we want to know how many pennies were minted within certain decades (1960–1969, 1970–1979, and so on).

Representative Sampling. One way to estimate the distribution of the dates on the pennies—without examining all 10,000—is to take a representative sample. This sample would be obtained by mixing the pennies up well and then removing a handful of them—perhaps 100 pennies. The distribution of dates might be as follows:

1960–1969: 5 percent
1970–1979: 5 percent
1980–1989: 20 percent
1990–1999: 30 percent
2000–present: 40 percent

If the pennies are very well mixed within the jar, and if you take a large enough sample, the resulting distribution will probably approach the actual distribution of the dates of all 10,000 coins.

The Principle of Randomness. The most important principle in sampling, or poll taking, is randomness. Every penny or every person should have a known chance, and especially an *equal chance*, of being sampled. If this happens, then a small sample should be representative of the whole group, both in demographic characteristics (age, religion, race, region, and the like) and in opinions. The ideal way to sample the voting population of the United States would be to put all voter names into a jar—or a computer—and randomly sample, say, 2,000 of them. Because this is too costly and inefficient, pollsters have developed other ways to obtain good samples. One technique is simply to choose a random selection of telephone numbers and interview the respective households. Prior to expanded cell phone use, this technique produced a relatively accurate sample at a low cost. However, in 2010 the proportion of people living in households without a landline grew to one in four (25 percent). For certain subgroups within the population the proportions are even higher; 30 percent of Latinos are cell-only, as are 30 percent of adults ages 18 to 24 and 49 percent of adults between the ages of 25 and 29. The percentage of households with only a landline continues to decrease but is estimated at about 10 percent. Only 2 percent of the U.S. population cannot be reached by a phone of any kind.

These rapid changes in use of phone technology increase the risk for what pollsters call "coverage error"; that is, the bias introduced when some portion of the population is not covered by the sample. If those missed in the sample differ substantially from those covered, the bias can lead to errors in reporting the results similar to the *Literary Digest* example described above. Whereas research in 2006 found that the likelihood of coverage bias in landline phone surveys was very small, a new study released by the Pew Research Center indicates that the size of the bias effect is increasing, as well as the likelihood of substantive consequences for social and political research reports.[23] Researchers continue to examine these issues as they develop new techniques such as address-based sampling frames to ensure that every person has a known and equal chance at being sampled. Yet more than 40 percent of households now use either caller ID or some other form of call screening. This has greatly reduced the number of households that polling organizations can reach. Calls may be automatically rejected, or the respondent may not take the call. Even when reached, researchers face additional challenges as fewer adults agree to be interviewed. According to the Pew Research Center, the percentage of households in a sample that are successfully interviewed has fallen dramatically. At Pew Research, for example, the response rate of a typical telephone survey was 36 percent in 1997 and is just 9 percent today.[24]

To ensure that the random samples include respondents from relevant segments of the population—rural, urban, northeastern, southern, and so on—most survey organizations randomly choose, say, urban areas that they will consider as representative of all urban areas. Then they randomly select their respondents within those areas. A generally less accurate technique is known as *quota sampling*. Here, survey researchers decide how many persons of certain types they need in the survey— such as minorities, women, or farmers— and then send out interviewers to find the necessary number of these types. Not only is this method often less accurate, but it also may be biased if, say, the interviewer refuses to go into certain neighborhoods or will not interview after dark.

23.   "Assessing the Cell Phone Challenge to Survey Research in 2010," Pew Research Center for the People and the Press, May 20, 2010.
24.   "Assessing the Representativeness of Public Opinion Surveys." The Pew Center for the People and the Press, May 15, 2012. Accessed at: http://www.people-press.org/2012/05/15/assessing-the-representativeness-of-public-opinion-surveys/

Generally, the national survey organizations take great care to select their samples randomly, because their reputations rest on the accuracy of their results. The Gallup and Roper polls usually interview about 1,500 individuals, and their results have a very high probability of being correct—within a margin of 3 percentage points.

Problems with Polls

Public opinion polls are snapshots of the opinions and preferences of the people at a specific moment in time and as expressed in response to a specific question. Given that definition, it is fairly easy to imagine situations in which the polls are wrong.

Sampling Errors. Polls may also report erroneous results because the pool of respondents was not chosen in a scientific manner; that is, the form of sampling and the number of people sampled may be too small to overcome **sampling error**, the difference between the sample result and the true result if the entire population had been interviewed. The sample would be biased, for example, if the poll interviewed people by telephone and did not correct for the fact that more women than men answer the telephone and that some populations (college students and very poor individuals, for example) cannot be found so easily by telephone. Unscientific mail-in polls, telephone call-in polls, Internet polls, and polls completed by the workers in a campaign office are not scientific and do not give an accurate picture of the public's views.

As pollsters get close to Election Day, they become even more concerned about their sample of respondents. Some pollsters continue to interview eligible voters, meaning those over age 18 and registered to vote. Many others use a series of questions in the poll and other weighting methods to try to identify "likely voters" so that they can be more accurate in their election eve predictions. When a poll changes its method from reporting the views of eligible voters to reporting those of likely voters, the results tend to change dramatically.

Poll Questions. It makes sense to expect that the results of a poll will depend on the questions asked. One problem with many polls is the yes/no answer format. For example, suppose the poll question asks, "Do you favor or oppose the war in Iraq?" Respondents might wish to answer that they favored the war at the beginning but not as it is currently being waged, or that they favor fighting terrorism but not a military occupation. They have no way of indicating their true position with a yes or no answer. Respondents also are sometimes swayed by the inclusion of certain words in a question: More respondents will answer in the affirmative if the question asks, "Do you favor or oppose the war in Iraq as a means of fighting terrorism?" Furthermore, respondents' answers are also influenced by the order in which questions are asked, by the possible answers from which they are allowed to choose, and, in some cases, by their interaction with the interviewer. To a certain extent, people try to please the interviewer. They answer questions about which they have no information and avoid some answers to try to measure up to the interviewer's expectations.

Push Polls. Some campaigns have begun using "push polls," in which the respondents are given misleading information in the questions asked to persuade them to vote against a candidate. For example, the interviewer might ask, "Do you approve or disapprove of Congressman Smith, who voted to raise

Sampling Error
The difference between a sample's results and the true result if the entire population had been interviewed.

your taxes 22 times?" Obviously, the answers given are likely to be influenced by such techniques. Push polls have been condemned by the polling industry and are considered to be unethical, but they are still used. In the 2000 Republican Party primary in South Carolina, for example, voters were asked, "Would you be more likely or less likely to vote for John McCain for president if you knew he had fathered an illegitimate black child?" Although no basis existed for the substance of the question, and George W. Bush's campaign disavowed any connection to the calls, thousands of Republican primary voters heard a message obviously designed to *push* them away from candidate McCain. In 2008, Jewish voters in Florida and Pennsylvania were targets of a push poll linking Barack Obama to the Palestine Liberation Organization. Other than complaining to the media about such efforts, candidates are largely defenseless against this abuse of polling.

Because of these problems with polls, you need to be especially careful when evaluating poll results. For some suggestions on how to be a critical consumer of public opinion polls, see the You Can Make a Difference feature at the end of this chapter.

Technology, Public Opinion, and the Political Process

Ironically, technological advances in communication have made gathering public opinion data more difficult in some ways. Federal law prohibits any sort of unsolicited calls to cell phones using "automated dialing devices" and because virtually all pollsters now conduct surveys using computerized systems, this presents a problem. Yet while cell phones make it easier for people to decline to be interviewed, they may also open new avenues to political participation. A 2010 study found that 26 percent of Americans used their cell phones to learn about or participate in the 2010 midterm elections.

Public Opinion and the Political Process

Public opinion affects the political process in many ways. Whether in office or in the midst of a campaign, politicians see public opinion as important to their success. The president, members of Congress, governors, and other elected officials realize that strong public support as expressed in opinion polls is a source of power in dealing with other politicians. It is far more difficult for a senator to say no to the president if the president is immensely popular and if polls show approval of the president's policies. Public opinion also helps political candidates identify the most important concerns among the people and may help them shape their campaigns successfully.

AP Photo/ Byron Rollins

President Harry Truman holds up the front page of the Chicago Daily Tribune issue that predicted his defeat on the basis of a Gallup poll. The poll had indicated that Truman would lose the 1948 contest for his reelection by a margin of 55.5 to 44.5 percent. The Gallup poll was completed more than a week before the election, so it missed a shift by undecided voters to Truman.

did you know?

When Americans were asked if they thought race relations were good or bad in the United States, 68 percent said that they were bad, but when asked about race relations in their own communities, 75 percent said that they were good.

Beyond Our Borders
WORLD OPINION OF THE UNITED STATES

■ **Learning Outcome 5:**
Assess the impact that world opinion of the United States has on the government's domestic and foreign policy decisions.

In the immediate aftermath of the September 11, 2001, terrorist attacks, most of the world expressed a great deal of sympathy toward the United States. Few nations objected to the subsequent American invasion of Afghanistan in 2001 to oust the Taliban government or to the Bush administration's vow to hunt down the terrorists responsible for the 9/11 attacks. When the United States announced plans to invade Iraq in 2003, however, world opinion was not supportive. By 2006, world opinion had become decidedly anti-American, as the United States' ongoing "war on terrorism" continued to offend other nations.

NEGATIVE VIEWS OF AMERICAN UNILATERALISM

The invasion of Iraq in 2003 marked a key turning point in world public opinion toward the United States. Most nations opposed the U.S. plan to attack Iraq. They were supportive of continuing inspections by the United Nations and did not agree that Iraq was a sponsor of terrorism. The willingness of American leaders to ignore world opinion with regard to the Iraq situation led to charges of arrogance on the part of the U.S. administration.

The Pew Global Attitudes Project regularly monitors public opinion toward the United States in more than 40 nations. By 2007, attitudes toward the United States had declined in many regions of the world. For example, the percentage of Canadians who had a favorable view of the United States fell from 71 percent in 2000 to 55 percent in 2007. Declines in favorable views were also found in Western Europe and in some South American countries. While the publics in many former Soviet states had been very supportive of the United States, their favorable views also declined during this period, although not as severely as in Western Europe.

ARAB AND MUSLIM OPINION TOWARD AMERICA AND ITS IDEALS

Among the majority of Middle Eastern states, approval of the United States is especially low among Muslims. This is true in such states as Egypt, Jordan, Pakistan, and Malaysia. However, divisions exist even among Muslims based on religious views. Sunni Muslims

in Lebanon are much more favorably inclined toward the United States than are their Shia countrymen and women. Many Muslim nations and their peoples are opposed to the U.S. action in Iraq and continued aggressive stance toward Iran. While those nations may not support the current regimes, they are more worried that the United States has destabilized the region, and they continue to see the United States as too supportive of the state of Israel. It is worth noting, however, that most Muslim states in Africa have favorable opinions of the United States.*

Many Arabs and Muslims resent U.S. interventionism in the Middle East. This does not mean that they reject all aspects of the United States or its ideals, however. The majority of Muslims do not support religious extremism or terrorism in their own nations. Nor are Arabs and Muslims dismissive of democracy. Recent polls

Muslim women examining a mosaic of stamps depicting the image of Barack Obama during the Asian International Stamp Exhibition held in Jakarta, Indonesia, in 2008.

*The Pew Global Attitudes Project, 2010 Survey, www.pewglobal.org.

(Continued)

(Continued)

have shown declining support for terrorist groups among Arabs and Muslims, with only 13 percent of Moroccans and 25 percent of Pakistani Muslims expressing positive views toward terrorism. There has also been broad support for democracy in the Middle East. Many individuals believe that democracy is a real possibility in their own country. Indeed, 83 percent of Lebanese and 80 percent of Jordanians believe that democracy could work in their respective nations. However, many are still suspicious of American motives in the region.

THE "OBAMA EFFECT"

A 2009–2010 poll conducted by the Program on International Policy Attitudes (PIPA) found that America's influence in the world is now seen as more positive than negative. The improved international standing coincides with Barack Obama's election as president. The survey, conducted among some 30,000 adults, found that the United States is viewed positively on balance in 20 of 28 countries, with an average of 46 percent of those surveyed now saying that the United States has a mostly positive influence in the world, while 34 percent say it has a negative influence. Germany is viewed most positively (with an average of 59 percent positive), and Iran is the least favorably viewed nation (15 percent). The Pew Global Attitudes project confirms these trends for the most part. Nations on the whole continue to be optimistic that the United States will do the right thing in world affairs, even though favorable attitudes declined during President Obama's first term. New challenges presented by continuing violence in Syria, troop withdrawl from Afghanistan, and the threat of nuclear weapons capability in Iran will certainly shape the world's view of the U.S. during a second term.

FOR CRITICAL ANALYSIS

1. *Pollsters do not know yet whether the "Obama effect" is temporary or lasting. Think back over the past year and identify events or actions taken by the government that might positively or negatively influence the world's opinion. Should the U.S. government keep world opinion in mind when making decisions? Why or why not?*

2. *Some polls have shown that younger Muslims and Arabs have a more positive opinion about the United States. Why might that be the case?*

During the presidential primary contests, polling becomes extremely important to candidates, contributors, and voters. Individuals who would like to make a campaign contribution to their favorite candidate may decide not to if the polls show that the candidate is unlikely to win. Voters do not want to waste their votes on the primary candidates who are doing poorly in the polls. In 2008, the two leading Democratic candidates, Senators Barack Obama and Hillary Clinton, used poll results to try to convince convention delegates of their respective strengths as the party nominee.

Nevertheless, surveys of public opinion are not equivalent to elections in the United States. Although opinion polls may influence political candidates or government officials, elections are the major vehicle through which Americans can bring about changes in their government.

Political Culture and Public Opinion

Americans are divided into a multitude of ethnic, religious, regional, and political subgroups. Given the diversity of American society and the wide range of opinions contained within it, how is it that the political process continues to function without being stalemated by conflict and dissension? One explanation is rooted in the concept of the American political culture, which can be described as a set of attitudes and ideas about the nation and the government. As discussed in Chapter 1, our political culture is widely shared by Americans of many different backgrounds. The elements of our political culture include certain shared beliefs about the most important values in the American political system, including (1) liberty, equality, and property; (2) support for religious freedom; and

(3) community service and personal achievement. The structure of the government—particularly federalism, separation of powers, and popular rule—is also an important value. When people share certain beliefs about the system and a reservoir of good feeling exists toward the institutions of government, the nation will be better able to weather periods of crisis. Such was the case after the 2000 presidential elections when, for several weeks, it was not certain who the next president would be and how that determination would be made. At the time, some argued that the nation was facing a true constitutional crisis. In fact, however, the broad majority of Americans did not believe that the uncertain outcome of the elections had created a constitutional crisis. Polls taken during this time found that, on the contrary, most Americans were confident in our political system's ability to decide the issue peaceably and in a lawful manner.[25]

Political Trust and Support for the Political System.   The political culture also helps Americans evaluate their government's performance. At times in our history, **political trust** in government has reached relatively high levels. At other times, political trust in government has fallen to low levels. For example, in the 1960s and 1970s, during the Vietnam War and the Watergate scandals, surveys showed that the overall level of political trust in government had declined steeply. Today people are expressing historically high levels of mistrust in government.[26] Majorities of Americans from both political parties are at times dissatisfied with the way the nation is governed (see Figure 6-6). Perhaps this can be attributed to divided power in Washington, with Democrats

Political Trust
The degree to which individuals express trust in the government and political institutions, usually measured through a specific series of survey questions.

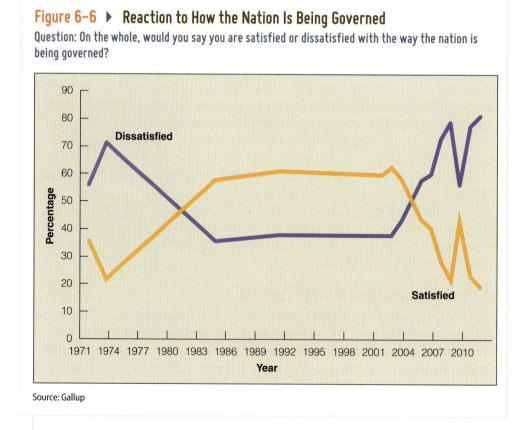

Figure 6–6 ▶ Reaction to How the Nation Is Being Governed

Question: On the whole, would you say you are satisfied or dissatisfied with the way the nation is being governed?

Source: Gallup

25. As reported in *Public Perspective*, March/April 2002, p. 11, summarizing the results of Gallup/CNN/*USA Today* polls conducted between November 11 and December 10, 2000.
26. Gallup's annual Governance survey, updated Sept. 8–11, 2011. Accessed at www.gallup.com/poll/149678/americans-express-historic-negativity-toward-government.aspx

How much confidence should we have in the opinions expressed by the public? This cartoonist believes that the public is gullible and not to be trusted. What about you? Do you trust the information reported in polls? Should policy-makers rely on polls when deciding the direction of the country?

controlling the White House and U.S. Senate and Republicans controlling the House of Representatives. Partisans on both sides can thus find fault with government without necessarily blaming their own party. The same poll shows record or near-record criticism of Congress, elected officials, government handling of domestic problems, the scope of government power, and government waste of tax dollars. Forty-nine percent of Americans believe the federal government has become so large and powerful that it poses an immediate threat to the rights and freedoms of ordinary citizens. In 2003, less than a third (30%) believed this. What does this indicate about the strength and viability of our shared political culture?

Researchers disagree over exactly how much importance varying levels of trust in government should be given. Some evidence indicates that the traditional measures of trust bias results negatively (in other words, trust is higher than polls show), and some scholars argue that democracy requires healthy skepticism rather than blind trust. Scholar Marc Hetherington demonstrates that declining levels of trust have policy implications. In his book, *Why Trust Matters*, he shows that the decline in Americans' political trust explains the erosion in public support for progressive policies such as welfare, food stamps, and health care.[27] As people have lost faith in the federal government, the delivery system for most redistributive policies, they have also lost faith in progressive ideas. The battle over health care reform offers a more recent example of this phenomenon.

Public Opinion about Government

A vital component of public opinion in the United States is the considerable ambivalence with which the public regards many major national institutions. Opinion polls over the last few decades show declining trends in the confidence Americans have in their institutions, such as government, banks, and the police. (See Chapter 1, Figure 1–1, for trends from 2002 to 2011.) The concern is that as confidence in government institutions falls, people will be less likely to embrace a shared political culture, adopt shared norms of political behavior, and as a consequence feel less constrained by government decisions.

Polling organizations such as Gallup regularly ask Americans to name the most important problem facing the country. Figure 6-7 reflects Gallup polls conducted from the years 2001 to 2011. It shows the relative importance Americans place on the economy versus other problems like war, terrorism, crime, or health care, among others. The public tends to emphasize problems that are immediate

27. Marc J. Hetherington, *Why Trust Matters: Declining Political Trust and the Demise of American Liberalism* (Princeton, NJ: Princeton University Press, 2006).

Figure 6–7 ▶ Perceived Most Important Problem Facing the U.S.

Question: "What do you think is the most important problem facing this country today?"

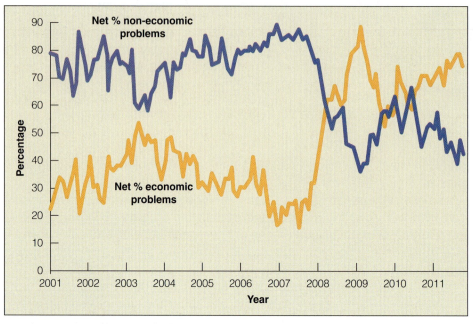

Source: Gallup, Monthly results, January 2001–2011.

and that have been the subject of many stories in the media. When coverage of a particular problem increases suddenly, the public is more likely to see that as the most important problem. Note the dramatic increase in attention to the economy and economic issues and corresponding decrease in attention to non-economic issues that correlates directly with the onset of the global recession in 2008.

When government does not respond adequately to a crisis, public reaction is swift and negative. For example, President George W. Bush's approval rating dropped precipitously following Hurricane Katrina because the majority of the public lacked confidence in the government's response to the devastating Gulf Coast hurricane. African Americans, in particular, believed the government would have responded more quickly if those affected by the storm had been wealthy and primarily white.[28] Similarly, as the economy faltered in the latest recession, individuals, businesses, and even the states looked to the federal government for answers and assistance. When an explosion at an offshore drilling rig operated by British Petroleum (BP) dumped unprecedented amounts of oil into the Gulf, the Obama administration took action to coordinate relief and cleanup efforts but still received criticism because it could not plug the leak. While Congress is best suited to investigate the nature of the problem, the president is best able to take action by mobilizing the resources of the federal bureaucracy.

In conclusion, how individuals and groups approach the political process has a tremendous impact on the country's ability to deal with new challenges, resolve conflicts, and guarantee to all citizens the opportunities afforded by peace and

28. Michael A. Fletcher and Richard Morin, "Bush's Approval Rating Drops to New Low in Wake of Storm," *The Washington Post*, September 13, 2005.

prosperity. The material we have reviewed in this chapter on political socialization and public opinion provides some basis for optimism about the future, but raises some caution flags as well.

Technology now connects us as a people in powerful new ways. Harnessing new forms of communication to promote political engagement, particularly among young people, is exciting. Yet access to technology is not equally distributed across society and, if not carefully monitored, these inequities have the potential to widen the gap between the two Americas. On the other hand, as communication technology advances, it becomes cheaper and more ubiquitous. The Arab Spring demonstrated how technology can advance revolutions and coalesce public opinion in support of new leaders and ideas. As oppressive regimes tried to maintain power, they banned mainstream media from reporting on the conflicts. Twitter, Facebook, and YouTube quickly emerged as a much more powerful force in accelerating social protest than traditional media.

Closer to home we find that lots of Americans are using social networks (66% of adults are regularly online) and that participants in social networking sites mirror the active and inactive political public in several ways. Those most likely to use social networks to urge political action are found at the farthest ends of the liberal and conservative spectrum—in other words, those most activated by their political ideologies. In this respect, they are no different from partisan activists. Political candidates, campaigns, and political organizations are actively reaching out to supporters and likely voters using all of the newest forms of communication technology. Campaign 2012 demonstrated that comfort with social media is key to reaching voters who do not watch television or read newspapers, particularly young voters. Twitter reported that people sent 31 million election-related tweets on election day alone (a 94 percent increase over election day 2008). President Obama announced his victory with a tweet "4 more years" that was re-tweeted over 714,000 times. Traditional network media outlets cited people's tweets as evidence of voting trends on live television. Facebook was joined by Tumblr, Spotify, Pinterest, and Instagram in extending the candidates' messages and images to voters. As these technologies mature and become more integrated into our daily lives, it remains important to carefully assess their impact on our political culture, our shared values, and our identity as a nation.

You Can Make a Difference

BEING A CRITICAL CONSUMER OF OPINION POLLS

iStockphoto.com/kyoshino

Americans are inundated with the results of public opinion polls. The polls purport to tell us a variety of things: whether the president's popularity is up or down, whether gun control is more in favor now than previously, or who is leading the pack for the next presidential nomination. What must be kept in mind with this blizzard of information is that all poll results are not equally good or equally believable.

WHY SHOULD YOU CARE?

As a critical consumer, you need to be aware of what makes one set of public opinion poll results valid and other results useless or even dangerously misleading. Knowing what makes a poll accurate is especially important if you plan to participate actively in politics. Successful participation depends on accurate information, and that includes knowing what your fellow citizens are thinking.

WHAT CAN YOU DO?

Pay attention only to opinion polls that are based on scientific, or random, samples. In these so-called *probability samples,* a known probability is used to select each person interviewed.

Do not give credence to the results of opinion polls that consist of shopping-mall interviews or the like. The main problem with this kind of opinion taking is that not everyone has an equal chance of being in the mall when the interview takes place. And it is almost certain that the people in the mall are not a reasonable cross section of a community's entire population.

Sometimes, even the most experienced pollsters have unreliable results. The "science" counted on for the 2008 presidential primary polling produced results that were wrong by wide margins. The evening before Super Tuesday 2008, the Reuters/C-SPAN/Zogby poll had Democrat Barack Obama with a 13-point lead over Hillary Clinton in the California primary. This same poll had Republican Mitt Romney with a 7-point lead over John McCain. The final voting results in the California primary showed Clinton ahead of Obama by 9 points; McCain held off Romney by almost 8. What happened?

© Sven Martson/The Image Works

Modern polling depends heavily on computerized telephone polling. The respondents are chosen by a random selection of telephone numbers. The interviewer inputs their responses directly into a computer for analysis.

Experts felt there were many reasons for such faulty results. The science of political polling tries to create a microcosm of the electorate; 833 Republicans and 895 Democrats were contacted and identified as "likely to vote." Apparently, the sample included too few Latinos and too many younger voters. Also, the "refusal rate" of people unwilling to talk to pollsters is rising. Pollsters have no way of knowing if these refusing voters represent the views of the majority. The 24/7 news cycle also influences the process. Results in the New Hampshire primary demonstrated that up to 15 percent of the voters decided whom to vote for over the weekend before the actual election. Pollsters missed most of those last-minute deciders.*

Pay attention as well to how people were contacted for the poll—by mail, by telephone, in person in their homes, or in some other way (such as via the Internet). Because of its lower cost, polling firms have turned more and more to telephone interviewing. This method can produce highly accurate results. Its disadvantage is that telephone interviews typically need to be short

*John Diaz, "Why the Polls Are So Wrong," *San Francisco Chronicle,* February 24, 2008, p. G4.

and to deal with questions that are fairly easy to answer. And, as noted earlier, it is difficult to get people to agree to participate. Interviews in person are better for getting useful information about why a particular response was given. They take much longer to complete, however. Results from mailed questionnaires should be taken with a grain of salt. Usually, only a small percentage of people send them back.

When viewers or listeners of television or radio shows are encouraged to call in their opinions to an 800 telephone number, the polling results are meaningless. Users of the Internet also have an easy way to make their views known. Only people who own computers and are interested in the topic will take the trouble to respond, however, and that group is not representative of the general public.

Check to see if your college or university has a polling center on campus. Often, polling centers are found in one or more of the social science departments, such as the political science, sociology, or communication department. These centers offer a good way for you to learn firsthand about the science of polling, as well as an opportunity to develop interviewing skills. At Quinnipiac University, a small liberal arts college in Connecticut, students staff a growing Polling Institute that has become well known for its Q-poll. Student interviewers use a computer-assisted telephone interviewing system to collect data from state and national residents. The poll is regularly cited during presidential primaries and general elections by major news outlets including the *Washington Post*, *The New York Times*, CNN, and Reuters.

Key Terms

agenda setting 186
consensus 181
divisive opinion 181
gender gap 192
generational effect 188

life cycle effect 188
managed news 186
media 186
nonopinion 182
opinion leader 185

opinion poll 195
peer group 185
political socialization 183
political trust 202
public opinion 181

sampling error 198
socioeconomic status 188
watergate break-in 188

Chapter Summary

1. Public opinion is defined as the aggregate of individual attitudes or beliefs shared by some portion of the adult population. A consensus exists when a large proportion of the public appears to express the same view on an issue. Divisive opinion exists when the public holds widely different attitudes on an issue. Sometimes, a poll shows a distribution of opinion, indicating that most people either have no information about an issue or are not interested enough in the issue to form a position on it. Public opinion impacts government actions by providing support for elected officials to adopt or fail to adopt policies. Public opinion can limit government activity if officials are unclear about the direction a majority of Americans support or if opinion is divided and the safest course of action is no action at all.

2. Most descriptions of public opinion are based on the results of opinion polls. The accuracy of polls depends on sampling techniques that include a representative sample of the population being polled and that ensure randomness in the selection of respondents. Problems with polls include sampling errors (which may occur when the pool of respondents is not chosen in a scientific manner), the difficulty of knowing the degree to which responses are influenced by the type and order of questions asked, the use of a yes/no format for answers, and the interviewer's techniques. Many are concerned about the use of "push polls" (in which the questions "push" the respondent toward a particular candidate).

3. People's opinions are formed through the political socialization process. Important factors in this process are the family, educational experiences, peer groups, opinion leaders, the media, and political events. The influence of the media as a socialization factor may be growing relative to the family. Voting behavior is influenced by demographic factors such as education, economic status, religion, race and ethnicity, gender, and region. It is also influenced by election-specific factors such as party identification, perception of the candidates, and issue preferences.

4. Technology is changing the way we communicate with one another. YouTube, Twitter, Twitpic, Facebook, and text messaging make it possible to share information with millions of people instantly. Social media have the power to shape political events (such as the Arab Spring uprisings) and influence support for or opposition to a political candidate. Candidates may learn too late that gaffes last in perpetuity because of new media. Republican presidential hopeful Rick Perry never recovered from his debate performances that were shared via Facebook and repeated endlessly on late-night comedy shows and on YouTube.

5. Public opinion also plays an important role in domestic and foreign policymaking. Although polling data show that a majority of Americans would like policy leaders to be influenced to a great extent by public opinion, politicians cannot always be guided by opinion polls. This is because the respondents often do not understand the costs and consequences of policy decisions or the trade-offs involved in making such decisions. Similarly, the actions of U.S. government officials can be encouraged or constrained by world opinion.

Selected Print, Media, and Online Resources

PRINT RESOURCES

Asher, Herbert. *Polling and the Public: What Every Citizen Should Know.* Washington, DC: CQ Press, 2007. This clearly written and often entertaining book explains what polls are, how they are conducted and interpreted, and how the wording and ordering of survey questions, as well as the interviewer's techniques, can significantly affect the respondents' answers.

Bardes, Barbara A., and Robert W. Oldendick. *Public Opinion: Measuring the American Mind,* 3rd ed. Belmont, CA: Wadsworth, 2006. This examination of public opinion polling looks at the uses of public opinion data and recent technological issues in polling in addition to providing excellent coverage of public opinion on important issues over a period of decades.

Clawson, Rosalee A., and Zoe M. Oxley. *Public Opinion: Democratic Ideals, Democratic Practice.* Washington, DC: CQ Press, 2008. This book begins with the premise that democratic theorists disagree about the degree to which citizens should play an active role in politics. Based on the research in public opinion, the authors explore how individuals come to know and understand politics and then how they think and behave politically.

Dalton, Russell J. *The Good Citizen: How a Younger Generation Is Reshaping American Politics.* Washington, DC: CQ Press, 2009. Contrary to the conventional wisdom that young people are politically disengaged, this book argues that in many ways today's youth are more engaged than those of previous generations, although the forms of engagement differ. Using public opinion surveys and other empirical research, Dalton analyzes modern citizenship norms that move away from duty-based engagement toward a more encompassing version of civic engagement.

Gimple, James G., J. Celeste Lay, and Jason E. Schuknecht. *Cultivating Democracy: Civic Environments and Political Socialization in America.* Washington, DC: Brookings Institution Press, 2003. This book examines the sources of political attitudes in adolescents by examining the characteristics of the local environments that shape their experiences as they come of age in a new century.

Sapiro, Virginia. "Not Your Parents' Political Socialization: Introduction for a New Generation." *Annual Review of Political Science.* 2004:7:1–23. This article reviews the newest research and research questions related to political socialization.

Smith, Christian. *Lost in Transition: The Dark Side of Emerging Adulthood.* New York: Oxford University Press, 2011. Based on over 200 in-depth interviews, this research explores the newest trends in the transition from adolescence to adulthood in the United States. Young people are waiting longer to marry, to have children, and to choose a career direction. The civic and social consequences for these trends are also addressed.

MEDIA RESOURCES

Blame It on Fidel—A 2007 French film in which Anna, a nine-year-old girl, must figure out her own beliefs in the confusion created as her parents become increasingly radicalized. This coming of age film explores themes of stereotyping, misinformation, the power of ideologies, and idealism.

Wag the Dog—A 1997 film that provides a very cynical look at the importance of public opinion. The film, which features Dustin Hoffman and Robert De Niro, follows the efforts of a presidential political consultant, who stages a foreign policy crisis to divert public opinion from a sex scandal in the White House.

ONLINE RESOURCES

Gallup has studied human attitudes and behavior for over 75 years. Although some of the data is only available by subscription, the Gallup Daily News regularly provides information and statistics on a variety of issues and current events: www.gallup.com

Latino Decisions conducts state-level polls, primarily in states with high Latino populations, to inform candidates and policymakers about concerns in the Latino community: www.latinodecisions.wordpress.com/

Pew Forum on Religion and Public Life part of the Pew Research Center. This forum conducts surveys, demographic analyses, and other social science research on important aspects of religion and public life in the United States and around the world. It also provides a neutral venue for discussions of timely issues through roundtables and briefings: www.pewforum.org/

Polling Report an up-to-date and easy-to-use Web site that offers polls and their results organized by topic: www.pollingreport.com

Real Clear Politics (RCP) daily digest of poll results, election analysis, and political commentary as well as an archive of past political polls: www.realclearpolitics.com

7 Interest Groups

Douglas Graham/roll call/Getty Images

The Occupy Wall Street protestors participate in a group meeting about strategy and logistics. At the core of the movement's philosophy was the belief that decisions should be made democratically, not by a small group of leaders.

LEARNING OUTCOMES

After reading this chapter, students will be able to:

■ **LO1** Define an interest group, and explain the constitutional and political reasons why so many groups are found in the United States.

■ **LO2** Explain why an individual may or may not decide to join an interest group and the benefits that membership can confer.

■ **LO3** Describe different types of interest groups and the sources of their political power.

■ **LO4** Identify the direct and indirect techniques that interest groups use to influence government decisions.

What If...

ALL INTEREST GROUPS WERE REGULATED BY THE GOVERNMENT?

BACKGROUND

You can start an interest group this afternoon in your class or at work or over the Internet or via Twitter. All it takes is inviting other people who share a common concern to join you to study the problem or take action to influence the government. You can meet in your home or a coffee shop or the public library. You can write letters to your congressperson or the president, or you can start a Web site promoting your interests. You can collect money for the effort or ask people to donate their time to the cause. All of these activities are protected by the First Amendment to the Constitution and need not involve any level of governmental oversight.

WHAT IF THE GOVERNMENT REGULATED ALL INTEREST GROUPS?

Let's look at what federal regulation of interest groups would mean. What if, when you started your group, you needed to get a license and report your group to the government? What if, when you contacted the public library to reserve a room, the librarian said, "What is your group's ID number? Do you have a license?" Americans currently join more interest groups than citizens of any other country. Would regulations like these discourage Americans from forming groups and limit their right to express themselves?

Currently, some aspects of interest groups are regulated, primarily through the Internal Revenue Service code and the limits on campaign contributions. If an interest group wants to accept donations, and those donations are to be tax deductible for the donor, it must prove that it is a nonprofit group. In that case, the group is severely restricted in its ability to take political action. Furthermore, such a nonprofit group must file a specific form with the IRS every year indicating its financial status and how it meets other requirements. Currently, groups that own property are permitted to seek nonprofit status to avoid paying local property taxes. Most religious institutions have this status.

Today, if your new interest group wants to hold a protest, some laws do apply. If the university or local government has a designated free speech zone, you may be able to speak and hold a protest with no permissions needed. Anti-abortion interest groups have regularly protested outside of Planned Parenthood centers and other institutions that provide abortion services. While the institutions and local governments have tried to restrain such protests, generally the Supreme Court has held that only restrictions based on safety concerns can be enforced. On the other hand, if you want to march down the street or pitch your tents on a public plaza, you will most likely need a permit.

At this time, most interest groups in the United States, whether nonprofit or for profit, exist without much government supervision. What would happen, though, if every interest group with 25 or more members were required to register with the government and report every contribution? Of course, such regulations would require reporting the names of all group members and, most likely, their Social Security numbers so that the IRS could make sure they were not avoiding taxes on their income. Once the group was registered, it could have access to public spaces for meetings and other public services, much like student groups that form on a campus.

WHAT WOULD BE THE IMPACT ON DEMOCRACY?

Regulating interest groups would be a huge, but not impossible, task for the government. Such regulation would have a chilling effect on free speech and the right to assembly in the United States. Individuals whose views are out of the mainstream or who are simply in the minority would be less likely to join groups and certainly less likely to take public actions. Fewer groups would form, and there would be a great advantage for the larger, highly organized interest groups in society. James Madison's fear that the majority could override the interests of minorities, expressed in Federalist #10, might come true. Social scientists have long known that the voices of elites in government and in interest groups get more attention in the media than do the voices of minorities, the poor, and new grassroots groups. As existing groups dominated political decision making, new views would have a difficult time finding a forum, and democratic debate would be diminished.

FOR CRITICAL ANALYSIS

1. *Could the government regulate groups more closely without violating the Constitution and the Bill of Rights?*

2. *Would you be more or less likely to join a group if your name would be supplied to local or federal government authorities?*

Interest Group
An organized group of individuals sharing common objectives who actively attempt to influence policymakers.

Lobbyist
An organization or individual who attempts to influence legislation and the administrative decisions of government.

■ Learning Outcome 1:
Define an interest group, and explain the constitutional and political reasons why so many groups are found in the United States.

Doctors, insurance companies, oil companies, environmentalists, older Americans, African American organizations, Native American tribes, small businesses, unions, gay and lesbian groups, and foreign governments all try to influence the political leaders and policymaking processes of the United States. The structure of American government and the freedoms guaranteed in the Bill of Rights invite the participation of **interest groups** at all stages of the policymaking process. One reason why so many different types of interest groups and other organized institutions attempt to influence our government is the many opportunities for them to do so. Interest groups can hire **lobbyists** to try to influence members of the House of Representatives, the Senate or any of its committees, or the president or any presidential officials. They can file briefs at the Supreme Court or challenge regulations issued by federal agencies. This ease of access to the government is sometimes known as the "multiple cracks" view of our political system. Interest groups can penetrate the political system through many, many entry points, and, as we will note, their right to do so is protected by the Constitution.

Interest Groups: A Natural Phenomenon

Alexis de Tocqueville observed in 1834 that "in no country of the world has the principle of association been more successfully used or applied to a greater multitude of objectives than in America."[1] The French traveler was amazed at the degree to which Americans formed groups to solve civic problems, establish social relationships, and speak for their economic or political interests. James Madison, when he wrote Federalist #10 (see Appendix C), foresaw the importance of having multiple organizations in the political system. He supported the creation of a large republic with many states to encourage the formation of multiple interests. The multitude of interests, in Madison's view, would protect minority views against the formation of an oppressive majority interest. Madison's belief in the power of groups to protect a democracy was echoed centuries later by the work of Robert A. Dahl,[2] a contributor to the pluralist theory of politics, as discussed in Chapter 1. Pluralism sees the political struggle pitting different groups against each other to reach a compromise in the public interest.

Surely, neither Madison nor de Tocqueville foresaw the formation of more than 100,000 associations in the United States or the spending of millions of dollars to influence legislation. Poll data show that more than two-thirds of all Americans belong to at least one group or association. Although the majority of these affiliations could not be classified as interest groups in the political sense, Americans do understand the principles of working in groups.

Today, interest groups range from the local clean water group to the state-wide association of teachers and the national chamber of commerce. They include small groups such as local environmental organizations and national groups such as the Boy Scouts of America, the American Civil Liberties Union, the National Education Association, and the American League of Lobbyists. The continuing increase in the number of groups that lobby governments and the multiple ways in which they are involved in the political process have been seen by some scholars as a detriment to an effective government. Sometimes called

1. Alexis de Tocqueville, *Democracy in America*, Vol. 1, edited by Phillips Bradley (New York: Knopf, 1980), p. 191.
2. Robert A. Dahl, *Who Governs? Democracy and Power in an American City* (New Haven, CT: Yale University Press, 1961).

hyperpluralism, the ability of interest groups to mandate policy or to defeat policies needed by the nation may work against the public good.[3]

Interest Groups and Social Movements

Interest groups are often spawned by mass **social movements**. Such movements represent demands by a large segment of the population for change in the political, economic, or social system. Social movements are often the first expression of latent discontent with the existing system. They may be the authentic voice of weaker or oppressed groups in society that do not have the means or standing to organize as interest groups. For example, most mainstream political and social leaders disapproved of the women's movement of the 1800s. Because women were unable to vote or take an active part in the political system, it was difficult for women who desired greater freedoms to organize formal groups. After the Civil War, when more women became active in professional life, the first real women's rights group, the National Woman Suffrage Association, came into being.

African Americans found themselves in an even more disadvantaged situation after the end of the Reconstruction period. They were unable to exercise their political rights in many Southern and border states, and their participation in any form of organization could lead to economic ruin, physical harassment, or even death. The civil rights movement of the 1950s and 1960s was clearly a social movement. Although the movement received support from several formal organizations—including the Southern Christian Leadership Conference, the National Association for the Advancement of Colored People, and the Urban League— only a social movement could generate the kinds of civil disobedience that took place in hundreds of towns and cities across the country.

In the mid-20th century, Hispanic or Latino Americans became part of a social movement to improve the treatment of immigrant workers. Cesar Chavez,

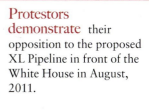

Social Movement
A movement that represents the demands of a large segment of the public for political, economic, or social change.

Rena Schild/Shutterstock.com

Protestors demonstrate their opposition to the proposed XL Pipeline in front of the White House in August, 2011.

3. Theodore Lowi, *The End of Liberalism* (New York: W. W. Norton, 1979).

Peter Silva/ZUMA Press/Newscom

Cesar Estrada Chavez, leader of the farmworker rights movement. He founded the National Farm Workers Association to secure the rights of migrant farmworkers to better wages and living conditions. One of the tactics he used was a consumer boycott against food producers.

did you know?

At least half of all lobbyists in Washington, D.C., are women, but they get paid only 80 percent of what the men earn.

a farmworker, organized the Mexican farm laborers in California and other western states to demand better working conditions, better treatment, and the right to form a union. At one point, the National Farm Workers Association initiated a strike against the grape growers in California and led a successful national boycott of table grapes for six years. Chavez became a national figure, and his work led to improved conditions for all farmworkers. By the 1960s, other leaders within the Hispanic American community founded the National Council of La Raza to improve educational and employment opportunities for their community. Chavez's social movement became a nationally recognized union, the United Farm Workers, while "La Raz" became recognized as an advocacy group that spoke for Hispanic Americans.

As you read in Chapter 5, the Stonewall riots in New York City were the beginning of the drive for greater rights and protections for gays and lesbians in the United States. This social movement began in New York City and San Francisco and then spread to gay communities throughout the nation. There is no doubt that gay, lesbian, and transgendered Americans have become a well-recognized interest group. At the national level, the groups lobby for equal rights under federal law, including the repeal of the "don't ask, don't tell" rule in the military, which was repealed in 2011, and the repeal of the Defense of Marriage Act. At the present time, the Human Rights Campaign is the largest lobbying group, with more than 1 million members. The work of gay, lesbian, and transgendered groups has been made more complicated by the fact that many issues of interest fall under the purview of state law. Thus, many gay, lesbian, and transgendered alliances work at the state and local level. Gay, lesbian, and transgendered groups frequently have chapters on college campuses and, in some areas, within high schools.

Social movements are often precursors of interest groups, some of which are listed in Table 7-1. It is too soon to know whether the nascent social movements targeting income inequality in the United States will become more like an interest group. Many of the local Occupy Wall Street groups ended up with lawyers and legal funds to protect their rights to protest in public places but, as a whole, they have intentionally avoided becoming an organized group. Other social movements, including those that support sustainable farming and making high-quality food more accessible may yet become interest groups if they find a need to recruit members through group incentives.

Why So Many?

Whether based in a social movement or created to meet an immediate crisis, interest groups continue to form and act in American society. One reason for the multitude of interest groups is that the right to join a group is protected by the First Amendment to the U.S. Constitution (see Chapter 4). Not only are all people guaranteed the right "peaceably to assemble," but they are also guaranteed the right "to petition the Government for a redress of grievances." This constitutional provision encourages Americans to form groups and to express their opinions to the government or to their elected representatives as members of a group. Group membership makes the individual's opinions appear more powerful and strongly conveys the group's ability to vote for or against a representative.

In addition, our federal system of government provides thousands of "pressure points" for interest group activity. Americans can form groups in their neighborhoods or cities and lobby the city council and their state government. They can join statewide groups or national groups and try to influence government policy through Congress or through one of the executive agencies or cabinet departments. Representatives of giant corporations may seek to influence the president personally at social events or fundraisers. When attempts to influence government through the executive and legislative branches fail, interest groups turn to the courts, filing suit in state or federal courts to achieve their political objectives. Pluralist theorists, as discussed in Chapter 1, point to the openness of the American political structure as a major factor in the power of groups in American politics.

Table 7–1 ▶ Social Movement Interest Groups

NAACP	www.naacp.org
Human Rights Campaign	www.hrc.org
The Urban League	www.nul.org
NOW	www.now.org
League of United Latin American Citizens	www.lulac.org
National Gay and Lesbian Task Force	www.ngltf.org

Why Do Americans Join Interest Groups?

One puzzle that has fascinated political scientists is why some people join interest groups, whereas many others do not. Everyone has some interest that could benefit from government action. For many individuals, however, those concerns remain unorganized interests, or **latent interests**.

According to political theorist Mancur Olson,[4] it simply may not be rational for individuals to join most groups. In his classic work on this topic, Olson introduced the idea of the "collective good." This concept refers to any public benefit that, if available to any member of the community, cannot be denied to any other member, whether or not he or she participated in the effort to gain the good.

Although collective benefits are usually thought of as coming from such public goods as clean air or national defense, benefits are also bestowed by the government on subsets of the public. Price subsidies to dairy farmers and loans to college students are examples. Olson used economic theory to propose that it is not rational for interested individuals to join groups that work for group benefits. In fact, it is often more rational for the individual to wait for others to procure the benefits and then share them. How many college students, for example, join the United States Student Association, an organization that lobbies the government for increased financial aid to students? The difficulty interest groups face in recruiting members when the benefits can be obtained without joining is referred to as the **free rider problem**.

■ **Learning Outcome 2:**
Explain why an individual may or may not decide to join an interest group and the benefits that membership can confer.

Latent Interests
Public-policy interests that are not recognized or addressed by a group at a particular time.

Free Rider Problem
The difficulty interest groups face in recruiting members when the benefits they achieve can be gained without joining the group.

---

4. Mancur Olson, *The Logic of Collective Action* (Cambridge, MA: Harvard University Press, 1965).

Incentives

If so little incentive exists for individuals to join together, why are there thousands of interest groups lobbying in Washington? According to the logic of collective action, if the contribution of an individual *will* make a difference to the effort, then it is worth it to the individual to join. Thus, smaller groups, which seek benefits for only a small proportion of the population, are more likely to enroll members who will give time and funds to the cause. Larger groups, which represent general public interests (the women's movement or the American Civil Liberties Union, for example), will find it relatively more difficult to get individuals to join. People need an incentive—material or otherwise—to participate.

Solidary Incentives Interest groups offer **solidary incentives** for their members. Solidary incentives include companionship, a sense of belonging, and the pleasure of associating with others. Although the National Audubon Society was originally founded to save the snowy egret from extinction, today most members join to learn more about birds and to meet and share their pleasure with other individuals who enjoy bird-watching as a hobby. The advent of social media has made the creation of solidary incentives much easier. An individual can make friends and exchange ideas with other members through Facebook or Twitter. Such exchanges make the connection to the organization even more worthwhile to the individual. Even though an individual may "join" a group for free through the social media, the interest group benefits from the attention garnered by these "fans." When the time comes to ask for a financial donation or to take local action, these social media participants will feel an enhanced loyalty to the group and may be willing to take action.

Material Incentives For other individuals, interest groups offer direct **material incentives**. A case in point is AARP (formerly the American Association of Retired Persons), which provides discounts, automobile insurance, and organized travel opportunities for its members. After Congress created the prescription drug benefit program supported by AARP, it became one of the larger insurers under that program. Because of its exceptionally low dues ($16 annually) and the benefits gained through membership, AARP has become the largest—and a very powerful—interest group in the United States. AARP can claim to represent the interests of millions of senior citizens and can show that 40 million actually have joined the group. For most seniors, the material incentives outweigh the membership costs.

Many other interest groups offer indirect material incentives for their members. Such groups as the American Dairy Association and the National Association of Automobile Dealers do not give discounts or freebies to their members, but they do offer indirect benefits and rewards by, for example, protecting the material interests of their members from government policymaking that is injurious to their industry or business.

Purposive Incentives Interest groups also offer the opportunity for individuals to pursue political, economic, or social goals through joint action. **Purposive incentives** offer individuals the satisfaction of taking action when the goals of a group correspond to their beliefs or principles. While the Occupy movement is a very new and fairly unformed interest, the individuals who took part in the tent camps and protests expressed very strong feelings about the economic imbalance in American life. The individuals who belong to a group focusing on the abortion issue, gun control, or environmental causes, for example, do so because they feel

---

Solidary Incentive
A reason or motive for supporting or participating in the activities of a group based on the desire to associate with others and to share with others a particular interest or hobby.

did you know?

The activities of interest groups at the state level have been growing much faster than in the nation's capital, with more than 44,000 registered state lobbyists in 2010 and a growth rate of 50 percent in California, Florida, and Texas in the last 10 years.

Material Incentive
A reason or motive for supporting or participating in the activities of a group based on economic benefits or opportunities.

Purposive Incentive
A reason for supporting or participating in the activities of a group based on agreement with the goals of the group. For example, someone with a strong interest in human rights might have a purposive incentive to join Amnesty International.

strongly enough about the issues to support the group's work with money and time. They are also the most likely members to have come out of a social movement and to see that joining the group will strengthen their influence on an issue of great personal importance.

Some scholars have argued that many people join interest groups simply for the discounts, magazine subscriptions, and other tangible benefits and are not really interested in the political positions taken by the groups. According to William P. Browne, however, research shows that people really do care about the policy stance of an interest group. Members of a group seek people who share the group's views and then ask them to join. As one group leader put it, "Getting members is about scaring the hell out of people."[5] People join the group and then feel that they are doing something about a cause that is important to them. Today, the use of social media makes sharing of views and goals even easier for a group.

Types of Interest Groups

Thousands of groups exist to influence government. Among the major types of interest groups are those that represent the main sectors of the economy. In addition, many public-interest organizations have been formed to represent the needs of the general citizenry, including some single-issue groups. The interests of foreign governments and foreign businesses are also represented in the American political arena.

■ **Learning Outcome 3:** Describe different types of interest groups and the sources of their political power.

Economic Interest Groups

More interest groups are formed to represent economic interests than any other set of interests. The variety of economic interest groups mirrors the complexity of the American economy. The major sectors that seek influence in Washington, D.C., include business, agriculture, labor unions and their members, government workers, and professionals.

Business Interest Groups. Thousands of business groups and trade associations work to influence government policies that affect their respective industries. Umbrella groups represent certain types of businesses or companies that deal in a particular type of product. The U.S. Chamber of Commerce, for example, is an umbrella group that represents businesses, and the National Association of Manufacturers is an umbrella group that represents only manufacturing concerns. These are two of the larger groups listed in Table 7-2. The American Pet Products Manufacturers Association works for the good of manufacturers of pet food, pet toys, and other pet products, as well as for pet shops. This group strongly opposes increased regulation of stores that sell animals and restrictions on importing pets. Other major organizations that represent business interests, such as the Better Business Bureaus, take positions on policies but do not actually lobby in Washington, D.C.[6]

Some business groups are decidedly more powerful than others. The U.S. Chamber of Commerce, which has more

Table 7–2 ▶ **Economic Interest Groups—Business**

U.S. Chamber of Commerce	www.uschamber.com
Better Business Bureau	www.bbb.org
National Association of Manufacturers	www.nam.com
National Federation of Independent Business	www.nifbonline.com

5. William P. Browne, *Groups, Interests, and U.S. Public Policy* (Washington, DC: Georgetown University Press, 1998), p. 23.
6. Charles S. Mack, *Business, Politics, and the Practice of Government Relations* (Westport, CT: Quorum Books, 1997), p. 14.

Table 7–3 ▶ Economic Interest Groups—Industries

American Bankers Association	www.aba.com
National Association of Home Builders	www.nahb.org
National Association of Realtors	www.realtor.com
National Beer Wholesalers Association	www.nbwa.org
National Restaurant Association	www.restaurant.org
America's Health Insurance Plans	www.ahip.org
Pharmaceutical Research and Manufacturers of America	www.phrma.org
American Hospital Association	www.aha.org

than 300,000 member companies, can bring constituent influence to bear on every member of Congress. Another powerful lobbying organization is the National Association of Manufacturers. With a staff of more than 60 people in Washington, D.C., the organization can mobilize dozens of well-educated, articulate lobbyists to work the corridors of Congress on issues of concern to its members.

Although business interest groups such as those listed in Table 7-3 are likely to agree on anything that reduces government regulation or taxation, they often do not concur on the specifics of policy, and the sector has been troubled by disagreement and fragmentation within its ranks. Large corporations have been far more concerned with federal regulation of their corporate boards and insider financial arrangements, whereas small businesses lobby for tax breaks for new equipment or new employees. One of the key issues on which businesses do not agree is immigration reform. It seems obvious that businesses that employ foreign workers should be responsible for reporting illegal immigrants, but smaller businesses, particularly in agriculture and construction, argue that checking everyone's immigration status and reporting to the government would be a heavy and expensive burden to bear. Large corporations that are normally under much greater governmental scrutiny and have very professional employment practices comply with immigration rules for their own good.

Agricultural Interest Groups. American farmers and their employees represent less than 2 percent of the U.S. population. Nevertheless, farmers' influence on legislation beneficial to their interests has been significant. Farmers have succeeded in their aims because they have very strong interest groups. Two of the largest are listed in Table 7-4. They are geographically dispersed and therefore have many representatives and senators to speak for them.

The American Farm Bureau Federation, established in 1919, has several million members (many of whom are not actually farmers) and is usually seen as conservative. It was instrumental in getting government guarantees of "fair" prices during the Great Depression in the 1930s.[7] Another important agricultural interest organization is the National Farmers Union (NFU), which represents smaller family farms. Generally the NFU holds more progressive policy positions than does the Farm Bureau. As farms have become larger and agribusiness has become a way of life, single-issue farm groups have emerged. The American Dairy Association, the Peanut Growers Group, and the National Soybean Association, for example, work to support their respective farmers and associated businesses. In recent years, agricultural interest groups have become active on many new issues. Among other things, they have opposed immigration restrictions and are very involved in international trade matters as

Table 7–4 ▶ Economic Interest Groups—Agriculture

American Farm Bureau Federation	www.fb.org
National Farmers Union	www.nfu.org

---

7. The Agricultural Adjustment Act of 1933 (declared unconstitutional) was replaced by the 1938 Agricultural Adjustment Act and was later changed and amended several times.

they seek new markets. One of the newest agricultural groups is the American Farmland Trust, which supports policies to conserve farmland and protect natural resources.

Labor Interest Groups. Interest groups representing the **labor movement** date back to at least 1886, when the American Federation of Labor (AFL) was formed. The largest American unions are listed in Table 7-5. In 1955, the AFL joined forces with the Congress of Industrial Organizations (CIO). Today, the combined AFL-CIO is a large union with a membership of nearly 9 million workers and an active political arm called the Committee on Political Education. In a sense, the AFL-CIO is a union of unions.

The AFL-CIO experienced severe discord within its ranks during 2005, however, when four key unions left the federation and formed the Change to Win Coalition. The new Change to Win Coalition represents about one-third of the 13 million workers who formerly belonged to the AFL-CIO. Many labor advocates fear that the split will further weaken organized labor's waning political influence. The role of unions in American society has declined in recent decades, as witnessed by the decrease in union membership (see Figure 7–1). In the age of automation and with the rise of the **service sector**, blue-collar workers in basic industries (autos, steel, and the like) represent an increasingly smaller percentage of the total working population. Although there was some growth in union membership in the early

Table 7–5 ▶ Economic Interest Groups—Labor

Change to Win Federation	www.changetowin.org
AFL-CIO	www.aflcio.org
SEIU	www.seiu.org
National Education Association	www.nea.org
International Brotherhood of Teamsters	www.teamster.org

Labor Movement

Generally, the economic and political expression of working-class interests; politically, the organization of working-class interests.

Service Sector

The sector of the economy that provides services—such as health care, banking, and education—in contrast to the sector that produces goods.

Figure 7–1 ▶ Decline in Union Membership, 1948 to Present

As shown in this figure, the percentage of the total workforce that is represented by labor unions has declined precipitously over the last 40 years. Note, however, that in contrast to the decline in union representation in the private sector, the percentage of government workers who are unionized has increased significantly since about 1960.

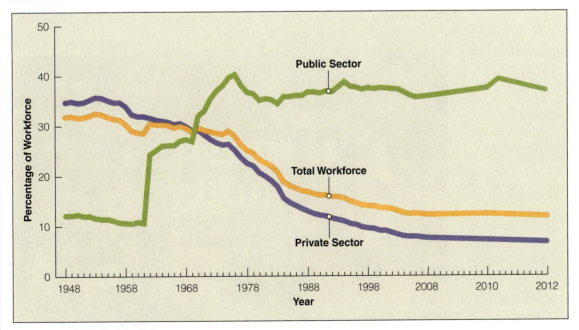

Source: Bureau of Labor Statistics, 2010.

2000s, the economic recession that began in 2008 took its toll on union workers as employees lost their jobs. At the end of 2011, total union membership in the United States stood at 14.8 million workers, or 11.8 percent of the workforce.

With the steady decline in employment in the industrial sector of the economy, national unions are looking to nontraditional areas for their membership, including migrant farmworkers, service workers, and, most recently, public employees— such as police officers, firefighting personnel, and teachers, including college professors and graduate assistants. By 2012, the number of individuals who belonged to public-sector unions outnumbered those in private-sector unions.

Although the proportion of the workforce that belongs to a union has declined over the years, American labor unions have not given up their efforts to support sympathetic candidates for Congress or for state office. Currently, the AFL-CIO, under the leadership of Richard L. Trumka, has a large political budget that it uses to help Democratic candidates nationwide. Although interest groups that favor Republicans continue to assist their candidates, the efforts of labor are more sustained and more targeted. Labor offers a candidate (such as President Obama) a corps of volunteers in addition to campaign contributions. A massive turnout by labor union members in critical elections can significantly increase the final vote totals for Democratic candidates.

Public-Employee Unions. The degree of unionization in the private sector has declined since 1965, but this has been partially offset by growth in the unionization of public employees. Figure 7–1 displays the growth in public-sector unionization. With a total membership of more than 7.1 million, public-sector unions are likely to continue expanding.

The American Federation of State, County, and Municipal Employees as well as the American Federation of Teachers are members of the AFL-CIO's Public Employee Department. Over the years, public-employee unions have become quite militant and are often involved in strikes or protests.

In 2011, the Republican governor and legislature in Wisconsin passed legislation limiting the ability of public-sector union members, including teachers, to bargain for benefits. Teachers, students, and their supporters occupied the Wisconsin statehouse for many weeks, but the law stood. An effort to recall the governor of

Thousands of Chicago teachers rally in Union Park in support of their leaders. The teachers were on strike for the first time in 19 years over a new contract and issues of pay and teacher evaluation.

© Todd Bannor/Alamy

the state was mounted in 2012. After an intense and expensive campaign, Governor Scott Walker defeated the Democratic challenger in the June, 2012, recall election and remained in office.

A powerful interest group lobbying on behalf of public employees is the National Education Association (NEA), a nationwide organization of about 2.8 million teachers and others connected with education. Many NEA locals function as labor unions. The NEA lobbies intensively for increased public funding of education.

Table 7—6 ▶ Professional Interest Groups

American Medical Association	www.ama-assm.org
American Dental Association	www.ada.org
American Bar Association	www.americanbar.org
American Library Association	www.ala.org
American Association for Justice	www.justice.org

Interest Groups of Professionals. Numerous professional organizations exist, including the American Bar Association, the Association of General Contractors of America, the Institute of Electrical and Electronic Engineers, and others. Some professional groups, such as those for lawyers and doctors (see Table 7-6), are more influential than others because of their members' social status. Lawyers have a unique advantage, because many members of Congress share their profession. Interest groups that represent lawyers include both the American Bar Association and the Association of Trial Lawyers of America, which has recently renamed itself the Association for Justice.[8] The trial lawyers have been very active in political campaigns and are usually one of the larger donors to Democratic candidates. In terms of money spent on lobbying, however, one professional organization stands head and shoulders above the rest—the American Medical Association (AMA). Founded in 1847, it is now affiliated with more than 2,000 local and state medical societies and has a total membership of about 300,000.

The Unorganized Poor. Some have argued that the system of interest group politics leaves out poor Americans or those without access to information. Americans who are disadvantaged economically cannot afford to join interest groups; if they are members of the working poor, they may hold two or more jobs just to survive, leaving them no time to participate in interest groups. They may not have access to the Internet and probably do not have time to join social networks online. Other groups in the population—including non-English-speaking groups, resident aliens, single parents, disabled Americans, and younger voters—probably do not have the time or expertise even to find out what group might represent them. Similarly, the millions of Americans affected by the mortgage default crisis, some poor and some middle class, have fought their battles against the banks and mortgage companies alone—no interest group exists or has formed to lobby for more effective policies to help these people. Consequently, some scholars suggest that interest groups and lobbyists are the privilege of upper-middle-class Americans and those who belong to unions or other special groups.

R. Allen Hays examines the plight of poor Americans in his book *Who Speaks for the Poor?*[9] Hays studied groups and individuals who have lobbied for public housing and other issues related to the poor and concluded that the poor depend largely on indirect representation. Most efforts on behalf of the poor come from a policy network of groups—including public housing officials, welfare workers and officials, religious groups, public-interest groups, and some liberal general-interest groups—that speak loudly and persistently for the poor. Poor Americans remain outside the interest group network and have little direct voice of their own.

---

8. www.opensecrets.org
9. R. Allen Hays, *Who Speaks for the Poor?* (New York: Routledge, 2001).

Politics with a Purpose

HOW TO ORGANIZE A GROUP

Within the last four years, two very different groups have organized to challenge the political status quo: the Tea Party and the Occupy movement. Although neither of these two groups can be said to have established itself as a true interest group, both have attracted a great deal of attention in the media and many supporters and critics. Both groups have formed and acted using 21st-century techniques for organizing, techniques that were impossible in decades past.

The Tea Party is an essentially political group that is fairly decentralized and has no top-down administration or bureaucracy. Critics suggest that it is really a faction of the Republican Party that is extremely conservative in its views. Members of Tea Party groups generally dispute that charge, although most of the candidates they back are Republicans. Survey data suggest that some of the members are, in fact, independent voters rather than Republicans.

The Occupy movement arose in the fall of 2011 as a protest movement against the distribution of wealth in the United States and an expression of alienation from corporate values and the current distribution of benefits in society. Occupy camps sprang up across American cities and in London and other European capitals as well. Supporters tended to be young and well educated or current students who were unemployed or underemployed, meaning that they could not find work in the field for which they had trained. The movement challenged local governments by using public spaces for its encampments and accepting the tickets issued by local police. Most camps were eventually disbanded due to public safety concerns, but then warmer weather encouraged them to sprout again.

So how do these groups organize? How could you organize a group to change society or improve your university? First, define your message. Work with a group of like-minded friends to identify your goals. Figure out what kind of a group structure will work and what tasks need to be done. Now, move into the 21st century: Set up your Web site, blog, or Facebook page. Get publicity so that others who agree with you can join your group. You might decide to demonstrate or post signs, or take some symbolic action to get on the news. Maximize the news exposure by posting a video on YouTube. Use any e-mail list available to you. Some of the Occupy groups were able to use lists of activists generated by volunteers in the Obama campaign of 2008. Tea Party members went to local Web sites for information about the next protest. Ask people to join your group by enrolling in your Web site and perhaps donating to the cause. Use all social media to attract followers, and inform them of your mission. Then use the media to let supporters know about your events.

Many organizing methods that seem so obvious to most Americans under 30 did not exist 10 years ago. Texting, cell phone apps, and tweeting are all new ways to keep in contact with like-minded Americans. Of course, getting a group started is one thing, but keeping it going and actually having an impact on public policy require building a more permanent structure and establishing a solid presence in the political arena. It will not be known for some years whether the Occupy movement or the Tea Party has such a future.

For an excellent source of ideas for starting a group, see the Web site: http://movements.org/how-to/

Environmental Groups

Environmental interest groups are not new. We have already mentioned the National Audubon Society, which was founded in 1905 to protect the snowy egret from the commercial demand for hat decorations. The patron of the Sierra Club, John Muir, worked for the creation of national parks more than a century ago. But the blossoming of national environmental groups with mass memberships did not occur until the 1970s. Since the first Earth Day, organized in 1970, many interest groups have sprung up to protect the environment in general or to save unique ecological niches. The groups, many of which are listed in Table 7-7, range from the National Wildlife Federation, with a membership of more than 5 million and an emphasis on education, to the more elite Environmental Defense Fund, with a membership of 300,000 and a focus on influencing federal policy. The National

Resources Defense Council is another very powerful environmental organization, one which has often used the law and lawsuits as part of its strategy. Other groups include the Nature Conservancy, which uses members' contributions to buy up threatened natural areas and either give them to state or local governments or manage them itself, and the more radical Greenpeace Society and Earth First. A more recent entry into the field of environmental groups is the Clean Water Network, which spun off from the National Resources Defense Council in 2008. The Clean Water Network is an alliance of local, state-level, and national groups that works to stop dangerous runoff and protect streams, lakes, and rivers. Many local groups engage in activities such as water sampling and stream monitoring to make sure that water protection standards are followed.

Table 7—7 ▶ Environmental Interest Groups

Sierra Club	www.sierraclub.org
The Nature Conservancy	www.nature.org
National Resources Defense Fund	www.nrdf.org
Clean Water Network	cleanwaternetwork.org
The World Wildlife Fund	www.wwf.org
The Audubon Society	www.audubon.org
National Wildlife Federation	www.nwf.org

Public-Interest Groups

Public interest is a difficult term to define because, as we noted in Chapter 6, there are many publics in our nation of about 320 million. It is almost impossible for one particular public policy to benefit everybody, which makes it practically impossible to define the public interest. Nonetheless, over the past few decades, a variety of lobbying organizations listed in Table 7-8 have been formed "in the public interest."

Public Interest
The best interests of the overall community; the national good, rather than the narrow interests of a particular group.

Young people work together to clean up a creek that has been polluted by run-off and flooding.

© Jim West/Alamy

Table 7—8 ▶ **Public-Interest Groups**

American Civil Liberties Union	www.aclu.org
League of Women Voters	www.lwv.org
Common Cause	www.commoncause.org
Consumer Federation of America	www.consumerfed.org
Amnesty International	www.amnesty.org

Nader Organizations. The best-known and perhaps the most effective public-interest groups are those organized under the leadership of consumer activist Ralph Nader. Nader's rise to the top began in 1965 with the publication of his book *Unsafe at Any Speed*, a lambasting critique of the purported attempt by General Motors (GM) to keep from the public detrimental information about its rear-engine Corvair. Partly as a result of Nader's book, Congress began to consider an automobile safety bill. GM made a clumsy attempt to discredit Nader's background. Nader sued the company, the media exploited the story, and when GM settled out of court for $425,000, Nader became a recognized champion of consumer interests. Since then, Nader has turned over much of his income to the more than 60 public-interest groups that he has formed or sponsored. Nader ran for president in 2000 on the Green Party ticket and again in 2004 and 2008 as an independent.

Other Public-Interest Groups. Partly in response to the Nader organizations, numerous conservative public-interest law firms have sprung up that are often pitted against the consumer groups in court. Some of these are the Mountain States Legal Defense Foundation, the Pacific Legal Foundation, the National Right-to-Work Legal Defense Foundation, the Washington Legal Foundation, the Institute for Justice, and the Mid-Atlantic Legal Foundation.

One of the first groups seeking political reform was Common Cause, founded in 1970. Its goal continues to be moving national priorities toward "the public" and to make governmental institutions more responsive to the needs of the public. Anyone willing to pay dues of $40 per year can become a member (student dues are only $15). Members are polled regularly to obtain information about local and national issues requiring reassessment. Some of the activities of Common Cause have been (1) helping to ensure the passage of the Twenty-sixth Amendment (giving 18-year-olds the right to vote), (2) achieving greater voter registration in all states, (3) supporting the complete withdrawal of all U.S. forces from South Vietnam in the 1970s, and (4) succeeding in passing campaign finance reform legislation.

While Common Cause has about 400,000 members and is still working for political reforms at the national and state level, it is not as well known today as MoveOn.org. Founded in 1998 by two entrepreneurs from California, the group's original purpose was to get millions of people to demand that President Clinton be censured instead of impeached and that the country should "move on" to deal with more important problems. What was strikingly different about this organization is that it was—and continues to be—an online interest group. MoveOn (www.moveon.org) has more than 5 million members and is now a family of organizations that are politically active in national campaigns and in pressuring government on specific issues.

The American Civil Liberties Union dates back to World War I (1914–1918), when, under a different name, it defended draft resisters. It generally enters into legal disputes related to Bill of Rights issues. The ACLU Web site has an excellent discussion of individuals' and groups' rights to express themselves and protest within the law. An international interest group with a strong presence on U.S. college campuses is Amnesty International. This organization, founded in 1961, spans the globe. The mission is to end human rights abuses wherever they are found. Sometimes under fire for unconventional methods, Amnesty has compiled an outstanding record of documenting human rights abuses and was awarded the Nobel Prize in 1977.

Other Interest Groups

Single-interest groups, being narrowly focused, may be able to call attention to their causes because they have simple, straightforward goals and because their members tend to care intensely about the issues. Thus, such groups can easily motivate their members to contact legislators or to organize demonstrations in support of their policy goals.

A number of interest groups focus on just one issue. The abortion debate has created various groups opposed to abortion, such as the National Right to Life Committee, and groups in favor of abortion rights, such as NARAL Pro-Choice America (see Table 7–9). Other single-issue groups are the National Rifle Association, the Right to Work Committee (an anti-union group), and the American Israel Public Affairs Committee (a pro-Israel group). Still other groups represent Americans who share a common characteristic, such as age or ethnicity. Such interest groups may lobby for legislation that benefits their members or upholds their rights or may just represent a viewpoint.

AARP, as mentioned earlier, is one of the most powerful interest groups in Washington, D.C., and, according to some, the strongest lobbying group in the United States. It is certainly the nation's largest interest group, with a membership of about 40 million. AARP has accomplished much for its members over the years. It played a significant role in the creation of Medicare and Medicaid, as well as in obtaining cost-of-living increases in Social Security payments. In 2003, AARP supported the Republican bill to add prescription drug coverage to Medicare. (The plan also made other changes to the system.) Some observers believe that AARP's support tipped the balance and allowed Congress to pass the measure on a closely divided vote. AARP also supported the Obama administration's health care reform legislation passed in 2010.

Foreign Governments

Homegrown interests are not the only players in the game. Washington, D.C., is also the center for lobbying by foreign governments as well as private foreign interests. The governments of the largest U.S. trading partners, such as Canada, European Union (EU) countries, Japan, and South Korea, maintain substantial research and lobbying staffs. Even smaller nations, such as those in the Caribbean, engage lobbyists when vital legislation affecting their trade interests is considered. Frequently, these foreign interests hire former representatives or former senators to promote their positions on Capitol Hill. To learn more about how foreign interests lobby the U.S. government, see this chapter's Beyond Our Borders feature.

What Makes an Interest Group Powerful?

At any time, thousands of interest groups are attempting to influence state legislatures, governors, Congress, and members of the executive branch of the U.S. government. What characteristics make some of those groups more powerful

Table 7–9 ▶ "One Issue" Interest Groups

National Right to Life Committee	www.nrlc.org
NARAL Pro-Choice America	www.naral.org
National Rifle Association	www.nra.org
Brady Campaign (handgun control)	www.bradycampaign.org
American Society for the Prevention of Cruelty to Animals	www.aspca.org
PETA	www.peta.org
MADD	www.madd.org
AARP	www.aarp.org

Figure 7.2 ▶ Profiles of Power—Four Influential Interest Groups

AARP, formerly the American Association of Retired People

Membership: 40 million Americans, mostly over 50

Location: Washington, D.C

Web site: www.aarp.org

The AARP began as an organization of retired teachers and has grown in the last three decades to a mass organization serving more than 40 million members. With a membership fee of only $16 per year, members are entitled to magazines and information, lobbying on their behalf, and access to purchase medical insurance, automobile insurance and travel services. AARP's political power derives from its huge membership, its ability to communicate to its members, and its mission to serve the needs of seniors. The group is now one of the best financed in Washington with an annual revenue base of more than $1 billion. Critics point out that AARP doesn't really offer insurance but lends its name and membership to other corporations which pay royalties of $600 billion a year to AARP. In 2011, AARP spent $15 million on lobbying Congress.

Source: Center for Responsive Politics, Christopher Georges, "Old money—finances of the American Association of Retired Persons," Washington Monthly, 1992.

The Nature Conservancy

Membership: 1 million through subscriptions to the magazine

Location: Fairfax, Virginia

Web site: www.nature.org

The Nature Conservancy is one of the largest and most successful environmental groups in the world, with total revenue for 2010 of more than $900 million. The Conservancy is often criticized by other environmental groups because it is very willing to partner with private property owners, corporations and the states to purchase and save specific tracts of land. It is seen as being more favorable to private ownership and capitalism than many other environmental interest groups. However, it has successfully purchased and preserved millions of acres of land, reefs, and seabed around the world. The organization has net assets of more than $4 billion.

Source: The Nature Conservancy Annual Report, Charity Navigator.

Pharmaceutical Research and Manufacturers of America (PhRMA)

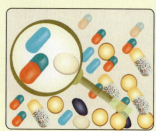

Membership: Only about 50 including all of the major drug-makers in the world. The list is available on PhRMA's website.

Location: Washington, D.C.

Web site: PhRMA.org

During the debate over the Patient Protection and Affordabilty Act (the Obama health care plan), PhRMA was considered one of the most influential players, working on the behalf of its corporate members to keep the government from regulating the cost of drugs. While the overall finances of the association are not public, the not-for-profit arm, PhRMA Foundation distributes hundreds of thousands of dollars to scholarship and research each year and the interest group itself spent more than $18 million for lobbying in 2009.

Source: Center for Responsive Politics.

Service Employees International Union (SEIU)

Membership: 2.1 million

Location: Washington, D.C.

Web site: www.seiu.org

One of the fastest growing unions in the country, the SEIU played an important role in the election of President Barack Obama. With its growth concentrated among public workers, the union saw the election of a progressive president as essential to the welfare of its members. SEIU has been a major campaign contributor to Democratic members of Congress, donating just under $9 million to individual campaigns. In addition the union spent about $15 million on "independent" expenditures for advertising and other communications in the 2010 campaign. The organization reported that it spent about $1.5 million on lobbying efforts in 2011.

Source: Center for Responsive Politics; U.S. Department of Labor.

than others and more likely to have influence over government policy? Generally, interest groups attain a reputation for being powerful through their membership size, financial resources, leadership, cohesiveness, and increasingly, their ability to rally public support behind their cause, whether through in-person demonstrations or via social media.

Size and Resources

No legislator can deny the power of an interest group that includes thousands of his or her own constituents among its members. Labor unions and organizations such as AARP and the American Automobile Association (AAA) are able to claim voters in every congressional district. Having a large membership—nearly 11 million in the case of the AFL-CIO—carries a great deal of weight with government officials. AARP now has about 40 million members and a budget of approximately $1 billion for its operations. In addition, AARP claims to represent all older Americans, who constitute close to 20 percent of the population, whether they join the organization or not.

Having a large number of members, even if the individual membership dues are relatively small, provides an organization with a strong financial base. Those funds pay for lobbyists, television advertisements, mailings to members, a Web site, and many other resources that help an interest group make its point to politicians. The business organization with the largest membership is probably the U.S. Chamber of Commerce, which has more than 300,000 members. The Chamber uses its members' dues to pay for staff and lobbyists, as well as a sophisticated communications network so that it can contact members in a timely way. All members can receive e-mail, use Facebook and Twitter, and check the Web site to get updates on the latest legislative proposals.

Other organizations may have fewer members but nonetheless be able to muster significant financial resources. The pharmaceutical industry is represented in Washington, D.C., by the Pharmaceutical Research Manufacturers of America (PhRMA), sometimes called Big Pharma. In 2009, this lobby poured resources into the fight over health reform legislation, seeking and getting limits on how much the new legislation would cost the pharmaceutical industry. The industry employed more than 1,200 lobbyists, according to estimates (2.3 for every member of Congress) and spent more than $200 million on lobbying.

Leadership

Money is not the only resource that interest groups need to have. Strong leaders who can develop effective strategies are also important. The National Resources Defense Council, formed in 1970 by a group of lawyers and law students who saw the need for a legal approach to environmental problems, is often cited as an outstanding environmental group. The leadership of the NRDC has led strong lobbying efforts for congressional action and planned superb strategies for bringing legal action against polluters and government agencies. Another example is the American Israel Public Affairs Committee (AIPAC), which has long benefited from strong leadership. AIPAC lobbies Congress and the executive branch on issues related to U.S.–Israeli relations, as well as general foreign policy in the Middle East. AIPAC has been successful in facilitating a close relationship between the two nations, which includes the $6 billion to $8 billion in foreign aid that the United States annually bestows on Israel. Despite its modest membership size, AIPAC has won bipartisan support for its agenda and is consistently ranked among the most influential interest groups in America.

Other interest groups, including some with few financial resources, succeed in part because they are led by individuals with charisma and access to power, such as Jesse Jackson of the Rainbow Coalition. Sometimes, choosing a leader with a particular image can be an effective strategy for an organization. The National Rifle Association (NRA) had more than organizational skills in mind when it elected the late Charlton Heston as its president. The strategy of using an actor who is identified with powerful roles as the spokesperson for the organization worked to improve its national image.

Beyond Our Borders

LOBBYING AND FOREIGN INTERESTS

Domestic groups are not alone in lobbying the federal government. Many foreign entities hire lobbyists to influence policy and spending decisions in the United States. American lobbying firms are often utilized by foreign groups seeking to advance their agendas. The use of American lobbyists ensures greater access and increases the possibility of success. In 2010, more than 130 countries spent about $460 billion lobbying the United States government and promoting their nations through public relations campaigns. Hundreds of foreign-owned firms also spent millions of dollars lobbying the Congress and the executive branch. With the United States holding such a dominant position in the global economy and world affairs, it is hardly surprising that foreign entities regularly attempt to influence the U.S. government.

FOREIGN CORPORATIONS AND THE GLOBAL ECONOMY

Economic globalization has had an incalculable impact on public policy worldwide. Given the United States' prominence in the global economy, international and multinational corporations have taken a keen interest in influencing the U.S. government. Foreign corporations spend millions of dollars each year on lobbying in an effort to create favorable business and trade conditions.

Consider several examples: In the list of top 20 spenders for lobbying in 2011 is Royal Dutch Shell, the largest oil company in the world. Based in the Netherlands, Shell Oil spent almost $15 million on lobbying in 2011. GlaxoSmithKline, one of the world's leading pharmaceutical firms, spent extensively on lobbying in the United States to influence health care legislation. Toyota Motors, by comparison, spent only about $4.5 million on lobbying.*

INFLUENCE FROM OTHER NATIONS

Foreign nations also lobby the U.S. government. After it became clear that several Saudi Arabian citizens had participated in the September 11, 2001, terrorist attacks, Saudi Arabia became very concerned about its image in the United States. The Saudi government hired Qorvis Communications, LLC, a public and government

*For reports on the expenditures of countries on lobbying efforts, go to the database at http://foreignlobbying.org, which is sustained by Propublica and the Sunlight Foundation, two not-for-profit organizations dedicated to making information about government more public. You can also go directly to the database maintained by the Department of Justice at www.fara.gov/.

The world headquarters of Royal Dutch Shell in The Hague, The Netherlands. The company spends millions of dollars annually to influence U.S. policy.

affairs consulting firm, to spread the message that Saudi Arabia backed the U.S.–led war on terrorism and was dedicated to peace in the Middle East. In 2002 alone, Saudi Arabia spent $14.6 million on lobbying and public relations services provided by Qorvis.

Individuals and firms who lobby as agents of foreign principals must register with the Department of Justice. Each year the DOJ sends a report to Congress on the registrants and their clients. Countries lobby to improve their trade relations with the United States, to gain relief from their debts, to increase tourism, to resist banking regulations, and to get help for their defense efforts. In 2011, Liberia, the fifth largest exporter of oil to the United States, spent more than $40 million on lobbying efforts. Iraq, lobbying for the reduction of its debts, spent about $5 million, half of what it spent the year before.

FOR CRITICAL ANALYSIS

1. *Should foreign governments and foreign corporations be permitted to lobby the members of Congress in the same way as American interest groups?*

2. *Should members of Congress and the executive branch have to report any contacts from a foreign nation or corporation?*

Cohesiveness

Regardless of an interest group's size or the amount of funds in its coffers, the motivation of its members is a key factor in determining how powerful it is. If the members of a group are committed to their beliefs strongly enough to e-mail or tweet their representatives, join a march on Washington, or work together to defeat a candidate, that group is considered powerful. As described earlier, the American labor movement's success in electing Democratic candidates made the labor movement a more powerful lobby.

In contrast, although groups that oppose abortion rights have had little success in influencing policy, they are considered powerful because their members are vocal and highly motivated. Other measures of cohesion include the ability of a group to get its members to contact Washington quickly or to give extra money when needed. The U.S. Chamber of Commerce excels at both of these strategies. In comparison, AARP cannot claim that it can get its 40 million members to contact their congressional representatives, but it does seem to influence the opinions of older Americans and their views of political candidates.

Interest Group Strategies

Interest groups employ a wide range of techniques and strategies to promote their policy goals. Although few groups are successful at persuading Congress and the president to completely endorse their programs, many are able to block— or at least weaken—legislation that is injurious to their members. The key to success for interest groups is access to government officials. To gain such access, interest groups and their representatives try to cultivate long-term relationships with legislators and government officials. The best of these relationships are based on mutual respect and cooperation. The interest group provides the officials with excellent sources of information and assistance, and the officials in turn give the group opportunities to express its views.

The techniques used by interest groups can be divided into direct and indirect techniques. With **direct techniques**, the interest group and its lobbyists approach the officials personally to present their case. With **indirect techniques**, in contrast, the interest group uses the general public or individual constituents to influence the government on its behalf.

Direct Techniques

Lobbying, publicizing ratings of legislative behavior, building coalitions, and providing campaign assistance are the four main direct techniques used by interest groups.

Lobbying Techniques. As might be guessed, the term *lobbying* comes from the activities of private citizens regularly congregating in the lobbies of legislative chambers before a session to petition legislators. In the latter part of the 1800s, railroad and industrial groups openly bribed state legislators to pass legislation beneficial to their interests, giving lobbying a well-deserved bad name. Most lobbyists today are professionals. They are either consultants to a company or interest group or members of one of the Washington, D.C., law firms that specialize in providing such services. Specialized law firms based in the capital region provide specialists in every sector of government policy to meet their clients' needs. One of the most successful firms is Patton Boggs, LLP, which received more than $47 million in fees for its efforts in 2011. You might wonder what Air France, the City of San Diego, Nissan North America, and the Waterways Council have in

■ **Learning Outcome 4:**
Identify the direct and indirect techniques that interest groups use to influence government decisions.

Direct Technique
An interest group activity that involves interaction with government officials to further the group's goals.

Indirect Technique
A strategy employed by interest groups that uses third parties to influence government officials.

common—all are using Patton Boggs, LLP, to do their lobbying. Additionally, the law firm represented 17 foreign entities, billing more than $3.4 million for those efforts. Among the firm's representatives are former congressman Thomas Boggs, Jr., and former senator Trent Lott.[10]

Lobbyists engage in an array of activities to influence legislation and government policy. These include the following:

1. Engaging in private meetings with public officials, including the president's advisers, to make known the interests of the lobbyists' clients. Although acting on behalf of their clients, lobbyists often furnish needed information to senators and representatives (and government agency appointees) that these officials could not easily obtain on their own. It is to the lobbyists' advantage to provide accurate information so that policymakers will rely on them as a source in the future.
2. Testifying before congressional committees for or against proposed legislation.
3. Testifying before executive rule-making agencies—such as the Federal Trade Commission or the Consumer Product Safety Commission—for or against proposed rules.
4. Assisting legislators or bureaucrats in drafting legislation or prospective regulations. Often, lobbyists furnish advice on the specific details of legislation.
5. Inviting legislators to social occasions, such as cocktail parties, boating expeditions, and other events, including conferences at exotic locations. Most lobbyists believe that meeting legislators in a relaxed social setting is effective.
6. Providing political information to legislators and other government officials. Often, the lobbyists have better information than the party leadership about how other legislators are going to vote. In this case, the political information they furnish may be a key to legislative success.
7. Supplying nominations for federal appointments to the executive branch.

The Ratings Game. Many interest groups attempt to influence the overall behavior of legislators through their rating systems. Each year, the interest group selects legislation that it believes is most important to its goals and then monitors how legislators vote on it. Each legislator is given a score based on the percentage of times that he or she voted in favor of the group's position. The usual scheme ranges from 0 to 100 percent. In the ratings scheme of the liberal Americans for Democratic Action, for example, a rating of 100 means that a member of Congress voted with the group on every issue and is, by that measure, very liberal.

Ratings are a shorthand way of describing members' voting records for interested citizens. They can also be used to embarrass members. For example, an environmental group identifies the 12 representatives it believes have the worst voting records on environmental issues and labels them "the Dirty Dozen," and a watchdog group describes those representatives who took home the most "pork" for their districts or states as the biggest "pigs."

Building Alliances. Another direct technique used by interest groups is to form a coalition with other groups that are concerned about the same legislation. Often, these groups will set up a paper organization with an innocuous name to represent their joint concerns. In the early 1990s, for example,

10. Andrew Ramonas, "Patton Boggs Tops in Foreign Country Lobbying," The Blog of the Legal Times. http://legaltimes.typepad.com/blt/2011/09/.

environmental, labor, and consumer groups formed an alliance called the Citizens Trade Campaign to oppose the passage of NAFTA.

Members of such a coalition share expenses and multiply the influence of their individual groups by combining their efforts. Other advantages of forming a coalition are that it blurs the specific interests of the individual groups involved and makes it appear that larger public interests are at stake. These alliances also are efficient devices for keeping like-minded groups from duplicating one another's lobbying efforts.

Another example of an alliance developed when the Republicans launched the K Street Project. The project, named for the street in Washington, D.C., where the largest lobbying firms have their headquarters, was designed to alter the lobbying community's pro-Democratic tilt. Republicans sought to pressure lobbying firms to hire Republicans in top positions, offering loyal lobbyists greater access to lawmakers in return.

Campaign Assistance. Interest groups have additional strategies to use in their attempts to influence government policies. Groups recognize that the greatest concern of legislators is to be reelected, so they focus on the legislators' campaign needs. Associations with large memberships, such as labor unions, are able to provide workers for political campaigns, including precinct workers to get out the vote, volunteers to put up posters and pass out literature, and people to staff telephone banks for campaign headquarters.

In many states where certain interest groups have large memberships, candidates vie for the groups' endorsements in the campaign. Gaining those endorsements may be automatic, or it may require that the candidates participate in debates or interviews with the interest groups. Endorsements are important, because an interest group usually publicizes its choices in its membership publication and because the candidate can use the endorsement in her or his campaign literature. Traditionally, labor unions have endorsed Democratic Party candidates. Republican candidates, however, often try to persuade union locals at least to refrain from any endorsement. Making no endorsement can then be perceived as disapproval of the Democratic Party candidate.

did you know?

Lobbying expenditures in the United States exceed the gross national product of 57 countries.

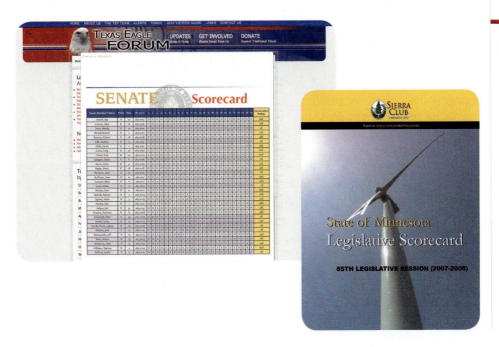

Interest groups from every imaginable ideological point of view issue scorecards of individual legislators' voting records as they relate to the organization's agenda. Shown here are two such scorecards. How much value can voters place on these kinds of ratings?

(Left: Courtesy of Pat Carlson, Texas Eagle Forum, http://www.texaseagle.org; Right: Courtesy of Sierra Club Minnesota North Star Chapter, http://minnesota.sierraclub.org))

Despite the passage of the Bipartisan Campaign Finance Act in 2002, the 2012 election boasted record campaign spending. The usual array of interest groups—labor unions, professional groups, and business associations— gathered contributions to their political action committees and distributed them to the candidates. Most labor contributions went to Democratic candidates, while a majority of business contributions went to Republicans. Some groups, such as real estate agents, gave evenly to both parties. At the same time, the newer campaign groups, the so-called 527 organizations—tax-exempt associations focused on influencing political elections—raised more than $350 million in unregulated contributions to support campaign activities, registration drives, and advertising. After seeing the success of these groups in raising and spending funds, hundreds of interest groups, private and non-profit, have founded their 527 organizations to spend funds for advertising and other political activities. The 2009 decision of the Supreme Court in *Citizens United v. FEC,* 558 U.S. (2010), makes it possible for unions, interest groups, and corporations to spend money directly on advertising for and against candidates in 2012.

Indirect Techniques

Interest groups can also try to influence government policy by working through others, who may be constituents or the general public. Indirect techniques mask the interest group's own activities and make the effort appear to be spontaneous. Furthermore, legislators and government officials are often more impressed by contacts from constituents than from an interest group's lobbyist.

Generating Public Pressure. In some instances, interest groups try to produce a groundswell of public pressure to influence the government. Such efforts may include advertisements in national magazines and newspapers, mass mailings, television publicity, and demonstrations. The Internet, YouTube, Twitter, and Facebook make communication efforts even more effective. "Like" Change to Win Federation or the Sierra Club or Occupy California on Facebook, and you will receive a constant set of updates, blogs, and links to videos. The Occupy movement gathered almost all of its strength and organizing power through the use of social networks.

Interest groups also may commission polls to find out what the public's sentiments are and then publicize the results. Of course, the questions in the polls are worded to get public responses that support the group's own position. The intent of this activity is to convince policymakers that public opinion overwhelmingly supports the group's position.

Some corporations and interest groups also engage in a practice that might be called **climate control**. With this strategy, public relations efforts are aimed at improving the public image of the industry or group and are not necessarily related to any specific political issue. Contributions by corporations and groups in support of public television programs, sponsorship of special events, and commercials extolling the virtues of corporate research are some ways of achieving climate control. For example, to improve its image in the wake of the Gulf Oil spill, British Petroleum launched a set of advertisements featuring individuals who work for the corporation talking about the cleanup, the good work done by BP, and their own pride in working for the corporation. In 2008, Home Depot advertised its commitment to hire and support the training of Olympic athletes, although economic pressures forced the company to end the program in 2009. By building a reservoir of favorable public opinion, groups

Climate Control

The use of public relations techniques to create favorable public opinion toward an interest group, industry, or corporation.

believe that their legislative goals will be less likely to encounter opposition from the public.

Using Constituents as Lobbyists.

Interest groups also use constituents to lobby for their goals. In the "shotgun" approach, the interest group tries to mobilize large numbers of constituents to e-mail, tweet, write, or phone their legislators or the president. These efforts are effective on Capitol Hill only with a very large number of responses, however, because legislators know that the voters did not initiate the communications on their own. Artificially manufactured grassroots activity has been aptly labeled *Astroturf lobbying*.

A more powerful variation of this technique uses only important constituents. With this approach, known as the "rifle" technique or the "Utah plant manager theory," the interest group might, for example, ask the manager of a local plant in Utah to contact the senator from Utah.[11] Because the constituent is seen as responsible for many jobs or other resources, the legislator is more likely to listen carefully to the constituent's concerns about legislation than to a paid lobbyist.

The importance of the electronic media cannot be understated for indirect lobbying. Whether Brad Pitt is speaking about the need to build housing in New Orleans for Katrina victims or George Clooney is staging a protest in front of an embassy, interest groups know that the most famous stars of the entertainment world get an audience. People recognize these individuals and want to see them, and thus receive a message about a public policy issue.

To protest a proposed law that would have placed new regulations on the internet, SOPA, Wikipedia shut its site down for one day. This screen shot captures the thank you message posted by Wikipedia after the black out concluded.

11. Kay Lehman Schlozman and John T. Tierney, *Organized Interests and American Democracy* (New York: Harper & Row, 1986), p. 293.

AP Photo/Cliff Owen

George Clooney and his father, Nick Clooney are arrested in March, 2012 for protesting outside of the Sudanese embassy in London. They staged the protest to call attention to the humanitaran crisis in the Sudan which killed thousands of Sudanese.

Boycott

A form of pressure or protest—an organized refusal to purchase a particular product or deal with a particular business.

Unconventional Forms of Pressure. Sometimes, interest groups may employ forms of pressure that are outside the ordinary political process. These can include marches, rallies, civil disobedience, or demonstrations. Such assemblies, as long as they are peaceful, are protected by the First Amendment. In Chapter 5, we described the civil disobedience techniques of the African American civil rights movement in the 1950s and 1960s. The 1963 March on Washington in support of civil rights was one of the most effective demonstrations ever organized. The women's suffrage movement of the early 1900s also employed marches and demonstrations to great effect.

Demonstrations, however, are not always peaceable. Violent demonstrations have a long history in America, dating back to the antitax Boston Tea Party described in Chapter 2. The Vietnam War (1964–1975) provoked many demonstrations, some of which were violent. In 1999, at a meeting of the World Trade Organization in Seattle, demonstrations against globalization turned violent. These demonstrations were repeated throughout the 2000s at various sites around the world. Still, violent demonstrations can be counterproductive—instead of putting pressure on the authorities, they may simply alienate the public. For example, historians continue to debate whether the demonstrations against the Vietnam War were effective or counterproductive.

Another unconventional form of pressure is the **boycott**—a refusal to buy a particular product or deal with a particular business. To be effective, boycotts must command widespread support. One example was the African American boycott of buses in Montgomery, Alabama, during 1955, described in Chapter 5. Another was the boycott of California grapes that were picked by nonunion workers, as part of a campaign to organize Mexican American farmworkers. The first grape boycott lasted from 1965 to 1970; a series of later boycotts was less effective. In recent years, *threats* of boycotts may have had more power than real ones: After Rush Limbaugh used inappropriate language about a Georgetown University law student, an immediate campaign using social media to threaten a boycott of advertiser products and services convinced a number of companies to drop their sponsorships of his program.

Regulating Lobbyists

Congress made its first attempt to control lobbyists and lobbying activities through Title III of the Legislative Reorganization Act of 1946, otherwise known as the Federal Regulation of Lobbying Act. The act actually provided for public disclosure more than for regulation, and it neglected to specify which agency would enforce its provisions. The 1946 legislation defined a *lobbyist* as any person or organization that received money to be used principally to influence legislation before Congress. Such persons and individuals were supposed to register their clients and the purposes of their efforts and report quarterly on their activities.

The legislation was tested in a 1954 Supreme Court case, *United States v. Harriss*,[12] and was found to be constitutional. The Court agreed that the lobbying law did not violate due process, freedom of speech or of the press, or the freedom to petition. The Court narrowly construed the act, however, holding that it applied only to lobbyists who were influencing federal legislation *directly*.

The Results of the 1946 Act

The immediate result of the act was that a minimal number of individuals registered as lobbyists. National interest groups, such as the National Rifle Association and the American Petroleum Institute, could employ hundreds of staff members who were, of course, working on legislation, but only register one or two lobbyists who were engaged *principally* in influencing Congress. There were no reporting requirements for lobbying the executive branch, federal agencies, the courts, or congressional staff.

According to the Center for Responsive Politics, approximately 12,654 individuals and organizations registered in 2011 as lobbyists, although most experts estimated that 10 times that number were actually employed in Washington to exert influence on the government.

While lobbying firms and individuals who represent foreign corporations must register with Congress, lobbyists who represent foreign governments must register with the Department of Justice under the Foreign Agent Registration Act of 1938. The Department of Justice publishes an annual report listing the lobbyists and the nations that have reported their activities. That report is available online at the Department of Justice Web site (www.usdoj .gov/criminal/fara).

The Reforms of 1995

The reform-minded Congress of 1995–1996 overhauled the lobbying legislation, fundamentally changing the ground rules for those who seek to influence the federal government. Lobbying legislation passed in 1995 included the following provisions:

1. A *lobbyist* is defined as anyone who spends at least 20 percent of his or her time lobbying members of Congress, their staffs, or executive branch officials.
2. Lobbyists must register with the clerk of the House and the secretary of the Senate within 45 days of being hired or of making their first contacts. The registration requirement applies to organizations that spend more than $20,000 in one year or to individuals who are paid more than $5,000 annually for lobbying work.
3. Semiannual (now quarterly and electronic) reports must disclose the general nature of the lobbying effort, specific issues and bill numbers, the estimated cost of the campaign, and a list of the branches of government contacted. The names of the individuals contacted need not be reported.
4. Representatives of U.S.–owned subsidiaries of foreign-owned firms and lawyers who represent foreign entities also are required to register.
5. The requirements exempt grassroots lobbying efforts and those of tax-exempt organizations, such as religious groups.

---

12. 347 U.S. 612 (1954).

As they debated the 1995 law, both the House and the Senate adopted new rules on gifts and travel expenses: The House adopted a flat ban on gifts, and the Senate limited gifts to $50 in value and to no more than $100 in total value from a single source in a year. There are exceptions for gifts from family members and for home-state products and souvenirs, such as T-shirts and coffee mugs. Both chambers banned all-expenses-paid trips, golf outings, and other such junkets. An exception applies for "widely attended" events, however, or if the member is a primary speaker at an event. These gift rules stopped the broad practice of taking members of Congress to lunch or dinner, but the various exemptions and exceptions have caused much controversy as the Senate and House Ethics Committees have considered individual cases.

Recent Lobbying Scandals

The regulation of lobbying activity again surfaced in 2005, when several scandals came to light. At the center of some publicized incidents was a highly influential and corrupt lobbyist, Jack Abramoff. Using his ties with numerous Republican (and a handful of Democratic) lawmakers, Abramoff brokered many deals for the special-interest clients that he represented in return for campaign donations, gifts, and various perks. In January 2006, Abramoff pled guilty to three criminal felony counts related to the defrauding of American Indian tribes and the corruption of public officials.

In 2007, both parties claimed that they wanted to reform lobbying legislation and the ethics rules in Congress. The House Democrats tightened the rules in that body early in the year, as did the Senate. The aptly named Honest Leadership and Open Government Act of 2007 was signed by President Bush in September 2007. The law tightened reporting requirements for lobbyists, extended the time period before ex-members can accept lobbying jobs (to two years for senators and one year for House members), set up rules for lobbying by members' spouses, and changed some campaign contribution rules for interest groups. The new rules adopted by the respective houses bar all members from receiving gifts or trips paid for by lobbyists unless preapproved by the Ethics Committee. Within three months after the bill took effect, a loophole was discovered that allows lobbyists to make a campaign contribution to a senator's campaign, for example, and then go to a fancy dinner where the campaign is allowed to pay the bill.[13] As with most other pieces of lobbying legislation, additional loopholes will be discovered and utilized by members and interest groups.

Interest Groups and Representative Democracy

The role played by interest groups in shaping national policy has caused many to question whether we really have a democracy at all. Most interest groups have a middle-class or upper-class bias. Members of interest groups can afford to pay the membership fees, are generally well educated, and normally participate in the political process to a greater extent than the "average" American. Furthermore, the majority of Americans do not actually join a group outside of

---

13.   Robert Pear, "Ethics Law Isn't Without Its Loopholes," *New York Times*, accessed April 20, 2008, from www.nytimes.com.

their religious congregation or a recreational group. They allow others who do join to represent them.

Furthermore, leaders of some interest groups may constitute an "elite within an elite," in the sense that they usually are from a different economic or social class than most of their members. Certainly, association executives are highly paid individuals who live in Washington, D.C., and associate regularly with the political elites of the country. The most powerful interest groups—those with the most resources and political influence—are primarily business, union, trade, or professional groups. In contrast, public-interest groups or civil rights groups make up only a small percentage of the interest groups lobbying Congress and may struggle to gain enough funds to continue to exist.

Thinking about the relatively low number of Americans who join them and their status as middle class or better leads one to conclude that interest groups are really an elitist phenomenon rather than, as discussed in Chapter 1, a manifestation of pluralism. Pluralist theory proposes that these many groups will try to influence the government and struggle to reach a compromise that will be advantageous to all sides. However, if most Americans are not represented by a group, say, on the question of farm subsidies or energy imports, is there any evidence that the final legislation improves life for ordinary Americans?

Interest Group Influence

The results of lobbying efforts—congressional legislation—do not always favor the interests of the most powerful groups, however. In part, this is because not all interest groups have an equal influence on government. Each group has a different combination of resources to use in the policymaking process. While some groups are composed of members who have high social status and significant economic resources, such as the National Association of Manufacturers, other groups derive influence from their large memberships. AARP's large membership allows it to wield significant power over legislators. Still other groups, such as environmentalist groups, have causes that can claim strong public support even from people who have no direct stake in the issue. Groups such as the National Rifle Association are well organized and have highly motivated members. This enables them to channel a stream of mail or electronic messages toward Congress with a few days' effort.

Even the most powerful interest groups do not always succeed in their demands. Whereas the U.S. Chamber of Commerce may understandably have a justified interest in the question of business taxes, many legislators might feel that the group should not engage in the debate over the future of Social Security. In other words, groups are seen as having a legitimate concern about the issues closest to their interests but not necessarily about broader issues. This may explain why some of the most successful groups are those that focus on very specific issues—such as tobacco farming, funding of abortions, or handgun control—and do not get involved in larger conflicts.

did you know?

As of 2012, the average salary for a lobbyist in Washington, D.C., is $177,000.

You Can Make a Difference

THE GUN CONTROL ISSUE

One of the issues on which Americans are clearly divided is gun control. The long-running debate over the right to own firearms has spawned numerous interest groups with a "single-issue" focus. Their passion is fueled by the 1 million gun incidents occurring in the United States each year—murders, suicides, assaults, accidents, and robberies in which guns are involved.

The Center to Prevent Youth Violence, whose Web site is shown here, is a group working to reduce gun violence against children and teens.

WHY SHOULD YOU CARE?

Research conducted by the National School Safety Center shows that more than 300 students have died in school shootings in the past 15 years. Student gunmen at Virginia Tech and Northern Illinois University in 2007 and 2008 served as traumatic reminders that campus populations seem increasingly vulnerable to gun violence at the hands of mentally unstable young people. In addition, hundreds of young people are killed by gun violence in urban areas and many more in accidental shootings.

To stop the shootings by mentally unstable individuals, many states are now sharing information about certain mentally unstable people with the National Instant Criminal Background Check system, prodded by a measure worked out by Congress and the National Rifle Association, one of the most powerful single-issue groups in the United States. About 32 states have started reporting mental health information to the federal database since the Virginia Tech tragedy, with other states considering laws to improve their reporting. However, people can still buy guns without anyone checking this database.

Gun control advocates would like to see a reinstatement of the Federal Assault Weapons Ban, which federal lawmakers allowed to expire in 2004. This law would ban the sale of military-style assault weapons and high-capacity ammunition magazines like those used by the Virginia Tech and Northern Illinois University killers. The leading group in these efforts continues to be the Brady Center to Prevent Gun Violence, an organization named for the press secretary who was wounded in the assassination attempt on President Reagan. Other organizations are focusing on the prevention of gun violence among youths and accidental shootings.

WHAT CAN YOU DO?

On campus, all students, staff, and faculty need to take responsibility for identifying and redirecting the energies of problematic people. Students take advantage of training offered by the university to identify individuals with problems and pay attention to information about personal safety. Short of installing metal detectors at every building entrance, experts think the majority of these violent events can be handled and prevented by behavioral awareness.

Like the Brady Center, the Center to Prevent Youth Violence grew out of a tragic shooting. After his brother was shot in the back of the head on the observation deck of the Empire State Building in 1997, Dan Gross quit his job to start the Center to Prevent Youth Violence (first named PAX). The center offers programs for young people and parents aimed at reducing gun violence. You can become part of a local group supporting this program. One of the programs sponsored by CPYV is the SPEAK UP hotline. Students who believe that someone is carrying a weapon, or has a gun available to them illegally, can call the SPEAK UP hotline and report their fear anonymously. The center also encourages young people to ask their friends' parents if there is a gun in their home when they visit and to not visit homes where guns are available to children and adults.

In direct contrast to these efforts to keep firearms and those who carry them far from young people, some Americans believe that students and educators should have the right to defend themselves, and that weapons on campus should be part of the plan. A nonprofit organization called Students for Concealed Carry on Campus has 42,000 members nationwide that include college students, faculty, and parents. This group advocates legislation that would allow licensed gun owners to carry concealed weapons on campus, believing that a well-trained citizen could stop a deranged shooter from committing mass murder. Thirteen states are currently considering a form of "concealed carry" legislation for college campuses. Proponents of the Brady Campaign to Prevent Gun Violence oppose the concealed carry legislation, believing that it would only heighten the danger on campuses, where young people drink heavily and live communally. However, a recent court decision in Colorado upheld the students' right under Colorado law to carry concealed licensed firearms on campus, striking down the Board of Regents rule against such action.

To learn about the position of a gun control advocate, contact the Brady Center to Prevent Gun Violence:

1225 Eye St. N.W., Suite 1100
Washington, DC 20005
Brady Center: 202-289-7319
Brady Campaign: 202-898-0792
www.bradycampaign.org

To learn about its efforts to stop gun violence, contact the Center to Prevent Youth Violence:

100 Wall Street, 2nd Floor
New York, NY 10005
212-269-5100
www.cpyv.org

To find out more about its positions, contact the National Rifle Association:

11250 Waples Mill Rd.
Fairfax, VA 22030
703-267-1000
www.nra.org

For more information about the rights of college students to carry weapons, contact Students for Concealed Carry on Campus: www.concealedcampus.org

REFERENCES

Daniel McGinn and Samantha Hening, "Spotting Trouble," *Newsweek*, accessed August 21, 2007, at www. newsweek.com.

Mitch Mitchell, "School-Shooting Expert Answers Tough Questions," *Fort Worth Star Telegram*, accessed February 15, 2008, at www.star-telegram.com/.

Matthew Phillips, "Not Yet Bulletproof," *Newsweek*, accessed October 12, 2007, at www.newsweek.com.

Amanda Ripley, "Ignoring Virginia Tech," *Time*, accessed April 15, 2008, at www.time.com.

Suzanne Smalley, "More Guns on Campus?" *Newsweek*, accessed February 15, 2008, at www.newsweek.com.

Key Terms

Boycott 234	**Indirect Technique** 229	**Lobbyist** 212	**Service Sector** 219
Climate Control 232	**Interest Group** 212	**Material Incentive** 216	**Social Movement** 213
Direct Technique 229	**Labor Movement** 219	**Public Interest** 223	**Solidary Incentive** 216
Free Rider Problem 215	**Latent Interests** 215	**Purposive Incentive** 216	

 # Chapter Summary

1. An interest group is an organization whose members share common objectives and actively attempt to influence government policy. Interest groups proliferate in the United States, because they can influence government at many points in the political structure and because their efforts are protected by the First Amendment to the Constitution. People join interest groups for solidary or emotional benefits, for material or financial reasons, or for purposive reasons. However, many individuals join no interests groups yet are able to benefit from the work of their members. This reality is called the "free rider" problem. Interest groups may grow from the participation of individuals in social movements.

2. Major types of interest groups include business, agricultural, labor, public employee, professional, and environmental groups. Other important groups may be considered public-interest groups. In addition, special-interest groups and foreign governments lobby the government. The relative power of interest groups can be estimated based on the size of their membership, their financial resources, leadership, cohesion, and support among the public

3. Interest groups use direct and indirect techniques to influence government. Direct techniques include testifying before committees and rule-making agencies, providing information to legislators, rating legislators' voting records, aiding political campaigns, and building alliances. Indirect techniques to influence government include campaigns to rally public sentiment, use of social media to generate public pressure, efforts to influence the climate of opinion, and the use of constituents to lobby for the group's interests. Unconventional methods of applying pressure include demonstrations and boycotts.

4. The 1946 Legislative Reorganization Act was the first attempt to control lobbyists and their activities through registration requirements. The United States Supreme Court narrowly construed the act as applying only to lobbyists who directly seek to influence federal legislation.

5. In 1995, Congress approved new legislation requiring anyone who spends 20 percent of his or her time influencing legislation to register. Also, any organization spending $20,000 or more and any individual who is paid more than $5,000 annually for his or her work must register. Quarterly reports must include the names of clients, the bills in which they are interested, and the branches of government contacted. The 2007 lobbying reform law tightened the regulations on lobbyists and imposed other rules on members who wish to become lobbyists after leaving office.

Selected Print, Media, and Online Resources

PRINT RESOURCES

Battista, Andrew. *The Revival of Labor Liberalism.* Champaign, IL: University of Illinois Press, 2008. While labor unions have lost members in recent decades, it is still true that few interest groups are as large as organized labor. Until the late 1960s, the labor movement and political liberalism were close allies. Battista, a political science professor, analyzes the political decline of labor and liberalism, especially after the breakup of the labor-liberal coalition. He also looks at recent attempts to put the coalition back together.

Baumgartner, Frank R., Jeffrey M. Berry, Marie Hojnacki, David C. Kimball, and Beth L. Leech. *Lobbying and Policy Change: Who Wins, Who Loses, and Why.* Chicago: University of Chicago Press, 2009. The authors explore the degree to which lobbying campaigns and intense interest group effort truly change public policy. Their somewhat surprising finding is that the majority of lobbying efforts fail in the face of the strong Washington bias toward the status quo.

Berry, Jeffrey M., and Clyde Wilcox. *Interest Group Society,* 5th ed. New York: Longman, 2009. This work examines the expanding influence of interest groups as well as their relationship to the party system.

Fleshler, Dan. *Transforming America's Israel Lobby: The Limits of Its Power and the Potential for Change.* Dulles, VA: Potomac Books, 2009. Fleshler contends that America's Israel lobby, like many other lobbies, is more resistant to compromise than the people it represents. He proposes strategies to encourage moderation and promote the peace process.

Kaiser, Robert G. *So Damn Much Money: The Triumph of Lobbying and the Corrosion of American Government.* New York: Knopf, 2009. A *Washington Post* journalist, Kaiser shows how lobbyists satisfy politicians' ever-growing need for campaign funds. He argues that behavior once considered corrupt has become commonplace.

Nownes, Anthony J. *Total Lobbying: What Lobbyists Want (and How They Try to Get It).* New York: Cambridge University Press, 2006. This well-written survey of lobbying covers state and local governments, in addition to lobbying at the federal level. It concentrates on public policy, land use, and procurement.

Tishnet, Mark V. *Out of Range: Why the Constitution Can't End the Battle over Guns.* New York: Oxford University Press, 2007. The author, a Harvard law professor, looks at the ongoing debate between the National Rifle Association and gun control groups and offers a thoughtful analysis of both sides of the debate.

MEDIA RESOURCES

Bowling for Columbine—Michael Moore's documentary won an Academy Award in 2003. Moore seeks to understand why the United States leads the industrialized world in firearms deaths. While the film is hilarious, it takes a strong position in favor of gun control and is critical of the National Rifle Association.

Casino Jack and the U.S. of Money—This 2010 documentary takes a scathing look at the machinations of Jack Abramoff and his colleagues. Beginning with his days as a College Republican, producer Alex Gibney traces Abramoff's rise to fame and the tremendous corruption that money brings to Congress.

Norma Rae—A 1979 Hollywood movie about an attempt by a northern union organizer to unionize workers in the southern textile industry; stars Sally Field, who won an Academy Award for her performance.

Organizing America: The History of Trade Unions—A 1994 documentary that incorporates interviews, personal accounts, and archival footage to tell the story of the American labor movement. The film is a Cambridge Educational Production.

ONLINE RESOURCES

AARP (formerly the American Association of Retired Persons)—a nonprofit, nonpartisan membership organization that helps people age 50 and over improve the quality of their lives: www.aarp.org

AFL-CIO (American Federation of Labor and Congress of Industrial Organizations)—a voluntary federation of 56 national and international labor unions: www.aflcio.org

The Center for Public Integrity—a nonprofit organization dedicated to producing original, responsible investigative journalism on issues of public concern; tracks lobbyists and their expenditures: www.publicintegrity.org/lobby

Center for Responsive Politics—a nonpartisan guide to money's influence on U.S. elections and public policy with data derived from Federal Election Commission reports: www.opensecrets.org

National Rifle Association—America's foremost defender of Second Amendment rights and firearms education organization in the world; provides information on the gun control issue: www.nra.org

8 Political Parties

The Democratic precinct chairwoman explains the rules to the voters at an Iowa Caucus in January of 2008 before beginning the debate over the candidates.

LEARNING OUTCOMES

After reading this chapter, students will be able to:

■ **LO1** Define the concept of a political party, and explain how political parties participate in the political system.

■ **LO2** Demonstrate an understanding of how the political parties originated in the United States and how their strength has increased or decreased over time.

■ **LO3** Explain the major differences in the demographics of the supporters of Republicans and Democrats, and discuss how the party positions differ on issues.

■ **LO4** Identify the three major components of the political party, and explain why these components are not necessarily consistent with each other.

■ **LO5** Explain the factors in the American political system that reinforce a two-party system, and discuss why minor or third parties are rarely successful.

What If...

POLITICAL PARTIES HAD ACTUAL MEMBERS?

BACKGROUND

American political parties are perhaps the loosest organizations in the political system. While they are responsible for nominating candidates for national, state, and local offices and deciding government policy, they have no true members. Any individual in the United States can declare himself or herself to be a Republican, a Democrat, a Libertarian, or any other party identification. Most people make that declaration in answer to a poll question asked by a survey researcher. People may also have to declare their party identification to the county clerk in order to vote in a primary election. However, party members do not carry identification cards, nor do they pay dues.

WHAT IF POLITICAL PARTIES IN THE UNITED STATES REQUIRED INDIVIDUALS TO ACTUALLY JOIN?

How would the political parties change if individuals had to actually join and become "real" members? Voters might register for the party online and charge the membership dues to their credit card or mail in a membership application. As with AARP, it is unlikely that anyone would be refused membership and it is likely dues would be very, very, low.

Why would an individual want to "join" a political party in the sense of joining an interest group or group of hobbyists? Political parties would probably offer benefits such as a magazine or newspaper to their members. They would most likely send out little presents such as T-shirts and pens. Imagine getting mail from a friend with an address label identifying her as a member of the Democratic Party. Individuals would receive solidary benefits such as knowing that they share the same views as millions of like-minded Americans.

For the political parties, having real members would give them reliable membership lists of their most likely voters. They could constantly send messages through the social media to the Americans who are most receptive to their policy positions and easily mobilize those members to vote in elections. Most likely, the political parties would try to recruit these members from those organizations where

they find the most support: The Democratic Party would recruit members from labor unions, campus political groups, and environmental groups; Republicans would recruit new members from small business organizations, members of the National Rifle Association, and professional groups. The parties would reap great financial rewards: If 10 million Americans joined each party at $10 annual dues, each party would add $100 million to its respective budget.

WHAT WOULD BE THE CONSEQUENCES FOR AMERICAN POLITICS?

If American political parties were supported by a broad base of members, would this change their policy positions and candidate choices? Becoming membership organizations could go one of two ways: Either the parties would become more cohesive, more polarized, and more exclusive, or they would become more moderate and broad-based. At the present time about one-third of Americans identify with either the Republicans or the Democrats. If only the most interested and most enthusiastic partisans joined the parties, it is likely they would become more cohesive and more polarized because their members would demand a set of core beliefs and candidates focused on those beliefs. Voters who are more moderate in their views would not want to join such an ideological group and would either become more independent in their views or start another party.

If, on the other hand, parties were to reach out to a broad spectrum of Americans, trying to become as large as possible, they would become more moderate in tone and action as they tried to keep their members happy and loyal to the cause.

FOR CRITICAL ANALYSIS

1. *Would a political party with 20 million dues-paying members all connected through Facebook be more powerful than parties are today?*

2. *What incentives might induce Americans under age 30 to actually join a political party?*

DURING NATIONAL ELECTION YEARS, whether for congressional seats, such as 2010, or the presidency, as in 2008 and 2012, political parties become a much more important feature in the political landscape of the United States. For the first six months of 2012, the big story was the Republican contest for the presidential nomination. Commentators argued over whether social issues such as abortion and gay marriage or Tea Party concerns about the size of government would "capture" the Republican Party. By early May, former Massachusetts governor Mitt Romney was the presumed nominee as all of his opponents dropped out of the race. Then, attention turned to the perennial question of whether all the Republican voters would unite to support him. President Obama spent this time period shoring up his support among the Democratic voters who backed him in 2008. For Republican voters, it became important to know when to vote and what restrictions might affect voting in the primary: Some states allow voters to choose either primary, whereas others restrict voting to declared or registered party "members." In some states, **independent** voters could vote in the primaries, but not in others.

Notice that in the previous paragraph, party "member" is placed in quotation marks. This is because Americans do not join a party, nor do they really become members. To become a member of a political party, you do not have to pay dues, pass an examination, or swear an oath of allegiance. Furthermore, individuals and groups of individuals switch their allegiance from one party to another during critical elections. Therefore, at this point, we can ask an obvious question: If nothing is required to be a member of a political party, what, then, is a political party?

What Is a Political Party?

A **political party** is a group of political activists who organize to win elections, operate the government, and determine public policy. This definition explains the difference between an interest group and a political party. Interest groups do not want to operate the government, and they do not put forth political candidates—even though they support candidates who will promote their interests if elected

Independent
A voter or candidate who does not identify with a political party.

■ **Learning Outcome 1:**
Define the concept of a political party, and explain how political parties participate in the political system.

Political Party
A group of political activists who organize to win elections, operate the government, and determine public policy.

A California Tea Party supporter holds her sign at the annual tax day rally on April 15, 2012. Why does the Tea Party claim that it is *not* a political party although it does endorse candidates and work for their election?

© ZUMA Press, Inc/Alamy

or reelected. Another important distinction is that interest groups tend to sharpen issues, whereas American political parties tend to blur their issue positions to attract voters.

Political parties differ from **factions**, which are smaller groups that are trying to obtain power or benefits.[1] Factions are subgroups within parties that may try to capture a nomination or get a position adopted by the party. A key difference between factions and parties is that factions do not have a permanent organization, whereas political parties do. Factions generally preceded the formation of political parties in American history, and the term is still used to refer to groups within parties that follow a particular leader or share a regional identification or an ideological viewpoint.

Political parties in the United States engage in a wide variety of activities, many of which are discussed in this chapter. Through these activities, parties perform several functions for the political system. These functions include the following:

1. *Recruiting candidates for public office.* Because it is the goal of parties to gain control of government, they must work to recruit candidates for all elective offices. Often, this means recruiting candidates to run against powerful incumbents. If parties did not search out and encourage political hopefuls, far more offices would be uncontested, and voters would have limited choices.

2. *Organizing and running elections.* Although elections are a government activity, political parties actually organize the voter-registration drives, recruit the volunteers to work at the polls, provide most of the campaign activity to stimulate interest in the election, and work to increase voter participation.

3. *Presenting alternative policies to the electorate.* In contrast to factions, which are often centered on individual politicians, parties are focused on a set of political positions. The Democrats or Republicans in Congress who vote together do so because they represent constituencies that have similar expectations and demands.

4. *Accepting responsibility for operating the government.* When a party elects the president or governor and members of the legislature, it accepts the responsibility for running the government. This includes staffing the executive branch with loyal party supporters and developing linkages among the elected officials to gain support for policies and their implementation.

5. *Acting as the organized opposition to the party in power.* The "out" party, or the one that does not control the government, is expected to articulate its own policies and oppose the winning party when appropriate. By organizing the opposition to the "in" party, the opposition party forces debate on the policy alternatives.

The major functions of American political parties are carried out by a small, relatively loose-knit nucleus of party activists. This arrangement is quite different from the more highly structured, mass-membership party organization typical of many European parties. American parties concentrate on winning elections rather than on signing up large numbers of deeply committed, dues-paying members who believe passionately in the party's program.

Factions
A group or bloc in a legislature or political party acting in pursuit of some special interest or position.

---

1. See James Madison's comments on factions in Chapter 2.

Two-Party System
A political system in which only two
parties have a reasonable chance of
winning.

did you
know?

The political party with the
most seats in the House of
Representatives chooses the
Speaker of the House, makes
any new rules it wants, gets
a majority of the seats on
each important committee
and chooses committee
chairs, and hires most of the
congressional staff.

A History of Political Parties in the United States

Although it is difficult to imagine a political system in the United States with four, five, six, or seven major political parties, other democratic systems have three-party, four-party, or even 10-party systems. In many nations, parties are clearly tied to ideological positions; parties that represent Marxist, socialist, liberal, conservative, and ultraconservative positions appear on the political continuum. Some nations have political parties representing regions of the nation that have separate cultural identities, such as the French-speaking and Flemish-speaking regions of Belgium. Some parties are rooted in religious differences. Parties also exist that represent specific economic interests—agricultural, maritime, or industrial—and some, such as monarchist parties, speak for alternative political systems.

The United States has a **two-party system**, and that system has been around since about 1800. The function and character of the political parties, as well as the emergence of the two-party system, have much to do with the unique historical forces operating from this country's beginning as an independent nation. James Madison (1751–1836) linked the emergence of political parties to the form of government created by the Constitution.

Generally, we can divide the evolution of the nation's political parties into seven periods:

1. The creation of parties, from 1789 to 1816.
2. The era of one-party rule, or personal politics, from 1816 to 1828.
3. The period from Andrew Jackson's presidency to just before the Civil War, from 1828 to 1860.
4. The Civil War and post–Civil War period, from 1860 to 1896.
5. The Republican ascendancy and the progressive period, from 1896 to 1932.
6. The New Deal period, from 1932 to about 1968.
7. The modern period, from approximately 1968 to the present.

The Formative Years: Federalists and Anti-Federalists

The first partisan political division in the United States occurred before the adoption of the Constitution. As you will recall from Chapter 2, the Federalists were those who pushed for adoption of the Constitution, whereas the Anti-Federalists were against ratification.

In September 1796, George Washington, who had served as president for almost two full terms, decided not to run again. In his farewell address, he made a somber assessment of the nation's future. Washington felt that the country might be destroyed by the "baneful [harmful] effects of the spirit of party." He viewed parties as a threat to both national unity and the concept of popular government. Early in his career, Thomas Jefferson did not like political parties either. In 1789, he stated, "If I could not go to heaven but with a party, I would not go there at all."[2]

Nevertheless, in the years after the ratification of the Constitution, Americans realized that something more permanent than a faction would be necessary to identify candidates for office and represent political differences among the people. The result was two political parties. One party was the Federalists, which

2. Letter to Francis Hopkinson written from Paris while Jefferson was minister to France. In John P. Foley, ed., *The Jeffersonian Cyclopedia* (New York: Russell & Russell, 1967), p. 677.

included John Adams, the second president (served 1797–1801). The Federalists represented commercial interests such as merchants and large planters. They supported a strong national government.

Thomas Jefferson led the other party, which came to be called the Republicans, or Jeffersonian Republicans. (These Republicans should not be confused with the later Republican Party of Abraham Lincoln. To avoid confusion, some scholars refer to Jefferson's party as the Democratic-Republicans, but this name was never used during the time that the party existed.) Jefferson's Republicans represented artisans and farmers. They strongly supported states' rights. In 1800, when Jefferson defeated Adams in the presidential contest, one of the world's first peaceful transfers of power from one party to another was achieved.

The Era of Good Feelings

From 1800 to 1820, a majority of U.S. voters regularly elected Republicans to the presidency and to Congress. By 1816, the Federalist Party had virtually collapsed, and two-party competition did not really exist. Although during elections the Republicans opposed the Federalists' call for a stronger, more active central government, they undertook such active government policies as acquiring the Louisiana Territory and Florida and establishing a national bank. Because the Republicans faced no real political opposition and little political debate was stirred, the administration of James Monroe (1817–1825) came to be known as the **era of good feelings**. Because political competition now took place among individual Republican aspirants, this period can also be called the *era of personal politics.*

Library of Congress, Prints & Photographs Division, Washington, D.C. LC-US262-387

Thomas Jefferson, founder of the first Republican Party. His election to the presidency in 1800 was one of the world's first transfers of power through a free election.

Era of Good Feelings
The years from 1817 to 1825, when James Monroe was president and had, in effect, no political opposition.

Democratic Party
One of the two major American political parties evolving out of the Republican Party of Thomas Jefferson.

Whig Party
A major party in the United States during the first half of the 19th century, formally established in 1836. The Whig Party was anti-Jackson and represented a variety of regional interests.

National Two-Party Rule: Democrats and Whigs

Organized two-party politics returned in 1824. With the election of John Quincy Adams as president, the Republican Party split into two entities. The followers of Adams called themselves National Republicans. The followers of Andrew Jackson, who defeated Adams in 1828, formed the **Democratic Party**. Later, the National Republicans took the name **Whig Party**, which had been a traditional name for British liberals. The Whigs stood for, among other things, federal spending on "internal improvements" such as roads. The Democrats opposed this policy. The Democrats, who were the stronger of the two parties, favored personal liberty and opportunity for the "common man." It was understood implicitly that the common man was a white man—hostility toward African Americans was an important force holding the disparate Democratic groups together.[3]

The Democrats' success was linked to their superior efforts to involve common citizens in the political process. Mass participation in politics and elections was a new phenomenon in the 1820s, as the political parties began to appeal to popular enthusiasm and themes. The parties adopted the techniques of mass campaigns, including rallies and parades. Lavishing food and drink on voters at polling

3. Edward Pessen, *Jacksonian America: Society, Personality, and Politics* (Homewood, IL: Dorsey Press, 1969). See especially pages 246–247. The small number of free blacks who could vote were overwhelmingly Whig.

places also became a common practice. Perhaps of greatest importance, however, was the push to cultivate party identity and loyalty. In large part, the spirit that motivated the new mass politics was democratic pride in participation. By making citizens feel that they were part of the political process, the parties hoped to win lasting party loyalty at the ballot box.

The Civil War Crisis and the Post–Civil War Period

In the 1850s, hostility between the North and South over the issue of slavery divided both parties. The Whigs were the first party to split apart. The Whigs had been the party of an active federal government, but Southerners had come to believe that a strong central government might use its power to free their slaves. The Southern Whigs therefore ceased to exist as an organized party. The Northern Whigs united with antislavery Democrats and members of the radical antislavery Free Soil Party to form the modern **Republican Party**.

After the Civil War, the Democratic Party was able to heal its divisions. Southern resentment of the Republicans' role in defeating the South and fears that the federal government would intervene on behalf of African Americans ensured that the Democrats would dominate the white South for the next century.

"Rum, Romanism, and Rebellion." Northern Democrats feared a strong government for other reasons. The Republicans thought that the government should promote business and economic growth, but many Republicans also wanted to use the power of government to impose evangelical Protestant moral values on society. Democrats opposed what they saw as culturally coercive measures. Many Republicans wanted to limit or even prohibit the sale of alcohol. They favored the establishment of public schools—with a Protestant curriculum. As a result, Catholics were strongly Democratic. In 1884, Protestant minister Samuel Burchard described the Democrats as the party of "rum, Romanism, and rebellion." This remark was offensive to Catholics, and Republican presidential candidate James Blaine later claimed that it cost him the White House. Offensive as it may have been, Burchard's characterization of the Democrats contained an element of truth.

The Triumph of the Republicans. In this period, the parties were evenly matched in strength. The abolition of the three-fifths rule, described in Chapter 2, meant that African Americans would be counted fully when allocating House seats and electoral votes to the South. The Republicans therefore had to carry almost every Northern state to win, and this was not always possible. In the 1890s, however, the Republicans gained a decisive edge. In that decade, the populist movement emerged in the West and South to champion the interests of small farmers, who were often heavily in debt. Populists supported inflation, which benefited debtors by reducing the real value of outstanding debts. In 1896, when William Jennings Bryan became the Democratic candidate for president, the Democrats embraced populism.

As it turned out, the few western farmers who were drawn to the Democrats by this step were greatly outnumbered by urban working-class voters who believed that inflation would reduce the purchasing power of their paychecks and who therefore became Republicans. William McKinley, the Republican candidate, was elected with a solid majority of the votes. Figure 8–1 shows the states taken by Bryan and

---

Republican Party

One of the two major American political parties. It emerged in the 1850s as an antislavery party and consisted of former Northern Whigs and antislavery Democrats.

Andrew Jackson, the seventh president of the United States, was known by the name, "Old Hickory," for his victories in the War of 1812. This is a painting done by Asher Brown Durand in 1835, during the last years of Jackson's second term.

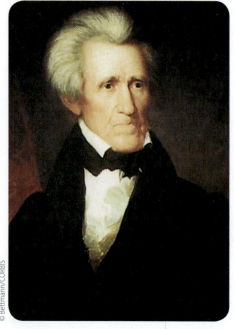

© Bettmann/CORBIS

Figure 8–1 ▶ The 1896 Presidential Election

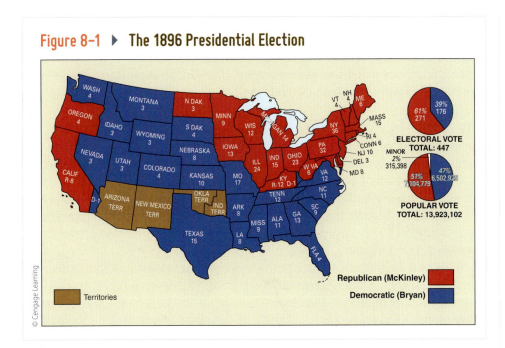

ELECTORAL VOTE TOTAL: 447

61% 271 / 39% 176

MINOR 2% 315,398

51% 7,104,779 / 47% 6,502,925

POPULAR VOTE TOTAL: 13,923,102

Republican (McKinley)
Democratic (Bryan)
Territories

© Cengage Learning

McKinley. This pattern of regional support persisted for many years. From 1896 until 1932, the Republicans were successfully able to present themselves as the party that knew how to manage the economy.

The Progressive Interlude

In the early 1900s, a spirit of political reform arose in both major parties. Called *progressivism*, this spirit was compounded by a fear of the growing power of great corporations and a belief that honest, impartial government could regulate the economy effectively. In 1912, the Republican Party temporarily split as former Republican president Theodore Roosevelt campaigned for the presidency on a third-party Progressive, or "Bull Moose," ticket. The Republican split permitted the election of Woodrow Wilson, the Democratic candidate, along with a Democratic Congress.

Like Roosevelt, Wilson considered himself a progressive, although he and Roosevelt did not agree on how progressivism ought to be implemented. Wilson's progressivism marked the beginning of a radical change in Democratic policies.

In 1912, Theodore Roosevelt campaigned for the presidency on a third-party Progressive, or Bull Moose, ticket. Here, you see a charter membership certificate showing Roosevelt and his vice-presidential candidate, Hiram W. Johnson. What was the main result of Roosevelt's formation of this third party?

© Bettmann/CORBIS

Dating back to its foundation, the Democratic Party had been the party of limited government. Under Wilson, the Democrats became for the first time at least as receptive as the Republicans to government action in the economy. (Wilson's progressivism did not extend to race relations—for African Americans, the Wilson administration was something of a disaster.)

The New Deal Era

The Republican ascendancy resumed after Wilson left office. It ended with the election of 1932, in the depths of the Great Depression. Republican Herbert Hoover was president when the Depression began in 1929. Although Hoover took some measures to fight the Depression, they fell far short of what the public demanded. Significantly, Hoover opposed federal relief for the unemployed and the destitute. In 1932, Democrat Franklin D. Roosevelt was elected president by an overwhelming margin.

The Great Depression shattered the working-class belief in Republican economic competence. Under Roosevelt, the Democrats began to make major interventions in the economy in an attempt to combat the Depression and to relieve the suffering of the unemployed. Roosevelt's New Deal relief programs were open to all citizens, both black and white. As a result, African Americans began to support the Democratic Party in large numbers—a development that would have stunned any American politician of the 1800s.

Roosevelt's political coalition was broad enough to establish the Democrats as the new majority party, in place of the Republicans. In the 1950s, Republican Dwight D. Eisenhower, the leading U.S. general during World War II, won two terms as president. Otherwise, with minor interruptions, the Democratic ascendancy lasted until 1968.

An Era of Divided Government

The New Deal coalition managed the unlikely feat of including both African Americans and southern whites who were hostile to African American advancement. This balancing act came to an end in the 1960s, a decade marked by the civil rights movement, by several years of race riots in major cities, and by increasingly heated protests against the Vietnam War. For many economically liberal, socially conservative voters (especially in the South), social issues had become more important than economic ones, and these voters left the Democrats. These voters outnumbered the new voters who joined the Democrats—newly enfranchised African Americans and former liberal Republicans in New England and the upper Midwest.

The Era of Shifting Majorities. The result, since 1968, has been an era in which neither party dominates. In presidential elections, the Republicans have had more success than the Democrats. Until 1994, Congress remained Democratic, but official party labels can be misleading. Some of the Democrats were southern conservatives who normally voted with the Republicans on issues. As these conservative Democrats retired, they were largely replaced by Republicans.

In the 42 years between the elections of 1968 and 2012, in only 14 years did one of the two major parties control the presidency, the House of Representatives, and the Senate. The Democrats controlled all three institutions during the presidency of Jimmy Carter (1977–1981), the first two years of Bill Clinton's presidency (1992–1994), and the first two years of Barack Obama's presidency (2008–2010). The Republicans controlled all three institutions during the third through

did you know?

The Democrats and Republicans each had exactly one woman delegate at their conventions in 1900.

Politics with a Purpose

SHIFTING PARTY COALITIONS

Have you ever heard the expression "politics makes strange bedfellows"? If so, then a coalition of Protestant conservative white voters and northeastern liberal urban voters from religious and ethnic groups as diverse as Jews, Irish Catholics, and African Americans would surely fit the description. This is exactly the New Deal coalition on which Democratic Party victories were based, starting with President Franklin D. Roosevelt's win in 1932. The name, New Deal coalition, refers to those groups who were most helped by President Roosevelt's New Deal programs to address the problems created by the Great Depression. This coalition of disparate groups was a stable electoral force that elected five Democrats to the White House over the next 58 years (Presidents Roosevelt, Truman, Kennedy, Johnson, and Carter).

The electoral landscape for the political parties changed a great deal from the early to middle 20th century. The Democratic Party, which had supported racial segregation in the South until the 1950s, advocated racial integration and other civil rights policies that drove white, Protestant, conservative southern voters who opposed these initiatives away. First Richard Nixon in 1972 and then Ronald Reagan in 1980 successfully drew these voters to the Republican Party. These voters were also drawn to the Republican Party's social conservatism and rejection of the cultural changes of the 1960s and 1970s. Often self-identifying as working class, these Reagan Democrats were attracted to President Reagan's policies. Motivated by belief in traditional family values, anti-communism, and a strong national defense, by the 1990s they had largely switched their allegiance to the Republican Party.

The 1980 presidential election also saw the first significant gender gap; that is, men and women voting in different patterns, with women voters less likely to support the Republican candidate. This trend has held in most presidential elections since. Additionally, immigration and differences in birthrates have increased the Latino proportion of the voting-age population and decreased the white proportion. Both parties have targeted Latino voters. While George W. Bush was somewhat successful with this group in 2000, with the exception of conservative Cuban Americans, Latinos supported Democrats and Barack Obama in 2008.

In addition to racial, religious, and ethnic groups, these changing party coalitions can be understood in geographic terms. As the previous discussion indicates, what was once a solidly Democratic region of the country as a vestige of the Civil War,[a] the South, has become a bastion of Republican electoral wins since the late 1980s. The Northeast, which had been moderate and Republican, is now a Democratic stronghold, as is immigrant-rich California. Additionally, the Pacific Northwest began to trend Democratic.[b] This left the Midwest and Central/Mountain West as battleground regions, especially the more populous states such as Ohio, Missouri, and Michigan, which are crucial to a presidential victory.

What happened in the 2008 presidential election? Turnout increased across the country in the primaries as well as in the general election. This was especially true in the Democratic primaries and caucuses, where many voters who were previously turned off by the system found appeal in the historic candidacies of Senator Obama and Senator Clinton (the first viable African American and female presidential candidates, respectively). Voters participated in the Democratic primaries and caucuses in record numbers.

Who were these new Democratic voters? This is a group of younger voters (under 30 years old); some are more affluent (making over $100,000) and more liberal; and they consist of mainly women, African Americans, and Latinos.[c]

The 2012 presidential election campaign illustrated the strength of the new Democratic coalition. While Republican candidate Mitt Romney gained a few more percentage points among women, the younger voters, and college graduates, the Republican ticket was unable to overcome the strong Democratic vote among African American voters (93%), Latino voters (71%) and women (55%). Younger voters were much more likely to vote for the Democratic ticket although they also tend to perceive themselves as Independents. The Democratic Party continued to see solid support among the most educated Americans and those in the highest income groups. What does this say for party politics in the future? Has the Democratic Party created a new majority party, or is this success tied to a very popular president? It would seem that unless the Republican Party can gain adherents among one or more of these demographic groups, it is unlikely to win the presidency in the elections to come.

[a] The Republican Party, the party of Lincoln, was associated with the "Yankees," or Union forces, long after the close of the Civil War. Local Republican candidates throughout the South were "sacrificial lambs," or candidates with no chance of winning the general election.

[b] Charles S. Bullock III, Donna R. Hoffman, and Ronald Keith Gaddie, "The Consolidation of the White Southern Vote," *Political Research Quarterly*, Vol. 58, no. 2, 2005, pp. 231–243.

[c] Ronald Brownstein, "A Party Transformed," *National Journal*, available at www3.nationaljournal.com/members/news/2008/02/0229nj1.htm.

sixth years of George W. Bush's presidency.[4] Before the 1992 elections, the electorate seemed to prefer, in most circumstances, to match a Republican president with a Democratic Congress. Under Bill Clinton, that state of affairs was reversed, with a Democratic president facing a Republican Congress. After the 2006 elections, a Republican president again faced a Democratic Congress. In 2008, Americans elected a Democrat, Barack Obama, as president, and gave the Democratic Party majorities in both houses of Congress, but the Democrats lost their majority in the House in 2010.

Red State, Blue State. The pattern of a Republican Congress and a Democratic president would have continued after the election of 2000 if Democratic presidential candidate Al Gore had prevailed. Gore won the popular vote, but he lost the electoral college by a narrow margin. Despite the closeness of the result, most states had voted in favor of either Bush or Gore by a fairly wide margin. To many observers, America had become divided between states that were solidly Republican or Democratic in their leanings, with a handful of "swing states." States that had shown strong support for a Republican candidate were deemed "red states" and so-called Democratic states were labeled "blue states." These labels have now become part of our political culture, and the outcome of any presidential race is portrayed in red and blue.

The outcome of the Bush-Gore contest in 2000 produced lingering bitterness in the political scene and may have increased general distrust of the electoral process. Although Bush was reelected over his Democratic opponent in 2006, a combination of Republican scandals, war-weariness, and anti-Bush sentiment cost the Republicans their majority in the House in 2006.

In 2008, the nation watched an unprecedented Democratic primary fight between a strong female candidate, Hillary Clinton, and a young African American senator, Barack Obama. Although many commentators felt that the party would

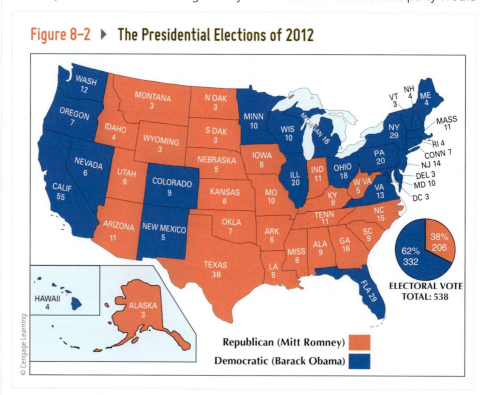

Figure 8–2 ▶ The Presidential Elections of 2012

ELECTORAL VOTE TOTAL: 538

62% 332

38% 206

Republican (Mitt Romney)
Democratic (Barack Obama)

© Cengage Learning

---

4. The Republicans also were in control of all three institutions for the first four months after Bush's inauguration. This initial period of control came to an end when Senator James Jeffords of Vermont left the Republican Party, giving the Democrats control of the Senate.

be weakened by the intense primary fight, Barack Obama easily won the election over Republican John McCain and the Democrats carried both houses of Congress. Analysts began to talk about a new realignment of voters and a progressive coalition that might last for some time in the future. However, the economic collapse of the banks began during the end of the 2008 campaign, and the effects of the recession lingered through much of President Obama's first term. By 2010, opponents of government debt and fears of the economic recession led to the Republicans re-capturing the House of Representatives.

Partisan Trends in the 2012 Elections

By the time the votes were all counted, it appeared that there was remarkably little change in the alignment of the voters in the 2012 elections. Perhaps the only real effect of the economic recession on the voters was an even split of Independent voters for the Republicans. The coalition that came together to elect President Obama in 2008 reappeared in 2012: African American voters, women, lower income voters, union voters, and Latino voters gave the president more than a majority of their votes. These groups reflect changes in the United States population, changes that will determine the direction of the nation in the future. The Republican coalition also remained unchanged: Well-educated voters, upper income voters, older voters, white men and women, and evangelical voters were more likely to vote for the Republicans. In some states, the Libertarian candidate polled 1% of the vote, ballots that might have been cast for Mitt Romney. The results of the Congressional elections were close to those of 2010: Republicans maintained a solid majority in the House of Representatives, and the Democrats gained two seats in the Senate to have a solid 53–45 majority in that chamber. Whether the Democratic Party has put together a coalition that will last for decades is yet to be seen, but the main groups in that coalition have been fairly consistent for the last two decades.

The Two Major U.S. Parties Today

It is sometimes said that the major American political parties are like Tweedledee and Tweedledum, the twins in Lewis Carroll's *Through the Looking-Glass.* Labels such as "Repubocrats" are especially popular among supporters of third parties, such as the Green Party and the Libertarian Party. Third-party advocates, of course, have an interest in claiming that no difference exists between the two major parties—their chances of gaining support are much greater if the major parties are seen as indistinguishable. Despite such allegations, the major parties do have substantial differences, both in their policies and in their constituents.

The Parties' Core Constituents

You learned in Chapter 6 how demographic factors affect support for the two parties. Democrats receive disproportionate support not only from the least well-educated voters but also from individuals with advanced degrees. Upper-income voters are generally more Republican than lower-income voters; businesspersons are much more likely to vote Republican than are labor union members. The Jewish electorate is heavily Democratic; white evangelical Christians who are regular churchgoers tend to be Republicans. Latinos are strongly Democratic; African Americans are overwhelmingly so. Women are somewhat more Democratic than men. City dwellers tend to be Democrats; suburbanites tend to be Republicans. In presidential elections, the South, the

■ **Learning Outcome 3:**
Explain the major differences in the demographics of the supporters of Republicans and Democrats, and discuss how the party positions differ on issues.

Rocky Mountain states, and the Great Plains states typically vote Republican; the West Coast and the Northeast are more likely to favor the Democrats. These tendencies represent the influences of economic interests and cultural values, which often conflict with each other.

Economic Beliefs

As discussed in the Politics with a Purpose on page 251, a coalition of the labor movement and various racial and ethnic minorities has been the core of Democratic Party support since the presidency of Franklin D. Roosevelt. The social programs and increased government intervention in the economy that made up Roosevelt's New Deal were intended to ease the pressure of economic hard times on these groups. This goal remains important for many Democrats today. In general, Democratic identifiers are more likely to approve of social-welfare spending, to support government regulation of business, to endorse measures to improve the situation of minorities, and to support assisting older adults with their medical expenses. Republicans are more supportive of the private marketplace, generally less favorable about central government action, and believe more strongly in an ethic of self-reliance and limited government.

Economic Directions. In his 1996 State of the Union address, Democratic president Bill Clinton announced that "the era of big government is over." One might conclude from this that both parties now favor limited government. However, up until 2010, it appeared that both parties were in favor of "big government." Deficits increased under both Ronald Reagan and George W. Bush (Republicans), and fell at the end of Bill Clinton's (a Democrat) presidency. Clinton, despite the protectionist beliefs of many Democrats in Congress, was in practice more supportive of free trade.[5] Barack Obama campaigned on a platform of social change, which he then began to enact in 2009 and 2010. As you have read, President Obama's health care bill became law in 2010, but his economic policies, while stopping a possible economic slide, did not end the high rate of unemployment among Americans.

By 2012, Americans had moved slightly closer to the Republican Party on some issues. As shown in Figure 8-3, while Americans were more likely to see Democrats as doing a better job on domestic policies, Republicans were seen as more likely to do a better job on the federal deficit.

Cultural Politics

In recent years, cultural values may have become more important than they previously were in defining the beliefs of the two major parties. For example, in 1987, Democrats were almost as likely to favor stricter abortion laws (40%) as Republicans were (48%). Today, Republicans are twice as likely to favor stricter abortion laws (50% to 25%). Of course, religious views also play a part in these cultural differences. As noted in Chapter 6, religiosity more likely is the difference between those who support liberal views and those who are more conservative; that is, those who attend services most often and are most involved with their church, synagogue, or mosque, are more socially conservative.

Cultural Politics and Socioeconomic Status.   Thomas Frank, a writer, returned to his home state of Kansas to find out why blue-collar Kansans were voting Republican. He noticed the following bumper sticker at a gun show in Kansas

5. Jeffrey Frankel, "Republican and Democratic Presidents Have Switched Economic Policies," *Milken Institute Review*, Vol. 5, No. 1, First Quarter 2003, pp. 18–25.

Figure 8-3 ▶ **Democratic Issues and Republican Issues, 2008 and 2012**

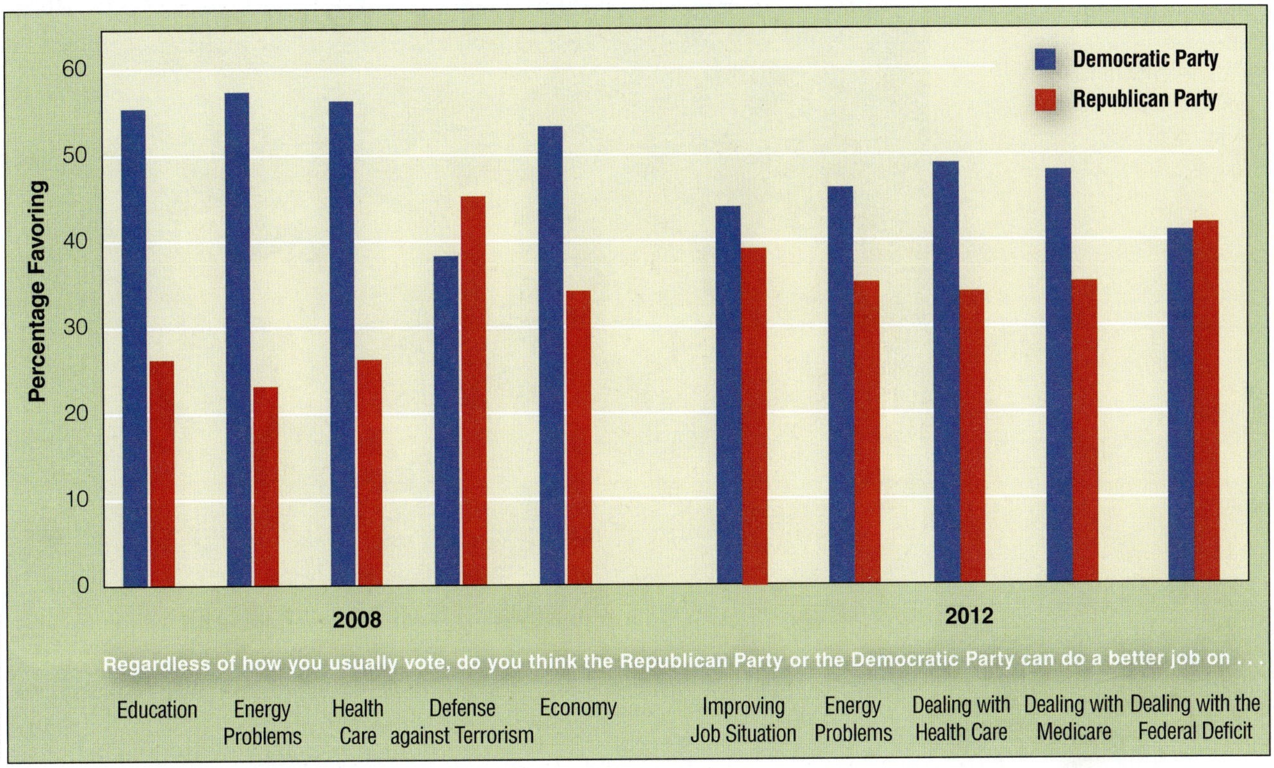

Democratic Party
Republican Party

Percentage Favoring

2008   2012

Regardless of how you usually vote, do you think the Republican Party or the Democratic Party can do a better job on . . .

| Education | Energy Problems | Health Care | Defense against Terrorism | Economy | Improving Job Situation | Energy Problems | Dealing with Health Care | Dealing with Medicare | Dealing with the Federal Deficit |

The Pew Research Center

Source: Pew Research Center for the People and the Press, a project of the Pew Research Center, March 11, 2012.

City: "A working person voting for the Democrats is like a chicken voting for Colonel Sanders." (Colonel Sanders is the iconic founder of Kentucky Fried Chicken, the chain of fried chicken restaurants.)

The bumper sticker highlights the fact that while economic conservatism is associated with higher incomes, social conservatism is relatively more common among lower-income groups. The individual who displayed the bumper sticker, therefore, was in effect claiming that cultural concerns—gun rights, religious views, less government—are far more important than economic ones. Frank argues that despite Republican control of the national government during the George W. Bush administration, cultural conservatives continued to view themselves as embattled "ordinary Americans" under threat from a liberal, cosmopolitan elite.[6]

Poll data have shown that many police officers, construction workers, military veterans, and rural residents began moving toward the Republican Party in the 1960s and 1970s, perhaps because they held more conservative social views. In contrast, many of America's rich and superrich elite, including financiers, media barons, software millionaires, and entertainers, started slowly but surely drifting toward the Democratic Party. In contrast, for the Republicans in the last two presidential elections, less than 10 percent of voters in pro-Bush counties earned more than $100,000 per year.

The Regional Factor in Cultural Politics. Conventionally, some parts of the country are viewed as culturally liberal and others as culturally conservative. On a regional basis, cultural liberalism (as opposed to economic liberalism) may be associated with economic dynamism. The San Francisco Bay Area can serve as an

did you know?

It took 103 ballots for John W. Davis to be nominated at the Democratic National Convention in 1924.

6. Thomas Frank, *What's the Matter with Kansas?* (New York: Macmillan, 2004).

Former Speaker Newt Gingrich and his wife Calista, greet supporters at an Idaho rally during the Republican presidential primaries in 2012.

example. The greater Bay Area contains Silicon Valley, the heart of the microcomputer industry; it has the highest per capita personal income of any metropolitan area in America. It also is one of the most liberal regions of the country.

To further illustrate this point, we can compare the political preferences of relatively wealthy states with relatively poor ones. Of the 10 states with the highest per capita personal incomes in 2004, eight voted for Democrat John Kerry in the presidential election of that year. Of the 25 states with the lowest per capita incomes in 2004, 23 voted for Republican George W. Bush.

Given these data, it seems difficult to believe that upper-income voters really are more Republican than lower-income ones. Within any given state or region, however, upscale voters are more likely to be Republican regardless of whether the area as a whole leans Democratic or Republican. States that vote Democratic are often northern states that contain large cities. At least part of this **reverse-income effect** may simply be that urban areas are more prosperous, culturally liberal, and Democratic than the countryside, and that the North is more prosperous, culturally liberal, and Democratic than the South.

Reverse-Income Effect
A tendency for wealthier states or regions to favor the Democrats and for less wealthy states or regions to favor the Republicans. The effect appears paradoxical because it reverses traditional patterns of support.

The 2012 Elections: Economics and Social Values

There is no doubt that the economy was the most important issue in the 2012 elections in almost every part of the nation. However, social issues, specifically, reproductive rights and abortion issues, were very important in races for the U.S. Senate and persuaded many women to vote for the Democratic ticket at the presidential level.

Although economic indicators suggested a very slow and less than robust recovery from the major recession of 2008–2009, unemployment rates fell to below 8% by October 2012, and there was evidence of growth in the construction of housing. While the majority of voters still said that the country was going in the wrong direction, the Democratic campaign emphasized the progress that had been made towards recovery. In contrast, the Republican campaign focused on the administration's record and promised a better approach. The Republican position appealed to small business owners, to Americans who were college-educated, and to many independent voters. The Democratic vote was certainly strengthened by the recovery of the automobile industry as a result of the Obama administration's policies, and blue collar voters kept their loyalty to the Democratic Party.

On issues important to women, the Democratic Party championed reproductive rights for women, health care initiatives for women, and their support for the right of women to choose an abortion. The Republican Party continued its stance as the party opposed a woman's right to choose. Their message, which officially allowed abortions under certain conditions, was completely undercut by Senate candidates who would not allow abortion in the case of rape and who made very peculiar statements about rape-caused pregnancies. The publicity accorded to these statements and the Democratic support for women secured a majority of votes for the ticket from women.

While the politics of immigration was rarely directly addressed in the campaign, it was clear that Latino voters saw the Democratic Party as more likely to pass immigration reform than the Republicans. The Republican ticket moved to the right on this issue, and Latino voters noted this. In 2012, the president announced a policy which allows undocumented young people who were brought to this country before the age of 16 to stay for two years if they meet educational, work, or military service requirements. Undoubtedly Latino voters viewed this action as proof of the Democratic Party's openness.

The Three Faces of a Party

Although American parties are known by a single name and, in the public mind, have a common historical identity, each party really has three major components. The first component is the **party-in-the-electorate**. This phrase refers to all those individuals who claim an attachment to the political party. They need not participate in election campaigns. Rather, the party-in-the-electorate is the large number of Americans who feel some loyalty to the party or who use partisanship as a cue to decide who will earn their vote. Party membership is not really a rational choice; rather, it is an emotional tie somewhat analogous to identifying with a region or a baseball team. Although individuals may hold a deep loyalty to or identification with a political party, members of the party-in-the-electorate do not need to speak out publicly, to contribute to campaigns, or to vote all Republican or all Democratic. Needless to say, the party leaders pay close attention to the affiliation of their members in the electorate.

The second component, the **party organization**, provides the structural framework for the political party by recruiting volunteers to become party leaders; identifying potential candidates; and organizing caucuses, conventions, and election campaigns for its candidates, as will be discussed in more detail shortly. The party organization and its active workers keep the party functioning between elections, as well as make sure that the party puts forth electable candidates and clear positions in the elections. If the party-in-the-electorate declines in numbers and loyalty, the party organization must try to find a strategy to rebuild the grassroots following.

The **party-in-government** is the third component of American political parties. The party-in-government consists of those elected and appointed officials who identify with a political party. Generally, elected officials do not also hold official party positions within the formal organization, although they often have the informal power to appoint party executives.

■ **Learning Outcome 4:**
Identify the three major components of the political party, and explain why these components are not necessarily consistent with each other.

Party-in-the-Electorate
Those members of the general public who identify with a political party or who express a preference for one party over another.

Party Organization
The formal structure and leadership of a political party, including election committees; local, state, and national executives; and paid professional staff.

Party-in-Government
All of the elected and appointed officials who identify with a political party.

Party Organization

Each of the American political parties is often seen as having a pyramid-shaped organization, with the national chairperson and committee at the top and the local precinct chairperson on the bottom. This structure, however, does not accurately reflect the relative power of the individual components of the party organization. If it did, the national chairperson of the Democratic Party or the Republican Party, along with the national committee, could simply dictate how the organization was to be run, just as if it were the ExxonMobil Corporation or Ford Motor Company. In reality, the political parties have a confederal structure, in which each unit has significant autonomy and is linked only loosely to the other units. The fact that these are not powerful national organizations can be seen in the uneven strength of local and state party organizations. In some states, parties receive significant contributions from individuals and interest groups for their operations, whereas in other states and localities political parties are very weak organizations with very little funding. This is particularly true of the minority party in a state or district where it has little chance to win a seat.

The National Party Organization

Each party has a national organization, the most clearly institutional part of which is the **national convention**, held every four years. The convention is used to nominate the presidential and vice presidential candidates. In addition, the **party platform** is developed at the national convention. The platform sets forth the party's position on the issues and makes promises to initiate certain policies if the party wins the presidency.

After the convention, the platform frequently is neglected or ignored by party candidates who disagree with it. Because candidates are trying to win votes from a wide spectrum of voters, it is counterproductive to emphasize the fairly narrow and sometimes controversial goals set forth in the platform. Political scientist Gerald M. Pomper discovered decades ago, however, that once elected, the parties do try to carry out platform promises, and that roughly three-fourths of the promises eventually become law.[7] Of course, some general goals, such as economic prosperity, are included in the platforms of both parties.

Convention Delegates. The party convention provides the most striking illustration of the difference between the ordinary members of a party, or party identifiers, and party activists. As a series of studies by *The New York Times* shows, delegates to the national party conventions are quite different from ordinary party identifiers. Delegates to the Democratic National Convention, as shown in Figure 8–4, are far more liberal than ordinary Democratic voters. Typically, delegates to the Republican National Convention are far more conservative than ordinary Republicans. Why does this happen? In part, it is because a person, to become a delegate, must gather votes in a primary election from party members who care enough to vote in a primary or be appointed by party leaders. Also, the primaries generally pit presidential candidates against each other on intraparty issues. Competition within each party tends to pull candidates away from the center, and delegates even more so. Often, the most important activity for the convention is making peace among the delegates who support different candidates and persuading them to accept a party platform that will appeal to the general electorate.

The National Committee. At the national convention, each of the parties formally chooses a national standing committee, elected by the individual state parties.

National Convention
The meeting held every four years by each major party to select presidential and vice presidential candidates, to write a platform, to choose a national committee, and to conduct party business.

Party Platform
A document drawn up at each national convention outlining the policies, positions, and principles of the party.

---

7. Gerald M. Pomper and Susan S. Lederman, *Elections in America: Control and Influence in Democratic Politics*, 2nd ed. (New York: Longman, 1980).

Figure 8-4 ▶ Convention Delegates and Voters: How Did They Compare on the Issues in 2008?

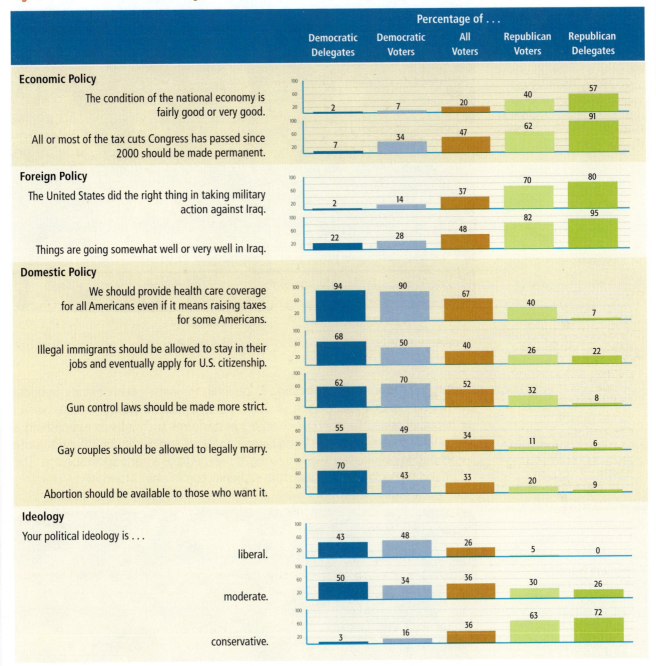

	Democratic Delegates	Democratic Voters	All Voters	Republican Voters	Republican Delegates
Economic Policy					
The condition of the national economy is fairly good or very good.	2	7	20	40	57
All or most of the tax cuts Congress has passed since 2000 should be made permanent.	7	34	47	62	91
Foreign Policy					
The United States did the right thing in taking military action against Iraq.	2	14	37	70	80
Things are going somewhat well or very well in Iraq.	22	28	48	82	95
Domestic Policy					
We should provide health care coverage for all Americans even if it means raising taxes for some Americans.	94	90	67	40	7
Illegal immigrants should be allowed to stay in their jobs and eventually apply for U.S. citizenship.	68	50	40	26	22
Gun control laws should be made more strict.	62	70	52	32	8
Gay couples should be allowed to legally marry.	55	49	34	11	6
Abortion should be available to those who want it.	70	43	33	20	9
Ideology					
Your political ideology is . . . liberal.	43	48	26	5	0
moderate.	50	34	36	30	26
conservative.	3	16	36	63	72

This **national committee** directs and coordinates party activities during the following four years. The Democrats include at least two members (a man and a woman) from each state, from the District of Columbia, and from the several territories. Governors, members of Congress, mayors, and other officials may be included as at-large members of the national committee. The Republicans, in addition, include state chairpersons from every state carried by the Republican Party in the preceding presidential, gubernatorial, or congressional elections. The selections of national committee members are ratified by the delegations to the national convention.

One of the jobs of the national committee is to ratify the presidential nominee's choice of a national chairperson, who (in principle) acts as the spokesperson for the party. The national chairperson and the national committee plan the next

National Committee
A standing committee of a national political party established to direct and coordinate party activities between national party conventions.

Two convention delegates from Colorado cheer as their governor, John Hickenlooper, addresses the convention. The Party conventions are intended to build enthusiasm among party members and supporters and to show off their political leaders, such as Governor Hickenlooper, to the American public.

The Washington Post/Getty Images

campaign and the next convention, obtain financial contributions, and publicize the national party.

Picking a National Chairperson. In general, the party's presidential candidate chooses the national chairperson. (If that candidate loses, however, the chairperson is often changed.) The national chairperson performs such jobs as establishing a national party headquarters, raising campaign funds and distributing them to state parties and to candidates, and appearing in the media as a party spokesperson. The national chairperson, along with the national committee, attempts to maintain

Republican convention delegates wave flags on the last day of the 2012 Republican National Convention in Tampa, Florida. They await the arrival of nominee Mitt Romney who will give his acceptance speech that night.

ROBYN BECK/Getty Images

some sort of liaison among the different levels of the party organization. The fact is, though, that the real strength and power of a national party are at the state level.

The State Party Organization

The Union has 50 states, plus the District of Columbia and the U.S. territories, and an equal number of party organizations for each major party. Thus, there are more than 100 state parties (and even more, if we include local parties and minor parties). Because every state party is unique, it is impossible to describe what an "average" state political party is like. Nonetheless, state parties have several organizational features in common.

Each state party has a chairperson, a committee, and local organizations. In theory, the role of the **state central committee**—the principal organized structure of each political party within each state—is similar in the various states. The committee, usually composed of members who represent congressional districts, state legislative districts, or counties, has responsibility for carrying out the policy decisions of the party's state convention. In some states, the state committee can issue directives to the state chairperson.

Also, like the national committee, the state central committee controls the use of party campaign funds during political campaigns. Usually, the state central committee has little, if any, influence on party candidates once they are elected. In fact, state parties are fundamentally loose alliances of local interests and coalitions of often bitterly opposed factions.

State parties are also important in national politics because of the **unit rule**, which awards electoral votes in presidential elections as an indivisible bloc (except in Maine and Nebraska). Presidential candidates concentrate their efforts in states in which voter preferences seem to be evenly divided or in which large numbers of electoral votes are at stake.

Local Party Machinery: The Grassroots

The lowest layer of party machinery is the local organization, supported by district leaders, precinct or ward captains, and party workers. Much of the work is coordinated by county committees and their chairpersons.

Patronage and City Machines.   In the 1800s, the institution of **patronage**— rewarding the party faithful with government jobs or contracts—held the local organization together. For immigrants and the poor, the political machine often furnished important services and protections. The big-city machine was the archetypal example. Tammany Hall, or the Tammany Society, which dominated New York City government for nearly two centuries, was perhaps the most notorious example of this political form.

The last big-city local political machine to exercise substantial power was run by Chicago's Mayor Richard J. Daley, who was also an important figure in national Democratic politics. Daley, as mayor, ran the Chicago Democratic machine from 1955 until his death in 1976. Machine politics in Chicago began to decline after Mayor Daley's death with the rise of independent Democrats in the city. Even Daley's own son, Richard M. Daley, who held the office from 1989 until 2011, did not control politics in Chicago as did his father. City machines are now dead, mostly because their function of providing social services (and reaping the reward of votes) has been taken over by state and national agencies. This trend began in the 1930s, when the social legislation of the New Deal established Social Security and unemployment insurance. The local party machine has little, if anything, to do with deciding who is eligible to receive these benefits.

State Central Committee
The principal organized structure of each political party within each state. This committee is responsible for carrying out policy decisions of the party's state convention.

Unit Rule
A rule by which all of a state's electoral votes are cast for the presidential candidate receiving a plurality of the popular vote in that state.

Patronage
Rewarding faithful party workers and followers with government employment and contracts.

Matt McClain for The Washington Post via Getty Images

Local Party Organizations Today, local political organizations—whether in cities, townships, or at the county level—still can contribute a great deal to local election campaigns. These organizations are able to provide the foot soldiers of politics—individuals who pass out literature and get out the vote on election day, which can be crucial in local elections. In many regions, local Democratic and Republican organizations still exercise some patronage, such as awarding courthouse jobs, contracts for street repair, and other lucrative construction contracts. The constitutionality of awarding (or not awarding) contracts on the basis of political affiliation has been subject to challenge, however. The United States Supreme Court has ruled that firing or failing to hire individuals because of their political affiliation is an infringement of the employees' First Amendment rights to free expression.[8] Local party organizations are also the most important vehicles for recruiting young adults into political work, because political involvement at the local level offers activists many opportunities to gain experience.

The local party organization is also the place where factions can gain a hold on the party machinery. Although the Tea Party groups throughout the nation have steadfastly maintained that they are *not a party,* many of these local groups have joined the county Republican organization, become the officers of the local Republican group, and made their endorsement part of a winning campaign. In 2012, for example, six-term senator Richard Lugar of Indiana was defeated in his primary election by the state treasurer, Richard Mourdock. The Tea Party claimed considerable success in unseating Lugar, and Mourdock did not deny their support. When local and state parties are taken over by more ideological factions, the relationship between Republican and Democratic elected officials becomes more polarized.

The Party-in-Government

After the election is over and the winners are announced, the focus of party activity shifts from getting out the vote to organizing and controlling the government. As you will learn in Chapter 12, party membership plays an important role in the day-to-day operations of Congress, with partisanship determining everything

did you know?

It takes about 700,000 signatures to qualify to be on the ballot as a presidential candidate in all 50 states.

---

8. *Rutan v. Republican Party of Illinois*, 497 U.S. 62 (1990).

from office space to committee assignments and power on Capitol Hill. For the president, the political party furnishes the pool of qualified applicants for political appointments to run the government. (Although it is uncommon to do so, presidents can and occasionally do appoint executive personnel, such as cabinet members, from the opposition party.) As we will note in Chapter 12, not as many of these appointed positions exist as presidents might like, and presidential power is limited by the permanent bureaucracy. Judicial appointments also offer a great opportunity to the winning party. For the most part, presidents are likely to appoint federal judges from their own party.

Divided Government.

All of these party appointments suggest that the winning political party, whether at the national, state, or local level, has a great deal of control in the American system. Because of the checks and balances and the relative lack of cohesion in American parties, however, such control is an illusion. One reason is that for some time, many Americans have seemed to prefer a **divided government**, with the executive and legislative branches controlled by different parties. The trend toward **ticket splitting**—splitting votes between the president and members of Congress—has increased sharply since 1952. This practice may indicate a lack of trust in government (as discussed in Chapter 6) or the relative weakness of party identification among many voters. Voters have often seemed comfortable with having a president affiliated with one party and a Congress controlled by the other.

The Limits of Party Unity.

Power of the parties is limited in other ways. Consider how major laws are passed in Congress. Traditionally, legislation has rarely been passed by a vote strictly along party lines. Although most Democrats may oppose a bill, for example, some Democrats may vote for it. Their votes, combined with the votes of Republicans, may be enough to pass the bill. Similarly, support from some Republicans may enable a bill sponsored by the Democrats to pass. This is not to say that Congress *never* votes along strict party lines. A notable example of such partisan voting occurred in the House of Representatives in 1998. The issue at hand was whether to impeach President Bill Clinton. Almost all votes were strictly along party lines—Democrats against, and Republicans for. In 2009 and 2010, partisan voting was again in vogue in the House of Representatives. Speaker Nancy Pelosi won a number of votes on Obama initiatives, including health care reform and an energy bill with almost all Democrats voting in favor and all Republicans opposed.

One reason that the political parties find it so hard to rally all of their members in Congress to vote along party lines is that parties have almost no control over who runs for office. In the United States, modern elections are "candidate centered," meaning that candidates choose to run, raise their own funds, build their own organizations, and win elections largely on their own, without significant help from a political party. This means, though, that the parties have very little control over the candidates who run under the party labels. For example, since 2010, the Republican Speaker of the House, John Boehner, has had a difficult time getting the new Tea Party–oriented members to follow the party line.

In addition, some votes always may be less favorable to a member's state or constituency. Democratic members of Congress who represent coal states have a difficult time supporting increased environmental regulations on that industry. Similarly, Republican senators Olympia Snowe and Susan Collins of Maine have often supported the Democratic majority on votes that they believe are important to their voters.

Divided Government
A situation in which one major political party controls the presidency and the other controls the chambers of Congress, or in which one party controls a state governorship and the other controls the state legislature.

Ticket Splitting
Voting for candidates of two or more parties for different offices. For example, a voter splits her ticket if she votes for a Republican presidential candidate and a Democratic congressional candidate.

Party Polarization.   Despite the forces that act against party-line voting, the two parties in Congress have been polarized at times, and defections from the party line have been rare. One such period was the mid-1990s, after the Republicans gained control of both the House and the Senate. Under House Speaker Newt Gingrich, the Republicans maintained strict discipline in an attempt to use their new majority to sponsor a specific legislative agenda. In 2003, polarization peaked again. "People genuinely hate each other," lamented Louisiana's Senator John Breaux, a moderate Democrat.[9]

One cause of polarization is the ability of the parties to create House districts that are **safe seats**. The creation of districts will be discussed further in Chapter 11. It is also true that the two parties are each more cohesive today than in many years. That means, for example, that the Republican Party leadership, many of its contributors, and its officeholders share beliefs about government and, to some extent, cultural values. Those beliefs are more conservative than those of the grassroots voter. Democratic leaders and politicians share more liberal views than those of the grassroots voter. This makes it easier for congresspeople and senators to vote together and support a common partisan position. With both parties becoming more cohesive, the debate over policies becomes more polarized and divisive.

Writers and advocates in the media, who find that stridency sells, also tend to encourage an atmosphere of polarization. Some commentators, however, do not believe that this spirit of polarization extends very far into the general electorate. They contend that a majority of Americans are strongly committed to tolerance of opposing political views. Supporting this view is Morris Fiorina, who argues that the American people are no more divided over their policy preferences than they have ever been.[10]

Safe Seat
A district that returns the legislator with 55 percent of the vote or more.

■ Learning Outcome 5:
Explain the factors in the American political system that reinforce a two-party system, and discuss why minor or third parties are rarely successful.

Why Has the Two-Party System Endured?

Two major parties have dominated the political landscape in the United States for almost two centuries for several reasons. These reasons have to do with (1) the historical foundations of the system, (2) political socialization and practical considerations, (3) the winner-take-all electoral system, and (4) state and federal laws favoring the two-party system.

The Historical Foundations of the Two-Party System

As we have seen, at many times in American history, one preeminent issue or dispute has divided the nation politically. In the beginning, Americans were at odds over ratifying the Constitution. After the Constitution went into effect, the power of the federal government became the major national issue. Thereafter, the dispute over slavery divided the nation by section, North versus South. At times—for example, in the North after the Civil War—cultural differences have been important, with advocates of government-sponsored morality (such as banning alcoholic beverages) pitted against advocates of personal liberty.

During much of the 1900s, economic differences were preeminent. In the New Deal period, the Democrats became known as the party of the working class, while the Republicans became known as the party of the middle and upper classes and commercial interests. When politics is based on an argument between

9.   Jackie Calmes, "Set This House on Fire," *The Wall Street Journal Europe*, December 1, 2003, p. A7.
10.   Morris Fiorina, *Culture War? The Myth of a Polarized America* (New York: Longman, 2005).

two opposing points of view, advocates of each viewpoint can mobilize most effectively by forming a single, unified party. Also, when a two-party system has been in existence for almost two centuries, it becomes difficult to imagine an alternative.

Political Socialization and Practical Considerations

Given that the majority of Americans identify with one of the two major political parties, it is not surprising that most children learn at a fairly young age to think of themselves as either Democrats or Republicans. This generates a built-in mechanism to perpetuate a two-party system. Also, many politically oriented people who aspire to work for social change consider that the only realistic way to capture political power in this country is to be either a Republican or a Democrat.

The Winner-Take-All Electoral System

At virtually every level of government in the United States, the outcome of elections is based on the **plurality**, winner-take-all principle. In a plurality system, the winner is the person who obtains the most votes, even if that person does not receive a majority (more than 50%) of the votes. Whoever gets the most votes gets everything. Most legislators in the United States are elected from single-member districts in which only one person represents the constituency, and the candidate who finishes second in such an election receives nothing for the effort.

Plurality
A number of votes cast for a candidate that is greater than the number of votes for any other candidate but not necessarily be a majority.

Presidential Voting.   The winner-take-all system also operates in the election of the U.S president. Recall that the voters in each state do not vote for a president directly but vote for **electoral college** delegates who are committed to the various presidential candidates. These delegates are called *electors*.

In all but two states (Maine and Nebraska), if a presidential candidate wins a plurality in the state, then *all* of the state's votes go to that candidate. For example, let us say that the electors pledged to a particular presidential candidate receive a plurality of 40 percent of the votes in a state. That presidential candidate will receive all of the state's votes in the electoral college. Minor parties have a difficult time competing under such a system. As shown in Table 8–1, American history has seen a number of national third-party campaigns. However, only Teddy Roosevelt, a former president who ran on a third-party ticket, received more than 88 electoral votes. In 1968, George Wallace, the segregationist former governor of Alabama, received 46 electoral votes, all from Deep South states. In recent decades, Ross Perot ran the most successful campaign, garnering 18.9 percent of the popular vote but no electoral votes at all. Because voters know such candidacies are doomed by the system, it is difficult to convince them to cast their vote for such candidates.

Electoral College
A group of persons, called electors, who are selected by the voters in each state. This group officially elects the president and the vice president of the United States.

Proportional Representation.   Many other nations use a system of proportional representation with multimember districts. If, during the national election, party X obtains 12 percent of the vote, party Y gets 43 percent of the vote, and party Z gets the remaining 45 percent of the vote, then party X gets 12 percent of the seats in the legislature, party Y gets 43 percent of the seats, and party Z gets 45 percent of the seats. Because even a minor party may still obtain at least a few seats in the legislature, the smaller parties have a greater incentive to organize under such electoral systems than they do in the United States. To read more about nations that utilize a proportional representation system, see this chapter's Beyond Our Borders feature.

The relative effects of proportional representation versus our system of single-member districts are so strong that many scholars have made them one

did you know?

The Reform Party, established in 1996, used a vote-by-mail process for the first step of its nominating convention and also accepted votes cast by e-mail.

TABLE 8–1 ▶ The Most Successful Third–Party Presidential Campaigns since 1864

The following list includes all third-party candidates winning more than 2 percent of the popular vote or any electoral votes since 1864. (We ignore isolated "unfaithful electors" in the electoral college who failed to vote for the candidate to which they were pledged.)

YEAR	MAJOR THIRD PARTY	THIRD–PARTY PRESIDENTIAL CANDIDATE	PERCENT OF THE POPULAR VOTE	ELECTORAL COLLEGE VOTES	WINNING PRESIDENTIAL CANDIDATE
1892	Populist	James Weaver	8.5	22	Grover Cleveland (D)
1904	Socialist	Eugene Debs	3.0	—	Theodore Roosevelt (R)
1908	Socialist	Eugene Debs	2.8	—	William Howard Taft (R)
1912	Progressive	Theodore Roosevelt	27.4	88	Woodrow Wilson (D)
1912	Socialist	Eugene Debs	6.0	—	Woodrow Wilson (D)
1920	Socialist	Eugene Debs	3.4	—	Warren G. Harding (R)
1924	Progressive	Robert LaFollette	16.6	13	Calvin Coolidge (R)
1948	States' Rights	Strom Thurmond	2.4	39	Harry Truman (D)
1960	Independent Democrat	Harry Byrd	0.4	15*	John Kennedy (D)
1968	American Independent	George Wallace	13.5	46	Richard Nixon (R)
1980	National Union	John Anderson	6.6	0	Ronald Reagan (R)
1992	Independent	Ross Perot	18.9	0	Bill Clinton (D)
1996	Reform	Ross Perot	8.4	0	Bill Clinton (D)

*Byrd received 15 electoral votes from unpledged electors in Alabama and Mississippi.
Source: *Dave Leip's Atlas of U.S. Presidential Elections*, www.uselectionatlas.org.

of the few "laws" of political science. Duverger's Law, named after French political scientist Maurice Duverger, states that electoral systems based on single-member districts tend to produce two parties, while systems of proportional representation produce multiple parties.[11] Still, many countries with single-member districts have more than two political parties—Britain and Canada are examples.

State and Federal Laws Favoring the Two Parties

Many state and federal election laws offer a clear advantage to the two major parties. In some states, the established major parties need to gather fewer signatures to place their candidates on the ballot than do minor parties or independent candidates. The criterion for determining how many signatures will be required is often based on the total party vote in the last general election, thus penalizing a new political party that did not compete in that election.

At the national level, minor parties face different obstacles. All of the rules and procedures of both houses of Congress divide committee seats, staff members, and other privileges on the basis of party membership. A legislator who is elected on a minor-party ticket, such as the Conservative Party of New York, must choose to be counted with one of the major parties to obtain a committee assignment.

11.   As cited in Todd Landman, *Issues and Methods in Comparative Politics* (New York: Routledge, 2003), p. 14.

The Federal Election Commission (FEC) rules for campaign financing also place restrictions on minor-party candidates. Such candidates are not eligible for federal matching funds in either the primary or the general election. In the 1980 election, John Anderson, running for president as an independent, sued the FEC for campaign funds. The commission finally agreed to repay part of his campaign costs after the election, in proportion to the votes he received. Giving funds to a candidate when the campaign is over is, of course, much less helpful than providing funds while the campaign is still under way.

The Role of Minor Parties in U.S. Politics

For the reasons just discussed, minor parties have a difficult (if not impossible) time competing within the American two-party political system. Nonetheless, minor parties have played an important role in our political life. Parties other than the Republicans or Democrats are usually called **third parties**. (Technically, of course, there could be fourth, fifth, or sixth parties as well, but we use the term *third party* because it has endured.) Third parties can come into existence in three ways: (1) They may be founded from scratch by individuals or groups who are committed to a particular interest, issue, or ideology; (2) they can split off from one of the major parties when a group becomes dissatisfied with the major party's policies; and (3) they can be organized around a particular charismatic leader and serve as that person's vehicle for contesting elections.

Third parties have acted as barometers of changes in the political mood. Such barometric indicators have forced the major parties to recognize new issues or trends in the thinking of Americans. Political scientists believe that third parties have acted as safety valves for dissident groups, preventing major confrontations and political unrest. In some instances, third parties have functioned as way stations for voters en route from one of the major parties to the other. Table 8–1 on page 266 lists significant third-party presidential campaigns in American history; Table 8–2 to the right provides a brief description of third-party beliefs.

Third Party
A political party other than the two major political parties (Republican and Democratic).

TABLE 8–2 ▸ **Policies of Selected American Third Parties since 1864**

Populist: This pro-farmer party of the 1890s advocated progressive reforms. It also advocated replacing gold with silver as the basis of the currency in hopes of creating a mild inflation in prices. (It was believed by many that inflation would help debtors and stimulate the economy.)

Socialist: This party advocated a "cooperative commonwealth" based on government ownership of industry. It was pro-labor, often antiwar, and in later years, anti-communist. It was dissolved in 1972 and replaced by nonparty advocacy groups (Democratic Socialists of America and Social Democrats USA).

Communist: This left-wing breakaway from the socialists was the U.S. branch of the worldwide communist movement. The party was pro-labor and advocated full equality for African Americans. It was also closely aligned with the Communist Party—led Soviet Union, which provoked great hostility among most Americans.

Progressive: This name was given to several successive splinter parties built around individual political leaders. Theodore Roosevelt, who ran in 1912, advocated federal regulation of industry to protect consumers, workers, and small businesses. Robert LaFollette, who ran in 1924, held similar viewpoints.

American Independent: Built around George Wallace, this party opposed any further promotion of civil rights and advocated a militant foreign policy. Wallace's supporters were mostly former Democrats who were soon to be Republicans.

Libertarian: This party believes that the individual and private marketplace will produce the best policies. The national government has a role in defending the nation and little else.

Reform: The Reform Party was initially built around businessman Ross Perot but later was taken over by others. Under Perot, the party was a middle-of-the-road group opposed to federal budget deficits. Under Patrick Buchanan, it came to represent right-wing nationalism and opposition to free trade.

Green: The Greens are a left-of-center pro-environmental party; they are also generally hostile to globalization.

Ralph Nader, a leader of the consumer protection movement, has run for president six times, once for the New Party, three times as the Green Party candidate, and twice as a pure independent.

Splinter Party
A new party formed by a dissident faction within a major political party. Often, splinter parties have emerged when a particular personality was at odds with the major party.

Ideological Third Parties

The longest-lived third parties have been those with strong ideological foundations that are typically at odds with the majority mind-set. The Socialist Party is an example. The party was founded in 1901 and lasted until 1972, when it was finally dissolved. (A smaller party later took up the name.)

Ideology has at least two functions. First, the members of the minor party regard themselves as outsiders and look to one another for support; ideology provides great psychological cohesiveness. Second, because the rewards of ideological commitment are partly psychological, these minor parties do not think in terms of immediate electoral success. A poor showing at the polls therefore does not dissuade either the leadership or the grassroots participants from continuing their quest for change in American government (and, ultimately, American society).

Currently active ideological parties include the Libertarian Party and the Green Party. The Libertarian Party supports a *laissez-faire* ("let it be") capitalist economic program, together with a hands-off policy on regulating matters of moral conduct. The Green Party began as a grassroots environmentalist organization with affiliated political parties across North America and Western Europe. It was established in the United States as a national party in 1996 and nominated Ralph Nader to run for president in 2000. Nader campaigned against what he called "corporate greed," advocated universal health insurance, and promoted environmental concerns.[12] He ran again for president as an independent in 2004 and in 2008.

Splinter Parties

Some of the most successful minor parties have been those that split from major parties. The impetus for these **splinter parties**, or factions, has usually been a situation in which a particular personality was at odds with the major party. The most successful of these splinter parties was the Bull Moose Progressive Party, formed in 1912 to support Theodore Roosevelt for president. The Republican National Convention of that year denied Roosevelt the nomination, although he had won most of the primaries. He therefore left the Republicans and ran against Republican "regular" William Howard Taft in the general election. Although Roosevelt did not win the election, he did split the Republican vote, enabling Democrat Woodrow Wilson to become president.

Third parties have also been formed to back individual candidates who were not rebelling against a particular party. Ross Perot, for example, who challenged Republican George H. W. Bush and Democrat Bill Clinton in 1992, had not previously been active in a major party. Perot's supporters, likewise, probably would have split

---

12. Ralph Nader offers his own entertaining account of his run for the presidency in 2000 in *Crashing the Party: How to Tell the Truth and Still Run for President* (New York: St. Martin's Press, 2002).

their votes between Bush and Clinton had Perot not been in the race. In theory, Perot ran in 1992 as a nonparty independent; in practice, he had to create a campaign organization. By 1996, Perot's organization was formalized as the Reform Party.

The Impact of Minor Parties

Third parties have rarely been able to affect American politics by actually winning elections. (One exception is that third-party and independent candidates have occasionally won races for state governorships—for example, Jesse Ventura was elected governor of Minnesota on the Reform Party ticket in 1998.) Instead, the impact of third parties has taken two forms. First, third parties can influence one of the major parties to take up one or more issues. Second, third parties can determine the outcome of a particular election by pulling votes from one of the major-party candidates in what is called the "spoiler effect."

H. Ross Perot, third-party candidate for president in 1992 and 1996, speaks before a California Senate committee in 2002.

Influencing the Major Parties. One of the most clear-cut examples of a major party adopting the issues of a minor party took place in 1896, when the Democratic Party took over the populist demand for "free silver"—that is, a policy of coining enough new money to create inflation. As you learned earlier, however, absorbing the populists cost the Democrats votes overall.

Affecting the Outcome of an Election. The presidential election of 2000 was one instance in which a minor party may have altered the outcome. Green candidate Ralph Nader received almost 100,000 votes in Florida, a majority of which would probably have gone to Democrat Al Gore if Nader had not been in the race. The real question, however, is not whether the Nader vote had an effect—clearly, it did—but whether the effect was important.

The problem is that in an election as close as the presidential election of 2000, *any* factor with an impact on the outcome can be said to have determined the results of the election. Discussing his landslide loss to Democrat Lyndon B. Johnson in 1964, Republican Barry Goldwater wrote, "When you've lost an election by that much, it isn't the case of whether you made the wrong speech or wore the wrong necktie. It was just the wrong time."[13] With the opposite situation, a humorist might speculate that Gore would have won the election had he worn a better tie! Nevertheless, given that Nader garnered almost 3 million votes nationwide, many people believe that the Nader campaign was an important reason for Gore's loss. Should voters ignore third parties to avoid spoiling the chances of a preferred major-party candidate?

Mechanisms of Political Change

What does the 21st century hold for the Democrats and the Republicans? Support for the two major parties is roughly balanced today. In the future, could one of the two parties decisively overtake the other and become the

---

13. Barry Goldwater, *With No Apologies* (New York: William Morrow, 1979).

Beyond Our Borders

MULTIPARTY SYSTEMS: THE RULE RATHER THAN THE EXCEPTION

The United States has a two-party system. Occasionally, a third-party candidate enters the race but really has little chance of winning. Throughout the world, though, most democracies have multiparty systems.

SOME EXAMPLES

In its first legislative elections ever, Afghanistan saw the emergence of six major parties and seven minor parties. The 2005 Iraqi national assembly election had a total of 15 parliamentary alliances and parties, plus 20 other parties. Any national election in India has six major parties, and a total of 30 parties in the states. (India also has more than 700 registered, but unrecognized, parties.)

The latest elections in Germany saw two major parties and several minor ones. Any given presidential election in France has even more parties. They include the National Front that represents the extreme right, anti-immigrant part of the electorate. But there was also a party supporting hunting, fishing, nature, and traditions and one supporting the Revolutionary Communist League. All in all, of the at least 15 French parties, most obtain some public funding.

After the Egyptian popular uprising which overthrew the authoritarian government of Hosni Mubarak, the leaders of the movement quickly moved to establish an election system. Within weeks, dozens of political parties formed and, as the first presidential election approached, at least 10 of these parties had candidates for that office. Parties ranged from conservative groups that had supported Mubarak to radical leftists to democratic liberals and Islamist groups who wanted a religious-based government.

PROPORTIONAL REPRESENTATION AND COALITIONS

Great Britain has often been described as having a two and one-half party system: The major parties, the Labour and Conservative parties, have alternated governing the nation for most of the time since World War II. The Liberal Democrat party, which has a long and distinguished history, usually came in third with not enough votes to make a difference.

In the 2010 parliamentary elections, neither major party won enough seats in Parliament to claim the right to form a government. As soon as the election results were announced, each of the two major parties began to "court" the Liberal Democrats, who had won enough seats to create a coalition. Within a week, Queen Elizabeth asked the head of the Conservative Party to become prime minister and he negotiated a coalition with the Liberal Democrats. In a surprising move, the two parties announced that while David Cameron, head of the Conservative Party, would be

Egyptian election officials check lists of voter names and prepare ballots for the November 2011 election.

prime minister, Nick Clegg, head of the Liberal Democrat Party, would be named deputy prime minister. Since the election, issues facing Britain have required the cooperation and consent of both parties, something that is not always easy to achieve.

Coalitions are almost a certainty in a multiparty system. Why? Because usually the leading party does not have a majority of votes in the legislature. The leading party therefore has to make compromises to obtain votes from other parties. These coalitions are subject to change due to the pressures of lawmaking. Often, a minor partner in a coalition finds itself unable to support the laws or policies proposed by its larger partners. Either a compromise will be found, or the coalition will be ended and new partners may be sought to form a government coalition. If we had a multiparty system in the United States, we might have a farmers' party, a Latino party, a western party, a labor party, and others. To gain support for her or his program, a president would have to build a coalition of several parties by persuading each that its members would benefit from the coalition. The major difficulty in a multiparty system is, of course, that the parties will withdraw from the coalition when they fail to benefit from it. Holding a coalition together for more than one issue is sometimes impossible.

FOR CRITICAL ANALYSIS

Are multiparty systems necessarily more representative than the two-party system in the United States? Why or why not?

"natural party of government"? The Republicans held this status from 1896 until 1932, and the Democrats enjoyed it for many years after the election of Franklin D. Roosevelt in 1932. Not surprisingly, political advisers in both parties dream of circumstances that could grant them lasting political hegemony, or dominance.

Realignment

One mechanism by which a party might gain dominance is called **realignment**. As described in the Politics with a Purpose feature, major constituencies shift their allegiance from one party to another, creating a long-term alteration in the political environment. Realignment has often been associated with particular elections, called *realigning elections*. The election of 1896, which established a Republican ascendancy, was clearly a realigning election. So was the election of 1932, which made the Democrats the leading party.

Realignment: The Myth of Dominance.

Several myths have grown up around the concept of realignment. One is that in realignment, a newly dominant party must replace the previously dominant party. Actually, realignment could easily strengthen an already dominant party. Alternatively, realignment could result in a tie. This has happened—twice. One example was the realignment of the 1850s, which resulted in Abraham Lincoln's election as president in 1860. After the Civil War, the Republicans and the Democrats were almost evenly matched nationally.

The most recent realignment—which also resulted in two closely matched parties—has sometimes been linked to the elections of 1968. Actually, the realignment was a gradual process that took place over many years. It is sometimes referred to as a "rolling realignment." In 1968, Democrat Hubert Humphrey, Republican Richard Nixon, and third-party candidate George Wallace of Alabama all vied for the presidency. Following the Republican victory in that election, Nixon adopted a "Southern strategy" aimed at drawing dissatisfied southern Democrats into the Republican Party.[14] At the presidential level, the strategy was an immediate success, although years would pass before the Republicans could gain dominance in the South's delegation to Congress or in state legislatures. Nixon's southern strategy helped create the political environment in which we live today. Another milestone in the progress of the Republicans was Ronald Reagan's sweeping victory in the presidential election of 1980.

Realignment: The Myth of Predictability.

A second myth concerning realignments is that they take place, like clockwork, every 36 years. Supposedly, there were realigning elections in 1860, 1896, 1932, and 1968, and therefore 2004 must have been a year for realignment. No such event took place. In fact, no force could cause political realignments at precise 36-year intervals. Further, as we observed earlier in this section, realignments are not always tied to particular elections. The most recent realignment, in which conservative southern Democrats became conservative southern Republicans, was not closely linked to a particular election. The realignment of the 1850s, following the creation of the modern Republican Party, also took place over a period of years.

Realignment
A process in which a substantial group of voters switches party allegiance, producing a long-term change in the political landscape.

---

14. The classic work on Nixon's southern strategy is Kirkpatrick Sales, *The Emerging Republican Majority* (New Rochelle, NY: Arlington House, 1969).

Is Realignment Still Possible? The nature of American political parties created the pattern of realignment in American history. The sheer size of the country, combined with the inexorable pressure toward a two-party system, resulted in parties made up of voters with conflicting interests or values. The pre–Civil War party system involved two parties—Whigs and Democrats—with support in both the North and the South. This system could survive only by burying, as deeply as possible, the issue of slavery. We should not be surprised that the structure eventually collapsed. The Republican ascendancy of 1896–1932 united capitalists and industrial workers under the Republican banner, despite serious economic conflicts between the two. The New Deal Democratic coalition after 1932 brought African Americans and ardent segregationists into the same party.

For realignment to occur, a substantial body of citizens must come to believe that their party can no longer represent their interests or values. The problem must be fundamental and not attributable to the behavior of an individual politician. Given the increasing cohesion of each of the parties today, it is unlikely that a realignment is in the offing. The values that unite each party are relatively coherent, and their constituents are reasonably compatible. Therefore, the current party system should be more stable than in the past, and a major realignment is not likely to take place in the foreseeable future.

Dealignment

Among political scientists, one common argument has been that realignment is no longer likely because voters are not as committed to the two major parties as they were in the 1800s and early 1900s. In this view, called **dealignment** theory, large numbers of independent voters may result in political volatility, but the absence of strong partisan attachments means that it is no longer easy to "lock in" political preferences for decades.

Independent Voters. Figure 8.5 shows trends in **party identification**, as measured by standard polling techniques from 1937 to the present. The chart displays a rise in the number of independent voters throughout the period, combined with a fall in support for the Democrats from the mid-1960s on. The decline in Democratic identification may be due to the consolidation of Republican support in the South since 1968, a process that by now may be substantially complete. In any event, the traditional Democratic advantage in party identification has vanished.

Not only has the number of independents grown over the last half-century, but voters are also less willing to vote a straight ticket—that is, to vote for all the candidates of one party. In the early 1900s, **straight-ticket voting** was nearly universal. By midcentury, 12 percent of voters engaged in ticket splitting. In recent presidential elections, between 20 and 40 percent of the voters engaged in split-ticket voting. This trend, along with the increase in the number of voters who call themselves independents, suggests that parties have lost much of their hold on the loyalty of the voters.

Not-So-Independent Voters. A problem with dealignment theory is that many "independent" voters are not all that independent. Polling organizations estimate that of the 33 percent of voters who identify themselves as independents, 11 percent vote as if they were Democrats in almost all elections, and 12 percent vote as if they were Republicans. If these "leaners" are deducted from

Dealignment
A decline in party loyalties that reduces long-term party commitment.

Party Identification
Linking oneself to a particular political party.

Straight-Ticket Voting
Voting exclusively for the candidates of one party.

the independent category, only 10 percent of the voters remain. These true independents are **swing voters**—they can swing back and forth between the parties. These voters are important in deciding elections. Some analysts believe, however, that swing voters are far less numerous today than they were two or three decades ago.

Tipping

Realignment is not the only mechanism that can alter the political landscape. Political transformation can also result from changes in the composition of the electorate. Even when groups of voters never change their party preferences, if one group becomes more numerous over time, it can become dominant for that reason alone. We call this kind of demographically based change **tipping**. Immigration is one cause of this phenomenon.

Tipping in Massachusetts. Consider Massachusetts, where for generations Irish Catholics confronted Protestant Yankees in the political arena. Most of the Yankees were Republican; most of the Irish were Democrats. The Yankees were numerically dominant from the founding of the state until 1928. In that year, for the first time, Democratic Irish voters came to outnumber the Republican Yankees. Massachusetts, which previously had been one of the most solidly Republican states, cast its presidential vote for Democrat Al Smith. Within a few years, Massachusetts became one of the most reliably Democratic states in the nation.

Tipping in California? California may have experienced a tipping effect during the 1990s. From 1952 until 1992, California consistently supported Republican presidential candidates, turning Democratic only in the landslide election of Lyndon Johnson in 1964. In 1992, however, the California electorate gave Democrat Bill Clinton a larger percentage of its votes than he received in the country as a whole. Since then, no Republican presidential candidate has managed to carry California.

The improved performance of the Democrats in California is almost certainly a function of demography. In 1999, California became the third state, after Hawaii and New Mexico, in which non-Latino whites do *not* make up a majority of the population. Latinos and African Americans both give most of their votes to the Democrats. Even before 1999, these groups were numerous enough to tip California into the Democratic column.

On to the Future

Some speculation about the future is reasonable, as long as we remember that unexpected events can make any prediction obsolete. We can anticipate that party advocates will continue to hope that events will propel their party into a dominant position. Either party could lose substantial support if it were identified with a major economic disaster. Noneconomic events could have an impact as well.

Republican strategists will seek to encourage substantial numbers of voters to abandon the Democrats, on the basis of cultural or economic issues. Some of these strategists believe that the relative conservatism of Hispanic Americans on cultural matters may provide an opening for the Republicans. Republicans are hopeful that their party can be seen as the party of economic recovery. Finally, Republicans look at the decline in Democratic Party identification since the 1960s (see Figure 8–5) and project that trend into the future.

Swing Voters
Voters who frequently swing their support from one party to another.

Tipping
A phenomenon that occurs when a group that is becoming more numerous over time grows large enough to change the political balance in a district, state, or country.

Figure 8–5 ▶ **Party Identification from 1937 to the Present**

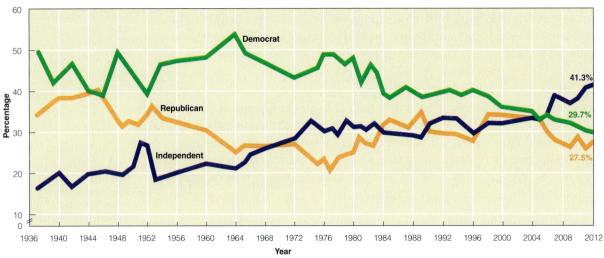

Source: The Gallup Poll, The Pew Research Center for the People and the Press, November 2003; and authors' updates.

Democratic strategists hope that the tolerant spirit of many younger voters (in attitudes toward gay rights, for example) may work to their advantage. The Democratic Party has worked hard in southwestern states and California to bring Latino voters to the fold, and the Obama administration has appealed, in particular, to female voters through its positions on health care. If the Democrats could add a significant majority of female and Latino voters to their numbers, it could offset some losses in the Middle West among blue-collar workers who are concerned about jobs and the economy.

Another possibility also exists: If the two parties continue their bitter rivalry on the campaign trail and gridlock persists in Congress, moderate voters and those who are weakly attached to a party may become true independents, deciding each election on the issues of concern to them and avoiding identification with a political party altogether.

You Can Make a Difference

ELECTING CONVENTION DELEGATES

The most exciting political party event, staged every four years, is the national convention. State conventions also take place on a regular basis. Surprising as it might seem, the individual voter has opportunities to become involved in nominating delegates to a state or national convention or to become a delegate.

Linh Hoang represented the state of Virginia as a delegate to the Democratic National Convention in 2012. His enthusiasm for the party and for the president is evident in this photo.

WHY SHOULD YOU CARE?

How would you like to exercise a small amount of real political power yourself—power that goes beyond simply voting in an election? You might be able to become a delegate to a county, district, or even state party convention. Many of these conventions nominate candidates for various offices. For example, in Michigan, the state party conventions nominate the candidates for the board of regents of the state's three top public universities. The regents set university policies, so these are nominations in which students have an obvious interest. In Michigan, if you are elected as a party precinct delegate, you can attend your party's state convention.

In much of the country, openings for district-level delegates outnumber people willing to serve. In such circumstances, almost anyone can become a delegate by collecting a handful of signatures on a nominating petition or by mounting a small-scale write-in campaign. You are then eligible to take part in one of the most educational political experiences available to an ordinary citizen. You will get a firsthand look at how political persuasion takes place, how resolutions are written and passed, and how candidates seek out support among their fellow party members. In some states, party caucuses bring debate even closer to the grassroots level.

WHAT CAN YOU DO?

When the parties choose delegates for the national convention, the process begins at the local level—either the congressional district or the state legislative district. Delegates may be elected in party primary elections or chosen in neighborhood or precinct caucuses. If the delegates are elected in a primary, persons who want to run for these positions must first file petitions with the board of elections. If you are interested in committing yourself to a particular presidential candidate and running for the delegate position, check with the local county committee or with the party's national committee about the rules you must follow.

It is even easier to get involved in the grassroots politics of presidential caucuses. In some states—Iowa being the earliest and most famous example—delegates are first nominated at the local precinct caucus. According to the rules of the Iowa caucuses, anyone can participate in a caucus if he or she is 18 years old, a resident of the precinct, and registered as a party member. These caucuses, in addition to being the focus of national media attention in January or February, select delegates to the county conventions who are pledged to specific presidential candidates. This is the first step toward the national convention.

At both the county caucus and the convention levels, both parties try to find younger members to fill some of the seats. Contact the state or county political party to find out when the caucuses or primaries will be held or check the Web sites of the Young Democrats or Young Republicans in your state. Then gather local supporters and friends, and prepare to join in an occasion during which political debate is at its best.

For further information about these opportunities (some states hold caucuses and state conventions in every election year), contact the state party office or your local state legislator for specific dates and regulations. You can also write to the national committee for information on how to become a delegate.

Republican National Committee
Republican National Headquarters
310 First Street SE
Washington, DC 20003
202-863-8500
www.rnc.org
Democratic National Committee
Democratic National Headquarters
430 S. Capitol St. SE
Washington, DC 20003
202-863-8000
www.democrats.org

Key Terms

Chapter Summary

1. A political party is a group of political activists who organize to win elections, operate the government, and determine public policy. Political parties recruit candidates for public office, organize and run elections, present alternative policies to the voters, assume responsibility for operating the government, and act as the opposition to the party in power.

2. The evolution of our nation's political parties can be divided into seven periods: (1) the creation and formation of political parties from 1789 to 1816; (2) the era of one-party rule, or personal politics, from 1816 to 1828; (3) the period from Andrew Jackson's presidency to the Civil War, from 1828 to 1860; (4) the Civil War and post–Civil War period, from 1860 to 1896; (5) the Republican ascendancy and progressive period, from 1896 to 1932; (6) the New Deal period, from 1932 to about 1968; and (7) the modern period, from approximately 1968 to the present.

3. Many of the differences between the two parties date from the time of Franklin D. Roosevelt's New Deal. The Democrats have advocated government action to help labor and minorities, and the Republicans have championed self-reliance and limited government. The constituents of the two parties continue to differ. A close look at policies actually enacted in recent years, however, suggests that despite rhetoric to the contrary, both parties are committed to a large and active government. Today, cultural differences are at least as important as economic issues in determining party allegiance.

4. A political party consists of three components: the party-in-the-electorate, the party organization, and the party-in-government. Each party component maintains linkages to the others to keep the party strong. Each level of the party— local, state, and national—has considerable autonomy. The national party organization is responsible for holding the national convention in presidential election years, writing the party platform, choosing the national committee, and conducting party business.

5. The party-in-government comprises all of the elected and appointed officeholders of a party. However, many officeholders may have won their seats with little or no help from the party, making them less susceptible to party control. If the political parties had more control over the candidates, they would be better able to carry out a cohesive program in government.

6. Two major parties have dominated the political landscape in the United States for almost two centuries. The reasons for this include (1) the historical foundations of the system, (2) political socialization and practical considerations, (3) the winner-take-all electoral system, and (4) state and federal laws favoring the two-party system. For these reasons, minor parties have found it extremely difficult to win elections. If the rules for getting candidates on the ballot were changed or states adopted more proportional voting systems, other political parties might form, such as an environmental party, an ultraconservative party, or a party based on religious affiliation. Such parties might do a better job of articulating certain interests than the two major parties do at the present time.

7. Minor (or third) parties have emerged from time to time, sometimes as dissatisfied splinter groups from within major parties, and have acted as barometers of changes in the political mood. Splinter parties have emerged when a particular personality was at odds with the major party, as when Theodore Roosevelt's differences with the Republican Party resulted in the formation of the Bull Moose Progressive Party. Other minor parties, such as the Socialist Party, have formed around specific issues or ideologies. Third parties can affect the political process (even if they do not win) if major parties adopt their issues or if they determine which major party wins an election.

8. One mechanism of political change is realignment, in which major blocs of voters switch allegiance from one party to another. Realignments were manifested in the elections of 1896 and 1932. Realignment need not leave one party dominant—it can result in two parties of roughly equal strength. Some scholars speak of dealignment—that is, the loss of strong party attachments. In fact, the share of the voters who describe themselves as independents has grown since the 1930s, and the share of self-identified Democrats has shrunk since the 1960s. Many independents actually vote as if they were Democrats or Republicans, however. Demographic change can also "tip" a district or state from one party to another.

Selected Print, Media, and Online Resources

PRINT RESOURCES

Abramowitz, Alan I. *The Disappearing Center: Engaged Citizens, Polarization, and American Democracy.* New Haven, CT: Yale University Press, 2011. Abramowitz argues that the number of moderate voters in the nation is decreasing as the two parties become more distant and more ideological, thus increasing the polarization of politics.

Amato, Theresa. *Grand Illusion: The Fantasy of Voter Choice in a Two-Party Tyranny.* New York: The New Press, 2009. As Ralph Nader's campaign manager during his 2000 and 2004 presidential runs, Amato was in an excellent position to see how the political system makes it almost impossible for third-party candidates to succeed. She also examines the experiences of other challengers, including John Anderson, Ross Perot, and Pat Buchanan.

Frank, Thomas. *What's the Matter with Kansas? How Conservatives Won the Heart of America.* New York: Henry Holt & Company, 2005. This book looks at how the Republican Party gained its current dominance in the American heartland. The author examines why so many Americans vote against their own economic interests.

Gould, Lewis. *Grand Old Party: A History of the Republicans.* New York: Random House, 2003. A companion volume to the history of the Democrats by Jules Witcover, listed below. Gould provides a sweeping history of the Republican Party from its origins as an anti-slavery coalition to the present. A major theme of the work is the evolution of the Republicans from a party of active government to the more conservative party that it is today.

McAuliffe, Terry. *What a Party! My Life among Democrats.* New York: St. Martin's Press, 2007. The former chairperson of the Democratic National Committee discusses his years of experience on the inside of a major political party.

Paul, Ron. *The Revolution: A Manifesto.* New York: Grand Central Publishing, 2008. Representative Paul (R.-Tex.) ran for president on the Libertarian ticket in 2004 and as a Republican in 2008 and in 2012. His concise political statement is an eloquent defense of the Libertarian cause. Among Paul's more striking proposals is the abolition of the Federal Reserve System, which, in his opinion, benefits only the rich.

Paulson, Arthur. *Electoral Realignment and the Outlook for American Democracy.* Boston: University Press of New England, 2006. Paulson seeks to understand recent realignments in the light of political geography and historical divisions.

Sager, Ryan. *The Elephant in the Room: Evangelicals, Libertarians, and the Battle to Control the Republican Party.* New York: Wiley, 2006. The author describes the current coalition of subgroups within the Republican Party and predicts an eventual splintering as the individual groups struggle for greater power within the party.

Schaller, Thomas F. *Whistling Past Dixie: How Democrats Can Win without the South.* New York: Simon & Schuster, 2008. Schaller, a professor of political science at the University of Maryland, argues that the Democrats are more likely to succeed by solidifying their support in northern states than by trying to rebuild their once-predominant position in the South.

Skocpol, Theda, and Vanessa Williamson. *The Tea Party and the Remaking of the Republican Party.* New York: Oxford University Press, 2011. Two political scientists report on their year-long investigation into the Tea Party. By spending long periods of time talking to these supporters, they are able to describe the goals and beliefs of Tea Party voters.

Witcover, Jules. *Party of the People: A History of the Democrats.* New York: Random House, 2003. A companion volume to the history of the Republicans by Lewis Gould, listed above. Witcover describes the transformation of the Democrats from a party of limited government to a party of national authority, but he also finds a common thread that connects modern Democrats to the past—a belief in social and economic justice.

MEDIA RESOURCES

The American President—A 1995 film starring Michael Douglas as a widowed president who must balance partisanship and friendship (Republicans in Congress promise to approve the president's crime bill only if he modifies an environmental plan sponsored by his liberal girlfriend).

The Best Man—A 1964 drama based on Gore Vidal's play of the same name. The film, which deals with political smear campaigns by presidential party nominees, focuses on political party power and ethics.

The Last Hurrah—A classic 1958 political film starring Spencer Tracy as a corrupt politician who seeks his fifth nomination for mayor of a city in New England.

A Third Choice—A film that examines America's experience with third parties and independent candidates throughout the nation's political history.

ONLINE RESOURCES

Democratic Party www.democrats.org

Green Party of the United States a federation of state Green Parties. Committed to environmentalism, nonviolence, social justice, and grassroots organizing: www.gp.org

Libertarian Party America's third largest and fastest-growing political party; calls itself the party of principle and supports smaller government, lower taxes, and more freedom: www.lp.org

The Pew Research Center for the People & the Press an independent, nonpartisan public opinion research organization that studies attitudes toward politics, the press, and public policy issues. Offers survey data online on how the parties fared during the most recent elections, voter typology, and numerous other issues: www.people-press.org/

Politics1.com a pioneering political blog and news site published as a nonpartisan public service to promote fully informed decision making by the American electorate. Offers extensive information on U.S. political parties, including the major parties and 50 minor parties: www.politics1.com/parties.htm

Republican Party www.gop.com

9 Voting and Elections

Republican voters cast their primary election ballots in New Orleans, Louisiana, in March, 2012.

SKIP BOLEN/EPA/Newscom

LEARNING OUTCOMES

After reading this chapter, students will be able to:

■ **LO1** Demonstrate an understanding of the electoral process in the United States, and explain how it relates to democratic theory.

■ **LO2** Discuss the factors that influence voter turnout in the United States, and compare American voter turnout to that of other nations.

■ **LO3** Describe historical restrictions on the vote in the United States, and explain how these restrictions have been ended.

■ **LO4** Describe the types of elections held in the United States, and explain the constitutional reasons for so many elections.

■ **LO5** Discuss the impact of the mechanics and technology of voting on voter turnout, vote fraud, and the ability of citizens to trust the process.

What If ...

VOTING ON THE INTERNET BECAME UNIVERSAL?

BACKGROUND

Today, you can do all your banking on your smartphone; use your smartphone as a boarding pass; watch movies, read books, and take photos on your smartphone; and order nearly anything imaginable over the Internet. Why can't you vote using a smartphone or the Internet? This seems to be the logical extension of today's technology. Instead, almost all local governments require the voter to vote in person on a specified day or seek an absentee ballot in advance. Some states allow advance voting in a specified place up to three weeks ahead of the vote, while Oregon has gone to mail-in ballots.

WHAT IF INTERNET VOTING BECAME UNIVERSAL?

Many people would find it very convenient to vote over the Internet, whether from a smartphone, desktop computer, or iPad. People traveling for business or pleasure would no longer need to request an absentee ballot or vote in advance of the election. Local governments would not have to invest millions in voting machines and cover the expense of operating polling places anymore. Even if local governments felt the need to honor the idea of a polling place, allowing voters to use laptops at polling places would be much less expensive and less trouble than today's voting booths.

Using today's technology for voting would likely increase voter turnout among younger Americans, the group least likely to vote. As you will read in this chapter, younger Americans are less likely to be settled in a community and less likely to have a deep interest in many political issues. But, if they received an e-mail alert and could vote instantly, voter turnout would likely increase among young people and perhaps among other groups in society.

Voting via the Internet would end the confusion over whether announcing the voting results of the eastern states affects turnout in the western states. A "window" for voting would open at a certain time, either in a state or across the nation, and all polls would open at the same time and close at the same time. Of course, no exit polling as we know it now could occur because voters would not be coming to the polling places. Results would be easily calculated and could be announced by a nonpartisan government agency at a specified time. No more hand recounts of spoiled ballots or visual inspections of punch-card ballots would occur.

WOULD INTERNET VOTING DISENFRANCHISE SOME VOTERS?

It is important to remember that not all Americans are "connected" to the Internet. Broadband service does not reach into many rural areas of the United States and, of course, many economically disadvantaged individuals do not have access to computers or to Internet services. Older Americans who do not have Internet services would most likely be discouraged from voting, as would poorer groups. Individuals who value their privacy might prefer not to vote via the Internet because the vote could be traced back to their computer or smartphone.

What would be the result if older Americans, less well-off Americans, and other groups were disenfranchised by Internet voting? Younger voters tend to be more liberal in their social views and, to some extent, in their views about government action. Increasing turnout among these voters would advantage Democratic Party candidates. However, lowering turnout among poorer, urban voters would cost those candidates votes as well. Republicans would work very hard to make sure that their older supporters had access to computers and assistance in voting, to be sure.

WHY HASN'T INTERNET VOTING BEEN ADOPTED?

The major issue with Internet voting is the security of the vote. In 2003, the U.S. Department of Defense announced that it planned to make Internet voting for the 2004 election available to all members of the armed forces serving overseas. At that time, more than 100,000 members of the military were in Iraq. By early 2004, the Pentagon announced that it had cancelled that plan due to the possibility of voter fraud. Stealing voter identification, hacking into the system, submitting thousands of fraudulent votes using hijacked computers—all of these are possibilities. In 2010, the District of Columbia announced a trial of an Internet voting system and invited hackers to try to "break into" the system. Within a few days, University of Michigan students hacked into the system, adding the Michigan fight song as a sound track for voting. The trial was cancelled.*

It is worth noting that the country of Estonia has adopted Internet voting, but it is optional there. Other nations are trying to solve the security problems in various ways. The real question is this: Why do people want to tamper with the vote? The answer is because the stakes in governing are so high.

FOR CRITICAL ANALYSIS

1. *Which groups would be most likely to vote over the Internet and which the least?*

2. *Would Internet voting increase citizens' trust in the voting process or make them even more suspicious of vote fraud?*

*Mike DeBonis, "Hacker infiltration ends D.C. online voting trial," Washington Post, October 12, 2010.

VOTING IN FREE and fair elections is the basis of any democracy. Whether the vote is an exercise in direct democracy, as in a referendum on an issue, or an exercise in representative democracy, a fair and trusted voting process ensures a majoritarian form of government. The United States is a representative democracy, meaning that the representatives who make policy decisions in Washington, D.C., are elected in free and open elections, and the candidate who gets the most votes wins. It is true that people are allowed to vote in China, Cuba, and North Korea, but there are no opposition candidates and no opposition campaign. In other nations, individuals are coerced into staying away from the polls by guerrilla fighters or, in some cases, by the government's own forces. In yet other nations, the incumbent government or candidate may alter the results of elections by fraudulent means. All of those cases fail the test of free and fair elections.

In the United States, it is often said that we have too many elections. In addition to voting for candidates, in some states, people can vote directly on laws. In California, often dozens of referenda are on the ballot at one time. Citizens are often asked to vote three times in one year—in a primary election to choose candidates, in elections for school taxes or other local matters, and in a general election. Americans often elect not only representatives to state and national legislatures and executive officers for the state, but also school superintendents, sheriffs, even the jailor. In addition, many states have elected judges, which can add 50 more offices in a city as large as Chicago.

Turning Out to Vote

In 2012, the voting-age population was about more than 240 million people. Of that number, 50 percent of the voting-age population, actually went to the polls. When only half of the voting-age population participates in elections, it means, among other things, that the winner of a close presidential election may be voted in by only about one-fourth of the voting-age population (see Table 9-1).

Learning Outcome 1:
Demonstrate an understanding of the electoral process in the United States, and explain how it relates to democratic theory.

Learning Outcome 2:
Discuss the factors that influence voter turnout in the United States, and compare American voter turnout to that of other nations.

Table 9-1 ▶ Elected by a Majority?

Most presidents have won a majority of the votes cast in the election. We generally judge the extent of their victory by whether they have won more than 51 percent of the votes. Some presidential elections have been proclaimed *landslides*, meaning that the candidates won by an extraordinary majority of votes cast. As indicated below, however, no modern president has been elected by more than 38 percent of the total voting-age population.

YEAR—WINNER (PARTY)	PERCENTAGE OF TOTAL POPULAR VOTE	PERCENTAGE OF VOTING-AGE POPULATION
1932—Roosevelt (D)	57.4	30.1
1936—Roosevelt (D)	60.8	34.6
1940—Roosevelt (D)	54.7	32.2
1944—Roosevelt (D)	53.4	29.9
1948—Truman (D)	49.6	25.3
1952—Eisenhower (R)	55.1	34.0

(continued)

Table 9-1 (continued)

YEAR—WINNER (PARTY)	PERCENTAGE OF TOTAL POPULAR VOTE	PERCENTAGE OF VOTING-AGE POPULATION
1956—Eisenhower (R)	57.4	34.1
1960—Kennedy (D)	49.7	31.2
1964—Johnson (D)	61.1	37.8
1968—Nixon (R)	43.4	26.4
1972—Nixon (R)	60.7	33.5
1976—Carter (D)	50.1	26.8
1980—Reagan (R)	50.7	26.7
1984—Reagan (R)	58.8	31.2
1988—Bush (R)	53.4	26.8
1992—Clinton (D)	43.3	23.1
1996—Clinton (D)	49.2	23.2
2000—Bush (R)	47.8	24.5
2004—Bush (R)	51.0	27.6
2008—Obama (D)	52.6	27.5
2012—Obama (D)	51.0	25.3

Sources: Congressional Quarterly Weekly Report, January 31, 1989, p. 137; New York Times, November 5, 1992; November 7, 1996; November 12, 2004; November 6, 2008; and author's update.

Voter Turnout
The percentage of citizens taking part in the election process; the number of eligible voters who actually "turn out" on election day to cast their ballots.

Figure 9-1 shows **voter turnout** for presidential and congressional elections from 1940 to 2012. According to these statistics, the last good year for voter turnout was 1960, when almost 65 percent of the voting-age population actually voted. Each of the peaks in the figure represents voter turnout in a presidential election. Thus, we can also see that turnout for congressional elections is influenced greatly by whether a presidential election occurs in the same year. Whereas voter turnout during the presidential elections of 2008 was more than 50 percent, it was only 42 percent in the midterm elections of 2010.

The same is true at the state level. When there is a race for governor, more voters participate both in the general election for governor and in the election for state representatives. Voter participation rates in gubernatorial elections are also greater in presidential election years. The average turnout in state elections is about 14 percentage points higher when a presidential election is held.

Now consider local elections: In races for mayor, city council, county auditor, and the like, it is fairly common for only 25 percent or less of the electorate to vote. Is something amiss here? It would seem that people should be more likely to vote in elections that directly affect them. At the local level, each person's vote counts more (because there are fewer voters). Furthermore, the issues—crime control, school bonds, sewer bonds, and so on—touch the immediate interests of the voters. The facts, however, do not fit the theory. Potential voters are most interested in national elections, when a presidential choice is involved. Otherwise, voter participation in our representative government is very low (and, as we have seen, it is not overwhelmingly great even in presidential elections).

The Effect of Low Voter Turnout

Two schools of thought concern low voter turnout. Some view low voter participation as a threat to representative democratic government. Too few individuals are deciding who wields political power in society. In addition, low voter participation

Figure 9-1 ▶ **Voter Turnout for Presidential and Congressional Elections, 1940–2012**

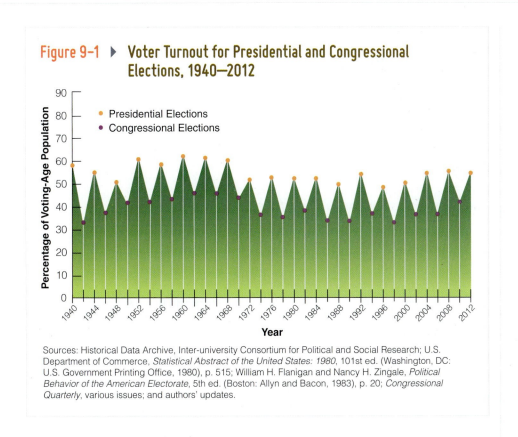

Sources: Historical Data Archive, Inter-university Consortium for Political and Social Research; U.S. Department of Commerce, *Statistical Abstract of the United States: 1980*, 101st ed. (Washington, DC: U.S. Government Printing Office, 1980), p. 515; William H. Flanigan and Nancy H. Zingale, *Political Behavior of the American Electorate*, 5th ed. (Boston: Allyn and Bacon, 1983), p. 20; *Congressional Quarterly*, various issues; and authors' updates.

presumably signals apathy or cynicism about the political system in general. It also may signal that potential voters simply do not want to take the time to learn about the issues or that the issues are too complicated. Some suggest that people do not vote because they do not believe that their vote will make any difference.

Others are less concerned about low voter participation. They believe that low voter participation simply indicates more satisfaction with the status quo. Also, they believe that representative democracy is a reality even if a very small percentage of eligible voters vote. If everyone who does not vote believes that the outcome of the election will accord with his or her own desires, then representative democracy is working. The nonvoters are obtaining the type of government—with the type of people running it—that they want to have anyway.

Is Voter Turnout Declining?

During many recent elections, the media have voiced concern that voter turnout is declining. Figure 9-1 appears to show somewhat lower voter turnout in recent years than during the 1960s. Pundits have blamed the low turnout on negative campaigning and broad public cynicism about the political process. But is voter turnout actually as low as it seems?

One problem with widely used measurements of voter turnout—as exemplified by Figure 9-1—is that they compare the number of people who actually vote with the voting-age population, not the population of *eligible voters*. These figures are not the same. The figure for the voting-age population includes felons and ex-felons who have lost the right to vote. Above all, it includes new immigrants who are not yet citizens. Finally, it does not include Americans living abroad, who can cast absentee ballots.

In 2008, the measured voting-age population included 3.2 million ineligible felons and ex-felons and an estimated 17.5 million noncitizens. It did not include

3.3 million Americans abroad. In 2008, the voting-age population was 225.5 million people. The number of eligible voters, however, was only 206.0 million. That means that voter turnout in 2008 was not 58 percent but about 64 percent of the truly eligible voters.

As you learned in Chapter 1, the United States has experienced high rates of immigration in recent decades. Political scientists Michael McDonald and Samuel Popkin argue that the apparent decline in voter turnout since 1972 is entirely a function of the increasing size of the ineligible population, chiefly due to immigration.[1]

Factors Influencing Who Votes

A clear association exists between voter participation and the following characteristics: age, educational attainment, minority status, income level, and the existence of two-party competition.

1. *Age.* Look at Figure 9-2, which shows the breakdown of voter participation by age group for the 2008 presidential election. It is very clear that the Americans who have the highest turnout rate are those reaching retirement. The reported turnout increases with each age group. Greater participation with age is very likely because older voters are more settled in their lives, are already registered, and have had more time to experience voting as an expected activity. Older voters may have more leisure time to learn about the campaign and the candidates, and communications, especially those from AARP, target this group.

   What is most striking about the turnout figures is that younger voters have the lowest turnout rate. Before 1971, the age of eligibility to vote was 21. Due to the prevailing sentiment that if a man was old enough to be drafted to fight in the Vietnam War, he should be old enough to vote, the U.S. Constitution was amended (via the Twenty-sixth Amendment) to lower the voting age to 18. However, young Americans have never exhibited a high turnout rate. In contrast to older Americans, young people are likely to change residence frequently, have few ties to the community, and perhaps not see election issues as relevant to them.

   Turnout among voters aged 18 to 24 increased significantly between 2000 and 2008, from 36 percent to 48.5 percent in the presidential elections. Evidence suggests that the candidates and political parties devoted much more attention to the younger voters. Candidates appeared on the television shows watched by younger voters, and campaigns began to utilize the Internet and social media to reach younger voters. Younger voters greatly increased their turnout in the 2008 primary elections, with many supporting Barack Obama's campaign for the presidency, although the increase in turnout for the general election was only 1.5 percent above 2004 levels.

Figure 9-2 ▶ Voting in the 2008 Presidential Elections by Age Group

Turnout is given as a percentage of the voting–age citizen population. The data given in this figure is from the Census Bureau. It has been gathered by polling the American public. Generally the Census data is not available for months after the election. The data from the 2008 polls indicates that turnout among older Americans remained high.

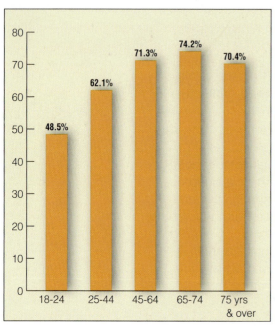

Source: U.S. Bureau of the Census, May 2010.

1. Michael P. McDonald and Samuel L. Popkin, "The Myth of the Vanishing Voter," *American Political Science Review,* Vol. 95, No. 4, December 2001, p. 963.

2. *Educational attainment.* Education also influences voter turnout. In general, the more education you have, the more likely you are to vote. This pattern is clearly evident in the 2008 election results, as you can see in Figure 9-3. Reported turnout was 30 percentage points higher for those who had some college education than it was for people who had never been to high school.

3. *Minority status.* Race and ethnicity are important, too, in determining the level of voter turnout. Non-Latino whites in 2008 voted at a 66.1 percent rate, whereas the non-Latino African American turnout rate was 64.7 percent, up almost 5 percent from 2004. For Latinos, the turnout rate was 49.9 percent, up 5 percent from 2004, and for Asian Americans the rate was 47.6 percent, up slightly from the previous presidential election. These low rates may occur because many Latino and Asian American immigrants are not yet citizens or due to language issues. The fact that the turnout increased 5 percent for African Americans and Latino voters is attributed to the voters' pride in President Obama's identity as an African American.

4. *Income level.* Differences in income also correlate with differences in voter turnout. Wealthier people tend to be overrepresented among voters who turn out on election day. In the 2008 presidential elections, voter turnout for those with the highest annual family incomes was almost twice the turnout for those with the lowest annual family incomes.

5. *Two-party competition.* Another factor in voter turnout is the extent to which elections are competitive within a state. More competitive states generally have higher turnout rates, and turnout increases considerably in states where an extremely competitive race occurs in a particular year. In addition, turnout can be increased through targeted get-out-the-vote drives among minority voters.

Figure 9-3 ▶ Voting in the 2008 Presidential Elections by Educational Level

These statistics reinforce one another. White voters are likely to be wealthier than African American voters, who are also less likely to have obtained a college education.

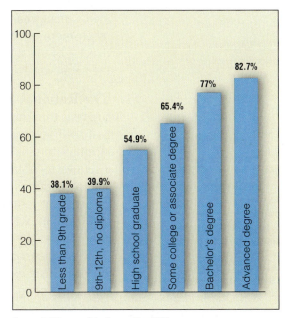

Source: U.S. Bureau of the Census, May 2010.

Why People Do Not Vote

For many years, political scientists believed that one reason why voter turnout in the United States was so much lower than in other Western nations was that it was very difficult to register to vote. In most states, registration required a special trip to a public office far in advance of elections. Today, all states are required to offer voter registration at a number of sites, including the driver's license bureau. In addition, many states offer advance voting at designated places on a walk-in basis up to three weeks before the election. These two innovations should have reduced barriers to registration and voting.

Uninformative Media Coverage and Negative Campaigning. Some scholars contend that one of the reasons why some people do not vote has to do with media coverage of campaigns. Many researchers have shown that the news media tend to provide much more news about "the horse race," or which candidates are ahead in the polls, than about the actual policy positions of the candidates. Thus, voters are not given the kind of information that would provide them with an incentive to go to the polls on election day.

did you know?

Computer software now exists that can identify likely voters and likely campaign donors by town, neighborhood, and street.

Additionally, negative campaigning is thought to have an adverse effect on voter turnout. By the time citizens are ready to cast their ballots, most of the information they have heard about the candidates has been so negative that no candidate is appealing.

According to a yearlong study conducted in 2000 by Harvard University's Center on the Press, Politics, and Public Policy, nonvoters and voters alike shared the same criticisms of the way the media cover campaigns: Most thought the media treated campaigns like theater or entertainment. Nonvoters, however, were much more cynical about government and politicians than were voters. As the director of the study put it, "All the polls, the spin, the attack ads, the money and the negative news have soured Americans on the way we choose our president."[2]

The Rational Ignorance Effect.

Rational Ignorance Effect
An effect produced when people purposely and rationally decide not to become informed on an issue because they believe that their vote on the issue is not likely to be a deciding one; a lack of incentive to seek the necessary information to cast an intelligent vote.

Another explanation of low voter turnout suggests that citizens are making a logical choice in not voting. If citizens believe that their votes will not affect the outcome of an election, then they have little incentive to seek the information they need to cast intelligent votes. The lack of incentive to obtain costly (in terms of time, attention, and so on) information about politicians and political issues has been called the **rational ignorance effect**. That term may seem contradictory, but it is not. Rational ignorance is a condition in which people purposely and rationally decide not to obtain information—to remain ignorant.[3]

Why, then, do even one-third to one-half of U.S. citizens bother to show up at the polls? One explanation is that most citizens receive personal satisfaction from the act of voting. It makes them feel that they are good citizens and that they are doing something patriotic, even though they are aware that their one vote will not change the outcome of the election.[4] Even among voters who are registered and who plan to vote, if the cost of voting goes up (in terms of time and inconvenience), the number of registered voters who actually vote will fall. In particular, bad weather on election day means that, on average, a smaller percentage of registered voters will go to the polls. It also appears that the greater the number of elections that are held, the smaller the turnout for primary and special elections. The Politics with a Purpose feature discusses the complexity of referenda elections across the states.

Plans for Improving Voter Turnout.

Mail-in voting in Oregon and easier access to registration are ideas that have been implemented in the hope of improving voter turnout. Nonetheless, voter turnout remains relatively low.

Two other ideas seemed promising. The first was to allow voters to visit the polls up to three weeks before election day. The second was to allow voters to vote by absentee ballot without having to give any particular reason for doing so. The Committee for the Study of the American Electorate discovered, however, that in areas that had implemented these plans, neither plan increased voter turnout. Indeed, voter turnout actually fell in those jurisdictions. In other words, states that did *not* permit early voting or unrestricted absentee voting had better turnout rates than states that did. Apparently, these two innovations appeal mostly to people who already intended to vote.

What is left? One possibility is to declare election day a national holiday or to hold elections on a Sunday, as is done in many other nations. Another is to adopt a registration method that places the responsibility on the government to make

2. Thomas E. Patterson, *The Vanishing Voter: Public Involvement in an Age of Uncertainty* (New York: Knopf, 2002). You can continue to track the Vanishing Voter Project at the study's Web site, www.hks.harvard.edu/presspol/vanishvoter.
3. Anthony Downs, *An Economic Theory of Democracy* (New York: Harper, 1957).
4. See Ilya Somin, "When Ignorance Isn't Bliss: How Political Ignorance Threatens Democracy," in *Policy Analysis,* September 22, 2004, Washington, DC: The Cato Institute, for a review of the rational ignorance theories.

Politics with a Purpose

LET'S PUT IT TO A VOTE

Have you ever heard someone say, usually in indignation, "There ought to be a law!"? Often this lawmaking happens in state legislatures or in Congress. However, in some states and localities, average citizens (or organized groups of "average citizens") can put an idea to a popular vote.

Why would citizens want to vote on laws themselves? The answer boils down to a debate over what type of democracy a society wants: direct or representative. While representative democracy is much more common, some states explicitly have created a means by which citizens can bypass the legislative process (through an initiative), revoke the actions of legislatures (via a referendum), or even remove elected officials from office (using recall).

While all states except Delaware require that amendments to the state constitutions go before the voters for final approval,[a] more than half of all states do not have any initiatives or referenda. In these 26 states, no mechanism exists for citizens to legislate through initiatives (enact laws by popular vote) or to overrule legislatures through referenda. The 24 states that do give citizens the ability to affect policy changes directly have seen vigorous debates over some of the most divisive and contentious issues of the day.

For example, both gay rights laws (domestic partnership laws, antidiscrimination laws) as well as laws defining marriage as a union between a man and a woman have been put to the direct democracy test. In 2006, an unsuccessful effort was made in Colorado by gay rights advocates to extend domestic partnership rights to same-sex couples through a referendum. In the same year, eight states had ballot issues to amend their constitutions to ban same-sex marriage; the amendment passed in all except one, Arizona.[b] However, in 2007, backers were unable to place on the ballot referenda on two Oregon laws that extended civil rights protections, including domestic partnership, to gays and lesbians.[c] In Maine, the law approving same-sex marriages was overturned by a referendum in 2009, although domestic partnerships remain legal. In 2012, advocates for same-sex marriage put another referendum on the ballot to overturn the 2009 vote. States choose the process by which a referendum, initiative, or recall effort is allowed on the ballot and the threshold of support necessary for winning. To get on the ballot, these efforts require that signatures be collected on a petition, and the petition is allowed to circulate for a set period of time. States also choose how many signatures are necessary for the effort to get on the ballot. Usually the minimum number is a percentage of either the total number of registered voters or the total turnout in the last general election. Sometimes states specify that the effort has to have support from across the state. Wyoming, for example, mandates that the signatures have to come from at least two-thirds of its counties.[d] Also, the signatures usually have to be from residents of that state who are registered voters. Often opponents of the effort use this stage to mount their attack. For example, in the 2007 Oregon referendum effort, supporters of gay rights were able to thwart the referendum both by challenging the validity of signatures and by effectively mobilizing in a "refuse to sign" campaign.[e]

Once it is on the ballot, the initiative, referendum, or recall must garner a certain percentage of votes. Often held in off-year elections, turnout for these votes may be very small. Some states go to great lengths, however, to ensure that the ballot issue has significant support not just from a majority of people voting in that election but also from the state's voting population. For example, Massachusetts requires that the measure receive a majority of the votes during that election and that those voting on the measure (either for or against) constitute in excess of 50 percent of those who voted in the previous general election.[f] Each of these examples illustrates the importance of each vote.

[a] M. Dane Waters, "Initiative and Referendum in the United States," a presentation to the Democracy Symposium, February 16–18, 2002, Williamsburg, VA; accessed at http://ni4d.us/library/waterspaper.pdf.
[b] www.cnn.com/ELECTION/2006/pages/results/ballot.measures; accessed April 11, 2008.
[c] www.basicrights.org/?p=84; accessed April 11, 2008.
[d] Jennifer Drage, "Initiative, Referendum, and Recall: The Process," *Journal of the American Society of Legislative Clerks and Secretaries*, Vol. 5, No. 2, 2000.
[e] www.basicrights.org/?p=84; accessed April 11, 2008.
[f] Drage, "Initiative, Referendum, and Recall: The Process."

sure all voters are registered. In Canada, a packet of information is mailed to each eligible voter. The citizen then returns the application to a federal office or applies online to be registered. After that act, a citizen is enrolled on the National Register of Electors (or citizens may opt out of having their name on the list). This registration activity takes place only once after the first registration—the voter would simply let the government know any future address changes. By making sure all

In 1944, the Georgia primary was opened to African American voters as the result of a Supreme Court decision. Registrars give instructions on how to cast a ballot.

AP Photos

eligible citizens are registered and informed about the polling place, the burden of registration and voting is lightened.

Legal Restrictions on Voting

■ **Learning Outcome 3:** Describe historical restrictions on the vote in the United States, and explain how these restrictions have been ended.

Legal restrictions on voter registration have existed since the founding of our nation when the franchise was granted to free, white males and occasionally to free African Americans. Since that time, groups have struggled to gain the franchise and to overcome voting restrictions in order to be represented at all levels of government.

Historical Restrictions

In most of the American colonies, only white males who owned property with a certain minimum value were eligible to vote, leaving a far greater number of Americans ineligible than eligible to take part in the democratic process.

Property Requirements. Many government functions concern property rights and the distribution of income and wealth, and some of the founders of our nation believed it was appropriate that only people who had an interest in property should vote on these issues. The idea of extending the vote to all citizens was, according to Charles Pinckney, a South Carolina delegate to the Constitutional Convention, merely "theoretical nonsense."

The logic behind the restriction of voting rights to property owners was questioned seriously by Thomas Paine in his pamphlet *Common Sense:*

Here is a man who today owns a jackass, and the jackass is worth $60. Today the man is a voter and goes to the polls and deposits his vote. Tomorrow the *jackass dies. The next day the man comes to vote without his jackass and cannot vote at all. Now tell me, which was the voter, the man or the jackass?*[5]

The writers of the Constitution allowed the states to decide who should vote. Thus, women were allowed to vote in Wyoming in 1870 but not in the entire nation until the Nineteenth Amendment was ratified in 1920. By about 1850, most white adult males in virtually all the states could vote without any property qualification. North Carolina was the last state to eliminate its property test for voting—in 1856.

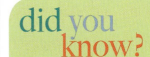

Further Extensions of the Franchise. Extension of the franchise to black males occurred with the passage of the Fifteenth Amendment in 1870. This enfranchisement was short lived, however, as the "redemption" of the South by white racists had rolled back these gains by the end of the century. As discussed in Chapter 5, African Americans, both male and female, were not able to participate in the electoral process in all states until the 1960s. The most recent extension of the franchise occurred when the voting age was reduced to 18 by the Twenty-sixth Amendment in 1971.

Is the Franchise Still Too Restrictive? Certain classes of people still do not have the right to vote. These include noncitizens and, in most states, convicted felons who have been released from prison. They also include current prison inmates, election law violators, and people who are mentally incompetent. Also, no one under the age of 18 can vote. Some political activists have argued that some of these groups should be allowed to vote. Most other democracies do not prevent persons convicted of a crime from voting after they have completed their sentences. In the 1800s, many states let noncitizen immigrants vote. In Nicaragua, the minimum voting age is 16.

One discussion concerns the voting rights of convicted felons who are no longer in prison or on parole. Some contend that voting should be a privilege, not a right, and we should not want the types of people who commit felonies participating in decision making. Others believe that it is wrong to further penalize those who have paid their debt to society. These people argue that barring felons from the polls injures minority groups because minorities make up a disproportionately large share of former prison inmates.

Current Eligibility and Registration Requirements

Voting generally requires **registration**, and to register, a person must satisfy the following voter qualifications, or legal requirements: (1) citizenship, (2) age (18 or older), and (3) residency—the duration varies widely from state to state and with types of elections. Since 1972, states cannot impose residency requirements of more than 30 days for voting in federal elections.

Each state has different qualifications for voting and registration. In 1993, Congress passed the "motor voter" bill, which requires that states provide voter-registration materials when people receive or renew driver's licenses, that all states allow voters to register by mail, and that voter-registration forms be made available at a wider variety of public places and agencies. In general, a person must register well in advance of an election, although voters in Idaho, Maine, Minnesota, Oregon, Wisconsin, and Wyoming are allowed to register up to, and on, election day. North Dakota has no voter registration at all.

Registration
The entry of a person's name onto the list of registered voters for elections. To register, a person must meet certain legal requirements of age, citizenship, and residency.

---

5. Thomas Paine, *Common Sense* (London: H. D. Symonds, 1792), p. 28.

Some argue that registration requirements are responsible for much of the nonparticipation in our political process. Certainly, since their introduction in the late 1800s, registration laws have reduced the voting participation of African Americans and immigrants. The question arises as to whether registration is really necessary. If it decreases participation in the political process, perhaps it should be dropped altogether. Still, as those in favor of registration requirements argue, such requirements may prevent fraudulent voting practices, such as multiple voting or voting by noncitizens.

In recent years, a number of states have passed stronger voter identification standards, although the actual requirements vary considerably. At the present time, at least seven states have strict photo-ID laws, requiring voters to show a government- issued photo ID to be able to vote. Another set of states requires either a photo ID or another, nonphoto ID or that someone at the polling place vouch for the individual personally. About 15 states have lists of acceptable forms of identification and another 19 have no ID requirement to vote. The Supreme Court found Indiana's strict photo-ID law constitutional in 2008,[6] although other states' laws have been found to be discriminatory by lower courts or by the U.S. Department of Justice. A study by the Brennan Center suggested that the stricter photo ID laws tended to decrease voting turnout in some precincts, while they increased turnout among older voters and higher income voters.[7] The question of whether a voter should have a photo ID is highly partisan: Republicans generally support such requirements as a way to make sure only eligible voters cast ballots; Democrats suggest that strict photo-ID laws are a handicap to poorer voters, elderly voters who do not drive, immigrants, young people, and others who do not have the time to get such an identification card.

Extension of the Voting Rights Act

In the summer of 2006, President Bush signed legislation that extended the Voting Rights Act for 25 more years. As discussed in Chapter 5, the Voting

Actor Bryan Greenberg shows his support for the "Rock the Vote" campaign at a pre-Grammy event in Los Angeles in Feburary, 2012. Celebrity spokespersons like Bryan Greenberg attract the attention of younger voters and help peruade them to participate in the political system through registering to vote and voting.

Angela Weiss/Getty Images

6. *Crawford v. Marion County Election Board,* 553 U.S. 181 (2008).
7. "ID at the Polls: Assessing the Impact of Recent State Voter ID Laws on Voter Turnout," *Harvard Law and Policy Review,* Vol. 3-1, 2007.

Rights Act was enacted to ensure that African Americans had equal access to the polls. Most of the provisions of the 1965 Voting Rights Act became permanent law. The 2006 act extended certain temporary sections and clarified certain amendments. For example, any new voting practices or procedures in jurisdictions with a history of discrimination in voting have to be approved by the U.S. Department of Justice or the federal district court in Washington, D.C., before being implemented. Section 203 of the 2006 act ensures that American citizens with limited proficiency in English can obtain the necessary assistance to enable them to understand and cast a ballot. Further, the act authorizes the U.S. attorney general to appoint federal election observers when evidence exists of attempts to intimidate minority voters at the polls. Those who supported the 2006 act believe that such provisions will ensure continuing voter participation by minority groups in America. However, it is difficult to overcome the anxieties that some individuals may feel about registration and voting. Naturalized citizens may be concerned that their legal status will be questioned, and this fear may overflow to other individuals of the same ethnic background even if they were born in the United States. Indeed, individuals with limited educational backgrounds or from very rural areas may also feel as if they are not welcome at the polls.

Primary Elections, General Elections, and More

One of the reasons often suggested for low voter turnout in the United States is the quantity of elections that are held. Because the United States has a federal system of government, elections are held at both the state and federal level. Additionally, most local units of government—towns, cities, counties—are staffed by officials who are elected at the local level. For the sake of convenience, the state organizes the federal elections for the House of Representatives, the Senate, and the presidency, but the county actually sets up and staffs the voting places and counts the vote.

As noted in Chapter 8, political parties in the United States do not have control over the candidates who run under their labels. Individuals who seek political office must be *nominated* in order to have their names placed on the ballot in the general election. The political party may nominate a candidate and endorse her, or another individual may submit appropriate petitions to make the nomination competitive. If two or more candidates are contesting the nomination for the party, voters will make the decision in a primary election.

Primary Elections

The purpose of a primary election is to choose a candidate who will become the party's nominee for the general election. This is true whether the primary election is for the nominee for state legislator, city council representative, or president of the United States. Primary elections were first mandated in 1903 in Wisconsin. The purpose of the primary was to open the nomination process to ordinary party members and to weaken the influence of party bosses in the nomination procedure. Today, all states have primary elections, which, in theory, are organized so that political party members can choose their own preferred candidate for office. As you will see, however, there are many different types of primary elections and many are not restricted to party members.

■ **Learning Outcome 4:**
Describe the types of elections held in the United States, and explain the constitutional reasons for so many elections.

AP Photo

AP Photo

During the 1968 Democratic convention, thousands of protesters gathered in front of the convention headquarters, the Hilton hotel in Chicago. National Guard troops and the Chicago police used military tactics to move the protesters away from the site.

Caucus
A meeting of party members designed to select candidates and propose policies.

Closed Primary
A type of primary in which the voter is limited to choosing candidates of the party of which he or she is a member.

Before discussing the types of primaries, we must first examine how some states use a party **caucus**. A caucus is typically a small, local meeting of party regulars who agree on a nominee. Sometimes the results of caucuses are voted on by a broader set of party members in a primary election. (If the party's chosen candidates have no opponents, however, a primary election may not be necessary.)

Alternatively, a slate of nominees of loyal party members may be chosen at a local or state party convention. In any event, the resulting primary elections differ from state to state. The most common types are discussed here.

Closed Primary. In a **closed primary**, only avowed or declared members of a party can vote in that party's primary. In other words, voters must declare their party affiliation, either when they register to vote or at the primary election. A closed-primary system tries to make sure that registered voters cannot cross over into the other party's primary in order to nominate the weakest candidate of the opposing party or to affect the ideological direction of that party.

Open Primary. In an **open primary**, voters can vote in either party primary without disclosing their party affiliation. Basically, the voter makes the choice in the privacy of the voting booth. The voter must, however, choose one party's list from which to select candidates. Open primaries place no restrictions on independent voters.

Blanket Primary. In a *blanket primary,* the voter can vote for candidates of more than one party. Alaska, Louisiana, and Washington have blanket primaries. Blanket-primary campaigns may be much more costly because each candidate for every office is trying to influence all of the voters, not just those in his or her party.

In 2000, the United States Supreme Court issued a decision that altered significantly the use of the blanket primary. The case arose when political parties in California challenged the constitutionality of a 1996 ballot initiative authorizing the use of the blanket primary in that state. The parties contended that the blanket primary violated their First Amendment right of association. Because the nominees represent the party, they argued, party members—not the general electorate—should have the right to choose the party's nominee. The Supreme Court ruled in favor of the parties, holding that the blanket primary violated parties' First Amendment associational rights.[8]

The Court's ruling called into question the constitutional validity of blanket primaries in other states as well. The question before these states is how to devise a primary election system that will comply with the Supreme

8. *California Democratic Party v. Jones,* 530 U.S. 567 (2000).

Court's ruling, yet offer independent voters a chance to participate in the primary elections.

Runoff Primary. Some states have a two-primary system. If no candidate receives a majority of the votes in the first primary, the top two candidates must compete in another primary, called a *runoff primary*.

General and Other Elections

What we commonly think of as "the election" is the general election, that is, the election that finally chooses the winner who will take office. In the United States, all federal general elections are held on the first Tuesday in November unless that is the first day of the month. The earliest date is thus November 2nd, and the latest is November 8th. To keep costs down, almost all states hold their elections on the same day even in years when there are no federal candidates. The interval between the primary and the general election may be more than six months or some shorter interval.

In addition to primary and general elections, states and localities often hold other types of elections. In a "special election," candidates vie for an office that has been left vacant due to death, resignation, or elevation to a higher office. Whether or not a special election is held for a representative or senator depends on state law and how much of the term remains. In some years, the nation's attention focuses on "recall elections," which are elections to remove an official from office and replace him or her with another candidate. Recall elections are held in response to petitions by the citizens, much like referenda. In 2003, the governor of California, who had just won a second term, was recalled and replaced by Arnold Schwarzenegger. In 2012, Governor Scott Walker of Wisconsin, who had championed legislation to limit the bargaining rights of public employees, faced a recall election. After the petition drive succeeded in putting a recall election on the calendar, the Democratic Party of Wisconsin held a primary to decide which candidate would oppose Walker in the recall election. In the actual recall election, Governor Walker retained his seat, defeating his opponent, 53 percent to 46 percent, in a victory that many saw as a defeat for the unions that campaigned for his recall.

Finally, local elections are held in many states to approve referenda or constitutional amendments, as discussed in the Politics with a Purpose in this chapter. Some state and local governments are required to seek public approval for any tax increase or bond issue beyond a constitutional limit. In a state such as Ohio, with a constitution dating back to 1803, almost all local taxes must be approved by the public. What this means is that school districts, park districts, and other public entities are constantly going to the public to get approval for tax increases of any kind. In a less-than-perfect economy or in the face of antitax sentiments, it is not easy to persuade voters to increase their own taxes.

How Are Elections Conducted?

The United States uses the **Australian ballot**—a secret ballot that is prepared, distributed, and counted by government officials at public expense. Since 1888, all states have used the Australian ballot. Before that, many states used the alternatives of oral voting and differently colored ballots prepared by the parties. Obviously, knowing which way a person was voting made it easy to apply pressure on the person to change his or her vote, and vote buying was common.

Open Primary
A primary in which any registered voter can vote (but must vote for candidates of only one party).

Australian Ballot
A secret ballot prepared, distributed, and tabulated by government officials at public expense. Since 1888, all U.S. states have used the Australian ballot rather than an open, public ballot.

■ **Learning Outcome 5:**
Discuss the impact of the mechanics and technology of voting on voting turnout, vote fraud, and the ability of citizens to trust the process.

Beyond Our Borders
WHY WOULD COMPULSORY VOTING INCREASE TURNOUT?

Most nations in the world are now democracies.* Some are very new and some are still unstable, but in every democracy the question of voter turnout is important. Some scholars have speculated that voting is a matter of historic behavior: Those countries, like the democracies of Western Europe, that had the most experience with democratic practice, would naturally have greater voter turnout. Turnout data from the United States would suggest that countries in which citizens are literate and better off economically would have higher turnout. However, turnout in many European nations has declined just as it has in the United States over the past several decades.

The data in Table 9-2 make the point that the United States has very low voter turnout compared to other nations, whether those nations are highly developed or not. Of the top 10 nations listed in the table, Australia, Belgium, and Italy have compulsory voting. The Netherlands had compulsory voting until 1967. After it became voluntary, voter turnout in the Netherlands dropped 20 percent. The same phenomenon occurred in Venezuela, which dropped compulsory voting in 1993 and saw turnout drop 30 percent.

Requiring citizens to vote sounds like a very serious and repressive measure. If citizens are unhappy with their government and, perhaps, with all the political parties, shouldn't they have the right not to vote? If people are highly suspicious of government and of the national police, couldn't there be recriminations over the vote? Generally speaking, those nations that have instituted the compulsory vote have also made accommodations to make voting easier: Voting is held on the weekend, those with illnesses are excused, registration for voting is maintained by the national government, and arrangements for early voting and mail-in ballots can be made.

The nations with compulsory voting believe that this practice makes sure that all voices are heard in the election. We know that those who are least educated and less well off are most likely not to vote. Proponents of compulsory voting argue that elections that try to include everyone are fairer. To those who say that being fined or otherwise penalized for not voting discriminates against the poor, they argue that citizens regularly are required to pay fees for drivers'

An Egyptian woman casts her ballot in the first free elections after the overthrow of Hosni Mubarak.

licenses, for parking tickets, and for car registrations, and that the penalty for not voting is very small.

In the United States, turnout has not been high since 1960, and it continues to decline. Arend Lijphart, a scholar of political participation, believes that the decline in turnout in the United States and in other European nations makes those societies less equal. In his address to the American Political Science Association, he suggested a number of remedies, including making registration easier and considering compulsory voting. According to Lijphart, requiring voting would increase turnout 7 to 16 percent.** More recently, when considering the severe decline in voting among younger Americans, Martin Wattenberg also proposed compulsory voting.*** He believes that this may be a necessary step to get younger Americans to pay more attention to political issues and to get more involved in the political system.

FOR CRITICAL ANALYSIS

1. *Why do you think U.S. voter turnout is so much lower than in many poorer, less developed nations?*

2. *Would compulsory voting change election outcomes in the United States?*

3. *Would uniform voting and election laws across the United States help increase turnout?*

---

*The Institute for Democracy and Electoral Assistance (IDEA), "What Affects Turnout?" www.idea.int/vt.

**Arend Lijphart, "Unequal Participation: Democracy's Unresolved Dilemma," *American Political Science Review* 91 (1): 8.

***Martin P. Wattenberg, *Is Voting for Young People?* 3rd ed., New York: Longman, 2012.

Office-Block and Party-Column Ballots

Two types of Australian ballots are used in the United States in general elections. The first, called an **office-block ballot**, or sometimes a **Massachusetts ballot**, groups all the candidates for a particular elective office under the title of that office. Parties dislike the office-block ballot because it places more emphasis on the office than on the party; it discourages straight-ticket voting and encourages split-ticket voting.

A **party-column ballot** is a form of general election ballot in which all of a party's candidates are arranged in one column under the party's label and symbol. It is also called the **Indiana ballot**. In some states, it allows voters to vote for all of a party's candidates for local, state, and national offices by simply marking a single "X" or by pulling a single lever. Most states use this type of ballot. As it encourages straight-ticket voting, the two major parties favor this form. When a party has an exceptionally strong presidential or gubernatorial candidate to head the ticket, the use of the party-column ballot increases the **coattail effect** (the influence of a popular candidate on the success of other candidates on the same party ticket).

Table 9–2 ▶ Turnout in Selected Countries, Most Recent National Election

COUNTRIES	VOTING–AGE POPULATION PERCENTAGE
Belgium	93.3
Denmark	83.2
Australia	81.0
Greece	79.2
New Zealand	77.8
Austria	75.6
Barbados	69.4
Germany	64.6
Bosnia and Herzegovina	58.7
United States (2008)	57.5
South Africa	56.6
India	56.4
Korea	46.6
Switzerland	39.8

Source: The Institute for Democracy and Electoral Assistance (IDEA), "What Affects Turnout?" www.idea.int/vt.

Voting by Mail

Although voting by mail has been accepted for absentee ballots for many decades (for example, for those who are doing business away from home or for members of the armed forces), only recently have several states offered mail ballots to all of their voters. The rationale for using the mail ballot is to make voting easier for the voters. A startling result came in a special election in Oregon in spring 1996: With the mail-only ballot, turnout was 66 percent, and the state saved more than $1 million. In the 2000 presidential elections, in which Oregon voters were allowed to mail in their ballots, voter participation was higher than 80 percent. Although voters in several states now have the option of voting by mail, Oregon is the only state to have abandoned precinct polling places completely.

Vote Fraud

Vote fraud is something regularly suspected but seldom proved. Voting in the 1800s, when secret ballots were rare and people had a cavalier attitude toward the open buying of votes, was probably much more conducive to fraud than are modern elections. Larry J. Sabato and Glenn R. Simpson, however, claim that the potential for vote fraud is high in many states, particularly through the use of phony voter registrations and absentee ballots.[9]

The Danger of Fraud. In California, for example, it is very difficult to remove a name from the polling list even if the person has not cast a ballot in the last two years. Thus, many persons are still on the rolls even though they no longer live in

Office-Block, or Massachusetts, Ballot
A form of general-election ballot in which candidates for elective office are grouped together under the title of each office. It emphasizes voting for the office and the individual candidate, rather than for the party.

Party-Column, or Indiana, Ballot
A form of general-election ballot in which all of a party's candidates for elective office are arranged in one column under the party's label and symbol. It emphasizes voting for the party, rather than for the office or individual.

Coattail Effect
The influence of a popular candidate on the electoral success of other candidates on the same party ticket. The effect is increased by the party-column ballot, which encourages straight-ticket voting.

9. Larry J. Sabato and Glenn R. Simpson, *Dirty Little Secrets: The Persistence of Corruption in American Politics* (New York: Random House, 1996).

Probate Court, Jefferson County, Alabama

SAMPLE	SAMPLE
OFFICIAL BALLOT	GENERAL AND CONSTITUTIONAL AMENDMENT ELECTION

JEFFERSON COUNTY | **GENERAL ELECTION** | **NOVEMBER 7, 2006**

INSTRUCTIONS TO VOTER
MARK THE OVAL TO THE
LEFT OF YOUR CHOICE
LIKE THIS.

STRAIGHT PARTY VOTING

○ ALABAMA DEMOCRATIC PARTY
○ ALABAMA REPUBLICAN PARTY

FOR GOVERNOR
VOTE FOR ONE

○ LUCY BAXLEY
Democrat
○ BOB RILEY
Republican
○ Write-in

FOR LIEUTENANT GOVERNOR
VOTE FOR ONE

○ JIM FOLSOM, JR.
Democrat
○ LUTHER STRANGE
Republican
○ Write-in

FOR UNITED STATES REPRESENTATIVE CONGRESSIONAL DISTRICT 6
VOTE FOR ONE

○ SPENCER BACHUS
Republican
○ Write-in

FOR ATTORNEY GENERAL
VOTE FOR ONE

○ JOHN TYSON, JR.
Democrat
○ TROY KING
Republican
○ Write-in

FOR STATE SENATOR DISTRICT NO. 95

FOR SUPREME COURT JUSTICE, PLACE NO. 3
VOTE FOR ONE

○ ALBERT L. "AL" JOHNSON
Democrat
○ LYN STUART
Republican
○ Write-in

FOR SUPREME COURT JUSTICE, PLACE NO.4
VOTE FOR ONE

○ JOHN H. ENGLAND, JR.
Democrat
○ GLENN MURDOCK
Republican
○ Write-in

FOR COURT OF CIVIL APPEALS JUDGE, PLACE NO. 1
VOTE FOR ONE

○ RAY VAUGHAN
Democrat
○ TERRY MOORE
Republican
○ Write-in

FOR COURT OF CIVIL APPEALS JUDGE, PLACE NO. 2
VOTE FOR ONE

○ KIMBERLY HARBISON DRAKE
Democrat
○ CRAIG PITTMAN
Republican
○ Write-in

FOR COURT OF CIVIL APPEALS, JUDGE, PLACE NO. 3
VOTE FOR ONE

○ JIM MCFERRIN
Democrat
○ TERRI WILLINGHAM THOMAS
Republican

FOR STATE AUDITOR
VOTE FOR ONE

○ JANIE BAKER CLARKE
Democrat
○ S. SAMANTHA "SAM" SHAW
Republican
○ Write-in

FOR COMMISSIONER OF AGRICULTURE AND INDUSTRIES
VOTE FOR ONE

○ RON SPARKS
Democrat
○ ALBERT LIPSCOMB
Republican
○ Write-in

FOR PUBLIC SERVICE COMMISSION, PLACE 1
VOTE FOR ONE

○ JAN COOK
Democrat
○ JOHN RICE
Republican
○ Write-in

FOR PUBLIC SERVICE COMMISSION, PLACE 2
VOTE FOR ONE

○ SUSAN PARKER
Democrat
○ PERRY O. HOOPER, JR.
Republican
○ Write-in

FOR STATE BOARD OF EDUCATION MEMBER DISTRICT NO. 06
VOTE FOR ONE

○ DAVID BYERS
Republican
○ Write-in

Many states allow paper or electronic ballots to have a "party circle" so the voter can vote for all the candidates of that party for local, state, and national offices with one mark.

Oregon is the only state that uses only a mail ballot. Special ballot boxes are set up where voters can deposit their ballots. Do you think that mail balloting would work for the entire United States?

California. Enterprising political activists could use these names for absentee ballots. Other states have registration laws meant to encourage easy registration and voting. Such laws can be taken advantage of by those who seek to vote more than once.

After the 2000 elections, Larry Sabato again emphasized the problem of voting fraud. "It's a silent scandal," said Sabato, "and the problem is getting worse with increases in absentee voting, which is the easiest way to commit fraud." He noted that in 2000, one-third of Florida's counties found that more than 1,200 votes were cast illegally by felons, and in one county alone nearly 500 votes were cast by unregistered voters. In two precincts, the number of ballots cast was greater than the number of people who voted.[10]

Mistakes by Voting Officials. Some observers claim, however, that errors leading to fraud are trivial in number, and that a few mistakes are inevitable in a system involving millions of voters. These people argue that an excessive concern with vote fraud makes it harder for minorities and poor people to vote.

For example, in 2000, Katherine Harris, Florida's top election official, oversaw a purge of the voter rolls while simultaneously serving as cochair of the Florida

REUTERS/Richard Clement/Landov

MULTNOMAH COUNTY
OFFICIAL BALLOT DROP SITE

---

10.   As cited in "Blind to Voter Fraud," *Wall Street Journal*, March 2, 2001, p. A10.

Bush campaign. According to *The New York Times,* when attempting to remove the names of convicted felons from the list of voters:

> *Ms. Harris's office overruled the advice of the private firm that compiled the felon list and called for removing not just names that were an exact match, but ones that were highly inexact. Thousands of Florida voters wound up being wrongly purged.... In Missouri, elected officials charged for years that large numbers of St. Louis residents were casting votes from vacant lots. A study conducted by The [St. Louis] Post Dispatch in 2001 found that in the vast majority of cases, the voters lived in homes that had been wrongly classified by the city.[11]*

In both the Florida and Missouri examples, a majority of the affected voters were African American.

As a result of the confusion generated by the 2000 elections, many states have improved their voting systems and procedures although, as discussed earlier in this chapter, the debate over requiring photo identification to vote is extremely controversial.

The Importance of the Voting Machine

The 2000 presidential election spurred a national debate on the mechanics of how people actually cast their ballots on election day. Up until 2000, states and counties moved from hand-counted paper ballots to mechanical voting machines or electronic touch-screen devices as they could afford the move or in response to local election difficulties. The outcome of the 2000 presidential election hinged on Florida's electoral votes. The biggest problem lay in Florida's use of punch-card ballots. Voters slipped their card into the voting book and then "punched" the number next to the name of the candidate they preferred. Because of the layout of the printed book in 2000, names were spread across two pages, resulting in a "butterfly" ballot. Voters could accidentally punch the wrong number and cast their vote for the wrong candidate.

did you know?

Each new voting machine costs more than $3,000 for the equipment alone.

Naples, Florida election workers study punch-card ballots in the state supreme court's ordered recount after the 2000 election. A few minutes after this photograph was taken, the U.S. Supreme Court stopped the recount and announced that it would hear the case. George W. Bush won Florida's electoral votes.

© COLIN BRALEY/Corbis

11.   "How America Doesn't Vote," *The New York Times: The News of the Week in Review,* February 15, 2004, p. 10.

As the election night came to a close, it was clear that the votes in Florida between George W. Bush and Al Gore were "too close to call." Ballot problems abounded: Some voters invalidated their ballots by voting for both candidates; some punch cards were not punched all the way through, resulting in no vote being counted; some had no vote for president at all. The Democratic Party and its candidates went to court to demand a recount of the votes. The Republican political leaders in Florida tried to stop recounts in fear of losing the election. After a series of dramatic legal battles, the U.S. Supreme Court settled the election by allowing a Florida decision favoring the Republicans to stand. However, the result was a seriously flawed election process that produced tremendous cynicism about the mechanics of voting.

In 2002, Congress passed the Help America Vote Act, which established the U.S. Election Assistance Commission. The charge of the commission is to set standards for voting machines; to distribute funds to help communities acquire new, easier-to-use machines; and to act as a clearinghouse of information for the states. As expected, several companies began to create new machines for use in the voting booth. Most of these depend on digital recording of votes. Given the mistakes that occurred in Florida, many citizens wanted a record of their votes so that a mistake in tallying votes could be checked against a paper record. Election officials are deeply concerned that recording and transmitting vote counts only digitally may be subject to hacking and vote fraud. To date, no system, including the use of the Internet, has been devised that is totally immune to some sort of fraud, and voters continue to be concerned about the security of our election system.[12]

The Electoral College

Many people who vote for the president and vice president think that they are voting directly for a candidate. In actuality, they are voting for **electors**, who will cast their ballots in the electoral college. Article II, Section 1, of the Constitution outlines in detail the method of choosing electors for president and vice president. The framers of the Constitution wanted to avoid the selection of president and vice president by the "excitable masses." Rather, they wished the choice to be made by a few supposedly dispassionate, reasonable men (but not women).

The Choice of Electors

Each state's electors are selected during each presidential election year. The selection is governed by state laws. After the national party convention, the electors normally are pledged to the candidates chosen. The total number of electors today is 538, equal to 100 senators, 435 members of the House, and three electors for the District of Columbia (the Twenty-third Amendment, ratified in 1961, added electors for the District of Columbia). Each state's number of electors equals that state's number of senators (two) plus its number of representatives. Figure 9-4 shows how the electoral votes are apportioned by state.

The Electors' Commitment

When a plurality of voters in a state chooses a slate of electors—except in Maine and Nebraska, where electoral votes are based on congressional districts—those electors are pledged to cast their ballots on the first Monday after the second

Elector
A member of the electoral college, which selects the president and vice president. Each state's electors are chosen in each presidential election year according to state laws.

did you know?

Forty-two states do not indicate on the ballot that the voter is casting a ballot for members of the electoral college rather than for the president and vice president directly.

---

12. The AEI-Brookings Election Reform Project collects data and provides reports on progress in securing the vote at its Web site: www.electionreformproject.org.

Figure 9-4 ▶ Electoral Votes by State

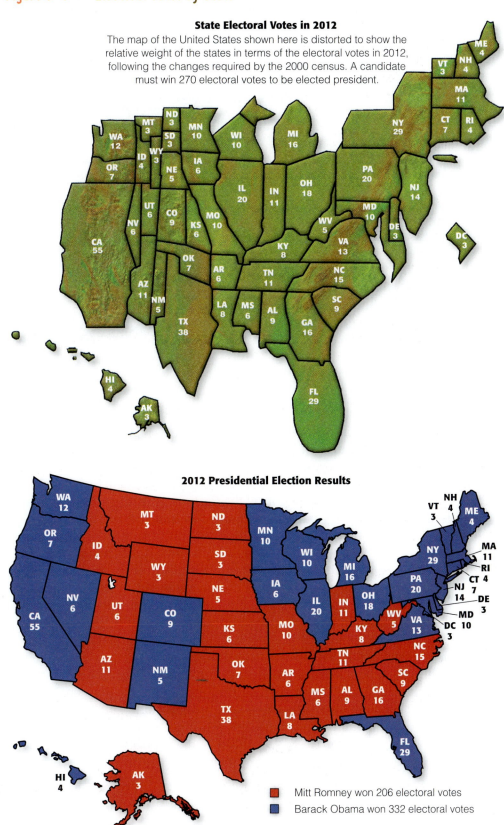

State Electoral Votes in 2012

The map of the United States shown here is distorted to show the relative weight of the states in terms of the electoral votes in 2012, following the changes required by the 2000 census. A candidate must win 270 electoral votes to be elected president.

2012 Presidential Election Results

■ Mitt Romney won 206 electoral votes
■ Barack Obama won 332 electoral votes

Wednesday in December in the state capital for the presidential and vice presidential candidates of their party. The Constitution does not, however, *require* the electors to cast their ballots for the candidates of their party.

The ballots are counted and certified before a joint session of Congress early in January. The candidates who receive a majority of the electoral votes (270) are certified as president-elect and vice president–elect. According to the Constitution, if no candidate receives a majority of the electoral votes, the election of the president is decided in the House from among the candidates with the three highest numbers of votes, with each state having one vote (decided by a plurality of each state delegation). The selection of the vice president is determined by the Senate in a choice between the two candidates with the most votes, each senator having one vote. Congress was required to choose the president and vice president in 1801 (Thomas Jefferson and Aaron Burr), and the House chose the president in 1825 (John Quincy Adams).[13]

It is possible for a candidate to become president without obtaining a majority of the popular vote. Many minority presidents are found in our history, including Abraham Lincoln, Woodrow Wilson, Harry Truman, John F. Kennedy, Richard Nixon (in 1968), Bill Clinton (1992, 1996), and George W. Bush (in 2000). Such an event becomes more likely when there are important third-party candidates.

Perhaps more distressing is the possibility of a candidate's being elected when an opposing candidate receives a plurality of the popular vote. This has occurred on four occasions—in the elections of John Quincy Adams in 1824, Rutherford B. Hayes in 1876, Benjamin Harrison in 1888, and George W. Bush in 2000, all of whom won elections in which an opponent received a plurality of the popular vote.

13.   For a detailed account of the process, see Michael J. Glennon, *When No Majority Rules: The Electoral College and Presidential Succession* (Washington, DC: Congressional Quarterly Press, 1993), p. 20.

Criticisms of the Electoral College

Besides the possibility of a candidate's becoming president even though an opponent obtains more popular votes, other complaints about the electoral college have emerged. The idea of the Constitution's framers was to have electors use their own discretion to decide who would make the best president. But electors no longer perform the selecting function envisioned by the founders, because they are committed to the candidate who has a plurality of popular votes in their state in the general election.[14]

One can also argue that the current system, which in most states gives all of the electoral votes to the candidate who has a statewide plurality, is unfair to other candidates and their supporters. The current system of voting also means that presidential campaigning will be concentrated in those states that have the largest number of electoral votes and in those states in which the outcome is likely to be close. The other states may receive second-class treatment during the presidential campaign. It can also be argued that something of a bias favors states with smaller populations, because including Senate seats in the electoral vote total partly offsets the edge of the more populous states in the House. Wyoming (with two senators and one representative) gets an electoral vote for roughly every 164,594 inhabitants (based on the 2000 census), for example, whereas Iowa gets one vote for every 418,046 inhabitants, and California has one vote for every 615,848 inhabitants. Note that many of the smallest states have Republican majorities.

Many proposals for reform of the electoral college system have been advanced, particularly after the turmoil resulting from the 2000 elections. The most obvious proposal is to eliminate the electoral college system completely and to elect candidates on a popular-vote basis; in other words, a direct election, by the people, of the president and vice president. Because abolishing the electoral college would require a constitutional amendment, however, the chances of electing the president by a direct vote are remote.

The major parties are not in favor of eliminating the electoral college, fearing that this would give minor parties a more influential role. Also, less populous states are not in favor of direct election of the president because they believe they would be overwhelmed by the large-state vote. In recent years, some states have begun to consider yet another way to make the electoral college more responsive to the popular vote. In 2007, the National Popular Vote (NPV) movement came to public attention. The movement creates a compact between the states that requires that electoral votes from NPV states will be cast for the candidate who wins the national popular vote regardless of the vote in that particular state. So far, two states have approved this law, and several more are considering it. In addition, Massachusetts, South Carolina, Virginia, and Wisconsin are among states considering adopting a district plan like that of Maine.

While the 2000 election caused considerable controversy and cynicism about the national electoral system, it also focused attention on issues that need to be resolved. Efforts to improve registration systems, to make voting easier and more secure, and to make changes to the electoral college all will work to make elections in the United States more trustworthy for the voters.

---

14. Note, however, that there have been revolts by so-called *faithless electors*—in 1796, 1820, 1948, 1956, 1960, 1968, 1972, 1976, 1988, and 2000.[Jen33]

You Can Make A Difference

REGISTERING AND VOTING

iStockphoto.com/kyoshino

© Jeff Greenberg/Alamy

Voter registration drive in Miami, Florida.

In nearly every state, before you are allowed to cast a vote in an election, you must first register. Registration laws vary considerably from state to state. Depending in part on how difficult a state's laws make it to register, some states have much lower rates of registration and voting participation than do others.

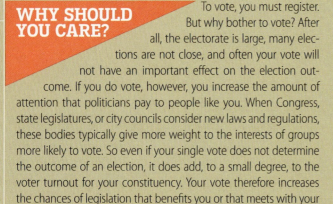

WHY SHOULD YOU CARE?

To vote, you must register. But why bother to vote? After all, the electorate is large, many elections are not close, and often your vote will not have an important effect on the election outcome. If you do vote, however, you increase the amount of attention that politicians pay to people like you. When Congress, state legislatures, or city councils consider new laws and regulations, these bodies typically give more weight to the interests of groups more likely to vote. So even if your single vote does not determine the outcome of an election, it does add, to a small degree, to the voter turnout for your constituency. Your vote therefore increases the chances of legislation that benefits you or that meets with your approval.

WHAT CAN YOU DO?

What do you have to do to register and cast a vote? In general, you must be a citizen of the United States, at least 18 years old on or before election day, and a resident of the state in which you intend to register. Most states require that you meet minimum-residency requirements. In other words, you must have lived in the state in which you plan to be registered for a specified period of time. If you have not lived in the state long enough to register before an upcoming election, you may retain your previous registration in another state and cast an absentee vote, if that state permits it. Minimum-residency requirements vary among the states. By a ruling of the United States Supreme Court, no state can require more than 30 days of residency. Some states require a much shorter period—for example, 10 days in Wisconsin and one day in Alabama. Thirty-one states do not have a minimum-residency requirement at all.

Can college students vote in their college town? Generally speaking, yes. Almost all students meet the 30 days of residency requirement, but states may have laws about the appropriate identification that make it more difficult to register and vote. Students should always check with the local board of elections or political party headquarters to get the right answer. And, remember, students who vote in their college town may not vote again in their parents' town.

Nearly every state also specifies a closing date by which you must be registered before an election. In other words, even if you have met a residency requirement, you still may not be able to vote if you register too close to the day of the election. The closing date is different in certain states (Connecticut and Delaware) for primary elections than for other elections. The closing date for registration varies from election day itself (Maine, Minnesota, Wisconsin, and Wyoming) to 30 days before the election in 13 states. In North Dakota, no registration is necessary.

In most states, your registration can be revoked if you do not vote within a certain number of years. This process of automatically "purging" the voter-registration lists of nonactive voters happens every two years in about a dozen states, every three years in Georgia, every four years in more than 20 other states, every five years in Maryland and Rhode Island, every eight years in North Carolina, and every 10 years in Michigan. Ten states do not require this purging at all.

Let us look at Iowa as an example. Iowa voters normally register through the local county auditor or when they obtain a driver's license (under the "motor voter" law of 1993). A voter who moves to a new address within the state must change his or her registration by contacting the auditor. Postcard registrations must be postmarked or delivered to the county auditor no later than the 15th day before an election. Voters can declare or change their party affiliation when they register or reregister, or they can change or declare a party when they go to the polls on election day. Postcard registration forms in Iowa are available at many public buildings, from labor unions, at political party headquarters, at the county auditors' offices, or from campus groups. Registrars who will accept registrations at other locations may be located by calling a party headquarters or a county auditor.

For more information on voting registration, contact your county or state officials, party headquarters, labor union, or local chapter of the League of Women Voters.*

*League of Women Voters, www.lwv.org

Key Terms

Australian ballot 293
caucus 292
closed primary 292
coattail effect 295

elector 298
office-block, or
   Massachusetts, ballot 295
open primary 293

party-column, or
   Indiana, ballot 295
rational ignorance
   effect 286

registration 289
voter turnout 282

Chapter Summary

1. The United States is a representative democracy with majoritarian elections, meaning that the candidate who wins the majority of the vote wins office. High voter turnout ensures that the government truly represents the will of the majority of the people.

2. Voter participation in the United States is low compared with that of other countries. Some view low voter turnout as a threat to representative democracy, whereas others believe it simply indicates greater satisfaction with the status quo. There is an association between voting and a person's age, education, minority status, and income level. Another factor affecting voter turnout is the extent to which elections are competitive within a state. It is also true that the number of eligible voters is smaller than the number of people of voting age because of ineligible felons and immigrants who are not yet citizens.

3. In the United States, only citizens have been able to vote. However, in the early years of the republic, only free white male citizens who owned property were eligible to vote. Over the years, laws have excluded women, citizens under 18 years of age, felons, ex-slaves, and others. By 1971 suffrage was extended to all citizens, male and female, aged 18 or older. However, questions remain: Should felons be excluded from voting? What about resident noncitizens or people who have difficulty getting registered? Each state has somewhat different registration processes and requirements for identification at the polls. Some claim that these requirements are responsible for much of the nonparticipation in the political process in the United States.

4. Because of the federal structure of the United States, citizens are asked to vote in federal, state, and local elections. To nominate candidates for office, voters participate in primary elections. The candidates are finally elected in the general election. In addition, voters may be asked to cast ballots on referenda, on constitutional amendments at the state level, for tax levies or in special elections to choose candidates for a vacated office.

5. The United States uses the Australian ballot, a secret ballot that is prepared, distributed, and counted by government officials. The office-block ballot groups candidates according to office. The party-column ballot groups candidates according to their party labels and symbols.

6. Vote fraud is often charged but not often proven. After the 2000 election, states and local communities adopted new forms of voting equipment, seeking to provide secure voting systems for elections. The federal government established a commission to test new technologies and provide a clearinghouse for information.

7. The voter technically does not vote directly for president but chooses between slates of presidential electors. In most states, the slate that wins the most popular votes throughout the state gets to cast all the electoral votes for the state. The candidate receiving a majority (270) of the electoral votes wins. Both the mechanics and the politics of the electoral college have been sharply criticized. Many proposed reforms include a proposal that the president be elected on a popular-vote basis in a direct election.

Selected Print, Media, and Online Resources

PRINT RESOURCES

Alvarez, R. Michael, and Thad E. Hall. *Electronic Elections: The Perils and Promises of Digital Democracy.* Princeton, NJ: Princeton University Press, 2008. Alvarez and Hall examine all past technologies in voting and look at the new voting machines and processes that are available in the digital age. They suggest standards by which voting systems can be improved.

Fortier, John C. *Absentee and Early Voting: Trends, Promises and Perils.* Washington, DC: AEI, 2006. The author looks at all of the efforts to encourage participation by making early voting and absentee voting easier and then discusses the advantages and disadvantages of these alternatives to going to the polls.

Green, Donald P., and Alan S. Gerber. *Get Out the Vote: How to Increase Voter Turnout.* Washington, DC: Brookings Institution Press, 2004. This volume is a practical guide for activists seeking to mount Get Out The Vote (GOTV) campaigns. It differs from other guides in that it is based on research and experiments in actual electoral settings— Green and Gerber are political science professors at Yale University. The authors discover that many widely used GOTV tactics are less effective than is often believed.

Herrnson, Paul S., Richard G. Niemi, Michael J. Hanmer, Benjamin B. Bederson, Frederick C. Conrad, and Michael W. Traugott. *Voting Technology: The Not-So-Simple Act of Casting a Ballot.* Washington, DC: Brookings Institution, 2008. This book summarizes the data collected by the Brookings Institution on how voting technology impacts voters' behavior.

Martinez, Michael D. *Does Turnout Matter?* Boulder, CO: Westview Press, 2009. Scholars have expended much effort in examining why voter turnout is lower in the United States than in many other countries, but the question of whether low turnout actually matters has received less attention. Martinez is a professor of political science at the University of Florida.

Piven, Frances Fox, Lori Minnite, and Margaret Groarke. *Keeping Down the Black Vote: Race and Demobilization of American Voters.* New York: The New Press, 2009. The authors claim that under the banner of election reform, leading operatives in the Republican Party have sought to affect elections by suppressing the black vote.

Poundstone, William. *Gaming the Vote: Why Elections Aren't Fair (and What We Can Do about It).* New York: Hill and Wang, 2009. America's first-past-the-post, winner-take-all voting system is not the only one possible, and Poundstone believes that it is actually one of the worst. In this volume, he provides a clear and witty tour of possible voting systems that may better reflect the will of the people.

Simons, Barbara, and Douglas W. Jones. *Who's Minding the Vote?* Sausalito, CA: Polipoint Press, 2008. This is a fascinating history of voting machines and technological methods that can be used to rig elections. The authors offer a scathing criticism of certain recently developed electronic voting systems.

MEDIA RESOURCES

American Blackout—A 2005 film starring former congresswoman Cynthia McKinney from Georgia as she investigates the ways in which African American voters can be challenged at the polls and kept from voting.

Election Day—This 2005 film was shot on election day in 2004 and looks at 14 different individuals who are trying to vote or who are working at the polls themselves.

Hacking Democracy—An HBO production that follows activist Bev Harris of Seattle and others as they take on Diebold, a company that makes electronic voting machines. The documentary argues that security lapses in Diebold's machines are a threat to the democratic process.

Mississippi Burning—This 1988 film, starring Gene Hackman and Willem Dafoe, is a fictional version of the investigation of the deaths of two civil rights workers who came to Mississippi to help register African Americans to vote in 1964.

Recount—A 2008 film nominated for an Emmy Award that chronicles the disputed 2000 presidential contest in Florida, where a mere 538 ballots separated Republican George W. Bush and Democrat Al Gore. The film makes out the victorious Republican operatives to be much more aggressive than the rather hapless Democrats.

Trouble in Paradise—Shot in Florida after the contested 2000 presidential election, the film follows Florida residents as they find out what laws have been changed and which aspects of voting are still troubling in their state. The film was released in 2004.

ONLINE RESOURCES

AEI–Brookings Election Reform Project—In response to the Help America Vote Act of 2002, this project aims to synthesize voting reform research and create a bridge between the research and policy communities. Discusses election technologies and their pros and cons: www.electionreformproject.org

The Center for Voting and Democracy—a source of analysis and perspective on improving how elections are held in the United States. Discusses the impact of different voting systems on election strategies and outcomes: www.fairvote.org

Institute for Democracy and Electoral Assistance (IDEA)—an intergovernmental organization that supports sustainable democracy worldwide. Provides information about voting and turnout around the world: www.idea.int

National Conference of State Legislatures—Find out what different states are doing to ensure the vote: www.ncsl.org/programs/legismgt/elect/elect.htm

Oregon Secretary of State Elections Division—includes frequently asked questions and a brief history of voting by mail: www.sos.state.or.us/elections/

10 Campaigning for Office

AP Photo/John Flesher

Senator Debbie Stabenow, Democrat of Michigan, speaks to cherry and apple farmers about her bid for reelection in 2012.

LEARNING OUTCOMES

After reading this chapter, students will be able to:

■ **LO1** Explain the eligibility requirements for president, senator, and representative, and discuss why an individual might choose to become a candidate for office.

■ **LO2** Produce a plan for a modern campaign for the United States Senate including the strategy, staff, and finances necessary for such an endeavor.

■ **LO3** Discuss the role of print, electronic, and social media in a political campaign including the news, debates, and paid advertising.

■ **LO4** Demonstrate an understanding of the evolution of campaign finance regulation, the development of political action committees (PACs), and the current state of such regulation.

■ **LO5** Describe the general outline of today's campaign for the presidency, and discuss the impact of the primary system on the outcome of the nomination process.

What If ...

SPENDING LIMITS WERE PLACED ON CAMPAIGNS?

BACKGROUND

After the 2012 presidential primary campaigns ended, less than $500,000 was distributed by the Federal Election Commission (FEC) to candidates who qualified for matching funds. In comparison, in 2008, the FEC dispersed more than $7 million. Only Buddy Roemer (former governor of Louisiana) and Gary Johnson (former governor of New Mexico) filed for matching funds. What this means is that all of the major Republican candidates competing for the presidential nomination—Michele Bachmann, Newt Gingrich, Jon Huntsman, Ron Paul, Rick Perry, Mitt Romney, and Rick Santorum—chose to raise funds on their own from individual donors and other sources and refused public funds. President Obama, who had no primary opponent, also refused public funds. The political parties each received a little more than $18 million from the FEC for their conventions. In addition, Congress appropriated $50 million to each convention city for help with security and police issues. Both Charlotte and Tampa had to raise another $50 million to $60 million from private funds to hold the conventions. For the general election, neither President Obama nor Republican nominee Mitt Romney accepted public funding, preferring to raise campaign funds without the restrictions that come with public funds. Clearly, the current public funding law is not relevant to today's presidential elections.

One of the most fundamental questions about campaign financing in the United States is the fairness of a system in which one candidate raises more money to finance a strong organization and to buy more media advertisements than others. Do voters have an equal chance to hear the positions and promises of all the candidates if some have greater financial resources? Should one candidate be able to buy five times more television time than another? The Supreme Court has said that individuals can spend their own funds for their campaigns as a practice of free speech. The same principle holds for interest groups that wish to express their views on the issues. So, the tension over regulating campaign finance lies between advocates of free speech and advocates of fairness.

WHAT IF SPENDING LIMITS WERE PLACED ON CAMPAIGNS?

If some limit on campaign spending were found to be constitutional, one consequence would be a decline in the number of candidates with "deep pockets." In other words, fewer of the very rich would attempt to run for office, because they would not be able to use their personal wealth in the effort to win.

A limit on campaign spending would also mean a limit on campaign contributions. Consequently, special-interest groups, corporations, and wealthy individuals would have less influence on campaigns. Limiting campaign spending might force a decline in the number of lobbyists in Washington, D.C., because lobbyists are often skilled at raising money for candidates. Newspapers and free electronic news sources could play a greater role in the campaign by providing information about the candidates.

Without so much campaign advertising, less information would be available to the voters. It is possible that turnout might decline if fewer voters were stimulated to vote by advertising. On the other hand, party organizations and grassroots campaigning would need to fill the void to get voters to the polls.

THE IMPACT ON TELEVISION AND SOCIAL MEDIA

Television and social media would also be affected. Just as the bulk of the public's entertainment time is spent on television, so too is the bulk of campaign spending. Consider that in just the month before the Iowa caucuses in 2012, $10 million was spent on television ads in Iowa. Voters in Iowa's capital saw thousands of ads for the candidates. While it may seem that the Internet is "free," candidates spend money to buy advertising on Google, Facebook, and other Web sites and to maintain large organizations to increase their presence on social networks. A limit on total campaign spending would, by necessity, dramatically reduce spending on all forms of advertising. Media companies, which count on increased profits in election years, would see a decline in their revenue, and overall advertising prices would decline.

WE HAVE ALREADY ATTEMPTED TO REFORM CAMPAIGNS

Complaints about excessive campaign spending are not new. Even sitting politicians have attempted to clean up elections. The BCRA of 2002 was one such attempt. The law became effective in January 2003. This law prohibited, among other things, so-called "soft money" contributions and expenditures that were clearly being used to influence federal elections. It also banned supposedly nonpartisan issue ads that were funded by corporations and labor unions. Such ads cannot appear 30 days prior to a primary election or 60 days before a general election. However, new forms of campaign organizations have been created and independent expenditures are an unregulated and major source of campaign funding. Without spending limits, it appears that campaign spending will continue to increase and the candidate with the most funding will have an advantage in persuading voters.

FOR CRITICAL ANALYSIS

1. *Why would it be extremely difficult to effectively limit campaign spending?*

2. *If campaign spending limits were effective, who would be hurt more—those politicians already in office or those attempting to win an election for the first time? Explain your answer.*

FREE ELECTIONS ARE the cornerstone of the American political system. Voters choose one candidate from a pool of candidates to hold political office by casting ballots in local, state, and federal elections. Voters are free from intimidation or coercion and are able to get easy access to information about the election, as provided for by a free press. In 2012, the voters chose Barack Obama and Joe Biden to be president and vice president of the United States for the next four years. In addition, voters elected all of the members of the House of Representatives and one-third of the members of the Senate. The campaigns were bitter, long, and extremely expensive, with the Democratic primary contest being the closest and most expensive in history. The total cost for all federal elections in the 2010–2012 cycle was estimated at more than $6 billion.

Voters and candidates frequently criticize the American electoral process. It is said to favor wealthier candidates, to further the aims of special-interest groups, and to be dominated by older voters and those with better educations and higher incomes. While the 2002 reform of the federal campaign finance law has had some effect on campaign strategy, new types of campaign organizations have been created to enable even greater private, independent fundraising. During the 2012 campaign, candidate advertising dominated the airwaves on radio and television as well as cable. Social media were used extensively to raise funds, register voters, and encourage participation in the campaign by supporters.

Who Wants to Be a Candidate?

Democratic political systems require competitive elections, meaning that opposition candidates for each office have a chance to win. If there is no competition for any office—president or local school superintendent—then the public has no ability to make a choice about its leadership or policies to be pursued. Who, then, are the people who seek to run for office?

The United States has thousands of elective offices. The political parties strive to provide a slate of candidates for every election. Recruiting candidates is easier for some offices than for others. Political parties may have difficulty finding candidates for the board of the local water control district, but they generally have a sufficient number of candidates for county commissioner or sheriff. The higher the office and the more prestige attached to it, the more candidates are likely to want to run. In many areas of the country, however, one political party may be considerably stronger than the other. In those situations, the minority party may have more difficulty finding nominees for elections in which victory is unlikely.

The presidential campaign provides the most colorful and exciting look at candidates and how they prepare to compete for office—in this instance, the highest office in the land. The men and women who wanted to be candidates in the 2012 presidential campaign faced a long and obstacle-filled path. First, they needed to raise sufficient funds to plan for the early campaigns in Iowa and New Hampshire. Then, they faced an unprecedented number of early **presidential primaries**, which determined if they could win in diverse states. The early primaries were followed by "Super Tuesday," with 10 primaries. Candidates and their campaign organizations needed to have strategies that maximized their strengths across the nation and, at the same time, raised enough donations to keep national campaigns going. They had to keep their organization alive for the primary season, plan to win caucus and primary votes, and, in the case of the Democrats in 2008, convince enough **superdelegates** to win the nomination before the convention. In that year, John McCain won his party's primaries early enough to

■ **Learning Outcome 1:**
Explain the eligibility requirements for president, senator, and representative, and discuss why an individual might choose to become a candidate for office.

Presidential Primary
A statewide primary election of delegates to a political party's national convention, held to determine a party's presidential nominee.

Superdelegate
A party leader or elected official who is given the right to vote at the party's national convention. Superdelegates are not elected at the state level.

John Moore/Getty Images

Mayor Cory Booker of Newark NJ, who ran for a second term in 2012, meets with British Prime Minister David Cameron and the Essex County Executive, Joe DiVincenzo, on the steps of Newark's City Hall.

begin raising funds for the general election, while Barack Obama and Hillary Clinton battled throughout the primary season, with Barack Obama ultimately receiving his party's nomination. In 2012, Mitt Romney wrapped up the Republican nomination in late spring and turned his attention to fundraising for the general election campaign.

Why They Run

People who choose to run for office can be divided into two groups—the self-starters and those who are recruited. The volunteers, or self-starters, get involved in political activities to further their careers, to carry out specific political programs, or in response to certain issues or events. Ralph Nader's campaigns for the presidency in 2000 and 2004 were rooted in his belief that the two major parties were ignoring vital issues, such as environmental protection and the influence of corporate wealth on American politics. Candidates such as Ron Paul, on the Republican side, and Dennis Kucinich, on the Democratic side, run for president to present their positions, even though they know that they have very little chance of winning.

Issues are important, but self-interest and personal goals—status, career objectives, prestige, and income—are central in motivating some candidates to enter political life. Political office is often seen as the stepping-stone to achieving certain career goals. A lawyer or an insurance agent may run for office only once or twice and then return to private life with enhanced status. Other politicians may aspire to long-term political office—for example, county offices such as commissioner or sheriff sometimes offer attractive opportunities for power, status, and income and are in themselves career goals. Finally, we think of ambition as the desire for ever-more-important offices and higher status. Politicians who run for lower offices and then set their sights on Congress or a governorship may be said to have "progressive" ambitions.[1]

The Nomination Process

Individuals become official candidates through the process of nomination. Generally, nominating processes for all offices are controlled by state laws and usually favor the two major political parties. For most minor offices, individuals become candidates by submitting petitions to the local election board. Political parties often help individuals obtain the petitions, pay whatever filing fee is required, and gather signatures. In most states, a candidate from one of the two major parties faces far fewer requirements to get on the ballot than a candidate who is an independent or who represents a minor or new party.

For higher-level offices, candidates may need to petition and then be nominated by a party convention at the state level. In other jurisdictions, party caucuses are empowered to nominate candidates. And, as will be discussed later, many contenders for office are nominated through a primary election in which two or more individuals contend for the party's nomination.

1. See the discussion of this topic in Linda Fowler, *Candidates, Congress, and the American Democracy* (Ann Arbor, MI: University of Michigan Press, 1993), pp. 56–59.

The American system of nominations and primary elections is one of the most complex in the world. In most European nations, the political party's choice of candidates is final, and no primary elections are ever held.

Who Is Eligible?

There are few constitutional restrictions on who can become a candidate in the United States. As set out in the Constitution, the formal requirements for national office are as follows:

1. *President.* Must be a natural-born citizen, have attained the age of 35 years, and be a resident of the country for 14 years by the time of inauguration.
2. *Vice president.* Must be a natural-born citizen, have attained the age of 35 years, and not be a resident of the same state as the candidate for president.[2]
3. *Senator.* Must be a citizen for at least nine years, have attained the age of 30 by the time of taking office, and be a resident of the state from which elected.
4. *Representative.* Must be a citizen for at least seven years, have attained the age of 25 by the time of taking office, and be a resident of the state from which elected.

The qualifications for state legislators are set by the state constitutions and likewise include age, place of residence, and citizenship. (Usually, the requirements for the upper chamber of a legislature are somewhat more stringent than those for the lower chamber.) The legal qualifications for running for governor or other state office are similar.

Who Runs?

Despite these minimal legal qualifications for office at both the national and state levels, a quick look at the slate of candidates in any election—or at the current members of the U.S. House of Representatives—will reveal that not all segments of the population take advantage of these opportunities. Holders of political office in the United States are overwhelmingly white and male. Until the 20th century, presidential candidates were of northern European origin and of Protestant heritage.[3] Laws that effectively denied voting rights made it impossible to elect African American public officials in many areas in which African Americans constituted a significant portion of the population. As a result of the passage of major civil rights legislation in the 1960s, however, the number of African American public officials has increased throughout the United States. By 2007, the number of African American elected officials was estimated at more than 9,500,[4] and 84 percent of Americans said they would be completely comfortable voting for an African American for president.[5]

Women as Candidates. Until recently, women generally were considered to be appropriate candidates only for lower-level offices, such as state legislator or school board member. It was thought that women would be more acceptable to the voting public if they were either running for an office that allowed them to continue their family duties, or were running for an office that focused on local affairs, such as city or school issues. The last 20 years have seen a tremendous

2. Technically, a presidential and vice presidential candidate can be from the same state, but if they are, one of the two must forfeit the electoral votes of his or her home state.
3. A number of early presidents were Unitarian. The Unitarian Church is not Protestant, but it is historically rooted in the Protestant tradition.
4. Ralph Everett, "Number of Black Elected Officials Increases, But Not by Much," *Joint Center Journal*, 2007.
5. Gallup Poll, February/March 2007.

Figure 10-1 ▶ Women Running for Congress (and Winning)

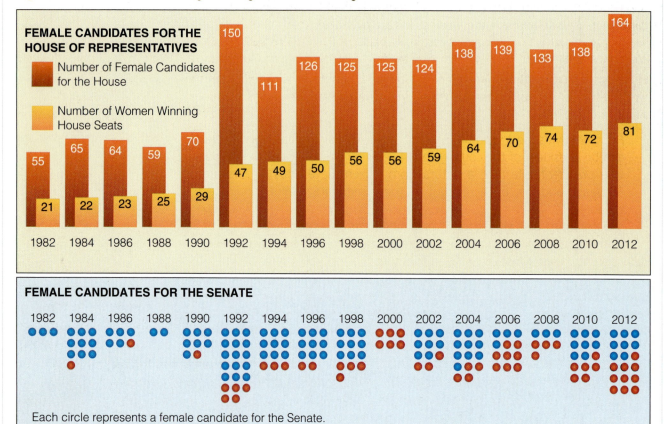

FEMALE CANDIDATES FOR THE HOUSE OF REPRESENTATIVES

- ■ Number of Female Candidates for the House
- ■ Number of Women Winning House Seats

FEMALE CANDIDATES FOR THE SENATE

Each circle represents a female candidate for the Senate.
A red circle denotes a winning candidate.

increase in the number of women who run for office, not only at the state level but for the U.S. Congress as well. Figure 10-1 shows the increase in female candidates. In 2012, 182 women ran for Congress, and 81 were elected. Noteworthy in the class of women elected to the Senate in 2012 are Tammy Baldwin, the first openly gay senator, and Mazie Hirono, Hawaii's first female senator.

In the past, women were not recruited because they had not worked their way up through the male-dominated party organization or because they were thought to have no chance of winning. Women also had a more difficult time raising campaign funds. Since the 1970s, there has been a focused effort to increase the number of women candidates. EMILY's List, a group that raises money to recruit and support liberal women candidates, has had a strong impact on the situation for women candidates. Other organizations with more conservative agendas also raise money for women. Recent elections have witnessed women candidates of either party raising millions of dollars and winning office; however, women voters are more likely to perceive gender bias and a harder path for women candidates. After the 2008 election, a majority of women saw gender bias in the treatment of Hillary Clinton and Sarah Palin.[6] According to the Gallup Poll, a vast majority of Americans (86 percent) would vote for a qualified woman for president.[7]

6. Jennifer Lawless and Richard L. Fox, "Men Rule: The Continued Underrepresentation of Women in U.S. Politics," Washington, DC: Women and Politics In statute, 2012.
7. Gallup Poll, September 8–11, 2005.

Lawyers as Candidates. Candidates are likely to be professionals, particularly lawyers. Political campaigning and officeholding are simply easier for some occupational groups than for others, and political involvement can make a valuable contribution to certain careers. Lawyers, for example, have more flexible schedules than do many other professionals, can take time off for campaigning, and can leave their jobs to hold public office full time. Furthermore, holding political office is good publicity for their professional practice, and they usually have partners or associates to keep the firm going while they are in office. Perhaps most important, many jobs that lawyers aspire to—federal or state judgeships, state attorney positions, or work in a federal agency—can be attained by political appointment. Such appointments often go to loyal partisans who have served their party by running for and holding office. For certain groups, then, participation in the political arena may further personal ambitions, whereas it could be a sacrifice for others whose careers demand full-time attention for many years.

The 21st Century Campaign

After the candidates have been nominated, the most exhausting and expensive part of the election process begins—the general election campaign. The contemporary political campaign is becoming more complex and more sophisticated with every election. Even with the most appealing of candidates, today's campaigns require a strong organization; expertise in political polling and marketing; professional assistance in fundraising, accounting, and financial management; and technological capabilities in every aspect of the campaign.

The Changing Campaign

The goal is the same for all campaigns—to convince voters to choose a candidate or a slate of candidates for office. Part of the reason for the increased intensity of campaigns in the last decade is that they are now centered on the candidate, not on the party. The candidate-centered campaign emerged in response to several developments: changes in the electoral system, the increased importance of television and other forms of electronic media in campaigns, the change in campaign funding, and technological advances in ways to reach potential voters, including social media and e-mail.

To run a successful and persuasive campaign, the candidate's organization must be able to raise funds for the effort; obtain coverage from the media; produce and pay for advertising, Web sites, and social media sites; schedule the candidate's time effectively; convey the candidate's position on the issues to the voters; conduct research on the opposing candidate; and get the voters to go to the polls. When party identification was stronger among voters and before the advent of television campaigning, a strong party organization at the local, state, or national level could furnish most of the services and expertise that the candidate needed. Political parties provided the funds for campaigning until the 1970s. Parties used their precinct organizations to distribute literature, register voters, and get out the vote on election day. Less effort was spent on advertising each candidate's positions and character, because the party label presumably communicated that information to many voters.

One of the reasons that campaigns no longer depend on parties is that fewer people identify with them (see Chapter 8), as is evident from the increased number of political independents. In 1952, about one-fifth of adults identified themselves as independents, whereas in 2012, almost 40 percent considered

■ **Learning Outcome 2:**
Produce a plan for a modern campaign for the United States Senate including the strategy, staff, and finances necessary for such an endeavor.

did you know?

EMILY's List means Early Money Is Like Yeast, referring both to needing money early in a campaign and to yeast for raising bread.

Political Consultant
A paid professional hired to devise a campaign strategy and manage a campaign.

Finance Chairperson
The campaign professional who directs fundraising, campaign spending, and compliance with campaign finance laws and reporting requirements.

Pollster
The person or firm who conducts public opinion polls for the campaign.

Communications Director
A professional specialist who plans the communications strategy and advertising campaign for the candidate.

Former senior White House adviser and campaign strategist for President Barack Obama, David Axelrod checks his wireless device for messages.

themselves to be independents. Political independents include not only adults who are well educated and issue oriented, but also many individuals who are not very interested in politics or well informed about candidates or issues.

The Professional Campaign Staff

Whether the candidate is running for the state legislature, for the governor's office, for the U.S. Congress, or for the presidency, every campaign has some fundamental tasks to accomplish. Today, in national elections, the lion's share of these tasks is handled by paid professionals, rather than volunteers or amateur politicians. Volunteers and amateurs are primarily used for the last-minute registration or voter turnout activities.

The most sought-after and possibly the most criticized campaign expert is the **political consultant**, who, for a large fee, devises a campaign strategy, creates a campaign theme, oversees the advertising, and possibly chooses the campaign colors and the candidate's official portrait. Political consultants began to displace volunteer campaign managers in the 1960s, about the same time that television became a force in campaigns. The paid consultant monitors the campaign's progress, plans all media appearances, and coaches the candidate for debates. The consultants and the firms they represent are not politically neutral; most will work only for candidates from one party. Consultants are on hand constantly to plan rebuttals to the opponent's charges and to recalibrate the campaign.

Under constant pressure to raise more campaign funds and to comply with the campaign finance laws, all campaigns need a **finance chairperson** who plans the fundraising strategy and finds the legal and accounting expertise needed for the organization. Of course, campaigns will either hire an in-house **pollster** or contract with a major polling firm for the tracking polls and focus groups discussed in Chapter 6.

Candidates need to have a clear strategy to gain public attention and to respond to attacks by their opponents. The campaign's **communications director** plans appearances, the themes to be communicated by the candidate at specific points in the campaign, and the responses to any attacks. The campaign's **press secretary** is responsible for dealing directly with the press. Perhaps the most famous example of a successful communication strategy was that of Bill Clinton in his 1992 victory. The campaign organized a "War Room" to instantly respond to any attack by his opponents. Today's candidates also need a communication strategy that utilizes social networks and the Internet. At the end of the campaign is the actual election. Campaigns need to find a way to recruit and organize volunteers for the **Get Out the Vote (GOTV)** drive to persuade voters to come to the polls on election day.

The Strategy of Winning

In the United States, unlike some European countries, the candidate who comes in second gets no reward; the winner takes all. A winner-take-all system is also known as a *plurality voting system.* In most situations, the winning candidate does not have to have a majority of the votes. If there are three candidates, the one who gets the most votes wins—that is, "takes it all"—and the other two candidates get nothing. Given this system, the campaign organization must plan a strategy that maximizes the candidate's chances of winning. In American politics, candidates seek to capture all of the votes of their party's supporters, to convince a majority of the independent voters to vote for them, and to gain a few votes from supporters of the other party. To accomplish these goals, candidates must consider their visibility, their message, and their campaign strategy.

Candidate Visibility and Appeal

One of the most important concerns is how well known the candidate is. If she or he is a highly visible incumbent, little campaigning may be needed except to remind the voters of the officeholder's good deeds. If, however, the candidate is an unknown challenger or a largely unfamiliar character attacking a well-known public figure, the campaign must devise a strategy to get the candidate before the public.

In the case of the independent candidate or the candidate representing a minor party, the problem of name recognition is serious. Such candidates must present an overwhelming case for the voter to reject the major-party candidates. Both Democratic and Republican candidates use the strategic ploy of labeling third-party candidates as "not serious"—and therefore not worth the voter's time.

Testing the Waters

In addition to measuring name recognition and "feelings" toward a candidate, today's campaigns rely heavily on other ways to find out how the electorate views the candidate and her message. Opinion polls are a major source of information for both the media and the candidates. Poll taking is widespread during the primaries. Presidential hopefuls have private polls taken to make sure that there is at least some chance they could be nominated and, if nominated, elected. During the presidential campaign, polling is even more frequent. Polls are taken not only by the regular pollsters—Gallup, Rasmussen, CBS News, and others—but also privately by the candidate and his or her campaign organization. As the election approaches, many candidates and commercial houses use **tracking polls**, which are polls taken almost every day, to find out how well they are competing for votes. Tracking polls enable consultants to fine-tune the advertising and the candidate's speeches in the last days of the campaign.

Another tactic is to use a **focus group** to gain insights into public perceptions of the candidate. Professional consultants organize a discussion of the candidate or of certain political issues among 10 to 15 ordinary citizens. The citizens are selected from specific target groups in the population—for example, working women, blue-collar men, senior citizens, or young voters. Recent campaigns have tried to reach groups such as "soccer moms," "Wal-Mart shoppers," or "NASCAR dads."[8] The group discusses personality traits of the candidate, political advertising, and other candidate-related issues. The conversation is digitally video recorded (and often observed from behind a mirrored wall). Focus groups are expected to reveal more emotional responses to candidates or the deeper anxieties of voters—feelings that consultants believe often are not tapped into by more impersonal telephone surveys. Indeed, some marketing organizations use

8. NASCAR stands for the National Association of Stock Car Auto Racing.

Press Secretary
The individual who interacts directly with the journalists covering the campaign.

Get Out the Vote (GOTV)
This phrase describes the multiple efforts expended by campaigns to get voters out to the polls on election day.

Tracking Poll
A poll taken for the candidate on a nearly daily basis as election day approaches.

Focus Group
A small group of individuals who are led in discussion by a professional consultant in order to gather opinions on and responses to candidates and issues.

did you know?
A candidate can buy lists of all the voters in a precinct, county, or state for only about two cents per name from a commercial firm.

handheld devices to measure how an audience responds to advertising or candidate statements. The campaign then can shape its messages to respond to these feelings and perceptions.

The Media and Political Campaigns

All forms of the media—television, newspapers, radio, magazines, blogs, and podcasts—have a significant political impact on American society. Media influence is most obvious during political campaigns. News coverage of a single event, such as the results of the Iowa caucuses or the New Hampshire primary, may be the most important factor in having a candidate be referred to in the media as the front-runner in a presidential campaign. It is not too much of an exaggeration to say that almost all national political figures, starting with the president, plan every public appearance and statement to attract media coverage.

Because television is still the primary news source for the majority of Americans, candidates and their consultants spend much of their time devising strategies that use television to their benefit. Three types of TV coverage are generally employed in campaigns for the presidency and other offices: advertising, management of news coverage, and campaign debates.

Advertising

Perhaps one of the most effective political ads of all time was a 30-second spot created by President Lyndon B. Johnson's media adviser in 1964. In this ad, a little girl stood in a field of daisies. As she held a daisy, she pulled the petals off and quietly counted to herself. Suddenly, when she reached number 10, a deep bass voice cut in and began a countdown: "10, 9, 8, 7, 6, …" When the voice intoned "zero," the unmistakable mushroom cloud of an atomic bomb began to fill the screen. Then President Johnson's voice was heard: "These are the stakes. To make a world in which all of God's children can live, or to go into the dark. We must

President Lyndon Johnson's "daisy girl" ad contrasted the innocence of childhood with the horror of an atomic attack. Johnson's opponent in the 1964 election was Senator Barry Goldwater, who was more likely to take a strong stance against the Soviet Union.

VOTE FOR PRESIDENT JOHNSON ON NOVEMBER 3.

A family watches the 1960 Kennedy-Nixon debates on television. After the debate, TV viewers thought Kennedy had won, whereas radio listeners thought Nixon had won.

bombards the news commentators with the "spin" they want on the event. Regardless of the risks of debating, the potential for gaining votes is so great that candidates undoubtedly will continue to seek televised debates. Of course, in today's Internet world, candidates also know that their performances will be "broadcast" on the Internet or posted on YouTube and that the bloggers will add their own interpretations to those of the mainstream media.

Political Campaigns and the Internet

Without a doubt, the Internet has become an important vehicle for campaign advertising and news coverage, as well as for soliciting campaign contributions. This first became clear during the 2004 presidential elections, when 7 percent of all Internet users participated in online campaign activities. (Internet users included about two-thirds of all American adults.) The Obama campaign in 2008 took the use of social media and the Internet to a new level, using it to raise millions of dollars in small contributions from social media "friends."

During the 2012 election campaigns, the Internet was used not only to advertise the candidates' positions, to solicit donations, and to podcast speeches and debates, but also to target messages. Candidates sought e-mail lists sorted by age, gender, and other demographic variables. Then they e-mailed messages to targeted groups. Members of union households received, for example, messages about lowering the number of jobs going overseas. Candidates used the Internet to recruit volunteers for Get Out the Vote campaigns. They also used e-mail and blogs to instruct citizens on how to participate in the political caucuses and how to persuade others to support their candidate of choice.

Today, the campaign staff of every candidate running for a significant political office includes an Internet campaign strategist—a professional hired to create and maintain the campaign Web site, blogs, and podcasts. The work of this strategist includes designing a user-friendly and attractive Web site for the candidate, managing the candidate's e-mail communications, and tracking campaign contributions made through the site. Additionally, virtually all major interest groups in the United States now use the Internet to promote their causes. Prior to elections, various groups engage in issue advocacy from their Web sites. At little or no cost, they can promote positions taken by favored candidates and solicit contributions.

Financing the Campaign

An old saying sums up the importance of financing a campaign: "Money is the mother's milk of politics." For any campaign to have a chance at success, it must raise enough funds to be competitive. In a book published in 1932 entitled *Money in Elections,* Louise Overacker had the following to say about campaign financing:

> The financing of elections in a democracy is a problem which is arousing increasing concern. Many are beginning to wonder if present-day methods of raising and spending campaign funds do not clog the wheels of our elaborately constructed mechanism of popular control, and if democracies do not inevitably become [governments ruled by small groups].[11]

Although writing more than 70 years ago, Overacker touched on a sensitive issue in American political campaigns—the connection between money and elections. As mentioned earlier, more than $6 billion was spent at all levels of campaigning during the 2011–2012 election cycle. Total spending by the presidential candidates in 2012 amounted to more than $2 billion. In the Connecticut Senate race in 2010, Linda McMann and Richard Blumenthal raised about $59 million, with $50 million coming from McMann's private fortune. Nevada, California, Florida, Wisconsin, and Washington saw senate races that cost between $27 million and $53 million. Traditionally, candidates spend much less to retain or obtain a seat in the House of Representatives, because representatives stand for seats in much smaller geographic areas; however, these races are heating up: In 2010, 10 races for the House of Representatives saw combined spending top $6 million. That would be about $10 for every man, woman, and child in the congressional district whether or not they were voters. Except for the presidential campaigns, all of these funds had to be provided by the candidates and their families, borrowed, or raised by contributions from individuals, political parties, or *political action committees,* described later in this chapter. For the presidential campaigns, some of the funds could come from the federal government, but both candidates in 2012 rejected those funds to raise their own.

Regulating Campaign Financing

The way campaigns are financed has changed dramatically in the last 25 years. Today, candidates and political parties must operate within the constraints imposed by complicated laws regulating campaign financing.

A variety of federal **corrupt practices acts** have been designed to regulate campaign financing. The first, passed in 1925, limited primary and general election expenses for congressional candidates. In addition, it required disclosure of election expenses and, in principle, put controls on contributions by corporations. The restrictions had many loopholes, and the acts proved to be ineffective.

The **Hatch Act** (Political Activities Act) of 1939 is best known for restricting the political activities of civil servants. The act also, however, made it unlawful for a political group to spend more than $3 million in any campaign and limited

Corrupt Practices Acts
A series of acts passed by Congress in an attempt to limit and regulate the size and sources of contributions and expenditures in political campaigns.

Hatch Act
An act passed in 1939 that restricted the political activities of government employees. It also prohibited a political group from spending more than $3 million in any campaign and limited individual contributions to a campaign committee to $5,000.

---

11. Louise Overacker, *Money in Elections* (New York: Macmillan, 1932), p. vii.

individual contributions to a political group to $5,000. Of course, such restrictions were easily circumvented by creating additional political groups.

In the 1970s, Congress passed additional legislation to reshape the nature of campaign financing. In 1971, it passed the Federal Election Campaign Act to reform the process. Then in 1974, in the wake of the Watergate scandal, Congress enacted further reforms.

The Federal Election Campaign Act

The Federal Election Campaign Act (FECA) of 1971, which became effective in 1972, essentially replaced all past laws. The act placed no limit on overall spending but restricted the amount that could be spent on mass-media advertising, including television, if the candidate took public money. It limited the amount that candidates could contribute to their own campaigns (a limit later ruled unconstitutional) and required disclosure of all contributions and expenditures over $100. In principle, the FECA limited the role of labor unions and corporations in political campaigns. It also provided for a voluntary $1 (now $3) check-off on federal income tax returns for general campaign funds to be used by major-party presidential candidates.

Further Reforms in 1974. For many, the 1971 act did not go far enough. Amendments to the FECA passed in 1974 did the following:

1. *Created the Federal Election Commission.* This commission consists of six nonpartisan administrators whose duties are to enforce compliance with the requirements of the act.
2. *Provided public financing for presidential primaries and general elections.* Any candidate running for president who is able to obtain sufficient contributions in at least 20 states can obtain a subsidy from the U.S. Treasury to help pay for primary campaigns. The Bush-Kerry race in 2004 was the last time both candidates accepted public money for the general election campaign.
3. *Limited presidential campaign spending.* Any candidate accepting federal support must agree to limit campaign expenditures to the amount prescribed by federal law.
4. *Limited contributions.* Under the 1974 amendments, citizens could contribute up to $1,000 to each candidate in each federal election or primary; the total limit on all contributions from an individual to all candidates was $25,000 per year. Groups could contribute a maximum of $5,000 to a candidate in any election. (As you will read shortly, some of these limits were changed by the 2002 campaign reform legislation.)
5. *Required disclosure.* Each candidate must file periodic reports with the FEC listing who contributed, how much was spent, and on what the funds were spent.

The 1971 and 1974 laws regulating campaign contributions and spending set in place the principles that have guided campaign finance ever since. The laws and those that have been enacted subsequently are guided by three principles: (1) set limits on what individuals and groups can give to individual candidates and within one election cycle; (2) provide some public funding for the presidential primaries, conventions, and the general election campaign; and (3) make all contributions and reports public. All contributions that are made to candidates under these laws and principles are usually called **hard money**. As will be detailed later, however, individuals and groups that wish to circumvent these principles have been successful in finding ways to do so. Other kinds of campaign donations are referred to as "soft money" or "outside spending."

Hard Money
This refers to political contributions and campaign spending that is recorded under the regulations set forth in law and by the Federal Election Commission.

Buckley v. Valeo. The 1971 act had limited the amount that each individual could spend on his or her own behalf. The Supreme Court declared the provision unconstitutional in 1976, in *Buckley v. Valeo*,[12] stating that it was unconstitutional to restrict in any way the amount congressional candidates could spend on their own behalf: "The candidate, no less than any other person, has a First Amendment right to engage in the discussion of public issues and vigorously and tirelessly to advocate his own election."

The *Buckley v. Valeo* decision, which has often been criticized, was directly countered by a 1997 Vermont law. The law, known as Act 64, imposed spending limits ranging from $2,000 to $300,000 (depending on the office sought) on candidates for state offices in Vermont. A number of groups, including the American Civil Liberties Union and the Republican Party, challenged the act, claiming that it violated the First Amendment's guarantee of free speech. In a landmark decision in August 2002, a federal appellate court disagreed and upheld the law.[13] In 2006, the U.S. Supreme Court declared that Vermont's campaign spending and donation limits were unconstitutional, thereby in a sense reaffirming the *Buckley v. Valeo* decision.

Interest Groups and Campaign Finance: Reaction to New Rules

In the last two decades, interest groups and individual companies worked tirelessly to find ways to support candidates through campaign donations. Candidates, in turn, have become dependent on these donations to run increasingly expensive campaigns. Interest groups and corporations funnel money to political candidates through several devices: **political action committees (PACs)**, **soft money** contributions, 527s, **issue advocacy advertising**, and, after soft money was outlawed, through "**Super PACs**." Every time legislation is passed at the federal or state level, interest groups, corporations, unions, and associations scramble to find new, legally allowable ways to influence campaigns. This activity has prompted commentators to label all campaign finance regulation as "whack the mole" law, meaning for every activity prohibited, another one pops up.

PACs and Political Campaigns

The 1974 and 1976 amendments to the Federal Election Campaign Act of 1971 allow corporations, labor unions, and other interest groups to set up PACs to raise funds for candidates. For a federal PAC to be legitimate, the funds must be raised from at least 50 volunteer donors and must be given to at least five candidates in the federal election. PACs can contribute up to $5,000 to each candidate in each election. Each corporation or each union is limited to one PAC. As you might imagine, corporate PACs obtain contributions from executives and managers in their firms, and unions obtain PAC funds from their members.

The number of PACs has grown significantly since 1976, as has the amount they spend on elections. PACs numbered about 1,000 in 1976; today, the number has grown to more than 4,600. Total spending by PACs grew from $19 million in 1973 to more than $1 billion in 2009–2010. About 35 percent of all campaign funds raised by House candidates in 2010 came from PACs.[14]

■ Learning Outcome 4:
Demonstrate an understanding of the evolution of campaign finance regulation, the development of political action committees (PACs), and the current state of such regulation.

Political Action Committee (PAC)
A committee set up by and representing a corporation, labor union, or special-interest group. PACs raise and give campaign donations.

Soft Money
Campaign contributions unregulated by federal or state law, usually given to parties and party committees to help fund general party activities.

Issue Advocacy Advertising
Advertising paid for by interest groups that support or oppose a candidate or a candidate's position on an issue without mentioning voting or elections.

Super PAC
A political committee that can accept unlimited contributions from individuals and corporations to spend supporting a candidate as long as its efforts are not coordinated with the candidate's own campaign.

12. 424 U.S. 1 (1976).
13. *Randell v. Vermont Public Interest Research Group*, 300 F.3d 129 (2d Cir. 2002).
14. Center for Responsive Politics, at www.opensecrets.org.

Figure 10-2 ▶ PAC Contributions to Congressional Candidates, 1991–2010

Campaign financing regulations clearly limit the amount that a PAC can give to any one candidate, but the amount that a PAC can spend on issue advocacy is limitless, whether on behalf of a candidate or party or in opposition to one.

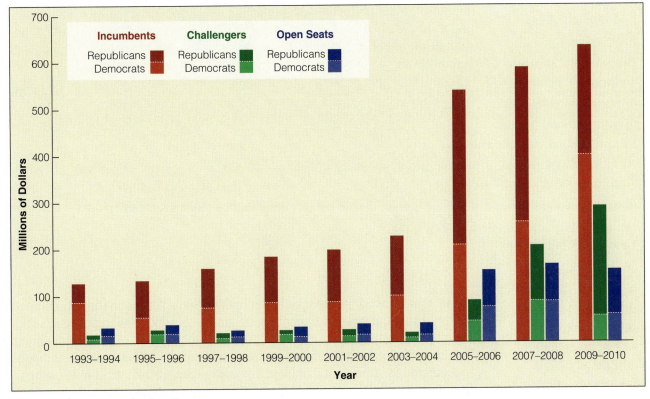

Source: Center for Responsive Politics, http://www.opensecrets.org.

Interest groups funnel PAC funds to the candidates they think can do the most good for them. Frequently, they make the maximum contribution of $5,000 per election to candidates who face little or no opposition. The summary of PAC contributions given in Figure 10-2 shows that the great bulk of campaign contributions goes to incumbent candidates rather than to challengers. Table 10-1 shows the amounts contributed by the top 10 PACs during the 2009–2010 election cycle.

As Table 10-1 also shows, many PACs give most of their contributions to candidates of one party. Other PACs, particularly corporate PACs, tend to give funds to Democrats in Congress as well as to Republicans, because, with both chambers of Congress so closely divided, predicting which party will be in control after an election is almost impossible. Why, you might ask, would members of the National Association of Realtors give to Democrats who may be more liberal than themselves? Interest groups see PAC contributions as a way to ensure *access* to powerful legislators, even though the groups may disagree with the legislators some of the time. PAC contributions are, in a way, an investment in a relationship.

Campaign Financing beyond the Limits

Within a few years after the establishment of the tight limits on contributions, new ways to finance campaigns were developed that skirted the reforms and made it possible for huge sums to be raised, especially by the major political parties.

Contributions to Political Parties. Candidates, PACs, and political parties found ways to generate *soft money*—that is, campaign contributions to political

did you know?

That Abraham Lincoln sold pieces of fence rail that he had split as political souvenirs to finance his campaign.

TABLE 10–1 ▶ The Top 10 PAC Contributors to Federal Candidates, 2009–2010 Election Cycle*

PAC NAME	TOTAL AMOUNT	DEM. (%)	REP. (%)
National Association of Realtors	$3,791,296	55	44
Honeywell International	$3,654,700	54	45
National Beer Wholesalers	$3,300,000	53	47
International Brotherhood of Electrical Workers	$2,993,373	98	2
American Bankers Association	$2,880,154	32	68
American Association for Justice (formerly, the Trial Lawyers Assn.)	$2,820,500	97	3
Operating Engineers Union	$2,799,220	88	11
National Auto Dealers Association	$2,483,400	44	5
International Association of Fire Fighters	$2,372,500	82	18
Credit Union National Assn.	$2,367,846	57	43
American Federation of Teachers	$2,361,250	99	0

*Includes subsidiaries and affiliated PACs, if any.

Source: Center for Responsive Politics, 2012.

parties that escaped the limits of federal election law. Although the FECA limited contributions that would be spent on elections, contributions to political parties for activities such as voter education and voter-registration drives had no limits. This loophole enabled the parties to raise millions of dollars from corporations and individuals. It was not unusual for some corporations to give more than $1 million to the Democratic National Committee or to the Republican Party.[15] Between 1993 and 2002, when soft money was banned, the amount raised for election activities quadrupled, increasing to more than $400 million. The parties spent these funds for their conventions, for registering voters, and for advertising to promote the general party position. The parties also sent a great deal to state and local party organizations, which used the soft money to support their own tickets.

Independent Expenditures
Nonregulated contributions from PACs, organizations, and individuals. The funds may be spent on advertising or other campaign activities, so long as those expenditures are not coordinated with those of a candidate.

Independent Expenditures. Corporations, labor unions, and other interest groups discovered that it was legal to make **independent expenditures** in an election campaign, so long as the expenditures were not coordinated with those of the candidate or political party. Hundreds of unique committees and organizations blossomed to take advantage of this campaign tactic. Although a 1990 United States Supreme Court decision, *Austin v. Michigan State Chamber of Commerce*,[16] upheld the right of the states and the federal government to limit independent, direct corporate expenditures (such as for advertisements) on behalf of *candidates*, the decision did not stop businesses and other types of groups from making independent expenditures on *issues*.

Issue Advocacy. Indeed, issue advocacy—spending unregulated funds on advertising that promotes positions on issues rather than candidates—has become a common tactic in recent years. Interest groups routinely wage their own issue campaigns. For example, the Christian Coalition, which is incorporated, annually raises millions of dollars to produce and distribute voter guidelines and other direct-mail literature

15. Paul Allen Beck, *Party Politics in America,* 8th ed. (New York: Longman, 1997), pp. 293–294.
16. 494 U.S. 652 (1990).

to describe candidates' positions on various issues and to promote its agenda. Issue advocacy ads frequently urge voters to contact their senator or representatives and tell him or her how to vote on a specific issue of concern to the interest group sponsoring the ad.

Although promoting issue positions is very close to promoting candidates who support those positions, the courts repeatedly have held, in accordance with the *Buckley v. Valeo* decision mentioned earlier, that interest groups have a First Amendment right to advocate their positions. In a 1996 decision,[17] the Supreme Court clarified this point, stating that political parties may also make independent expenditures on behalf of candidates—as long as the parties do so *independently* of the candidates. In other words, the parties must not coordinate such expenditures with the candidates' campaigns.

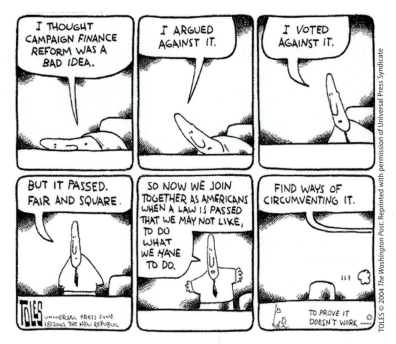

The Bipartisan Campaign Reform Act of 2002

While both Democrats and Republicans argued for campaign reform legislation during the 1990s, the bill cosponsored by Senators John McCain, a Republican, and Russ Feingold, a Democrat, finally became the Bipartisan Campaign Reform Act (BCRA) in 2002. This act, which amended the 1971 FECA, took effect on the day after the congressional elections of November 5, 2002.

Key Elements of the New Law. The 2002 law bans the large, unlimited contributions to national political parties that are known as soft money. It places curbs on, but does not entirely eliminate, the use of campaign ads by outside special-interest groups advocating the election or defeat of specific candidates. Such ads are allowed up to 60 days before a general election and up to 30 days before a primary election.

In 1974, contributions by individuals to federal candidates were limited to $1,000 per individual. The 2002 act increased this limit to $2,000, with annual increases. In addition, the maximum amount that an individual can give to all federal candidates was raised from $25,000 per year to $95,000 over a two-year election cycle. The act did not ban soft money contributions to state and local parties. These parties can accept such contributions, as long as they are limited to $10,000 per year per individual. Although the provisions of the act were challenged by groups that saw it as a threat to their influence in elections, the Supreme Court, in a series of decisions, upheld most of the law. However, remember that the law pertains to direct contributions to candidates and funds spent that are coordinated with the candidate's own campaign.

The Rise of the 527s. Interest groups that previously gave soft money to the parties responded to the 2002 BCRA by setting up new organizations outside the parties, called 527 organizations after the section of the tax code that provides for them. These tax-exempt organizations, which rely on soft money

17.   *Colorado Republican Federal Campaign Committee v. Federal Election Commission*, 518 U.S. 604 (1996).

Politics with a Purpose

CAMPAIGN FUNDS:
HOW MANY SOURCES ARE THERE?

Money is the lifeblood of elections. Candidates for office raise and spend hundreds of millions of dollars. For example, the presidential campaign in 2012 saw more than $2 billion in expenditures. However, not all that money was spent by the Romney and Obama campaigns or by the Republican or Democratic parties. With the changes in campaign finance laws and the court decisions in *Citizens United v. FEC* and *Freedomnow.org v. FEC*, the number of sources for campaign funds to be spent on behalf of candidates multiplied rapidly.

At the beginning of every campaign, the candidate for federal office, whether the presidency, the Senate, or the House of Representatives, establishes a political action committee, a PAC. This organization can receive donations from individuals and other PACs and from the political party, within the FEC's specified limits. Many kinds of PACs are currently in existence: candidate PACs that support the candidate's campaign directly; leadership PACs that are often founded by the Speaker of the House or Minority Leader of the Senate and distribute campaign funds to other candidates; connected PACs, meaning those connected to a union or corporation or trade association; and nonconnected PACs, which have no such affiliation. All of these are subject to FEC regulations regarding limits and disclosure, and all may spend funds under the direction of the candidate's campaign.

However, the amount of funds not regulated by the FEC continues to grow, mostly through the establishment of 527s and Super PACs. Before the 2002 Bipartisan Campaign Reform Act (BCRA), donors could give unlimited or "soft" money to parties as long as the parties did not explicitly use that money to aid particular candidates. The BCRA outlawed that particular form of soft money, but in its place have risen so-called 527 groups, named for the section of the U.S. Tax Code that provides for these nonprofits to collect donations without having to pay taxes on the money.

The rise of these 527 groups is important for many reasons. By closing the soft money loophole, the BCRA stopped the flow of money from corporations, unions, and wealthy individuals to the political parties. One of the effects of the BCRA was that these donors avoided the provisions of BCRA by redirecting their giving to a relatively new form of organization, the 527. Since the 2002 law, corporations, unions, and wealthy individuals are among the top financial contributors to 527 groups. These groups are not limited in how much money they may accept, nor are they limited in the source of the money. This behavior is related to the way in which they spend their money. The Federal Election Commission (FEC) has ruled that if these groups wish to remain unregulated in

fundraising, they may not coordinate with any candidate for a federal election (such as for president or congressperson). This means they may not actively campaign for someone running for these offices, nor may they use the "magic words" "vote for" or "vote against" a particular federal candidate in advertisements they finance. If they violate these rules, they may become subject to fines. However, they can support issue ads that make clear which issues and, by the way, which candidates they are supporting or opposing.[a]

Despite these limits, these groups are very important players in campaigns. Although the tax status has existed for many years and some groups had limited exposure in 2000,[b] the presidential election of 2004 marked a turning point, making 527 groups a topic of discussion in the mainstream media. One of the more famous, although not the most financially active, groups was the Swift Boat Veterans for Truth. This group was highly critical of the Democratic nominee, Senator John Kerry, attacking his Vietnam War record. By 2008 standards, this group's financial footprint was relatively small; it raised only $158,750 in 2004. Of that sum, Bob J. Perry, a Houston, Texas–based builder, contributed $100,000. In the 2004 cycle, Mr. Perry was the fifth-highest donor to 527 groups (giving $8,085,199), and in 2006, he gave the most money ($9,750,000) to 527s. All of this information is publicly accessible either through the FEC or through public-interest groups such as the Center for Responsive Politics, which runs a searchable Web site, www.opensecrets.org.

Some public-interest watchdog groups, such as Democracy 21, the Campaign Legal Center, and the Center for Responsive Politics, are highly critical of the burgeoning influence of 527s. In 2004, they filed a complaint with the FEC against America Coming Together, charging that it had violated the ban on candidate advocacy. This is a Democratic-leaning group whose largest individual contributor, George Soros, donated $7.5 million in 2004.[c] In 2007, the FEC ruled against the 527, levying a fine of $775,000 against it for making more than $100 million in inappropriate contributions.[d] The public-interest groups protested that the fine was not sufficiently large to deter future 527 actions. As the 2008 primary season progressed, it became obvious that 527s were raising money and running advertisements as they did in 2004.

In 2009, the Supreme Court decision in *Citizens United v. FEC* changed the campaign finance game once again. The decision allowed corporations, individuals, and any association to collect unlimited contributions and spend funds for advertising as long as the activities were not coordinated with the candidate's campaign. *The Freedomnow.org v. FEC* case allowed the so-called Super PACs to collect unlimited contributions and spend money in campaigns without FEC regulation of what may be said and when. For wealthy individuals, corporations, and interest groups, the rise of the 527s and the Super PACs provide great advantages. Corporations do not want their names and products tied to a candidate endorsement because it may alienate their customers. But, if a corporation—say, an oil company—can give unlimited funds to a Super PAC with a patriotic name, the company's reputation will incur little damage. Congress and future court decisions will decide what limits to place on what these "outside spenders" can do.

[a] www.clcblog.org, accessed April 17, 2008.
[b] In the Republican presidential nominating contest in 2000, Senator John McCain was highly criticized by a 527 group, Republicans for Clean Air. The group was funded in part by individuals who supported then–Governor Bush's candidacy; www.dallasobserver.com/2000-04-06/news/clearing-the-air, accessed April 17, 2008.
[c] www.opensecrets.org/527s/527cmtedetail.asp?cycle=2004&format=&ein=200094706&tname=America%20Coming% 20Together, accessed April 17, 2008.
[d] www.democracy21.org/index.asp?Type=B_PR&SEC=%7B7248831A-87CA-4C2D-B873-60C64918C920%7D, accessed April 17, 2008.

contributions for their funding and generally must report their contributions and expenditures to the Internal Revenue Service, are discussed in more detail in the Politics with a Purpose feature. What started out as a device to circumvent the campaign finance limits on donations has now grown into a complicated web of unregulated campaign financing. As noted in the box, 527 groups can be a vehicle for a particular point of view, such as the Swift Boat Veterans for Truth campaign against Senator John Kerry; however, powerful interest groups now use 527s in addition to their existing political action committees to receive monies for voter registration drives and other activities. The top names in Table 10-2 might look familiar. EMILY's List, for example, has been a longstanding PAC that supports women candidates, mostly Democrats. It still has a PAC that receives regulated contributions and makes direct limited donations to candidates. Yet EMILY's List also has a 527 organization that can accept unlimited donations and spend the funds on "uncoordinated advertising." The list of top 2010 groups includes labor unions, groups linked to business, groups headed by well-known politicians, and others that maintain both PACs and 527 organizations. This tactic gives the groups greater ability than a PAC to raise and spend money.

TABLE 10-2 ▶ Top Ten 527 Committees in Expenditures in 2010

COMMITTEE	2010 EXPENDITURES	VIEWPOINT	AFFILIATION
American Solutions Winning the Future	$28.4 million	Republican	Newt Gingrich
Service Employees International Union	$15.5 million	Democratic	SEIU
Citizens United	$9.2 million	Conservative	
EMILY's List	$10.4 million	Progressive	Supports women candidates
America Votes	$11.2 million	Democratic	Union
College Republican National Committee	$8.6 million	Republican	Republican Party
National Education Association	$7.5 million	Democratic	Teachers' union
Citizens for Strength and Security	$7.2 million	Democratic	
American Crossroads	$1.4 million	Republican	Karl Rove
ActBlue	$5.4 million	Democratic	Democratic Party

Source: OpenSecrets.org, "Top 50 Federally Focused Organizations," Center for Responsive Politics. www.opensecrets.org/527s/.

Overall, 527 groups spent more than $540 million in the 2009–2010 election cycle, with the top 10 spending more than $5 million each, as shown in Table 10-2. Note the wholesome and patriotic titles of the 527 committees in the table. A few are independent, but the vast majority of these groups have a partisan preference, regardless of what they call themselves.

In contrast to the 527s, charities and true not-for-profit organizations are not allowed to participate directly in any type of political activity. If they do so, they risk fines and the loss of their charitable tax-exempt status. In 2005, the IRS reviewed more than 80 churches, charities, and other tax-exempt organizations. The IRS looked for such banned activities as the distribution of printed materials encouraging members to vote for a specific candidate, contributions of cash to candidates' campaigns, and ministers' use of their pulpits to oppose or endorse specific candidates.

The IRS found that churches played a particularly important role in the 2004 elections. For example, well-known fundamentalist Baptist minister Jerry Falwell used his Web site to endorse President Bush and to urge visitors to the site to donate $5,000 to the Campaign for Working Families. At the All Saints Church in Pasadena, California, a pastor gave a sermon in which he imagined a debate among Senator John Kerry, President George Bush, and Jesus Christ. Although Jesus won, the press reported that the hypothetical debate came out in favor of John Kerry.

Of the 82 churches, charities, and other tax-exempt organizations that the IRS examined, more than 75 percent engaged in prohibited political activity during the 2003–2004 election cycle. The IRS proposed to revoke the tax-exempt status of at least three of these organizations.

Campaign Financing and the 2008 Elections

In 2008, the current campaign financing laws were put to the test and may have failed. Senator John McCain, who authored the most recent revision of the laws, chose not to accept private donations during the general election campaign. As a result, the total amount he raised during 2008 was about $350 million. He did, however, accept about $1 million in PAC contributions. He ran his fall campaign on the $84 million of federal campaign funds granted to him under law. In addition, the Republican National Committee was able to raise and spend funds toward his election.

Taking the completely opposite approach, Senator Barack Obama chose not to accept public funds for the general election campaign. During the 2008 campaign, he raised more than $630 million but accepted no PAC donations. The Obama campaign pioneered new ways for individuals to make contributions over the Internet, and millions of individuals chose to give in that manner. One result of the disparity in funds available was the ability of the Obama campaign to mount an exceptional Get Out the Vote campaign and to purchase four times more advertising time than did McCain. At the end of the campaign came many calls for a reexamination of campaign finance laws to fit these new realities.

Citizens United, Freedom Now, and the Future of Campaign Finance Regulation

The Supreme Court decision in *Citizens United v. FEC* shook the political world like no other since *Buckley v. Valeo*.[18] In many ways, the case continued the struggle of outside groups and groups not affiliated with political parties to play a bigger

---

18. *Citizens United v. Federal Election Commission*, 558 U.S. (2010).

role in political campaigns. Although three decades of campaign finance laws and regulation had been passed to contain the influence of groups on the political process and to limit the contributions of individuals, political action committees, and corporations, the *Citizens United* decision, on its face, lifted many of those restrictions. The decision allows corporations, unions, groups such as Citizens United, and others to spend money in campaign advertising without limit as long as it is not coordinated with a campaign. Indeed, the restriction against using direct campaign language such as "vote for Mr. Smith" has been lifted as well. President Obama expressed his disagreement with the decision during his State of the Union speech, and most Democrats applauded his remarks. The Democratic leadership of the Congress pledged to write new laws to counteract this decision, but no action was taken before the 2010 election.

While public attention was focused on the *Citizens United* decision, a federal appeals court granted even more freedom to corporations, unions, individuals, and interest groups to spend money on campaigns. In the case *FreedomNow.org v. FEC,* an interest group that represents conservative economic views charged that the FEC regulations barring individuals and groups from spending as much as they want on campaigns was unconstitutional due to the decision in *Citizens United.* The appeals court agreed, and that decision has opened the doors for the creation of Super PACs, which can raise and spend unlimited amounts of money as long as their campaigns are not coordinated with those of the candidates. Individuals can give unlimited amounts of money to a Super PAC, as can corporations, unions, or other groups. In contrast to the 527 organizations, these campaign PACs must report their donors to the FEC either quarterly or monthly. As shown in Table 10-3, the top 10 Super PACs in the first half of 2012 all had adopted innocuous names that make it difficult for voters to know who they represent unless they look up their donor list from the FEC.

With the creation of 527s and Super PACs, what a millionaire or corporation can spend on an election has no limit, which means that campaign spending will soar until some way to regulate this spending can be created. While the campaigns of the presidential and senatorial candidates may be more restrained in their attacks on opponents and less clear about the ideological issues at stake in an election, 527s and Super PACs are able to say whatever they want. We can

Table 10-3 ▶ Top 10 Super PACs in Expenditures in First Six Months of 2012

Super PAC	Supports/Opposes	Leans	Expenditures
Restore Our Future	Romney	Conservative	$46.5 million
Winning Our Future	Gingrich	Conservative	$17.0 million
Priorities USA Action	Obama	Liberal	$9.5 million
Red, White and Blue	Santorum	Conservative	$7.5 million
Club for Growth		Conservative	$5.4 million
Endorse Liberty	Paul	Conservative	$4.1 million
Make Us Great Again	Perry	Conservative	$3.9 million
House Majority PAC	Democratic candidates	Democratic	$3.5 million
Our Destiny PAC	Huntsman	Conservative	$2.8 million
Majority PAC	Democratic candidates	Democratic	$2.7 million

Source: "Super PACs." OpenSecrets.org. www.opensecrets.org/pacs/superpacs.php, accessed June 17, 2012.

expect to see the most explosive charges and the most negative ads come from these organizations in the future, perhaps making the polarization of the voters even stronger and creating even more cynicism among the electorate.

Running for President: The Longest Campaign

"Beauty Contest"
A presidential primary in which contending candidates compete for popular votes but the results do not control the selection of delegates to the national convention.

The American presidential election is the culmination of two different campaigns linked by the parties' national conventions. The presidential primary campaign lasts from January until June of the election year. Traditionally, the final campaign heats up around Labor Day, although if the nominees are known, it will begin even before the conventions.

Until 1968, however, there were fewer than 20 primary elections for the presidency. They were often "**beauty contests**" in which the candidates competed for popular votes, but the results had little or no impact on the selection of delegates to the national convention. National conventions were meetings of the party elite—legislators, mayors, county chairpersons, and loyal party workers—who were mostly appointed to their delegations. National conventions saw numerous trades and bargains among competing candidates, and the leaders of large blocs of delegates could direct their delegates to support a favorite candidate.

Reforming the Primaries

In recent decades, the character of the primary process and the makeup of the national convention have changed dramatically. The public, rather than party elites, now generally controls the nomination process. In 1968, after President Lyndon B. Johnson declined to run for another term, the Democratic Party nomination race was dominated by candidates who opposed the war in Vietnam. After Robert F. Kennedy was assassinated in June 1968, antiwar Democrats faced a convention that would nominate LBJ's choice regardless of popular votes. After the extraordinary disruptive riots outside the doors of the 1968 Democratic Convention in Chicago, many party leaders pushed for serious reforms of the convention process. They saw the general dissatisfaction with the convention, and the riots in particular, as being caused by the inability of the average party member to influence the nomination system.

The Democratic National Committee appointed a special commission to study the problems of the primary system. Called the McGovern-Fraser Commission, the group formulated new rules for delegate selection over the next several years that had to be followed by state Democratic parties.

The reforms instituted by the Democratic Party, which were imitated in part by the Republicans, revolutionized the nomination process for the presidency. The most important changes require that a majority of the Democratic convention delegates not be nominated by party elites; they must be elected by the voters in primary elections, in caucuses held by local parties (discussed later), or at state conventions. No delegates can be awarded on a "winner-take-all" basis; all must be proportional to the votes for the contenders. Delegates are normally pledged to a particular candidate, although the pledge is not always formally binding at the convention.

The delegation from each state must also include a proportion of women, younger party members, and representatives of the minority groups within the party. At first, virtually no special privileges were given to elected party officials,

© Bettmann/Corbis

Senator Robert F. Kennedy tells a press conference on April 1, 1968, that he will pursue the Democratic nomination for president. He was assassinated after winning the California primary election. Then–Vice President Hubert Humphrey won the nomination for president that year but lost the election to Richard Nixon.

such as senators and governors. After the conventions chose candidates who were not as strong as the party hoped for, the Democratic Party invented super-delegates, who are primarily elected Democratic officeholders and state leaders. Superdelegates comprise less than 20 percent of the delegate votes.

Front-Loading the Primaries

As soon as politicians and potential presidential candidates realized that winning as many primary elections as possible guaranteed them the party's nomination for president, their tactics changed dramatically. For example, candidates running in the 2012 primaries, such as Governor Mitt Romney, concentrated on building organizations in states that held early, important primary elections. Candidates realized that winning early contests, such as the Iowa caucuses or the New Hampshire primary election (both in January), meant that the media instantly would label the winner as the **front-runner**, thus increasing the candidate's media exposure and escalating the pace of contributions to his or her campaign fund.

The Rush to Be First. The states and state political parties began to see that early primaries had a much greater effect on the outcome of the presidential election and, accordingly, began to hold their primaries earlier in the season to secure that advantage. While New Hampshire held on to its claim to be the first primary, other states moved theirs to the following week. A group of mostly southern states decided to hold their primaries on the same date, known as Super Tuesday, in the hope of nominating a moderate southerner at the Democratic convention. When California, which had held the last primary (in June), moved its primary to March, the primary season was curtailed drastically. Due to this process of **front-loading** the primaries, in 2000 the presidential nominating process was over in March, with both George W. Bush and Al Gore having enough convention delegate votes to win their nominations. This meant that the campaign was essentially without news until the conventions in August, a gap that did not appeal to the politicians or the media. Both parties discussed whether more changes in the primary process were necessary.

did you know?

That David Leroy Gatchell changed his middle name to None of the Above, but when he ran for the U.S. Senate representing Tennessee, a court ruled that he could not use his middle name on the ballot.

Front-Runner
The presidential candidate who appears to be ahead at a given time in the primary season.

Front-Loading
The practice of moving presidential primary elections to the early part of the campaign to maximize the impact of these primaries on the nomination.

Beyond Our Borders
HOW SHORT CAN A CAMPAIGN BE?

Consider the difference between U.S. presidential campaigns and the British system of elections for Parliament and prime minister. In the United States, candidates for president begin traveling the country and building up support about two years before the general election. The primary election season starts just after January 1st of the election year, and the campaigns continue nonstop for almost 11 months.

In the United Kingdom, the prime minister makes the decision to hold elections for Parliament, or the House of Commons. In any case, parliamentary elections must be held at least every five years by law. The prime minister asks the queen to call elections either when the party's support is declining or when an advantage exists to the majority party to hold elections. In one year, there were two general elections due to the instability of the party's majority. When the queen issues the proclamation dissolving the Parliament, the date for the general election is set, and it must be held within 17 days of the proclamation. From that moment until the election is held, the parliamentary buildings are closed to the public, and government administrators may not make any announcements of new initiatives or new decisions on policy.*

In less than three weeks, the political parties assemble their candidates for each constituency, name their leaders as contenders for the prime minister's position, and do all their campaigning, both locally and nationally. With each new election in Great Britain, more American practices have come into play. American political consultants are regularly hired to help with developing the message for the parties and planning the advertising campaign. Survey research and political polling are also well developed in Great Britain, and pre-election polls are widely read. In the 2010 election, the three major party candidates held a live debate on television, American-style, for the first time in British history. Generally, the debate seemed to highlight the performance of the third party candidate, the leader of the Liberal Democratic Party.

So, how do the parties use that time, and how much money is spent during this short campaign period? British law has focused on spending limits for the campaign rather than on donation limits. Each party is limited in its expenditures during the year before the election. The spending limits are set on a constituency basis. In 2005, each major party was limited to spending about $30,000 per seat in the House of Commons. Compare that with the United States' average expenditure of more than $1 million for each seat in the House of Representatives. Altogether, the expenditures of the three contending parties in 2010 were about $125 million, compared to the billions spent in the United States for a similar period.**

BEN STANSALL/AFP/Getty Images

With neither party winning a clear majority of the seats in Parliament, David Cameron of the Conservative Party and Nick Clegg of the Liberal Democratic Party formed a partnership to govern the United Kingdom. Cameron became the prime minister, while Clegg took the title of deputy prime minister. Here they walk to the opening parliamentary session together.

Finally, after the votes were counted in 2010, no party held a majority of seats in the House of Commons, meaning that none of the three contenders for prime minister would be named leader of the government. (The leader of the government in Great Britain is an elected member of Parliament and the leader of the majority party.) The Labor Party won more seats than the Conservative Party, while the Liberal Democratic Party won enough seats to form a coalition. Several days after the election, the Liberal Democratic Party agreed to a deal with the Conservative Party, and a government was formed. It was an interesting arrangement because the Liberal Democratic Party is actually closer to the Labor Party on many issues, but its platform insisted on electoral reform, which its new partner, the Conservative Party, agreed to.

Could the United States face a similar situation in congressional elections or even the presidential election? Yes, if a third party became strong enough. Conceivably, a third party could win enough seats in Congress to deny the majority to either the Democrats or the Republicans. It is much more difficult in America for a third party to win

*See the excellent Web site maintained by the British Parliament for more information: www.parliament.uk.
**Library of Congress: www.loc.gov/law/help/campaign-finance/uk.php.

iStockphoto.com/Ayeshna iStockphoto.com/mattjeacock

enough electoral votes to send the presidential election into the House of Representatives, as discussed in Chapter 9.

The larger question is whether the United States could adopt some electoral reforms to reduce the cost of our campaigns (and the possible influence of donors) and shorten the season. While a six-week window and 17-day campaign seem very short, most Americans would like to see a shorter election season and less campaign advertising in their lives.

In 2005, a private commission headed by former president Jimmy Carter and former secretary of state James A. Baker III proposed a number of steps to avoid the consequences of early primaries. The Commission on Federal Election Reform was organized by American University. The commission argued in favor of keeping the Iowa caucuses and New Hampshire's early primary because "they test the candidates by genuine retail, door-to-door campaigning." After that, though, the commission had a radical suggestion—eliminate the state primaries and hold four regional presidential primaries. These regional primaries would be held at monthly intervals in March, April, May, and June, with the order rotated every four years. Neither party acted on that suggestion although both allowed the Iowa caucus and the New Hampshire primary to hold their places in the calendar. Instead, both parties allowed states to set primary dates between January and June, with multiple primary elections on many Tuesdays through the spring. Super Tuesday, in early March, normally attracts the primaries of eight to ten states, scattered across the nation.

The 2008 Primary Contest. The contest for the Democratic nomination drew a large and diverse field of candidates in 2008. Senator Hillary Rodham Clinton, former First Lady, started out as the strongest candidate due to her early fundraising and organizational strengths. Many observers saw former vice presidential candidate John Edwards of North Carolina as the real challenger to Clinton. While other candidates were in the race, Senator Barack Obama of Illinois quickly emerged as a talented and formidable candidate. Obama showed his strength early, winning the Iowa caucuses while Clinton pulled out a victory in New Hampshire, confounding the polling organizations. The two battled throughout the spring, with Clinton winning in the Midwest and Obama in the South and West. Finally, in early June, Senator Obama achieved the goal of having a majority of delegates and Senator Clinton accepted the voters' decision. On the Republican side, there were a number of candidates for the presidency in 2008, but Senator John McCain secured the nomination by the end of March.

The 2012 Primary Season

By early fall of 2011, many Republican voters believed that a few strong candidates were available to challenge President Obama for the 2012 election. However, by the end of 2011, the Republican field was crowded with candidates who participated in multiple debates during the late fall pre-primary season.

Mitt Romney campaigns in New Hampshire in November, 2011 with the support of former Minnesota governor, Tim Pawlenty, who had dropped out of the race by then.

Former Massachusetts governor Mitt Romney began his second campaign for the nomination in 2011, as did Ron Paul, who had run as a Libertarian in the past. Other candidates who attracted an early following were Congresswoman Michele Bachmann, former governor Tim Pawlenty, former Speaker Newt Gingrich, Texas governor Rick Perry, Ambassador Jon Huntsman, Jr., and former senator Rick Santorum. Most of the candidates competed in the Iowa caucuses and, to the surprise of many, Rick Santorum narrowly won the contest. Romney won the New Hampshire primary, and the race was on. One by one, the Republican candidates dropped out of the race, leaving Santorum, Paul, and Governor Romney, who finally clinched the nomination in late May. As the primaries unfolded in the Republican Party, it was clear that a large and vocal minority of those voters were more conservative than Mr. Romney, but they were split between social conservatives who supported Senator Santorum and anti-tax, anti-government voters who favored Ron Paul. On the Democratic side, primaries were held and delegates selected, but because President Obama was not challenged, he received all the delegates.

On to the National Convention

Presidential candidates have been nominated by the convention method in every election since 1832. The delegates are sent from each state and are apportioned on the basis of state representation. Extra delegates are allowed to attend from states that had voting majorities for the party in the preceding elections. Parties also accept delegates from the District of Columbia, the territories, and certain overseas groups.

Seating the Delegates. At the convention, each political party uses a **credentials committee** to determine which delegates may participate. The credentials committee usually prepares a roll of all delegates entitled to be seated. Controversy may arise when rival groups claim to be the official party organization for a county, district, or state. The Mississippi Democratic Party split along racial lines in 1964 at the height of the civil rights movement in the Deep South.

Credentials Committee
A committee used by political parties at their national conventions to determine which delegates may participate. The committee inspects the claim of each prospective delegate to be seated as a legitimate representative of his or her state.

STEVE NESIUS/Reuters/Landov

President Barack Obama prepares to give his acceptance speech at the Democratic National Convention in 2012. His speech was intended to build support and enthusiasm among Democrats and independent voters for his reelection.

Separate all-white and mixed white/African American sets of delegates were selected, and both factions showed up at the national convention. After much debate on party rules, the committee decided to seat the pro–civil rights delegates and exclude those who represented the traditional "white" party.

Convention Activities. The typical convention lasts only a few days. The first day consists of speech making, usually against the opposing party. During the second day, there are committee reports, and during the third day, there is presidential balloting. Because delegates generally arrive at the convention committed to presidential candidates, no convention since 1952 has required more than one ballot to choose a nominee, and since 1972, candidates have usually come into the convention with enough committed delegates to win. On the fourth day, a vice presidential candidate is usually nominated, and the presidential nominee gives the acceptance speech.

In 2012, the Democratic and Republican conventions were scheduled within one week of one another—the Republican convention right before Labor Day and the Democratic convention immediately after. The Democratic National Convention was held in Charlotte, North Carolina, and planned to increase support for the Democratic ticket in that state and neighboring Virginia.

The Republican National Convention was shortened by one day due to the possible arrival of a hurricane in Tampa, Florida, where the event was held. However, events were re-scheduled and the party completed the business of nominating Mitt Romney and Paul Ryan in three days. The Republicans spent much of their time showcasing young, conservative speakers who echoed their candidates' views on supporting business and the private sector of the economy. Both Governor Romney and his wife used their speeches to provide more personal information about themselves and the nominee's accomplishments.

The Democratic National Convention was held the following week in Charlotte, North Carolina. In contrast to the earlier Republican event, the Democratic National Convention dedicated an entire evening to supporting women's issues and concerns. Leading female office-holders spoke in support of the Obama record on women's rights. Former President Bill Clinton spoke on the second night, nominating President Obama for a second term. It is worth noting that the prime time networks restricted their coverage of both conventions to about two to three hours per night and that few of the speeches or events drew huge numbers of viewers.

On to the General Election

Even though the voters may think the presidential election process has gone on for years, the general election campaign actually begins after the two party conventions, when the nominees are officially proclaimed. The general election campaign strategies for each candidate are similar to those used during the primaries, except that each candidate now tries to articulate his or her differences from the opposition in terms of party issues. As noted in Chapter 6, voters respond to the campaigns on the basis of partisanship, the candidates' personalities, and the issues of the day.

Candidates plan their campaigns to use media advertising, debates, social media strategies, and Get Out the Vote (GOTV) campaigns. In addition, campaign strategists must constantly plan to win enough electoral votes to receive the majority. Campaign managers quickly identify those states where their candidate will almost certainly win the popular vote. As illustrated in the endpapers of this book, certain states will quickly line up in the Republican or Democratic column. Those states see relatively light campaign activity and advertising. However, those states that are likely to be close in the popular vote have been tagged **battleground states** and will see intense campaigning up to the very day of the election.

In 2000 and 2004, Florida was such a state. States such as Ohio and Wisconsin, which have closely divided electorates, are often in the battleground column. However, it is important to note that the states that will be closely fought change with every presidential election, because the issues and appeals of the two candidates determine race dynamics. In any case, the votes will be counted, the exit polls will be tallied, and the commentators will be heard on election night. In 2012, polls released just before election day suggested that the presidential election was a dead heat and too close to predict. Both candidates campaigned until voting started and then awaited the results. Early in the evening, Romney posted a win in North Carolina, but Obama won the electoral votes of Virginia, a key battleground state. By later in the evening, several other battleground states had swung to President Obama, and the election was almost decided. Ohio also voted for the president and although the election results in Florida were not final until days after the balloting, President Obama and Vice President Biden secured enough electoral votes to win on election night.

Battleground State
A state likely to be so closely fought that the campaigns devote exceptional effort to winning the popular and electoral vote there.

You Can Make a Difference

STUDENTS ON THE CAMPAIGN TRAIL

iStockphoto.com/kyoshino

The U.S. Congress has 535 members; other elected officials across the nation include more than 7,000 state legislators; 53 governors, attorneys general, treasurers, and secretaries of state; and thousands of mayors and city council members. None of these leaders could run political campaigns without the volunteer efforts of students. What do you believe in? Some students view campaign work as a civic duty. Causes and candidates across the nation would benefit from a volunteer's time and talent.

BRIAN KERSEY/UPI/Newscom

Campaign workers at the Chicago, Illinois headquarters for the 2012 Obama reelection campaign discuss their assignments for the day.

WHY SHOULD YOU CARE?

The 2008 presidential race sparked interest in many young voters, with 70 percent of 18- to 24-year-olds following the campaign closely, according to a Harvard University survey.

With the promise of change coming from all candidates in this presidential race, young voters seemed to be inspired to get involved. Turnout among young voters did increase a few percentage points, although not as much as it increased (9%) between 2000 and 2004. Knocking on doors and manning phone banks may not be glamorous work, but these experiences can provide a glimpse into a community that you might not get even by living in the neighborhood. You can talk to people face to face about issues that are important to them. Many students feel that college is the perfect time to work for a candidate or issue, when flexible school schedules and summers lend themselves to the time necessary to devote to a campaign.

You hear much discussion in the media concerning the youth vote but rarely find the opportunity for young people to speak for themselves concerning issues of the day. When you are volunteering for a campaign, opportunities to meet candidates, attend rallies, and engage in debate allow you to voice your opinion firsthand in the context of our political system. Opinions can be diverse even among volunteers with the same campaign affiliation, with some motivated by economic policy and fiscal issues and others by social issues.

WHAT CAN YOU DO?

Most people envision presidential races when first considering campaign volunteer work, but local elections or national hot-button issues such as gun control and local ballot initiatives in your own community feature some form of a campaign. How do you decide which campaign is right for you? Take into consideration how much time you can devote to the work, how close to home you want to stay, and how much responsibility you are willing to take on.

Campaign work can take many forms for first-time volunteers. You might help with fundraising, weekend door-to-door canvassing, or the effort to get people out to vote as election day approaches. You might work for one of the party organizations such as the Democratic National Committee or the Republican National Committee, or join a campus branch of College Democrats or College Republicans. These clubs host candidates to address students, hold voter registration drives, volunteer at local political events, and work phone banks for candidates and issues. You might also volunteer for an independent political entity, such as an issue-oriented nonprofit group or a 527 organization, advocating for candidates and voter mobilization.

Political campaigns offer many opportunities to develop a wide range of skills in a very fast-paced and exciting environment. You get a front-row seat to the electoral process; the work can be grueling but rarely boring. Satisfaction comes from working for a candidate or a cause that you respect and support and knowing that your individual efforts can make a difference.

For further information on volunteering for political campaigns, please contact one of the following organizations:

The Democratic National Committee
430 South Capitol Street SE
Washington, DC 20003
202-863-8000
www.democrats.org
College Democrats of America
430 South Capitol Street SE
Washington, DC 20003
202-863-8000
www.collegedems.com

The Republican National Committee
310 First Street SE
Washington, DC 20003
202-863-8500
www.gop.com
College Republican National Committee
600 Pennsylvania Ave. SE, Suite 215
Washington, DC 20003
888-765-3564
www.crnc.org

REFERENCES

Sharon Kelly, Justin Levitt, and Amanda Tammen Peterson, "One State, Two State, Red State, Blue State: A Quick Guide to Working on Political Campaigns," Cambridge, MA: Bernard Koteen Office of Public Interest Advising, Harvard Law School, 2007.

Mike Maciag, "BU Students Spread the Word for Candidates," *Peoria Journal Star*, May 4, 2008.

Emily Schultheis, "Students Plan to Hit the Campaign Trail," *Politico*, May 1, 2008.

Mercedes Suarez, "American College Students Embracing U.S. Political Process," America.gov, October 26, 2007.

Key Terms

battleground state 334

"beauty contest" 328

communications director 312

corrupt practices acts 318

credentials committee 332

finance chairperson 312

focus group 313

front-loading 329

front-runner 329

Get Out the Vote (GOTV) 313

hard money 319

Hatch Act 318

independent expenditures 322

issue advocacy advertising 320

political action committee (PAC) 320

political consultant 312

pollster 312

presidential primary 307

press secretary 313

soft money 320

spin 316

spin doctors 316

superdelegate 307

Super PAC 320

tracking poll 313

Chapter Summary

1. Free and fair elections are the basis for the continuation of a democratic form of government. To qualify as free and fair, elections should be fairly administered, information about the candidates and issues must be available through a free press, and voters must be free from coercion and intimidation.

2. People may choose to run for political office to further their careers, to carry out specific political programs, or in response to certain issues or events. The legal qualifications for holding political office are minimal at both the state and local levels, but holders of political office still are predominantly white and male and are likely to be from the professional class.

3. American political campaigns are lengthy and extremely expensive. In the last decade, they have become more candidate centered rather than party centered in response to technological innovations and decreasing party identification. Candidates have begun to rely less on the party and more on paid professional consultants to perform the various tasks necessary to wage a political campaign. The crucial task of professional political consultants is image building. The campaign organization devises a campaign strategy to maximize the candidate's chances of winning. Candidates use public opinion polls and focus groups to gauge their popularity and to test the mood of the country.

4. Political campaigns have well-thought-out strategies to use the media to the advantage of their candidates. Campaigns want to maximize exposure of the candidate through free coverage on the news, paid advertising, and success in candidate debates. Not only do campaigns plan how to get media coverage but they interpret events and news for the media, hoping to influence voters to think positively of the candidate.

5. The amount of money spent in financing campaigns is increasing steadily. A variety of corrupt practices acts have been passed to regulate campaign finance. The Federal Election Campaign Act of 1971 and its amendments in 1974 and 1976 instituted major reforms by limiting spending and contributions; the acts allowed corporations, labor unions, and interest groups to set up political action committees (PACs) to raise money for candidates. Additionally, public matching funds were made available to primary campaigns if certain criteria were met. The intent was to help candidates be competitive in the primaries. New techniques, including "soft money" contributions to the parties and independent expenditures, were later developed. The Bipartisan Campaign Reform Act (BCRA) of 2002 banned soft money contributions to the national parties, limited advertising by interest groups, and increased the limits on individual contributions. By 2008, most of the major candidates refused public funding in the primary campaigns, as did the Obama campaign in the general election, resulting in very large differences between the campaigns in financial resources. The idea of "leveling the playing field" for candidates in either the primaries or the general election seemed to be obsolete.

6. After the Democratic Convention of 1968, the McGovern-Fraser Commission formulated new rules for primaries, which were adopted by all Democrats and by Republicans in many states. These reforms opened up the nomination process for the presidency to all voters. The new system effectively removed control of the nomination process from the political party members and gave it to the voting public. Sometimes this produces a great party leader, and other years it produces a candidate who is not well supported by party loyalists and who cannot win the election.

7. A presidential primary is a statewide election to help a political party determine its presidential nominee at the national convention. Some states use the caucus method of choosing convention delegates. The primary campaign recently has been shortened to the first few months of the election year.

8. The party conventions are held to finalize the nomination of a candidate for president. Normally, the convention is used to unite the party and to introduce the winning candidate to the public. It marks the beginning of the general election campaign. Contested conventions have been rare in the last 50 years.

9. The general election campaign begins after Labor Day in September. Presidential candidates and their campaign organizations use advertising, appearances, speeches, and debates to win support from voters. In recent years, attention has been lavished on battleground states where presidential contests were closely fought.

Selected Print, Media, and Online Resources

PRINT RESOURCES

Karpf, David. *The MoveOn Effect: The Unexpected Transformation of American Political Advocacy.* New York: Oxford University Press, 2012. The author examines how today's organizations use the Internet and social media to gain supporters and motivate followers to join others in a common cause. His work addresses the new ways that organizations arise, organize, fundraise, and operate across the country, utilizing the capacity of the Internet to connect their followers.

Lau, Richard R., et al., eds. *How Voters Decide: Information Processing in Election Campaigns.* Cambridge, MA: Cambridge University Press, 2006. The researchers who wrote this book attempted to get "inside the heads" of citizens who confront huge amounts of information during modern presidential campaigns. The researchers argued that we should care not just about which candidates receive the most votes, but also about how many citizens voted "correctly"—that is, in accordance with their own interests.

MoveOn. *MoveOn's 50 Ways to Love Your Country: How to Find Your Political Voice and Become a Catalyst for Change.* Makawao, Maui, HI: Inner Ocean Publishing, 2004. This book contains 50 short chapters in which individuals describe how they sought to make a difference by getting involved in the political process. MoveOn has been called a "shadow party" to the Democrats. Nevertheless, the techniques described here could be used just as easily by Republicans. The volume is also available on audiotape.

Nelson, Michael, ed. *The Elections of 2008.* Washington, DC: CQ Press, 2009. This collection of essays by well-known political scientists comments on all aspects of the 2008 campaign, from the primaries through the general election.

Plouffe, David. *The Audacity to Win: The Inside Story and Lesson of Barack Obama's Historic Victory.* New York: Viking, 2009. David Plouffe, one of the president's closest advisers, and political consultants tell the inside story of the Obama campaign's strategy for winning in 2008. This is a good look at the inside of a high-powered campaign apparatus.

Smidt, Corwin, Kevin den Dulk, Bryan Froehle, James Penning, Stephen Monsma, and Douglas L. Koopman. *The Disappearing God Gap? Religion in the 2008 Presidential Election.* New York: Oxford University Press, 2010. After two elections in which religious conservatives seemed to have played a strong role, religion and religious views were much less important in the election of 2008. The authors examine the role of religion in American elections and comment on how that role changed in the Obama election.

Dja65/Shutterstock.com

Thurber, James A., and Candice J. Nelson, eds. *Campaigns and Elections American Style: Transforming American Politics*. New York: Westview Press, 2004. The articles in this book consider the basics of American campaigns and discuss practical campaign politics. They examine the evolution of campaigns over time, including town meetings, talk radio, infomercials, and focus groups. In this book, you will discover how campaign themes and strategies are determined.

Wayne, Stephen J. *The Road to the White House, 2008: The Politics of Presidential Elections*. Belmont, CA: Wadsworth Publishing, 2008. Stephen Wayne examines the changes in the election process since 1996 and provides an excellent analysis of the presidential selection process.

MEDIA RESOURCES

Bulworth—A 1998 satirical film starring Warren Beatty and Halle Berry. Jay Bulworth, a senator who is fed up with politics and life in general, hires a hit man to carry out his own assassination. He then throws political caution to the wind in campaign appearances by telling the truth and behaving the way he really wants to behave.

The Candidate—A 1972 film, starring a young Robert Redford, that effectively investigates and satirizes the decisions that a candidate for the U.S. Senate must make. It's a political classic.

Game Change—Released in 2012, this movie portrays the Republican campaign in 2008 with an emphasis on the introduction of Sarah Palin as the vice presidential candidate. It stars Ed Harris, Julianne Moore, and Woody Harrelson.

If You Can't Say Anything Nice—Negative campaigning seems to have become the norm in recent years. This 1999 program looks at the resulting decline in popularity of politics among the electorate and suggests approaches to restoring faith in the process. It is part of the series *Politics as Usual*, available from the Films Media Group.

Money Talks: The Influence of Money on American Politics—Bill Moyers reports on the influence of money on our political system. Produced in 1994.

Primary Colors—A 1998 film starring John Travolta as a southern governor who is plagued by a sex scandal during his run for the presidency.

ONLINE RESOURCES

Center for Responsive Politics a nonpartisan, independent, and nonprofit research group that tracks money in U.S. politics and its effect on elections and public policy: www.opensecrets.org

Federal Election Commission an independent regulatory agency created by Congress in 1975 to administer and enforce the Federal Election Campaign Act (FECA)—the statute that governs the financing of federal elections; contains detailed information about current campaign financing laws and the latest filings of finance reports: www.fec.gov

Project Vote Smart investigates voting records and campaign financing information: www.vote-smart.org

11 The Congress

TIM SLOAN/AFP/Getty Images

Speaker of the House John Boehner (R., Ohio) holds up his gavel as he calls the House to order in January 2012.

LEARNING OUTCOMES

After reading this chapter, students will be able to:

■ **LO1** Describe the major powers of the Congress as granted by the U.S. Constitution.

■ **LO2** Explain the differences between the House of Representatives and the Senate with regard to their constituencies, terms of office, powers, and political processes.

■ **LO3** Describe the processes of reapportionment and redistricting.

■ **LO4** Discuss the importance of committees to the lawmaking process and to the ability of members of Congress to do their jobs.

■ **LO5** Describe the leadership structure in each house of Congress, noting the differences between the House and the Senate.

■ **LO6** Demonstrate how a bill becomes a law, and explain how the different processes in the House and the Senate influence legislating.

What If ...

CONGRESS HAD TIME LIMITS?

BACKGROUND

The first year of the 1st Congress, held from 1789 to 1791, the members met from March to September, passing necessary legislation and organizing the government. In the second year, they met from January to August, and then reconvened from December to March. During the next five decades, Congress conducted most of its business in short sessions, with long recess periods for the members to maintain their farms and businesses back home.

Today, the U.S. Congress is still organized as two one-year sessions. The respective houses adjourn at the very end of one year and then reconvene about three weeks later. The House calendar clearly designates the days that members can spend in their districts meeting with constituents and, in many cases, fundraising. It is worth noting that the House calendar generally shows no sessions for Fridays or Mondays and long periods around legal holidays for "district work." Today's House and Senate do not want to adjourn formally in part because they fear the executive branch will take action while they are not in session. This work pattern allows for difficult issues such as raising the debt ceiling to go unresolved for many months. Other measures, such as tax relief or the extension of unemployment benefits, may persist for short periods with no attempt to resolve underlying issues. Finally, Congress may, by its own procedures, avoid such unpleasant tasks as finalizing a fiscal year budget. The government can run on a series of continuing resolutions. The low 2012 public approval ratings of Congress, along with the recent lack of congressional productivity, might make one wonder about an admittedly radical idea.

WHAT IF CONGRESS HAD TIME LIMITS?

In contrast to the U.S. Congress, many state constitutions limit the days and weeks that state legislatures can meet. For example, the Kentucky legislature may only meet for 60 "legislative days" in even-numbered years and 30 days in odd-numbered years. In Nevada, the legislature may meet for 120 calendar days, while in Missouri, the legislature must conclude its business by May 30th. Additionally, most state constitutions require that the state's budget must be balanced and the government cannot continue without a budget for the fiscal year. In some states, if the legislature does not complete the work on a budget, the governor may complete the task.

If the U.S. Congress were limited by a constitutional amendment to meeting for only six months, could the body be effective? Six months to work, followed by six months to be in one's home state, would increase pressure to complete the year's business, including the budget and tax issues, before adjournment. Both political parties might feel pressure to compromise and pass legislation before going home to explain their votes to their constituents. Given the large amount of work to do, members could easily spend as much time in daily floor sessions as they do now. Communication with their constituents back home could be handled by live conferences over the Internet.

Depending on the wording of the amendment, it would now be possible to consider membership in the House or Senate a part-time job, as in many state legislatures. This would mean, perhaps, paying the members a part-time or reduced salary and expecting them to maintain a career in the working world. That change, in itself, would make individuals less likely to see election to Congress as a career. Congress might return to a legislature of citizen-legislators much as the founders envisioned. The expenses of supporting the Congress could be greatly decreased because the large amount of staff on Capitol Hill would no longer be necessary, and congresspersons would not be constantly traveling back and forth to Washington.

DISADVANTAGES OF A PART-TIME CONGRESS

Obviously, a part-time Congress would have little ability to deal with domestic or international crises. Generally, in the states, the governor has the ability to call the legislature back to the capitol in special session. The president can also call Congress into special session to deal with emergencies.

Would making membership a part-time job cost the body in terms of expertise and effectiveness? Scholars who have studied the effects of term limits on state legislatures say that having more frequent turnover of members reduces the knowledge available to make good decisions. It takes several years for a member of Congress to become well versed in public policy in any one specific area or to understand the budget, say, of the Defense Department. Making their jobs part time would make it harder for congresspersons to gain the expertise necessary to offset the expertise of either bureaucrats or lobbyists for special interests. Both of those groups would be engaged in fighting for their interests full time. Finally, the executive would likely gain power if the Congress worked only six months a year. The president would be free to make more interim appointments without congressional scrutiny and to dominate the media with his or her agenda. Members of Congress would be playing "catch-up" when they returned to Washington after their six months at home.

FOR CRITICAL ANALYSIS

1. *Would forcing members of Congress to adjourn at a specified time motivate them to pass legislation or to leave decisions to the president?*

2. *How can members of Congress be encouraged to retire sooner and give more opportunities to younger Americans to run for the House and the Senate?*

MOST AMERICANS VIEW Congress in a less than flattering light. In recent years, Congress has appeared to be deeply split, highly partisan in its conduct, and not very responsive to public needs. Polls show that public approval of the Congress rarely reaches more than 40 percent; in fact, approval rates of the Congress are often very low. Yet individual members of Congress often receive much higher approval ratings from the voters in their districts. This is one of the paradoxes of the relationship between the people and Congress. Members of the public hold the institution in relatively low regard compared with the satisfaction they express with their individual representatives.

Part of the explanation for these seemingly contradictory appraisals is that members of Congress spend considerable time and effort serving their **constituents**. If the federal bureaucracy makes a mistake, the senator's or representative's office tries to resolve the issue. The members of the Congress spend considerable time and effort developing what is sometimes called a **"homestyle"** to gain the trust and appreciation of their constituents through service, local appearances, and the creation of local offices.

Congress, however, was created to work not just for local constituents but also for the nation as a whole. The representatives and senators in their Washington work are creating what might be called a **"hillstyle,"** which refers to their work on legislation and in party leadership to create laws and policies for our nation.[1] In this chapter, we describe the functions of Congress, including constituent service, representation, lawmaking, and oversight of the government. We review how the members of Congress are elected and how Congress organizes itself when it meets. We also examine how bills pass through the legislative process.

Constituent
One of the persons represented by a legislator or other elected or appointed official.

Homestyle
The actions and behaviors of a member of Congress aimed at the constituents and intended to win the support and trust of the voters at home.

Hillstyle
The actions and behaviors of a member of Congress in Washington, D.C., intended to promote policies and the member's own career aspirations.

The Functions of Congress

The founders of the American republic believed that the bulk of the power that would be exercised by a national government should be in the hands of the legislature because the members were elected by the people, or, in the case of the Senate, by the states. The leading role envisioned for Congress in the new government is apparent from its primacy in the Constitution. Article I deals with the structure, the powers, and the operation of Congress, beginning in Section 1 with an application of the basic principle of separation of powers: "All legislative Powers herein granted shall be vested in a Congress of the United States, which shall consist of a Senate and House of Representatives." These legislative powers are spelled out in detail in Article I and elsewhere.

The **bicameralism** of Congress—its division into two legislative houses—was in part the result of the Connecticut Compromise, which tried to balance the large-state population advantage, reflected in the House, and the small-state demand for equality in policymaking, which was satisfied in the Senate. Beyond that, the two chambers of Congress also reflected the social-class biases of the founders. They wished to balance the interests and the numerical superiority of the common citizens with the property interests of the less numerous landowners, bankers, and merchants. They achieved this goal by providing in Sections 2 and 3 of Article I that members of the House of Representatives should be elected directly by "the People," whereas members of the Senate were to be chosen by the elected representatives sitting in state legislatures, who were more likely to be members of the elite. (In 1913, the passage of the Seventeenth Amendment,

Bicameralism
The division of a legislature into two separate assemblies.

---

1. Richard Fenno, *Home Style: House Members in Their Districts* (Boston: Little, Brown, 1978).

which provides that senators also are to be elected directly by the people, resulted in the change of the latter provision.)

The logic of separate constituencies and separate interests underlying the bicameral Congress was reinforced by differences in length of tenure. Members of the House are required to face the electorate every two years, whereas senators can serve for a much more secure term of six years—even longer than the four-year term provided for the president. Furthermore, the senators' terms are staggered so that only one-third of the senators face the electorate every two years, along with all of the House members.

The bicameral structure of Congress was designed to enable the legislative body and its members to perform certain functions for the political system. These functions include lawmaking, representation, service to constituents, oversight, public education, and conflict resolution. Of these, the two most important and the ones most often in conflict are lawmaking and representation.

The Lawmaking Function

The principal and most obvious function of any legislature is **lawmaking**. Congress is the highest elected body in the country, charged with making binding rules for all Americans. Lawmaking requires decisions about the size of the federal budget, about health care reform and gun control, and about the long-term prospects for war or peace. This does not mean, however, that Congress initiates most of the ideas for legislation that it eventually considers. A majority of the bills that Congress acts on originate in the executive branch, and many other bills are traceable to interest groups and political party organizations. Through the processes of compromise and **logrolling** (offering to support a fellow member's bill in exchange for that member's promise to support your bill in the future), as well as debate and discussion, backers of legislation attempt to fashion a winning majority coalition to create policies for the nation.

The Representation Function

Representation includes both representing the desires and demands of the constituents in the member's home district or state and representing larger national interests such as farmers or the environment. Because the interests of constituents in a specific district may be in conflict with the demands of national policy, the representation function is often at variance with the lawmaking function for individual lawmakers and sometimes for Congress as a whole. For example, although it may be in the interest of the nation to reduce defense spending by closing military bases, such closures are not in the interest of the states and districts that will lose jobs and local spending. Every legislator faces votes that set representational issues against lawmaking realities.

How should the legislators fulfill the representation function? There are several views on how this should be accomplished.

The Trustee View of Representation. The first approach to the question of how representation should be achieved is that legislators should act as **trustees** of the broad interests of the entire society. They should vote against the narrow interests of their constituents if their conscience and their perception of national needs so dictate. For example, several Republican legislators have supported strong laws regulating the tobacco industry despite the views of some of their constituents.

Lawmaking
The process of establishing the legal rules that govern society.

Logrolling
An arrangement in which two or more members of Congress agree in advance to support each other's bills.

Representation
The function of members of Congress as elected officials representing the views of their constituents.

Trustee
A legislator who acts according to her or his conscience and the broad interests of the entire society.

AP Photo/Seth Perlman

State representative Aaron Schock (R.-Ill.), left, greets a voter at a diner in Peoria, Illinois, after winning the Republican primary race for the congressional nomination. Schock, who was only 26 at the time, became the youngest member of Congress when he won his seat in the November 2008 election.

The Instructed-Delegate View of Representation. Directly opposed to the trustee view of representation is the notion that the members of Congress should behave as **instructed delegates**; that is, they should mirror the views of the majority of the constituents who elected them to power in the first place. On the surface, this approach is plausible and rewarding. For it to work, however, we must assume that constituents actually have well-formed views on the issues that are decided in Congress and, further, that they have clear-cut preferences about these issues. Neither condition is likely to be satisfied very often.

Generally, most legislators hold neither a pure trustee view nor a pure instructed-delegate view. Typically, they combine both perspectives in a pragmatic mix that is often called the "politico" style.

Service to Constituents

Individual members of Congress are expected by their constituents to act as brokers between private citizens and the imposing, often faceless federal government. This function of providing service to constituents usually takes the form of **casework**. As noted previously, legislators make choices about their "hillstyle," deciding how much time they and their staff will spend on casework activities, such as tracking down a missing Social Security check, explaining the meaning of particular bills to people who may be affected by them, promoting a local business interest, or interceding with a regulatory agency on behalf of constituents who disagree with proposed agency regulations.

Legislators and many analysts of congressional behavior regard this **ombudsperson** role as an activity that strongly benefits the members of Congress. A government characterized by a large, confusing bureaucracy and complex public programs offers innumerable opportunities for legislators to assist (usually) grateful constituents. Morris P. Fiorina once suggested, somewhat mischievously, that senators and representatives prefer to maintain bureaucratic confusion to

did you know?

Fewer than 3 in 10 people can name the House member from their district, and fewer than half can name even one of the two senators from their state.

Instructed Delegate
A legislator who is an agent of the voters who elected him or her and who votes according to the views of constituents regardless of personal beliefs.

Casework
Personal work for constituents by members of Congress.

Ombudsperson
A person who hears and investigates complaints by private individuals against public officials or agencies.

Former chief executive officer of British Petroleum Tony Hayward listens to statements by members of the House Subcommittee on Oversight and Investigations after the oil spill in the Gulf of Mexico.

Jeff Malet/Newscom

maximize their opportunities for performing good deeds on behalf of their constituents:

> *Some poor, aggrieved constituent becomes enmeshed in the tentacles of an evil bureaucracy and calls upon Congressman St. George to do battle with the dragon.... In dealing with the bureaucracy, the congressman is not merely one vote of 435. Rather, he is a nonpartisan power, someone whose phone call snaps an office to attention. He is not kept on hold. The constituent who receives aid believes that his congressman and his congressman alone got results.*[2]

Although the political parties in Congress disagree on most issues, they find it difficult to vote against benefits for their constituents. As the economic downturn continued in 2009, the administration proposed a reduction in the percentage of wages withheld from workers' paychecks for Social Security as a way to put more money in their pockets. While Republicans did point out the long-term consequences of the plan—setting even less money aside for Social Security—they could not vote against a tax cut. Democrats spoke to the benefit of this temporary action for ordinary workers. Both parties chose to ignore the fact that this action makes it likely that Social Security will be insolvent even earlier than has been predicted.

The Oversight Function

Oversight of the bureaucracy is essential if the decisions made by Congress are to have any force. **Oversight** is the process by which Congress follows up on the laws it has enacted to ensure that they are being enforced and administered in the way Congress intended. This is done by holding committee hearings and investigations, changing the size of an agency's budget, and cross-examining high-level presidential nominees to head major agencies. Sometimes Congress

Oversight
The process by which Congress follows up on laws it has enacted to ensure that they are being enforced and administered in the way Congress intended.

---

2. Morris P. Fiorina, *Congress: Keystone of the Washington Establishment*, 2nd ed. (New Haven, CT: Yale University Press, 1989), pp. 44, 47.

establishes a special commission to investigate a problem. For example, after Hurricane Katrina devastated New Orleans and parts of surrounding states in 2005, Congress created a commission to determine how and why the federal government, particularly the Federal Emergency Management Agency (FEMA), had mishandled government aid both during and after that natural disaster. Oversight can, of course, be partisan in nature, as when House Republicans grilled administration officials over national security leaks in 2012.

Senators and representatives increasingly see their oversight function as a critically important part of their legislative activities. In part, oversight is related to the concept of constituency service, particularly when Congress investigates alleged arbitrariness or wrongdoing by bureaucratic agencies.

The Public-Education Function

Educating the public is a function that is performed whenever Congress holds public hearings, exercises oversight over the bureaucracy, or engages in committee and floor debate on such major issues and topics as political assassinations, aging, illegal drugs, and the concerns of small businesses. In so doing, Congress presents a range of viewpoints on pressing national questions. In recent years, members of Congress and the committees of Congress have greatly improved access to information through their use of the Internet and Web sites. Congress also decides what issues will come up for discussion and decision; this agenda setting is a major facet of its public-education function.

The Conflict-Resolution Function

Congress is commonly seen as an institution for resolving conflicts within American society. Organized interest groups and representatives of different racial, religious, economic, and ideological interests look on Congress as an access point for airing their grievances and seeking help. This puts Congress in the position of trying to resolve the differences among competing points of view by passing laws to accommodate as many interested parties as possible. To the extent that Congress meets pluralist expectations in accommodating competing interests, it tends to build support for the entire political process.

The Powers of Congress

The Constitution is both highly specific and extremely vague about the powers that Congress may exercise. The first 17 clauses of Article I, Section 8, specify most of the **enumerated powers** of Congress—that is, powers expressly given to that body.

Enumerated Powers

The enumerated, or expressed, powers of Congress include the right to impose taxes and import tariffs; borrow funds; regulate interstate commerce and international trade; establish procedures for naturalizing citizens; make laws regulating bankruptcies; coin (and print) money and regulate its value; establish standards of weights and measures; punish counterfeiters; establish post offices and postal routes; regulate copyrights and patents; establish the federal court system; punish illegal acts on the high seas; declare war; raise and regulate an army and a navy; call up and regulate the state militias to enforce laws, to suppress insurrections, and to repel invasions; and govern the District of Columbia.

■ **Learning Outcome 1:**
Describe the major powers of the Congress as granted by the U.S. Constitution.

Enumerated Power
A power specifically granted to the national government by the Constitution. The first 17 clauses of Article I, Section 8, specify most of the enumerated powers of Congress.

Politics with a Purpose
KEEPING TABS ON CONGRESS

What if we told you that we would decide whether your privacy on Facebook would be protected? Or what you would spend for your connection to the Internet? What if we were to tell you that for every dollar you earned, we were going to take 28 cents and decide how to spend it?[a] And that our actions would influence how much it cost you to fill up your gas tank? You would probably think that if you gave us all this power, you should pay attention to see if we are making the "right" choices, especially since you have a say in whether we keep our jobs.

Congress has these kinds of powers. Along with the president, Congress sets tax law—including gas taxes—and regulates interstate commerce (the Internet), among many other activities. In fact, in any given week early in the legislative session, at least a hundred bills and resolutions are introduced in the U.S. Senate. How is the average citizen supposed to keep track of all of these pieces of potential legislation, any one of which may have an impact on his or her life? And, as you consider voting for your representative or the challenger, how can you know if your member voted as you preferred? Substantive representation, the extent to which an elected official's actions match the interests of his or her constituency, can be assessed in a variety of ways. The Congressional Record[b] is the official source of information on everything that has happened in Congress. The Library of Congress provides access to the Congressional Record and provides links to other data, such as congressional committees, government reports, and presidential nominations (http://thomas.loc.gov).

A quick perusal of these sites illustrates that in addition to the sheer volume of all the bills introduced, the legislative process is extremely complex. There are 22 House committees, 20 Senate committees, and four joint committees (where membership is shared between the chambers). These bodies all have subcommittees, where the real work of writing laws and holding hearings occurs. So how can you keep track of legislation that is important to you? You can become familiar with organizations that are vital to the democratic process by making sense of and tracking legislation.

For example, certain nonprofit organizations gather information from advocacy groups, such as those discussed in Chapter 7. These nonprofits examine the groups' preferences on legislation pending before Congress and then compare them with how the members of Congress vote. One nonprofit organization, Voter Information Services, hosts a Web site that allows users to create report cards on members of Congress by choosing from a list of advocacy groups.[c]

A closer examination of these report cards illustrates the differences in how particular groups assess the actions of members of Congress. Take, for example, the votes on which NARAL ProChoice America and the National Right to Life Committee (NRLC) "score" or record whether the member votes as the group wants. In 2006, Congress debated S. 403, the Child Custody Protection Act. NARAL described it as a bill making it a crime for anyone other than a parent "including a grandparent, adult sibling or religious counselor" to take a "young woman across state lines for abortion care." The NRLC described the same portion of the bill in very different terms, arguing that "abortion clinics' out-of-state advertising in non-notification states … frequently highlights the avoidance of parental notification as a selling point. In other cases, young girls are subjected to tremendous pressure from much older males and others who do not have their best interests at heart."[d] Organizations like Voter Information Services allow you to examine these groups' assessments of members of Congress side-by-side. You can decide which groups' positions best match yours and whose assessments of members of Congress you most trust.

Whether you visit advocacy groups online or use the Congressional Record, journalistic sources such as *Congressional Quarterly* or *The National Journal*, or specialized tracking agencies like GalleryWatch.com or CongressNow.com, the information on what our Congress does is readily available. Our role as citizens is to pay attention.

[a] www.irs.gov/pub/irs-pdf/n1036.pdf
[b] http://thomas.loc.gov/home/r110query.html
[c] www.vis.org/crc/groupsincrc.aspx
[d] www.nrlc.org/Federal/CCPA/CCPASenateLetter092806.html

The most important of the domestic powers of Congress, listed in Article I, Section 8, are the rights to collect taxes, to spend, and to regulate commerce. The most important foreign policy power is the power to declare war. Other sections of the Constitution allow Congress to establish rules for its own members, to regulate the electoral college, and to override a presidential veto. Congress may also regulate the extent of the Supreme Court's authority to review cases decided by the lower courts, regulate relations among states, and propose amendments to the Constitution.

Powers of the Senate. Some functions are restricted to one chamber. The Senate must advise on, and consent to, the ratification of treaties and must accept or reject presidential nominations of ambassadors, Supreme Court justices, and "all other Officers of the United States." During the first two years of President Barack Obama's term, two Supreme Court vacancies occurred through the retirements of Justices David Souter in 2009 and John Paul Stevens in 2010. The president nominated Appellate Judge Sonia Sotomayor to fill Souter's seat in 2009. Although the Republicans in the Senate would have liked to object to the appointment, Judge Sotomayor had been confirmed in her appellate seat as an appointee of George W. Bush. In 2010, President Obama made another somewhat controversial appointment but, given the outstanding qualifications of Solicitor General Elena Kagan, she too was confirmed. In contrast, the president had more difficulty with lower judicial appointments and ambassadorial appointments.

While the Republicans in the Senate slowed the approval process for lower court judges in the first year of the Obama presidency, eventually the majority of his judicial appointments were approved. However, several of those appointments—including Judge Robert Chatigny of Connecticut, who had given a stay of execution to a serial killer; Judge Goodwin Liu, a supporter of gay marriage; and Edward C. Dumont, who would have been the first openly gay appellate judge—were killed by the filibuster, and the individuals withdrew their nominations. Republicans in the Senate were particularly angered by the president's decision to make recess appointments to the National Labor Relations Board and the new Consumer Protection Agency during the Christmas holiday in 2011. To prevent such appointments, the Senate did not recess but held symbolic sessions for a few moments each day. Although a federal court refused to stop the appointments to the NLRB, commentators debated whether the Obama appointments made while the Senate was technically in session were constitutional.[3] The Senate Republicans then retaliated by holding up further judicial and executive nominees.

Constitutional Amendments. Amendments to the Constitution provide for other congressional powers. Congress must certify the election of a president and a vice president or choose these officers if no candidate has a majority of the electoral vote (Twelfth Amendment). It may levy an income tax (Sixteenth Amendment) and determine who will be acting president in case of the death or incapacity of the president or vice president (Twentieth Amendment and Twenty-fifth Amendment). In addition, Congress explicitly is given the power to enforce, by appropriate legislation, the provisions of several other amendments.

The Necessary and Proper Clause

Beyond these numerous specific powers, Congress enjoys the right under Article I, Section 8 (the "elastic" or "necessary and proper" clause), "[t]o make all Laws which shall be necessary and proper for carrying into Execution the foregoing Powers [of Article I], and all other Powers vested by this Constitution in the Government of the United States, or in any Department or Officer thereof." As discussed in Chapter 3, this vague statement of congressional responsibilities provided, over time, the basis for a greatly expanded national government. It also constituted, at least in theory, a check on the expansion of presidential powers.

---

3. Manu Raju and Scott Wong, "Obama Recess Appointment Power Is Murky," *Politico*, January 4, 2012. www.politico.com/news/stories/0112/71089.html.

Checks on the Congress

When you consider all of the powers of Congress and its ability to override a presidential veto, it is undoubtedly the most powerful branch of government. However, because of the diversity of the United States and the corresponding diverse interests of members of the Congress, rarely does enough unanimity exist to override presidential vetoes. So, one check on the Congress is the veto of the president. Another constitutional check is the power of the Supreme Court to hold a law passed by the Congress as unconstitutional. Additionally, the members of the House face election every two years. If the Congress were to exercise too much power in the eyes of the public, it is likely that many members would be voted out of office. And on the other side of Capitol Hill sits the Senate, which often curbs the House by not agreeing with proposals from the "other house."

House-Senate Differences

■ **Learning Outcome 2:**
Explain the differences between the House of Representatives and the Senate with regard to their constituencies, terms of office, powers, and political processes.

Congress is composed of two markedly different—but coequal—chambers. Although the Senate and the House of Representatives exist within the same legislative institution, each has developed certain distinctive features that clearly distinguish it from the other. Table 11–1 summarizes these differences.

Size and Rules

The central difference between the House and the Senate is simply that the House is much larger than the Senate. The House has 435 representatives, plus delegates from the District of Columbia, Puerto Rico, Guam, American Samoa, and the Virgin Islands, compared with just 100 senators. This size difference means that a greater number of formal rules are needed to govern activity in the House, whereas correspondingly looser procedures can be followed in the less crowded Senate.

The effect of the difference in size is most obvious in the rules governing debate on the floors of the two chambers. The House operates with an elaborate system to control the agenda and allot time fairly in such a large assembly. For each major bill, the **Rules Committee** normally proposes a **Rule** for debate that includes time limitations for the debate, divides the time between the majority and the minority, and specifies whether amendments can be proposed. The House debates and approves the Rule, which will govern the debate on that specific legislation. As a consequence of its stricter time limits on debate, the House, despite its greater size, often is able to act on legislation more quickly than the Senate.

Rules Committee
A standing committee of the House of Representatives that provides special rules under which specific bills can be debated, amended, and considered by the House.

Rule
The proposal by the Rules Committee of the House that states the conditions for debate for one piece of legislation.

Debate and Filibustering

In the Senate, the rules governing debate are much less limiting. In fact, for legislation to reach the floor of the Senate, the body must have approved the rules of debate by a **Unanimous Consent Agreement**, which means that the entire body agrees to the rules of debate. The Senate tradition of the **filibuster**, or the use of unlimited debate as a blocking tactic, dates back to 1790. In that year, a proposal to move the U.S. capital from New York to Philadelphia was stalled by such time-wasting maneuvers. This unlimited-debate tradition—which also existed in the House until 1811—is not absolute, however.

Beginning in 2009, the use of the filibuster became the usual way of doing business in the Senate. At the beginning of the session, the Democratic majority

Unanimous Consent Agreement
An agreement on the rules of debate for proposed legislation in the Senate that is approved by all the members.

Filibuster
The use of the Senate's tradition of unlimited debate as a delaying tactic to block a bill.

plus the two independent senators (Sanders, Vt., and Lieberman, Conn.), could muster 60 votes to support President Obama's initiatives in health care reform and financial reform. The Republican strategy was to force a cloture vote against their filibuster on almost every issue, betting that some Democrats might not be able to support every initiative. The strategy forced the administration into deal-making on some votes, which may have increased public disapproval of some of the legislation. When Senator Scott Brown won election from Massachusetts in early 2010, Republicans had 41 seats and Democrats could be forced into more compromises to get the 60 votes to stop the filibuster. The use of such tactics has increased tremendously over the last two decades, leading to the concept of **unorthodox lawmaking**, meaning the use of obscure parliamentary procedures to get laws passed in the face of strong opposition.[4] Such tactics, however, are difficult to explain to the public and seem possibly undemocratic.

Table 11–1 ▶ **Differences between the House and the Senate**

HOUSE*	SENATE*
Constitutional Differences	
Members chosen from local districts	Members chosen from an entire state
Two-year term	Six-year term
Originally elected by voters	Originally (until 1913) elected by state legislatures
May impeach (indict) federal officials	May convict federal officials of impeachable offenses
Process and Culture	
Larger (435 voting members)	Smaller (100 members)
More formal rules	Fewer rules and restrictions
Debate limited	Debate extended
Less prestige and less individual notice	More prestige and more media attention
More partisan	More individualistic
Specific Powers	
Originates bills for raising revenues	Has power to advise the president on, and to consent to, presidential appointments and treaties

*Some of these differences, such as the term of office, are provided for in the Constitution. Others, such as debate rules, are not.

Under Senate Rule 22, debate may be ended by invoking *cloture*. Cloture shuts off discussion on a bill. Amended in 1975 and 1979, Rule 22 states that debate may be closed off on a bill if 16 senators sign a petition requesting it and if, after two days have elapsed, three-fifths of the entire membership (60 votes, assuming no vacancies) vote for cloture. After cloture is invoked, each senator may speak on a bill for a maximum of one hour before a vote is taken.

In 1979, the Senate refined Rule 22 to ensure that a final vote must take place within 100 hours of debate after cloture has been imposed. It further limited the use of multiple amendments to stall post-cloture final action on a bill.

Unorthodox Lawmaking
The use of out-of-the-ordinary parliamentary tactics to pass legislation.

Prestige

As a consequence of the greater size of the House, representatives generally cannot achieve as much individual recognition and public prestige as can members of the Senate. Senators are better able to gain media exposure and to establish careers as spokespersons for large national constituencies. To obtain recognition for his or her activities, a member of the House generally must do one of two things. He or she might survive in office long enough to join the ranks of the leadership on committees or within the party. Alternatively, the representative could become an expert on some specialized aspect of legislative policy, such as tax laws, the environment, or education.

4. Barbara Sinclair, *Unorthodox Lawmaking: New Legislative Processes in the U.S. Congress.* 3rd ed. (Washington, DC: CQ Press, 2007).

Congresspersons and the Citizenry: A Comparison

Members of the U.S. Senate and the U.S. House of Representatives are not typical American citizens. Members of Congress are older than most Americans, partly because of constitutional age requirements and partly because a good deal of political experience normally is an advantage in running for national office. Members of Congress are also disproportionately white, male, and trained in high-status occupations. Lawyers are by far the largest occupational group among congresspersons, although the proportion of lawyers in the House is lower now than it was in the past. Compared with the average American citizen, members of Congress are well paid. In 2012, annual congressional salaries were $174,000. Increasingly, members of Congress are also much wealthier than the average citizen. Whereas less than 1 percent of Americans have assets exceeding $1 million, about 40 percent of the members of Congress are millionaires. Table 11–2 summarizes selected characteristics of the members of Congress.

Compared with the composition of Congress over the past 200 years, however, the House and Senate today are significantly more diverse in gender and ethnicity than ever before. There are 76 women in the House of Representatives (17 percent) and 17 women in the U.S. Senate (17 percent). Minority group members fill over 17 percent of the seats in the House; they include 44 African American members, 25 Hispanic members, 7 Asian or Pacific Islander Americans, and 1 Native American, Tom Cole of Oklahoma. The Senate has 2 Hispanic members and 2 Asian Americans but no African Americans. The 112th Congress has significant numbers of members born in 1946 or later, the so-called baby boomers.

Table 11–2 ▸ Characteristics of the 112th Congress, 2011–2013

	U.S. POPULATION, 2010	HOUSE	SENATE
Age (average)	36.8	57	62
Percent minority	28%	17.7%	4%
Religion			
Percent church members	60%	93%	92%
Percent Catholic	25.1%	31%	24%
Percent Protestant	51.3%	56%	55%
Percent Jewish	1.2%	7.3%	13%
Percent female	50.9%	17.5%	17%
Lawyers	0.4%	23.9%	37%
Blue-collar occupations	30%	1.6%	3%
Military veteran	7.6%	21.4%	28.9%
Percent households earning more than $50,000	42%	100%	100%
Assets more than $1 million	1%	42%	66%

Sources: E. Eric Petersen, "Representatives and Senators: Trends in Member Characteristics Since 1945," Washington, D.C.: Congressional Research Service, 2012. Tom Shine, "47% of Congress Members Millionaires—a Status Shared by Only 1% of Americans," ABC News, November 16, 2011.

A majority of House members and Senators belong to this postwar generation. This shift in the character of Congress may prompt consideration of the issues that will affect the boomers, such as Social Security and Medicare.

Congressional Elections

The process of electing members of Congress is decentralized. Congressional elections are conducted by the individual state governments. The states, however, must conform to the rules established by the U.S. Constitution and by national statutes. The Constitution states that representatives are to be elected every second year by popular ballot, and the number of seats awarded to each state is to be determined every 10 years by the results of the census. It is important to note that the decennial census is viewed as crucial by members of Congress and by the states. If the census is not accurate, perhaps undercounting individuals living in a state, then that state might lose a representative in Congress. Each state has at least one representative, with most congressional districts having about 650,000 residents. Senators are elected by popular vote (since the passage of the Seventeenth Amendment) every six years; approximately one-third of the seats are chosen every two years. Each state has two senators. Under Article I, Section 4, of the Constitution, state legislatures are given control over "[t]he Times, Places and Manner of holding Elections for Senators and Representatives"; however, "the Congress may at any time by Law make or alter such Regulations."

Only states can elect members of Congress. Therefore, territories such as Puerto Rico and Guam are not represented, though they do elect nonvoting delegates who sit in the House. The District of Columbia is also represented only by a nonvoting delegate. The District is not represented in the Senate at all. Several proposals have been made to give D.C. voting representation in Congress. In 1978, Congress approved a constitutional amendment to give the District the representation it would have if it were a state, including two senators. The amendment was not ratified, however. More recently, District citizens have campaigned to make D.C. a state. New states can be admitted to the union without amending the Constitution. Another proposal is to allow District citizens to vote either with Maryland or Virginia, as they did in the 18th century. However, this solution would not give the citizens of the District the attention they believe is necessary to meet their interests. Democrats in Congress have generally supported more representation for the District because the majority of its citizens are African American and vote overwhelmingly Democratic. Republicans are generally not supportive of giving voting powers to D.C.'s representative.

Candidates for Congressional Elections

Candidates for House and Senate seats may be self-selected. The qualifications for the two houses do differ: Members of the House must be at least 25 years old, a citizen for seven years, and live in the state they will represent; whereas senators must be 30 years old, a citizen for nine years, and a resident of the state they represent. In congressional districts where one party is very strong, however, there may be a shortage of candidates willing to represent the weaker party. In such circumstances, leaders of the weaker party must often actively recruit candidates. Candidates may resemble the voters of the district in ethnicity or religion, but they are also likely to be very successful individuals who have been active in politics before. House candidates are especially likely to have local ties to their districts. Candidates usually choose to run because they believe they would enjoy the job and its accompanying status. They also may be thinking of a House seat as a stepping-stone to future political office as a senator, governor, or president. Individuals who seek Senate seats may also have plans to run for governor in their home state or be considering a run for the presidency.

Congressional Campaigns and Elections. Congressional campaigns have changed considerably in the past two decades. Like all other campaigns, they are much more expensive, with the average cost of a winning Senate campaign now $9.7 million and a winning House campaign more than $1.4 million. Campaign funds include direct contributions by individuals, contributions by political action committees (PACs), and "soft money" funneled through state party committees. As you read in Chapter 10, all of these contributions are regulated by laws, including the Federal Election Campaign Act of 1971, as amended, and most recently the Bipartisan Campaign Reform Act of 2002. Once in office, legislators spend time almost every day raising funds for their next campaign.

Most candidates for Congress must win the nomination through a **direct primary**, in which **party identifiers** vote for the candidate who will be on the party ticket in the general election. To win the primary, candidates may take more liberal or more conservative positions to get the votes of party identifiers. In the general election, they may moderate their views to attract the votes of independents and voters from the other party.

Direct Primary
An intraparty election in which the voters select the candidates who will run on a party's ticket in the subsequent general election.

Party Identifier
A person who identifies with a political party.

Presidential Effects. Congressional candidates are always hopeful that a strong presidential candidate on the ticket will have "coattails" that will sweep in senators and representatives of the same party. In fact, coattail effects have been quite limited, and in recent presidential elections have not materialized at all. One way to measure the coattail effect is to look at the subsequent midterm elections, held in the even-numbered years following the presidential contests. In these years, voter turnout falls sharply. In the past, the party controlling the White House normally lost seats in Congress in the midterm elections, in part because the coattail effect ceased to apply. Members of Congress who were from contested districts or who were in their first term were more likely not to be reelected.

Table 11–3 shows the pattern for midterm elections since 1942. The president's party lost seats in every election from 1942 to 1998. In that year, with President Bill Clinton under the threat of impeachment, voters showed their displeasure with the Republicans by voting in five more Democrats. In 2002, Republicans bucked the normal slump by winning five more Republican seats in the House. Most commentators believed that these midterm victories were based on public support for the president after the September 11 attacks. In 2006, the Republicans suffered a fairly normal midterm defeat, comparable to the midterm defeat in 1958, the sixth year of the Eisenhower presidency.

The 2010 midterm elections were a sweeping win by the Republicans, aided by the newly energized members

Table 11–3 ▶ Midterm Gains and Losses by the Party of the President, 1942–2010

SEATS GAINED OR LOST BY THE PARTY OF THE PRESIDENT IN THE HOUSE OF REPRESENTATIVES	
1942	−45 (D.)
1946	−55 (D.)
1950	−29 (D.)
1954	−18 (R.)
1958	−47 (R.)
1962	−4 (D.)
1966	−47 (D.)
1970	−12 (R.)
1974	−48 (R.)
1978	−15 (D.)
1982	−26 (R.)
1986	−5 (R.)
1990	−8 (R.)
1994	−52 (D.)
1998	+5 (D.)
2002	+5 (R.)
2006	−30 (R.)
2010	−62 (D.)

of the Tea Party movement. Republicans gained more than 60 seats in the House of Representatives, thus gaining majority control in that body. Although it is normal for the "out party" to gain seats in the midterms, the size of the Republican victory was the largest ever in modern times.

The Power of Incumbency

The power of incumbency in the outcome of congressional elections cannot be overemphasized. Once members are elected and survive the second election, they build up considerable loyalty among their constituents, and they are frequently reelected as long as they wish to serve. Table 11–4 shows that more than 90 percent of representatives and a slightly smaller proportion of senators who decide to run for reelection are successful. This conclusion holds for both presidential-year and midterm elections. Several scholars contend that the pursuit of reelection is the strongest motivation behind the activities of members of Congress. The reelection goal is pursued in several ways. Incumbents develop their homestyle, using the mass media, making personal appearances with constituents, and sending newsletters—all to produce a favorable image and to make their name a household word. Members of Congress generally try to present themselves as informed, experienced, and responsive to people's needs. Legislators also can point to things that they have done to benefit their constituents—by fulfilling the congressional casework function or by bringing money for mass transit to the district, for example. Finally, incumbents can demonstrate the positions that they have taken on key issues by referring to their voting records in Congress.

Table 11–4 ▶ The Power of Incumbency

	ELECTION YEAR											
	1990	1992	1994	1996	1998	2000	2002	2004	2006	2008	2010	2012
HOUSE												
Number of incumbent candidates	406	368	387	384	402	403	393	404	405	389	393	382
Reelected	390	325	349	361	395	394	383	397	382	372	336	345
Percentage of total	96.0	88.3	90.2	94.0	98.3	97.8	97.5	98.3	94.3	95.6	85.4	90.0
Defeated	16	43	38	23	7	9	10	7	23	17	57	37
In primary	1	19	3	2	1	3	3	1	2	3	4	5
In general election	15	24	34	21	6	6	7	6	21	17	53	32
SENATE												
Number of incumbent candidates	32	28	26	21	29	29	28	26	29	32	25	22
Reelected	31	23	24	19	26	23	24	25	23	23	21	21
Percentage of total	96.9	82.1	92.3	90.5	89.7	79.3	85.7	96.2	79.3	81.3	84	95.0
Defeated	1	5	2	2	3	6	4	1	6	3	4	2
In primary	0	1	0	1	0	0	1	0	1*	0	2	1
In general election	1	4	2	1	3	6	3	1	6	3	2	1

*Joe Lieberman of Connecticut lost the Democratic primary but won the general election as an independent. He chose to organize with the Senate Democrats.

Sources: Norman Ornstein, Thomas E. Mann, and Michael J. Malbin, *Vital Statistics on Congress, 2001–2002* (Washington, DC: The AEI Press, 2002); and authors' update.

Party Control of Congress after the 2012 Elections

While a number of members of Congress retired before the election and a few were defeated in primaries, the majority of incumbent members ran for another term, and more than 90% were reelected. By the time the votes were counted, it was clear that the two houses were divided by party: The House Republicans maintained their majority, although they lost seven seats. Senate Democrats increased their margin by two with the division in the Senate as 53 Democrats, 45 Republicans, and 2 Independents, Bernie Sanders of Vermont and Angus King of Maine.

■ **Learning Outcome 3:**
Describe the processes of reapportionment and redistricting.

Reapportionment
The allocation of seats in the House of Representatives to each state after each census.

Redistricting
The redrawing of the boundaries of the congressional districts within each state.

Justiciable Question
A question that may be raised and reviewed in court.

Gerrymandering
The drawing of legislative district boundary lines to obtain partisan or factional advantage. A district is said to be gerrymandered when its shape is manipulated by the dominant party in the state legislature to maximize electoral strength at the expense of the minority party.

Congressional Apportionment

Two of the most complicated aspects of congressional elections are apportionment issues—**reapportionment** (the allocation of seats in the House to each state after each census) and **redistricting** (the redrawing of the boundaries of the districts within each state). In a landmark 6-2 vote in 1962, the United States Supreme Court made the apportionment of state legislative districts a **justiciable** (that is, a reviewable) **question**.[5] The Court did so by invoking the Fourteenth Amendment principle that no state can deny to any person "the equal protection of the laws." In 1964, the Court held that *both* chambers of a state legislature must be apportioned so that all districts are equal in population.[6] Later that year, the Court applied this "one person, one vote" principle to U.S. congressional districts on the basis of Article I, Section 2, of the Constitution, which requires that members of the House be chosen "by the People of the several States."[7]

Severe malapportionment of congressional districts before 1964 resulted in some districts containing two or three times the populations of other districts in the same state, thereby diluting the effect of a vote cast in the more populous districts. This system generally benefited the conservative populations of rural areas and small towns and harmed the interests of the more heavily populated and liberal cities. In fact, suburban areas have benefited the most from the Court's rulings, as suburbs account for an increasingly larger proportion of the nation's population, while cities include a correspondingly smaller segment of the population.

Gerrymandering

Although the general issue of apportionment has been dealt with fairly successfully by the one person, one vote principle, the **gerrymandering** issue has not yet been resolved. This term refers to the legislative boundary-drawing tactics that were used under Elbridge Gerry, the governor of Massachusetts, in the 1812 elections (see Figure 11–1). A district is said to have been gerrymandered when its shape is altered substantially by the dominant party in a state legislature to maximize its electoral strength at the expense of the minority party.

In 1986, the Supreme Court heard a case that challenged gerrymandered congressional districts in Indiana. The Court ruled for the first time that redistricting for the political benefit of one group could be challenged on constitutional grounds. In this specific case, Davis v. Bandemer,[8] however, the Court did not agree that the districts were drawn unfairly, because it could not be proved that a group of voters would consistently be deprived of influence at the polls as a result of the new districts.

---

5. *Baker v. Carr*, 369 U.S. 186 (1962). The term *justiciable* is pronounced "juhs-tish-a-buhl."
6. *Reynolds v. Sims*, 377 U.S. 533 (1964).
7. *Wesberry v. Sanders*, 376 U.S. 1 (1964).
8. 478 U.S. 109 (1986).

Figure 11-1 ▶ The Original Gerrymander

The practice of "gerrymandering"——the excessive manipulation of the shape of a legislative district to benefit a certain incumbent or party——is probably as old as the Republic, but the name originated in 1812. In that year, the Massachusetts legislature carved out of Essex County a district that historian John Fiske said has a "dragonlike contour." When the painter Gilbert Stuart saw the misshapen district, he penciled in a head, wings, and claws and exclaimed, "That will do for a salamander!" Editor Benjamin Russell replied, "Better say a Gerrymander" (after Elbridge Gerry, then-governor of Massachusetts).

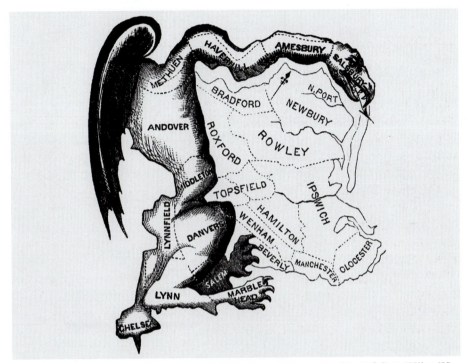

Source: *Congressional Quarterly's Guide to Congress*, 3rd ed. (Washington, DC: Congressional Quarterly Press, 1982), p. 695.

Redistricting after the 2010 Census

Not only did Republicans win a majority of seats in the House of Representatives in 2010, but they captured a majority of statehouses and governorships, which meant that they would have the upper hand in the drawing of new congressional districts after the release of the results of the 2010 Census. Take the case of Ohio as an illustration: Ohio lost enough population between 2000 and 2010 to lose two congressional seats. That meant all the districts in the state would be redrawn to adjust for the lower number of congressional districts. Ohio is generally regarded as a "battleground state" that is almost evenly divided between Democratic and Republican voters. Through the redistricting process, which was supposedly bipartisan, Ohio Republicans managed to put two sitting Democratic members of Congress—Marcy Kaptur and Dennis Kucinich—in one district and, through the drawing of district boundaries, make it possible for Republicans to win 12 of the 16 districts. For an example of a Republican-leaning district, look at Figure 11–2, showing Ohio's First Congressional District. While this district included half of Hamilton County and half of the city of Cincinnati for many years, it now looks like "crossed signal flags." The district joins the traditional western Hamilton County districts with Warren County to the northeast with an odd-shaped bridge. The intent is to add enough Republican voters to the district to offset the majority Democratic vote in Cincinnati.

Redistricting decisions are often made by a small group of political leaders within a state legislature. Typically, their goal is to shape voting districts in such a

Figure 11–2 ▶ The First Congressional District of Ohio

Effective Beginning with the Election in 2012 for the 113th U.S. Congress

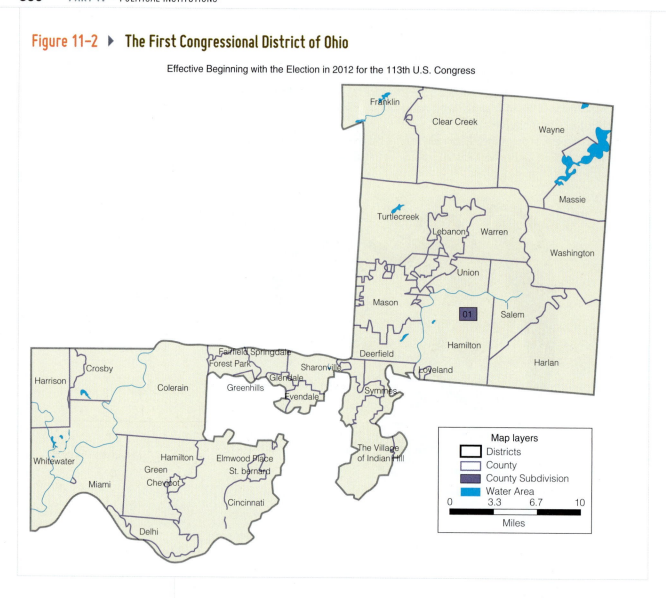

way as to maximize their party's chances of winning state legislative seats as well as seats in Congress. Two of the techniques they use are called "packing" and "cracking." With the use of powerful computers and software, they *pack* voters supporting the opposing party into as few districts as possible or *crack* the opposing party's supporters into different districts.

Clearly, partisan redistricting aids incumbents. The party that dominates a state's legislature will be making redistricting decisions. Through gerrymandering tactics such as packing and cracking, districts can be redrawn in such a way as to ensure that party's continued strength in the state legislature or Congress. As pointed out before, some have estimated that only between 30 and 50 of the 435 seats in the House of Representatives were open for any real competition in the most recent elections.

In 2004, the United States Supreme Court reviewed an obviously political redistricting scheme in Pennsylvania. The Court concluded, however, that the federal judiciary would not address purely political gerrymandering claims.[9] Two years later, the Supreme Court reached a similar conclusion with respect to most of the new congressional districts created by the Republicans in the Texas legislature in 2003. Again, except for one district in Texas, the Court refused to intervene in what was clearly a political gerrymandering plan.[10]

9. *Vieth v. Jubelirer*, 541 U.S. 267 (2004).
10. *League of United Latin American Citizens v. Perry*, 399 F.Supp. 2nd 756 (2006).

Figure 11–3 ▸ Congressional Districts of Iowa

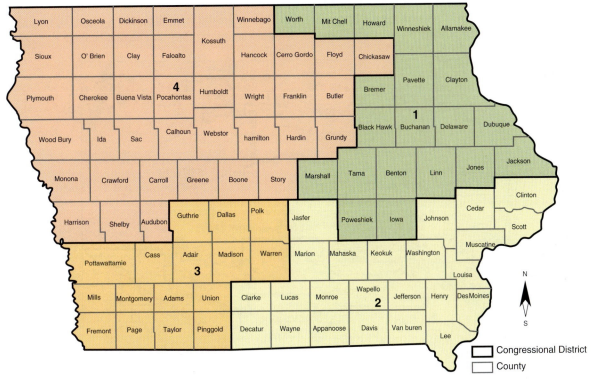

IOWA CONGRESSIONAL DISTRICTS

Effective Beginning with the Election in 2012 for the 113th U.S. Congress

▢ Congressional District
▢ County

Prepared by the Iowa Legislative Services Agency

Nonpartisan Redistricting

Several states, including Arizona, Iowa, and Minnesota, have adopted non-partisan redistricting procedures. As you will see if you compare the First District of Ohio with the map of the Iowa districts (Figure 11–3, nonpartisan districts usually respect county lines and divide the state into fairly cleanly shaped districts that share geographic characteristics. Research has shown that nonpartisan districts tend to be more competitive, no doubt because they have not been drawn to favor one party over the other.

"Minority-Majority" Districts

In the early 1990s, the federal government encouraged a type of gerrymandering that made possible the election of a minority representative from a "minority-majority" area. Under the mandate of the Voting Rights Act of 1965, the Justice Department issued directives to states after the 1990 census instructing them to create congressional districts that would maximize the voting power of minority groups—that is, create districts in which minority voters were the majority. The result was several creatively drawn congressional districts—see, for example, the depiction of the Illinois Fourth Congressional District in Figure 11–4, which is commonly described as "a pair of earmuffs."

Constitutional Challenges

Many of these "minority-majority" districts were challenged in court by citizens who claimed that creating districts based on race or ethnicity alone violates the

did you know?

The most recently constructed dormitory for Senate pages cost about $8 million, or $264,200 per bed, compared with the median cost of a university dormitory of $22,600 per bed.

Figure 11-4 ▶ The Fourth Congressional District of Illinois

The 4th district is outlined here in blue. It stretches from the near north side of Chicago out to the western suburbs and then turns east through the south side of Chicago. Why is the district drawn this way? The district includes a majority of Hispanic Americans and meets the criteria for a majority minority district. However, the northern portion of the district contains many Puerto Rican Americans while many Mexican Americans live in the southern portion. The western link between the two is a super highway where no one resides. The question is whether the people in this district have much in common other than Hispanic heritage.

Source: www.nationalatlas.gov

equal protection clause of the Constitution. In 1995, the Supreme Court agreed with this argument when it declared that Georgia's new Eleventh Congressional District was unconstitutional. The district stretched from Atlanta to the Atlantic, splitting eight counties and five municipalities along the way. The Court referred to the district as a "monstrosity" linking "widely spaced urban centers that have absolutely nothing to do with each other." The Court went on to say that when a state assigns voters on the basis of race, "it engages in the offensive and demeaning assumption that voters of a particular race, because of their race, think alike, share the same political interests, and will prefer the same candidates at the polls." The Court also chastised the Justice Department for concluding that race-based districting was mandated under the Voting Rights Act of 1965: "When the Justice Department's interpretation of the Act compels race-based districting, it by definition raises a serious constitutional question."[11] In subsequent rulings, the Court affirmed its position that when race is the dominant factor in the drawing of congressional district lines, the districts are unconstitutional.

Changing Directions

In the early 2000s, the Supreme Court seemed to take a new direction on racial redistricting challenges. In a 2000 case, the Court limited the federal government's authority to invalidate changes in state and local elections on the basis that the changes were discriminatory. The case involved a proposed school redistricting

11. *Miller v. Johnson,* 515 U.S. 900 (1995).

plan in Louisiana. The Court held that federal approval for the plan could not be withheld simply because the plan was discriminatory. Rather, the test was whether the plan left racial and ethnic minorities worse off than they were before.[12]

In 2001, the Supreme Court reviewed, for a second time, a case involving North Carolina's Twelfth District. The district was 165 miles long, following Interstate 85, for the most part. According to a local joke, the district was so narrow that a car traveling down the interstate highway with both doors open would kill most of the voters in the district. In 1996, the Supreme Court had held that the district was unconstitutional because race had been the dominant factor in drawing its boundaries. Shortly thereafter, the boundaries were redrawn, but the district was again challenged as a racial gerrymander. A federal district court agreed and invalidated the new boundaries as unconstitutional. In 2001, however, the Supreme Court held that there was insufficient evidence for the lower court's conclusion that race had been the dominant factor when the boundaries were redrawn.[13] The Twelfth District's boundaries remained as drawn.

Perks and Privileges

Legislators have many benefits that are not available to most workers. For example, members of Congress are granted generous **franking** privileges that permit them to mail newsletters, surveys, and other correspondence to their constituents. The annual cost of congressional mail has risen from $11 million in 1971 to more than $70 million today. Typically, the costs for these mailings rise substantially during election years.

Franking
A policy that enables members of Congress to send material through the mail by substituting their facsimile signature (frank) for postage.

Permanent Professional Staffs

More than 30,000 people are employed in the Capitol Hill bureaucracy. About half of them are personal and committee staff members. The personal staff includes office clerks and secretaries; professionals who deal with media relations, draft legislation, and satisfy constituency requests for service; and staffers who maintain local offices in the member's home district or state.

The average Senate office on Capitol Hill employs about 30 staff members, and twice that number work on the personal staffs of senators from the most populous states. House office staffs typically are limited to 18 employees. The number of staff members has increased dramatically since 1960. With the bulk of those increases coming in assistants to individual members, some scholars question whether staff members are really advising on legislation or are primarily aiding constituents and gaining votes in the next election.

Congress also benefits from the expertise of the professional staffs of agencies created to produce information for members of the House and Senate. For example, the Congressional Research Service, the Government Accountability Office, and the Congressional Budget Office all provide reports, audits, and policy recommendations for review by members of Congress.

Privileges and Immunities under the Law

Members of Congress also benefit from some special constitutional protections. Under Article I, Section 6, of the Constitution, they "shall in all Cases, except Treason, Felony and Breach of the Peace, be privileged from Arrest during their Attendance at the Session of their respective Houses, and in going to and returning from the same;

---

12. *Reno v. Bossier Parish School Board*, 528 U.S. 320 (2000).
13. *Easley v. Cromartie*, 532 U.S. 234 (2001).

Members of the Congressional Black Caucus applaud their chairman, Representative Emanuel Cleaver, as he makes remarks at a town hall meeting in California.

© ZUMA Wire Service/Alamy

and for any Speech or Debate in either House, they shall not be questioned in any other Place." The arrest immunity clause is not really an important provision today. The "speech or debate" clause, however, means that a member may make any allegations or other statements he or she wishes in connection with official duties and normally not be sued for libel or slander or otherwise be subject to legal action.

Congressional Caucuses: Another Source of Support

All members of Congress are members of one or more caucuses. The most important caucuses are those established by the parties in each chamber. These Democratic and Republican meetings provide information to the members and devise legislative strategy for the party. Other caucuses bring together members who have similar political views, such as the moderate Democratic Study Group, while some have a constituency focus, such as the Rust Belt Caucus or the Potato Caucus. Some of the most important and influential caucuses are those for minority and underrepresented groups in Congress.

The Congressional Women's Caucus has long provided support for the relatively few women who were elected to the Congress and has provided a forum for discussing issues that women members find important. Among the other minority or ethnic-based caucuses, two of the most important are the Congressional Black Caucus and the Hispanic Congressional Caucus. Both of these associations have grown in the last two decades as the numbers of African American and Hispanic members grew. These organizations, which are now funded by businesses and special interests, provide staff assistance and information for members of Congress and help them build support among specific groups of voters. Additionally, the caucuses provide internships and scholarships for students as a way to recruit political leaders for the future.

■ **Learning Outcome 4:**
Discuss the importance of committees to the lawmaking process and to the ability of members of Congress to do their jobs.

The Committee Structure

Most of the actual work of legislating is performed by the committees and subcommittees within Congress. Thousands of bills are introduced in every session of Congress, and no single member can possibly be adequately informed on all the issues that arise. The committee system is a way to provide for specialization, or a division of the legislative labor. Members of a committee can concentrate on just one area or topic—such as taxation or energy—and develop sufficient expertise to draft appropriate legislation when needed. The flow of legislation through both the House and the Senate is determined largely by the speed with which the members of these committees act on bills and resolutions.

The Power of Committees

Sometimes called "little legislatures," committees usually have the final say on pieces of legislation.[14] Committee actions may be overturned on the floor by the House or Senate, but this rarely happens. Legislators normally defer to the expertise of the chairperson and other members of the committee who speak on the floor in defense of a committee decision. Chairpersons of committees exercise control over the scheduling of hearings and formal action on a bill. They also decide which subcommittee will act on legislation falling within their committee's jurisdiction.

Committees only very rarely are deprived of control over a bill—although this kind of action is provided for in the rules of each chamber. In the House, if a bill has been considered by a standing committee for 30 days, the signatures of a majority (218) of the House membership on a **discharge petition** can pry a bill out of an uncooperative committee's hands. From 1909 to 2007, however, although more than 900 such petitions were initiated, only slightly more than two dozen resulted in successful discharge efforts. Of those, 20 resulted in bills that passed the House.[15]

Types of Congressional Committees

Over the past two centuries, Congress has created several different types of committees, each of which serves particular needs of the institution.

Standing Committees. By far the most important committees in Congress are the **standing committees**— permanent bodies that are established by the rules of each chamber of Congress and that continue from session to session. A list of the standing committees of the 112th Congress is presented in Table 11–5. In addition, most of the standing committees have created subcommittees to carry out their work. For example, the 110th Congress had 68 subcommittees in the Senate and 88 in the House.[16] Each standing committee is given a specific area of legislative policy jurisdiction, and almost all legislative measures are considered by the appropriate standing committees.

Discharge Petition
A procedure by which a bill in the House of Representatives may be forced (discharged) out of a committee that has refused to report it for consideration by the House. The petition must be signed by an absolute majority (218) of representatives and is used only on rare occasions.

Standing Committee
A permanent committee in the House or Senate that considers bills within a certain subject area.

Representative Nydia M. Velazquez, D., N.Y., the first Puerto Rican woman elected to Congress, praises the achievements of Supreme Court Justice Sonia Sotomayor, the first Latina member of the Court.

AP Photo/J. Scott Applewhite

---

14. The term *little legislatures* is from Woodrow Wilson, *Congressional Government* (New York: Meridian Books, 1956 [first published in 1885]).
15. Congressional Quarterly, Inc., *Guide to Congress*, 5th ed. (Washington, DC: CQ Press, 2000); and authors' update.
16. *Congressional Directory* (Washington, DC: U.S. Government Printing Office, various editions).

Table 11–5 ▶ **Standing Committees of the 112th Congress, 2011–2013**

HOUSE COMMITTEES	SENATE COMMITTEES
Agriculture	Agriculture, Nutrition, and Forestry
Appropriations	Appropriations
Armed Services	Armed Services
Budget	Banking, Housing, and Urban Affairs
Education and the Workforce	Budget
Energy and Commerce	Commerce, Science, and Transportation
Financial Services	Energy and Natural Resources
Foreign Affairs	Environment and Public Works
Homeland Security	Finance
House Administration	Foreign Relations
Judiciary	Health, Education, Labor, and Pensions
Natural Resources	Homeland Security and Governmental Affairs
Oversight and Government Reform	Judiciary
Rules	Rules and Administration
Science, Space and Technology	Small Business and Entrepreneurship
Small Business	Veterans Affairs
Transportation and Infrastructure	
Veterans Affairs	
Ways and Means	

did you know?

Samuel Morse demonstrated his telegraph to Congress in 1843 by stretching wire between two committee rooms.

Select Committee
A temporary legislative committee established for a limited time period and for a special purpose.

Joint Committee
A legislative committee composed of members from both chambers of Congress.

Because of the importance of their work and the traditional influence of their members in Congress, certain committees are considered to be more prestigious than others. Seats on standing committees that handle spending issues are especially sought after because members can use these positions to benefit their constituents. Committees that control spending include the Appropriations Committee in either chamber and the Ways and Means Committee in the House. Members also normally seek seats on committees that handle matters of special interest to their constituents. A member of the House from an agricultural district, for example, will have an interest in joining the House Agriculture Committee.

Select Committees. In principle, a **select committee** is created for a limited time and for a specific legislative purpose. For example, a select committee may be formed to investigate a public problem, such as child nutrition or aging. In practice, a select committee, such as the Select Committee on Intelligence in each chamber, may continue indefinitely. Select committees rarely create original legislation.

Joint Committees. A **joint committee** is formed by the concurrent action of both chambers of Congress and consists of members from each chamber. Joint committees, which may be permanent or temporary, have dealt with the economy, taxation, and the Library of Congress.

Conference Committees. Special joint committees—**conference committees**—are formed to achieve agreement between the House and the Senate on the exact wording of legislative acts when the two chambers pass legislative proposals in different forms. The bill is reported out of the conference committee if it is approved by the majority of members from both houses who sit on the committee. It is then returned to the House and Senate for final votes. No bill can be sent to the White House to be signed into law unless it first passes both chambers in identical form. Sometimes called the "third house" of Congress, conference committees are in a position to make significant alterations to legislation and frequently become the focal point of policy debates.

Conference Committee
A special joint committee appointed to reconcile differences when bills pass the two chambers of Congress in different forms.

The House Rules Committee. Because of its special "gatekeeping" power over the terms on which legislation will reach the floor of the House of Representatives, the House Rules Committee holds a uniquely powerful position. A special committee rule sets the time limit on debate and determines whether and how a bill may be amended. This practice dates back to 1883. The Rules Committee has the unusual power to meet while the House is in session, to have its resolutions considered immediately on the floor, and to initiate legislation on its own.

The Selection of Committee Members

In both chambers, members are appointed to standing committees by the Steering Committee of their party. The majority-party member with the longest term of continuous service on a standing committee can be given preference when the leadership nominates chairpersons. Newt Gingrich, during his time as Speaker in the House, restricted chairpersons' terms to six years. Additionally, he bypassed seniority to appoint chairpersons loyal to his own platform.

Respecting seniority is an informal, traditional process, and it applies to other significant posts in Congress as well. The **seniority system,** although it deliberately treats members unequally, provides a predictable means of assigning positions of power within Congress. The most senior member of the minority party is called the *ranking committee member* for that party.

Seniority System
A custom followed in both chambers of Congress specifying that the member of the majority party with the longest term of continuous service will be given preference when a committee chairperson (or a holder of some other significant post) is selected.

The general pattern until the 1970s was that members of the House or Senate who represented **safe seats** would be reelected continually and eventually would accumulate enough years of continuous committee service to enable them to become the chairpersons of their committees. In the 1970s, a number of reforms in the chairperson selection process somewhat modified the seniority system. The reforms introduced the use of a secret ballot in electing House committee chairpersons and allowed for the possibility of choosing a chairperson on a basis other than seniority. The Democrats immediately replaced three senior chairpersons who were out of step with the rest of their party. The Republican leadership in the House has also taken more control over the selection of committee chairpersons.

Safe Seat
A district that returns a legislator with 55 percent of the vote or more.

The Formal Leadership

The limited amount of centralized power that exists in Congress is exercised through party-based mechanisms. Congress is organized by party. When the Democratic Party, for example, wins a majority of seats in either the House or the Senate, Democrats control the official positions of power in that chamber, and every important committee has a Democratic chairperson and a majority of Democratic members. The same process holds when Republicans are in the

■ Learning Outcome 5:
Describe the leadership structure in each house of Congress, noting the differences between the House and the Senate.

Speaker of the House
The presiding officer in the House of Representatives. The Speaker is always a member of the majority party and is the most powerful and influential member of the House.

majority. For a complete list of the current leadership of both parties in the House of Representatives, go to www.house.gov.

Generally speaking, the leadership organizations in the House and the Senate look alike on paper. However, leaders in the House of Representatives have more control over the agenda of the body and, often, over their own party's members. Senate leaders, due to the power of individual members, must work closely with the other party's leaders to achieve success. Although the party leaders in both the House and the Senate are considered to be the most powerful members of the Congress, their powers pale compared to those given to the leaders in true "party government" legislatures. The differences between those legislatures and the U.S. Congress are detailed in the Beyond Our Borders feature.

Leadership in the House

The House leadership is made up of the Speaker, the majority and minority leaders, and the party whips.

The Speaker. The foremost power holder in the House of Representatives is the **Speaker of the House.** The Speaker's position is technically a nonpartisan one, but in fact, for the better part of two centuries, the Speaker has been the official leader of the majority party in the House. When a new Congress convenes in January of odd-numbered years, each party nominates a candidate for Speaker. All Democratic members of the House are expected to vote for their party's nominee, and all Republicans are expected to support their candidate. The vote to organize the House is the one vote in which representatives must vote with their party. In a sense, this vote defines a member's partisan status.

The influence of modern-day Speakers is based primarily on their personal prestige, persuasive ability, and knowledge of the legislative process—plus the acquiescence or active support of other representatives. In recent years, both the Republican and Democratic parties in the House have given their leaders more power in making appointments and controlling the agenda. The major formal powers of the Speaker include the following:

1. Presiding over meetings of the House.
2. Appointing members of joint committees and conference committees.
3. Scheduling legislation for floor action.
4. Deciding points of order and interpreting the rules with the advice of the House parliamentarian.
5. Referring bills and resolutions to the appropriate standing committees of the House.

A Speaker may take part in floor debate and vote, as can any other member of Congress, but recent Speakers usually have voted only to break a tie. Since 1975, the Speaker, when a Democrat, has also had the power to appoint the Democratic Steering Committee, which determines new committee assignments for House party members.

In general, the powers of the Speaker are related to his or her control over information and communications channels in the House and the degree of support received from members. This is a significant power in a large, decentralized institution in which information is a very important resource. Since the Speakership of Newt Gingrich (R., Ga.) in 1994, the leadership of the House has held significant power to control the agenda and provide rewards to the members. During the same time period, the degree of polarization between the majority and minority parties has increased, and cohesion within each party has grown stronger.

Beyond Our Borders
SHOULD PARTIES CONTROL LEGISLATURES (AND GOVERNMENTS)?

The Congress of the United States is, as you know, a bicameral legislature. The American-style legislature differs from most of the legislatures in the world in several significant ways. Because the U.S. government is composed of three branches, separate structures sharing powers, we frequently have "divided" government, meaning that the party that controls one or both houses of Congress does not control the presidency. Does this mean that the government is hopelessly deadlocked? Not usually. Members of Congress, especially in the House, frequently support their party leaders, but on many other votes, they "cross the aisle" to vote with members of the other side, thinking it best for their constituency or for their reelection.

Most Americans think that our legislature is modeled on the British parliament. However, the parliament of Great Britain, as well as that of many other Western nations, is based on the idea of "party government." No separation of powers exists between the legislature and the executive branch. What does this mean? When a political party wins a majority of seats in the House of Parliament (the lower and only powerful house), that party then selects the prime minister, who is also the party leader. The prime minister and his or her cabinet members actually sit in Parliament during debates, where they play an active role. The party, which may have promised "lemonade in every drinking fountain" or a better welfare system, votes the new law into effect, and the prime minister implements the new policy.*

Similar systems with two major parties and some minor parties are in effect in Canada and other nations as well. Another variation on this type of party government occurs when a nation such as Germany, Italy, or Israel has a multiparty system. In that case, no party wins a majority of seats. The party with the plurality of seats chooses the leader and then negotiates with other parties to form a coalition to constitute a government and pass new legislation. Governing as part of a coalition is much more difficult, however, because if one partner does not agree with the proposed policy, the coalition may fall apart, and new elections may be necessary.

Consider the important relationship between the executive (prime minister or president) and the legislature. In the U.S. system, even if the Congress and the president are of the same party, this does not guarantee that the president's agenda will be fully carried out. Although George W. Bush was able to get much of his legislation passed in the early years of his administration, he could not get

support for reforming Social Security in 2005. Mr. Obama, who came into office with a very large majority in the House of Representatives, received speedy and cohesive support for his initiatives in his first year, but legislation often bogged down in the Senate due to its procedural rules. In fact, both the Democrats and the Republicans in the House were so cohesive throughout much of those years that some scholars believed it was a form of "conditional party government."** In a true party government system, everything on the Democrats' agenda would become law, and the president would be selected by the Congress.

Although Americans complain bitterly about ineffective Congresses, they generally prefer divided government due to fear that one party will have too much power.

Press Association via AP Images

Deputy Prime Minister Nick Clegg (5th from right) and Prime Minister David Cameron of Great Britain respond to members of Parliament during the Question Hour in May, 2010.

FOR CRITICAL ANALYSIS

1. *Would the United States ever give the kind of power to the president to achieve his or her agenda that is given to the prime minister of Great Britain?*

2. *What is more important—controlling government power or having a more effective legislature?*

3. *How would the United States Congress be different if three or four parties were represented there?*

*For information on the world's legislatures, go to the Web site of the Inter-Parliamentary Union at www.ipu.org.
**The "conditional party government" thesis has been developed by David Rohde, *Parties and Leaders in the Postreform House* (Chicago: University of Chicago Press, 1991).

Scholars suggest that this is the result of increased ideological makeup within the congressional delegation of both parties and the election of fewer moderate or centrist members to the House of Representatives.

The Majority Leader. The **majority leader of the House** is elected by a caucus of the majority party to foster cohesion among party members and to act as a spokesperson for the party. The majority leader influences the scheduling of debate and acts as the chief supporter of the Speaker. The majority leader cooperates with the Speaker and other party leaders, both inside and outside Congress, to formulate the party's legislative program and to guide that program through the legislative process in the House. The Democrats often recruit future Speakers from those who hold that position.

The Minority Leader. The **minority leader of the House** is the candidate nominated for Speaker by a caucus of the minority party. Like the majority leader, the leader of the minority party has as her or his primary responsibility the maintaining of cohesion within the party's ranks. The minority leader works for cohesion among the party's members and speaks on behalf of the president if the minority party controls the White House. In relations with the majority party, the minority leader consults with both the Speaker and the majority leader on recognizing members who wish to speak on the floor, on House rules and procedures, and on the scheduling of legislation. Minority leaders have no actual power in these areas, however.

Whips. The leadership of each party includes assistants to the majority and minority leaders, known as whips. The **whips** are members of Congress who assist the party leaders by passing information down from the leadership to party members and by ensuring that members show up for floor debate and cast their votes on important issues. Whips conduct polls among party members about the members' views on legislation, inform the leaders about whose vote is doubtful and whose is certain, and may exert pressure on members to support the leaders' positions. In the House, serving as a whip is the first step toward positions of higher leadership.

Leadership in the Senate

The Senate is less than one-fourth the size of the House. This fact alone probably explains why a formal, complex, and centralized leadership structure is not as necessary in the Senate as it is in the House. For a list of the current leaders of both parties in the U.S. Senate, go to www.senate.gov.

The two highest-ranking formal leadership positions in the Senate are essentially ceremonial in nature. Under the Constitution, the vice president of the United States is the president (that is, the presiding officer) of the Senate and may vote to break a tie. The vice president, however, is only rarely present for a meeting of the Senate. The Senate elects instead a **president pro tempore** ("pro tem") to preside over the Senate in the vice president's absence. Ordinarily, the president pro tem is the member of the majority party with the longest continuous term of service in the Senate. The president pro tem is mostly a ceremonial position. Junior senators take turns actually presiding over the sessions of the Senate.

The real leadership power in the Senate rests in the hands of the **Senate majority leader,** the **Senate minority leader,** and their respective whips. The Senate majority and minority leaders have the right to be recognized first in debate on the floor and generally exercise the same powers available to the

Majority Leader of the House
A legislative position held by an important party member in the House of Representatives. The majority leader is selected by the majority party in caucus or conference to foster cohesion among party members and to act as spokesperson for the majority party in the House.

Minority Leader of the House
The party leader elected by the minority party in the House.

Whip
A member of Congress who aids the majority or minority leader of the House or the Senate.

President Pro Tempore
The temporary presiding officer of the Senate in the absence of the vice president.

Senate Majority Leader
The chief spokesperson of the majority party in the Senate, who directs the legislative program and party strategy.

Senate Minority Leader
The party officer in the Senate who commands the minority party's opposition to the policies of the majority party and directs the legislative program and strategy of his or her party.

House majority and minority leaders. They control the scheduling of debate on the floor in conjunction with the majority party's Policy Committee, influence the allocation of committee assignments for new members or for senators attempting to transfer to a new committee, influence the selection of other party officials, and participate in selecting members of conference committees. The leaders are expected to mobilize support for partisan legislative initiatives or for the proposals of a president who belongs to their party. The leaders act as liaisons with the White House when the president is of their party, try to obtain the cooperation of committee chairpersons, and seek to facilitate the smooth functioning of the Senate through the senators' unanimous consent. The majority and minority leaders are elected by their respective party caucuses.

Senate party whips, like their House counterparts, maintain communication within the party on platform positions and try to ensure that party colleagues are present for floor debate and important votes. The Senate whip system is far less elaborate than its counterpart in the House, simply because there are fewer members to track.

AP Photo/Pablo Martinez Monsivais

Senate Majority Leader Harry Reid of Nevada, left, and Senate Minority Leader Mitch McConnell of Kentucky arrive at a meeting with the president on health care reform in 2010.

How Members of Congress Decide

Each member of Congress casts hundreds of votes in each session. Each member compiles a record of votes during the years that he or she spends in the national legislature. Any particular vote is cast for several different reasons. Research shows that the best predictor of a member's vote is party affiliation. Obviously, party members do have common opinions on some, if not all, issues facing the nation. In addition, the party leadership in each house works hard to build cohesion and agreement among the members through the activities of the party caucuses and conferences. In recent years, the increase in partisanship in both the House and the Senate has meant that most Republicans are voting in opposition to most Democrats.

■ **Learning Outcome 6:**
Demonstrate how a bill becomes a law, and explain how the different processes in the House and the Senate influence legislating.

The Conservative Coalition

Political parties are not always unified. In the 1950s and 1960s, the Democrats in Congress were often split between northern liberals and southern conservatives. This division gave rise to the **conservative coalition,** a voting bloc made up of conservative Democrats and conservative (which is to say, most) Republicans. This coalition was able to win many votes over the years. Today, however, most southern conservatives are Republicans, so the coalition has almost disappeared. Some Democrats in Congress, however, represent more moderate states or districts. The votes of these members, who are known as **Blue Dog Democrats,** are frequently sought after by Republican leaders.

"Crossing Over"

On some votes, individual representatives and senators will vote against their party, "crossing over to the other side" because the interests of their states or districts differ from the interests that prevail within the rest of their party. In some

Conservative Coalition
An alliance of Republicans and southern Democrats that can form in the House or the Senate to oppose liberal legislation and support conservative legislation.

Blue Dog Democrats
Members of Congress from more moderate states or districts who sometimes "cross over" to vote with Republicans on legislation.

Earmarks
Funding appropriations that are specifically designated for a named project in a member's state or district.

Pork
Special projects or appropriations that are intended to benefit a member's district or state; slang term for earmarks.

cases, members vote a certain way because of the influence of regional or national interests. Other voting decisions are based on the members' religious or ideological beliefs. Votes on issues such as abortion or gay rights may be motivated by a member's religious views.

With so many voting decisions, every member cannot be fully informed on each issue. Research suggests that many voting decisions are based on cues provided by trusted colleagues or the party leadership. A member who sits on the committee that wrote a law may become a reliable source of information about that law. Alternatively, a member may turn to a colleague who represents a district in the same state or one who represents a similar district for cues on voting. Cues may also come from fellow committee members, leaders, and the administration.

Logrolling, Earmarks, and "Pork"

Sometimes, leaders on either side of the aisle will offer incentives to get needed votes for the passage of legislation. Even the president has been known to offer opportunities for the member to better serve his or her district through "bringing home the bacon." When a member "trades" his or her vote on a particular bill with another member in exchange for his or her vote on other legislation, the practice is known as logrolling, described earlier in the chapter. Often members request that special appropriations for projects back home are attached to a bill to gain their votes. If the actual project is named, this is referred to as an **earmark.** The term comes from the V-shaped mark that is cut in a pig's ear to identify the animal. The special projects that are so identified are often referred to as **pork,** as in bringing home the bacon or pork. Although the practice of special appropriations has a long history, the amounts now being earmarked equal more than $30 billion in most years. Efforts have been made to force lawmakers to reveal all of their special projects, but new methods have been found to hide these special appropriations from the public eye.

Politicians and reformers often rail against the practice of earmarks, and some projects seem absolutely silly to everyone except the people or state that will benefit. In some cases, earmarks truly are needed; in others, they are seen as the key to keeping a member of Congress in office. As the late Senator Robert Byrd of West Virginia was known to remark, "One man's pork is another man's job."[17]

How a Bill Becomes Law

Each year, Congress and the president propose and approve many laws. Some are budget and appropriations laws that require extensive bargaining but must be passed for the government to continue to function. Other laws are relatively free of controversy and are passed with little dissension. Still other proposed legislation is extremely controversial and reaches to the roots of differences between Democrats and Republicans and between the executive and legislative branches.

As detailed in Figure 11–5, each law begins as a bill, which must be introduced in either the House or the Senate. Often, similar bills are introduced in both chambers. A "money bill," however, must start in the House. In each chamber, the bill follows similar steps. It is referred to a committee and its subcommittees for study, discussion, hearings, and rewriting ("markup"). When the bill is reported out to the full chamber, it must be scheduled for debate (by the Rules Committee in the House and by the leadership in the Senate). After the bill has been passed

17. "Just Say No to Earmarks," *Wall Street Journal,* editorial, October 4, 2006.

Figure 11-5 ▶ How a Bill Becomes Law

This illustration shows the most typical way in which proposed legislation is enacted into law. Most legislation begins as similar bills introduced into the House and the Senate. The process is illustrated here with two hypothetical bills, House bill No. 100 (HR 100) and Senate bill No. 200 (S 200). The path of HR 100 is shown on the left, and that of S 200, on the right.

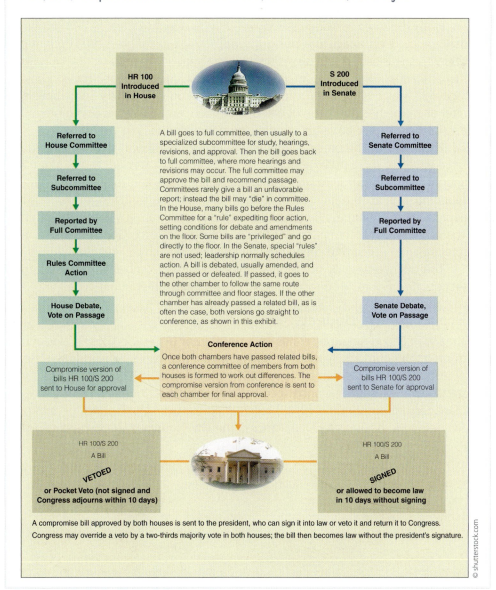

HR 100 Introduced in House

S 200 Introduced in Senate

Referred to House Committee

Referred to Subcommittee

Reported by Full Committee

Rules Committee Action

House Debate, Vote on Passage

A bill goes to full committee, then usually to a specialized subcommittee for study, hearings, revisions, and approval. Then the bill goes back to full committee, where more hearings and revisions may occur. The full committee may approve the bill and recommend passage. Committees rarely give a bill an unfavorable report; instead the bill may "die" in committee. In the House, many bills go before the Rules Committee for a "rule" expediting floor action, setting conditions for debate and amendments on the floor. Some bills are "privileged" and go directly to the floor. In the Senate, special "rules" are not used; leadership normally schedules action. A bill is debated, usually amended, and then passed or defeated. If passed, it goes to the other chamber to follow the same route through committee and floor stages. If the other chamber has already passed a related bill, as is often the case, both versions go straight to conference, as shown in this exhibit.

Referred to Senate Committee

Referred to Subcommittee

Reported by Full Committee

Senate Debate, Vote on Passage

Conference Action
Once both chambers have passed related bills, a conference committee of members from both houses is formed to work out differences. The compromise version from conference is sent to each chamber for final approval.

Compromise version of bills HR 100/S 200 sent to House for approval

Compromise version of bills HR 100/S 200 sent to Senate for approval

HR 100/S 200
A Bill
VETOED
or Pocket Veto (not signed and Congress adjourns within 10 days)

HR 100/S 200
A Bill
SIGNED
or allowed to become law in 10 days without signing

A compromise bill approved by both houses is sent to the president, who can sign it into law or veto it and return it to Congress. Congress may override a veto by a two-thirds majority vote in both houses; the bill then becomes law without the president's signature.

© shutterstock.com

in each chamber, if it contains different provisions, a conference committee is formed to write a compromise bill, which must be approved by both chambers before it is sent to the president to sign or veto.

Another form of congressional action, the *joint resolution*, differs little from a bill in how it is proposed or debated. Once it is approved by both chambers and signed by the president, it has the force of law.[18] A joint resolution to amend the Constitution, however, after it is approved by two-thirds of both chambers, is sent not to the president but to the states for ratification.

---

18. In contrast, *simple resolutions* and *concurrent resolutions* do not carry the force of law, but rather are used by one or both chambers of Congress, respectively, to express facts, principles, or opinions. For example, a concurrent resolution is used to set the time when Congress will adjourn.

How Much Will the Government Spend?

The Constitution is very clear about where the power of the purse lies in the national government: All taxing or spending bills must originate in the House of Representatives. Today, much of the business of Congress is concerned with approving government expenditures through the budget process and with raising the revenues to pay for government programs.

From 1922, when Congress required the president to prepare and present to the legislature an **executive budget,** until 1974, the congressional budget process was so disjointed that it was difficult to visualize the total picture of government finances. The president presented the executive budget to Congress in January. It was broken down into 13 or more appropriations bills. Some time later, after all of the bills had been debated, amended, and passed, it was more or less possible to estimate total government spending for the next year.

Frustrated by the president's ability to impound, or withhold, funds and dissatisfied with the entire budget process, Congress passed the Budget and Impoundment Control Act of 1974 to regain some control over the nation's spending. The act required the president to spend the funds that Congress had appropriated, ending the president's ability to kill programs by withholding funds. The other major accomplishment of the act was to force Congress to examine total national taxing and spending at least twice in each budget cycle.

The budget cycle of the federal government is described in the rest of this section. (See Figure 11–6 for a graphic illustration of the budget cycle.)

Preparing the Budget

The federal government operates on a **fiscal year (FY)** cycle. The fiscal year runs from October through September, so that fiscal 2009, or FY09, runs from October 1, 2008, through September 30, 2009. Eighteen months before a fiscal year starts, the executive branch begins preparing the budget. The Office of Management and Budget (OMB) receives advice from the Council of Economic Advisers and the Treasury Department. The OMB outlines the budget and then

Executive Budget
The budget prepared and submitted by the president to Congress.

Fiscal Year (FY)
A 12-month period that is used for bookkeeping, or accounting, purposes. Usually, the fiscal year does not coincide with the calendar year. For example, the federal government's fiscal year runs from October 1 through September 30.

Figure 11–6 ▶ The Budget Cycle

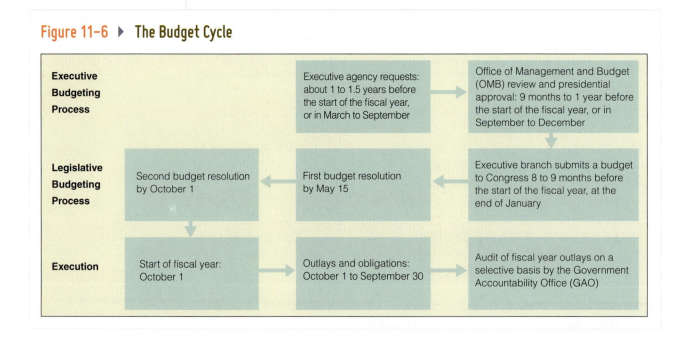

Executive Budgeting Process		Executive agency requests: about 1 to 1.5 years before the start of the fiscal year, or in March to September	Office of Management and Budget (OMB) review and presidential approval: 9 months to 1 year before the start of the fiscal year, or in September to December
Legislative Budgeting Process	Second budget resolution by October 1	First budget resolution by May 15	Executive branch submits a budget to Congress 8 to 9 months before the start of the fiscal year, at the end of January
Execution	Start of fiscal year: October 1	Outlays and obligations: October 1 to September 30	Audit of fiscal year outlays on a selective basis by the Government Accountability Office (GAO)

sends it to the various departments and agencies. Bargaining follows, in which—to use only two of many examples—the Department of Health and Human Services argues for more welfare spending, and the armed forces argue for more defense spending.

Even though the OMB has only 600 employees, it is one of the most powerful agencies in Washington. It assembles the budget documents and monitors federal agencies throughout each year. Every year, it begins the budget process with a **spring review,** in which it requires all of the agencies to review their programs, activities, and goals. At the beginning of each summer, the OMB sends out a letter instructing agencies to submit their requests for funding for the next fiscal year. By the end of the summer, each agency must submit a formal request to the OMB.

In actuality, the "budget season" begins with the **fall review.** At this time, the OMB looks at budget requests and, in almost all cases, routinely cuts them back. Although the OMB works within guidelines established by the president, specific decisions often are left to the OMB director and the director's associates. By the beginning of November, the director's review begins. The director meets with cabinet secretaries and budget officers. Time becomes crucial. The budget must be completed by January so that it can be included in the *Economic Report of the President.*

Congress Faces the Budget

In January, nine months before the fiscal year starts, the president takes the OMB's proposed budget, approves it, and submits it to Congress. Then the congressional budgeting process takes over. The budgeting process involves two steps. First, Congress must authorize funds to be spent. The **authorization** is a formal declaration by the appropriate congressional committee that a certain amount of funding may be available to an agency. Congressional committees and subcommittees look at the proposals from the executive branch and the Congressional Budget Office in making the decision to authorize funds. After the funds are authorized, they must be appropriated by Congress. The appropriations committees of both the House and the Senate forward spending bills to their respective bodies. The **appropriation** of funds occurs when the final bill is passed.

The budget process involves large sums. For example, President Barack Obama's proposed budget for fiscal year 2011 called for expenditures of $3.83 trillion, or $3,830,000,000,000. When forming the budget for a given year, Congress and the president must take into account revenues, primarily in the form of taxes, as well as expenditures to balance the budget. If spending exceeds the amount brought in by taxes, the government runs a budget deficit (and increases the public debt). For example, although President Obama's proposed budget for fiscal year 2013 called for expenditures of approximately $3.7 trillion, projected revenues from taxes amounted to only about $2.56 trillion, leaving a deficit of just under $1 billion.

With these large sums in play, representatives and senators who chair key committees find it relatively easy to slip spending proposals into a variety of bills. These proposals may have nothing to do with the ostensible purpose of the bill. Are such earmarked appropriations good policy?

Budget Resolutions

The **first budget resolution** by Congress is scheduled to be passed in May of each year. It sets overall revenue goals and spending targets. During the summer,

---

Spring Review
The annual process in which the Office of Management and Budget requires federal agencies to review their programs, activities, and goals and submit their requests for funding for the next fiscal year.

Fall Review
The annual process in which the Office of Management and Budget, after receiving formal federal agency requests for funding for the next fiscal year, reviews the requests, makes changes, and submits its recommendations to the president.

Authorization
A formal declaration by a legislative committee that a certain amount of funding may be available to an agency. Some authorizations terminate in a year; others are renewable automatically, without further congressional action.

Appropriation
The passage, by Congress, of a spending bill specifying the amount of authorized funds that actually will be allocated for an agency's use.

First Budget Resolution
A resolution passed by Congress in May that sets overall revenue and spending goals for the following fiscal year.

President Barack Obama meets with Republican and Democratic Congressional leaders to solve the debt ceiling crisis of 2011.

© White House Photo/Alamy

Second Budget Resolution
A resolution passed by Congress in September that sets "binding" limits on taxes and spending for the following fiscal year.

Continuing Resolution
A temporary funding law that Congress passes when an appropriations bill has not been decided by the beginning of the new fiscal year on October 1.

bargaining among all the concerned parties takes place. Spending and tax laws that are drawn up during this period are supposed to be guided by the May congressional budget resolution.

By September, Congress is scheduled to pass its **second budget resolution,** one that will set "binding" limits on taxes and spending for the fiscal year beginning October 1. Bills passed before that date that do not fit within the limits of the budget resolution are supposed to be changed.

In actuality, between 1978 and 1996 Congress did not pass a complete budget by October 1. Even more striking is the fact that the Congress did not pass a budget at all in 2009, 2010, or 2011. In other words, generally, Congress does not follow its own rules. In each fiscal year that starts without a budget, every agency operates on the basis of a **continuing resolution,** which enables the agency to keep on doing whatever it was doing the previous year with the same amount of funding. Even continuing resolutions have not always been passed on time.

You Can Make a Difference

WHY SHOULD YOU CARE ABOUT CONGRESS?

The legislation that Congress passes can directly affect your life. Consider, for example, the major reform of American health policy and health insurance passed in 2010. For the time being, this bill will make it possible for young people under 26 to stay on their parents' health insurance policy. When you enter the workplace, the health insurance options that may be offered to you by your employer will be regulated by the new policies. If you have a medical condition that makes obtaining health insurance difficult, the new law will, eventually, prohibit discrimination against you in obtaining health insurance. And, finally, it is likely that these new rules will make health insurance more expensive than it is today.

Additionally, congressional legislation will affect the kind of car you buy, your use of the Internet, your access to cable or satellite TV, and how much you pay for gas for your car. Recent changes in law will make the federal government your source for student loans. So you had better pay attention to what Congress is doing and what your representative or senator is voting for.

You can make a difference in our democracy simply by going to the polls on election day and voting for the candidates you would like to represent you in Congress. It goes without saying, though, that to cast an informed vote, you need to know how your congressional representatives stand on the issues and, if they are incumbents, how they have voted on bills that are important to you.

WHAT CAN YOU DO?

To contact a member of Congress, start by going to the Web sites of the U.S. House of Representatives (www.house.gov) and the U.S. Senate (www.senate.gov). For the House, finding your representative is easy: Just type in your zip code and you will be directed to the member's Web site. For the Senate, look for your state.

Not all congressional Web sites are equally informative. Often, they post pictures of lawmakers, state flags, and events from their districts. Many sites contain congressional biographies, constituent services, sponsored legislation, and contact information. Some congressional sites have interactive polls and regularly updated blogs. In 2007, the Sunlight Foundation conducted the

Courtesy of Congresswoman Sheila Jackson Lee/United States House of Representatives

Congresswoman Sheila Jackson Lee lists her voting record on her Web site, making it easy for constituents to track her positions on issues they care about.

Congressional Web Site Investigation Project. This group wanted to examine how well members of Congress spend taxpayer money to maintain official Web sites. They used everyday citizens to evaluate their own congressional representatives' sites for transparency and accountability. Do these Web sites allow responsible citizens to exercise oversight over their representatives and hold them accountable for their performance? Go to www.sunlightlabs.com to find the project's results.

You can also contact your representatives using one of the following addresses or phone numbers:

United States House of Representatives
Washington, DC 20515
202-224-3121
United States Senate
Washington, DC 20510
202-224-3121

Interest groups also track the voting records of members of Congress and rate the members on the issues. Project Vote Smart is supported by thousands of volunteers, conservative and liberal, who research the backgrounds and records of thousands of political candidates and elected officials to provide citizens with their voting records, campaign contributions, public statements, biographical data, and evaluations from more than 150 competing special-interest groups. You can contact Project Vote Smart at

Project Vote Smart
One Common Ground
Philipsburg, MT 59858
1-888-VOTE-SMART (1-888-868-3762)
www.votesmart.org

Nonpartisan, independent, and nonprofit, the Center for Responsive Politics (CRP) educates voters through research that tracks campaign contributions and lobbying data. They "count cash to make change" in government and strive to inform voters about how money in politics affects their lives. You can contact the CRP at

The Center for Responsive Politics

1101 14th St. NW, Suite 1030
Washington, DC 20005-5635
202-857-0044
www.opensecrets.org

REFERENCES

Kelly McCormack, "Congressional Websites: The Bright, Bland and Bizarre," The Hill.com, accessed June 20, 2007.

Conor Kenny, "Participatory Democracy: Rate Your Senator's and Representative's Web Pages," PRWatch.org, accessed February 21, 2007.

"About Project Vote Smart," http://votesmart.org/about.

Key Terms

appropriation 371

authorization 371

bicameralism 341

Blue Dog Democrats 367

casework 343

conference committee 363

conservative coalition 367

constituent 341

continuing resolution 372

direct primary 352

discharge petition 361

earmarks 368

enumerated power 345

executive budget 370

fall review 371

filibuster 348

first budget resolution 371

fiscal year (FY) 370

franking 359

gerrymandering 354

hillstyle 341

homestyle 341

instructed delegate 343

joint committee 362

justiciable question 354

lawmaking 342

logrolling 342

majority leader of the House 366

minority leader of the House 366

ombudsperson 343

oversight 344

party identifier 352

pork 368

president pro tempore 366

reapportionment 354

redistricting 354

representation 342

Rule 348

Rules Committee 348

safe seat 363

second budget resolution 372

select committee 362

Senate majority leader 366

Senate minority leader 366

seniority system 363

Speaker of the House 364

spring review 371

standing committee 361

trustee 342

Unanimous Consent Agreement 348

unorthodox lawmaking 349

whip 366

Chapter Summary

1. The authors of the Constitution believed that the bulk of national power should be in the legislature because it represents the voters most directly. All legislative power rests in the Congress. The Constitution states that Congress will consist of two chambers. A result of the Connecticut Compromise, this bicameral structure established a balanced legislature, with the membership in the House of Representatives based on population and the membership in the Senate based on the equality of states.

2. Members of the House and the Senate cultivate votes in their constituencies through providing services, visiting,

and bringing home federal dollars for projects. At the same time, they must participate in debate and lawmaking for the nation as a whole, including casting votes for legislation that may be of no interest to their constituents or may, in fact, not be beneficial to them. The career of a legislator is determined both by his or her reelection and by the party leadership in Congress, so fulfilling both roles is necessary.

The functions of Congress include (1) lawmaking, (2) representation, (3) service to constituents, (4) oversight, (5) public education, and (6) conflict resolution.

3. The first 17 clauses of Article I, Section 8, of the Constitution specify most of the enumerated, or expressed, powers of Congress, including the right to impose taxes, to borrow money, to regulate commerce, and to declare war. Besides its enumerated powers, Congress enjoys the right to "make all Laws which shall be necessary and proper for carrying into Execution the foregoing Powers, and all other Powers vested by this Constitution in the Government of the United States, or in any Department or Officer thereof." This is called the elastic, or necessary and proper, clause.

4. The House of Representatives has 435 members, and the Senate has 100 members. Owing to its larger size, the House has more formal rules. The Senate tradition of unlimited debate (filibustering) dates back to 1790 and has been used over the years to frustrate the passage of bills. Under Senate Rule 22, cloture can be used to shut off debate on a bill.

5. Members of Congress are not typical American citizens. They are older and wealthier than most Americans, disproportionately white and male, and more likely to be trained in professional occupations.

6. Congressional elections are operated by the individual state governments, which must abide by rules established by the Constitution and national statutes. Most candidates for Congress must win nomination through a direct primary. The overwhelming majority of incumbent representatives and a smaller proportion of senators who run for reelection are successful. A complicated aspect of congressional elections is apportionment—the allocation of legislative seats to constituencies. The Supreme Court's "one person, one vote" rule has been applied to equalize the populations of congressional and state legislative districts.

7. Members of Congress are well paid and enjoy benefits such as franking privileges. Members of Congress have personal and committee staff members available to them and also receive many legal privileges and immunities.

8. Most of the actual work of legislating is performed by committees and subcommittees within Congress. Legislation introduced into the House or Senate is assigned to the appropriate standing committees for review. Select committees are created for a limited time for a specific purpose. Joint committees are formed by the concurrent action of both chambers and consist of members from each chamber. Conference committees are special joint committees set up to achieve agreement between the House and the Senate on the exact wording of legislative acts passed by both chambers in different forms. The seniority rule, which is usually followed, specifies that the longest-serving member of the majority party will be the chairperson of a committee.

9. The foremost power holder in the House of Representatives is the Speaker of the House. Other leaders are the House majority leader, the House minority leader, and the majority and minority whips. Formally, the vice president is the presiding officer of the Senate, with the most senior member of the majority party serving as the president pro tempore to preside when the vice president is absent. Actual leadership in the Senate rests with the majority leader, the minority leader, and their whips.

10. A bill becomes law by progressing through both chambers of Congress and their appropriate standing and joint committees to the president. Members are usually most influenced in their voting decisions by their party affiliation, their constituency's interests, their own interests, and cues given by other legislators.

11. The budget process for a fiscal year begins with the preparation of an executive budget by the president. This is reviewed by the Office of Management and Budget and then sent to Congress, which is supposed to pass a final budget by the end of September. Since 1978, Congress generally has not followed its own time rules.

Selected Print, Media, and Online Resources

PRINT RESOURCES

Barone, Michael, and Grant Ujifusa. *The Almanac of American Politics, 2012.* Washington, DC: National Journal, 2012. This book, published biannually, is a comprehensive summary of current political information on each member of Congress, his or her state or congressional district, recent congressional election results, key votes, ratings by various organizations, sources of campaign contributions, and records of campaign expenditures.

Davidson, Roger H., and Walter J. Oleszek. *Congress and Its Members,* 13th ed. Washington, DC: CQ Press, 2011. This classic looks carefully at the "two Congresses," the one in Washington and the role played by congresspersons at home.

Draper, Robert. *Do Not Ask What Good We Do.* New York: The Free Press, 2012. Draper, a *New York Times* writer, reveals an insider's view of the Congress and some of its colorful members and criticizes both houses for their ineffectiveness.

Just, Ward S. *The Congressman Who Loved Flaubert.* New York: Carrol and Graf Publishers, 1990. This fictional account of a career politician was first published in 1973 and is still a favorite with students of political science. Ward Just is renowned for his political fiction, and particularly for his examination of character and motivation.

Mann, Thomas B., and Norman J. Ornstein. *The Broken Branch: How Congress Is Failing America and How to Get It Back on Track.* New York: Oxford University Press, 2006. These two political scientists believe that Congress is more dysfunctional now than ever before. They claim excessive partisan bickering and internal rancor are to blame. These two scholars of government and politics present a blueprint for reform.

Rangel, Charles B., and Leon Wynter. *And I Haven't Had a Bad Day Since: The Memoir of Charles B. Rangel's Journey from the Streets of Harlem to the Halls of Congress.* New York: Scribner, 2007. This biographical account of one of Congress's most flamboyant members tells his story (obviously), from the streets of Harlem to the halls of Congress. Rangel, a high school dropout, became a lawyer and then a member of Congress. He helped create the earned-income tax credit for working families.

MEDIA RESOURCES

Charlie Wilson's War: One of the best movies of 2007, starring Tom Hanks and Julia Roberts. This hilarious film is based on the true story of how Wilson, a hard-living, hard-drinking representative from Texas, almost single-handedly won a billion dollars in funding for the Afghans, who were fighting a Russian invasion. When equipped with heat-seeking missiles, the Afghans win. Philip Seymour Hoffman steals the show, portraying a rogue CIA operative.

The Congress—In one of his earliest efforts (1988), filmmaker Ken Burns profiles the history of Congress. Narration is by David McCullough, and those interviewed include David Broker, Alistair Cooke, and Cokie Roberts. PBS Home Video rereleased this film on DVD in 2003.

Congress: A Day in the Life of a Representative—From political meetings to social functions to campaigning, this 1995 program examines what politicians really do. Featured representatives are Tim Roemer (a Democrat from Indiana) and Sue Myrick (a Republican from North Carolina).

Mr. Smith Goes to Washington—A 1939 film in which Jimmy Stewart plays the naïve congressman who is quickly educated in Washington. A true American political classic.

Porked: Earmarks for Profit—A 2008 release from Fox News Channel that investigates congressional earmarks. Fox reporters contend that pork wastes tax dollars. Beyond that, the network also claims that some members of Congress have funded projects that benefited their own bank accounts.

The Seduction of Joe Tynan—A 1979 film in which Alan Alda plays a young senator who must face serious decisions about his political role and his private life.

ONLINE RESOURCES

Congressional Budget Office—provides Congress with nonpartisan analyses for economic and budget decisions and with estimates required for the congressional budget process: www.cbo.gov

Congressional Quarterly—a publication that reports on Congress: www.cq.com

GPO Access—a service of the U.S. Government Printing Office that provides free electronic access to a wealth of important information products produced by the federal government: www.gpoaccess.gov

The Hill—a congressional newspaper that publishes daily when Congress is in session, with a special focus on business and lobbying, political campaigns, and goings-on on Capitol Hill: http://thehill.com/

Roll Call—the newspaper of the Capitol that provides an inside view into what's going on in Washington, D.C.: www.rollcall.com

United States Congress—To view the schedule of activities taking place in Congress and utilize a wealth of other resources, use the following Web sites: www.senate. gov and www.house.gov

12 The President

On October 29, 2012, President Barack Obama speaks in the White House briefing room after hearing the preliminary damage reports on Hurricane Sandy, which had hit the East Coast. He cancelled his campaign events to travel to New Jersey to view the damage after this appearance.

Brendan Hoffman/Getty Images

LEARNING OUTCOMES

After reading this chapter, students will be able to:

■ **LO1** Explain the formal and informal roles played by the president, and discuss the constitutional or political origins of those roles.

■ **LO2** Discuss the president's role in the legislative process including tools to initiate or block legislation.

■ **LO3** Explain the emergency powers of the president and the executive powers of the president.

■ **LO4** Describe the executive offices that support the president.

■ **LO5** Describe the job of the vice president, and explain the circumstances under which the vice president becomes president.

377

What If...

THERE WERE NO EXECUTIVE PRIVILEGE?

BACKGROUND

When a U.S. president wishes to keep information secret, he or she can invoke executive privilege. Although executive privilege is not mentioned in the Constitution, presidents from George Washington to George W. Bush invoked this privilege in response to perceived encroachments on the executive branch by Congress and by the judiciary. Generally, executive privilege is the claim set forth by the president that certain communications must be kept secret for the good of the nation, whether for domestic interests or national security interests. The trouble begins when other branches suspect the executive is claiming this right to save embarrassment for the president or presidential subordinates. For example, in 2006, when two congressional committees were investigating the federal government's response to Hurricane Katrina, the Bush administration cited the need for confidentiality of executive-branch communications as justification for refusing to turn over certain documents, including e-mail correspondence involving White House staff members. The administration had previously refused to release the names of oil company executives who had advised Vice President Cheney on energy policy.

Nonetheless, Congress could try to prohibit the use of executive privilege by passing a law. Alternatively, the Supreme Court could hold that executive privilege as a right is an unconstitutional exercise of executive power.

IF EXECUTIVE PRIVILEGE WERE ELIMINATED

If there were no executive privilege, a president would have to be aware that all of his or her words, documents, and actions could be made public. We know from 20th century history that when a president does not have full executive privilege to protect information, the results can be devastating.

President Richard Nixon (served 1969–1974) had tape-recorded hundreds of hours of conversations in the Oval Office. During a scandal involving a cover-up (the Watergate scandal), Congress requested those tapes. Nixon invoked executive privilege and refused to turn them over. Ultimately, the Supreme Court ordered him to do so, however, and the tapes provided damning information about Nixon's role in the purported cover-up of illegal activities. Rather than face impeachment, Nixon resigned the presidency.

Clearly, if executive privilege were eliminated, it is unlikely that conversations between the president and other members of the executive branch ever would be recorded or otherwise documented. As a result, we would have fewer records of an administration's activities than we do today.

EXECUTIVE PRIVILEGE IN A WORLD FILLED WITH TERRORISM

Following the terrorist attacks on September 11, 2001, Attorney General John Ashcroft advised federal agencies "to lean toward withholding information whenever possible." Often, the Bush administration attempted to withhold information from Congress and the courts, not just the public. In matters of national security, when the president and the president's advisers are discussing attacks on Al Qaeda's leaders or Iranian nuclear plants, the claim of executive privilege to prevent leaks to America's enemies would likely be justified. In 2012, the Obama administration claimed executive privilege for communications in the Department of Justice operation known as "Fast and Furious," which involved illegal gun transfers with Mexican drug lords. While no details were given, the operation likely involved relationships with the Mexican government that the president felt could not be disclosed.

Congress itself can be a source of leaks. While Congress has procedures that can be used to guard sensitive information, it is unaccustomed to keeping secrets and often finds it hard to do so. The very size of the Congress and its staff makes it difficult to keep secrets.

PAST, PRESENT, AND FUTURE PRESIDENTIAL PAPERS

The Bush administration attempted to control not only its own records but also those of former presidents, even against their wishes. Soon after September 11, 2001, President Bush signed Executive Order 13233, which provided that former presidents' private papers can be released only with the approval of both the former president in question and the current one. Former president Bill Clinton publicly objected, saying that he wanted all of his papers released to the public. Nevertheless, the Bush administration denied access to documents surrounding the 177 pardons that Clinton granted in the last days of his presidency.

If executive privilege were eliminated, the White House would have a difficult time regulating the flow of past and present presidential records into the public forum. The behavior of presidents and their administrations would certainly change. They might simply insist that no record of sensitive conversations may exist. If so, future Americans would lose much of the historical background for America's domestic and international actions.

FOR CRITICAL ANALYSIS

1. *The history of executive privilege dates back to 1796, when President George Washington refused a request by the House for certain documents. Given the changes that have taken place since that time, should executive privilege be eliminated—or is it even more necessary today than it was at that time?*

2. *What would be the costs to the nation if executive privilege were eliminated?*

THE WRITERS OF the Constitution created the presidency of the United States without any models to follow. Nowhere else in the world was there a democratically selected chief executive. What the founders did not want was a king. In fact, given their previous experience with royal governors in the colonies, many of the delegates to the Constitutional Convention wanted to create a very weak executive who could not veto legislation. Other delegates, especially those who had witnessed the need for a strong leader in the Revolutionary army, believed a strong executive would be necessary for the new republic.

Overall, however, the delegates did not spend much time discussing the actual powers to be granted to the president, leaving those questions to the Committee on Detail. The delegates, in the end, created a chief executive who had enough powers granted in the Constitution to balance those of Congress.[1]

The power exercised by each president who has held the office has been scrutinized and judged by historians, political scientists, the media, and the public. The personalities and foibles of each president have also been investigated and judged by many. Indeed, it would seem that Americans are fascinated by presidential power and by the persons who hold the office. In this chapter, after looking at who can become president and at the process involved, we will examine closely the nature and extent of the constitutional powers held by the president, including whether the president can decide which records can be made public and which aides might testify before Congress, as discussed in the What if … feature opening this chapter.

Who Can Become President?

The requirements for becoming president, as outlined in Article II, Section 1, of the Constitution, are not overwhelmingly stringent:

> No person except a natural born Citizen, or a Citizen of the United States, at the time of the Adoption of this Constitution, shall be eligible to the Office of President; neither shall any Person be eligible to that Office who shall not have attained to the Age of thirty-five Years, and been fourteen Years a Resident within the United States.

The only question that arises about these qualifications relates to the term *natural-born citizen*. Does that mean only citizens born in the United States and its territories? What about a child born to a U.S. citizen (or to a couple who are U.S. citizens) visiting or living in another country? Although the Supreme Court has never directly addressed the question, it is reasonable to expect that someone would be eligible if her or his parents were Americans. The first presidents, after all, were not even American citizens at birth, and others were born in areas that did not become part of the United States until later. These questions were debated when George Romney, who was born in Chihuahua, Mexico, made a serious bid for the Republican presidential nomination in the 1960s.[2] Similar questions were raised about the 2008 Republican candidate, John McCain, who was born in Panama on an American military base. Those questions were quickly dismissed because it is clear that children born abroad to American citizens are considered natural-born Americans. From time to time, movements arise to

did you know?
George Washington's salary of $25,000 in 1789 was the equivalent of about $600,000 in today's dollars.

did you know?
The salary of the president did not increase from 1969 until 2001, when it was raised to $400,000.

1. Forrest McDonald, *The American Presidency: An Intellectual History* (Lawrence, KS: University Press of Kansas, 1994), p. 179.
2. George Romney was governor of Michigan from 1963 to 1969. Romney was not nominated for the presidency, and the issue remains unresolved.

Harry Truman, left, is shown when he was the proprietor of a Kansas City, Missouri, men's clothing store, about 1920. Ronald Reagan, right, is shown as a frontier marshal in the movie *Law and Order*, released in 1953. Compared to members of Congress, presidents have had more varied backgrounds. How would varied life experiences benefit a president?

Truman, courtesy of Truman Presidential Library and Museum; Reagan, AP Photo

allow *naturalized* citizens to be eligible to run for the presidency, but these have had no success.

The American dream is symbolized by the statement that "anybody can become president of this country." It is true that in modern times, presidents have included a haberdasher (Harry Truman—for a short period of time), a peanut farmer (Jimmy Carter), and an actor (Ronald Reagan). But if you examine the list of presidents in the appendix, you will see that the most common previous occupation of presidents in this country has been that of lawyer. Out of 43 presidents, 26 have been lawyers, and many have been wealthy. (Fewer lawyers have become president in the last century, in part because senators, who are likely to be lawyers, have had a difficult time being elected president. Senators have often faced the problem of defending their voting records.)

Although the Constitution states that the minimum-age requirement for the presidency is 35 years, most presidents have been much older than that when they assumed office. John F. Kennedy, at the age of 43, was the youngest elected president, and the oldest was Ronald Reagan, at age 69. The average age at inauguration has been 54. The selection of presidents reflects a clear demographic bias. Until 2009, all had been white, male, and from the Protestant tradition, except for John F. Kennedy, who was a Roman Catholic. The inauguration of Barack Obama, a man of mixed race—and, indeed, of Kenyan and American ancestry—was an extraordinary milestone in American history. Presidents have been men of great stature (such as George Washington) and men in whom leadership qualities were not so pronounced (such as Warren Harding; served 1921–1923). A presidential candidate usually has experience as a vice president, senator, or state governor. Former governors have been especially successful at winning the presidency, because they can make the legitimate claims to have executive experience and to be electable.

The Process of Becoming President

Major and minor political parties nominate candidates for president and vice president at national conventions every four years. As discussed earlier the nation's voters do not elect a president and vice president directly, but rather cast ballots for presidential electors, who then vote for president and vice president in the electoral college.

Because winning the election requires winning the majority of electoral votes, it is conceivable that someone could be elected to the office of the presidency without having a majority of the popular vote cast. In four cases, candidates won elections even though their major opponents received more popular votes. One of those cases occurred in 2000, when George W. Bush won the electoral college vote and became president even though his opponent, Al Gore, won the popular vote. In elections when more than two candidates were running for office, many presidential candidates have won with less than 50 percent of the total popular votes cast for all candidates—including Abraham Lincoln, Woodrow Wilson, Harry Truman, John F. Kennedy, Richard Nixon, and, in 1992, Bill Clinton. Independent candidate Ross Perot garnered a surprising 19 percent of the vote in 1992. Remember from Chapter 9 that no president has won a majority of votes from the entire voting-age population.

Twice, the electoral college has failed to give any candidate a majority. At this point, the election is thrown into the House of Representatives. The president is then chosen from among the three candidates having the most electoral college votes, as noted in Chapter 9. Thomas Jefferson and Aaron Burr tied in the electoral college in 1800. This happened because the Constitution had not been explicit in indicating which of the two electoral votes were for president and which were for vice president. In 1804, the **Twelfth Amendment** clarified the matter by requiring that the president and vice president be chosen separately. In 1824, the House again had to make a choice, this time among William H. Crawford, Andrew Jackson, and John Quincy Adams. It chose Adams, even though Jackson had more electoral and popular votes.

Twelfth Amendment
An amendment to the Constitution, adopted in 1804, that specifies the separate election of the president and vice president by the electoral college.

The Many Roles of the President

The Constitution speaks briefly about the duties and obligations of the president. Based on this brief list of powers and on the precedents of history, the presidency has grown into a very complicated job that requires balancing at least five constitutional roles: (1) head of state, (2) chief executive, (3) commander in chief of the armed forces, (4) chief diplomat, and (5) chief legislator of the United States. Here we examine each of these significant presidential functions, or roles. It is worth noting that one person plays all these roles simultaneously and that these roles may at times come into conflict.

■ Learning Outcome 1:
Explain the formal and informal roles played by the president, and discuss the constitutional or political origins of those roles.

Head of State

Every nation has at least one person who is the ceremonial head of state. In most democratic governments, the role of **head of state** is given to someone other than the chief executive, who leads the executive branch of government. In Britain, for example, the head of state is the queen. In much of Europe, the prime minister is the chief executive, and the head of state is the president. But in the

Head of State
The role of the president as ceremonial head of the government.

President Barack Obama discusses global economic issues with other world leaders at the G8 summit held at Camp David, Maryland in May, 2012. Do you think such face-to-face meetings produce tangible results or just reinforce personal relationships?

© White House Photo/Alamy

United States, the president is both chief executive and head of state. According to William Howard Taft, as head of state the president symbolizes the "dignity and majesty" of the American people.

As head of state, the president engages in many activities that are largely symbolic or ceremonial, such as the following:

- Decorating war heroes.
- Throwing out the first pitch to open the baseball season.
- Dedicating parks and post offices.
- Receiving visiting heads of state at the White House.
- Going on official state visits to other countries.
- Making personal telephone calls to astronauts.
- Representing the nation at times of national mourning, such as after the terrorist attacks of September 11, 2001; after the loss of the space shuttle *Columbia* in 2003; and after the destruction from Hurricane Katrina in 2005.

Some students of the American political system believe that having the president serve as both the chief executive and the head of state drastically limits the time available to do "real" work. Not all presidents have agreed with this conclusion, however—particularly those presidents who have skillfully blended these two roles with their role as politician. Being head of state gives the president tremendous public exposure, which can be an important asset in a campaign for reelection. When that exposure is positive, it helps the president deal with Congress over proposed legislation and increases the chances of being reelected—or getting the candidates of the president's party elected.

Chief Executive

According to the Constitution, "The executive Power shall be vested in a President of the United States of America. ... [H]e may require the Opinion, in writing, of the principal Officer in each of the executive Departments, upon any Subject relating to the Duties of their respective Offices ... and he shall nominate, and by and with the Advice and Consent of the Senate, shall appoint ... Officers of the United States. ... [H]e shall take Care that the Laws be faithfully executed."

As **chief executive**, the president is constitutionally bound to enforce the acts of Congress, the judgments of federal courts, and treaties signed by the United States. The duty to "faithfully execute" the laws has been a source of constitutional power for presidents. Is the president allowed to reject certain parts of legislation if he or she believes that they are unconstitutional? This question relates to so-called **signing statements**, which are written declarations made by presidents that accompany legislation.

For at least 175 years, presidents have used signing statements to make substantive constitutional pronouncements on the bill being signed. In 1830, President Andrew Jackson created a controversy when he signed a bill and at the same time sent to Congress a message that restricted the reach of the statute. In 1842, President John Tyler expressed misgivings in a signing statement about the constitutionality and policy of an entire act. Presidents Abraham Lincoln, Andrew Johnson, Theodore Roosevelt, Woodrow Wilson, and Franklin Roosevelt all used signing statements.

As for the legality of the practice, the Department of Justice has advised the last four administrations that the Constitution provides the president with the authority to decline to enforce a clearly unconstitutional law. Four justices of the Supreme Court joined in an opinion that the president may resist laws that encroach upon presidential powers by "disregarding them when they're unconstitutional."[3]

After George W. Bush took office, he issued signing statements on more than 800 statutes, more than all of the previous presidents combined. He also tended to use the statements for a different purpose. When earlier presidents issued signing statements, they were normally used to instruct agencies on how to execute the laws or for similar purposes. In contrast, many (if not most) of Bush's signing statements served notice that he believed parts of bills that he signed were unconstitutional or might violate national security. President Obama has continued the practice of issuing signing statements to indicate his intentions with regard to legislation.

Some members of Congress are not so concerned about Bush's signing statements. Senator John Cornyn (R.-Tex.) said that Bush's signing statements are only "expressions of presidential opinion" and carry no legal weight. According to Cornyn, federal courts would be unlikely to consider the statements when interpreting the laws with which they were issued.[4]

The Powers of Appointment and Removal.

To assist in the various tasks of the chief executive, the president has a federal bureaucracy (see Chapter 13), which consists of more than 2.7 million federal civilian employees. You might think that the president, as head of the largest bureaucracy in the United States, wields enormous power. The president, however, only nominally runs the executive bureaucracy. Most government positions are filled by **civil service** employees, who generally gain government employment through a merit system rather than presidential appointment.[5] Therefore, even though the president has important **appointment power** it is limited to cabinet and subcabinet

Chief Executive
The role of the president as head of the executive branch of the government.

Signing Statement
A written declaration that a president may make when signing a bill into law. Usually, such statements point out sections of the law that the president deems unconstitutional.

did you know?
Thomas Jefferson was the first president to be inaugurated in Washington, D.C., where he walked to the Capitol from a boardinghouse, took the oath, made a brief speech in the Senate chamber, and then walked back home.

Civil Service
A collective term for the body of employees working for the government. Generally, civil service is understood to apply to all those who gain government employment through a merit system.

Appointment Power
The authority vested in the president to fill a government office or position. Positions filled by presidential appointment include those in the executive branch and the federal judiciary, commissioned officers in the armed forces, and members of the independent regulatory commissions.

---

3. *Freytag v. C.I.R.,* 501 U.S. 868 (1991).
4. T. J. Halstead, "Presidential Signing Statements: Constitutional and Institutional Implications" (Washington, DC: Congressional Research Service, September 17, 2007).
5. See Chapter 14 for a discussion of the Civil Service Reform Act.

jobs, federal judgeships, agency heads, and several thousand lesser jobs. For example, of the more than 600,000 civilian jobs in the Department of Defense, the president may appoint fewer than 700. The largest number of jobs available for presidential appointments is in the State Department (more than 1,200), but many of those are ambassadorships, usually given to major donors and supporters of the president. Soon after each presidential election, the government publishes a list of these specific jobs in a volume titled, "The Plum Book: Policy and Supporting Positions." It is so-called because these have long been considered "plum jobs."

The president's power to remove from office those officials who are not doing a good job or who do not agree with the president is not explicitly granted by the Constitution and has been limited with regard to certain agencies. In 1926, however, a Supreme Court decision prevented Congress from interfering with the president's ability to fire those executive-branch officials whom the president had appointed with Senate approval.[6] Ten agencies have directors whom the president can remove at any time, including the Arms Control and Disarmament Agency, the Commission on Civil Rights, the Environmental Protection Agency, the General Services Administration, and the Small Business Administration. In addition, the president can remove all heads of cabinet departments, all individuals in the Executive Office of the President, and all political appointees.

Harry Truman spoke candidly of the difficulties a president faces in trying to control the executive bureaucracy. On leaving office, he referred to the problems that Dwight Eisenhower, as a former general of the army, was going to have: "He'll sit here and he'll say do this! do that! and nothing will happen. Poor Ike—it won't be a bit like the Army. He'll find it very frustrating."[7]

The Power to Grant Reprieves and Pardons. Section 2 of Article II of the Constitution gives the president the power to grant **reprieves** and **pardons** for offenses against the United States except in cases of impeachment. All pardons are administered by the Office of the Pardon Attorney in the Department of Justice. In principle, a pardon is granted to remedy a mistake made in a conviction.

The United States Supreme Court upheld the president's power to grant reprieves and pardons in a 1925 case concerning a pardon granted by the president to an individual convicted of contempt of court. The judiciary had contended that only judges had the authority to convict individuals for contempt of court when court orders were violated and that the courts should be free from interference by the executive branch. The Court simply stated that the president could grant reprieves or pardons for all offenses "either before trial, during trial, or after trial, by individuals, or by classes, conditionally or absolutely, and this without modification or regulation by Congress."[8]

The power to pardon can also be used to apply to large groups of individuals who may be subject to indictment and trial. In 1977, President Jimmy Carter extended amnesty to all of the Vietnam War resisters who avoided the military draft by fleeing to Canada. More than 50,000 individuals were allowed to come back to the United States, free from the possibility of prosecution. The power to

Reprieve
A formal postponement of the execution of a sentence imposed by a court of law.

Pardon
A release from the punishment for or legal consequences of a crime; a pardon can be granted by the president before or after a conviction.

---

6. *Meyers v. United States,* 272 U.S. 52 (1926).
7. Quoted in Richard E. Neustadt, *Presidential Power: The Politics of Leadership* (New York: Wiley, 1960), p. 9. Truman may not have considered the amount of politics involved in decision making in the upper echelon of the army.
8. *Ex parte Grossman,* 267 U.S. 87 (1925).

reprieve individuals allows the president to extend clemency to federal prisoners, usually on humanitarian grounds. However, in 1999, President Bill Clinton extended a conditional offer of clemency to a group of Puerto Rican nationalists who had been tried for planning terrorist attacks in the United States. The condition was for them to renounce the use of terrorist tactics and to not associate with other nationalists who advocate violence. Twelve accepted the offer, while two refused to accept the conditions.

In a controversial decision, President Gerald Ford pardoned former president Richard Nixon for his role in the Watergate affair before any charges were brought in court. Just before George W. Bush's inauguration in 2001, President Clinton announced pardons for almost 200 persons. Some of these pardons were controversial and appeared to be political favors.

Commander in Chief

The president, according to the Constitution, "shall be Commander in Chief of the Army and Navy of the United States, and of the Militia of the several States, when called into the actual Service of the United States." In other words, the armed forces are under civilian, rather than military, control.

Wartime Powers. Certainly, those who wrote the Constitution had George Washington in mind when they made the president the **commander in chief**. The founders did not, however, expect presidents to lead the country into war without congressional authorization. Remember from Chapters 2 and 11 that Congress is given the power to declare war. As the United States grew in military power and global reach, presidents became much more likely to send troops into armed combat either in crisis situations or with an authorizing resolution short of a declaration of war. The last war to be fought under a congressional declaration was World War II.

Although we do not expect our president to lead the troops into battle, presidents as commanders in chief have wielded dramatic power. Harry Truman made the difficult decision to drop atomic bombs on Hiroshima and Nagasaki in 1945 to force Japan to surrender and thus bring World War II to an end. Lyndon B. Johnson ordered bombing missions against North Vietnam in the 1960s, and he personally selected some of the targets. Richard Nixon decided to invade Cambodia in 1970, which was widely condemned as going beyond his power as commander in chief.

The president is the ultimate decision maker in military matters and, as such, has the final authority to launch a nuclear strike using missiles or bombs. Everywhere the president goes, so too goes the "football"—a briefcase filled with all the codes necessary to order a nuclear attack. Only the president has the power to order the use of nuclear force.

The use of military force by presidents has raised some very thorny issues for the balance between Congress and the presidency. Harry Truman sent U.S. troops to Korea under a United Nations resolution, and Lyndon Johnson escalated the U.S. involvement in Vietnam under the quickly passed Gulf of Tonkin Resolution. George W. Bush invaded Iraq with congressional authorization. In none of these cases did Congress and the public expect extended wars with many casualties.

Presidents have also used military force without any congressional authorization, particularly in emergency situations. Ronald Reagan sent troops to Grenada to stop a supposedly communist coup, and Lyndon Johnson invaded the

Commander in Chief
The role of the president as supreme commander of the military forces of the United States and of the state National Guard units when they are called into federal service.

Dominican Republic. George H. W. Bush sent troops to Panama, and numerous presidents have ordered quick air strikes on perceived enemies.

The War Powers Resolution. In an attempt to gain more control over such military activities, in 1973 Congress passed the **War Powers Resolution**— over President Nixon's veto—requiring that the president consult with Congress when sending American forces into action. Once they are sent, the president must report to Congress within 48 hours. Unless Congress approves the use of troops within 60 days or extends the 60-day time limit, the forces must be withdrawn. The War Powers Resolution was tested in the fall of 1983, when Reagan requested that troops be left in Lebanon. The resulting compromise was a congressional resolution allowing troops to remain there for 18 months. Shortly after the resolution was passed, however, more than 240 sailors and marines were killed in a suicide bombing of a U.S. military housing compound in Beirut. That event provoked a furious congressional debate over the role that American troops were playing in the Middle East, and all troops were withdrawn shortly thereafter.

Despite the War Powers Resolution, the powers of the president as commander in chief have continued to expand. The attacks of September 11, 2001, were the first on U.S. soil since Pearl Harbor. The imminent sense of threat supported passage of legislation that gave the president and the executive branch powers that had not been seen since World War II. President Bush's use of surveillance powers and other powers granted by the PATRIOT Act have caused considerable controversy. In the face of continued terrorist threats, President Obama has signed extensions of the PATRIOT Act and continued many of the actions of the Bush administration. In addition, the Obama administration has ordered drone strikes on a number of terrorist leaders. This is an interesting tactic that avoids the War Powers Act in that no American troops are involved in a combat situation when drones are used.

Chief Diplomat

The Constitution gives the president the power to recognize foreign governments; to make treaties, with the **advice and consent** of the Senate; and to make special agreements with other heads of state that do not require congressional approval. In addition, the president nominates ambassadors. As **chief diplomat**, the president dominates American foreign policy, a role that has been supported many times by the Supreme Court.

Diplomatic Recognition. An important power of the president as chief diplomat is that of **diplomatic recognition**, or the power to recognize—or refuse to recognize—foreign governments. In the role of ceremonial head of state, the president has always received foreign diplomats. In modern times, the simple act of receiving a foreign diplomat has been equivalent to accrediting the diplomat and officially recognizing his or her government. Such recognition of the legitimacy of another country's government is a prerequisite to diplomatic relations or treaties between that country and the United States.

Deciding when to recognize a foreign power is not always simple. The United States, for example, did not recognize the Soviet Union until 1933—16 years after the Russian Revolution of 1917. It was only after all attempts to reverse the effects of that revolution—including military invasion of Russia and diplomatic isolation—had proved futile that Franklin Roosevelt extended recognition to the Soviet government. U.S. presidents faced a similar problem with the Chinese

---

War Powers Resolution
A law passed in 1973 spelling out the conditions under which the president can commit troops without congressional approval.

Advice and Consent
Terms in the Constitution describing the U.S. Senate's power to review and approve treaties and presidential appointments.

Chief Diplomat
The role of the president in recognizing foreign governments, making treaties, and effecting executive agreements.

Diplomatic Recognition
The formal acknowledgment of a foreign government as legitimate.

AP Photo

communist revolution. In December 1978, long after the communist victory in China in 1949, Jimmy Carter granted official recognition to the People's Republic of China.[9]

A diplomatic recognition issue that faced the Clinton administration involved recognizing a former enemy—the Republic of Vietnam. Many Americans, particularly those who believed that Vietnam had not been forthcoming in the efforts to find the remains of missing American soldiers or to find out about former prisoners of war, opposed any formal relationship with that nation. After the U.S. government had negotiated with the Vietnamese government for many years over the missing-in-action issue and engaged in limited diplomatic contacts for several years, President Clinton announced on July 11, 1995, that the United States would recognize the government of Vietnam and move to establish normal diplomatic relations.

Proposal and Ratification of Treaties. The president has the sole power to negotiate treaties with other nations. These treaties must be presented to the Senate, where they may be modified and must be approved by a two-thirds vote. After ratification, the president can approve the senatorial version of the treaty. Approval poses a problem when the Senate has tacked on substantive amendments or reservations to a treaty, particularly when such changes may require reopening negotiations with the other signatory governments. Sometimes a president may decide to withdraw a treaty if the senatorial changes are too extensive, as Woodrow Wilson did with the Versailles Treaty in 1919. Wilson believed that the senatorial reservations would weaken the treaty so much that it would be ineffective. His refusal to accept the senatorial version of the treaty led to the eventual refusal of the United States to join the League of Nations.

did you know?

John F. Kennedy was the youngest elected president, taking office at the age of 43, but Theodore Roosevelt assumed office at the age of 42 after the assassination of President William McKinley.

---

9. The Nixon administration first encouraged new relations with the People's Republic of China by allowing a cultural exchange of Ping-Pong teams.

President Carter was successful in lobbying for the treaties that provided for the return of the Panama Canal to Panama by the year 2000 and for neutralizing the canal. President Bill Clinton won a major political and legislative victory in 1993 by persuading Congress to ratify the North American Free Trade Agreement (NAFTA). In so doing, he had to overcome opposition from Democrats and most of organized labor. In 1998, he worked closely with Senate Republicans to ensure Senate approval of a treaty governing the use of chemical weapons. In 2000, President Clinton won another major legislative victory when Congress voted to normalize trade relations with China permanently.

Before September 11, 2001, President George W. Bush indicated his intention to steer the United States in a more unilateral direction on foreign policy. He rejected the Kyoto Agreement on global warming and proposed ending the 1972 Anti-Ballistic Missile (ABM) Treaty that was part of the first Strategic Arms Limitation Treaty (SALT I). After the terrorist attacks of September 11, 2001, however, President Bush sought cooperation from U.S. allies in the war on terrorism. Bush's return to multilateralism was exemplified in the signing of a nuclear weapons reduction treaty with Russia in 2002. Nonetheless, his attempts to gain international support for a war against Iraq to overthrow that country's government were not as successful as he had hoped. During the continuing occupation of Iraq, the Bush administration saw even more erosion in other countries' support of his actions.

The Obama administration quickly signaled a new outlook in foreign policy, with the president making multiple trips overseas, including to Egypt, in his first year in office. President Obama's stated goals in foreign policy included a more cooperative approach to world affairs and the reduction of nuclear weapons for all nations. In 2010, the president signed a treaty with Russia for a joint reduction of long-range nuclear weapons. The new START treaty was ratified by the U.S. Senate late in that year.

Executive Agreement
An international agreement made by the president, without senatorial ratification, with the head of a foreign state.

Executive Agreements. Presidential power in foreign affairs is enhanced greatly by the use of **executive agreements** made between the president and other heads of state. Such agreements do not require Senate approval, although the House and Senate may refuse to appropriate the funds necessary to implement them. Whereas treaties are binding on all succeeding administrations, executive agreements require each new president's consent to remain in effect.

Among the advantages of executive agreements are speed and secrecy. The former is essential during a crisis; the latter is important when the administration fears that open senatorial debate may be detrimental to the best interests of the United States or to the interests of the president.[10] Executive agreements (about 13,000) greatly outnumber treaties (about 1,300). Many executive agreements contain secret provisions calling for American military assistance or other support. For example, Franklin Roosevelt (served 1933–1945) used executive agreements to bypass congressional isolationists when he traded American destroyers for British Caribbean naval bases and when he arranged diplomatic and military affairs with Canada and Latin American nations.

■ **Learning Outcome 2:**
Discuss the president's role in the legislative process including tools to initiate or block legislation.

Chief Legislator

Chief Legislator
The role of the president in influencing the making of laws.

Constitutionally, presidents must recommend to Congress legislation that they judge necessary and expedient. Not all presidents have wielded their powers as **chief legislator** in the same manner. Some presidents have been almost completely unsuccessful in getting their legislative programs implemented by Congress.

---

10. The Case Act of 1972 requires that all executive agreements be transmitted to Congress within 60 days after the agreement takes effect. Secret agreements are transmitted to the foreign relations committees as classified information.

Presidents Franklin Roosevelt and Lyndon Johnson, however, saw much of their proposed legislation put into effect. Each year, the *Congressional Quarterly Weekly Review* publishes an analysis of presidential success in terms of legislation passed that the president has publicly supported. As illustrated by the graph in Figure 12-1, presidents tend to have a high success rate at the beginning of their administration, with a steep decline toward the end of their term. George W. Bush had more than a 70 percent success rate during the years he had a Republican-controlled Congress, but it fell to 34 percent after the Democrats won control of Congress in the 2006 elections. President Barack Obama found extraordinary support for his initiatives from the large Democratic majorities in both the House and the Senate, earning the highest success score ever recorded for a president in his first year, 96.7 percent. In his second year as president, Mr. Obama's success rate remained very high at 85.8 percent, but after the Republicans won the House of Representatives in 2010, his legislative success rate for 2011 fell to 57.1 percent, about the same as Ronald Reagan's for the third year of his presidency.

In modern times, the president has played a dominant role in creating the congressional agenda. In the president's annual **State of the Union message**, which is required by the Constitution (Article II, Section 3) and is usually given in late January, shortly after Congress reconvenes, the president, as chief legislator, presents a program. The message gives a broad, comprehensive view of what the president wishes the legislature to accomplish during its session. Originally, presidents simply sent a written memo to the Congress, which clearly satisfies the constitutional requirement. In modern times, however, presidents see the State of the Union address as a tool to advance their policy agenda. The president is able

State of the Union Message

An annual message to Congress in which the president proposes a legislative program. The message is addressed not only to Congress but also to the American people and to the world.

Figure 12–1 ▶ Presidential Success Rate by Year of Presidency

The graph illustrates the president's success rate on bills on which he had taken a position. Note that presidents do very well at the beginning of their terms, especially when they have control of Congress. When the other party controls Congress, the presidential success rate falls.

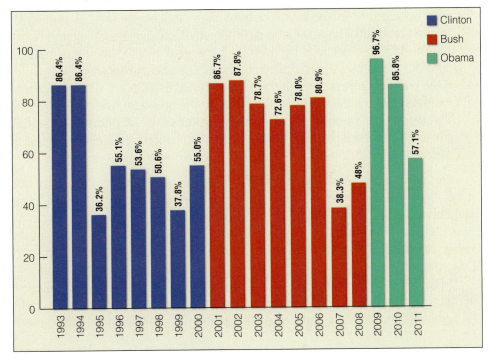

Source: *Congressional Quarterly Weekly Report*, January 14, 2008, p.137.

Veto Message
The president's formal explanation of a veto when legislation is returned to Congress.

Pocket Veto
A special veto exercised by the chief executive after a legislative body has adjourned. Bills not signed by the chief executive die after a specified period of time. If Congress wishes to reconsider such a bill, it must be reintroduced in the following session of Congress.

to command the media stage and set out his or her goals. President Ronald Reagan began the practice of referring to ordinary citizens and bringing the subjects of those stories to sit in the balcony during the speech. Today, the president, the opposition party, and the commentators all recognize the impact of the State of the Union message on public opinion.

Getting Legislation Passed. The president can propose legislation. Congress, however, is not required to pass—or even introduce—any of the administration's bills. How, then, does the president get those proposals made into law? One way is by exercising the power of persuasion. The president writes to, telephones, and meets with various congressional leaders; makes public announcements to influence public opinion; and, as head of the party, exercises legislative leadership through the congresspersons of that party. Most presidents also have an Office of Congressional Liaison within the White House Office. Such an office is staffed by individuals with extensive Washington experience, including former members of the Congress, who lobby the Congress on behalf of the president and monitor the progress of legislation on Capitol Hill. Presidents may also decide to use social events to lobby the Congress, inviting the members and their spouses to parties at the White House. A more negative strategy is for the president to threaten to veto legislation if it does not correspond to his or her position.

Saying No to Legislation. The president has the power to say no to legislation through use of the veto, by which the White House returns a bill unsigned to Congress with a **veto message** attached.[11] Because the Constitution requires that every bill passed by the House and the Senate be sent to the president before it becomes law, the president must act on each bill.

1. If the bill is signed, it becomes law.
2. If the bill is not sent back to Congress after 10 congressional working days, it becomes law without the president's signature.
3. The president can reject the bill and send it back to Congress with a veto message setting forth objections. Congress then can change the bill, hoping to secure presidential approval and pass it again. Or, Congress can simply reject the president's objections by overriding the veto with a two-thirds roll-call vote of the members present in both the House and the Senate.
4. If the president refuses to sign the bill and Congress adjourns within 10 working days after the bill has been submitted to the president, the bill is killed for that session of Congress. This is called a **pocket veto**. If Congress wishes the bill to be reconsidered, the bill must be reintroduced during the following session.

Presidents employed the veto power infrequently until after the Civil War, but it has been used with increasing vigor since then (see Table 12-1). The total number of vetoes from George Washington through the middle of George W. Bush's second term in office was 2,552, with about two-thirds of those vetoes being exercised by Grover Cleveland, Franklin Roosevelt, Harry Truman, and Dwight Eisenhower.

Millard Fillmore (served 1850-1853) was the last president to serve a full term in office without exercising the veto power. George W. Bush, who had the benefit of a Republican Congress that passed legislation he was willing to sign, did not

---

11. *Veto* in Latin means "I forbid."

TABLE 12-1 ▶ Presidential Vetoes, 1789 to the Present

YEARS	PRESIDENT	REGULAR VETOES	VETOES OVERRIDDEN	POCKET VETOES	TOTAL VETOES
1789–1797	Washington	2	0	0	2
1797–1801	J. Adams	0	0	0	0
1801–1809	Jefferson	0	0	0	0
1809–1817	Madison	5	0	2	7
1817–1825	Monroe	1	0	0	1
1825–1829	J. Q. Adams	0	0	0	0
1829–1837	Jackson	5	0	7	12
1837–1841	Van Buren	0	0	1	1
1841–1841	W. Harrison	0	0	0	0
1841–1845	Tyler	6	1	4	10
1845–1849	Polk	2	0	1	3
1849–1850	Taylor	0	0	0	0
1850–1853	Fillmore	0	0	0	0
1853–1857	Pierce	9	5	0	9
1857–1861	Buchanan	4	0	3	7
1861–1865	Lincoln	2	0	5	7
1865–1869	A. Johnson	21	15	8	29
1869–1877	Grant	45	4	48	93
1877–1881	Hayes	12	1	1	13
1881–1881	Garfield	0	0	0	0
1881–1885	Arthur	4	1	8	12
1885–1889	Cleveland	304	2	110	414
1889–1893	B. Harrison	19	1	25	44
1893–1897	Cleveland	42	5	128	170
1897–1901	McKinley	6	0	36	42
1901–1909	T. Roosevelt	42	1	40	82
1909–1913	Taft	30	1	9	39
1913–1921	Wilson	33	6	11	44
1921–1923	Harding	5	0	1	6
1923–1929	Coolidge	20	4	30	50
1929–1933	Hoover	21	3	16	37
1933–1945	F. Roosevelt	372	9	263	635
1945–1953	Truman	180	12	70	250
1953–1961	Eisenhower	73	2	108	181
1961–1963	Kennedy	12	0	9	21
1963–1969	L. Johnson	16	0	14	30
1969–1974	Nixon	26*	7	17	43
1974–1977	Ford	48	12	18	66
1977–1981	Carter	13	2	18	31
1981–1989	Reagan	39	9	39	78
1989–1993	George H. W. Bush	29	1	15	44
1993–2001	Clinton	37**	2	1	38
2001–2008	George W. Bush	11	4	1	12
2009–2012	Obama	2	0	0	2
TOTAL		**1,497**	**110**	**1,067**	**2,565**

*Two pocket vetoes by President Nixon, overruled in the courts, are counted here as regular vetoes. **President Clinton's line-item vetoes are not included.

Source: Office of the Clerk.

Beyond Our Borders
DO WE NEED A PRESIDENT AND A KING?

In the United States, the president is the head of state and the head of government. In many democratic societies, the government has a head of government, who actually guides government policy and is the political leader, and a head of state, who is the symbolic head of government. As noted in Chapter 11, in parliamentary systems the head of government is actually elected by his or her peers in the majority party in the legislature. In Great Britain, after the election, the leader of the majority party is asked by the queen of England (in her role as head of state) if he or she will serve as the prime minister. The queen has no political power whatsoever. She cannot refuse to name the leader of the majority party. When she opens the parliamentary session, she reads a speech written for her by the prime minister. Similar political systems with royal families and parliamentary leadership are found in Denmark, Sweden, Spain, and a few smaller European nations. The advantage of this system is that the head of state, the monarch, symbolically represents the nation. Public fascination with the royal family and the queen generally means that the prime minister can do his or her job without all the gossip and journalistic coverage that surrounds the president of the United States.

Other democracies, including Italy, France, and Germany, have no royal families. The president of the nation is separately elected for a longer term but has little political power. He or she is the head of state and may counsel the head of the government, but political and executive power rests with the prime minister or premier. In some democratic states, the president and the premier are elected, although with different terms.

Until 2008, Vladimir Putin was the president of Russia, but his two terms were limited by the 1993 constitution. After his second term, his chosen successor, Dmitry Medvedev, was elected for one term. Soon after the election, Medvedev named Putin as the premier, still leaving him with considerable power. After Medvedev served one term, Putin was elected to the presidency again because his ability to serve two more terms was constitutional. So, in the case of Russia and some other states, the head of state is the president (who is elected) and who then can name the premier and the

cabinet ministers. The intent of this system is for the president to be popularly elected and to exercise political leadership, while the premier runs the everyday operations of government and leads the legislative branch. But such a system can develop into a rivalry or collusion between the president and the premier. How can citizens know which one really has the power of the leader?

Russian president Putin chairs a meeting on inter-ethnic relations in Moldova, a former Soviet republic. In this role, Putin is both the foreign policy leader of Russia and the symbolic head of state as he shores up relationships with the independent nation of Moldova.

FOR CRITICAL ANALYSIS

1. *Why is it important to separate the roles of head of state and head of government?*

2. *Can the existence of a symbolic head of state, such as a monarch, make the elected leader more effective?*

3. *Does the U.S. president, who is both head of state and head of government, carry too heavy a burden?*

veto any legislation during his first term. Only in the summer of 2006 did Bush finally issue a veto, saying "no" to stem-cell research legislation passed by Congress. He occasionally threatened to use the veto and certainly used it when he was governor of Texas. After the Democrats took control of Congress in 2006, Bush used the veto more frequently, even on bills with bipartisan majorities.

The Line-Item Veto. Ronald Reagan lobbied strenuously for Congress to give to the president another tool, the **line-item veto**, which would allow the president to veto *specific* spending provisions of legislation that was passed by Congress. In 1996, Congress passed the Line Item Veto Act, which provided for the line-item veto. Signed by President Clinton, the law granted the president the power to rescind any item in an appropriations bill unless Congress passed a resolution of disapproval. Of course, the congressional resolution could be, in turn, vetoed by the president. The law did not take effect until after the 1996 election.

The act was soon challenged in court as an unconstitutional delegation of legislative powers to the executive branch. In 1998, by a 6-3 vote, the United States Supreme Court agreed and overturned the act. The Court stated that "there is no provision in the Constitution that authorizes the president to enact, to amend or to repeal statutes."[12]

President Dwight D. Eisenhower prepares for a nationwide radio and television address in 1959. In that address he called for new labor legislation "to protect the American people from the gangsters, racketeers, and other corrupt elements that have invaded the labor-management field."

Congress's Power to Override Presidential Vetoes. A veto is a clear-cut indication of the president's dissatisfaction with congressional legislation. Congress, however, can override a presidential veto, although it rarely exercises this power. Consider that two-thirds of the members of each chamber who are present must vote to override the president's veto in a roll-call vote. This means that if only one-third plus one of the members voting in one of the chambers of Congress do not agree to override the veto, the veto holds. Congress first overrode a presidential veto during the administration of John Tyler (served 1841–1845). In the first 65 years of American federal government history, out of 33 regular vetoes, Congress overrode only one, or about 3 percent. Overall, only about 7 percent of all regular vetoes have been overridden.

Other Presidential Powers

The powers of the president just discussed are called **constitutional powers**, because their basis lies in the Constitution. In addition, Congress has established by law, or statute, numerous other presidential powers, such as the ability to declare national emergencies. These are called **statutory powers**. Both constitutional and statutory powers have been labeled the **expressed powers** of the president, because they are expressly written into the Constitution or into law.

Presidents also have what have come to be known as **inherent powers**. These depend on the statements in the Constitution that "the executive Power shall be vested in a President" and that the president should "take Care that the Laws be faithfully executed." The most common example of inherent powers are those emergency powers invoked by the president during wartime. Franklin Roosevelt, for example, used his inherent powers to move the Japanese and Japanese Americans living in the United States into internment camps for the duration of World War II.

Line-Item Veto
The power of an executive to veto individual lines or items within a piece of legislation without vetoing the entire bill.

Constitutional Power
A power vested in the president by Article II of the Constitution.

Statutory Power
A power created for the president through laws enacted by Congress.

Expressed Power
A power of the president that is expressly written into the Constitution or into statutory law.

Inherent Powers
Powers of the president derived from the statements in the Constitution that "the executive Power shall be vested in a President" and that the president should "take Care that the Laws be faithfully executed"; defined through practice rather than through law.

12. *Clinton v. City of New York,* 524 U.S. 417 (1998).

Patronage
The practice of rewarding faithful party workers and followers with government employment and contracts.

Clearly, modern U.S. presidents have many powers at their disposal. According to some critics, among the powers exercised by modern presidents are certain powers that rightfully belong to Congress but that Congress has yielded to the executive branch.

The President as Party Chief and Superpolitician

Presidents are by no means above political partisanship, and one of their many roles is that of chief of party. Although the Constitution says nothing about the function of the president within a political party (the mere concept of political parties was abhorrent to most of the authors of the Constitution), today presidents are the actual leaders of their parties.

The President as Chief of Party

As party leader, the president chooses the national committee chairperson and can try to discipline party members who fail to support presidential policies. One way of exerting political power within the party is through **patronage**—appointing political supporters to government or public jobs. This power was more extensive in the past, before the establishment of the civil service in 1883 (see Chapter 13), but the president retains important patronage power. As noted earlier, the president can appoint several thousand individuals to jobs in the cabinet, the White House, embassies, and the federal regulatory agencies.

Perhaps the most important partisan role that the president played in the late 1900s and early 2000s was that of fundraiser. The president is able to raise large amounts for the party through appearances at dinners, speaking engagements, and other social occasions. President Clinton may have raised more than half a billion dollars for the Democratic Party during his two terms. President George W. Bush was even more successful than Clinton.

Presidents have other ways of exerting influence as party chief. The president may make it known that a particular congressperson's choice for federal judge will not be appointed unless that member of Congress is more supportive of the president's legislative program.[13] The president may agree to campaign for a particular program or for a particular candidate. Presidents also reward loyal members of Congress with support for the funding of local projects, tax breaks for regional industries, and other forms of "pork."

The President's Power to Persuade

According to political scientist Richard E. Neustadt, without the power to persuade, no president can lead very well. After all, even though the president is in the news virtually every day, the Constitution gives Congress most of the authority in the U.S. political system. The Constitution does not give the executive branch enough constitutional power to keep the president constantly in a strong leadership position. Therefore, the president must establish a "professional reputation" that will convince Congress, the bureaucracy, and the public to support what the president wants. As Neustadt argues, "presidential power is the power to persuade."[14]

---

13. "Senatorial courtesy" (see Chapter 15) often puts the judicial appointment in the hands of the Senate, however.
14. Richard E. Neustadt, *Presidential Power and the Modern Presidents: The Politics of Leadership from Roosevelt to Reagan*, rev. ed. (New York: Free Press, 1991).

Constituencies and Public Approval

All politicians worry about their constituencies, and presidents are no exception. Presidents with high approval ratings are able to leverage those ratings with the members of Congress who would prefer not to vote against the opinions of their own constituents.

Presidential Constituencies. According to Neustadt, presidents have not just one constituency, but many. In principle, they are beholden to the entire electorate—the public of the United States—even those who did not vote. They are certainly beholden to their party because its members helped to put them in office. The president's constituencies also include members of the opposing party, whose cooperation the president needs. Finally, the president must take into consideration a constituency that has come to be called the **Washington community**. This community consists of individuals who—whether in or out of political office—are intimately familiar with the workings of government, thrive on gossip, and measure on a daily basis the political power of the president.

Public Approval. All of these constituencies are impressed by presidents who maintain a high level of public approval, partly because this is very difficult to accomplish. Presidential popularity, as measured by national polls, gives the president an extra political resource to use in persuading legislators or bureaucrats to pass legislation. As you will note from Figure 12-2, patterns for almost all presidents are common. Presidential approval ratings tend to be very high when a new president takes office (the honeymoon period), and they certainly decline to a low in the last two years of the second term. Spikes in public approval apart from that cycle tend to occur when the United States sends troops in harm's way. This is called the "rally 'round the flag" effect. Take a look at George H. W. Bush's ratings. Popular approval of the president reached a new high at the beginning of the Persian Gulf War, but that approval had no staying power, and his ratings declined precipitously in the year following the victory. Bill Clinton defied all tradition by having high ratings even while he was fighting impeachment.

Washington Community
Individuals regularly involved with politics in Washington, D.C.

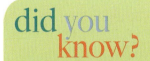

did you
know?

Four United States presidents have been awarded the Nobel Prize for Peace—Theodore Roosevelt, Woodrow Wilson, Jimmy Carter, and Barack Obama.

Figure 12-2 ▶ Public Popularity of Modern Presidents

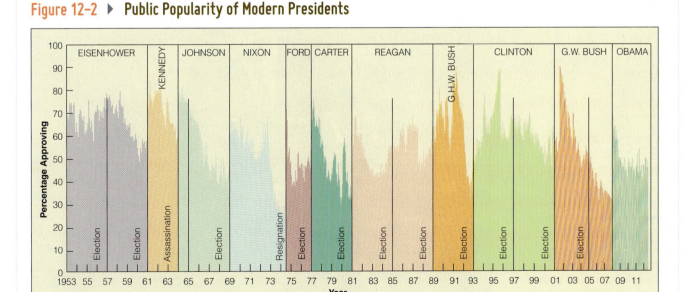

Source: The Roper Center for Public Opinion Research; Gallup and USA Today/CNN Polls, March 1992 through June 2012.

George W. Bush and the Public Opinion Polls. The impact of popular approval on a president's prospects was placed in sharp relief by the experiences of President Bush. Immediately after September 11, 2001, Bush had the highest approval ratings ever recorded. His popularity then entered a steep decline that was interrupted only briefly by high ratings during the early phases of the Second Gulf War. During his second term, Bush's approval ratings reached new lows, falling to 31 percent before the midterm elections in 2006 and then declining further to less than 30 percent by 2008. Without doubt, the economic crisis of fall 2008 contributed to the final low ebb of his approval ratings.

Barack Obama and Popular Approval

Like most presidents who win office with a substantial margin of victory, President Barack Obama entered the office with very high approval ratings. Voters, as usual, were willing to give the new president high marks for his first year in office. Additionally, Mr. Obama's youth, energy, and new outlook seemed to enhance his positive image. As the economic crisis deepened and various government measures failed to improve the unemployment figures, Mr. Obama began to experience some decline in his approval ratings. By the middle of his second year in office, his approval ratings had stabilized at about 50 percent, a level similar to that achieved by many other presidents in their first term in office.

"Going Public." Since the early 1900s, presidents have spoken more to the public and less to Congress. In the 1800s, only 7 percent of presidential speeches were addressed to the public; since 1900, 50 percent have been addressed to the public. One scholar, Samuel Kernell, has proposed that the style of presidential leadership has changed since World War II, owing partly to the influence of

President John F. Kennedy discusses the Berlin crisis at a news conference in 1961. Kennedy continues to be considered the master of such events.

AP Photo/Bill Chaplis

television, with a resulting change in the balance of national politics.[15] Presidents frequently go over the heads of Congress and the political elites, taking their cases directly to the people.

This strategy, which Kernell dubbed "going public," gives the president additional power through the ability to persuade and manipulate public opinion. By identifying their own positions so clearly, presidents make compromises with Congress much more difficult and weaken the legislators' positions. Given the increasing importance of the media as the major source of political information for citizens and elites, presidents will continue to use public opinion as part of their arsenal of weapons to gain support from Congress and to achieve their policy goals.

Special Uses of Presidential Power

■ **Learning Outcome 3:**
Explain the emergency powers of the president and the executive powers of the president.

Presidents have at their disposal a variety of special powers and privileges not available in the other branches of the U.S. government: (1) emergency powers, (2) executive orders, and (3) executive privilege.

Emergency Powers

If you read the Constitution, you will find no mention of the additional powers that the executive office may exercise during national emergencies. The Supreme Court has indicated that an "emergency does not create power."[16] But it is clear that presidents have used their inherent powers during times of emergency, particularly in the realm of foreign affairs. The **emergency powers** of the president were first enunciated in the Supreme Court's decision in *United States v. Curtiss-Wright Export Corp.*[17] In that case, President Franklin Roosevelt, without authorization by Congress, ordered an embargo on the shipment of weapons to two warring South American countries. The Court recognized that the president may exercise inherent powers in foreign affairs and that the national government has primacy in these affairs.

Emergency Powers
Inherent powers exercised by the president during a period of national crisis.

Examples of emergency powers are abundant, coinciding with crises in domestic and foreign affairs. Abraham Lincoln suspended civil liberties at the beginning of the Civil War (1861–1865) and called the state militias into national service. These actions and his subsequent governance of conquered areas and even of areas of Northern states were justified by claims that they were essential to preserve the Union. Franklin Roosevelt declared an "unlimited national emergency" following the fall of France in World War II (1939–1945) and mobilized the federal budget and the economy for war.

President Harry Truman authorized the federal seizure of steel plants and their operation by the national government in 1952 during the Korean War. Truman claimed that he was using his inherent emergency power as chief executive and commander in chief to safeguard the nation's security, as an ongoing strike by steelworkers threatened the supply of weapons to the armed forces. The Supreme Court did not agree, holding that the president had no authority under the Constitution to seize private property or to legislate such action.[18] According to legal scholars, this was the first time a limit was placed on the exercise of the president's emergency powers.

did you know?
The shortest inaugural address was George Washington's second one at 135 words.

15. Samuel Kernell, *Going Public: New Strategies of Presidential Leadership,* 3rd ed. (Washington, DC: Congressional Quarterly Press, 1997).
16. *Home Building and Loan Association v. Blaisdell,* 290 U.S. 398 (1934).
17. 299 U.S. 304 (1936).
18. *Youngstown Sheet and Tube Co. v. Sawyer,* 343 U.S. 579 (1952).

After September 11, the Bush administration pushed several laws through the Congress that granted more power to the Department of Justice and other agencies to investigate possible terrorists. Many of these provisions of the PATRIOT Act and other laws have been reaffirmed by Congress in subsequent years, while others have been revised. In 2006, it became clear that President Bush had also authorized federal agencies to eavesdrop on international telephone calls without a court order when the party overseas was suspected of having information about terrorism or might be a suspect in a terrorist plot. This eavesdropping had not been authorized under the legislation. Many scholars claimed that this exercise of presidential power was far beyond what could be claimed an emergency power.[19] The Bush administration claimed that it was entirely within the president's power to make such an authorization, although it did not claim the authorization to be within the Supreme Court's definition of "emergency power." Following these disclosures, the administration pursued an expanded law to allow such wiretapping, but provisions of that new bill proved too controversial to pass in 2008.

Executive Orders

Executive Order

A rule or regulation issued by the president that has the effect of law. Executive orders can implement and give administrative effect to provisions in the Constitution, to treaties, and to statutes.

Congress allows the president (as well as administrative agencies) to issue **executive orders** that have the force of law. These executive orders can do the following: (1) enforce legislative statutes, (2) enforce the Constitution or treaties with foreign nations, and (3) establish or modify rules and practices of executive administrative agencies.

An executive order, then, represents the president's legislative power. The only requirement is that under the Administrative Procedure Act of 1946, all executive orders must be published in the ***Federal Register***, a daily publication of the U.S. government. Executive orders have been used to establish procedures to appoint non-career administrators, to implement national affirmative action regulations, to restructure the White House bureaucracy, to ration consumer goods and to administer wage and price controls under emergency conditions, to classify government information as secret, to regulate the export of restricted items, and to establish military tribunals for suspected terrorists.

Federal Register

A publication of the U.S. government that prints executive orders, rules, and regulations.

It is important to note that executive orders can be revoked by succeeding presidents. George H. W. Bush issued an order to ban foreign aid to countries that included abortion in their family planning strategies, because that provision (known as the Hyde Amendment) could not make it through Congress as legislation. President Clinton revoked the order. The George W. Bush administration revoked many of the thousands of executive orders and regulations issued in the last months of the Clinton administration. Not surprisingly, the Obama administration revoked a number of the Bush orders and issued new orders in support of stronger environmental regulations, food safety, consumer safety, and many other areas.

Executive Privilege

Executive Privilege

The right of executive officials to withhold information from or refuse to appear before a legislative committee.

Another inherent executive power that has been claimed by presidents concerns the ability of the president and the president's executive officials to withhold information from or refuse to appear before Congress or the courts. This is called **executive privilege**, and it relies on the constitutional separation of powers for its basis.

Presidents have frequently invoked executive privilege to avoid having to disclose information to Congress on actions of the executive branch. For example,

---

19. Elizabeth Drew, "Power Grab," *New York Review of Books,* Vol. 53, No. 11, June 22, 2006.

Politics With A Purpose

"FOR THE RECORD" VERSUS "THAT'S PRIVILEGED INFORMATION"

Do we have a right to know everything our government does? What circumstances might justify the president keeping his or her activities or those of the administration secret? These questions raise complex issues, and common sense says the answers lie somewhere in between the two extremes. How this balance is struck has been the subject of intense political debate.

After the Watergate scandal (see the "Abuses of Executive Power and Impeachment" section for an explanation of these events), Congress passed the Presidential Records Act of 1978 (PRA) to address control of the historical record of a presidential administration.[a] Immediately upon the inauguration of the successor, the National Archives physically takes control of all presidential and vice presidential records. For a period of 12 years, the National Archives is responsible for processing these papers and reviewing and examining each document for national security issues or other reasons that would preclude it from being made public. Under the PRA, after the 12-year period and as the archivists finish their work, the records are released to the presidential libraries. Each library— staffed by archivists employed by the federal government—houses all of the papers of that administration.[b] However, current or former presidents can request that certain documents not be released, claiming executive privilege (discussed in the "Special Uses of Presidential Power" section).[c]

President Reagan's records were the first to be processed under the PRA. In February 2001, President Bush was notified that one of the first batches of Reagan documents was scheduled for release, as the 12-year period was set to expire. The president's subsequent Executive Order (E.O. 13233) in November 2001 significantly altered the PRA. Under E.O. 13233, instead of the process described previously, the National Archives now cannot release documents until the current and former presidents have approved their release. Researchers who may want access to these records bear the burden of arguing before a federal court that the president has no reason to withhold the records. The burden of proof has shifted away from the current or former presidents, who formerly had to demonstrate a compelling reason to keep the public away from the records. Now the burden is on the public to substantiate their need to know. A coalition of scholars, researchers, journalists, and public-interest lobby groups joined in a suit to stop the implementation of President Bush's executive order. Among the groups joining the 2002 suit filed by a public-interest group called Public Citizen were the Association of American University Presses (AAUP), the Association of American Publishers, the Society of American Historians, and the Society of Professional Journalists. The group won a partial victory in October 2007 when a federal court struck down the portion of E.O. 13233 allowing current and former presidents to screen the release of documents.[d]

In 2007, congressional partisan control reverted to the Democrats, and Representative Henry Waxman (D.-Ca.) became chair of the House Government and Oversight Committee. He coauthored the Presidential Records Act Amendments of 2007, which then passed the House and died in the Senate. Immediately after President Obama's inauguration, he signed an Executive Order that countermanded the Bush rules, although it did allow former presidents the opportunity to claim executive privilege for any requested documents. Around the same time, the House passed another, stronger version of the 2007 bill, but the two houses have not yet agreed upon a new version of the law. The issue of executive privilege often comes into play when the Senate is considering nominations to the federal courts. In early 2010, President Obama nominated Elena Kagan for the Supreme Court. Immediately, the Senate Judiciary Committee requested access to memos that Ms. Kagan wrote as an aide in the Clinton White House. Although President Clinton's papers are not supposed to be available until 2013, the former president has raised no objection to releasing the Kagan memos. However, the Clinton library contains more than 77 million pages of documents, and most have not yet been catalogued.

[a] www.archives.gov/presidential-libraries/laws/1978-act.html.
[b] For a complete list of the presidential libraries, see www.archives.gov/presidential-libraries.
[c] If someone wants access to an unreleased document, the person can file a Freedom of Information Act (FOIA) request. Archivists trained with an understanding of the PRA, FOIA, and any other governing statutes determine whether to release the documents. This process remains in place today.
[d] http://aaupnet.org/news/press/PRAamicus.pdf.

AP Photo/Bob Daughterty

Richard Nixon says goodbye outside the White House after his resignation on August 9, 1974, as he prepares to board a helicopter for a flight to nearby Andrews Air Force Base. Nixon addressed members of his staff in the East Room prior to his departure. Was Nixon impeached?

President George W. Bush claimed executive privilege to keep the head of the newly established Office of Homeland Security, Tom Ridge, from testifying before Congress. Bush, like presidents before him, claimed that a certain degree of secrecy is essential to national security. Critics of executive privilege believe that it can be used to shield from public scrutiny actions of the executive branch that should be open to Congress and to the American citizenry.

Limiting Executive Privilege. Limits to executive privilege went untested until the Watergate affair in the early 1970s. Five men had broken into the headquarters of the Democratic National Committee and were caught searching for documents that would damage the candidacy of the Democratic nominee, George McGovern. Later investigation showed that the break-in was planned by members of Richard Nixon's campaign committee and that Nixon and his closest advisers had devised a strategy for impeding the investigation of the crime. After it became known that all of the conversations held in the Oval Office had been tape-recorded on a secret system, Nixon was ordered to turn over the tapes to the special prosecutor.

Nixon refused to do so, claiming executive privilege. He argued that "no president could function if the private papers of his office, prepared by his personal staff, were open to public scrutiny." In 1974, in one of the Supreme Court's most famous cases, *United States v. Nixon,*[20] the justices unanimously ruled that Nixon had to hand over the tapes. The Court held that executive privilege could not be used to prevent evidence from being heard in criminal proceedings.

Clinton's Attempted Use of Executive Privilege. The claim of executive privilege was also raised by the Clinton administration as a defense against the aggressive investigation of Clinton's relationship with White House intern Monica Lewinsky by Independent Counsel Kenneth Starr. The Clinton administration claimed executive privilege for several presidential aides who might have discussed the situation with the president. In addition, President Clinton asserted that his White House counsel did not have to testify before the Starr grand jury due to attorney-client privilege. Finally, the Department of Justice claimed that members of the Secret Service who guard the president could not testify about his activities due to a "protective function privilege" inherent in their duties. The federal judge overseeing the case denied the claims of privilege, however, and the decision was upheld on appeal.

Abuses of Executive Power and Impeachment

Presidents normally leave office either because their first term has expired and they have not sought (or won) reelection or because, having served two full terms, they are not allowed to be elected for a third term (owing to the

---

20.   318 U.S. 683 (1974).

Twenty-second Amendment, passed in 1951). Eight presidents have died in office. But a president may leave office in another way—by **impeachment** and conviction. Articles I and II of the Constitution authorize the House and Senate to remove the president, the vice president, or other civil officers of the United States for committing "Treason, Bribery, or other high Crimes and Misdemeanors." According to the Constitution, the impeachment process begins in the House, which impeaches (accuses) the federal officer involved. If the House votes to impeach the officer, it draws up articles of impeachment and submits them to the Senate, which conducts the actual trial.

In the history of the United States, no president has ever actually been impeached and also convicted—and thus removed from office—by means of this process.

President Andrew Johnson (served 1865–1869), who succeeded to the office after the assassination of Abraham Lincoln, was impeached by the House but acquitted by the Senate. More than a century later, the House Judiciary Committee approved articles of impeachment against President Richard Nixon for his involvement in the cover-up of the Watergate break-in of 1972. Informed by members of his own party that he had no hope of surviving the trial in the Senate, Nixon resigned on August 9, 1974, before the full House voted on the articles. Nixon is the only president to have resigned from office.

The second president to be impeached by the House but not convicted by the Senate was President Bill Clinton. In September 1998, Independent Counsel Kenneth Starr sent to Congress the findings of his investigation of the president on the charges of perjury and obstruction of justice. The House approved two charges against Clinton: lying to the grand jury about his affair with Monica Lewinsky and obstruction of justice. The articles of impeachment were then sent to the Senate, which acquitted Clinton.

The Executive Organization

Gone are the days when presidents answered their own mail, as George Washington did. It was not until 1857 that Congress authorized a private secretary for the president, to be paid by the federal government. Woodrow Wilson typed most of his correspondence, even though he did have several secretaries. At the beginning of Franklin Roosevelt's long tenure in the White House, the entire staff consisted of 37 employees. With the New Deal and World War II, however, the presidential staff became a sizable organization.

Today, the executive organization includes a White House office staff of about 600, including some workers who are part-time employees and others who are borrowed from their departments by the White House. The more than 360 employees who work in the White House Office are closest to the president. The employees who work for the numerous councils and advisory groups are supposed to advise the president on policy and coordinate the work of departments. The group of appointees perhaps most helpful to the president are the cabinet members, each of whom is the principal officer of a government department.

The Cabinet

Although the Constitution does not include the word *cabinet,* it does state that the president "may require the Opinion, in writing, of the principal Officer in each of the executive Departments." Since the time of George Washington, the president has turned to an advisory group, or **cabinet**, for counsel.

Impeachment
An action by the House of Representatives to accuse the president, vice president, or other civil officers of the United States of committing "Treason, Bribery, or other high Crimes and Misdemeanors."

■ **Learning Outcome 4:**
Describe the executive offices that support the president.

Cabinet
An advisory group selected by the president to aid in making decisions. The cabinet includes the heads of 15 executive departments and others named by the president.

Kitchen Cabinet
The informal advisers to the president.

Members of the Cabinet. Originally, the cabinet consisted of only four officials—the secretaries of state, treasury, and war, and the attorney general. Today, the cabinet numbers 14 department secretaries and the attorney general. (See Chapter 13 for a detailed discussion of these cabinet departments.) The cabinet may include others as well. The president can, at his or her discretion, ascribe cabinet rank to the vice president, the head of the Office of Management and Budget, the national security adviser, the ambassador to the United Nations, or others.

Often, a president will use a **kitchen cabinet** to replace the formal cabinet as a major source of advice. The term *kitchen cabinet* originated during the presidency of Andrew Jackson, who relied on the counsel of close friends who often met with him in the kitchen of the White House. A kitchen cabinet is a very informal group of advisers; usually, they are friends with whom the president worked before being elected.

Presidential Use of Cabinets. Because neither the Constitution nor statutory law requires the president to consult with the cabinet, its use is purely discretionary. Some presidents have relied on the counsel of their cabinets more than others. Dwight Eisenhower was used to the team approach to solving problems from his experience as supreme Allied commander during World War II, and therefore he frequently turned to his cabinet for advice on a wide range of issues. More often, presidents have solicited the opinions of their cabinets and then done what they wanted to do anyway. Lincoln supposedly said—after a cabinet meeting in which a vote was seven nays against his one aye—"Seven nays and one aye; the ayes have it." In general, few presidents have relied heavily on the advice of their cabinet members.

It is not surprising that presidents tend not to rely on their cabinet members' advice. Often, the departmental heads are more responsive to the wishes of their own staffs or to their own political ambitions than they are to the president. They may be more concerned with obtaining resources for their departments than with achieving the goals of the president. So a strong conflict of interest between presidents and their cabinet members often exists.

The Executive Office of the President

Executive Office of the President (EOP)
An organization established by President Franklin D. Roosevelt to assist the president in carrying out major duties.

When President Franklin Roosevelt appointed a special committee on administrative management, he knew that the committee would conclude that the president needed help. The committee proposed a major reorganization of the executive branch. Congress did not approve the entire reorganization, but it did create the **Executive Office of the President (EOP)** to provide staff assistance for the chief executive and to help coordinate the executive bureaucracy. Since that time, many agencies have been created within the EOP to supply the president with advice and staff help. These agencies include the following:

- White House Office
- White House Military Office
- Office of the Vice President
- Council of Economic Advisers
- Office of National Drug Control Policy
- Office of Science and Technology Policy
- Office of the United States Trade Representative
- Council on Environmental Quality
- President's Critical Infrastructure Protection Board

- Office of Management and Budget
- National Security Council
- President's Foreign Intelligence Advisory Board
- Office of National AIDS Policy

Several of the offices within the EOP are especially important, including the White House Office, the Office of Management and Budget, and the National Security Council.

The White House Office.
The **White House Office** includes most of the key personal and political advisers to the president. Among the jobs held by these aides are those of legal counsel to the president, secretary, press secretary, and appointments secretary. In all recent administrations, one member of the White House Office has been named **chief of staff**. This person, who is responsible for coordinating the office, is also one of the president's chief advisers.

Often, the individuals who hold these positions are recruited from the president's campaign staff. Their duties—mainly protecting the president's political interests—are similar to campaign functions. In fact, most observers of the presidency agree that contemporary presidents continue their campaigning after inauguration. The **permanent campaign** is a long-term strategy planned by the White House Office of Communications with the press secretary to keep the president's approval ratings high and to improve his or her support in Congress. The campaign includes staged events, symbolic actions, and controlled media appearances. During the Obama presidency this function rose to a new height with the adoption of all forms of electronic media. Anyone who had worked in the 2008 campaign or who signed up for presidential updates received e-mails from the president or Joe Biden or the First Lady on a weekly basis with information about the president's initiatives. The White House also sent out tweets and posted information on all social media sites.

The president may establish special advisory units within the White House to address topics the president finds especially important. Under George W. Bush, these units also included the Office of Faith-Based and Community Initiatives and the USA Freedom Corps. The White House Office also includes the staff members who support the First Lady.

In addition to civilian advisers, the president is supported by a large number of military personnel, who are organized under the White House Military Office. These members of the military provide communications, transportation, medical care, and food services to the president and the White House staff.

Employees of the White House Office have been both envied and criticized. The White House Office, according to most former staffers, grants its employees access and power. They are able to use the resources of the White House to contact virtually anyone in the world by telephone, text, fax, satellite telephone, or e-mail, as well as to use the influence of the White House to persuade legislators and citizens. Because of this influence, staffers are often criticized for overstepping the bounds of the office. The appointments secretary is able to grant or deny senators, representatives, and cabinet secretaries access to the president. The press secretary grants the press and television journalists access to any information about the president.

White House staff members are closest to the president and may have considerable influence over the administration's decisions. When presidents are under fire for their decisions, the staff is often accused of keeping the chief executive too isolated from criticism or help. Presidents insist that they will not allow the

White House Office
The personal office of the president, which tends to presidential political needs and manages the media.

Chief of Staff
The person who is named to direct the White House Office and advise the president.

Permanent Campaign
A coordinated and planned strategy carried out by the White House to increase the president's popularity and support.

did you know?
The 2008 presidential elections were the first since 1952 without an incumbent president or vice president running.

staff to become too powerful, but, given the difficulty of the office, each president eventually turns to staff members for loyal assistance and protection.

The Office of Management and Budget.

Office of Management and Budget (OMB)
A division of the Executive Office of the President. The OMB assists the president in preparing the annual budget, clearing and coordinating departmental agency budgets, and supervising the administration of the federal budget.

The **Office of Management and Budget (OMB)** was originally the Bureau of the Budget, which was created in 1921 within the Department of the Treasury. Recognizing the importance of this agency, Franklin Roosevelt moved it into the White House Office in 1939. Richard Nixon reorganized the Bureau of the Budget in 1970 and changed its name to reflect its new managerial function. It is headed by a director, who must make up the annual federal budget that the president presents to Congress each January for approval. In principle, the director of the OMB has broad fiscal powers in planning and estimating various parts of the federal budget, because all agencies must submit their proposed budget to the OMB for approval. In reality, it is not so clear that the OMB truly can affect the greater scope of the federal budget. Rather, the OMB may be more important as a clearinghouse for legislative proposals initiated in the executive agencies.

The National Security Council.

National Security Council (NSC)
An agency in the Executive Office of the President that advises the president on national security.

The **National Security Council (NSC)** is a link between the president's key foreign and military advisers and the president. Its members consist of the president, the vice president, and the secretaries of state and defense, plus other informal members. Included in the NSC is the president's special assistant for national security affairs. In 2001, Condoleezza Rice became the first woman to serve as a president's national security adviser.

"Policy Tsars."

policy tsar
A high-ranking member of the Executive Office of the President appointed to coordinate action in one specific policy area.

For many decades presidents have created positions within the Executive Office of the President that were focused on one special policy area. Many of these positions have been titled "senior policy coordinator" or "senior adviser," and most of them have been appointments that do not require Senate confirmation. In general, these positions last only as long as the president. Each new president decides which domestic or foreign policy issues need special attention from an individual who can report directly to the chief executive. In recent administrations, the nickname "**policy tsar**" has been attached to these positions.

If the president has special councils on problems such as drugs or the environment and cabinet departments or independent agencies designated to handle an area of government policy, why does the president need yet another individual to supervise government action? What presidents expect when they appoint a policy tsar is a unique focus on the problem, along with the ability to coordinate the efforts of all the other government agencies that have some authority in that policy area. Additionally, the individuals named to these positions are often well-regarded experts who can bring an outsider's point of view both to the president and to the agencies involved in dealing with an issue. George W. Bush, over the two terms of his presidency, appointed more than 30 individuals to these positions.

President Obama created more than 40 positions in the Executive Office of the President to advise him on specific issue areas and to coordinate the work of cabinet departments on such topics as health care reform, climate change, and urban initiatives. Criticism of his decision to create so many special advisers ranged from the cost to the effectiveness of having people in place to oversee the work of cabinet secretaries[21], but his ability to do so was unquestionable. The president

---

21. Aaron J. Saiger, "Obama's "Czar's" for Domestic Policy and the Law of the White House Staff," *Fordham Law Review* 79 (2011): 2576–2616.

explained his need for experts in areas on which he wished to focus his administration's policymaking efforts.

The Vice Presidency

The Constitution does not give much power to the vice president. The only formal duty is to preside over the Senate, which is rarely necessary. This obligation is fulfilled when the Senate organizes and adopts its rules and when the vice president is needed to decide a tie vote. In all other cases, the president pro tem manages parliamentary procedures in the Senate. The vice president is expected to participate only informally in senatorial deliberations, if at all.

The Vice President's Job

Vice presidents have traditionally been chosen by presidential nominees to balance the ticket to attract groups of voters or appease party factions. If a presidential nominee is from the North, it is not a bad idea to have a vice presidential nominee who is from the South. If the presidential nominee is from a rural state, perhaps someone with an urban background would be most suitable as a running mate. Presidential nominees who are strongly conservative or strongly liberal would do well to have vice presidential nominees who are more in the middle of the political road.

Strengthening the Ticket. In recent presidential elections, vice presidents have often been selected for other reasons. Bill Clinton picked Al Gore to be his running mate in 1992, even though both were southerners and moderates. The ticket appealed to southerners and moderates, both of whom were crucial to the election. In 2000, both vice presidential selections were intended to shore up the respective presidential candidates' perceived weaknesses. Republican George W. Bush, who was subject to criticism for his lack of federal government experience and his "lightweight" personality, chose Dick Cheney, a former

Vice President Joe Biden lays a wreath at the Tomb of the Unknowns in Arlington National Cemetery on Memorial Day 2010.

JEWEL SAMAD/AFP/Getty Images/Newscom

member of Congress who had also served as secretary of defense. Democrat Al Gore chose Senator Joe Lieberman of Connecticut, whose reputation for moral integrity (as an Orthodox Jew) could help counteract the effects of Bill Clinton's sex scandals. Both presidential candidates in 2008 sought to balance their perceived weaknesses with their vice presidential choices. Barack Obama chose Senator Joseph Biden to add experience and foreign policy knowledge to his ticket, and John McCain chose Sarah Palin to add youth and an appeal to the Christian right to his ticket. In 2012, Republican nominee Mitt Romney selected Representative Paul Ryan of Wisconsin to be his running mate. Ryan, a well-known fiscal conservative, was selected to persuade Tea Party members and conservative Republicans to vote for the ticket.

Supporting the President. The job of vice president is not extremely demanding, even when the president gives some specific task to the vice president. Typically, vice presidents spend their time supporting the president's activities. During the Clinton administration (1993–2001), however, Vice President Al Gore did much to strengthen the position of vice president by his aggressive support for environmental protection policies on a global basis. He also took a special interest in areas of emerging technology and lobbied Congress to provide subsidies to public schools for Internet use.

Vice President Dick Cheney, as one of President George W. Bush's key advisers, clearly was an influential figure in the Bush administration. Although many of the Washington elite were happy to see Dick Cheney as vice president because of his intelligence and wide range of experience, he quickly became a controversial figure due to his outspoken support for a tough foreign and military policy and for having encouraged Bush to attack Iraq.

Vice President Joe Biden, the former senator from Delaware, was a popular choice for vice president among Democrats and voters. He had many years of experience in the Senate, thus balancing President's Obama's relative lack of experience on Capitol Hill. Once the Obama administration took office, Biden's role became somewhat clearer. His experiences in the Senate prepared him to be a senior adviser to the president on foreign policy issues, although he certainly was not as controversial a figure as Cheney had been. Of course, the vice presidency takes on more significance if the president becomes disabled or dies in office and the vice president becomes president.

Vice presidents sometimes have become elected presidents in their own right. John Adams and Thomas Jefferson were the first two vice presidents to do so. Richard Nixon was elected president in 1968 after he had served as Dwight D. Eisenhower's vice president from 1953 to 1961. In 1988, George H. W. Bush was elected to the presidency after eight years as Ronald Reagan's vice president.

Presidential Succession

Eight vice presidents have become president because of the death of the president. John Tyler, the first to do so, took over William Henry Harrison's position after only one month. No one knew whether Tyler should simply be a caretaker until a new president could be elected three and a half years later or whether he actually should be president. Tyler assumed that he was supposed to be the chief executive and he acted as such, although he was commonly referred to as "His Accidency." Since then, vice presidents taking over the position of the presidency because of the incumbent's death have assumed the presidential powers.

did you know?

President Richard Nixon served 56 days without a vice president, and President Gerald Ford served 132 days without a vice president.

But what should a vice president do if a president becomes incapable of carrying out necessary duties while in office? When James Garfield was shot in 1881, he remained alive for two and a half months. What was Vice President Chester Arthur's role? This question was not addressed in the original Constitution. Article II, Section 1, says only that "[i]n Case of the Removal of the President from Office, or of his Death, Resignation, or Inability to discharge the Powers and Duties of the said Office, the same shall devolve on [the same powers shall be exercised by] the Vice President." Many instances of presidential disability have occurred. When Dwight Eisenhower became ill a second time in 1958, he entered into a pact with Richard Nixon specifying that the vice president could determine whether the president was incapable of carrying out his duties if the president could not communicate. John F. Kennedy and Lyndon Johnson entered into similar agreements with their vice presidents. Finally, in 1967, the **Twenty-fifth Amendment** was ratified, establishing procedures in case of presidential incapacity.

The Twenty-fifth Amendment

According to the Twenty-fifth Amendment, when a president believes that he or she is incapable of performing the duties of office, the president must inform Congress in writing. Then the vice president serves as acting president until the president can resume normal duties. When the president is unable to communicate, a majority of the cabinet, including the vice president, can declare that fact to Congress. Then the vice president serves as acting president until the president resumes normal duties. If a dispute arises over the return of the president's ability, a two-thirds vote of Congress is required to decide whether the vice president shall remain acting president or whether the president shall resume normal duties.

In 2002, President George W. Bush formally invoked the Twenty-fifth Amendment for the first time by officially transferring presidential power to Vice President Dick Cheney while the president underwent a colonoscopy, a 20-minute procedure. He commented that he undertook this transfer of power "because we're at war," referring to the war on terrorism. The only other time the provisions of the Twenty-fifth Amendment have been used was during President Reagan's colon surgery in 1985, although Reagan did not formally invoke the amendment.

Twenty-fifth Amendment
A 1967 amendment to the Constitution that establishes procedures for filling presidential and vice presidential vacancies and makes provisions for presidential disability.

An attempted assassination of Ronald Reagan occurred on March 31, 1981. In the foreground, two men bend over Press Secretary James Brady, who lies seriously wounded. In the background, President Reagan is watched over by a U.S. Secret Service agent with an automatic weapon. A Washington, D.C., police officer, Thomas Delahanty, lies to the left after also being shot.

AP Photo/Ron Edmonds

When the Vice Presidency Becomes Vacant

The Twenty-fifth Amendment also addresses the issue of how the president should fill a vacant vice presidency. Section 2 of the amendment simply states, "Whenever there is a vacancy in the office of the Vice President, the President shall nominate a Vice President who shall take office upon confirmation by a majority vote of both Houses of Congress." This is exactly what occurred when Richard Nixon's vice president, Spiro Agnew, resigned in 1973 because of his alleged receipt of construction contract kickbacks during his tenure as governor of Maryland. Nixon turned to Gerald Ford as his choice for vice president. After extensive hearings, both chambers of Congress confirmed the appointment. Then, when Nixon resigned on August 9, 1974, Ford automatically became president and nominated Nelson Rockefeller as his vice president. Congress confirmed Ford's choice. For the first time in the history of the country, neither the president nor the vice president had been elected to that position.

The question of who shall be president if both the president and vice president die is answered by the Succession Act of 1947. If the president and vice president die, resign, or are disabled, the Speaker of the House will become president, after resigning from Congress. Next in line is the president pro tem of the Senate, followed by the cabinet officers in the order of the creation of their departments (see Table 12-2).

Table 12-2 ▶ Line of Succession to the Presidency of the United States

1.	Vice President
2.	Speaker of the House of Representatives
3.	Senate President Pro Tempore
4.	Secretary of State
5.	Secretary of the Treasury
6.	Secretary of Defense
7.	Attorney General (head of the Justice Department)
8.	Secretary of the Interior
9.	Secretary of Agriculture
10.	Secretary of Commerce
11.	Secretary of Labor
12.	Secretary of Health and Human Services
13.	Secretary of Housing and Urban Development
14.	Secretary of Transportation
15.	Secretary of Energy
16.	Secretary of Education
17.	Secretary of Veterans Affairs
18.	Secretary of Homeland Security

You Can Make a Difference

Jewel Samad/AFP/Getty Images

WATCHING THE WHITE HOUSE

As our head of state, chief executive, commander in chief, and chief legislator, the president of the United States wields massive power over matters at home and abroad. However, the times we live in also present major challenges to this individual, and it is up to us as citizens to monitor our president's performance and balance our country's place in the world.

Former Prime Minister of Australia John Howard created a YouTube video to communicate to constitutents. Here a journalist reviews his video.

WHY SHOULD YOU CARE?

A recent panel convened at the Center for Public Leadership at Harvard's John F. Kennedy School of Government to discuss the challenges facing the president-elect in the 2008 election. Foreign policy issues topped concerns cited, with the continued U.S. presence in Iraq debated and the nuclear potential of Iran and North Korea studied. President Obama inherited the largest ongoing deployment of U.S. military forces in combat since the Vietnam War, while trying to overcome the unprecedented unpopularity of America in the world.

Domestically, five challenges were listed as needing resolution: (1) reforming America's financial institutions, (2) lessening inequality between society's richest 1 percent and the bottom 80 percent on the income scale, (3) improving the health care system, (4) creating a more open global economy, and (5) providing energy security while reducing climate change. This is a daunting to-do list for any president and, to make things even more complex, what needs to be done in each of these areas is not completely clear.

WHAT CAN YOU DO?

As you will remember, President Obama garnered a majority of votes from younger voters and more than expected from highly educated Americans. You can maintain a connection to the White House and keep informed on the president's initiatives by monitoring the home page of the White House, www.whitehouse.gov. This Web site has current news; links to the Web pages of the president, vice president, and First Lady; categories for public policy; pages for the president's cabinet; and interactive links where you can register your comments. You can sign up for e-mail from the White House or the president's political campaign to receive constant updates on policy initiatives or appointments. You can also sign up for Facebook or Twitter updates. Link to the White House's YouTube site, where you can watch videos from the president and other government officials. You can, of course, use "snail mail" to write to President Obama at this address:

The President of the United States
The White House
1600 Pennsylvania Avenue N.W.
Washington, DC 20500

Countless Web sites provide daily updates focusing on the president and the White House. White House Watch, www.washingtonpost.com/whitehousewatch, is published every weekday and includes White House–related items from newspapers, magazines, broadcast Web sites, and blogs. The White House Watch Links on the site include the latest White House salary list, a map of the West Wing, presidential approval polls, and a list of correspondents covering the White House for major news outlets. Politicalticker, a blog for CNNPolitics.com, features the latest political news and has a special category devoted to the president. Beltway Confidential, http://blogs.chron.com/beltwayconfidential, is a blog run by the *Houston Chronicle* that features "The President of America," with daily updates from media sources around the country and opportunities to post your comments.

Finally, if you would like to check the factual accuracy of statements made by the president or about him or her in the media, you can go to www.factcheck.org, a project of the Annenberg Public Policy Center (APPC) of the University of Pennsylvania. The APPC was established in 1994 to create a community of scholars to address public policy issues at the local, state, and federal levels.

What is most important is that you stay interested in the president and his or her initiatives whether you agree with them or not and keep up with the policy debates in Washington, D.C. By keeping up with the debates, you will be able to be an opinion leader among your friends and family and ensure their continued engagement with our political system.

REFERENCES

Glenn Greenwald, "Trust Us Government," Salon.com, accessed January 29, 2008, at www.salon.com.

Jeffrey Jones, "Low Trust in Federal Government Rivals Watergate Era Levels," Gallup News Service, accessed September 26, 2007, at www.gallup.com.

http://blogs.chron.com/beltwayconfidential/the_president_of_america.

http://politicalticker.blogs.cnn.com.

www.factcheck.org.

www.washingtonpost.com/whitehousewatch.

www.whitehouse.gov.

Key Terms

advice and consent 386

appointment power 383

cabinet 401

chief diplomat 386

chief executive 383

chief legislator 388

chief of staff 403

civil service 383

commander in chief 385

constitutional powers 393

diplomatic recognition 386

emergency powers 397

executive agreement 388

Executive Office of the President (EOP) 402

executive order 398

executive privilege 398

expressed powers 393

Federal Register 398

head of state 381

impeachment 401

inherent powers 393

kitchen cabinet 402

line-item veto 393

National Security Council (NSC) 404

Office of Management and Budget (OMB) 404

pardon 384

patronage 394

permanent campaign 403

pocket veto 390

policy tsar 404

reprieve 384

signing statement 383

State of the Union message 389

statutory powers 393

Twelfth Amendment 381

Twenty-fifth Amendment 407

veto message 390

War Powers Resolution 386

Washington community 395

White House Office 403

 Chapter Summary

1. The office of the presidency in the United States, combining as it does the functions of head of state and chief executive, was unique when it was created. The framers of the Constitution were divided over whether the president should be a weak or a strong executive.

2. The requirements for the office of the presidency are outlined in Article II, Section 1, of the Constitution. The president's roles include both formal and informal duties. The roles of the president include head of state, chief executive, commander in chief, chief diplomat, chief legislator, and party chief.

3. As head of state, the president is ceremonial leader of the government. As chief executive, the president is bound to enforce the acts of Congress, the judgments of the federal courts, and treaties. The chief executive has the power of appointment and the power to grant reprieves and pardons.

4. As commander in chief, the president is the ultimate decision maker in military matters. As chief diplomat, the president recognizes foreign governments, negotiates treaties, signs agreements, and nominates and receives ambassadors.

5. The role of chief legislator includes recommending legislation to Congress, lobbying for the legislation, approving laws, and exercising the veto power. In addition to constitutional and inherent powers, the president has statutory powers written into law by Congress.

6. Presidents are also the political leaders of their party, naming the leadership of the party and being the chief fundraiser for future elections. To become effective leaders and to gain support for their policies, presidents try to maintain strong approval ratings from the public, as measured by frequent polls. The White House Office works tirelessly to improve the president's image and reputation through its relationship with the media. Presidents who maintain their popularity are likely to have more success in their legislative programs.

7. Presidents have a variety of special powers not available to other branches of the government. These include

emergency power, which is most frequently used during war or a national crisis, and the power to issue executive orders and invoke executive privilege.

8. Abuses of executive power are dealt with by Articles I and II of the Constitution, which authorize the House and Senate to impeach and remove the president, vice president, or other officers of the federal government for committing "Treason, Bribery, or other high Crimes and Misdemeanors."

9. The president fulfills the role of chief executive by appointing individuals of his or her choice to positions in the departments and agencies of government, as well as various advisers in the White House Office and the Executive Office of the President. Some of the offices within the EOP were established by law while others are appointed as the president desires. All appointees are supposed to be working for the president's initiatives and making sure that the larger bureaucracy is also supportive of the president's programs.

10. The vice president is the constitutional officer assigned to preside over the Senate and to assume the presidency in the event of the death, resignation, removal, or disability of the president. The Twenty-fifth Amendment, passed in 1967, established procedures to be followed in case of presidential incapacity and when filling a vacant vice presidency.

Selected Print, Media, and Online Resources

PRINT RESOURCES

Clinton, Bill. *My Life*. New York: Knopf, 2004. President Clinton's autobiography devotes ample space to illuminating stories from his childhood. In contrast, some may find the account of his presidential years excessively detailed. Still, the book is essential source material on one of the most important and controversial political figures of our time.

Crenson, Matthew, and Benjamin Ginsberg. *Presidential Power: Unchecked and Unbalanced*. New York: W. W. Norton, 2007. The authors return to the idea that the president has become too powerful and show how presidents over the last 30 years have expanded the power of the office.

Mann, James. *Rise of the Vulcans: The History of Bush's War Cabinet*. New York: Viking Books, 2004. This is a collective biography of the foreign policy team (not all of whom were actually in the cabinet) during George W. Bush's first term. The self-described Vulcans included Donald Rumsfeld, secretary of defense; Vice President Dick Cheney; Colin Powell, secretary of state; Paul Wolfowitz, deputy secretary of defense; Richard Armitage, deputy secretary of state; and Condoleezza Rice, national security adviser. While these individuals were never in perfect agreement, they shared basic values.

Rockman, Bert A., Andrew Rudalevige, and Colin Campbell. *The Obama Presidency: Appraisals and Prospects*. Washington, D.C.: CQ Press College, 2011. Three of the leading scholars of the presidency examine the successes and failures of the first two years of the Obama presidency.

Skowronek, Stephen. *Presidential Leadership in Political Time: Reprise and Reappraisal*. Lawrence, KS: University Press of Kansas, 2008. In this updating of a well-known book, the author expands on his thesis that presidents' successes are, in part, constrained by the political events of the day. He includes both Bill Clinton and George W. Bush in his analysis.

MEDIA RESOURCES

Fahrenheit 9/11—Michael Moore's scathing 2004 critique of the Bush administration has been called "one long political attack ad." It is also the highest-grossing documentary ever made. While the film may be biased, it is—like all of Moore's productions—entertaining.

The Guns of October—This film explores the Cuban Missile Crisis of 1962. It portrays the Kennedy decision-making process in deciding not to attack Cuba.

LBJ: A Biography—An acclaimed biography of Lyndon Johnson that covers his rise to power, his presidency, and the events of the Vietnam War, which ended his presidency; produced in 1991 as part of PBS's *The American Experience* series.

Nixon—An excellent 1995 film exposing the events of Richard Nixon's troubled presidency. Anthony Hopkins plays the embattled but brilliant chief executive.

Sunrise at Campobello—An excellent portrait of one of the greatest presidents, Franklin Delano Roosevelt; produced in 1960 and starring Ralph Bellamy.

ONLINE RESOURCES

The American Presidency Project at the University of California at Santa Barbara—a wonderful collection of presidential photographs, documents, audio, and video: www.presidency.ucsb.edu

Bartleby.com—Internet publisher of literature, reference, and verse providing unlimited access to books and information. Includes inaugural addresses of American presidents from George Washington to Barack Obama: www.bartleby.com/124

Dave Leip's Atlas of U.S. Presidential Elections— offers an excellent collection of data and maps describing all U.S. presidential elections: www.uselectionatlas.org

The White House—extensive information on the White House and the presidency: www.whitehouse.gov

13 The Bureaucracy

Internal Revenue Service workers sort individual returns at the IRS center in Covington, Kentucky. Similar centers operate in different regions of the country.

LEARNING OUTCOMES

After reading this chapter, students will be able to:

■ **LO1** Define the concept of the bureaucracy, and explain why such an organization is necessary.

■ **LO2** Compare the structure and function of executive departments, executive agencies, independent regulatory agencies, and government corporations.

■ **LO3** Explain how individuals get positions in the federal bureaucracy, and discuss the history of attempts to reform that process.

■ **LO4** Describe the tools and powers that bureaucratic agencies have to shape policies and regulations.

What If ...

EVERY FEDERAL AGENCY REPORTED TO THE PEOPLE?

BACKGROUND

Each year, every federal department, commission, and agency meets with the Office of Management and Budget (OMB) to propose a budget. The General Accountability Office (GAO) may investigate an agency for wrongdoing or simply audit its financial statements. Although the Congress does approve the budget for every agency, appropriations committees do not have enough time to look at the work of the entire federal government. And today, many federal agencies post a great deal of their work on the Internet, so why not have every federal agency report to the people?

WHAT IF EVERY FEDERAL AGENCY REPORTED TO THE PEOPLE?

While most agencies must produce some sort of report to Congress or to the GAO or OMB, no simple report exists showing what the federal government is doing for the people of the United States. Some agencies post their annual reports on the Internet for all to see, but they are generally glossy, slick presentations that highlight their accomplishments and gloss over the less successful ventures. Other agencies post detailed statistical reports such as the Agriculture Department's monthly corn production prediction. The results of other agencies' work turn up in the various censuses conducted by the Department of Commerce—the Census of Farm Owners, the Census of Hospitals, or the Census of Small Business, for instance.

What if every agency had to produce, on a specified day, a five-page report of its work? The contents would be specified by law: What were its revenues and expenses? How many people did it serve? What exactly are its programs and how were its services delivered? In the case of the U.S. Postal Service, for example, what did it actually cost to deliver a first-class letter or a heavy catalog, and did the postal service make or lose money on each? Anyone could read the reports on the Internet, and copies could be downloaded and printed at every public library.

WHAT WOULD THE REPORTS ACCOMPLISH?

Annual reports for all federal agencies could accomplish two important tasks: First, they could make citizens more aware of what their tax dollars purchase in goods and services. Citizens might find that they approve of the services being provided. While it is likely to

become clear that some services provided by the government are pretty expensive, the people will likely decide that they are essential. Consider, for example, medical care and rehabilitation for wounded veterans returning from Afghanistan. The extreme cost of such care should surprise no one. On the other hand, public awareness of some of the fraudulent schemes perpetrated by individuals or organizations to get Medicare dollars might help citizens stop waste.

Annual reports, produced in very consistent ways, would surely make agencies more accountable to the president, to the Congress, and to the citizens. Currently, government agencies seek either the same amount of or increased funding each year on the basis that their work is stellar and important. However, most agencies do not need to explain what they do to the public. They assume their continued existence. Short, fact-based reports would be nonpolitical, unlike the current glossy brochures. In fact, it might be a good idea for a panel of citizens and journalists to draw up the format and occasionally check that agencies are complying with the reporting requirements.

ANNUAL REPORTS COULD BE A WASTE OF TIME AND MONEY

Very few Americans would likely read annual agency reports. Most citizens do not think too much about government or the political process unless a presidential election looms. Downloading and reading through rather dry bureaucratic reports demands a high interest in government. For the agencies, these new reports would be yet another paperwork requirement that consumes time and money. Currently Congress requires all sorts of reports from agencies, reports that some say waste time and produce only controversy, such as the annual report on terrorist groups. Many career government workers would likely find it futile to produce an annual report to the people that few would read.

FOR CRITICAL ANALYSIS

1. *What specific items should be included in the annual report of each agency?*

2. *Name several government organizations that you might be interested in knowing about. Do you think others would have a similar list?*

FACELESS BUREAUCRATS—this image provokes a negative reaction from many, if not most, Americans. Polls consistently report that the majority of Americans support "less government." The same polls, however, report that the majority of Americans support almost every specific program that the government undertakes. The conflict between the desire for small government and the benefits that only a large government can provide has been a constant feature of American politics. For example, the goal of preserving endangered species has widespread support. At the same time, many people believe that restrictions imposed under the Endangered Species Act violate the rights of landowners. Helping the elderly pay their medical bills is a popular objective, but hardly anyone enjoys paying the Medicare tax that supports this effort.

In addition, everyone complains about the inefficiency and wastefulness of government in general and at federal, state, and local levels. The media regularly uncover examples of failures in governmental programs. Inadequate, slow, or bungled responses to crises such as Hurricane Katrina or the 2010 oil spill become the "face" of government through the news media. In this chapter, we describe the size, organization, and staffing of the federal bureaucracy. We review modern attempts at bureaucratic reform and the process by which Congress exerts ultimate control over the bureaucracy. We also discuss the bureaucracy's role in making rules and setting policy.

The Nature of Bureaucracy

■ **Learning Outcome 1:**
Define the concept of the bureaucracy, and explain why such an organization is necessary.

Every modern president, at one time or another, has proclaimed that his administration was going to "fix the government." All modern presidents also have put forth plans to end government waste and inefficiency. For instance, Bill Clinton's plan was called Reinventing Government, followed by Performance-Based Budgeting under George W. Bush. Within a few months of his inauguration, President Obama issued a call to his departments to "cut what doesn't work."[1] The success of plans such as these has been, in a word, underwhelming. Presidents generally have been powerless to affect the structure and operation of the federal bureaucracy significantly.

A **bureaucracy** is the name given to a large organization that is structured hierarchically to carry out specific functions. Generally, most bureaucracies are characterized by an organization chart. The units of the organization are divided according to the specialization and expertise of the employees.

Bureaucracy
A large organization that is structured hierarchically to carry out specific functions.

Public and Private Bureaucracies

We should not think of bureaucracy as unique to government. Any large corporation or university can be considered a bureaucratic organization. The fact is that the handling of complex problems requires a division of labor. Individuals must concentrate their skills on specific, well-defined aspects of a problem and depend on others to solve the rest of it.

Public or government bureaucracies differ from private organizations in some important ways, however. A private corporation, such as Microsoft, has a single set of leaders—its board of directors. Public bureaucracies, in contrast, do not have a single set of leaders. Although the president is the chief administrator of the federal system, all bureaucratic agencies are subject to Congress for their

---

1. President Barack Obama, Weekly Radio Address, April 25, 2009. http//www.whitehouse.gov

AP Photo/Patrick Semansky

funding, staffing, and their continued existence. Furthermore, public bureaucracies supposedly serve the citizenry.

One other important difference between private corporations and government bureaucracies is that government bureaucracies are not organized to make a profit. Rather, they are supposed to perform their functions as efficiently as possible to conserve the taxpayers' dollars. Perhaps this ideal makes citizens hostile toward government bureaucracy when they experience inefficiency and red tape.

Models of Bureaucracy

Several theories have been offered to help us better understand the ways in which bureaucracies function. Each of these theories focuses on specific features of bureaucracies.

Weberian Model. The classic model, or **Weberian model**, of the modern bureaucracy was proposed by the German sociologist Max Weber.[2] He argued that the increasingly complex nature of modern life, coupled with the steadily growing demands placed on governments by their citizens, made the formation of bureaucracies inevitable. According to Weber, most bureaucracies—whether in the public or private sector—are organized hierarchically and governed by formal procedures. The power in a bureaucracy flows from the top downward. Decision-making processes in bureaucracies are shaped by detailed technical rules that promote similar decisions in similar situations. Bureaucrats are specialists who attempt to resolve problems through logical reasoning and data analysis instead of instinct and guesswork. Individual advancement in bureaucracies is supposed to be based on merit rather than political connections. The modern bureaucracy, according to Weber, should be an apolitical organization.

Acquisitive Model. Other theorists do not view bureaucracies in terms as benign as Weber's. Some believe that bureaucracies are acquisitive in nature. Proponents of the **acquisitive model** argue that top-level bureaucrats will always

Weberian Model
A model of bureaucracy developed by the German sociologist Max Weber, who viewed bureaucracies as rational, hierarchical organizations in which decisions are based on logical reasoning.

Acquisitive Model
A model of bureaucracy that views top-level bureaucrats as seeking to expand the size of their budgets and staffs to gain greater power.

2. Max Weber, *Theory of Social and Economic Organization*, Talcott Parsons, ed. (New York: Oxford University Press, 1974).

try to expand, or at least to avoid any reductions in, the size of their budgets. Although government bureaucracies are not-for-profit enterprises, bureaucrats want to maximize the size of their budgets and staffs, because these things are the most visible trappings of power in the public sector. These efforts are also prompted by the desire of bureaucrats to "sell" their products—national defense, public housing, agricultural subsidies, and so on—to both Congress and the public.

Monopolistic Model
A model of bureaucracy that compares bureaucracies to monopolistic business firms. Lack of competition in either circumstance leads to inefficient and costly operations.

Monopolistic Model. Because government bureaucracies seldom have competitors, some theorists have suggested that these bureaucratic organizations may be explained best by a **monopolistic model**. The analysis is similar to that used by economists to examine the behavior of monopolistic firms. Monopolistic bureaucracies—like monopolistic firms—essentially have no competitors and act accordingly. Because monopolistic bureaucracies usually are not penalized for chronic inefficiency, they have little reason to adopt cost-saving measures or to use their resources more productively. Some economists have argued that such problems can be cured only by privatizing certain bureaucratic functions.

Bureaucracies Compared

The federal bureaucracy in the United States enjoys a greater degree of autonomy than do federal or national bureaucracies in many other nations. Much of the insularity that is commonly supposed to characterize the bureaucracy in this country may stem from the sheer size of the government organizations needed to implement an annual budget that is about $3 trillion. Because the lines of authority often are not well defined, some bureaucracies may be able to operate with a significant degree of autonomy.

The federal government spends more than $1 billion every five hours, every day of the year.

The federal nature of the American government also means that national bureaucracies regularly provide financial assistance to their state counterparts. Both the Department of Education and the Department of Housing and Urban Development, for example, distribute funds to their counterparts at the state level. In contrast, most bureaucracies in European countries have a top-down command structure so that national programs may be implemented directly at the lower level. This is due not only to the smaller size of most European countries but also to the fact that public ownership of such businesses as telephone companies, airlines, railroads, and utilities is far more common in Europe than in the United States.

The fact that the U.S. government owns relatively few enterprises does not mean, however, that its bureaucracies are comparatively powerless. Many **administrative agencies** in the federal bureaucracy—such as the Environmental Protection Agency, the Nuclear Regulatory Commission, and the Securities and Exchange Commission—regulate private companies.

Administrative Agency
A federal, state, or local government unit established to perform a specific function. Administrative agencies are created and authorized by legislative bodies to administer and enforce specific laws.

The Size of the Bureaucracy

In 1789, the new government's bureaucracy was minuscule. There were three departments—State (with nine employees), War (with two employees), and Treasury (with 39 employees)—and the Office of the Attorney General (which later became the Department of Justice). The bureaucracy was still small in 1798. At that time, the secretary of state had seven clerks and spent a total of $500 (about $8,545 in 2008 dollars) on stationery and printing. In that same year, the Appropriations Act allocated $1.4 million to the War Department (or $23.9 million in 2008 dollars).[3]

---

3. Leonard D. White, *The Federalists: A Study in Administrative History, 1789–1801* (New York: Free Press, 1948).

Figure 13-1 ▸ **Federal Agencies and Their Respective Numbers of Civilian Employees**

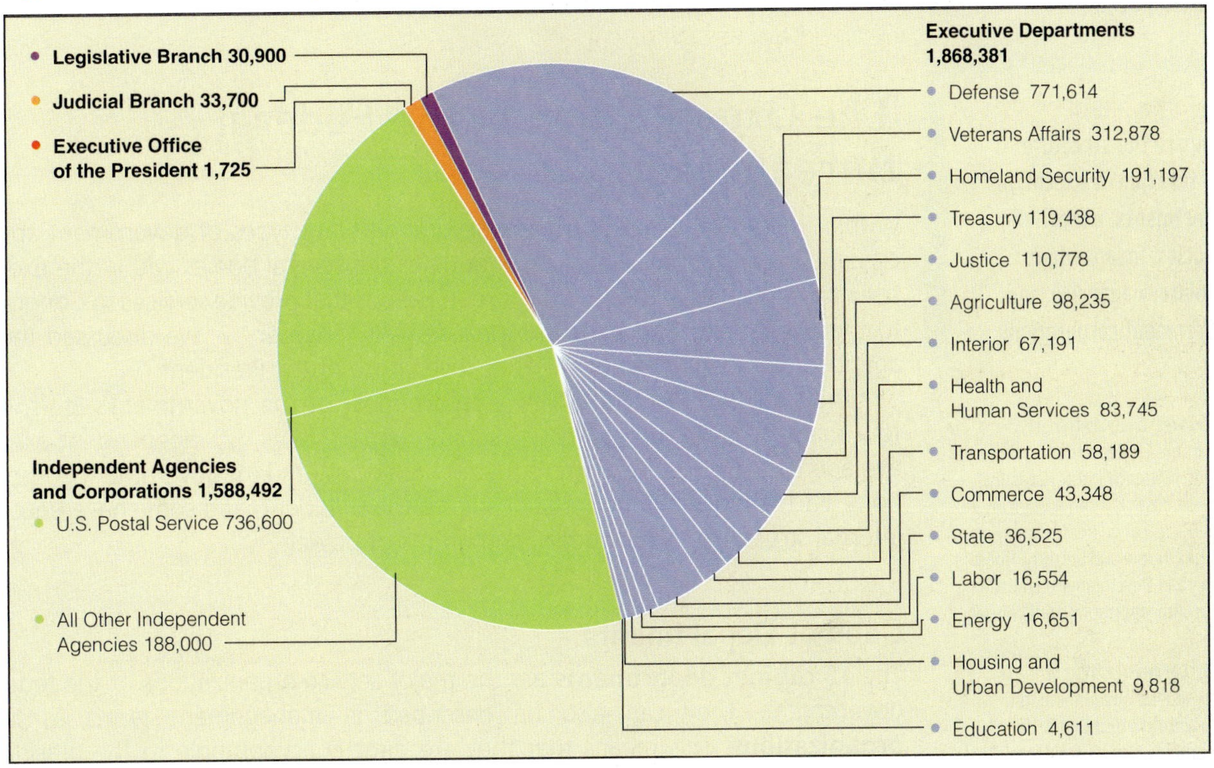

Legislative Branch 30,900
Judicial Branch 33,700
Executive Office of the President 1,725
Independent Agencies and Corporations 1,588,492
U.S. Postal Service 736,600
All Other Independent Agencies 188,000
Executive Departments 1,868,381
Defense 771,614
Veterans Affairs 312,878
Homeland Security 191,197
Treasury 119,438
Justice 110,778
Agriculture 98,235
Interior 67,191
Health and Human Services 83,745
Transportation 58,189
Commerce 43,348
State 36,525
Labor 16,554
Energy 16,651
Housing and Urban Development 9,818
Education 4,611

Source: Curtis W. Copeland, "The Federal Workforce: Characteristics and Trends," Washington, D.C.: Congressional Research Service, 2011.

Times have changed, as we can see in Figure 13-1, which lists the various federal agencies and the number of civilian employees in each. Excluding the military, the federal bureaucracy includes approximately 2.7 million government employees. That number has remained relatively stable for the last several decades. It is somewhat deceiving, however, because many other individuals work directly or indirectly for the federal government as subcontractors or consultants and in other capacities. Experts estimate that the number of individuals employed through private contractors for the federal government grew from 4.4 million in 1999 to more than 7.6 million in 2005. Much of this growth resulted from the decision to employ private contractors in many support roles in Iraq and Afghanistan.[4]

The figures for federal government employment are only part of the story. Figure 13-2 shows the growth in government employment at the federal, state, and local levels. Since 1970, this growth has been mainly at the state and local levels. If all government employees are included, more than 16 percent of all civilian employment is accounted for by government. The costs of the bureaucracy are commensurately high. The share of the gross domestic product accounted for by all government spending was only 8.5 percent in 1929. Today, it exceeds 40 percent. Could we reduce the cost of government by eliminating unnecessary spending? We look at one example of

Figure 13-2 ▸ **Government Employment at the Federal, State, and Local Levels**

There are more local government employees than federal or state employees combined.

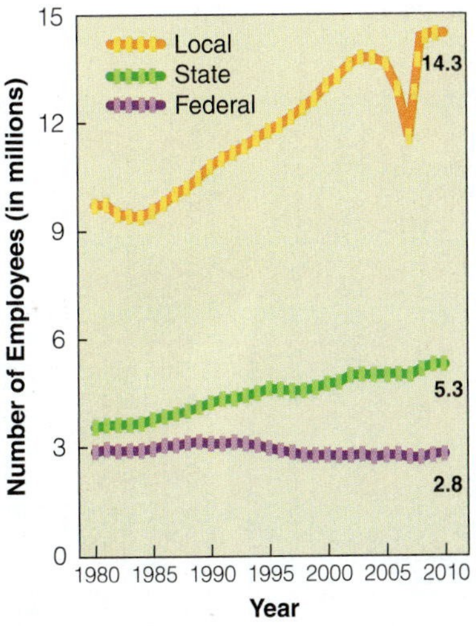

15
12
9
6
3
0
Local
State
Federal
14.3
5.3
2.8
Number of Employees (in millions)
1980 1985 1990 1995 2000 2005 2010
Year

Source: U.S. Bureau of the Census, 2011.

4. See, for example, Paul C. Light, *The New True Size of Government* (Robert F. Wagner Graduate School of Public Service, New York University, 2006).

questionable spending in the discussion of AMTRAK in the "Government Corporations" section.

The Organization of the Federal Bureaucracy

Within the federal bureaucracy are several different types of government agencies and organizations. Figure 13-3 outlines the several bodies within the executive branch, as well as the separate organizations that provide services to Congress, to the courts, and directly to the president. In Chapter 12, we discussed those agencies considered part of the Executive Office of the President.

The executive branch, which employs most of the government's staff, has four major types of structures: (1) cabinet departments, (2) independent executive agencies, (3) independent regulatory agencies, and (4) government corporations. Each has a distinctive relationship to the president, and some have unusual internal structures, overall goals, and grants of power.

Cabinet Departments

The 15 **cabinet departments** are the major service organizations of the federal government. They can also be described in management terms as **line organizations**. This means that they are directly accountable to the president and are responsible for performing government functions, such as printing money and training troops. These departments were created by Congress when the need for each department arose. The first department to be created was State, and the most recent one was Homeland Security, established in 2003. The difficulties faced in creating that new department are discussed in the "Reorganizing to Stop Terrorism" section. A president might ask that a new department be created or an old one abolished, but the president has no power to do so without legislative approval from Congress.

Each department is headed by a secretary (except for the Justice Department, which is headed by the attorney general). Each also has several levels of undersecretaries, assistant secretaries, and so on.

Presidents theoretically have considerable control over the cabinet departments, because presidents are able to appoint or fire all of the top officials. As discussed in Chapter 12, these positions are listed in the Plum Book. Even cabinet departments do not always respond to the president's wishes, though. One reason that presidents are frequently unhappy with their departments is that the entire bureaucratic structure below the top political levels is staffed by permanent employees, many of whom are committed to established programs or procedures and who resist change. Table 13-1 on page 461 shows that each cabinet department employs thousands of individuals, only a handful of whom are under the control of the president. The table also describes some of the functions of each department.

■ **Learning Outcome 2:**
Compare the structure and function of executive departments, executive agencies, independent regulatory agencies, and government corporations.

Cabinet Department
One of the 15 departments of the executive branch (State, Treasury, Defense, Justice, Interior, Agriculture, Commerce, Labor, Health and Human Services, Homeland Security, Housing and Urban Development, Education, Energy, Transportation, and Veterans Affairs).

Line Organization
In the federal government, an administrative unit that is directly accountable to the president.

Attorney General Eric Holder responds to questions during a meeting. He is the nation's chief prosecutor and the chief executive of the Department of Justice and a member of the president's cabinet.

EdStock/iStockphoto.com

Figure 13-3 ▶ Organization Chart of the Federal Government

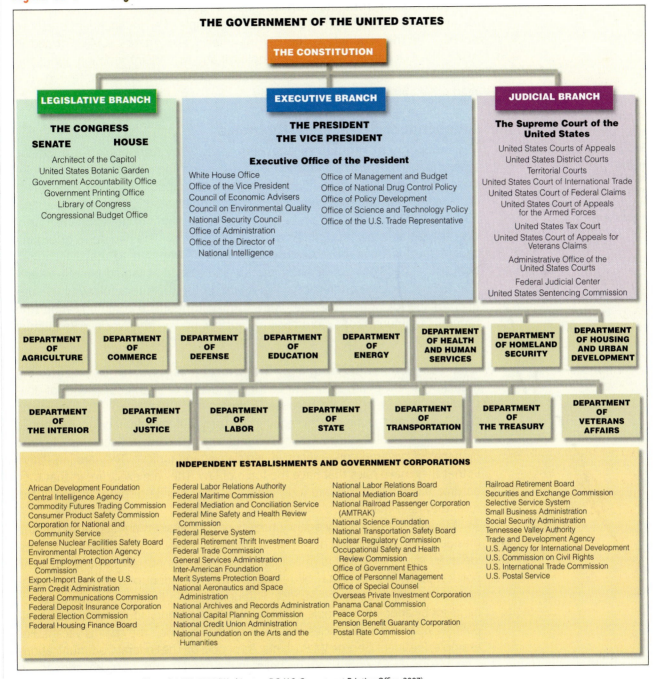

Source: United States Government Manual, 2007–2008 (Washington, DC: U.S. Government Printing Office, 2007).

Independent Executive Agencies

Independent executive agencies are bureaucratic organizations that are not located within a department but report directly to the president, who appoints their chief officials. When a new federal agency is created—the Environmental Protection Agency, for example—Congress decides where it will be located in the bureaucracy. In recent decades, presidents often have asked that a new organization be kept separate or independent rather than added to an existing

Independent Executive Agency
A federal agency that is not part of a cabinet department but reports directly to the president.

department, particularly if a department may be hostile to the agency's creation. The Smithsonian Institution, which runs the government's museums and the National Zoo, was formed in 1846 and is an example of an independent executive agency. Another example is the Central Intelligence Agency (CIA). Formed in 1947, the CIA gathers and analyzes political and military information about foreign countries and conducts covert operations outside the United States. You can read more about the CIA in Chapter 17.

Independent Regulatory Agencies

Independent Regulatory Agency
An agency outside the major executive departments charged with making and implementing rules and regulations.

The **independent regulatory agencies** are typically responsible for a specific type of public policy. Their function is to make and implement rules and regulations in a particular sphere of action to protect the public interest. The earliest such agency was the Interstate Commerce Commission (ICC), which was established in 1887 when Americans began to seek some form of government control over the rapidly growing business and industrial sector. This new form of organization, the independent regulatory agency, was supposed to make technical, nonpolitical decisions about rates, profits, and rules that would benefit all and that did not require congressional legislation. In the years that followed the creation of the ICC, other agencies were formed to regulate communication (the Federal Communications Commission), nuclear power (the Nuclear Regulatory Commission), and so on. (The ICC was abolished on December 30, 1995.)

The Purpose and Nature of Regulatory Agencies.
In practice, the regulatory agencies are administered independently of all three branches of government. They were set up because Congress felt it was unable to handle the complexities and technicalities required to carry out specific laws in the public interest. The regulatory commissions in fact combine some functions of all three branches of government—executive, legislative, and judicial. They are legislative in that they make rules that have the force of law. They are executive in that they enforce those rules. They are judicial in that they decide disputes involving the rules they have made.

Members of regulatory agency boards or commissions are appointed by the president with the consent of the Senate, although they do not report to the president. By law, the members of regulatory agencies cannot all be from the same political party. Members may be removed by the president only for causes specified in the law creating the agency. Presidents can influence regulatory agency behavior by appointing people of their own parties or individuals who share their political views when vacancies occur—in particular, when the chair is vacant. For example, President George W. Bush placed people on the Federal Communications Commission (FCC) who shared his belief in the need to curb obscene language in the media. Not surprisingly, the FCC soon thereafter started to "crack down" on obscenities on the air. One victim of this regulatory effort was Howard Stern, a nationally syndicated radio and television personality. His response was to switch from commercial radio and TV to unregulated satellite radio, where he can be heard every day on Sirius.

Agency Capture.
Over the last several decades, some observers have concluded that these agencies, although nominally independent, may in fact not always be so. They contend that many independent regulatory agencies have been **captured** by the very industries and firms they were supposed to regulate. The results have been less competition rather than more competition, higher prices rather than lower prices, and less choice rather than more choice for

Capture
The act by which an industry being regulated by a government agency gains direct or indirect control over agency personnel and decision makers.

TABLE 13–1 ▶ Executive Departments

DEPARTMENT AND YEAR ESTABLISHED	PRINCIPAL FUNCTIONS
State (1789) (36,525 employees)	Negotiates treaties; develops foreign policy; protects citizens abroad
Treasury (1789) (119,438 employees)	Pays all federal bills; borrows money; collects federal taxes; mints coins and prints paper currency; supervises national banks
Interior (1849) (67,191 employees)	Supervises federally owned lands and parks; supervises Native American affairs
Justice (1870)* (110,778 employees)	Furnishes legal advice to the president; enforces federal criminal laws; supervises federal prisons
Agriculture (1889) (98,235 employees)	Assists farmers and ranchers; conducts agricultural research; works to protect forests
Commerce (1913)** (43,348 employees)	Grants patents and trademarks; conducts national census; monitors weather; protects interests of businesses (Note: The Commerce Department houses the Census Bureau, which increased its workforce from several thousand employees to more than a half million between early 2009 and summer 2010. Most of these workers were short-term temporary employees.)
Labor (1913)** (16,554 employees)	Administers federal labor laws; promotes interests of workers
Defense (1947)*** (771,614 employees)	Manages the armed forces; operates military bases; oversees civil defense
Housing and Urban Development (1965) (9,818 employees)	Deals with nation's housing needs; develops and rehabilitates urban communities; oversees resale of mortgages
Transportation (1967) (58,189 employees)	Finances improvements in mass transit; develops and administers programs for highways, railroads, and aviation
Energy (1977) (16,651 employees)	Promotes energy conservation; analyzes energy data; conducts research and development
Health and Human Services (1979)*** (83,745 employees)	Promotes public health; enforces pure food and drug laws; conducts and sponsors health-related research
Education (1979)*** (4,611 employees)	Coordinates federal education programs and policies; administers aid to education; promotes educational research
Veterans Affairs (1988) (312,878 employees)	Promotes welfare of U.S. veterans
Homeland Security (2003) (191,197 employees)	Attempts to prevent terrorist attacks within the United States; controls U.S. borders; minimizes damage from natural disasters

*Formed from the Office of the Attorney General (created in 1789).

**Formed from the Department of Commerce and Labor (created in 1903).

***Formed from the Department of War (created in 1789) and the Department of the Navy (created in 1798).

****Formed from the Department of Health, Education, and Welfare (created in 1953).

Employment figures from Curtis W. Copeland, "The Federal Workforce: Characteristics and Trends," Washington, D.C.: Congressional Research Service, 2011.

consumers. One of the accusations made after the BP oil spill in 2010 was that the appropriate regulatory agency, the Minerals and Mining Administration, had become too lax in enforcing the safety regulations on the drilling rigs because it favored the oil companies.

Deregulation and Reregulation. During the presidency of Ronald Reagan (served 1981–1989), some significant deregulation (the removal of regulatory restraints—the opposite of regulation) occurred, much of which had started under President Jimmy Carter (served 1977–1981). For example, President Carter appointed a chairperson of the Civil Aeronautics Board (CAB), who gradually eliminated regulation of airline fares and routes. Then, under Reagan, the CAB was eliminated on January 1, 1985.

During the administration of George H. W. Bush (served 1989–1993), calls for reregulation of many businesses increased. During that administration, the Americans with Disabilities Act of 1990, the Civil Rights Act of 1991, and the Clean Air Act Amendments of 1991, all of which increased or changed the regulation of many businesses, were passed. Additionally, the Cable Re-regulation Act of 1992 was passed.

Under President Bill Clinton (served 1993–2001), the Interstate Commerce Commission was eliminated, and the banking and telecommunications industries, along with many other sectors of the economy, were deregulated. At the same time, extensive regulation protected the environment. In the wake of the mortgage crisis of 2007 and failure of several large investment houses in 2008, the Congress passed the Dodd-Frank bill, which tightened regulations on banks and almost all financial institutions.

Government Corporations

Another form of bureaucratic organization in the United States is the **government corporation**. Although the concept is borrowed from the world of business, distinct differences exist between public and private corporations.

Government Corporation
An agency of government that administers a quasi-business enterprise. These corporations are used when activities are primarily commercial.

A private corporation has shareholders (stockholders) who elect a board of directors, who in turn choose the corporate officers, such as president and vice president. When a private corporation makes a profit, it must pay taxes (unless it avoids them through various legal loopholes). It either distributes part or all of the after-tax profits to shareholders as dividends or plows the profits back into the corporation to make new investments.

A government corporation has a board of directors and managers, but it does not have any stockholders. We cannot buy shares of stock in a government corporation. If the government corporation makes a profit, it does not distribute the profit as dividends. Also, if it makes a profit, it does not have to pay taxes; the profits remain in the corporation.

Two of the best-known government corporations are the U.S. Postal Service and AMTRAK, the domestic passenger railroad corporation. Thirty-five years ago, after several private rail companies went bankrupt, Congress created a public railway system called AMTRAK. Today, AMTRAK links 500 American towns and cities in 46 states with more than 22,000 miles of rail. It has many critics both inside and outside of Congress.

During AMTRAK's existence, American taxpayers have subsidized it to the tune of more than $25 billion. Current subsidies typically exceed $1 billion per year—$1.6 billion was requested in 2010, and $1.4 billion was requested for 2007. As Republican Representative Harold Rogers of Kentucky has pointed out, "Every time a passenger boards a train, Uncle Sam writes a check for $138.71, on average." Those in favor of the AMTRAK subsidies argue that AMTRAK provides essential transportation for the poor. However, the majority of daily passengers are middle-class commuters on the eastern corridor routes.

For many years, critics of this government corporation have said that the benefits of AMTRAK, including reducing congestion on the highways, do not outweigh the costs. Some have suggested that the passenger service be privatized—that is, sold to a private corporation. However, as the price of gasoline rose in 2008 and the issue of the future supply of oil became critical, AMTRAK became more popular with travelers. Faced with skyrocketing gas prices, rail transportation may see expansion rather than contraction in the next decade.

The U.S. Postal Service, which is the second largest employer in the United States (after Walmart), has more than 550,000 employees. On paper, the postal service appears to be "breaking even" in terms of costs and revenues for its primary business. However, critics note that this government corporation has the right to borrow funds from the federal government at a very low interest rate and has borrowed about $13 billion so far to support its operations. Recently, the U.S. Postal Service has proposed several strategies for cutting costs including eliminating Saturday delivery and closing large bulk-mail centers. Additionally, the post office is collaborating with a private corporation, UPS, to deliver packages to home addresses.

Challenges to the Bureaucracy

With cabinet departments, independent executive agencies, independent regulatory agencies, and government corporations, the federal bureaucracy is both complex and very specialized. Each agency, corporation, or line department has its own mission, its own goals, and, in many cases, its own constituents either at home or, in the case of the State Department, abroad. However, some problems and crises require the attention of multiple agencies. In these cases, overlapping jurisdictions can cause confusion, or problems may arise that no agency has the authority to solve.

A famous story about the Carter administration makes this point: President Jimmy Carter believed he smelled something dead behind his Oval Office wall—probably a mouse. His staff called the General Services Administration, which has responsibility for the White House, but those bureaucrats claimed it was not their problem. They had fumigated recently, so the mouse must have come in from outside. The Department of the Interior, which has responsibility for the gardens and grounds, refused to help since the mouse was now inside. Eventually, an interagency task force was created to remove the mouse. If solving this small problem was complicated for the federal bureaucracy, consider larger issues such as terrorism and natural disasters.

Reorganizing to Stop Terrorism

After September 11, 2001, the nation saw that no single agency was responsible for coordinating antiterrorism efforts. Nor was one person able to muster a nationwide response to a terrorist attack. Fighting terrorism involves so many different aspects—screening baggage at airports, inspecting freight shipments, and protecting the border, to name just a few—that coordinating them would be impossible unless all of these functions were combined into one agency.

The creation of the Department of Homeland Security (DHS) in 2003 was the largest reorganization of the U.S. government since 1947. Twenty-two agencies with responsibilities for preventing terrorism were merged into a single department. The Congress and the president agreed that combining the Federal Emergency Management Agency (FEMA), Customs and Border Protection, the Coast Guard, the Secret Service, and many other organizations into a single agency would promote efficiency and improve coordination. This sprawling agency now has more than 190,000 employees and an estimated budget of $47 billion (as of 2012).

One of the main challenges facing the new department was integrating agencies whose missions were very different. Some commentators suggested that the bureaucratic cultures of agencies focused on law enforcement, such as the Secret Service and the Border Patrol, would be difficult to mesh with the agencies that focus on problems faced by citizens in a time of natural disasters, such as the Federal Emergency Management Agency (FEMA). Indeed, when FEMA became part of the DHS, not only was its funding reduced, but more importantly, it received less attention because the focus of the DHS has been on fighting terrorism, not on responding to natural disasters.

Perhaps even more importantly, the DHS did not actually unify all U.S. antiterrorism efforts. The most important antiterrorist agencies are the Federal Bureau of Investigation (FBI) and the Central Intelligence Agency (CIA), but neither is part of the DHS. Many believe that the number one problem in addressing terrorism is the failure of the FBI and CIA to exchange information with each other. To address this problem, President Bush created a Terrorist Threat Integration Center in *addition* to the DHS, the FBI, and the CIA. In 2004, Congress established the new Office of the Director of National Intelligence to coordinate the nation's intelligence efforts, and in 2005, President Bush appointed John Negroponte to be the director of national intelligence to try once again to coordinate the nation's intelligence agencies. This position, however, has been difficult to establish. In 2010, President Barack Obama named the fourth director in five years, General James R. Clapper. Many Washington insiders note that the authority of the director is often undercut by other appointees who may be closer to the president, including the director of the CIA and the national security adviser, making this a very difficult position to hold.

Dealing with Natural Disasters

As George H. W. Bush faced a tough reelection campaign in 1992, Hurricane Andrew struck southern Florida, one of only three Category 5 storms to hit the United States in the 20th century. Hurricane Andrew destroyed many communities south of Miami, Florida, leaving hundreds of thousands of people without power and without homes. Although the total death toll was only 65, the storm cost more than $25 billion in damage and losses. The Bush administration was widely criticized for not getting aid to the victims quickly enough, and the president was chided for not putting in a personal appearance.

Supposedly, FEMA was strengthened and improved after Hurricane Andrew. FEMA did deal with hundreds of natural disasters in the years that followed, including tornados, floods, and blizzards. However, in 2005, a year in which

The U.S. Coast Guard patrols the waters of Boston Harbor in preparation for the 2004 Democratic convention. Since September 11, 2001, such precautions have become normal in the United States.

REUTERS/William B. Plowman/Landov

five major hurricanes made landfall in the United States, FEMA again proved unable to meet the challenges of a massive natural disaster. When Hurricane Katrina headed toward New Orleans, all authorities warned of a possible flooding situation. No one dreamed of flooding that would trap thousands of residents in their homes for a week or more and destroy whole neighborhoods in New Orleans. No one had planned to evacuate thousands of people with no transportation of their own or to house them for years after the storm.

A natural disaster such as Hurricane Katrina can only be met by coordinated action from local, state, and federal authorities. Clearly, miscommunication occurred among all those levels of government in the case of Katrina. Responding to Hurricane Katrina involved the Army Corps of Engineers (responsible for the New Orleans levees), FEMA, the National Guard, the departments of Energy (oil rigs and refineries), Health and Human Services (hospitals, health services, vaccines), Housing and Urban Development (housing and rebuilding), and Education (schools destroyed throughout Louisiana). While FEMA is charged with emergency management, it does not have any direct control over these other federal agencies. The sitting president, George W. Bush, was severely criticized for not acting quickly enough in this crisis. In 2010, an oil-drilling rig in the Gulf of Mexico exploded, triggering a massive oil spill. Again, within days, the media and local government officials were calling for faster and more effective federal government assistance even though the technology for dealing with such a spill is only available in the petroleum industry. President Barack Obama was accused of not visiting the region quickly enough and not demonstrating enough anger at the oil company.

What Hurricane Katrina illustrates is the huge challenge faced by bureaucracies when dealing with natural disasters. So many agencies and levels of government must be coordinated that sometimes responses are delayed and aid does not get to the victims in a timely way. Media coverage of these tragedies focuses on the struggles of citizens, while the struggles of the bureaucrats take place in back rooms as officials strive to find the right equipment and personnel to meet unique disasters. At times, no president can be successful in dealing with the public relations aspect of these events.

Staffing the Bureaucracy

■ **Learning Outcome 3:**
Explain how individuals get positions in the federal bureaucracy, and discuss the history of attempts to reform that process.

The two categories of bureaucrats are political appointees and civil servants. As noted earlier, the president is able to make political appointments to most of the top jobs in the federal bureaucracy. The president can also appoint ambassadors to foreign posts. As noted in Chapter 12, these jobs are listed in the Plum Book. The rest of the national government's employees belong to the civil service and obtain their jobs through a much more formal process.

Political Appointees

To fill the positions listed in the Plum Book, the president and the president's advisers solicit suggestions from politicians, businesspersons, and other prominent individuals. Appointments to these positions offer the president a way to pay off outstanding political debts. But the president must also consider such things as the candidate's work experience, intelligence, political affiliations, and personal characteristics. Presidents have differed in the importance they attach to appointing women and minorities to plum positions. Presidents often use ambassadorships, however, to reward individuals for their campaign contributions.

Secretary of State
Hillary Clinton speaks during a joint press conference with her British counterpart, William Hague, at the State Department building in Washington, D.C.

AFP PHOTO/Mandel/Newscom

We should note here that even though the president has the power to appoint a government official, this does not mean an appointment will pass muster. Before making any nominations, the administration requires potential appointees to undergo a detailed screening process and answer questions such as the following: What are your accomplishments? Did you ever *not* pay taxes for your nannies or housekeepers? What kinds of investments have you made? What have your past partisan affiliations been?

Such a process takes months, and after completing it, the appointees must be confirmed by the Senate. Even with such a screening process, the Bush administration made some serious errors. For example, the president's appointment of Michael Brown to head FEMA turned out to be a big mistake, because Brown had no experience in emergency planning and relief efforts. Several Obama appointees were either not confirmed or left the government quickly after difficulties with their resumes or political activities prior to taking office were uncovered.

The Aristocracy of the Federal Government.   Political appointees are in some sense the aristocracy of the federal government. But their powers, although formidable on paper, are often exaggerated. Like the president, a political appointee will occupy her or his position for a comparatively brief time. Political appointees often leave office before the president's term actually ends. In fact, the average term of service for political appointees is less than two years. As a result, most appointees have little background for their positions and may be mere figureheads. Often, they only respond to the paperwork that flows up from below. Additionally, the professional civil servants who make up the permanent civil service may not feel compelled to carry out their current boss's directives quickly, because they know that he or she will not be around for very long.

The Difficulty in Firing Civil Servants.   This inertia is compounded by the fact that it is very difficult to discharge civil servants. In recent years, less than one-tenth of 1 percent of federal employees have been fired for incompetence. Because discharged employees may appeal their dismissals, many months or even years can pass before the issue is resolved conclusively. This occupational rigidity helps ensure that most political appointees, no matter how competent or driven, will not be able to exert much meaningful influence over their subordinates, let alone implement dramatic changes in the bureaucracy itself.

History of the Federal Civil Service

When the federal government was formed in 1789, it had no career public servants but rather consisted of amateurs who were almost all Federalists. When Thomas Jefferson took over as president, few people in his party were holding federal administrative jobs, so he fired more than 100 officials and replaced them with his own supporters. Then, for the next 25 years, a growing body of federal administrators gained experience and expertise, becoming in the process professional public servants. These administrators stayed in office regardless of who was elected president. The bureaucracy had become a self-maintaining, long-term element within government.

To the Victor Belong the Spoils. When Andrew Jackson took over the White House in 1828, he could not believe how many appointed officials (appointed before he became president, that is) were overtly hostile toward him and his Democratic Party. Because the bureaucracy was reluctant to carry out his programs, Jackson did the obvious: He fired federal officials—more than had all his predecessors combined. The **spoils system**—an application of the principle that to the victor belong the spoils—became the standard method of filling federal positions. Whenever a new president was elected from a different party, the staffing of the federal government would almost completely turn over.

Spoils System
The awarding of government jobs to political supporters and friends.

The Civil Service Reform Act of 1883. Jackson's spoils system survived for several years, but it became increasingly corrupt. Also, as the size of the bureaucracy increased by 300 percent between 1851 and 1881, the cry for civil service reform became louder. Reformers began to look to the example of several

WASHINGTON, D. C.—THE ATTACK ON THE PRESIDENT'S LIFE—SCENE IN THE LADIES' ROOM OF THE BALTIMORE AND OHIO RAILROAD DEPOT—THE ARREST OF THE ASSASSIN.

On September 19, 1881, President James A. Garfield was assassinated by a disappointed office seeker, Charles J. Guiteau. The long-term effect of this event was to replace the spoils system with a permanent career civil service. This process began with the passage of the Pendleton Act in 1883, which established the Civil Service Commission.

Merit System
The selection, retention, and promotion of government employees on the basis of competitive examinations.

Pendleton Act (Civil Service Reform Act)
An act that established the principle of employment on the basis of merit and created the Civil Service Commission to administer the personnel service.

Civil Service Commission
The initial central personnel agency of the national government, created in 1883.

did you know?

Federal officials spent $333,000 building a deluxe, earthquake-proof outhouse for hikers in Pennsylvania's remote Delaware Water Gap recreation area.

European countries, Germany in particular, which had established a professional civil service that operated under a **merit system**, in which job appointments were based on competitive examinations.

In 1883, the **Pendleton Act**—or **Civil Service Reform Act**—was passed, placing the first limits on the spoils system. The act established the principle of employment on the basis of open, competitive examinations and created the **Civil Service Commission** to administer the personnel service. Initially, only 10 percent of federal employees were covered by the merit system. Later laws, amendments, and executive orders, however, increased the coverage to more than 90 percent of federal employees. The effects of these reforms were felt at all levels of government.

The Supreme Court strengthened the civil service system in *Elrod v. Burns*[5] in 1976 and *Branti v. Finkel*[6] in 1980. In those two cases, the Court used the First Amendment to forbid government officials from discharging or threatening to discharge public employees solely for *not* being supporters of the political party in power unless party affiliation is an appropriate requirement for the position. Additional enhancements to the civil service system were added in *Rutan v. Republican Party of Illinois*[7] in 1990. The Court's ruling effectively prevented the use of partisan political considerations as the basis for hiring, promoting, or transferring most public employees. An exception was permitted, however, for senior policy-making positions, which usually go to officials who will support the programs of the elected leaders.

The Civil Service Reform Act of 1978. In 1978, the Civil Service Reform Act abolished the Civil Service Commission and created two new federal agencies to perform its duties. To administer the civil service laws, rules, and regulations, the act created the Office of Personnel Management (OPM), which is empowered to recruit, interview, and test potential government workers and determine who should be hired. The OPM makes recommendations to the individual agencies as to which persons meet the standards (typically, the top three applicants for a position), and the agencies then decide whom to hire. To oversee promotions, employees' rights, and other employment matters, the act created the Merit Systems Protection Board (MSPB), which evaluates charges of wrongdoing, hears employee appeals of agency decisions, and can order corrective action against agencies and employees.

Federal Employees and Political Campaigns. In 1933, when President Franklin D. Roosevelt set up his New Deal, a virtual army of civil servants was hired to staff the numerous new agencies that were created. Because the individuals who worked in these agencies owed their jobs to the Democratic Party, it seemed natural for them to campaign for Democratic candidates. The Democrats controlling Congress in the mid-1930s did not object. But in 1938, a coalition of conservative Democrats and Republicans took control of Congress and forced through the Hatch Act—or Political Activities Act—of 1939. The act prohibited federal employees from actively participating in the political management of campaigns. It also forbade the use of federal authority to influence nominations and elections and outlawed the use of bureaucratic rank to pressure federal employees to make political contributions.

The Hatch Act created a controversy that lasted for decades. Many contended that the act deprived federal employees of their First Amendment freedoms of

---

5. 427 U.S. 347 (1976).
6. 445 U.S. 507 (1980).
7. 497 U.S. 62 (1990).

speech and association. In 1972, a federal district court declared it unconstitutional. The United States Supreme Court, however, reaffirmed the challenged portion of the act in 1973, stating that the government's interest in preserving a nonpartisan civil service was so great that the prohibitions should remain.[8] Twenty years later, Congress addressed the criticisms of the Hatch Act by passing the Federal Employees Political Activities Act of 1993. This act, which amended the Hatch Act, lessened the harshness of the 1939 act in several ways. Among other things, the 1993 act allowed federal employees to run for office in nonpartisan elections, participate in voter-registration drives, make campaign contributions to political organizations, and campaign for candidates in partisan elections.

Modern Attempts at Bureaucratic Reform

As long as the federal bureaucracy exists, attempts to make it more open, efficient, and responsive to the needs of U.S. citizens will continue. The most important actual and proposed reforms in the last several decades include sunshine and sunset laws, privatization, incentives for efficiency, and more protection for so-called whistleblowers.

Sunshine Laws before and after September 11

In 1976, Congress enacted the **Government in the Sunshine Act**. It required for the first time that all multiheaded federal agencies—agencies headed by a committee instead of an individual—hold their meetings regularly in public session. The bill defined *meetings* as almost any gathering, formal or informal, of agency members, including a conference telephone call. The only exceptions to this rule of openness are discussions of matters such as court proceedings or personnel problems, and these exceptions are specifically listed in the bill. Sunshine laws now exist at all levels of government.

Government in the Sunshine Act
A law that requires all committee-directed federal agencies to conduct their business regularly in public session.

Information Disclosure. Sunshine laws are consistent with the policy of information disclosure supported by the government for decades. For example, beginning in the 1960s, several consumer protection laws have required that certain information be disclosed to consumers when purchasing homes, borrowing funds, and so on. In 1966, the federal government passed the Freedom of Information Act, which required federal government agencies, with certain exceptions, to disclose to individuals, on their request, any information about them contained in government files.

Curbs on Information Disclosure. Since September 11, 2001, the trend toward government in the sunshine and information disclosure has been reversed at both the federal and state levels. Within weeks after September 11, 2001, numerous federal agencies removed hundreds, if not thousands, of documents from Internet sites, public libraries, and reading rooms found in various federal government departments. Information contained in some of the documents included diagrams of power plants and pipelines, structural details on dams, and safety plans for chemical plants. The military also immediately started restricting information about its current and planned activities, as did the FBI. These agencies were concerned that terrorists could use this information to plan attacks. The federal government has also gone back into the archives to remove an increasing quantity of not only sensitive information but also sometimes seemingly unimportant information.

8. *United States Civil Service Commission v. National Association of Letter Carriers,* 413 U.S. 548 (1973).

In making some public documents inaccessible to the public, the federal government was ahead of state and local governments, but they quickly followed suit. State and local governments control and supervise police forces, dams, electricity sources, and water supplies. Consequently, it is not surprising that many state and local governments followed in the footsteps of the federal government in curbing access to certain public records and information. Most local agencies, however, do include the public in their planning for emergencies.

Sunset Laws

Sunset Legislation
Laws requiring that existing programs be reviewed regularly for their effectiveness and be terminated unless specifically extended as a result of these reviews.

It has often been suggested that the federal government be subject to **sunset legislation**, which places government programs on a definite schedule for congressional consideration. Unless Congress specifically reauthorizes a particular federally operated program at the end of a designated period, it is automatically terminated; that is, its sun sets.

The idea of sunset legislation was initially suggested by Franklin D. Roosevelt when he created the plethora of New Deal agencies in the 1930s. His assistant, William O. Douglas, recommended that each agency's charter should include a provision allowing for its termination in 10 years. Only an act of Congress could revitalize it. The proposal was never adopted. It was not until 1976 that a state legislature—Colorado's—adopted sunset legislation for state regulatory commissions, giving them a life of six years before their suns set. Today, most states have some type of sunset law.

Privatization

Privatization
The replacement of government services with services provided by private firms.

Another approach to bureaucratic reform is **privatization**, which occurs when government services are replaced by services from the private sector. For example, the government might contract with private firms to operate prisons. Supporters of privatization argue that some services could be provided more efficiently by the private sector. Another scheme is to furnish vouchers to "clients" in lieu of services. For example, instead of supplying housing, the government could offer vouchers that recipients could use to "pay" for housing in privately owned buildings.

An armed nuclear security officer patrols the coastal area of the Diablo Canyon nuclear power plant on May 5, 2004, in Avila Beach, California. Since September 11, all American utilities have increased the security at their facilities. Do you think that the increased awareness of a possible terrorist attack has actually prevented such an event?

AP Photo/Michael A. Mariant

Beyond Our Borders
PRIVATIZING THE U.S. MILITARY ABROAD

Privatization has been a hot topic for several decades now, at least domestically. All levels of government—federal, state, and local—have privatized at least some activities. Less well known, however, is that for more than two decades, the U.S. military has been employing private companies abroad to perform several functions previously done by military personnel. After the American military was downsized following the fall of the Berlin Wall in 1989, the military responded by outsourcing many functions to the private sector. Before the First Gulf War, the Pentagon was already spending about 8 percent of its overall budget on private companies.

PRIVATE CONTRACTORS GALORE

In the last decade, the military has been supported by private contractors in Iraq and Afghanistan. By 2006, more than 100,000 private contractors/workers were on the ground in Iraq employed in some capacity by the U.S. government. By mid-2008, the number reached more than 160,000, about as many as there were U.S. military personnel. What do all these private contractors actually do? They provide food and water for the troops, transport supplies for the coalition troops and for civilians stationed in Iraq, repair equipment, and are employed as guards for prisoners. In addition, most major construction on American bases and air fields is done by contractors.

THE NUMBERS TELL IT ALL

One of the reasons that the U.S. military has felt obligated to hire private contractors in Iraq and elsewhere is that the army in particular has been downsized. During the First Gulf War, active-duty troops in the army numbered 711,000. Today, that number has been reduced by almost one-third, to only about 550,000. As a result, the Pentagon says that it has to fill ancillary jobs and programs by contracting with private companies that either send their workers abroad or hire workers there. The Army Corps of Engineers and the Navy Seabees did a great deal of the construction in World War II, but today, neither of these forces has the manpower to do similar work in Iraq. Additionally, there are political reasons for using contractors: Remember that many of the military troops deployed in Iraq and Afghanistan are members of the reserves or National Guard. Would it be efficient and acceptable to call up family members to go to Afghanistan to cook meals for the other troops?

As the war in Iraq wound down, the American military presence was downsized along with the contractors who supported it. By 2011, there were more than 60,000 contractors in Iraq but only 45,000 troops, and most of the military forces would be leaving by 2014. However, the war in Afghanistan was ramped up in 2009–2010 with an increase in the level of military personnel and contractors. By 2011, about 90,000 contractors were employed there to support just over 99,000 troops. Under orders from General Petraeus, the United States hired as many local contractors as

REUTERS/Sabine Siebold/LANDOV

American soldiers discuss the upcoming operation with their Afghan interpreter who is a private contractor as are thousands of other Afghan personnel assisting the American military there.

possible. By 2011, about half of all the contracted employees in Afghanistan were citizens of that nation.[*]

Hiring private contractors to work in a combat zone has some real complications. First, private contractors are often subject to combat conditions resulting in the risk of capture, injury, or death. Several contractors, both American and European, have been captured and held as hostages. A few of these have been murdered. More than 1,500 civilian contractors have been killed in their line of work. In addition, private contractors can commit crimes against Iraqi or Afghani civilians or against other contractors. In accordance with a recently approved amendment to the Uniform Code of Military Justice, contractors accused of crimes are tried in military courts-martial.

Who is hiring these contractors, and where are they being hired? Large international firms, some of which are based in the United States, are the major employers. Kellogg, Brown and Root, a firm based in Houston, Texas, is the largest employer of contractors on the ground in Iraq. Booz Allen Hamilton, based in Fairfax, Virginia, also has multiple contracts with the Department of Defense as well as various intelligence agencies. These two firms are generally considered private military companies, PMCs, of which there are hundreds operating on a worldwide basis.

FOR CRITICAL ANALYSIS

Does using thousands of private contractors in active war zones increase or decrease the public's support for the conflict?

[*]Moshe Schartz and Joyprada Swain, "Department of Defense Contractors in Afghanistan and Iraq: Background and Analysis," Washington, D.C.: Congressional Research Service, 2011.

iStockphoto.com/Ayoshino iStockphoto.com/mattjeacock

The privatization, or contracting out, strategy has been most successful at the local level. Municipalities, for example, can form contracts with private companies for such things as trash collection. This approach is not a cure-all, however, as many functions, particularly on the national level, cannot be contracted out in any meaningful way. For example, the federal government could not contract out most of the Defense Department's functions to private firms. Nonetheless, the U.S. military has contracted out many services in Iraq and elsewhere, as discussed in this chapter's Beyond Our Borders feature.

Incentives for Efficiency and Productivity

An increasing number of state governments are beginning to experiment with a variety of schemes to run their operations more efficiently and capably. They focus on maximizing the efficiency and productivity of government workers by providing incentives for improved performance.[9] For example, many governors, mayors, and city administrators are considering ways in which government can be made more entrepreneurial. Some of the most promising measures have included such tactics as permitting agencies that do not spend their entire budgets to keep some of the difference and rewarding employees with performance-based bonuses.

Government Performance and Results Act. At the federal level, the Government Performance and Results Act of 1997 was designed to improve efficiency in the federal workforce. The act required that all government agencies (except the CIA) describe their new goals and establish methods for determining whether those goals are met. Goals may be broadly crafted (e.g., reducing the time it takes to test a new drug before allowing it to be marketed) or narrowly crafted (e.g., reducing the number of times a telephone rings before it is answered).

The performance-based budgeting implemented by President George W. Bush took this results-oriented approach a step further. Performance-based budgeting links agency funding to actual agency performance. Agencies are given specific performance criteria to meet, and the Office of Management and Budget rates each agency to determine how well it has performed. In theory, the amount of funds that each agency receives in the next annual budget should be determined by the extent to which it has met the performance criteria.

Bureaucracy Has Changed Little, Though. Efforts to improve bureaucratic efficiency are supported by the assertion that although society and industry have changed enormously in the past century, the form of government used in Washington, D.C., and in most states has remained the same. Some observers believe that the nation's diverse economic base cannot be administered competently by traditional bureaucratic organizations. Consequently, the government must become more responsive to cope with the increasing demands placed on it. Political scientists Joel Aberbach and Bert Rockman take issue with this contention. They argue that the bureaucracy has changed significantly over time in response to changes desired by various presidential administrations. In their opinion, many of the problems attributed to the bureaucracy are, in fact, a result of the political decision-making process. Therefore, attempts to reinvent government by reforming the bureaucracy are misguided.[10] Public assessment of bureaucratic services would provide another way to get more feedback from the public.

9.   See, for example, David Osborne and Ted Gaebler, *Reinventing Government: How the Entrepreneurial Spirit Is Transforming the Public Sector* (Reading, MA: Addison-Wesley, 1992); and David Osborne and Peter Plastrik, *Banishing Bureaucracy: The Five Strategies for Reinventing Government* (Reading, MA: Addison-Wesley, 1997).

10.   Joel D. Aberbach and Bert A. Rockman, *In the Web of Politics: Three Decades of the U.S. Federal Executive* (Washington, DC: Brookings Institution Press, 2000).

Other analysts have suggested that the problem lies not so much with traditional bureaucratic organizations as with the people who run them. According to policy specialist Taegan Goddard and journalist Christopher Riback, what needs to be reinvented is not the machinery of government, but public officials. After each election, new appointees to bureaucratic positions may find themselves managing complex, multimillion-dollar enterprises, yet they often are untrained for their jobs. According to these authors, if we want to reform the bureaucracy, we should focus on preparing newcomers for the task of "doing" government.[11]

Saving Costs through E-Government. Many contend that the communications revolution brought about by the Internet has not only improved the efficiency with which government agencies deliver services to the public but also reduced the cost of government. Agencies can now communicate with members of the public, as well as other agencies, via e-mail. Additionally, every federal agency now has a Web site citizens can access to find information about agency services instead of calling or appearing in person at a regional agency office. Since 2003, federal agencies have also been required by the Government Paperwork Elimination Act of 1998 to use e-commerce whenever it is practical to do so and will save on costs.

Helping Out the Whistleblowers

The term **whistleblower** as applied to the federal bureaucracy has a special meaning: It is someone who blows the whistle on a gross governmental inefficiency or illegal action. Whistleblowers may be clerical workers, managers, or even specialists, such as scientists.

Laws Protecting Whistleblowers. The 1978 Civil Service Reform Act prohibits reprisals against whistleblowers by their superiors, and it set up the Merit Systems Protection Board as part of this protection. Many federal agencies also have toll-free hotlines that employees can use anonymously to report bureaucratic waste and inappropriate behavior. About 35 percent of all calls result in agency action or follow-up.

Further protection for whistleblowers was provided in 1989, when Congress passed the Whistle-Blower Protection Act. That act established an independent agency, the Office of Special Counsel (OSC), to investigate complaints brought by government employees who have been demoted, fired, or otherwise sanctioned for reporting government fraud or waste. Congress is currently considering legislation that would extend whistleblower protections to civil servants at national security agencies, employees of government contractors, and federal workers who expose the distortion of scientific data for political reasons.

Some state and federal laws encourage employees to blow the whistle on their employers' wrongful actions by providing monetary incentives to the whistleblowers. At the federal level, the False Claims Act of 1986 allows a whistleblower who has disclosed information about a fraud against the U.S. government to receive a monetary award. If the government chooses to prosecute the case and wins, the whistleblower receives between 15 and 25 percent of the

did you know?

Each year, federal administrative agencies produce rules that fill 7,500 pages in the *Code of Federal Regulations*.

Whistleblower
Someone who brings to public attention gross governmental inefficiency or an illegal action.

---

11. Taegan D. Goddard and Christopher Riback, *You Won—Now What? How Americans Can Make Democracy Work from City Hall to the White House* (New York: Scribner, 1998).

proceeds. If the government declines to intervene, the whistleblower can bring suit on behalf of the government, and if the suit is successful, will receive between 25 and 30 percent of the proceeds.

The Problem Continues. Despite these endeavors to help whistleblowers, little evidence indicates that potential whistleblowers truly have received more protection. More than 40 percent of the employees who turned to the OSC for assistance in a recent three-year period stated that they were no longer employees of the government agencies on which they blew the whistle.

Additionally, in a significant 2006 decision, the U.S. Supreme Court placed restrictions on lawsuits brought by public workers. The case, *Garcetti v. Ceballos*,[12] involved an assistant district attorney, Richard Ceballos, who wrote a memo asking if a county sheriff's deputy had lied in a search warrant affidavit. Ceballos claimed that he was subsequently demoted and denied a promotion for trying to expose the lie. The outcome of the case turned on an interpretation of an employee's right to freedom of speech—whether it included the right to criticize an employment-related action. In a close (5-4) and controversial decision, the Supreme Court held that when public employees make statements relating to their official duties, they are not speaking as citizens for First Amendment purposes. The Court deemed that when he wrote his memo, Ceballos was speaking as an employee, not a citizen, and was thus subject to his employer's disciplinary actions. The ruling will affect millions of governmental employees.

Bureaucrats as Politicians and Policymakers

■ **Learning Outcome 4:**
Describe the tools and powers that bureaucratic agencies have to shape policies and regulations.

Because Congress is unable to oversee the day-to-day administration of its programs, it must delegate certain powers to administrative agencies. Congress delegates the power to implement legislation to agencies through what is called **enabling legislation**. For example, the Federal Trade Commission was created by the Federal Trade Commission Act of 1914, the Equal Employment Opportunity Commission was created by the Civil Rights Act of 1964, and the Occupational Safety and Health Administration was created by the Occupational Safety and Health Act of 1970. The enabling legislation generally specifies the name, purpose, composition, functions, and powers of the agency.

Enabling Legislation
A statute enacted by Congress that authorizes the creation of an administrative agency and specifies the name, purpose, composition, functions, and powers of the agency being created.

In theory, the agencies should put into effect laws passed by Congress. Laws are often drafted in such vague and general terms, however, that they provide relatively little guidance to agency administrators as to how the laws should be implemented. This means that the agencies must decide how best to carry out the wishes of Congress.

The discretion given to administrative agencies is not accidental. Congress has long realized that it lacks the technical expertise and the resources to monitor the implementation of its laws. Hence, the administrative agency is created to fill the gaps. This gap-filling role requires the agency to formulate administrative rules (regulations) to put flesh on the bones of the law. But it also forces the agency to become an unelected policymaker.

12. 126 S. Ct. 1951 (2006).

The Rule-Making Environment

Rule making does not occur in a vacuum. Suppose that Congress passes a new air pollution law. The Environmental Protection Agency (EPA) might decide to implement the new law through a technical regulation on factory emissions. This proposed regulation would be published in the *Federal Register,* a daily government publication, so that interested parties would have an opportunity to comment on it. Individuals and companies that opposed the rule (or parts of it) might then try to convince the EPA to revise or redraft the regulation. Some parties might try to persuade the agency to withdraw the proposed regulation altogether. In any event, the EPA would consider these comments in drafting the final version of the regulation following the expiration of the comment period.

Waiting Periods and Court Challenges. Once the final regulation has been published in the *Federal Register,* the rule can be enforced after a 60-day waiting period. During that period, businesses, individuals, and state and local governments can ask Congress to overturn the regulation. After that 60-day period has lapsed, the regulation can still be challenged in court by a party having a direct interest in the rule, such as a company that expects to incur significant costs in complying with it. The company could argue that the rule misinterprets the applicable law or goes beyond the agency's statutory purview. An allegation by the company that the EPA made a mistake in judgment probably would not be enough to convince the court to throw out the rule. The company instead would have to demonstrate that the rule was "arbitrary and capricious." To meet this standard, the company would have to show that the rule reflected a serious flaw in the EPA's judgment.

Controversies. How agencies implement, administer, and enforce legislation has resulted in controversy. Decisions made by agencies charged with administering the Endangered Species Act have led to protests from farmers, ranchers, and others whose economic interests have been harmed. For example, the government decided to cut off the flow of irrigation water from Klamath Lake in Oregon in the summer of 2001. That action, which affected irrigation water for more than 1,000 farmers in southern Oregon and northern California, was undertaken to save endangered suckerfish and salmon. It was believed that the lake's water level was so low that further use of the water for irrigation would harm these fish. The results of this decision were devastating for many farmers.

One of the agencies that seems to be most sensitive to a change in presidential administration is the Environmental Protection Agency, created by Congress in 1970. Over the years, Congress has passed several laws to improve air quality in the United States and given the EPA the authority to carry out this legislation. Presidents differ, however, in how they interpret these congressional mandates. During the George W. Bush administration, the EPA issued decisions that seemed to weaken the enforcement of air pollution laws. In 1999, several environmental groups petitioned the EPA to set new standards for automobiles to reduce greenhouse gas emissions. In 2003, the EPA refused to do so, claiming that it did not have the legal authority to do this. Massachusetts and other states that passed laws regulating automobiles in their own states sued the EPA. In 2007, the Supreme Court ruled, by a 5-4 majority, that the EPA cannot refuse to assess environmental hazards and issue appropriate regulations. As Justice John Paul Stevens wrote, "This is the Congressional design. EPA has refused to comply with this clear statutory command."[13] This was an unusual situation in that the states actually challenged a regulatory agency to issue stronger regulations. Often, challenges to regulatory agencies are intended to weaken new regulations.

When Barack Obama became president, his administration took a much firmer stand on the enforcement of air pollution regulations. While the president was committed to the passage of a new energy bill that would reduce the United States' contribution to greenhouse gases, by spring of 2010 it seemed that major new legislation might not pass quickly. The Environmental Protection Administration issued new gas mileage requirements and new rules regulating tailpipe emissions for cars and trucks in April 2010. A Republican-led attempt in the Senate to veto these new regulations was defeated in June of that year. Under the Obama administration, the EPA also issued new regulations for coal mining and for emissions from coal-burning power plants. In all of these cases, the executive agency noted that it had the authority to issue such rules under prior legislation such as the Clean Air Act.

Negotiated Rule Making

Since the end of World War II (1939–1945), companies, environmentalists, and other special-interest groups have challenged government regulations in court. In the 1980s, however, the sheer wastefulness of attempting to regulate through litigation became more and more apparent. Today, a growing number of federal agencies encourage businesses and public-interest groups to become directly involved in drafting regulations. Agencies hope that such participation may help prevent later courtroom battles over the meaning, applicability, and legal effect of the regulations.

Congress formally approved such a process, which is called *negotiated rule making,* in the Negotiated Rule-making Act of 1990. The act authorizes agencies to allow those who will be affected by a new rule to participate in the rule-drafting process. If an agency chooses to engage in negotiated rule making, it must publish in the *Federal Register* the subject and scope of the rule to be developed, the parties affected significantly by the rule, and other information. Representatives of the affected groups and other interested parties then may apply to be members of the negotiating committee. The agency is represented on the committee, but a neutral third party (not the agency) presides over the proceedings. Once the committee members have reached agreement on the terms of the proposed rule, a notice is published in the *Federal Register,* followed by a period for comments by any person or organization interested in the proposed rule. Negotiated rule making often is conducted under the condition that the participants promise not to challenge in court the outcome of any agreement to which they were a party.

Bureaucrats Are Policymakers

Theories of public administration once assumed that bureaucrats do not make policy decisions but only implement the laws and policies promulgated by the president and legislative bodies. Many people continue to make this assumption. A more realistic view, now held by most bureaucrats and elected officials, is that the agencies and departments of government play important roles in policymaking. As we have seen, many government rules, regulations, and programs are in

---

13. *Commonwealth of Massachusetts v. EPA,* 127 S. Ct. 1438 (2007).

fact initiated by bureaucrats, based on their expertise and scientific studies. How a law passed by Congress eventually is translated into concrete action—from the forms to be filled out to decisions about who gets the benefits—usually is determined within each agency or department. Even the evaluation of whether a policy has achieved its purpose usually is based on studies commissioned and interpreted by the agency administering the program.

The bureaucracy's policymaking role has often been depicted by what traditionally has been called the "iron triangle." Recently, the concept of an "issue network" has been viewed as a more accurate description of the policymaking process.

Iron Triangles. In the past, scholars often described the bureaucracy's role in the policymaking process by using the concept of an **iron triangle**—a three-way alliance among legislators in Congress, bureaucrats, and interest groups. Consider as an example the development of agricultural policy. Congress, as one component of the triangle (as illustrated in Figure 13-4), includes two major committees concerned with agricultural policy, the House Committee on Agriculture and the Senate Committee on Agriculture, Nutrition, and Forestry. The Department of Agriculture, the second component of the triangle, has more than 95,000 employees, plus thousands of contractors and consultants. Agricultural interest groups, the third component of the iron triangle in agricultural policymaking, include many large and powerful associations, such as the American Farm Bureau Federation, the National Cattleman's Association, and the Corn Growers Association. These three components of the iron triangle work together, formally or informally, to create policy.

For example, the various agricultural interest groups lobby Congress to develop policies that benefit their interests. Members of Congress cannot afford

Iron Triangle
The three-way alliance among legislators, bureaucrats, and interest groups to make or preserve policies that benefit their respective interests.

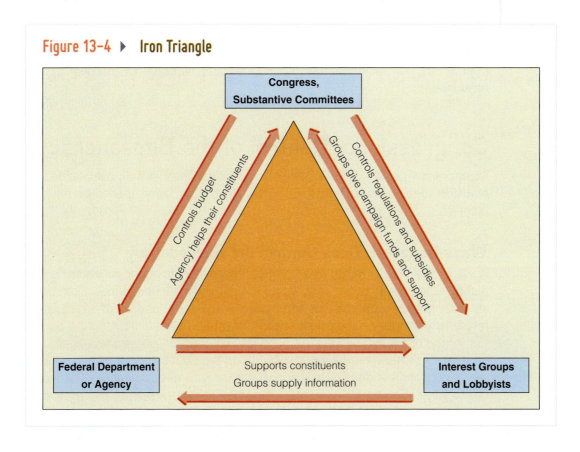

Figure 13-4 ▸ Iron Triangle

Congress, Substantive Committees

Controls budget
Agency helps their constituents

Controls regulations and subsidies
Groups give campaign funds and support

Federal Department or Agency

Supports constituents
Groups supply information

Interest Groups and Lobbyists

to ignore the wishes of interest groups, because they are potential sources of voter support and campaign contributions. The legislators in Congress also work closely with the Department of Agriculture, which, in implementing a policy, can develop rules that benefit—or at least do not hurt—certain industries or groups. The Department of Agriculture, in turn, supports policies that enhance the department's budget and powers. In this way, according to theory, agricultural policy is created that benefits all three components of the iron triangle.

Issue Networks. To be sure, the preceding discussion presents a simplified picture of how the iron triangle works. With the growth in the complexity of government, policymaking also has become more complicated. The bureaucracy is larger, Congress has more committees and subcommittees, and interest groups are more powerful than ever. Although iron triangles still exist, often they are inadequate as descriptions of how policy is actually made. Frequently, different interest groups concerned about a certain area of policy have conflicting demands, making agency decisions difficult. Additionally, divided government in some years has meant that departments are sometimes pressured by the president to take one approach and by Congress to take another.

Many scholars now use the term *issue network* to describe the policymaking process. An **issue network** consists of individuals or organizations that support a particular policy position on the environment, taxation, consumer safety, or some other issue. Typically, an issue network includes legislators and/or their staff members, interest groups, bureaucrats, scholars and other experts, and representatives from the media. Members of a particular issue network work together to influence the president, members of Congress, administrative agencies, and the courts to affect public policy on a specific issue. Each policy issue may involve conflicting positions taken by two or more issue networks. During the Obama administration, issue networks concerned with the health industry, the energy industry, and public education ramped up their efforts to be influential in the sweeping legislation proposed by the president.

Issue Network

A group of individuals or organizations—which may consist of legislators and legislative staff members, interest group leaders, bureaucrats, the media, scholars, and other experts—that supports a particular policy position on a given issue.

Congressional Control of the Bureaucracy

Many political pundits doubt whether Congress can meaningfully control the federal bureaucracy. Nevertheless, Congress does have some means of exerting control.

Ways Congress Does Control the Bureaucracy

These commentators forget that Congress specifies in an agency's "enabling legislation" the powers of the agency and the parameters within which it can operate. Additionally, Congress has the power of the purse and theoretically could refuse to authorize or appropriate funds for a particular agency (see the discussion of the budgeting process in Chapter 11). Whether Congress would actually take such a drastic measure would depend on the circumstances. It is clear, however, that Congress does have the legal authority to decide whether to fund or not to fund administrative agencies. Congress can also exercise oversight over agencies through investigations and hearings.

Politics with a Purpose

HOLDING GOVERNMENT ACCOUNTABLE

If $17 million were stolen from the federal government, the thieves should be held to account.[a] If our nation's airport security system were not keeping pace with emerging terrorist threats, policymakers in a position to act should be informed.[b] If sensitive U.S. military equipment such as F-13 antennae, nuclear biological chemical gear, and pieces of body armor plates could be bought freely on Internet auction sites, an investigation should be launched to shut this practice down.[c] Keeping all aspects of government accountable and investigating possible fraud, waste, and abuse are among the key responsibilities of the Government Accountability Office (GAO).

Created by Congress in 1921, the GAO (originally named the General Accounting Office) was designed to audit and review executive branch agencies.[d] Sometimes called Congress's watchdog, GAO is part of the legislative branch and is headed by the comptroller general, who is appointed by the president and confirmed by the Senate for a 12-year, nonrenewable term. The size, responsibilities, and reach of GAO have changed over time, hitting their zenith in the early 1990s. In 2004, the agency's name was changed to the Government Accountability Office to reflect the way it had expanded from its original mission. The examples cited earlier are just a few of the many investigations it launches each year. With a staff of more than 3,100 people and a budget of more than $489 million, GAO conducts reviews, writes reports, and investigates (often undercover) alleged wrongdoing on the part of individuals within the federal government.[e]

One of the ways GAO keeps tabs on government is to list areas within the federal government that are at high risk for "fraud, waste, abuse, and mismanagement."[f] Some agencies, such as the Medicare Program and the Department of Defense Supply Chain Management, have remained on the list since 1990. An example of an agency recently removed from the list is the U.S. Postal Service. The Postal Service was originally added to the list because of concerns about its fiscal health. The GAO determined that significant changes, including retiring its debt and implementing $5 billion in cost savings, were made to justify removing it from the list.

The information GAO provides is critical in a democracy, where citizens need to be informed about the actions of government. The GAO issues many reports each year on such topics as understanding how the government spends taxpayers' dollars, the safety of our food supply, and successful strategies for monitoring convicted sex offenders. Many reports are available online, through your college or university library, or may be ordered directly from GAO (www.gao.gov/cgi-bin/ordtab.pl).

If this sort of investigative and analysis work sounds interesting, you might consider employment with GAO or another similar agency among the many you will discover in this chapter. Students can intern with these organizations to gain valuable work experience.[g] Those close to graduating should visit www.usajobs.opm.gov, which is a gateway to government employment opportunities. Whether you plan to be a chemist or are studying animal husbandry or criminal justice, the federal bureaucracy needs your talents.

[a] www.gao.gov/new.items/d07724t.pdf.
[b] http://oversight.house.gov/documents/20071114175647.pdf.
[c] www.gao.gov/new.items/d08644t.pdf.
[d] Frederick M. Kaiser, CRS Report for Congress (GAO: Government Accountability Office and General Accounting Office, 2007), updated June 22, 2007, Order Code RL30349, www.fas.org/sgp/crs/misc/RL30349.pdf, accessed May 15, 2007.
[e] www.gao.gov/about/gglance.html.
[f] www.gao.gov/new.items/d07310.pdf.
[g] www.studentjobs.gov/searchvol.asp.

Congressional committees conduct investigations and hold hearings to oversee an agency's actions, reviewing them to ensure compliance with congressional intentions. The agency's officers and employees can be ordered to testify before a committee about the details of an action. Through these oversight activities, especially in the questions and comments of members of the House or Senate during the hearings, Congress indicates its positions on specific programs and issues.

Congress can ask the Government Accountability Office (GAO) to investigate particular agency actions as well. The Congressional Budget Office (CBO) also conducts oversight studies. The results of a GAO or CBO study may encourage Congress to hold further hearings or make changes in the law. Even if a law is not changed explicitly by Congress, however, the views expressed in any investigations and hearings are taken seriously by agency officials, who often act on those views.

In 1996, Congress passed the Congressional Review Act. The act created special procedures that can be employed to express congressional disapproval of particular agency actions. These procedures have rarely been used, however. Since the act's passage, the executive branch has issued more than 15,000 regulations. Yet only eight resolutions of disapproval have been introduced, and none of these was passed by either chamber.

Reasons Why Congress Cannot Easily Oversee the Bureaucracy

Despite the powers just described, one theory of congressional control over the bureaucracy suggests that Congress cannot possibly oversee all of the bureaucracy. Consider two possible approaches to congressional control—(1) the "police patrol" and (2) the "fire alarm" approach. Certain congressional activities, such as annual budget hearings, fall under the police patrol approach. This regular review occasionally catches *some* deficiencies in a bureaucracy's job performance, but it usually fails to detect most problems.

In contrast, the fire alarm approach is more likely to discover gross inadequacies in a bureaucracy's job performance. In this approach, Congress and its committees react to scandal, citizen disappointment, and massive negative publicity by launching a full-scale investigation into whatever agency is suspected of wrongdoing. Clearly, this is what happened when Congress investigated the inadequacies of the CIA after the terrorist attacks of September 11, 2001. Congress was also responding to an alarm when it investigated the failures of FEMA after Hurricane Katrina. Fire alarm investigations will not catch all problems, but they will alert bureaucracies that they need to clean up their procedures before a problem arises in their own agencies.[14]

---

14.   Matthew D. McCubbins and Thomas Schwartz, "Congressional Oversight Overlooked: Police Patrols versus Fire Alarms," *American Journal of Political Science*, February 28, 1984, pp. 165–179.

You Can Make a Difference

WHAT THE GOVERNMENT KNOWS ABOUT YOU

The federal government collects billions of pieces of information on tens of millions of Americans each year. These data are stored in files and sometimes are exchanged among agencies. You are probably the subject of several federal records (e.g., in the Social Security Administration, the Internal Revenue Service, and, if you are a male, the Selective Service).

Source: U.S. Department of Homeland Security

The Department of Homeland Security web site provides guidance on making an FOIA request. Visit www.dhs.gov/xfoia/ editorial_0316.shtm.

WHY SHOULD YOU CARE?

Verifying the information that the government has on you can be important. On several occasions, the records of two people with similar names have become confused. Sometimes innocent persons have had the criminal records of other persons erroneously inserted into their files. Such disasters are not always caused by bureaucratic error. One of the most common crimes in today's world is identity theft, in which one person uses another person's personal identifiers (such as a Social Security number) to commit fraud. In some instances, identity thieves have been arrested or even jailed under someone else's name.

WHAT CAN YOU DO?

The 1966 Freedom of Information Act (FOIA) requires that the federal government release, at your request, any identifiable information it has about you or about any other subject. Ten categories of material are exempted, however (classified material, confidential material on trade secrets, internal personnel rules, personal medical files, and the like). To request material, write directly to the FOIA officer at the agency in question (say, the Department of Education). You must

have a relatively specific idea about the document or information you want to obtain.

A second law, the Privacy Act of 1974, gives you access specifically to information the government may have collected about you. This law allows you to review records on file with federal agencies and to check those records for possible inaccuracies. If you want to look at any records or find out if an agency has a record on you, write to the agency head or Privacy Act officer, and address your letter to the specific agency. State that "under the provisions of the Privacy Act of 1974, 5 U.S.C. 522a, I hereby request a copy of (or access to) ___." Then describe the record that you wish to investigate.

The American Civil Liberties Union (ACLU) has published a manual, called *Your Right to Government Information*, that guides you through the steps of obtaining information from the federal government. You can order it online at www.aclu.org. Alternatively, you can order the manual from the ACLU at the following address:

ACLU Publications
P.O. Box 4713
Trenton, NJ 08650-4713
1-800-775-ACLU

Key Terms

acquisitive model 415
administrative
    agency 416
bureaucracy 414
cabinet department 418
capture 420
Civil Service
    Commission 428

enabling legislation 434
government
    corporation 422
Government in the
    Sunshine Act 429
independent executive
    agency 419

independent regulatory
    agency 420
iron triangle 437
issue network 438
line organization 418
merit system 428
monopolistic model 416

Pendleton Act (Civil Service
    Reform Act) 428
privatization 430
spoils system 427
sunset legislation 430
Weberian model 415
whistleblower 433

Chapter Summary

1. Bureaucracies are hierarchical organizations characterized by a division of labor and extensive procedural rules. Bureaucracy is the primary form of organization of most major corporations and universities as well as governments. These organizations are developed to carry out complex policies and procedures or to deliver multiple services or products in a fair, consistent, and effective manner.

2. Several theories have been offered to explain bureaucracies. The Weberian model posits that bureaucracies are rational, hierarchical organizations in which decisions are based on logical reasoning. The acquisitive model views top-level bureaucrats as pressing for ever-larger budgets and staffs to augment their own sense of power and security. The monopolistic model focuses on the environment in which most government bureaucracies operate, stating that bureaucracies are inefficient and excessively costly to operate because they have no competitors.

3. Since the founding of the United States, the federal bureaucracy has grown from 50 to about 2.7 million employees (excluding the military). Federal, state, and local employees together make up more than 16 percent of the nation's civilian labor force. The federal bureaucracy consists of 15 cabinet departments, as well as a large number of independent executive agencies, independent regulatory agencies, and government corporations. These entities enjoy varying degrees of autonomy, visibility, and political support.

4. A federal bureaucracy of career civil servants was formed during Thomas Jefferson's presidency. Andrew Jackson implemented a spoils system through which he appointed his own political supporters. A civil service based on professionalism and merit was the goal of the Civil Service Reform Act of 1883. Concerns that the civil service be freed from the pressures of politics prompted the passage of the Hatch Act in 1939. Significant changes in the administration of the civil service were made by the Civil Service Reform Act of 1978.

5. Bureaucracies, due to their very size and complexity, may become inefficient and slow. Presidents try to manage the bureaucracy through political appointments to top positions. Congress also becomes frustrated when it receives reports of corruption or malfeasance in the bureaucracy. To solve some of these problems, many attempts have been made to make the federal bureaucracy more open, efficient, and responsive to the needs of U.S. citizens. The most important reforms have included sunshine and sunset laws, privatization, strategies to provide incentives for increased productivity and efficiency, and protection for whistleblowers.

6. The bureaucracy has a complex relationship with the political branches of the government. While it reports to the president, the Congress oversees the bureaucracy and provides its budget. In addition, Congress delegates much of its authority to federal agencies when it creates new laws. The bureaucrats who run these agencies become important policymakers, because Congress has neither the time nor the technical expertise to oversee the administration of its laws. In the agency rule-making process, a proposed regulation is published. A comment period follows, during which interested parties may offer suggestions for changes. Because companies and other organizations have challenged many regulations in court, federal agencies now are authorized to allow parties that will be affected by new regulations to participate in the rule-drafting process.

7. Congress exerts ultimate control over all federal agencies because it controls the federal government's purse strings. It also establishes the general guidelines by which regulatory agencies must abide. The appropriations process may provide a way to send messages of approval or disapproval to particular agencies, as do congressional hearings and investigations of agency actions.

Selected Print, Media, and Online Resources

PRINT RESOURCES

Alexander, David. *The Pentagon: The People, the Building, and the Mission.* Osceola, WI: Zenith Press, 2008. Veteran defense writer and novelist David Alexander delivers the inside story on the people who have brought the Pentagon to life, from its initial construction during World War II to its restoration after the terrorist attacks on September 11, 2001.

Freeman, Jody, and Martha Minow. *Government by Contract: Outsourcing and American Democracy.* Cambridge, MA: Harvard University Press, 2009. Outsourcing raises questions about costs, quality, and democratic oversight. Harvard law professors Freeman and Minow describe the scope of government contracting and the issues that result.

Goodsell, Charles T. *The Case for Bureaucracy: A Public Administration Polemic,* 4th ed. Washington, DC: CQ Press, 2003. Goodsell argues for the excellence of the federal bureaucracy, introducing all types of performance measures and examining numerous public opinion polls that demonstrate satisfaction with government agencies.

Government Jobs News, Info Tech Employment, and Partnerships for Community, editors, *Government Jobs in America: Jobs in U.S. States and Cities and U.S. Federal Agencies with Job Titles, Salaries, and Pension Estimates—Why You Want One, What Jobs are Available, How to Get One.* Washington, D.C.: Partnerships for Community, 2011.

If you are interested in applying for a job with any U.S. government agency, this comprehensive guide will lead you through the process, from reviewing the qualifications necessary to the final interview.

Haymann, Philip, B. *Living the Policy Process.* New York: Oxford University Press, 2008. Haymann uses case studies to examine how policymakers struggle to affect governmental decisions. His detailed accounts range from the cabinet level down to the middle tiers of the federal bureaucracy. Examples include providing support to anti-Soviet Afghan rebels and attempting to restrict smoking.

Kinsey, Christopher, and Malcolm Patterson. *Contractors and War: The Transformation of United States' Expeditionary Operations.* The authors trace the move from using members of the military for support operations to the almost total reliance on private contractors since the 1990s.

Osborne, David, and Peter Plastrik. *Banishing Bureaucracy: The Five Strategies for Reinventing Government.* San Francisco: David Osborne Publishing, 2006. In 1992, David Osborne (with Ted Gaebler) wrote a best seller entitled *Reinventing Government. Banishing Bureaucracy* is his sequel, which goes one step further—it outlines specific strategies that can help transform public systems and organizations into engines of efficiency. The book focuses on clarifying a bureaucracy's purpose, creating incentives, improving accountability, redistributing power, and nurturing the correct culture.

Weiner, Tim. *Legacy of Ashes: The History of the CIA.* New York: Doubleday, 2007. The author has written a very readable account of the CIA with the general view that many of its directors and major players have been less than competent. The book provides real insight into the CIA's role in recent American history.

MEDIA RESOURCES

The Bureaucracy of Government: John Lukacs—In a 1988 Bill Moyers special, historian John Lukacs discusses the common political lament over the giant but invisible mechanism called bureaucracy.

King Corn—A 2007 documentary that demonstrates the impact of corn growing on modern America. Ian Cheney and Curt Ellis learn that corn is in almost everything they eat. They move to Iowa for a year to grow corn and find out what happens to it. Inevitably, they come face to face with America's farm policy and its subsidies.

When the Levees Broke: A Requiem in Four Acts—A strong treatment of Hurricane Katrina's impact on New Orleans by renowned African American director Spike Lee. We learn about the appalling performance of authorities at every level and the suffering that could have been avoided. Lee's anger at what he sees adds spice to the 2006 production.

Yes, Minister—A new member of the British cabinet bumps up against the machinations of a top civil servant in a comedy of manners. This popular 1980 BBC comedy is now available on DVD.

ONLINE RESOURCES

Federal Register—the official publication for executive branch documents: www.gpoaccess.gov/fr/browse.html

The Plum Book—lists the bureaucratic positions that can be filled by presidential appointment: www.gpoaccess.gov/plumbook/index.html

United States Government Manual—describes the origins, purposes, and administrators of every federal department and agency: www.gpoaccess.gov/gmanual/index.html

USA.gov—the United States government's official Web portal, which makes it easy for the public to get government information and services on the Web, such as telephone numbers for government agencies and personnel: www.USA.gov

14 The Courts

JONATHAN ERNST/Reuters/Landov

The lawyers who are members of the Supreme Court bar line up outside the lawyer's entrance to the court on the first day of the oral arguments on the constitutionality of the Affordable Health Care Act in 2012.

LEARNING OUTCOMES

After reading this chapter, students will be able to:

■ **LO1** Explain how judges in the American system decide cases, and define *stare decisis*.

■ **LO2** Define *judicial review* and explain the constitutional and judicial origins of this power.

■ **LO3** Produce a graphic illustration of the federal court system, and explain how a case moves from the trial court to the highest court of appeals, the Supreme Court.

■ **LO4** Explain how judges are nominated and confirmed for the Supreme Court.

■ **LO5** Compare the concepts of judicial activism and judicial restraint, and link these concepts to the decisions of the Supreme Court in the last few decades.

What If...

SUPREME COURT JUSTICES HAD TERM LIMITS?

BACKGROUND

The nine justices who sit on the Supreme Court are not elected officials. Rather, they are appointed by the president (and confirmed by the Senate). Barring gross misconduct, they also hold their offices for life. Given the long life span of Americans, it is not unusual for justices to be actively serving on the court after they turn 80 years old. Would the justices be more in tune with the ideas of Americans and less likely to use their power to make policy if they did not hold permanent seats? One way to make the justices even more responsive to public opinion might be to limit their tenure in office.

WHAT IF SUPREME COURT JUSTICES HAD TERM LIMITS?

If Supreme Court justices had term limits, what should be the length of the term? Perhaps an appropriate one would be the average time on the bench from the founding of our nation until 1970—15 years. In other words, after confirmation by the Senate, a person could serve only 15 years on the bench and then would have to retire. Perhaps the most important result of term limits would be a reduction in the rancor surrounding confirmation hearings. Today, the confirmation of a Supreme Court nominee—one chosen by the president to fit his or her views—is a major political event because that person may be on the Court for the next three decades.

Consider the current chief justice, John Roberts. When he took the Supreme Court bench at age 50, Americans could potentially anticipate that his conservative ideology would influence Supreme Court decisions for as long as 30 years. Knowing this, those who did not share his views or philosophy opposed his confirmation. If term limits had been in existence, in contrast, less would have been at stake—probably about half as many years of his influence.

TERM LIMITS WOULD PUT THE UNITED STATES IN LINE WITH OTHER DEMOCRACIES

In having no term limits for federal judges, the United States is somewhat out of step. Not only does just one state—Rhode Island—appoint state supreme court justices for life, but virtually every other major democratic nation has age or term limits for judges. Thus, term limits in the United States for federal judges would not be an anomaly. Even with term limits, Supreme Court justices would still be independent, which is what the framers of the Constitution desired.

MORE INFUSION OF NEW BLOOD

With term limits of, say, 15 years, vacancies would be created on a more or less regular basis. Consequently, Supreme Court justices would have less temptation to time their retirements for political purposes. Thus, liberal-leaning justices would not necessarily delay their retirements until a Democratic president was in office, and conservative-leaning justices would not necessarily wait for a Republican. In other words, fewer justices would follow the example of Justice Thurgood Marshall, who often said that he was determined to hang on to his judicial power until a Democratic president was in office to appoint his successor. After many years on the bench, he joked, "I have instructed my clerks that if I should die, they should have me stuffed—and continue to cast my votes."

In short, virtually every president, whether he or she was a Republican or Democrat, would get a chance to fill a Supreme Court vacancy every few years. As a result, "new blood" would be infused into the Supreme Court more often. We would no longer face the risk of having Supreme Court justices who become less than enthusiastic about their work and less willing to examine new intellectual arguments. Term limits would also avoid the decrepitude that has occurred with several very old Supreme Court justices. In the last 30 years, some truly have stayed until the last possible minute. The public might prefer at least to have a mandatory retirement age.

FOR CRITICAL ANALYSIS

1. What are the benefits of having lifetime appointments to the Supreme Court?

2. Just because a president can appoint whomever he or she wishes to the Supreme Court, does that necessarily mean that the successful nominee will always reflect the president's political philosophy? Explain your answer.

THE JUSTICES OF the Supreme Court are not elected, but rather are appointed by the president and confirmed by the Senate. The same is true for all other federal court judges. It is a fact that many federal judges and Supreme Court justices sit on the bench for 30 years or more. As discussed in the What if…, some critics of the court suggest that lifetime appointments for judges guarantee that some will be out of touch with current political and social debates.

As Alexis de Tocqueville, a French commentator on American society in the 1800s, noted, "scarcely any political question arises in the United States that is not resolved, sooner or later, into a judicial question."[1] Our judiciary forms part of our political process. The instant that judges interpret the law, they become actors in the political arena—policymakers working within a political institution. The most important political force within our judiciary is the United States Supreme Court.

How do courts make policy? Why do the federal courts play such an important role in American government? The answers to these questions lie, in part, in our colonial heritage. Most of American law is based on the English system, particularly the English *common-law tradition*. In that tradition, the decisions made by judges constitute an important source of law. In the United States, the Supreme Court has extraordinary power to shape the nation's policies through the practice of **judicial review**, first explicated by Justice Marshall in the *Marbury v. Madison* case in 1803. We open this chapter with an examination of this tradition and of the various sources of American law. We then look at the federal court system—its organization, how its judges are selected, how these judges affect policy, and how they are restrained by our system of checks and balances.

Sources of American Law

In 1066, the Normans conquered England, and William the Conqueror and his successors began the process of unifying the country under their rule. One of the ways they did this was to establish king's courts. Before the conquest, disputes had been settled according to local custom. The king's courts sought to establish a common or uniform set of rules for the whole country. As the number of courts and cases increased, portions of the most important decisions of each year were compiled in *Year Books*. Judges settling disputes similar to ones that had been decided before used the *Year Books* as the basis for their decisions. If a case was unique, judges had to create new laws, but they based their decisions on the general principles suggested by earlier cases. The body of judge-made law that developed under this system is still used today and is known as the **common law**.

The practice of deciding new cases with reference to former decisions—that is, according to **precedent**—became a cornerstone of the English and American judicial systems and is embodied in the doctrine of *stare decisis* (pronounced *ster-ay dih-si-ses*), a Latin phrase that means "to stand on decided cases." The doctrine of **stare decisis** obligates judges to follow the precedents set previously by their own courts or by higher courts that have authority over them.

For example, a lower state court in California would be obligated to follow a precedent set by the California Supreme Court. That lower court, however, would

did you know?

The Supreme Court was not provided with a building of its own until 1935, in the 146th year of its existence.

Judicial Review

The power of the Supreme Court or any court to hold a law or other legal action as unconstitutional.

■ **Learning Outcome 1:**

Explain how judges in the American system decide cases, and define *stare decisis*.

Common Law

Judge-made law that originated in England from decisions shaped according to prevailing custom. Decisions were applied to similar situations and gradually became common to the nation.

Precedent

A court rule bearing on subsequent legal decisions in similar cases. Judges rely on precedents in deciding cases.

Stare Decisis

To stand on decided cases; the judicial policy of following precedents established by past decisions.

---

1. Alexis de Tocqueville, *Democracy in America* (New York: Harper & Row, 1966), p. 248.

not be obligated to follow a precedent set by the supreme court of another state, because each state court system is independent. Of course, when the United States Supreme Court decides an issue, all of the nation's other courts are obligated to abide by the Court's decision, because the Supreme Court is the highest court in the land.

The doctrine of *stare decisis* provides a basis for judicial decision making in all countries that have common-law systems. Today, the United States, Britain, and several dozen other countries have common-law systems. Generally, those countries that were once British colonies, such as Australia, Canada, and India, have retained their English common-law heritage. An alternative legal system based on Muslim *sharia* is discussed in this chapter's Beyond Our Borders feature.

The body of American law includes the federal and state constitutions, statutes passed by legislative bodies, administrative law, and case law—the legal principles expressed in court decisions. The power of case law rests in the principle of judicial review.

Constitutions

The constitutions of the federal government and the states set forth the general organization, powers, and limits of government. The U.S. Constitution is the supreme law of the land. A law in violation of the Constitution, no matter what its source, may be declared unconstitutional and thereafter cannot be enforced. Similarly, the state constitutions are supreme within their respective borders (unless they conflict with the U.S. Constitution or federal laws and treaties made in accordance with it). The Constitution thus defines the political playing field on which state and federal powers are reconciled. The idea that the Constitution should be supreme in certain matters stemmed from widespread dissatisfaction with the weak federal government that had existed previously under the Articles of Confederation adopted in 1781.

Statutes and Administrative Regulations

Although the English common law provides the basis for both our civil and criminal legal systems, statutes (laws enacted by legislatures) increasingly have become important in defining the rights and obligations of individuals. Federal statutes may relate to any subject that is a concern of the federal government and may apply to areas ranging from hazardous waste to federal taxation. State statutes include criminal codes, commercial laws, and laws covering a variety of other matters. Cities, counties, and other local political bodies also pass statutes, which are called ordinances. These ordinances may deal with such issues as zoning proposals and public safety. Rules and regulations issued by administrative agencies are another source of law. Today, much of the work of the courts consists of interpreting these laws and regulations and applying them to circumstances in cases before the courts.

AP Photo

Judge Tom Colbert is the first African American to be appointed to the Supreme Court of Oklahoma. Prior to that appointment, he served on the Oklahoma Court of Civil Appeals.

Beyond Our Borders
THE LEGAL SYSTEM BASED ON *SHARIA*

Hundreds of millions of Muslims throughout the world are governed by a system of law called *sharia*. In this system, religious laws and precepts are combined with practical laws relating to common actions, such as entering into contracts and borrowing funds.

THE AUTHORITY OF *SHARIA*

It is said that *sharia*, or Islamic law, is drawn from two major sources and one lesser source. The first major source is the Qur'an (Koran) and the specific guidelines laid down in it. The second major source, called *sunnah*, is based on the way the Prophet Muhammad lived his life. The lesser source is called *ijma*; it represents the consensus of opinion in the community of Muslims. *Sharia* law is comprehensive in nature. All possible actions of Muslims are divided into five categories: obligatory, meritorious, permissible, reprehensible, and forbidden.

THE SCOPE OF *SHARIA* LAW

Sharia law covers many aspects of daily life, including the following:

- Dietary rules
- Relations between married men and women
- The role of women
- Holidays
- Dress codes, particularly for women
- Speech with respect to the Prophet Muhammad
- Crimes, including adultery, murder, and theft
- Business dealings, including the borrowing and lending of funds

WHERE *SHARIA* LAW IS APPLIED

The degree to which *sharia* is used varies throughout Muslim societies today. Several of the countries with the largest Muslim populations (e.g., Bangladesh, India, and Indonesia) do not have Islamic law. Other Muslim countries have dual systems of *sharia* courts and secular courts. In 2008, many British citizens were surprised by the remarks of the Archbishop of Canterbury, the religious leader of all Episcopalians, that there was a need for accommodation of *sharia* law in Great Britain.* He was referring to a system of *sharia* courts that has been functioning in Muslim neighborhoods for the last 20 years. The comments followed news that a *sharia* court had

A Sharia court judge in Great Britain confers with two Muslim women about their court case.

released some Somali youths who had stabbed another young man after ordering the assailants to compensate the victim and apologize. This incident led to national debate over whether the *sharia* court was performing functions that should be reserved for criminal and civil courts. In other parts of England, *sharia* courts deal mainly with Islamic laws regarding divorce and the rights of women, much in the same way the Catholic Church decides the status of its own members.**

Canada, which has a *sharia* arbitration court in Ontario, is the first North American country to establish a *sharia* court. Some countries, including Iran and Saudi Arabia, maintain religious courts for all aspects of jurisprudence, including civil and criminal law. Recently, Nigeria has reintroduced *sharia* courts.

*"Sharia Law Courts Are Already Dealing with Crime on the Streets of London, It Has Emerged," *Evening Standard*, London, February 8, 2008.
**"The View from Inside a Sharia Court," BBC News, February 11, 2008.

FOR CRITICAL ANALYSIS

1. *Do you think that a nation can have two different systems of law at the same time?*
2. *How should decisions about religious law be regarded by civil legal systems?*

Case Law

Because we have a common-law tradition, in which the doctrine of *stare decisis* (described earlier) plays an important role, the decisions rendered by the courts also form an important body of law, collectively referred to as **case law**. Case law includes judicial interpretations of common-law principles and doctrines, as well as interpretations of the types of law just mentioned—constitutional provisions, statutes, and administrative agency regulations. As you learned in previous chapters, it is up to the courts—and particularly the Supreme Court—to decide what a constitutional provision or a statutory phrase means. In doing so, the courts, in effect, establish law.

Judicial Review

The process for deciding whether a law is contrary to the mandates of the Constitution is known as judicial review. This power is nowhere mentioned in the U.S. Constitution. Rather, this judicial power was first established in the famous case of *Marbury v. Madison* (as discussed in the Politics with a Purpose on the next page). In that case, Chief Justice Marshall insisted that the Supreme Court had the power to decide that a law passed by Congress violated the Constitution:

> *It is emphatically the province and duty of the Judicial Department to say what the law is. Those who apply the rule to a particular case must, of necessity, expound and interpret that rule. If two laws conflict with each other, the courts must decide on the operation of each.*[2]

The Supreme Court has ruled parts or all of acts of Congress to be unconstitutional fewer than 200 times in its history. State laws, however, have been declared unconstitutional by the court much more often—more than 1,000 times. The court has been more active in declaring federal or state laws unconstitutional since the beginning of the 20th century.

The Supreme Court, through its power of judicial review, can effectively define the separation of powers between the branches. In 1983, for example, the Court outlawed the practice of the legislative veto by which one or both chambers of Congress could overturn decisions made by the president or by executive agencies. This single decision overturned dozens of separate statutes and reinforced the Court's position as the arbiter of institutional power.

The Federal Court System

The United States has a dual court system. There are state courts and federal courts. Each of the 50 states, as well as the District of Columbia, has its own independent system of courts. This means that there are 52 court systems in total. The federal court derives its power from the U.S. Constitution, Article III, Section 1, and is organized according to congressional legislation. State courts draw their authority from state constitutions and laws. Court cases that originate in state court systems reach the Supreme Court only after they have been appealed to the highest possible state court. Figure 14–1 shows the basic components of the state and federal court systems.

Basic Judicial Requirements

In any court system, state or federal, before a case can be brought before a court, certain requirements must be met. Two important requirements are jurisdiction and standing to sue.

Case Law
Judicial interpretations of common-law principles and doctrines, as well as interpretations of constitutional law, statutory law, and administrative law.

■ **Learning Outcome 2:**
Define *judicial review* and explain the constitutional and judicial origins of this power.

■ **Learning Outcome 3:**
Produce a graphic illustration of the federal court system, and explain how a case moves from the trial court to the highest court of appeals, the Supreme Court.

---

2. 5 U.S. (1 Cranch) 137 (1803).

Politics with a Purpose
POLITICAL STRUGGLES FOUGHT IN THE COURT

Complaints about activist judges, a hotly contested election with partisan opponents hurling nasty insults, and debates about big government. One might argue that this is a description of politics in the 21st century. However, it also describes the presidential election of 1800, the aftermath of which led to *Marbury v. Madison,* one of the most important Supreme Court cases, whose influence is felt today.

Marbury v. Madison established the doctrine of judicial review, or the ability of the Court to rule an act of government to be unconstitutional. It was precipitated by the presidential election of 1800, in which the incumbent president, John Adams, was defeated by his vice president, Thomas Jefferson. Not only did this event mark the first election where issues divided the emerging political parties, but the election was also intensely and personally fought. President Adams was a member of the Federalist Party, which had emerged victorious in the fights over ratification of the Constitution. Jefferson was an Anti-Federalist and the leader of the ascendant Jeffersonian Republicans. These two groups disagreed on the power of the federal government. In addition, the two men bitterly disagreed with each other's politics.

While Thomas Jefferson would eventually win the election, he would not take office until March 1801.[a] In the interim between the election and inauguration, the Federalist-controlled Congress passed a series of laws creating additional judicial positions that would be staffed with Federalist appointments. One of these positions was District of Columbia Justice of the Peace, a relatively low-level judicial appointment whose term would expire in five years. William Marbury was confirmed as one of these appointments. The day before inauguration, the appointment papers were signed and sealed, but not delivered. John Marshall was to deliver the appointment, but he had his own appointment to become chief justice of the Supreme Court. Upon taking office, President Jefferson ordered his secretary of state, James Madison, not to deliver the commissions. Marbury and two others brought suit to the Supreme Court, asking that the Court force Jefferson to deliver the commissions.

Some accounts argue that Marbury took this action, not because he wanted the appointment, but because he wanted to provoke a fight with Jefferson. Marbury was a committed Federalist who believed that the Jeffersonian argument to reduce federal government control and give power back to state governments was deeply flawed. These Federalists were very unhappy with the outcome of the election and were seeking mechanisms to remain influential.[b]

By then, the chief justice of the Supreme Court was John Marshall, a Federalist appointed by the former President Adams. Marshall had a real dilemma to resolve in this case. He knew that if he ordered Jefferson to honor the commission, the president would likely ignore the order, resulting in an unacceptably dangerous constitutional crisis for the young country, and the Supreme Court would be weakened. Marshall, writing for the Court, issued a decision that found Marbury's rights had been denied but that the law passed by Congress that would have granted the Court the power of redress was unconstitutional. In other words, Marshall said that the Supreme Court was not where Marbury should have sought a solution, arguing for the first time that the Court had the power to "say what the law is."[c]

John Marshall's role and the legal arguments he used in deciding the case have many interpretations.[d] Without dispute, however, this case marked the formal articulation of judicial review, a power that in the 20th century would touch Americans' most basic liberties and rights. Even more significantly, the case illustrates that the intense battles waged by groups to make a difference in contemporary politics (e.g., *Roe v. Wade* and *Bush v. Gore)* are as old as the Republic.

[a] This election was also noteworthy for illustrating the flaw in the electoral college that resulted in a tie between Jefferson and his running mate, Aaron Burr. Breaking the tie in the House of Representatives took six days and 36 ballots. www.historynow.org/09_2004/historian4b.html, accessed May 16, 2008.
[b] www.claremont.org/publications/crb/id.1183/article_detail.asp#, accessed May 17, 2008.
[c] *Marbury v. Madison,* 5 U.S. 137 (1803).
[d] See, for example, Alexander M. Bickel, *The Least Dangerous Branch: The Supreme Court at the Bar of Politics* (New Haven, CT: Yale University Press, 1986); and William E. Nelson, *Marbury v. Madison: The Origins and Legacy of Judicial Review* (Lawrence, KS: University Press of Kansas, 2000).

Jurisdiction

The authority of a court to decide certain cases. Not all courts have the authority to decide all cases. Two jurisdictional issues are where a case arises as well as its subject matter.

Jurisdiction. A state court can exercise **jurisdiction** (the authority of the court to hear and decide a case) over the residents of a particular geographic area, such as a county or district. A state's highest court, or supreme court, has jurisdictional authority over all residents within the state. Because the Constitution established a federal government with limited powers, federal jurisdiction is also limited.

Figure 14–1 ▶ Dual Structure of the American Court System

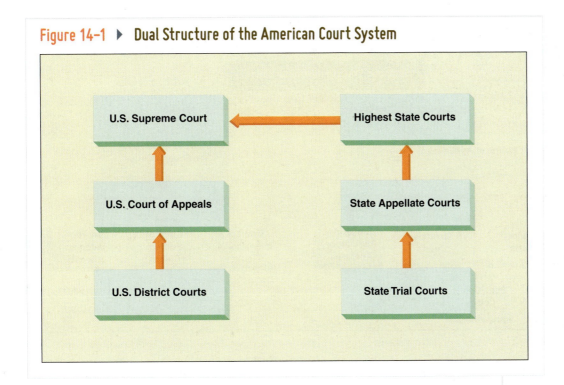

Article III, Section 1, of the U.S. Constitution limits the jurisdiction of the federal courts to cases that involve either a federal question or diversity of citizenship. A **federal question** arises when a case is based, at least in part, on the U.S. Constitution, a treaty, or a federal law. A person who claims that her or his rights under the Constitution, such as the right to free speech, have been violated could bring a case in a federal court. **Diversity of citizenship** exists when the parties to a lawsuit are from different states, or (more rarely) when the suit involves a U.S. citizen and a government or citizen of a foreign country. The amount in controversy must be at least $75,000 before a federal court can take jurisdiction in a diversity case, however.

Standing to Sue. Another basic judicial requirement is standing to sue, or a sufficient "stake" in a matter to justify bringing suit. The party bringing a lawsuit must have suffered a harm, or have been threatened by a harm, as a result of the action that led to the dispute in question. Standing to sue also requires that the controversy at issue be a justiciable controversy. A *justiciable controversy* is a controversy that is real and substantial, as opposed to hypothetical or academic. In other words, a court will not give advisory opinions on hypothetical questions.

Types of Federal Courts

As you can see in Figure 14–2, the federal court system is basically a three-tiered model consisting of (1) U.S. district courts and various specialized courts of limited jurisdiction (not all of the latter are shown in the figure); (2) intermediate U.S. courts of appeals; and (3) the United States Supreme Court. Other specialized courts in the federal system are discussed in a later section. In addition, the U.S. military has its own system of courts, which are established under the Uniform Code of Military Justice. Cases from these other federal courts may also reach the Supreme Court.

Federal Question
A question that has to do with the U.S. Constitution, acts of Congress, or treaties. A federal question provides a basis for federal jurisdiction.

Diversity of Citizenship
The condition that exists when the parties to a lawsuit are citizens of different states, or when the parties are citizens of a U.S. state and citizens or the government of a foreign country. Diversity of citizenship can provide a basis for federal jurisdiction.

Figure 14–2 ▶ The Federal Court System

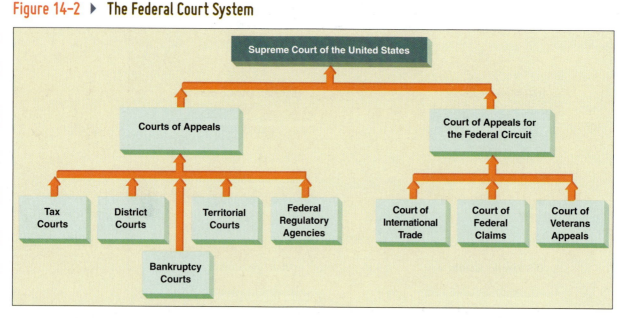

U.S. District Courts. The U.S. district courts are trial courts. A **trial court** is what the name implies—a court in which trials are held and testimony is taken. The U.S. district courts are courts of **general jurisdiction**, meaning that they can hear cases involving a broad array of issues. Federal cases involving most matters typically are heard in district courts. The other courts on the lower tier of the model shown in Figure 14–2 are courts of **limited jurisdiction**, meaning that they can try cases involving only certain types of claims, such as tax claims or bankruptcy petitions.

Every state has at least one federal district court. The number of judicial districts can vary over time as a result of population changes and corresponding caseloads. Currently, there are 94 federal judicial districts. A party who is dissatisfied with the decision of a district court can appeal the case to the appropriate U.S. court of appeals, or federal **appellate court**. Figure 14–3 shows the jurisdictional boundaries of the district courts (which are state boundaries, unless otherwise indicated by dotted lines within a state) and of the U.S. courts of appeals.

U.S. Courts of Appeals. The 13 U.S. courts of appeals are also referred to as U.S. circuit courts of appeals. Twelve of these courts, including the U.S. Court of Appeals for the District of Columbia, hear appeals from the federal district courts located within their respective judicial circuits (geographic areas over which they exercise jurisdiction). The Court of Appeals for the Thirteenth Circuit, called the Federal Circuit, has national appellate jurisdiction over certain types of cases, such as cases involving patent law and those in which the U.S. government is a defendant.

Note that when an appellate court reviews a case that was decided in a district court, the appellate court does not conduct another trial. Rather, a panel of three or more judges reviews the record of the case on appeal, which includes a transcript of the trial proceedings, and determines whether the trial court committed an error. Usually, appellate courts do not look at questions of *fact* (such as whether a party did, in fact, commit a certain action, such as burning a flag) but

Figure 14-3 ▶ Geographic Boundaries of Federal District Courts and Circuit Courts of Appeals

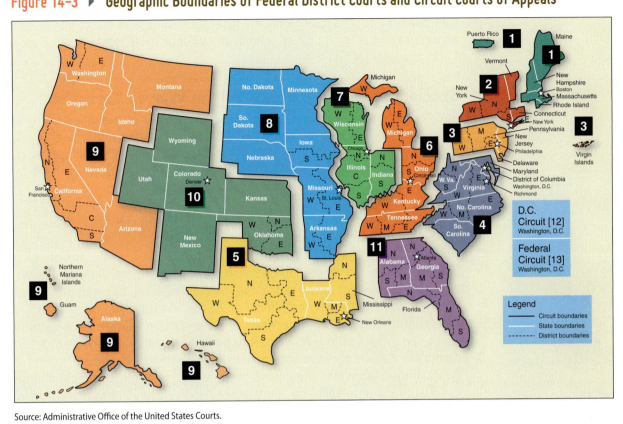

Source: Administrative Office of the United States Courts.

at questions of *law* (such as whether the act of burning a flag is a form of speech protected by the First Amendment to the Constitution). An appellate court will challenge a trial court's finding of fact only when the finding is clearly contrary to the evidence presented at trial or when no evidence supports the finding.

A party can petition the United States Supreme Court to review an appellate court's decision. The likelihood that the Supreme Court will grant the petition is slim, however, because the Court reviews very few of the cases decided by the appellate courts. This means that decisions made by appellate judges are usually final.

The United States Supreme Court. The highest level of the three-tiered model of the federal court system is the United States Supreme Court. When the Supreme Court came into existence in 1789, it had five justices. Congress passes laws that determine the number of justices and other aspects of the court. In the following years, more justices were added. Since 1869, nine justices have been on the Court at any given time.

According to the language of Article III of the U.S. Constitution, there is only one national Supreme Court. All other courts in the federal system are considered "inferior." Congress is empowered to create other inferior courts as it deems necessary. The inferior courts that Congress has created include the district courts, the federal courts of appeals, and the federal courts of limited jurisdiction.

Although the Supreme Court can exercise original jurisdiction (that is, act as a trial court) in certain cases, such as those affecting foreign diplomats and those in which a state is a party, most of its work is as an appellate court. The Court hears appeals not only from the federal appellate courts but also from the highest state courts. Note, though, that the United States Supreme Court can review a state supreme court decision only if a federal question is involved. Because of its importance in the federal court system, we will look more closely at the Supreme Court in a later section.

Specialized Federal Courts and the War on Terrorism

As noted, the federal court system includes a variety of trial courts of limited jurisdiction, dealing with matters such as tax claims, patent law, Native American claims, bankruptcy, or international trade. The government's attempts to combat terrorism have drawn attention to certain specialized courts that meet in secret.

The FISA Court. The federal government created the first secret court in 1978. In that year, Congress passed the Foreign Intelligence Surveillance Act (FISA), which established a court to hear requests for warrants for the surveillance of suspected spies. Officials can request warrants without having to reveal to the suspect or the public the information used to justify the warrant. The FISA court has approved almost all of the thousands of requests for warrants that the U.S. attorney general's office and other officials have submitted. The seven judges on the FISA court (who are also federal district judges from across the nation) meet in secret, with no published opinions or orders. The public has no access to the court's proceedings or records. Hence, when the court authorizes surveillance, most suspects do not even know that they are under scrutiny. Additionally, during the Clinton administration, the court was given the authority to approve physical as well as electronic searches, which means that officials may search a suspect's property without obtaining a warrant in open court and without notifying the subject.

In the aftermath of the terrorist attacks on September 11, 2001, the Bush administration expanded the powers of the FISA court. Previously, the FISA allowed secret domestic surveillance only if the target was spying as an agent of another nation. Post–September 11 amendments allow warrants if a "significant purpose" of the surveillance is to gather foreign intelligence and allow surveillance of groups who are not agents of a foreign government.

The prison at Guantánamo Bay, Cuba, where the detainees from the Afghanistan and Iraq wars were held until their military trials or their release to another country. Why did the United States create the prison at Guantánamo Bay?

AP Photo/Brennan Linsley

Alien "Removal Courts." The FISA court is not the only court in which suspects' rights have been reduced. In response to the Oklahoma City bombing in 1995, Congress passed the Anti-Terrorism and Effective Death Penalty Act of 1996. The act included a provision creating an alien "removal court" to hear evidence against suspected "alien terrorists." The judges rule on whether there is probable cause for deportation. If so, a public deportation proceeding is held in a U.S. district court. The prosecution does not need to follow procedures that normally apply in criminal cases. In addition, the defendant cannot see the evidence that the prosecution used to secure the hearing.

In some cases, the United States Supreme Court ruled against the George W. Bush administration's efforts to use secret legal proceedings in dealing with suspected terrorists. In 2004, the Supreme Court ruled that enemy combatants who are U.S. citizens and who have been taken prisoner by the United States cannot be denied due process rights. Justice Sandra Day O'Connor wrote that "due process demands that a citizen held in the United States as an enemy combatant be given a meaningful opportunity to contest the factual basis of that detention before a neutral decision maker. . . . A state of war is not a blank check for the president when it comes to the rights of the nation's citizens."[3] The Court also found that noncitizen detainees held at Guantánamo Bay in Cuba were entitled to challenge the grounds for their confinement.[4]

In response to the court rulings, the Bush administration asked Congress to enact a law establishing military tribunals to hear the prisoners' cases at Guantánamo. In 2006, the Court held that these tribunals did not meet due-process requirements for a fair hearing. The central issue in the case was whether the entire situation at the prison camp violated the prisoners' right of *habeas corpus*—the right of a detained person to challenge the legality of his or her detention before a judge or other neutral party. Congress then passed the Military Commissions Act of 2006, which eliminated federal court jurisdiction over *habeas corpus* challenges by enemy combatants. This law was also tested in court, but the Supreme Court refused to hear the case, so the law, as upheld by an appellate court, stands.[5]

Finally, in 2008, the Supreme Court, by a 5-4 majority, held that enemy combatants have the right to challenge their detention in front of a federal court if they have not been charged with a crime. This ruling essentially grants the detainees at Guantánamo Bay the right of *habeas corpus,* a right that the majority said Congress cannot restrict.[6] After President Obama took office in 2009, he announced that the prison at Guantánamo would be closed within a year; however, Congress has been unwilling to fund a prison in the United States to hold suspected terrorists and the administration has let the prison continue to exist. In addition, it has been difficult to find countries to accept some of the remaining prisoners who might be released. As of 2012 about 170 prisoners remained in the Cuban facility awaiting either trial or release.

Parties to Lawsuits

In most lawsuits, the parties are the plaintiff (the person or organization that initiates the lawsuit) and the defendant (the person or organization against whom the lawsuit is brought). Numerous plaintiffs and defendants may be in a single lawsuit. In the last several decades, many lawsuits have been brought by interest groups (see Chapter 7). Interest groups play an important role in our judicial system, because they **litigate**—bring to trial—or assist in litigating most cases of racial or gender-based discrimination, virtually all civil liberties cases, and more than one-third of the cases involving business matters. Interest groups also file *amicus curiae* (pronounced ah-*mee*-kous *kur*-ee-eye) briefs, or "friend of the court" briefs, in more than 50 percent of these kinds of cases.

Litigate
To engage in a legal proceeding or seek relief in a court of law; to carry on a lawsuit.

---

3. *Hamdi v. Rumsfeld,* 542 U.S. 507 (2004).
4. Hamdi was eventually released following a settlement with the government under which he agreed to renounce his U.S. citizenship and return to Saudi Arabia.
5. *Boumediene v. Bush,* 476 F.3d 981 (D.C. Cir. 2007).
6. *Boumediene v. Bush,* 553 U.S. 723 (2008).

Class-Action Suit
A lawsuit filed by an individual seeking damages for "all persons similarly situated."

Sometimes interest groups or other plaintiffs will bring a **class-action suit**, in which whatever the court decides will affect all members of a class similarly situated (such as users of a particular product manufactured by the defendant in the lawsuit). The strategy of class-action lawsuits was pioneered by such groups as the National Association for the Advancement of Colored People (NAACP), the Legal Defense Fund, and the Sierra Club, whose leaders believed that the courts would offer a more sympathetic forum for their views than would Congress.

Procedural Rules

Both the federal and the state courts have established procedural rules that shape the litigation process. These rules are designed to protect the rights and interests of the parties, to ensure that the litigation proceeds in a fair and orderly manner, and to identify the issues that must be decided by the court, thus saving court time and costs. Court decisions may also apply to trial procedures. For example, the Supreme Court has held that the parties' attorneys cannot discriminate against prospective jurors on the basis of race or gender. Some lower courts have also held that people cannot be excluded from juries because of their sexual orientation or religion.

The parties must comply with procedural rules and with any orders given by the judge during the course of the litigation. When a party does not follow a court's order, the court can cite him or her for contempt. A party who commits *civil* contempt (failing to comply with a court's order for the benefit of another party to the proceeding) can be taken into custody, fined, or both, until the party complies with the court's order. A party who commits *criminal* contempt (obstructing the administration of justice or bringing the court into disrespect) also can be taken into custody and fined but cannot avoid punishment by complying with a previous order.

Throughout this book, you have read about how technology is affecting all areas of government. The judiciary is no exception. Today's courts continue to place opinions and other information online. Increasingly, lawyers are expected to file court documents electronically. There is little doubt that in the future we will see more court proceedings being conducted through use of the Internet.

A courtroom artist's rendering of the sentencing trial for Zacarias Moussaoui at the federal courthouse. The confessed September 11 conspirator testified he knew about the terrorist plot when he was arrested a month before the attacks and lied to FBI agents because he wanted the mission to go forward.

© Art Lein/epa/Corbis

The Supreme Court at Work

The Supreme Court begins its regular annual term on the first Monday in October and usually adjourns in late June or early July of the next year. Special sessions may be held after the regular term ends, but only a few cases are decided in this way. More commonly, cases are carried over until the next regular session.

Of the total number of cases that are decided each year, those reviewed by the Supreme Court represent less than one-half of 1 percent. Included in these, however, are decisions that profoundly affect our lives. In recent years, the United States Supreme Court has decided issues involving the Obama health reform legislation, capital punishment, affirmative action programs, religious freedom, assisted suicide, abortion, property rights, sexual harassment, pornography, states' rights, limits on federal jurisdiction, and many other matters with significant consequences for the nation. Because the Supreme Court exercises a great deal of discretion over the types of cases it hears, it can influence the nation's policies by issuing decisions in some types of cases and refusing to hear appeals in others, thereby allowing lower court decisions to stand.

Justice Ruth Bader Ginsburg being interviewed in 2008. She noted the presence of two Jewish justices on the court and that their religion plays no role in their decisions.

Which Cases Reach the Supreme Court?

Many people are surprised to learn that in a typical case, there is no absolute right of appeal to the United States Supreme Court. The Court's appellate jurisdiction is almost entirely discretionary; the Court can choose which cases it will decide. The justices never explain their reasons for hearing certain cases and not others, so it is difficult to predict which case or type of case the Court might select. Former chief justice William Rehnquist, in his description of the selection process in *The Supreme Court: How It Was, How It Is,*[7] said that the decision of whether to accept a case "strikes me as a rather subjective decision, made up in part of intuition and in part of legal judgment."

Factors That Bear on the Decision. Factors that bear on the decision include whether a legal question has been decided differently by various lower courts and needs resolution by the highest court, whether a lower court's decision conflicts with an existing Supreme Court ruling, and whether the issue could have significance beyond the parties to the dispute.

Another factor is whether the solicitor general is pressuring the Court to take a case. The solicitor general, a high-ranking presidential appointee within the Justice Department, represents the national government before the Supreme Court and promotes presidential policies in the federal courts. He or she decides what cases the government should ask the Supreme Court to review and what position the government should take in cases before the Court.

Granting Petitions for Review. If the Court decides to grant a petition for review, it will issue a **writ of *certiorari*** (pronounced sur-shee-uh-*rah*-ree). The writ orders a lower court to send the Supreme Court a record of the case for

Writ of *Certiorari*
An order issued by a higher court to a lower court to send up the record of a case for review.

7. William H. Rehnquist, *The Supreme Court: How It Was, How It Is* (New York: Morrow, 1987).

review. More than 90 percent of the petitions for review are denied. A denial is not a decision on the merits of a case, nor does it indicate agreement with the lower court's opinion. (The judgment of the lower court remains in force, however.) Therefore, denial of the writ has no value as a precedent. The Court will not issue a writ unless at least four justices approve of it. This is called the **rule of four**.[8]

Rule of Four
A United States Supreme Court procedure by which four justices must vote to grant a petition for review if a case is to come before the full court.

Deciding Cases

Once the Supreme Court grants *certiorari* in a particular case, the justices do extensive research on the legal issues and facts involved in the case. (Of course, some preliminary research is necessary before deciding to grant the petition for review.) Each justice is entitled to four law clerks, who undertake much of the research and preliminary drafting necessary for the justice to form an opinion.[9]

The Court normally does not hear any evidence, as is true with all appeals courts. The Court's consideration of a case is based on the abstracts, the record, and the briefs. The attorneys are permitted to present **oral arguments**. All statements and the justices' questions are recorded during these sessions. Unlike the practice in most courts, lawyers addressing the Supreme Court can be (and often are) questioned by the justices at any time during oral argument.

Oral Arguments
The verbal arguments presented in person by attorneys to an appellate court. Each attorney presents reasons to the court why the court should rule in her or his client's favor.

The justices meet to discuss and vote on cases in conferences held throughout the term. In these conferences, in addition to deciding cases currently before the Court, the justices determine which new petitions for *certiorari* to grant. These conferences take place in the oak-paneled chamber and are strictly private—no stenographers, tape recorders, or video cameras are allowed. Two pages used to be in attendance to wait on the justices while they were in conference, but fear of information leaks caused the Court to stop this practice.[10]

Decisions and Opinions

When the Court has reached a decision, its opinion is written. The **opinion** contains the Court's ruling on the issue or issues presented, the reasons for its decision, the rules of law that apply, and other information. In many cases, the decision of the lower court is **affirmed**, resulting in the enforcement of that court's judgment or decree. If the Supreme Court believes that a reversible error was committed during the trial or that the jury was instructed improperly, however, the decision will be **reversed**. Sometimes the case will be **remanded** (sent back to the court that originally heard the case) for a new trial or other proceeding. For example, a lower court might have held that a party was not entitled to bring a lawsuit under a particular law. If the Supreme Court holds to the contrary, it will remand (send back) the case to the trial court with instructions that the trial proceed.

Opinion
The statement by a judge or a court of the decision reached in a case. The opinion sets forth the applicable law and details the reasoning on which the ruling was based.

Affirm
To declare that a court ruling is valid and must stand.

Reverse
To annul or make void a court ruling on account of some error or irregularity.

Remand
To send a case back to the court that originally heard it.

The Court's written opinion sometimes is unsigned; this is called an opinion *per curiam* ("by the court"). Typically, the Court's opinion is signed by all the justices who agree with it. When in the majority, the chief justice assigns the opinion

8. The "rule of four" is modified when seven or fewer justices participate, which occurs from time to time. When that happens, as few as three justices can grant *certiorari*.
9. For a former Supreme Court law clerk's account of the role these clerks play in the high court's decision-making process, see Edward Lazarus, *Closed Chambers: The First Eyewitness Account of the Epic Struggles inside the Supreme Court* (New York: Times Books, 1998).
10. It turned out that one supposed information leak came from lawyers making educated guesses.

and often writes it personally. When the chief justice is in the minority, the senior justice on the majority side decides who writes the opinion.

When all justices unanimously agree on an opinion, the opinion is written for the entire Court (all the justices) and can be deemed a **unanimous opinion**. When there is not a unanimous opinion, a **majority opinion** is written, outlining the views of the majority of the justices involved in the case. Often, one or more justices who feel strongly about making or emphasizing a particular point that is not made or emphasized in the unanimous or majority written opinion will write a **concurring opinion**. That means the justice writing the concurring opinion agrees (concurs) with the conclusion given in the majority written opinion, but for different reasons. Finally, in other than unanimous opinions, one or more **dissenting opinions** are usually written by those justices who do not agree with the majority. The dissenting opinion is important because it often forms the basis of the arguments used years later if the Court reverses the previous decision and establishes a new precedent.

Shortly after the opinion is written, the Supreme Court announces its decision from the bench. At that time, the opinion is made available to the public at the office of the clerk of the Court. The clerk also releases the opinion for online publication. Ultimately, the opinion is published in the *United States Reports*, which is the official printed record of the Court's decisions.

Some have complained that the Court reviews too few cases each term, thus giving the lower courts less guidance on important issues. The number of signed opinions issued by the Court has dwindled notably since the 1980s. For example, in its 1982–1983 term, the Court issued signed opinions in 141 cases. By 2010, this number dropped to between 80 and 100 per term.

Some scholars suggest that one of the reasons why the Court hears fewer cases today than in the past is the growing conservatism of the judges sitting on lower courts. More than half of these judges have now been appointed by Republican presidents. As a result, the government loses fewer cases in the lower courts, which lessens the need for the government to appeal the rulings through the solicitor general's office. Some support for this conclusion is given by the fact that the number of petitions filed by that office declined by more than 50 percent after George W. Bush became president.

The Selection of Federal Judges

All federal judges are appointed. The Constitution, in Article II, Section 2, states that the president appoints the justices of the Supreme Court with the advice and consent of the Senate. Congress has provided the same procedure for staffing other federal courts. This means that the Senate and the president jointly decide who shall fill every vacant judicial position, no matter what the level.

Federal judgeships in the United States number more than 870. Once appointed to such a judgeship, a person holds that job for life. Judges serve until they resign, retire voluntarily, or die. Federal judges who engage in blatantly illegal conduct may be removed through impeachment, although such action is rare.

Judicial Appointments

Judicial candidates for federal judgeships are suggested to the president by the Department of Justice, senators, other judges, the candidates, and lawyers'

Unanimous Opinion
A court opinion or determination on which all judges agree.

Majority Opinion
A court opinion reflecting the views of the majority of the judges.

Concurring Opinion
A separate opinion prepared by a judge who supports the decision of the majority of the court but who wants to make or clarify a particular point or to voice disapproval of the grounds on which the decision was made.

Dissenting Opinion
A separate opinion in which a judge dissents from (disagrees with) the conclusion reached by the majority on the court and expounds his or her own views about the case.

■ **Learning Outcome 4:**
Explain how judges are nominated and confirmed for the Supreme Court.

Ryan Kelly/Getty Images

Associate Justice Sonia Sotomayor arrives in the House of Representatives for the President's State of the Union Address in 2010.

Senatorial Courtesy
In federal district court judgeship nominations, a tradition allowing a senator to veto a judicial appointment in his or her state.

associations and other interest groups. In selecting a candidate to nominate for a judgeship, the president considers not only the person's competence but also other factors, including the person's political philosophy (as will be discussed shortly), ethnicity, and gender.

The nomination process—no matter how the nominees are obtained—always works the same way. The president makes the actual nomination, transmitting the name to the Senate. The Senate then either confirms or rejects the nomination. To reach a conclusion, the Senate Judiciary Committee (operating through subcommittees) invites testimony, both written and oral, at its various hearings. A practice used in the Senate, called **senatorial courtesy**, is a constraint on the president's freedom to appoint federal district judges. Senatorial courtesy allows a senator of the president's political party to veto a judicial appointment in her or his state by way of a "blue slip." Traditionally, the senators from the nominee's state are sent a blue form on which to make comments. They may return the "blue slip" with comments or not return it at all. Not returning the blue slip is a veto of the nomination.[11] During much of American history, senators from the "opposition" party (the party to which the president did not belong) also have enjoyed the right of senatorial courtesy, although their veto power has varied over time.

Federal District Court Judgeship Nominations. Although the president officially nominates federal judges, in the past the nomination of federal district court judges actually originated with a senator or senators of the president's party from the state in which there was a vacancy. In effect, judicial appointments were a form of political patronage. President Jimmy Carter (served 1977–1981) ended this tradition by establishing independent commissions to oversee the initial nomination process. President Ronald Reagan (served 1981–1989) abolished Carter's nominating commissions and established complete presidential control of nominations.

Federal Courts of Appeals Appointments. Appointments to the federal courts of appeals are far less numerous than federal district court appointments, but they are more important. This is because federal appellate judges handle more important matters, at least from the point of view of the president, and therefore presidents take a keener interest in the nomination process for such judgeships. Also, the U.S. courts of appeals have become stepping-stones to the Supreme Court.

Supreme Court Appointments. As we have described, the president nominates Supreme Court justices.[12] As you can see in Table 14–1, which summarizes the background of all Supreme Court justices to 2012 the most common

11.   Mitchell A. Sollenberger, "The Blue Slip Process in the Senate Committee on the Judiciary: Background, Issues, and Options," Congressional Research Service, November 21, 2003.

12.   For a discussion of the factors that may come into play during the process of nominating Supreme Court justices, see David A. Yalof, *Pursuit of Justices: Presidential Politics and the Selection of Supreme Court Nominees* (Chicago: University of Chicago Press, 1999).

occupational background of the justices at the time of their appointment has been private legal practice or state or federal judgeship. Those nine justices who were in federal executive posts at the time of their appointment held the high offices of secretary of state, comptroller of the treasury, secretary of the navy, postmaster general, secretary of the interior, chairman of the Securities and Exchange Commission, and secretary of labor. In the "Other" category under "Occupational Position before Appointment" in Table 14–1 are two justices who were professors of law (including William H. Taft, a former president) and one justice who was a North Carolina state employee with responsibility for organizing and revising the state's statutes.

The Special Role of the Chief Justice.

Although ideology is always important in judicial appointments, as described next, when a chief justice is selected for the Supreme Court, other considerations must also be taken into account. The chief justice is not only the head of a group of nine justices who interpret the law. He or she is also in essence the chief executive officer (CEO) of a large bureaucracy that includes all of the following: 1,200 judges with lifetime tenure, more than 850 magistrates and bankruptcy judges, and more than 30,000 staff members.

The chief justice is also the chair of the Judicial Conference of the United States, a policymaking body that sets priorities for the federal judiciary. That means that the chief justice also indirectly oversees the $5.5 billion budget of this group.

Finally, the chief justice appoints the director of the Administrative Office of the United States Courts. The chief justice and this director select judges who sit on judicial committees that examine international judicial relations, technology, and a variety of other topics.

Partisanship and Judicial Appointments

Ideology plays an important role in the president's choices for judicial appointments. In most circumstances, the president appoints judges or justices who belong to the president's own political party. Presidents see their federal judiciary appointments as the one sure way to institutionalize their political views long after they have left office. By 1993, for example, presidents Ronald Reagan and George H. W. Bush together had appointed nearly three-quarters of all federal court judges. This preponderance

Table 14–1 ▶ Background of U.S. Supreme Court Justices to 2012; Number of Justices = 112 Total)

OCCUPATIONAL POSITION BEFORE APPOINTMENT	
Private legal practice	25
State judgeship	21
Federal judgeship	31
U.S. attorney general	7
Deputy or assistant U.S. attorney general	2
U.S. solicitor general	3
U.S. senator	6
U.S. representative	2
State governor	3
Federal executive post	9
Other	3
RELIGIOUS BACKGROUND	
Protestant	83
Roman Catholic	14
Jewish	7
Unitarian	7
No religious affiliation	1
AGE ON APPOINTMENT	
Under 40	5
41–50	34
51–60	59
61–70	14
POLITICAL PARTY AFFILIATION	
Federalist (to 1835)	13
Jeffersonian Republican (to 1828)	7
Whig (to 1861)	1
Democrat	46
Republican	44
Independent	1
EDUCATIONAL BACKGROUND	
College graduate	96
Not a college graduate	16
GENDER	
Male	108
Female	4
RACE	
White	109
African American	2
Hispanic American	1

Source: Congressional Quarterly, *Congressional Quarterly's Guide to the U.S. Supreme Court* (Washington, DC: Congressional Quarterly Press, 1996); and authors' updates.

On August 7, 2010, Elena Kagan is sworn in as the 112th U.S. Supreme Court justice and the Court's fourth woman ever.

of Republican-appointed federal judges strengthened the legal moorings of the conservative social agenda on a variety of issues, ranging from abortion to civil rights. Nevertheless, President Bill Clinton had the opportunity to appoint about 200 federal judges, thereby shifting the ideological makeup of the federal judiciary.

During the first two years of his second term, President George W. Bush was able to nominate two relatively conservative justices to the Supreme Court—John Roberts, who became chief justice, and Samuel Alito. Both are Catholics and have relatively, but not consistently, conservative views. In fact, during his first term as chief justice, Roberts voted most of the time with the Court's most conservative justices, Antonin Scalia and Clarence Thomas. Nonetheless, Roberts and Alito did not cause the Supreme Court to "tilt to the right" as much as some people anticipated. The reason is that the two Bush appointees replaced justices who were moderate to conservative. Interestingly, some previous conservative justices have shown a tendency to migrate to a more liberal view of the law. Sandra Day O'Connor, the first female justice and a conservative, gradually shifted to the left on several issues, including abortion. In 1981, during her confirmation hearing before the Senate Judiciary Committee, she said, "I am opposed to it [abortion], as a matter of birth control or otherwise." By 1992, she was part of a 5-4 majority that agreed that the Constitution protects a woman's right to an abortion.

Similarly, Justice John Paul Stevens, who was appointed by Gerald Ford, was expected to be a moderate or conservative in his views but, over time, became a member of the liberal bloc on the Court. Stevens, who retired in 2010, was renowned for his ability to find a compromise between the justices and to build a voting majority. President Obama nominated Solicitor General Elena Kagan, former dean of the law school at Harvard University, to fill Stevens's seat. His first nominee to the Court, Associate Justice Sonia Sotomayor, who replaced Justice David Souter, became the first Hispanic American to serve on the Court. Both of President Obama's appointments were to seats formerly held by more liberal justices, so the balance of ideology on the Supreme Court remained the same as it had been during the George W. Bush administration.

The Senate's Role

Ideology also plays a large role in the Senate's confirmation hearings, and presidential nominees to the Supreme Court have not always been confirmed. In fact, almost 20 percent of presidential nominations to the Supreme Court have been either rejected or not acted on by the Senate. Many acrimonious battles over Supreme Court appointments have occurred when the Senate and the president have not seen eye to eye about political matters.

The U.S. Senate had a long record of refusing to confirm the president's judicial nominations extending from the beginning of Andrew Jackson's presidency in 1829 to the end of Ulysses Grant's presidency in 1877. From 1894 until 1968, however, only three nominees were not confirmed. Then, from 1968 through

1987, four presidential nominees to the highest court were rejected. One of the most controversial Supreme Court nominations was that of Clarence Thomas, who underwent an extremely volatile confirmation hearing in 1991, replete with charges against him of sexual harassment. He was ultimately confirmed by the Senate, however, and has been a stalwart voice for conservatism ever since.

President Bill Clinton had little trouble gaining approval for both of his nominees to the Supreme Court: Ruth Bader Ginsburg and Stephen Breyer. President George W. Bush's nominees faced hostile grilling in their confirmation hearings, and various interest groups mounted intense media advertising blitzes against them. Bush had to forgo one of his nominees, Harriet Miers, when he realized that she could not be confirmed by the Senate. President Obama's two nominations, Sonia Sotomayor and Elena Kagan, while seen as too liberal by some senators, were eminently qualified for the Court and were approved by the Senate with little incident.

Both Clinton and Bush had trouble securing Senate approval for their judicial nominations to the lower courts. In fact, during the late 1990s and early 2000s, the duel between the Senate and the president aroused considerable concern about the consequences of the increasingly partisan and ideological tension over federal judicial appointments. On several occasions, presidents have appointed federal judges using a temporary "recess appointment." This procedure is always used for the same reason—to avoid the continuation of an acrimonious and perhaps futile Senate confirmation process.

Although the confirmation hearings on Supreme Court nominees get all of the media attention, the hearings on nominees for the lower federal courts are equally bitter, leading some to ask whether the politicization of the confirmation process has gone too far. According to Fifth Circuit Court Judge Edith Jones, judicial nominations have turned into battlegrounds because so many federal judges now view the courts as agents of social change. Jones argues that when judge-made law (as opposed to legislature-made law) enters into sensitive topics, it provokes a political reaction. Thus, the ideology and political views of the potential justices should be a matter of public concern and political debate.[13]

Politics has played a role in selecting judges since the administration of George Washington. The classic case cited earlier, *Marbury v. Madison*, was rooted in partisan politics. Nonetheless, most nominees are confirmed without dispute. As of 2006, the vacancy rate on the federal bench was at its lowest point in 14 years. Those nominees who run into trouble are usually the most conservative Republican nominees or the most liberal Democratic ones. It is legitimate to evaluate a candidate's judicial ideology when that ideology is strongly held and likely to influence the judge's rulings.

Policymaking and the Courts

The partisan battles over judicial appointments reflect an important reality in today's American government: the importance of the judiciary in national politics. Because appointments to the federal bench are for life, the ideology of judicial appointees can affect national policy for years to come. Although the primary function of judges in our system of government is to interpret and apply the laws, inevitably judges make policy when carrying out this task. One of the major policymaking tools of the federal courts is their power of judicial review.

---

13. Cited by John Leo, "A Judge with No Agenda," *Jewish World Review*, July 5, 2005.

Do you ever have one of those days when everything seems un-Constitutional?"

Judicial Review

If a federal court declares that a federal or state law or policy is unconstitutional, the court's decision affects the application of the law or policy only within that court's jurisdiction. For this reason, the higher the level of the court, the greater the impact of the decision on society. Because of the Supreme Court's national jurisdiction, its decisions have the greatest impact. For example, when the Supreme Court held that an Arkansas state constitutional amendment limiting the terms of congresspersons was unconstitutional, laws establishing term limits in 23 other states were also invalidated.[14]

Some claim that the power of judicial review gives unelected judges and justices on federal court benches too much influence over national policy. Others argue that the powers exercised by the federal courts, particularly the power of judicial review, are necessary to protect our constitutional rights and liberties. Built into our federal form of government is a system of checks and balances. If the federal courts did not have the power of judicial review, no governmental body could check Congress's lawmaking authority.

Judicial Activism and Judicial Restraint

Judicial scholars like to characterize different judges and justices as being either "activist" or "restraintist." The doctrine of **judicial activism** rests on the conviction that the federal judiciary should take an active role by using its powers to check the activities of Congress, state legislatures, and administrative agencies when those governmental bodies exceed their authority. One of the Supreme Court's most activist eras was the period from 1953 to 1969, when the Court was headed by Chief Justice Earl Warren. The Warren Court propelled the civil rights movement forward by holding, among other things, that laws permitting racial segregation violated the equal protection clause.

In contrast, the doctrine of **judicial restraint** rests on the assumption that the courts should defer to the decisions made by the legislative and executive branches, because members of Congress and the president are elected by the people, whereas members of the federal judiciary are not. Because administrative agency personnel normally have more expertise than the courts do in the areas regulated by the agencies, the courts likewise should defer to agency rules and decisions. In other words, under the doctrine of judicial restraint, the courts should not thwart the implementation of legislative acts and agency rules unless they are clearly unconstitutional.

Judicial activism sometimes is linked with liberalism, and judicial restraint with conservatism. In fact, though, a conservative judge can be activist, just as a liberal judge can be restraintist. In the 1950s and 1960s, the Supreme Court was activist and liberal. Some observers believe that the Rehnquist Court, with its conservative majority, became increasingly activist during the early 2000s. Some go even

■ **Learning Outcome 5:**
Compare the concepts of judicial activism and judicial restraint, and link these concepts to the decisions of the Supreme Court in the last few decades.

Judicial Activism
A doctrine holding that the Supreme Court should take an active role by using its powers to check the activities of governmental bodies when those bodies exceed their authority.

Judicial Restraint
A doctrine holding that the Supreme Court should defer to the decisions made by the elected representatives of the people in the legislative and executive branches.

---

14. *U.S. Term Limits v. Thornton*, 514 U.S. 779 (1995).

further and claim that the federal courts, including the Supreme Court, wield too much power in our democracy.

Strict versus Broad Construction

Other terms that are often used to describe a justice's philosophy are *strict construction* and *broad construction*. Justices who believe in **strict construction** look to the "letter of the law" when they attempt to interpret the Constitution or a particular statute. Those who favor **broad construction** try to determine the context and purpose of the law.

As with the doctrines of judicial restraint and judicial activism, strict construction is often associated with conservative political views, whereas broad construction is often linked with liberalism. These traditional political associations sometimes appear to be reversed, however. Consider the Eleventh Amendment to the Constitution, which rules out lawsuits in federal courts "against one of the United States by Citizens of another State, or by Citizens or Subjects of any Foreign State." Nothing is said about citizens suing their *own* states, and strict construction would therefore find such suits to be constitutional. Conservative justices, however, have construed this amendment broadly to deny citizens the constitutional right to sue their own states in most circumstances. John T. Noonan, Jr., a federal appellate court judge who was appointed by a Republican president, has described these rulings as "adventurous."[15]

Broad construction is often associated with the concept of a "living constitution." Supreme Court Justice Antonin Scalia has said that "the Constitution is not a living organism, it is a legal document. It says something and doesn't say other things." Scalia believes that jurists should stick to the plain text of the Constitution "as it was originally written and intended."[16]

Ideology and the Rehnquist Court

William H. Rehnquist became the 16th chief justice of the Supreme Court in 1986, after 14 years as an associate justice. He was known as a strong anchor of the Court's conservative wing until his death in 2005. With Rehnquist's appointment as chief justice, it seemed to observers that the Court would necessarily become more conservative.

Indeed, that is what happened. The Court began to take a rightward shift shortly after Rehnquist became chief justice, and the Court's rightward movement continued as other conservative appointments to the bench were made during the Reagan and George H. W. Bush administrations. During the late 1990s and early 2000s, three of the justices (William Rehnquist, Antonin Scalia, and Clarence Thomas) were notably conservative in their views. Four of the justices (John Paul Stevens, David Souter, Ruth Bader Ginsburg, and Stephen Breyer) held moderate-to-liberal views. The middle of the Court was occupied by two moderate-to-conservative justices, Sandra Day O'Connor and Anthony Kennedy. O'Connor and Kennedy usually provided the swing votes on the Court in controversial cases.

Although the Court seemed to become more conservative under Rehnquist's leadership, its decisions were not always predictable. Many cases were decided by very close votes, and results seemed to vary depending on the issue. For example, the Court ruled in 1995 that Congress had overreached its powers under the commerce clause when it attempted to regulate the possession of guns in

Strict Construction
A judicial philosophy that looks to the "letter of the law" when interpreting the Constitution or a particular statute.

Broad Construction
A judicial philosophy that looks to the context and purpose of a law when making an interpretation.

---

15. John T. Noonan, Jr., *Narrowing the Nation's Power: The Supreme Court Sides with the States* (Berkeley, CA: University of California Press, 2002).
16. Speech given at the Woodrow Wilson Center, Washington, D.C., March 14, 2005.

schoolyards. According to the Court, the possession of guns in school zones had nothing to do with the commerce clause.[17] Yet in 2005, the Court upheld Congress's power under the commerce clause to ban marijuana use even when a state's law permitted such use.[18] In other areas such as civil rights, the Court generally issued conservative opinions.

The Roberts Court

In 2006, a new chief justice was appointed to the court. John Roberts had a distinguished career as an attorney in Washington, D.C. He had served as a clerk to the Supreme Court while in law school and was well liked by the justices. The confirmation process had been quite smooth, and many hoped that he would be a moderate leader of the Court.

During John Roberts's first term (2005–2006) as chief justice, the Court ruled on several important issues, but no clear pattern was discernible in the decisions. In the years following his appointment, Roberts was more likely to vote with the conservative justices—Scalia, Thomas, and Alito—than with the moderate-to-liberal bloc. Thus, several important decisions were handed down with close votes. In an important case for environmentalist groups, the Court held that the Environmental Protection Agency (EPA) did have the power under the Clean Air Act to regulate greenhouse gases. The vote was 5-4, with the chief justice on the minority side.[19] Similarly, when the Court upheld the 2003 federal law banning partial-birth abortions, Roberts was on the conservative side in a 5-4 vote.[20]

Later in 2007, the Supreme Court issued a very important opinion on school integration. By another 5-4 vote, the Court ruled that school district policies that included race as a determining factor in admission to certain schools were unconstitutional on the ground that they violated the equal protection clause of the Constitution.[21] After Justices Sonia Sotomayor and Elena Kagan joined the court early in the Obama adminstration, court-watchers believed that the Roberts Court would make conservative decisions but that the majority often would be razor-thin. Indeed, in 2012, the Court announced two decisions that supported this appraisal: The Court overturned four provisions of Arizona's controversial law regarding illegal immigrants but upheld the central provision allowing police officers to check the immigration status of those individuals who had been arrested or stopped on other charges. A few days later, the Supreme Court upheld the individual mandate to buy health insurance under the Affordable Health Care Act (Obama's health care legislation) by a 5-4 margin, with the chief

Attorneys General Pam Bondi of Florida and Luther Strange of Alabama, both Republicans, depart the Supreme Court building after the third day of oral arguments on the constitutionality of the Affordable Health Care Act.

RON SACHS/DPA/Landov

17. *United States v. Lopez,* 514 U.S. 549 (1995)
18. *Gonzales v. Raich,* 545 U.S. 1 (2005).
19. *Massachusetts v. EPA,* 127 St. Ct. 1438 (2007).
20. *Gonzales v. Carhart,* 127 St. Ct. 1610 (2007).
21. *Parents Involved in Community Schools v. Seattle School District,* N. 1, 127 St. Ct. 2162 (2007).

justice supporting the law as legal under the commerce clause of the Constitution.

What Checks Our Courts?

Our judicial system is one of the most independent in the world, but the courts do not have absolute independence, for they are part of the political process. Political checks limit the extent to which courts can exercise judicial review and engage in an activist policy. These checks are exercised by the executive branch, the legislature, the public, and, finally, the judiciary.

Executive Checks

President Andrew Jackson was once supposed to have said, after Chief Justice John Marshall made an unpopular decision, "John Marshall has made his decision; now let him enforce it."[22] This purported remark goes to the heart of **judicial implementation**—the enforcement of judicial decisions in such a way that those decisions are translated into policy. The Supreme Court simply does not have any enforcement powers, and whether a decision will be implemented depends on the cooperation of the other two branches of government. Rarely, though, will a president refuse to enforce a Supreme Court decision, as President Jackson did. To take such an action could mean a significant loss of public support because of the Supreme Court's stature in the eyes of the nation.

More commonly, presidents exercise influence over the judiciary by appointing new judges and justices as federal judicial seats become vacant. Additionally, as mentioned earlier, the U.S. solicitor general plays a significant role in the federal court system, and the person holding this office is a presidential appointee.

Executives at the state level may also refuse to implement court decisions with which they disagree. A notable example of such a refusal occurred in Arkansas after the Supreme Court ordered schools to desegregate "with all deliberate speed" in 1955.[23] Arkansas Governor Orval Faubus refused to cooperate with the decision and used the state's National Guard to block the integration of Central High School in Little Rock. Ultimately, President Dwight Eisenhower had to federalize the Arkansas National Guard and send federal troops to Little Rock to quell the violence that had erupted.

Legislative Checks

Courts may make rulings, but often the legislatures at local, state, and federal levels are required to appropriate funds to carry out the courts' rulings. A court, for example, may decide that prison conditions must be improved, but the

Time & Life Pictures/Getty Images

Federal troops
were sent by President Eisenhower to guard Little Rock High School and to ensure the safety of the African American students who were going to attend that school.

Judicial Implementation
The way in which court decisions are translated into action.

---

22. The decision referred to was *Cherokee Nation v. Georgia,* 30 U.S. 1 (1831).
23. *Brown v. Board of Education,* 349 U.S. 294 (1955)—the second *Brown* decision.

legislature authorizes the funds necessary to carry out the ruling. When such funds are not appropriated, the court that made the ruling, in effect, has been checked.

Constitutional Amendments. Courts' rulings can be overturned by constitutional amendments at both the federal and state levels. Many of the amendments to the U.S. Constitution (such as the Fourteenth, Fifteenth, and Twenty-sixth Amendments) check the state courts' ability to allow discrimination, for example. Proposed constitutional amendments that were created in an effort to reverse courts' decisions on school prayer and abortion have failed.

Rewriting Laws. Finally, Congress or a state legislature can rewrite (amend) old laws or enact new ones to overturn a court's rulings if the legislature concludes that the court is interpreting laws or legislative intentions erroneously. For example, Congress passed the Civil Rights Act of 1991 in part to overturn a series of conservative rulings in employment-discrimination cases. In 1993, Congress enacted the Religious Freedom Restoration Act (RFRA), which broadened religious liberties, after Congress concluded that a 1990 Supreme Court ruling restricted religious freedom to an unacceptable extent.[24]

According to political scientist Walter Murphy, "A permanent feature of our constitutional landscape is the ongoing tug and pull between elected government and the courts."[25] Certainly, over the last few decades, the Supreme Court has been in conflict with the other two branches of government. Congress at various times has passed laws that, among other things, made it illegal to burn the American flag and attempted to curb pornography on the Internet. In each instance, the Supreme Court ruled that those laws were unconstitutional. The Court also invalidated the RFRA.

Whenever Congress does not like what the judiciary does, it threatens to censure the judiciary for its activism. One member of the Senate Judiciary Committee, John Cornyn (R.-Tex.), claimed that judges are making "political decisions yet are unaccountable to the public." He went on to say that violence against judges in the courtroom can be explained by the public's distress at such activism.

The states can also negate or alter the effects of Supreme Court rulings, when such decisions allow it. A good case in point is *Kelo v. City of New London*.[26] In that case, the Supreme Court allowed a city to take private property for redevelopment by private businesses. Since that case was decided, a majority of states have passed legislation limiting or prohibiting such takings.

Public Opinion

Public opinion plays a significant role in shaping government policy, and certainly the judiciary is not exempt from this rule. For one thing, persons affected by a Supreme Court decision that is noticeably at odds with their views may simply ignore it. Officially sponsored prayers were banned in public schools in 1962, yet it was widely known that the ban was (and still is) ignored in many southern districts. What can the courts do in this situation? Unless someone complains about the prayers and initiates a lawsuit, the courts can do nothing. The public can also pressure state and local government officials to refuse to enforce a certain decision. As already mentioned, judicial implementation requires the cooperation of

24.   *Employment Division, Department of Human Resources of Oregon v. Smith,* 494 U.S. 872 (1990).
25.   As quoted in Neal Devins, "The Last Word Debate: How Social and Political Forces Shape Constitutional Values," *American Bar Association Journal,* October 1997, p. 48.
26.   545 U.S. 469 (2005).

government officials at all levels, and public opinion in various regions of the country will influence whether such cooperation is forthcoming.

Additionally, the courts necessarily are influenced by public opinion to some extent. After all, judges are not isolated in our society; their attitudes are influenced by social trends, just as the attitudes and beliefs of all persons are. Courts generally tend to avoid issuing decisions that they know will be noticeably at odds with public opinion.[27] In part, this is because the judiciary, as a branch of the government, prefers to avoid creating divisiveness among the public. Also, a court—particularly the Supreme Court—may lose stature if it decides a case in a way that markedly diverges from public opinion. For example, in 2002, the Supreme Court ruled that the execution of mentally retarded criminals violates the Eighth Amendment's ban on cruel and unusual punishment. In its ruling, the Court indicated that the standards of what constitutes cruel and unusual punishment are influenced by public opinion and that there is "powerful evidence that today our society views mentally retarded offenders as categorically less culpable than the average criminal."[28]

Judicial Traditions and Doctrines

Supreme Court justices (and other federal judges) typically exercise self-restraint in fashioning their decisions. In part, this restraint stems from their knowledge that the other two branches of government and the public can exercise checks on the judiciary, as previously discussed. To a large extent, however, this restraint is mandated by various judicially established traditions and doctrines. When reviewing a case, the Supreme Court typically narrows its focus to just one issue or one aspect of an issue involved in the case. The Court rarely makes broad, sweeping decisions on issues. Furthermore, the doctrine of *stare decisis* acts as a restraint because it obligates the courts, including the Supreme Court, to follow established precedents when deciding cases. Only rarely will courts overrule a precedent.

Hypothetical and Political Questions.

Other judicial doctrines and practices also act as restraints. As already mentioned, the courts will hear only what are called justiciable disputes, which arise out of actual cases. In other words, a court will not hear a case that involves a merely hypothetical issue. Additionally, if a political question is involved, the Supreme Court often will exercise judicial restraint and refuse to rule on the matter. A **political question** is one that the Supreme Court declares should be decided by the elected branches of government—the executive branch, the legislative branch, or those two branches acting together. For example, the Supreme Court has refused to rule on the controversy regarding the rights of gays and lesbians in the military, preferring instead to defer to the executive branch's decisions on the matter. Generally, fewer questions are deemed political questions by the Supreme Court today than in the past.

Political Question
An issue that a court believes should be decided by the executive or legislative branch.

The Impact of the Lower Courts.

Higher courts can reverse the decisions of lower courts. Lower courts can act as a check on higher courts, too. Lower courts can ignore—and have ignored—Supreme Court decisions. Usually, this is done indirectly. A lower court might conclude, for example, that the precedent set by the Supreme Court does not apply to the exact circumstances in the case before the court; or the lower court may decide that the Supreme Court's decision was ambiguous with respect to the issue before the lower court. The fact that the Supreme Court rarely makes broad and clear-cut statements on any issue makes it easier for the lower courts to interpret the Supreme Court's decisions in a different way.

---

27.   One striking counterexample is the *Kelo v. City of New London* decision mentioned earlier.
28.   *Atkins v. Virginia,* 536 U.S. 304 (2002).

You Can Make a Difference

VOLUNTEER IN THE COURTS

© iStockphoto.com/brocreative

This young man may have been observing a court proceeding or volunteering in the court system. Explore such opportunities where you live or attend school.

Almost everyone has a legal problem at some point in his or her life. As a student, you may be dealing with a traffic ticket, an accident citation, a drunk driving arrest, or a domestic dispute. Or you might have difficulty getting back a security deposit or forcing your landlord to fix your apartment. Every citizen has a right to be treated fairly when such issues bring him or her into the court system, whether it is a municipal court, a state court, or the federal district court. However, all court systems in the United States are overburdened with too many cases and too few employees to provide needed services. How can you make a difference in improving the court system and, perhaps, helping fellow students?

First, everyone should experience the courts at work. All local courts are open to the public to watch arraignments and first pleas. Check the Web site of your local court system and find out the place and time of municipal or other local court proceedings. Spend time as a visitor to the court to observe how individuals who are being charged with a crime are treated. Is it obvious that their rights are being respected? Do attorneys represent them in felony cases? Try to understand the wide variety of cases that come before a court.

HELP YOUR FELLOW STUDENTS

Most large universities have some type of office to help students who need legal services. Check your college's Web site for "Student Legal Services." These offices are often staffed with attorneys who will consult with registered students if they are going to face charges either on campus or in the local community. Most of the student legal services offices also provide opportunities for student workers, either in paid positions or as volunteers, to assist students who need legal advice and counseling. This is an opportunity to become much more familiar with your rights as a student and the way to approach the legal system.

HELP IN YOUR COMMUNITY

Some American cities and states have volunteer opportunities and internships in the local court system for undergraduate students as well as for law students. In New York State, numerous volunteer opportunities can be found in the court system helping victims and providing assistance in divorce and immigration court or other legal systems. San Diego, California, seeks student volunteers in its court system for such positions as helping at the information desk, providing services to jurors, working in the business office, providing tours, and assisting in the children's waiting rooms. In Los Angeles, California, where more than 300,000 litigants annually do not have lawyers, the courts seek college students from the southern California universities to become "volunteer lawyers," helping individuals in completing forms, applying to the right court, and dealing with court processes. Each student volunteer receives about 60 hours of training before he or she can become part of "the Justice Corps" of the Los Angeles courts.

Working in the court system will help you learn your own rights and, if you are interested in becoming an attorney, give you real experience in the field.

For information on campus-based student legal services, go to your university's Web site and search for "Legal Services" or "Student Legal Services."

For volunteer opportunities, check the Web site of your local court system.

Key Terms

Chapter Summary

1. American law is rooted in the common-law tradition, which is part of our heritage from England. Fundamental sources of American law include the U.S. Constitution and state constitutions, statutes enacted by legislative bodies, regulations issued by administrative agencies, and case law. The common-law doctrine of *stare decisis* (which means "to stand on decided cases") obligates judges to follow precedents established previously by their own courts or by higher courts that have authority over them. Precedents established by the United States Supreme Court, the highest court in the land, are binding on all lower courts. The justices of the Supreme Court as well as those in all federal courts are appointed for life terms, making them invulnerable to political pressure or the need for reelection. Thus, appointed judges are, in fact, able to make decisions that have a lasting impact on American society.

2. Article III, Section 1, of the U.S. Constitution limits the jurisdiction of the federal courts to cases involving (1) a federal question, which is a question based, at least in part, on the U.S. Constitution, a treaty, or a federal law; or (2) diversity of citizenship, which arises when parties to a lawsuit are from different states or when the lawsuit involves a foreign citizen or government. The federal court system is a three-tiered model consisting of (1) U.S. district (trial) courts and various lower courts of limited jurisdiction; (2) U.S. courts of appeals; and (3) the United States Supreme Court. Cases may be appealed from the district courts to the appellate courts. In most cases, the decisions of the federal appellate courts are final because the Supreme Court hears relatively few cases.

3. The Supreme Court's decision to review a case is influenced by many factors, including the significance of the issues involved and whether the solicitor general is pressing the Court to take the case. After a case is accepted, the justices undertake research (with the help of their law clerks) on the issues involved in the case, hear oral arguments from the parties, meet in conference to discuss and vote on the issue, and announce the opinion, which is then released for publication.

4. Federal judges are nominated by the president and confirmed by the Senate. Once appointed, they hold office for life, barring gross misconduct. The nomination and confirmation process, particularly for Supreme Court justices, is often extremely politicized. Democrats and Republicans alike realize that justices may occupy seats on the Court for decades and naturally want to have persons appointed who share their basic views. Nearly 20 percent of all Supreme Court appointments have been either rejected or not acted on by the Senate.

5. In interpreting and applying the law, judges inevitably become policymakers. The most important policymaking tool of the federal courts is the power of judicial review. This power was not mentioned specifically in the Constitution, but John Marshall claimed the power for the Court in his 1803 decision in *Marbury v. Madison*.

6. Judges who take an active role in checking the activities of the other branches of government sometimes are characterized as "activist" judges, and judges who defer to the other branches' decisions sometimes are regarded as "restraint-ist" judges. The Warren Court of the 1950s and 1960s was activist in a liberal direction, whereas the Rehnquist Court became increasingly activist in a conservative direction. Several politicians and scholars argue that judicial activism has gotten out of hand. One of the criticisms of the Court is that it should not "make law" but should defer to the legislative branch in deciding policy issues. However, in the

interpretation of previously written laws, it has often fallen to the Supreme Court to make a final determination. The Court has also taken on policy issues such as school segregation that no political branch would address.

7. Checks on the powers of the federal courts include executive checks, legislative checks, public opinion, and judicial traditions and doctrines.

Selected Print, Media, and Online Resources

PRINT RESOURCES

Foskett, Ken. *Judging Thomas: The Life and Times of Clarence Thomas.* New York: William Morrow, 2004. Foskett, an Atlanta journalist, delves into the intellectual development of Justice Thomas, one of the nation's most prominent African American conservatives.

Greenburg, Jan Crawford. *Supreme Conflict: The Inside Story of the Struggle for the Control of the United States Supreme Court.* New York: Penguin Books, 2008. A newspaper and PBS reporter, Greenburg developed close relationships with justices and staff at the Supreme Court. She tells the inside story of which justices were really powerful and which were the followers.

Klarman, Michael J. *From Jim Crow to Civil Rights: The Supreme Court and the Struggle for Racial Equality.* New York: Oxford University Press, 2004. Klarman, a professor of constitutional law, provides a detailed history of the Supreme Court's changing attitudes toward equality. Klarman argues that the civil rights movement would have revolutionized the status of African Americans even if the Court had not outlawed segregation.

O'Connor, Sandra Day. *The Majesty of the Law: Reflections of a Supreme Court Justice.* New York: Random House, 2003. As the Supreme Court's most prominent swing vote during her years on the bench, Justice O'Connor may have been the most powerful member of that body. O'Connor gives a basic introduction to the Court, reflects on past discrimination against women in the law, tells amusing stories about fellow justices, and calls for improving the treatment of jury members.

Peppers, Todd C., and Artemus Ward, editors. *In Chambers: Stories of Supreme Court Law Clerks and Their Justices.* Charlottesville, VA: University of Virginia Press, 2011. Young attorneys who have completed their positions as "clerks" to the Supreme Court justices write about their experiences and about the everyday life of the court behind the scenes.

Roosevelt, Kermit. *The Myth of Judicial Activism: Making Sense of Supreme Court Decisions.* New Haven, CT: Yale University Press, 2008. Roosevelt, a University of Pennsylvania professor, defends the Court against charges of undue judicial activism. Roosevelt finds the Court's decisions to be reasonable, although he disagrees with some of them.

Teles, Stephen. *The Rise of the Conservative Legal Movement: The Battle for Control of the Law.* Princeton, NJ: Princeton University Press, 2012. Teles provides an account of how conservative foundations and institutions fostered ways to support the education and later networking of the conservative legal scholars who have challenged liberal policies before the court.

Zimmerman, Joseph F. *Interstate Disputes: The Supreme Court's Original Jurisdiction.* Buffalo, NY: State University of New York, 2006. This well-researched study examines the role of the Court in settling disputes between the states. The author concludes that states should enter into more interstate compacts rather than taking their disputes to the Supreme Court.

MEDIA RESOURCES

Amistad—A 1997 movie, starring Anthony Hopkins, about a slave ship mutiny in 1839. Much of the story revolves around the prosecution, ending at the Supreme Court, of the slave who led the revolt.

Gideon's Trumpet—A 1980 film, starring Henry Fonda as the small-time criminal James Earl Gideon, which makes clear the path a case takes to the Supreme Court and the importance of cases decided there.

Justice Sandra Day O'Connor—In a 1994 program, Bill Moyers conducts Justice O'Connor's first television interview. Topics include women's rights, O'Connor's role as the Supreme Court's first female justice, and her difficulties breaking into the male-dominated legal profession. O'Connor defends her positions on affirmative action and abortion.

The Magnificent Yankee—A 1950 movie, starring Louis Calhern and Ann Harding, that traces the life and philosophy of Oliver Wendell Holmes, Jr., one of the Supreme Court's most brilliant justices.

Marbury v. Madison—A 1987 video on the famous 1803 case that established the principle of judicial review. This is the first in a four-part series, *Equal Justice Under Law: Landmark Cases in Supreme Court History,* produced by the Judicial Conference of the United States.

The Supreme Court—A four-part PBS series that won a 2008 Parents' Choice Gold Award. The series follows the history of the Supreme Court from the first chief justice, John Marshall, to the earliest days of the Roberts Court. Some of the many topics are the Court's dismal performance in the Civil War era, its conflicts with President Franklin D. Roosevelt, its role in banning the segregation of African Americans, and the abortion controversy.

truTV—This TV channel covers high-profile trials, including those of O. J. Simpson, the Unabomber, British nanny Louise Woodward, and Timothy McVeigh. (You can learn below how to access truTV from your area via its Web site.)

ONLINE RESOURCES

FindLaw searchable database of Supreme Court decisions since 1970: www.findlaw.com

Legal Information Institute at Cornell University Law School offers an easily searchable index to Supreme Court opinions, including some important historic decisions: www.law.cornell.edu/supct/index.html

The Oyez Project a multimedia archive devoted to the Supreme Court of the United States and its work: www.oyez.org/oyez/frontpage

Supreme Court of the United States Supreme Court decisions are available here within hours of their release: supremecourtus.gov

truTV.com Web site dedicated to the television station (formerly Court TV) that focuses on real-life stories told from a first-person perspective. The site offers the program lineup, which features six hours of daily trial coverage; a Crime Library, which includes case histories as well as selected documents filed with the court and court transcripts; and a link to CNN Crime for trial news: www.trutv.com

United States Courts The home page of the federal courts is a good starting point for learning about the federal court system in general. At this site, you can even follow the path of a case as it moves through the federal court system: www.uscourts.gov

15 Domestic Policy

© Jim West/Alamy

Oberlin College students picket an injection well as a tank truck unloads the waste generated by hydraulic fracking to produce natural gas.

LEARNING OUTCOMES

After reading this chapter, students will be able to:

■ **LO1** Describe the policymaking process as it applies to American national government.

■ **LO2** Explain the principles underlying the American health care system and the issues facing that system.

■ **LO3** Describe the environmental policies of the United States and the role of the Environmental Protection Agency in implementing these policies.

■ **LO4** Analyze American energy policy, and discuss how it encourages energy independence.

■ **LO5** Describe the national policies for ending

What If...

WE HAD UNIVERSAL HEALTH CARE?

BACKGROUND

In the United States, we have a private health care system with about 40 percent of Americans using government programs to pay for their health insurance. That includes the senior citizens under Medicare, military veterans, permanently disabled Americans, children insured under the state-federal partnership program, and the poorest Americans who are covered under Medicaid, another joint state-federal program. The Patient Protection and Affordable Care Act, hereafter referred to as the Affordable Care Act, is a step toward universal health care, but it maintains the private health care system. While it requires that all Americans have health insurance, either purchased privately or through the federal or state government, it does not take control of private physicians, the prescription drug industry, or hospitals. Even after all provisions of the ACA come into plan, the United States will remain the only major industrialized democratic nation without a health care system that guarantees equal access to basic health care for all citizens.

WHAT IF WE HAD UNIVERSAL HEALTH CARE?

With universal health care, everyone in need of basic medical care would have access to physicians, clinics, and hospital services. Every legal resident of the United States would receive free or nearly free medical examinations, routine physician visits, well-baby care, and required tests. Most likely, prescription drugs would be available at very low cost to all Americans regardless of their income or where they obtain their insurance. Such a health care system would likely be paid for by a combination of taxes on workers and their employers and income taxes on all. Such a system might include the option for additional private insurance available for extra cost. Doctors might work for the state or national government, or they could remain as private practitioners.

THE SAN FRANCISCO EXPERIMENT

To understand how universal health care might work, we can go to San Francisco, California, where a universal health care plan was approved in the summer of 2006. The San Francisco Health Access Plan, as it is called, is financed by local government, mandatory contributions from employers, and income-adjusted premiums from users. It is open to anyone who makes $54,000 per year or less. Individuals who have private insurance purchased on their own or through their employer are encouraged to keep that coverage.

Enrollment fees range from $3 to $201, and most participants will pay $35 per month. Uninsured San Franciscans can then seek comprehensive primary care in the city's public and private clinics and hospitals. San Francisco Mayor Gavin Newsom described the city's historic undertaking as a "moral obligation."

Four years after the plan was initiated, "Healthy San Francisco" was nominated for a national prize for innovative policies. While most patients are very satisfied with the service they receive, the cost of the program has continued to grow, and the city of San Francisco, facing a deficit like many American cities, may need to change the plan.

The situation in San Francisco raises a difficult problem for the adoption of universal health care in the United States. As a federal system, the states and local governments have considerable control of health care within their boundaries. The ACA mandate for individual insurance is one step toward a national policy; however, wide differences will remain in the availability of the best physicians and best practices across states and cities in the United States because some states may offer better incentives to doctors than others.

HOW DOES UNIVERSAL HEALTH CARE AFFECT THE INDIVIDUAL PATIENT?

The National Audit Office of the United Kingdom (Great Britain, Scotland, and Wales) conducted a study of the health systems in 10 major industrialized nations in 2011. The study underscored the fact that all of these nations except the United States guaranteed access to health care to all. However, a wide variety of systems in place range from the British system of state-employed doctors and state-run hospitals to the French system with national health insurance but private physicians who "bill" the state for their services.

Generally, studies of universal systems show that for the average individual, good basic care is available. Infant mortality tends to decrease because all pregnant women have access to prenatal care. Other basic medical conditions are well covered. Most nations cover most of the cost of prescriptions so that no individual is denied an expensive but necessary medication. However, in some nations there are long waits for advanced procedures and less availability of some of the more expensive tests and scans performed routinely in the United States. To this point, Americans have made clear their desire to keep their private physicians, private hospitals, and the right to access very expensive and advanced treatments. Whether Americans will be willing to trade these practices for a universal health system is a question yet to be decided even when the ACA is fully implemented.

FOR CRITICAL ANALYSIS

1. *What are the advantages and disadvantages of a universal health care system?*

2. *How could the United States implement a universal health care system and retain some of the features of the current system that are desired by citizens?*

Domestic Policy
Public plans or courses of action that concern internal issues of national importance, such as poverty, health care, and the environment.

■ **Learning Outcome 1:**
Describe the policymaking process as it applies to American national government institutions.

WHEN PEOPLE ARE ASKED what the national government is supposed to do for them, generally they will answer that the government should defend our nation and solve our national problems. Americans expect the federal government to pay attention to the issues that impact the lives of American citizens. The legislation and regulations passed to address these problems are usually called "domestic policy." **Domestic policy** can be defined as all of the laws, government planning, and government actions that affect each individual's daily life in the United States. Consequently, the span of such policies is enormous. Domestic policies range from relatively simple issues, such as what the speed limit should be on interstate highways, to more complex ones, such as how best to reduce our nation's contribution to climate change or how to improve the performance of schools across the nation.

As noted in the What if … that opens this chapter, the question of providing health care to all Americans is a consuming national issue. In 2010, the United States adopted a major reform of our health policies, but the Congress did not adopt a universal health care system. The complex nature of the health policy reform legislation and the debate that accompanied that reform effort reflect the fact that the reform will touch virtually all Americans. Like many other domestic policies, this one was formulated and implemented by the federal government but will involve efforts of federal, state, and local governments and the private sector.

In this chapter, we look at domestic policy issues involving health care, the environment and energy, poverty and welfare, immigration, and others. Before we start our analysis, though, we must look at how public policies are made.

The Policymaking Process

How does any issue get resolved? First, the issue must be identified as a problem. Often, policymakers simply have to turn on the news or look at the Internet or hear from a constituent to discover that a problem is brewing. On rare occasions, a crisis, such as that brought about by the terrorist attacks of September 11, 2001, or the flooding caused by Hurricane Katrina, creates the need to formulate policy. Like most Americans, however, policymakers receive much of their information from the national media. Of course, interest groups are always bringing issues to the attention of the Congress in hopes of influencing policy outcomes.

As an example of policymaking, consider the Affordable Care Act. President Obama set the agenda for this bill by making it a priority of his first year in office. The law, which was passed about 14 months later, requires all Americans to have health insurance either through their employer, state insurance exchanges, or a federal program such as Medicaid. Some provisions of the law took effect almost immediately, including the one that requires insurance companies to allow parents to keep their children on their policies until age 26. The law will not be fully implemented for a decade.

No matter how simple or how complex the problem, those who make policy follow several steps. We can divide the process of policymaking into at least five steps: agenda building, policy formulation, policy adoption, policy implementation, and policy evaluation (see Figure 15-1).

Agenda Building

First, the issue must get on the agenda. In other words, Congress must become aware that an issue requires congressional action. Agenda building may occur as the result of a crisis, technological change, or mass media campaigns, as well as through the efforts of strong political personalities and effective lobbying groups.

Advocates for improved health care in this nation had advocated for a massive reform of the system for years. As noted above, President Obama chose to put health care reform on the top of his presidential agenda. The Democratic majorities in both the House and the Senate supported his priority as they, under the leadership of the late Senator Ted Kennedy, had pushed for health system reform for many years.

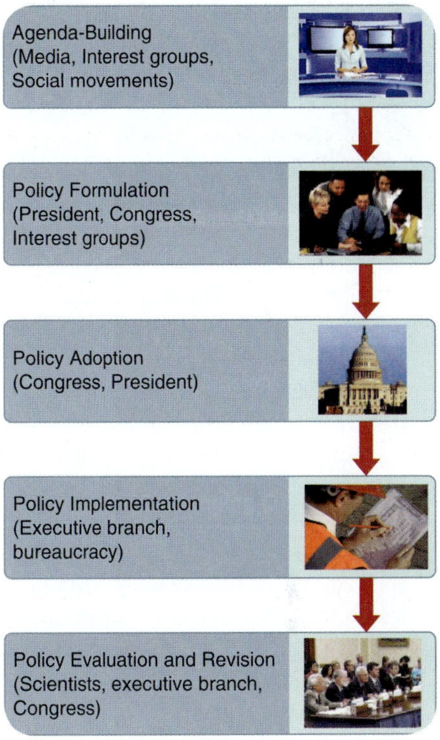

Policy Formulation

During the next step in the policymaking process, various policy proposals are discussed among government officials and the public. Such discussions may take place in the printed media, on television, and in the halls of Congress. Congress holds hearings, the president voices the administration's views, and the topic may even become a campaign issue.

With the Democratic majorities in Congress beginning work on the legislation, Republicans quickly took the position that they opposed the reform bill but they lacked the votes in either house to change the momentum. Interest groups, seeing that the bill had a chance to become law, offered their own proposals. As the policy was being formulated, groups representing America's doctors, hospitals, pharmacies, medical appliance makers, pharmaceutical manufacturers, and every other part of the medical industry offered proposals and commented on the draft legislation. In some cases, groups agreed to not oppose the law if their interests were protected. It is important to note, however, that the input of these groups into the policy formulation process is invaluable: They know more about the American system of health care then any member of the Congress.

Policy Adoption

The third step in the policymaking process involves choosing a specific policy from among the proposals that have been discussed. In the end, the bill passed both houses, although the margin in the Senate was very small. The progress of the bill through Congress revealed some of the intense partisan behavior that has become common in recent years. Republicans put forward alternate proposals and claimed that they were ignored by the administration and the Democrats. Democrats used all parliamentary means to pass the bill, including keeping the Republicans out of the final negotiations between the House and the Senate. This, of course, was exactly how Republicans had treated Democrats in passing the Medicare drug prescription bill in 2006.

Policy Implementation

The fourth step in the policymaking process involves the implementation of the policy alternative chosen by Congress. Government action must be implemented by bureaucrats, the courts, police, and individual citizens. In the example of the Affordable Care Act, the main portion of the legislation was not to come into effect until 2014. For the most part, therefore, implementation did not begin immediately. Some sections of the bill did become effective in 2011, however.

Figure 15-1 ▶ The Policy Process

Agenda-Building
(Media, Interest groups,
Social movements)

Policy Formulation
(President, Congress,
Interest groups)

Policy Adoption
(Congress, President)

Policy Implementation
(Executive branch,
bureaucracy)

Policy Evaluation and Revision
(Scientists, executive branch,
Congress)

did you know?

In the mid-1930s, during the Great Depression, Senator Huey P. Long of Louisiana proposed that the government confiscate all personal fortunes of more than $5 million and all incomes of more than $1 million and use the funds to give every American family a house, a car, and an annual income of $2,000 or more (about $25,000 in today's dollars).

Politics with a Purpose
DEFINING PROBLEMS AND FINDING SOLUTIONS IN EDUCATION

What's in a name? Policymakers often choose names for legislation as a way of directing attention to a particular policy problem. For example, President George W. Bush's No Child Left Behind (NCLB) landmark education bill[a] was designed to focus on specific problems the president had identified: inadequate accountability of schools to the public; tax dollars not having their intended effect on education; and disturbing trends showing disparate rates of success in school among children of different socioeconomic groups.

As governor of Texas, President Bush had been a proponent of the reforms that had grown in popularity during the late 1980s and early 1990s. Accountability advocates favored standardized testing throughout a child's educational career to measure concretely the progress schools were making toward specific educational goals. The results of these tests would factor significantly into teacher raises and funding for particular schools and school districts across the state.[b]

The president also identified what he called the "soft bigotry of low expectations," referring to the lower test scores of specific groups of children.[c] In an effort to close these gaps, the law mandated that test scores be reported separately for specific racial and ethnic groups, for low-income children, for children for whom English is a second language, and for children with disabilities. States were charged with setting educational goals, assessing how close to the goals schools were at the time of passage of the law, and using the differential to determine "adequate yearly progress" (AYP) benchmarks the schools must hit each year. If any one of the subgroups listed does not make AYP, the entire school is listed as "needs improvement"; NCLB allows children in these schools to transfer to better-performing schools.

NCLB passed Congress with bipartisan support and without major opposition from teachers' groups and unions. Interestingly, these groups had been an active part of the dialogue on school reform for several decades. The immediate response of the American Federation of Teachers (AFT) to NCLB was similar to its response in the 1980s—to embrace goals to close the gaps between groups of children. The National Education Association (NEA), on the other hand, has been vocal in its opposition to NCLB, even threatening to sue to overturn the law.[d] In recent years, both

groups have been critical of the testing, arguing that its high-stakes nature drives curriculum, creating a "teaching to the test" mentality.

These teacher groups have been joined by others in opposition to the implementation of the law. Disability and immigration advocates argue that NCLB does not meet the special needs of children with disabilities and immigrant children[e] Some conservative groups are frustrated by what they see as an inappropriate growth of federal government power.

With the election of President Barack Obama, a number of groups believed that they had an ally in the White House. The teachers' unions, the AFT and NEA, were surprised to see the president choose Arne Duncan, former superintendent of the Chicago schools, as secretary of education. Duncan had been the chief administrator for the Chicago schools and an outspoken supporter of teacher accountability and school reform. The Obama administration has continued the push for more accountability for teachers, for charter schools, and for improvements in student learning. A multibillion-dollar fund, the Race to the Top, was established for competitive grants to states for improvement. To even qualify to compete for the grants, teachers, administrators, and boards of education must agree to support the innovations funded by the grants. By 2012, more than 20 states had received funding.

No Child Left Behind remains the law of the land, but many states have been unable to meet the goals of this ambitious legislation. To avoid penalizing them, the Obama administration has given temporary waivers to 37 states and the District of Columbia so they will have more time to reach the standards set out by the law and not lose federal funding.

[a]Signed by the president on January 8, 2002, PL 107–110.
[b]E. DeBray, K. McDermott, and P. Wohlstetter, "Introduction to the Special Issue on Federalism Reconsidered: The Case of the No Child Left Behind Act," *Peabody Journal of Education*, Vol. 80, 2005, pp. 1–18.
[c]The president used this phrase many times in the lead-up to the legislation and during its implementation. An example of the latter is in a speech made to the National Association for the Advancement of Colored People (NAACP) in June 2006, available at www.whitehouse.gov/news/releases/2006/07/20060720.html.
[d]J. Koppich, "A Tale of Two Approaches—The AFT, the NEA, and NCLB," *Peabody Journal of Education*, Vol. 80, 2005, pp. 137–155.
[e]www.ncd.gov/newsroom/news/2003/r03-419.htm; www.urban.org/publications/411469.html.

These included the creation of insurance pools for people with existing conditions, new taxes on wealthier retirees for their prescription drug coverage, coverage of children up to age 26, and support for the creating of electronic medical records. Republican opposition to the law did not abate and it became a major campaign issue in 2010. Although Republicans did gain a majority in the House of Representatives in that election, they could not overturn the bill without gaining control of the Senate. However, a number of states elected Republican administrations and 26 Republican attorneys general filed suit against the bill, challenging the individual mandate to buy insurance and the provision requiring states to expand their Medicaid rolls. As you have read, the individual mandate was upheld by the Supreme Court in 2012 but the Medicaid mandate to the states was overturned, leaving that part of the law unenforceable.

Policy Evaluation

After a policy has been implemented, it is evaluated. Groups inside and outside the government conduct studies to determine what actually happens after a policy has been in place for a given period of time. Based on this feedback and the perceived success or failure of the policy, a new round of policymaking initiatives will be undertaken to improve on the effort. Because the Affordable Care Act has not been fully implemented, there has been little evaluation of the policy's outcomes. Some health industry economists and the Congressional Budget Office have suggested that the cost will be far higher than originally estimated while other sources predict it will save billions over the long term. Some experts believe that many small businesses will drop insurance coverage for their employees due to the high cost of the new program, but these are simply predictions for the future. As you read in Politics with a Purpose, the landmark education legislation passed by the Bush administration, No Child Left Behind, has been implemented and the outcome of the legislation is being monitored. While many states cannot meet the goals of the legislation and have requested more time to do so, test scores have improved at several grade levels and across ethnic groups in some areas. Most education analysts believe that progress is being made although the law should be revised, but not repealed, to make it more effective.

Health Care

Undoubtedly, one of the most important problems facing the nation is how to guarantee affordable health care for all Americans at a cost the nation can bear. Spending for health care is estimated to account for almost 20 percent of the total U.S. economy. In 1965, about 6 percent of our income was spent on health care, and that percentage has been increasing ever since, exceeding 17 percent by 2011 and projected to reach 20 percent by 2020. Per capita spending on health care is greater in the United States than almost anywhere else in the world. Measured by the percentage of the gross domestic product (GDP) devoted to health care, America spends almost twice as much as Australia or Canada (see Figure 15-2 on the next page). (The GDP is the dollar value of all final goods and services produced in a one-year period.)

The Rising Cost of Health Care

Numerous explanations exist for why health care costs have risen so much. At least one has to do with changing demographics—the U.S. population is

■ **Learning Outcome 2:**
Explain the principles underlying the American health care system and the issues facing that system.

Figure 15–2 ▶ **Cost of Health Care in Economically Advanced Nations**
Cost is given as a percentage of total gross domestic product (GDP).

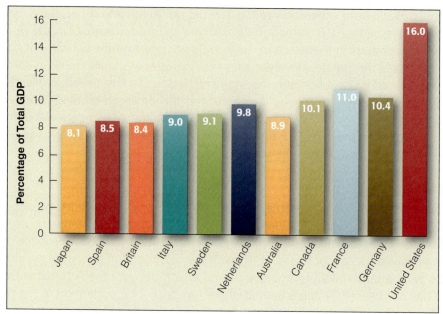

Source: Organization for Economic Cooperation and Development, *OECD Health Data*, 2009.

getting older. Life expectancy has gone up, as shown in Figure 15-3. The top 5 percent of those using health care incur more than 50 percent of all health care costs. The bottom 70 percent of health care users account for only 10 percent of health care expenditures. Not surprisingly, the elderly make up most of the top users of health care services, including nursing home care and long-term care for those suffering from debilitating diseases.

Advanced Technology. Another reason why health care costs have risen so dramatically is advancing technology. A computerized tomography (CT) scanner costs around $1 million. A magnetic resonance imaging (MRI) scanner can cost more than $2 million. A positron emission tomography (PET) scanner costs approximately $4 million. All of these machines have become increasingly available in recent decades and are in demand around the country. Typical fees for procedures using these scanners range from $300 to $500 for a CT scan to as high as $2,000 for a PET scan. The development of new technologies that help physicians and hospitals prolong human life is an ongoing process in an ever-advancing industry. New procedures and drugs that involve even greater costs can be expected in the future. It is also true that these advanced procedures are more readily available in the United States than anywhere else in the world.

The Government's Role in Financing Health Care. Currently, government spending on health care constitutes about 45 percent of total health care spending. Private insurance accounts for about 35 percent of payments for health care. The remainder—less than 20 percent—is paid directly by individuals or by philanthropy. Medicare and Medicaid have been the main sources of hospital and other medical benefits for 35 million U.S. residents, most of whom are age 65 and older.

Medicare is specifically designed to support the elderly, regardless of income. **Medicaid**, a joint state-federal program, is in principle a program to subsidize

Medicare
A federal health insurance program that covers U.S. residents age 65 and older. The costs are met by a tax on wages and salaries.

Medicaid
A joint state–federal program that provides medical care to the poor (including indigent elderly persons in nursing homes). The program is funded out of general government revenues.

Figure 15-3 ▶ Life Expectancy in the United States

Along with health-care spending, life expectancy has gone up. The health care system and high nutrition are two factors in this increase in life expectancy, but as more Americans live to their mid-80s or longer, their medical costs go up as well.

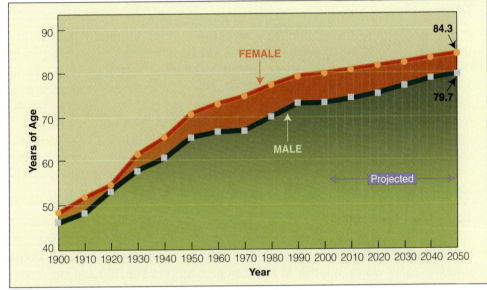

Source: Social Security Administration, Office of the Chief Actuary.

health care for the poor. In practice, it often provides long-term health care to persons living in nursing homes. (To become eligible for Medicaid, these individuals must first exhaust their financial assets.) Medicare, Medicaid, and private insurance companies are called *third parties*. Caregivers and patients are the two primary parties. When third parties pay for medical care, the demand for such services increases; health care recipients have no incentive to restrain their use of health care. One result is some degree of wasted resources.

Medicare

The Medicare program, created in 1965 under President Lyndon B. Johnson (served 1963–1969), pays hospital and physicians' bills for U.S. residents age 65 and older. As already mentioned, beginning in 2006, Medicare also pays for at least part of the prescription drug expenses of the elderly. In return for paying a tax on their earnings (currently set at 2.9 percent of wages and salaries) while in the workforce, retirees are assured that the majority of their hospital and physicians' bills will be paid for with public funds.

Over the past 40 years, Medicare has become the second-largest domestic spending program, after Social Security. Government expenditures on Medicare have routinely turned out to be far in excess of the expenditures forecast at the time the program was put into place or expanded. In Chapter 16, you will learn about Medicare's impact on the current federal budget and the impact it is likely to have in the future. For now, consider only that the total outlays on Medicare are high enough to create substantial demands to curtail its costs.

One response by the federal government to soaring Medicare costs has been to impose arbitrary reimbursement caps on specific procedures. To avoid going over Medicare's reimbursement caps, however, hospitals have an incentive to discharge patients quickly. The government has also cut rates of reimbursement to individual physicians and physician groups, such as health maintenance organizations (HMOs).

One consequence has been a nearly 15 percent reduction in the amount the government pays for Medicare services provided by physicians. Some medical practices are reluctant to add new Medicare patients although they cannot drop those who are already being treated.

Medicaid

In a few short years, the joint federal-state taxpayer-funded Medicaid program for the "working poor" has generated one of the biggest expansions of government entitlements in the last 50 years. In 1997, Medicaid spending was around $150 billion. Ten years later, it exceeded $300 billion. At the end of the last decade, 34 million people were enrolled in the program. Today, there are more than 46 million. The increase in unemployment after the financial crisis of 2008 added almost 4 million people to the Medicaid program. When you add Medicaid coverage to Medicare and the military and federal employee health plans, the government has clearly become the nation's primary health insurer. More than 100 million people—one in three—in the United States has government coverage.

Why Has Medicaid Spending Exploded? One of the reasons Medicaid has become such an important health insurance program is that the income ceiling for eligibility for families has increased to more than $46,100 per year in most states. In other words, a family of four can earn around $46,100 and still obtain health insurance through Medicaid for its children. Indeed, many low-income workers choose Medicaid over health insurance offered by employers. Why? The reason is that Medicaid is less costly and sometimes covers more medical expenses. For most recipients, Medicaid is either free or almost free.

Medicaid and the States. On average, the federal government pays almost 60 percent of Medicaid's cost; the states pay the rest. Certain states, particularly in the South, receive even higher reimbursements. In general, such states are not complaining about the expansion of Medicaid. Other states, however, such as New York, have been overwhelmed by the rate of increase in Medicaid spending. Even with the federal government's partial reimbursement, the portion paid by

Family members and patients wait in the emergency room at Children's Hospital Central California in 2004. Many families use the emergency room for routine treatments because they are uninsured. Why is this a very ineffective way to treat patients?

AP Photo/Gary Kazanjian

the states has increased so rapidly that the states are becoming financially strapped. Florida, for example, had to drastically revise its Medicaid eligibility rules to reduce the number of families using Medicaid. Otherwise, the state projected a budget deficit that it would not be able to handle.

The Uninsured

More than 49 million Americans—about 18.5 percent of the population—do not have health insurance. Because about half of all working Americans have health insurance through their employers, the recession of 2008 and the loss of jobs added about 4 million Americans to the ranks of the uninsured. The proportion of the population that is uninsured varies from one part of the country to another and between different groups. According to a study by the Kaiser Family Foundation, among all age groups, young people under 25 are most likely to be uninsured.[1] While only 14 percent of white, nonelderly Americans are uninsured, more than 30 percent of Hispanic Americans and 22 percent of African Americans are uninsured. The Kaiser report suggests that the individuals most likely to be uninsured are the working poor because they are likely to hold jobs that do not pay enough to purchase health insurance even if the employer shares the cost. It is worth noting that in 2010, the average health insurance premium per employee for a private business was more than $12,000.

According to surveys, being uninsured has negative health consequences. People without coverage are less likely to get basic preventive care, such as mammograms; less likely to have a personal physician; and more likely to rate their own health as only poor or fair.

A further problem faced by the uninsured is that when they do seek medical care, they must usually pay much higher fees than would be paid on their behalf if they had insurance coverage. Large third-party insurers, private or public, normally strike hard bargains with hospitals and physicians over how much they will pay for procedures and services. The uninsured have less bargaining power. As a result, hospitals attempt to recover from the uninsured the revenues they lost in paying third-party insurers.

In any given year, most people do not require expensive health care. Young, healthy people in particular can be tempted to do without insurance. One benefit of insurance coverage, however, is that it protects the insured against catastrophic costs resulting from unusual events. Medical care for life-threatening accidents or diseases can run into thousands or even hundreds of thousands of dollars. An uninsured person who requires this kind of medical care may be forced into bankruptcy.

The 2010 Health Care Reform Legislation

On March 23, 2010, after a long and intense battle in Congress, President Obama signed the Patient Protection and Affordable Care Act, the biggest reform of the American health care and health insurance system since the approval of Medicare in 1965. The new legislation relies on a combination of private insurance, public programs such as Medicare and Medicaid, and new state-based nonprofit health exchanges to provide health insurance coverage to almost all Americans. The program, as it passed the Congress, is not like the types of programs adopted in many European countries or in Canada.

---

1. Kaiser Commission on Medicaid and the Uninsured. "The Uninsured: A Primer," Washington, D.C.: Kaiser Family Foundation, 2011.

National Health Insurance
A plan under which the government provides basic health care coverage to all citizens. Most such plans are funded by taxes on wages or salaries.

Single-Payer Plan
A plan under which one entity has a monopoly on issuing a particular type of insurance. Typically, the entity is the government, and the insurance is basic health coverage.

Western Europe, Japan, Canada, and Australia all provide systems of universal coverage. Such coverage is provided through **national health insurance**. In effect, the government takes over the economic function of providing basic health care coverage. Private insurers are excluded from this market. The government collects premiums from employers and employees on the basis of their ability to pay and then pays physicians and hospitals for basic services to the entire population. Because the government provides all basic insurance coverage, national health insurance systems are often called **single-payer plans** or called *socialized medicine.* It should be noted, though, that only health insurance is socialized. The government does not employ most physicians, and in many countries the hospitals are largely private as well.[2]

What are the major provisions of the new health policy legislation? The new act requires all Americans who earn wages to have a health insurance policy either through their employer or through one of the new nonprofit health exchanges. Taxpayers who do not have health insurance may face a fine if they do not qualify for government help to buy insurance. Employers may purchase private insurance as they do currently or, by 2017, participate in the state-based exchanges as well. However, the types of insurance that employers may offer employees will be regulated to ensure certain coverage and to limit employee contributions. Additionally, eligibility for Medicaid will be expanded, as will insurance options for children of low-income families. Prescription costs for seniors will be discounted gradually until all their costs are covered. The health insurance industry also received new mandates to insure younger Americans, up to age 26, on their parents' policies, to not drop coverage for those who become ill, and to eliminate lifetime limits on coverage. The legislation also includes more than 100 new programs to improve the delivery of health services to patients and to make medical systems more efficient.[3]

Environmental Policy

■ **Learning Outcome 3:**
Describe the environmental policies of the United States and the role of the Environmental Protection Agency in implementing these policies.

Fifty years ago, Rachel Carson published *Silent Spring*[4], the book that can be credited with starting the contemporary environmental movement in the United States. Carson's book called attention to the consequences of widespread use of pesticides and other chemicals that are dispersed into the waterways and have deadly effects on fish and wildlife. Eight years later, the first Earth Day was celebrated. Later that same year, President Nixon proposed and the Congress approved the creation of the Environmental Protection Agency, an independent executive agency charged with protecting the environment and human health. Since that time, Americans have paid increasing attention to environmental issues and the federal government has enacted a number of specific policies intended to improve our environment.

The Environmental Movement

Environmental issues are not limited to concerns about pollution and its health effects but include the desire to save and protect natural resources. The environmental movement looks to the early part of the 20th century for its beginnings, when President Theodore Roosevelt, an enthusiastic hunter and

---

2. Britain is an exception. Under the British "National Health," most (but not all) physicians are employed by the government.
3. There are many good summaries of the new legislation. Among these is one provided by the Georgetown University Health Institute, http://ccf.georgetown.edu; and the Kaiser Family Foundation, http://kff.org.
4. Rachel Carson, *Silent Spring,* Boston: Houghton Mifflin, 1962; repr., Boston: Mariner Books, 2002.

outdoorsman, created five national parks and expanded federal protection to a vast area near Yellowstone National Park. The movement to protect the environment has been based on two major strands of thought since its beginnings in the early 1900s. One point of view calls for *conservation*—that is, a policy under which natural resources should be used, but not abused. America's national forests, which are the responsibility of the Department of Agriculture, are an example of conservation in that the forests can be timbered with appropriate permits, hunting and fishing are usually permitted, and, in the West, farmers may obtain licenses to use public lands for their cattle. A second view advocates *preservation*. Under this policy, natural preserves are established that are isolated from the effects of human activity. The national parks and national wilderness areas exemplify this view, with all human activity except hiking and climbing restricted.

In the 1960s, an environmentalist movement arose that was much more focused on pollution issues than the previous conservation movement. A series of high-profile events including the publication of *Silent Spring*; a massive oil spill off the coast of Santa Barbara, California, in 1969; and, in the same year, the fire on the Cuyahoga River caused by flammable chemicals awakened a new movement to control air and water pollution. Established conservation groups like the Audubon Society and the Sierra Club were joined by new groups including Greenpeace, Friends of the Earth, and the Wilderness Society to pressure the government to take greater action against pollution and the destruction of our environment.

The environmentalist movement focused public attention on the damage that an industrialized society can bring to the environment. Whether people are more concerned about preservation of natural places and endangered species or, as in urban areas, about smog, water pollution, and exposure to chemicals, the goals of the environmental movement have a wide base of support. In general, people are very supportive of efforts to improve the environment: A Gallup Poll taken in 2012 reported that more than 70 percent of Americans supported higher emission standards for business and industry, 69 percent favored spending more government money on wind and solar power, and 64 percent supported strongly enforcing federal environmental regulations.[5] However, when asked whether they would prioritize environmental protection over economic growth, only 41 percent agreed, continuing a trend that began with the recession of 2008. From 1985 until 2009, a majority of Americans prioritized environmental protection over economic growth.[6]

Cleaning Up the Air and Water

The government has been responding to pollution problems since before the American Revolution, when the Massachusetts Bay Colony issued regulations to try to stop the pollution of Boston Harbor. In the 1800s, states passed laws controlling water pollution after scientists and medical researchers convinced most policymakers that dumping sewage into drinking and bathing water caused disease. At the national level, the Federal Water Pollution Control Act of 1948 provided research and assistance to the states for pollution-control efforts, but little was done.

5. Frank Newport, "Americans Endorse Various Energy, Environment Proposals," The Gallup Poll, April 9, 2012.
6. Dennis Jacobe, "Americans Still Prioritize Economic Growth over Environment," The Gallup Poll, March 29, 2012.

The Cuyahoga River in 1969—firefighters extinguish a fire that started on the river and spread to a wooden trestle bridge.

Photo courtesy of the Environmental Protection Agency

Environmental Impact Statement (EIS)
A report that must show the costs and benefits of major federal actions that could significantly affect the quality of the environment.

The National Environmental Policy Act. The year 1969 marked the start of the most concerted national government involvement in solving pollution problems. As mentioned, in that year, the conflict between oil exploration interests and environmental interests literally erupted when an oil well six miles off the coast of Santa Barbara, California, exploded, releasing 235,000 gallons of crude oil. The result was an oil slick that covered an area of 800 square miles and washed up on the city's beaches and killed plant life, birds, and fish. Hearings in Congress revealed that the Interior Department had no guidance in the energy-environment trade-off. Congress soon passed the National Environmental Policy Act of 1969. This landmark legislation established, among other things, the Council on Environmental Quality. It also mandated that an **environmental impact statement (EIS)** be prepared for all major federal actions that could significantly affect the quality of the environment. The act gave citizens and public-interest groups who were concerned with the environment a weapon against the unnecessary and inappropriate use of natural resources by the government.

Curbing Air Pollution. Beginning in 1975, the government began regulating tailpipe emissions from cars and light trucks in an attempt to curb air pollution. After years of lobbying by environmentalists, Congress passed the Clean Air Act of 1990. The act established tighter standards for emissions of nitrogen dioxide (NO_2) and other pollutants by newly built cars and light trucks. California was allowed to establish its own, stricter standards. By 1994, the maximum allowable NO_2 emissions (averaged over each manufacturer's "fleet" of vehicles) were about one-fifth of the 1975 standard. The "Tier 2" system, phased in between 2004 and 2007, reduced maximum fleet emissions by cars and light trucks to just over 2 percent of the 1975 standard. In 2008–2009, the standards were extended to trucks weighing between 6,000 and 8,500 pounds.

Stationary sources of air pollution were also subjected to more regulation under the 1990 act. The act required 110 of the oldest coal-burning power plants in the United States to cut their emissions by 40 percent by 2001. Controls were placed on other factories and businesses in an attempt to reduce ground-level ozone pollution in 96 cities to healthful levels by 2005 (except in Los Angeles, which had until 2010 to meet the standards). The act also required that the production of chlorofluorocarbons (CFCs) be stopped completely by 2002. CFCs are thought to deplete the ozone layer in the upper atmosphere and increase the levels of harmful radiation reaching the earth's surface. CFCs were formerly used in air-conditioning and other refrigeration units.

In 1997, in light of evidence that very small particles (2.5 microns, or millionths of a meter, across) of soot might be dangerous to our health, the Environmental Protection Agency (EPA) issued new particulate standards for motor vehicle exhaust systems and other sources of pollution. The EPA also established a more rigorous standard for ground-level ozone, which is formed when sunlight combines with pollutants from cars and other sources. Ozone is a major component of smog.

The United States is making fairly substantial strides in the war on toxic emissions. According to the EPA, in the last 30 years U.S. air pollution has been cut in half. Airborne lead is 3 percent of what it was in 1975, and the lead content of the average American's blood is one-fifth of what it was in that year. Airborne sulfur dioxide concentrations are one-fifth of the levels found in the 1960s. Carbon monoxide concentrations are one-quarter of what they were in 1970. Water pollution is also down. Levels of six persistent pollutants in U.S. freshwater fish are about one-fifth of their 1970 levels. One reason for these successes is that the American public is increasingly aware of the need for environmental protection. To a large extent, this increased awareness has resulted from the efforts of various environmental interest groups, which have also exerted pressure on Congress to take action.

Water Pollution.

One of the most important acts regulating water pollution is the Clean Water Act of 1972, which amended the Federal Water Pollution Control Act of 1948. The Clean Water Act established the following goals: (1) make waters safe for swimming; (2) protect fish and wildlife; and (3) eliminate the discharge of pollutants into the water. The act set specific time schedules, which were subsequently extended by further legislation. Under these schedules, the EPA establishes limits on discharges of types of pollutants based on the technology available for controlling them. The 1972 act also required municipal and industrial polluters to apply for permits before discharging wastes into navigable waters.

The Clean Water Act also prohibits the filling or dredging of wetlands unless a permit is obtained from the Army Corps of Engineers. The EPA defines *wetlands* as "those areas that are inundated or saturated by surface or ground water at a frequency and duration sufficient to support, and that under normal circumstances do support, a prevalence of vegetation typically adapted for life in saturated soil conditions." In recent years, the broad interpretation of what constitutes a wetland that is subject to the regulatory authority of the federal government has generated substantial controversy.

Perhaps one of the most controversial regulations concerning wetlands was the "migratory-bird rule" issued by the Army Corps of Engineers. Under this rule, any bodies of water that could affect interstate commerce, including seasonal ponds or waters "used or suitable for use by migratory birds" that fly over state borders, were "navigable waters" subject to federal regulation under the Clean Water Act as wetlands. In 2001, after years of controversy, the United States Supreme Court struck down the rule. The Court stated that it was not prepared to hold that isolated and seasonal ponds, puddles, and "prairie potholes" become "navigable waters of the United States" simply because they serve as a habitat for migratory birds.[7]

---

7. *Solid Waste Agency of Northern Cook County v. U.S. Army Corps of Engineers,* 531 U.S. 159 (2001).

The Endangered Species Act

Inspired by the plight of disappearing species, Congress passed the Endangered Species Preservation Act in 1966. In 1973, Congress passed a completely new Endangered Species Act (ESA), which made it illegal to kill, harm, or otherwise "take" a species listed as endangered or threatened. The government could purchase habitat critical to the survival of a species or prevent landowners from engaging in development that would harm a listed species.

The ESA proved to be a powerful legal tool for the ecology movement. In a famous example, environmental groups sued to stop the Tennessee Valley Authority from completing the Tellico Dam on the grounds that it threatened habitat critical to the survival of the snail darter, a tiny fish. In 1978, the United States Supreme Court ruled in favor of the endangered fish.[8] Further controversy erupted in 1990, when the Fish and Wildlife Service listed the spotted owl as a threatened species. The logging industry blamed the ESA for a precipitous decline in national forest timber sales in subsequent years. A more recent controversy erupted when the Fish and Wildlife Service proposed removing the protected status of wolves in some western states. While cattlemen and hunters praised the idea of shooting wolves that preyed on cattle and sheep, environmental groups claimed that the wolf population was not yet strong enough to allow hunting.

The ESA continues to be a major subject of debate. However, signs indicate that the government and environmentalists may be seeking common ground. Both sides are shifting toward incentives for landowners who participate in protection programs. "Regulatory incentives really do result in landowners doing good things for their land," said William Irvin of the World Wildlife Fund.[9]

Sustainability

Before the mid-1980s, environmental politics seemed to be couched in terms of "them against us." "Them" was everyone involved in businesses that cut down rain forests, poisoned rivers, and created oil spills. "Us" was the government, and it was the government's job to stop "them." Today, most Americans support legislation to cut down on pollution, to save green areas, and to encourage the recycling of waste. Around the globe, individuals, governments, and businesses have come to believe that the earth's resources are limited and that the survival of the planet depends on moving toward a sustainable society.

What does **sustainability** mean? Sustainability means achieving a balance between economic and social activities and nature that will permit the healthy existence of both. In terms of public policy, it means that societies act in such a way as to maintain healthy supplies of air, water, and the natural resources that make modern life possible. The United States government adopted a policy of sustainability beginning in 2007 with an executive order that requires all federal agencies to "conduct their environmental, transportation, and energy-related activities … in an environmentally sound, economically and fiscally sound, integrated, continuously improving, efficient, and sustainable manner."[10]

At the federal government level, this order directed agencies to buy efficient vehicles, recycle products, and enforce legislation aimed at increasing sustainability. The order was reinforced by another in 2009 issued by President Obama to increase efforts to reduce greenhouse emissions. At the state and local level,

Sustainability
Achieving a balance between society and nature that will permit both to exist in harmony.

---

8. *Tennessee Valley Authority v. Hill,* 437 U.S. 153 (1978). In 1979, Congress exempted the snail darter from the ESA. In 1980, snail darters were discovered elsewhere, and the species turned out not to be in danger.
9. "Endangered Species Act Turns 30 as Environmental Strategy Shifts," *The Charleston Post and Courier,* Charleston, SC, January 2, 2004.
10. "Sustainability," Environmental Protection Agency statement, www.epa.gov/sustainability/

Beyond Our Borders
HOW GREEN IS EUROPE?

The European Community has shown a remarkable ability to agree on energy conservation and environmental goals for all of its members and make considerable progress towards attaining these goals. Following the publication of the European Commission's report on sustainable energy in 2006, the European Parliament began considering the situation and acting upon it in 2007. This confederation of nations agreed to cut greenhouse gases by 20 percent by 2020 and to work for a new treaty to follow the Kyoto accords that would further decrease such emissions by 2030. In addition, the European Community has taken a number of steps to help its citizens to make "green decisions" to conserve energy in the home and on the road.

All appliances of almost every type that are sold in Europe are tagged with an Energy Efficiency Rating. These easy-to-read tags grade the appliance on a scale of A to G on energy efficiency and carbon dioxide impact. The nations agreed that all new buildings and those undergoing substantial remodeling should be more energy efficient and install the most energy-efficient heating and air-conditioning systems available. In future years, Europeans will be able to buy cars and trucks that are increasingly efficient and better for the environment as well. The agreement among the nations sets carbon dioxide emissions standards for all new cars and requires manufacturers to further cut emissions by 1 percent per year every year until 2020.

What about the day-to-day habits of European citizens? Countries have differing standards, but all of the European Union members have agreed to try to reduce waste and increase recycling. If you live in Germany, for example, your neighbors have strong expectations that you will reuse, recycle, and sort your garbage. Virtually every German neighborhood or apartment building has five different bins outside, all color-coded to help you dispose of your waste properly. You will use the yellow bin for any kind of food packaging, the blue bin for paper and cardboard, the "bio" bin for leftover food waste, and separate bins for clear, brown, and green glass. A black bin is also available for those who are too lazy to separate or have something that doesn't fit the system. Switzerland and Denmark also have extremely high rates of recycling waste products from households. In some nations, there are complaints that the government does not provide enough bins for trash or does not pick up

These recycling bins in Wales, United Kingdom, are typical of those found in many European countries. Citizens are asked, at the minimum, to sort their waste into paper, plastic, glass, and compostable food items.

the materials properly while in other nations, citizens are fined for not separating their trash.

Not only do the European nations pride themselves on their "green" habits, but the European Commission makes public everyone's results on the various measures it has adopted. For example, if you go to the Web site Europe's Energy Portal, www. energy.eu/, you will find scorecards for gas and oil prices, energy dependency, CO_2 emissions, and renewable energy production for each nation. Imagine a report card on the American states that would give the same kind of measures!

FOR CRITICAL ANALYSIS

1. *Why do you think the European nations have been able to agree on such progressive measures in energy efficiency and environmental protections?*

2. *Do you think government regulations and fines are the best way to gain citizen compliance with energy and environmental goals?*

sustainability means increased recycling efforts, legislation which has banned the use of non-recyclable plastic bags, efforts to increase composting and reduction of waste for landfills. Both in Europe and the United States, corporations have responded to the call for a more sustainable society by developing more compostable or degradable products.

Global Climate Change

A major source of concern for the general public has been the emission of pollutants into the air and water. Each year, the world atmosphere receives 20 million metric tons of sulfur dioxide, 18 million metric tons of ozone pollutants, and 60 million metric tons of carbon monoxide. A majority of climate scientists believe that these pollutants are the cause of global climate change and a warming climate will represent a major threat to human survival on the planet. Christine Todd Whitman, who headed the EPA from 2001 to 2003, called global warming "one of the greatest environmental challenges we face, if not the greatest." International efforts to limit the output of pollutants, especially carbon dioxide from vehicles and power plants, have been controversial but are widely supported by citizens throughout the world.

The Kyoto Protocol. In 1997, delegates from around the world gathered in Kyoto, Japan, for a global climate conference sponsored by the United Nations. The conference issued a proposed treaty aimed at reducing emissions of greenhouse gases to 5.2 percent below 1990 levels by 2012. Only 38 developed nations were mandated to reduce their emissions, however—developing nations including China and India faced only voluntary limits. The U.S. Senate voted unanimously in 1997 that it would not accept a treaty that exempted developing countries, and in 2001 President Bush announced that he would not submit the Kyoto protocol to the Senate for ratification. By 2007, 124 nations had ratified the protocol. Its rejection by the United States, however, raised the question of whether it could ever be effective.

Even in those European countries that most enthusiastically supported the Kyoto protocol and signed it, the results have not been overly positive. By 2008, it became clear that 13 of the 15 original European Union signatories would miss their 2010 emission targets. At the same time, two nations that are considered to be "developing nations," China and India, have seen their emissions increase dramatically, but they were not required to abide by the protocol. In May 2011, the potential impact of the Kyoto agreement was severely diminished when Canada, Russia, and France announced that they were withdrawing from the agreement.

The Global Warming Debate. While the majority of scientists who perform research on the world's climate believe that global warming will be significant, there is considerable disagreement as to how much warming will actually occur. It is generally accepted that world temperatures have already increased by at least 0.6 degree Celsius over the last century. Scenarios by the United Nations Intergovernmental Panel on Climate Change predict increases ranging from 2.0 to 4.5 degrees Celsius by the year 2100. More conservative estimates, such as those by climate experts James Hansen and Patrick Michaels, average around 0.75 degree Celsius.[11]

Global warming has become a major political football to be kicked back and forth by conservatives and liberals. Some conservatives have seized on the work

11. J. E. Hansen, "Can We Defuse the Global Warming Time Bomb?" *Scientific American,* March 2004, pp. 69–77. This article is also online at www.sciam.com/media/pdf/hansen.pdf.

The water seeping from an abandoned coal mine on Kayford Mountain in West Virginia contains sulphur and other waste products that pollute local streams such as this one.

of scientists who believe that global warming does not exist at all. (Some of these researchers work for oil companies.) If this were true, there would be no reason to limit emissions of carbon dioxide and other greenhouse gases. A more sophisticated argument by conservatives is that major steps to limit emissions in the near future would not be cost effective. Bjørn Lomborg, a critic of the environmental movement, believes that it would be more practical to take action against global warming later in the century, when the technology to do so is more highly developed and when renewable energy sources have become more competitive in price.[12]

Energy Policy

The United States has always had enormous energy resources, whether from coal, oil, natural gas, or alternative sources such as wind or solar power. However, for most of the last 150 years, the American economy has been primarily dependent on fossil fuels, namely oil, coal, and natural gas. When we think about the use of energy in the United States, it is important to think beyond our homes with all their appliances and our cars. Energy is necessary to power all factories in the United States and to keep trucks, trains, airplanes, and all other forms of transportation moving. In some cases, fossil fuel is the raw material for objects in our daily lives. Plastics, polystyrene, the case for your iPad—all are made from petroleum products. While support for alternative sources of energy is very strong across the nation, becoming less dependent on fossil fuel products will require a long-term strategy. If you look at Figure 15-4, you can see the percentage of energy used by the various sectors of the American economy.

Energy policy—that is, laws concerned with how much energy is needed and used—and the regulation of energy producers tend to become important only during a crisis. In 1973, the Organization of Petroleum Exporting Countries (OPEC), the cartel of oil-producing nations, instituted an embargo on shipments

■ **Learning Outcome 4:** Analyze American energy policy, and discuss how it encourages energy independence.

Energy Policy
Laws concerned with how much energy is needed and used.

12. Bjørn Lomborg, *The Skeptical Environmentalist* (Cambridge, England: Cambridge University Press, 2001), pp. 258–324.

Figure 15-4 ▶ U.S. Energy Consumption by Economic Sector, 2010
Although transportation uses 28% of energy in the U.S., the generation of electric power is the greatest consumer of energy.

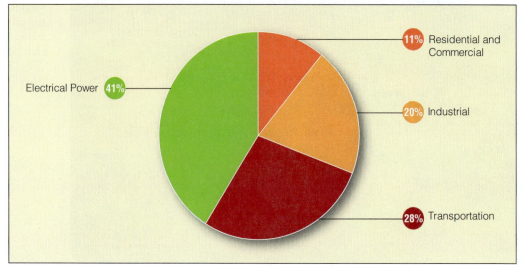

Source: "Energy Consumption Estimates by Sector, 1948–2010," U.S. Energy Information Administration, 2012.

of petroleum to the United States because of our support of Israel in the Arab-Israeli conflict of that year. President Nixon declared that the United States would achieve energy independence through reducing speed limits and meeting Corporate Average Fuel Economy (CAFE) standards by a certain time.

In 1977, President Carter also found himself facing shortages of oil and natural gas. The Department of Energy was created, and numerous programs were instituted to assist citizens in buying more energy-efficient appliances and improving the energy profile of their homes. In addition, legislation created the National Petroleum Reserve, and incentives for researching alternative forms of energy were instituted. However, over time, Americans sought to replace their smaller, more efficient cars with sport utility vehicles (SUVs) and light trucks. Airline traffic grew. Suburbs were built farther from cities and jobs. America's dependence on foreign oil has grown, as has the nation's overall appetite for energy.

In 2010, the United States consumed about 19 million barrels of petroleum per day, with half of this used as gasoline for transportation. Of those 19 million barrels per day, about 50 percent was imported. As has been the case for many decades, the United States is the third largest producer of oil but the largest consumer among the major producers. In fact, the United States has increased domestic production by about 1 million barrels a day over the last three years as prices increased around the world. From the 1970s until about 2003, the price of crude oil averaged less than $40 per barrel, with the exception of the spike in prices during the oil embargo in 1973. In the last 10 years, the price of crude oil per barrel has often reached more than $100 per barrel as demand for the product around the world has grown. What happens when the price of crude rises? First, it becomes economically feasible for less productive wells in the United States to begin pumping oil again, individual consumers look for ways to cut their use of gasoline and drive down demand for oil, and, most importantly, industries that use oil to produce energy or other products switch to less expensive fuels. If you look at Figure 15-5, Sources of Electricity Generation 2011, you will see that 22 percent

Figure 15–5 ▶ Sources of Electricity Generation 2011

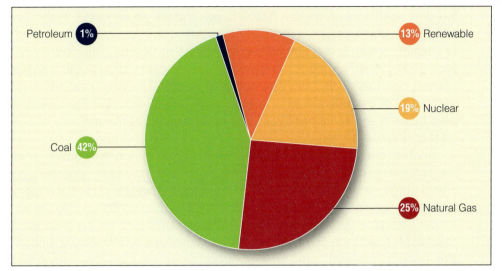

Petroleum **1%**
13% Renewable
19% Nuclear
Coal **42%**
25% Natural Gas

Source: "How much of our electricity is generated from renewable energy?" U.S. Energy Information Administration, June 27, 2012.

of the nation's energy came from natural gas in 2011. As natural gas has become more abundant, the cost has fallen and a number of power- generating plants have switched from burning oil to burning natural gas to produce electricity.

Energy and the Environment

Because of the effects of producing energy and burning fuels, energy policy is deeply entangled with environmental policy.[13] Using gasoline to power a car is the normal practice. However, burning gasoline produces serious emissions that contribute to the buildup of smog in the atmosphere. As noted previously, through a series of laws passed over the last 20 years, the EPA has forced cities to implement procedures to reduce smog and to require cleaner-burning gasoline. In addition, Congress has mandated that 10 percent of fuels sold in the years to come include ethanol as an ingredient. In response, the production of corn, which is used to make ethanol, has shot up, but still not enough is being grown to overcome the accompanying rise in price.

The United States continues to pump oil from existing wells and offshore platforms. However, more areas exist where oil could be found and extracted, but in most cases, environmental risks would be incurred. Following the oil spill in Santa Barbara, California, from an offshore drilling rig, most Americans welcomed laws that forbade drilling in new areas off Florida, Louisiana, Texas, and California. In addition, large areas of the Arctic National Wilderness Reserve (ANWR) have also been protected from oil exploration. Drilling in the ANWR is an extremely controversial issue because of the pristine nature of the land and the potential danger to native wildlife in that area of Alaska. In 2010, the clash between environmental protection and the need for energy sources came to a head in the Gulf of Mexico at a drilling rig named the Deepwater Horizon. The rig, leased by

In the last three years, production of natural gas has increased dramatically due to the use of "fracking" to release gas from layers of shale deep beneath the earth's surface. This hydro-fracking well is being drilled in Pennsylvania.

© Philip Scalia/Alamy

---

13. For a comprehensive look at all energy resources in the United States, go to the Web site of the Department of Energy: www.energy.gov/energysources.

British Petroleum, was drilling for oil more than a mile deep in the ocean when a "blowout" of oil and gas occurred. The blowout preventer—a multimillion-dollar, five-story apparatus on the sea floor—failed, and the rig exploded. In the weeks and months that followed, millions of gallons of oil and gas spewed from the well as attempts to cap it met limited success. President Obama convinced BP to set aside $20 billion in a fund to compensate Gulf residents for losses in wages and business revenues. Gulf state governors and mayors expressed great anger at the inefficiency of the federal response and the perceived neglect of their states' polluted beaches and economic losses, but the aftermath of the spill may not be as great as originally feared.

Another dilemma facing the United States involves domestic power production and the need for cleaner air. The majority of electric power generated in the United States comes from coal-fired plants in the Midwest and central regions of the nation. For many years, these plants spewed carbon emissions into the air. As scientists became aware of the impact of these emissions on the environment, new laws required the plants to reduce their emissions by installing scrubbers or, after reaching the legal "cap" on their carbon emissions, buying or trading for the right to produce more. The EPA, under the Bush administration, issued regulations for coal-burning plants that reduced their burden of meeting the standards. States that felt they received the most damage from some of these emissions sued to make the EPA issue standards that meet the letter of the Clean Air Act. The Supreme Court agreed with these states, and the EPA began to prepare stricter standards. After President Obama was elected, the EPA moved ahead with great energy to enforce stricter standards both for power plants and for the emissions of cars and trucks, including a mandate for average fuel efficiency of 35 miles per gallon for cars and light trucks by 2019.

Nuclear Power—An Unpopular Solution

One strategy for reducing carbon emissions of coal-fired plants and also the environmental and human risks of coal mining is to increase the number of

Japanese journalists inspect what remains of the Fukushima Dai-ichi nuclear power plant which was destroyed by the 2011 tsunami. The release of radiation from the plant after its destruction has forced Japan to reconsider its dependency on nuclear energy.

nuclear power plants in the United States. Nuclear power plants are very efficient and emit very low levels of greenhouse gases.[14] However, the accident at the Three Mile Island plant in Pennsylvania in 1979 and the disaster at Chernobyl in the Soviet Union in 1986 have almost destroyed any support for nuclear power in the United States. Not only do people fear the possibility of an accident at such a plant, but nuclear plants also provide a superb target for terrorist attacks.

Finally, nuclear plants produce spent fuel, which must be stored until it is safe. No state wants to be the repository for nuclear waste, and few citizens want the waste trucked through their neighborhoods. The United States for many decades was alone among industrialized nations in its fear of nuclear power, but given the concern about carbon emissions from the coal-fired plants, the United States was beginning to license the construction of new nuclear plants in the early 2000s. However, after a tsunami destroyed a huge coastal area of Japan in 2011 and caused the meltdown of a nuclear plant, the Japanese have begun to have serious concerns about their dependence on nuclear power. Even in Europe and the former Soviet Union, where hundreds of nuclear plants have operated safely for decades, the radiation release from the Japanese plant has renewed the demand to reduce the number of nuclear plants in operation.

Alternative Approaches to the Energy Crisis

Several alternative sources of energy can be used to reduce the nation's dependence on fossil fuels. Huge wind farms in California generate energy for cities there. Research continues on harnessing the power of the ocean waves to produce electricity and the most efficient ways to use geothermal energy from below the surface of the earth.[15] However, the technology does not yet exist to use any of these sources to produce the quantity of energy needed to replace our coal plants or other current energy sources. And, in some areas, citizens consider wind farms extremely disturbing to the environment and area wildlife.

The rising price of gasoline in 2008 spurred a much greater demand for hybrid automobiles and for smaller, more fuel-efficient cars. In addition, people began to ride motor scooters for city commutes and increased their use of mass transit. Homes closer to the city center became somewhat more attractive, although it will be many years before the trend of living in the suburbs will be reversed. Both political parties seemed supportive of new legislation encouraging energy efficiency in home building, using energy-efficient light bulbs, and giving incentives to buy hybrid vehicles. The Obama administration has sought comprehensive energy legislation from the Congress since the president's inauguration. Members of the administration and of Congress realize that both energy needs and environmental concerns must be addressed in the same legislation. Proponents of a "cap and trade" system want industries to account for their carbon emissions through a market system, as in Europe, as described in the Beyond Our Borders in this chapter. The opponents of such a system believe that it will drive up energy costs for everyone because costs will be passed down to the ultimate consumer. Energy legislation stalled in the Congress in 2010 and no new plan has been passed.

---

14. Larry Parker and Mark Holt, "Nuclear Power: Outlook for New U.S. Reactors" (Washington, DC: Congressional Research Service, March 9, 2007).
15. For a discussion of these new technologies, see Jay Inslee and Bracken Henricks, *Apollo's Fire* (Washington, D.C.: Island Press, 2007).

Many environmentalists and commentators suggest that a much greater use of wind power could reduce the nation's dependence on fossil fuels. This California windmill farm produces energy for Palm Springs. However, windmill farms cannot be successful everywhere in the United States.

Johnny Habell/Shutterstock.com

■ **Learning Outcome 5:**
Describe the national policies for ending poverty in the United States and alleviating the issues caused by economic downturns.

Income Transfer
A transfer of income from some individuals in the economy to others, generally by government action.

Poverty and Welfare

Throughout the world, poverty has historically been accepted as inevitable. The United States and other industrialized nations, however, have sustained enough economic growth in the past several hundred years to eliminate mass poverty. In fact, considering the wealth and high standard of living in the United States, the persistence of poverty here appears bizarre and anomalous. How can so much poverty exist in a nation of so much abundance? And what can be done about it?

A traditional solution has been **income transfers**. These are methods of transferring income from relatively well-to-do to relatively poor groups in society, and as a nation, we have been using such transfers for a long time. Before we examine these efforts, let us look at the concept of poverty in more detail and at the characteristics of the poor.

The Low-Income Population

We can see in Figure 15-6 that the number of people classified as poor fell steadily from 1961 to 1968—that is, during the presidencies of John Kennedy and Lyndon Johnson. The number remained level until the recession of 1981–1982, during Ronald Reagan's presidency, when it increased substantially. The number fell during the Internet boom of 1994–2000, but then it started to rise again. Over the last 50 years, the number of Americans who are classified as poor has ranged from a high of 40 million in 1959 to a low of 25 million. The percentage generally has been below 15 percent. In 2011, about 46.2 million Americans, or about 16.3 percent, were classified as poor. The economic downturn and increase in unemployment sent the rate to the highest it has been since 1997. Even though economists declared that the recession had ended and recovery was beginning, the number of poor increased by more than 6 million between 2009 and 2011. For many of these Americans, family savings were exhausted, unemployment benefits had expired, and the hope of a job was fading. Many Americans who turned 62 applied for early retirement and their reduced Social Security benefits, while others claimed permanent disability.

Figure 15-6 ▸ The Official Number of Poor in the United States

The number of individuals classified as poor fell steadily from 1961 through 1968. It then increased during the 1981–1982 recession. After 1994, the number fell steadily until 2000, when it started to rise again. The recession that began in 2008 spurred an increase to a fifty–year high in the number of poor Americans.

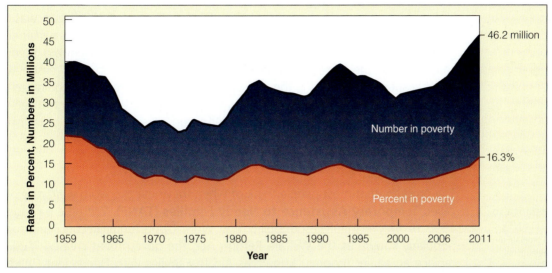

Note: The data points represent the midpoints of the respective years.
Source: U.S. Census Bureau, Current Population Reports, *Income, Poverty, and Health Insurance Coverage in the United States: 2007*, Washington, D.C.: Government Printing Office (2007) and authors' update.

The threshold income level that is used to determine who falls into the poverty category was originally based on the cost of a nutritionally adequate food plan designed by the U.S. Department of Agriculture in 1963. The threshold was determined by multiplying the food-plan cost times three, on the assumption that food expenses constitute approximately one-third of a poor family's expenditures. Until 1969, annual revisions of the threshold level were based only on changes in food prices. After 1969, the adjustments were made on the basis of changes in the consumer price index (CPI). The CPI is based on the average prices of a specified set of goods and services bought by wage earners in urban areas.

The low-income poverty threshold thus represents the income needed to maintain a specified standard of living as of 1963, with the purchasing-power value increased year by year to reflect the general increase in prices. For 2012, for example, the official poverty level for a family of four was about $23,050.

The official poverty level is based on pretax income, including cash but not **in-kind subsidies**—food stamps, housing vouchers, and the like. If we correct poverty levels for such benefits, the percentage of the population that is below the poverty line drops dramatically. To put the official U.S. poverty level in perspective, consider that this income level for the United States is twice as high as the world's average per capita income level. According to the World Bank, only 26 countries have per capita incomes higher than the poverty income threshold defined by the U.S. government.

In-Kind Subsidy
A good or service—such as food stamps, housing, or medical care—provided by the government to low-income groups.

The Antipoverty Budget

It is not always easy to determine how much the government spends to combat poverty. In part, this is because it can be difficult to decide whether a particular program is an antipoverty program. Are grants to foster parents an antipoverty measure? What about job-training programs? Are college scholarships for low-income students an antipoverty measure?

President Obama's 2012 budget allocated more than $1 trillion, or about one-third of all federal expenditures, to federal programs that support persons of limited income (scholarships included).[16] Of this amount, $233 billion was for Medicaid, which funds medical services for the poor, as discussed earlier. The states were expected to contribute an additional $150 billion to Medicaid. Medical care is by far the largest portion of the antipoverty budget. One reason why medical spending is high is the widespread belief that everyone should receive medical care that at least approximates the care received by an average person. No such belief supports spending for other purposes, such as shelter or transportation. Elderly people receive 60 percent of Medicaid spending.

Basic Welfare

The program that most people think of when they hear the word *welfare* is now called **Temporary Assistance to Needy Families (TANF)**. With the passage in 1996 of the Personal Responsibility and Work Opportunity Reconciliation Act, popularly known as the Welfare Reform Act, the government created TANF to replace an earlier program known as Aid to Families with Dependent Children (AFDC). The AFDC program provided "cash support for low-income families with dependent children who have been deprived of parental support due to death, disability, continued absence of a parent, or unemployment."

Under the TANF program, the U.S. government turned over to the states, in the form of block grants, funds targeted for welfare assistance. The states, not the national government, now bear the burden of any increased welfare spending. For example, if a state wishes to increase the amount of TANF payments over what the national government supports, the state has to pay the additional costs.

One of the aims of the Welfare Reform Act was to reduce welfare spending. To do this, the act made two significant changes in the basic welfare program. One change was to limit most welfare recipients to only two years of assistance at a time. The second change was to impose a lifetime limit on welfare assistance of five years. The Welfare Reform Act has largely met its objectives. During the first five years after the act was passed, the number of families receiving welfare payments was cut in half. The 2010 federal budget allocated $22 billion to the TANF block grants.

Welfare Controversies

Whether known as AFDC or TANF, the basic welfare program has always been controversial. Conservative and libertarian voters often object to welfare spending as a matter of principle, believing that it reduces the incentive to find paid employment. Because AFDC and TANF have largely supported single-parent households, some also believe that such programs are antimarriage. Finally, certain people object to welfare spending out of a belief that welfare recipients are "not like us." In fact, non-Hispanic whites made up only 30 percent of TANF recipients in the mid-2000s. As a result of all these factors, basic welfare payments in the United States are relatively low when compared with similar payments in other industrialized nations. In 2012, the average monthly TANF payment nationwide was about $700, with a national maximum of $1,500 for a family of four.

Temporary Assistance to Needy Families (TANF)
A state-administered program in which grants from the national government are used to provide welfare benefits. The TANF program replaced the Aid to Families with Dependent Children (AFDC) program.

did you know?

The Greenville County Department of Social Services in South Carolina wrote to a food stamp recipient, "Your food stamps will be stopped ... because we received notice that you passed away. May God bless you. You may reapply if there is a change in your circumstances."

---

16.   This sum does not include the earned income tax credit, which is not part of the federal budget.

Other Forms of Government Assistance

The **Supplemental Security Income (SSI)** program was established in 1974 to provide a nationwide minimum income for elderly persons and persons with disabilities who do not qualify for Social Security benefits. The 2012 budget allocated $52 billion to this program.

The government also issues **food stamps**, benefits that can be used to purchase food; they are usually provided electronically through a card similar to a debit card. Food stamps are available to low-income individuals and families. Recipients must prove that they qualify by showing that they have a low income (or no income at all). Food stamps go to a much larger group of people than do TANF payments, including the unemployed and single adults, groups which have expanded during the recession. President Obama's 2012 budget allocated $75 billion to the food stamp program. The food stamp program has become a major part of the welfare system in the United States, although it was started in 1964 mainly to benefit farmers by distributing surplus food through retail channels.

The **earned income tax credit (EITC) program** was created in 1975 to help low-income workers by giving back part or all of their Social Security taxes. Currently, about 15 percent of all taxpayers claim an EITC, and an estimated $49 billion per year is rebated to taxpayers through the program.

Homelessness—Still a Problem

The plight of the homeless remains a problem. Some observers argue that the Welfare Reform Act of 1996 has increased the number of homeless persons. No hard statistics on the homeless are available, but estimates of the number of people without a home on any given night in the United States range from a low of 230,000 to as many as 750,000 people.

It is difficult to estimate how many people are homeless because the number depends on how the homeless are defined. There are *street people*—those who sleep in bus stations, parks, and other areas. Many of these people are youthful runaways. There are also the so-called *sheltered homeless*—those who sleep in government-supported or privately funded shelters. Many of these individuals used to live with their families or friends. Whereas street people are almost always single, the sheltered homeless include many families with children. Homeless families are the fastest-growing subgroup of the homeless population. The homeless problem pits liberals against conservatives. Conservatives argue that there are not really that many homeless people and that most of them are alcoholics, drug users, or the mentally ill. Conservatives contend that these individuals should be dealt with by either the mental health system or the criminal justice system. In contrast, many liberals argue that homelessness is caused by a reduction in welfare benefits and by excessively priced housing.

Some cities have "criminalized" homelessness. Many municipalities have outlawed sleeping on park benches and sidewalks, as well as panhandling and leaving personal property on public property. In some cities, police sweeps remove the homeless, who then become part of the criminal justice system. In general, northern cities have assumed a responsibility to shelter the homeless in bad weather. Cities in warmer climates are most concerned with a year-round homeless problem. No new national policies on the homeless have been initiated, in part because of disagreement about the causes of and solutions for the problem.

Since 1993, the U.S. Department of Housing and Urban Development has spent billions of dollars on programs designed to combat homelessness. Yet

Supplemental Security Income (SSI)
A federal program established to provide assistance to elderly persons and persons with disabilities.

Food Stamps
Benefits issued by the federal government to low-income individuals to be used for the purchase of food; originally provided as coupons, but now typically provided electronically through a card similar to a debit card.

Earned Income Tax Credit (EITC) Program
A government program that helps low-income workers by giving back part or all of their Social Security taxes.

because of the intense disagreement about the number of homeless persons, the reasons for homelessness, and the possible cures for the problem, no consistent government policy has resulted. Whatever policies have been adopted usually have been attacked by one group or another.

Immigration

Time and again, this nation has been challenged and changed—and culturally enriched—by immigrant groups. All of these immigrants have faced the problems involved in living in a new and different political and cultural environment. Most of them have had to overcome language barriers, and many have had to deal with discrimination in one form or another because of their skin color, their inability to speak English fluently, or their customs. The civil rights legislation passed during and since the 1960s has done much to counter the effects of prejudice against immigrant groups by ensuring that they obtain equal rights under the law.

One of the questions facing Americans and their political leaders today is the effect of immigration on American politics and government. Other issues are whether immigration is having a positive or negative impact on the United States and the form immigration reform should take.

The Continued Influx of Immigrants

Today, immigration rates are among the highest they have been since their peak in the early 20th century. Every year, more than 1 million people immigrate to this country, and people who were born on foreign soil now constitute more than 10 percent of the U.S. population—twice the percentage of 30 years ago.

Minority Groups' Importance on the Rise. Since 1977, four out of five immigrants have come from Latin America or Asia. Hispanics have overtaken African Americans as the nation's largest minority. If current immigration rates continue, by the year 2060, minority groups collectively will constitute the "majority" of Americans. If Hispanics, African Americans, and perhaps Asians were to form coalitions, they could increase their political power dramatically and would have the numerical strength to make significant changes. Many commentators predict that the longtime white majority will no longer dominate American politics.

The Advantages of High Rates of Immigration. Some regard the high rate of immigration as a plus for America, because it offsets the low birthrate and aging population. Immigrants expand the workforce and help support, through their taxes, government programs that benefit older Americans, such as Medicare and Social Security. If it were not for immigration, contend these observers, the United States would be facing even more serious problems than it already does with funding these programs (see Chapter 16). In contrast, nations that do not have high immigration rates, such as Japan, are experiencing serious fiscal challenges due to their aging populations.

Attempts at Immigration Reform

A significant number of U.S. citizens, however, believe that immigration—both legal and illegal—negatively affects America. They argue, among other things, that the large number of immigrants seeking work results in lower wages for Americans, especially those with few skills. They also worry about the cost of providing immigrants with services such as schools and medical care.

Not surprisingly, before the 2006 elections, members of Congress were in favor of enacting a sweeping immigration reform bill, but the two houses could not agree on what it should do. Some versions of the bill in the House would have made every illegal immigrant in the United States a felon. The Senate, in contrast, came up with a much softer immigration reform system, one that was similar to a proposal made by President Bush. The Senate bill in its various forms in 2006 would have allowed illegal immigrants to gradually become citizens. None of these immigration reform bills came to fruition. Later in the year, however, Congress did pass legislation authorizing the construction of a 700-mile-long fence between the United States and Mexico. The fence is to be a real fence in some areas and a "virtual fence" using cameras and surveillance technologies in other areas. Although a combination of physical fence and "virtual" fence has been completed from San Diego, California to Yuma, Arizona, President Obama ended any further construction in 2010.

Conservative radio talk show hosts took up the cause of defeating the Senate's comprehensive immigration bill because it was seen to offer "amnesty" for illegal immigrants. Members of Congress were content to let the bill die rather than face unhappy constituents in an election year. By 2008, the debate seemed to have changed, with virtually all of the candidates for president, except the most conservative, supporting legislation that would tighten the borders, force employers to check the papers of their workers, and eventually build a path to citizenship. As the recession deepened in 2008–2009, many undocumented workers left the United States to return to their homes in Central America, and the problem of a "flood" of undocumented workers seemed to dissipate. Comprehensive immigration reform, while supported by President Obama, was not a priority on his first term agenda. However, a number of states began to pass laws to curtail the activities of undocumented workers. In 2010, Arizona passed

A college student demonstrates his support for the DREAM Act, legislation which would provide a way for young people who were brought to the United States by their parents and who are undocumented residents to apply for legal residency after satisfying work, military service, or education requirements.

© Jim West/Alamy

a law requiring state and local police and law enforcement officers to check individuals' citizenship or residency papers if they had been stopped on suspicion of an offense. The law, which requires local officials to enforce federal law, sparked a national debate. President Obama ordered the Justice Department to investigate whether the Arizona law was constitutional, and demonstrations against the law took place in many cities. National public opinion supported the Arizona law and the governor claimed that the law was necessary to limit crime and violence related to illegal border crossings. In July 2010, Federal District Court Judge Susan Bolton issued a preliminary injunction blocking the most controversial parts of the law while allowing others to take effect, including one that bans cities from refusing to cooperate with federal immigration officials. The case was appealed by the state of Arizona and reached the Supreme Court in 2011. In June 2012, the Supreme Court held that a number of the provisions of the law were unconstitutional, although the decision upheld the portion of the law allowing police officers who had stopped an individual on suspicion of a crime to ask for proof of citizenship or residency if they suspected the person was undocumented. The Obama administration announced that the federal offices in Arizona might not cooperate with police who made such arrests.

In general, the Obama administration followed a two-pronged approach to dealing with undocumented workers. For the first few years, the administration stepped up raids on companies suspected of employing a number of such individuals and, if they were found, deported the workers. However, by 2011 the administration announced a policy that suspended deportations of individuals who had not committed crimes. In 2012, the president, by executive order, suspended for one year any deportation of a young adult who had been illegally brought to this country by parents before the child was 16 if that young person had finished high school or was in post-secondary school or the military or gainfully employed. He ordered federal agencies to issue work permits to such individuals if they were under 30 years old and had no serious criminal record. His legislative proposal to allow such young adults to become residents, the DREAM Act, had not been passed by Congress but the president's order gave students at least a year to stay in the United States.

The Range of Federal Public Policies

In this chapter, we have looked at federal health policies, at environmental and energy issues, at poverty, welfare, and immigration issues. In Chapter 16, we will look more closely at the entitlement programs, Social Security, Medicare, and Medicaid.

The United States government implements policies that have been legislated by Congress across the entire spectrum of American life. For example, think about federal policies that impact colleges and universities: Title IX programs ensure that women have equal opportunities to play intercollegiate sports, while programs from the Department of Veterans Affairs provide tuition benefits for returning military veterans and for members of the reserves and the National Guard. Almost all aspects of the federal student loan program are regulated by the federal government, from eligibility for a subsidized loan to the requirement that colleges keep accurate records of student attendance date of withdrawal from class.

Public policies at the national level have an enormous impact on cities and the housing market. Not only does the national government guarantee most mortgages approved in this country, but federal programs provide a range of support

You Can Make a Difference

DOING YOUR PART: SUSTAIN THE PLANET

Engineering students at the University of Texas organize an "E-waste" drive to recycle computers, printers, and other electronic items.

For the first time in human history on the planet, most peoples and nations in the world are recognizing that the earth, our planet, has finite resources. If we are able to sustain the existing resources of air, water, earth, oceans, rivers, and forests, the planet will be able to support human endeavors for a much longer period of time. Maintaining the earth's ecological balance will reduce the impact of misuse on human society. For example, continuing to burn down the rain forest to provide cropland for subsistence farming may feed a family in South America or Africa for a few years, but the soil is poor and will be quickly exhausted of nutrients. Deforestation will add to global temperature increases, greatly increase the likelihood of floods and landslides, and of course destroy the habitats of plants and animals. Finding ways for people to farm in environmentally safer ways or to harvest and sell other types of crops and starting other local industries will also feed families, but without the long-term effects of deforestation.

In a completely different setting, urban America, supporting the recycling of metal, paper, glass, and plastic has multiple good effects: It reduces landfills, it reduces municipal costs for collecting trash and maintaining the landfills, it encourages reuse of resources instead of the creation of throwaway objects, and, in the long run, it saves energy. The movement toward sustainability improves earth's balance while being good for human society.

WHY SHOULD YOU CARE?

The answer is simple: You need the earth's resources to live out your life with the quality of life you expect and so do your descendants. The young "inherit the earth," in every way. While past generations may have generated smog over big cities, deforested large areas of the country, disrupted the ecology of regions by damming rivers, and erected levees that actually increase the destructiveness of floods, the earth has shown a remarkable ability to heal itself if given time and better treatment. Dams are removed and rivers become healthy. London has clean air instead of the smoke-filled haze of past generations. Areas of New England are returning to their original forested state.

WHAT CAN YOU DO?

Individuals can support sustainability at a number of levels. If you want to become politically active, then join a group on campus that supports sustainability. Almost all campuses have an environmental group pushing for more sustainable practices at the university and throughout the local area. Of course, you can join and participate in the efforts of many national interest groups, many of which are detailed in Chapter 7. To find more groups, go to www.ecoearth.info/links/Sustainability/. You will find lists of organizations that support sustainability efforts around the globe.

At another level, every individual can adopt sustainable practices in his or her own life. What would these look like? One set of practices involves conserving fossil fuels and reducing your contribution to air pollution by owning a fuel-efficient car, learning to drive in a more fuel-efficient way, combining trips, not driving during smog alerts, and putting the transmission of your car in neutral at stoplights to save more than 5 percent of your fuel. Recycle all of your paper, glass, metal, and plastic, and most importantly, recycle all your old electronics to dispose of them properly. Think about how you eat: Visit a local farmers' market, and buy fresh produce and meat. Eating locally produced food accomplishes many goals, including reducing transportation costs, eating healthier and better food, and reducing our dependence on imported food.

Individuals can do hundreds of "little things" to practice sustainability without changing their lifestyle or increasing their costs. For one very helpful list of suggestions, go to "50 Ways to Help the Planet," posted by Wire and Twine at www.50waystohelp.com. Other helpful Web sites on the topic of sustainability include the following:

United States Environmental Protection Agency: www.epa.gov/sustainability

Worldwatch Institute: www.worldwatch.org

Smart Communities Network: www.smartcommunities.ncat.org

Center for a Sustainable Economy: www.sustainable-economy.org

services for individuals who are poor or cannot afford to own or rent a home. The goal of national policy is for every American to have a safe place to live. To achieve that goal, the federal government provides support to cities for their own housing programs, vouchers for individuals to choose their own apartments, and guarantees to developers who build homes for low-income Americans.

The national government implements important policies to support the agricultural industry in this country, to keep the treatment of labor unions fair, to support school systems in their reform efforts, to assist states to build and maintain highways and bridges. In these times of rising public deficits and seemingly expanding federal programs, a majority of Americans say that government spending and programs should be cut, but the only program a majority of Americans agree should be cut is foreign aid to other nations, one of the smallest government programs in existence. One of the advantages of the explosion of information on the Internet is that today, you can learn about the programs of almost all federal agencies (with the exception of the intelligence agencies) by visiting their Web sites.

Key Terms

domestic policy 476

earned income tax credit (EITC) program 499

energy policy 491

environmental impact statement (EIS) 486

food stamps 499

income transfer 496

in-kind subsidy 497

Medicaid 480

Medicare 480

national health insurance 484

single-payer plan 484

Supplemental Security Income (SSI) 499

Sustainability 488

Temporary Assistance to Needy Families (TANF) 498

Chapter Summary

1. Domestic policy consists of all of the laws, government planning, and government actions that affect the lives of American citizens. Policies are created in response to public problems or public demand for government action. Major policy problems discussed in this chapter include health care, poverty and welfare, immigration, environmental and energy policy.

2. The policymaking process is initiated when policymakers become aware—through the media or from their constituents—of a problem that needs to be addressed by the legislature and the president. The process of policymaking includes five steps: agenda building, policy formulation, policy adoption, policy implementation, and policy evaluation. As the proposed policy is formulated and debated during the adoption process, the views of the public, interest groups, and the government are heard. All policy actions necessarily result in both costs and benefits for society.

3. Health care spending is about 18 percent of the U.S. economy and is growing. Reasons for this growth include the increasing number of elderly persons, advancing technology, and higher demand because costs are picked up by third-party insurers. A major third party is Medicare, the federal program that pays health care expenses of U.S. residents age 65 and older. The federal government has tried to restrain the growth in Medicare spending, but it has also expanded the program to cover prescription drugs.

4. About 15 percent of the population does not have health insurance—a major political issue. Most uninsured adults work for employers that cannot afford to offer health benefits. Hospitals tend to charge the uninsured higher rates than they charge insurance companies or the government. One proposal for addressing this problem is a national health insurance system under which the government provides basic coverage to all citizens. The United States has chosen to continue with a plan that combines government-required health insurance, private and public insurers, and private provision of services. Most Americans prefer this approach because they wish to choose their own medical

providers. Whether this approach will result in cost control and better health for Americans is yet to be seen.

5. Pollution problems continue to plague the United States and the world. Since the 1800s, several significant federal acts have been passed in an attempt to curb the pollution of our environment. The National Environmental Policy Act of 1969 established the Council on Environmental Quality. That act also mandated that environmental impact statements be prepared for all legislation or major federal actions that might significantly affect the quality of the environment. The Clean Water Act of 1972 and the Clean Air Act amendments of 1990 constituted the most significant government attempts at cleaning up our environment. With the recent Gulf oil spill, the conflict between protecting the environment and keeping energy cheap in the United States has become more intense.

6. Energy policy in the United States has generally sought to stabilize the supply of cheap energy to meet the demands of Americans. When energy sources are threatened, new policies have been adopted, such as increasing efficiency standards for automobiles, funding research on new technologies, and supporting the use of alternative energy. All energy policies are deeply interconnected with environmental issues, because the use of fossil fuels contributes to air pollution and climate change. Reducing the use of energy and using new technologies for cleaner energy make all energy more expensive for Americans. However, reduced future supplies are likely to mean more reforms in the future. Whether Americans will choose to pay more for their everyday needs to provide for a cleaner environment is a question that will be resolved in the future.

7. Despite the wealth of the United States as a whole, a significant number of Americans live in poverty or are homeless. The poverty threshold represents the income needed to maintain a specified standard of living as of 1963, with the purchasing-power value increased year by year based on the general increase in prices. The official poverty level is based on pretax income, including cash, and does not take into consideration in-kind subsidies (food stamps, housing vouchers, and so on).

8. The 1996 Welfare Reform Act transferred more control over welfare programs to the states, limited the number of years people can receive welfare assistance, and imposed work requirements on welfare recipients. The act succeeded in reducing the number of welfare recipients in the United States by at least 50 percent.

9. America has always been a land of immigrants and continues to be so. Today, more than 1 million immigrants from other nations enter the United States each year, and more than 10 percent of the U.S. population consists of foreign-born persons. The civil rights legislation of the 1960s and later has helped immigrants to overcome some of the effects of prejudice and discrimination against them. Today, the controversy centers on a reform of our immigration legislation that will improve our system for temporary workers and enable undocumented immigrants to have a path to citizenship.

Selected Print, Media, and Online Resources

PRINT RESOURCES

Dja65/Shutterstock.com

Blundell, Katherine, and Fraser Armstrong. *Energy… Beyond Oil.* Cambridge, England: Oxford University Press, 2007. Written by two British scientists, the book reviews all of the major new technologies for energy generation and discusses whether or when the technologies can make a contribution to world energy needs.

Edwards, Andres R. *The Sustainability Revolution: Portrait of a Paradigm Shift.* Gabriola Island, British Columbia, Canada: New Society Publishers, 2005. The author clearly explains the concept of sustainability and demonstrates how it applies in five sectors: community, commerce, resource extraction, design and structures, and the biosphere.

Ehrenreich, Barbara. *Nickel and Dimed: On (Not) Getting By in America.* New York: Owl Books, 2002. Released on audio CD in 2004. What is life like for the working poor? Commentator and humorist Barbara Ehrenreich sought to live for a few months working at minimum-wage jobs. Here, she describes her experiences.

Hage, Dave. *Reforming Welfare by Rewarding Work: One State's Successful Experiment.* Minneapolis, MN: University of Minnesota Press, 2004. Hage describes the Minnesota Family Investment Program, a pilot program in welfare reform. He illustrates the story with firsthand accounts of three families.

Laufer, Peter, and Markos Kounalakis. *Calexico: Hope and Hysteria in the California Borderlands.* Sausalito, CA: PoliPointPress, 2009. Calexico is a news-gathering travelogue that explores the California-Mexico border region, a land of its own inhabited by people who experience the immigration crisis in all its dimensions, every day. Laufer is a foreign affairs journalist and radio commentator; Kounalakis is the editor of the *Washington Monthly.*

Miller, Roger LeRoy, et al. *The Economics of Public Issues*, 15th ed. Reading, MA: Addison-Wesley, 2005. Chapters 4, 8, 11, 13, 19, 20, 22, 24, and 27 are especially useful. The authors use short essays of three to seven pages to explain the purely economic aspects of numerous social problems, including health care, the environment, and poverty.

Schellenberger, Michael, and Ted Nordhaus. *Break Through: From the Death of Environmentalism to the Politics of Possibility*. New York: Houghton-Mifflin, 2007. The authors argue that the environmentalist movement is no longer useful nor effective. A new approach to policy embracing research and societal needs will succeed, in their view.

Sered, Susan Starr, and Rushika Fernandopulle. *Uninsured in America: Life and Death in the Land of Opportunity*. Berkeley, CA: University of California Press, 2006. Based on interviews with 120 uninsured individuals and numerous policymakers and medical providers, this book looks at the growing ranks of Americans lacking health insurance and the problems with the nation's current health care policies.

Zuberi, Dan. *Differences That Matter: Social Policy and the Working Poor in the United States and Canada*. Ithaca, NY: Cornell University Press, 2006. The author takes a comparative approach to the lives of the working poor in the United States and Canada, looking at vital issues ranging from health care to labor policies.

MEDIA RESOURCES

A Day's Work, A Day's Pay——This 2002 documentary by Jonathan Skurnik and Kathy Leichter follows three welfare recipients in New York City from 1997 to 2000. When forced to work at city jobs for well below the prevailing wage and not allowed to go to school, the three fight for programs that will help them get better jobs.

America's Promise: Who's Entitled to What?——A four-part series that examines the current state of welfare.

An Inconvenient Truth——A 2006 Paramount Classics production of former vice president Al Gore's Oscar-winning documentary on global warming and actions that can be taken in response to this challenge.

Sicko——Michael Moore's 2007 effort, which takes on the U.S. health care industry. Rather than focusing on the plight of the uninsured, Moore addresses the troubles of those who have been denied coverage by their insurance companies. In his most outrageous stunt ever, Moore assembles a group of 9/11 rescue workers who have been denied proper care and takes them to Cuba, where the government, perfectly aware of the propaganda implications, is more than happy to arrange for their treatment.

Traffic——A 2001 film, starring Michael Douglas and Benicio Del Toro, that offers compelling insights into the consequences of failed drug policies. (*Authors' note*: Be aware that this film contains material of a violent and sexual nature that may be offensive.)

Young Criminals, Adult Punishment——An ABC program that examines the issue of whether the harsh sentences given out to adult criminals, including capital punishment, should also be applied to young violent offenders.

ONLINE RESOURCES

Department of Energy, Energy Information Agency compiles every possible statistic on energy use, mining, drilling for oil, etc. www.eia.gov.

Environmental Protection Agency implements the federal regulations regarding air and water pollution. Its Web site documents current programs and gives valuable information about many environmental topics: www.epa.gov

Institute for Research on Poverty offers information on poverty in the United States and the latest research on this topic: www.ssc.wisc.edu/irp

National Governors Association bipartisan organization of the nation's governors that promotes visionary state leadership, shares best practices, and speaks with a unified voice on national policy, such as the current status of welfare reform: www.nga.org

U.S. Census Bureau reports current statistics on poverty in the United States: www.census.gov/hhes/www/poverty.html

16 Economic Policy

Scott Olson/Getty Images

President Barack Obama greets workers at the Master Lock plant in Milwaukee, Wisconsin in February, 2012. He cited the company for bringing one hundred jobs back from China to the United States.

aplia

LEARNING OUTCOMES

After reading this chapter, students will be able to:

■ **LO1** Explain how the financial crisis that began in 2008 has affected a range of national and state policies and how it is having a long-term impact on the lives of citizens.

■ **LO2** Define fiscal and monetary policy, and explain the tools used by the institutions of the national government to shape economic policy.

■ **LO3** Discuss the annual deficit and the total national debt, and explain the impact of these two concepts on American life and policies.

■ **LO4** Define entitlement programs, and describe how these programs are related to economic policies.

■ **LO5** Describe the role of the Federal Reserve Bank and its Board of Governors in influencing the economy.

What If...

THE FEDERAL GOVERNMENT WERE REQUIRED TO BALANCE ITS BUDGET?

BACKGROUND

Except for the wartime periods of the Civil War and World War II, the U.S. government has normally run a very low budget deficit. Of course, up until the Great Depression, the number of government spending programs was very low. From the end of World War II until the present, the national government has operated at a deficit most of the time, although there was a surplus in 1998–2001. However, all states are required by their constitutions to balance their budgets. Let's assume that an amendment requiring a balanced budget is added to the U.S. Constitution. Initially, the two possible ways to balance the federal budget would be to raise taxes and increase user fees or to reduce the amount of federal government spending. Alternatively, a combination of these two actions could be undertaken.

INCREASED TAXES

On the revenue side of the equation, one way to balance the budget is to increase taxes on individuals and corporations. If the government increased taxes on individuals, then the tax rates paid by the middle class would have to rise significantly. Why? The reason is simple: The middle class is the source of most federal tax revenues. The rich and the superrich are currently required to pay a higher tax rate than the middle class, although certain provisions in the tax code may allow them to pay less. Even raising taxes on the rich to 90 percent or more would not balance the federal budget. Thus, taxes would need to be increased among all income groups to raise significantly larger revenues. Middle-class Americans would see their taxes go up rather dramatically. Another way to increase tax revenues is, of course, to strengthen economic growth. The more people who are working for good wages, the more tax money is collected at every level of government.

Taxes on corporations could also be increased significantly. This might raise more revenue in the short run, but in a global economy, American corporations might decide to move even more of their operations to countries with more advantageous tax structures. This would deprive the government of revenue and Americans of jobs.. In addition, increased taxes on corporations will reduce dividends to stockholders, many of whom depend on that income for their own needs. Finally, increasing taxes on corporations may cause them to raise the cost of their products to make up that revenue.

It would also be possible to increase user fees for all federal government services, perhaps to keep them more in line with the actual costs of the federal government. The fees to visit national parks would likely be raised, as one example.

REDUCED FEDERAL GOVERNMENT SPENDING

On the spending side of the equation, a reduction in federal government spending could mean dramatic changes for many Americans.

In theory, it seems easy to cut some federal programs, such as the pork-barrel spending projects so beloved by members of Congress. And, of course, particular federal departments are always the target of budget-cutters: the Department of Energy, the Departments of Education, Commerce, and Labor, and the Environmental Protection Agency are among those often mentioned as superfluous by critics. However, these are very small departments with relatively few employees and fairly small budgets.

Many budget critics have suggested that the budget be reduced "across the board" to the levels of the 1990s, for example. While this is a simple concept to understand, the strategy would require cuts to every budget within the federal government. Would citizens really want a 10 percent reduction in the pay of soldiers in Afghanistan or the reduction of residential mail service to four or five days a week? What about the increases in spending due to inflation or increased energy costs?

The deepest and most difficult cuts would need to come from entitlements, that is, programs that have promised certain benefits to certain classes of citizens, including Social Security to retired citizens, aid to disabled Americans, pensions to military veterans, and the Medicare health insurance program for seniors. Entitlement programs account for about half of the entire national budget, so these must be cut; but reducing benefits to Social Security recipients or veterans is politically impossible.

THE UPSIDE OF BALANCING THE BUDGET

Although balancing the federal budget every year would be an extremely difficult and painful process, in the long run it could be a healthy practice. For one thing, the government would not need to sell bonds to foreign countries such as China to fund its debt. In fact, a reduction in debt would improve the nation's budget status because less interest would need to be paid on the public debt, freeing up those funds for other important programs. However, actually getting to a balanced budget has proved difficult for all modern nations.

FOR CRITICAL ANALYSIS

1. *Of the two methods of reducing the deficit to zero—raising taxes or decreasing government spending—which method do you believe would be perceived by most people to be less painful? Why?*

2. *How can the federal government spend more than it receives every year, whereas a family would have a hard time doing the same thing year in and year out?*

THE ECONOMIC RECESSION of 2007–2008 is a prime example of how the good intentions of governments, corporations, and citizens can go terribly wrong. The housing bubble and the economic collapse that followed it exemplify the ways in which the government impacts the economy through laws, regulations, well-intentioned policies, bureaucratic decision making, and sheer politics.

The recession was caused by a complex of political and economic decisions that came together as a perfect storm of unintended consequences. For the past two decades or so, the federal government had tried to widen opportunities for all Americans to buy homes. Some of the policies enacted were intended to end discrimination by banks against minority or poor borrowers. Other policies aimed to encourage home building and home buying in order to stimulate economic growth. Americans responded by building more homes and condominiums, buying more residences, furnishing them, and borrowing the money to do so. At the same time, two other developments occurred—one in the world of high finance and investment and the other in the global economy. Assuring lawmakers that they would be responsible and that the crash of 1929 could never happen again, banks pressured Congress to repeal the **Glass-Steagall Act** of 1933, which forbade banks from partnering with investment firms and limited their ability to speculate in stocks and bonds. In 1998, the Congress obliged. This change in banking regulation encouraged banks, insurance companies, and all kinds of investment companies to create and invest in forms of credit never before imagined. The riskiest turned out to be "bundles" of home mortgages, a substantial proportion of which were given to people who could not afford the monthly payments when interest rates rose. The second development was the globalization of this market: Banks and investment firms in the United States traded such bundles to their equals in Europe and throughout the world and they, in turn, invested in U.S. mortgages. When interest rates rose and unemployment began to increase, many homeowners could no longer pay back their loans, and those mortgages went into default. The investment instruments collapsed because there were not enough reserves to cover the losses, and in October 2008, Lehman Brothers, a stalwart Wall Street investment company, failed entirely. Quickly, the Bush administration and the Congress realized that other huge banks would fail and a worldwide economic collapse would follow. The first rescue package was passed before the election of 2008. After the Obama administration came into office a stimulus bill titled the American Recovery and Reinvestment Act of 2009 was passed, the government assumed control of General Motors and the Chrysler Corporation, and other banks were put under strict federal control until their debts were paid. However, the recession's effects lingered for four years, with unemployment rising to 9 percent. Congress passed and the president signed numerous pieces of legislation to try to encourage growth, but after the 2010 midterm election, the debate over how to do this became even more intensely political. In this chapter we examine the ways in which the federal government influences the economy and the political differences that underlie all economic policies.

Prosperity Is the Goal

Everyone wants prosperity for the American people. Democrats and Republicans agree that the goals of the nation's economic policy should be low unemployment, low rates of **inflation** (rapidly rising prices and wages), strong growth in the gross domestic product, and increasing incomes for American families.

■ **Learning Outcome 1:**
Explain how the financial crisis that began in 2008 has affected a range of national and state policies and how it is having a long-term impact on the lives of citizens.

Glass-Steagall Act
A law passed in 1933 to regulate the banking industry which prohibited banks from engaging in speculative investments or becoming investment houses.

Inflation
A sustained rise in the general price level of goods and services.

Recession
Two or more successive quarters in which the economy shrinks instead of grows.

Furthermore, the economy should be stable—not growing too fast and not slowing down too much.

Like any economy that is fundamentally capitalist, the U.S. economy experiences ups and downs. Good times—booms—are followed by lean years. If a slowdown is so severe that the economy actually shrinks for six or more months, it is called a **recession**. Recessions bring increased unemployment, stagnation in household income, and, sometimes, the permanent loss of jobs. Because the consequences of recessions affect individuals directly and therefore influence the voter's view of how well the economy is doing, poor economic conditions disadvantage the sitting president, the president's party, and its members in Congress. Political science research has made clear the importance of economic perceptions to American voters: Ronald Reagan's campaign in 1980 asked voters, "Are you better off today than you were four years ago?" and the voters replied by denying Jimmy Carter a second term. Incumbent presidents and members of Congress try frequently to influence the economy, although they may not have as much power as the voters believe they do.

Unemployment

Unemployment
The inability of those who are in the labor force to find a job; defined as the total number of those actively looking for a job but unable to find one.

Full Employment
An arbitrary level of unemployment that corresponds to "normal" friction in the labor market. In 1986, a 6.5 percent rate of unemployment was considered full employment. Today, it is assumed to be around 5 percent.

One political goal of any administration is to keep the rate of unemployment down. **Unemployment** is the inability of those who are in the workforce to find jobs. Individuals may become unemployed for several reasons. Some people enter the labor force for the first time and have to look for a job. Some people are fired or laid off and have to look for a job. Others just want to change occupations. **Full employment** is defined as a level of unemployment that makes allowances for normal movement between jobs. The Full Employment Act of 1947 set that level at 4 percent. During recessions, unemployment rises well above the full employment level. For example, during the business slowdown of 2001–2002, following the 9/11 attack, the rate of unemployment increased from 4 to 6.5 percent. By late 2005, the unemployment rate fell to less than 5 percent and stayed there until spring 2008, when it reached 5.5 percent. As the financial crisis of 2008 grew in size and scope, the stock markets plunged and business activity throughout the world weakened. The average unemployment rate for 2009 was more than 9 percent, and the rate did not begin to decrease until late 2011.

Unemployment Becomes an Issue. For much of American history, unemployment was not a problem that the federal government was expected to address. In the early years of the republic, most people would have thought that the national government could not do much about unemployment. By the late 1800s, many people had come to believe that as a matter of principle, the government should not fight unemployment. This belief followed from an economic philosophy that was dominant in those years—*laissez-faire economics*. (You learned about the concept of *laissez-faire*—French for "let it be"—in Chapter 1.) Advocates of this philosophy believed then (and now) that government intervention in the economy is almost always misguided and likely to lead to negative results. A second barrier to any federal government action against unemployment was the doctrine of *dual federalism*, described in Chapter 3. Under this theory, only state governments had the right to address a problem such as unemployment. For the most part, however, ups and downs in the economy were seen as a consequence of the capitalist system and not a matter for government.

The Great Depression of the 1930s ended popular support for dual federalism and *laissez-faire* economics. As the Depression took hold, unemployment initially exceeded 25 percent. Relatively high rates of unemployment—more than 15 percent—persisted for more than 10 years. One of the methods that the Roosevelt administration adopted to combat the effects of the Depression was direct government employment of those without jobs through such programs as the Civilian Conservation Corps and the Works Progress Administration.

Since the passage of the Social Security Act of 1935, the federal government has also offered a program of unemployment insurance. The program is the government's single most important source of assistance to the jobless. Not all unemployed workers are eligible, however. In fact, only about one-third of the unemployed receive benefits. Benefits are not available to employees who quit their jobs voluntarily or are fired for cause (for example, constantly showing up late for work). They are also not paid to workers who are entering the labor force for the first time but cannot find a job. Unemployment insurance is a joint state-federal program, and the state portion is paid for by a tax on employers. In 2009 and 2010, facing the highest unemployment rate in decades, Congress extended benefits to 99 weeks from the standard 26 weeks for some of the most affected states and pumped more federal dollars into the fund.

Measuring Unemployment. Estimates of the number of unemployed are prepared by the U.S. Department of Labor. The Bureau of the Census also generates estimates using survey research data. Figure 16–1 shows how unemployment has fluctuated over the course of American history.

Critics of the published unemployment rate calculated by the federal government believe that it fails to reflect the true numbers of discouraged workers and "hidden unemployed." Although no exact definition of discouraged workers or a way to measure them exists, the Department of Labor defines them as people who have dropped out of the labor force and are no longer looking for a job because they believe that the job market has little to offer them.

> **did you know?**
>
> The median household income in the United States is about $64,000, but the median National Basketball Association player's salary is about $5 million.

Figure 16–1 ▶ More than a Century of Unemployment

Unemployment reached lows during World Wars I and II of less than 2 percent and a high during the Great Depression of more than 25 percent.

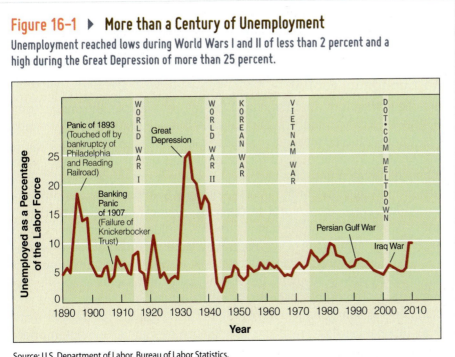

Source: U.S. Department of Labor, Bureau of Labor Statistics.

Inflation

Rising prices, or inflation, can also be a serious political problem for any sitting administration, especially if prices are rising quickly. As previously stated, inflation is a sustained upward movement in the average level of prices. Inflation can also be defined as a decline in the purchasing power of money over time. The government measures inflation using the **Consumer Price Index (CPI)**. The Bureau of Labor Statistics (BLS) identifies a market basket of goods and services purchased by the typical consumer and regularly checks the price of that basket. Over a period of many years, inflation can add up. For example, today's dollar is worth (very roughly) one-twentieth of what a dollar was worth a century ago. While interest rates overall have not increased in the past four years, the increase in the price of oil and, thus, all transportation costs, has begun to drive up all consumer goods. Inflation is always a concern for the nation; however, the economic downturn of 2007–2012 has seen very low or negative inflation, mostly due to very low interest rates. Economists worry that a quick recovery would lead to increased inflation. To keep this in perspective, consider the interest rate on a home mortgage. In 2012, rates were extremely low, with some mortgages available at 4 percent. In 1979, the interest rate on a mortgage was more than 12 percent.

> **Consumer Price Index (CPI)**
> A measure of the change in price over time of a specific group of goods and services used by the average household.

The Business Cycle

As noted above, the capitalist economy normally passes through times of expansion and contraction known as the **business cycle**. This means that economies expand in times of growth, creating more jobs and producing more goods and services. The businesses may overexpand and consumers may overspend, and at some point, the economy will cease to grow and begin a period of recession.

An extremely severe recession is called a *depression*, as in the example of the Great Depression. By 1933, actual output was 35 percent below the nation's productive capacity. Between 1929 and 1932, more than 5,000 banks (one out of every five) failed, and their customers' deposits vanished. Compared to that catastrophe, most modern recessions have been less severe, in part because the American government and all governments of democratic countries have tried to reduce the effects of recession on their people and encourage growth by every means available.

> **Business Cycle**
> A term that describes fluctuations in the nation's economic activity including periods of economic expansion and contraction

The Economic Toolkit

When the first signs of a recession appear—say, for example, the unemployment rate ticks up a notch and the stock market falls—the president of the United States turns to the administration's economic team for advice. The president's team consists of the secretary of the Treasury, the Council of Economic Advisers, the budget director, and possibly, the U.S. trade representative. In the Obama administration, Secretary of the Treasury Timothy Geithner led the effort to meet the economic crisis. The Council of Economic Advisers reviews all the data and suggests strategies to the president and the president's political team. At the same time, the members of Congress, well aware of the political consequences of an economic downturn, begin to investigate ways to stimulate the economy through **fiscal policy**, meaning the use of taxing and spending to effect economic activity. The other major player in this situation is the chairman of the Federal Reserve Bank, Ben Bernanke. As we will discuss later in this chapter, the Federal Reserve has its own sphere of influence over the economy—**monetary policy**, or the regulation of changes in the supply of money to influence interest rates, credit availability, employment, and the rate of inflation.

> **Fiscal Policy**
> The federal government's use of taxation and spending policies to affect overall business activity.
>
> **Monetary Policy**
> The utilization of changes in the amount of money in circulation to alter credit markets, employment, and the rate of inflation.

The strategies chosen by the president and the Congress are both economic and political. Whether the sitting administration is Republican or Democratic, presidential team members want to be successful and retain their offices. However, the choices they make to influence economic strategy will likely depend on their political party, their ideological framework—that is, liberal, moderate, or conservative—and which economic theory they believe will generate economic growth.

Economic Theory Guides Policy

Since the Great Depression of the 1930s, the federal government has grown much larger and taken a much larger role in the economy. At the same time, citizens have come to expect that the government will seek to stabilize the economy so that ordinary people can improve their standard of living. A number of theories argue which strategies are most likely to cushion or reduce the impact of an economic downturn and restart the economy on the road to growth and stability. Policymakers base their recommendations for government intervention and legislation on one or more of these economic theories.

Laissez-Faire Economics

As mentioned earlier, the founders of the American republic did not envision a government that regulated most aspects of the economy. Indeed, John Locke, the theorist of natural rights, used the example of the small farmer who grows enough for himself and then trades or sells for what he needs as the example of a free man who needs little government. Articulated by Adam Smith in *The Wealth of Nations*[1] in 1776, *laissez-faire* theory believes that the actions of each individual person and business will best be regulated through free competition. If an individual prices his or her merchandise too high, it will not sell. A competitor will force the price down. This theory sees government regulation and intervention in the marketplace as mistaken: Such interference will upset the free market and will eventually be costly to the economy. Although most modern political leaders support some government regulation of the economy, such as keeping unsafe drugs from the market and prohibiting child labor, libertarians and some conservatives often express the view that the government has no business taking over a company such as General Motors or regulating the compensation of bank executives.

Keynesian Economic Theory

The British economist John Maynard Keynes (1883–1946) originated the school of thought called **Keynesian economics**, which supports the use of government spending and taxing to help stabilize the economy. (*Keynesian* is pronounced kayn-zee-un.) Keynes believed that a need for government intervention in the economy existed in part because, after falling into a recession or depression, a modern economy may become trapped in an ongoing state of less than full employment.

Keynes developed his fiscal policy theories during the Great Depression. He believed that the forces of supply and demand operated too slowly on their own in such a serious recession. Unemployment meant people had less to spend, and because they could not buy things, more businesses failed, creating additional unemployment. It was a vicious cycle. Keynes's idea was simple: In such circumstances, the

Keynesian Economics
A school of economic thought that tends to favor active federal government policymaking to stabilize economy-wide fluctuations, usually by implementing discretionary fiscal policy.

---

1. Adam Smith, *The Wealth of Nations. 1776,* available in many editions.

government should step in and undertake the spending that is needed to return the economy to a more normal state.[2] Since World War II, Keynesian theory has supported the policies of many presidents, Republican and Democratic. The stimulus bill passed in the first months of the Obama administration is a clear example of the government providing funding for infrastructure projects such as roads and bridges to increase employment in the construction sector. The bill also provided billions in assistance to state and local governments so that they did not need to lay off teachers and police and fire personnel.

Supply-Side Economics

When Ronald Reagan took office in 1981, the country was suffering both a recession and extremely high inflation or rising prices. High inflation hurts the ordinary citizen by requiring her to spend a great deal more for gas, groceries, clothing, and energy at a time when wages and salaries are not rising at the same rate. The Reagan administration embraced an economic theory called "supply-side economics," which holds that the answer to inflation is to reduce government regulation and cut taxes so that businesses will produce more products. The oversupply of production and services will drive down prices through competition. Meanwhile, the theory holds that this increasing growth will produce more government revenue through the increased taxes generated by businesses and individuals. Supply-side economics shares a great deal with *laissez-faire* economics in terms of reducing government's role in the economy, but it maintains the government safety net programs. Although Reagan's strategy did curb inflation and stimulate growth, it did not produce the amount of tax revenue that had been predicted, and his administration incurred large budget deficits, as have many others.

While *laissez-faire* economics generally has little role for government in its strategies, both Keynesian theory and supply-side economics see the president, the Congress, and the Federal Reserve System using the tools of fiscal and monetary policy to influence the economy. Democrats tend to subscribe to the "percolate-up" view of the economy, meaning that the government should aid economically disadvantaged citizens, and the improvement of their household income will eventually produce more wealth for everyone. Republicans are said to believe in the "trickle-down" approach to economic policy, meaning that with less government and fewer taxes, the owners of businesses and the rich will do well, and their wealth will generate jobs and income for the less well off. The tools of fiscal policy and monetary policy described below can be used to support either approach.

Fiscal Policy

■ **Learning Outcome 2:**
Define fiscal and monetary policy, and explain the tools used by the institutions of the national government to shape economic policy.

To smooth out the ups and downs of the national economy, the government has several policy options. One is to change the level of taxes or government spending. The other possibility involves influencing interest rates and the money side of the economy. We will examine taxing and spending, or fiscal policy, first. Fiscal policy is the domain of Congress and the president. Generally, the incumbent president and the president's party are blamed by the public for an economic downturn. However, any real changes in fiscal policy are likely to be initiated by the president and then passed by the Congress. In general, these are Keynesian policies.

---

2. Robert Skidelsky, *John Maynard Keynes: The Economist as Savior, 1920–1937: A Biography* (New York: Penguin USA, 1994).

Government Borrowing

Government spending can be financed in several ways, including by increasing taxes and borrowing. For government spending to have the effect Keynes wanted, however, it was essential that it be financed by borrowing, not taxes. In other words, the government should run a **budget deficit:** It should spend more than it receives. If government spending during a recession is funded by increased taxes, those higher taxes will make the impact of the recession even worse for citizens. During a recession, the government borrows money through debt to spend more on stimulus projects and unemployment. This spending should make up for the reduced spending by businesses and consumers.

Budget Deficit
Government expenditures that exceed receipts.

Discretionary Fiscal Policy

Keynes originally developed his fiscal theories as a way of lifting an economy out of a major disaster such as the Great Depression. Beginning with the presidency of John F. Kennedy (served 1961–1963), however, policymakers have attempted to use Keynesian methods to fine-tune the economy. This is discretionary fiscal policy (*discretionary* means left to the judgment or discretion of a policymaker). Kennedy was the first American president to explicitly adopt Keynesian economics. In 1963, during a mild business slowdown, Kennedy proposed a tax cut. Congress did not actually pass the necessary legislation until early 1964, after Kennedy had been assassinated. The economy picked up—and the tax cut was a success.

President George W. Bush pushed his tax cuts of 2001 and 2003 as a method of stimulating the economy to halt the economic slowdown of those years. During 2006, Bush repeatedly pointed out that since his tax cuts had been put into effect, the economy had grown so much that federal tax revenues had increased more than anticipated, thereby reducing the federal budget deficit below the level predicted. As Bush approached the end of his second term, he noted that his proposed 2008 budget submitted to Congress would reduce the budget deficit and produce a surplus by 2012. However, the financial crisis of 2008 intervened and the government increased its deficit spending at a rapid rate, producing the likelihood of unbalanced budgets for the next decade.

The Obama administration has consistently followed a Keynesian path as it has attempted to speed the economic recovery. Extending unemployment benefits, extending the food stamp program, sending stimulus monies to state and local governments, reducing the Social Security tax paid by workers on their earnings—all of these efforts qualify as discretionary fiscal policy. The economic recovery has been very slow, however, and the Republican opposition has claimed that increasing government regulation at the same time and creating programs that are very expensive to implement have instead hampered the recovery.

did you know?

An aide to President George W. Bush gave this succinct description of federal priorities: "It helps to think of the government as an insurance company with an army."

The Thorny Problem of Timing

Attempts to fine-tune the economy face a timing problem. Have you ever turned on the hot water to take a shower, had cold water come out, and then, in frustration, given the hot water faucet another turn and gotten scalded? What happened was a lag between the time you turned on the faucet and the time the hot water actually reached the showerhead. Policymakers concerned with short-run stabilization face similar difficulties.

It takes a while to collect and assimilate economic data. There will be a time lag between the recognition of an economic problem and the implementation of policy to solve it. Getting Congress to act can easily take a year or two. Finally, after

An unemployed worker applies for benefits at the Los Angeles, California, Job Service office. Many construction workers lost their jobs as the subprime mortgage crisis continued.

AP Photo/Damian Dovarganes

fiscal policy is enacted, it takes time for the policy to act on the economy. Because fiscal policy time lags are long and variable, a policy designed to combat a recession may not produce results until the economy is already out of the recession.

Deficit Spending and the Public Debt

U.S. Treasury Bond
Debt issued by the federal government.

The federal government typically borrows by selling **U.S. Treasury bonds**. The sale of these federal government bonds to corporations, private individuals, pension plans, and foreign governments, businesses, and individuals adds to this nation's *public debt*. In the last few years, foreigners have come to own about 50 percent of the U.S. public debt. Thirty years ago, the share of the U.S. public debt held by foreigners was only 15 percent.

The Public Debt in Perspective

Did you know that the federal government has accumulated more than $15 trillion in debt, or $49,999 for every man, woman, and child in the United States? Does that scare you? It certainly would if you thought that we had to pay it back tomorrow, but we do not.[3] As long as the U.S. government can borrow money from its citizens and others and make the interest payments, there is no need to pay off the entire debt.

There are two types of public debt—gross and net. The **gross public debt** includes all federal government interagency borrowings, which really do not matter. This is similar to your taking an IOU ("I owe you") out of your left pocket and putting it into your right pocket. What is important is the **net public debt**— the public debt that does not include interagency borrowing. Figure 16–2 shows the net public debt of the federal government since 1940.

This figure does not consider two very important variables: inflation and increases in population. A better way to examine the relative importance of the public debt is to compare it to the **gross domestic product (GDP)**, as is done in Figure 16–3. (The *gross domestic product* is the dollar value of all final goods and services produced in a one-year period.) There you see that the public debt reached

Learning Outcome 3:
Discuss the annual deficit and the total national debt, and explain the impact of these two concepts on American life and policies.

Gross Public Debt
The net public debt plus interagency borrowings within the government.

Net Public Debt
The accumulation of all past federal government deficits; the total amount owed by the federal government to individuals, businesses, and foreigners.

Gross Domestic Product (GDP)
The dollar value of all final goods and services produced in a one-year period.

3. If you would like to see the minute-by-minute calculation of the debt as well as other real-time government statistics, go to: www.usdebtclock.org.

Figure 16–2 ▶ Net Public Debt of the Federal Government

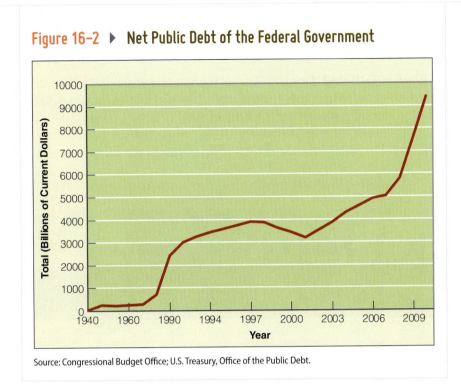

Source: Congressional Budget Office; U.S. Treasury, Office of the Public Debt.

its peak during World War II and fell thereafter. Since about 1960, the net public debt as a percentage of GDP has ranged between 30 and 50 percent; however, the recent spending to combat the financial crisis and new federal programs such as the health care reform bill suggest that our future net public debt could reach a "normal level" of more than 70 percent of the GDP. In the summer of 2011, the national debt actually equaled 100 percent of the GDP for a short time. Sustained high levels of national debt can be managed but, in another economic crisis, a high

Figure 16–3 ▶ Net Public Debt as a Percentage of the Gross Domestic Product

During World War II, the net public debt as a percentage of GDP grew dramatically. It fell thereafter but rose again from 1975 to 1995. The percentage fell after 1995, began to rise again after the events of September 11, 2001, and then fell again, starting in 2004.

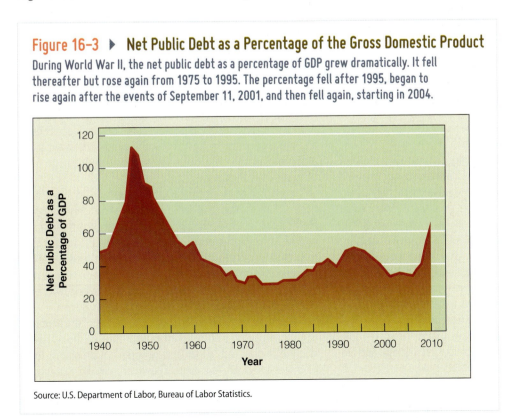

Source: U.S. Department of Labor, Bureau of Labor Statistics.

level could lead to a weakening of the nation's credit in the world and serious economic problems such as those being experienced in Greece, Spain, and Portugal.

Are We Always in Debt? From 1960 until the last few years of the 20th century, the federal government spent more than it received in all but two years. Some observers consider these ongoing budget deficits to be the negative result of Keynesian policies. Others argue that the deficits actually result from the abuse of Keynesianism. Politicians have been more than happy to run budget deficits in

Politics with a Purpose

MANAGING OUR MONEY

iStockphoto.com/kyoshino iStockphoto.com/Daniel Laflor

Have you ever worried that your paycheck will not cover your monthly expenses, about how you are going to pay your bills, or about repaying your college loans? Most of us experience these concerns at one time or another and are forced to find solutions. Maybe we become more fiscally disciplined, give up texting, reduce our cable TV bill, and stick to a budget. Maybe we take a second job to increase revenue. Maybe one of your motivations for going to college is economic security. Similarly, many Americans have become concerned over the rising national debt and wonder if it can be sustained.

The national debt is so huge and the budget is so complicated that it is tempting to just ignore the problem or to refuse to deal with the numbers. But a number of advocacy groups and organizations provide research, blogs, reports, and easy tools to allow anyone to understand the revenue, spending, and debt problems faced by the United States in the current era.

For instance, the Concord Coalition (www.concordcoalition.org) is a bipartisan organization advocating a "generationally responsible fiscal policy." As an advocacy group (see Chapter 7), its mission involves creating public awareness and lobbying government for reduced spending, fiscal discipline, and balanced budgets. The Concord Coalition encourages public awareness of government spending and advocates for a federal budget that will eventually be balanced, arguing that the nation cannot sustain large budget deficits forever. Its budget simulation is intended to involve college students in setting priorities for the budget and trying out ways to reduce the national debt. If you would like to try a version of this simulation, go to www.concordcoalition.org/penny-game and set the budget priorities yourself. Get 100 pennies and distribute them in the way you prefer to maintain our national programs and sustain benefits to those who need them. Don't forget to pay the interest on the national debt.

The Concord Coalition's conservative approach is not the only possibility: There is a wide range of opinions on this topic and are many respectable think tanks and advocacy groups that study the problem. Another organization, the Committee for a Responsible Federal Budget, takes a bipartisan, moderate approach. The committee's board includes Erskine Bowles and Alan Simpson, two former members of Congress who cochaired the Simpson-Bowles Commission on the budget in 2009, as well as former Democratic and Republican budget directors, members of Congress, and Treasury secretaries. The Web site for the center includes a wide range of documents, research reports, and blogs about the budget. If you go to its "Stabilize the Debt" online exercise, you can try various solutions to stabilize the nation debt and begin to reduce it in the future (www.crfb.org/stabilizethedebt/). In another interactive exercise, you can compare the myriad plans for reducing the deficit, ranging from the Obama administration's plan to those of very conservative policymakers, and look at how each would impact the activities of government ranging from the military to Medicare.

For a different point of view, visit the Web site of the Center on Budget and Policy Priorities, a nonpartisan advocacy group with a more progressive stance (www.cbpp.org). The center analyzes a great variety of budget data on its Web site and provides excellent research reports on income, taxation, the federal deficit, and policy priorities. To see an array of easy-to-understand charts that summarize income, taxes, and spending priorities, go to its blog: www.offthechartsblog.org.

As a candidate, Senator Obama's platform included fiscal reform, citing the debt and deficit spending as barriers to "responsible fiscal policies." However, upon becoming president, he was faced with an extraordinary economic crisis and needed to use the fiscal tools of stimulus spending and aid to the unemployed to stabilize the economy. From the beginning, his administration has called for an increase in taxes on the wealthiest Americans, to help reduce the budget deficit and to add more fairness to the tax system.

Clearly, all of these advocacy groups and all of the members of Congress and the administration want the country to have a stable economy with sustainable government programs. These Web sites reflect different approaches to accomplishing this goal.

recessions, but they have often refused to implement the other side of Keynes's recommendations—to run a budget surplus during boom times.

In 1993, however, President Bill Clinton (served 1993–2001) obtained a tax increase as the nation emerged from a mild recession. For the first time, the federal government implemented the more painful side of Keynesianism. In any event, between the tax increase and the dot-com boom, the United States had a budget surplus each year from 1998 to 2002. Some commentators predicted that we would be running federal government surpluses for years to come. All of those projections went by the wayside because of several events.

One event was the dot-com bust, followed by the 2001–2002 recession, which was caused by the terrorist attacks on September 11, 2001. These events lowered not only the rate of growth of the economy but also the federal government's tax receipts. Another event was a series of large tax cuts passed by Congress in 2001 and 2003 at the urging of President George W. Bush. Finally, the government had to pay for the war in Iraq in 2003 and the occupation of that country thereafter, which turned out to be far more costly than ever imagined. The federal budget deficit for 2007 was close to $270 billion. Then the financial crisis of 2008 occurred, plunging the nation into recession and unemployment. Congress reacted by creating bailout funds and passing stimulus spending, thus increasing the debt. The Obama administration, faced with a long-lasting recession and high levels of unemployment, continued to increase government spending on benefits and on program in hopes the economy would improve. After the Republicans took control of the House of Representatives in 2011, legislative gridlock prevented the passage of either tax increases or serious spending reductions.

What will happen if our public debt remains at such a high level? The aftermath of the recession of 2008 will linger for a long time. As you read in the Politics with a Purpose box in this chapter, many nonpartisan advocacy groups are also considering our future economic situation. First, it will be necessary to stabilize the debt, meaning to reach a level of taxation and revenue that keeps the debt from increasing. At the same time, the president and Congress should be making a long-term plan to slowly reduce the debt to more manageable levels. The two greatest fears are that inflation and interest rates could begin to rise, thus increasing our payments on the debt, and that another deep recession would occur, requiring the government to step in and issue more debt to sustain the economy.

The Politics of Taxes

Another major tool to influence economic activity in the United States is taxation. Your state may have changed its tax structure, perhaps by reducing corporate taxes to entice companies to bring their jobs and businesses there. Or, faced with a looming budget deficit, your state may have increased income or business taxes. Taxes and tax exclusions and deductions are used by virtually every government body in the United States to give incentives to some sectors of the economy and to discourage other sectors.

Americans pay a variety of different taxes. At the federal level, the income tax is levied on most sources of income. Social Security and Medicare taxes are assessed on wages and salaries. There is an income tax for corporations, and an estate tax is collected from property left behind by those who have died. Excise taxes are paid on gasoline and on certain goods and services at federal, state, and local levels. State and local governments also assess taxes on income, sales, and land. Altogether, the value of all taxes collected by the federal government and by state and local governments is about 30 percent of GDP. This is a substantial sum, but it is less than many other countries collect.

Federal Income Tax Rates

Individuals and businesses pay taxes based on tax rates. Not all of your income is taxed at the same rate. The first few dollars you make are not taxed at all. The highest rate is imposed on the "last" dollar you make. This highest rate is the *marginal* tax rate. Table 16–1 shows the 2012 marginal tax rates for individuals and married couples. The higher the tax rate, the greater the public's reaction to that tax rate. If the highest tax rate you pay on the income you make is 15 percent, then any method you can use to reduce your taxable income by $1 saves you 15¢ in tax liabilities that you owe the federal government. Individuals paying a 15 percent rate have a relatively small incentive to avoid paying taxes, but consider the individuals who faced a marginal tax rate of 94 percent in the 1940s. They had a tremendous incentive to find legal ways to reduce their taxable incomes. For every $1 of income that was somehow deemed nontaxable, these taxpayers would reduce their tax liability by 94¢.

Loopholes and Lowered Taxes

Loophole
A legal method by which individuals and businesses are allowed to reduce the tax liabilities owed to the government.

Individuals and corporations facing high tax rates will adjust their earning and spending behavior to reduce their taxes. They will also make concerted attempts to get Congress to add **loopholes** to the tax law that allow them to reduce their taxable incomes. When Congress imposed very high tax rates on high incomes, it also provided for more loopholes than it does today. For example, special provisions enabled investors in oil and gas wells to reduce their taxable incomes.

In recent years, a great deal of attention has been paid to the billionaire Warren Buffet, CEO of Berkshire Hathaway Inc. Buffet told President Obama that it seemed unfair that he paid a lower rate of taxation than his secretary. How could that possibly occur when Buffet earns hundreds of millions of dollars each year? While Buffet's secretary earns a six-figure income and thus pays nearly 30 percent per year in federal taxes, Buffet's income comes from dividends on the stock he holds in the corporation. The tax rate on dividend income is 15 percent. Like many other very wealthy individuals, his tax rate is about the same as the

---

Table 16–1 ▶ **Marginal Tax Rates for Single Persons and Married Couples (2010)**

SINGLE PERSONS		MARRIED COUPLES FILING JOINTLY	
MARGINAL TAX BRACKET	MARGINAL TAX RATE	MARGINAL TAX BRACKET	MARGINAL TAX RATE
$0–$8,700	10%	$0–$17,400	10%
$8,700–$35,350 plus	15%	$17,400–$70,700	15%
$35,350–$85,650	25%	$70,700–$142,700	25%
$85,650–$178,650	28%	$142,700–$217,450	28%
$178,650–$388,350	33%	$217,450–$388,350	33%
$388,350 plus	35%	$388,350	35%

average blue-collar household's. Thus, Buffet and the president question whether such a tax rate is fair. Many billionaires agree, and the Obama administration and the Democrats have made a number of efforts to pass a "Buffet rule" raising taxes on the wealthiest Americans to at least 30 percent, regardless of the source of their income.

In 2001, President George W. Bush fulfilled a campaign pledge by persuading Congress to enact new legislation lowering tax rates for a period of several years. In 2003, rates were lowered again, retroactive to January 2003; these rates are reflected in Table 16–1. As a result of other changes in the new tax laws, the U.S. tax code became even more complicated than it was before. President Bush tried several times to make his tax rate cuts permanent, but after the Democrats took over Congress in 2006, that became an impossibility. President Obama has announced his intention to let the tax cuts for the wealthiest taxpayers expire, while keeping some of the cuts for middle-income and lower-income Americans.

President Obama confers with Warren Buffet, billionaire business leader. Buffet supported Mr. Obama's efforts to raise taxes on the very wealthy.

Progressive and Regressive Taxation. As Table 16–1 shows, the greater your income, the higher the marginal tax rate. Persons with large incomes pay a larger share of their income in income tax. A tax system in which rates go up with income is called a **progressive tax** system. The federal income tax is clearly progressive.

The income tax is not the only tax you must pay. For example, the federal Social Security tax is levied on wage and salary income at a flat rate of 6.2 percent. (Employers pay another 6.2 percent, making the total effective rate 12.4 percent.) In 2012, however, there was no Social Security tax on wages and salaries in excess of $110,100. (This threshold changes from year to year.) And, due to legislation passed to stimulate the economy, the percentage of wages paid to Social Security is temporarily reduced to 4.2 percent for employees. Persons with very high salaries therefore pay no Social Security tax on much of their wages. In addition, the tax is not levied on investment income (including capital gains, rents, some royalties, interest, dividends, or profits from a business). The wealthy receive a much greater share of their income from these sources than do the poor. As a result, the wealthy pay a much smaller portion of their income in Social Security taxes than do the working poor. As Table 16-2 shows, the Social Security tax is therefore a **regressive tax**.

Progressive Tax
A tax that rises in percentage terms as incomes rise.

Regressive Tax
A tax that falls in percentage terms as incomes rise.

Who Pays? The question of whether the tax system should be progressive—and if so, to what degree—is subject to vigorous political debate. Democrats in general and liberals in particular favor a tax system that is significantly progressive. Republicans and conservatives are more likely to prefer a tax

Table 16–2 ▶ Progressive versus Regressive Taxes

PROGRESSIVE TAXES	REGRESSIVE TAXES
Federal income tax	Social Security tax
State income taxes	Medicare tax
Federal corporate income tax	State sales taxes
Estate tax	Local real estate taxes

Figure 16–4 ▶ Federal Income Tax Burden by Income Group, 2012

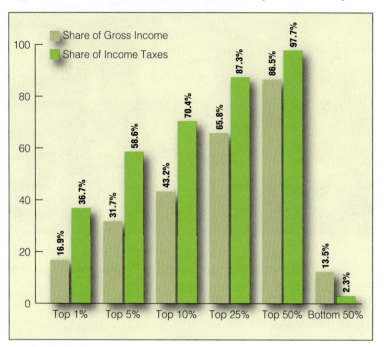

Source: The Tax Foundation, 2011. www.taxfoundation.org.

system that is proportional or even regressive. For example, President Bush's tax cuts made the federal system somewhat less progressive, largely because they significantly reduced taxes on nonsalary income. If you look at Figure 16–4, you will see that almost half of all American households pay no federal income taxes at all, while the top 25 percent of all households pay more than 87 percent of all income taxes. Thus, the federal income tax is progressive, but the tax burden overall is much more complicated.

Overall, what kind of tax system do we have? The various taxes Americans pay pull in different directions. The Medicare tax, as applied to wages and salaries, is entirely flat—that is, neither progressive nor regressive. Because it is not levied on investment income, however, it is regressive overall. Sales taxes are regressive because the wealthy spend a relatively smaller portion of their income on items subject to the sales tax. Table 16–2 lists the characteristics of major taxes. Add everything up, and the tax system as a whole is probably slightly progressive.[4]

■ **Learning Outcome 4:**
Define entitlement programs, and describe how these programs are related to economic policies.

Entitlements: The Big Budget Item

As we have seen, the overall tax structure of the United States is tilted toward a progressive tax system, in which wealthier taxpayers pay a higher percentage of the taxes. Many lower income workers, however, pay a huge share of the regressive taxes. Consider a long-haul independent trucker and the regressive federal and state taxes that he pays on diesel fuel. Republicans and Democrats argue vehemently about the tax system. Many Democrats, including President Obama, believe that wealthy Americans are not paying their fair share.

However, lower income workers in the United States are far more dependent on the programs that have been created to sustain incomes and provide for retirement income. These programs include Social Security, Medicare, unemployment insurance, disability insurance, and medical care and pensions for veterans. All of these programs have broad support from the public and are widely seen as "promises" made to all Americans.

These programs are known as "entitlements" because they are guaranteed to the respective recipients and because they are not approved through the regular budget process. They are automatically paid and automatically adjusted for cost of living increases. All of these programs together amount to almost

---

4. Brian Roach, "GDAE Working Paper No. 03–10: Progressive and Regressive Taxation in the United States: Who's Really Paying (and Not Paying) Their Fair Share?" (Medford, MA: Global Development and Environment Institute, Tufts University, 2003). This paper is online at www.ase.tufts.edu/gdae/Pubs/wp/03-10-Tax_Incidence.pdf.

Figure 16–5 ▶ Federal Income and Outlays for Fiscal Year 2009

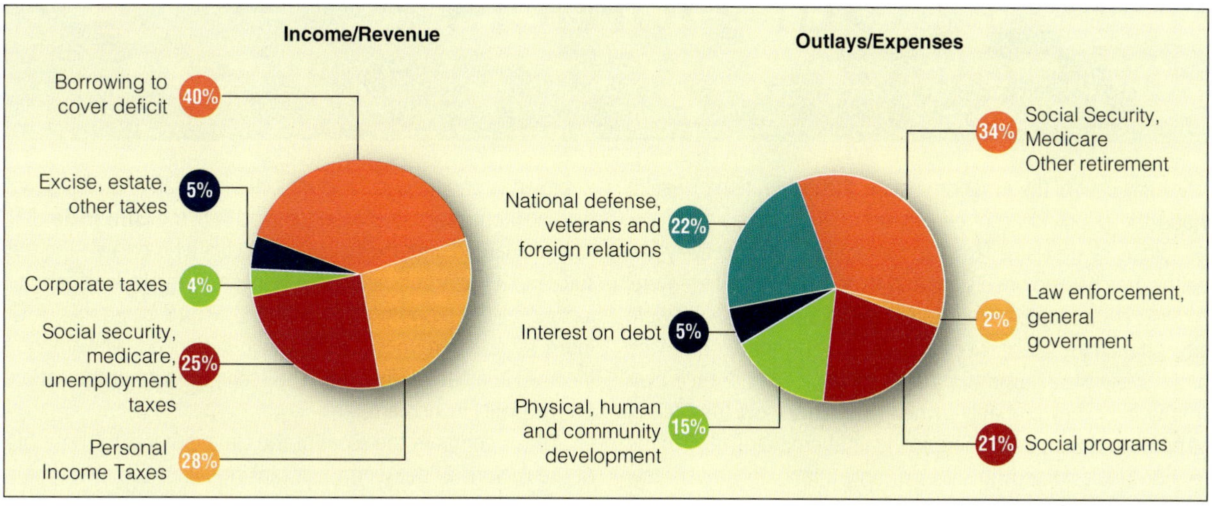

Income/Revenue

- Borrowing to cover deficit **40%**
- Excise, estate, other taxes **5%**
- Corporate taxes **4%**
- Social security, medicare, unemployment taxes **25%**
- Personal Income Taxes **28%**

Outlays/Expenses

- Social Security, Medicare Other retirement **34%**
- Law enforcement, general government **2%**
- Social programs **21%**
- Physical, human and community development **15%**
- Interest on debt **5%**
- National defense, veterans and foreign relations **22%**

Source: Internal Revenue Service. Citizen's Guide to the Federal Budget www.irs.gov.

two-thirds of the federal budget. As shown in Figure 16–5, the taxes collected by the federal government in 2011 amounted to only about two-thirds of what it spent. Therefore, in order to pay these entitlement benefits in the future, we can either eliminate all other federal programs, including defense, or these programs will need to be revised in some way.

Social Security and Medicare

Closely related to the question of taxes in the United States is the viability of the Social Security system. Social Security taxes came into existence when the Federal Insurance Contribution Act (FICA) was passed in 1935. Social Security was established as a means of guaranteeing a minimum level of pension benefits to all persons. Today, many people regard Social Security as a kind of "social compact"—a national promise to successive generations that they will receive support in their old age.

To pay for Social Security, as of 2012, a 6.2 percent tax rate is imposed on each employee's wages up to a maximum of $110,200, although a temporary reduction of 2 percent has been passed to help workers during the recession. Employers must pay in ("contribute") an equal percentage. In addition, a combined employer/employee 2.9 percent tax rate is assessed for Medicare on all wage income, with no upper limit. (Medicare is a federal program, begun in 1965, that pays hospital and physicians' bills for persons age 65 and older. See Chapters 7 and 15.)

Social Security Is Not a Pension Fund

One of the problems with the Social Security system is that people who pay into Social Security think that they are actually paying into a fund, perhaps with their name on it. This is what you do when you pay into a private pension plan. It is not

Beyond Our Borders
HOW UNEQUAL IS AMERICAN SOCIETY?

In the early days of the American nation, the distribution of wealth among the people was, of course, unequal. Relatively few large landholders owned large farms and plantations, and relatively few wealthy merchants owned ships and traded in goods. There were, of course, craftspeople, lawyers, and other professionals who were better off than the rest of the citizens. Most of the free people of the United States were farmers or craftspeople working in their own communities. They probably owned their land, tools, furnishings, and products, but nothing more. In the southern states, most of the free individuals owned no slaves or only a few. Only a very few wealthy individuals owned a large number of enslaved persons. Wealth, at the levels known today, was unheard of. As the United States developed economically, many individuals did well enough to form a strong middle class.

Many commentators and economists believe that the United States today is a much less equal society than it was only a few decades ago. Due to the recession, the median income today for American families, in inflation-adjusted dollars, is less than it was 10 years ago. Many families have lost their savings or their homes due to unemployment. On the other hand, the wealthiest Americans have continued to increase their worth due both to their ability to keep their tax bills relatively low and their ability to earn more wealth through investments, even during a recession. Technological developments have created many billionaires: Among those are Mark Zuckerberg, founder of Facebook, and the creators of Instagram, a smart-phone app that was sold to Facebook for more than $1 billion only two years after it entered the business scene. While it is true that the wealthiest 1 percent of Americans pay a proportionately large share of income taxes, about 38 percent of all taxes paid, their average income is 18 times the median, and their wealth is growing.

How does the United States compare to the rest of the world in terms of this income inequality? We all know large numbers of truly impoverished individuals exist in many nations, but is overall income equality more likely in those nations? The Organization for Economic Cooperation and Development (OECD), an international agency dedicated to improving conditions in all nations, publishes an annual report on income inequality based on a statistic called "the **Gini Index**." The index is named after the Italian statistician who created the measure, and it measures the degree of income equality in a nation by looking at the proportions in different income categories. A Gini Index score of zero means that there is perfect equality among all incomes in a nation. The larger the score, the further the nation is from equality in incomes.

If we compare the score of the United States to those of all of the nations of the world, our ranking is not too low: In 2011, the United States ranked 43rd in income inequality among the 104 nations for which data were available.[a] The nation with the most inequality was Namibia and that with the least was Sweden. Most of the nations with higher levels of income inequality were underdeveloped nations that may have a small group of very wealthy households and a multitude of very poor citizens. However, the OECD also published the index only for its own members, mostly developed Western nations. Among this group of 22 nations, the United States is the third most unequal nation, although its ranking is close to those of Israel, the United Kingdom, Italy, and Australia. Mexico has the highest Gini score in this group and Denmark the lowest.

The issue of income inequality in America has also been the subject of the research of two French economists who currently teach in the United States.[b] Both Emmanuel Saez and Thomas Piketty claim to love the United States and admire greatly the free and entrepreneurial nature of the country. What they find in their research is that the United States is quickly becoming more unequal than at any time in its history. Piketty says, "The United States is getting accustomed to a completely crazy level of inequality."[c] He continues, "The United States is becoming like Old Europe, which is very strange in historical perspective…[it]used to be very egalitarian, not just in spirit but in actuality." The work of these two economists, according to the *New York Times*, is being read in Washington, D.C., as well as in economic journals.

Gini Index
A statistical measure of the distribution of income in a nation. A higher number indicates more inequality in incomes within a nation.

[a]Organization for Economic Development and Cooperation, "Divided We Stand: Why Inequality Keeps Rising," 2011.
[b]Emmanuel Saez and Thomas Piketty, cited in "Income Distribution in the U.S.," www.wealthandwant.com/income/income_distribution.html.
[c]Annie Lowry, "French Duo See (Well) Past Tax Rise for the Richest," *New York Times*, April 17, 2012, A1.

FOR CRITICAL ANALYSIS

1. *Do you think that Americans think of the nation as one of income equality or one of great inequality?*

2. *What kinds of actions could be taken to increase income equality in the United States?*

the case, however, with the federal Social Security system, which is basically a pay-as-you-go transfer system in which those who are working are paying benefits to those who are retired.

Currently, the number of people who are working relative to the number of people who are retiring is declining. Therefore, for the system to continue as it is structured now, those who work will have to pay more in Social Security taxes to fund the benefits of those who retire. Projections of retirees suggest that by 2030, there will only be two employed workers for every Social Security recipient and, unless there are changes in the system, they will pay a very large part of their paychecks to the federal government to fund the retirement benefits of other Americans.

The growing number of people claiming the Social Security retirement benefit may pose less of a problem than the ballooning cost of Medicare. In the first place, an older population will require greater expenditures on medical care. In addition, however, medical expenditures *per person* are also increasing rapidly. Given continuing advances in medical science, Americans may logically wish to devote an ever greater share of the national income to medical care. This choice puts serious pressure on federal and state budgets, however, because a large part of the nation's medical bill is funded by the government. With the adoption of the new health care reform legislation and the increase in the number of Americans who will likely be covered either by Medicaid or a state-sponsored program, it is very difficult to predict the future expenditures for these three programs. It is possible that the three combined will total more than 20 percent of the nation's gross domestic product, with a corresponding increase in taxes to fund the benefits provided.

What Will It Take to Salvage Social Security?

These facts illustrate why efforts to reform Social Security and Medicare have begun to dominate the nation's public agenda. What remains to be seen is how the government ultimately will resolve the problem. What, if anything, might be done?

Raise Taxes. One option is to raise the combined Social Security and Medicare payroll tax rate. A 2.2 percentage point hike in the payroll tax rate, to an overall rate of 16.8 percent, would yield an $80 billion annual increase in contributions. Such a tax increase would keep current taxes above current benefits until 2020, after which the system would again technically be in deficit. Another option is to eliminate the current cap on the level of wages to which the Social Security payroll tax is applied; this measure would also generate about $80 billion per year in additional tax revenues. Nevertheless, even a combined policy of eliminating the wage cap and implementing a 2.2 percentage point tax increase would not keep tax collections above benefit payments over the long run.

Consider Other Options. Proposals are also on the table to increase the age of full benefit eligibility, perhaps to as high as 70. In addition, many experts believe that increases in immigration offer the best hope of dealing with the tax burdens and workforce shrinkage of the future. Unless Congress changes the existing immigration system to permit the admission of a much larger number of working-age immigrants with useful skills, however, immigration is unlikely to fully relieve the pressure building due to our aging population.

Privatize Social Security. Still another proposal calls for partially privatizing the Social Security system in the hope of increasing the rate of return on individuals' retirement contributions. Privatization would allow workers to invest a specified portion of their Social Security payroll taxes in the stock market and possibly in other investment options, such as bonds or real estate. If the economy is good and the stock market grows, then the increased value of these investments would provide more benefits to individuals when they retire. President George W. Bush's proposal that Social Security be partially privatized in this way drew significant support from younger Americans but total opposition from most members of Congress and the AARP.

Several groups oppose the concept of partial privatization. These groups fear that the diversion of Social Security funds into individual investment portfolios could jeopardize the welfare of future retirees, who could be at the mercy of the volatile stock market. Opponents of partial privatization point out that such a plan might mean that workers would have to pay for two systems for many years—the benefits for today's retirees cannot simply be abolished.

Obviously, solving the problem of increasing Social Security and Medicare obligations is a task for future presidents and Congresses. While it will be a controversial issue, most Americans are aware that it must be solved.

Monetary Policy

One of the major tools for stabilizing the economy, as noted earlier in the chapter, is *monetary policy*—controlling the rate of growth of the money supply. This policy is the domain of the **Federal Reserve System**, also known simply as **the Fed**. The Fed is the most important regulatory agency in the U.S. monetary system.

The Fed performs several important functions. Perhaps the Fed's most important ability is that it is able to regulate the amount of money in circulation, which can be defined loosely as checkable account balances and currency. The Fed also provides a system for transferring checks from one bank to another. In addition, it holds reserves deposited by most of the nation's banks, savings and loan associations, savings banks, and credit unions.

Organization of the Federal Reserve System

A board of governors manages the Fed. This board consists of seven full-time members appointed by the president with the approval of the Senate. The 12 Federal Reserve district banks have 25 branches. The most important unit within the Fed is the **Federal Open Market Committee**. This is the body that actually determines the future growth of the money supply and other important economy-wide financial variables. This committee is composed of the members of the Board of Governors, the president of the New York Federal Reserve Bank, and presidents of four other Federal Reserve banks, rotated periodically.

The Board of Governors of the Federal Reserve System is independent. The president can attempt to influence the board, and Congress can threaten to merge the Fed into the Treasury Department, but as long as the Fed retains its independence, its chairperson and governors can do what they please. Hence, any talk about "the president's monetary policy" or "Congress's monetary policy" is inaccurate. To be sure, the Fed has, on occasion, yielded to presidential pressure, and for a while the Fed's chairperson had to observe a congressional

■ Learning Outcome 5:

Describe the role of the Federal Reserve Bank and its Board of Governors in influencing the economy.

Federal Reserve System (the Fed)
The most important regulatory agency in the U.S. monetary system. The Fed performs several important functions such as regulating the amount of money in circulation and providing a system for transferring checks from one bank to another.

Federal Open Market Committee
The most important body within the Federal Reserve System. The Federal Open Market Committee decides how monetary policy should be carried out.

resolution requiring him to report monetary targets over each six-month period. But now more than ever before, the Fed remains one of the truly independent sources of economic power in the government.[5]

Loose and Tight Monetary Policies

The Federal Reserve System seeks to stabilize nationwide economic activity by controlling the amount of money in circulation. Changing the amount of money in circulation is a major aspect of monetary policy. You may have read a news report in which a business executive complained that money is "too tight." This means that the Federal Reserve has increased the interest rate that it charges banks, making it more expensive to borrow money. You may have run across a story about an economist who has warned that money is "too loose." In this instance, the Fed has lowered the interest rate in hopes of stimulating borrowing by businesses and individuals. The businesses will then use that money to invest in new equipment and create new jobs. When the interest rate is lowered, it is easier, theoretically, for businesses and individuals to borrow money, thus stimulating the economy.

How do the actions of the Federal Reserve affect the life of the ordinary citizen? The answer to that question depends on what kinds of loans an individual might have. If you have a 30-year fixed-rate mortgage on your home, for example, nothing the Fed does will change the interest rate of your loan. However, if you have a low adjustable-rate mortgage, the rate will increase as the Fed increases the prime rate. This happened to millions of homeowners and investors between 2005 and 2007, with payments increasing so much that many homes were foreclosed on by the banks. Generally, interest on credit cards remains high no matter what the Fed does. It is important to remember that the Fed is more interested in stimulating business activity than it is in stimulating individuals to buy more homes.[6]

Chairman of the Federal Reserve Board Ben Bernanke testifies on the state of the economy before the House Financial Services Committee in 2010.

KEVIN DIETSCH/UPI/Newscom

5. Axel Krause, "The American Federal Reserve System: Functioning and Accountability" (Paris, France: Groupement d'études et de recherches, Notre Europe, Research and Policy Paper No. 7, 1999). This paper is available online at www.notre-europe.eu/en/axes.
6. For data on Federal Reserve prime rates and mortgage rates, see the Historical Data series from the Federal Reserve Board of Governors at www.federalreserve.gov.

Time Lags for Monetary Policy

You learned earlier that policymakers who implement fiscal policy—the manipulation of budget deficits and the tax system—experience problems with time lags. The Fed faces similar problems when it implements monetary policy. Sometimes accurate information about the economy is not available for months. Once the state of the economy is known, time may elapse before any policy can be put into effect. Still, the time lag when implementing monetary policy is usually much shorter than the lag involved in fiscal policy. The Federal Open Market Committee meets eight times per year and can put a policy into effect relatively quickly. Nevertheless, a change in the money supply may not have an effect for several months.

In the early years of the 21st century, the United States experienced a housing boom and a rapid increase in the values of homes and condominiums. Credit was easily available, and the Fed, seeking to keep the economy growing, kept rates low. Then rates began to increase to stop inflation, and many millions of Americans found themselves with mortgages that were becoming more expensive. The housing market declined, values of homes declined, and people ended up owning homes that were not worth their mortgage value. Some people lost their homes, whereas others simply let the bank take over their investments. As the crisis continued, Congress struggled to create legislation to help homeowners who found themselves in this situation. Some analysts criticized the Fed for lowering interest rates too far and stimulating borrowing, whereas other commentators blamed the lending institutions and financial houses that borrowed funds against overvalued mortgages. The mortgage crisis was not limited to the United States: European banks shared the banking crisis.[7]

Monetary versus Fiscal Policy

A tight monetary policy is effective as a way of taming inflation. (Some would argue that, ultimately, a tight monetary policy is the only way that inflation can be fought.) If interest rates go high enough, people *will* stop borrowing. How effective, though, is a **loose monetary policy** at ending a recession?

Under normal conditions, a loose monetary policy will spur growth in economic activity. At any given time, many businesses are considering whether to borrow. If interest rates are low, they are more likely to do so. Low interest rates also reduce the cost of new houses or cars and encourage consumers to spend.

Recall from earlier in the chapter, however, that in a serious recession like that of 2008–2009, businesses may not want to borrow, no matter how low the interest rate falls. Likewise, consumers who fear losing their jobs or homes are not going to make major purchases either. In these circumstances, monetary policy is ineffective. Using monetary policy in this situation has been described as "pushing on a string," because the government has no power to *make* people borrow

Globalization and World Trade

Most of the consumer electronic goods you purchase—flat-screen television sets, portable media players, cell phones, and digital cameras—are made in other countries. Many of the raw materials used in manufacturing in this

Tight Monetary Policy
Monetary policy that makes credit expensive in an effort to slow the economy.

Loose Monetary Policy
Monetary policy that makes credit inexpensive and abundant, possibly leading to inflation.

---

7. "CSI: Credit Crunch," *The Economist*, October 18, 2007, www.economist.com/specialreports.

country are also purchased abroad. Globalization, which means worldwide distribution of production, marketing, and sales of goods and services, has made it possible for many of the corporations that are familiar to Americans such as Coca-Cola, Apple, and Procter & Gamble to sell their products worldwide, manufacture products in many different nations, and employ hundreds of thousands of people around the globe. When you go into a store to buy clothing, electronics, or furniture for your home, you do not usually think about where the item was manufactured or whose hands manufactured it.

Items appear in-store with English labels and the appropriate price tags and care labels you would expect to see if they were manufactured in the next county. However, they are likely to have been shipped to the United States in a container and comprised of parts manufactured in many different nations. Many "American-made" cars and trucks contain parts manufactured in Korea or Mexico or Canada.

While world trade has made our lives easier and products cheaper for consumers, it is a controversial topic. Since 1999, meetings of major trade bodies such as the World Trade Organization have been marked by large and sometimes violent demonstrations against globalization. Opponents of globalization often refer to "slave" wages in developing countries as a reason to restrict imports from those nations. Others argue that we should restrict imports from countries that do not enforce the same environmental standards as the United States. There are those who worry that the United States is no longer able to manufacture some products, such as computer monitors, and that this could endanger the nation in a time of war. Most vocal are those who see jobs lost, workers displaced, and towns in economic decline after a factory moves its production overseas. The United States, at one time, had flourishing furniture, textile, and leather industries. Most of those products are now made overseas.

Chinese workers assembling Apple products at a factory in Linghua in the Guangdong province of China. American groups charge Apple with unfair labor practices for such plants, and after an investigation, Apple announced plans to improve the conditions for its workers in China.

Imports and Exports

Imports are those goods (and services) that we purchase from outside the United States. Today, imports make up about 15 percent of the goods and services that we buy. Imports include everything from computers to cars to the petroleum that we refine for gasoline for our cars.

The United States not only imports goods and services from abroad, but also sells goods and services abroad, called **exports**. Exports include corn, soybeans, wheat, cars, airplanes, tractors, locomotives, and weapons. The United States exports about 13 percent of the GDP. Like our imports, our exports are a relatively small part of our economy compared with many other countries. In world trade, imports are paid for by exports. For a number of years, the United States has run a negative **balance of trade**, meaning the difference in value between our imports and our exports. In 2010, for example, the United States exported $1.3 trillion in goods and services while importing $1.9 trillion.

Imports
Goods and services produced outside a country but sold within its borders.

Exports
Goods and services produced domestically for sale abroad.

Balance of Trade
The difference between the value of a nation's exports of goods and the value of its imports of goods.

About $270 billion, or almost half of that trade deficit, was due to imports of petroleum from other nations.

The Impact of Import Restrictions on Exports

Economists point out that if we restrict the ability of the rest of the world to sell goods and services to us, then the rest of the world will not be able to purchase all of the goods and services that we want to sell to them. This argument runs contrary to the beliefs of people who want to restrict foreign competition to protect domestic jobs. Although it is certainly possible to preserve jobs in certain sectors of the economy by restricting foreign competition, there is evidence that import restrictions actually reduce the total number of jobs in the economy. Why? The reason is that ultimately such restrictions lead to a reduction in employment in export industries.

One of the best examples of how import restrictions raise prices to consumers has been in the automobile industry, where "voluntary" restrictions on Japanese car imports were in place for more than a decade. As Japanese cars gained in popularity in the 1980s, U.S. automakers and the United Automobile Workers lobbied for protection for their products. The United States and Japan entered into a "voluntary agreement" to reduce imports of Japanese cars from 1981 into the late 1990s. The result was more demand for Japanese cars than supply, and their prices went up. Domestic carmakers then increased their prices to match those of the imported cars. The estimated cost in one year to consumers was $6.5 billion, or $250,000 for each of the 26,000 American jobs saved. To become even more competitive, the major Japanese and Korean car companies now assemble cars in the United States, employing thousands of Americans in their plants.

Quotas and Tariffs. The U.S. government uses two key tools to restrict foreign trade: import quotas and tariffs. An **import quota** is a restriction imposed on the value or number of units of a particular good that can be brought into the United States. **Tariffs** are taxes specifically on imports. Tariffs can be set as a particular dollar amount per unit—say, 10¢ per pound—or as a percentage of the value of the imported commodity.

Free-Trade Areas and Common Markets. To lower or even eliminate restrictions on free trade among nations, some nations and groups of nations have created free-trade areas, sometimes called "common markets." The oldest and best-known common market is today called the European Union (EU). As of 2012, the EU consisted of 27 member nations. These countries have eliminated almost all restrictions on trade in both goods and services among themselves.

On our side of the Atlantic, the best-known free-trade zone consists of Canada, the United States, and Mexico. This free-trade zone was created by the North American Free Trade Agreement (NAFTA), approved by Congress in 1993. A more recent trade agreement is the Central American–Dominican Republic Free Trade Agreement (CAFTA-DR), which was signed into law by President George W. Bush in 2005. This agreement was formed by Costa Rica, the Dominican Republic, El Salvador, Guatemala, Honduras, Nicaragua, and the United States. CAFTA-DR was implemented on a rolling basis as the trade partners agreed to various provisions. By 2007, almost all of the nations were part of the agreement. The CAFTA agreement is still opposed by many members of American textile workers' unions, which see it as a threat to their jobs.

Import Quota
A restriction imposed on the value or number of units of a particular good that can be brought into a country. Foreign suppliers are unable to sell more than the amount specified in the import quota.

Tariffs
Taxes on imports.

© Sean Masterson/epa/Corbis

The World Trade Organization

Since 1997, the principal institution overseeing tariffs throughout the world has been the World Trade Organization (WTO). The goal of the nations that created the WTO was to lessen trade barriers throughout the world, so that all nations can benefit from freer international trade.

What the WTO Does. The WTO's many tasks include administering trade agreements, acting as a forum for trade negotiations, settling trade disputes, and reviewing national trade policies. Today, the WTO has more than 140 member nations, accounting for more than 97 percent of world trade. Another 30 countries are negotiating to obtain membership. Since the WTO came into being, it has settled many trade disputes between countries, sometimes involving the United States. For example, the United States took a case against the European Union to the WTO, charging that the EU imposed unfair tariffs on bananas from the Western Hemisphere. In that case the WTO ruled in the favor of the United States and its Central American partners. In other cases, the United States has not fared as well.

The WTO continues to work to lower trade barriers across the world, but the negotiations are slow and difficult. Some countries do not want to be flooded with cheap products from other nations that will destroy their own industries. Almost every nation and region works to protect its own agricultural sector and its small farmers. Even within the EU, the winemakers of France and Italy fight over trade policy.

Sending Work Overseas

For hundreds of years, nations have bought goods and services from abroad. Nonetheless, Americans have always perceived the purchase of services from other countries as a way of allowing those countries to "steal" American jobs.

Today, such activity is called either *offshoring* or *outsourcing*. During the 2008 presidential campaigns, outsourcing continued to be a hot topic, particularly as factories continued to close in the United States.

The latest data about outsourcing from the McKinsey Global Institute show that about 300,000 jobs per year are lost to overseas outsourcing firms. This may sound like a lot, but we must put that number in perspective: The U.S. labor market has close to 140 million workers! In any one month, more than 4 million U.S. residents start new jobs with new employers.

Outsourcing is here to stay, but the countries to which jobs are outsourced may change. India and China were the leading "villains" in the outsourcing debate a few years ago, but other countries may soon take their place. Why? Wages for outsourcing services are rising rapidly in both of those countries. This means that other low-wage countries, such as the Philippines and Indonesia, may become larger providers of services. When the real need is for customer service or highly skilled workers, companies such as Dell Computers have moved jobs home, a process that can be called "insourcing." Indeed, as a consequence of the worldwide recession and the lowering of some costs in the United States compared to other nations, the degree of insourcing has increased.

Facing the Future

Even though American economic growth has slowed over the last four years and millions of Americans have lost their jobs, the economy of the United States is still the strongest in the world, and the American dollar remains the currency of world trade. The people of the United States are envied for their freedom, for their access to education, and for their ability to innovate. These qualities will keep the United States a strong economy for many decades in the future.

However, the economic recession of 2007–2008 and the long economic slowdown that followed will have lasting effects on several generations of Americans. Students who graduated from college during this period may have had a harder time getting a job, paying off their student loans, and moving into their own homes. Many middle-class and middle-aged Americans either lost their homes or saw the value of their homes decline due to the mortgage crisis. Many baby boomers saw the value of their retirement savings greatly diminish and must plan to work longer before they can retire. These effects are not only personal: The debt incurred by the government to stimulate the economy and carry people through the recession will need to be repaid over time. To do this, political leaders must come together and work out plans for future sources of revenue and reform spending programs to keep the nation's economy strong.

You Can Make a Difference

HOW TO PLAN FOR YOUR FUTURE

If you are between 20 and 40 today, you may likely live to be 100 years old. How do you plan for a retirement that could last 40 years? Retirement is probably the last thing on your mind right now, with college loans and credit card debt to be paid. Today's college graduates kick off their careers more than $20,000 in debt, on average. College costs have soared; tuition has increased 28 percent for private colleges and 38 percent for public colleges in the past 10 years. Meanwhile, average earnings have not kept pace; men with a bachelor's degree today earn only 5.45 percent more than they did a decade ago, with women earning about 10.4 percent more.

Financial adviser working with a young couple to plan their future.

WHY SHOULD YOU CARE?

As the common saying goes, a comfortable retirement is based on a "three-legged stool" of Social Security, pensions, and savings. Several trends are working against today's college graduates. Unless reforms are enacted to shore up the system, Social Security benefits for future retirees, who are now in their twenties, could be cut by more than 20 percent and reduced even further as funding runs out. The traditional pension is disappearing from the workplace, with more employers favoring 401(k) plans that allow workers to save with pretax contributions. Today's young employees are expected to invest in these employer-sponsored retirement plans, which allow them to choose from a mix of investment options and may have matching employer contributions. You may also choose to save through individual retirement accounts (IRAs), stocks, bonds, mutual funds, and cash accounts such as bank savings accounts, certificates of deposit (CDs), and money market funds.

The point is that, when it comes to retirement, young workers are on their own and need a plan for future financial security.

WHAT CAN YOU DO?

Money compounds over time, so the earlier you invest, the greater your yield will be. Compound interest means that you earn interest on the original amount you've saved, and you continue to earn interest on the interest. The longer your money is invested, the more compounding can work for you. The earlier you start, the less you have to save to reach your goal. The longer you wait, the harder it is to make up for lost interest earnings.

For example, if you have a goal to save $100,000 and have 20 years to do so, at a conservative 4 percent rate of return, you would need to invest $3,272 per year; compounding will do the rest of the work for you. If you needed to save the same $100,000 and had only 10 years to do so, you would have to save more and take more risk. Even with an 8 percent rate of return, you would need to save $6,559 each year.

When you make saving money a part of your lifestyle at a young age, it will become a habit, not an option. As you begin your career, make sure you take advantage of all savings options at your disposal. Here are a few key questions you should ask any potential or current employer:

- Is there a traditional benefit pension plan?
- Is there a 401(k) or other contribution plan and, if so, are your contributions matched?
- How soon can you join the plan?
- What are the plan's vesting rules, and what happens to your money if you leave the company?

Your employer may have plans to help you save for your future, but the responsibility really lies with you. Financial experts agree on a few simple rules to keep you on track to reach your goals: avoid credit card debt, track expenses and spend within a monthly budget, maintain three to six months of savings equivalent to living expenses in a short-term account, contribute the maximum allowed to your 401(k), take advantage of any "free

(Continued)

(Continued)

money" company matches, and maintain savings beyond employer-sponsored plans, such as individual retirement accounts (IRAs).

Choose to Save, a program of the nonprofit Employee Benefit Research Institute and the American Savings Education Council, was created in 1996 to promote individual savings. Its Web site, www.choosetosave.org, provides free savings tools and information to help plan for financial security. Retirement planning worksheets, interactive financial calculators, DVDs, and other materials are available. You can also contact this organization at:

Choose to Save
1100 13th St. NW, Suite 878
Washington, DC 20005
202-659-0670

To monitor reforms in Social Security, contact:

Social Security Administration
Office of Public Inquiries
Windsor Park Bldg.
6401 Security Blvd.
Baltimore, MD 21235
800-772-1213
www.ssa.gov

REFERENCES
Aleksandra Todorova, "What Will Retirement Be Like for Gens X and Y?" *Smart Money*, May 15, 2007. www.smartmoney.com.
www.choosetosave.org.
www.ssa.gov.

Key Terms

balance of trade 529	fiscal policy 512	imports 529	progressive tax 521
budget deficit 515	full employment 510	inflation 509	recession 510
business cycle 512	Gini index 524	Keynesian economics 513	regressive tax 521
Consumer Price Index (CPI) 512	Glass-Steagall Act 509	loophole 520	tariffs 530
exports 529	gross domestic product (GDP) 516	loose monetary policy 528	tight monetary policy 528
Federal Open Market Committee 526	gross public debt 516	monetary policy 512	unemployment 510
Federal Reserve System (the Fed) 526	import quota 530	net public debt 516	U.S. Treasury bond 516

Chapter Summary

1. The recession of 2008 was caused by a multitude of factors including the relaxing of regulations on banks and investment houses, increasing numbers of mortgages in default, excessive speculation by some investors, and a housing bubble that saw the price of housing reach unsustainable levels. These factors came together as a recession began and caused a crisis in the economic system. The government's attempts to stop a worldwide depression and then to get the economy restarted included the TARP bailout fund, stimulus programs, extended unemployment benefits, reductions in Social Security taxes, and an increase in the national debt.

2. One of the most important policy goals of the federal government is to maintain economic growth without falling into either excessive unemployment or inflation (rising prices).

Inflation is commonly measured using the Consumer Price Index (CPI) published by the U.S. Bureau of Labor Statistics. The regular fluctuations in the economy are called business cycles. If the economy fails to grow for six months or more, the nation is experiencing a recession. The president, the Congress, and the Federal Reserve System all have tools to help stabilize the economy. Generally, the two major strategies are fiscal policy and monetary policy.

3. Fiscal policy is the use of taxes and spending to affect the overall economy. Economist John Maynard Keynes is credited with developing a theory under which the government should run budget deficits during recessions to stimulate the economy. Keynes also advocated budget surpluses in boom times, but political leaders have been reluctant to implement this side of the policy. Time lags in implementing fiscal policy can create serious difficulties.

4. The federal government has run a deficit in most years since the 1930s. The deficit is met by U.S. Treasury borrowing. This adds to the public debt of the U.S. government. Although the budget was temporarily in surplus from 1998 to 2002, deficits now seem likely for many years to come.

5. Monetary policy is controlled by the Federal Reserve System, or the Fed. Monetary policy involves changing the rate of growth of the money supply in an attempt to either stimulate or cool the economy. A loose monetary policy, in which more money is created, encourages economic growth. A tight monetary policy, in which less money is created, may be the only effective way of ending an inflationary spiral. Monetary policy may, however, be ineffectual in pulling the economy out of a severe recession—fiscal policy may be required.

6. The United States imports and exports goods as well as services from and to nations around the world. While economists of all persuasions strongly support world trade, the public is less enthusiastic. Restrictions on imports to protect jobs are often popular. Ultimately, however, imports are paid for by exports. Restricting imports restricts exports as well, with resulting loss of employment in export industries. Trade restrictions also increase the cost of the affected goods to consumers.

7. Groups of nations have established free-trade blocs to encourage trade among themselves. Examples include the European Union and the North American Free Trade Association (NAFTA). The World Trade Organization (WTO) is an international organization that oversees trade disputes and provides a forum for negotiations to reduce trade restrictions. The WTO has been a source of controversy in American politics.

8. The current account balance includes the balance of trade, which is limited to goods, and also the balance in the trade of services and other items. A possible problem for the future is the growing size of the U.S. current account deficit, which is funded by foreign investments in the United States.

9. The various types of taxes levied by the federal, state, and local governments have different goals and different impacts on citizens. U.S. taxes amount to about 30 percent of the gross domestic product, which is not particularly high by international standards. Individuals and corporations that pay taxes at the highest rates will try to pressure Congress into creating exemptions and tax loopholes, which allow high-income earners to reduce their taxable incomes. The federal income tax is progressive; that is, tax rates increase as income increases. Some other taxes, such as the Social Security tax and state sales taxes, are regressive—they take a larger share of the income of poorer people. As a whole, the tax system is slightly progressive.

10. One of the issues facing the United States is the viability of such entitlement programs as Social Security and Medicare. These programs are actually "promises" of benefits that must be paid to their respective recipients. As the number of people who are retired increases relative to the number of people who are working, those who are working may have to pay more for the benefits of those who retire. Proposed solutions to the problem include raising taxes, reducing benefits, allowing more immigration, and partially privatizing the Social Security system in hopes of obtaining higher rates of return on contributions.

Selected Print, Media, and Online Resources

PRINT RESOURCES

Bernstein, Michael. *A Splendid Exchange: How Trade Shaped the World.* New York: Atlantic Monthly Press, 2008. The author does a superb job of tracing the history of trade between nations and demonstrates how trade changed the way societies live.

Friedman, Milton, and Walter Heller. *Monetary versus Fiscal Policy.* New York: Norton, 1969. This is a classic presentation of the pros and cons of monetary and fiscal policy given by a noninterventionist (Friedman) and an advocate of federal government intervention in the economy (Heller).

Hira, Ron, and Anil Hira. *Outsourcing America: The True Cost of Shipping Jobs Overseas and What Can Be Done about It.* New York: AMACON, 2008. The authors look closely at the effects of outsourcing on the American economy and make suggestions to political leaders on how to bring jobs back to the United States.

Kotlikoff, Laurence J., and Scott Burns. *The Coming Generational Storm: What You Need to Know about America's Economic Future.* Cambridge, MA: MIT Press, 2004. The authors explain how an aging population will create a crisis in Social Security and Medicare funding. One possible flaw in the authors' argument is their unquestioning use of very long-term demographic projections, which are inherently uncertain.

Lewis, Michael. *The Big Short: Inside the Doomsday Machine.* New York: Norton, 2010. A former Wall Street investor and longtime financial reporter explains the derivative business and the reasons for the financial crisis.

Mortensen, Gretchen, with Joshua Rosner. *Reckless Endangerment: How Outsized Ambition, Greed and Corruption Led to Economic Armageddon.* New York: Times Books, 2011.

Phillips, Kevin. *Bad Money, Reckless Finance, Failed Politics, and the Global Crisis of American Capitalism.* New York: Viking, 2008. This best-selling author and former reporter for the *New York Times* investigates the deterioration of U.S. influence in the world and the causes of the subprime mortgage crisis.

Sorkin, Andrew Ross. *Too Big to Fail: How Washington and Wall Street Fought to Save the Financial System and Themselves.* New York: Viking, 2009. This absorbing book traces the day-to-day decisions that led to the government bailout of the major banks and averted a worldwide depression.

MEDIA RESOURCES

Alan Greenspan—This rather laudatory biography of the former chair of the Federal Reserve was released in 1999. Using Greenspan as an example, the film looks at factors that influence the world and national economies.

Enron: The Smartest Guys in the Room—The risk-taking culture of the Enron Corporation led to its fall and the trials of many of its executives, even though, as this 2005 documentary shows, they were the smartest guys in the room.

Frontline: The Warning—This 2010 *Frontline* program interviews many individuals from the 1980s onward to analyze decisions that led to the mortgage crisis of 2008.

Outsourced—A 2008 satiric comedy starring Josh Hamilton that examines the experience of an American manager who is sent to India to manage a call center.

ONLINE RESOURCES

Federal Reserve Bank of San Francisco keeps up with actions taken by the Federal Reserve: www.frbsf.org

Office for Management and Budget at the White House OMB'spredominant mission is to assist the president in overseeing the preparation of the federal budget and to supervise its administration in executive branch agencies. Visit OMB's Web site to view recent budgets and budget factsheets: www.whitehouse.gov/omb/budget/fy2009

Organization for Economic Cooperation and Development This multinational research group works to increase development and improve the quality of governance among all nations. Its statistical reports are a valuable source of comparative information. www.oecd.org

Social Security Administration delivers services through a nationwide network of over 1,400 offices. Information and services available online: www.ssa.gov

Tax Foundation The mission of the Tax Foundation is to educate taxpayers about sound tax policy and the size of the tax burden borne by Americans at all levels of government. Read about federal tax policy, including several studies on its impact, at the Web site of this nonpartisan educational organization: www.taxfoundation.org

World Trade Organization provides a set of rules and a negotiating forum for trade between nations at a global or near-global level: www.wto.org

17 Foreign Policy and National Security

© Everett Collection Inc/Alamy

An unmanned aerial vehicle or drone flies over the aircraft carrier, USS Carl Vinson.

LEARNING OUTCOMES

After reading this chapter, students will be able to:

■ **LO1** Define foreign policy, diplomacy, and national security policy, and explain how these policies shape the position of the United States in the world.

■ **LO2** Explain the role of the president in setting foreign policy and national security policy, and compare those powers to the powers of the Congress.

■ **LO3** Trace the evolution of United States foreign policy from isolationism to global leadership.

■ **LO4** Explain the origins of the war on terror and how it has influenced domestic policy and relations with other nations.

■ **LO5** Discuss the security and diplomatic challenges facing the United States today.

What If...

THE UNITED STATES DISPOSED OF ALL OF ITS NUCLEAR WEAPONS?

BACKGROUND

At the height of the Cold War, both the United States and the Soviet Union possessed more than 10,000 nuclear warheads ready for missile launch. In addition to land-based missiles, both nations had fleets of submarines fully armed with nuclear missiles that could be launched in a matter of minutes. As you will read in this chapter, efforts to limit these weapons began in the Nixon administration and, following the fall of the Soviet Union, several agreements have been signed by the United States and Russia to destroy significant numbers of these weapons.

WHAT IF THE UNITED STATES DISPOSED OF ALL OF ITS NUCLEAR WEAPONS?

According to the Arms Control Association, the United States still maintains about 5,500 active and reserve nuclear warheads and more than 4,000 "retired" warheads waiting for disposal in some form or another. The Soviet Union has about 5,500 active and reserve warheads and more than 5,000 "retired" warheads waiting for disposal. What would happen if the United States declared unilaterally that it was proceeding to dismantle and destroy all of its nuclear weapons? It is likely that the other major Western nations that have nuclear weapons—the United Kingdom and France— would do likewise. Russia, which has agreed to a mutual plan for destroying part of its arsenal, might agree, in principle, to do so as well. China, which is estimated to hold 250 warheads, may or may not agree to do so. The nations thought to have nuclear arms but which do not admit to it include Israel, India, and Pakistan. Iran, North Korea, and Syria are developing or have developed the capacity to make such weapons.

Why wouldn't China, Russia, India, Pakistan, and Israel be quick to dispose of their weapons and thus reduce the possibility of a nuclear war that would threaten the existence of all life on earth? The answer lies in each nation's perception of its most immediate threat. Israel fears attacks from neighboring Arab nations, attacks that would be devastating if a nuclear weapon were used. Pakistan, India, China, and Russia share common borders and also are concerned about being vulnerable to attack. The nations that are secretly developing weapons are doing so, supposedly, for self-defense and protection against their enemies. For these nations to dispose of their weapons requires the establishment of peace in their respective regions of the globe.

CAN WE EASILY DISPOSE OF THESE WEAPONS?

In 2010, the United States and Russia agreed to dispose of a large proportion of their stockpiles of nuclear material in addition to reducing their actual warheads. This agreement follows up on a 2000 agreement between the nations to get rid of 34 tons of plutonium each. That amount of plutonium is enough to make 17,000 bombs. Imagine how much other "spare" nuclear material is available around the world! The material has not been disposed of to date because other nations had not donated the promised $2 billion to help Russia fulfill its end of the bargain. Disposing of nuclear materials and dismantling nuclear warheads is an extremely expensive and difficult business.

Some of the ways that nuclear material can be destroyed include "burning" it as fuel for energy, diluting it with waste from nuclear power plants, destroying the material in accelerators, disposing of waste in deep holes bored in the earth, burying it beneath the seabed, or sending it to outer space. At the present time, any excess material from the destruction of nuclear warheads is "capsulized" in secure containers for permanent storage. Each method entails enormous problems involving the transport and secure storage of the material at every step. It would take several decades to actually dismantle and destroy all the material currently owned by the United States alone.

WHAT ARE THE POLITICS OF THIS PROPOSAL?

Some arms control advocates have been pushing for a nuclear-free world for many decades. In 2007, four prominent American statesmen including George Shultz and Henry Kissinger, both former secretaries of state, called for more effort to eliminate nuclear weapons globally. They noted that the "rogue" states and those worried about their own security might be convinced to give up their weapons if the United States and the world's strongest nations agreed to a multilateral approach that reduced the threat of nuclear weapons and provided a secure way to get rid of them together. Arms control advocates point to such an essay as the right idea but suggest that the American nuclear industry and the weapons industry are dragging their feet and slowing down the process of agreeing to the end of the nuclear era because it would destroy their businesses. Conservatives who believe that a strong military posture is essential to American foreign policy point to dangers in the world to the United States and support keeping some nuclear capability. All in all, there does not seem to be enough trust in the world to begin this process.

FOR CRITICAL ANALYSIS

1. *Do you think the United States would be safe from attack if it disposed of its nuclear arsenal?*

2. *How can the United States and Russia be sure that they have each disposed of all their weapons and that other nations have done so as well?*

ON ANY MORNING, Americans may see the world on their televisions or telephones. They might see President Obama meeting with G8 leaders in France, Pakistani villagers mourning the deaths of civilians killed by American drones, Egyptian students rallying for their new democracy in Tahrir Square, or American students held hostage in Iran. The world is probably "smaller" and more accessible to Americans than at any time in history although Americans are, in general, not better informed about events abroad.

Not only are world events more visible to Americans, but the world has become an even more complex place for the United States as a nation. It is not clear who might be the enemy or enemies of the United States or what role the United States should play in global affairs. At the end of World War II, the United States was the undisputed leader of the "free world" and a military and economic superpower. Today, the U.S. economy is deeply intertwined with the world economy, our military is not welcome in many nations, and our motives may be suspect to many of the world's freedom fighters. Yet, when a crisis occurs abroad, such as the uprising in Libya against Muammar Gaddafi, the nations of Europe often turn to the United States to lead the effort to support the rebels.

In this chapter, we examine the tools of foreign policy and national security policy in light of the many challenges facing the United States in the world today, including the threat of nuclear weapons, as discussed in the opening What if.

Facing the World: Foreign and Defense Policy

The United States is only one nation in a world with more than 200 independent countries, each of which has its own national goals and interests. What tools does our nation have to deal with the many challenges to its peace and prosperity? One tool is **foreign policy**. By this term, we mean both the goals the government wants to achieve in the world and the techniques and strategies used to achieve them. For example, if one national goal is to achieve stability in the Middle East and to encourage the formation of pro-American governments there, U.S. foreign policy in that area may be carried out through **diplomacy, economic aid, technical assistance**, or military intervention. Sometimes foreign policies are restricted to statements of goals or ideas, such as ending the HIV/AIDs epidemic in Africa, whereas at other times foreign policies are comprehensive efforts to achieve particular objectives, such as changing the regime in Iraq.

As you will read later in this chapter, in the United States, the **foreign policy process** usually originates with the president and those agencies that provide advice on foreign policy matters. Congressional action and national public debate often affect foreign policy formulation.

National Security Policy

As one aspect of overall foreign policy, **national security policy** is designed primarily to protect the independence and the political integrity of the United States. It concerns itself with the defense of the United States against actual or potential (real or imagined) enemies, domestic or foreign.

U.S. national security policy is based on determinations made by the Department of Defense, the Department of State, and many other federal agencies, including the National Security Council (NSC). The NSC acts as an advisory body to the president, but it has increasingly become a rival to the State Department in influencing the foreign policy process.

Foreign Policy
A nation's external goals and the techniques and strategies used to achieve them.

■ **Learning Outcome 1:**
Define foreign policy, diplomacy, and national security policy, and explain how these policies shape the position of the United States in the world.

Diplomacy
The process by which states carry on political relations with each other; settling conflicts among nations by peaceful means.

Economic Aid
Assistance to other nations in the form of grants, loans, or credits to buy the assisting nation's products.

Technical Assistance
The practice of sending experts in such areas as agriculture, engineering, or business to aid other nations.

Foreign Policy Process
The steps by which foreign policy goals are decided and acted on.

National Security Policy
Foreign and domestic policy designed to protect the nation's independence and political and economic integrity; policy concerned with the safety and defense of the nation.

© DOD Photo/Alamy

Secretary of State Hillary Clinton briefs the press after the April 2012 NATO meetings in Brussels. At that meeting, the member states agreed on the terms and conditions for the troop drawdown in Afghanistan.

Defense Policy
A subset of national security policies having to do with the U.S. armed forces.

Defense policy is a subset of national security policy. Generally, defense policy refers to the set of policies that direct the scale and size of the U.S. armed forces. Among the questions defense policymakers must consider is the number of major wars the United States should be prepared to fight simultaneously. Defense policy also considers the types of armed forces units we need to have, such as Rapid Defense Forces or Marine Expeditionary Forces, and the types of weaponry that should be developed and maintained for the nation's security. Defense policies are proposed by the leaders of the nation's military forces and the secretary of defense and are greatly influenced by congressional decision makers and by the companies that manufacture weapons, aircraft, and ships.

Diplomacy

Diplomacy is another aspect of foreign policy. Diplomacy includes all of a nation's external relationships, from routine diplomatic communications to summit meetings among heads of state. More specifically, diplomacy refers to the settling of disputes and conflicts among nations by peaceful methods. Diplomacy is the set of negotiating techniques by which a nation attempts to carry out its foreign policy.

Diplomacy can be carried out by individual nations, by groups of nations, or by international organizations. The United Nations often spearheads diplomatic actions in the interests of maintaining peace in certain areas. For example, in 2012, after Mohamed Morsi became president following Egypt's first democratic election in decades, Secretary of State Hillary Clinton traveled to Egypt to meet Mr. Morsi. Her conversations, as the leader of the American diplomatic team, conveyed American support for the new democratic regime, assurances of continued American assistance, and, most likely, concerns over any attempt to repress the Christian population of that predominantly Muslim nation.

Over the past 50 years, American presidents have often exercised diplomacy to encourage peace in the Middle East. The most successful example was President Jimmy Carter's efforts in 1978 to get Israel and Egypt to agree to a path to peaceful relations. The Camp David Accords were negotiated in the United States by the leaders of Egypt and Israel, with the direct mediation of President Carter. The two countries agreed to work toward peace between them, including mutual recognition.[1] Diplomacy can be successful only if the parties are willing to negotiate. Diplomacy clearly failed before the First Gulf War and perhaps before the second (some observers believe that the United States did not give diplomacy a long enough time to work to avoid the Second Gulf War). The United States continues to work with European allies to pressure Iran to reject the development of nuclear weapons and—through talks including Russia, China, Japan, South Korea, and North Korea—to persuade North Korea to end its weapons

---

1. To read the text of the Camp David Accords, go to: www.jimmycarterlibrary.org/documents/campdavid/accords/phtml.

development. In the summer of 2008, North Korea agreed to hand over its long-awaited nuclear program declaration (description of its program) to Chinese officials, and it blew up a cooling tower at one of its nuclear facilities to demonstrate its desire to move forward in ending its weapons program. However, in the spring of 2009, North Korea proceeded to test a nuclear weapon and has rejected all further talks.

Who Makes Foreign Policy?

■ **Learning Outcome 2:**
Explain the role of the president in setting foreign policy and national security policy, and compare those powers to the powers of the Congress.

Given the vast array of challenges in the world, developing a comprehensive U.S. foreign policy is a demanding task. Does this responsibility fall to the president, to Congress, or to both acting jointly? There is no easy answer to this question, because, as constitutional authority Edwin S. Corwin once observed, the U.S. Constitution created an "invitation to struggle" between the president and Congress for control over the foreign policy process. Let us look first at the powers given to the president by the Constitution.

Constitutional Powers of the President

The Constitution confers on the president broad powers that are either explicit or implied in key constitutional provisions. Article II vests the executive power of the government in the president. The presidential oath of office given in Article II, Section 1, requires that the president "solemnly swear" to "preserve, protect and defend the Constitution of the United States."

War Powers. In addition, and perhaps more importantly, Article II, Section 2, designates the president as "Commander in Chief of the Army and Navy of the United States." Starting with Abraham Lincoln, all presidents have interpreted this authority dynamically and broadly. Since George Washington's administration, the United States has been involved in at least 125 undeclared wars conducted under presidential authority. For example, in 1950, Harry Truman ordered U.S. armed forces in the Pacific to counter North Korea's invasion of South Korea. Dwight Eisenhower threatened China and North Korea with nuclear weapons if the Korean peace talks were not successfully concluded. Bill Clinton sent troops to Haiti and Bosnia. In 2001, George W. Bush authorized an attack against the al Qaeda terrorist network and the Taliban government in Afghanistan. In 2003, after receiving authorization to use force from Congress, Bush sent military forces to Iraq to destroy Saddam Hussein's government.

The president's "war powers" as commander in chief also include the ability to approve covert operations by the military or intelligence agencies and the use of surveillance technologies outside the United States. While a candidate, Barack Obama decried some of President Bush's decisions, including opening the prison at Guantánamo Bay and holding some prisoners abroad in unspecified locations. After a short time in office, the new president began using his war powers to make similar decisions. One of the most striking decisions made by President Obama was to increase the use of unmanned drones to assassinate the leadership of al Qaeda wherever they could be found. According to David Sanger,[2] the president personally approved each target for the drone strikes. Collateral civilian deaths from some of the strikes in Pakistan aggravated U.S.-Pakistan relations, as did the raid on Osama bin Laden's compound in May 2011. Again, the president

---

2. David E. Sanger, *Confront and Conceal: Obama's Secret Wars and Surprising Use of American Power* (New York: Crown, 2012).

President Obama, Vice President Biden, Secretary of State Hillary Clinton and other members of the national security team monitor the Navy SEAL raid on the home of Osama Bin Laden.

PETE SOUZA/Reuters/Landov

personally approved the raid, in which Navy Seal teams were helicoptered into a Pakistani city, attacked bin Laden's compound, killed the al Qaeda leader, and took the body to a Navy ship for burial at sea.

Treaties and Executive Agreements.   Article II, Section 2, of the Constitution also gives the president the power to make treaties, provided that two-thirds of the senators present concur. Presidents usually have been successful in getting treaties through the Senate. In addition to this formal treaty-making power, the president uses executive agreements (discussed in Chapter 12). Since World War II (1939–1945), executive agreements have accounted for almost 95 percent of the understandings reached between the United States and other nations.

Executive agreements have a long and important history. During World War II, Franklin Roosevelt reached several agreements with the Soviet Union and other

President Jimmy Carter greets the president of Panama after signing the treaty that returned control of the Panama Canal to the nation of Panama.

© CORBIS/Kightlinger

countries. One agreement with long-term results was concluded at Yalta in the Soviet Crimea. In other important agreements, presidents Eisenhower, Kennedy, and Johnson all promised support to the government of South Vietnam. In all, since 1946, more than 8,000 executive agreements with foreign countries have been made. There is no way to obtain an accurate count, because perhaps as many as several hundred of these agreements have been secret.

Other Constitutional Powers. An additional power conferred on the president in Article II, Section 2, is the right to appoint ambassadors, other public ministers, and consuls. In Section 3 of that article, the president is given the power to recognize foreign governments by receiving their ambassadors.

Informal Techniques of Presidential Leadership

Other broad sources of presidential power in the U.S. foreign policy process are tradition, precedent, and the president's personality. The president can employ a host of informal techniques that give the White House overwhelming superiority within the government in foreign policy leadership.

First, the president has access to information. The Central Intelligence Agency (CIA), the State Department, and the Defense Department make more information available to the president than to any other governmental official. This information carries with it the ability to make quick decisions—and the president uses that ability often. Second, the president is a legislative leader who can influence the funds that are allocated for different programs. Third, the president can influence public opinion. President Theodore Roosevelt once made the following statement:

> People used to say to me that I was an astonishingly good politician and divined what the people are going to think.... I did not "divine" how the people were going to think; I simply made up my mind what they ought to think and then did my best to get them to think it.[3]

Presidents are without equal with respect to influencing public opinion, partly because of their ability to command the media. Depending on their skill in appealing to patriotic sentiment (and sometimes fear), they can make people believe that their course in foreign affairs is right and necessary. During the first year of his presidency, Barack Obama made a very deliberate decision to change the tone of American policy in the world, visiting a number of nations to express support for democracy and to signal that the United States would not intervene militarily in the affairs of other nations. World public opinion responded to these declarations with an increase in approval for the United States in many nations. American public opinion often seems to be impressed by the president's decision to make a national commitment abroad. President George W. Bush's speech to Congress shortly after the September 11 attacks rallied the nation and brought new respect for his leadership. It is worth noting that presidents normally, although certainly not always, receive the immediate support of the American people in a foreign policy crisis.

Finally, the president can commit the nation morally to a course of action in foreign affairs. Because the president is the head of state and the leader of one of the most powerful nations on earth, once the president has made a commitment for the United States, it is difficult for Congress or anyone else to back down on that commitment.

did you know?

It is estimated that the Central Intelligence Agency has more than 16,000 employees, with about 5,000 in the clandestine services.

3. Sidney Warren, *The President as World Leader* (New York: McGraw-Hill, 1964), p. 23.

Other Sources of Foreign Policymaking

In addition to the president, there are at least four foreign policymaking sources within the executive branch: (1) the Department of State, (2) the National Security Council, (3) the intelligence community, and (4) the Department of Defense.

The Department of State. In principle, the State Department is the executive agency that has primary authority over foreign affairs. It supervises U.S. relations with the more than 200 independent nations around the world and with the United Nations and other multinational groups, such as the Organization of American States. It staffs embassies and consulates throughout the world. It has about 32,000 employees. This number may sound impressive, but it is small compared with, say, the 67,000 employees of the Department of Health and Human Services. Also, the State Department had an annual budget of only $9.1 billion in fiscal year 2009, one of the smallest budgets of the cabinet departments.

Newly elected presidents usually tell the American public that the new secretary of state is the nation's chief foreign policy adviser. Hillary Clinton, has, without doubt, been the chief diplomat for the Obama White House. Nonetheless, the State Department's preeminence in foreign policy has declined since World War II. The State Department's image within the White House Executive Office and Congress (and even with foreign governments) is quite poor—a slow, plodding, bureaucratic maze of inefficient, indecisive individuals. Reportedly, Premier Nikita Khrushchev of the Soviet Union urged President John F. Kennedy to formulate his own views rather than rely on State Department officials who, according to Khrushchev, "specialized in why something had not worked forty years ago."[4] In any event, since the days of Franklin Roosevelt, the State Department has often been bypassed or ignored when crucial decisions are made.

It is not surprising that the State Department has been overshadowed in foreign policy. It has no natural domestic constituency as does, for example, the Department of Defense, which can call on defense contractors for support. Instead, the State Department has what might be called **negative constituents**—U.S. citizens who openly oppose the government's policies. One of the State Department's major functions, administering foreign aid, often elicits criticisms. There is a widespread belief that the United States spends much more on foreign aid than it actually does. For 2012, Congress approved about $52 billion for the State Department and foreign aid, or about 1.5 percent of total federal spending.

The National Security Council. The job of the National Security Council (NSC), created by the National Security Act of 1947, is to advise the president on the integration of "domestic, foreign, and military policies relating to the national security." Its larger purpose is to provide policy continuity from one administration to the next. As it has turned out, the NSC—consisting of the president, the vice president, the secretaries of state and defense, the director of emergency planning, and often the chairperson of the joint chiefs of staff and the director of the CIA—is used in just about any way the president wants to use it.

The role of national security adviser to the president seems to adjust to fit the player. Some advisers have come into conflict with heads of the State Department. Henry A. Kissinger, Nixon's flamboyant and aggressive national security adviser, rapidly gained ascendancy over William Rogers, the secretary of state. More recently, Condoleezza Rice played an important role as national security adviser during George W. Bush's first term. Rice eventually became secretary of state.

Negative Constituents
Citizens who openly oppose the government's policies.

---

4. Theodore C. Sorensen, *Kennedy* (New York: Harper & Row, 1965), pp. 554–555.

Politics with a Purpose

THINK TANKS

Why is the price of gasoline so high? What is the effect of the demand for oil from emerging markets like China? Should the United States empty out its Strategic Petroleum Reserves to combat the low production from oil-producing nations?[a] Would that have a detrimental effect on our ability to respond should we need to send troops and ships into a military situation? Can the United States meet the oil price crisis alone, or would a coalition of nations have more influence on oil producers?

Policymakers need experts to help them answer these questions, and they often turn to think tanks for this expertise. Former State Department adviser Richard Haass called the influence of these "idea factories" "among the most important and least appreciated."[b] Emerging at the beginning of the 20th century, think tanks were named for the small rooms in which research scientists and military strategists plotted the conduct of World War II. They have proliferated; more than 2,000 of these organizations are based in the United States alone. Most are nonprofit and nonpartisan, although many advocate particular ideological perspectives. Some are so-called legacy organizations, like the Carter Center, the Hoover Institute, or the Nixon Center for Peace and Freedom. Some are attached to universities, like the Harvard Kennedy School, and some are independent, like the RAND Corporation.[c] Throughout the 1960s and 1970s, advocacy think tanks emerged, such as the conservative Heritage Foundation (1973) and the libertarian Cato Institute (1977), named for the libertarian pamphlets written during the American Revolution.[d]

In addition to governments' seeking ideas from think tanks, there is a revolving door between think tanks and government.[e] Many U.S. government officials have worked for think tanks, often after having served as officials in previous presidential administrations. For example, Zbigniew Brzezinski, who was President Carter's national security adviser, is a counselor for the Center for Strategic and International Studies. Lee Feinstein has been a senior fellow for U.S. Foreign Policy and International Law at the Council on Foreign Relations and was a senior official in President Clinton's Department of State. James Baker was the secretary of state under George H. W. Bush and now is the honorary head of the James A. Baker III Institute for Public Policy at Rice University.[f] Aside from providing personnel for executive branch policy positions, think tanks also try to influence opinion through publications, press releases, opinion editorials (op-eds), and media appearances.

Returning to the questions posed earlier about rising oil prices, in a 2006 op-ed in the *Washington Times*, an analyst for RAND argued that the United States has little control over oil prices and that the government should encourage alternative fuels such as ethanol and increase supply by opening up drilling in the protected Arctic National Wildlife Reserve (ANWR),[g] a move opposed by some environmental groups. Similarly, in 2008, representatives from the Cato Institute recommended drilling in ANWR as well as opening up federally protected land in the Mountain West to oil shale development. Cato also advocates draining the Strategic Petroleum Reserves, arguing that threats to our national security from worldwide oil embargoes against us are exaggerated.[h] While the American Enterprise Institute places the "blame" for high oil prices on increased demand from emerging markets,[i] George Soros (whose foundation has funded several advocacy groups and think tanks) has argued the cause involves the complex relationship among competing and complicated factors.[j] As the Obama administration made appointments to powerful positions in national security and defense, scholars and commentators from several think tanks moved into the administration, while other Republican-connected or more conservative thinkers moved back to the private sector.

[a] The Strategic Petroleum Reserves is a large stockpile of emergency petroleum, controlled by the U.S. Department of Energy, created after the 1973–1974 oil embargo. www.fossil.energy.gov/programs/reserves/#Strategic%20Petroleum%20Reserve, accessed June 4, 2008.

[b] Richard Haass, "Think Tanks and U.S. Foreign Policy: A Policy-Maker's Perspective," *U.S. Foreign Policy Agenda, An Electronic Journal of the U.S. Department of State*, Vol. 7, 2000, pp. 5–8, accessed June 1, 2008, at http://usinfo.state.gov/journals/itps/1102/ijpe/ijpe1102.pdf.

[c] Donald E. Abelson, "Think Tanks and U.S. Foreign Policy: An Historical View," *U.S. Foreign Policy Agenda, An Electronic Journal of the U.S. Department of State*, Vol. 7, 2000, pp. 9–12.

[d] www.cato.org/about.php, accessed June 5, 2008.

[e] *U.S. Foreign Policy Agenda, An Electronic Journal of the U.S. Department of State*, Vol. 7, 2000, pp. 39–40, accessed June 1, 2008, at http://usinfo.state.gov/journals/itps/1102/ijpe/ijpe1102.pdf.

[f] *Ibid.*

[g] www.rand.org/commentary/051906WT.html.

[h] www.cato.org/pub_display.php?pub_id=9438.

[i] www.aei.org/publications/pubID.27426,filter.all/pub_detail.asp.

[j] He argues that subsidies foreign countries place on their production of oil, the profit margins on oil exploration and development, and speculative buying on world commodities markets have all driven the price of oil upward. www.salon.com/tech/htww/2008/06/03/soros_oil_bubble_2/.

Intelligence Community
The government agencies that gather information about the capabilities and intentions of foreign governments or that engage in covert actions.

The Intelligence Community. No discussion of foreign policy would be complete without some mention of the **intelligence community**, the 40 or more government agencies or bureaus involved in intelligence activities. They include the following:

1. Central Intelligence Agency (CIA)
2. National Security Agency (NSA)
3. Defense Intelligence Agency (DIA)
4. Offices within the Department of Defense
5. Bureau of Intelligence and Research in the Department of State
6. Federal Bureau of Investigation (FBI)
7. Army intelligence
8. Air force intelligence
9. Drug Enforcement Administration (DEA)
10. Department of Energy
11. Directorate of Information Analysis and Infrastructure Protection in the Department of Homeland Security
12. Office of the Director of National Intelligence

The CIA, created as part of the National Security Act of 1947, is the lead organization of the intelligence community.

Covert Actions. Intelligence activities consist mostly of overt information gathering, but covert actions also are undertaken. Covert actions, as the name implies, are carried out in secret, and the American public rarely finds out about them. The CIA covertly aided in the overthrow of the Mossadegh regime of Iran in 1953 and the Arbenz government of Guatemala in 1954. The agency was instrumental in destabilizing the Allende government in Chile from 1970 to 1973.

During the mid-1970s, the "dark side" of the CIA was partly uncovered when the Senate undertook an investigation of its activities. One of the major findings of the Senate Select Committee on Intelligence was that the CIA had routinely spied on American citizens domestically—supposedly a prohibited activity. Consequently, the CIA was scrutinized by oversight committees within Congress, which restricted the scope of its operations. By 1980, however, the CIA had regained much of its lost power to engage in covert activities.

Criticisms of the Intelligence Community. By 2001, the CIA had come under fire for several lapses, including the discovery that one of its agents was spying on behalf of a foreign power, the failure to detect the nuclear arsenals of India and Pakistan, and, above all, the failure to obtain advance knowledge about the September 11 terrorist attacks. With the rise of terrorism as a threat, the intelligence agencies have received more funding and enhanced surveillance powers, but these moves have also provoked fears of civil liberties violations. In 2004, the bipartisan September 11 Commission called for a new intelligence czar to oversee the entire intelligence community, with full control of all agency budgets. After initially balking at this recommendation, President Bush eventually called for a partial implementation of the commission's report. Legislation enacted in 2004 established the Office of the Director of National Intelligence to oversee the intelligence community. In 2005, Bush appointed John Negroponte to be the first director. In 2009, President Obama named the fourth director in five years to the position. It seemed apparent that infighting with the CIA chief and other national security advisers makes this a very difficult position to hold.

Johnny Bivera, U.S. Navy

The Department of Defense. The Department of Defense (DoD) was created in 1947 to bring all of the various activities of the American military establishment under the jurisdiction of a single department headed by a civilian secretary of defense. At the same time, the joint chiefs of staff, consisting of the commanders of the various military branches and a chairperson, was created to formulate a unified military strategy.

Although the Department of Defense is larger than any other federal department, it declined in size after the fall of the Soviet Union in 1991. In the subsequent 10 years, the total number of civilian employees was reduced by about 400,000, to about 665,000. Military personnel were also reduced in number. The defense budget remained relatively flat for several years, but with the advent of the war on terrorism and the use of military forces in Afghanistan and Iraq, funding has again been increased.

Congress Balances the Presidency

A new interest in the balance of power between Congress and the president on foreign policy questions developed during the Vietnam War (1964–1975). Sensitive to public frustration over the long and costly war and angry at Richard Nixon for some of his other actions as president, Congress attempted to establish limits on the power of the president in setting foreign and defense policy. In 1973, Congress passed the War Powers Resolution over President Nixon's veto. The act limited the president's use of troops in military action without congressional approval (see Chapter 12). Most presidents, however, have not interpreted the "consultation" provisions of the act as meaning that Congress should be consulted before military action is taken. Instead, presidents Ford, Carter, Reagan, George H. W. Bush, and Clinton ordered troop movements and then informed congressional leaders. Critics note that it is quite possible for a president to commit troops to a situation from which the nation

An aerial view of the Pentagon, the headquarters of the U.S. Department of Defense (DoD), located between the Potomac River and Arlington National Cemetery. The Pentagon employs approximately 23,000 military and civilian personnel and is one of the world's largest office buildings, with three times the floor space of the Empire State Building in New York City. In the background, the obelisk of the Washington Monument is visible. When the media refer to the Pentagon, what do they mean?

could not withdraw without incurring heavy losses, whether or not Congress is consulted.

Congress has also exerted its authority by limiting or denying presidential requests for military assistance to various groups (such as Angolan rebels and the government of El Salvador) and requests for new weapons (such as the B-1 bomber). In general, Congress has been cautious in supporting the president in situations in which military involvement of American troops for a long period of time is possible. Like most members of the American public, members of Congress do not want to see American troops in harm's way unnecessarily.

Congress has its limits, of course, and often these are based on political considerations about election campaigns. Prior to the 2006 elections, Democrats found that antiwar platforms could be very effective during their campaigns. Certainly, the Iraq War and the future foreign policy direction of the United States were very important issues in the presidential and congressional elections of 2008; however, when the Democratic Party won control of the Congress and the presidency in 2008, it then assumed leadership of our national security policy. As is normally the case, the party of the president tends to support the commander in chief even when its members may have personal doubts about the use of military force.

Domestic Sources of Foreign Policy

The making of foreign policy is often viewed as a presidential prerogative because of the president's constitutional power in that area and the resources of the executive branch that the president controls. Foreign policymaking is also influenced by various other sources, however, including elite and mass opinion and the *military-industrial complex*, described in a following section.

Elite and Mass Opinion

Public opinion influences the making of U.S. foreign policy through several channels. Elites in American business, education, communications, labor, and religion try to influence presidential decision making through several strategies. A number of elite organizations, such as the Council on Foreign Relations and the Trilateral Commission, work to increase international cooperation and to influence foreign policy through conferences, publications, and research. The members of the American elite establishment also exert influence on foreign policy through the general public by encouraging debate about foreign policy positions, publicizing the issues, and using the media.

Generally, the efforts of the president and the elites are most successful with the segment of the population called the **attentive public**. This sector of the mass public, which probably constitutes 10 to 20 percent of all citizens, is more interested in foreign affairs than are most other Americans, and members of the attentive public are likely to transmit their opinions to the less interested members of the public through conversation and local leadership.

Interest Group Politics in Global Affairs

Attentive Public
That portion of the general public that pays attention to policy issues.

Civilian fear of the relationship between the defense establishment and arms manufacturers (the **military-industrial complex**) dates back many years. During President Eisenhower's eight years in office, the former five-star general of the army experienced firsthand the kind of pressure that could be brought against him and other policymakers by arms manufacturers. Eisenhower decided to give

Military-Industrial Complex
The mutually beneficial relationship between the armed forces and defense contractors.

the country a solemn and—as he saw it—necessary warning of the consequences of this influence. On January 17, 1961, in his last official speech, he said:

> *In the councils of government, we must guard against the acquisition of unwarranted influence, whether sought or unsought, by the military-industrial complex. The potential for the disastrous rise of misplaced power exists and will persist.... Only an alert and knowledgeable citizenry can compel the proper meshing of the huge industrial and military machinery of defense with our peaceful methods and goals, so that security and liberty may prosper together.[5]*

The Pentagon has supported a large sector of our economy through defense contracts. It has also supplied retired army officers as key executives to large defense-contracting firms. Perhaps the Pentagon's strongest allies have been members of Congress whose districts or states benefit economically from military bases or contracts. After the Cold War ended in the late 1980s, the defense industry looked abroad for new customers. The United States is, at this point in history, the world's largest arms supplier.

Arms suppliers and defense contractors are not the only groups pressing Congress and the president to act on foreign policy issues. Corn and soybean farmers want trade policies that favor the exportation of their products; General Electric, Caterpillar, and John Deere want assistance to sell their machinery overseas; and, at home, Serbian Americans, Greek Americans and many other groups lobby for foreign policies that address their home nation's issues.

The Major Themes of American Foreign Policy

From the earliest years of the republic, Americans have felt that their nation had a special destiny. The American experiment in democratic government and capitalism, it was thought, would provide the best possible life for men and women and be a model for other nations. As the United States assumed greater status as a power in world politics, Americans came to believe that the nation's actions on the world stage should be guided by American political and moral principles. As Harry Truman stated, "The United States should take the lead in running the world in the way that it ought to be run." Truman's statement is a classic expression of a **moralist foreign policy**, one that bases foreign policy decisions on the morally right decision. George W. Bush defended his invasion of Iraq as a moral decision to rid the world of a bad ruler, while Barack Obama supported the Libyan and Egyptian democracy movements on the moral grounds that democracy is the right of the people. At other times, and sometimes simultaneously, the United States may make decisions based on a **realist foreign policy** perspective, one that puts the nation's economic and security interests ahead of morality. The increased use of drones to track down and dispose of terrorists appears to be a clearly realist decision.

Although some observers might suggest that U.S. foreign policy is inconsistent and changes with each occupant of the White House, the long view of American diplomatic ventures does reveal major themes underlying foreign policy. In the early years of the nation, presidents and the people generally agreed that the United States should avoid foreign entanglements and concentrate instead

■ **Learning Outcome 3:**
Trace the evolution of United States foreign policy from isolationism to global leadership.

Moralist Foreign Policy
A foreign policy based on values and moral beliefs.

Realist Foreign policy
A foreign policy based on an understanding of the nation's economic and security interests.

5. *Congressional Almanac* (Washington, DC: Congressional Quarterly Press, 1961), pp. 938–939.

on its own development. From the beginning of the 20th century until today, however, a major theme has been increasing global involvement. The theme of the post–World War II years was the containment of communism. One of the themes for the first decade of the 21st century has been the battle against terrorism and, under President Obama, support for democracy movements in the Middle East.

The Formative Years: Avoiding Entanglements

Foreign policy was largely nonexistent during the formative years of the United States. Remember that the new nation was operating under the Articles of Confederation. The national government had no right to levy or collect taxes, no control over commerce, no right to make commercial treaties, and no power to raise an army (the Revolutionary army was disbanded in 1783). The government's lack of international power was made clear when Barbary pirates seized American hostages in the Mediterranean. The United States was unable to rescue the hostages and ignominiously had to purchase them in a treaty with Morocco.

The founders of this nation had a basic mistrust of European governments. George Washington said it was the U.S. policy "to steer clear of permanent alliances," and Thomas Jefferson echoed this sentiment when he said America wanted peace with all nations but "entangling alliances with none." This was also a logical position at a time when the United States was so weak militarily that it could not influence European development directly. Moreover, being protected by oceans that took weeks to traverse certainly allowed the nation to avoid entangling alliances. During the 1800s, therefore, the United States generally stayed out of European conflicts and politics. In this hemisphere, however, the United States pursued an actively **expansionist policy.** The nation purchased Louisiana in 1803, annexed Texas in 1845, gained substantial territory from Mexico in 1848, purchased Alaska in 1867, and annexed Hawaii in 1898.

The Monroe Doctrine. President James Monroe, in his message to Congress on December 2, 1823, stated that the United States would not accept foreign intervention in the Western Hemisphere. In return, the United States would not meddle in European affairs. The **Monroe Doctrine** was the underpinning of the U.S. **isolationist foreign policy** toward Europe, which continued throughout the 1800s.

The Spanish-American War and World War I. The end of the isolationist policy started with the Spanish-American War in 1898. Winning the war gave the United States possession of Guam, Puerto Rico, and the Philippines (which gained independence in 1946). On the heels of that war came World War I (1914–1918). In his reelection campaign of 1916, President Woodrow Wilson ran on the slogan "He kept us out of war." Nonetheless, the United States declared war on Germany on April 6, 1917, because that country refused to give up its campaign of sinking all ships headed for Britain, including passenger ships. (Large passenger ships of that time commonly held more than a thousand people, so the sinking of such a ship was a disaster comparable to the attack on the World Trade Center.)

In the 1920s, the United States went "back to normalcy," as President Warren G. Harding urged it to do. U.S. military forces were largely disbanded, defense spending dropped to about 1 percent of total annual national income, and the nation returned to a period of isolationism.

Expansionist Policy
A policy that embraces the extension of American borders as far as possible.

Monroe Doctrine
A policy statement made by President James Monroe in 1823, which set out three principles: (1) European nations should not establish new colonies in the Western Hemisphere; (2) European nations should not intervene in the affairs of independent nations of the Western Hemisphere; and (3) the United States would not interfere in the affairs of European nations.

Isolationist Foreign Policy
A policy of abstaining from an active role in international affairs or alliances, which characterized U.S. foreign policy toward Europe during most of the 1800s.

The Era of Internationalism

Isolationism was permanently shattered by the bombing of the U.S. naval base at Pearl Harbor, Hawaii, on December 7, 1941. The surprise attack by the Japanese caused the deaths of 2,403 American servicemen and wounded 1,143 others. Eighteen warships were sunk or seriously damaged, and 188 planes were destroyed at the airfields. The American public was outraged. President Franklin Roosevelt asked Congress to declare war on Japan immediately, and the United States entered World War II. This unequivocal response was certainly due to the nature of the provocation. American soil had not been attacked by a foreign power since the occupation of Washington, D.C., by the British in 1814.

The United States was the only major participating country to emerge from World War II with its economy intact, and even strengthened. Britain, France, Germany, Italy, Japan, the Soviet Union, and several minor participants in the war were economically devastated. The United States was also the only country to have control over operational nuclear weapons. President Harry Truman had made the decision to use two atomic bombs, on August 6 and August 9, 1945, to end the war with Japan. (Historians still argue over the necessity of this action, which ultimately killed more than 100,000 Japanese and left an equal number permanently injured.) The United States truly had become the world's superpower.

The Cold War. The United States had become an uncomfortable ally of the Soviet Union after Adolf Hitler's invasion of that country. Soon after World War II ended, relations between the Soviet Union and the West deteriorated. The Soviet Union wanted a weakened Germany, and to achieve this, it insisted that Germany be divided in two, with East Germany becoming a buffer against the West. Little by little, the Soviet Union helped install communist governments in Eastern

Library of Congress Prints & PhotographsDivision, Washington, D.C.

British Prime Minister Winston Churchill, U.S. President Franklin Roosevelt, and Soviet leader Joseph Stalin met at Yalta from February 4 to 11, 1945, to resolve their differences over the shape that the international community would take after World War II.

Soviet Bloc
The Soviet Union and the Eastern European countries that installed communist regimes after World War II and were dominated by the Soviet Union.

Cold War
The ideological, political, and economic confrontation between the United States and the Soviet Union following World War II.

Iron Curtain
The term used to describe the division of Europe between the Soviet bloc and the West; coined by Winston Churchill.

Containment
A U.S. diplomatic policy adopted by the Truman administration to contain communist power within its existing boundaries.

Truman Doctrine
The policy adopted by President Harry Truman in 1947 to halt communist expansion in southeastern Europe.

European countries, which began to be referred to collectively as the **Soviet bloc**. In response, the United States encouraged the rearming of Western Europe. The **Cold War** had begun.[6]

In Fulton, Missouri, on March 5, 1946, Winston Churchill, in a striking metaphor, declared that from the Baltic to the Adriatic Sea "an iron curtain has descended across the [European] continent." The term **iron curtain** became even more appropriate when Soviet-dominated East Germany built a wall separating East Berlin from West Berlin in August 1961.

Containment Policy. In 1947, a remarkable article was published in *Foreign Affairs*. The article was signed by "X." The actual author was George F. Kennan, chief of the policy-planning staff for the State Department. The doctrine of **containment** set forth in the article became—according to many—the bible of Western foreign policy. The author, "X," argued that whenever and wherever the Soviet Union could successfully challenge the West, it would do so. He recommended that our policy toward the Soviet Union be "firm and vigilant containment of Russian expansive tendencies."[7]

The containment theory was expressed clearly in the **Truman Doctrine**, which was enunciated by President Harry Truman in his historic address to Congress on March 12, 1947. In that address, he announced that the United States must help countries in which a communist takeover seemed likely. Later that year, he backed the Marshall Plan, an economic assistance plan for Europe that was intended to prevent the expansion of communist influence there. By 1950, the United States had entered into a military alliance with the European nations commonly called the North Atlantic Treaty Organization (NATO). The combined military power of the United States and the European nations worked to contain Soviet influence to Eastern Europe and to maintain a credible response to any Soviet military attack on Western Europe.

Superpower Relations

During the Cold War, there was never any direct military conflict between the United States and the Soviet Union. Rather, confrontations among "client" nations were used to carry out the policies of the superpowers. Only on occasion did the United States directly enter a conflict in a significant way. Two such occasions were in Korea and in Vietnam.

After the end of World War II, northern Korea was occupied by the Soviet Union, and southern Korea was occupied by the United States. The result was two rival Korean governments. In 1950, North Korea invaded South Korea. Under United Nations authority, the United States entered the war, which prevented an almost certain South Korean defeat. When U.S. forces were on the brink of conquering North Korea, however, China joined the war on the side of the North, resulting in a stalemate. An armistice signed in 1953 led to the two Koreas that exist today. U.S. forces have remained in South Korea ever since.

The Vietnam War (1964–1975) also involved the United States in a civil war between a communist North Vietnam and pro-Western South Vietnam. When the French army in Indochina was defeated by the communist forces of Ho Chi Minh and the two Vietnams were created in 1954, the United States assumed the role of supporting the South Vietnamese government against North Vietnam. President John Kennedy sent 16,000 "advisers" to help South Vietnam, and after Kennedy's death in 1963, President Lyndon B. Johnson greatly increased the

---

6. See John Lewis Gaddis, *The United Nations and the Origins of the Cold War* (New York: Columbia University Press, 1972).
7. X, "The Sources of Soviet Conduct," *Foreign Affairs*, July 1947, p. 575.

scope of that support. More than 500,000 American troops were in Vietnam at the height of the U.S. involvement. More than 58,000 Americans were killed and 300,000 were wounded in the conflict. A peace agreement in 1973 allowed U.S. troops to leave the country, and in 1975 North Vietnam easily occupied Saigon (the South Vietnamese capital) and unified the nation. The debate over U.S. involvement in Vietnam became extremely heated and, as mentioned previously, spurred congressional efforts to limit the ability of the president to commit forces to armed combat. The military draft was also a major source of contention during the Vietnam War.

The Cuban Missile Crisis. Perhaps the closest the two superpowers came to a nuclear confrontation was the Cuban missile crisis in 1962. The Soviets installed missiles in Cuba, 90 miles off the U.S. coast, in response to Cuban fears of an American invasion and to try to balance an American nuclear advantage. President Kennedy and his advisers rejected the option of invading Cuba and set up a naval blockade around the island instead. When Soviet vessels appeared near Cuban waters, the tension reached its height. After intense negotiations between Washington and Moscow, the Soviet ships turned around on October 25, and on October 28, the Soviet Union announced the withdrawal of its missile operations from Cuba. In exchange, the United States agreed not to invade Cuba in the future and to remove some of its own missiles that were located near the Soviet border in Turkey.

A Period of *Détente*. The French word ***détente*** means "a relaxation of tensions." By the end of the 1960s, it was clear that some efforts had to be made to reduce the threat of nuclear war between the United States and the Soviet Union. The Soviet Union gradually had begun to catch up in the building of strategic nuclear delivery vehicles in the form of bombers and missiles, thus balancing the nuclear scales between the two countries. Each nation acquired the military capacity to destroy the other with nuclear weapons.

As the result of lengthy negotiations under Secretary of State Henry Kissinger and President Nixon, the United States and the Soviet Union signed the **Strategic Arms Limitation Treaty (SALT I)** in May 1972. That treaty "permanently" limited the development and deployment of antiballistic missiles (ABMs) and limited the number of offensive missiles each country could deploy. To further reduce tensions, new scientific and cultural exchanges were arranged with the Soviets, as well as new opportunities for Jewish emigration out of the Soviet Union.

The policy of *détente* was not limited to the U.S. relationship with the Soviet Union. Seeing an opportunity to capitalize on increasing friction between the Soviet Union and the People's Republic of China, Kissinger secretly began negotiations to establish a new relationship with that nation. President Nixon eventually visited China in 1972. The visit set the stage for the formal diplomatic recognition of that country, which occurred during the Carter administration (1977–1981).

The Reagan-Bush Years. President Ronald Reagan took a hard line against the Soviet Union during his first term, proposing the strategic defense initiative (SDI), or "Star Wars," in 1983. The SDI was designed to serve as a space-based defense against enemy missiles. Reagan and others in his administration argued that the program would deter nuclear war by shifting the emphasis of defense strategy from offensive to defensive weapons systems.

In November 1985, however, President Reagan and Mikhail Gorbachev, the Soviet leader, began to work on an arms reduction compact. The negotiations resulted in a historic agreement signed by Reagan and Gorbachev in Washington,

Détente
A French word meaning a relaxation of tensions. The term characterized U.S.-Soviet relations as they developed under President Richard Nixon and Secretary of State Henry Kissinger.

Strategic Arms Limitation Treaty (SALT I)
A treaty between the United States and the Soviet Union to stabilize the nuclear arms competition between the two countries. SALT I talks began in 1969, and agreements were signed on May 26, 1972.

did you know?

Russia suffered more battle deaths in putting down the rebellion in Chechnya than the Soviet Union experienced in its decades-long attempt to subdue Afghanistan.

■ **Learning Outcome 4:**
Explain the origins of the war on terror and how it has influenced domestic policy and relations with other nations.

D.C., on December 8, 1987. The terms of the Intermediate-Range Nuclear Force (INF) Treaty, which was ratified by the Senate, required the superpowers to dismantle a total of 4,000 intermediate-range missiles within the first three years of the agreement.

Beginning in 1989, President George H. W. Bush continued the negotiations with the Soviet Union to reduce the number of nuclear weapons and the number of armed troops in Europe. Subsequent events, including developments in Eastern Europe, the unification of Germany, and the dissolution of the Soviet Union (in December 1991), changed the world order. American and other Western leaders now worked to find and control the weapons that had formerly been in the inventory of the Soviet Union. Agreements were signed with Russia and with other former Soviet republics to reduce the weapons threat.

The Dissolution of the Soviet Union. After the fall of the Berlin Wall in 1989, it was clear that the Soviet Union had relinquished much of its political and military control over the states of Eastern Europe that formerly had been part of the Soviet bloc. Since 1991, Russia has struggled to develop a democratic system of government. Boris Yeltsin, president of Russia from 1991 to 1999, attempted to lead needed reforms of the government and electoral system. In 2000, Yeltsin, whose health was failing, named Vladimir Putin as acting president. After completing his terms as an elected president, Putin became the premier of Russia in 2008 and then, in 2012, was elected president again. Although Mr. Putin publicly declares his faith in a democratic regime, his actions, including unresolved murders of journalists and the jailing of his opponents, generate suspicion about his intentions.

The War on Terror

In 2001, terrorism came home to the United States in ways that few Americans could have imagined. In a well-coordinated attack, 19 terrorists hijacked four airplanes and crashed three of them into buildings—two into the World Trade Center towers in New York City and one into the Pentagon in Washington, D.C. The fourth airplane crashed in a field in Pennsylvania, after the passengers fought the hijackers. Why did the al Qaeda network plan and launch attacks on the United States? Apparently, the leaders of the network, including Osama bin Laden, were angered by the presence of U.S. troops on the soil of Saudi Arabia, which they regard as sacred. They also saw the United States as the primary defender of Israel against the Palestinians and as the defender of the royal family that governs Saudi Arabia. The attacks were intended to so frighten and demoralize the American people that they would convince their leaders to withdraw American troops from the Middle East.

After September 11, President George W. Bush implemented stronger security measures to protect homeland security and U.S. facilities and personnel abroad. The president sought and received congressional support for heightened airport security, new laws allowing greater domestic surveillance of potential terrorists, and new funding for the military. The Bush administration has also conducted two military efforts as part of the war on terrorism.

The first military response to the attacks was directed against al Qaeda camps in Afghanistan and the Taliban regime, which had ruled that country since 1996. In late 2001, after building a coalition of international allies and anti-Taliban rebels within Afghanistan, the United States defeated the Taliban and fostered the creation of an interim government that did not support terrorism. In 2003, the Bush administration launched a war to remove Saddam Hussein from Iraq that embroiled the United States in a decade-long conflict.

Terrorism has posed a unique challenge for U.S. foreign policymakers. The Bush administration's response was unique. In September 2002, President Bush enunciated what has since become known as the "Bush doctrine," or the doctrine of preemption:

> We will ... [defend] the United States, the American people, and our interests at home and abroad by identifying and destroying the threat before it reaches our borders. While the United States will constantly strive to enlist the support of the international community, we will not hesitate to act alone, if necessary, to exercise our right of self-defense by acting preemptively against such terrorists, to prevent them from doing harm against our people and our country.[8]

The concept of "**preemptive war**" as a defense strategy was a new element in U.S. foreign policy. The concept is based on the assumption that in the war on terrorism, self-defense must be *anticipatory*. As President Bush stated on March 17, 2003, just before launching the invasion of Iraq, "Responding to such enemies only after they have struck first is not self-defense, it is suicide."

Preemptive War
A military engagement fought to stop an enemy before that enemy attacks the United States.

The Bush doctrine was not without its critics. Some pointed out that preemptive wars against other nations have traditionally been waged by dictators and rogue states—not democratic nations. By employing such tactics, the United States would seem to be contradicting its basic values. In his campaign for president, Barack Obama repudiated this approach to national security policy and, in the first year of his presidency, made a number of speeches abroad in which he signaled a new, more conciliatory approach to other nations.

The Iraq and Afghanistan Wars

On August 2, 1990, the Persian Gulf became the setting for a major challenge to the international system set up after World War II (1939–1945). President Saddam Hussein of Iraq sent troops into the neighboring oil sheikdom of Kuwait, occupying that country. This was the most clear-cut case of aggression against an independent nation in half a century.

The Persian Gulf—The First Gulf War. At the formal request of the king of Saudi Arabia, American troops were dispatched to set up a defensive line at the Kuwaiti border. After the United Nations (UN) approved a resolution authorizing the use of force if Saddam Hussein did not respond to sanctions, the U.S. Congress reluctantly also approved such an authorization. On January 17, 1991, two days after a deadline for Hussein to withdraw, U.S.-led coalition forces launched a massive air attack on Iraq. After several weeks, the ground offensive began. Iraqi troops retreated from Kuwait a few days later, and the First Gulf War ended, although many Americans criticized President George H. W. Bush for not sending troops to Baghdad to depose Saddam Hussein.

As part of the cease-fire that ended the Gulf War, Iraq agreed to abide by all UN resolutions and to allow UN weapons inspectors to search for and oversee the destruction of its medium-range missiles and all weapons of mass destruction, including any chemical and nuclear weapons, and related research facilities. Economic sanctions were to be imposed on Iraq until the weapons inspectors finished their work. In 1999, however, Iraq placed so many obstacles in the path of the UN inspectors that they withdrew from the country.

---

8. George W. Bush, September 17, 2002. The full text of the document from which this statement is taken can be accessed at www.whitehouse.gov/nsc/nssall.html.

The Iraq War. After the terrorist attacks on the United States on September 11, 2001, President George W. Bush called Iraq and Saddam Hussein part of an "axis of evil" that threatened world peace. In 2002 and early 2003, Bush called for a "regime change" in Iraq and began assembling an international coalition that might support further military action in Iraq.

Having tried and failed to convince the UN Security Council that the UN should take action to enforce its resolutions, Bush created a coalition of 35 other nations, including Britain, to join the United States to invade Iraq. Within three weeks, the coalition forces had toppled Hussein's decades-old dictatorship and were in control of Baghdad and most of the other major Iraqi cities.

The process of establishing order and creating a new government in Iraq turned out to be extraordinarily difficult, however. In the course of the fighting, the Iraqi army, rather than surrendering, disbanded. Soldiers simply took off their uniforms and made their way home. As a result, the task of maintaining law and order fell on the shoulders of a remarkably small coalition expeditionary force that faced disorder across the nation. Saddam Hussein was found and later tried and executed by an Iraqi court for crimes against the Kurdish people, but that did not stop the insurgent resistance movement against the coalition forces.

Occupied Iraq. The people of Iraq are divided into three principal groups by ethnicity and religion. The Kurdish-speaking people of the north, who had in practice been functioning as an American-sponsored independent state since the First Gulf War, were overjoyed by the invasion. The Arabs adhering to the Shiite branch of Islam live principally in the south and constitute a majority of the population. The Shiites were glad that Saddam Hussein, who had murdered many thousands of Shiites, was gone. They were deeply skeptical of U.S. intentions, however. The Arabs belonging to the Sunni branch of Islam live in the center of the country, west of Baghdad. Although the Sunnis constituted only a minority of the population, they had controlled the government under Hussein. Many of them considered the occupation a disaster. Figure 17–1 shows the distribution of major ethnic and religious groups in Iraq.

The Situation Worsens. In April 2004, four non-Iraqi civilian security personnel were murdered in the Sunni city of Fallujah, and their bodies were publicly defiled. U.S. Marines entered the city to locate and arrest the perpetrators. In the months and years that followed, sectarian violence between the various ethnic and religious groups continued. Some sectors of Iraq fell under the control of local clerics such as Muqtada al Sadr, who had his own militia. To make matters worse, in May 2004, graphic photographs were published showing that U.S. guards at Abu Ghraib prison in Baghdad had subjected prisoners to physical and sexual abuse.

While coalition forces were able to maintain control of the country, they were now suffering monthly casualties comparable to those experienced during the initial invasion. Casualties continued to increase in the years that followed, and the unpopularity of the war among the American people dragged President Bush's approval rating to historic lows.

The Bush Surge. By 2007, it was clear that al Qaeda terrorist cells were also participating in the attacks against both coalition forces and the emerging Iraqi government. In spring 2007, President Bush and his commanders in the field requested additional troops for a "surge" of military activity to defeat the insurgency. Although many in Congress and the public did not believe that the surge

Figure 17-1 ▶ Ethnic/Religious Groups in Iraq

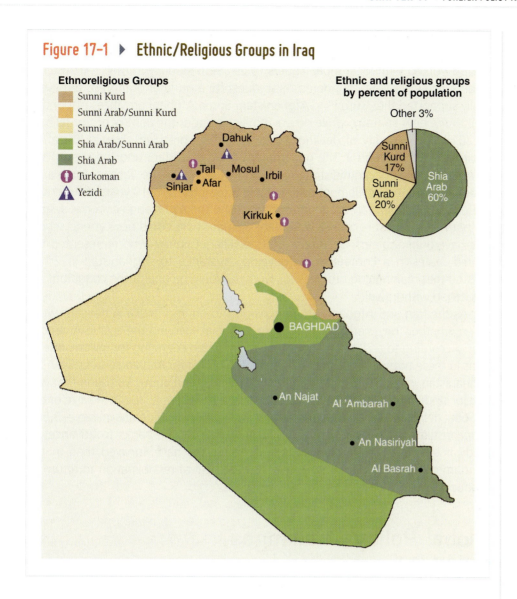

would be successful, by late 2007, violence in many parts of Iraq had decreased, and the Iraqi military forces were taking the lead in operations against the insurgents. By the time President Obama came into office, the new chief executive could confidently schedule troop withdrawals over the next two years and move into continued negotiations with the Iraqi government about future relationships with the United States.

The "Necessary" War

As the Bush administration came to an end in early 2009, it was clear that the situation in Afghanistan was far from resolved. The Taliban regrouped in the provinces and corruption spread through the government. President Obama had campaigned on the premise that Afghanistan was a "necessary" war, so he was faced, in 2009, with a serious decision on how to proceed with the American mission in that nation. After several months of internal discussions, the administration agreed to a type of "surge" in Afghanistan and a planned withdrawal beginning in 2011. Policy seemed to be in disarray, however, in 2010, when the commanding officer, General Stanley McChrystal, was fired and General David Petraeus was asked to take over the situation in the theater of war.

The new commander argued that it was necessary to increase troop levels in Afghanistan and to change the American strategy to one in which American troops worked with local tribal leaders to establish stability in their regions. The Obama administration considered this request for a number of months but eventually supported the "surge" in Afghanistan. Some Afghani provinces responded well to the new strategy, while others remained under the control of the Taliban. By 2012, the difficulty of dealing with the Afghani president, Hamid Karzai, of coping with corruption in the government of Afghanistan, and the cost of the war led the Obama administration to begin talks with the Taliban and Karzai about a negotiated settlement of the war. It is clear that the 10 years of American presence in Afghanistan did produce progress in the social and economic system of that nation, most notably for Afghani women, who could now attend school and have public careers. Secretary of State Hillary Clinton, who represented the United States in a conference to develop assistance to Afghanistan in 2012, insisted that maintaining progress for women would be one of the conditions for U.S. troop withdrawal.[9]

As the Iraq and Afghanistan wars wound to an end, many Americans wondered whether they were worth both the financial cost and the cost in American lives. According to a 2011 analysis, the accumulated spending for military operations in these two nations since 9/11 was $806 billion for Iraq and $444 billion for Afghanistan, plus $29 billion for enhanced security and about $6 billion that was unallocated. The grand total was $1.2 trillion over 10 years, about the size of the national deficit in 2012.[10] The human toll was about 4,500 deaths in Iraq— 3,500 from hostile action—and almost 1,900 in Afghanistan. Thanks to advances in medical technology, far more wounded Americans have survived than in the Vietnam conflict, although many need a great deal of rehabilitation to return to productive lives.

Global Policy Challenges

The foreign and national security policies of the United States are formulated to deal with world conditions at a particular period in history. Early in its history, the United States was a weak, new nation facing older nations well equipped for world domination. In the 21st century, the United States faces different challenges. Now it must devise foreign and defense policies that will enhance its security in a world in which it is the global superpower and has no equal. Among the challenges that must be faced are the growth of new economic and military powers, the threat of terrorism, the explosion in technological warfare, the proliferation of nuclear weapons, and numerous regional conflicts, including the ongoing violence in the Middle East.

The Emerging World Order

From 1945 until 1989, the world watched as two superpowers, the United States and the Soviet Union, dueled for power in the world. Both nations had their allies and fought wars through their surrogates. Both nations built up huge arsenals of nuclear weapons and were militarily prepared to destroy each other and the world itself. After the Berlin Wall fell in 1989, the entire Soviet bloc disintegrated

---

9. "Hillary Clinton Puts Conditions on U.S. Portion of $16 Billion Afghan Assistance Pledge," CBS News, July 9, 2012. www.cbsnews.com.

10. Amy Belasco, "The Cost of Iraq, Afghanistan and Other Global War on Terror Operations since 9/11," Washington, DC: Congressional Research Service, 2011.

with surprising speed. East Germany, one of the strongest allies of the Soviet Union, merged with West Germany to become one nation, democratic and capitalistic. All of the other Eastern bloc nations became truly independent states, and a new Russian state emerged.

After the Persian Gulf War in 1991, it was clear that the American military was the finest in the world and that U.S. advances in technology and weaponry were far superior to those of any other nation. What this meant was that the United States was the sole military global superpower. Under the Clinton administration, the Pentagon tried to plan for a post–Cold War world. What should be the national security objectives of the nation? How should the military be structured? How many wars should the United States be equipped to handle at one time? What kinds of intelligence gathering would be important now that the Soviets were no longer a threat? All of these questions and more needed to be answered in terms of American foreign and national security policy.

The Clinton administration, with the approval of Congress, began to change the size and scope of the American military. By 2001, the active-duty military was one-third smaller than it had been in 1990, dropping from 2.1 million in 1989 to 1.4 million in 1999.[11] Fewer appropriations were made to build new ships and acquire new equipment. The Central Intelligence Agency was ordered to focus more on economic intelligence and less on military intelligence. The United States has continued to lead NATO and maintain this military alliance of European nations. Although Russia objects to the continued existence of this alliance, many of the former Soviet bloc nations, beginning with Poland, expressed interest in joining NATO. By 2008, the alliance included the 28 members who joined at the beginning of or before the fall of the Soviet Union, as well as the Czech Republic, Hungary, Poland, Bulgaria, Estonia, Latvia, Lithuania, Romania, Slovakia, and Slovenia, all former allies of the Soviet Union. At the same time, other developments in the world challenged American policy. The European Union became a single economic unit, competing with American exports around the world. China began to become an economic force in the world and, a few years later, India followed suit. By 2008, China was a major trading partner of the United States and, with its newly generated cash, a major holder of the securities of the U.S. government. China became a major military power as well, with nuclear weapons and missile capabilities. Other nations such as Brazil and Australia became important economic players in the world.

By 2001, when terrorists attacked the World Trade Center in New York, the United States was focused more on economic growth and economic competition in the world. The United States military was prepared for crisis situations and technologically sophisticated warfare, but not for a long engagement on the ground. The wars in Iraq and Afghanistan have drained our military resources. One of the questions that Americans must face in the future is whether to plan for strengthening the military to face global threats or to place our hopes in a more peaceful world.

The Threat of Terrorism

Dissident groups, rebels, and other revolutionaries have long engaged in terrorism to gain attention and to force their enemies to the bargaining table. Over the last two decades, however, terrorism has increasingly threatened world peace and the lives of ordinary citizens.

---

11. Edward F. Bruner, "Military Forces: What Is the Appropriate Size for the United States?" *Congressional Research Service Report for Congress*, updated February 10, 2005.

Terrorism and Regional Strife. Terrorism can be a weapon of choice in regional or domestic strife. The conflict in the Middle East between Israel and the Arab states is an example. Until recently, the conflict had been lessened by a series of painfully negotiated agreements between Israel and some of the Arab states. Those opposed to the peace process, however, have continued to disrupt the negotiations through assassinations, mass murders, and bomb blasts in the streets of major cities within Israel. Other regions have also experienced terrorism. In September 2004, terrorists acting on behalf of Chechnya, a breakaway republic of Russia, seized a school at Beslan in the nearby Russian republic of North Ossetia. In the end, at least 330 people—most of them children—were dead.

Terrorist Attacks against Foreign Civilians. In other cases, terrorist acts are planned against civilians of foreign nations traveling abroad, to make an international statement. One of the most striking attacks was launched by Palestinian terrorists against Israeli athletes at the Munich Olympics in 1972, during which 11 athletes were murdered. Other attacks have included ship and airplane hijackings, as well as bombings of embassies. For example, in 1998, terrorist bombings of two American embassies in Africa killed 257 people, including 12 Americans, and injured more than 5,500 others.

London Bombings. On July 7, 2005, terrorists carried out synchronized bombings of the London Underground (subway) and bus network. Four suicide bombers, believed to have been of Middle Eastern descent, claimed the lives of 52 people and wounded hundreds more in the attacks. On July 21, a second group of bombers attempted to carry out a similar plot, but no one was killed. Following the attacks, security was heightened in Britain and elsewhere (including New York City).

In August 2006, British authorities foiled a plot to bring down 10 planes scheduled to leave London's Heathrow Airport for the United States. If successful, it would have been the largest terrorist attack since September 11. The alleged bombers planned to blow up the airplanes with liquid chemicals that could be combined to make a bomb. Many planned attacks have been stopped in the United States and abroad since 9/11. Some, like the underwear bomber on the flight to Detroit and the Times Square bomber in New York, are publicly arrested and tried. Other plots are stopped before execution and little public knowledge is available. As the Olympic Games were about to begin in London in 2012, extensive preparations were made to stop any possible terrorist attacks.

Nuclear Weapons

In 1945, the United States was the only nation to possess nuclear weapons. Several nations quickly joined the "nuclear club," however, including the Soviet Union in 1949, Great Britain in 1952, France in 1960, and China in 1964. Few nations have made public their nuclear weapons programs since China's successful test of nuclear weapons in 1964. India and Pakistan, however, detonated nuclear devices within a few weeks of each other in 1998, and North Korea conducted an underground nuclear explosive test in October 2006. Several other nations are suspected of possessing nuclear weapons or the capability to produce them in a short time.

The United States and the Soviet Union. More than 12,000 nuclear warheads are known to be stocked worldwide, although the exact number is uncertain, because some countries do not reveal the extent of their nuclear stockpiles. Although the United States and Russia have dismantled some of their nuclear weapons systems since the end of the Cold War and the dissolution of the Soviet Union in 1991, both still retain sizable nuclear arsenals. Even more troublesome is nuclear proliferation—that is, the development of nuclear weapons by additional nations.

Nuclear Proliferation. The United States has attempted to influence late arrivals to the nuclear club through a combination of rewards and punishments. In some cases, the United States has promised aid to a nation to gain cooperation. In other cases, such as those of India and Pakistan, it has imposed economic sanctions as a punishment for carrying out nuclear tests. In the end, Pakistan demonstrated its ability to explode nuclear bombs in 1998. Despite the United States' disagreement with these countries, President Bush signed a new nuclear pact with India in March 2006.

In 1999, President Bill Clinton presented the Comprehensive Nuclear Test Ban Treaty to the Senate for ratification. The treaty, formed in 1996, prohibits all nuclear test explosions worldwide and established a global network of monitoring stations. Ninety-three nations have ratified the treaty. Among those that have not are China, Israel, India, and Pakistan. In a defeat for the Clinton administration, the U.S. Senate rejected the treaty in 1999.

The United States has suspected for some time that nations such as North Korea and Iran might supply nuclear materials to terrorists or to nations that want to have nuclear capability. In addition, Israel is known to possess more than 100 nuclear warheads. South Africa developed six nuclear warheads in the 1980s but dismantled them in 1990. In 2003, Libya announced that it was abandoning a secret nuclear weapons program. Also, since the dissolution of the Soviet Union in 1991, the security of its nuclear arsenal has declined. There have been reported thefts, smugglings, and illicit sales of nuclear material from the former Soviet Union in the past 20 years.

For years, the United States, the European Union, and the UN have tried to prevent Iran from becoming a nuclear power. Today, though, many observers believe that Iran has already developed nuclear capability or is close to doing so. Continued diplomatic attempts to at least slow down Iran's quest for a nuclear bomb have proved ineffectual at best.

With nuclear weapons, materials, and technology available worldwide, it is conceivable that terrorists could develop a nuclear device and use it in a terrorist act. In fact, a U.S. federal indictment filed in 1998, after the attack on the American embassies in Kenya and Tanzania, charged Osama bin Laden and his associates with trying to buy components for a nuclear bomb "at various times" since 1992.

did you
know?

Including the Civil War, more than 1 million American soldiers have been killed in the nation's wars.

The United States and Regional Conflicts

The United States has played a role—sometimes alone, sometimes with other powers—in many regional conflicts during the 1990s and 2000s. In other situations, tensions exist between the United States and another nation over trade, weapons acquisition, or political differences. The tense relationships between the United States and Iran and between the United States and North Korea have already been discussed. It is important to note, however, that both of those states play important roles in their own regions of the globe. The United States is just one player in the situation and often must work with other global powers such as China or Russia in that region.

The Middle East

For many decades, the question of the continued existence and development of the state of Israel has been the predominant issue for the United States in the Middle East. As a longtime supporter of Israel, the United States has undertaken to persuade the Israelis to negotiate with the Palestinian Arabs who live in the territories occupied by the state of Israel. The conflict, which began in 1948, has

© Picture Contact BV/Alamy

To protect Israeli civilians from terrorism, Israel has built a wall to separate Palestinian settlements from Jewish neighborhoods.

been extremely difficult to resolve. The internationally recognized solution is for Israel to yield the West Bank and the Gaza Strip to the Palestinians in return for effective security commitments and abandonment by the Palestinians of any right of return to Israel proper. Unfortunately, the Palestinians have been unable to stop all terrorist attacks on Israel, and Israel has been unwilling to dismantle its settlements in the occupied territories. Furthermore, the two parties have been unable to come to an agreement on how much of the West Bank should go to the Palestinians and on what compensation (if any) the Palestinians should receive for abandoning all claims to settlement in Israel proper.

In December 1988, the United States began talking directly to the Palestine Liberation Organization (PLO), and in 1991, under great pressure from the United States, the Israelis opened talks with representatives of the Palestinians and other Arab states. In 1993, both parties agreed to set up Palestinian self-government in the West Bank and the Gaza Strip. The historic agreement, signed in Cairo on May 4, 1994, put in place a process by which the Palestinians would assume self-rule in the Gaza Strip and in the town of Jericho. In the months that followed, Israeli troops withdrew from much of the occupied territory, the new Palestinian Authority assumed police duties, and many Palestinian prisoners were freed by the Israelis.

President Bush attempted to renew Israeli-Palestinian negotiations in 2003 by sponsoring a "road map" for peace. First, the road map called for an end to terrorism by the Palestinians. Later, it held out hopes for a Palestinian state alongside Israel. In its weakened condition, however, the Palestinian Authority was unable to make any commitments, and the road map process ground to a halt. In February 2004, Israeli prime minister Ariel Sharon announced a plan under which

Israel would withdraw from the Gaza Strip regardless of whether a deal could be reached with the Palestinians. Sharon's plan met with strong opposition within his own political party, but ultimately the withdrawal took place.

After the death of Palestinian leader Yasser Arafat in 2004, a moderate prime minister was elected. In January 2006, however, the militant group Hamas won a majority of the seats in the Palestinian legislature. American and European politicians hoped that after it became part of the legitimate government, Hamas would agree to rescind its avowed desire to destroy Israel, but so far, it has not done so.

The Arab Spring. The situation in the Middle East including the fate of Israel has been destabilized by the demands for democracy that arose in 2011 and 2012. Popular movements have replaced the authoritarian regimes in Egypt, Libya, and Tunisia, Yemen. The Assad government in Syria is engaged in a civil war with the opposition forces there. These "Arab Spring" movements could mark very positive change for the United States as new democratically elected governments come into power (see Figure 17-2). Democratic nations are less likely to go to war and are more stable. The United States has encouraged the development of democracy throughout the world but, when a movement arises, must decide whether to support the movement with more than words.

In the case of Egypt, the Obama administration encouraged the democracy movement through diplomacy and by refusing to offer any assistance to the old regime of Hosni Mubarak. Since it was a peaceful uprising and supported by many members of Egypt's military establishment, the United States played no role militarily. Libya was a very different situation. With a democracy movement growing in power, the United States led a NATO-created military force to provide bombing strikes in aid of the opposition movement. The Libyan leader, Muammar Gaddafi, was captured and killed. The situation in Libya is very unsettled with the continued existence of militia groups include one that attacked the U.S. embassy in September, 2012, and killed the ambassador and three other Americans. The circumstances in Syria are extremely complicated. The United States supports the rebel movement through United Nations–imposed sanctions on the regime but has offered no military assistance to the rebels even as the Assad regime is slaughtering civilians.

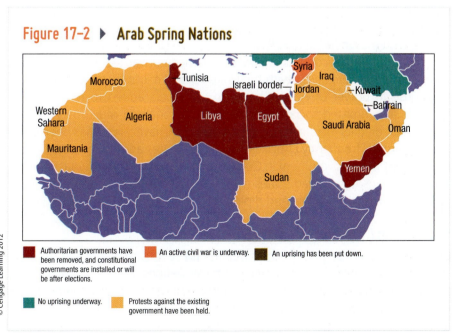

Figure 17–2 ▶ Arab Spring Nations

■ Authoritarian governments have been removed, and constitutional governments are installed or will be after elections.

■ An active civil war is underway.

■ An uprising has been put down.

■ No uprising underway.

■ Protests against the existing government have been held.

© Cengage Learning 2012

Why doesn't the United States intervene in Syria? The Russians support the Assad regime and are completely opposed to U.S. intervention. Intervention is also daunting because Syria has a stockpile of chemical and biological weapons, some of which might be left over from Saddam Hussein's ventures in Iraq.

Iranian Ambitions.   Another important nation in the Middle East is Iran, which has been a religious state since the overthrow of the former shah and the uprising in support of the Ayatollah Khomeini. After the American embassy was captured and its staff held hostage during the Carter administration, the United States and Iran have had a very difficult relationship. It is important to note, however, that Iran is not a closed society and Iranians travel to Europe frequently and have business relationships with companies throughout the world. The major issue between the United States and Iran is that nation's secret development of a nuclear capability. Although the United States and other nations have imposed strong sanctions on Iran, there seems to be no reduction in the effort to possess a nuclear weapon. Iran's possession of such a weapon and the missiles to deliver it established a strong threat to the state of Israel and the potential for generating a major conflict in the region.

Central and South America

As noted above, the United States has had a protective attitude toward the rest of the Western Hemisphere since the Monroe Doctrine was announced in 1823. Having stable, democratic governments in Central and South American nations provides the United States with economic partnerships and with a stable "neighborhood." Of course, at many times in the past, the United States has operated under a realist policy of dealing with authoritarians to achieve stability in this region. During the Cold War years, the United States was particularly concerned about the rise of socialist or communist regimes in Central and South America.

Tensions between the United States and Cuba have frequently erupted since Fidel Castro took power in Cuba in 1959. Relations with Cuba continue to be politically important in the United States, because the Cuban American population can influence election outcomes in Florida, a state that all presidential candidates try to win. When Fidel Castro became seriously ill and underwent surgery in the summer of 2006, his brother, Raul, temporarily assumed power. In 2008, Fidel named his brother as his official successor. Although no major changes have occurred in relationships with the United States, Raul Castro immediately legalized cell phones for Cuban citizens. Some economic activities have been privatized in Cuba, although no one knows when relations with the United States might be normalized.

The rise to power of Hugo Chavez in Venezuela added to tensions in the region. As a committed socialist, Chavez has nationalized much of Venezuela's industry, including its lucrative oil export business. Chavez, who has been elected by wide margins, frequently criticizes the United States and, to increase tensions, supports the Castro government in Cuba and the Assad regime in Syria. Regardless of these tensions, the United States continues to import almost 1 million barrels of oil per day from Venezuela and diplomatic relations have been maintained.

War and HIV/AIDS in Africa

The continent of Africa presents many extremely serious challenges to the United States and the rest of the world. Many African nations are still underdeveloped, with enormous health problems and unstable regimes. Tribal rivalries lead to civil wars and, in the worst cases, genocide. The United States has worked with the United Nations to try to end conflicts and improve the situation on the continent.

Beyond Our Borders

CHINA: A SUPERPOWER UNDER THE SPOTLIGHT

China has experienced rapid economic growth for the last 30 years and today is one of the world's great economic powers. Adjusted for purchasing power, China's gross domestic product (GDP) is now second only to that of the United States and is almost double that of Japan. This fact does not mean that all Chinese are rich. Per capita income in China is well below that of the United States and Europe.

Between 2001 and 2007, China's industrial output increased by almost 50 percent. China now produces more steel than America and Japan combined. Such rapid growth requires massive amounts of raw materials. China consumes 40 percent of the world's output of cement, for example. China's growing demand for raw materials has contributed to dramatic increases in the world prices of many commodities, including oil. Although the worldwide recession of 2008–2009 had some impact on China's economy, mostly because consumers in Western nations purchased fewer Chinese exports, the Chinese economy held steady throughout the entire period.

The city of Shanghai, China, is known for its beautiful skyline. New buildings are constructed each year in this growing metropolis.

CHINA'S ECONOMIC PROSPECTS

U.S. economists have projected that China's GDP will surpass that of the United States by 2039, making China's economy the largest in the world. In fact, this projection may underestimate China's prospects, because it uses substantially lower growth rates than the actual rates China has posted during the last 30 years.

CHINESE-AMERICAN RELATIONS

Since Richard Nixon's visit to China in 1972, American policy has been to gradually engage the Chinese in diplomatic and economic relationships in the hope of turning the nation in a more pro-Western direction. In 1989, however, when Chinese students engaged in extraordinary demonstrations against the government, the Chinese government crushed the demonstrations, killing several students and protesters and imprisoning others. The result was a distinct chill in Chinese-American relations.

After initially criticizing the administration of George H. W. Bush (served 1989–1993) for not being hard enough on China, President Bill Clinton came around to a policy of diplomatic outreach to the Chinese. An important reason for this change was the large and growing trade ties between the two countries. China was granted most-favored-nation status for tariffs and trade policy on a year-to-year basis. In 2000, Congress granted China permanent **Normal Trade Relations (NTR) status**, thus endorsing China's admission to the World Trade Organization (WTO). For a country that is officially communist, China already permits a striking degree of free enterprise, and the rules China must follow as a WTO member will further increase the role of the private sector in China's economy.

Normal Trade Relations (NTR) Status
A status granted through an international treaty by which each member nation must treat other members at least as well as it treats the country that receives its most favorable treatment. This status was formerly known as most-favored-nation status.

In recent years, China did support the American efforts against terrorists but did not support the war in Iraq. Although the two nations have had diplomatic differences, China has joined the six-party talks, working with the United States, Japan, Russia, South Korea, and North Korea to negotiate with North Korea to end its pursuit of nuclear weapons.

CHINA IN THE SPOTLIGHT

In 2008, China became the center of world attention. First, an enormous earthquake struck the area near Chengdu, causing thousands of deaths and billions of dollars of destruction. For the first time since World War II, the Chinese government chose to be open to the media and to allow foreign journalists to report the tragedy. The Chinese government used every resource possible to help the people in the region and to encourage truthful

(continued)

(continued)

reporting. The openness shown by China in this situation may well have been related to China's pride in hosting the 2008 Olympics in Beijing. Although already an economic and military superpower, the Chinese government and the Chinese people placed a great deal of importance on enhancing the nation's standing in the world by producing the most successful Olympic games ever seen.

FOR CRITICAL ANALYSIS

1. *How does China's status as an authoritarian state impact relationships with the United States?*
2. *Why does China want to keep a good relationship with the United States?*

During the early 2000s, the disease AIDS (acquired immune deficiency syndrome) spread throughout southern Africa. This disease infects one-fourth of the populations of Botswana and Zimbabwe and is endemic in most other nations in the southernmost part of the continent. Millions of adults are dying from AIDS, leaving orphaned children. The epidemic is taking a huge economic toll on the affected countries because of the cost of caring for patients and the loss of skilled workers. The disease may be the greatest single threat to world stability emanating from Africa. The Bush administration put in place a special aid package directed at this problem amounting to $15 billion over five years, which has been very successful in reducing the deaths from this disease.

Revolutions and tribal warfare have occurred in several African nations. In 1994, the nation of Rwanda was torn apart by a tribal civil war. Almost a million civilians were massacred during the course of the conflict. The nation of France has been deeply involved with Rwanda, a former colony, and the United States has had little involvement regardless of the humanitarian issues.

In 2004, the world woke up to a growing disaster in Darfur, a western province of Sudan. In the spring of 2004, Sudan had reached a tenuous agreement with rebels in the southern part of the country, but the agreement did not cover a separate rebellion in Darfur. Government-sponsored militias drove more than a million inhabitants of Darfur from their homes and into refugee camps, where they faced starvation. By 2012, Darfur was subject to somewhat less violence but groups from Sudan and from the newly formed nation of South Sudan continued to attack Darfur occasionally.

Civil wars have occurred in Zaire and in Angola. Currently, there is unrest in Mali and extreme economic distress in Zimbabwe. Generally, the United States has preferred to work through the United Nations to aid in reaching peace in these African nations. In addition, an African Union now exists which succeeds an earlier organization known as the Organization of African Unity. The African Union has a membership of 54 states and exists to further the economic and political development of all African countries. It has taken action during civil wars and has fielded peacekeeping forces in Darfur, for example. For the United States, supporting the actions of the AU is greatly preferable to intervening directly in African conflicts.

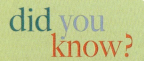

did you know?

The United States invaded and occupied part of Russia in 1919.

You Can Make a Difference

WORKING FOR HUMAN RIGHTS

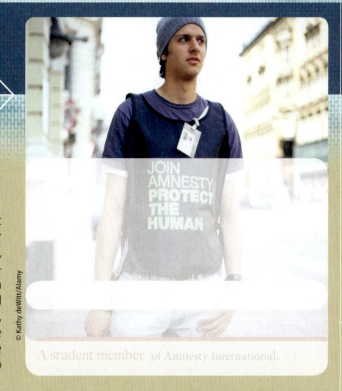

A student member of Amnesty International.

In many countries throughout the world, human rights are not protected. In some nations, people are imprisoned, tortured, or killed because they oppose the current regime. In other nations, certain ethnic or racial groups are oppressed by the majority population. Monks in Myanmar, lawyers in Pakistan, food rioters in Bangladesh, Egypt, and Haiti, and women activists in Iran have all landed on the front pages of our newspapers in the past year, fighting for the basic human rights of millions of people in the world. More than 200,000 people in Darfur alone have died since 2003, as a direct result of the Sudanese government's actions to displace an entire population.

WHY SHOULD YOU CARE?

The strongest reason for involving yourself with human rights issues in other countries is simple moral altruism— unselfish regard for the welfare of others. The defense of human rights is unlikely to put a single dollar in your pocket. A broader consideration, however, is that human rights abuses are often associated with the kind of dictatorial regimes that are likely to provoke wars. To the extent that the people of the world can create a climate in which human rights abuses are unacceptable, they may also create an atmosphere in which national leaders believe that they must display peaceful conduct generally. This, in turn, might reduce the frequency of wars, some of which could involve the United States. Fewer wars would mean preserving peace and human life, not to mention reducing the financial burden of warfare.

WHAT CAN YOU DO?

What can you do to work for the improvement of human rights in other nations? One way is to join an organization that attempts to keep watch over human rights violations. Two such organizations are listed at the end of this feature, and several support student chapters on college campuses. By publicizing human rights violations, such organizations try to pressure nations into changing their practices. Sometimes, these organizations are able to apply enough pressure and cause enough embarrassment that victims may be freed from prison or allowed to emigrate.

Another way to work for human rights is to keep informed about the state of affairs in other nations and to write personally to governments that violate human rights or to their embassies, asking them to cease these violations.

If you want to receive general information about the position of the United States on human rights violations, you can contact the State Department:

U.S. Department of State
Bureau of Democracy, Human Rights, and Labor
2201 C St. NW
Washington, DC 20520
202-647-4000
www.state.gov/g/drl/hr

The following organizations are well known for their watchdog efforts in countries that violate human rights for political reasons:

Amnesty International U.S.A.
5 Penn Plaza
New York, NY 10001
212-807-8400
www.amnestyusa.org

American Friends Service Committee
1501 Cherry St.
Philadelphia, PA 19102
215-241-7000
www.afsc.org

Key Terms

attentive public 548
Cold War 552
containment 552
defense policy 540
détente 553
diplomacy 539
economic aid 539

expansionist policy 550
foreign policy 539
foreign policy process 539
intelligence community 546
iron curtain 552
isolationist foreign
  policy 550

military-industrial
  complex 548
Monroe Doctrine 550
moralist foreign policy 549
national security policy 539
negative constituents 544
Normal Trade Relations
  (NTR) status 565

preemptive war 555
realist foreign policy 549
Soviet bloc 552
Strategic Arms Limitation
  Treaty (SALT I) 553
technical assistance 539
Truman Doctrine 552

Chapter Summary

1. Foreign policy includes national goals and the techniques used to achieve them. National security policy, which is one aspect of foreign policy, is designed to protect the independence and the political and economic integrity of the United States. Diplomacy involves the nation's external relationships and is an attempt to resolve conflict without resort to arms. U.S. foreign policy is sometimes based on moral idealism and sometimes on political realism. The goals of U.S. foreign policy have shifted over the two centuries of the nation's existence as our place in global affairs also changed from minor ex-colony to superpower.

2. The formal power of the president to make foreign policy derives from the U.S. Constitution, which designates the president as commander in chief of the army and navy. Presidents have interpreted this authority broadly. They also have the power to make treaties and executive agreements. In principle, the State Department is the executive agency with primary authority over foreign affairs. The National Security Council also plays a major role. The intelligence community consists of government agencies engaged in activities varying from information gathering to covert operations. In response to presidential actions in the Vietnam War, Congress attempted to establish some limits on the power of the president to intervene abroad by passing the War Powers Resolution in 1973.

3. Three major themes have guided U.S. foreign policy. In the early years of the nation, isolationism was the primary strategy. With the start of the 20th century, isolationism gave way to global involvement. From the end of World War II through the 1980s, the major goal was to contain communism and the influence of the Soviet Union.

4. During the 1800s, the United States had little international power and generally stayed out of European conflicts and politics, and so these years have been called the period of isolationism. The Monroe Doctrine of 1823 stated that the United States would not accept foreign intervention in the Western Hemisphere and would not meddle in European affairs. The United States pursued an actively expansionist policy in the Americas and the Pacific area, however.

5. The end of the policy of isolationism toward Europe started with the Spanish-American War of 1898. U.S. involvement in European politics became more extensive when the United States entered World War I on April 6, 1917. World War II marked a lasting change in American foreign policy. The United States was the only major country to emerge from the war with its economy intact and the only country with operating nuclear weapons.

6. Soon after the close of World War II, the uncomfortable alliance between the United States and the Soviet Union ended, and the Cold War began. A policy of containment, which assumed an expansionist Soviet Union, was enunciated in the Truman Doctrine. Following the frustrations of the Vietnam War and the apparent arms equality of the United States and the Soviet Union, the United States adopted a policy of *détente*. Although President Reagan took a tough stance toward the Soviet Union during his first term, his second term saw serious negotiations toward arms reduction, culminating in the signing of the Intermediate-Range Nuclear Force Treaty in 1987. After the fall of the Soviet Union, Russia emerged as a less threatening state and signed the Strategic Arms Reduction Treaty with the United States in 1992.

7. After the dissolution of the Soviet Union, the United States assumed the position of global superpower without a military competitor. However, the United States has maintained the NATO alliance with its European allies and has added several former Soviet bloc states to the alliance. Russia has remained a powerful nation, one that is becoming increasingly a one-party state. The European Union continues to increase its influence as an economic superpower and competitor to the United States, while the rapidly developing economies of India and China continue to push those nations into the global power structure.

8. Terrorism has become a major challenge facing the United States and other nations. The United States waged war on terrorism after the September 11 attacks. U.S. armed forces occupied Afghanistan in 2001 and Iraq in 2003.

9. Nuclear proliferation continues to be an issue as a result of the breakup of the Soviet Union and loss of control over its nuclear arsenal, along with the continued efforts of other nations to gain nuclear warheads. More than 20,000 nuclear warheads are known to exist worldwide. The United States is a signatory to the Nuclear Non-proliferation Treaty and the Comprehensive Test Ban Treaty and works actively with other nations to reduce the threat of nuclear arms. Recently, the United States and Russia signed a treaty to further reduce each nation's supply of nuclear missiles.

10. Ethnic tensions and political instability in many regions of the world provide challenges to the United States. Support for Israel has been at the center of U.S. foreign policy in the Middle East, as well as support for the installation of democratic governments in Israel's neighboring countries. Iran has continued to develop nuclear weapons in the face of sanctions imposed by the United Nations. Civil wars have erupted in a number of African states in the last two decades, but the United States has preferred to work through the United Nations or African Union in bringing peace to these nations. In Central and South America, the United States has encouraged economic development and democracy throughout the continent. Tensions remain between the United States and the communist government of Cuba and with the government of Hugo Chavez in Venezuela.

Selected Print, Media, and Online Resources

PRINT RESOURCES

Chomsky, Noam, and Gilbert Achcar. *Perilous Power: The Middle East and U.S. Foreign Policy Dialogues on Terror, Democracy, War, and Justice.* Boulder, CO: Paradigm, 2006. Chomsky is one of the most vocal critics of U.S. foreign policy, and he shows it in the essays in this book. Achcar is a specialist in Middle Eastern affairs who has lived in the region. These authors examine key questions relating to terrorism, conspiracies, democracy, anti-Semitism, and anti-Arab racism. This book can serve as an introduction to understanding the Middle East today.

Hoffmann, Stanley. *Chaos and Violence: What Globalization, Failed States, and Terrorism Mean for U.S. Foreign Policy.* Lanham, MD: Rowman & Littlefield, 2006. What is the proper place of the United States in a world that has been defined by the terrorist acts of September 11, 2001? What are the ethics of intervention, and what is the morality of human rights? These are questions the author answers. He also attempts to show how our broken relationship with Europe can be repaired. He believes that America has engaged in too much unilateralism.

Hook, Steven W. *U.S. Foreign Policy: The Paradox of World Power,* 3rd ed. Washington, DC: CQ Press, 2010. In his third edition of this survey of American foreign policy, Hook adds the first two years of the Obama administration and its initiatives in foreign policy to his account.

Kang, David. *China Rising: Peace, Power, and Order in East Asia.* New York: Columbia University Press, 2007. Kang examines the history of China and suggests that the ascendance of China to great power status is not a destabilizing force in the world, but that the Chinese rise to power will be peaceful and an asset to other Asian nations.

O'Hanlon, Michael, and Mike M. Mochizuki. *Crisis in the Korean Peninsula: How to Deal with a Nuclear North Korea.* New York: McGraw-Hill,

2003. The authors provide a comprehensive introduction to the dangers posed by North Korea, which could become a greater threat to world peace than the current terrorist movements. They also offer a possible "grand bargain" to defuse the crisis.

Power, Samantha. *A Problem from Hell: America and the Age of Genocide.* New York: HarperCollins, 2007. This well-known former journalist, who is now the executive director of Harvard's Carr Center for Human Rights, looks at U.S. responses to genocide in Rwanda, Darfur, and other areas of the world during the last century. She argues that U.S. intervention has been woefully inadequate.

Ricks, Thomas E. *The Gamble: General David Petraeus and the American Military Adventure in Iraq, 2006–2008.* New York: Penguin Press, 2009. In 2007, Ricks released *Fiasco: The American Military Adventure in Iraq, 2003 to 2005.* This was one of the most well received and scathing accounts of disastrous U.S. policies and practices in that country and became a number-one *New York Times* best seller. In *The Gamble,* Ricks returns to Iraq to find out whether America's new counterinsurgency strategy can rescue a seemingly impossible situation.

Sanger, David E. *Confront and Conceal: Obama's Secret Wars and Surprising Use of American Power.* New York: Crown, 2012. The author, a reporter for *The New York Times,* reveals the degree to which the president personally is involved in decision making on the U.S. pursuit of terrorists.

Zakaria, Fareed. *The Post-American World.* New York: W. W. Norton, 2008. Zakaria, a *Newsweek* editor and television commentator, does not write about the decline of America, but about the rise of other nations, especially China and India. An optimist despite the current terror crisis, Zakaria contends that the world is richer and more peaceful than it has ever been and that these trends are likely to continue. He concludes with a critique of the U.S. foreign policy process, which he believes is designed for partisan battles rather than problem solving.

MEDIA RESOURCES

Black Hawk Down—This 2002 film recounts the events in Mogadishu, Somalia, in October 1993, during which two U.S. Black Hawk helicopters were shot down. The film, based on reporter Mark Bowden's best-selling book by the same name, contains graphic scenes of terrifying urban warfare.

The Fall of Milosevic—A highly acclaimed 2003 documentary by Norma Percy and Brian Lapping, this film covers the final years of the crisis in the former Yugoslavia, including the war in Kosovo and the fall of Slobodan Milosevic, the Serb nationalist leader and alleged war criminal. Except for Milosevic, almost all top Serb and Albanian leaders are interviewed, as are President Bill Clinton and British prime minister Tony Blair.

The 50 Years War—Israel and the Arabs—This is a two-volume PBS Home Video released in 2000. More balanced than some accounts, this film includes interviews with many leaders involved in the struggle, including (from Israel) Yitzhak Rabin, Shimon Peres, Benjamin Netanyahu, and Ariel Sharon; (from the Arab world) Egypt's Anwar al-Sadat, Jordan's King Hussein, and Yasser Arafat; and (from the United States) presidents Jimmy Carter, George H. W. Bush, and Bill Clinton.

The Hurt Locker—This Academy Award–winning film traces the work of an American bomb squad in Iraq and brings home the intensity of these soldiers' work in identifying Iraqi attackers.

No End in Sight: Iraq's Descent into Chaos—Packed with interviews of officials, generals, and soldiers, this 2007 film argues that insufficient troop levels, the disbanding of Iraq's army, and the dismantling of the Iraqi government led to the insurgency and chaos that have bedeviled the country. *No End in Sight* is a shocking portrait of arrogance and incompetence, laced with terrifying war footage.

Senator Obama Goes to Africa—A documentary of Barack Obama's 2006 trip to Kenya, South Africa, and Chad. Despite the many questions Americans have had about Barack Obama, he has been more open about his unusual past than most politicians. One source of information is this film, which shows some of the advantages and disadvantages of Obama's international fame. In the end, he can do little about the suffering that he sees.

United 93—A 2006 documentary about the fourth airplane hijacked on 9/11. When they learned the fate of the other three planes through cell phones, the passengers decided to fight back, with the result that the flight crashed in a Pennsylvania field, far from its intended target. *United 93* takes places in real time and is almost unbearably moving. Several critics named it the best film of the year.

ONLINE RESOURCES

Arms Control Association a national nonpartisan membership organization dedicated to promoting public understanding of and support for effective arms control policies. The Web site of the ACA lists each country's status in terms of signing arms control treaties and its inventory of weapons: www.armscontrol.org

Brookings a nonprofit public policy organization based in Washington, D.C. Access the research reports of this think tank: www.brookings.edu

Center for Security Studies (CSS) an academic institute at ETH Zurich specializing in research, teaching, and the provision of services in international and national security policy. Provides information about human rights, national security, and other issues from a European point of view: www.css.ethz.ch/index_EN

Central Intelligence Agency created in 1947 with the signing of the National Security Act by President Harry S Truman. Learn more about this independent agency responsible for providing national security intelligence to senior U.S. policymakers: www.cia.gov

Freedom House an organization that promotes its vision of democracy around the world and rates all nations on their democratic practices: www.freedomhouse.org

U.S. Department of State provides access to hundreds of Web sites on foreign and defense policies of the U.S. government and the governments of other nations and includes information about visas, passports, and individual countries: www.state.gov

18 State and Local Government

KAMIL KRZACZYNSKI/EPA/Landov

Chicago Mayor Rahm Emmanuel marches in the 2012 St. Patrick's Day parade with the Prime Minister of Ireland, Enda Kenny.

LEARNING OUTCOMES

After reading this chapter, students will be able to:

■ **LO1** Discuss the relationship of state laws and constitutions to the U.S. Constitution and federal law.

■ **LO2** Explain why counties, cities, and other units of local government are limited in their power and their autonomy.

■ **LO3** Discuss the issues raised by corruption and patronage in local and state governments.

■ **LO4** Describe the most important sources of revenue for states and local governments and their biggest expenditures, and contrast them with those of the federal government.

What If...

ALL STATES OFFERED SCHOOL VOUCHERS?

BACKGROUND

All public education systems in the United States are funded by and controlled by local and state governments. These entities set policies, raise taxes and distribute them to schools, and regulate all aspects of the public school system. Many observers argue that the low achievement of American students requires drastic changes. They propose that the easiest way to improve the system is to make schools compete with each other. Currently, parents normally are required to send their children to a public school in the particular district where the family's home is located. Generally, only families that are willing to spend from $3,000 to $10,000 per year for tuition at private schools (in addition to the property taxes they pay to support their local public school districts) have a choice as to which school their children will attend.

WHAT IF STATES GAVE PARENTS MONEY TO CHANGE SCHOOLS?

School choice can involve open districts, meaning that parents can choose to send their children to public schools outside of their districts. The type of school choice that generates controversy, however, usually involves giving families vouchers, representing state funds that can be used at any school, public or private. In other words, a voucher is worth some specified amount of money, such as $5,000, but only if it is redeemed by a bona fide public or private school. Any such plan has to be set up by state or local government, because that is where the responsibility for education currently lies.

Under such a system, parents determine where their children go to school. The children may attend the same local public school, a public school in another district, or a private school anywhere. Private schools can accept the vouchers as full payment for tuition fees or require that additional fees be paid.

COMPETITION WOULD BECOME EVIDENT

Certainly, with a voucher system, competition for students would develop. Public schools would have to compete not only among themselves (as they currently do in areas that have open districts) but also with private schools. Private schools would have to compete with all schools.

Some critics of school choice, particularly public school teachers and administrators, are uncomfortable with treating public education like a business. Because of the competitive environment that would be created by school choice, some public schools might not be able to keep and attract enough students to survive. These schools, unless further subsidized by state and local governments, would go bankrupt and disappear. Still, in Milwaukee, Wisconsin, where the first voucher program was established in 1990, the program has raised test scores at both private and public schools. School board members and some liberals who formerly opposed the plan now accept it.

THE CONSTITUTIONAL ISSUE

Other critics of school vouchers claim that such programs violate the federal Constitution or state constitutions because they allow state funds to be used for education at religious schools. For example, in Cleveland, Ohio, children from low-income families received state funds, in the form of vouchers, to attend the schools of their choice. Most of the 4,000 children in the program left public schools to attend Catholic educational institutions.

According to opponents, the use of tax dollars to support religious education violated the establishment clause of the First Amendment to the Constitution, which requires the separation of church and state (see Chapter 4). In 2002, however, the Supreme Court held that the voucher program was constitutional because families theoretically could use the vouchers to send their children not only to religious schools but also to secular private academies, suburban public schools, or charter schools. Therefore, the program did not unconstitutionally entangle church and state.

FOR CRITICAL ANALYSIS

1. *Why are teachers' unions, such as the National Education Association, so adamantly against vouchers?*

2. *Do you see school choice as hurting or helping students from low-income families?*

FOR MOST AMERICANS, state and local governments have the most day-to-day impact on their lives. To get a driver's license, you must meet directly with a representative of the state government and complete state-required forms and tests. You probably attended elementary and secondary schools provided by local governmental units, typically called school boards. Local governments determine the cost of a traffic ticket and the day that your street is cleaned. Because they shape the environments in which all Americans live, the more than 89,000 local governmental units in the United States play a vital role in our federal system. However, as you read in Chapter 3, many state government functions are paid for, in part, by federal grants. More and more, federal programs shape or control state programs that directly affect citizens.

From a practical point of view, it is impossible to understand American politics and government today without knowledge of how state and local governments operate—the topic of this chapter. We begin by examining the constitutional powers of the states as set forth by the founders in the U.S. Constitution. As you will see, local governments were not mentioned in the Constitution. The founders left their existence in the hands of state government. The What If … that opens this chapter looks at the role of state and local governments in allowing parents to choose an alternative to the public school system. The issue of school vouchers is complex, involving federal rules and the Supreme Court, state rules, and local school boards.

The U.S. Constitution and the State Governments

■ **Learning Outcome 1:**
Discuss the relationship of state laws and constitutions to the U.S. Constitution and federal law.

We live in a federal system in which there are 50 separate state governments and one national government. The U.S. Constitution reserves a broad range of powers for state governments. It also prohibits state governments from engaging in certain activities. The U.S. Constitution does not say explicitly what the states actually may do. Rather, state powers are simply reserved, or residual: States may do anything that is not prohibited by the Constitution or anything that is not expressly within the realm of the national government.

The major reserved powers of the states are the powers to tax, spend, and regulate intrastate commerce (commerce within a given state). The states also have general police power, meaning that they can impose their will on their citizens in the areas of safety (through, say, traffic laws), health (immunizations), welfare (child-abuse laws), and morals (regulation of pornographic materials).

Restrictions on state and local governmental activity are implied by the Constitution in Article VI, Clause 2:

> *This Constitution, and the Laws of the United States which shall be made in Pursuance thereof; and all Treaties made, or which shall be made, under the Authority of the United States, shall be the supreme Law of the Land; and the Judges in every State shall be bound thereby, any Thing in the Constitution or Laws of any State to the Contrary notwithstanding.*

In other words, the U.S. Constitution is the supreme law of the land. No state or local law can be in conflict with the Constitution, with laws made by the national Congress, or with treaties entered into by the national government. State and local governments, however, will create policies that are at odds with federal policies or adopt policies that the federal government has not yet adopted. In recent

David Santiago/El Nuevo Herald/MCT/Newscom

Carlos Gimenez, mayor of Miami-Dade County, won the mayor's race after the recall of the prior mayor. Gimenez, the former fire chief for Miami-Dade, came to the United States from Cuba as a child and won the mayor's position in an 11-candidate election.

years, states, especially those along the Mexican border, have passed their own policies to deal with illegal immigrants, in part because the Congress has not yet agreed on a new immigration policy. Arizona, Alabama, South Carolina and Utah are among those states that have passed laws to discourage the residency of undocumented immigrants. The Arizona law, signed by Governor Jan Brewer in 2010, required all immigrants to carry their papers, banned immigrants from soliciting work in public places, and required police to ask the immigration status of individuals detained for other crimes if the police suspected that they were illegal immigrants. In a landmark Supreme Court case, many aspects of the Arizona law were found to be unconstitutional, but the provision allowing police officers to ask for proof of legal residency when a suspect is detained was upheld.[1] Alabama has passed a law making all contracts signed by undocumented immigrants illegal, including apartment leases and possibly utility contracts. That law and many others are being tested in the federal courts. If, in the future, the U.S. Congress passes legislation that conflicts with the Arizona law, the United States Supreme Court would be the final arbiter of any conflict between the Arizona laws and the federal law.

The U.S. Constitution is a model of brevity, although at the cost of specificity. State constitutions, however, typically are excessively long and detailed. The U.S. Constitution has endured for 200 years and has been amended only 27 times. State constitutions are another matter. Louisiana has had 11 constitutions; Georgia, 9; and Virginia, 7. The number of amendments submitted to voters borders on the absurd. For example, the citizens of Alabama have adopted 827 amendments to their state constitution; this outlandish number is due to the fact that even local governments must have a state constitutional amendment to engage in certain activities. An amendment might specify the salary for a particular local official or authorize gambling casinos for specified counties.

Why Are State Constitutions So Long?

According to historians, the length and mass of detail of many state constitutions reflect the loss of popular confidence in state legislatures between the end of the Civil War and the early 1900s. During that period, 42 states adopted or revised their constitutions. Those constitutions adopted before or after that period are shorter and contain fewer restrictions on the powers of state legislatures. Another equally important reason for the length and detail of state constitutions is that state constitution makers apparently have had a difficult time distinguishing between constitutional and statutory law. Does the Louisiana constitution need an amendment to declare Huey Long's birthday a legal holiday? Is it necessary for the constitution of South Dakota to authorize a cordage and twine plant at the state penitentiary? Does the California constitution need to discuss the tax-exempt status of the Huntington Library and Art Gallery? The U.S. Constitution contains no such details. It leaves to the legislature the nuts-and-bolts activity of making specific statutory laws.

---

1. *Arizona v. U.S.*, 567 U.S. ___(2012).

In all fairness to the states, their courts do not interpret their constitutions as freely as the United States Supreme Court interprets the U.S. Constitution. Therefore, the states feel compelled to be more specific in their own constitutions. Additionally, the framers of state constitutions may feel obliged to fill in the gaps left by the very brief federal Constitution.

The Constitutional Convention and the Constitutional Initiative

Two of the several ways to effect constitutional changes are the state constitutional convention and the constitutional initiative. As of 2007, more than 230 state constitutional conventions had been used to write an entirely new constitution or to attempt to amend an existing one. In 18 states, the constitution can be amended by **constitutional initiative**.[2] An initiative allows citizens to place a proposed amendment on the ballot without calling a constitutional convention. The number of signatures required to get a constitutional initiative on the ballot varies from state to state; it is usually between 5 and 10 percent of the total number of votes cast for governor in the last election. The initiative process has been used most frequently in California and Oregon. Relatively few initiative amendments are approved by the electorate.

The State Executive Branch

All state governments in the United States have executive, legislative, and judicial branches. Here the similarity with the federal government ends. State governments do not always have strong executive branches.

A Weak Executive

During the colonial period, governors were appointed by the Crown and had the power to call the colonial assembly (the colonial legislative body) into session, recommend legislation, exercise veto power, and dissolve the assembly. The colonial governor acted as commander in chief of the colony's military forces and was also the head of the judiciary.

Not surprisingly, the colonies' revolt against British rule centered on the all-powerful colonial governors. When the first states were formed after the Declaration of Independence, hostility toward the governor's office ensured a weak executive branch and an extremely strong legislative branch. By the 1830s, however, the state executive office had become more important. Since Andrew Jackson's presidency, all governors (except in South Carolina) have been elected directly by the people. Simultaneously, there was an effort to democratize state government by popularly electing other state government officials as well.

Under the tenets of Jacksonian democracy, the more public officials who are elected (and not appointed), the more democratic (and better) the system will be. Even today, some states have many state offices with independently elected officials. The direct election of so many executive officials makes it likely that no one will have much power, because each official is working to secure his or her own political support. Only if the elected officials happen to be able to work together cohesively can they get much done.

Constitutional Initiative
An electoral device whereby citizens can propose a constitutional amendment through petitions signed by the required number of registered voters.

---

2. These states are Arizona, Arkansas, California, Colorado, Florida, Illinois, Massachusetts, Michigan, Mississippi, Missouri, Montana, Nebraska, Nevada, North Dakota, Ohio, Oklahoma, Oregon, and South Dakota.

Wisconsin governor Scott Walker talks with the media on the night before he successfully retained his office in a recall election.

A slight majority of the states require that the candidates for governor and lieutenant governor run for election as a team. In some states where this is not required, however, the voters have at times chosen a governor from one political party and a lieutenant governor from another. In a few states, this has actually created a situation in which the governor is unwilling to leave the state in order to prevent the lieutenant governor from exerting power during the governor's absence.

Reforming the System

Most states follow the practice of electing numerous executive officials. Nonetheless, governors have exercised the authority of their office with increasing frequency in recent years. Governors, for example, have become a significant force in legislative policymaking. In theory, the governor enjoys the same advantage that the president has over Congress in his or her ability to make policy decisions and to embody them in a program on which the state legislative body can act. How the governor exercises this ability often depends on her or his powers of persuasion. A strong personality can make for a strong executive office. Personal skill, the strength of political parties and special-interest groups, and the governor's use of the media can affect how much actual power she or he has.

Reorganization of the state executive branch to achieve greater efficiency has been attempted many times and in many states. There are some obstacles to reorganizing state executive branches, however. Voters do not want to lose their ability to influence politics directly. Both the voters and the legislators fear that reorganization will concentrate too much authority in the hands of the governor. Finally, many believe that numerous governmental functions, such as control of the highway program, should remain administrative rather than political.

Despite the fragmentation of executive power and doubts about the concentration of power in an executive's hands, the trend toward modernization has increased the powers of many of the states' highest executives. Based on a governor's ability to make major appointments, formulate a state budget, veto legislation, and exercise other powers, the National Governors Association ranks the governors of at least 25 states as powerful or very powerful executives. Only 11 states are assessed as giving their executives little or very little power.

Moreover, state governors—as well as legislators—are playing increasingly important roles as the states assume more authority over programs, such as welfare, that for decades were controlled by the national government. The trend toward states' rights during the 1990s and 2000s has allowed governors to become models of leadership on several issues affecting national politics, including crime, welfare, and education. A state governorship may also be a stepping-stone to the U.S. presidency. Seventeen of the nation's 43 presidents (39%), including several recent presidents (Jimmy Carter, Ronald Reagan, Bill Clinton, and George W. Bush), served as state governors before assuming the presidential office. For these reasons, elections to state governorships tend to receive more national attention than in the past.

The Governor's Veto Power

The veto power gives the president of the United States immense leverage. Simply the threat of a presidential veto often means that legislation will not be passed by Congress. In some states, governors have strong veto power, but in other states, governors have no veto power at all. Some states give the governor veto power but allow only five days in which to exercise it. Thirteen states give the governor pocket veto power.

In 43 states, the governor has some form of **item veto** power on appropriations, which gives the governor an opportunity to decrease legislative spending. If the governor in such a state does not like one item, or line, in an appropriations bill, he or she can veto that item. In 12 states, the governor can reduce the amount of the appropriation but cannot eliminate it altogether. Nineteen states give governors the ability to use the item veto on more than just appropriations.

Item Veto
The power exercised by the governors of most states to veto particular sections or items of an appropriations bill, while signing the remainder of the bill into law.

The State Legislature

Although a move in recent years has increased the power of governors, state legislatures are still an important force in state politics and state governmental decision making. The task of these assemblies is to legislate on such matters as taxes and the regulation of business and commerce, highways, school systems and the funding of education, and welfare payments. Allocation of funds and program priorities are vital issues to local residents and communities, and conflicts between regions within the state or between the cities and the rural areas are common.

State legislatures have been criticized for being unprofessional and less than effective. It is true that state legislatures sometimes spend their time considering trivial legislation (such as the official state pie in Florida), and lobbyists often have too much influence in state capitals. At the same time, state legislators are often given few resources with which to work. In many states, legislatures are limited to meeting only part of the year, and in some the pay is a disincentive to real service. In 20 states, state legislators are paid less than $15,000 per year. The National Council of State Legislatures actually categorizes state legislatures as fully professional, hybrid, or volunteer/part time, according to the characteristics discussed here. A complete list of state legislators' salaries, as well as other characteristics of state legislatures, is given in Table 18–1.

We have seen earlier (Chapter 11) how a bill becomes a law in the U.S. Congress. A similar process occurs at the state level. Figure 18–1 on page 620 traces how an idea becomes a law in the Florida legislature. Similar steps are followed in other states (note that Nebraska has a unicameral legislature, however, so it has no second chamber process).

did you know?

Missouri state legislators approved a five-pound, 1,012-page bill aimed at reducing state paperwork.

Legislative Apportionment

Drawing up legislative districts—state as well as federal—has long been subject to gerrymandering (creative cartography designed to guarantee that one political party maintains control of a particular voting district). Malapportionment is the skewed distribution of voters in a state's legislative districts. The United States Supreme Court ruled in 1962 that malapportioned state legislatures violate the equal protection clause of the Fourteenth Amendment.[3] In a series of cases that followed, the Court held that legislative districts must be as nearly equal as

---

3. *Baker v. Carr*, 369 U.S. 186 (1962).

Table 18—1 ▸ Characteristics of State Legislatures 2012

	SEATS IN SENATE	LENGTH OF TERM	SEATS IN HOUSE	LENGTH OF TERM	YEARS SESSIONS ARE HELD	SALARY*
Alabama	35	4	105	4	Annual	$10(d)†
Alaska	20	4	40	2	Annual	$50,400†
Arizona	30	2	60	2	Annual	$24,000†
Arkansas	35	4	100	2	Odd	$15,851†
California	40	4	80	2	Even**	$95,291†
Colorado	35	4	65	2	Annual	$30,000†
Connecticut	36	2	151	2	Annual	$28,000
Delaware	21	4	41	2	Annual	$42,750
Florida	40	4	120	2	Annual	$29,687†
Georgia	56	2	180	2	Annual	$17,342†
Hawaii	25	4	51	2	Annual	$46,273†
Idaho	35	2	70	2	Annual	$16,116†
Illinois	59	‡	118	2	Annual	$67,836†
Indiana	50	4	100	2	Annual	$22,616†
Iowa	50	4	100	2	Annual	$25,000†
Kansas	40	4	125	2	Annual	$88.66(d)†
Kentucky	38	4	100	2	Annual	$188.22(d)†
Louisiana	39	4	105	4	Annual	$16,800†
Maine	35	2	151	2	Even	$13,526§†
Maryland	47	4	141	4	Annual	$43,500†
Massachusetts	40	2	160	2	Biennial**	$61,133†
Michigan	38	4	110	2	Annual	$71,685†
Minnesota	67	4	134	2	Biennial	$31,140†
Mississippi	52	4	122	4	Annual	$10,000†
Missouri	34	4	163	2	Annual	$35,915†
Montana	50	4	100	2	Odd	$82.64(d)†
Nebraska	49	4	—	—	Annual	$12,000"
Nevada	21	4	42	2	Odd	$146.29(d)†
New Hampshire	24	2	400	2	Annual	$200(b)
New Jersey	40	4	80	2	Biennial	$49,000
New Mexico	42	4	70	2	Annual	—†
New York	62	2	150	2	Annual	$79,500†
North Carolina	50	2	120	2	Odd††	$13,951†
North Dakota	47	4	94	4	Odd	$152(d)†
Ohio	33	4	99	2	Biennial	$60,584
Oklahoma	48	4	101	2	Annual	$38,400†
Oregon	30	4	60	2	Odd	$21,936†
Pennsylvania	50	4	203	2	Odd**	$82,026†
Rhode Island	38	2	75	2	Annual	$13,089
South Carolina	46	4	124	2	Biennial	$10,400†

	SEATS IN SENATE	LENGTH OF TERM	SEATS IN HOUSE	LENGTH OF TERM	YEARS SESSIONS ARE HELD	SALARY*
South Dakota	35	2	70	2	Annual	$12,000[†]
Tennessee	33	4	99	2	Biennial	$19,009[†]
Texas	31	4	150	2	Odd	$7,200[†]
Utah	29	4	75	2	Annual	$117(d)[†]
Vermont	30	2	150	2	Annual	$604.79(w)[†]
Virginia	40	4	100	2	Annual	$18,000[‡‡]
Washington	49	4	98	2	Annual	$42,106[†]
West Virginia	34	4	100	2	Annual	$20,000[†]
Wisconsin	33	4	99	2	Biennial	$49,943[†]
Wyoming	30	4	60	2	Biennial	$150(d)[†]

*Salaries annual unless otherwise noted as (d)—per day, (b)—per biennium, or (w)—per week.
[†]Plus *per diem* living expenses.
[‡]Terms vary from two to four years.
[§]For odd year; $8,655 for even year.
["]Unicameral legislature.
[**]Two-year session (that is, it meets every year).
[††]Annual at option of legislature.
[‡‡]Senate; House is $17,640.
Source: Council of State Governments, *Book of the States* (2012 Edition).

possible in terms of population, and the grossest examples of state legislative malapportionment were eliminated.[4] The Supreme Court, however, allowed "benevolent, bipartisan gerrymandering" in certain states.

Minority Representation. In 1977, the Supreme Court held that a state had an obligation under the 1965 Voting Rights Act to draw district boundaries to maximize minority legislative representation.[5] Thus, each decade, state and federal legislative districts must be redrawn to ensure that every person's vote is roughly equal and that minorities are represented adequately.

By the mid-1990s, the Supreme Court had reversed its position on what has been called "racial gerrymandering." In a series of cases, the Court held that voting districts that are redrawn solely with the goal of maximizing the electoral strength and representation of minority groups violate the equal protection clause.[6] (See Chapter 11 for a more detailed discussion of this issue.)

Political Gerrymandering. In recent years, political gerrymandering that benefits both of the major political parties has become a significant issue. Using sophisticated computer programs, legislators can draw district lines that virtually guarantee the reelection of incumbents. In many states, Republican and Democratic legislators conspire to ensure the safety of incumbents, regardless of party. In 2004, for example, not a single seat in the California state legislature changed hands. Some have said that instead of the voters choosing their legislators, the legislators now choose their voters. The Supreme Court has not blocked this practice. In 1986, the Court did hold that it was at least conceivable that an instance of political gerrymandering might be unconstitutional.[7] In 2004 and

4. *Reynolds v. Sims*, 377 U.S. 533 (1964); and other cases.
5. *United Jewish Organizations of Williamsburg v. Cary*, 430 U.S. 144 (1977).
6. *Miller v. Johnson*, 515 U.S. 900 (1995); *Shaw v. Hunt*, 517 U.S. 899 (1996); and *Bush v. Vera*, 517 U.S. 952 (1996).
7. *Davis v. Bandemer*, 478 U.S. 109 (1986).

Figure 18–1 ▶ How an Idea Becomes a Law

A simplified chart showing the route a bill takes through the Florida legislature. Bills may originate in either house. This bill originated in the House of Representatives.

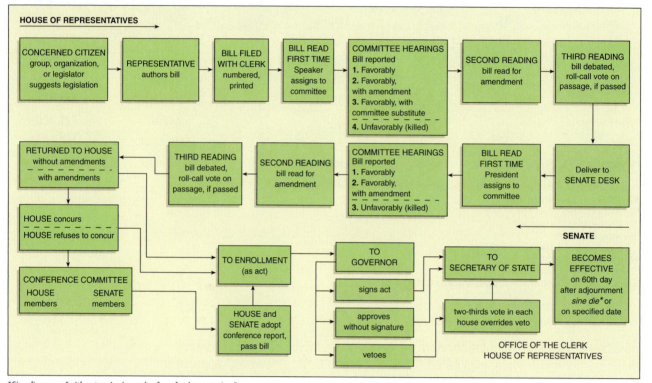

*Sine die means "without assigning a day for a further meeting."
Source: Allen Morris and Joan Perry Morris, compilers, *The Florida Handbook, 2005–2006*, 30th ed. (Tallahassee, FL: Peninsular Books, 2005).

2006, however, the Court in effect withdrew the possibility that it might ever issue such a ruling.[8]

Citizens in states ranging from Massachusetts to California have organized campaigns to win new laws that curb political gerrymandering. Iowa and Arizona already use nonpartisan commissions to draw district lines instead of leaving the job to the legislature and the governor. In 2012 Ohio voters will decide whether a nonpartisan system will be adopted for their state. Some experts believe that regional political loyalties have become so entrenched that nonpartisan plans can create only a handful of competitive districts.[9]

Term Limits for State Legislators

For more than a decade, many states have agreed that a legislator's tenure should be limited. Although the restrictions vary, 15 states have laws restricting the number of terms a legislator can serve. In four other states—Massachusetts, Oregon, Washington, and Wyoming—term-limit laws were thrown out by the respective state supreme courts, while Idaho's and Utah's legislatures repealed their own term-limit laws. Advocates of term limits argue that lawmakers who have not spent years in public office will best represent the interests of voters. Special-interest groups will have less chance to influence a politician who does not have

8. *Vieth v. Jubelirer*, 541 U.S. 267 (2004); *League of Latin American Citizens v. Perry*, 126 S.Ct. 2594 (2006).
9. Ann Sanner, "Voter Coalition to Submit Signatures in Ballot Effort to Change How Ohio Draws Political Lines," Associated Press, July 3, 2012.

a future campaign to finance. Opponents of term limits argue that the same newly elected lawmakers who are less likely to be swayed by special interests are also more likely to lack the experience required to understand state policy. Ironically, such opponents include current politicians who once voted for term limits but are now subject to their consequences.

Making service in the legislature a part-time job rather than a full-time one is another way states try to keep legislators in tune with their fellow citizens. In some states, especially large states such as California and New York, state legislators receive a salary that is large enough to live on. In these states, service in the legislature is considered a full-time job, and the members of the statehouse and senate are referred to as professional legislators. In a majority of the states, however, legislative service is considered part-time work, and salaries reflect this expectation. Such states are said to have citizen legislators. New Hampshire is an extreme example of this system. The 400 members of its house are paid only $200 per session, with no allowance for expenses. New Hampshire has only about 1.3 million people, so it is relatively easy for a political activist to become part of the legislature.

Advocates of a professional legislature recognize that this system would be a hard sell in a state with a small population, such as Montana. Still, these advocates believe that a part-time legislature creates significant problems and that larger states such as Texas should not rely on such a system. Paid only $7,200 per year, Texas legislators have a powerful incentive to represent and take payments from corrupt special interests. Paying legislators a living wage would actually make it easier for ordinary citizens to run for office. Service should not be limited to the retired, the wealthy, and lawyers who represent the powerful. Those who support a citizen legislature do not believe that states with professional legislators have better laws. They contend that much of the extra time spent by professional legislators is likely to be wasted and that making legislators full-time professionals encourages careerism and a lack of responsiveness to the voters.

Ethics and Campaign Finance Reform in the States

Regulations for campaign contributions and the disclosure of contributors for all federal offices, including representatives, senators, and the president, are the result of legislation passed by the Congress and rules put forward by the Federal Election Commission. However, regulations that affect candidates for office at the state level are the responsibility of state legislatures and the governor. States differ a great deal in the degree to which they regulate campaign contributions and the disclosure of donors. For example, while most states require that all contributions be disclosed to the public through some sort of quarterly reporting system, the amount of information disclosed about the donors varies widely, as does the public's access to the information. Some states require that the donor's name, occupation, address, and employer be disclosed, whereas 14 states do not require either the donor's occupation or employer to be disclosed, thus hiding contributions from those industries that might benefit from legislation. Almost all states require that candidates report expenditures, but several do not require the amount or purpose of the expenditure to be revealed. More than 40 states now post all information that is reported on their Web sites, but not all require candidates to file electronically, so information is not available to the public quickly.[10]

Similarly, states have struggled to enact and enforce ethics legislation. If a legislature is composed of volunteer legislators meeting, perhaps, for four or five months per year and being paid less than $15,000, it seems unlikely that the

---

10. "Grading Campaign Disclosure 2008," The Campaign Disclosure Project, www.campaigndisclosure.org.

legislators depend on their elected position for their livelihood. Most part-time legislators have real careers and earn their livings through those positions. However, there are always questions of conflicts of interest, lobbying gifts and parties, and opportunities for a legislator or the staff to benefit from a particular piece of legislation. There are numerous examples of legislators and governors who have suffered legal action from lapses in ethical decision making. Generally, states have tried to adopt ethics codes that would prohibit legislators and other officeholders from accepting gifts or free dinners from lobbyists or require them to disclose gifts over a minimum amount. In Tennessee, legislators must disclose any contribution over $250. In addition, states are passing ethics laws that prohibit former legislators from becoming lobbyists at the state capitol for a certain period of time. Six states have a two-year period before a legislator can become a lobbyist, whereas 20 states require sitting out for only one year.[11] Sometimes, it appears that ethics rules can go too far. A Colorado amendment to the constitution passed by voters in 2006 prevented any state official's child from receiving a college scholarship or any Colorado college professor from accepting the Nobel Prize.[12]

Direct Democracy: The Initiative, Referendum, and Recall

There is a major difference between the legislative process as outlined in the U.S. Constitution and the legislative process as outlined in the various state constitutions. Many states exercise a type of direct democracy through the initiative, the referendum, and the recall—procedures that allow voters to control the government directly.

The Initiative. One technique lets citizens bypass legislatures by proposing new statutes or changes in government for citizen approval. Most states that permit the citizen legislative initiative require that the initiative's backers circulate a petition to place the issue on the ballot and that a certain percentage of the registered voters in the last gubernatorial election sign the petition. Twenty-four states use the legislative initiative, typically those states in which political parties are relatively weak and nonpartisan groups are strong. Legislative initiatives have involved a range of issues, including crime victims' rights, campaign contributions, corporate spending on ballot questions, affirmative action, physician-assisted suicide, and the medical use of marijuana. In some instances, voters have passed state initiatives that are contrary to federal policy. For example, several states passed initiatives legalizing the use of marijuana for medical purposes, a policy that conflicts with federal law.

The Referendum. The referendum is similar to the initiative, except that the issue (or constitutional change) is proposed first by the legislature and then directed to the voters for their approval. The referendum is most often used for approval of local school bond issues and for amendments to state constitutions. In several states that provide for the referendum, a bill passed by the legislature may be suspended by obtaining the required number of voters' signatures on petitions. A statewide referendum election is then held. If a majority of the voters disapprove of the bill, it is no longer valid.

The referendum was not initially intended for regular use, and it was employed infrequently in the past. Its opponents argue that it is an unnecessary check on representative government and that it weakens legislative responsibility. In recent

---

11. "Ethics Reform," Center for Policy Alternatives, National Council of State Legislatures, www.cfpa.org.
12. Karl Kurtz, "Colorado Ethics Initiative Blocked by Court," *The Thicket at State Legislatures*, July 1, 2007, http://ncsl.typepad .com/the_thicket.

years, the referendum has become increasingly popular as citizens have attempted to control their state and local governments. Interest groups have been active in sponsoring the petition drives necessary to force a referendum. More than two-thirds of the states provide for the referendum.

The Recall. The right of citizens to recall (or remove) elected officials is not exercised frequently. Recall is a provision written into the constitutions of 15 states. It allows voters to remove elected state officials, including the governor, before the expiration of their terms of office. In the case of judges, the recall can terminate a lifetime appointment.

Citizens begin the recall process by circulating petitions demanding a statewide vote to remove the offending officeholder. The number of signatures required to bring about the election ranges from 10 to 40 percent of the last vote for the office in question. In some states, the recall election is held concurrently with an election to pick the official's successor in office. In 2012, Wisconsin held a recall election for Governor Scott Walker, who had proposed and implemented severe changes in the rights of public employees to collectively bargain. Walker became the only American governor to survive a recall election, defeating his opponent handily.

The recall and the initiative are examples of "pure democracy," in which the people as a whole vote directly on important issues. Such measures are distinct in theory and in practice from the norms of "representative democracy," in which the people govern only indirectly through their elected representatives.

The State Judiciary

In addition to the federal courts, each of the 50 states, as well as the District of Columbia, has its own separate court system. Figure 18–2 shows a sample state court system. Like the federal court system, it has several tiers, including trial courts, intermediate courts of appeals, and a supreme court.

Trial Courts

All states have major trial courts, commonly called circuit courts, district courts, or superior courts. The number of judges and their terms in office vary widely. As in the federal court system, the trial courts are of two types: those having limited jurisdiction and those having general jurisdiction.[13] Cases heard before these courts can be appealed to the state intermediate appellate court and ultimately to the state supreme court.

Appellate Courts

About three-fourths of the states have intermediate appellate courts between the trial courts of original jurisdiction and the highest state appellate court, or the supreme court. These are usually called courts of appeals. Salaries of state judges vary widely, but higher pay is given to appellate and supreme court members.

The highest state appellate courts are usually called simply supreme courts, although they are also labeled the supreme judicial court (Maine and Massachusetts), the court of appeals (Maryland and New York), the court of criminal appeals (Oklahoma and Texas, which also have separate supreme courts for appeals in noncriminal cases), or the supreme court of appeals (West Virginia). The decisions of each state's highest court on all questions of state law are final.

---

13. See Chapter 14 for a definition of these terms.

Figure 18-2 ▶ **A Sample State Court System**

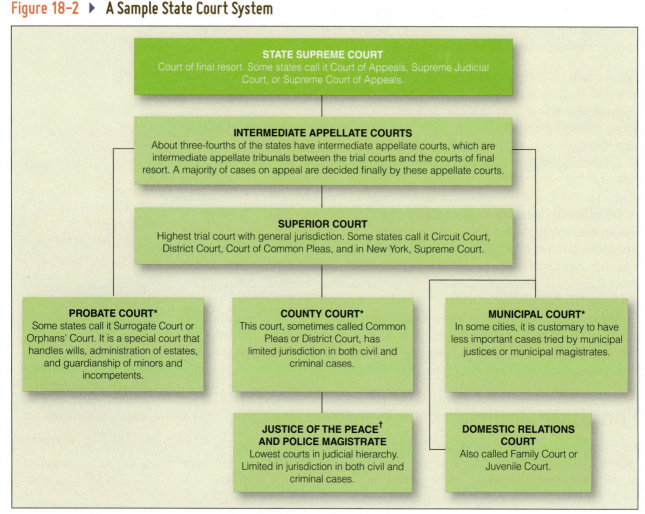

*Courts of special jurisdiction, such as probate, family, or juvenile courts, and the so-called inferior courts, such as common pleas or municipal courts, may be separate courts or may be part of the trial court of general jurisdiction.
†Justices of the peace do not exist in all states. Their jurisdiction varies greatly from state to state when they do exist.
Source: William P. Statsky, *Essentials of Paralegalism: Perspectives, Problems, and Skills*, 4th ed. (Clifton Park, NY: Thomson Delmar Learning, 2006).

Only when issues of federal law are involved can a decision made by a state's highest court be overruled by the United States Supreme Court.

Judicial Elections and Appointments

State court judges are either elected or appointed, depending on the state and (often) on the level of court involved—the procedures vary widely from state to state. In some states, including Delaware, the procedure is similar to the way federal judges are appointed: The judges are appointed by the governor and confirmed by the upper chamber of the legislature. In other states, all state court judges are elected, either on a partisan ballot (as in Alabama) or on a nonpartisan ballot (as in Kentucky). In several states, judges in some of the lower courts are elected, while those in the appellate courts are appointed. Additionally, depending on the state, judges who are appointed may have to run for reelection if they wish to serve a second term.

In the 38 states that elect judges, many of these elections are turning into hard-fought political battles. This is happening even in states with nonpartisan elections. A little-noted Supreme Court decision has changed the old rules for judicial campaigning. In 2002, the Court overturned a state law that barred judicial candidates from commenting on controversies they might have to resolve.[14] Now groups with strong opinions on abortion or same-sex marriage can grill candidates on these issues. In some states, judicial races have turned into fights between trial lawyers who sue businesses and the businesses that they sue. Some judges now advocate replacing judicial elections with an appointive system. The American Bar Association has called for public financing of judicial campaigns so that candidates will not have to seek private contributions.

How Local Government Operates

Local governments are difficult to describe because of their great dissimilarities and because, if we include municipalities, counties, towns, townships, and special districts, there are so many of them. We limit the discussion here to the most important types and features of local governments.

The Legal Existence of Local Government

As mentioned earlier, the U.S. Constitution makes no mention of local governments. Article IV, Section 4, merely states that "[t]he United States shall guarantee to every State in this Union a Republican Form of Government." Actually, then, the states do not even need to have local governments. Consequently, every local government is a creature of the state. The state can create a local government, and the state can terminate the right of a local government to exist. States often have abolished entire counties, school districts, cities, and special districts. Since World War II (1939–1945), almost 20,000 school districts have gone out of existence as they were consolidated with other school districts.

Because the local government is the legal creation of the state, does that mean the state can dictate everything the local government does? For many years, that seemed to be the case. The narrowest possible view of the legal status of local governments follows **Dillon's rule**, outlined by Judge John F. Dillon in his *Commentaries on the Law of Municipal Corporations* in 1872. He stated that municipal corporations may possess only powers "granted in express words … [that are] necessarily or fairly implied in or incident to the powers expressly granted."[15] Cities governed under Dillon's rule have sometimes been dominated by the state legislatures, depending on the extent of the authority granted to the cities by the legislatures. Those communities wishing to obtain the status of a municipal corporation have petitioned the state legislature for a **charter**.

In a revolt against state legislative power over municipalities, the home rule movement began. It was based on **Cooley's rule**, derived from an 1871 decision by Michigan judge Thomas Cooley stating that cities should be able to govern themselves.[16] Since 1900, about four-fifths of the states have allowed **municipal home rule**, but only with respect to local concerns for which no statewide interests are involved. A municipality must choose to become a **home rule city**; otherwise, it operates as a **general law city**. In the latter case, the state makes certain general laws relating to cities of different sizes, which are designated as first-class cities, second-class cities, or towns. Once a city, by virtue of its

■ **Learning Outcome 2:**
Explain why counties, cities, and other units of local government are limited in their power and their autonomy.

Dillon's Rule
The narrowest possible interpretation of the legal status of local governments, outlined by Judge John E. Dillon, who in 1872 stated that a municipal corporation can exercise only those powers expressly granted by state law.

Charter
A document issued by a government that grants to a person, a group of persons, or a corporation the right to carry on one or more specific activities. A state government can grant a charter to a municipality.

Cooley's Rule
The view that cities should be able to govern themselves, presented in an 1871 Michigan decision by Judge Thomas Cooley.

Municipal Home Rule
The power vested in a local unit of government to draft or change its own charter and to manage its own affairs.

Home Rule City
A city permitted by the state to let local voters frame, adopt, and amend their own charter.

General Law City
A city operating under general state laws that apply to all local governmental units of a similar type.

---

14. *Republican Party of Minnesota v. White*, 536 U.S. 765 (2002).
15. John F. Dillon, *Commentaries on the Law of Municipal Corporations*, 5th ed. (Boston: Little, Brown, 1911), Vol. 1, Sec. 237.
16. *People v. Hurlbut*, 24 Mich. 44 (1871).

Beyond Our Borders
EVERYONE HAS A MAYOR!

As long as humans have lived in communities, there have been community leaders, individuals who bear responsibility for the welfare of others in the community or who must bring the members of the community to a decision or lead them into war. Local governments today are the governments closest to the people of a nation. They may have democratically elected leaders, or the leadership may be appointed by the central government. In more primitive societies, the local leader acquires his or her title through birth into a leading family or is named by a religious leader. Why do people need local governments today? What services can the town or village provide that a nation cannot?

While the nation's central government can promise clean water and a sanitary sewer system to every citizen of the country, someone has to make sure that the water and sewers actually reach every individual household. Local governments typically are charged with ensuring the health and safety of the people, by providing fire, police, and health services. Standards may be set at the provincial or state level or in unitary states at the national level, but only firefighters at the local firehouse know the neighborhood and the quickest way to reach a fire.

How are local governments organized in different nations? In most European nations, Australia, and New Zealand, local governments are elected. Responsibilities often involve planning, economic development, water, sewer and health issues, and public safety. The terms of local officials may be two, four, or six years. In some nations, like France, the mayor of a city is not elected directly but is the choice of the political party that wins the most seats in the city council. Nations with strong central governments such as France make policy decisions in the capital, but local services are increasingly decentralized. A large federal nation like India has a variety of local forms of government, ranging from the most modern city to small villages where basic services are lacking and financial resources are few.

China is a not a democratic government, and local government officials are chosen by regional governments. The Chinese Communist Party carefully monitors the work of local officials to make sure national policies are followed. In the last two years, the corruption of local government officials has led to protests and uprisings by local citizens. In Afghanistan, where the United States and NATO allies have worked to bring peace and reduce the influence of the Taliban, most villages are organized by traditional tribal affiliations, and the village chief is chosen by his tribe, not elected.

Village elder Mohammad Zaher of Asmar leaves a meeting with U.S. Marines in Afghanistan. The meeting of tribal leaders, called a "jirga," was held to discuss ways for the Marines to cooperate with local officials.

When the United States increased its troop commitment to the Afghanistan war in 2011, one goal of that increase was closer collaboration with local leaders to provide support for village needs, thus building more trust between the allied military and Afghani civilians. Afghan local governments, however, have very few resources to serve their people, much less the refugees from other parts of the nation who have settled there. Writer Anna Badkhen reported that the Afghan government welcomed hundreds of thousands of refugees back from Pakistan in 2008–2009.[a] A local official told her, though, that the government provided no food, no electricity, no housing, and no health care for these people and as a result, many became bitter toward the local government and turned to the Taliban for such help.

FOR CRITICAL ANALYSIS

1. *While most local governments have elected leaders, given the types of services provided by towns, cities, and villages, why shouldn't an appointed leader be just as effective?*

2. *Discuss whether you think individuals are more likely to know more about their local leaders or their national leaders.*

[a] Anna Badkhen, "Helpless to Help in Afghanistan's Local Government," *Foreign Policy*, April 22, 2010. www.foreignpolicy.com/articles/2010/04/22.

population, receives such a ranking, it follows the general law established by the state. Only if it chooses to be a home rule city can it avoid such state government restrictions. In many states, only cities with populations of 2,500 or more can choose home rule.

Local Governmental Units

The four major types of local governmental units are municipalities, counties, towns and townships, and special districts.

Municipalities. A municipality is a political entity created by the people of a city or town to govern themselves locally. Currently, there are more than 19,000 municipalities within the 50 states. Almost all municipalities are fairly small cities. Only about 200 cities have populations more than 100,000, and only nine cities (Chicago, Dallas, Houston, Los Angeles, New York, Philadelphia, Phoenix, San Antonio, and San Diego) have populations more than 1 million. City expenditures are primarily for water supply and other utilities, police and fire protection, and education. About three-fourths of municipal tax revenues come from property taxes. Municipalities often rely heavily on financial assistance from both the federal and state governments.

Counties. The difference between a **county** and a municipality is that a county is usually not created at the behest of its inhabitants. The state sets up counties on its own initiative to serve as political extensions of the state government. Counties apply state law and administer state business at the local level.

> **County**
> The chief governmental unit set up by the state to administer state law and business at the local level. Counties are drawn up by area, rather than by rural or urban criteria.

The United States has more than 3,000 counties, which vary greatly in both size and population. San Bernardino County in California is the largest geographically, with 20,102 square miles. New York County in New York is possibly the smallest, with fewer than 22 square miles. County populations within California alone range from millions of residents, as in Los Angeles County, to barely a thousand, as in Alpine County.

County governments' responsibilities include zoning, building regulations, health, hospitals, parks, recreation, highways, public safety, justice, and record-keeping. Typically, when a municipality is established within a county, the county withdraws most of its services from the municipality; for example, the municipal police force takes over from the county police force. County governments are extremely complex entities, a product of the era of Jacksonian democracy and its effort to bring government closer to the people. There is no easy way to describe their operation in summary form. The county has been called by one scholar "the dark continent of American politics."[17]

Towns and Townships. A unique governmental creation in the New England states is the **New England town**—not to be confused with the word *town* (meaning a small city). In Connecticut, Maine, Massachusetts, New Hampshire, and Vermont, the unit called the town combines the roles of city and county in one governing unit. A New England town typically consists of one or more urban settlements and the surrounding rural areas. Consequently, counties have little importance in New England. In Connecticut, for example, they are simply geographic units.

> **New England Town**
> A governmental unit in the New England states that combines the roles of city and county in one unit.

From the New England town is derived the tradition of the **town meeting**, an annual meeting at which direct democracy was—and continues to be—practiced. Each resident of a town is summoned to the annual meeting at the

> **Town Meeting**
> The governing authority of a New England town. Qualified voters may participate in the election of officers and the passage of legislation.

17. Henry S. Gilbertson, *The County, the "Dark Continent of American Politics"* (New York: National Short Ballot Association, 1917).

town hall. Those who attend levy taxes, pass laws, elect town officers, and appropriate money for different activities.

Normally, few residents show up for town meetings today unless an item of high interest is on the agenda or unless family members want to be elected to office. The town meeting takes a day or more, and few citizens are able to set aside such a large amount of time. Because of the declining interest in town meetings, many New England towns have adopted a **town manager system**: The voters simply elect three **selectpersons**, who then appoint a professional town manager. The town manager in turn appoints other officials.

Townships operate somewhat like counties, though on a lower level. Where they exist, there may be several dozen within a county. They perform some of the functions that the county would otherwise perform. Most midwestern states have townships, and they are also found in New Jersey, New York, and Pennsylvania. A township is not the same thing as a New England town, because it is meant to be a rural government rather than a city government. Moreover, it is never the principal unit of local government, as are New England towns. The boundaries of most townships are based on federal land surveys that began in the 1780s, mapping the land into six-square-mile blocks called townships. They were then subdivided into 36 blocks of one square mile each, called sections. Typically, a road was built along the boundaries of each section.

Although townships have few functions in many parts of the nation, they are still politically important in others. In some metropolitan areas, townships are the political unit that provides most public services to residents who live in suburban **unincorporated areas**.

Special Districts and School Districts. The most numerous local government units are special districts. Currently, there are more than 35,000 special districts (see Table 18–2). Special districts are one-function governments that usually are created by the state legislature and governed by a board of directors. Special districts may be called authorities, boards, corporations, or simply districts.

One important feature of special districts is that they cut across geographic and governmental boundaries. Sometimes special districts even cut across state lines. For example, the Port Authority of New York and New Jersey was established by an interstate compact between the two states in 1921 to develop and operate the harbor facilities in the area. A mosquito control district may cut across both municipal and county lines. A metropolitan transit district may provide bus service to dozens of municipalities and to several counties.

Town Manager System
A form of town government in which voters elect three selectpersons, who then appoint a professional town manager, who in turn appoints other officials.

Selectperson
A member of the governing group of a town.

Township
A rural unit of government based on federal land surveys of the American frontier in the 1780s. Townships have declined significantly in importance.

Unincorporated Area
An area not located within the boundary of a municipality.

Table 18–2 ▶ Local Governments in the United States

Counties	3,033
Municipalities (mainly cities and towns)	19,492
Townships (less extensive powers)	16,519
Special districts (water supply, fire protection, hospitals, libraries, parks and recreation, highways, sewers, and the like)	37,381
School districts	13,051
Total	**89,476**

Source: U.S. Census Bureau, 2007 Census of Governments.

School districts, although listed separately in Table 18–2, are essentially a type of special district. Except for school districts, the typical citizen is not very aware of most special districts. Most citizens do not know who furnishes their weed control, mosquito abatement, water, or sewage service. Part of the reason for the low profile of special districts is that most special district administrators are appointed, not elected, and therefore receive little public attention.

Consolidation of Governments

With more than 80,000 separate and often overlapping governmental units within the United States, the trend toward consolidation in recent years is understandable. **Consolidation** is the union of two or more governmental units to form a single unit. Typically, a state constitution or a state statute will designate consolidation procedures.

Consolidation is often recommended for metropolitan-area problems, but to date few consolidations have occurred within metropolitan areas. The most successful consolidations have been **functional consolidations**, particularly of city and county police, health, and welfare departments. In some situations, functional consolidation is a satisfactory alternative to the complete consolidation of governmental units. One of the most successful examples of functional consolidation was started in 1957 in Dade County, Florida. The county government, now called Miami-Dade, is a union of 26 municipalities. Each municipality has its own governmental entity, but the county government has the authority to furnish water, planning, mass transit, and police services and to set minimum standards of performance. The governing body of Miami-Dade is an elected board of county commissioners, which appoints an executive mayor.

A special type of consolidation is the **council of governments (COG)**, a voluntary organization of counties and municipalities that attempts to deal with area-wide problems. More than 200 COGs have been established, mainly since 1966. The impetus for their establishment was, and continues to be, federal government grants. COGs are an alternative means of treating major regional problems that various communities are unwilling to tackle on a consolidated basis, either by true consolidation of governmental units or by functional consolidation.

The power of COGs is advisory only. Each member unit simply selects its council representatives, who report back to the unit after COG meetings. Nonetheless, today several COGs have gained considerable influence on regional policy. These include the Metropolitan Washington Council of Governments in Washington, D.C., the Supervisors' Inter-County Commission in Detroit, and the Association of Bay Area Governments in the San Francisco Bay area.

How Municipalities Are Governed

We can divide municipal representative governments into four general types of plans: (1) the commission plan, (2) the council-manager plan, (3) the mayor-administrator plan, and (4) the mayor-council plan.

The Commission Plan. The commission form of municipal government consists of a commission of three to nine members who have both legislative and executive powers. The salient aspects of the commission plan are as follows:

1. Executive and legislative powers are concentrated in a small group of individuals, who are elected at large on a (normally) nonpartisan ballot.
2. Each commissioner is individually responsible for heading a particular municipal department, such as the department of public safety.

Consolidation
The union of two or more governmental units to form a single unit.

Functional Consolidation
Cooperation by two or more units of local government in providing services to their inhabitants. This is generally done by unifying a set of departments (e.g., the police departments) into a single agency.

Council of Governments (COG)
A voluntary organization of counties and municipalities concerned with area-wide problems.

3. The commission is collectively responsible for passing ordinances and controlling spending.
4. The mayor (an office that is only ceremonial) is selected from the members of the commission.

The commission plan, originating in Galveston, Texas, in 1901, had its greatest popularity during the first 20 years of the 20th century. It appealed to municipal government reformers. They looked on it as a type of business organization that

Politics with a Purpose

WHO SHOULD RUN THE CITY, "PROFESSIONALS" OR POLITICIANS?

Who is the mayor of your city or town? Does she or he have executive branch powers such as the ability to make appointments, propose a city budget, and manage day-to-day business? If your mayor is well known and has this kind of authority, your town likely has a strong mayor system. In this type of system, the mayor is elected independently of the town or city council, as opposed to being chosen from the council. Large cities tend to have a strong mayor system, so-called for the executive-type powers the office controls.

Contrast this with a system where the city council is the most powerful elected municipal body. The council members might vie for the mayor's spot, which is usually ceremonial. In this council-manager system, the council will appoint a professional city manager, who will take on the daily management of the municipality.

Cities and towns must make choices about municipal government while considering how best to provide essential services (e.g., water, police, waste management) with limited resources. Advocates for the city manager system say it is more economical. They argue that trained professionals are able to hire and fire staff unencumbered by political patronage and have the educational and vocational background to eliminate waste and inefficiency.[a]

Many city manager systems were created during the Progressive Era, which fostered a meritocracy over patronage. These Progressive reformers at the turn of the 20th century valued expertise and skill and formed the modern bureaucracy we see at all levels of government: city, state, and national. A professionalized city management assumed that "scientific management" was superior to political control, which would lead to "cronyism … and inferior standards."[b]

On the other side are proponents of the strong mayor system, where the mayor is elected and has the power to run the

day-to-day operations of the municipality, including budget creation, management of personnel, and responsibility for delivery of essential goods and services. While almost half of all cities with more than 2,500 people use a council-manager system,[c] moderate to large-sized cities with city manager systems sometimes flirt with this strong mayor system. Though the larger the city, the greater likelihood of adopting this system, the reasons for success or failure of strong mayor initiatives seem to be specific to the particular city. For example, Miami-Dade, Florida, passed a strong mayor initiative in 2007, moving away from the council-manager system with a weak mayor, despite the strong opposition from some labor groups and city council members.[d] The popularity of the then mayor and general public support paved the way for the change.[e]

By contrast, the efforts of the pro–strong mayor groups in Dallas, Texas, were stymied by a coalition of community activists, African American and Latino civic leaders, and some leaders in the business community. A long history of political wrangling among these groups, as well as between the groups and the mayor, resulted in tensions that served as a contentious backdrop, making the strong mayor proposal even less likely to pass.

So, what has happened to cities that have switched from a weak mayor/council-manager system to a strong mayor form of government? Little systematic evidence exists. Our federal system allows local governments to decide what structure of leadership they want at the helm of their municipality, and these decisions are examined on a case-by-case basis.

[a]www.council-manager.org/index.php, accessed June 5, 2008.
[b]www.hogriver.org/issues/v02n04/politics.htm, accessed June 5, 2008.
[c]www.council-manager.org/index.php, accessed June 5, 2008.
[d]"Strong Mayor Isn't a Cure-all," *St. Petersburg Times* (Florida), February 1, 2007, p. 16A.
[e]http://metropolitan.fiu.edu/downloads/HeraldStrongMayor.pdf, accessed June 5, 2008.

would eliminate the problems they believed to be inherent in the long ballot and in partisan municipal politics. Unfortunately, vesting both legislative and executive power in the hands of a small group of individuals means that there are no checks and balances on administration and spending. Also, because the mayoral office is ceremonial, there is no provision for strong leadership. Not surprisingly, only about 100 cities today use the commission plan—Atlantic City, Mobile, Salt Lake City, Topeka, and Tulsa are a few of them.

The Council-Manager Plan. In the council-manager form of municipal government, a city council appoints a professional manager, who acts as the chief executive. He or she typically is called the city manager. In principle, the manager is there simply to see that the general directions of the city council are carried out. The important features of the council-manager plan are as follows:

1. A professional, trained manager can hire and fire subordinates and is responsible to the council.
2. The council or commission consists of five to seven members, elected at large on a nonpartisan ballot.
3. The mayor may be chosen from within the council or from outside, but he or she has no executive function. As with the commission plan, the mayor's job may be largely ceremonial, or it may be limited to chairing council meetings. The city manager works for the council, not the mayor (unless, of course, the mayor is part of the council).

Today, about 2,000 cities use the council-manager plan. About one-third of the cities with populations of more than 5,000 and about one-half of the cities with populations of more than 25,000 operate with this type of plan. Only three large cities—Cincinnati, Dallas, and San Antonio—are still using this form.

The major defect of the council-manager scheme, as with the commission plan, is that there is no single, strong political executive leader. It is therefore not surprising that large cities rarely use such a plan or that some cities strengthen the mayor's position while keeping a manager.

The Mayor-Administrator Plan. The mayor-administrator plan is often used in large cities without a strong mayor. It is similar to the council-manager plan except that the political leadership is vested in the mayor. The mayor is an elected chief executive. She or he appoints an administrative officer, whose function is to free the mayor from routine administrative tasks, such as personnel direction and budget supervision.

The Mayor-Council Plan. The mayor-council form of municipal government is the oldest and most widely used. The mayor is an elected chief executive, and the council is the legislative body. Virtually all councils are unicameral. The council typically has five to nine members, except in very large cities. For example, in Chicago, the council has 50 members. Council members are popularly elected for terms as long as six, but normally four, years.

Sheryl Sculley, city manager of San Antonio, Texas, meets with her city's Public Affairs Department director.

The mayor-council plan can either be a strong mayor type or a weak mayor type. In the *strong mayor–council plan*, the mayor is the chief executive and has virtually complete control over hiring and firing employees, as well as preparing the budget. The mayor exercises strong and positive leadership in the formation of city policies. The *weak mayor–council plan* separates executive and legislative functions completely. The mayor is elected as chief executive officer; the council is elected as the legislative body. This traditional division of powers allows for checks and balances on spending and administration.

About 50 percent of American cities use some form of the mayor-council plan. Most recently, the mayor-council plan has lost ground to the council-manager plan in small and middle-sized cities.

■ **Learning Outcome 3:**
Discuss the issues raised by corruption and patronage in local and state governments.

Machine versus Reform in City Politics

For much of the late 19th and early 20th centuries, many major cities were run by "the machine." The machine was an integrated political organization. Each city block within the municipality had an organizer, each neighborhood had a political club, each district had a leader, and all of these parts of the machine had a boss—such as William Tweed in New York, Richard Daley in Chicago, Edward Crump in Memphis, or Tom Pendergast in Kansas City. The machine became a popular form of city political organization in the 1840s, when the first waves of European immigrants came to the United States to work in urban factories. Those individuals, often lacking the ability to communicate in English, needed help—and the machine was created to help them.[18] The urban machine drew on the support of the dominant ethnic groups to forge a strong political institution that was able to keep the boss (usually the mayor) in office year after year. The machine was oiled by patronage—rewarding faithful party workers and followers with government employment and contracts. The party in power was often referred to as the patronage party.[19]

According to sociologist Robert Merton, the machine offered personalized assistance to the needy, helped establish local businesses, opened avenues of upward social mobility for the underprivileged, and afforded a locus of strong political authority and responsibility.[20] Others, however, viewed party machines and the behind-the-scenes government that they often involved as contrary to our principles of government. In their classic work on city politics, Edward Banfield and James Q. Wilson also gave a critical appraisal of machine politics:

> [M]achine government is, essentially, a system of organized bribery. The destruction of machines … permit[s] government on the basis of appropriate motives, that is, public-regarding ones. In fact it has other highly desirable consequences—especially greater honesty, impartiality, and (in routine matters) efficiency.[21]

Library of Congress Prints & Photographs Division, Washington, D.C. [LC-USZ6-787]

THE "BRAINS"
THAT ACHIEVED THE TAMMANY VICTORY AT THE ROCHESTER DEMOCRATIC CONVENTION.

A Thomas Nast cartoon shows Boss Tweed represented as having a money-bag face. The caption reads, "The 'Brains' that achieved the Tammany Victory at the Rochester Democratic Convention." Another identifying feature is a famous $15,500 diamond stickpin. Why are there no true big-city "machine" bosses anymore in the United States?

18.   See Harvey W. Zorbaugh, *The Gold Coast and the Slum: A Sociological Study of Chicago's Near North Side* (Chicago: University of Chicago Press, 1929).
19.   See, for example, Harold F. Gosnell, *Machine Politics: Chicago Model* (Chicago: University of Chicago Press, 1937).
20.   Robert Merton, *Social Theory and Social Structure* (Glencoe, IL: Free Press, 1957), pp. 71–81.
21.   Edward C. Banfield and James Q. Wilson, *City Politics* (New York: Vintage Books, 1963), p. 12.

When the last of the big-city bosses, Mayor Richard Daley of Chicago, died in December 1976, an era died with him. The big-city machine began to be in serious trouble in the 1960s, when community activists organized to work for a more professional and efficient municipal government. Soon, governments of administrators rather than politicians began to appear. Fewer offices were elective; more were appointive.

Switching from a political to an administrative form of urban government was a way to break up the centralized urban political machine. In some cities, the results have been beneficial to most citizens. In others, decentralization has gone so far that no strong leader exists to pull together discordant factions to create and follow a coherent policy. Consequently, in cities with a highly decentralized government typified by numerous independent commissions and boards, much that should be done does not get done, particularly when an area-wide concern is involved. This is an especially severe problem for less economically privileged people, who used to be able to rely on machine-sponsored activities and on the machine's political clout to help them compete against wealthier citizens for a share of the city's services. Reform is in some ways a middle-class preoccupation, whereas the less advantaged may believe they are better served by machine politics.

Governing Metropolitan Areas

Large cities are often faced with problems that develop in part from a shrinking employment base. When employers move out of a city, there is a smaller tax base, and more people are out of work. Less tax revenue means fewer funds to pay for schools and to meet other municipal obligations, including fighting crime and assisting those who are unemployed. These developments feed on themselves, leading to more crime, more poverty, an even smaller job base, and other problems.

But crime, as well as problems such as traffic congestion and pollution, is not contained within municipal political boundaries. For this reason, solutions are sometimes sought for a metropolitan area as a whole. Annexation by a city of the surrounding suburbs is one solution; consolidation of city and county governments into a single government is another. People who live in the suburbs often oppose such measures, however, particularly when they and the residents of a city are of different races or social classes, or have different political agendas.

A third possible solution to problems that spread beyond limited political boundaries is to set up a system of metropolitan government. With this method, a single entity, such as a county, concerns itself with the problems of an entire metropolitan area, and smaller entities, such as individual city governments, concern themselves with local matters. People who live in the suburbs often oppose this solution, however, for the same reasons that they oppose other measures: They want to preserve their communities and lifestyles as they are.

A fourth solution is the creation of special districts, each of which is concerned with a specific service—an area's water supply or public transportation system, for example. Special districts are more popular than the other solutions, in part because they can deal with a single matter relatively more efficiently without concern for social issues or class conflict.

did you know?

"Boss" William Tweed of New York City's political machine, Tammany Hall, once offered cartoonist Thomas Nast $500,000 to stop his "attacks" on Tweed in *Harper's Weekly*.

AP Photo/Matt Rourke

Members of Philadelphia's Community Preservation Network protest the City of Philadelphia's use of eminent domain to take property. After the Supreme Court decision in 2005 to allow cities to use the right of eminent domain for economic development, citizens created protest groups across the United States, and some states then banned the practice.

■ **Learning Outcome 4:**
Describe the most important sources of revenue for states and local governments and their biggest expenditures, and contrast them with those of the federal government.

Paying for State and Local Government

Examining the spending habits of a household often gives relevant information about the personalities and priorities of the household members. Examination of the expenditure patterns of state and local governments likewise can be illuminating.

State and Local Government Expenditures

Table 18–3 shows state expenditures, by function, in percentages. Table 18–4 shows these data for local governments. Education and highways are major expenses at both the state and local level. (Most state spending on education is for colleges and universities; most local spending is for elementary and secondary schools.) Because of the growth of Medicaid—the health care program for the poor—welfare is now the leading expense at the state level. Local governments, in contrast, spend heavily on utilities such as water, electricity, gas, sewers, and garbage collection.

Compare state and local spending on education with spending by the federal government, which allocates only about 4 percent of its budget to education. Despite high expenditures, state and local governments are finding that their educational programs are not always producing well-educated students. The failings of state and local educational systems led the Congress to pass President Bush's No Child Left Behind legislation in 2001. Although the Obama administration wants to reform that legislation, it has not backed a repeal of the law, which requires states to have more consistent standards for schools and to test student achievement.

State and Local Government Revenues

State and local expenditures have to be paid for somehow. Until the 20th century, almost all state and local expenditures were paid for by state and local revenues raised within state borders. Starting in the 20th century, however, federal grants to state and local governmental units began to pay some of these costs.

Figure 18–3 shows the percentages of revenues in various categories received by state and local governments. The most important tax at the state level is the **general sales tax**. Whereas the federal government obtains about 45 percent of its total revenues from the personal income tax, states obtain only about 11 percent in this way. In 2010, seven states still did not have a personal income tax. Other taxes assessed by states include corporate income taxes and fees, fees for permits and licenses at both the state and local governmental levels, as well as

General Sales Tax
A tax levied as a proportion of the retail price of a commodity at the point of sale.

Table 18–3 ▶ State Expenditures (in percentages)

EXPENDITURE	PERCENTAGE
Welfare, including Medicaid	12
Education	18
Employee retirement	12
Highways	8
Governmental administration	2
Health care (includes hospitals and Medicaid)	31
Protection (includes police, fire, prisons)	7
Interest on general debt	3
Other	7

Source: Census of Government 2009.

Table 18–4 ▶ Local Expenditures (in percentages)

EXPENDITURE	PERCENTAGE
Education	38
Welfare	5
Protection (includes fire and police)	11
Transportation	8
Governmental administration	3
Health care (includes hospitals)	8
Pensions	2
Interest on general debt	4
Other	21

Source: Census of Government 2009.

Figure 18-3 ▶ State and Local Government Revenues

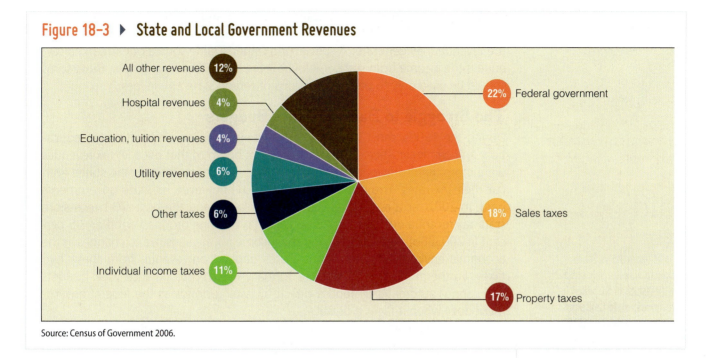

All other revenues **12%**
Hospital revenues **4%**
Education, tuition revenues **4%**
Utility revenues **6%**
Other taxes **6%**
Individual income taxes **11%**
22% Federal government
18% Sales taxes
17% Property taxes

Source: Census of Government 2006.

inheritance and gift taxes at the state level. At the local level, the most important tax is the **property tax**. More than 95 percent of property tax revenues are raised by local governments.

Because states vary in the types and amounts of taxes collected, there is considerable competition between them to attract businesses or certain populations. States compete to offer a better climate for business by giving incentives such as a 20-year reduction in property taxes to a new employer or creating bonds to help a new business build a facility in the state. Why do states do this? They intend to recoup their investment or lost tax revenue through taxes on the employees' income and on the company in the future. States also compete for new residents. It should be no surprise that many individuals choose Florida as their permanent residence during their retirement years: Compare paying no income taxes to paying more than 7 percent of your income in taxes in New York. Changing residency does not usually mean people must give up their home in their former state of residence; simply being absent from that state for a specified number of days will qualify them as nonresidents, but they may still maintain a home there. States also compete to have the lowest sales tax, gasoline tax, and estate tax. The overall state and local tax burden for an individual can vary from more than 10 percent of income in New York; Washington, D.C.; and New Jersey to 6 percent in Alaska.

Nontax revenue includes federal grants to state and local governments. Today, federal grants to state and local governments provide about 22 percent of state government income. The grants are not always without "strings," however. Federal programs in such areas as education, highway construction, health care, and law enforcement may dispense cash subject to certain conditions (see Chapter 3).

Revenues from publicly operated services and businesses are additional sources of income for state and local governments. Publicly operated services include universities and hospitals, as well as municipal utilities such as water, electric power, and bus systems. More than one-third of the states sell liquor at a profit through state-operated stores. Other state-run businesses include Washington's ferries and North Dakota's commercial banks. Further nontax revenue sources include court fines and interest on loans and investments. In the 1980s, state lotteries became an increasingly popular way to raise revenues.

Property Tax
A tax on the value of real estate. This tax is a particularly important source of revenue for local governments.

Most revenue from publicly operated services and businesses is earmarked for the services that earned it. Tuition goes only to colleges, and state hospitals keep the revenue they generate. A special and rather sizable source of earmarked revenue is the income from state employee retirement plans. In principle, these sums should be used only to pay the pensions of retired state employees.

The Struggle to Balance State Budgets

During the 1990s, most states expanded their spending on health care, education, and criminal justice. During the dot-com boom of that decade, tax revenues were more than sufficient to fund the increases in most states. Some states even cut their tax rates. The dot-com bust of 2001, however, hit state governments hard. In 2002, as a result of the dot-com collapse and the post–9/11 recession, state tax revenue dropped by 7.8 percent. Tax revenue dropped another 3.5 percent in 2003. Both the sales tax and the income tax are sensitive to changes in the economic environment, and many states depend on revenue from these two taxes. Furthermore, most states are formally required to balance their budgets and cannot automatically fund a deficit by issuing bonds as the federal government does when it faces a deficit.

State economies recovered from 2004 through mid-2008. But then, the economic crisis of 2008 and the recession that followed sent state tax collections into free fall. By 2010, a number of the larger and wealthier states—Texas, California, New York—found themselves facing huge budget deficits. As the economy slowly began to recover, states faced huge budget shortfalls. Remember, except for Vermont, states cannot actually run a budget deficit. By 2012, states' revenues remained more than 5 percent lower than pre-recession levels, while their obligations to educate millions of K–12 students and support public universities grew at normal rates. The state shortfalls for 2013, projected to exceed $540 billion, have been closed by raising taxes in some states, cutting services, laying off employees, cutting preschool programs, and delaying necessary construction projects. California, for example, had to close a $15 billion gap, while some energy-rich states like North Dakota and Alaska had no gap to close.[22] The state of Michigan has never recovered from the recession of 2002 and has considered ending the state fair, in existence since 1849. Hawaii cut its school year by 17 days to reduce its expenditures on teachers' salaries.

What caused these budget deficits? First and foremost, a decline in state revenues of 8.9 percent occurred in 2009 due to the loss of income taxes from workers and from businesses. Only five states saw slight increases in their revenues. Governors and state legislators found themselves caught between two highly vocal groups—those who opposed cutting spending on education, health care, and other services and those who opposed higher taxes, including the new Tea Party adherents.

Getting into Trouble: Borrowing Too Much. Although every state constitution except that of Vermont requires the state to balance its budget, states have shown great ingenuity in evading this requirement. Even if states cannot automatically borrow to meet a budget deficit, their legislatures can still find ways to borrow. Such practices only postpone the problem, though; eventually, the debt must be repaid.

New York is an example of a state that has engaged in what many consider excessive borrowing despite constitutional restrictions. New York's constitution ostensibly requires that voters approve state borrowing. Nevertheless, by 2004, New York's debt had reached $46.9 billion, or $2,420 for every inhabitant of the

---

22. Phil Oliff, Chris Mai, and Vincent Palacios, "States Continue to Feel Recession's Impact," Washington, DC: Center for Budget and Policy Priorities, June 27, 2012.

state. In 2000, the state had adopted a new law designed to curb borrowing, but despite the law, borrowing actually accelerated. According to many observers, New York was falling into a pattern of borrowing to fund day-to-day expenses rather than long-term capital improvements such as roads or bridges.

Getting into Trouble: Poor Productivity. An additional problem for the states is that the tasks they perform are somewhat resistant to productivity improvements. Over the years, America's farms and factories have posted dramatic improvements in the volume of goods produced by the labor of each individual farmer or worker—in other words, these industries have improved their productivity. It is more difficult to attain such improvements in service industries. Some services, notably education and law enforcement, require face-to-face interaction with the public. It is difficult to cut the amount of such interaction without reducing the quality of the service. Still, from 1993 to 2000, productivity in a typical private-sector service industry rose by about 20 percent. The productivity of government services rose by much less.

Getting into Trouble: Health Care Costs. Increased health care costs were a major part of the states' budget problems in the early 2000s, and they continue to be a major threat to the solvency of state governments. One problem is the rising cost of health insurance premiums for state and local government employees. Nationwide, the cost of health insurance premiums rose by 50 percent from 2000 to 2007, and such costs for state employees grew as well. A much greater problem is Medicaid, the program that provides health care services to the poor. State Medicaid spending rose by 9 percent per year on average between 2000 and 2007. The economic recession sent even more individuals to the Medicaid program, and burdens on the states increased correspondingly. The new federal health care reforms will also enroll more individuals in Medicaid in the future, although the actual costs to the states cannot yet be predicted. All in all, the recession of 2008–2009 is "the worst situation in 50 years," according to Susan Urahn, director of the Pew Center for the States.[23]

States as Policy Pioneers. State budgets are also influenced by the mix of public policies adopted by the state to serve the citizens. Over the past two centuries, states have often pioneered innovative policies that were later adopted by the federal government. For example, several states have experimented with requiring all residents to have health insurance either through their employer, their school, or through state-run insurance plans. Massachusetts was the most recent state to adopt such a plan, and many other states are watching the implementation of the plan to see if it is successful.

States are also in the forefront of environmental policies, in part because of their unique geographic and demographic situations. California, with its immense population growth and propensity to develop smog in the coastal areas, has been much stricter about emission controls for automobiles than the federal government for more than 30 years. Recently, the California Air Resources Board released a draft plan for reducing greenhouse gas emissions to 1990 levels by creating a carbon credit trading system, using landfills to produce methane, reducing urban sprawl, and changing the law for automobile emissions. The comprehensive plan would impact virtually every industry in California. While the draft plan needs much more analysis and would need implementation from the legislature, it illustrates the degree to which states can create innovative new policies and experiment with new ways to address public issues.

23.　Devin Dwyer, "Top 10 States in Fiscal Peril," *ABC News*, November 16, 2009.

You Can Make a Difference

LEARNING ABOUT LOCAL POLITICS AND GOVERNMENT IN YOUR COMMUNITY

Your local government bodies are usually close by. If you would like to learn how government operates, local government is a logical place to start.

WHY SHOULD YOU CARE?

What government does or fails to do in the areas of education, health, employment, and crime affects you, your family, and your friends. Your sense of adventure, concern, curiosity, or injustice may urge you to take an active part in the government of a society with which you might not be particularly content. Yet getting involved on the national level may seem complicated, and national issues may not be of immediate concern. You may not even know exactly where you stand on many of those issues.

Every week, however, decisions are being made in your community that directly affect your local environment, transportation, education, health, employment, rent, schools, utility rates, freedom from crime, and overall quality of life. The local level is a good place to begin discovering who you are politically.

WHAT CAN YOU DO?

Many neighborhoods have formed neighborhood associations to protect their interests. One way to learn about issues that directly affect you (such as whether a street in your neighborhood should be widened or a park created) is to attend a local neighborhood association meeting. Another way to familiarize yourself with local political issues is to attend a city council meeting. Think about the issues being discussed. How do these issues and their outcomes concern you as an individual? What is your position on each issue?

If you are interested in education and educational reform, you can attend a school board meeting. Typically, the board will devote a substantial amount of time to budgetary decisions. Pay close attention to how the board believes school funds should be allocated. What are the board's primary concerns and priorities? Do you agree with the board's views? Find out if the school district is considering proposals to implement innovative educational programs.

Tashua Allman, the elected mayor of Glenville, West Virginia.

Getting involved in a campaign for a local or state office is another way to learn about political issues that affect your community or your state. You can also participate at the local level in campaigns by candidates seeking national office, such as candidates running for Congress. Working at the grassroots level for a political candidate gives you firsthand knowledge of how the politics of democracy actually works. You could even run for office. Many young people have run for and won office as city council members, state legislators, or mayors. Aaron Schock, the youngest member of the House of Representatives, was elected to the school board at the age of 18.

Finally, to observe the judicial branch of government at work, you can watch the proceedings in your local courts. An important court at the local level is the small claims court. Small claims courts hear disputes involving claims under a certain amount, such as $2,500 or $5,000 (the amount varies from state to state). Lawyers are not required, and many small claims courts do not permit lawyers. Other local courts are described in Figure 18–2. For information on your local courts and on when you can attend court proceedings, call the courthouse clerk.

Key Terms

Chapter Summary

1. The United States has more than 89,000 separate governmental units. State and local governments perform a wide variety of highly visible functions and services, such as education, health care, police and fire protection, parks and recreation, highway safety and maintenance, insurance, and professional licensing.

2. Under the U.S. Constitution, powers not delegated expressly to the federal government are reserved to the states. The states may exercise taxing, spending, and general police powers. State constitutions are often very long. One reason for their length is that a loss of popular confidence in state legislatures in the late 1800s caused the framers of the constitutions to include many provisions that would normally be considered statutory law. Other reasons include state courts' reluctance to interpret state constitutions as freely as the United States Supreme Court interprets the U.S. Constitution.

3. In colonial America, the governors of the colonies were vested with extensive powers. Following the Revolutionary War, most states established forms of government in which the governor received very limited powers. After Andrew Jackson's presidency, however, all governors (except in South Carolina) were elected directly by the people. Most governors have the right to exercise some sort of veto power; many enjoy item veto power.

4. State legislatures deal with matters such as taxes, schools, highways, and welfare. They must also redraw state and federal legislative districts each decade to ensure that every person's vote is roughly equal to that of others and that minorities are adequately represented in both the state legislature and Congress. Voters may exercise some direct control over state government through the use of the initiative, referendum, and recall. Every state has its own court system. Most such systems have several levels of courts, including trial courts, intermediate courts of appeals, and a supreme court.

5. The United States has more than 19,000 municipalities, most of which are small cities. The more than 3,000 counties in this country are merely extensions of state authority and apply state laws at the local level. In New England, many of the functions of municipalities and counties are combined in towns. Municipalities may be governed by a commission consisting of members with executive and legislative powers, or they may be administered according to a council-manager, mayor-administrator, or mayor-council plan. Most major cities used to be run by political machines, which freely dispensed favors to supporters. In recent decades, however, political machines have become almost completely extinct.

6. State spending is funded by sales, property, corporate, and personal income taxes and is concentrated on welfare (including Medicaid), higher education, and highways. Local spending, which is mainly funded by property taxes, goes largely to the public schools and to utility services such as water, electricity, gas, sewers, and garbage collection. States compete for businesses and residents by lowering tax rates or giving rebates. States show considerable variation in their policies and programs. They may have different models of funding their operations and they may have very different laws and policies. States have long been seen as models of experimentation. If a program works at the state level, it may be copied by other states or enacted into federal law.

Selected Print, Media, and Online Resources

PRINT RESOURCES

Deckman, Melissa M. *School Board Battles: The Christian Right in Local Politics*. Washington, DC: Georgetown University Press, 2004. Deckman, a college professor, provides a judicious look at a controversial topic. She contends that members of the Christian Right and their opponents tend to demonize each other in local races and that the Christian Right is more complicated than it is usually portrayed.

Ehrenhalt, Alan. *The Great Inversion and the Future of the American City*. New York: Knopf, 2012. A well-known sociologist describes the new urbanism, meaning the movement of the young professionals and highly educated back to the urban core while the economically less well-off citizens are moving to the suburbs. While this creates new vibrancy for cities, it makes living more expensive for the poor.

Gray, Virginia, and Russell Hanson, eds. *Politics in the American States*, 8th ed. Washington, DC: CQ Press, 2007. Twenty authors compare policies and processes as well as the political climate across the states.

Grunwald, Michael. *The Swamp: The Everglades, Florida, and the Politics of Paradise*. New York: Simon & Schuster, 2006. Grunwald, a *Washington Post* reporter, tells the story of how local Florida interests first sought to drain the Everglades and then to restore it. The book contains entertaining vignettes on the environmental activists who sought to turn back the "march of progress" beginning in the 1960s.

Karch, Andrew. *Democratic Laboratories: Policy Diffusion among the American States*. Ann Arbor, MI: University of Michigan Press, 2007. In this scholarly book, the author examines the process by which policy ideas from one state are translated to another and how some federal policies may be resisted by states.

Siegel, Fred. *The Prince of the City: Giuliani, New York and the Genius of American Life*. New York: Encounter Books, 2005. This work is as much a history of late 20th-century New York City as a biography of Rudolph Giuliani, the city's mayor during the September 11 terrorist attacks. Crime rates went down under Giuliani, and he was also unusually successful in curbing spending. But his leadership during September 11 made him the national figure he is today.

MEDIA RESOURCES

Can the States Do It Better?—This is a program examining devolution—shifting federal powers back to the states—and what this means for the states with respect to, among other things, school reform.

City Hall—A 1996 drama about corruption at city hall in New York and a mayor, played by Al Pacino, who is willing to break the law to fulfill his presidential aspirations.

The Last Hurrah—A film based, in part, on the career of James Curley (1874–1958) of Massachusetts, who played a leading role in creating and running Boston's political machine in the first half of the 20th century. When Curley was convicted of mail fraud and sent to prison in 1947, he refused to resign as mayor and maintained his office while in jail.

Our Town—A 1980 film based on Thornton Wilder's play about day-to-day life and politics in a small, picturesque community—Peterborough ("Grover's Corners" in the play) in New Hampshire.

ONLINE RESOURCES

Campaign Finance Information Center This nonprofit organization gathers campaign finance policies and information from across the nation. Find out how to get information on campaign contributions and expenditures for your state: www.campaignfinance.org

The Council of State Governments a region-based forum that fosters the exchange of insights and ideas to help state officials shape public policy; an excellent source for information on state governments: www.csg.org

FindLaw searchable database of state law codes (statutes) and state court cases: www.findlaw.com/casecode/state.html

National Conference of State Legislatures a bipartisan organization that serves the legislators and staffs of the nation's 50 states, its commonwealths, and territories. NCSL provides research, technical assistance, and opportunities for policymakers to exchange ideas on the most pressing state issues: www.ncsl.org

National Governors Association The bipartisan organization of the nation's governors offers a wide variety of information on issues and data relating to state governments: www.nga.org

Project Vote Smart: This mostly volunteer, independent research group provides information on state governments, including their constitutional powers, education, and finances: www.vote-smart.org/resource_govt101_09.php

State and Local Government on the Net a directory of official state, county, and city government Web sites: www.statelocalgov.net

Tax Foundation The mission of the Tax Foundation is to educate taxpayers about sound tax policy and the size of the tax burden borne by Americans at all levels of government. For information on comparative tax collections and revenue expenditures by states or by the federal government, go to the extensive data collection of this nonpartisan educational organization: www.taxfoundation.org

U.S. Census Bureau State and County QuickFacts Find a wealth of data on state and local governments by simply clicking on states and counties on the maps: quickfacts.census.gov/qfd/index.html

THE DECLARATION OF INDEPENDENCE

In Congress, July 4, 1776

A Declaration by the Representatives of the United States of America, in General Congress assembled. When in the Course of human Events, it becomes necessary for one People to dissolve the Political Bands which have connected them with another, and to assume among the Powers of the Earth, the separate and equal Station to which the Laws of Nature and of Nature's God entitle them, a decent Respect to the Opinions of Mankind requires that they should declare the causes which impel them to the Separation.

We hold these Truths to be self-evident, that all Men are created equal, that they are endowed by their Creator with certain unalienable Rights, that among these are Life, Liberty, and the Pursuit of Happiness—That to secure these Rights, Governments are instituted among Men, deriving their just Powers from the Consent of the Governed, that whenever any Form of Government becomes destructive of these Ends, it is the Right of the People to alter or to abolish it, and to institute new Government, laying its Foundation on such Principles, and organizing its Powers in such Forms, as to them shall seem most likely to effect their Safety and Happiness. Prudence, indeed, will dictate that Governments long established should not be changed for light and transient Causes; and accordingly all Experience hath shewn, that Mankind are more disposed to suffer, while Evils are sufferable, than to right themselves by abolishing the Forms to which they are accustomed. But when a long Train of Abuses and Usurpations, pursuing invariably the same Object, evinces a Design to reduce them under absolute Despotism, it is their Right, it is their Duty, to throw off such Government, and to provide new Guards for their future Security. Such has been the patient Sufferance of these Colonies; and such is now the Necessity which constrains them to alter their former Systems of Government. The History of the present King of Great-Britain is a History of repeated Injuries and Usurpations, all having in direct Object the Establishment of an absolute Tyranny over these States. To prove this, let Facts be submitted to a candid World.

He has refused his Assent to Laws, the most wholesome and necessary for the public Good.

He has forbidden his Governors to pass Laws of immediate and pressing Importance, unless suspended in their Operation till his Assent should be obtained; and when so suspended, he has utterly neglected to attend to them.

He has refused to pass other Laws for the Accommodation of large Districts of People, unless those People would relinquish the Right of Representation in the Legislature, a Right inestimable to them, and formidable to Tyrants only.

He has called together Legislative Bodies at Places unusual, uncomfortable, and distant from the Depository of their Public Records, for the sole Purpose of fatiguing them into Compliance with his Measures.

He has dissolved Representative Houses repeatedly, for opposing with manly Firmness his Invasions on the Rights of the People.

He has refused for a long Time, after such Dissolutions, to cause others to be elected; whereby the Legislative Powers, incapable of Annihilation, have returned to the People at large for their exercise; the State remaining in the mean time exposed to all the Dangers of Invasion from without, and Convulsions within.

He has endeavoured to prevent the Population of these States; for that Purpose obstructing the Laws for Naturalization of Foreigners; refusing to pass others to encourage their Migrations hither, and raising the Conditions of new Appropriations of Lands.

He has obstructed the Administration of Justice, by refusing his Assent to Laws for establishing Judiciary Powers.

He has made Judges dependent on his Will alone, for the Tenure of their offices, and the Amount and payment of their Salaries.

He has erected a Multitude of new Offices, and sent hither Swarms of Officers to harass our People, and eat out their Substance.

He has kept among us, in Times of Peace, Standing Armies, without the consent of our Legislatures.

He has affected to render the Military independent of, and superior to the Civil Power.

He has combined with others to subject us to a Jurisdiction foreign to our Constitution, and unacknowledged by our Laws; giving his Assent to their Acts of pretended Legislation:

For quartering large Bodies of Armed Troops among us:

For protecting them, by a mock Trial, from Punishment for any Murders which they should commit on the Inhabitants of these States:

For cutting off our Trade with all Parts of the World:

For imposing Taxes on us without our Consent:

For depriving us, in many cases, of the Benefits of Trial by Jury:

For transporting us beyond Seas to be tried for pretended Offences:

For abolishing the free System of English Laws in a neighbouring Province, establishing therein an arbitrary Government, and enlarging its Boundaries, so as to render it at once an Example and fit Instrument for introducing the same absolute Rule into these Colonies:

For taking away our Charters, abolishing our most valuable Laws, and altering fundamentally the Forms of our Governments:

For suspending our own Legislatures, and declaring themselves invested with Power to legislate for us in all Cases whatsoever.

He has abdicated Government here, by declaring us out of his Protection and waging War against us.

He has plundered our Seas, ravaged our Coasts, burnt our towns, and destroyed the Lives of our People.

He is, at this Time, transporting large Armies of foreign Mercenaries to compleat the works of Death, Desolation, and Tyranny, already begun with circumstances of Cruelty and Perfidy, scarcely paralleled in the most barbarous Ages, and totally unworthy the Head of a civilized Nation.

He has constrained our fellow Citizens taken Captive on the high Seas to bear Arms against their Country, to become the Executioners of their Friends and Brethren, or to fall themselves by their Hands.

He has excited domestic Insurrections amongst us, and has endeavoured to bring on the Inhabitants of our Frontiers, the merciless Indian Savages, whose known Rule of Warfare, is an undistinguished Destruction, of all Ages, Sexes and Conditions.

In every state of these Oppressions we have Petitioned for Redress in the most humble Terms: Our repeated Petitions have been answered only by repeated Injury. A Prince, whose Character is thus marked by every act which may define a Tyrant, is unfit to be the Ruler of a free People.

Nor have we been wanting in Attentions to our British Brethren. We have warned them from Time to Time of Attempts by their Legislature to extend an unwarrantable Jurisdiction over us. We have reminded them of the Circumstances of our Emigration and Settlement here. We have appealed to their native Justice and Magnanimity, and we have conjured them by the Ties of our common Kindred to disavow these Usurpations, which, would inevitably interrupt our Connections and Correspondence. They too have been deaf to the Voice of Justice and of Consanguinity. We must, therefore, acquiesce in the Necessity, which denounces our Separation, and hold them, as we hold the rest of Mankind, Enemies in War, in Peace, Friends.

We, therefore, the Representatives of the UNITED STATES OF AMERICA, in General Congress Assembled, appealing to the Supreme Judge of the World for the Rectitude of our Intentions, do, in the Name, and by the Authority of the good People of these Colonies, solemnly Publish and Declare, That these United Colonies are, and of Right ought to be, Free and Independent States; that they are absolved from all Allegiance to the British Crown, and that all political Connection between them and the State of Great-Britain, is and ought to be totally dissolved; and that as Free and Independent States, they have full Power to levy War, conclude Peace, contract Alliances, establish Commerce, and to do all other Acts and Things which Independent States may of right do. And for the support of this declaration, with a firm Reliance on the Protection of divine Providence, we mutually pledge to each other our lives, our Fortunes, and our sacred Honor.

THE CONSTITUTION OF THE UNITED STATES*

The Preamble

We the People of the United States, in Order to form a more perfect Union, establish Justice, insure domestic Tranquility, provide for the common defence, promote the general Welfare, and secure the Blessings of Liberty to ourselves and our Posterity, do ordain and establish this *Constitution* for the United States of America.

The Preamble declares that "We the People" are the authority for the Constitution (unlike the Articles of Confederation, which derived their authority from the states). The Preamble also sets out the purposes of the Constitution.

Article I. (*Legislative Branch*)

The first part of the Constitution, Article I, deals with the organization and powers of the lawmaking branch of the national government, the Congress.

Section 1. *Legislative Powers*

All legislative Powers herein granted shall be vested in a Congress of the United States, which shall consist of a Senate and House of Representatives.

Section 2. *House of Representatives*

Clause 1: Composition and Election of Members. The House of Representatives shall be composed of Members chosen every second Year by the People of the several States, and the Electors in each State shall have the Qualifications requisite for Electors of the most numerous Branch of the State Legislature.

Each state has the power to decide who may vote for members of Congress. Within each state, those who may vote for state legislators may also vote for members of the House of Representatives (and, under the Seventeenth Amendment, for U.S. senators). When the Constitution was written, nearly all states limited voting rights to white male property owners or taxpayers at least 21 years old. Subsequent amendments granted voting power to African American men, all women, and everyone at least 18 years old.

Clause 2: Qualifications. No Person shall be a Representative who shall not have attained to the Age of twenty five Years, and been seven Years a Citizen of the United States, and who shall not, when elected, be an Inhabitant of that State in which he shall be chosen.

Each member of the House must be at least 25 years old, a citizen of the United States for at least seven years, and a resident of the state in which she or he is elected.

Clause 3: Apportionment of Representatives and Direct Taxes. Representatives [and direct Taxes][1] shall be apportioned among the several States which may be included within this Union, according to their respective Numbers [which shall be determined by adding to the whole Number of free Persons, including those bound to Service for a Term of Years, and excluding Indians not taxed, three fifths of all other Persons].[2] The actual Enumeration shall be made within three Years after the first Meeting of the Congress of the United States, and within every subsequent Term of ten Years, in such Manner as they shall by Law direct. The Number of Representatives shall not exceed one for every thirty Thousand, but each State shall have at Least one Representative; and until such enumeration shall be made, the State of New Hampshire shall be entitled to chuse three, Massachusetts eight, Rhode Island and Providence Plantations one, Connecticut five, New York six, New Jersey four, Pennsylvania eight, Delaware one, Maryland six, Virginia ten, North Carolina five, South Carolina five, and Georgia three.

A state's representation in the House is based on the size of its population. Population is counted in each decade's census, after which Congress reapportions House seats. Since early in the 20th century, the number of seats has been limited to 435.

Clause 4: Vacancies. When vacancies happen in the Representation from any State, the Executive Authority thereof shall issue Writs of Election to fill such Vacancies.

The "Executive Authority" is the state's governor. When a vacancy occurs in the House, the governor calls a special election to fill it.

Clause 5: Officers and Impeachment. The House of Representatives shall chuse their Speaker and other Officers; and shall have the sole Power of Impeachment.

The power to impeach is the power to accuse. In this case, it is the power to accuse members of the executive or judicial branch of wrongdoing or abuse of power. Once a bill of impeachment is issued, the Senate holds the trial.

Section 3. The Senate

Clause 1: Term and Number of Members. The Senate of the United States shall be composed of two Senators from each State [chosen by the Legislature thereof],[3] for six Years; and each Senator shall have one Vote.

Every state has two senators, each of whom serves for six years and has one vote in the upper chamber. Since the Seventeenth Amendment in 1913, all senators have been elected directly by voters of the state during the regular election.

Clause 2: Classification of Senators. Immediately after they shall be assembled in Consequence of the first Election, they shall be divided as equally as may be into three Classes. The Seats of the Senators of the first Class shall be vacated at the Expiration of the

---

*The spelling, capitalization, and punctuation of the original have been retained here. Brackets indicate passages that have been altered by amendments to the Constitution. We have added article titles (in parentheses), section titles, and clause designations. We have also inserted annotations in blue italic type.

1. Modified by the Sixteenth Amendment.
2. Modified by the Fourteenth Amendment.
3. Repealed by the Seventeenth Amendment.

second Year, of the second Class at the Expiration of the fourth Year, and of the third Class at the Expiration of the sixth Year, so that one third may be chosen every second Year; [and if Vacancies happen by Resignation, or otherwise, during the Recess of the Legislature of any State, the Executive thereof may make temporary Appointments until the next Meeting of the Legislature, which shall then fill such Vacancies].[4]

One-third of the Senate's seats are open to election every two years (in contrast, all members of the House are elected simultaneously).

Clause 3: Qualifications. No Person shall be a Senator who shall not have attained to the Age of thirty Years, and been nine Years a Citizen of the United States, and who shall not, when elected, be an Inhabitant of that State for which he shall be chosen.

Every senator must be at least 30 years old, a citizen of the United States for a minimum of nine years, and a resident of the state in which he or she is elected.

Clause 4: The Role of the Vice President. The Vice President of the United States shall be President of the Senate, but shall have no Vote, unless they be equally divided.

The vice president presides over meetings of the Senate but cannot vote unless there is a tie. The Constitution gives no other official duties to the vice president.

Clause 5: Other Officers. The Senate shall chuse their other Officers, and also a President pro tempore, in the Absence of the Vice President, or when he shall exercise the Office of President of the United States.

The Senate votes for one of its members to preside when the vice president is absent. This person is usually called the president pro tempore because of the temporary nature of the position.

Clause 6: Impeachment Trials. The Senate shall have the sole Power to try all Impeachments. When sitting for that Purpose, they shall be on Oath or Affirmation. When the President of the United States is tried, the Chief Justice shall preside: And no Person shall be convicted without the Concurrence of two thirds of the Members present.

The Senate conducts trials of officials that the House impeaches. The Senate sits as a jury, with the vice president presiding if the president is not on trial.

Clause 7: Penalties for Conviction. Judgment in Cases of Impeachment shall not extend further than to removal from Office, and disqualification to hold and enjoy any Office of honor, Trust, or Profit under the United States: but the Party convicted shall nevertheless be liable and subject to Indictment, Trial, Judgment, and Punishment, according to Law.

On conviction of impeachment charges, the Senate can only force an official to leave office and prevent him or her from holding another office in the federal government. The individual, however, can still be tried in a regular court.

Section 4. *Congressional Elections: Times, Manner, and Places*

Clause 1: Elections. The Times, Places and Manner of holding Elections for Senators and Representatives, shall be prescribed in each State by the Legislature thereof; but the Congress may at any time by Law make or alter such Regulations, except as to the Places of chusing Senators.

Congress set the Tuesday after the first Monday in November in even-numbered years as the date for congressional elections. In states with more than one seat in the House, Congress requires that representatives be elected from districts within each state. Under the Seventeenth Amendment, senators are elected at the same places as other officials.

Clause 2: Sessions of Congress. [The Congress shall assemble at least once in every Year, and such Meeting shall be on the first Monday in December, unless they shall by Law appoint a different Day.][5]

Congress has to meet every year at least once. The regular session now begins at noon on January 3 of each year, subsequent to the Twentieth Amendment, unless Congress passes a law to fix a different date. Congress stays in session until its members vote to adjourn. Additionally, the president may call a special session.

Section 5. *Powers and Duties of the Houses*

Clause 1: Admitting Members and Quorum. Each House shall be the Judge of the Elections, Returns, and Qualifications of its own Members, and a Majority of each shall constitute a Quorum to do Business; but a smaller Number may adjourn from day to day, and may be authorized to compel the Attendance of absent Members, in such Manner, and under such Penalties as each House may provide.

Each chamber may exclude or refuse to seat a member-elect.

The quorum rule requires that 218 members of the House and 51 members of the Senate be present to conduct business. This rule normally is not enforced in the handling of routine matters.

Clause 2: Rules and Discipline of Members. Each House may determine the Rules of its Proceedings, punish its Members for disorderly Behaviour, and, with the Concurrence of two thirds, expel a Member.

The House and the Senate may adopt their own rules to guide their proceedings. Each may also discipline its members for conduct that is deemed unacceptable. No member may be expelled without a two-thirds majority vote in favor of expulsion.

Clause 3: Keeping a Record. Each House shall keep a Journal of its Proceedings, and from time to time publish the same, excepting such Parts as may in their Judgment require Secrecy; and the Yeas and Nays of the Members of either House on any question shall, at the Desire of one fifth of those Present, be entered on the Journal.

The journals of the two chambers are published at the end of each session of Congress.

---

4. Modified by the Seventeenth Amendment.
5. Changed by the Twentieth Amendment.

Clause 4: Adjournment. Neither House, during the Session of Congress, shall, without the Consent of the other, adjourn for more than three days, nor to any other Place than that in which the two Houses shall be sitting.

Congress has the power to determine when and where to meet, provided, however, that both chambers meet in the same city. Neither chamber may recess for more than three days without the consent of the other.

Section 6. *Rights of Members*

Clause 1: Compensation and Privileges. The Senators and Representatives shall receive a Compensation for their services, to be ascertained by Law, and paid out of the Treasury of the United States. They shall in all Cases, except Treason, Felony and Breach of the Peace, be privileged from Arrest during their Attendance at the Session of their respective Houses, and in going to and returning from the same; and for any Speech or Debate in either House, they shall not be questioned in any other Place.

Congressional salaries are to be paid by the U.S. Treasury rather than by the members' respective states. The original salaries were $6 per day; in 1857 they were $3,000 per year. Both representatives and senators were paid $165,200 in 2006.

Treason is defined in Article III, Section 3. A felony is any serious crime. A breach of the peace is any indictable offense less than treason or a felony. Members cannot be arrested for things they say during speeches and debates in Congress. This immunity applies to the Capitol Building itself and not to their private lives.

Clause 2: Restrictions. No Senator or Representative shall, during the Time for which he was elected, be appointed to any civil Office under the Authority of the United States, which shall have been created, or the Emoluments whereof shall have been encreased during such time; and no Person holding any Office under the United States, shall be a Member of either House during his Continuance in Office.

During the term for which a member was elected, he or she cannot concurrently accept another federal government position.

Section 7. *Legislative Powers: Bills and Resolutions*

Clause 1: Revenue Bills. All Bills for raising Revenue shall originate in the House of Representatives; but the Senate may propose or concur with Amendments as on other Bills.

All tax and appropriation bills for raising money have to originate in the House of Representatives. The Senate, though, often amends such bills and may even substitute an entirely different bill.

Clause 2: The Presidential Veto. Every Bill which shall have passed the House of Representatives and the Senate, shall, before it becomes a Law, be presented to the President of the United States; If he approve he shall sign it, but if not he shall return it, with his Objections to the House in which it shall have originated, who shall enter the Objections at large on their Journal, and proceed to reconsider it. If after such Reconsideration two thirds of that House shall agree to pass the Bill, it shall be sent together with the Objections, to the other House, by which it shall likewise be reconsidered, and if approved by two thirds of that House, it shall become a Law. But in all such Cases the Votes of both Houses shall be determined by Yeas and Nays, and the Names of the Persons voting for and against the Bill shall be entered on the Journal of each House respectively. If any Bill shall not be returned by the President within 10 Days (Sundays excepted) after it shall have been presented to him, the Same shall be a Law, in like Manner as if he had signed it, unless the Congress by their Adjournment prevent its Return in which Case it shall not be a Law.

When Congress sends the president a bill, he or she can sign it (in which case it becomes law) or send it back to the chamber in which it originated. If it is sent back, a two-thirds majority of each chamber must pass it again for it to become law. If the president neither signs it nor sends it back within 10 days, it becomes law anyway, unless Congress adjourns in the meantime.

Clause 3: Actions on Other Matters. Every Order, Resolution, or Vote to which the Concurrence of the Senate and House of Representatives may be necessary (except on a question of Adjournment) shall be presented to the President of the United States; and before the Same shall take Effect, shall be approved by him, or being disapproved by him, shall be repassed by two thirds of the Senate and House of Representatives, according to the Rules and Limitations prescribed in the Case of a Bill.

The president must have the opportunity to either sign or veto everything that Congress passes, except votes to adjourn and resolutions not having the force of law.

Section 8. *The Powers of Congress*

Clause 1: Taxing. The Congress shall have Power to lay and collect Taxes, Duties, Imposts and Excises, to pay the Debts and provide for the common Defence and general Welfare of the United States; but all Duties, Imposts and Excises shall be uniform throughout the United States;

Duties are taxes on imports and exports. Impost is a generic term for tax. Excises are taxes on the manufacture, sale, or use of goods.

Clause 2: Borrowing. To borrow Money on the credit of the United States;

Congress has the power to borrow money, which is normally carried out through the sale of U.S. treasury bonds on which interest is paid. Note that the Constitution places no limit on the amount of government borrowing.

Clause 3: Regulation of Commerce. To regulate Commerce with foreign Nations, and among the several States, and with the Indian Tribes; Gibbons v. Ogden

This is the commerce clause, which gives to Congress the power to regulate interstate and foreign trade. Much of the activity of Congress is based on this clause.

Clause 4: Naturalization and Bankruptcy. To establish an uniform Rule of Naturalization, and uniform Laws on the subject of Bankruptcies throughout the United States;

Only Congress may determine how aliens can become citizens of the United States. Congress may make laws with respect to bankruptcy.

McCullough v. Maryland

Clause 5: Money and Standards. To coin Money, regulate the Value thereof, and of foreign Coin, and fix the Standard of Weights and Measures;

Congress mints coins and prints and circulates paper money. Congress can establish uniform measures of time, distance, weight, and so on. In 1838, Congress adopted the English system of weights and measurements as our national standard.

Clause 6: Punishing Counterfeiters. To provide for the Punishment of counterfeiting the Securities and current Coin of the United States;

Congress has the power to punish those who copy American money and pass it off as real. Currently, the fine is up to $5,000 and/or imprisonment for up to 15 years.

Clause 7: Roads and Post Offices. To establish Post Offices and post Roads;

Post roads include all routes over which mail is carried— highways, railways, waterways, and airways.

Clause 8: Patents and Copyrights. To promote the Progress of Science and useful Arts, by securing for limited Times to Authors and Inventors the exclusive Right to their respective Writings and Discoveries;

Authors' and composers' works are protected by copyrights established by copyright law, which currently is the Copyright Act of 1976, as amended. Copyrights are valid for the life of the author or composer plus 70 years. Inventors' works are protected by patents, which vary in length of protection from 14 to 20 years. A patent gives a person the exclusive right to control the manufacture or sale of her or his invention.

Clause 9: Lower Courts. To constitute Tribunals inferior to the supreme Court;

Congress has the authority to set up all federal courts, except the Supreme Court, and to decide what cases those courts will hear.

Clause 10: Punishment for Piracy. To define and punish Piracies and Felonies committed on the high Seas, and Offences against the Law of Nations;

Congress has the authority to prohibit the commission of certain acts outside U.S. territory and to punish certain violations of international law.

Clause 11: Declaration of War. To declare War, grant Letters of Marque and Reprisal, and make Rules concerning Captures on Land and Water;

Only Congress can declare war, although the president, as commander in chief, can make war without Congress's formal declaration. Letters of marque and reprisal authorized private parties to capture and destroy enemy ships in wartime. Since the middle of the 19th century, international law has prohibited letters of marque and reprisal, and the United States has honored the ban.

Clause 12: The Army. To raise and support Armies, but no Appropriation of Money to that Use shall be for a longer Term than two Years;

Congress has the power to create an army; the money used to pay for it must be appropriated for no more than two-year intervals. This latter restriction gives ultimate control of the army to civilians.

Clause 13: Creation of a Navy. To provide and maintain a Navy;

This clause allows for the maintenance of a navy. In 1947, Congress created the U.S. Air Force.

Clause 14: Regulation of the Armed Forces. To make Rules for the Government and Regulation of the land and naval Forces;

Congress sets the rules for the military mainly by way of the Uniform Code of Military Justice, which was enacted in 1950 by Congress.

Clause 15: The Militia. To provide for calling forth the Militia to execute the Laws of the Union, suppress Insurrections and repel Invasions;

The militia is known today as the National Guard. Both Congress and the president have the authority to call the National Guard into federal service.

Clause 16: How the Militia Is Organized. To provide for organizing, arming, and disciplining the Militia, and for governing such Part of them as may be employed in the Service of the United States, reserving to the States respectively, the Appointment of the Officers, and the Authority of training the Militia according to the discipline prescribed by Congress;

This clause gives Congress the power to "federalize" state militia (National Guard). When called into such service, the National Guard is subject to the same rules that Congress has set forth for the regular armed services.

Clause 17: Creation of the District of Columbia. To exercise exclusive Legislation in all Cases whatsoever, over such District (not exceeding ten Miles square) as may, by Cession of particular States, and the Acceptance of Congress, become the Seat of the Government of the United States, and to exercise like Authority over all Places purchased by the Consent of the Legislature of the State in which the Same shall be, for the Erection of Forts, Magazines, Arsenals, dock-Yards, and other needful Buildings;—And

Congress established the District of Columbia as the national capital in 1791. Virginia and Maryland had granted land for the District, but Virginia's grant was returned because it was believed it would not be needed. Today, the District covers 69 square miles.

Clause 18: The Elastic Clause. To make all Laws which shall be necessary and proper for carrying into Execution the foregoing Powers, and all other Powers vested by this Constitution in the Government of the United States, or in any Department or Officer thereof.

This clause—the necessary and proper clause, or the elastic clause—grants no specific powers, and thus it can be stretched to fit different circumstances. It has allowed Congress to adapt the government to changing needs and times.

Section 9. *The Powers Denied to Congress*

Clause 1: Question of Slavery. The Migration or Importation of such Persons as any of the States now existing shall think proper to admit, shall not be prohibited by the Congress prior to the Year one thousand eight hundred and eight, but a Tax or duty may be imposed on such Importation, not exceeding ten dollars for each Person.

"Persons" referred to slaves. Congress outlawed the slave trade in 1808.

Clause 2: Habeas Corpus. The privilege of the Writ of Habeas Corpus shall not be suspended, unless when in Cases of Rebellion or Invasion the public Safety may require it.

A writ of habeas corpus is a court order directing a sheriff or other public officer who is detaining another person to "produce the body" of the detainee so the court can assess the legality of the detention.

Clause 3: Special Bills. No Bill of Attainder or ex post facto Law shall be passed.

A bill of attainder is a law that inflicts punishment without a trial. An ex post facto law is a law that inflicts punishment for an act that was not illegal when it was committed.

Clause 4: Direct Taxes. [No Capitation, or other direct, Tax shall be laid, unless in Proportion to the Census or Enumeration herein before directed to be taken.][6]

A capitation is a tax on a person. A direct tax is a tax paid directly to the government, such as a property tax. This clause was intended to prevent Congress from levying a tax on slaves per person and thereby taxing slavery out of existence.

Clause 5: Export Taxes. No Tax or Duty shall be laid on Articles exported from any State.

Congress may not tax any goods sold from one state to another or from one state to a foreign country. (Congress does have the power to tax goods that are bought from other countries, however.)

Clause 6: Interstate Commerce. No Preference shall be given by any Regulation of Commerce or Revenue to the Ports of one State over those of another: nor shall Vessels bound to, or from, one State, be obliged to enter, clear, or pay Duties in another.

Congress may not treat different ports within the United States differently in terms of taxing and commerce powers. Congress may not give one state's port a legal advantage over the ports of another state.

Clause 7: Treasury Withdrawals. No Money shall be drawn from the Treasury, but in Consequence of Appropriations made by Law; and a regular Statement and Account of the Receipts and Expenditures of all public Money shall be published from time to time.

Federal funds can be spent only as Congress authorizes. This is a significant check on the president's power.

Clause 8: Titles of Nobility. No Title of Nobility shall be granted by the United States: And no Person holding any Office of Profit or Trust under them, shall, without the Consent of the Congress, accept of any present, Emolument, Office, or Title, of any kind whatever, from any King, Prince, or foreign State.

No person in the United States may hold a title of nobility, such as duke or duchess. This clause also discourages bribery of American officials by foreign governments.

Section 10. *Those Powers Denied to the States*

Clause 1: Treaties and Coinage. No State shall enter into any Treaty, Alliance, or Confederation; grant Letters of Marque and Reprisal; coin Money; emit Bills of Credit; make any Thing but gold and silver Coin a Tender in Payment of Debts; pass any Bill of Attainder, ex post facto Law, or Law impairing the Obligation of Contracts, or grant any Title of Nobility.

Prohibiting state laws "impairing the Obligation of Contracts" was intended to protect creditors. (Shayss' Rebellion—an attempt to prevent courts from giving effect to creditors' legal actions against debtors—occurred only one year before the Constitution was written.)

Clause 2: Duties and Imposts. No State shall, without the Consent of the Congress, lay any Imposts or Duties on Imports or Exports, except what may be absolutely necessary for executing its inspection Laws; and the net Produce of all Duties and Imposts, laid by any State on Imports or Exports, shall be for the Use of the Treasury of the United States; and all such Laws shall be subject to the Revision and Controul of the Congress.

Only Congress can tax imports. Further, the states cannot tax exports.

Clause 3: War. No State shall, without the Consent of Congress, lay any Duty of Tonnage, keep Troops, or Ships of War in time of Peace, enter into any Agreement or Compact with another State, or with a foreign Power or engage in War, unless actually invaded, or in such imminent Danger as will not admit of delay.

A duty of tonnage is a tax on ships according to their cargo capacity. No states may tax ships according to their cargo unless Congress agrees. Additionally, this clause forbids any state to keep troops or warships during peacetime or to make a compact with another state or foreign nation unless Congress so agrees. A state, in contrast, can maintain a militia, but its use has to be limited to disorders that occur within the state—unless, of course, the militia is called into federal service.

ARTICLE II. (*Executive Branch*)

Section 1. *The Nature and Scope of Presidential Power*

Clause 1: Four-Year Term. The executive Power shall be vested in a President of the United States of America. He shall hold his Office during the Term of four Years, and, together with the Vice President, chosen for the same Term, be elected, as follows.

The president has the power to carry out laws made by Congress, called the executive power. He or she serves in office for a four-year term after election. The Twenty-second Amendment limits the number of times a person may be elected president.

Clause 2: Choosing Electors from Each State. Each State shall appoint, in such Manner as the Legislature thereof may direct, a Number of Electors, equal to the whole Number of Senators and Representatives to which the State may be entitled in the Congress; but no Senator or Representative, or Person holding an Office of Trust or Profit under the United States, shall be appointed an Elector.

The "Electors" are known more commonly as the "electoral college." The president is elected by electors—that is, representatives chosen by the people—rather than by the people directly.

6. Modified by the Sixteenth Amendment.

Clause 3: The Former System of Elections. [The Electors shall meet in their respective States, and vote by Ballot for two Persons, of whom one at least shall not be an Inhabitant of the same State with themselves. And they shall make a List of all the Persons voted for, and of the Number of Votes for each; which List they shall sign and certify, and transmit sealed to the Seat of the Government of the United States, directed to the President of the Senate. The President of the Senate shall, in the Presence of the Senate and House of Representatives, open all the Certificates, and the Votes shall then be counted. The Person having the greatest Number of Votes shall be the President, if such Number be a Majority of the whole Number of Electors appointed; and if there be more than one who have such Majority, and have an equal Number of Votes, then the House of Representatives shall immediately chuse by Ballot one of them for President; and if no Person have a Majority, then from the five highest on the List the said House shall in like Manner chuse the President. But in chusing the President, the Votes shall be taken by States, the Representation from each State having one Vote; A quorum for this Purpose shall consist of a Member or Members from two thirds of the States, and a Majority of all the States shall be necessary to a Choice. In every Case, after the Choice of the President, the Person having the greater Number of Votes of the Electors shall be the Vice President. But if there should remain two or more who have equal Votes, the Senate shall chuse from them by Ballot the Vice President.][7]

The original method of selecting the president and vice president was replaced by the Twelfth Amendment. Apparently, the framers did not anticipate the rise of political parties and the development of primaries and conventions.

Clause 4: The Time of Elections. The Congress may determine the Time of chusing the Electors, and the Day on which they shall give their Votes; which Day shall be the same throughout the United States.

Congress set the Tuesday after the first Monday in November every fourth year as the date for choosing electors. The electors cast their votes on the Monday after the second Wednesday in December of that year.

Clause 5: Qualifications for President. No person except a natural born Citizen, or a Citizen of the United States, at the time of the Adoption of this Constitution, shall be eligible to the Office of President; neither shall any Person be eligible to that Office who shall not have attained to the Age of thirty five Years, and been fourteen Years a Resident within the United States.

The president must be a natural-born citizen, be at least 35 years of age when taking office, and have been a resident within the United States for at least 14 years.

Clause 6: Succession of the Vice President. [In Case of the Removal of the President from Office, or of his Death, Resignation or Inability to discharge the Powers and Duties of the said Office, the same shall devolve on the Vice President, and the Congress may by Law provide for the Case of Removal, Death, Resignation or Inability,

both of the President and Vice President, declaring what Officer shall then act as President, and such Officer shall act accordingly, until the Disability be removed, or a President shall be elected.][8]

This section provided for the method by which the vice president was to succeed to the presidency, but its wording is ambiguous. It was replaced by the Twenty-fifth Amendment.

Clause 7: The President's Salary. The President shall, at stated Times, receive for his Services, a Compensation, which shall neither be encreased nor diminished during the Period for which he shall have been elected, and he shall not receive within that Period any other Emolument from the United States, or any of them.

The president maintains the same salary during each four-year term. Moreover, she or he may not receive additional cash payments from the government. Originally set at $25,000 per year, the salary is currently $400,000 a year plus a $50,000 nontaxable expense account.

Clause 8: The Oath of Office. Before he enter on the Execution of his Office, he shall take the following Oath or Affirmation: "I do solemnly swear (or affirm) that I will faithfully execute the Office of President of the United States, and will to the best of my Ability, preserve, protect and defend the Constitution of the United States."

The president is "sworn in" prior to beginning the duties of the office. The taking of the oath of office occurs on January 20, following the November election. The ceremony is called the inauguration. The oath of office is administered by the chief justice of the United States Supreme Court.

Section 2. *Powers of the President*

Clause 1: Commander in Chief. The President shall be Commander in Chief of the Army and Navy of the United States, and of the Militia of the several States, when called into the actual Service of the United States; he may require the Opinion, in writing, of the principal Officer in each of the executive Departments, upon any Subject relating to the Duties of their respective Offices, and he shall have Power to grant Reprieves and Pardons for Offences against the United States, except in Cases of Impeachment.

The armed forces are placed under civilian control because the president is a civilian but still commander in chief of the military. The president may ask for the help of the head of each of the executive departments (thereby creating the Cabinet). The Cabinet members are chosen by the president with the consent of the Senate, but they can be removed without Senate approval.

The president's clemency powers extend only to federal cases. In those cases, he or she may grant a full or conditional pardon, or reduce a prison term or fine.

Clause 2: Treaties and Appointment. He shall have Power, by and with the Advice and Consent of the Senate, to make Treaties, provided two thirds of the Senators present concur; and he shall nominate, and by and with the Advice and Consent of the Senate,

---

7. Changed by the Twelfth Amendment.
8. Modified by the Twenty-fifth Amendment.

shall appoint Ambassadors, other public Ministers and Consuls, Judges of the supreme Court, and all other Officers of the United States, whose Appointments are not herein otherwise provided for, and which shall be established by Law; but the Congress may by Law vest the Appointment of such inferior Officers, as they think proper, in the President alone, in the Courts of Law, or in the Heads of Departments.

Many of the major powers of the president are identified in this clause, including the power to make treaties with foreign governments (with the approval of the Senate by a two-thirds vote) and the power to appoint ambassadors, Supreme Court justices, and other government officials. Most such appointments require Senate approval.

Clause 3: Vacancies. The President shall have Power to fill up all Vacancies that may happen during the Recess of the Senate, by granting Commissions which shall expire at the end of their next Session.

The president has the power to appoint temporary officials to fill vacant federal offices without Senate approval if the Congress is not in session. Such appointments expire automatically at the end of Congress's next term.

Section 3. *Duties of the President*

He shall from time to time give to the Congress Information of the State of the Union, and recommend to their Consideration such Measures as he shall judge necessary and expedient; he may, on extraordinary Occasions, convene both Houses, or either of them, and in Case of Disagreement between them, with Respect to the Time of Adjournment, he may adjourn them to such Time as he shall think proper; he shall receive Ambassadors and other public Ministers; he shall take Care that the Laws be faithfully executed, and shall Commission all the Officers of the United States.

Annually, the president reports on the state of the union to Congress, recommends legislative measures, and proposes a federal budget. The State of the Union speech is a statement not only to Congress but also to the American people. After it is given, the president proposes a federal budget and presents an economic report. At any time, the president may send special messages to Congress while it is in session. The president has the power to call special sessions, to adjourn Congress when its two chambers do not agree on when to adjourn, to receive diplomatic representatives of other governments, and to ensure the proper execution of all federal laws. The president further has the ability to empower federal officers to hold their positions and to perform their duties.

Section 4. *Impeachment*

The President, Vice President and all civil Officers of the United States, shall be removed from Office on Impeachment for, and Conviction of, Treason, Bribery, or other high Crimes and Misdemeanors.

Treason denotes giving aid to the nation's enemies. The phrase "high crimes and misdemeanors" is usually considered to mean serious abuses of political power. In either case, the president or vice president may be accused by the House (called an impeachment) and then removed from office if convicted by the Senate. (Note that impeachment does not mean removal but rather refers to an accusation of treason or high crimes and misdemeanors.)

ARTICLE III. *(Judicial Branch)*

Section 1. *Judicial Powers, Courts, and Judges*

The judicial Power of the United States, shall be vested in one supreme Court, and in such inferior Courts as the Congress may from time to time ordain and establish. The Judges, both of the supreme and inferior Courts, shall hold their Offices during good Behaviour, and shall, at stated Times, receive for their Services a Compensation, which shall not be diminished during their Continuance in Office.

The Supreme Court is vested with judicial power, as are the lower federal courts that Congress creates. Federal judges serve in their offices for life unless they are impeached and convicted by Congress. The payment of federal judges may not be reduced during their time in office.

Section 2. *Jurisdiction*

Clause 1: Cases under Federal Jurisdiction. The judicial Power shall extend to all Cases, in Law and Equity, arising under this Constitution, the Laws of the United States, and Treaties made, or which shall be made, under their Authority;—to all Cases affecting Ambassadors, other public Ministers and Consuls;—to all Cases of admiralty and maritime Jurisdiction;—to Controversies to which the United States shall be a Party;—to Controversies between two or more States; [—between a State and Citizens of another State;—][9] between Citizens of different States;—between Citizens of the same State claiming Lands under Grants of different States, [and between a State, or the Citizens thereof, and foreign States, Citizens or Subjects.][10]

The federal courts take on cases that concern the meaning of the U.S. Constitution, all federal laws, and treaties. They also can take on cases involving citizens of different states and citizens of foreign nations.

Clause 2: Cases for the Supreme Court. In all Cases affecting Ambassadors, other public Ministers and Consuls, and those in which a State shall be a Party, the supreme Court shall have original Jurisdiction. In all the other Cases before mentioned, the supreme Court shall have appellate Jurisdiction, both as to Law and Fact, with such Exceptions, and under such Regulations as the Congress shall make.

In a limited number of situations, the Supreme Court acts as a trial court and has original jurisdiction. These cases involve a representative from another country or involve a state. In all other situations, the cases must first be tried in the lower courts and then can be appealed to the Supreme Court. Congress may, however, make exceptions. Today, the Supreme Court acts as a trial court of first instance on rare occasions.

9. Modified by the Eleventh Amendment.
10. Modified by the Eleventh Amendment.

Clause 3: The Conduct of Trials. The Trial of all Crimes, except in Cases of Impeachment, shall be by Jury; and such Trial shall be held in the State where the said Crimes shall have been committed; but when not committed within any State, the Trial shall be at such Place or Places as the Congress may by Law have directed.

Any person accused of a federal crime is granted the right to a trial by jury in a federal court in that state in which the crime was committed. Trials of impeachment are an exception.

Section 3. *Treason*

Clause 1: The Definition of Treason. Treason against the United States, shall consist only in levying War against them, or, in adhering to their Enemies, giving them Aid and Comfort. No Person shall be convicted of Treason unless on the Testimony of two Witnesses to the same overt Act, or on Confession in open Court.

Treason is the making of war against the United States or giving aid to its enemies.

Clause 2: Punishment. The Congress shall have Power to declare the Punishment of Treason, but no Attainder of Treason shall work Corruption of Blood, or Forfeiture except during the Life of the Person attainted.

Congress has provided that the punishment for treason ranges from a minimum of five years in prison and/or a $10,000 fine to a maximum of death. "No Attainder of Treason shall work Corruption of Blood" prohibits punishment of the traitor's heirs.

ARTICLE IV. (*Relations among the States*)

Section 1. *Full Faith and Credit*

Full Faith and Credit shall be given in each State to the public Acts, Records, and judicial Proceedings of every other State. And the Congress may by general Laws prescribe the Manner in which such Acts, Records and Proceedings shall be proved, and the Effect thereof.

All states are required to respect one another's laws, records, and lawful decisions. There are exceptions, however. A state does not have to enforce another state's criminal code. Nor does it have to recognize another state's grant of a divorce if the person obtaining the divorce did not establish legal residence in the state in which it was given.

Section 2. *Treatment of Citizens*

Clause 1: Privileges and Immunities. The Citizens of each State shall be entitled to all Privileges and Immunities of Citizens in the several States.

A citizen of a state has the same rights and privileges as the citizens of another state in which he or she happens to be.

Clause 2: Extradition. A Person charged in any State with Treason, Felony, or other Crime, who shall flee from Justice, and be found in another State, shall on Demand of the executive Authority of the State from which he fled, be delivered up, to be removed to the State having Jurisdiction of the Crime.

Any person accused of a crime who flees to another state must be returned to the state in which the crime occurred.

Clause 3: Fugitive Slaves. [No Person held to Service or Labour in one State, under the Laws thereof, escaping into another, shall, in Consequence of any Law or Regulation therein, be discharged from such Service or Labour, but shall be delivered up on Claim of the Party to whom such Service or Labour may be due.][11]

This clause was struck down by the Thirteenth Amendment, which abolished slavery in 1865.

Section 3. *Admission of States*

Clause 1: The Process. New States may be admitted by the Congress into this Union; but no new State shall be formed or erected within the Jurisdiction of any other State; nor any State be formed by the Junction of two or more States, or Parts of States, without the Consent of the Legislatures of the States concerned as well as of the Congress.

Only Congress has the power to admit new states to the union. No state may be created by taking territory from an existing state unless the state's legislature so consents.

Clause 2: Public Land. The Congress shall have Power to dispose of and make all needful Rules and Regulations respecting the Territory or other Property belonging to the United States; and nothing in this Constitution shall be so construed as to Prejudice any Claims of the United States, or of any particular State.

The federal government has the exclusive right to administer federal government public lands.

Section 4. *Republican Form of Government*

The United States shall guarantee to every State in this Union a Republican Form of Government, and shall protect each of them against Invasion; and on Application of the Legislature, or of the Executive (when the Legislature cannot be convened) against domestic Violence.

Each state is promised a republican form of government—that is, one in which the people elect their representatives. The federal government is bound to protect states against any attack by foreigners or during times of trouble within a state.

ARTICLE V. (*Methods of Amendment*)

The Congress, whenever two thirds of both Houses shall deem it necessary, shall propose Amendments to this Constitution, or on the Application of the Legislatures of two thirds of the several States, shall call a Convention for proposing Amendments, which, in either Case, shall be valid to all Intents and Purposes, as Part of this Constitution, when ratified by the Legislatures of three fourths of the several States, or by Conventions in three fourths thereof, as the one or the other Mode of Ratification may be proposed by the Congress; Provided that no Amendment which may be made prior to the Year One thousand eight hundred and eight shall in any Manner affect the first and fourth Clauses in the Ninth Section of the First Article; and that no State, without its Consent, shall be deprived of its equal Suffrage in the Senate.

Amendments may be proposed in either of two ways: a two-thirds vote of each chamber (Congress) or at the request of two-thirds

11.   Repealed by the Thirteenth Amendment.

of the states. Ratification of amendments may be carried out in two ways: by the legislatures of three-fourths of the states or by the voters in three-fourths of the states. No state may be denied equal representation in the Senate.

ARTICLE VI. (National Supremacy)

Clause 1: Existing Obligations. All Debts contracted and Engagements entered into, before the Adoption of this Constitution shall be as valid against the United States under this Constitution, as under the Confederation.

During the Revolutionary War and the years of the Confederation, Congress borrowed large sums. This clause pledged that the new federal government would assume those financial obligations.

Clause 2: Supreme Law of the Land. This Constitution, and the Laws of the United States which shall be made in Pursuance thereof; and all Treaties made, or which shall be made, under the Authority of the United States, shall be the supreme Law of the Land; and the Judges in every State shall be bound thereby, any Thing in the Constitution or Laws of any State to the Contrary notwithstanding.

This is typically called the supremacy clause; it declares that federal law takes precedence over all forms of state law. No government at the local or state level may make or enforce any law that conflicts with any provision of the Constitution, acts of Congress, treaties, or other rules and regulations issued by the president and his or her subordinates in the executive branch of the federal government.

Clause 3: Oath of Office. The Senators and Representatives before mentioned, and the Members of the several State Legislatures, and all executive and judicial Officers, both of the United States and of the several States, shall be bound by Oath or Affirmation, to support this Constitution; but no religious Test shall ever be required as a Qualification to any Office or public Trust under the United States.

Every federal and state official must take an oath of office promising to support the U.S. Constitution. Religion may not be used as a qualification to serve in any federal office.

ARTICLE VII. (Ratification)

The Ratification of the Conventions of nine States shall be sufficient for the Establishment of this Constitution between the States so ratifying the Same.

Nine states were required to ratify the Constitution. Delaware was the first and New Hampshire the ninth.

Done in Convention by the Unanimous Consent of the States present the Seventeenth Day of September in the Year of our Lord one thousand seven hundred and Eighty seven and of the Independence of the United States of America the Twelfth. In witness whereof we have hereunto subscribed our Names,

Go. WASHINGTON
Presid't.
and deputy from Virginia

Attest William Jackson Secretary

Delaware {	Geo. Read Gunning Bedford jun John Dickinson Richard Bassett Jaco. Broom	New Hampshire {	John Langdon Nicholas Gilman
Maryland {	James McHenry Dan of St. Thos. Jenifer Danl. Carroll	Massachusetts {	Nathaniel Gorham Rufus King
Virginia {	John Blair James Madison Jr.	Connecticut {	Wm. Saml. Johnson Roger Sherman
North Carolina {	Wm. Blount Richd. Dobbs Spaight Hu. Williamson	New York {	Alexander Hamilton
South Carolina {	J. Rutledge Charles Cotesworth Pinckney Charles Pinckney Pierce Butler	New Jersey {	Wh. Livingston David Brearley Wm. Paterson Jona. Dayton
Georgia {	William Few Abr. Baldwin	Pennsylvania {	B. Franklin Thomas Mifflin Robt. Morris Geo. Clymer Thos. FitzSimons Jared Ingersoll James Wilson Gouv. Morris

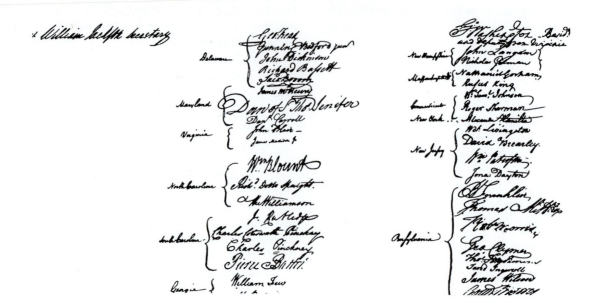

AMENDMENTS TO THE CONSTITUTION OF THE UNITED STATES (The Bill of Rights)[12]

Articles in addition to, and amendment of, the Constitution of the United States of America, proposed by Congress and ratified by the Legislatures of the several states, pursuant to the Fifth Article of the original Constitution.

AMENDMENT I. (Religion, Speech, Assembly, and Petition)

Congress shall make no law respecting an establishment of religion, or prohibiting the free exercise thereof; or abridging the freedom of speech, or of the press; or the right of the people peaceably to assemble, and to petition the Government for a redress of grievances.

Congress may not create an official church or enact laws limiting the freedom of religion, speech, the press, assembly, and petition. These guarantees, like the others in the Bill of Rights (the first 10 amendments), are not absolute—each may be exercised only with regard to the rights of other persons.

AMENDMENT II. (Militia and the Right to Bear Arms)

A well regulated Militia, being necessary to the security of a free State, the right of the people to keep and bear Arms, shall not be infringed.

To protect itself, each state has the right to maintain a volunteer armed force. States and the federal government regulate the possession and use of firearms by individuals.

AMENDMENT III. (The Quartering of Soldiers)

No Soldier shall, in time of peace be quartered in any house, without the consent of the Owner, nor in time of war, but in a manner to be prescribed by law.

Before the Revolutionary War, it had been common British practice to quarter soldiers in colonists' homes. Military troops do not have the power to take over private houses during peacetime.

AMENDMENT IV. (Searches and Seizures)

The right of the people to be secure in their persons, houses, papers, and effects, against unreasonable searches and seizures, shall not be violated, and no Warrants shall issue, but upon probable cause, supported by Oath or affirmation, and particularly describing the place to be searched, and the persons or things to be seized.

Here the word warrant *means "justification" and refers to a document issued by a magistrate or judge indicating the name, address, and possible offense committed. Anyone asking for the warrant, such as a police officer, must be able to convince the magistrate or judge that an offense probably has been committed.*

AMENDMENT V. (Grand Juries, Self-Incrimination, Double Jeopardy, Due Process, and Eminent Domain)

No person shall be held to answer for a capital, or otherwise infamous crime, unless on a presentment or indictment of a Grand Jury, except in cases arising in the land or naval forces, or in the Militia, when in actual service in time of War or public danger; nor shall any person be subject for the same offence to be twice put in jeopardy of life or limb; nor shall be compelled in any criminal case to be a witness against himself, nor be deprived of life, liberty, or property, without due process of law; nor shall private property be taken for public use, without just compensation.

There are two types of juries. A grand jury considers physical evidence and the testimony of witnesses and decides whether there is sufficient reason to bring a case to trial. A petit jury hears the case at trial and decides it. "For the same offence to be twice put in jeopardy of life or limb" means to be tried twice for the same crime. A person may not be tried for the same crime twice or forced to give evidence against herself or himself. No person's right to life, liberty, or property may be taken away except by lawful means, called the due process of law. Private property taken for use in public purposes must be paid for by the government.

AMENDMENT VI. (Criminal Court Procedures)

In all criminal prosecutions, the accused shall enjoy the right to a speedy and public trial, by an impartial jury of the State and district wherein the crime shall have been committed, which district shall have been previously ascertained by law, and to be informed of the nature and cause of the accusation; to be confronted with the witnesses against him; to have compulsory process for obtaining witnesses in his favor, and to have the Assistance of Counsel for his defence.

Any person accused of a crime has the right to a fair and public trial by a jury in the state in which the crime took place. The charges against that person must be indicated. Any accused person has the right to a lawyer to defend him or her and to question those who testify against him or her, as well as the right to call people to speak in his or her favor at trial.

AMENDMENT VII. (Trial by Jury in Civil Cases)

In Suits at common law, where the value in controversy shall exceed twenty dollars, the right of trial by jury shall be preserved, and no fact tried by jury, shall be otherwise re-examined in any Court of the United States, than according to the rules of the common law.

A jury trial may be requested by either party in a dispute in any case involving more than $20. If both parties agree to a trial by a judge without a jury, the right to a jury trial may be put aside.

AMENDMENT VIII. (Bail, Cruel and Unusual Punishment)

Excessive bail shall not be required, nor excessive fines imposed, nor cruel and unusual punishments inflicted.

Bail is that amount of money that a person accused of a crime may be required to deposit with the court as a guaranty that she or he will appear in court when requested. The amount of bail required or the fine imposed as punishment for a crime must be reasonable compared with the seriousness of the crime involved. Any punishment judged to be too harsh or too severe for a crime shall be prohibited.

AMENDMENT IX. (The Rights Retained by the People)

The enumeration in the Constitution, of certain rights, shall not be construed to deny or disparage others retained by the people.

Many civil rights that are not explicitly enumerated in the Constitution are still held by the people.

AMENDMENT X. (Reserved Powers of the States)

The powers not delegated to the United States by the Constitution, nor prohibited by it to the States, are reserved to the States respectively, or to the people.

Those powers not delegated by the Constitution to the federal government or expressly denied to the states belong to the states and to the people. This amendment in essence allows the states to pass laws under their "police powers."

AMENDMENT XI. (Ratified on February 7, 1795—Suits against States)

The Judicial power of the United States shall not be construed to extend to any suit in law or equity, commenced or prosecuted against one of the United States by Citizens of another State, or by Citizens or Subjects of any Foreign State.

This amendment has been interpreted to mean that a state cannot be sued in federal court by one of its own citizens, by a citizen of another state, or by a foreign country.

AMENDMENT XII. (Ratified on June 15, 1804—Election of the President)

The Electors shall meet in their respective states, and vote by ballot for President and Vice-President, one of whom, at least, shall not be an inhabitant of the same State with themselves; they shall name in their ballots the person voted for as President, and in distinct ballots the person voted for as Vice-President, and they shall make distinct lists of all persons voted for as President, and of all persons voted for as Vice-President, and of the number of votes for each, which lists they shall sign and certify, and transmit sealed to the seat of the government of the United States, directed to the President of the Senate;—The President of the Senate shall, in the presence of the Senate and House of Representatives, open all the certificates and the votes shall then be counted;—The person having the greatest number of votes for President, shall be the President, if such number be a majority of the whole number of Electors appointed; and if no person have such majority, then from the persons having the highest numbers not exceeding three on the list of those voted for as President, the House of Representatives shall choose immediately, by ballot, the President. But in choosing the President, the votes shall be taken by States, the representation from each State having one vote; a quorum for this purpose shall consist of a member or members from two-thirds of the States, and a majority of all States shall be necessary to a choice. [And if the House of Representatives shall not choose a President whenever the right of choice shall devolve upon them, before the fourth day of March next following, then the Vice-President shall act as President, as in the case of the death or other constitutional disability of the President.][13]—The person having the greatest number of votes as Vice-President, shall be the Vice-President, if such number be a majority of the whole number of Electors appointed, and if no person have a majority,

---

13. Changed by the Twentieth Amendment.

then from the two highest numbers on the list, the Senate shall choose the Vice-President; a quorum for the purpose shall consist of two-thirds of the whole number of Senators, and a majority of the whole number shall be necessary to a choice. But no person constitutionally ineligible to the office of President shall be eligible to that of Vice-President of the United States.

The original procedure set out for the election of president and vice president in Article II, Section 1, resulted in a tie in 1800 between Thomas Jefferson and Aaron Burr. It was not until the next year that the House of Representatives chose Jefferson to be president. This amendment changed the procedure by providing for separate ballots for president and vice president.

AMENDMENT XIII. (Ratified on December 6, 1865—Prohibition of Slavery)

Section 1.

Neither slavery nor involuntary servitude, except as a punishment for crime whereof the party shall have been duly convicted, shall exist within the United States, or any place subject to their jurisdiction.

Some slaves had been freed during the Civil War. This amendment freed the others and abolished slavery.

Section 2.

Congress shall have power to enforce this article by appropriate legislation.

AMENDMENT XIV. (Ratified on July 9, 1868—Citizenship, Due Process, and Equal Protection of the Laws)

Section 1.

All persons born or naturalized in the United States, and subject to the jurisdiction thereof, are citizens of the United States and of the State wherein they reside. No State shall make or enforce any law which shall abridge the privileges or immunities of citizens of the United States; nor shall any State deprive any person of life, liberty, or property, without due process of law; nor deny to any person within its jurisdiction the equal protection of the laws.

Under this provision, states cannot make or enforce laws that take away rights given to all citizens by the federal government. States cannot act unfairly or arbitrarily toward, or discriminate against, any person.

Section 2.

Representatives shall be apportioned among the several States according to their respective numbers, counting the whole number of persons in each State, excluding Indians not taxed. But when the right to vote at any election for the choice of electors for President and Vice President of the United States, Representatives in Congress, the Executive and Judicial officers of a State, or the members of the Legislature thereof, is denied to any of the male inhabitants of such State, being [twenty-one][14] years of age, and citizens of the United

States, or in any way abridged, except for participation in rebellion, or other crime, the basis of representation therein shall be reduced in the proportion which the number of such male citizens shall bear to the whole number of male citizens twenty-one years of age in such State.

Section 3.

No person shall be a Senator or Representative in Congress, or elector of President and Vice President, or hold any office, civil or military, under the United States, or under any State, who having previously taken an oath, as a member of Congress, or as an officer of the United States, or as a member of any State legislature, or as an executive or judicial officer of any State, to support the Constitution of the United States, shall have engaged in insurrection or rebellion against the same, or given aid or comfort to the enemies thereof. But Congress may by a vote of two-thirds of each House, remove such disability.

This provision forbade former state or federal government officials who had acted in support of the Confederacy during the Civil War to hold office again. It limited the president's power to pardon those persons. Congress removed this "disability" in 1898.

Section 4.

The validity of the public debt of the United States, authorized by law, including debts incurred for payment of pensions and bounties for services in suppressing insurrection or rebellion, shall not be questioned. But neither the United States nor any State shall assume or pay any debt or obligation incurred in aid of insurrection or rebellion against the United States, or any claim for the loss or emancipation of any slave, but all such debts, obligations and claims shall be held illegal and void.

Section 5.

The Congress shall have power to enforce, by appropriate legislation, the provisions of this article.

AMENDMENT XV. (Ratified on February 3, 1870—The Right to Vote)

Section 1.

The right of citizens of the United States to vote shall not be denied or abridged by the United States or by any State on account of race, color, or previous condition of servitude.

No citizen can be refused the right to vote simply because of race or color or because that person was once a slave.

Section 2.

The Congress shall have power to enforce this article by appropriate legislation.

AMENDMENT XVI. (Ratified on February 3, 1913—Income Taxes)

The Congress shall have power to lay and collect taxes on incomes, from whatever source derived, without apportionment among the several States, and without regard to any census or enumeration.

---

14. Changed by the Twenty-sixth Amendment.

This amendment allows Congress to tax income without sharing the revenue so obtained with the states according to their population.

AMENDMENT XVII. *(Ratified on April 8, 1913—The Popular Election of Senators)*

Section 1.

The Senate of the United States shall be composed of two Senators from each State, elected by the people thereof, for six years; and each Senator shall have one vote. The electors in each State shall have the qualifications requisite for electors of the most numerous branch of the State legislatures.

Section 2.

When vacancies happen in the representation of any State in the Senate, the executive authority of such State shall issue writs of election to fill such vacancies: *Provided,* That the legislature of any State may empower the executive thereof to make temporary appointments until the people fill the vacancies by election as the legislature may direct.

Section 3.

This amendment shall not be so construed as to affect the election or term of any Senator chosen before it becomes valid as part of the Constitution.

This amendment modified portions of Article I, Section 3, that related to election of senators. Senators are now elected by the voters in each state directly. When a vacancy occurs, either the state may fill the vacancy by a special election, or the governor of the state involved may appoint someone to fill the seat until the next election.

AMENDMENT XVIII. *(Ratified on January 16, 1919—Prohibition)*

Section 1.

After one year from the ratification of this article the manufacture, sale, or transportation of intoxicating liquors within, the importation thereof into, or the exportation thereof from the United States and all territory subject to the jurisdiction thereof for beverage purposes is hereby prohibited.

Section 2.

The Congress and the several States shall have concurrent power to enforce this article by appropriate legislation.

Section 3.

This article shall be inoperative unless it shall have been ratified as an amendment to the Constitution by the legislatures of the several States, as provided in the Constitution, within seven years from the date of the submission hereof to the States by the Congress.[15]

This amendment made it illegal to manufacture, sell, and transport alcoholic beverages in the United States. It was repealed by the Twenty-first Amendment.

AMENDMENT XIX. *(Ratified on August 18, 1920—Women's Right to Vote)*

Section 1.

The right of citizens of the United States to vote shall not be denied or abridged by the United States or by any State on account of sex.

Section 2.

Congress shall have power to enforce this article by appropriate legislation.

Women were given the right to vote by this amendment, and Congress was given the power to enforce this right.

AMENDMENT XX. *(Ratified on January 23, 1933—The Lame Duck Amendment)*

Section 1.

The terms of the President and Vice President shall end at noon on the 20th day of January, and the terms of Senators and Representatives at noon on the 3d day of January, of the years in which such terms would have ended if this article had not been ratified; and the terms of their successors shall then begin.

This amendment modified Article I, Section 4, Clause 2, and other provisions relating to the president in the Twelfth Amendment. The taking of the oath of office was moved from March 4 to January 20.

Section 2.

The Congress shall assemble at least once in every year, and such meeting shall begin at noon on the 3rd day of January, unless they shall by law appoint a different day.

Congress changed the beginning of its term to January 3. The reason the Twentieth Amendment is called the Lame Duck Amendment is that it shortens the time between when a member of Congress is defeated for reelection and when he or she leaves office.

Section 3.

If, at the time fixed for the beginning of the term of the President, the President elect shall have died, the Vice President elect shall become President. If a President shall not have been chosen before the time fixed for the beginning of his term, or if the President elect shall have failed to qualify, then the Vice President elect shall act as President until a President shall have qualified; and the Congress may by law provide for the case wherein neither a President elect nor a Vice President elect shall have qualified, declaring who shall then act as President, or the manner in which one who is to act shall be selected, and such person shall act accordingly until a President or Vice President shall have qualified.

This part of the amendment deals with problem areas left ambiguous by Article II and the Twelfth Amendment. If the president dies before January 20 or fails to qualify for office, the presidency is to be filled as described in this section.

---

15. The Eighteenth Amendment was repealed by the Twenty-first Amendment.

Section 4.

The Congress may by law provide for the case of the death of any of the persons from whom the House of Representatives may choose a President whenever the rights of choice shall have devolved upon them, and for the case of the death of any of the persons from whom the Senate may choose a Vice President whenever the right of choice shall have devolved upon them.

Congress has never created legislation pursuant to this section.

Section 5.

Sections 1 and 2 shall take effect on the 15th day of October following the ratification of this article.

Section 6.

This article shall be inoperative unless it shall have been ratified as an amendment to the Constitution by the legislatures of three-fourths of the several States within seven years from the date of its submission.

AMENDMENT XXI. *(Ratified on December 5, 1933—The Repeal of Prohibition)*

Section 1.

The eighteenth article of amendment to the Constitution of the United States is hereby repealed.

Section 2.

The transportation or importation into any State, Territory, or possession of the United States for delivery or use therein of intoxicating liquors, in violation of the laws thereof, is hereby prohibited.

Section 3.

This article shall be inoperative unless it shall have been ratified as an amendment to the Constitution by conventions in the several States, as provided in the Constitution, within seven years from the date of the submission hereof to the States by the Congress.

The amendment repealed the Eighteenth Amendment but did not make alcoholic beverages legal everywhere. Rather, they remained illegal in any state that so designated them. Many such "dry" states existed for a number of years after 1933. Today, there are still "dry" counties within the United States, in which the sale of alcoholic beverages is illegal.

AMENDMENT XXII. *(Ratified on February 27, 1951—Limitation of Presidential Terms)*

Section 1.

No person shall be elected to the office of the President more than twice, and no person who has held the office of President, or acted as President, for more than two years of a term to which some other person was elected President shall be elected to the office of President more than once. But this Article shall not apply to any person holding the office of President when this Article was proposed by the Congress, and shall not prevent any person who may be holding the office of President, or acting as President, during the term within which this Article becomes operative from holding the office of President or acting as President during the remainder of such term.

Section 2.

This article shall be inoperative unless it shall have been ratified as an amendment to the Constitution by the legislatures of three-fourths of the several States within seven years from the date of its submission to the States by the Congress.

No president may serve more than two elected terms. If, however, a president has succeeded to the office after the halfway point of a term in which another president was originally elected, then that president may serve for more than eight years, but not to exceed 10 years.

AMENDMENT XXIII. *(Ratified on March 29, 1961—Presidential Electors for the District of Columbia)*

Section 1.

The District constituting the seat of Government of the United States shall appoint in such manner as the Congress may direct:

A number of electors of President and Vice President equal to the whole number of Senators and Representatives in Congress to which the District would be entitled if it were a State, but in no event more than the least populous State; they shall be in addition to those appointed by the States, but they shall be considered, for the purposes of the election of President and Vice President, to be electors appointed by a State; and they shall meet in the District and perform such duties as provided by the twelfth article of amendment.

Section 2.

The Congress shall have power to enforce this article by appropriate legislation.

Citizens living in the District of Columbia have the right to vote in elections for president and vice president. The District of Columbia has three presidential electors, whereas before this amendment it had none.

AMENDMENT XXIV. *(Ratified on January 23, 1964—The Anti–Poll Tax Amendment)*

Section 1.

The right of citizens of the United States to vote in any primary or other election for President or Vice President, for electors for President or Vice President, or for Senator or Representative in Congress, shall not be denied or abridged by the United States, or any State by reason of failure to pay any poll tax or other tax.

Section 2.

The Congress shall have power to enforce this article by appropriate legislation.

No government shall require a person to pay a poll tax to vote in any federal election.

AMENDMENT XXV. *(Ratified on February 10, 1967—Presidential Disability and Vice Presidential Vacancies)*

Section 1.

In case of the removal of the President from office or of his death or resignation, the Vice President shall become President.

Whenever a president dies or resigns from office, the vice president becomes president.

Section 2.

Whenever there is a vacancy in the office of the Vice President, the President shall nominate a Vice President who shall take office upon confirmation by a majority vote of both Houses of Congress.

Whenever the office of the vice presidency becomes vacant, the president may appoint someone to fill this office, provided Congress consents.

Section 3.

Whenever the President transmits to the President pro tempore of the Senate and the Speaker of the House of Representatives his written declaration that he is unable to discharge the powers and duties of his office, and until he transmits to them a written declaration to the contrary, such powers and duties shall be discharged by the Vice President as Acting President.

Whenever the president believes she or he is unable to carry out the duties of the office, she or he shall so indicate to Congress in writing. The vice president then acts as president until the president declares that she or he is again able to carry out the duties of the office.

Section 4.

Whenever the Vice President and a majority of either the principal officers of the executive departments or of such other body as Congress may by law provide, transmit to the President pro tempore of the Senate and the Speaker of the House of Representatives their written declaration that the President is unable to discharge the powers and duties of his office, the Vice President shall immediately assume the powers and duties of the office as Acting President.

Thereafter, when the President transmits to the President pro tempore of the Senate and the Speaker of the House of Representatives his written declaration that no inability exists, he shall resume the powers and duties of his office unless the Vice President and a majority of either the principal officers of the executive department or of such other body as Congress may by law provide, transmit within four days to the President pro tempore

of the Senate and the Speaker of the House of Representatives their written declaration that the President is unable to discharge the powers and duties of his office. Thereupon Congress shall decide the issue, assembling within forty-eight hours for that purpose if not in session. If the Congress, within twenty-one days after receipt of the latter written declaration, or, if Congress is not in session, within twenty-one days after Congress is required to assemble, determines by two-thirds vote of both Houses that the President is unable to discharge the powers and duties of his office, the Vice President shall continue to discharge the same as Acting President; otherwise, the President shall resume the powers and duties of his office.

Whenever the vice president and a majority of the members of the Cabinet believe that the president cannot carry out her or his duties, they shall so indicate in writing to Congress. The vice president shall then act as president. When the president believes that she or he is able to carry out her or his duties again, she or he shall so indicate to the Congress. However, if the vice president and a majority of the Cabinet do not agree, Congress must decide by a two-thirds vote within three weeks who shall act as president.

AMENDMENT XXVI. *(Ratified on July 1, 1971—The 18-Year-Old Vote)*

Section 1.

The right of citizens of the United States, who are eighteen years of age or older, to vote shall not be denied or abridged by the United States or by any State on account of age.

No one 18 years of age or older can be denied the right to vote in federal or state elections by virtue of age.

Section 2.

The Congress shall have power to enforce this article by appropriate legislation.

AMENDMENT XXVII. *(Ratified on May 7, 1992—Congressional Pay)*

No law, varying the compensation for the services of the Senators and Representatives, shall take effect, until an election of representatives shall have intervened.

This amendment allows the voters to have some control over increases in salaries for congressional members. Originally submitted to the states for ratification in 1789, it was not ratified until 203 years later, in 1992.

THE FEDERALIST PAPERS
Nos. 10 and 51

In 1787, after the newly drafted U.S. Constitution was submitted to the 13 states for ratification, a major political debate ensued between the Federalists (who favored ratification) and the Anti-Federalists (who opposed ratification). Anti-Federalists in New York were particularly critical of the Constitution, and in response to their objections, Federalists Alexander Hamilton, James Madison, and John Jay wrote a series of 85 essays in defense of the Constitution. The essays were published in New York newspapers and reprinted in other newspapers throughout the country.

For students of American government, the essays, collectively known as the Federalist Papers, are particularly important because they provide a glimpse of the founders' political philosophy and intentions in designing the Constitution—and, consequently, in shaping the American philosophy of government.

We have included in this appendix two of these essays: Federalist Papers No. 10 and No. 51. Each essay has been annotated by the authors to indicate its importance in American political thought and to clarify the meaning of particular passages.

Federalist Paper No. 10

Federalist Paper No. 10, penned by James Madison, has often been singled out as a key document in American political thought. In this essay, Madison attacks the Anti-Federalists' fear that a republican form of government will inevitably give rise to "factions"—small political parties or groups united by a common interest—that will control the government. Factions will be harmful to the country because they will implement policies beneficial to their own interests but adverse to other people's rights and to the public good. In this essay, Madison attempts to lay to rest this fear by explaining how, in a large republic such as the United States, there will be so many different factions, held together by regional or local interests, that no single one of them will dominate national politics.

Madison opens his essay with a paragraph discussing how important it is to devise a plan of government that can control the "instability, injustice, and confusion" brought about by factions.

Among the numerous advantages promised by a well-constructed Union, none deserves to be more accurately developed than its tendency to break and control the violence of faction. The friend of popular governments never finds himself so much alarmed for their character and fate as when he contemplates their propensity to this dangerous vice. He will not fail, therefore, to set a due value on any plan which, without violating the principles to which he is attached, provides a proper cure for it. The instability, injustice, and confusion introduced into the public councils have, in truth, been the mortal diseases under which popular governments have everywhere perished, as they continue to be the favorite

and fruitful topics from which the adversaries to liberty derive their most specious declamations. The valuable improvements made by the American constitutions on the popular models, both ancient and modern, cannot certainly be too much admired; but it would be an unwarrantable partiality to contend that they have as effectually obviated the danger on this side, as was wished and expected. Complaints are everywhere heard from our most considerate and virtuous citizens, equally the friends of public and private faith and of public and personal liberty, that our governments are too unstable, that the public good is disregarded in the conflicts of rival parties, and that measures are too often decided, not according to the rules of justice and the rights of the minor party, but by the superior force of an interested and overbearing majority. However anxiously we may wish that these complaints had no foundation, the evidence of known facts will not permit us to deny that they are in some degree true. It will be found, indeed, on a candid review of our situation, that some of the distresses under which we labor have been erroneously charged on the operation of our governments; but it will be found, at the same time, that other causes will not alone account for many of our heaviest misfortunes; and, particularly, for that prevailing and increasing distrust of public engagements and alarm for private rights which are echoed from one end of the continent to the other. These must be chiefly, if not wholly, effects of the unsteadiness and injustice with which a factious spirit has tainted our public administration.

Madison now defines what he means by the term faction.

By a faction I understand a number of citizens, whether amounting to a majority or minority of the whole, who are united and actuated by some common impulse of passion, or of interest, adverse to the rights of other citizens, or the permanent and aggregate interests of the community.

Madison next contends that there are two methods by which the "mischiefs of faction" can be cured: by removing the causes of faction or by controlling their effects. In the following paragraphs, Madison explains how liberty itself nourishes factions. Therefore, to abolish factions would involve abolishing liberty—a cure "worse than the disease."

There are two methods of curing the mischiefs of faction: the one, by removing its causes; the other, by controlling its effects.

There are again two methods of removing the causes of faction: the one, by destroying the liberty which is essential to its existence; the other, by giving to every citizen the same opinions, the same passions, and the same interests.

It could never be more truly said than of the first remedy that it was worse than the disease. Liberty is to faction what air is to fire, an aliment without which it instantly expires. But it could not be a less folly to abolish liberty, which is essential to political life, because it nourishes faction than it would be to wish the annihilation of air, which is essential to animal life, because it imparts to fire its destructive agency.

The second expedient is as impracticable as the first would be unwise. As long as the reason of man continues fallible, and he is at liberty to exercise it, different opinions will be formed. As long as the connection subsists between his reason and his self-love, his opinions and his passions will have a reciprocal influence on each other; and the former will be objects to which the latter will attach themselves. The diversity in the faculties of men, from which the rights of property originate, is not less an insuperable obstacle to a uniformity of interests. The protection of these faculties is the first object of government. From the protection of different and unequal faculties of acquiring property, the possession of different degrees and kinds of property immediately results; and from the influence of these on the sentiments and views of the respective proprietors ensues a division of the society into different interests and parties.

The latent causes of faction are thus sown in the nature of man; and we see them everywhere brought into different degrees of activity, according to the different circumstances of civil society. A zeal for different opinions concerning religion, concerning government, and many other points, as well of speculation as of practice; an attachment to different leaders ambitiously contending for pre-eminence and power; or to persons of other descriptions whose fortunes have been interesting to the human passions, have, in turn, divided mankind into parties, inflamed them with mutual animosity, and rendered them much more disposed to vex and oppress each other than to co-operate for their common good. So strong is this propensity of mankind to fall into mutual animosities that where no substantial occasion presents itself the most frivolous and fanciful distinctions have been sufficient to kindle their unfriendly passions and excite their most violent conflicts. But the most common and durable source of factions has been the various and unequal distribution of property. Those who hold and those who are without property have ever formed distinct interests in society. Those who are creditors, and those who are debtors, fall under a like discrimination. A landed interest, a manufacturing interest, a mercantile interest, a moneyed interest, with many lesser interests, grow up of necessity in civilized nations, and divide them into different classes, actuated by different sentiments and views. The regulation of these various and interfering interests forms the principal task of modern legislation and involves the spirit of party and faction in the necessary and ordinary operations of government.

No man is allowed to be a judge in his own cause, because his interest would certainly bias his judgment, and, not improbably, corrupt his integrity. With equal, nay with greater reason, a body of men are unfit to be both judges and parties at the same time; yet what are many of the most important acts of legislation but so many judicial determinations, not indeed concerning the rights of single persons, but concerning the rights of large bodies of citizens? And what are the different classes of legislators but advocates and parties to the causes which they determine? Is a law proposed concerning private debts? It is a question to which the creditors are parties on one side and the debtors on the other.

Justice ought to hold the balance between them. Yet the parties are, and must be, themselves the judges; and the most numerous party, or in other words, the most powerful faction must be expected to prevail. Shall domestic manufacturers be encouraged, and in what degree, by restrictions on foreign manufacturers? [These] are questions which would be differently decided by the landed and the manufacturing classes, and probably by neither with a sole regard to justice and the public good. The apportionment of taxes on the various descriptions of property is an act which seems to require the most exact impartiality; yet there is, perhaps, no legislative act in which greater opportunity and temptation are given to a predominant party to trample on the rules of justice. Every shilling with which they overburden the inferior number is a shilling saved to their own pockets.

It is in vain to say that enlightened statesmen will be able to adjust these clashing interests and render them all subservient to the public good. Enlightened statesmen will not always be at the helm. Nor, in many cases, can such an adjustment be made at all without taking into view indirect and remote considerations, which will rarely prevail over the immediate interest which one party may find in disregarding the rights of another or the good of the whole.

The inference to which we are brought is that the *causes* of faction cannot be removed and that relief is only to be sought in the means of controlling its *effects*.

Having concluded that "the causes of faction cannot be removed," Madison now looks in some detail at the other method by which factions can be cured—by controlling their effects. This is the heart of his essay. He begins by positing a significant question: How can you have self-government without risking the possibility that a ruling faction, particularly a majority faction, might tyrannize over the rights of others?

If a faction consists of less than a majority, relief is supplied by the republican principle, which enables the majority to defeat its sinister views by regular vote. It may clog the administration, it may convulse the society; but it will be unable to execute and mask its violence under the forms of the Constitution. When a majority is included in a faction, the form of popular government, on the other hand, enables it to sacrifice to its ruling passion or interest both the public good and the rights of other citizens. To secure the public good and private rights against the danger of such a faction, and at the same time to preserve the spirit and the form of popular government, is then the great object to which our inquiries are directed. Let me add that it is the great desideratum by which alone this form of government can be rescued from the opprobrium under which it has so long labored and be recommended to the esteem and adoption of mankind.

Madison now sets forth the idea that one way to control the effects of factions is to ensure that the majority is rendered incapable of acting in concert in order to "carry into effect schemes of oppression." He goes on to state that in a democracy, in which all citizens participate personally in government decision making, there is no way to prevent the majority from communicating with each other and, as a result, acting in concert.

By what means is this object attainable? Evidently by one of two only. Either the existence of the same passion or interest in a majority at the same time must be prevented, or the majority, having such coexistent passion or interest, must be rendered, by their number and local situation, unable to concert and carry into effect schemes of oppression. If the impulse and the opportunity be suffered to coincide, we well know that neither moral nor religious motives can be relied on as an adequate control. They are not found to be such on the injustice and violence of individuals, and lose their efficacy in proportion to the number combined together, that is, in proportion as their efficacy becomes needful.

From this view of the subject it may be concluded that a pure democracy, by which I mean a society consisting of a small number of citizens, who assemble and administer the government in person, can admit of no cure for the mischiefs of faction. A common passion or interest will, in almost every case, be felt by a majority of the whole; a communication and concert results from the form of government itself; and there is nothing to check the inducements to sacrifice the weaker party or an obnoxious individual. Hence it is that such democracies have ever been spectacles of turbulence and contention; have ever been found incompatible with personal security or the rights of property; and have in general been as short in their lives as they have been violent in their deaths. Theoretic politicians, who have patronized this species of government, have erroneously supposed that by reducing mankind to a perfect equality in their political rights, they would at the same time be perfectly equalized and assimilated in their possessions, their opinions, and their passions.

Madison now moves on to discuss the benefits of a republic with respect to controlling the effects of factions. He begins by defining a republic and then pointing out the "two great points of difference" between a republic and a democracy: a republic is governed by a small body of elected representatives, not by the people directly; and a republic can extend over a much larger territory and embrace more citizens than a democracy can.

A republic, by which I mean a government in which the scheme of representation takes place, opens a different prospect and promises the cure for which we are seeking. Let us examine the points in which it varies from pure democracy, and we shall comprehend both the nature of the cure and the efficacy which it must derive from the Union.

The two great points of difference between a democracy and a republic are: first, the delegation of the government, in the latter, to a small number of citizens elected by the rest; secondly, the greater number of citizens and greater sphere of country over which the latter may be extended.

In the following four paragraphs, Madison explains how in a republic, particularly a large republic, the delegation of authority to elected representatives will increase the likelihood that those who govern will be "fit" for their positions and that a proper balance will be achieved between local (factional) interests and national interests. Note how he stresses that the new federal Constitution, by dividing powers between state governments and the national government, provides a "happy combination in this respect."

The effect of the first difference is, on the one hand, to refine and enlarge the public views by passing them through the medium of a chosen body of citizens, whose wisdom may best discern the true interest of their country and whose patriotism and love of justice will be least likely to sacrifice it to temporary or partial considerations. Under such a regulation it may well happen that the public voice, pronounced by the representatives of the people, will be more consonant to the public good than if pronounced by the people themselves, convened for the purpose. On the other hand, the effect may be inverted. Men of factious tempers, of local prejudices, or of sinister designs, may, by intrigue, by corruption, or by other means, first obtain the suffrages, and then betray the interests of the people. The question resulting is, whether small or extensive republics are most favorable to the election of proper guardians of the public weal; and it is clearly decided in favor of the latter by two obvious considerations.

In the first place, it is to be remarked that however small the republic may be the representatives must be raised to a certain number in order to guard against the cabals of a few; and that however large it may be, they must be limited to a certain number in order to guard against the confusion of a multitude. Hence, the number of representatives in the two cases not being in proportion to that of the constituents, and being proportionally greater in the small republic, it follows that if the proportion of fit characters be not less in the large than in the small republic, the former will present a greater option, and consequently a greater probability of a fit choice.

In the next place, as each representative will be chosen by a greater number of citizens in the large than in the small republic, it will be more difficult for unworthy candidates to practice with success the vicious arts by which elections are too often carried; and the suffrages of the people being more free, will be more likely to center on men who possess the most attractive merit and the most diffusive and established characters.

It must be confessed that in this, as in most other cases, there is a mean, on both sides of which inconveniencies will be found to lie. By enlarging too much the number of electors, you render the representative too little acquainted with all their local circumstances and lesser interests; as by reducing it too much, you render him unduly attached to these, and too little fit to comprehend and pursue great and national objects. The federal Constitution forms a happy combination in this respect; the great and aggregate interests being referred to the national, the local and particular to the State legislatures.

Madison now looks more closely at the other difference between a republic and a democracy—namely, that a republic can encompass a larger territory and more citizens than a democracy can. In the remaining paragraphs of his essay, Madison concludes that in a large republic, it will be difficult for factions to act in concert. Although a factious group—religious, political, economic, or otherwise—may control a local or regional government, it will have little chance of gathering a national following. This is because in a large republic, there will be numerous factions whose work will offset the work of any one particular faction ("sect"). As Madison phrases it, these numerous factions will "secure the national councils against any danger from that source."

The other point of difference is the greater number of citizens and extent of territory which may be brought within the compass of republican than of democratic government; and it is this circumstance principally which renders factious combinations less to be dreaded in the former than in the latter. The smaller the society, the fewer probably will be the distinct parties and interests composing it; the fewer the distinct parties and interests, the more frequently will a majority be found of the same party; and the smaller the number of individuals composing a majority, and the smaller the compass within which they are placed, the more easily will they concert and execute their plans of oppression. Extend the sphere and you take in a greater variety of parties and interests; you make it less probable that a majority of the whole will have a common motive to invade the rights of other citizens; or if such a common motive exists, it will be more difficult for all who feel it to discover their own strength and to act in unison with each other. Besides other impediments, it may be remarked that, where there is a consciousness of unjust or dishonorable purposes, communication is always checked by distrust in proportion to the number whose concurrence is necessary.

Hence, it clearly appears that the same advantage which a republic has over a democracy in controlling the effects of faction is enjoyed by a large over a small republic—is enjoyed by the Union over the States composing it. Does this advantage consist in the substitution of representatives whose enlightened views and virtuous sentiments render them superior to local prejudices and to schemes of injustice? It will not be denied that the representation of the Union will be most likely to possess these requisite endowments. Does it consist in the greater security afforded by a greater variety of parties, against the event of any one party being able to outnumber and oppress the rest? In an equal degree does the increased variety of parties comprised within the Union increase this security. Does it, in fine, consist in the greater obstacles opposed to the concert and accomplishment of the secret wishes of an unjust and interested majority? Here again the extent of the Union gives it the most palpable advantage.

The influence of factious leaders may kindle a flame within their particular States but will be unable to spread a general conflagration through the other States. A religious sect may degenerate into a political faction in a part of the Confederacy; but the variety of sects dispersed over the entire face of it must secure the national councils against any danger from that source. A rage for paper money, for an abolition of debts, for an equal division of property, or for any other improper or wicked project, will be less apt to pervade the whole body of the Union than a particular member of it, in the same proportion as such a malady is more likely to taint a particular county or district than an entire State.

In the extent and proper structure of the Union, therefore, we behold a republican remedy for the diseases most incident to republican government. And according to the degree of pleasure and pride we feel in being republicans ought to be our zeal in cherishing the spirit and supporting the character of federalists.

Publius

(James Madison)

Federalist Paper No. 51

Federalist Paper No. 51, also authored by James Madison, is another classic in American political theory. Although the Federalists wanted a strong national government, they had not abandoned the traditional American view, particularly notable during the revolutionary era, that those holding powerful government positions could not be trusted to put national interests and the common good above their own personal interests. In this essay, Madison explains why the separation of the national government's powers into three branches—executive, legislative, and judicial—and a federal structure of government offer the best protection against tyranny.

To what expedient, then, shall we finally resort, for maintaining in practice the necessary partition of power among the several departments as laid down in the Constitution? The only answer that can be given is that as all these exterior provisions are found to be inadequate the defect must be supplied, by so contriving the interior structure of the government as that its several constituent parts may, by their mutual relations, be the means of keeping each other in their proper places. Without presuming to undertake a full development of this important idea I will hazard a few general observations which may perhaps place it in a clearer light, and enable us to form a more correct judgment of the principles and structure of the government planned by the convention.

In the next two paragraphs, Madison stresses that for the powers of the different branches (departments) of government to be truly separated, the personnel in one branch should not be dependent on another branch for their appointment or for the "emoluments" (compensation) attached to their offices.

In order to lay a due foundation for that separate and distinct exercise of the different powers of government, which to a certain extent is admitted on all hands to be essential to the preservation of liberty, it is evident that each department should have a will of its own; and consequently should be so constituted that the members of each should have as little agency as possible in the appointment of the members of the others. Were this principle rigorously adhered to, it would require that all the appointments for the supreme executive, legislative, and judiciary magistracies should be drawn from the same fountain of authority, the people, through channels having no communication whatever with one another. Perhaps such a plan of constructing the several departments would be less difficult in practice than it may in contemplation appear. Some difficulties, however, and some additional expense would attend the execution of it. Some deviations, therefore, from the principle must be admitted. In the constitution of the judiciary department in particular, it might be inexpedient to insist rigorously on the principle: first, because peculiar qualifications being essential in the members, the primary consideration ought to be to select that mode of choice which best secures these qualifications; second, because the permanent tenure by which the appointments are held in that department must soon destroy all sense of dependence on the authority conferring them.

It is equally evident that the members of each department should be as little dependent as possible on those of the others for the emoluments annexed to their offices. Were the executive magistrate, or the judges, not independent of the legislature in this particular, their independence in every other would be merely nominal.

In the following passages, which are among the most widely quoted of Madison's writings, he explains how the separation of the powers of government into three branches helps to counter the effects of personal ambition on government. The separation of powers allows personal motives to be linked to the constitutional rights of a branch of government. In effect, competing personal interests in each branch will help to keep the powers of the three government branches separate and, in so doing, will help to guard the public interest.

But the great security against a gradual concentration of the several powers in the same department consists in giving to those who administer each department the necessary constitutional means and personal motives to resist encroachments of the others. The provision for defense must in this, as in all other cases, be made commensurate to the danger of attack. Ambition must be made to counteract ambition. The interest of the man must be connected with the constitutional rights of the place. It may be a reflection on human nature that such devices should be necessary to control the abuses of government. But what is government itself but the greatest of all reflections on human nature? If men were angels, no government would be necessary. If angels were to govern men, neither external nor internal controls on government would be necessary. In framing a government which is to be administered by men over men, the great difficulty lies in this: you must first enable the government to control the governed; and in the next place oblige it to control itself. A dependence on the people is, no doubt, the primary control on the government; but experience has taught mankind the necessity of auxiliary precautions.

This policy of supplying, by opposite and rival interests, the defect of better motives, might be traced through the whole system of human affairs, private as well as public. We see it particularly displayed in all the subordinate distributions of power, where the constant aim is to divide and arrange the several offices in such a manner as that each may be a check on the other—that the private interest of every individual may be a sentinel over the public rights. These inventions of prudence cannot be less requisite in the distribution of the supreme powers of the State.

Madison now addresses the issue of equality between the branches of government. The legislature will necessarily predominate, but if the executive is given an "absolute negative" (absolute veto power) over legislative actions, this also could lead to an abuse of power. Madison concludes that the division of the legislature into two "branches" (parts, or chambers) will act as a check on the legislature's powers.

But it is not possible to give to each department an equal power of self-defense. In republican government, the legislative authority necessarily predominates. The remedy for this inconveniency is to divide the legislature into different branches; and to render them, by different modes of election and different principles of action, as little connected with each other as the nature of their common functions and their common depen-

dence on the society will admit. It may even be necessary to guard against dangerous encroachments by still further precautions. As the weight of the legislative authority requires that it should be thus divided, the weakness of the executive may require, on the other hand, that it should be fortified. An absolute negative on the legislature appears, at first view, to be the natural defense with which the executive magistrate should be armed. But perhaps it would be neither altogether safe nor alone sufficient. On ordinary occasions it might not be exerted with the requisite firmness, and on extraordinary occasions it might be perfidiously abused. May not this defect of an absolute negative be supplied by some qualified connection between this weaker department and the weaker branch of the stronger department, by which the latter may be led to support the constitutional rights of the former, without being too much detached from the rights of its own department?

If the principles on which these observations are founded be just, as I persuade myself they are, and they be applied as a criterion to the several State constitutions, and to the federal Constitution, it will be found that if the latter does not perfectly correspond with them, the former are infinitely less able to bear such a test.

In the remainder of the essay, Madison discusses how a federal system of government, in which powers are divided between the states and the national government, offers "double security" against tyranny.

There are, moreover, two considerations particularly applicable to the federal system of America, which place that system in a very interesting point of view.

First. In a single republic, all the power surrendered by the people is submitted to the administration of a single government; and the usurpations are guarded against by a division of the government into distinct and separate departments. In the compound republic of America, the power surrendered by the people is first divided between two distinct governments, and then the portion allotted to each subdivided among distinct and separate departments. Hence a double security arises to the rights of the people. The different governments will control each other, at the same time that each will be controlled by itself.

Second. It is of great importance in a republic not only to guard the society against the oppression of its rulers, but to guard one part of the society against the injustice of the other part. Different interests necessarily exist in different classes of citizens. If a majority be united by a common interest, the rights of the minority will be insecure. There are but two methods of providing against this evil: the one by creating a will in the community independent of the majority—that is, of the society itself; the other, by comprehending in the society so many separate descriptions of citizens as will render an unjust combination of a majority of the whole very improbable, if not impracticable. The first method prevails in all governments possessing an hereditary or self-appointed authority. This, at best, is but a precarious security; because a power independent of the society may as well espouse the unjust views of the major as the rightful interests of the minor party, and may possibly be turned against both parties. The second method will be exemplified in the federal republic of the United States. Whilst all authority in it will be derived from and dependent on the society, the society itself will be broken into so many parts, interests and classes of citizens, that the rights of individuals, or of the minority, will be in little danger from interested combinations of the majority.

In a free government the security for civil rights must be the same as that for religious rights. It consists in the one case in the multiplicity of interests, and in the other in the multiplicity of sects. The degree of security in both cases will depend on the number of interests and sects; and this may be presumed to depend on the extent of country and number of people comprehended under the same government. This view of the subject must particularly recommend a proper federal system to all the sincere and considerate friends of republican government, since it shows that in exact proportion as the territory of the Union may be formed into more circumscribed Confederacies, or States, oppressive combinations of a majority will be facilitated; the best security, under the republican forms, for the rights of every class of citizen, will be diminished; and consequently the stability and independence of some member of the government, the only other security, must be proportionally increased. Justice is the end of government. It is the end of civil society. It ever has been and ever will be pursued until it be obtained, or until liberty be lost in the pursuit. In a society under the forms of which the stronger faction can readily unite and oppress the weaker, anarchy may as truly be said to reign as in a state of nature, where the weaker individual is not secured against the violence of the stronger; and as, in the latter state, even the stronger individuals are prompted, by the uncertainty of their condition, to submit to a government which may protect the weak as well as themselves; so, in the former state, will the more powerful factions or parties be gradually induced, by a like motive, to wish for a government which will protect all parties, the weaker as well as the more powerful.

It can be little doubted that if the State of Rhode Island was separated from the Confederacy and left to itself, the insecurity of rights under the popular form of government within such narrow limits would be displayed by such reiterated oppressions of factious majorities that some power altogether independent of the people would soon be called for by the voice of the very factions whose misrule had proved the necessity of it. In the extended republic of the United States, and among the great variety of interests, parties, and sects which it embraces, a coalition of a majority of the whole society could seldom take place on any other principles than those of justice and the general good; whilst there being thus less danger to a minor from the will of a major party, there must be less pretext, also, to provide for the security of the former, by introducing into the government a will not dependent on the latter, or, in other words, a will independent of the society itself. It is no less certain than it is important, notwithstanding the contrary opinions which have been entertained, that the larger the society, provided it lie within a practicable sphere, the more duly capable it will be of self-government. And happily for the republican cause, the practicable sphere may be carried to a very great extent by a judicious modification and mixture of the *federal principle*.

Publius
(James Madison)

GLOSSARY

A

Acquisitive Model   A model of bureaucracy that view stop-level bureaucrats as seeking to expand the size of their budgets and staffs to gain greater power.

Actual Malice   Either knowledge of a defamatory statement's falsity or a reckless disregard for the truth.

Administrative Agency   A federal, state, or local government unit established to perform a specific function. Administrative agencies are created and authorized by legislative bodies to administer and enforce specific laws.

Advice and Consent   Terms in the Constitution describing the U.S. Senate's power to review and approve treaties and presidential appointments.

Affirm   To declare that a court ruling is valid and must stand.

Affirmative Action   A policy in educational admissions or job hiring that gives special attention or compensatory treatment to traditionally disadvantaged groups in an effort to overcome present effects of past discrimination.

Agenda Setting   Determining which public policy questions will be debated or considered.

Anarchy   The absence of any form of government or political authority.

Anti-Federalist   An individual who opposed the ratification of the new Constitution in 1787. The Anti-Federalists were opposed to a strong central government.

Appellate Court   A court having jurisdiction to review cases and issues that were originally tried in lower courts.

Appointment Power   The authority vested in the president to fill a government office or position. Positions filled by presidential appointment include those in the executive branch and the federal judiciary, commissioned officers in the armed forces, and members of the independent regulatory commissions.

Appropriation   The passage, by Congress, of a spending bill specifying the amount of authorized funds that actually will be allocated for an agency's use.

Aristocracy   Rule by the "best"; in reality, rule by an upper class.

Attentive Public   That portion of the general public that pays attention to policy issues.

Australian Ballot   A secret ballot prepared, distributed, and tabulated by government officials at public expense. Since 1888, all U.S. states have used the Australian ballot rather than an open, public ballot.

Authoritarianism   A type of regime in which only the government is fully controlled by the ruler. Social and economic institutions exist that are not under the government's control.

Authorization   A formal declaration by a legislative committee that a certain amount of funding may be available to an agency. Some authorizations terminate in a year; others are renewable automatically, without further congressional action.

B

Balance of Trade   The difference between the value of a nation's exports of goods and the value of its imports of goods.

Battleground State   A state that is likely to be so closely fought that the campaigns devote exceptional effort to winning the popular and electoral vote there.

"Beauty Contest"   A presidential primary in which contending candidates compete for popular votes but the results do not control the selection of delegates to the national convention.

Bicameral Legislature   A legislature made up of two parts, called chambers. The U.S. Congress, composed of the House of Representatives and the Senate, is a bicameral legislature.

Bicameralism   The division of a legislature into two separate assemblies.

Black Codes   Laws passed by Southern states immediately after the Civil war denying most legal rights to freed slaves.

Block Grants   Federal programs that provide funds to state and local governments for general functional areas, such as criminal justice or mental health programs.

Blue Dog Democrats   Members of Congress from more moderate states or districts who sometimes "cross over" to vote with Republicans on legislation.

Boycott   A form of pressure or protest—an organized refusal to purchase a particular product or deal with a particular business.

Broad Construction   A judicial philosophy that looks to the context and purpose of a law when making an interpretation.

Budget Deficit   Government expenditures that exceed receipts.

Bureaucracy   A large organization that is structured hierarchically to carry out specific functions.

Business Cycle   A term that describes fluctuations in the nation's economic activity including   periods of economic expansion and contraction

Busing   In the context of civil rights, the transportation of public school students from areas where they live to schools in other areas to eliminate school segregation based on residential racial patterns.

C

Cabinet   An advisory group selected by the president to aid in making decisions. The Cabinet includes the heads of 15 executive departments and others named by the president.

Cabinet Department   One of the 15 departments of the executive branch (State, Treasury, Defense, Justice, Interior, Agriculture, Commerce, Labor, Health and Human Services, Homeland Security, Housing and Urban Development, Education, Energy, Transportation, and Veterans Affairs).

Capitalism   An economic system characterized by the private ownership of wealth-creating assets, free markets, and freedom of contract.

Capture   The act by which an industry being regulated by a government agency gains direct or indirect control over agency personnel and decision makers.

Case Law   Judicial interpretations of common-law principles and doctrines, as well as interpretations of constitutional law, statutory law, and administrative law.

Casework   Personal work for constituents by members of Congress.

Categorical Grants   Federal grants to states or local governments that are for specific programs or projects.

Caucus   A meeting of party members designed to select candidates and propose policies.

Charter   A document issued by a government that grants to a person, a group of persons, or a corporation the right to carry on one or more specific activities. A state government can grant a charter to a municipality.

Checks and Balances A major principle of the American system of government whereby each branch of the government can check the actions of the others.

Chief Diplomat The role of the president in recognizing foreign governments, making treaties, and effecting executive agreements.

Chief Executive The role of the president as head of the executive branch of the government.

Chief Legislator The role of the president in influencing the making of laws.

Chief of Staff The person who is named to direct the White House Office and advise the president.

Civil Disobedience A nonviolent, public refusal to obey allegedly unjust laws.

Civil Liberties Those personal freedoms that are protected for all individuals. Civil liberties typically involve restraining the government's actions against individuals.

Civil Rights All rights rooted in the Fourteenth Amendment's guarantee of equal protection under the law.

Civil Service A collective term for the body of employees working for the government. Generally, civil service is understood to apply to all those who gain government employment through a merit system.

Civil Service Commission The initial central personnel agency of the national government, created in 1883.

Class-Action Suit A lawsuit filed by an individual seeking damages for "all persons similarly situated."

Clear and Present Danger Test The test proposed by Justice Oliver Wendell Holmes for determining when government may restrict free speech. Restrictions are permissible, he argued, only when speech creates a *clear and present danger* to the public order.

Climate Control The use of public relations techniques to create favorable public opinion toward an interest group, industry, or corporation.

Closed Primary A type of primary in which the voter is limited to choosing candidates of the party of which he or she is a member.

Coattail Effect The influence of a popular candidate on the electoral success of other candidates on the same party ticket. The effect is increased by the party-column ballot, which encourages straight-ticket voting.

Cold War The ideological, political, and economic confrontation between the United States and the Soviet Union following World War II.

Commander in Chief The role of the president as supreme commander of the military forces of the United States and of the state National Guard units when they are called into federal service.

Commerce Clause The section of the Constitution in which Congress is given the power to regulate trade among the states and with foreign countries.

Commercial Speech Advertising statements, which increasingly have been given First Amendment protection.

Common Law Judge-made law that originated in England from decisions shaped according to prevailing custom. Decisions were applied to similar situations and gradually became common to the nation.

Communications Director A professional specialist who plans the communications strategy and advertising campaign for the candidate.

Concurrent Powers Powers held jointly by the national and state governments.

Concurring Opinion A separate opinion prepared by a judge who supports the decision of the majority of the court but who wants to make or clarify a particular point or to voice disapproval of the grounds on which the decision was made.

Confederal System A system consisting of a league of independent states, each having essentially sovereign powers. The central government created by such a league has only limited powers over the states.

Confederation A political system in which states or regional governments retain ultimate authority except for those powers they expressly delegate to a central government. A voluntary association of independent states, in which the member states agree to limited restraints on their freedom of action.

Conference Committee A special joint committee appointed to reconcile differences when bills pass the two chambers of Congress in different forms.

Consensus General agreement among the citizenry on an issue.

Conservatism A set of beliefs that includes a limited role for the national government in helping individuals, support for traditional values and lifestyles, and a cautious response to change.

Conservative Coalition An alliance of Republicans and Southern Democrats that can form in the House or the Senate to oppose liberal legislation and support conservative legislation.

Consolidation The union of two or more governmental units to form a single unit.

Constituent One of the persons represented by a legislator or other elected or appointed official.

Constitutional Initiative An electoral device whereby citizens can propose a constitutional amendment through petitions signed by the required number of registered voters.

Constitutional Power A power vested in the president by Article II of the Constitution.

Consumer Price Index (CPI) A measure of the change in price over time of a specific group of goods and services used by the average household.

Containment A U.S. diplomatic policy adopted by the Truman administration to contain communist power within its existing boundaries.

Continuing Resolution A temporary funding law that Congress passes when an appropriations bill has not been decided by the beginning of the new fiscal year on October 1.

Cooley's Rule The view that cities should be able to govern themselves, presented in an 1871 Michigan decision by Judge Thomas Cooley.

Cooperative Federalism The theory that the states and the national government should cooperate in solving problems.

Corrupt Practices Acts A series of acts passed by Congress in an attempt to limit and regulate the size and sources of contributions and expenditures in political campaigns.

Council of Governments (COG) A voluntary organization of counties and municipalities concerned with area-wide problems.

County The chief governmental unit set up by the state to administer state law and business at the local level. Counties are drawn up by area, rather than by rural or urban criteria.

Credentials Committee A committee used by political parties at their national conventions to determine which delegates may participate. The committee inspects the claim of each prospective delegate to be seated as a legitimate representative of his or her state

D

De Facto Segregation Racial segregation that occurs because of past social and economic conditions and residential racial patterns.

De Jure Segregation Racial segregation that occurs because of laws or administrative decisions by public agencies.

Dealignment A decline in party loyalties that reduces long-term party commitment.

Defamation of Character   Wrongfully hurting a person's good reputation. The law imposes a general duty on all persons to refrain from making false, defamatory statements about others.

Defense Policy   A subset of national security policies having to do with the U.S. armed forces.

Democracy   A system of government in which political authority is vested in the people. Derived from the Greek words *demos* ("the people") and *kratos* ("authority").

Democratic Party   One of the two major American political parties evolving out of the Republican Party of Thomas Jefferson.

Democratic Republic   A republic in which representatives elected by the people make and enforce laws and policies.

Détente   A French word meaning a relaxation of tensions. The term characterized U.S.-Soviet relations as they developed under President Richard Nixon and Secretary of State Henry Kissinger.

Devolution   The transfer of powers from a national or central government to a state or local government.

Dillon's Rule   The narrowest possible interpretation of the legal status of local governments, outlined by Judge John E. Dillon, who in 1872 stated that a municipal corporation can exercise only those powers expressly granted by state law.

Diplomacy   The process by which states carry on political relations with each other; settling conflicts among nations by peaceful means.

Diplomatic Recognition   The formal acknowledgment of a foreign government as legitimate.

Direct Democracy   A system of government in which political decisions are made by the people directly, rather than by their elected representatives; probably attained most easily in small political communities.

Direct Primary   An intraparty election in which the voters select the candidates who will run on a party's ticket in the subsequent general election.

Direct Technique   An interest group activity that involves interaction with government officials to further the group's goals.

Discharge Petition   A procedure by which a bill in the House of Representatives may be forced (discharged) out of a committee that has refused to report it for consideration by the House. The petition must be signed by an absolute majority (218) of representatives and is used only on rare occasions.

Dissenting Opinion   A separate opinion in which a judge dissents from (disagrees with) the conclusion reached by the majority on the court and expounds his or her own views about the case.

Diversity of Citizenship   The condition that exists when the parties to a lawsuit are citizens of different states, or when the parties are citizens of a U.S. state and citizens or the government of a foreign country. Diversity of citizenship can provide a basis for federal jurisdiction.

Divided Government   A situation in which one major political party controls the presidency and the other controls the chambers of Congress, or in which one party controls a state governorship and the other controls the state legislature.

Divine Right of Kings   A political and religious doctrine that asserts a monarchy's legitimacy is conferred directly by God and as such a king is not subject to any earthly authority, including his people or the church.

Divisive Opinion   Public opinion that is polarized between two quite different positions.

Domestic Policy   Public plans or courses of action that concern internal issues of national importance, such as poverty, crime, and the environment.

Dual Federalism   A system in which the states and the national government each remains supreme within its own sphere. The doctrine looks on nation and state as coequal sovereign powers. Neither the state government nor the national government should interfere in the other's sphere.

E

Earmarks   Funding appropriations that are specifically designated for a named project in a member's state or district.

Earned-Income Tax Credit (EITC) Program   A government program that helps low-income workers by giving back part or all of their Social Security taxes.

Economic Aid   Assistance to other nations in the form of grants, loans, or credits to buy the assisting nation's products.

Elastic Clause, or Necessary and Proper Clause   The clause in Article I, Section 8, that grants Congress the power to do whatever is necessary to execute its specifically delegated powers.

Elector   A member of the electoral college, which selects the president and vice president. Each state's electors are chosen in each presidential election year according to state laws.

Electoral College   A group of persons called *electors* selected by the voters in each state and the District of Columbia; this group officially elects the president and vice president of the United States. The number of electors in each state is equal to the number of each state's representatives in both chambers of Congress.

Elite Theory   A perspective holding that society is ruled by a small number of people who exercise power to further their self-interest.

Emergency Power   An inherent power exercised by the president during a period of national crisis.

Eminent Domain   A power set forth in the Fifth Amendment to the U.S. Constitution that allows government to take private property for public use under the condition that compensation is offered to the landowner.

Enabling Legislation   A statute enacted by Congress that authorizes the creation of an administrative agency and specifies the name, purpose, composition, functions, and powers of the agency being created.

Energy Policy   Laws concerned with how much energy is needed and used.

Enumerated Power   A power specifically granted to the national government by the Constitution. The first 17 clauses of Article I, Section 8, specify most of the enumerated powers of Congress.

Environmental Impact Statement (EIS)   A report that must show the costs and benefits of major federal actions that could significantly affect the quality of the environment.

Equality   As a political value, the idea that all people are of equal worth.

Era of Good Feelings   The years from 1817 to 1825, when James Monroe was president and there was, in effect, no political opposition.

Establishment Clause   The part of the First Amendment prohibiting the establishment of a church officially supported by the national government. It is applied to questions of state and local government aid to religious organizations and schools, the legality of allowing or requiring school prayers, and the teaching of evolution versus intelligent design.

Exclusionary Rule   A policy forbidding the admission at trial of illegally seized evidence.

Executive Agreement   An international agreement made by the president, without senatorial ratification, with the head of a foreign state.

Executive Budget   The budget prepared and submitted by the president to Congress.

Executive Office of the President (EOP)   An organization established by President Franklin D. Roosevelt to assist the president in carrying out major duties.

Executive Order   A rule or regulation issued by the president that has the effect of law. Executive orders can implement and give administrative effect to provisions in the Constitution, to treaties, and to statutes.

Executive Privilege   The right of executive officials to withhold information from or to refuse to appear before a legislative committee.

Expansionist Policy   A policy that embraces the extension of American borders as far as possible.

Exports   Goods and services produced domestically for sale abroad.

Expressed Power   A power of the president that is expressly written into the Constitution or into statutory law.

Extradite   To surrender an accused or convicted criminal to the authorities of the state from which he or she has fled; to return a fugitive criminal to the jurisdiction of the accusing state.

F

Faction   A group or bloc in a legislature or political party acting in pursuit of some special interest or position.

Fall Review   The annual process in which the Office of Management and Budget, after receiving formal federal agency requests for funding for the next fiscal year, reviews the requests, makes changes, and submits its recommendations to the president.

Federal Mandate   A requirement in federal legislation that forces states and municipalities to comply with certain rules.

Federal Open Market Committee   The most important body within the Federal Reserve System. The Federal Open Market Committee decides how monetary policy should be carried out.

Federal Question   A question that has to do with the U.S. Constitution, acts of Congress, or treaties. A federal question provides a basis for federal jurisdiction.

Federal Register   A publication of the U.S. government that prints executive orders, rules, and regulations.

Federal Reserve System (the Fed)   The agency created by Congress in 1913 to serve as the nation's central banking organization.

Federal System   A system of government in which power is divided between a central government and regional, or subdivisional, governments. Each level must have some domain in which its policies are dominant and some genuine political or constitutional guarantee of its authority.

Federalism   A system of government in which power is divided by a written constitution between a central government and regional or subdivisional governments. Each level must have some domain in which its policies are dominant and some genuine constitutional guarantee of its authority.

Federalist   The name given to one who was in favor of the adoption of the U.S. Constitution and the creation of a federal union with a strong central government.

Feminism   The philosophy of political, economic, and social equality for women and the gender consciousness sufficient to mobilize women for change.

Filibuster   The use of the Senate's tradition of unlimited debate as a delaying tactic to block a bill.

Finance Chairperson   The campaign professional who directs fundraising, campaign spending, and compliance with campaign finance laws and reporting requirements.

First Budget Resolution   A resolution passed by Congress in May that sets overall revenue and spending goals for the following fiscal year.

Fiscal Policy   The federal government's use of taxation and spending policies to affect overall business activity.

Fiscal Year (FY)   A 12-month period that is used for bookkeeping, or accounting purposes. Usually, the fiscal year does not coincide with the calendar year. For example, the federal government's fiscal year runs from October 1 through September 30.

Focus Group   A small group of individuals who are led in discussion by a professional consultant in order to gather opinions on and responses to candidates and issues.

Food Stamps   Benefits issued by the federal government to low-income individuals to be used for the purchase of food; originally provided as coupons, but now typically provided electronically through a card similar to a debit card.

Foreign Policy   A nation's external goals and the techniques and strategies used to achieve them.

Foreign Policy Process   The steps by which foreign policy goals are decided and acted on.

Franking   A policy that enables members of Congress to send material through the mail by substituting their facsimile signature (frank) for postage.

Free Exercise Clause   The provision of the First Amendment guaranteeing the free exercise of religion.

Free Rider Problem   The difficulty interest groups face in recruiting members when the benefits they achieve can be gained without joining the group.

Front-Loading   The practice of moving presidential primary elections to the early part of the campaign to maximize the impact of these primaries on the nomination.

Front-Runner   The presidential candidate who appears to be ahead at a given time in the primary season.

Full Employment   An arbitrary level of unemployment that corresponds to "normal" friction in the labor market. In 1986, a 6.5 percent rate of unemployment was considered full employment. Today, it is assumed to be around 5 percent.

Full Faith and Credit Clause   This section of the Constitution requires states to recognize one another's laws and court decisions. It ensures that rights established under deeds, wills, contracts, and other civil matters in one state will be honored by other states.

Functional Consolidation   Cooperation by two or more units of local government in providing services to their inhabitants. This is generally done by unifying a set of departments (e.g., the police departments) into a single agency.

G

Gag Order   An order issued by a judge restricting the publication of news about a trial or a pretrial hearing to protect the accused's right to a fair trial.

Gender Discrimination   Any practice, policy, or procedure that denies equality of treatment to an individual or to a group because of gender.

Gender Gap   The difference between the percentage of women who vote for a particular candidate and the percentage of men who vote for the candidate.

General Jurisdiction   Exists when a court's authority to hear cases is not significantly restricted. A court of general jurisdiction normally can hear a broad range of cases.

General Law City   A city operating under general state laws that apply to all local governmental units of a similar type.

General Sales Tax   A tax levied as a proportion of the retail price of a commodity at the point of sale.

Generational Effect   A long-lasting effect of the events of a particular time on the political opinions of those who came of political age at that time.

Gerrymandering   The drawing of legislative district boundary lines to obtain partisan or factional advantage. A district is said to be gerrymandered when its shape is manipulated by the dominant party in the state legislature to maximize electoral strength at the expense of the minority party.

Get Out the Vote (GOTV)   This phrase describes the multiple efforts expended by campaigns to get voters out to the polls on election day.

Gini Index A statistical measure of the distribution of income in a nation. A higher number indicates more inequality in incomes within a nation.

Glass-Steagall Act A law passed in 1933 to regulate the banking industry which prohibited banks from engaging in speculative investments or becoming investment houses.

Government The preeminent institution in which decisions are made that resolve conflicts or allocate benefits and privileges. It is unique because it has the ultimate authority within society.

Government Corporation An agency of government that administers a quasi-business enterprise. These corporations are used when activities are primarily commercial.

Government in the Sunshine Act A law that requires all committee-directed federal agencies to conduct their business regularly in public session.

Grandfather Clause A device used by Southern states to disenfranchise African Americans. It restricted voting to those whose grandfathers had voted before 1867.

Great Compromise The compromise between the New Jersey and Virginia plans that created one chamber of the Congress based on population and one chamber representing each state equally; also called the Connecticut Compromise.

Gross Domestic Product (GDP) The dollar value of all final goods and services produced in a one-year period.

Gross Public Debt The net public debt plus interagency borrowings within the government.

H

Hard Money This refers to political contributions and campaign spending that is recorded under the regulations set forth in law and by the Federal Election Commission.

Hatch Act An act passed in 1939 that restricted the political activities of government employees. It also prohibited a political group from spending more than $3 million in any campaign and limited individual contributions to a campaign committee to $5,000.

Hate Crime A criminal offense committed against a person or property that is motivated, in whole or in part, by the offender's bias against a race, color, ethnicity, national origin, sex, gender identity or expression, sexual orientation, disability, age, or religion.

Head of State The role of the president as ceremonial head of the government.

Hillstyle The actions and behaviors of a member of Congress in Washington, D.C., intended to promote policies and the member's own career aspirations.

Hispanic Someone who can claim a heritage from a Spanish-speaking country other than Spain. This is the term most often used by government agencies to describe this group. Citizens of Spanish-speaking countries do not use this term to describe themselves.

Home Rule City A city permitted by the state to let local voters frame, adopt, and amend their own charter.

Homestyle The actions and behaviors of a member of Congress aimed at the constituents and intended to win the support and trust of the voters at home.

I

Ideology A comprehensive set of beliefs about the nature of people and about the role of an institution or government.

Impeachment An action by the House of Representatives to accuse the president, vice president, or other civil officers of the United States of committing "Treason, Bribery, or other high Crimes and Misdemeanors."

Import Quota A restriction imposed on the value or number of units of a particular good that can be brought into a country. Foreign suppliers are unable to sell more than the amount specified in the import quota.

Imports Goods and services produced outside a country but sold within its borders.

Income Transfer A transfer of income from some individuals in the economy to other individuals. This is generally done by government action.

Incorporation Theory The view that most of the protections of the Bill of Rights apply to state governments through the Fourteenth Amendment's due process clause.

Independent A voter or candidate who does not identify with a political party.

Independent Executive Agency A federal agency that is not part of a Cabinet department but reports directly to the president.

Independent Expenditures Nonregulated contributions from PACs, organizations, and individuals. The funds may be spent on advertising or other campaign activities, so long as those expenditures are not coordinated with those of a candidate.

Independent Regulatory Agency An agency outside the major executive departments charged with making and implementing rules and regulations.

Indirect Technique A strategy employed by interest groups that uses third parties to influence government officials.

Inflation A sustained rise in the general price level of goods and services.

Inherent Power A power of the president derived from the statements in the Constitution that "the executive Power shall be vested in a President" and that the president should "take Care that the Laws be faithfully executed"; defined through practice rather than through law.

Initiative A procedure by which voters can propose a law or constitutional amendment.

In-Kind Subsidy A good or service—such as food stamps, housing, or medical care—provided by the government to low-income groups.

Institution An ongoing organization that performs certain functions for society.

Instructed Delegate A legislator who is an agent of the voters who elected him or her and who votes according to the views of constituents regardless of personal beliefs.

Intelligence Community The government agencies that gather information about the capabilities and intentions of foreign governments or that engage in covert actions.

Interest Group An organized group of individuals sharing common objectives who actively attempt to influence policy makers.

Interstate Compact An agreement between two or more states. Agreements on minor matters are made without congressional consent, but any compact that tends to increase the power of the contracting states relative to other states or relative to the national government generally requires the consent of Congress. Such compacts serve as a means by which states can solve regional problems.

Iron Curtain The term used to describe the division of Europe between the Soviet bloc and the West; coined by Winston Churchill.

Iron Triangle The three-way alliance among legislators, bureaucrats, and interest groups to make or preserve policies that benefit their respective interests.

Isolationist Foreign Policy A policy of abstaining from an active role in international affairs or alliances, which characterized U.S. foreign policy toward Europe during most of the 1800s.

Issue Advocacy Advertising Advertising paid for by interest groups that support or oppose a candidate or a candidate's position on an issue without mentioning voting or elections.

Issue Network A group of individuals or organizations—which may consist of legislators and legislative staff members, interest group leaders, bureaucrats, the media, scholars, and other experts—that supports a particular policy position on a given issue.

Item Veto The power exercised by the governors of most states to veto particular sections or items of an appropriations bill, while signing the remainder of the bill into law.

J

Jim Crow Laws Laws enacted by Southern states that enforced segregation in schools, on transportation, and in public accommodations.

Joint Committee A legislative committee composed of members from both chambers of Congress.

Judicial Activism A doctrine holding that the Supreme Court should take an active role by using its powers to check the activities of governmental bodies when those bodies exceed their authority.

Judicial Implementation The way in which court decisions are translated into action.

Judicial Restraint A doctrine holding that the Supreme Court should defer to the decisions made by the elected representatives of the people in the legislative and executive branches.

Judicial Review The power of the Supreme Court or any court to hold a law or other legal action as unconstitutional.

Jurisdiction The authority of a court to decide certain cases. Not all courts have the authority to decide all cases. Two jurisdictional issues are where a case arises as well as its subject matter.

Justiciable Question A question that may be raised and reviewed in court.

K

Keynesian Economics A school of economic thought that tends to favor active federal government policy making to stabilize economy-wide fluctuations, usually by implementing discretionary fiscal policy.

Kitchen Cabinet The informal advisers to the president.

L

Labor Movement Generally, the economic and political expression of working-class interests; politically, the organization of working-class interests.

Latent Interests Public-policy interests that are not recognized or addressed by a group at a particular time.

Latino Preferred term for referring to individuals who claim a heritage from a Spanish-speaking country other than Spain.

Lawmaking The process of establishing the legal rules that govern society.

Legislature A governmental body primarily responsible for the making of laws.

Libel A written defamation of a person's character, reputation, business, or property rights.

Liberalism A set of beliefs that includes the advocacy of positive government action to improve the welfare of individuals, support for civil rights, and tolerance for political and social change.

Libertarianism A political ideology based on skepticism or opposition toward almost all government activities.

Liberty The greatest freedom of individuals that is consistent with the freedom of other individuals in the society.

Life Cycle Effect People change as they grow older because of age-specific experiences and thus people are likely to hold age-specific attitudes.

Limited Government The principle that the powers of government should be limited, usually by constitutional checks.

Limited Jurisdiction Exists when a court's authority to hear cases is restricted to certain types of claims, such as tax claims or bankruptcy petitions.

Line Organization In the federal government, an administrative unit that is directly accountable to the president.

Line-Item Veto The power of an executive to veto individual lines or items within a piece of legislation without vetoing the entire bill.

Literacy Test A test administered as a precondition for voting, often used to prevent African Americans from exercising their right to vote.

Litigate To engage in a legal proceeding or seek relief in a court of law; to carry on a lawsuit.

Lobbyist An organization or individual who attempts to influence legislation and the administrative decisions of government.

Logrolling An arrangement in which two or more members of Congress agree in advance to support each other's bills.

Loophole A legal method by which individuals and businesses are allowed to reduce the tax liabilities owed to the government.

Loose Monetary Policy Monetary policy that makes credit inexpensive and abundant, possibly leading to inflation.

M

Madisonian Model A structure of government proposed by James Madison in which the powers of the government are separated into three branches: executive, legislative, and judicial.

Majoritarianism A political theory holding that in a democracy, the government ought to do what the majority of the people want.

Majority More than 50 percent.

Majority Leader of the House A legislative position held by an important party member in the House of Representatives. The majority leader is selected by the majority party in caucus or conference to foster cohesion among party members and to act as spokesperson for the majority party in the House.

Majority Opinion A court opinion reflecting the views of the majority of the judges.

Majority Rule A basic principle of democracy asserting that the greatest number of citizens in any political unit should select officials and determine policy.

Managed News Information generated and distributed by the government in such a way as to give government interests priority over candor.

Material Incentive A reason or motive having to do with economic benefits or opportunities.

Media Channels of mass communication.

Medicaid A joint state–federal program that provides medical care to the poor (including indigent elderly persons in nursing homes). The program is funded out of general government revenues.

Medicare A federal health insurance program that covers U.S. residents age 65 and older. The costs are met by a tax on wages and salaries.

Merit System The selection, retention, and promotion of government employees on the basis of competitive examinations.

Military-Industrial Complex The mutually beneficial relationship between the armed forces and defense contractors.

Minority Leader of the House The party leader elected by the minority party in the House.

Monetary Policy The utilization of changes in the amount of money in circulation to alter credit markets, employment, and the rate of inflation.

Monopolistic Model A model of bureaucracy that compares bureaucracies to monopolistic business firms. Lack of competition in either circumstance leads to inefficient and costly operations.

Monroe Doctrine A policy statement made by President James Monroe in 1823, which set out three principles: (1) European nations should not establish new colonies in the Western Hemisphere; (2) European nations should not intervene in the affairs of independent nations of the Western Hemisphere; and (3) the United States would not interfere in the affairs of European nations.

Moralist Foreign Policy A foreign policy based on values and moral beliefs.

Municipal Home Rule The power vested in a local unit of government to draft or change its own charter and to manage its own affairs.

N

National Committee A standing committee of a national political party established to direct and coordinate party activities between national party conventions.

National Convention The meeting held every four years by each major party to select presidential and vice presidential candidates, to write a platform, to choose a national committee, and to conduct party business.

National Health Insurance A plan to provide universal health insurance under which the government provides basic health care coverage to all citizens. In most such plans, the program is funded by taxes on wages or salaries.

National Security Council (NSC) An agency in the Executive Office of the President that advises the president on national security.

National Security Policy Foreign and domestic policy designed to protect the nation's independence and political and economic integrity; policy that is concerned with the safety and defense of the nation.

Natural Rights Rights held to be inherent in natural law, not dependent on governments. John Locke stated that natural law, being superior to human law, specifies certain rights of "life, liberty, and property." These rights, altered to become "life, liberty, and the pursuit of happiness," are asserted in the Declaration of Independence.

Negative Constituents Citizens who openly oppose the government's policies.

Net Public Debt The accumulation of all past federal government deficits; the total amount owed by the federal government to individuals, businesses, and foreigners.

New England Town A governmental unit in the New England states that combines the roles of city and county in one unit.

Nonopinion The lack of an opinion on an issue or policy among the majority.

Normal Trade Relations (NTR) Status A status granted through an international treaty by which each member nation must treat other members at least as well as it treats the country that receives its most favorable treatment. This status was formerly known as most-favored-nation status.

O

Office of Management and Budget (OMB) A division of the Executive Office of the President. The OMB assists the president in preparing the annual budget, clearing and coordinating departmental agency budgets, and supervising the administration of the federal budget.

Office-Block, or Massachusetts, Ballot A form of general-election ballot in which candidates for elective office are grouped together under the title of each office. It emphasizes voting for the office and the individual candidate, rather than for the party.

Oligarchy Rule by the few in their own interests.

Ombudsperson A person who hears and investigates complaints by private individuals against public officials or agencies.

Open Primary A primary in which any registered voter can vote (but must vote for candidates of only one party).

Opinion Leader One who is able to influence the opinions of others because of position, expertise, or personality.

Opinion Poll A method of systematically questioning a small, selected sample of respondents who are deemed representative of the total population.

Opinion The statement by a judge or a court of the decision reached in a case. The opinion sets forth the applicable law and details the reasoning on which the ruling was based.

Oral Arguments The verbal arguments presented in person by attorneys to an appellate court. Each attorney presents reasons to the court why the court should rule in her or his client's favor.

Order A state of peace and security. Maintaining order by protecting members of society from violence and criminal activity is the oldest purpose of government.

Oversight The process by which Congress follows up on laws it has enacted to ensure that they are being enforced and administered in the way Congress intended.

P

Pardon A release from the punishment for or legal consequences of a crime; a pardon can be granted by the president before or after a conviction.

Party Identification Linking oneself to a particular political party.

Party Identifier A person who identifies with a political party.

Party Organization The formal structure and leadership of a political party, including election committees; local, state, and national executives; and paid professional staff.

Party Platform A document drawn up at each national convention outlining the policies, positions, and principles of the party.

Party-Column, or Indiana, Ballot A form of general-election ballot in which all of a party's candidates for elective office are arranged in one column under the party's label and symbol. It emphasizes voting for the party, rather than for the office or individual.

Party-in-Government All of the elected and appointed officials who identify with a political party.

Party-in-the-Electorate Those members of the general public who identify with a political party or who express a preference for one party over another.

Patronage The practice of rewarding faithful party workers and followers with government employment and contracts.

Peer Group A group consisting of members sharing common social characteristics. These groups play an important part in the socialization process, helping to shape attitudes and beliefs.

Pendleton Act (Civil Service Reform Act) An act that established the principle of employment on the basis of merit and created the Civil Service Commission to administer the personnel service.

Permanent Campaign A coordinated and planned strategy carried out by the White House to increase the president's popularity and support.

Picket-Fence Federalism A model of federalism in which specific programs and policies (depicted as vertical pickets in a picket fence) involve all levels of government—national, state, and local (depicted by the horizontal boards in a picket fence).

Pluralism A theory that views politics as a conflict among interest groups. Political decision making is characterized by bargaining and compromise.

Plurality A number of votes cast for a candidate that is greater than the number of votes for any other candidate but not necessarily a majority.

Pocket Veto A special veto exercised by the chief executive after a legislative body has adjourned. Bills not signed by the chief executive die after a specified period of time. If Congress wishes to reconsider such a bill, it must be reintroduced in the following session of Congress.

Police Power The authority to legislate for the protection of the health, morals, safety, and welfare of the people. In the United States, most police power is reserved to the states.

Policy Tsar A high-ranking member of the Executive Office of the President appointed to coordinate action in one specific policy area.

Political Action Committee (PAC) A committee set up by and representing a corporation, labor union, or special-interest group. PACs raise and give campaign donations.

Political Consultant A paid professional hired to devise a campaign strategy and manage a campaign.

Political Culture The set of ideals, values, and ways of thinking about government and politics that is shared by all citizens.

Political Party A group of political activists who organize to win elections, operate the government, and determine public policy.

Political Question An issue that a court believes should be decided by the executive or legislative branch.

Political Socialization The process through which individuals learn a set of political attitudes and form opinions about social issues. Families and the educational system are two of the most important forces in the political socialization process.

Political Trust The degree to which individuals express trust in the government and political institutions, usually measured through a specific series of survey questions.

Politics The process of resolving conflicts and deciding "who gets what, when, and how." More specifically, politics is the struggle over power or influence within organizations or informal groups that can grant or withhold benefits or privileges.

Poll Tax A special tax that must be paid as a qualification for voting. The Twenty-fourth Amendment to the Constitution outlawed the poll tax in national elections, and in 1966, the Supreme Court declared it unconstitutional in all elections.

Pollster The person or firm who conducts public opinion polls for the campaign.

Pork Special projects or appropriations that are intended to benefit a member's district or state; slang term for earmarks.

Precedent A court rule bearing on subsequent legal decisions in similar cases. Judges rely on precedents in deciding cases.

Preemptive War A military engagement fought to stop an enemy before that enemy attacks the United States.

President Pro Tempore The temporary presiding officer of the Senate in the absence of the vice president.

Presidential Primary A statewide primary election of delegates to a political party's national convention, held to determine a party's presidential nominee.

Press Secretary The individual who interacts directly with the journalists covering the campaign.

Press Secretary The presidential staff member responsible for handling White House media relations and communications.

Prior Restraint Restraining an action before the activity has actually occurred. When expression is involved, this means censorship.

Privatization The replacement of government services with services provided by private firms.

Privileges and Immunities Special rights and exceptions provided by law. States may not discriminate against one another's citizens.

Progressive Tax A tax that rises in percentage terms as incomes rise.

Property Anything that is or may be subject to ownership. As conceived by the political philosopher John Locke, the right to property is a natural right superior to human law (laws made by government).

Property Tax A tax on the value of real estate. This tax is a particularly important source of revenue for local governments.

Public Figure A public official, movie star, or other person known to the public because of his or her position or activities.

Public Interest The best interests of the overall community; the national good, rather than the narrow interests of a particular group.

Public Opinion The aggregate of individual attitudes or beliefs shared by some portion of the adult population.

Purposive Incentive A reason for supporting or participating in the activities of a group that is based on agreement with the goals of the group. For example, someone with a strong interest in human rights might have a purposive incentive to join Amnesty International.

R

Ratification Formal approval.

Rational Ignorance Effect An effect produced when people purposely and rationally decide not to become informed on an issue because they believe that their vote on the issue is not likely to be a deciding one; a lack of incentive to seek the necessary information to cast an intelligent vote.

Realignment A process in which a substantial group of voters switches party allegiance, producing a long-term change in the political landscape.

Realist Foreign Policy A foreign policy based on an understanding of the nation's economic and security interests.

Reapportionment The allocation of seats in the House of Representatives to each state after each census.

Recall A procedure allowing people to vote to dismiss an elected official from state office before his or her term has expired.

Recession Two or more successive quarters in which the economy shrinks instead of grows.

Redistricting The redrawing of the boundaries of the congressional districts within each state.

Referendum An electoral device whereby legislative or constitutional measures are referred by the legislature to the voters for approval or disapproval.

Registration The entry of a person's name onto the list of registered voters for elections. To register, a person must meet certain legal requirements of age, citizenship, and residency.

Regressive Tax A tax that falls in percentage terms as incomes rise.

Remand To send a case back to the court that originally heard it.

Reparation Compensation, monetary or nonmonetary (e.g., formal apology), to make amends for a past transgression or harm.

Representation The function of members of Congress as elected officials representing the views of their constituents.

Representative Assembly A legislature composed of individuals who represent the population.

Representative Democracy A form of government in which representatives elected by the people make and enforce laws and policies; may retain the monarchy in a ceremonial role.

Reprieve   A formal postponement of the execution of a sentence imposed by a court of law.

Republic   A form of government in which sovereignty rests with the people, as opposed to a king or monarch.

Republican Party   One of the two major American political parties. It emerged in the 1850s as an antislavery party and consisted of former Northern Whigs and antislavery Democrats.

Reverse Discrimination   The charge that an affirmative action program discriminates against those who do not have minority status.

Reverse   To annul or make void a court ruling on account of some error or irregularity.

Reverse-Income Effect   A tendency for wealthier states or regions to favor the Democrats and for less wealthy states or regions to favor the Republicans. The effect appears paradoxical because it reverses traditional patterns of support.

Rule of Four   A United States Supreme Court procedure by which four justices must vote to grant a petition for review if a case is to come before the full court.

Rule   The proposal by the Rules Committee of the House that states the conditions for debate for one piece of legislation.

Rules Committee   A standing committee of the House of Representatives that provides special rules under which specific bills can be debated, amended, and considered by the House.

S

Safe Seat   A district that returns the legislator with 55 percent of the vote or more.

Sampling Error   The difference between a sample's results and the true result if the entire population had been interviewed.

Second Budget Resolution   A resolution passed by Congress in September that sets "binding" limits on taxes and spending for the following fiscal year.

Select Committee   A temporary legislative committee established for a limited time period and for a special purpose.

Selectperson   A member of the governing group of a town.

Senate Majority Leader   The chief spokesperson of the majority party in the Senate, who directs the legislative program and party strategy.

Senate Minority Leader   The party officer in the Senate who commands the minority party's opposition to the policies of the majority party and directs the legislative program and strategy of his or her party.

Senatorial Courtesy   In federal district court judgeship nominations, a tradition allowing a senator to veto a judicial appointment in his or her state.

Seniority System   A custom followed in both chambers of Congress specifying that the member of the majority party with the longest term of continuous service will be given preference when a committee chairperson (or a holder of some other significant post) is selected.

Separate-but-Equal Doctrine   The 1896 doctrine holding that separate-but-equal facilities do not violate the equal protection clause.

Separation of Powers   The principle of dividing governmental powers among different branches of government.

Service Sector   The sector of the economy that provides services—such as health care, banking, and education—in contrast to the sector that produces goods.

Sexual Harassment   Unwanted physical or verbal conduct or abuse of a sexual nature that interferes with a recipient's job performance, creates a hostile work environment, or carries with it an implicit or explicit threat of adverse employment consequences.

Signing Statement   A written declaration that a president may make when signing a bill into law. Usually, such statements point out sections of the law that the president deems unconstitutional.

Single-Payer Plan   A plan under which one entity has a monopoly on issuing a particular type of insurance. Typically, the entity is the government, and the insurance is basic health coverage.

Slander   The public uttering of a false statement that harms the good reputation of another. The statement must be made to, or within the hearing of, persons other than the defamed party.

Social Contract   A theory of politics that asserts that individuals form political communities by a process of mutual consent, giving up a measure of their individual liberty in order to gain the protection of government.

Social Movement   A movement that represents the demands of a large segment of the public for political, economic, or social change.

Socialism   A political ideology based on strong support for economic and social equality. Socialists traditionally envisioned a society in which major businesses were taken over by the government or by employee cooperatives

Socioeconomic Status   The value assigned to a person due to occupation or income. An upper-class person, for example, has high socioeconomic status.

Soft Money   Campaign contributions unregulated by federal or state law, usually given to parties and party committees to help fund general party activities.

Solidary Incentive   A reason or motive having to do with the desire to associate with others and to share with others a particular interest or hobby.

Soviet Bloc   The Soviet Union and the Eastern European countries that installed communist regimes after World War II and were dominated by the Soviet Union.

Speaker of the House   The presiding officer in the House of Representatives. The Speaker is always a member of the majority party and is the most powerful and influential member of the House.

Spin   An interpretation of campaign events or election results that is favorable to the candidate's campaign strategy.

Spin Doctor   A political campaign adviser who tries to convince journalists of the truth of a particular interpretation of events.

Splinter Party   A new party formed by a dissident faction within a major political party. Often, splinter parties have emerged when a particular personality was at odds with the major party.

Spoils System   The awarding of government jobs to political supporters and friends.

Spring Review   The annual process in which the Office of Management and Budget requires federal agencies to review their programs, activities, and goals and submit their requests for funding for the next fiscal year.

Standing Committee   A permanent committee in the House or Senate that considers bills within a certain subject area.

Stare Decisis   To stand on decided cases; the judicial policy of following precedents established by past decisions.

State   A group of people occupying a specific area and organized under one government; may be either a nation or a subunit of a nation.

State Central Committee   The principal organized structure of each political party within each state. This committee is responsible for carrying out policy decisions of the party's state convention.

State of the Union Message   An annual message to Congress in which the president proposes a legislative program. The message is addressed not only to Congress but also to the American people and to the world.

Statutory Power   A power created for the president through laws enacted by Congress.

Straight-Ticket Voting   Voting exclusively for the candidates of one party.

Strategic Arms Limitation Treaty (SALT I)   A treaty between the United States and the Soviet Union to stabilize the nuclear arms competition between the two countries. SALT I talks began in 1969, and agreements were signed on May 26, 1972.

Strict Construction   A judicial philosophy that looks to the "letter of the law" when interpreting the Constitution or a particular statute.

Subpoena   A legal writ requiring a person's appearance in court to give testimony.

Suffrage   The right to vote; the franchise.

Sunset Legislation   Laws requiring that existing programs be reviewed regularly for their effectiveness and be terminated unless specifically extended as a result of these reviews.

Super PAC   A political committee that can accept unlimited contributions from individuals and corporations to spend supporting a candidate as long as its efforts are not coordinated with the candidate's own campaign.

Superdelegate   A party leader or elected official who is given the right to vote at the party's national convention. Superdelegates are not elected at the state level.

Supplemental Security Income (SSI)   A federal program established to provide assistance to elderly persons and persons with disabilities.

Supremacy Clause   The constitutional provision that makes the Constitution and federal laws superior to all conflicting state and local laws.

Supremacy Doctrine   A doctrine that asserts the priority of national law over state laws. This principle is rooted in Article VI of the Constitution, which provides that the Constitution, the laws passed by the national government under its constitutional powers, and all treaties constitute the supreme law of the land.

Sustainability   Achieving a balance between society and nature that will permit both to exist in harmony.

Swing Voters   Voters who frequently swing their support from one party to another.

Symbolic Speech   Nonverbal expression of beliefs, which is given substantial protection by the courts.

T

Tariffs   Taxes on imports.

Technical Assistance   The practice of sending experts in such areas as agriculture, engineering, or business to aid other nations.

Temporary Assistance to Needy Families (TANF)   A state-administered program in which grants from the national government are used to provide welfare benefits. The TANF program replaced the Aid to Families with Dependent Children (AFDC) program.

Third Party   A political party other than the two major political parties (Republican and Democratic).

Ticket Splitting   Voting for candidates of two or more parties for different offices. For example, a voter splits her ticket if she votes for a Republican presidential candidate and a Democratic congressional candidate.

Tight Monetary Policy   Monetary policy that makes credit expensive in an effort to slow the economy.

Tipping   A phenomenon that occurs when a group that is becoming more numerous over time grows large enough to change the political balance in a district, state, or country.

Totalitarian Regime   A form of government that controls all aspects of the political and social life of a nation.

Town Manager System   A form of town government in which voters elect three selectpersons, who then appoint a professional town manager, who in turn appoints other officials.

Town Meeting   The governing authority of a New England town. Qualified voters may participate in the election of officers and the passage of legislation.

Township   A rural unit of government based on federal land surveys of the American frontier in the 1780s. Townships have declined significantly in importance.

Tracking Poll   A poll taken for the candidate on a nearly daily basis as election day approaches.

Trial Court   The court in which most cases begin.

Truman Doctrine   The policy adopted by President Harry Truman in 1947 to halt communist expansion in southeastern Europe.

Trustee   A legislator who acts according to her or his conscience and the broad interests of the entire society.

Twelfth Amendment   An amendment to the Constitution, adopted in 1804, that specifies the separate election of the president and vice president by the electoral college.

Twenty-fifth Amendment   A 1967 amendment to the Constitution that establishes procedures for filling presidential and vice presidential vacancies and makes provisions for presidential disability.

Two-Party System   A political system in which only two parties have a reasonable chance of winning.

U

U.S. Treasury Bond   Debt issued by the federal government.

Unanimous Consent Agreement   An agreement on the rules of debate for proposed legislation in the Senate that is approved by all the members.

Unanimous Opinion   A court opinion or determination on which all judges agree.

Unemployment   The inability of those who are in the labor force to find a job; defined as the total number of those in the labor force actively looking for a job but unable to find one.

Unicameral Legislature   A legislature with only one legislative chamber, as opposed to a bicameral (two-chamber) legislature, such as the U.S. Congress. Today, Nebraska is the only state in the Union with a unicameral legislature.

Unincorporated Area   An area not loca-ted within the boundary of a municipality.

Unit Rule   A rule by which all of a state's electoral votes are cast for the presidential candidate receiving a plurality of the popular vote in that state.

Unitary System   A centralized governmental system in which local or subdivisional governments exercise only those powers given to them by the central government.

Universal Suffrage   The right of all adults to vote for their representative.

Unorthodox Lawmaking   The use of out-of-the-ordinary parliamentary tactics to pass legislation.

V

Veto Message   The president's formal explanation of a veto when legislation is returned to Congress.

Voter Turnout   The percentage of citizens taking part in the election process; the number of eligible voters who actually "turn out" on election day to cast their ballots.

W

War Powers Resolution   A law passed in 1973 spelling out the conditions under which the president can commit troops without congressional approval.

Washington Community   Individuals regularly involved with politics in Washington, D.C.

Watergate Break-in   The 1972 illegal entry into the Democratic National Committee offices by participants in President Richard Nixon's reelection campaign.

Weberian Model   A model of bureaucracy developed by the German sociologist Max Weber, who viewed bureaucracies as rational, hierarchical organizations in which decisions are based on logical reasoning.

Whig Party   A major party in the United States during the first half of the 19th century, formally established in 1836. The Whig Party was anti-Jackson and represented a variety of regional interests.

Whip   A member of Congress who aids the majority or minority leader of the House or the Senate.

Whistleblower   Someone who brings to public attention gross governmental inefficiency or an illegal action.

White House Office   The personal office of the president, which tends to presidential political needs and manages the media.

White Primary   A state primary election that restricts voting to whites only; outlawed by the Supreme Court in 1944.

Writ of *Certiorari*   An order issued by a higher court to a lower court to send up the record of a case for review.

INDEX